MICROSOFT®
VISUAL BASIC® 2010:
RELOADED

FOURTH EDITION

MICROSOFT® VISUAL BASIC® 2010: RELOADED

DIANE ZAK

COURSE TECHNOLOGY
CENGAGE Learning™

Australia • Brazil • Japan • Korea • Mexico • Singapore • Spain • United Kingdom • United States

COURSE TECHNOLOGY
CENGAGE Learning™

Microsoft® Visual Basic® 2010: RELOADED, Fourth Edition
Diane Zak

Executive Editor: Marie Lee
Acquisitions Editor: Amy Jollymore
Freelance Product Manager: Tricia Coia
Senior Content Project Manager: Jill Braiewa
Editorial Assistant: Jacqueline Lacaire
Art Director: Faith Brosnan
Quality Assurance: Green Pen QA
Text Designer: Shawn Girsberger
Cover Designer: Cabbage Design Company
Print Buyer: Julio Esperas
Proofreader: Suzanne Huizenga
Indexer: Rich Carlson
Compositor: Integra Software Services

Library of Congress Control Number: 2010930342

ISBN-13: 978-1-111-22179-9

ISBN-10: 1-111-22179-0

Course Technology
20 Channel Center Street
Boston, MA 02210
USA

Printed in the United States of America
1 2 3 4 5 6 7 16 15 14 13 12 11 10

Brief Contents

The following appendix is located in the VbReloaded2010\AppE folder:

Contents

Preface

Microsoft Visual Basic 2010: RELOADED, Fourth Edition uses Visual Basic 2010, an object-oriented language, to teach programming concepts. This book is designed for a beginning programming course; however, it assumes students are familiar with basic Windows skills and file management.

Organization and Coverage

Microsoft Visual Basic 2010: RELOADED, Fourth Edition contains 14 chapters and four appendices (A through D). An additional appendix on locating syntax and logic errors is contained in the VbReloaded2010\AppE folder, which is included in the data files that accompany this book. In the chapters, students with no previous programming experience learn how to plan and create their own interactive Windows applications. By the end of the book, students will have learned how to use TOE charts, pseudocode, and flowcharts to plan an application. They also will learn how to work with objects and write Visual Basic statements such as If...Then...Else, Select Case, Do...Loop, For...Next, and For Each...Next. Students also will learn how to manipulate variables, constants, strings, sequential access files, structures, and arrays. In Chapter 12, they will learn how to connect an application to a Microsoft Access database, and then use Language Integrated Query (LINQ) to query the database. Chapter 13 shows students how to create simple Web applications, and Chapter 14 shows them how to create their own classes and objects.

Approach

Like the previous editions, *Microsoft Visual Basic 2010: RELOADED, Fourth Edition* is distinguished from other textbooks because of its unique approach, which motivates students by demonstrating why they need to learn the concepts and skills presented. Each chapter begins with an introduction to one or more programming concepts. The concepts are illustrated with code examples and sample programs. The sample programs are provided to students to allow them to observe how the current concept can be utilized before they are introduced to the next concept. Following the concept portion in each chapter are two Programming Tutorials. Each Programming Tutorial guides students through the process of creating an application using the concepts covered in the chapter. A Programming Example follows the Programming Tutorials in each chapter. The Programming Example contains a completed application that demonstrates the chapter concepts. Following the Programming Example are the Summary, Key Terms, Review Questions, Exercises, and Case Projects sections.

Features

Microsoft Visual Basic 2010: RELOADED, Fourth Edition is an exceptional textbook because it also includes the following features:

READ THIS BEFORE YOU BEGIN This section is consistent with Course Technology's unequaled commitment to helping instructors introduce technology into the classroom. Technical considerations and assumptions about hardware, software, and default settings are listed in one place to help instructors save time and eliminate unnecessary aggravation.

HOW TO BOXES The How To boxes in each chapter summarize important concepts and provide a quick reference for students. The How To boxes that introduce new statements, functions, or methods contain the syntax and examples of using the syntax. Many of the How To boxes contain the steps for performing common tasks.

TIPS These notes provide additional information about the current concept. Examples include alternative ways of writing statements or performing tasks, as well as warnings about common mistakes made when using a particular command and reminders of related concepts learned in previous chapters.

PROGRAMMING EXAMPLE A Programming Example follows the Programming Tutorials in each chapter. The Programming Example shows the TOE chart and pseudocode used to plan the program. It also shows the user interface and Visual Basic code.

SUMMARY Each chapter contains a Summary section that recaps the concepts covered in the chapter.

KEY TERMS Following the Summary section in each chapter is a listing of the key terms introduced throughout the chapter, along with their definitions.

REVIEW QUESTIONS Each chapter contains Review Questions designed to test a student's understanding of the chapter's concepts.

CASE PROJECTS At the end of each chapter are four Case Projects, one of which is a Think Tank Case Project. The Case Projects give the student the opportunity to independently synthesize and evaluate information, examine potential solutions, and make recommendations. Most of the Case Projects include a sample interface.

THINK TANK CASE PROJECTS The last Case Project in each chapter is designated by the "Think Tank" icon. The Think Tank Case Projects are more challenging than the other Case Projects.

New to This Edition!

DESIGNED FOR THE DIFFERENT LEARNING STYLES The three most common learning styles are visual, auditory, and kinesthetic. This book contains videos for visual and auditory learners, and Try It! files for kinesthetic learners.

VIDEOS Each chapter has accompanying videos that demonstrate and explain the concepts covered in the chapter. The videos can be found on the Course Technology Web site at *www.cengage.com/coursetechnology*.

TRY IT! FILES Each chapter has accompanying Try It! files that allow the student to practice a concept before moving on to the next concept.

MINI-QUIZZES Mini-Quizzes are strategically placed to test students' knowledge at various points in the chapter. Answers to the quiz questions are provided in Appendix A, allowing students to determine whether they have mastered the material covered thus far before continuing with the chapter.

PROGRAMMING TUTORIALS In this edition of the book, each chapter contains two Programming Tutorials (rather than one, as in the previous edition). The Programming Tutorials provide step-by-step instructions for using the chapter's concepts in an application. In most cases, the first tutorial in each chapter is easier than the second because it contains more detailed steps. Typically, one of the tutorial applications is a simple game, while the other is a business application. Game applications are used because research shows that the fun and exciting nature of games helps motivate students to learn.

STRING MANIPULATION String manipulation is now in its own chapter (Chapter 10) along with menus.

WEB APPLICATIONS Web applications are now covered in Chapter 13 rather than in an online appendix.

SEQUENTIAL ACCESS FILES Sequential access files, which are covered in Chapter 11, are now manipulated using StreamReader and StreamWriter objects. The Split function is also covered in the chapter.

CHAPTER 2 Chapter 2 now includes the Font and Color dialog boxes and the PrintForm control. It also shows students how an application can play audio files during run time.

CHECK BOXES Check boxes are now covered in Chapter 4.

IMAGE LIST CONTROL The ImageList control is now covered in Chapter 7.

PENCIL AND PAPER EXERCISES Following the Review Questions in each chapter are Pencil and Paper Exercises. The Exercises are designated as Modify This, Introductory, Intermediate, Advanced, Discovery, and Swat the Bugs. The Advanced and Discovery Exercises provide practice in applying cumulative programming knowledge. They also allow students to explore alternative solutions to programming tasks. The Swat the Bugs Exercises provide an opportunity for students to detect and correct errors in one or more lines of code.

COMPUTER EXERCISES The Computer Exercises, which follow the Pencil and Paper Exercises in each chapter, provide students with additional practice of the skills and concepts they learned in the chapter. The Exercises are designated as Modify This, Introductory, Intermediate, Advanced, Discovery, and Swat the Bugs. The Advanced and Discovery Exercises provide practice in applying cumulative programming knowledge. They also allow students to explore alternative solutions to programming tasks. The Swat the Bugs Exercises provide an opportunity for students to detect and correct errors in an existing application.

NEW EXAMPLES, SAMPLE PROGRAMS, TUTORIALS, AND EXERCISES Each chapter has been updated with new examples, sample programs, tutorials, and exercises.

Instructor Resources and Supplements

All of the resources available with this book are provided to the instructor on a single CD-ROM. Many also can be found on the Course Technology Web site (*www.cengage.com/coursetechnology*).

ELECTRONIC INSTRUCTOR'S MANUAL The Instructor's Manual that accompanies this textbook includes additional instructional material to assist in class preparation, including items such as Sample Syllabi, Chapter Outlines, Technical Notes, Lecture Notes, Quick Quizzes, Teaching Tips, Discussion Topics, and Additional Case Projects.

EXAMVIEW® This textbook is accompanied by ExamView, a powerful testing software package that allows instructors to create and administer printed, computer (LAN-based), and Internet exams. ExamView includes hundreds of questions that correspond to the topics covered in this text, enabling students to generate detailed study guides that include page references for further review. The computer-based and Internet testing components allow students to take exams at their computers, and also save the instructor time by grading each exam automatically.

MICROSOFT® POWERPOINT® PRESENTATIONS This book offers Microsoft PowerPoint slides for each chapter. These are included as a teaching aid for classroom presentation, to make available to students on the network for chapter review, or to be printed for classroom distribution. Instructors can add their own slides for additional topics they introduce to the class.

DATA FILES Data files are necessary for completing many of the Programming Tutorials and Computer Exercises in this book. They also are associated with the Try It! elements. The data files are provided on the Instructor Resources CD-ROM and may also be found on the Course Technology Web site at *www.cengage.com/coursetechnology*.

SOLUTION FILES Solutions to the Review Questions, Pencil and Paper Exercises, Computer Exercises, and Case Projects, as well as to the sample programs that appear in the figures throughout the book, are provided on the Instructor Resources CD-ROM. They also may be found on the Course Technology Web site at *www.cengage.com/coursetechnology.* The solutions are password protected.

DISTANCE LEARNING Course Technology offers online WebCT, Blackboard, and Angel courses for this text to provide the most complete and dynamic learning experience possible. When you add online content to one of your courses, you're adding a lot: automated tests, topic reviews, quick quizzes, and additional case projects with solutions. For more information on how to bring distance learning to your course, contact your local Course Technology sales representative.

Acknowledgments

Writing a book is a team effort rather than an individual one. I would like to take this opportunity to thank my team, especially Sreejith Govindan (Full Service Project Manager), Jill Braiewa (Senior Content Project Manager), Tricia Coia (Freelance Product Manager), Suzanne Huizenga (Proofreader), and Nicole Ashton (Quality Assurance). Thank you for your support, enthusiasm, patience, and hard work. Last, but certainly not least, I want to thank the following reviewers for their invaluable ideas and comments: Judy Scholl, Austin Community College; Wendy Ceccucci, Quinnipiac University; and Hyder Ali, California State University—Northridge.

Diane Zak

Read This Before You Begin

Technical Information

Data Files

You will need data files to complete some of the tutorials and exercises in this book. You also will need data files for the solutions mentioned in the Try It! elements. Your instructor may provide the data files to you. You may obtain the files electronically on the Course Technology Web site (*www.cengage.com/coursetechnology*).

Each chapter in this book has its own set of data files, which are stored in a separate folder within the VbReloaded2010 folder. The files for Chapter 1 are stored in the VbReloaded2010\Chap01 folder. Similarly, the files for Chapter 2 are stored in the VbReloaded2010\Chap02 folder. Throughout this book, you will be instructed to open files from or save files to these folders.

You can use a computer in your school lab or your own computer to complete the computer activities in this book.

Using Your Own Computer

To use your own computer to complete the computer activities in this book, you will need the following:

- A Pentium® 4 processor, 1.6 GHz or higher, personal computer running Microsoft Windows. This book was written and Quality Assurance tested using Microsoft Windows 7.
- Either Microsoft Visual Studio 2010 or the Express Edition of Microsoft Visual Basic 2010 installed on your computer. This book was written using Microsoft Visual Studio 2010 Professional Edition, and Quality Assurance tested using the Express Edition of Microsoft Visual Basic 2010. At the time of this writing, you can download a free copy of Visual Basic 2010 Express Edition at *www.microsoft.com/express/downloads*. If necessary, use the following information when installing the Professional or Express Editions of the software:

    1. If the Choose Default Environment Settings dialog box appears when you start Visual Studio, select the Visual Basic Development Settings option.

2. Start either Visual Studio or the Express Edition of Visual Basic. Click Tools on the menu bar and then click Options to open the Options dialog box. If necessary, deselect the Show all settings check box, which appears in the lower-left corner of the dialog box. Click the Projects and Solutions node. Use the information shown in Figure 1-6 in Chapter 1 to select and deselect the appropriate check boxes, and then close the dialog box.
3. If you are using the Express Edition of Visual Basic 2010, click Tools on the menu bar, point to Settings, and then select Expert Settings.

- If you are using the Express Edition of Visual Basic 2010, you won't be able to complete Chapter 13 unless Visual Web Developer 2010 Express is installed on your computer. At the time of this writing, you can download a free copy of Visual Web Developer 2010 Express from *http://www.microsoft.com/express/Downloads/#2010-Visual-Web-Developer*. Figure 13-5 in Chapter 13 contains the instructions for starting and configuring Visual Web Developer 2010 Express. Chapter 13 was written using Microsoft Visual Studio 2010 Professional Edition, and Quality Assurance tested using the Express Edition of Microsoft Visual Web Developer 2010.

Figures

The figures in this book reflect how your screen will look if you are using Microsoft Visual Studio 2010 Professional Edition and a Microsoft Windows 7 system. Your screen may appear slightly different in some instances if you are using another version of Microsoft Visual Studio, Microsoft Visual Basic, or Microsoft Windows.

Visit Our Web Site

Additional materials designed for this textbook might be available through the Course Technology Web site, *www.cengage.com/coursetechnology*. Search this site for more details.

To the Instructor

To complete the computer activities in this book, your students must use a set of data files. The files are included on the Instructor's Resource CD. They also may be obtained electronically through the Course Technology Web site at *www.cengage.com/coursetechnology*.

The material in this book was written using Microsoft Visual Studio 2010 Professional Edition and Quality Assurance tested using the Express Edition of Microsoft Visual Basic 2010 and Microsoft Visual Web Developer 2010 on a Microsoft Windows 7 operating system.

Course Technology Data Files

You are granted a license to copy the data files to any computer or computer network used by individuals who have purchased this book.

OVERVIEW

An Introduction to Programming

After studying this Overview, you should be able to:

- Define the terminology used in programming
- Explain the tasks performed by a programmer
- Describe the qualities of a good programmer
- Understand the employment opportunities for programmers and software engineers
- Understand how to use the chapters effectively
- Run a Visual Basic 2010 application

Programming a Computer

In essence, the word **programming** means *giving a mechanism the directions to accomplish a task*. If you are like most people, you've already programmed several mechanisms. For example, at one time or another, you probably programmed your digital video recorder (DVR) in order to schedule a timed recording of a movie. You also may have programmed the speed dial feature on your cell phone. Or you may have programmed your coffee maker to begin the brewing process before you wake up in the morning. Like your DVR, cell phone, and coffee maker, a computer also is a mechanism that can be programmed. The directions given to a computer are called **computer programs** or, more simply, **programs**. The people who write programs are called **programmers**. Programmers use a variety of special languages, called **programming languages**, to communicate with the computer. Some popular programming languages are Visual Basic, C#, C++, and Java. In this book, you will use the Visual Basic programming language.

The Programmer's Job

When a company has a problem that requires a computer solution, typically it is a programmer that comes to the rescue. The programmer might be an employee of the company; or he or she might be a freelance programmer, which is a programmer who works on temporary contracts rather than for a long-term employer. First the programmer meets with the user, which is the person (or persons) responsible for describing the problem. In many cases, this person also will eventually use the solution. Depending on the complexity of the problem, multiple programmers may be involved, and they may need to meet with the user several times. The purpose of the initial meetings is to determine the exact problem and to agree on the desired solution. After the programmer and user agree on the solution, the programmer begins converting the solution into a computer program. During the conversion phase, the programmer meets periodically with the user to determine whether the program fulfills the user's needs and to refine any details of the solution. When the user is satisfied that the program does what he or she wants it to do, the programmer rigorously tests the program with sample data before releasing it to the user. In many cases, the programmer also provides the user with a manual that explains how to use the program. As this process indicates, the creation of a good computer solution to a problem—in other words, the creation of a good program—requires a great deal of interaction between the programmer and the user.

Programming teams often contain subject matter experts, who may or may not be programmers. For example, an accountant might be part of a team working on a program that requires accounting expertise.

Do I Have What It Takes to Be a Programmer?

According to the 2008–09 Edition of the Occupational Outlook Handbook (OOH), published by the U.S. Department of Labor's Bureau of Labor Statistics, "When hiring programmers, employers look for people with the necessary programming skills who can think logically and pay close attention to detail. Programming calls for patience, persistence, and the ability to work on exacting analytical work, especially under pressure. Ingenuity and creativity also are particularly important when programmers design solutions and test their work for potential failures.... Because programmers are expected to work in teams and interact directly with users, employers want programmers who are able to communicate with nontechnical personnel. Business skills are also important, especially for those wishing to advance to managerial positions." If this description sounds like you, then you probably have what it takes to be a programmer. But if it doesn't sound like you, it's still worth your time to understand the programming process, especially if you are planning a career in business. Knowing even a little bit about the programming process will allow you, the manager of a department, to better communicate your department's needs to a programmer. It also will give you the confidence to question the programmer when he or she claims that the program modification you requested can't be made. In addition, it will help you determine whether the $15,000 quote you received from a freelance programmer seems reasonable. Lastly, understanding the process a computer programmer follows when solving a problem can help you solve problems that don't require a computer solution.

Employment Opportunities

But if, after reading this book, you are excited about the idea of working as a computer programmer, here is some information on employment opportunities. When searching for a job in computer programming, you will encounter ads for "computer programmers" as well as for "computer software engineers." Although job titles and descriptions vary, computer software engineers typically are responsible for designing an appropriate solution to a user's problem, while computer programmers are responsible for translating the solution into a language that the computer can understand. The process of translating the solution is called **coding**. Keep in mind that, depending on the employer and the size and complexity of the user's problem, the design and coding tasks may be performed by the same employee, no matter what his or her job title is. In other words, it's not unusual for a software engineer to code her solution, just as it's not unusual for a programmer to have designed the solution he is coding. Typically, computer software engineers are expected to have at least a bachelor's degree in computer engineering or computer science, along with practical work experience. Computer programmers usually need at least an associate's degree in computer science, mathematics, or information systems, as well as proficiency in one or more programming languages. Computer programmers and software engineers are employed in almost every industry, such as telecommunications companies, software publishers, financial institutions, insurance carriers, educational institutions, and government agencies. According to the May 2008 Occupational Employment Statistics, programmers held about 394,230 jobs and had a mean annual wage of $73,470. Software engineers, on the other hand, held about 494,160 jobs with a mean annual wage of $87,900. The Bureau of Labor Statistics predicts that employment of programmers will decline slowly, decreasing by 4% from 2006 to 2016. However, the employment of computer software engineers is projected to increase by 38% over the same period. There is a great deal of competition for programming and software engineering jobs, so jobseekers will need to keep up to date with the latest programming languages and technologies. More information about computer programmers and computer software engineers can be found on the Bureau of Labor Statistics Web site at *www.bls.gov*.

Using the Chapters Effectively

The chapters in this book teach you how to write programs using the Visual Basic programming language. Each chapter focuses on programming concepts, which are first introduced using simple examples and then utilized in larger applications at the end of the chapter. Two Programming Tutorials follow the concepts section in each chapter. Each Programming Tutorial guides you through the process of creating an application using the concepts covered in the chapter. Many of the applications created in the Programming Tutorials are simple games, while others are business applications. A Programming Example follows the Programming Tutorials in each chapter. The Programming Example contains a completed application that demonstrates the chapter concepts. You should be sure to complete one or more of the Programming Tutorials and Programming Example after reading the concepts section, because doing so will help you complete the Computer Exercises and Case Projects at the end of the chapter. In addition, some of the Computer Exercises require you to make changes to the applications created in the Programming Tutorials and Programming Example.

To run a sample application that you will create in this book:

The Windows logo key looks like this: .

1. Press and hold down the **Windows logo** key on your keyboard as you tap the letter **r**, and then release the logo key. The Run dialog box opens.
2. Click the **Browse** button to open the Browse dialog box. Locate and then open the VbReloaded2010\Overview folder on your computer's hard disk or on the device designated by your instructor. Click **TicTacToe** (**TicTacToe.exe**) in the list of filenames. (Depending on how Windows is set up on your computer, you may see the .exe extension on the filename.) Click the **Open** button to close the Browse dialog box.
3. Click the **OK** button in the Run dialog box. After a few moments, the Tic-Tac-Toe application's user interface appears on the screen. Click the **middle square**. See Figure O-1.

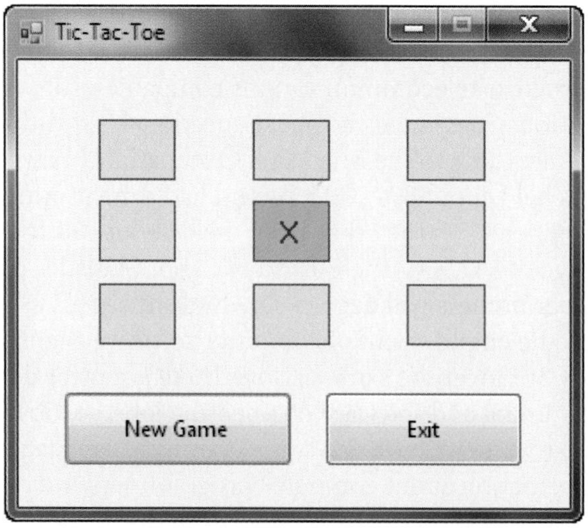

Figure O-1 Tic-Tac-Toe application

4. Click the **first square in the top row**, then click the **middle square in the top row**, and then click the **last square in the top row**.
5. Finally, click the **middle square in the bottom row**. The "Game over! X wins." message appears in a message box. Click the **OK** button to close the message box. See Figure O-2.

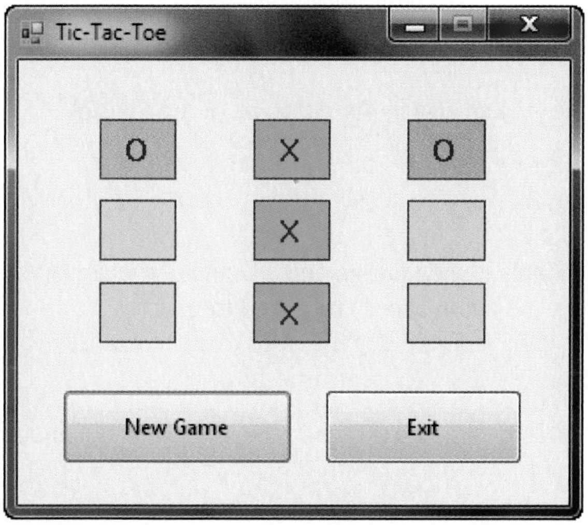

Figure O-2 Os and Xs in the interface

6. If you want to play the game again, click the **New Game** button. Otherwise, click the **Exit** button.

Throughout each chapter, you will find How To boxes. Some How To boxes, like the one in Figure O-3, contain steps that show you how to accomplish a task, such as how to start Visual Studio 2010 or Visual Basic 2010 Express Edition. You are not expected to follow the steps in these How To boxes while you are reading the chapter. Rather, these How To boxes are intended to provide a quick reference that you can use when completing the end-of-chapter Programming Tutorials, Programming Example, Computer Exercises, and Case Projects. Feel free to skim these How To boxes and use them only if and when you need to do so. The same holds true for How To boxes containing bulleted items.

HOW TO Start Visual Studio 2010 or Visual Basic 2010 Express Edition

1. Click the Start button on the Windows 7 taskbar, and then point to All Programs.
2. *If you are using Visual Studio 2010,* click Microsoft Visual Studio 2010 on the Start menu, and then click Microsoft Visual Studio 2010. If the Choose Default Environment Settings dialog box appears, click Visual Basic Development Settings, and then click Start Visual Studio.

   If you are using Visual Basic 2010 Express Edition, click Microsoft Visual Basic 2010 Express on the Start menu.

Figure O-3 How to start Visual Studio 2010 or Visual Basic 2010 Express Edition

Other How To boxes, like the one in Figure O-4, contain information pertaining to a Visual Basic instruction, such as the instruction's syntax and examples of using the instruction. You should study the information in these How To boxes while you are reading the chapter.

HOW TO Declare a Variable

Syntax
{**Dim** | **Private** | **Static**} *variableName* **As** *dataType* [= *initialValue*]

Example 1
```
Dim hours As Integer
Dim payRate As Double
```
declares an Integer variable named `hours` and a Double variable named `payRate`; the variables are automatically initialized to 0

Example 2
```
Dim discount As Decimal
```
declares a Decimal variable named `discount`; the variable is automatically initialized to 0

Example 3
```
Dim isDataOk As Boolean = True
```
declares a Boolean variable named `isDataOk` and initializes it using the keyword `True`

Example 4
```
Dim message As String = "Good Morning"
```
declares a String variable named `message` and initializes it using the string "Good Morning"

Figure O-4 How to declare a variable

The three most common learning styles are visual, auditory, and kinesthetic. Briefly, visual learners learn by watching, auditory learners learn by listening, and kinesthetic learners learn by doing. This book contains special elements designed specifically for each of the different learning styles. For example, each chapter contains videos for visual and auditory learners. The videos demonstrate and explain the concepts covered in the chapter. In addition to the Programming Tutorials, each chapter contains Try It! files for kinesthetic learners. The Try It! files allow the learner to practice with a concept before moving on to the next concept.

Summary

- Programs are the step-by-step instructions that tell a computer how to perform a task.
- Programmers use various programming languages to communicate with the computer.

- In most cases, a programmer meets with the user several times to determine the exact problem to be solved and to agree on a solution. He or she also gets together periodically with the user to verify that the solution meets the user's needs and to refine any details.
- Programmers rigorously test a program with sample data before releasing the program to the user.
- All business people should know at least a little about the programming process.
- It's not unusual for the same person to perform the duties of both a software engineer and a programmer.

Key Terms

Coding—the process of translating a solution into a language that the computer can understand

Computer programs—the directions given to computers; also called programs

Programmers—the people who write computer programs

Programming—the process of giving a mechanism the directions to accomplish a task

Programming languages—languages used to communicate with a computer

Programs—the directions given to computers; also called computer programs

CHAPTER 1

An Introduction to Visual Basic 2010

After studying Chapter 1, you should be able to:

- Create a Visual Basic 2010 Windows application
- Manage the windows in the integrated development environment (IDE)
- Set the properties of an object
- Add a control to a form
- Use the Label, Button, and PictureBox tools
- Use the options on the Format menu
- Enter code in the Code Editor window
- Save a solution
- Start and end an application
- Write an assignment statement
- Print an application's code and interface
- Close and open an existing solution
- Find and correct a syntax error

Visual Basic 2010

In this book, you will learn how to create programs using the Visual Basic programming language. At the time of this writing, the most recent version of the language is called Visual Basic 2010 (scheduled for release in April 2010). Visual Basic 2010 is an **object-oriented programming language**, which is a language that allows the programmer to use objects to accomplish a program's goal. An **object** is anything that can be seen, touched, or used. In other words, an object is nearly any *thing*. The objects used in an object-oriented program can take on many different forms. Programs written for the Windows environment typically use objects such as check boxes, list boxes, and buttons. A payroll program, on the other hand, might utilize objects found in the real world, such as a time card object, an employee object, and a check object. Every object used in an object-oriented program is created from a **class**, which is a pattern that the computer uses to create the object. The class contains the instructions that tell the computer how the object should look and behave. An object created from a class is called an **instance** of the class and is said to be **instantiated** from the class. An analogy involving a cookie cutter and cookies is often used to describe a class and its objects: the class is the cookie cutter, and the objects instantiated from the class are the cookies. You will learn more about classes and objects throughout this book.

Visual Basic 2010 is available either as a stand-alone product, called Visual Basic 2010 Express Edition, or as part of Visual Studio 2010. Both products include an **integrated development environment (IDE)**, which is an environment that contains all of the tools and features you need to create, run, and test your programs. However, unlike the Visual Basic 2010 Express Edition, which contains only the Visual Basic language, Visual Studio 2010 contains four different languages: Visual Basic, Visual C++, Visual C#, and Visual F#.

You can download a free copy of Visual Basic 2010 Express Edition at *www.microsoft.com/express/downloads*.

You can use Visual Basic to create programs, called applications, for the Windows environment or for the Web. A Windows application has a Windows user interface and runs on a personal computer. A **user interface** is what the user sees and interacts with while an application is running. Examples of Windows applications include graphics programs, data-entry systems, and games. A Web application, on the other hand, has a Web user interface and runs on a server. You access a Web application using your computer's browser. Examples of Web applications include e-commerce applications available on the Internet, and employee handbook applications accessible on a company's intranet. You also can use Visual Basic to create applications for mobile devices, such as pocket PCs, cell phones, and PDAs (personal digital assistants). In this chapter, you will learn how to create Windows applications. Web and smart device applications are covered later in this book.

You can view the Ch01Video1 file and then skim the sections from *Creating a Visual Basic Windows Application* to *The Toolbox Window*. However, be sure to pay particular attention to the boldface keywords in those sections.

Creating a Visual Basic Windows Application

Windows applications created in Visual Studio 2010 are composed of solutions, projects, and files. A **solution** is a container that stores the projects and files for an entire application. A **project** also is a container, but it stores files associated with that particular project. Although the idea of solutions, projects, and files may sound confusing, the concept of placing things in containers is nothing new to you. Think of a solution as being similar to a drawer in

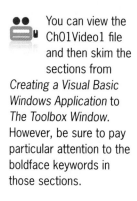

None of the solutions created in this book will contain more than one project.

a filing cabinet. A project then is similar to a file folder that you store in the drawer, and a file is similar to a document that you store in the file folder. You can place many file folders in a filing cabinet drawer, just as you can place many projects in a solution. You also can store many documents in a file folder, similar to the way you can store many files in a project. Figure 1-1 illustrates this analogy.

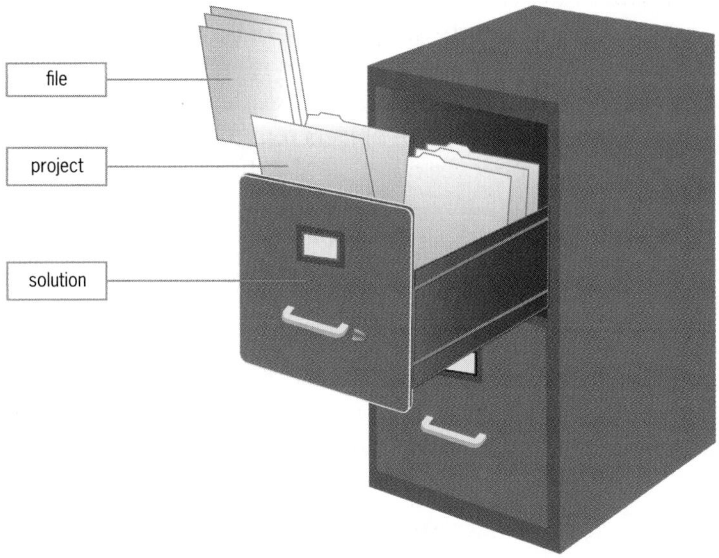

Figure 1-1 Illustration of a solution, project, and file

Before you can create a Windows application in Visual Basic, you first must start either Visual Studio or the Express Edition of Visual Basic. The steps for starting both products are listed in the How To box shown in Figure 1-2. As mentioned in the Overview, you are not expected to follow the steps listed in a How To box right now. Rather, the steps are intended to be used as a quick reference when you are completing the Programming Tutorials, Programming Example, Exercises, and Case Projects located at the end of each chapter.

HOW TO Start Visual Studio 2010 or Visual Basic 2010 Express Edition

1. Click the Start button on the Windows 7 taskbar, and then point to All Programs.
2. *If you are using Visual Studio 2010,* click Microsoft Visual Studio 2010 on the All Programs menu, and then click Microsoft Visual Studio 2010. If the Choose Default Environment Settings dialog box appears, click Visual Basic Development Settings, and then click Start Visual Studio.

   If you are using Visual Basic 2010 Express Edition, click Microsoft Visual Basic 2010 Express on the All Programs menu.

Figure 1-2 How to start Visual Studio 2010 or Visual Basic 2010 Express Edition

When you start the Professional Edition of Visual Studio 2010, your screen will appear similar to Figure 1-3. (If you are using a different edition of Visual Studio, your startup screen might look slightly different than the one shown in Figure 1-3.) When you start the Express Edition of Visual Basic 2010, on the other hand, your screen will appear similar to Figure 1-4. In either case, your Recent Projects list might include the names of projects or solutions with which you have recently worked. As Figures 1-3 and 1-4 indicate, the IDE (integrated development environment) contains four windows: Start Page, Toolbox, Solution Explorer, and Team Explorer. (The Toolbox window in both figures is auto-hidden. You will learn how to auto-hide a window in the *Managing the Windows in the IDE* section of this chapter.)

Important note: You can reset the window layout by clicking Window on the menu bar, then clicking Reset Window Layout, and then clicking the Yes button. To select a different window layout, click Tools on the menu bar, click Import and Export Settings, select the Reset all settings radio button, and then click the Next button. Select the appropriate radio button in the Save Current Settings pane, click the Next button, click the preferred settings collection (such as Visual Basic Development Settings), and then click the Finish button.

Your startup screen may not contain the Team Explorer window.

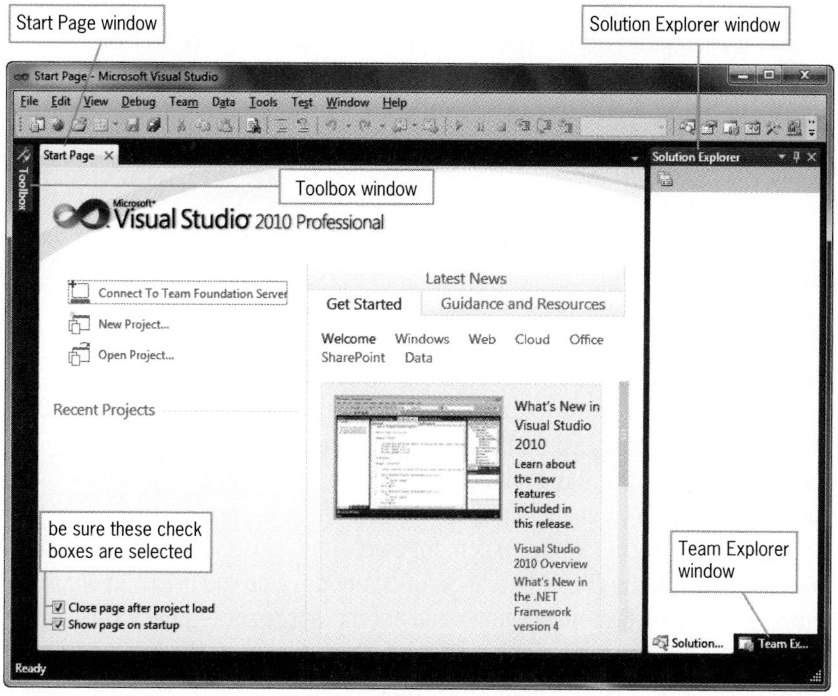

Figure 1-3 Microsoft Visual Studio 2010 Professional startup screen

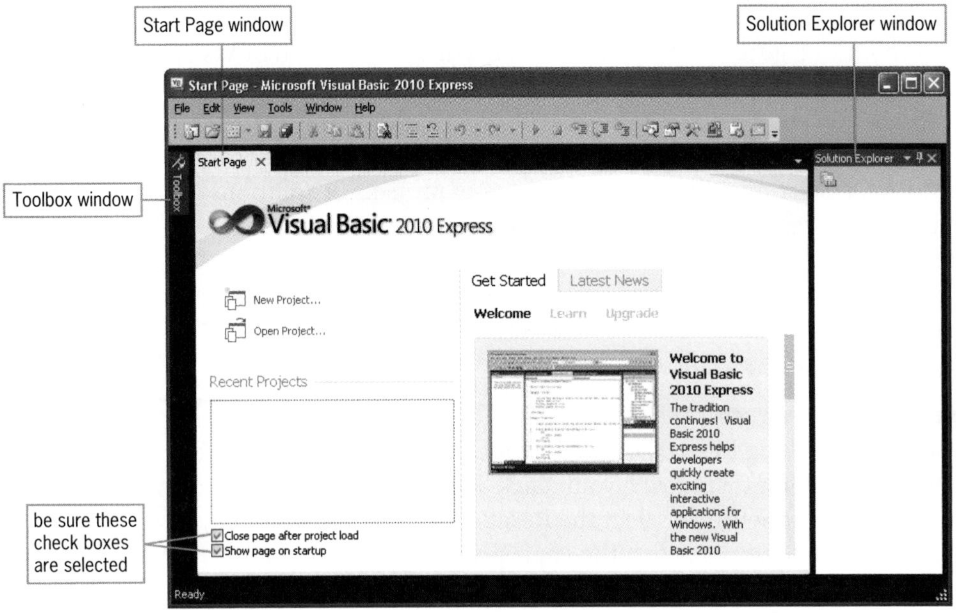

Figure 1-4 Microsoft Visual Basic 2010 Express startup screen

Figure 1-5 shows the steps you follow to create a Visual Basic 2010 Windows application. Here again, you don't need to perform the steps right now. Figure 1-6 shows an example of the Options dialog box mentioned in the steps. Figures 1-7 and 1-8 show an example of a completed New Project dialog box in Visual Studio 2010 and Visual Basic 2010 Express Edition, respectively.

HOW TO Create a Visual Basic 2010 Windows Application

1. If necessary, start either Visual Studio 2010 or Visual Basic 2010 Express Edition.
2. This step is necessary so that your screen agrees with the figures and tutorial instructions in this book. Click Tools on the menu bar, and then click Options to open the Options dialog box. If necessary, deselect the Show all settings check box, which appears in the lower-left corner of the dialog box. Click the Projects and Solutions node. Use the information shown in Figure 1-6 to select and deselect the appropriate check boxes. (Your dialog box will look slightly different if you are using the Express Edition.) When you are finished, click the OK button to close the Options dialog box.
3. Click File on the menu bar, and then click New Project to open the New Project dialog box.
4. If necessary, click Visual Basic in the Installed Templates list, and then (if necessary) click Windows Forms Application in the middle column of the dialog box.

Figure 1-5 How to create a Visual Basic 2010 Windows application *(continues)*

(continued)

5. Enter an appropriate name and location in the Name and Location boxes, respectively. (You can use the Browse button to enter the location.)
6. If necessary, select the Create directory for solution check box.
7. Enter an appropriate name in the Solution name box. Examples of completed New Project dialog boxes are shown in Figures 1-7 (Visual Studio 2010) and 1-8 (Visual Basic 2010 Express Edition).
8. Click the OK button.

Figure 1-5 How to create a Visual Basic 2010 Windows application

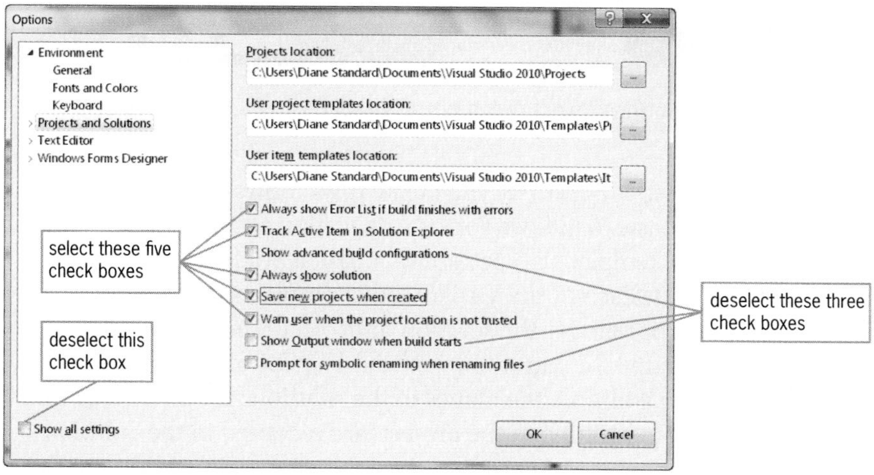

Figure 1-6 Options dialog box

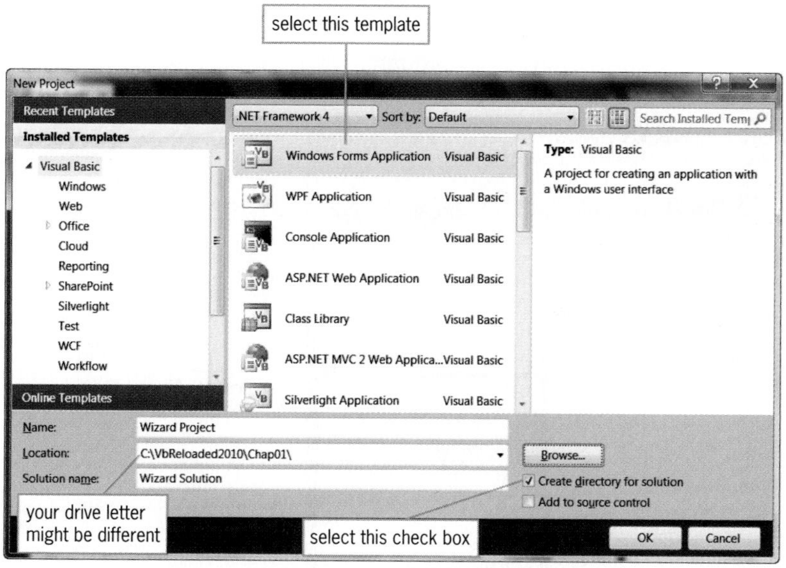

Figure 1-7 Completed New Project dialog box in Visual Studio 2010

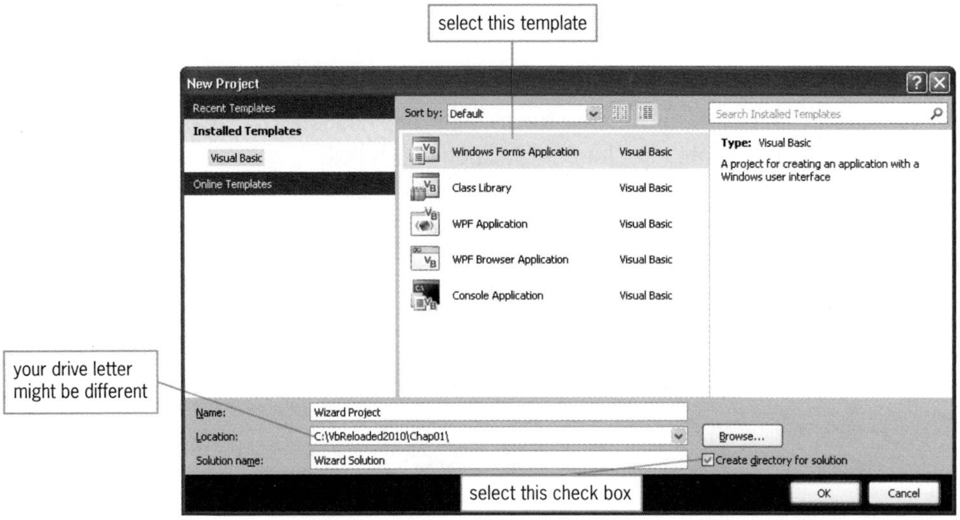

Figure 1-8 Completed New Project dialog box in Visual Basic 2010 Express Edition

As indicated in Figures 1-7 and 1-8, you create a Windows application by selecting the Visual Basic Windows Forms Application template in the New Project dialog box. A template is a pattern that Visual Studio uses to create solutions and projects. Each of the Visual Studio templates includes a set of folders and files appropriate for the solution or project. The folders and files are automatically created for you when you click the OK button in the New Project dialog box. In addition, the names of the solution and project, as well as other information pertaining to the project, are recorded in the Solution Explorer window, as shown in Figure 1-9. Also notice that, in addition to the windows mentioned earlier, three other windows appear in the IDE: Windows Form Designer, Properties, and Data Sources.

Your screen may not contain the Team Explorer or Data Sources windows.

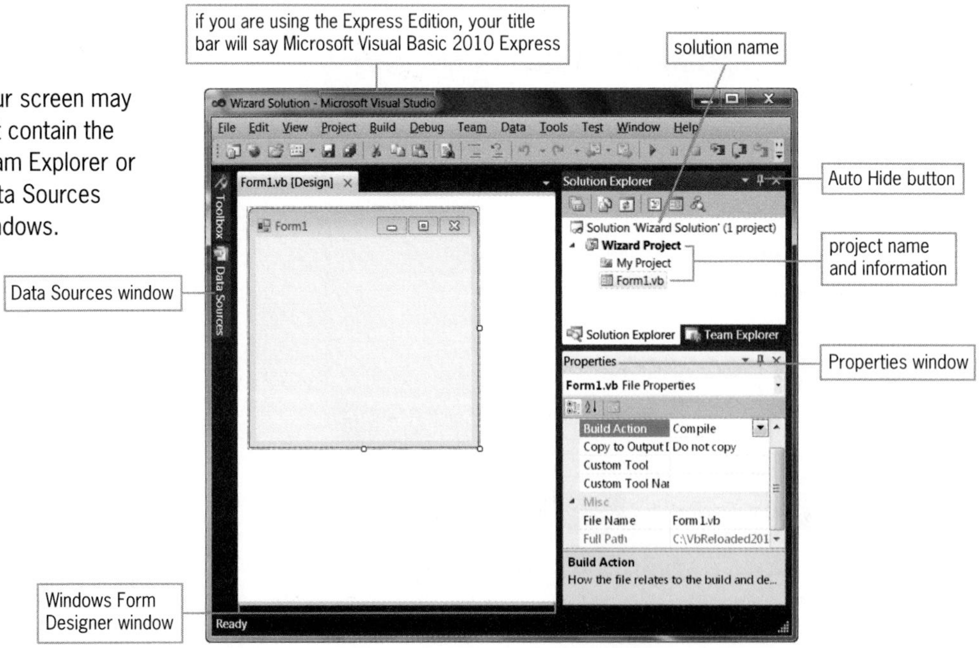

Figure 1-9 Solution and Visual Basic project

Managing the Windows in the IDE

In most cases, you will find it easier to work in the IDE if you either close or auto-hide the windows you are not currently using. The easiest way to close an open window is to click the Close button on the window's title bar. In most cases, the View menu provides an appropriate option for opening a closed window. Rather than closing a window, you also can auto-hide it. You auto-hide a window using the Auto Hide button (shown earlier in Figure 1-9) on the window's title bar. The Auto Hide button is a toggle button: clicking it once activates it, and clicking it again deactivates it. The Toolbox window shown earlier in Figure 1-9 is an example of an auto-hidden window. Figure 1-10 lists various ways of managing the windows in the IDE. As mentioned in the Overview, you don't need to read every bulleted item in a How To box right now. But you should browse the How To box to get familiar with its contents.

HOW TO Manage the Windows in the IDE

- To close an open window, click the Close button on its title bar.
- To open a window, use an option on the View menu.
- To auto-hide a window, click the Auto Hide (vertical pushpin) button on its title bar. When you do this, the window is minimized and appears as a tab on the edge of the IDE. (The Toolbox window shown earlier in Figure 1-9 is an example of an auto-hidden window.)
- To temporarily display an auto-hidden window, place your mouse pointer on the window's tab.
- To permanently display an auto-hidden window, click the Auto Hide (horizontal pushpin) button on its title bar.
- To reset the window layout, click Window on the menu bar, then click Reset Window Layout, and then click the Yes button.
- To select a different window layout, click Tools on the menu bar, click Import and Export Settings, select the Reset all settings radio button, and then click the Next button. Select the appropriate radio button in the Save Current Settings pane, click the Next button, click the preferred settings collection (such as Visual Basic Development Settings), and then click the Finish button.

Figure 1-10 How to manage the windows in the IDE

In the next several sections, you will take a closer look at the Windows Form Designer, Solution Explorer, Properties, and Toolbox windows.

The Windows Form Designer Window

Figure 1-11 shows the **Windows Form Designer window**, where you create (or design) the graphical user interface, referred to as a **GUI**, for your project. Recall that a user interface is what the user sees and interacts with while an application is running. Only a Windows Form object appears in the designer window shown in Figure 1-11. A **Windows Form object**, or **form**, is the foundation for the user interface in a Windows application. You create the user interface by adding other objects, such as buttons and text boxes, to the form. Notice that a title bar appears at the top of the form. The title bar contains a default caption—in this case, Form1—as well as Minimize, Maximize, and Close buttons. At the top of the designer window is a tab labeled Form1.vb [Design]. [Design] identifies the window as the designer window. Form1.vb is the name of the file (on your computer's hard disk or on the device designated by your instructor or technical support person) that contains the Visual Basic instructions associated with the form.

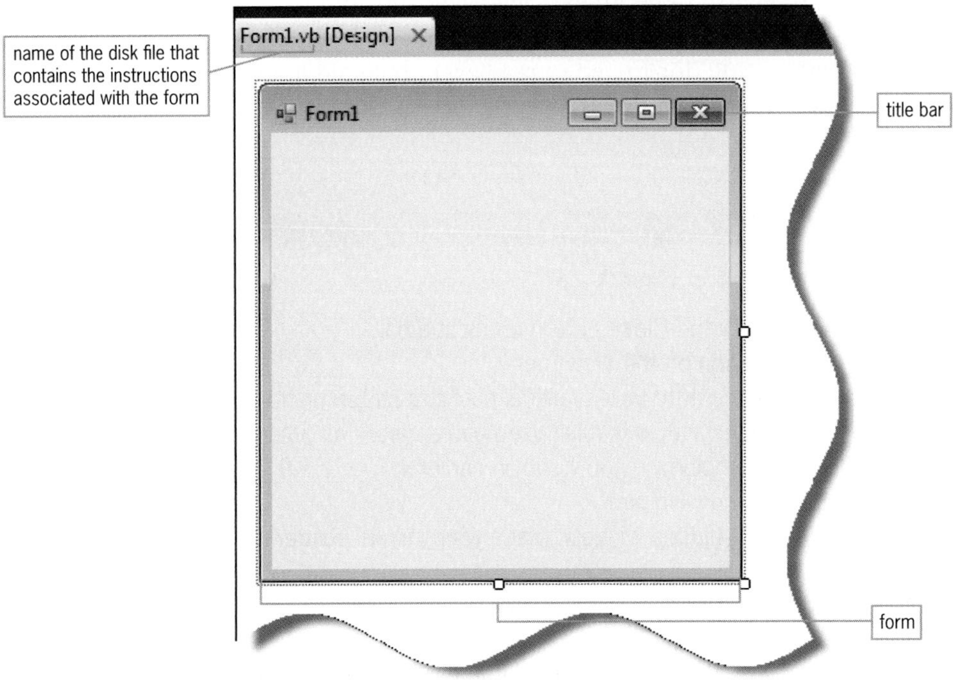

Figure 1-11 Windows Form Designer window

Recall that a class is a pattern that the computer uses to create an object.

As you learned earlier in this chapter, all objects in an object-oriented program are instantiated (created) from a class. A form, for example, is an instance of the Windows Form class. The form is automatically instantiated for you when you create a Windows application.

The Solution Explorer Window

The **Solution Explorer window** displays a list of the projects contained in the current solution and the items contained in each project. Figure 1-12 shows the Solution Explorer window for the Wizard Solution, which contains one project named Wizard Project. Within the Wizard Project are a My Project folder and a file named Form1.vb. The project also contains other items, which typically are kept hidden. However, you can display the additional items by clicking the Show All Files button. You would click the button again to hide the items. The .vb on the Form1.vb filename indicates that the file is a Visual Basic source file. A **source file** is a file that contains program instructions, called **code**. The Form1.vb file contains the code associated with the form displayed in the designer window. You can view the code using the Code Editor window, which you will learn about in *The Code Editor Window* section of this chapter.

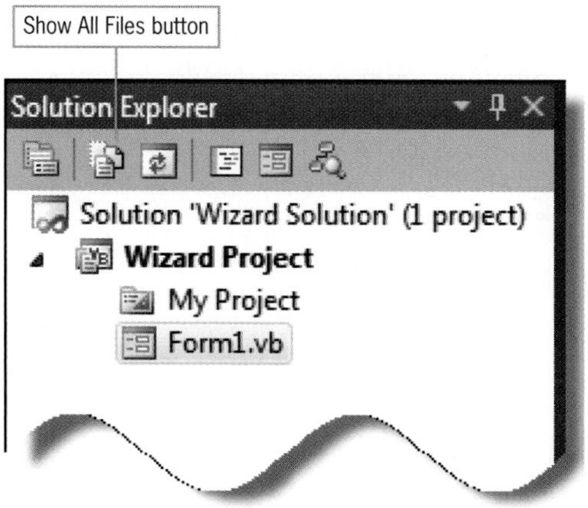

Figure 1-12 Solution Explorer window

The Form1.vb source file is referred to as a **form file**, because it contains the code associated with a form. The code associated with the first form included in a project is automatically stored in a form file named Form1.vb. The code associated with the second form in the same project is stored in a form file named Form2.vb, and so on. Because a project can contain many forms and, therefore, many form files, it is a good practice to give each form file a more meaningful name. Doing this will help you keep track of the various form files in the project. You can use the Properties window to change the filename.

The Properties Window

As is everything in an object-oriented language, a file is an object. Each object has a set of attributes that determine its appearance and behavior. The attributes are called **properties** and are listed in the **Properties window**. When an object is created, a default value is assigned to each of its properties. The Properties window shown in Figure 1-13 lists the default values assigned to the properties of the Form1.vb file. As indicated in the figure, the Properties window has an Object box and a Properties list. The **Object box** contains the name of the selected object. In this case, it contains Form1.vb, which is the name of the form file. The **Properties list** has two columns. The left column displays the names of the selected object's properties. You can use the Alphabetical and Categorized buttons to display the names either alphabetically or by category, respectively. However, it's usually easier to work with the Properties window when the properties are listed in alphabetical order, as they are in Figure 1-13. The right column in the Properties list is called the **Settings box** and displays the current value (or setting) of each of the properties. As the figure indicates, the current value of the File Name property is Form1.vb. To change the value of a property, you first select the property in the Properties list. You then either type the new value in the property's Settings box or select the new value from a list or dialog box. For example, to change the value of the File Name property from Form1.vb to Main Form.vb, you click File Name in the Properties list and then type Main Form.vb in the Settings box. Notice that a brief description of the selected property appears in the Description pane, which is located at the bottom of the Properties window.

In the context of object-oriented programming (OOP), the Properties window "exposes" an object's attributes (properties) to the programmer, allowing the programmer to change one or more default values.

To display the properties of the Form1.vb file, Form1.vb must be selected in the Solution Explorer window. You also can change the File Name property's value by right-clicking Form1.vb in the Solution Explorer window, and then clicking Rename on the context menu.

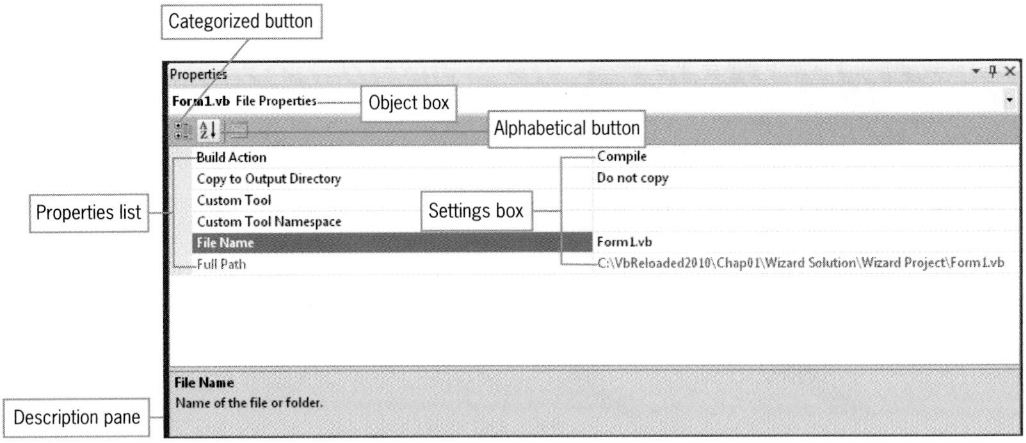

Figure 1-13 Properties window showing the Form1.vb file's properties

Properties of a Windows Form

Like a file, a Windows form also has a set of properties. The form's properties will appear in the Properties window when you select the form in the designer window. The Properties window in Figure 1-14 shows a partial listing of the properties of a Windows form. The vertical scroll bar on the Properties window indicates that there are more properties to view. Notice that Form1 System.Windows.Forms.Form appears in the Object box in the figure. Form1 is the name of the form. The name is automatically assigned to the form when the form is instantiated (created). In System.Windows.Forms.Form, Form is the name of the class (pattern) used to instantiate the form. System.Windows.Forms is the namespace that contains the Form class definition. A **class definition** is a block of code that specifies (or defines) an object's appearance and behavior. All class definitions in Visual Basic 2010 are contained in namespaces, which you can picture as blocks of memory cells inside the computer. Each **namespace** contains the code that defines a group of related classes. The System.Windows.Forms namespace contains the definition of the Windows Form class. It also contains the class definitions for objects you add to a form, such as buttons and text boxes. The period that separates each word in System.Windows.Forms.Form is called the **dot member access operator**. Similar to the backslash (\) in a folder path, the dot member access operator indicates a hierarchy, but of namespaces rather than folders. In other words, the backslash in the path C:\VbReloaded2010\Chap01\Wizard Solution\Wizard Project\Form1.vb indicates that the Form1.vb file is contained in (or is a member of) the Wizard Project folder, which is a member of the Wizard Solution folder, which is a member of the Chap01 folder, which is a member of the VbReloaded2010 folder, which is a member of the C: drive. Likewise, the name System.Windows.Forms.Form indicates that the Form class is a member of the Forms namespace, which is a member of the Windows namespace, which is a member of the System namespace. The dot member access operator allows the computer to locate the Form class in the computer's internal memory, similar to the way the backslash (\) allows the computer to locate the Form1.vb file on your computer's disk.

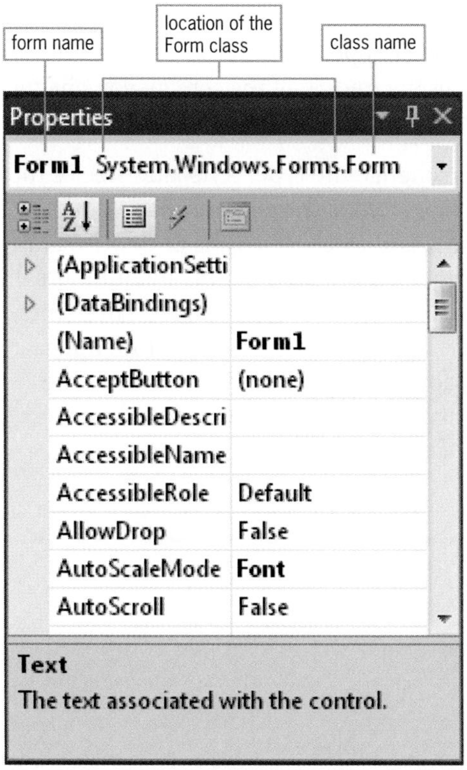

Figure 1-14 Properties window showing a partial listing of the form's properties

As you do to a form file, you should assign a more meaningful name to a Windows form because doing so will help you keep track of the various forms in a project. Unlike a file, a form has a Name property rather than a File Name property. You use the name entered in an object's Name property to refer to the object in code, so each object must have a unique name. The name you assign to an object must begin with a letter and contain only letters, numbers, and the underscore character. The name cannot include punctuation characters or spaces. There are several conventions for naming objects in Visual Basic. In this book, you will use a naming convention that begins each object's name with the object's purpose, followed by its class. In addition, form names will be entered using **Pascal case**, which capitalizes the first letter in the name and the first letter of each subsequent word in the name. Following this naming convention, you would assign the name `MainForm` to the main form in an application. "Main" reminds you of the form's purpose, and "Form" indicates the class used to create the form. Similarly, a secondary form used to access an employee database might be named `EmployeeDataForm` or `PersonnelForm`. In addition to changing the form's Name property, you also should change its Text property, which controls the text displayed in the form's title bar. The text also appears when you hover your mouse pointer over the application's button on the Windows 7 taskbar while the application is running. Form1 is the default value assigned to the Text property of the first form in a project. Better, more descriptive values for the Text property include "Wizard Viewer", "Commission Calculator", and "Employee Information". The Name and Text properties of a form should always be changed to more meaningful values. The Name property is used by the programmer when coding. The Text property, on the other hand, is read by the user while the application is running.

Pascal is a programming language created by Niklaus Wirth in the late 1960s. It was named in honor of the seventeenth-century French mathematician Blaise Pascal and is used to develop scientific applications.

Another popular naming convention is Hungarian notation, which combines the object's type (form, button, and so on) with its purpose. Using this naming convention, you would assign the name `frmMain` to the main form. The "frm" identifies the object as a form.

To restore a property to its default value, right-click the property in the Properties list, and then click Reset on the context menu.

At times, you may want to change the form's StartPosition property, which controls the location of the form when it first appears on the screen after the application is started. To display a form in the middle of the screen, you change its StartPosition property from WindowsDefaultLocation to CenterScreen.

You can use the form's Font property to change the type, style, and size of the font used to display the text on the form. A **font** is the general shape of the characters in the text. Segoe UI, Tahoma, and Microsoft Sans Serif are examples of font types. Font styles include regular, bold, and italic. The numbers 9, 12, and 18 are examples of font sizes, which typically are measured in points, with one **point** equaling 1/72 of an inch. The recommended font for applications created for systems running Windows 7 (or Windows Vista) is Segoe UI, because it offers improved readability. Segoe is pronounced SEE-go, and UI stands for user interface. For most of the elements in the interface, you will use the 9-point size of the font.

The answers to Mini-Quiz questions are located in Appendix A.

Mini-Quiz 1-1

1. Windows applications created in Visual Studio 2010 are composed of ______________.
   a. solutions
   b. projects
   c. files
   d. all of the above
2. How do you auto-hide a window?
3. How do you temporarily display an auto-hidden window?
4. How do you reset the windows in the IDE?
5. The value assigned to a form's ______________ property appears in the form's title bar.
   a. Caption
   b. Name
   c. Text
   d. Title
6. You can display a form in the middle of the screen by setting the form's ______________ property to CenterScreen.
   a. StartPosition
   b. ScreenLocation
   c. StartLocation
   d. CenterScreen

The Toolbox Window

Figure 1-15 shows the Toolbox window that appears when you are using the Windows Form designer. The **Toolbox window**, referred to more simply as the **toolbox**, contains the tools you use when creating your application's user interface. The toolbox tabs allow you to view the tools either by category or in alphabetical order by name. When you rest your mouse pointer on either the tool's name or its icon, the tool's purpose appears in a box, as shown in Figure 1-15. Each tool in the toolbox represents a class from which an object, such as a button or check box, can be instantiated. The objects, called **controls**, will appear on the form. Figure 1-16 lists the steps for adding a control to a form.

You can view the Ch01Video2 file and then skim the sections from *The Toolbox Window* to *The Code Editor Window*. However, be sure to pay particular attention to the boldface keywords in those sections.

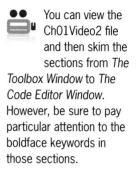

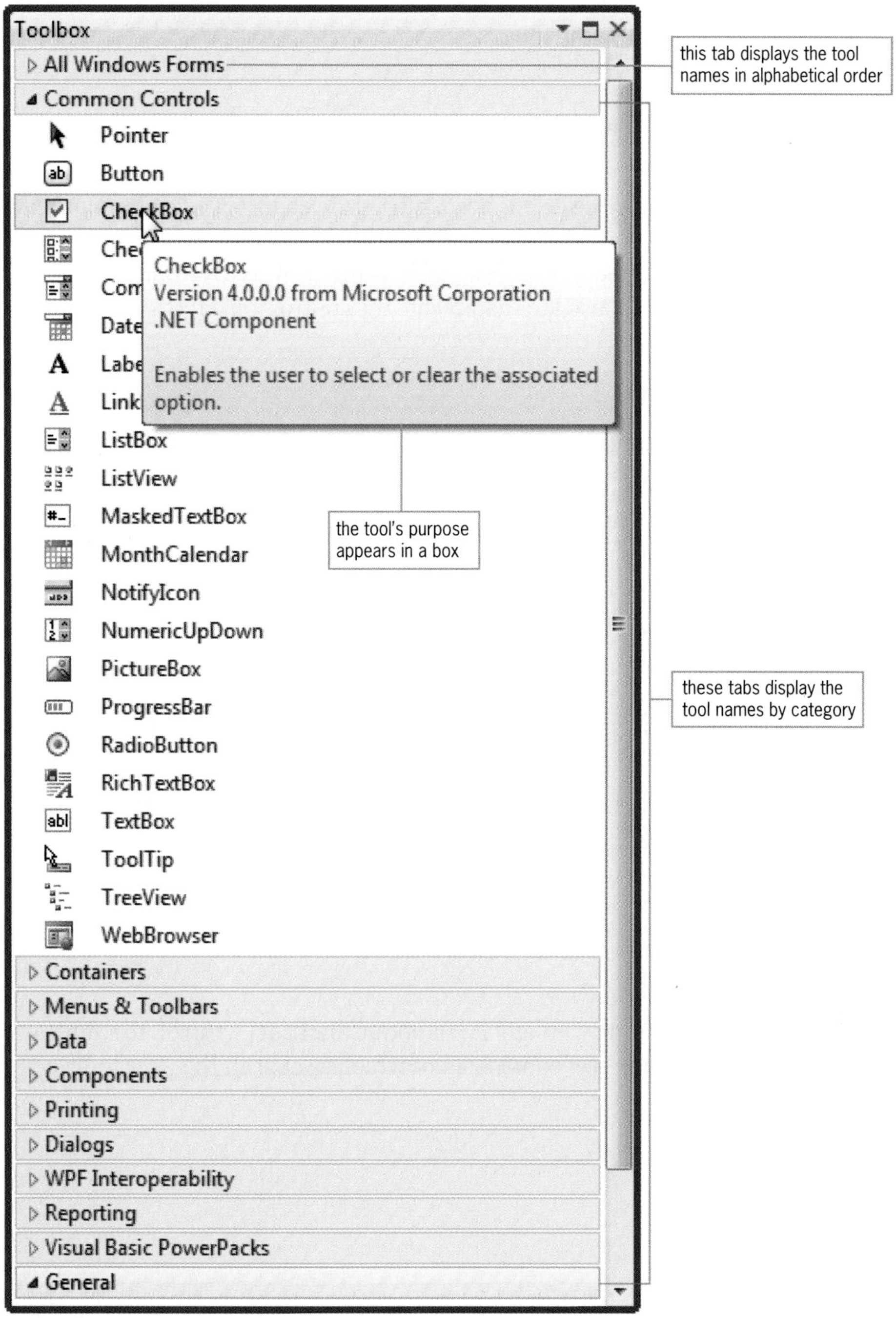

Figure 1-15 Toolbox window

HOW TO Add a Control to a Form

1. Click a tool in the toolbox, but do not release the mouse button.
2. Hold down the mouse button as you drag the mouse pointer to the form. You will see a solid box, as well as an outline of a rectangle and a plus box, following the mouse pointer.
3. Release the mouse button.

Additional ways:

- Click a tool in the toolbox and then click the form.
- Click a tool in the toolbox, then place the mouse pointer on the form, and then press the left mouse button and drag the mouse pointer until the control is the desired size.
- Double-click a tool in the toolbox.

Figure 1-16 How to add a control to a form

Controls on a form can be selected, sized, moved, deleted, locked, and unlocked. Locking a control prevents it from being moved inadvertently. When a control is locked, a small lock appears in the upper-left corner of the control. Figure 1-17 summarizes the methods used to manipulate the controls on a form.

HOW TO Manipulate the Controls on a Form

- To select a control, click it in the designer window. You also can use the list arrow button in the Properties window's Object box.
- To size a control, use the sizing handles that appear on the control when it is selected.
- To move a control, drag the control to the desired location.
- To delete a control, select the control in the designer window, and then press the Delete key on your keyboard.
- To lock and unlock the controls, right-click the form (or any control on the form), and then click Lock Controls on the Context menu. The Lock Controls option is a toggle option: clicking it once activates it, and clicking it again deactivates it. You also can use the Lock Controls command on the Format menu.

Figure 1-17 How to manipulate the controls on a form

In the next three sections, you will learn about the Label control, the Button control, and the Picture box control, all of which appear in the user interface shown in Figure 1-18.

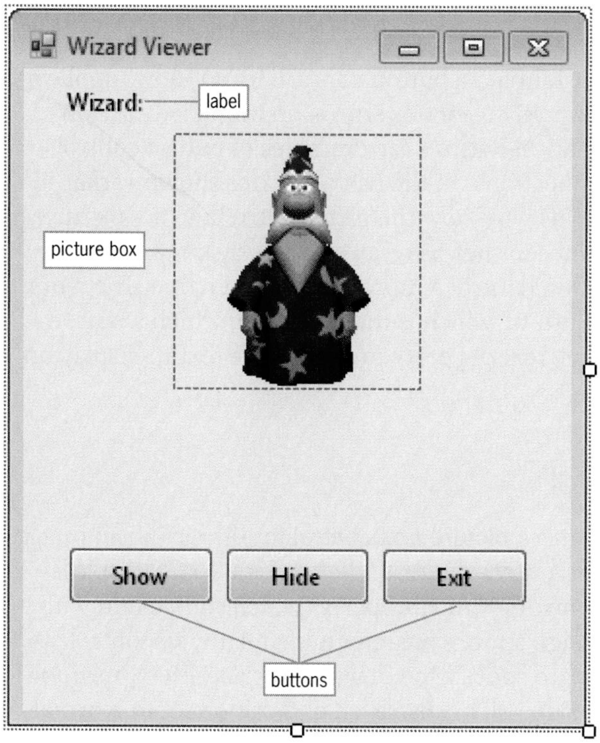

Figure 1-18 Wizard application's user interface

The Label Control

You use the Label tool to add a label control to a form. The purpose of a **label control** is to display text that the user is not allowed to edit while the application is running. Label controls are used in an interface to identify the contents of other controls, such as the contents of text boxes and list boxes. The label control in Figure 1-18 identifies the contents of a picture box control. Label controls also are used to display program output, such as the result of a calculation.

You use the Name property to give a label control a more meaningful name. You use the Text property to specify the text to display inside a label control. The Name property is used by the programmer when coding the application, whereas the Text property is read by the user while the application is running. Some programmers assign meaningful names to all of the label controls in an interface, while others do so only for label controls that display program output; this book follows the latter practice. In the naming convention used in this book, control names are made up of the control's purpose followed by the control's class (in this case, Label). Unlike form names, which are entered using Pascal case, control names are entered using **camel case**. This means that you enter the first word in the control's name in lowercase and then capitalize the first letter of each subsequent word in the name, like this: `salesTaxLabel`. Camel case refers to the fact that the uppercase letters appear as "humps" in the name because they are taller than the lowercase letters.

The Button Control

You use the Button tool to instantiate a button control. In Windows applications, a **button control** is commonly used to perform an immediate action when clicked. The OK and Cancel buttons are examples of button controls found in many Windows applications. In the user interface shown earlier in Figure 1-18, the button controls will show the picture box, hide the picture box, and exit the application when they are clicked. Here again, you use the Name property to give a button control a more meaningful name. The name should end with the word "Button," which is the class from which a button control is created. You use the Text property to specify the text to display on the button's face.

The Picture Box Control

The PictureBox tool instantiates a **picture box control** for displaying an image on the form. The picture box control shown earlier in Figure 1-18 displays an image of a wizard. The control's Name property (which should end with PictureBox) allows you to assign a more meaningful name to the control, and its Image property allows you to specify the image to display. The SizeMode property handles how the image will be displayed and can be set to Normal, StretchImage, AutoSize, CenterImage, or Zoom.

Using the Format Menu

The Format menu provides options for manipulating the controls on the form. The Align option, for example, allows you to align two or more controls by their left, right, top, or bottom borders. You can use the Make Same Size option to make two or more controls the same width and/or height. Before you can use the Format menu to change the alignment or size of two or more controls, you first must select the controls. You select the first control by clicking it. You select the second and subsequent controls by pressing and holding down the Control (Ctrl) key as you click the control. The first control you select should always be the one whose size and/or location you want to match. For example, to align the left border of the Label2 control with the left border of the Label1 control, you first select the Label1 control and then select the Label2 control. However, to make the Label1 control the same size as the Label2 control, you must select the Label2 control before selecting the Label1 control. The first control you select is referred to as the **reference control**. The reference control will have white sizing handles, whereas the other selected controls will have black sizing handles. The Format menu also has a Center in Form option that centers one or more controls either horizontally or vertically on the form. You will experiment with the Format menu in both Programming Tutorials at the end of this chapter.

The answers to Mini-Quiz questions are located in Appendix A.

Mini-Quiz 1-2

1. How do you delete a control from the form?
2. Amounts calculated by an application should be displayed in a ______________ control on the form.

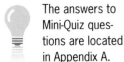

a. button

b. form

c. label

d. text

3. Using the naming convention you learned in this book, which of the following is a valid name for a control?

   a. calcButton

   b. salesTaxLabel

   c. birthdayPictureBox

   d. all of the above

4. Which of the following properties determines the image that appears in a picture box?

   a. Icon

   b. Image

   c. Picture

   d. all of the above

5. If you want to align the top border of the Label5 control with the top border of the Label4 control, which of the two controls should you select first?

The Code Editor Window

After creating your application's user interface, you can begin entering the Visual Basic instructions (code) that tell the controls how to respond to the user's actions. Those actions—such as clicking, double-clicking, and scrolling—are called **events**. You tell a control how to respond to an event by writing an **event procedure**, which is a set of Visual Basic instructions that are processed only when the event occurs. You enter an event procedure's code in the **Code Editor window**. Figure 1-19 lists various ways to open the Code Editor window, and Figure 1-20 shows the Code Editor window opened in the IDE. The Code Editor window contains the Class statement, which is used to define a class in Visual Basic. The Class statement in Figure 1-20 begins with the `Public Class MainForm` clause and ends with the `End Class` clause. Within the Class statement you enter the code to tell the form and its objects how to react to the user's actions. The Code Editor window also contains a Class Name list box and a Method Name list box. The **Class Name list box** lists the names of the objects included in the user interface. The **Method Name list box** lists the events to which the selected object is capable of responding.

You can view the Ch01Video3 file and then skim the sections from *The Code Editor Window* to *Opening an Existing Solution*. However, be sure to pay particular attention to the boldface keywords in those sections.

In object-oriented programming (OOP), an event is considered a behavior of an object because it represents an action to which the object can respond. The Code Editor window "exposes" an object's behaviors to the programmer.

HOW TO Open the Code Editor Window

- Right-click the form, and then click View Code on the context menu.
- Verify that the designer window is the active window, then click View on the menu bar, and then click Code.
- Verify that the designer window is the active window, and then press the F7 key on your keyboard.
- Click the form or a control on the form, then click the Events button in the Properties window, and then double-click the desired event.
- Double-click the form or a control on the form.

Figure 1-19 How to open the Code Editor window

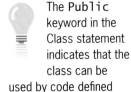

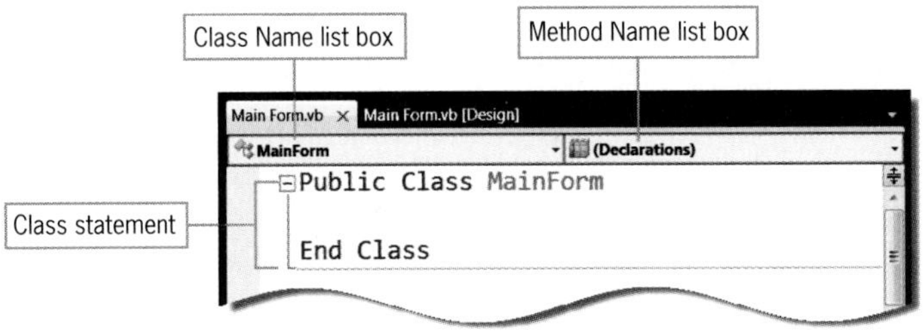

Figure 1-20 Code Editor window

The `Public` keyword in the Class statement indicates that the class can be used by code defined outside of the class.

You use the Class Name and Method Name list boxes to select the object and event, respectively, that you want to code. For example, to code the exitButton's Click event, you first select exitButton in the Class Name list box and then select Click in the Method Name list box. When you do this, a code template for the exitButton's Click event procedure appears in the Code Editor window, as shown in Figure 1-21. The code template helps you follow the rules of the Visual Basic language. The rules of a programming language are called its **syntax**. The first line in the code template is called the **procedure header**, and the last line is called the **procedure footer**. The procedure header begins with the two keywords `Private Sub`. A **keyword** is a word that has a special meaning in a programming language. Keywords appear in a different color from the rest of the code. The `Private` keyword in Figure 1-21 indicates that the button's Click event procedure can be used only within the current Code Editor window. The `Sub` keyword is an abbreviation of the term **sub procedure**, which is a block of code that performs a specific task. Following the `Sub` keyword is the name of the object, an underscore, the name of the event, and parentheses containing some text. For now, you do not have to be concerned with the text that appears between the parentheses. After the closing parenthesis is `Handles exitButton.Click`. This part of the procedure header indicates that the procedure handles (or is associated with) the exitButton's Click event. It tells the computer to process the procedure only when the exitButton is clicked. The code template ends with the procedure footer, which contains the keywords `End Sub`. You enter your Visual Basic instructions at the location of the insertion point, which appears between the `Private Sub` and `End Sub` clauses in Figure 1-21. The Code Editor automatically indents the line between the procedure header and footer. Indenting the lines within a procedure makes the instructions easier to read and is a common programming practice.

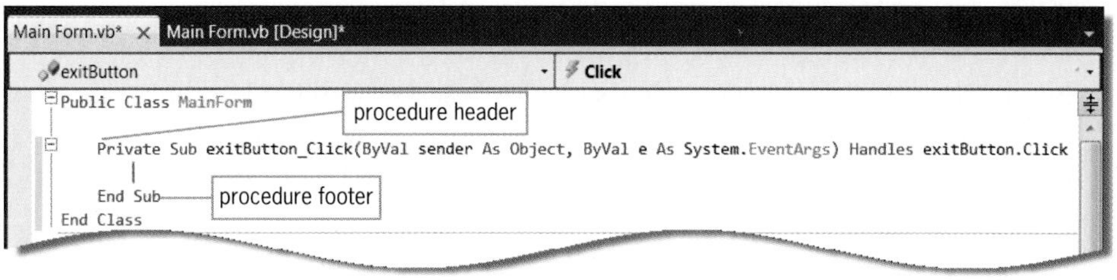
Main Form.vb*
Main Form.vb [Design]*
exitButton
Click
Public Class MainForm
procedure header
Private Sub exitButton_Click(ByVal sender As Object, ByVal e As System.EventArgs) Handles exitButton.Click
End Sub
procedure footer
End Class

Figure 1-21 Code template for the exitButton's Click event procedure

When the user clicks an Exit button on a form, it usually indicates that he or she wants to end the application. You can stop an application using the `Me.Close()` instruction.

The Me.Close() Instruction

The `Me.Close()` instruction tells the computer to close the current form. If the current form is the only form in the application, closing it terminates the entire application. In the instruction, `Me` is a keyword that refers to the current form, and Close is one of the methods available in Visual Basic. A **method** is a predefined procedure that you can call (or invoke) when needed. For example, if you want the computer to close the current form when the user clicks the Exit button, you enter the `Me.Close()` instruction in the exitButton's Click event procedure, as shown in Figure 1-22. Notice the empty set of parentheses after the method's name in the instruction. The parentheses are required when calling some Visual Basic methods. However, depending on the method, the parentheses may or may not be empty. If you forget to enter the parentheses, the Code Editor will enter them for you when you move the insertion point to another line in the Code Editor window. When the user clicks the Exit button while the application is running, the computer processes the instructions shown in the exitButton_Click procedure one after another in the order in which they appear in the procedure. In programming, this is referred to as **sequential processing** or as the **sequence structure**. (You will learn about two other programming structures, called selection and repetition, in later chapters.)

To display line numbers in the Code Editor window, click Tools and then click Options. Select the Show all settings check box, if necessary. Expand the Text Editor node, and then click Basic. Select the Line numbers check box, and then click the OK button.

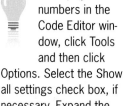

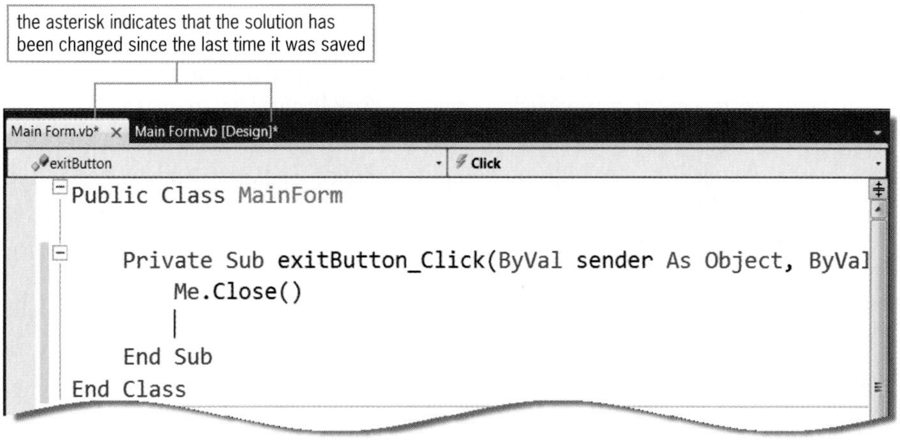
the asterisk indicates that the solution has been changed since the last time it was saved
Main Form.vb*
Main Form.vb [Design]*
exitButton
Click
Public Class MainForm
Private Sub exitButton_Click(ByVal sender As Object, ByVal
Me.Close()
End Sub
End Class

Figure 1-22 `Me.Close()` instruction entered in the Click event procedure

Saving a Solution

Notice the asterisk (*) that appears on the designer and Code Editor tabs in Figure 1-22. The asterisk indicates that a change was made to the solution since the last time it was saved. It is a good practice to save the current solution every 10 or 15 minutes so that you will not lose a lot of your work if the computer loses power. When you save a solution, the computer saves any changes made to the files included in the solution. Saving the solution also removes the asterisk that appears on the designer and Code Editor tabs. Figure 1-23 lists two ways to save a solution.

HOW TO Save a Solution

- Click File on the menu bar, and then click Save All.
- Click the Save All button on the Standard toolbar.

Figure 1-23 How to save a solution

Starting and Ending an Application

When you are finished coding the application, you need to start it to make sure that it is working correctly. Before you start an application for the first time, you should verify the name of the **startup form**, which is the form that the computer automatically displays each time the application is started. The name appears in the Startup form list box in the Project Designer window. Figure 1-24 shows the steps you follow to specify the startup form's name, and Figure 1-25 shows the name of the startup form (in this case, MainForm) selected in the Project Designer window.

HOW TO Specify the Startup Form

1. Open the Project Designer window. You can open the window by right-clicking My Project in the Solution Explorer window, and then clicking Open on the context menu. You also can click Project on the menu bar, and then click <project name> Properties on the menu. In addition, you can right-click the project's name in the Solution Explorer window, and then click Properties.
2. Click the Application tab, if necessary.
3. If the startup form's name does not appear in the Startup form list box, click the Startup form list arrow, and then click the appropriate form name in the list.
4. Click the Close button on the Project Designer window's tab.

Figure 1-24 How to specify the startup form

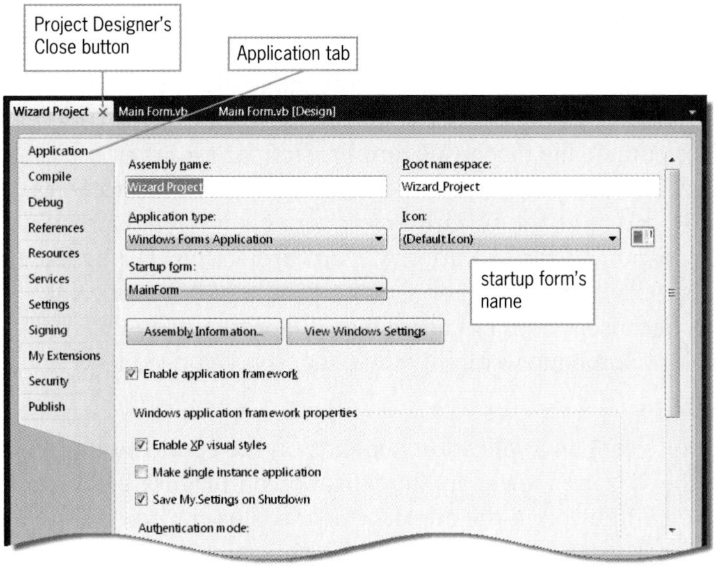

Figure 1-25 Project Designer window

Figure 1-26 shows various ways to start an application, and Figure 1-27 shows the result of starting the Wizard Viewer application. The computer automatically displays the startup form, which in this case is the MainForm. (At this point, you do not need to be concerned about the window that appears at the bottom of the screen.)

HOW TO Start an Application

- Save the solution. Click Debug on the menu bar, and then click Start Debugging.
- Save the solution, and then press the F5 key on your keyboard.
- Save the solution, and then click the Start Debugging button on the Standard toolbar.

Figure 1-26 How to start an application

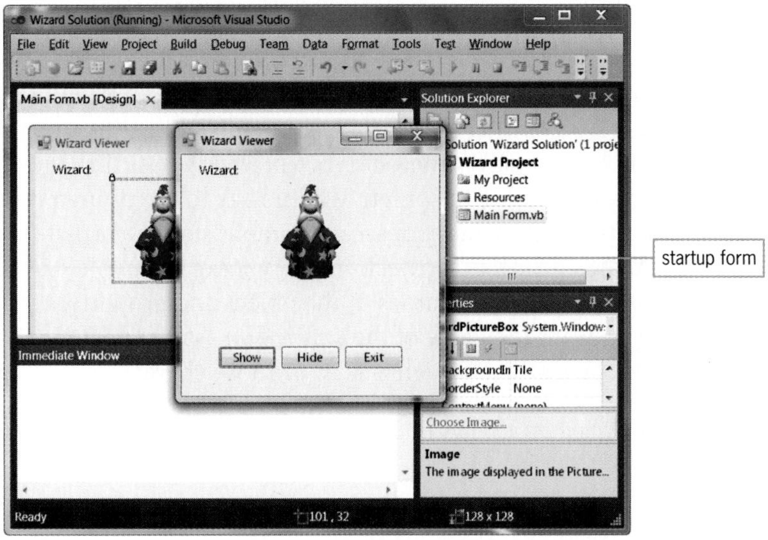

Figure 1-27 Result of starting the Wizard Viewer application

You can change the name of the executable file by opening the Project Designer window and then entering the new name in the Assembly name box on the Application tab. Or, you can use Windows to rename the file before giving it to the user.

When you start a Visual Basic application, the computer automatically creates a file that can be run outside of the IDE (such as from the Run dialog box in Windows). The file is referred to as an **executable file**. The executable file's name is the same as the project's name, except it ends with .exe. The name of the executable file for the Wizard Project, for example, is Wizard Project.exe. The computer stores the executable file in the project's bin\Debug folder. In this case, the Wizard Project.exe file is stored in the VbReloaded2010\Chap01\Wizard Solution\Wizard Project\bin\Debug folder. When you are finished with an application, you typically give the user only the executable file, because it does not allow him or her to modify the application's code. To allow someone to modify the code, you will need to provide the entire solution.

The way you end (or close) an application depends on the application's interface. To end the Wizard Viewer application shown in Figure 1-27, you can click either the Exit button in the interface or the Close button on the application's title bar. To close Visual Studio 2010, you can use either the Exit option on Visual Studio's File menu or the Close button on its title bar. Figure 1-28 lists various ways of ending an application.

HOW TO End an Application

- Click an Exit button in the interface.
- Click File on the application's menu bar, and then click Exit.
- Click the Close button on the application's title bar.
- Click the designer window to make it the active window. Click Debug on the menu bar, and then click Stop Debugging.
- Click the Stop Debugging button on the Standard toolbar.

Figure 1-28 How to end an application

Assigning a Value to a Property During Run Time

Earlier, you learned how to use the Properties window to set an object's properties during design time, which is when you are building the interface. You also can set an object's properties during run time, which occurs while an application is running; you do this using an assignment statement. An **assignment statement** is one of many different types of Visual Basic instructions. Its purpose is to assign a value to something (such as to the property of an object) during run time. The syntax of an assignment statement that assigns a value to an object's property is *object.property = expression*. In the syntax, *object* and *property* are the names of the object and property, respectively, to which you want the value of the *expression* assigned. The *expression* can be a number, a **string** (which is zero or more characters enclosed in quotation marks), a calculation, or a keyword. You use a period to separate the object name from the property name. Recall that the period is the dot member access operator. In this case, the operator indicates that the *property* is a member of the *object.* You use an equal sign between the *object.property* information and the *expression.* The equal sign in an assignment statement is called the **assignment operator**. When the computer processes an assignment statement, it assigns the value of the expression that appears on the right side of the assignment operator to the object and property that appear on the left side of the assignment operator. The assignment statement `greetingLabel.Text = "Hello"`, for example, assigns the string "Hello" to the Text property of the greetingLabel. Recall that a control's Text property specifies the text to display inside the control. Likewise, to assign the keyword `True` to the Visible property of the wizardPictureBox, you use the assignment statement `wizardPictureBox.Visible = True`. When a control's Visible property is set to True, the control is visible on the form while the application is running. To make a control invisible during run time, you set its Visible property to False, like this: `wizardPictureBox.Visible = False`. Figure 1-29 shows the appropriate assignment statements entered in the Wizard application's Code Editor window.

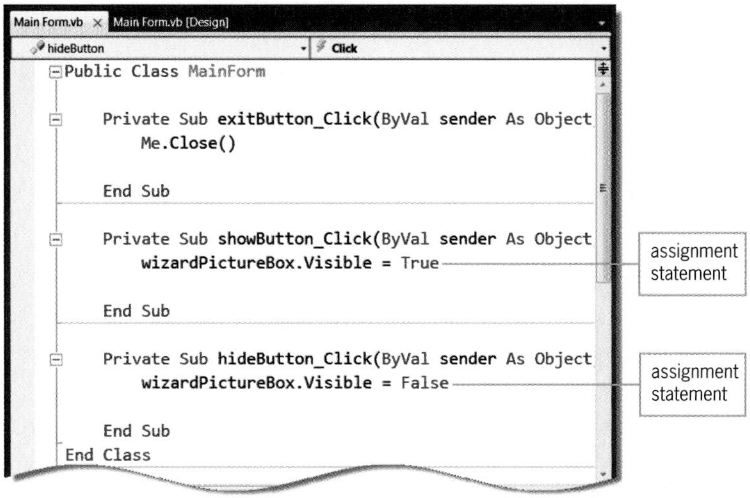

Figure 1-29 Assignment statements entered in the Code Editor window

Printing the Code and User Interface

You should always print a copy of your application's code, because the printout will help you understand and maintain the application in the future. You also should print a copy of the application's user interface. Figure 1-30 shows the steps you follow to print the code and the interface during design time. (In Chapter 2, you will learn how to print the interface during run time.)

HOW TO Print the Code and Interface During Design Time

To print the code:

1. Make the Code Editor window the active window, and then collapse any code that you do not want to print. You collapse the code by clicking the minus box that appears next to the code.
2. Click File on the menu bar, and then click Print. If you don't want to print the collapsed code, select the Hide collapsed regions check box. To print line numbers, select the Include line numbers check box. Click the OK button to begin printing.

To print the interface during design time:

1. Make the designer window the active window. Press and hold down the Alt key on your keyboard as you tap the Print Screen (or Prnt Scrn or PrtSc) key, and then release the Alt key. Doing this places a picture of the interface on the Clipboard.
2. Start Microsoft Word (or any application that can display a picture) and open a new document (if necessary). Press Control (or Ctrl) + v to paste the contents of the Clipboard in the document. Press Control (or Ctrl) + p to open the Print dialog box, and then click the OK button.

Figure 1-30 How to print the code and interface during design time

Closing the Current Solution

When you are finished working on a solution, you should close it. Closing a solution closes all projects and files contained in the solution. If unsaved changes were made to the solution, project, or form, a dialog box opens and prompts you to save the appropriate files. The steps you follow to close a solution are listed in Figure 1-31. Be careful to use the Close Solution (or Close Project) option on the File menu, rather than the menu's Close option. The Close option does not close the solution. Instead, it closes only the open windows, such as the designer and Code Editor windows, in the IDE.

HOW TO Close a Solution

1. Click File on the menu bar.
2. Click Close Solution (or Close Project).

Figure 1-31 How to close a solution

Opening an Existing Solution

Figure 1-32 shows the steps you follow to open an existing solution. If a solution is already open in the IDE, it is closed before another solution is opened. In other words, only one solution can be open in the IDE at any one time.

HOW TO Open an Existing Solution

1. Click File on the menu bar, and then click Open Project to open the Open Project dialog box.
2. Locate and then click the solution filename, which is contained in the application's solution folder. The solution filename has an .sln filename extension, which stands for "solution."
3. Click the Open button in the Open Project dialog box.
4. If the Windows Form Designer window is not displayed, click View on the menu bar, and then click Designer.

Figure 1-32 How to open an existing solution

Coding Errors

As the amount of code you need to enter increases, so does the likelihood for errors. An error in a program's code is referred to as a **bug**. The process of locating and correcting any bugs in a program is called **debugging**. Program bugs typically are caused by either syntax errors or logic errors. In this chapter, you'll learn about syntax errors only. Logic errors are covered later in this book. A **syntax error** occurs when you break one of the programming language's rules. Most syntax errors are a result of typing errors that occur when entering instructions, such as typing `Me.Clse()` instead of `Me.Close()`. The Code Editor detects most syntax errors as you enter the instructions. Figure 1-33 shows the result of typing `Me.Clse()` in the exitButton's Click event procedure. The jagged blue line indicates that the code contains a syntax error.

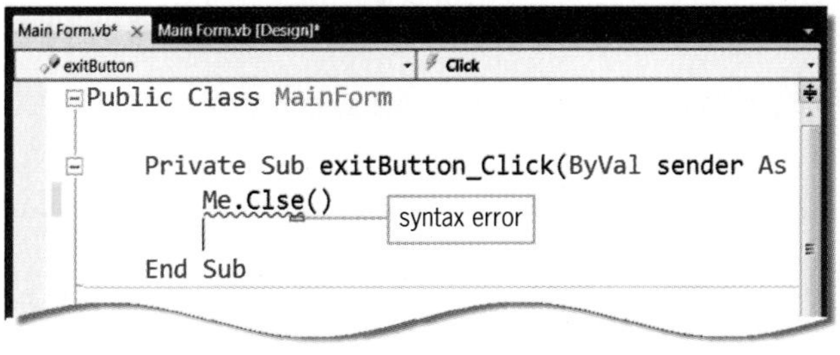

Figure 1-33 Syntax error in the exitButton's Click event procedure

You can find out more information about the syntax error by positioning your mouse pointer on the mistyped instruction. When you do so, the Code Editor displays a box that contains an appropriate error message, as shown in Figure 1-34. In this case, the message indicates that the Code Editor does not recognize `Clse`.

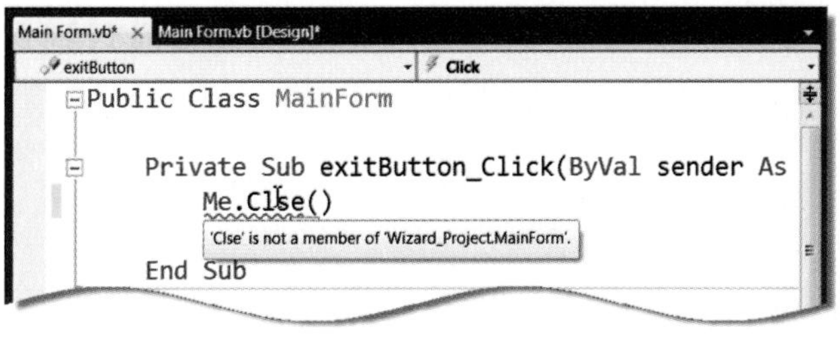

Figure 1-34 Syntax error message

Usually, you correct any syntax errors before starting an application. However, if you inadvertently start an application that contains a syntax error, the dialog box shown in Figure 1-35 will appear. Clicking the No button opens the Error List window shown in Figure 1-36. The window provides both the description and location of the error in the code.

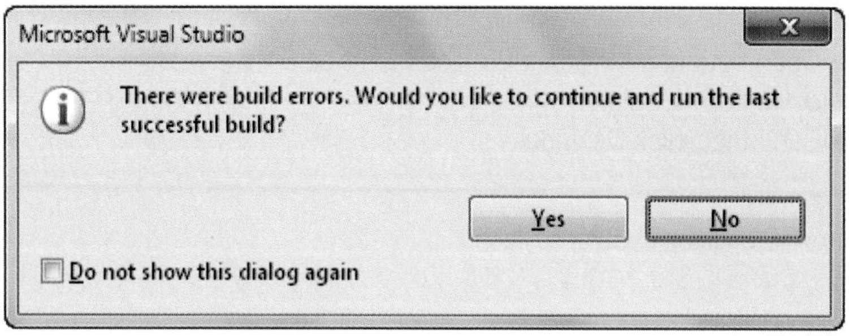

Figure 1-35 Dialog box

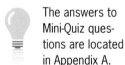

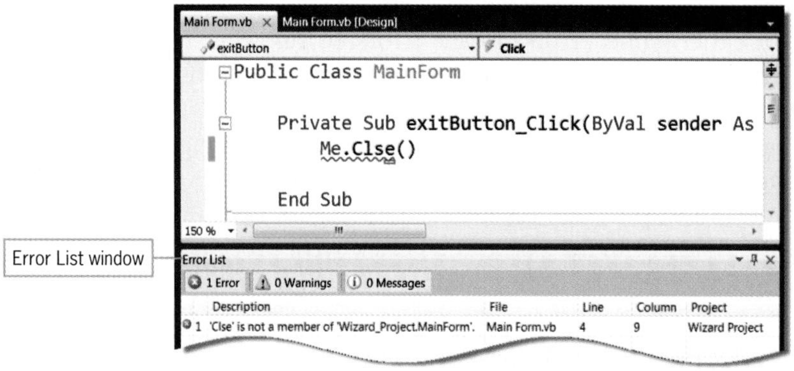

Figure 1-36 Result of starting an application that contains a syntax error

The answers to Mini-Quiz questions are located in Appendix A.

Mini-Quiz 1-3

1. What is the proper way to close a solution?
   a. click the Close option on the File menu
   b. click the Close Solution option on the File menu
   c. click the Close All option on the File menu
   d. either a or b

2. The form that appears automatically when an application is started is called the ______________ form.
   a. beginning
   b. main
   c. startup
   d. none of the above

3. Which of the following instructions can be used to end an application?
   a. `Close.Me()`
   b. `Me.Close()`
   c. `Me.End()`
   d. `Me.Stop()`

4. Which of the following assigns the string "Las Vegas" to the cityLabel control?
   a. `cityLabel.Label = "Las Vegas"`
   b. `cityLabel.String = "Las Vegas"`
   c. `cityLabel.Text = "Las Vegas"`
   d. none of the above

5. The process of locating and fixing any errors in a program is called ______________.
   a. bug-proofing
   b. bug-eliminating
   c. debugging
   d. error removal

You have completed the concepts section of Chapter 1. The next section is the Programming Tutorial section, which contains two tutorials. The tutorials give you step-by-step instructions for completing applications that use the chapter's concepts. In most cases, the first tutorial in each chapter is easier than the second tutorial because it contains more detailed step-by-step instructions. A Programming Example follows the tutorials. The Programming Example is a completed program that demonstrates the concepts taught in the chapter. Following the Programming Example are the Summary, Key Terms, Review Questions, Exercises, and Case Projects sections.

PROGRAMMING TUTORIAL 1

Creating the Wizard Viewer Application

The Ch01Video4 file demonstrates all of the steps in Programming Tutorial 1.

In this tutorial, you create the Wizard Viewer application from the chapter. The interface contains a label, a picture box, and three buttons. The first button displays the picture box on the form, and the second button hides the picture box. The third button ends the application.

Creating a Visual Basic Windows Application

Before you can create a Windows application in Visual Basic, you first must start either Visual Studio or the Express Edition of Visual Basic.

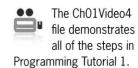

To create a Visual Basic Windows application:

1. Click the **Start** button on the Windows 7 taskbar, and then point to **All Programs**.
2. *If you are using Visual Studio 2010,* click **Microsoft Visual Studio 2010** on the All Programs menu, and then click **Microsoft Visual Studio 2010**. If the Choose Default Environment Settings dialog box appears, click **Visual Basic Development Settings**, and then click **Start Visual Studio**.

   If you are using Visual Basic 2010 Express Edition, click **Microsoft Visual Basic 2010 Express** on the All Programs menu.
3. Click **Window** on the menu bar, then click **Reset Window Layout**, and then click the **Yes** button. If you are using the Professional Edition of Visual Studio 2010, your screen will appear similar to Figure 1-37. If you are using the Express Edition of Visual Basic 2010, your screen will appear similar to Figure 1-38. (Do not be concerned if your screen does not have the Team Explorer window.)

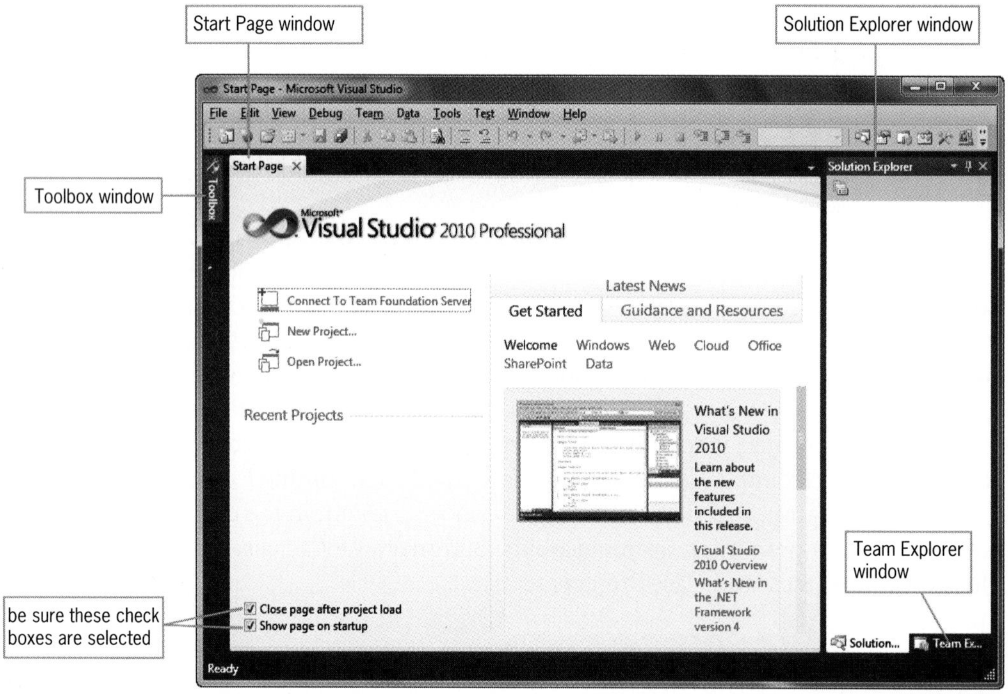

Figure 1-37 Microsoft Visual Studio 2010 Professional startup screen

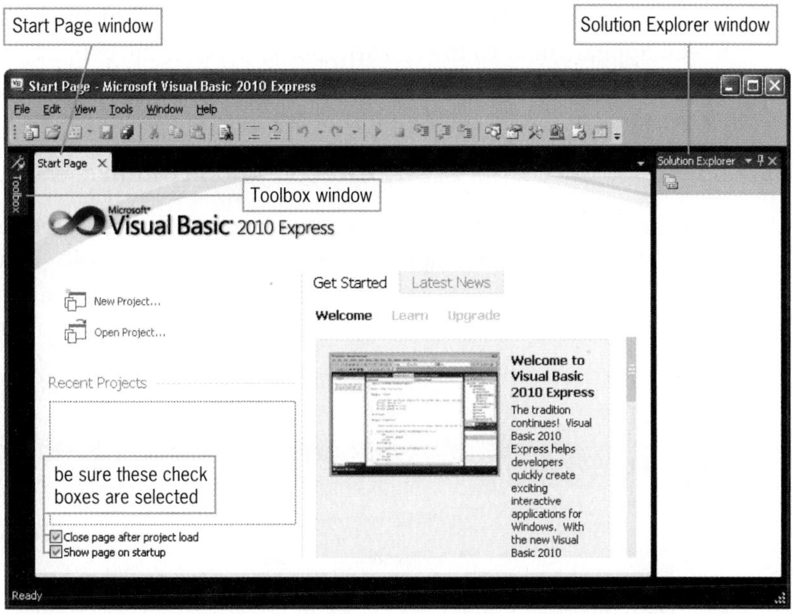

Figure 1-38 Microsoft Visual Basic 2010 Express startup screen

4. Click **Tools** on the menu bar, and then click **Options**. If necessary, deselect the **Show all settings** check box, which appears in the lower-left corner of the Options dialog box. Click the **Projects and Solutions** node. Use the information shown in Figure 1-39 to select and deselect the appropriate check boxes. (Your dialog box will look slightly different if you are using the Express Edition.)

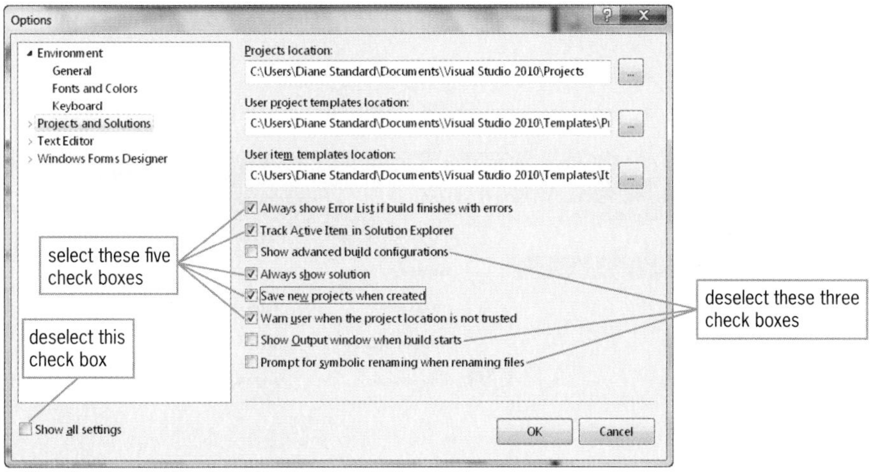

Figure 1-39 Options dialog box

5. Click the **OK** button to close the Options dialog box.
6. Click **File** on the menu bar, and then click **New Project** to open the New Project dialog box.
7. If necessary, click **Visual Basic** in the Installed Templates list, and then (if necessary) click **Windows Forms Application** in the middle column of the dialog box.

8. Type **Wizard Project** in the Name box. Click the **Browse** button, which appears next to the Location box, to open the Project Location dialog box. Locate and then click the **VbReloaded2010\Chap01** folder, and then click the **Select Folder** button.

9. If necessary, select the **Create directory for solution** check box.

10. Change the name in the Solution name box to **Wizard Solution**. The completed New Project dialog box is shown in Figure 1-40 (Visual Studio 2010) and Figure 1-41 (Visual Basic 2010 Express Edition).

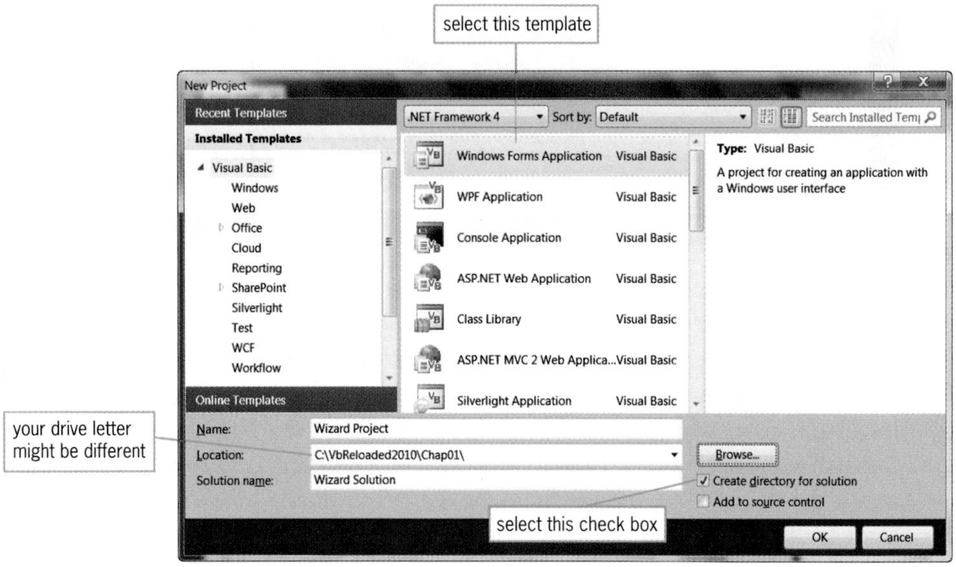

Figure 1-40 Completed New Project dialog box in Visual Studio 2010

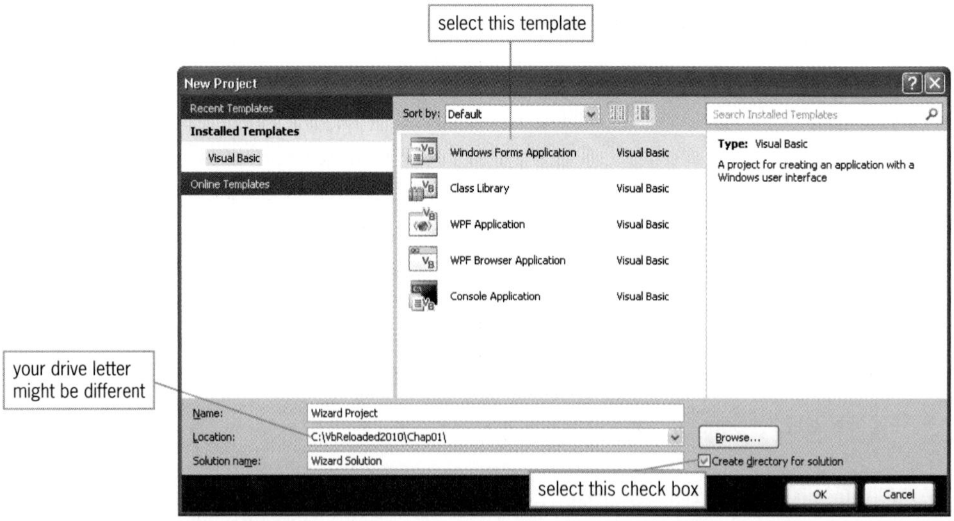

Figure 1-41 Completed New Project dialog box in Visual Basic 2010 Express Edition

11. Click the **OK** button to close the New Project dialog box. When you click the OK button, Visual Studio creates a solution and adds a Visual Basic project to the solution, as shown in Figure 1-42. (Do not

be concerned if your screen does not have the Data Sources or Team Explorer windows.)

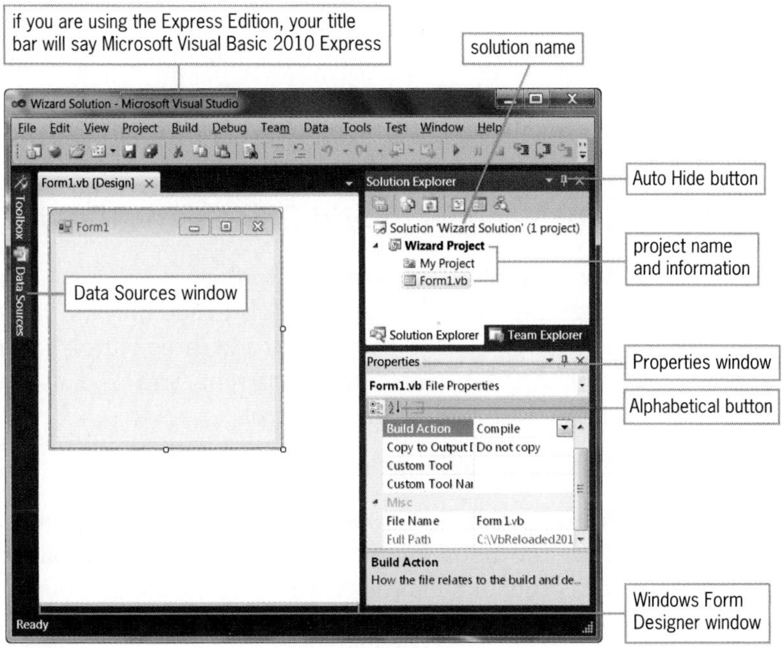

Figure 1-42 Solution and Visual Basic project

12. If necessary, click the **Alphabetical** button in the Properties window to display the property names in alphabetical order.

Managing the Windows in the IDE

In the next set of steps, you practice closing, opening, auto-hiding, and displaying the windows in the IDE.

To close, open, auto-hide, and display the windows in the IDE:

1. Click the **Close** button on the Properties window's title bar to close the window. To open the window, click **View** on the menu bar, and then click **Properties Window** (or point to **Other Windows** and then click **Properties Window**).
2. If necessary, click the **Team Explorer window's** tab, and then click the **Close** button on its title bar.
3. Click the **Auto Hide** button (the vertical pushpin) on the Solution Explorer window's title bar. The Solution Explorer window is minimized and appears as a tab on the right edge of the IDE.
4. To temporarily display the Solution Explorer window, place your mouse pointer on the Solution Explorer tab. The Solution Explorer window slides into view. Notice that the Auto Hide button is now a horizontal pushpin rather than a vertical pushpin.
5. Move your mouse pointer away from the Solution Explorer window. The window is minimized and appears as a tab again.

6. To permanently display the Solution Explorer window, place your mouse pointer on the Solution Explorer tab, and then click the **Auto Hide** button (the horizontal pushpin) on its title bar. The vertical pushpin button replaces the horizontal pushpin button.

7. On your own, close the Data Sources window (if necessary) and permanently display the Toolbox window. If necessary, click the **Common Controls** tab in the Toolbox window.

Using the Toolbox Window to Add Objects to a Form

The Toolbox window, or toolbox, contains the tools you use when creating your application's user interface. You use the tools to add objects, called controls, to a form. In the next set of steps, you will add three button controls, a label control, and a picture box control to the current form. You also practice sizing, moving, deleting, and undeleting a control.

To add controls to the form and then manipulate the controls:

1. Click the **Button** tool in the toolbox, but do not release the mouse button. Hold down the mouse button as you drag the mouse pointer to the lower-left corner of the form. As you drag the mouse pointer, you will see a solid box, as well as an outline of a rectangle and a plus box, following the mouse pointer. See Figure 1-43. Notice that a blue line appears between the form's left border and the control's left border, and between the control's bottom border and the form's bottom border. The blue lines are called margin lines, because their size is determined by the contents of the control's Margin property. The purpose of the margin lines is to assist you in spacing the controls properly on a form.

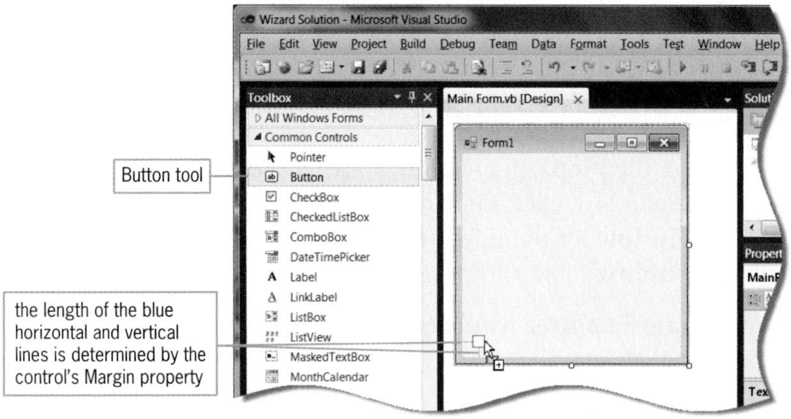

Figure 1-43 Button tool being dragged to the form

2. Release the mouse button. A button control appears on the form. See Figure 1-44. Notice that an asterisk (*) appears on the Form1.vb [Design] tab in the designer window. The asterisk indicates that the form has been changed since the last time it was saved. The sizing handles on the button control indicate that the control is selected. You can use the sizing handles to make a control bigger or smaller.

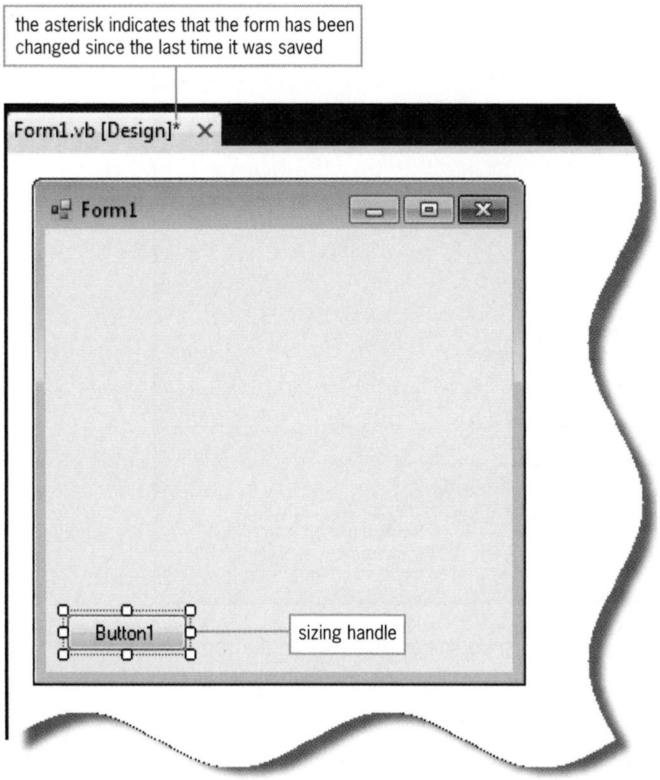
the asterisk indicates that the form has been changed since the last time it was saved
Form1.vb [Design]*
Form1
Button1
sizing handle

Figure 1-44 Button control added to the form

3. Use the middle sizing handle at the top of the button control to make the button control taller.

4. Now you will practice repositioning a control on the form. Place your mouse pointer on the center of the button control, then press the left mouse button and drag the control to another area of the form. Release the mouse button.

5. Next, you will practice deleting and then restoring a control. Press the **Delete** key on your keyboard to delete the button control. Click **Edit** on the menu bar, and then click **Undo** to reinstate the button control.

6. Drag the button control back to its original location in the lower-left corner of the form.

7. You also can add a control to a form by clicking the appropriate tool and then clicking the form. Click the **Button** tool in the toolbox, then click anywhere on the **form**.

8. Drag the second button control until the top of the control is aligned with the top of the first button control, but don't release the mouse button. When the tops of both controls are aligned, the designer displays a blue snap line, as shown in Figure 1-45.

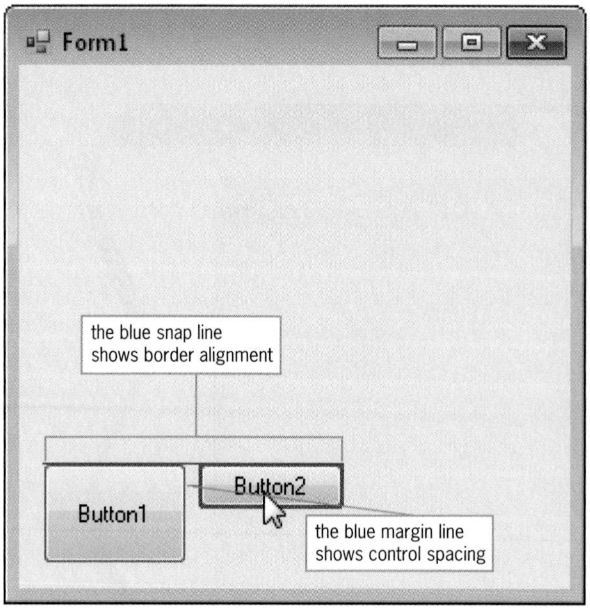

Figure 1-45 A blue snap line appears when the top borders of both controls are aligned

9. Now drag the second button control down slightly, until the Button2 text is aligned with the Button1 text, but don't release the mouse button. When the text in both controls is aligned, the designer displays a pink snap line, as shown in Figure 1-46.

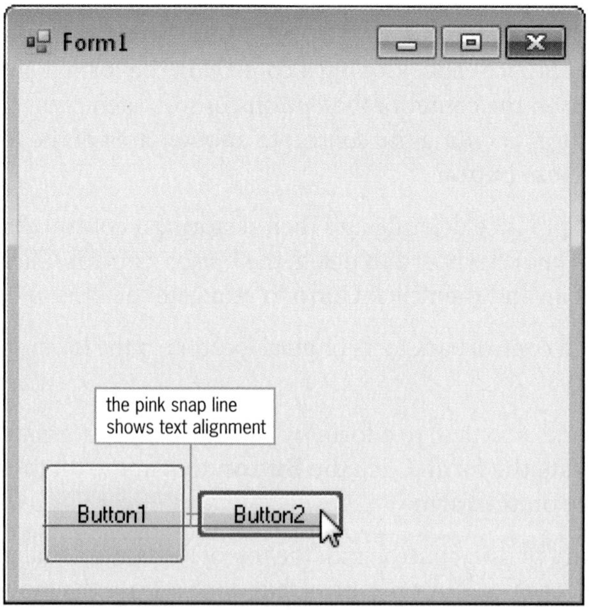

Figure 1-46 A pink snap line appears when the text in both controls is aligned

10. Release the mouse button.

11. Another way to add a control to a form is by clicking the appropriate tool, then placing the mouse pointer on the form, and then pressing the left mouse button and dragging the mouse pointer until the

control is the desired size. Click the **Button** tool in the toolbox, then place the mouse pointer on the form. Press the left mouse button and drag the mouse pointer until the control is the desired size, and then release the mouse button. (You do not need to worry about the exact location and size of the button.)

12. Drag the third button control until the Button3 text is aligned with the Button2 text, and then release the mouse button.
13. Add a label control and a picture box control to the form. Position the controls as shown in Figure 1-47. (You do not need to worry about the exact location and size of the controls in the interface.)

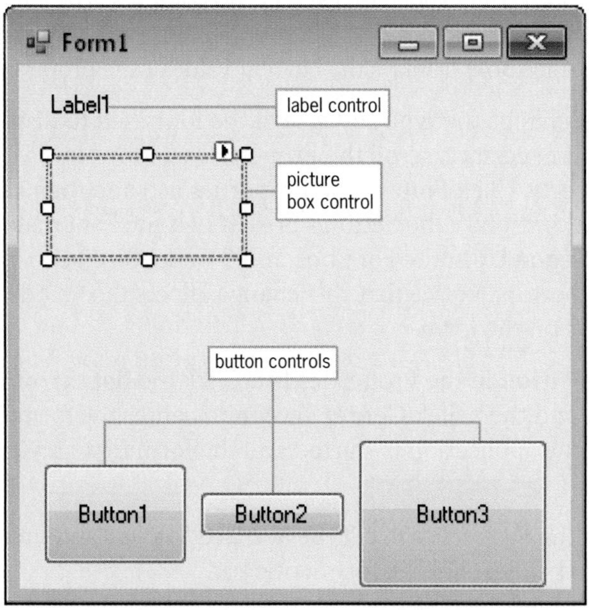

Figure 1-47 Controls added to the form

14. Save the solution by clicking **File** on the menu bar, and then clicking **Save All**.
15. Auto-hide the Toolbox window.

Using the Properties Window to Change an Object's Properties

Each object in Visual Basic has a set of properties that determine its appearance and behavior. Each property has a default value assigned to it when the object is created. You can use the Properties window to assign a different value to a property. First, you will change the File Name property of the form file object from Form1.vb to Main Form.vb.

To change the name of the form file object:

1. Right-click **Form1.vb** in the Solution Explorer window, and then click **Properties**.
2. Click **File Name** in the Properties list, and then type **Main Form.vb** and press **Enter**.

In the next set of steps, you will assign values to some of the properties of the form.

To assign values to some of the properties of the form:

1. Click the **form** (but not a control on the form). Sizing handles appear on the form to indicate that the form is selected, and the form's properties appear in the Properties window. If the property names do not appear in alphabetical order, click the **Alphabetical** button in the Properties window. As you learned in the chapter, the Properties window contains an Object box and a Properties list. The Object box contains the name of the selected object, as well as the class from which the object was instantiated. In this case, the Object box contains "Form1 System.Windows.Forms.Form". The Properties list has two columns. The left column shows the names of the selected object's properties. The right column (called the Settings box) displays the current value of the property.
2. First, you will change the type and size of the font used to display text on the form. If necessary, scroll the Properties window until you see the Font property. Click **Font** in the Properties list, and then click the **...** (ellipsis) button in the Settings box. When the Font dialog box opens, click **Segoe UI** in the Font box and **9** in the Size box, and then click the **OK** button. Notice that this change affects the text displayed in the controls on the form.
3. Click **StartPosition** in the Properties list. Click the **list arrow** in the Settings box, and then click **CenterScreen** to center the form on the screen when the application is started and the form first appears on the screen.
4. Click **Text** in the Properties list. Type **Wizard Viewer** and press **Enter**. The text appears in the form's title bar.
5. Now give the form a more meaningful name. Scroll to the top of the Properties window, then click **(Name)** in the Properties list. Type **MainForm** and press **Enter**.

In the next set of steps, you assign values to some of the properties of the Label1 control.

To assign values to some of the properties of the Label1 control:

1. Click the **Label1** control on the form. Click **Text** in the Properties list, then type **Wizard:** and press **Enter**. The text appears inside the label control. Notice that the label control automatically sizes to fit its current contents. This occurs because the control's AutoSize property is set to True.
2. Now you will set the label control's Location property, which determines the position of the control's upper-left corner on the form. Click **Location** in the Properties list. The first number in the Settings box refers to the control's horizontal location on the form; the second number refers to its vertical location. Type **19, 9** and press **Enter**. (Rather than setting the Location property, you can simply drag a control to the desired location.)

In the next set of steps, you assign values to some of the properties of the button controls.

To assign values to some of the properties of the button controls:

1. Click the **Button1** control on the form. Set the Name property to **showButton** and set the Text property to **Show**. If necessary, set the Location property to **23, 239**.
2. Click the **Button2** control on the form. Set the Name property to **hideButton** and set the Text property to **Hide**. If necessary, set the Size property to **75, 29**.
3. Click the **Button3** control on the form. Set the Name property to **exitButton** and set the Text property to **Exit**.

Using the Format Menu

If you want to make the Show and Exit buttons the same size as the Hide button, you can do so by individually setting the Show and Exit buttons' Size properties to the same value as the Hide button's Size property. However, an easier way is to use the Format menu. Before you can use the Format menu, you need to select the appropriate controls. The first control you select should always be the one whose size and/or location you want to match. In this case, you want the size of the Show and Exit buttons to match the size of the Hide button. Therefore, you should select the Hide button first. Recall that the first control selected is referred to as the reference control.

To make the Show and Exit buttons the same size as the Hide button:

1. Click the **Hide** button in the form. Press and hold down the **Control** (**Ctrl**) key as you click the **Show** button and then the **Exit** button, and then release the Control key. The three buttons are now selected. Notice that the sizing handles on the reference control (the Hide button) are white, whereas the sizing handles on the Show and Exit buttons are black. See Figure 1-48.

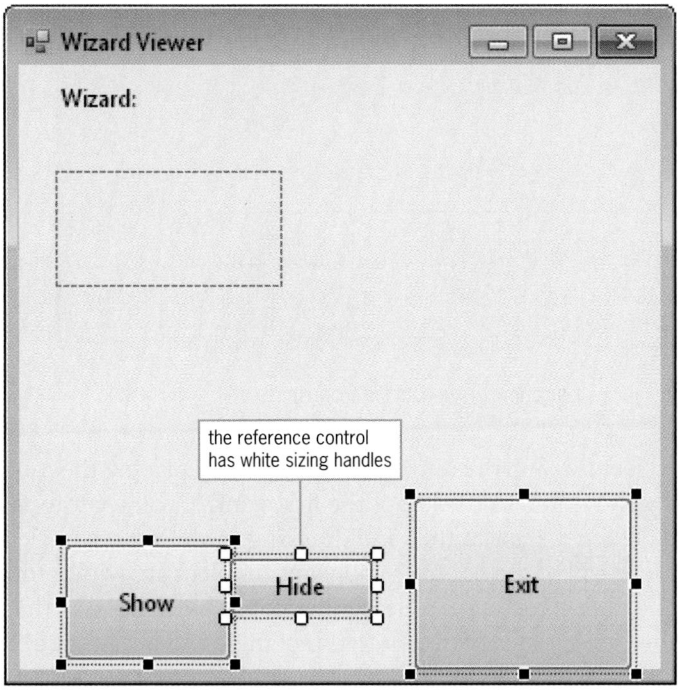

Figure 1-48 Buttons selected on the form

2. Click **Format** on the menu bar. Point to **Make Same Size**, and then click **Both**. The Show and Exit buttons are now the same size as the Hide button.
3. Click the **form** to deselect the buttons.

Next, you will use the Format menu to align the top borders of the Hide and Exit buttons with the top border of the Show button. In this case, the Show button should be the reference control.

To align the top borders of the buttons:

1. Click the **Show** button on the form. Press and hold down the **Control** (**Ctrl**) key as you click the **Hide** button and the **Exit** button, and then release the Control key.
2. Click **Format** on the menu bar. Point to **Align**, and then click **Tops**. The top borders of the Hide and Exit buttons are now aligned with the top border of the Show button.
3. Click the **form** to deselect the buttons.
4. If necessary, position the buttons to match those shown in Figure 1-49.

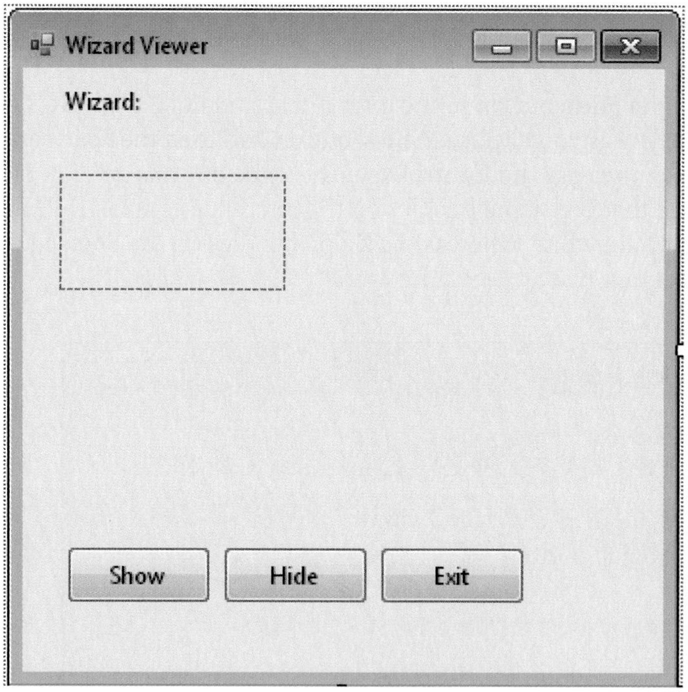

Figure 1-49 Location of the buttons on the form

You also can select a group of controls on the form by placing the mouse pointer slightly above and to the left of the first control you want to select, then pressing the left mouse button and dragging. A dotted rectangle appears as you drag. When all of the controls you want to select are within (or at least touched by) the dotted rectangle, release the mouse button. All of the controls surrounded or touched by the dotted rectangle will be selected. You will try this next.

To center the buttons horizontally on the form:

1. Place the mouse pointer slightly above and to the left of the Show button. Press the left mouse button and drag until the controls are within the dotted rectangle. See Figure 1-50.

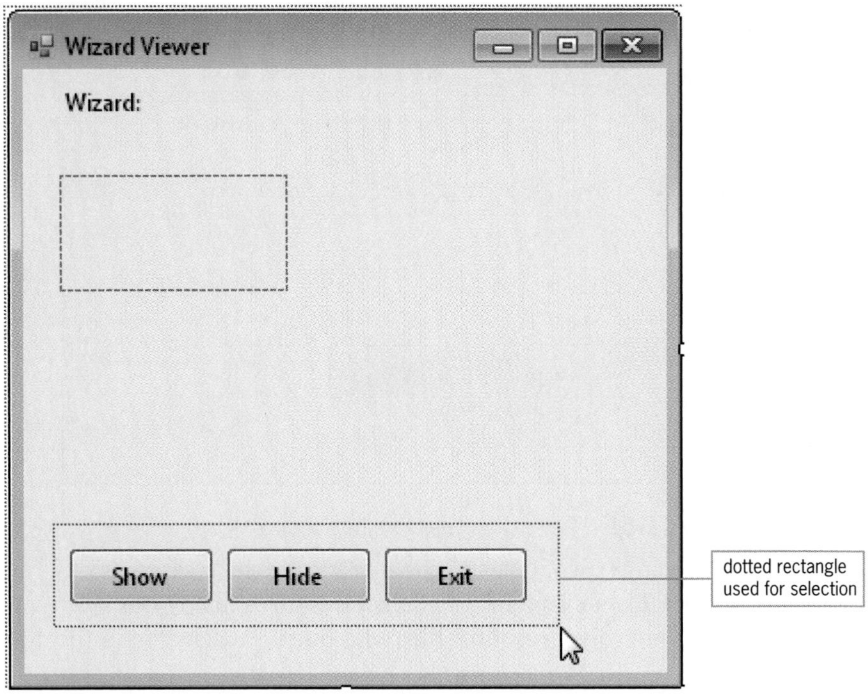

Figure 1-50 Buttons within the dotted rectangle

2. Release the mouse button. The three buttons are now selected. Click **Format** on the menu bar, point to **Center in Form**, and then click **Horizontally**.
3. Click the **form** to deselect the buttons.

Displaying an Image in a Picture Box Control

You can use a picture box control to display an image. The image you will display in the current interface is stored in the Wizard_appears (Wizard_appears.gif) file contained in the VbReloaded2010\Chap01 folder. The Wizard_appears image file was downloaded from the Animation Library site. You can browse and optionally download other free image files at *www.animationlibrary.com*.

To display an image in a picture box control:

1. Click the **PictureBox1** control on the form. A box containing a triangle appears in the upper-right corner of the control. The box is referred to as the task box because, when you click it, it displays a list of the tasks associated with the control. Each task in the list is associated with one or more properties. You can set the properties using the task list or the Properties window.
2. Click the **task box** on the PictureBox1 control. See Figure 1-51.

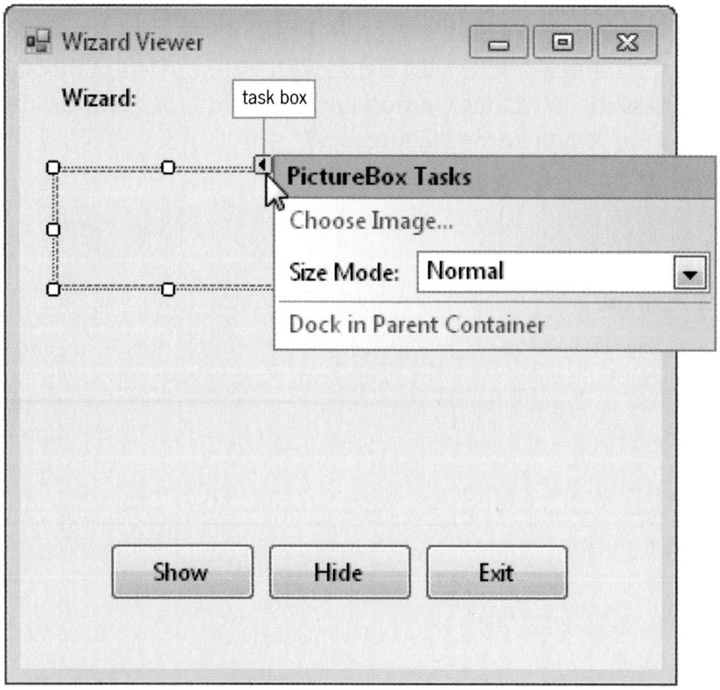

Figure 1-51 Task list for a picture box control

3. Click **Choose Image**. The Select Resource dialog box opens. Verify that the Project resource file radio button is selected in the dialog box.
4. Click the **Import** button. The Open dialog box opens.
5. Open the VbReloaded2010\Chap01 folder, then click **Wizard_appears** (**Wizard_appears.gif**) in the list of filenames. Click the **Open** button. The completed Select Resource dialog box is shown in Figure 1-52.

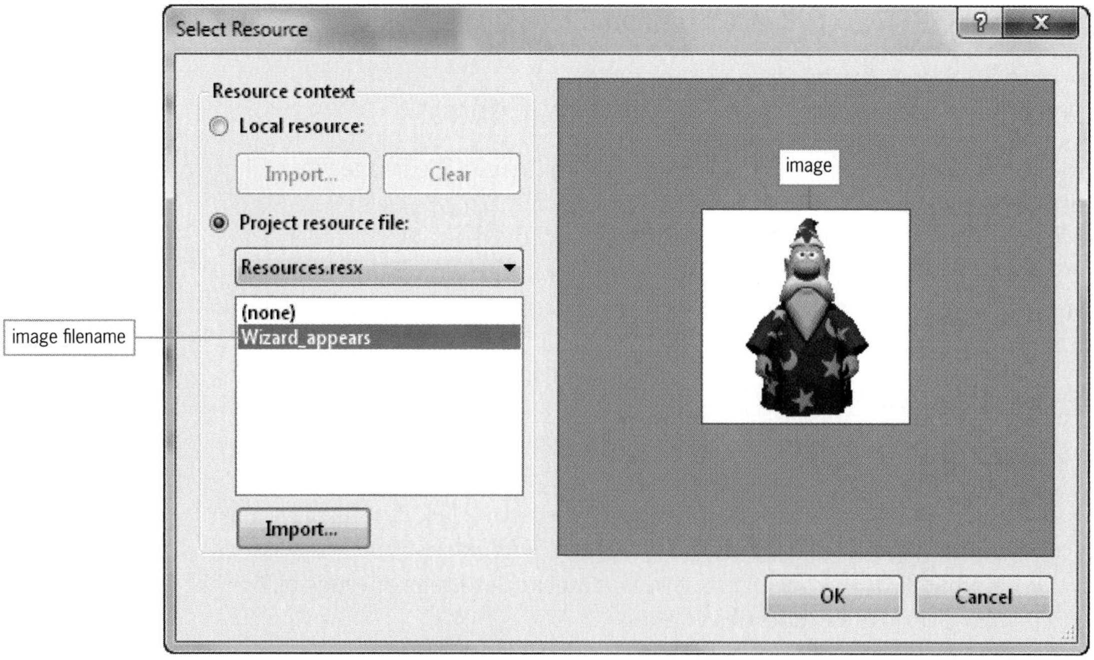

Figure 1-52 Completed Select Resource dialog box

6. Click the **OK** button. A portion of the image appears in the picture box control on the form.
7. Click the **Size Mode** list arrow in the task list, and then click **AutoSize**. The picture box control automatically sizes to fit its contents. However, don't be concerned if the entire image does not appear in the control. (You also can set the SizeMode property in the Properties window.)
8. Click the **picture box** control to close the task list.
9. Use the Properties window to set the picture box's Name property to **wizardPictureBox** and its Location property to **23, 32**.
10. Click the **picture box** control to return to the designer window. Now use the Format menu to center the picture box horizontally on the form. The completed interface is shown in Figure 1-53. (Don't be concerned if the entire image does not appear in the control.)

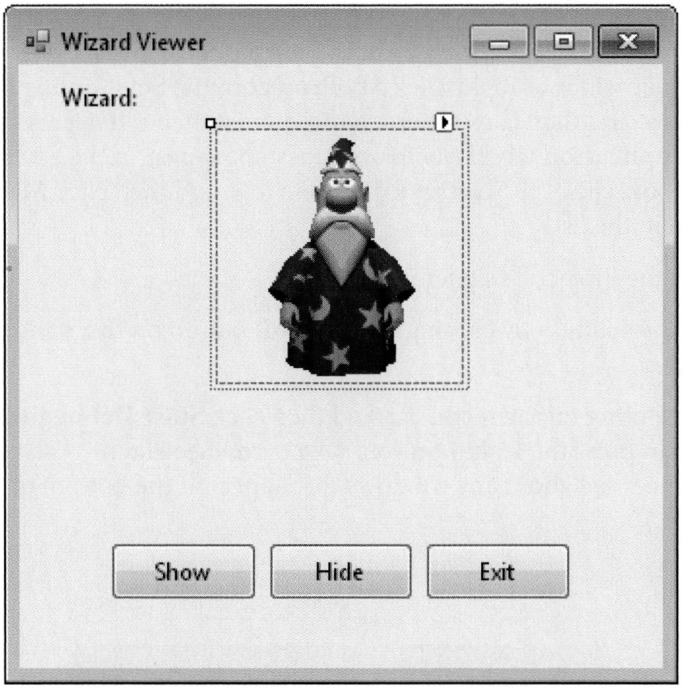

Figure 1-53 Completed interface

11. Save the solution by clicking **File** on the menu bar, and then clicking **Save All**.

In the next set of steps, you will lock the controls in place on the form. Locking the controls prevents them from being moved inadvertently as you work in the IDE.

To lock the controls:

1. Right-click the **form**, and then click **Lock Controls** on the context menu. Notice that a small lock appears in the upper-left corner of the form. (You also can lock the controls by clicking Format on the menu bar, and then clicking Lock Controls.)

2. Click the **Show** button. The small lock in the upper-left corner of the control indicates that the control is locked.

3. Try dragging one of the controls to a different location on the form. You will not be able to do so.

If you need to move a control after you have locked the controls in place, you can change the control's Location property setting in the Properties window. You also can unlock the control by changing its Locked property to False. Or, you can unlock all of the controls by clicking Format on the menu bar, and then clicking Lock Controls. The Lock Controls option is a toggle option: clicking it once activates it, and clicking it again deactivates it.

Starting and Ending an Application

Now that the interface is complete, you can start the application to see how it will look to the user.

To start and end the current application:

1. First, you will verify the name of the startup form in the Project Designer window. Right-click **My Project** in the Solution Explorer window, and then click **Open** on the context menu. If necessary, click the **Application** tab. If MainForm does not appear in the Startup form box, click the **Startup form** list arrow, and then click **Main-Form** in the list.

2. Close the Project Designer window.

3. Save the solution by clicking the **Save All** button on the Standard toolbar.

4. Click **Debug** on the menu bar, and then click **Start Debugging**. (You also can press the F5 key on your keyboard.) See Figure 1-54. (Do not be concerned about any windows that appear at the bottom of the screen.)

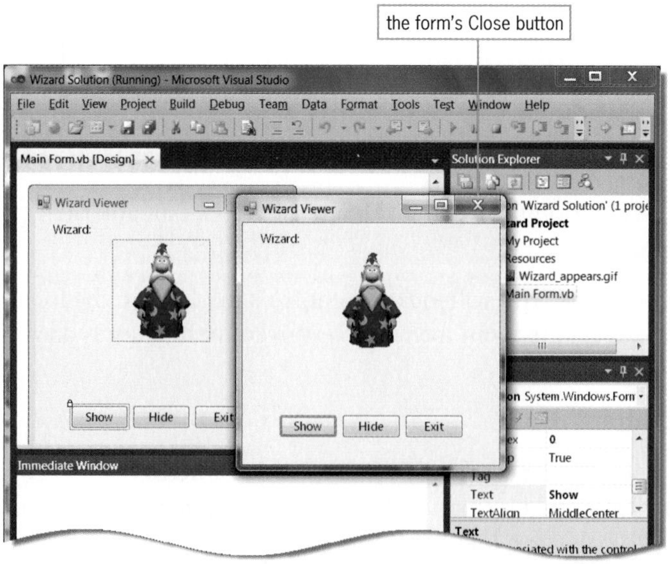

Figure 1-54 Result of starting the Wizard Viewer application

5. Click the **Hide** button, then click the **Show** button, and then click the **Exit** button. Currently, the buttons do not perform any tasks when clicked. This is because you have not yet entered the instructions that tell them the tasks to perform.
6. Click the **Close** button on the form's title bar.

Coding the Wizard Viewer Application

At this point, the buttons in the interface do not know the tasks they should perform when they are clicked by the user. You tell a button what to do by writing an event procedure for it. You write the event procedure in the Code Editor window.

To open the Code Editor window, and then code the Exit button's Click event procedure:

1. Auto-hide the Solution Explorer and Properties windows.
2. Right-click the **form**, and then click **View Code** to open the Code Editor window. Click the **Class Name** list arrow, and then click **exit-Button** in the list. Click the **Method Name** list arrow, and then click **Click** in the list. The code template for the exitButton's Click event procedure appears in the Code Editor window. See Figure 1-55. Notice the sizing list box in the lower-left corner of the window. You can use the list box to increase or decrease the size of the font used to display the code.

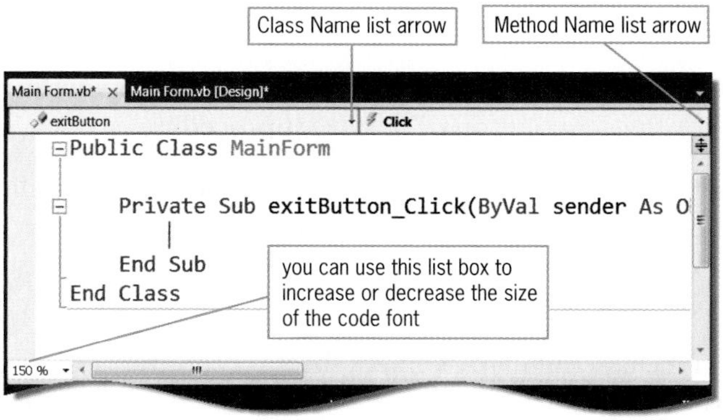

Figure 1-55 Code template for the exitButton's Click event procedure

3. The Exit button should end the application when it is clicked. The appropriate instruction to enter in the button's Click event procedure is `Me.Close()`. You can type the instruction on your own or use the Code Editor window's IntelliSense feature. In this set of steps, you will use the IntelliSense feature. Type **me.** (but don't press Enter). When you type the period, the IntelliSense feature displays a list of properties, methods, and so on from which you can select.

   Important note: If the list of choices does not appear, the IntelliSense feature may have been turned off on your computer system. To turn it on, click Tools on the menu bar, and then click Options. If necessary, select the Show all settings check box. Expand the Text Editor node in the Options dialog box, and then click Basic. Select the Auto list members check box. Click the OK button to close the Options dialog box.

4. If necessary, click the **Common** tab. The Common tab displays the most commonly used items, whereas the All tab displays all of the items. Type **cl** (but don't press Enter). The IntelliSense feature highlights the Close method in the list. See Figure 1-56.

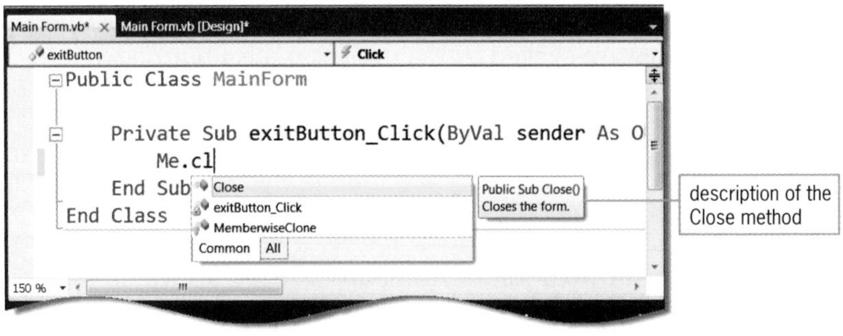

Figure 1-56 Close method highlighted in the Common tab's list

5. Press the **Enter** key on your keyboard to select the Close method. The Code Editor enters the `Me.Close()` instruction in the procedure.

When the user clicks the Show and Hide buttons, the buttons' Click event procedures should make the wizardPictureBox control visible and invisible, respectively. You can use assignment statements to accomplish both tasks.

To code the Show and Hide buttons' Click event procedures:

1. Use the Class Name and Method Name list boxes to open the code template for the showButton's Click event procedure.

2. You make a picture box visible by setting its Visible property to True. Type **wiz** and then click **wizardPictureBox** in the list.

3. Now you can either press the Tab key to enter wizardPictureBox in the procedure, or you can press the character that follows wizardPictureBox in the assignment statement. In this case, the next character is the period. Type **.** (a period), then type the letter **v**. The IntelliSense feature highlights Visible in the list.

4. Here again, you can either press the Tab key or type the next character in the assignment statement. In this case, the next character is the equal sign. Type = (an equal sign), then type **t** to select the `True` keyword in the list, and then press **Enter**. The Code Editor enters the `wizardPictureBox.Visible = True` statement in the procedure.

5. Open the code template for the hideButton's Click event procedure. On your own, use the IntelliSense feature to enter the following assignment statement into the procedure: `wizardPictureBox.Visible = False`. Figure 1-57 shows the code entered in the Code Editor window.

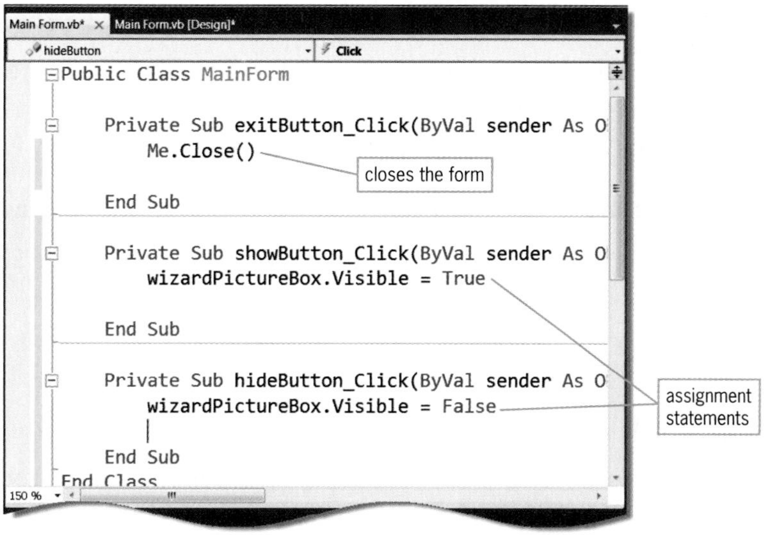

Figure 1-57 Code entered in the Code Editor window

At times, you may want to display line numbers in the Code Editor window.

To display line numbers in the Code Editor window:

1. Click **Tools** on the menu bar, and then click **Options**. If necessary, select the **Show all settings** check box.
2. If necessary, expand the **Text Editor** node in the Options dialog box, and then click **Basic**. Select the **Line numbers** check box.
3. At this point, you can either deselect the Show all settings check box or leave it selected. Click the **OK** button to close the Options dialog box. See Figure 1-58.

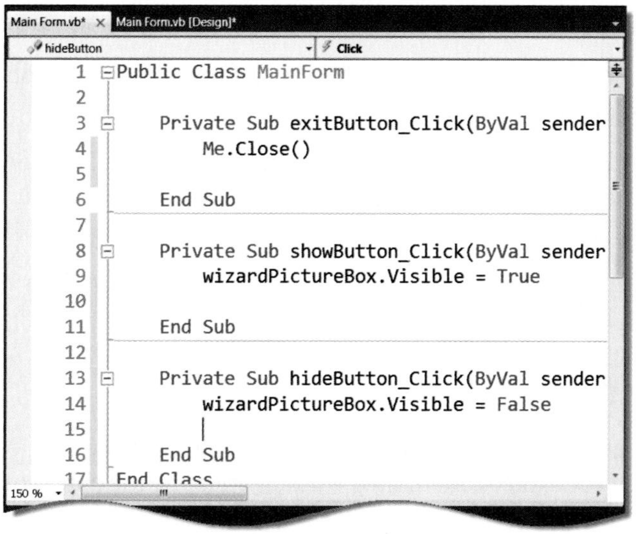

Figure 1-58 Line numbers shown in the Code Editor window

In the next set of steps, you save the solution and then start and test the application.

To save the solution and then start and test the application:

1. Click the **Close** button on the Code Editor window's title bar to close the window.
2. Click **File** on the menu bar, and then click **Save All**.
3. Click **Debug** on the menu bar, and then click **Start Debugging**.
4. Click the **Hide** button. The picture box disappears. Click the **Show** button. The picture box reappears.
5. Click the **Exit** button to end the application.

Closing the Current Solution

You should close a solution when you are finished working with it. You close a solution using the Close Solution (or Close Project) option on the File menu. When you close a solution, all projects and files contained in the solution also are closed.

To close the current solution:

1. Click **File** on the menu bar, and then click **Close Solution** (or **Close Project**).
2. Temporarily display the Solution Explorer window to verify that no solutions are open in the IDE.

Opening an Existing Solution

You can use the File menu to open an existing solution. If a solution is already open in the IDE, it is closed before another solution is opened.

To open the Wizard Solution:

1. If necessary, permanently display the Solution Explorer window.
2. Click **File** on the menu bar, and then click **Open Project** to open the Open Project dialog box.
3. Locate and then open the VbReloaded2010\Chap01\Wizard Solution folder. If necessary, click **Wizard Solution** (**Wizard Solution.sln**) in the list of filenames, and then click the **Open** button.
4. If you do not see the form in the designer window, click **View** on the menu bar, and then click **Designer**.

Printing the Application's Code

For your future reference, you should always print a copy of the application's code. To print the code, the Code Editor window must be the active (current) window.

To print the current application's code:

1. Right-click the **form**, and then click **View Code** to open the Code Editor window.
2. Click **File** on the menu bar, and then click **Print** to open the Print dialog box. If you select the Include line numbers check box, line

numbers will be printed even if they do not appear in the Code Editor window. If the Include line numbers check box is not selected, no line numbers will appear on the printout, even though they may appear in the Code Editor window.

3. Select the **Include line numbers** check box.

4. If your computer is connected to a printer, click the **OK** button to begin printing; otherwise, click the **Cancel** button. If you clicked the OK button, your printer prints the code.

Printing the Application's Interface

To print the application's interface during design time, the Windows Form designer window must be the active window.

To print the Wizard Viewer application's interface:

1. If necessary, click the **Main Form.vb [Design]** tab to make the designer window the active window, then press **Alt + Print Screen** (Prnt Scrn or PrtSc) to place a picture of the interface on the Clipboard.

2. Start an application that can display a picture, such as the Microsoft Word application, and open a new document (if necessary). Press **Control** (Ctrl) + **v** to paste the contents of the Clipboard in the document. Press **Control** (Ctrl) + **p** to open the Print dialog box.

3. If your computer is connected to a printer, click the **OK** button; otherwise, click the **Cancel** button. If you clicked the OK button, your printer prints the document.

4. Close the Microsoft Word (or other) application without saving the changes to the document.

Syntax Errors in Code

In this section, you will introduce a syntax error in the Hide button's Click event procedure. You then will debug the procedure by locating and fixing the error.

To introduce a syntax error in the code:

1. Click the **Main Form.vb** tab to make the Code Editor window the active window, and then auto-hide the Solution Explorer window.

2. Locate the hideButton's Click event procedure. Change the word `False` in the assignment statement to **Flse**, and then click the **blank line below the assignment statement**. The jagged blue line that appears below the mistyped word indicates that the instruction contains a syntax error.

3. Position your mouse pointer on the mistyped word, `Flse`. An error message appears in a box. See Figure 1-59. The message indicates that the Code Editor does not recognize the name, `Flse`. (Don't be concerned if your error message is slightly different than the one shown in the figure.)

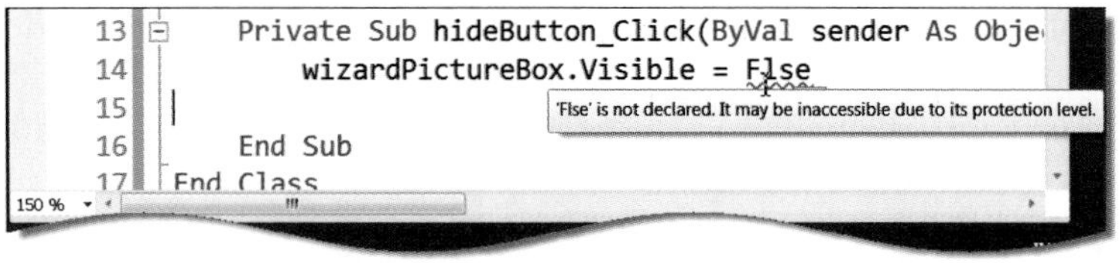

Figure 1-59 Jagged blue line and box indicate a syntax error

4. Now observe what happens when you start an application without correcting a syntax error. Save the solution, and then start the application. The message box shown in Figure 1-60 appears.

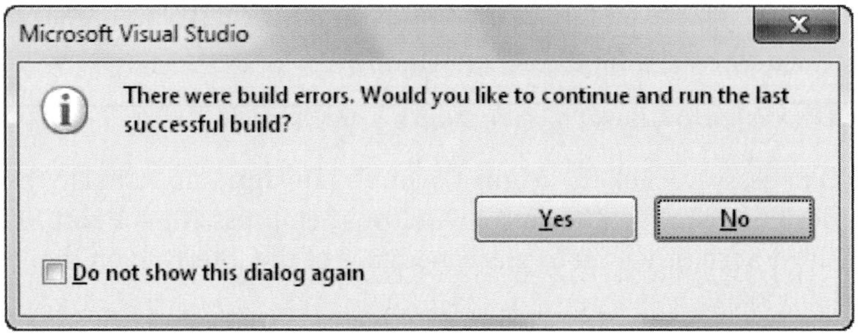

Figure 1-60 The message indicates that the code contains errors

5. Click the **No** button. The Error List window shown in Figure 1-61 opens. Notice that the Error List window indicates that the code has one error, which occurs on Line 14: Name 'Flse' is not declared.

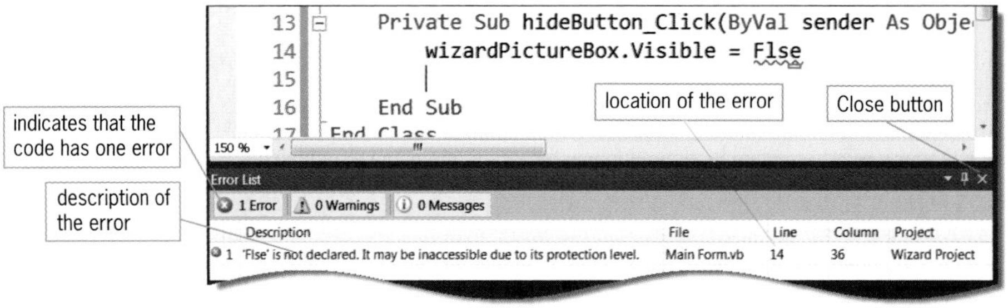

Figure 1-61 Error List window

6. Correct the syntax error by changing `Flse` in Line 14's assignment statement to **False**, and then click the **blank line below the assignment statement**. The Error List window shows that the code is now free of any errors.
7. Close the Error List window. Save the solution, and then start the application. Click the **Hide** button to verify that it is working correctly.
8. Click the **Exit** button to end the application, and then close the Code Editor window.

Exiting Visual Studio 2010 or Visual Basic 2010 Express Edition

You can exit Visual Studio or Visual Basic Express Edition using either the Close button on the title bar or the Exit option on the File menu.

To exit Visual Studio or Visual Basic Express Edition:

1. Click **File** on the menu bar.
2. Click **Exit** on the menu.

Running the Application's Executable File

Earlier you learned that when you start a Visual Basic application, the computer automatically creates a file that can be run outside of the IDE. The file has the same name as the project, but with an .exe filename extension. The computer stores the file in the project's bin\Debug folder.

To run the Wizard Project.exe file:

1. Press and hold down the **Windows logo** key on your keyboard as you tap the letter **r**, and then release the logo key. The Run dialog opens.
2. Click the **Browse** button to open the Browse dialog box. Locate and then open the VbReloaded2010\Chap01\Wizard Solution\Wizard Project\bin\Debug folder. Click **Wizard Project** (**Wizard Project.exe**) in the list of filenames. (Depending on how Windows is set up on your computer, you may see the .exe extension on the filename.) Click the **Open** button to close the Browse dialog box.
3. Click the **OK** button in the Run dialog box. After a few moments, the Wizard Viewer application's interface appears on the screen. Click the **Hide** and **Show** buttons to test the application, and then click the **Exit** button.

The Windows logo key looks like this: .

PROGRAMMING TUTORIAL 2

Creating the Horse Auction Application

In this tutorial, you create the Horse Auction application shown in Figure 1-62. The interface contains a label, three picture boxes, and three buttons. The abbyPictureBox and rascalPictureBox controls contain pictures of horses. The pictures are stored in the abby.jpg and rascal.jpg files, which are contained in the VbReloaded2010\Chap01 folder. The abbyButton and rascalButton controls display one of the horse pictures in the displayPictureBox. Each also displays the name of its respective horse (either Abby or Rascal) in the nameLabel control. The exitButton ends the application.

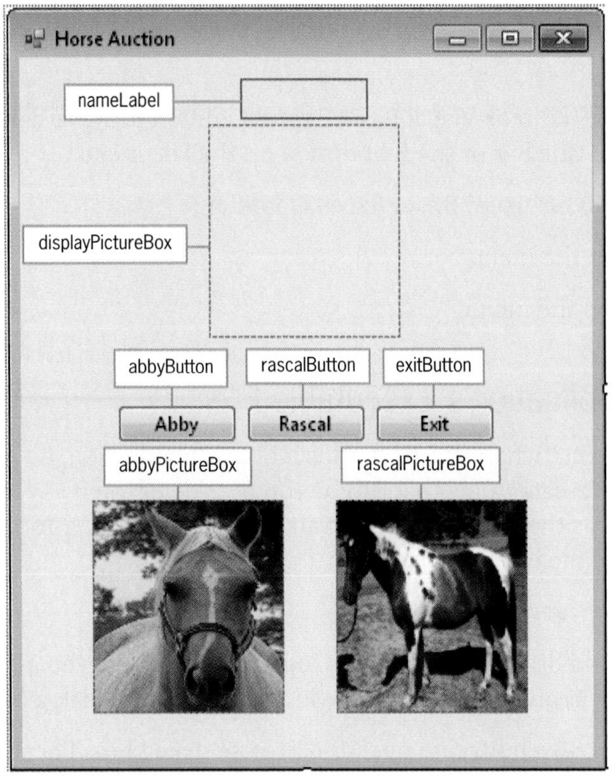

Figure 1-62 Horse Auction application's user interface

To begin creating the Horse Auction application:

1. Start Visual Studio 2010 or Visual Basic 2010 Express Edition. If you need help, refer to the How To box shown earlier in Figure 1-2.
2. Click **Window** on the menu bar, then click **Reset Window Layout**, and then click the **Yes** button.
3. Click **Tools** on the menu bar, and then click **Options** to open the Options dialog box. Use the information shown earlier in Figure 1-6 to select and deselect the appropriate check boxes, and then close the dialog box.
4. Use the New Project option on the File menu to create a new Visual Basic Windows application. Use the following names for the solution and project: Horse Solution and Horse Project. Save the solution in the VbReloaded2010\Chap01 folder. If you need help, refer to the How To box shown earlier in Figure 1-5.
5. Use the Properties window to change the form file's name from Form1.vb to **Main Form.vb**. (If you do not see the form file's properties in the Properties window, click Form1.vb in the Solution Explorer window.)
6. Click the **form**. Change the form's name to **MainForm**. Also change the form's Font property to **Segoe UI, 9 pt**.
7. Change the form's StartPosition property so that the form will be centered on the screen when the application is started.
8. Change the form's Text property so that "Horse Auction" (without the quotes) appears in its title bar.

Managing the Windows in the IDE

In the next set of steps, you practice closing, opening, auto-hiding, and displaying the windows in the IDE. If you need help while performing the steps, refer to the How To box shown earlier in Figure 1-10.

To close, open, auto-hide, and display the windows in the IDE:

1. Close the Properties window, and then open the Properties window.
2. If necessary, close the Team Explorer and Data Sources windows.
3. Auto-hide the Solution Explorer window, and then temporarily display the window.
4. Permanently display the Solution Explorer and Toolbox windows.

Using the Toolbox Window to Add Objects to a Form

In the next set of steps, you add the seven controls to the form. You also size, move, delete, and undelete a control.

To add controls to the form, and then manipulate the controls:

1. Use the Label tool in the toolbox to add a label to the form. If you need help, refer to the How To box shown earlier in Figure 1-16.
2. Next, add three picture boxes and three buttons to the form. Position the controls as shown in Figure 1-63. You can make the form larger by dragging one of its sizing handles, which appear on its right and bottom borders. If you need help, refer to the How To box shown earlier in Figure 1-17.

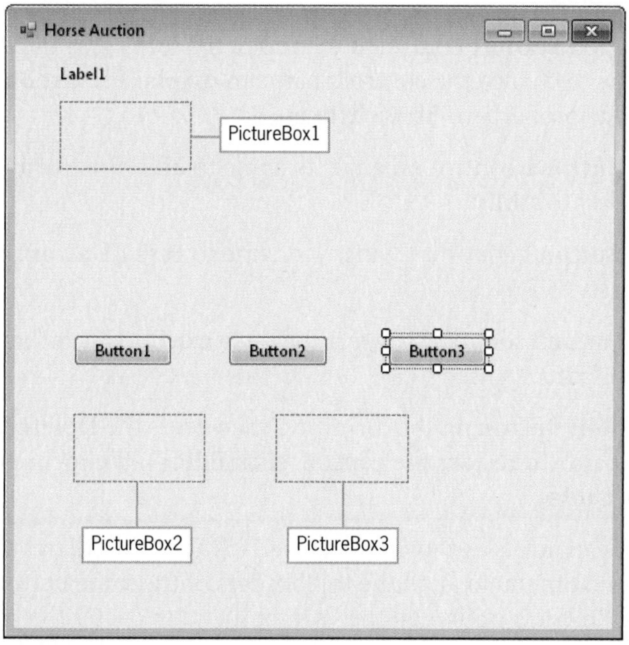

Figure 1-63 Controls added to the form

3. Click the **Label1** control. Change the label's name to **nameLabel**. Set the label's BorderStyle property to **FixedSingle**, and set its AutoSize property to **False**.

4. Click **Text** in the label's Properties list, then press the **Backspace** key on your keyboard, and then press **Enter** to remove the Label1 text from the control. Now change the label's Size property to **80, 25**.
5. Click **TextAlign** in the Properties list, then click the **list arrow** in the Settings box, and then click the **rectangle located in the second row, second column**. This will center the text within the label control.
6. Click the **PictureBox2** control at the bottom of the form. Change its name to **abbyPictureBox**. Click the control's **task box**, and then use its task list to display the image stored in the **abby.jpg** file, which is contained in the VbReloaded2010\Chap01 folder. Also use the task list to set the Size Mode to **StretchImage**. If you need help, refer to the *Displaying an Image in a Picture Box Control* section in Programming Tutorial 1.
7. Use the Properties window to set the abbyPictureBox control's Size property to **120, 130**.
8. Use the Make Same Size option on the Format menu to make the other two picture boxes the same size as the abbyPictureBox. If you need help, refer to the *Using the Format Menu* section in either the chapter or Programming Tutorial 1.
9. Click the **form** to deselect the three picture box controls.
10. Click the **PictureBox3** control at the bottom of the form. Change its name to **rascalPictureBox**. Use the control's task list to display the image stored in the **rascal.jpg** file, which is contained in the VbReloaded2010\Chap01 folder. Also use the task list to set the Size Mode to **StretchImage**.
11. Click the **PictureBox1** control at the top of the form. Use the Properties window to change the control's name to **displayPictureBox** and its SizeMode property to **StretchImage**.
12. Click the **Button1** control. Change its name to **abbyButton** and its Text property to **Abby**.
13. Click the **Button2** control. Change its name to **rascalButton** and its Text property to **Rascal**.
14. Click the **Button3** control. Change its name to **exitButton** and its Text property to **Exit**.
15. Click the **abbyButton** on the form, and then press the **Delete** key on your keyboard. To restore the control, click **Edit** on the menu bar, and then click **Undo**.
16. Position the controls as shown in Figure 1-64. Use the Align option on the Format menu to align the top borders of the three buttons. Use the Center in Form option on the Format menu to center the label, horizontally, on the form. Then use it to center the displayPictureBox, horizontally, on the form. Select the three buttons and then use the Center in Form option to center them, horizontally, on the form.

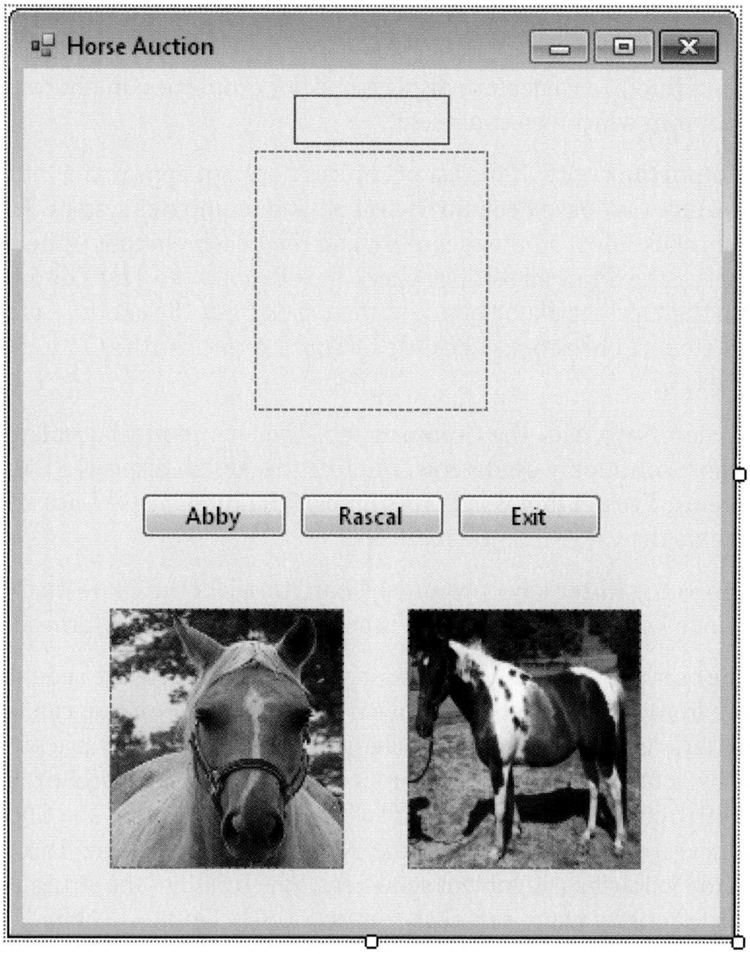

Figure 1-64 Location of controls on the form

17. Lock the controls on the form by right-clicking the **form**, and then clicking **Lock Controls** on the context menu.

18. Save the solution. If you need help, refer to the How To box shown earlier in Figure 1-23.

Coding the Horse Auction Application

At this point, the Abby, Rascal, and Exit buttons in the interface do not know the tasks they should perform when they are clicked by the user. You tell a button what to do by writing an event procedure for it. You write the event procedure in the Code Editor window.

To open the Code Editor window, and then code the Exit button's Click event procedure:

1. Auto-hide the Toolbox, Solution Explorer, and Properties windows.
2. Open the Code Editor window. If you need help, refer to the How To box shown earlier in Figure 1-19.
3. Use the Class Name and Method Name list boxes to open the code template for the exitButton's Click event procedure.

4. The Exit button should end the application when it is clicked. Type **me.** (but don't press Enter). When you type the period, the Code Editor's IntelliSense feature displays a list of properties, methods, and so on from which you can select.

   Important note: If the list of choices does not appear, the IntelliSense feature may have been turned off on your computer system. To turn it on, click Tools on the menu bar, and then click Options. If necessary, select the Show all settings check box. Expand the Text Editor node in the Options dialog box, and then click Basic. Select the Auto list members check box. Click the OK button to close the Options dialog box.

5. If necessary, click the **Common** tab. The Common tab displays the most commonly used items, whereas the All tab displays all of the items. Type **cl** (but don't press Enter). The IntelliSense feature highlights the Close method in the list.

6. Press the **Enter** key on your keyboard to select the Close method. The Code Editor enters the `Me.Close()` instruction in the procedure.

When the user clicks the Abby button, its Click event procedure should display the image from the abbyPictureBox in the displayPictureBox. You can accomplish this task using an assignment statement that assigns the Image property of the abbyPictureBox to the Image property of the displayPictureBox, like this: `displayPictureBox.Image = abbyPictureBox.Image`. The Click event procedure also should display the name "Abby" in the nameLabel. This task requires the following assignment statement, which assigns the string "Abby" to the Text property of the nameLabel: `nameLabel.Text = "Abby"`.

To code the Abby button's Click event procedure:

1. Open the code template for the abbyButton's Click event procedure.

2. Type **displ** to highlight displayPictureBox in the list. (If displayPictureBox is not highlighted in the list, click displayPictureBox.) Press the **Tab** key to enter displayPictureBox in the procedure.

3. Type `.` (a period). The Image property should be highlighted in the list. (If the Image property is not highlighted in the list, click Image.)

4. Press the **Tab** key to enter Image in the procedure.

5. Type **=abbyp** to highlight abbyPictureBox in the list. (If abbyPictureBox is not highlighted in the list, click abbyPictureBox.)

6. Type `.` (a period). The Image property should be highlighted in the list. Press **Enter**. The Code Editor enters the `displayPictureBox.Image = abbyPictureBox.Image` statement in the procedure.

7. Next, use the IntelliSense feature to type the **nameLabel.Text = "Abby"** statement in the procedure. Press **Enter** after typing the statement.

When the user clicks the Rascal button, its Click event procedure should display the image from the rascalPictureBox in the displayPictureBox. It also should display the name "Rascal" in the nameLabel.

To code the Rascal button's Click event procedure:

1. Open the code template for the rascalButton's Click event procedure, and then enter the appropriate assignment statements.

2. If line numbers do not appear in the Code Editor window, click **Tools** on the menu bar, and then click **Options**. If necessary, select the **Show all settings** check box.

3. If necessary, expand the **Text Editor** node in the Options dialog box, and then click **Basic**. Select the **Line numbers** check box.

4. At this point, you can either deselect the Show all settings check box or leave it selected. Click the **OK** button to close the Options dialog box. The completed code is shown in Figure 1-65.

```
Main Form.vb*  ×  Main Form.vb [Design]*

MainForm                          ▼  (Declarations)
    1 ⊟Public Class MainForm
    2
    3 ⊟    Private Sub exitButton_Click(ByVal sender As Object, ByV
    4            Me.Close()
    5
    6        End Sub
    7
    8 ⊟    Private Sub abbyButton_Click(ByVal sender As Object, ByV
    9            displayPictureBox.Image = abbyPictureBox.Image
   10            nameLabel.Text = "Abby"
   11
   12        End Sub
   13
   14 ⊟    Private Sub rascalButton_Click(ByVal sender As Object, B
   15            displayPictureBox.Image = rascalPictureBox.Image
   16            nameLabel.Text = "Rascal"
   17
   18        End Sub
   19 End Class
```

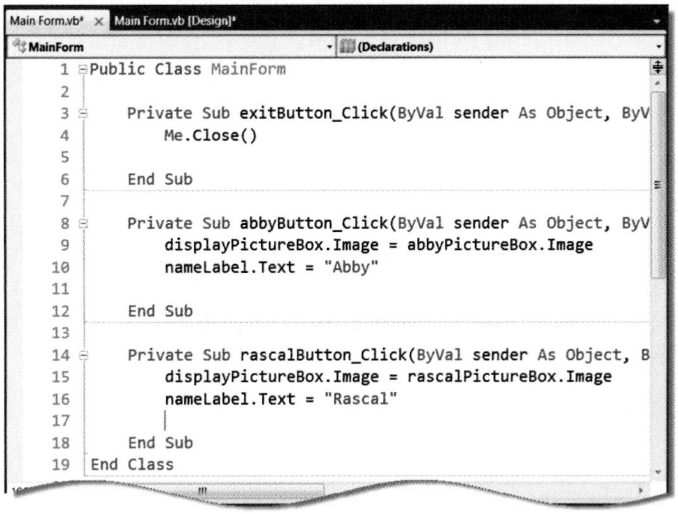

Figure 1-65 Completed code for the Horse Auction application

Testing an Application

In the following set of steps, you will test the application to determine whether the buttons respond correctly to the user.

To start and end the current application:

1. Verify that MainForm is the name of the startup form in the Project Designer window, and then close the window. If you need help, refer to the How To box shown earlier in Figure 1-24.

2. Save the solution.

3. Start the application. If you need help, refer to the How To box shown earlier in Figure 1-26. (Do not be concerned about any windows that appear at the bottom of the screen.)

4. Click the **Abby** button. The picture of Abby appears in the displayPictureBox, and the name "Abby" appears in the label control.

5. Click the **Rascal** button. The picture of Rascal appears in the display-PictureBox, and the name "Rascal" appears in the label control.

6. Click the **Exit** button.

Printing the Application's Code and Interface

For your future reference, you should always print a copy of the application's code and its interface. To print the code, the Code Editor window must be the active (current) window. To print the interface during design time, the Windows Form designer window must be the active window.

To print the current application's code:

1. If necessary, click the **Main Form.vb** tab to make the Code Editor window the active window.
2. If your computer is connected to a printer, print the code with line numbers. If you need help, refer to the How To box shown earlier in Figure 1-30.
3. If your computer is connected to a printer, print the application's interface. If you need help, refer to the How To box shown earlier in Figure 1-30.

Closing and Opening a Solution

You should close a solution when you are finished working with it. You close a solution using the Close Solution (or Close Project) option on the File menu. When you close a solution, all projects and files contained in the solution also are closed. You can open an existing solution using the Open Project option on the File menu.

To close and then open the current solution:

1. Close the Horse solution. If you need help, refer to the How To box shown earlier in Figure 1-31.
2. Temporarily display the Solution Explorer window to verify that no solutions are open.
3. Now, open the Horse solution. If you need help, refer to the How To box shown earlier in Figure 1-32.
4. Temporarily display the Solution Explorer window to verify that the solution is open.

Syntax Errors in Code

In this section, you will introduce a syntax error in the Rascal button's Click event procedure. You then will debug the procedure by locating and fixing the error.

To introduce a syntax error in the code:

1. If necessary, click the **Main Form.vb** tab to make the Code Editor window the active window.
2. Locate the rascalButton's Click event procedure. Delete **.Text** in the second assignment statement, and then click the **blank line** below the assignment statement. The jagged blue line that appears below the string "Rascal" indicates that the assignment statement contains a syntax error.

3. Position your mouse pointer on the jagged blue line. An error message appears in a box, as shown in Figure 1-66. The message indicates that the string "Rascal" cannot be converted to a label. In other words, it cannot be assigned to the label itself; rather, it must be assigned to one of the label's properties. In this case, it should be assigned to the label's Text property.

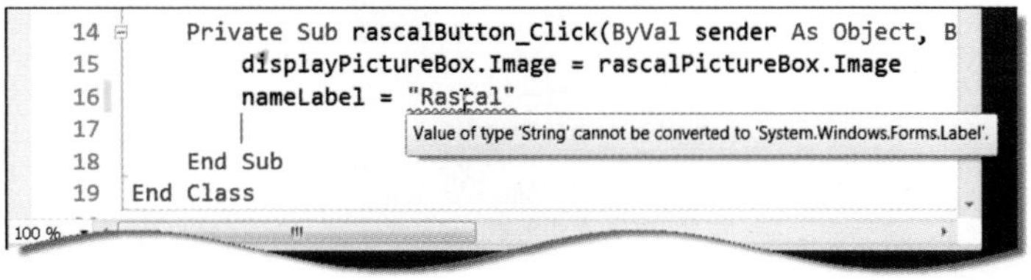
14 Private Sub rascalButton_Click(ByVal sender As Object, B
15 displayPictureBox.Image = rascalPictureBox.Image
16 nameLabel = "Rascal"
17
18 End Sub
19 End Class
Value of type 'String' cannot be converted to 'System.Windows.Forms.Label'.
100 %

Figure 1-66 Jagged line and error message indicate a syntax error

4. Now observe what happens when you start the application without correcting the syntax error. Save the solution, and then start the application. A message box appears and indicates that the code contains errors. The message asks whether you want to continue.
5. Click the **No** button. The Error List window opens at the bottom of the IDE. The Error List window indicates that the code has one error, which occurs on Line 16.
6. Correct the syntax error by retyping **.Text** after nameLabel, and then click the **blank line below the assignment statement**. The Error List window shows that the code is now free of errors.
7. Close the Error List window. Save the solution, and then start the application. Click the **Rascal** button to verify that it is working correctly.
8. Click the **Exit** button to end the application, and then close the Code Editor window.

Modifying the Interface

In this set of steps, you will modify the interface so that the two picture boxes at the bottom of the form do not appear when the application is started.

To modify the interface:

1. Right-click the **form**, and then click **Lock Controls** to unlock the controls.
2. Place your mouse pointer on the sizing handle that appears at the bottom of the form. Press and hold down the left mouse button as you drag the bottom border up. When you no longer see the picture boxes at the bottom of the form, release the mouse button.
3. Lock the controls on the form.
4. Save the solution, and then start the application. Click the **Abby** button. See Figure 1-67.

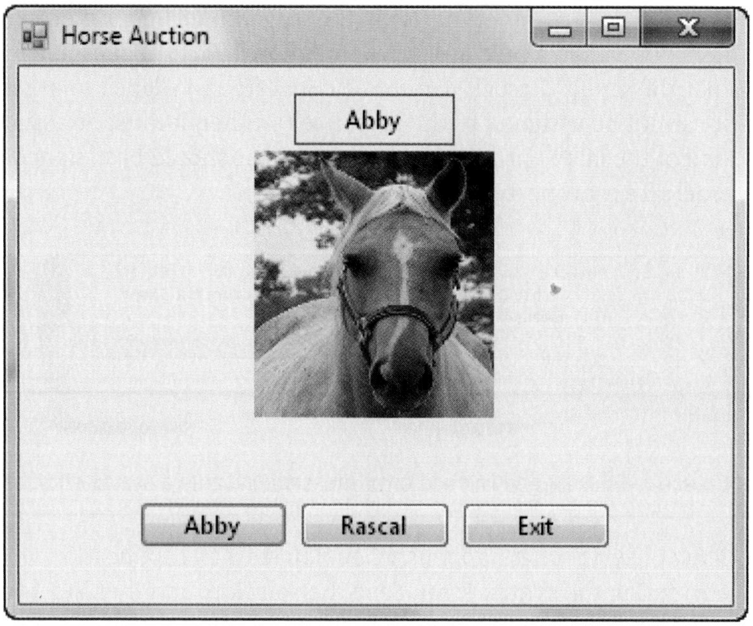

Figure 1-67 Result of clicking the Abby button

5. Click the **Rascal** button, and then click the **Exit** button.
6. Close the solution.

Exiting Visual Studio 2010 or Visual Basic 2010 Express Edition

You can exit Visual Studio or Visual Basic Express Edition using either the Close button on the title bar or the Exit option on the File menu.

To exit Visual Studio or Visual Basic Express Edition:

1. Click **File** on the menu bar.
2. Click **Exit** on the menu.

Running the Application's Executable File

Earlier you learned that when you start a Visual Basic application, the computer automatically creates a file that can be run outside of the IDE. The file has the same name as the project, but with an .exe filename extension. The computer stores the file in the project's bin\Debug folder.

To run the Horse Project.exe file:

The Windows logo key looks like this: ⊞.

1. Press and hold down the **Windows logo** key on your keyboard as you tap the letter **r**, and then release the logo key. The Run dialog opens.
2. Click the **Browse** button to open the Browse dialog box. Locate and then open the VbReloaded2010\Chap01\Horse Solution\Horse Project\bin\Debug folder. Click **Horse Project** (**Horse Project.exe**) in the list of filenames. (Depending on how Windows is set up on your computer, you may see the .exe extension on the filename.) Click the **Open** button to close the Browse dialog box.
3. Click the **OK** button in the Run dialog box. After a few moments, the Horse Auction application's interface appears on the screen.

Click the **Abby** and **Rascal** buttons to test the application, and then click the **Exit** button.

PROGRAMMING EXAMPLE
State Capitals

Create an application that displays the state capital in a label when a button with the state's name is clicked. Use the following state names: Alabama, Alaska, Arizona, and Arkansas. Use the following names for the solution, project, and form file: State Capital Solution, State Capital Project, and Main Form.vb. Save the files in the VbReloaded2010\Chap01 folder. Remember to lock the controls in the interface. See Figures 1-68 through 1-70.

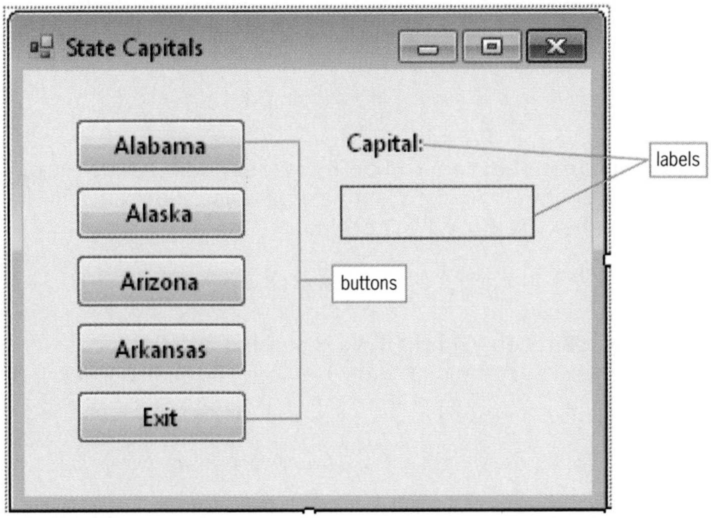

Figure 1-68 User interface

Object	Property	Setting
Form1	Name	MainForm
	Font	Segoe UI, 9pt
	StartPosition	CenterScreen
	Text	State Capitals
Button1	Name	alabamaButton
	Text	Alabama
Button2	Name	alaskaButton
	Text	Alaska
Button3	Name	arizonaButton
	Text	Arizona
Button4	Name	arkansasButton
	Text	Arkansas
Button5	Name	exitButton
	Text	Exit
Label1	Text	Capital:
Label2	Name	capitalLabel
	AutoSize	False
	BorderStyle	FixedSingle
	Text	(empty) (Hint: Delete the text in the Settings box.)
	TextAlign	MiddleCenter

Figure 1-69 Objects, properties, and settings

```
Public Class MainForm

    Private Sub alabamaButton_Click(ByVal sender As Object,
    ByVal e As System.EventArgs) Handles alabamaButton.Click
          capitalLabel.Text = "Montgomery"

    End Sub

    Private Sub alaskaButton_Click(ByVal sender As Object,
    ByVal e As System.EventArgs) Handles alaskaButton.Click
          capitalLabel.Text = "Juneau"

    End Sub

    Private Sub arizonaButton_Click(ByVal sender As Object,
    ByVal e As System.EventArgs) Handles arizonaButton.Click
          capitalLabel.Text = "Phoenix"

    End Sub

    Private Sub arkansasButton_Click(ByVal sender As Object,
    ByVal e As System.EventArgs) Handles arkansasButton.Click
          capitalLabel.Text = "Little Rock"

    End Sub

    Private Sub exitButton_Click(ByVal sender As Object,
    ByVal e As System.EventArgs) Handles exitButton.Click
          Me.Close()

    End Sub
End Class
```

Figure 1-70 Code

Summary

- An object-oriented programming language, such as Visual Basic 2010, allows programmers to use objects to accomplish a program's goal.
- An object is anything that can be seen, touched, or used. Every object has attributes, called properties, that control its appearance and behavior.
- Every object in an object-oriented program is instantiated (created) from a class, which is a pattern that tells the computer how the object should look and behave. An object is referred to as an instance of the class.
- Applications created in Visual Studio 2010 are composed of solutions, projects, and files.
- You create your application's GUI in the Windows Form Designer window.
- A form is the foundation for the user interface in a Windows application.
- A Windows Form object is instantiated from the Windows Form class.

- The Solution Explorer window displays the names of projects and files contained in the current solution.
- The Properties window lists the selected object's properties.
- All class definitions are contained in namespaces.
- The System.Windows.Forms namespace contains the definition of the Windows Form class, as well as the class definitions for objects you add to a form.
- You use the value stored in an object's Name property to refer to the object in code.
- The value stored in the form's Text property displays in the form's title bar and on the Windows 7 taskbar when you hover your mouse pointer over the application's button.
- The form's StartPosition property determines the position of the form when it first appears on the screen when the application is started.
- The recommended font for applications created for the Windows 7 (or Windows Vista) environment is the 9-point size of the Segoe UI font.
- The Toolbox window contains the tools you use when creating your application's GUI.
- The value stored in a control's Text property displays inside the control.
- Controls on a form can be selected, sized, moved, deleted, or locked and unlocked.
- A label control displays text that the user is not allowed to edit while the application is running.
- Button controls are commonly used to perform an immediate action when clicked.
- You use a picture box control to display an image on the form.
- The Format menu provides options for aligning and sizing the controls on a form.
- You tell an object how to respond to an event by coding an event procedure. You enter the code in the Code Editor window.
- You use the Class Name and Method Name list boxes in the Code Editor window to select the object and event that you want to code.
- The Code Editor provides a code template for each of an object's event procedures. The code template begins with the `Private Sub` clause and ends with the `End Sub` clause. You enter your Visual Basic instructions between those clauses.
- You can use the `Me.Close()` instruction to terminate an application.
- You should save the solution every 10 or 15 minutes.
- When you start a Visual Basic application, the computer automatically creates an executable file. This is the file typically given to the user. You can run this file from the Windows Run dialog box. To open the dialog box, press and hold down the Windows logo key on your keyboard as you tap the letter r, and then release the logo key.

- You can use an assignment statement to assign a value to a property while an application is running.
- You should print an application's code and its user interface.
- Closing a solution closes all projects and files contained in the solution.
- The process of locating and correcting the errors (bugs) in a program is called debugging.

Key Terms

Assignment operator—the equal sign in an assignment statement

Assignment statement—an instruction that assigns a value to something, such as to the property of an object

Bug—an error in a program's code

Button control—the control commonly used to perform an immediate action when clicked

Camel case—the practice of entering the first word in an object's name in lowercase and then capitalizing the first letter of each subsequent word in the name

Class—the term used in object-oriented programming (OOP) to refer to a pattern that the computer uses to instantiate an object

Class definition—a block of code that specifies (or defines) an object's appearance and behavior

Class Name list box—appears in the Code Editor window; lists the names of the objects included in the user interface

Code—program instructions

Code Editor window—the window in which you enter your application's code

Controls—objects (such as a label, picture box, or button) added to a form

Debugging—the process of locating and correcting the errors (bugs) in a program

Dot member access operator—a period; used to indicate a hierarchy

Event procedure—a set of Visual Basic instructions that tell an object how to respond to an event

Events—actions to which an object can respond; examples include clicking, double-clicking, and scrolling

Executable file—a file that can be run outside of the Visual Studio IDE, such as from the Run dialog box in Windows; the file has an .exe extension on its filename

Font—the general shape of the characters used to display text

Form—the foundation for the user interface in a Windows application; also called a Windows form object

Form file—a file that contains the code associated with a Windows form

GUI—graphical user interface

IDE—integrated development environment

Instance—the term used in object-oriented programming (OOP) to refer to an object instantiated (created) from a class

Instantiated—the term used in object-oriented programming (OOP) to refer to the process of creating an object from a class

Integrated development environment—an environment that contains all of the tools and features you need to create, run, and test your programs; also called an IDE

Keyword—a word that has a special meaning in a programming language

Label control—the control used to display text that the user is not allowed to edit during run time

Method—a predefined Visual Basic procedure that you can call (or invoke) when needed

Method Name list box—appears in the Code Editor window; lists the events to which the selected object is capable of responding

Namespace—a block of memory cells inside the computer; contains the code that defines a group of related classes

Object—in object-oriented programming (OOP), anything that can be seen, touched, or used

Object box—the section of the Properties window that contains the name of the selected object

Object-oriented programming language—a language that allows the programmer to use objects to accomplish a program's goal

Pascal case—the practice of capitalizing the first letter in a form's name and the first letter of each subsequent word in the name

Picture box control—the control used to display an image on a form

Point—used to measure font size; 1/72 of an inch

Procedure footer—the last line in a code template

Procedure header—the first line in a code template

Project—a container that stores files associated with that particular project

Properties—the attributes that control an object's appearance and behavior

Properties list—the section of the Properties window that lists the names of the properties associated with the selected object, as well as each property's value

Properties window—the window that lists an object's attributes (properties)

Reference control—the first control selected in a group of controls; this is the control whose size and/or location you want the other selected controls to match

Sequence structure—refers to the fact that the computer processes a procedure's instructions one after another in the order in which they appear in the procedure; also referred to as sequential processing

Sequential processing—refers to the fact that the computer processes a procedure's instructions one after another in the order in which they appear in the procedure; also referred to as the sequence structure

Settings box—the right column of the Properties list; displays the current value (setting) of each property

Solution—a container that stores the projects and files for an entire application

Solution Explorer window—the window that displays a list of the projects contained in the current solution and the items contained in each project

Source file—a file that contains code

Startup form—the form that appears automatically when an application is started

String—zero or more characters enclosed in quotation marks

Sub procedure—a block of code that performs a specific task

Syntax—the rules of a programming language

Syntax error—occurs when an instruction in your code breaks one of a programming language's rules

Toolbox—Toolbox window

Toolbox window—the window that contains the tools used when creating an interface; each tool represents a class; referred to more simply as the toolbox

User interface—what the user sees and interacts with while an application is running

Windows Form Designer window—the window in which you create your application's GUI

Windows Form object—the foundation for the user interface in a Windows application; referred to more simply as a form

Review Questions

1. When a form has been modified since the last time it was saved, what appears on its tab in the designer window?

   a. an ampersand (&)

   b. an asterisk (*)

   c. a percent sign (%)

   d. a plus sign (+)

2. Which of the following assigns the string "785.23" to the amountLabel control?

   a. `amountLabel = "785.23"`

   b. `amountLabel.String = "785.23"`

   c. `amountLabel.Text = '785.23'`

   d. `amountLabel.Text = "785.23"`

3. Which of the following is a pattern for creating an object?

   a. an attribute

   b. a behavior

   c. a class

   d. an instance

4. You use the _______________ window to set the characteristics that control an object's appearance and behavior.

   a. Characteristics

   b. Object

   c. Properties

   d. Toolbox

5. Which of the following instructions makes the soLongLabel invisible?

   a. `soLongLabel.Visible = False`

   b. `soLongLabel.Visible = True`

   c. `soLongLabel.Invisible = False`

   d. `soLongLabel.Invisible = True`

6. The text that appears on the face of a button control is stored in the control's _______________ property.

   a. Caption

   b. Label

   c. Name

   d. Text

7. Actions such as clicking and double-clicking are called _______________.

   a. actionEvents

   b. events

   c. happenings

   d. procedures

8. The equal sign in an assignment statement is called the _______________ operator.

   a. assignment

   b. dot member access

   c. equality

   d. equation

9. If a project is stored in the F:\Chap01\First Solution\First Project folder, the computer will store the project's executable file in the _______________ folder.

   a. F:\Chap01\First Solution\First Project

   b. F:\Chap01\First Solution\First Project\bin\Debug

   c. F:\Chap01\First Solution\First Project\bin\Executable

   d. F:\Chap01\First Solution\First Project\Executable

10. When coding, you use the value in an object's ______________ property to refer to the object in code.

   a. Caption

   b. Label

   c. Name

   d. Text

Exercises

Pencil and Paper

INTRODUCTORY

1. Explain the difference between a Windows application and a Web application.

INTRODUCTORY

2. Explain the difference between a form's Text property and its Name property.

INTERMEDIATE

3. Explain the process of using the Format menu to align the left border of the Button1 and Button2 controls with the left border of the Button3 control.

INTERMEDIATE

4. Write an assignment statement to assign the string "Visual Basic" to the languageLabel control.

ADVANCED

5. Write an assignment statement to assign the contents of the firstLabel control to the secondLabel control.

SWAT THE BUGS

6. Correct the errors in the following line of code:

```
myButton.Visibel = Yes
```

Computer

MODIFY THIS

7. If necessary, create the Horse Auction application from this chapter's Programming Tutorial 2. Add another button and picture box to the form. Name the controls starButton and starPictureBox. In the starPictureBox control, display the picture stored in the star.jpg file. The file is contained in the VbReloaded2010\Chap01 folder. When the user clicks the starButton, the button's Click event procedure should assign the Image property of the starPictureBox to the Image property of the displayPictureBox. It also should assign the name "Star" to the nameLabel. Make the appropriate modifications to the application's interface and code. Save the solution and then start and test the application. Close the solution. Locate the application's .exe file. Run the file from the Run dialog box in Windows.

8. If necessary, create the State Capitals application from this chapter's Programming Example. Add another label control to the form. Assign the name signingOrderLabel to the control. Modify the application so that it displays a message indicating the state's U.S. Constitution signing order. For example, when the user clicks the Alabama button, the button's Click event procedure should display the message "Alabama was the 22nd state to sign the U.S. Constitution." (Alaska was the 49th state to sign the Constitution, Arizona was the 48th state, and Arkansas was the 25th state.) Save the solution and then start and test the application. Close the solution. Locate the application's .exe file. Run the file from the Run dialog box in Windows.

MODIFY THIS

9. In this exercise, you add label and button controls to a form. You also change the properties of the form and its controls.

INTRODUCTORY

   a. Open the Mechanics Solution (Mechanics Solution.sln) file, which is contained in the VbReloaded2010\Chap01\Mechanics Solution folder.
   b. Assign the filename Main Form.vb to the form file object. Assign the name MainForm to the form.
   c. The form's title bar should say IMA. Set the appropriate property.
   d. The form should be centered on the screen when it first appears. Set the appropriate property.
   e. Change the form's Font property to Segoe UI, 9 point.
   f. Add a label control to the form. Change the label control's name to companyLabel.
   g. The label control should display the caption "International Mechanics Association" (without the quotation marks). Set the appropriate property.
   h. Display the label control's text in italics. Change the size of the text to 12 points.
   i. Center the label control horizontally and vertically on the form.
   j. Add a button control to the form. Change the button control's name to exitButton.
   k. The button control's face should say "Exit" (without the quotation marks). Set the appropriate property.
   l. Lock the controls on the form.
   m. The Exit button should terminate the application when clicked. Enter the appropriate code in the Code Editor window.
   n. Verify that the MainForm is the project's startup form.
   o. Save the solution and then start and test the application. Close the solution.

INTERMEDIATE

10. Create a Windows application. Use the following names for the solution, project, and form file: Costello Solution, Costello Project, and Main Form.vb. Save the application in the VbReloaded2010\Chap01 folder. Create the user interface shown in Figure 1-71. (You will need to set the messageLabel control's BorderStyle and AutoSize properties.) The Exit button should terminate the application when it is clicked. When the Display button is clicked, it should display the message "We have the best deals in town!" in the messageLabel control. Enter the appropriate code in the Code Editor window. Save the solution and then start and test the application. Close the solution.

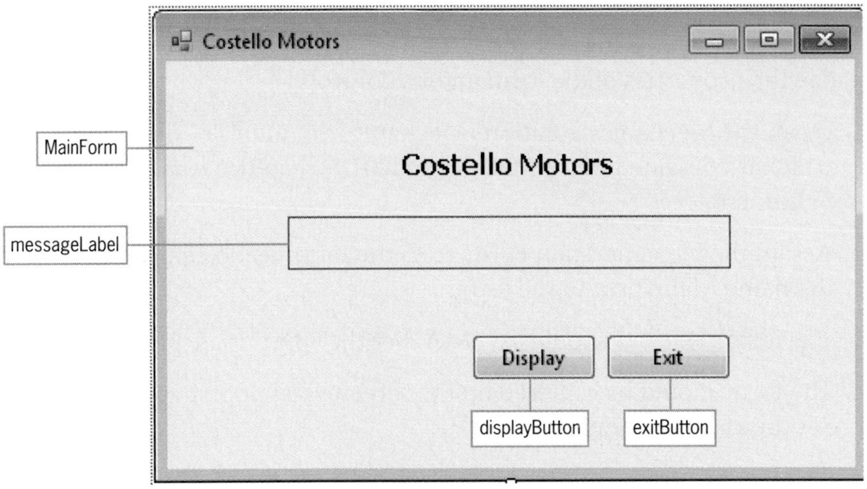

Figure 1-71 Interface for the Costello Motors application

SWAT THE BUGS

11. Open the Debug Solution (Debug Solution.sln) file, which is contained in the VbReloaded2010\Chap01\Debug Solution folder. Start the application. Click the Exit button. Notice that the Exit button does not end the application. Click the Close button on the form's title bar to end the application. Open the Code Editor window. Locate and then correct the error. Save the solution and then start and test the application. Close the solution.

Case Projects

Castle's Ice Cream Parlor

Create an application that displays the price of an item in a label when a button with the item's name is clicked. Use button and label controls in the interface. Include a button control that allows the user to terminate the application. Be sure to assign meaningful names to the form, the button controls, and the label control that contains the price. Name the solution, project, and form file Castle Solution, Castle Project, and Main Form.vb, respectively. Save the application in the VbReloaded2010\Chap01 folder. You can create either your own interface or the one shown in Figure 1-72. The item names are shown in the figure. Use your own prices for each item.

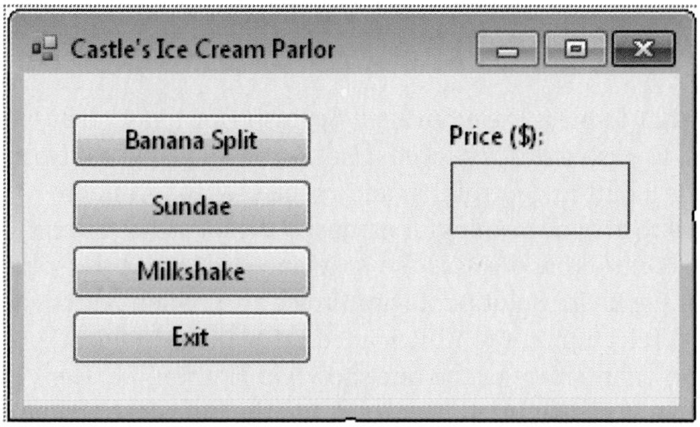

Figure 1-72 Sample interface for the Castle's Ice Cream Parlor application

Allen School District

Create an application that displays the name of the principal and the school's phone number in labels when a button with the school's name is clicked. Use button and label controls in the interface. Include a button control that allows the user to terminate the application. Be sure to assign meaningful names to the form, the button controls, and the label controls that contain the name and phone number. Name the solution, project, and form file Allen Solution, Allen Project, and Main Form.vb, respectively. Save the application in the VbReloaded2010\Chap01 folder. You can create either your own interface or the one shown in Figure 1-73. The school names are shown in the figure. You provide the names for the principals and the phone numbers for the schools.

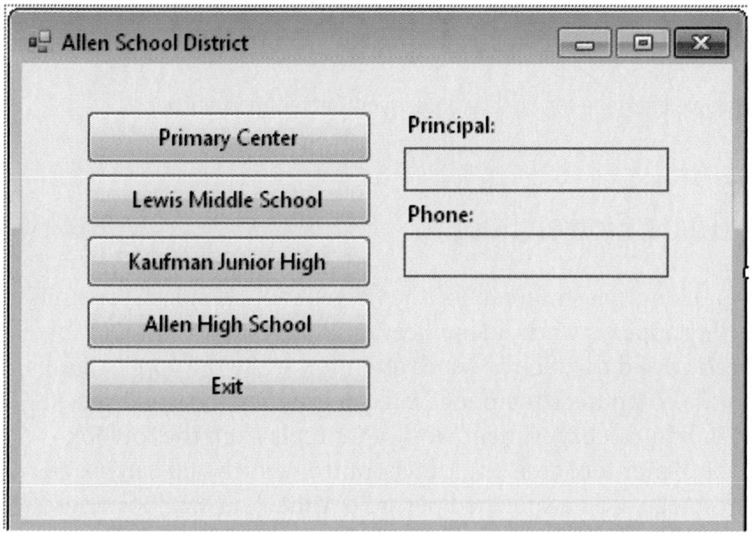

Figure 1-73 Sample interface for the Allen School District application

Elvira Learning Center

Create an application that displays the equivalent Spanish word in a label when a button with an English word is clicked. Use button and label controls in the interface. Include a button control that allows the user to terminate the application. Be sure to assign meaningful names to the form, the button controls, and the label control that displays the Spanish word. Name the solution, project, and form file Elvira Solution, Elvira Project, and Main Form.vb, respectively. Save the application in the VbReloaded2010\Chap01 folder. You can create either your own interface or the one shown in Figure 1-74. The English words are shown in the figure. If necessary, use the Internet to determine the equivalent Spanish words.

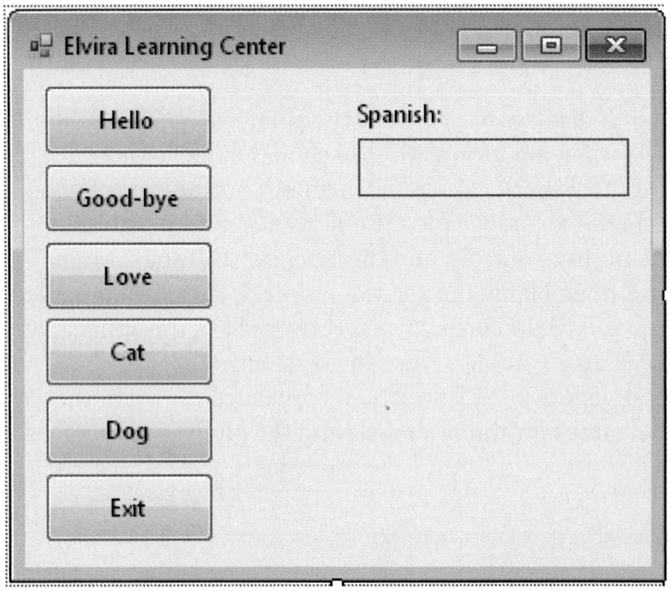

Figure 1-74 Sample interface for the Elvira Learning Center application

Mary Golds Flower Shop

Create an eye-catching splash screen for the flower shop. A splash screen is the first image that appears when an application is started. It is used to introduce the application and to hold the user's attention while the application is being read into the computer's memory. You can use the tools you learned in this chapter, or you can experiment with other tools from the toolbox. (For example, the Timer tool creates a timer control, which you can use to close the splash screen after a specified period of time. You can look ahead to Chapter 8 to learn how to use a timer control.) Name the solution, project, and form file Mary Golds Solution, Mary Golds Project, and Main Form.vb, respectively. Save the application in the VbReloaded2010\Chap01 folder.

CHAPTER 2

Creating a User Interface

After studying Chapter 2, you should be able to:

- Plan an application using a TOE chart
- Use a text box and table layout panel
- Follow the Windows standards regarding the layout and labeling of controls
- Follow the Windows standards regarding the use of graphics, fonts, and color
- Assign access keys to controls
- Set the tab order
- Add a splash screen to a project
- Use the Font and Color dialog boxes
- Designate a default button
- Print the interface during run time
- Play an audio file

Planning an Application

Before you can create the user interface for a Visual Basic Windows application, you need to plan the application. The plan should be developed jointly with the user to ensure that the application meets the user's needs. It cannot be stressed enough that the only way to guarantee the success of an application is to actively involve the user in the planning phase. Figure 2-1 lists the steps to follow when planning an application.

HOW TO Plan an Application

1. Identify the tasks the application needs to perform.
2. Identify the objects to which you will assign those tasks.
3. Identify the events required to trigger an object into performing its assigned tasks.
4. Design the user interface.

Figure 2-1 How to plan an application

You can use a TOE (Task, Object, Event) chart to record the application's tasks, objects, and events, which are identified in the first three steps of the planning phase. In the next several sections, you will complete a TOE chart for the Sunshine Cellular Company.

Sunshine Cellular Company

The Sunshine Cellular Company takes orders for cell phones by phone. The cell phones are priced at $100 each and are available in two colors: silver and blue. The company employs 10 salespeople to answer the phones. The salespeople record each order on a form that contains the customer's name and address, and the number of silver and blue phones ordered. The salespeople then calculate the total number of phones ordered and the total price of the phones, including a 5% sales tax. The company's sales manager feels that having the salespeople manually perform the necessary calculations is much too time-consuming and prone to errors. She wants you to create a computerized application that will solve the problems of the current order-taking system. The first step in planning this application is to identify the application's tasks.

Identifying the Application's Tasks

Realizing that it is essential to involve the user when planning the application, you meet with the sales manager to determine her requirements. You ask the sales manager to bring the form the salespeople currently use to record the orders. Viewing the current forms and procedures will help you gain a better understanding of the application. You also may be able to use the current form as a guide when designing the user interface. Figure 2-2 shows the current order form used by Sunshine Cellular.

Sunshine Cellular Order Form

Customer name: ______________________

Address: ______________________

City: ______________ State: __________ ZIP: ______

Number of silver phones ordered	Number of blue phones ordered	Total number of phones ordered	Total price

Figure 2-2 Current order form used by Sunshine Cellular

When identifying the tasks an application needs to perform, it is helpful to ask the questions italicized in the following bulleted items. The answers pertaining to the Sunshine Cellular application follow each question.

- *What information will the application need to display on the screen and/or print on the printer?* The Sunshine Cellular application should display the customer's name, street address, city, state, ZIP code, number of silver phones ordered, number of blue phones ordered, total number of phones ordered, and total price of the order. In this case, the application does not need to print anything on the printer.
- *What information will the user need to enter into the user interface to display and/or print the desired information?* In the Sunshine Cellular application, the salesperson (the user) must enter the customer's name, street address, city, state, ZIP code, and the number of silver and blue phones ordered.
- *What information will the application need to calculate to display and/or print the desired information?* The Sunshine Cellular application needs to calculate the total number of phones ordered and the total price of the order.
- *How will the user end the application?* All applications should provide a way for the user to end the application. The Sunshine Cellular application will use an Exit button for this task.
- *Will previous information need to be cleared from the screen before new information is entered?* After the salesperson enters and calculates an order, he or she will need to clear the order's information from the screen before entering the next order.

Figure 2-3 shows the Sunshine Cellular application's tasks listed in a TOE chart. The tasks do not need to be listed in any particular order. In this case, the data entry tasks are listed first, followed by the calculation tasks, display tasks, application ending task, and screen clearing task.

Task	Object	Event
Get the following order information from the user: Customer's name Street address City State ZIP code Number of silver phones ordered Number of blue phones ordered		
Calculate total phones ordered and total price		
Display the following information: Customer's name Street address City State ZIP code Number of silver phones ordered Number of blue phones ordered Total phones ordered Total price		
End the application		
Clear screen for the next order		

Figure 2-3 Tasks entered in a TOE chart

You can draw a TOE chart by hand or use the table feature in a word processor (such as Microsoft Word).

Identifying the Objects

After completing the Task column of the TOE chart, you then assign each task to an object in the user interface. For this application, the only objects you will use besides the Windows form itself are the button, label, and text box controls. As you already know, you use a label control to display information that you do not want the user to change while the application is running, and you use a button control to perform an action immediately after the user clicks it. You use a **text box** to give the user an area in which to enter data.

The first task listed in Figure 2-3 is to get the order information from the user. For each order, the salesperson will need to enter the customer's name, address, city, state, and ZIP code, as well as the number of silver phones ordered and the number of blue phones ordered. Because you need to provide the salesperson with areas in which to enter the information, you will assign the first task to seven text boxes—one for each item of information. The names of the text boxes will be nameTextBox, addressTextBox, cityTextBox, stateTextBox, zipTextBox, silverTextBox, and blueTextBox.

The second task listed in the TOE chart is to calculate both the total number of phones ordered and the total price. So that the salesperson can calculate these amounts at any time, you will assign the task to a button named calcButton.

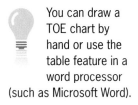

The third task listed in the TOE chart is to display the order information, the total number of phones ordered, and the total price. The order information is displayed automatically when the user enters that information in the seven text boxes. The total phones ordered and total price, however, are not entered by the user. Instead, those amounts are calculated by the calcButton. Because the user should not be allowed to change the calculated results, you will have the calcButton display the total phones ordered and total price in two label controls named totalPhonesLabel and totalPriceLabel. Notice that the task of displaying the total phones ordered involves two objects (calcButton and totalPhonesLabel). The task of displaying the total price also involves two objects (calcButton and totalPriceLabel).

The last two tasks listed in the TOE chart are "End the application" and "Clear screen for the next order." You will assign the tasks to buttons named exitButton and clearButton; doing this gives the user control over when the tasks are performed. Figure 2-4 shows the TOE chart with the Task and Object columns completed.

Task	**Object**	**Event**
Get the following order information from the user:		
Customer's name	nameTextBox	
Street address	addressTextBox	
City	cityTextBox	
State	stateTextBox	
ZIP code	zipTextBox	
Number of silver phones ordered	silverTextBox	
Number of blue phones ordered	blueTextBox	
Calculate total phones ordered and total price	calcButton	
Display the following information:		
Customer's name	nameTextBox	
Street address	streetTextBox	
City	cityTextBox	
State	stateTextBox	
ZIP code	zipTextBox	
Number of silver phones ordered	silverTextBox	
Number of blue phones ordered	blueTextBox	
Total phones ordered	calcButton, totalPhonesLabel	
Total price	calcButton, totalPriceLabel	
End the application	exitButton	
Clear screen for the next order	clearButton	

Figure 2-4 Tasks and objects entered in a TOE chart

Identifying the Events

After defining the application's tasks and assigning the tasks to objects in the interface, you then determine which event (if any) must occur for an object to carry out its assigned task. The seven text boxes listed in the TOE chart in Figure 2-4 are assigned the task of getting and displaying the order information. Text boxes accept and display information automatically, so no special event is necessary for them to carry out their assigned task. The two label controls listed in the TOE chart are assigned the task of displaying the total number of phones ordered and the total price of the order. Label controls automatically display their contents; so, here again, no special event needs to occur. (Recall that the two label controls will get their values from the calcButton.) The remaining objects listed in the TOE chart are the three buttons. You will have the buttons perform their assigned tasks when the user clicks them. Figure 2-5 shows the completed TOE chart for the Sunshine Cellular application.

Task	**Object**	**Event**
Get the following order information from the user:		
Customer's name	nameTextBox	None
Street address	addressTextBox	None
City	cityTextBox	None
State	stateTextBox	None
ZIP code	zipTextBox	None
Number of silver phones ordered	silverTextBox	None
Number of blue phones ordered	blueTextBox	None
Calculate total phones ordered and total price	calcButton	Click
Display the following information:		
Customer's name	nameTextBox	None
Street address	streetTextBox	None
City	cityTextBox	None
State	stateTextBox	None
ZIP code	zipTextBox	None
Number of silver phones ordered	silverTextBox	None
Number of blue phones ordered	blueTextBox	None
Total phones ordered	calcButton, totalPhonesLabel	Click, None
Total price	calcButton, totalPriceLabel	Click, None
End the application	exitButton	Click
Clear screen for the next order	clearButton	Click

Figure 2-5 Completed TOE chart ordered by task

If the application you are creating is small, as is the Sunshine Cellular application, you can use the TOE chart in its current form to help you write the Visual Basic code. When the application is large, however, it is often helpful to rearrange the TOE chart so that it is ordered by object rather than by task. To do so, you list all of the objects in the Object column of a new TOE chart, being sure to list each object only once. You then list each object's tasks and events in the Task and Event columns, respectively. Figure 2-6 shows the rearranged TOE chart ordered by object rather than by task.

Task	Object	Event
1. Calculate total phones ordered and total price 2. Display total phones ordered and total price in totalPhonesLabel and totalPriceLabel	calcButton	Click
Clear screen for the next order	clearButton	Click
End the application	exitButton	Click
Display total phones ordered (from calcButton)	totalPhonesLabel	None
Display total price (from calcButton)	totalPriceLabel	None
Get and display the order information	nameTextBox, addressTextBox, cityTextBox, stateTextBox, zipTextBox, silverTextBox, blueTextBox	None

Figure 2-6 Completed TOE chart ordered by object

Mini-Quiz 2-1

The answers to Mini-Quiz questions are located in Appendix A.

1. When planning an application, you first identify the necessary ________________.
   a. code
   b. events
   c. objects
   d. tasks

2. Every object in a user interface needs an event to occur in order for it to perform its assigned task.
   a. True
   b. False

3. The task of getting a sales tax rate from the user should be assigned to a ________________ control.
   a. button
   b. label
   c. text box
   d. either b or c

Designing the User Interface

After completing the TOE chart, the next step is to design the user interface. Although the TOE chart lists the objects included in the application's interface, it does not tell you *where* to place the objects on the form. While the design of an interface is open to creativity, there are some guidelines to which you should adhere so that your application is consistent with the Windows standards. This consistency will make your application easier to both learn and use, because the interface will have a familiar look to it. The guidelines are referred to as GUI guidelines, because they pertain to graphical user interfaces. The first GUI guidelines you will learn in this chapter relate to the placement of the controls on a form.

Some companies have their own standards for interfaces used within the company.

Arranging the Controls on a Form

In Western countries, you should organize the user interface so that the information flows either vertically or horizontally, with the most important information always located in the upper-left corner of the screen. In a vertical arrangement, the information flows from top to bottom: the essential information is located in the first column of the screen, while secondary information is placed in subsequent columns. In a horizontal arrangement, on the other hand, the information flows from left to right: the essential information is placed in the first row of the screen, with secondary information placed in subsequent rows. Related controls should be grouped together using either white (empty) space or one of the tools located in the Containers section of the toolbox. Examples of tools found in the Containers section include the GroupBox, Panel, and TableLayoutPanel tools. The difference between a panel and a group box is that, unlike a group box, a panel can have scroll bars. However, unlike a panel, a group box has a Text property that you can use to indicate the contents of the control. Unlike the panel and group box controls, the table layout panel provides a table structure in which you place other controls. You will learn how to use a table layout panel in this chapter's Programming Tutorial 1.

The Ch02ContainerControls video demonstrates how to use the group box, panel, and table layout panel controls.

Figures 2-7 and 2-8 show two different interfaces for the Sunshine Cellular application. In Figure 2-7 the information is arranged vertically, and white space is used to group related controls together. In Figure 2-8 the information is arranged horizontally, with related controls grouped together using a group box, panel, and table layout panel. Each text box and button in both interfaces is labeled so the user knows the control's purpose. The Name: label that identifies the nameTextBox tells the user the type of information to enter in the text box. Similarly, the Calculate Order text on the calcButton's face indicates the action the button will perform when it is clicked.

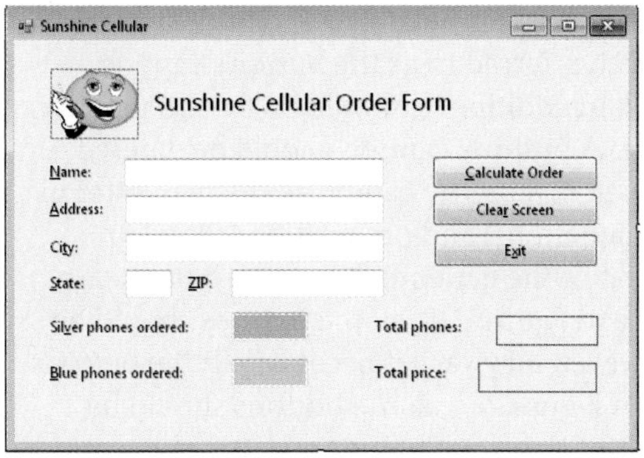

Figure 2-7 Vertical arrangement of the Sunshine Cellular interface

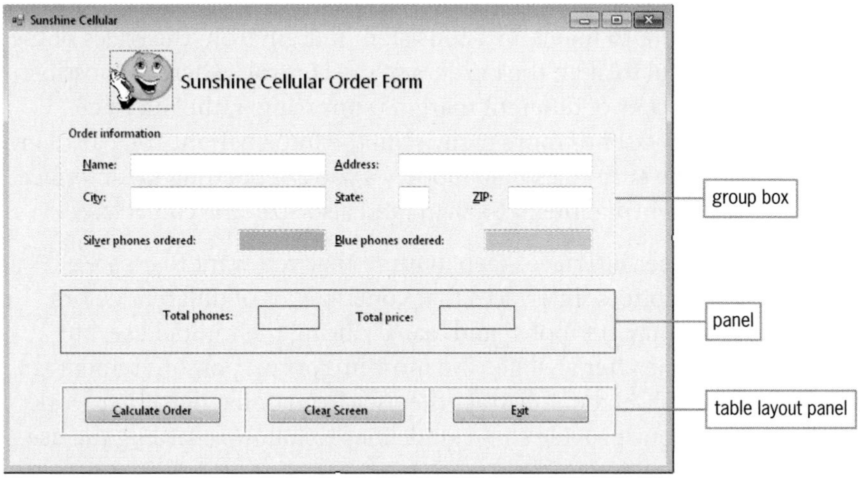

Figure 2-8 Horizontal arrangement of the Sunshine Cellular interface

Most times, program output (such as the result of calculations) is displayed in a label control in the interface. Label controls that display program output should be labeled to make their contents obvious to the user. In the interfaces shown in Figures 2-7 and 2-8, the "Total phones:" and "Total price:" labels identify the contents of the totalPhonesLabel and totalPriceLabel controls, respectively. The text contained in an identifying label should be meaningful and left-aligned within the label. In most cases, an identifying label should be from one to three words only and appear on one line. In addition, the identifying label should be positioned either above or to the left of the control it identifies. An identifying label should end with a colon (:). The colon distinguishes an identifying label from other text in the user interface, such as the heading text "Sunshine Cellular Order Form". Some assistive technologies, which are technologies that provide assistance to individuals with disabilities, rely on the colons to make this distinction. The Windows standard is to use sentence capitalization for identifying labels. **Sentence capitalization** means you capitalize only the first letter in the first word and in any words that are customarily capitalized.

As you learned in Chapter 1, buttons are identified by the text that appears on the button's face. The text is often referred to as the button's caption. The caption should be meaningful. In addition, it should be from one to three words only and appear on one line. A button's caption should be entered using **book title capitalization,** which means you capitalize the first letter in each word, except for articles, conjunctions, and prepositions that do not occur at either the beginning or end of the caption. When the buttons are positioned horizontally, as they are in Figure 2-8, all the buttons should be the same height; their widths, however, may vary if necessary. If the buttons are stacked vertically, as they are in Figure 2-7, all the buttons should be the same height and the same width. In a group of buttons, the most commonly used button typically appears first—either on the left (in a horizontal arrangement) or on the top (in a vertical arrangement).

When positioning the controls in the interface, place related controls close to each other and be sure to maintain a consistent margin from the edges of the form. Also, it's helpful to align the borders of the controls wherever possible to minimize the number of different margins appearing in the interface. Doing this allows the user to more easily scan the information. You can align the borders using the snap lines that appear as you are building the interface. Or, you can use the Format menu to align (and also size) the controls.

When designing a user interface, keep in mind that you want to create a screen that no one notices. Interfaces that contain a lot of different colors, fonts, and graphics may get "oohs" and "aahs" during their initial use, but they become tiresome after a while. The most important point to remember is that the interface should not distract the user from doing his or her work. The next three sections provide some guidelines to follow regarding the use of these elements in an interface.

The graphics, font, and color guidelines do not pertain to game applications.

Including Graphics in the User Interface

The human eye is attracted to pictures before text, so use graphics sparingly. Designers typically include graphics to either emphasize or clarify a portion of the screen. However, a graphic also can be used merely for aesthetic purposes, as long as it is small and placed in a location that does not distract the user. The small graphic in the Sunshine Cellular interfaces is included for aesthetics only. The graphic is purposely located in the upper-left corner of each interface, which is where you want the user's eye to be drawn first anyway. The graphic adds a personal touch to the order form without being distracting to the user.

Including Different Fonts in the User Interface

An object's Font property determines the type, style, and size of the font used to display the object's text. Recall that Segoe UI, Tahoma, and Microsoft Sans Serif are examples of font types. Font styles include regular, bold, and italic. The numbers 9, 12, and 18 are examples of font sizes. You should use only one font type for all of the text in the interface. As you learned in Chapter 1, the Segoe UI font is recommended for Windows 7 (or Windows Vista) applications. You should use no more than two different font sizes in an interface. In addition, avoid using italics and underlining in an interface, because both font styles make text difficult to read. The use of bold text should be limited to titles, headings, and key items that you want to emphasize.

When you add a control to the form, the value stored in the form's Font property is automatically assigned to the control's Font property. Therefore, if you set the form's Font property *before* adding the controls to the form, you will not need to set each control's Font property separately. If you set the form's Font property *after* adding the controls, all of the existing controls whose Font properties have not been set individually will assume the form's setting.

Including Color in the User Interface

The human eye is attracted to color before black and white; therefore, use color sparingly in an interface. It is a good practice to build the interface using black, white, and gray first, and then add color only if you have a good reason to do so. Keep the following three points in mind when deciding whether to include color in an interface:

1. Many people have some form of either color blindness or color confusion, so they will have trouble distinguishing colors.
2. Color is very subjective: a color that looks pretty to you may be hideous to someone else.
3. A color may have a different meaning in a different culture.

You can change the background color of a text box by setting its BackColor property.

Usually, it is best to use black text on a white, off-white, or light gray background, because dark text on a light background is the easiest to read. You should never use a dark color for the background or a light color for the text, because a dark background is hard on the eyes, and light-colored text can appear blurry. If you are going to include color in the interface, limit the number of colors to three, not including white, black, and gray. Be sure that the colors you choose complement each other. Although color can be used to identify an important element in the interface, you should never use it as the only means of identification. In the Sunshine Cellular interfaces, for example, the two colored text boxes help the salesperson quickly identify where to enter the order for silver and blue phones. However, color is not the only means of identifying the purpose of those text boxes; each also has an identifying label.

Borders and Sizing of Controls

A control's BorderStyle property determines the style of its border and can be set to None, FixedSingle, or Fixed3D. In most cases, a text box's BorderStyle property should be left at its default setting: Fixed3D. The Fixed3D setting gives the control a three-dimensional appearance. The appropriate setting for a label control's BorderStyle property depends on the control's purpose. For label controls that identify other controls (such as those that identify text boxes), the BorderStyle setting should be None, which is the default setting. However, you typically set to FixedSingle the BorderStyle property of label controls that display program output, such as those that display the result of a calculation. The FixedSingle setting surrounds the control with a thin line.

If a label's AutoSize and BorderStyle properties are set to True and None, and you remove the contents of its Text property, you will not see the label on the form. You will need to use the Properties window's Object box to access the label.

Whether a label control automatically sizes to fit its current contents is determined by the control's AutoSize property. Here too, the appropriate setting depends on the label's purpose. In most cases, the setting is True (the default) for labels that identify other controls and False for labels that display program output.

The answers to Mini-Quiz questions are located in Appendix A.

Mini-Quiz 2-2

1. The text on a button's face should be entered using ______________.
   a. book title capitalization
   b. lowercase letters
   c. sentence capitalization
   d. uppercase letters
2. Which of the following controls can be used to group together other controls?
   a. group box
   b. panel
   c. table layout panel
   d all of the above
3. Label controls that identify text boxes usually have their BorderStyle and AutoSize properties set to ______________ and ______________, respectively.
   a. None, False
   b. None, True
   c. False, No
   d. FixedSingle, Yes

Assigning Access Keys

The text in many of the controls shown in Figure 2-9 contains an underlined letter. The underlined letter is called an **access key**, and it allows the user to select an object using the Alt key in combination with a letter or number. In Visual Studio, for example, you can select the File menu by pressing Alt+F, because the letter F is the File menu's access key. Access keys are not case sensitive; therefore, you can select the File menu by pressing either Alt+F or Alt+f. Similarly, you can select the Calculate Order button in the Sunshine Cellular interface by pressing either Alt+C or Alt+c.

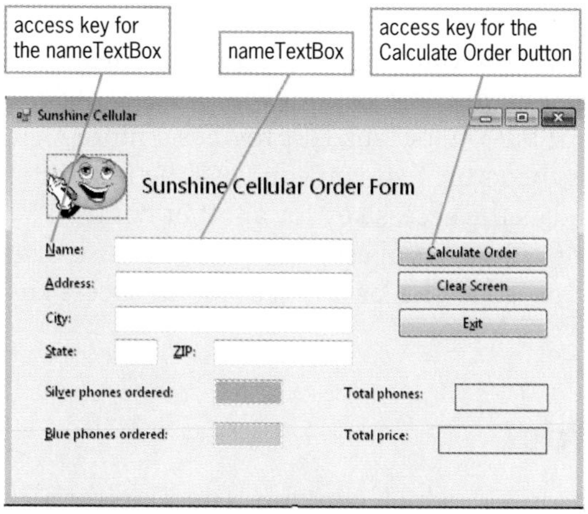

Figure 2-9 Sunshine Cellular interface

To always display access keys, refer to the Summary section at the end of the chapter.

Depending on your system's settings, the access keys may or may not appear underlined while an application is running. If you do not see the underlined access keys, you can show them temporarily by pressing the Alt key. You can subsequently hide them by pressing the Alt key again.

You should assign access keys to each of the controls (in the interface) that can accept user input. Examples of such controls include text boxes and buttons, because the user can enter information in a text box and click a button. The only exceptions to this rule are the OK and Cancel buttons, which typically do not have access keys in Windows applications. It is important to assign access keys to controls for the following three reasons:

1. They allow a user to work with the application even when the mouse becomes inoperative.
2. They allow users who are fast typists to keep their hands on the keyboard.
3. They allow people with disabilities, which may prevent them from working with a mouse, to use the application.

You assign an access key by including an ampersand (&) in the control's caption or identifying label. If the control is a button, you include the ampersand in the button's Text property, which is where a button's caption is stored. If the control is a text box, you include the ampersand in the Text property of its identifying label. (As you will learn later in this chapter, you also must set the TabIndex properties of the text box and its identifying label appropriately.) You enter the ampersand to the immediate left of the character you want to designate as the access key. For example, to assign the letter C as the access key for the Calculate Order button, you enter &Calculate Order in the button's Text property. To assign the letter N as the access key for the nameTextBox control, you enter &Name: in the Text property of its identifying label. Notice that the Total phones: and Total price: labels in Figure 2-9 do not have access keys. This is because the labels do not identify controls that accept user input; rather, they identify other label controls. Recall that users cannot access label controls while an application is running, so it is inappropriate to assign an access key to the controls.

Each access key in the interface should be unique. The first choice for an access key is the first letter of the caption or identifying label, unless another letter provides a more meaningful association. For example, the letter x is the access key for an Exit button, because it provides a more meaningful association than does the letter E. If you can't use the first letter (perhaps because it already is used as the access key for another control) and no other letter provides a more meaningful association, then use a distinctive consonant in the caption or label. The last choices for an access key are a vowel or a number.

Controlling the Tab Order

When a text box has the focus, an insertion point appears inside it. When a button has the focus, it has a darkened border.

Most controls have a TabIndex property, which contains a number that represents the order in which the control was added to the form. The first control added to a form has a TabIndex value of 0. The second control has a TabIndex of 1, and so on. The TabIndex values determine the tab order, which is the order that each control receives the **focus** when the user either presses the Tab key or employs an access key while an application is running. A control whose TabIndex is 2 will receive the focus immediately after the control whose TabIndex is 1. Likewise, a control with a TabIndex of 18 will receive the focus immediately after the control whose TabIndex is 17. When a control has the focus, it can accept input from the user. Most times you will need to reset the TabIndex values for an interface, because controls rarely are added to a form in the desired tab order. To determine the appropriate TabIndex values, you first make a list of the controls that can accept user input. The list should reflect the order in which the user will want to access the controls. In the Sunshine Cellular interface, the user typically will want to access the nameTextBox first, followed by the addressTextBox, cityTextBox, and so on. If a control that accepts user input is identified by a label control, you also include the label control in the list. (A text box is an example of a control that accepts user input and is identified by a label control.) You place the name of the label control immediately above the name of the control it identifies in the list. In the Sunshine Cellular interface, the Label1 control (which contains Name:) identifies the nameTextBox. Therefore, Label1 should appear immediately above nameTextBox in the list. The names of controls that do not accept user input and are not used to identify controls that do should be placed at the bottom of the list; these controls do not need to appear in any specific order. After listing the control names, you then assign each control in the list a TabIndex value, beginning with the number 0. If a control does not have a TabIndex property, you do not assign it a TabIndex value in the list. You can tell whether a control has a TabIndex property by viewing its Properties list.

Figure 2-10 shows the list of controls and TabIndex values for the Sunshine Cellular interface. Notice that the TabIndex value assigned to each text box's identifying label is one number less than the value assigned to the text box itself. For example, the Label1 control has a TabIndex value of 0 and its corresponding text box (nameTextBox) has a TabIndex value of 1. For a text box's access key (which is defined in the identifying label) to work appropriately, you must be sure to set the identifying label's TabIndex property to a value that is one number less than the value stored in the text box's TabIndex property.

Controls that accept user input, along with their identifying labels	**TabIndex value**
Label1 (Name:)	0
nameTextBox	1
Label2 (Address:)	2
addressTextBox	3
Label3 (City:)	4
cityTextBox	5
Label4 (State:)	6
stateTextBox	7
Label5 (ZIP:)	8
zipTextBox	9
Label6 (Silver phones ordered:)	10
silverTextBox	11
Label7 (Blue phones ordered:)	12
blueTextBox	13
calcButton	14
clearButton	15
exitButton	16
Other controls	
Label10 (Sunshine Cellular Order Form)	17
Label8 (Total phones:)	18
Label9 (Total price:)	19
totalPhonesLabel	20
totalPriceLabel	21
PictureBox1	N/A

Figure 2-10 List of controls and TabIndex values

If you want to try setting the tab order, open the solution contained in the Try It 1! folder. Then use the information in Figures 2-11 and 2-12.

Although you can use the Properties window to set each control's TabIndex property, it is easier to use the Tab Order option on the View menu. Figure 2-11 shows the steps for using that option, and Figure 2-12 shows the correct TabIndex values for the Sunshine Cellular interface.

HOW TO Set the TabIndex Property Using the Tab Order Option

1. If necessary, make the designer window the active window.
2. Click View on the menu bar, and then click Tab Order. The current TabIndex values appear in blue boxes on the form. (If you are using the Express Edition, the Tab Order option might not be available until you click Tools on the menu bar, point to Settings, and then click Expert Settings.)
3. Click the first control you want in the tab order. The color of the box changes to white, and the number 0 appears in the box.
4. Click the second control you want in the tab order, and so on. If you make a mistake when specifying the tab order, press the Esc key to remove the boxes from the form, and then start over again.
5. When you have finished setting all of the TabIndex values, the color of the boxes will automatically change from white to blue. See Figure 2-12.
6. Press the Esc key to remove the blue boxes from the form. (You also can click View on the menu bar, and then click Tab Order.)

Figure 2-11 How to set the TabIndex property using the Tab Order option

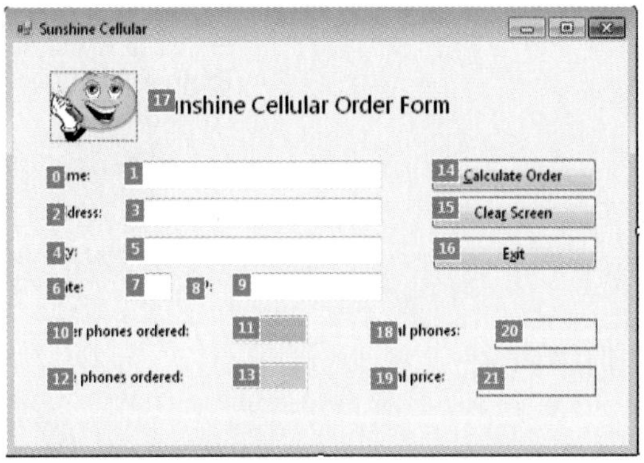

Figure 2-12 Correct TabIndex values

If you make a mistake when specifying the tab order, press the Esc key to remove the boxes from the form, and then start over again.

The answers to Mini-Quiz questions are located in Appendix A.

Mini-Quiz 2-3

1. TabIndex values begin with the number _______________.
   a. 0
   b. 1

2. If a label's TabIndex value is 2, the TabIndex value of the text box it identifies should be _______________.
   a. 1
   b. 2
   c. 3

3. If a button contains the caption Calculate Tax, you can select the button by pressing _______________.
   a. Shift+t
   b. Ctrl+t
   c. Alt+t
   d. none of the above

4. Every control in an interface has a TabIndex property.
   a. True
   b. False

Splash Screens

Many times, a splash screen appears when an application is started. Developers use a splash screen to both introduce the application and hold the user's attention as the application is being read into the computer's internal memory. Figure 2-13 shows the splash screen that appears when you start the Professional Edition of Visual Studio 2010.

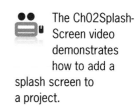

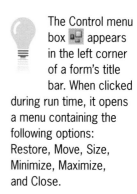

Figure 2-13 Visual Studio 2010 splash screen

The Ch02SplashScreen video demonstrates how to add a splash screen to a project.

Figure 2-14 lists the steps for adding a new splash screen to a project, and Figure 2-15 shows an example of a completed Add New Item dialog box. You can use the templates listed in the dialog box to add many different items to a project. The Splash Screen template adds a Windows form that is already configured for use as a splash screen. If you prefer to create your splash screen from scratch, you can use the Windows Form template to add a blank Windows form to the project. You then would set the form's FormBorderStyle property to either None or FixedSingle. If you set it to FixedSingle, you also would need to set the form's ControlBox property to False and then remove the text from the form's Text property. Setting the ControlBox property to False removes the Control menu box, as well as the Minimize, Maximize, and Close buttons, from the title bar.

The Control menu box appears in the left corner of a form's title bar. When clicked during run time, it opens a menu containing the following options: Restore, Move, Size, Minimize, Maximize, and Close.

HOW TO Add a New Splash Screen to a Project

1. Click Project on the menu bar, and then click Add New Item to open the Add New Item dialog box.
2. *If you are using Visual Studio 2010*, expand the Common Items node in the Installed Templates list (if necessary), and then click Windows Forms.
3. *If you are using Visual Basic 2010 Express Edition*, scroll the middle column of the dialog box until you see Splash Screen.
4. Click Splash Screen in the middle column of the dialog box. (If you want to create your own splash screen, click Windows Form instead.)
5. Enter an appropriate name in the Name box. Figure 2-15 shows an example of a completed Add New Item dialog box in Visual Studio 2010. Your dialog box will look slightly different if you are using Visual Basic 2010 Express Edition.
6. Click the Add button. See Figure 2-16.

Figure 2-14 How to add a new splash screen to a project

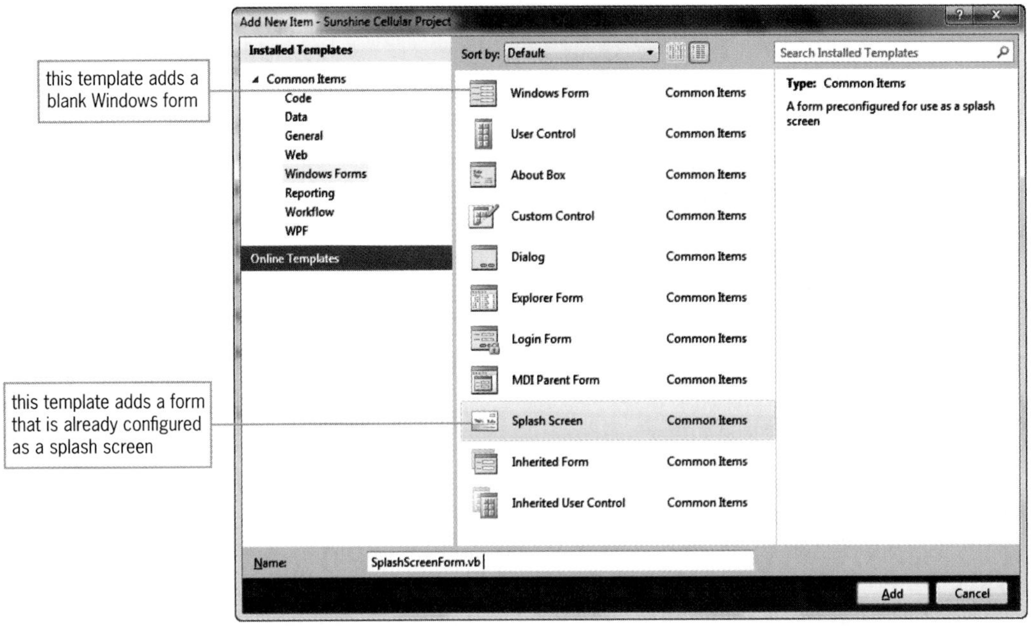

Figure 2-15 Completed Add New Item dialog box in Visual Studio 2010

Figure 2-16 shows the form created by the Splash Screen template during design time. The form contains five controls: two table layout panels and three labels. You can modify the form by adding controls to it or deleting controls from it. You also can use the Properties window to change the properties of the form and its controls.

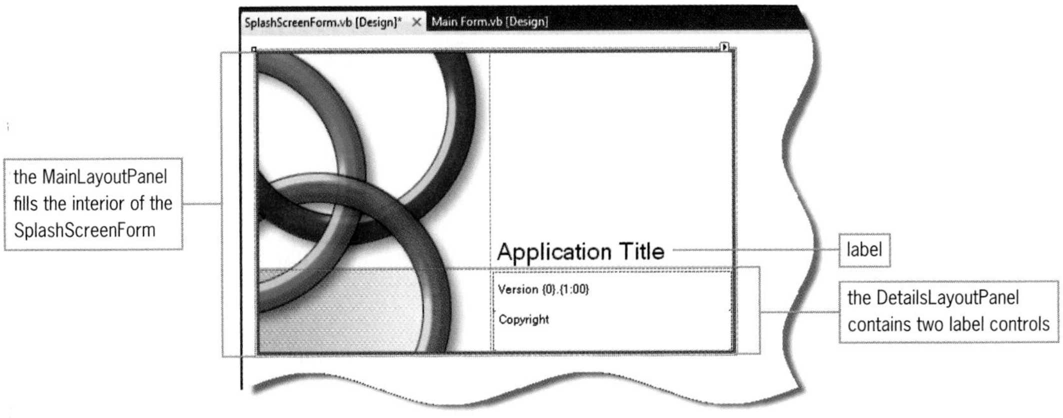

Figure 2-16 Splash screen created by the Splash Screen template

In Chapter 1 you learned that the computer automatically displays an application's startup form each time the application is started. It also automatically displays an application's splash screen; however, you first must specify the splash screen's name in the Project Designer window. Figure 2-17 shows the steps you follow to indicate the name of the splash screen, and Figure 2-18 shows the name (in this case, SplashScreenForm) selected in the Project Designer window. When the application is started, the splash screen will appear first. After a few seconds, the splash screen will disappear automatically and the startup form will appear.

HOW TO Specify the Splash Screen

1. Open the Project Designer window. You can open the window by right-clicking My Project in the Solution Explorer window, and then clicking Open on the context menu. You also can click Project on the menu bar, and then click <project name> Properties on the menu. In addition, you can right-click the project's name in the Solution Explorer window, and then click Properties.
2. Click the Application tab, if necessary, and then click the Splash screen list arrow in the Application pane.
3. Click the name of the splash screen in the list. Figure 2-18 shows an example of the Project Designer window.
4. Click the Close button on the Project Designer window.

Figure 2-17 How to specify the splash screen

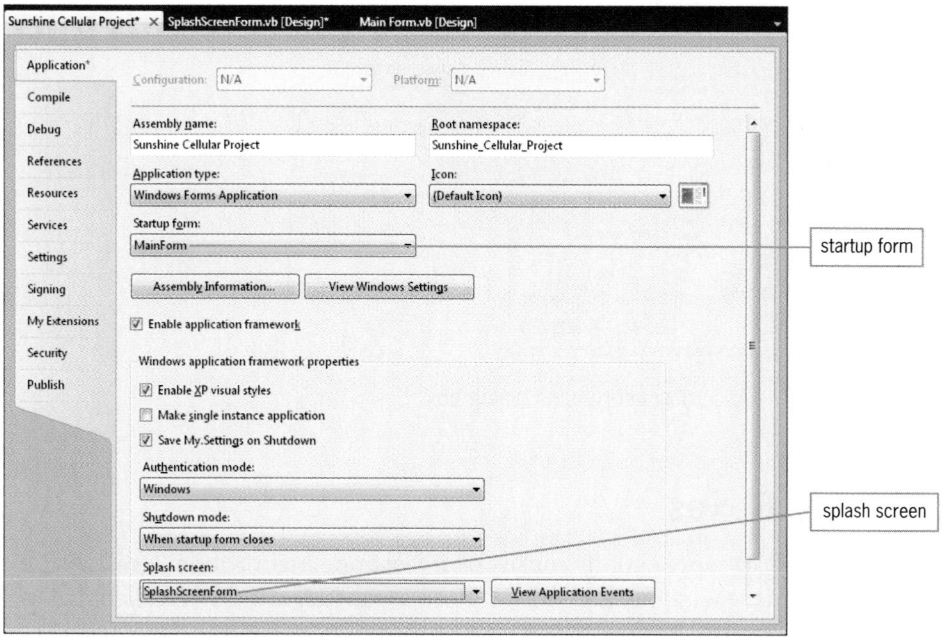

Figure 2-18 Project Designer window

Figure 2-19 shows the SplashScreenForm during run time. The values that appear in the three labels are determined by the entries in the Assembly Information dialog box, which is shown in Figure 2-20. You would need to use this dialog box, rather than the Properties window, to make changes to those values. To open the dialog box, you first open the Project Designer window by right-clicking My Project in the Solution Explorer window and then clicking Open on the context menu. You then click the Assembly Information button in the Application pane.

Figure 1-24 in Chapter 1 mentions other ways of opening the Project Designer window.

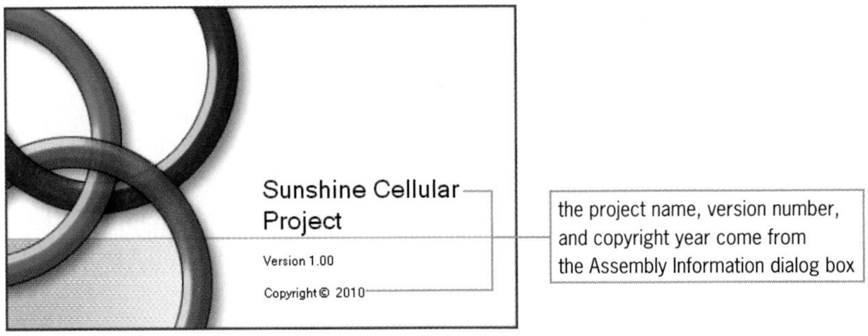

Figure 2-19 SplashScreenForm during run time

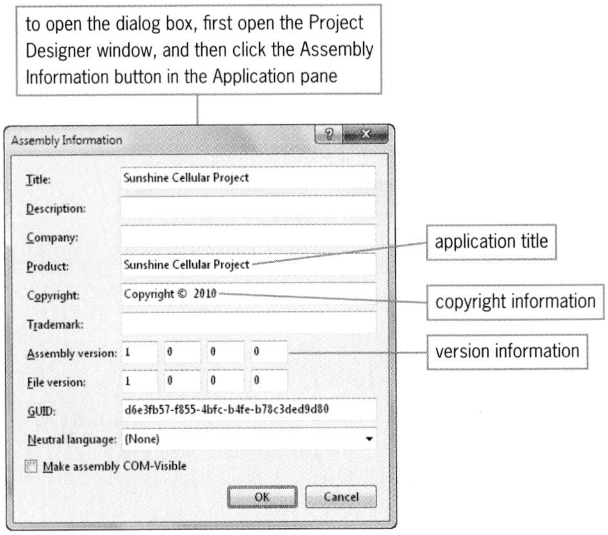

Figure 2-20 Assembly Information dialog box

If you want to try adding a splash screen to a project, open the solution contained in the Try It 2! folder. Then use the information in Figures 2-14 and 2-17.

Dialog Boxes

Most Windows applications consist of at least one main window (referred to as a primary window) and one or more secondary windows (called dialog boxes). The primary viewing and editing of your application's data take place in a **primary window**. The primary window shown in Figure 2-21, for example, allows you to view and edit documents created using the Notepad application. **Dialog boxes**, on the other hand, support and supplement a user's activities in a primary window. For instance, you can use the Font dialog box in Figure 2-21 to specify the font of the text selected in the primary window.

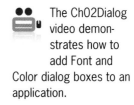

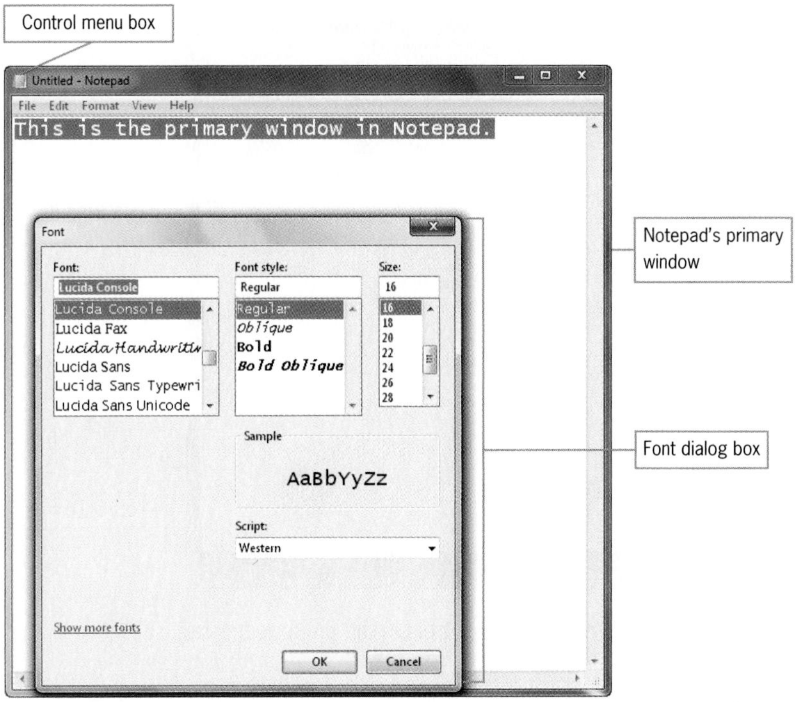

Figure 2-21 Primary window and Font dialog box in Notepad

The Dialog template in the Add New Item dialog box creates a Windows form that is already configured for use as a dialog box. If you prefer to create your dialog box from scratch, you can use the Windows Form template to add a blank Windows form to the project. You then would set the form's FormBorderStyle property to FixedDialog. The FixedDialog setting draws a fixed border around the form, and it removes the Control menu box from the form's title bar. The Windows standard is that dialog boxes contain only a Close button and, in some cases, a Help button. Therefore, you also would need to remove the Minimize and Maximize buttons from the title bar by setting the form's MinimizeBox and MaximizeBox properties to False.

In addition to the Dialog template, Visual Basic also provides several tools for creating commonly-used dialog boxes, such as the Color, Font, and Save As dialog boxes. The tools are located in the Dialogs section of the toolbox. When you drag one of these tools to the form, its instantiated control does not appear on the form. Instead, the control is placed in the component tray in the IDE. The component tray stores controls that do not appear in the user interface during run time. The component tray shown in Figure 2-22 contains the font and color dialog controls.

The Ch02Dialog video demonstrates how to add Font and Color dialog boxes to an application.

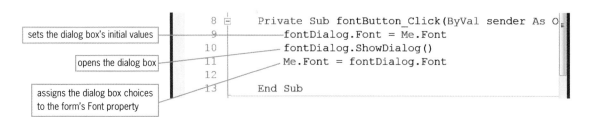

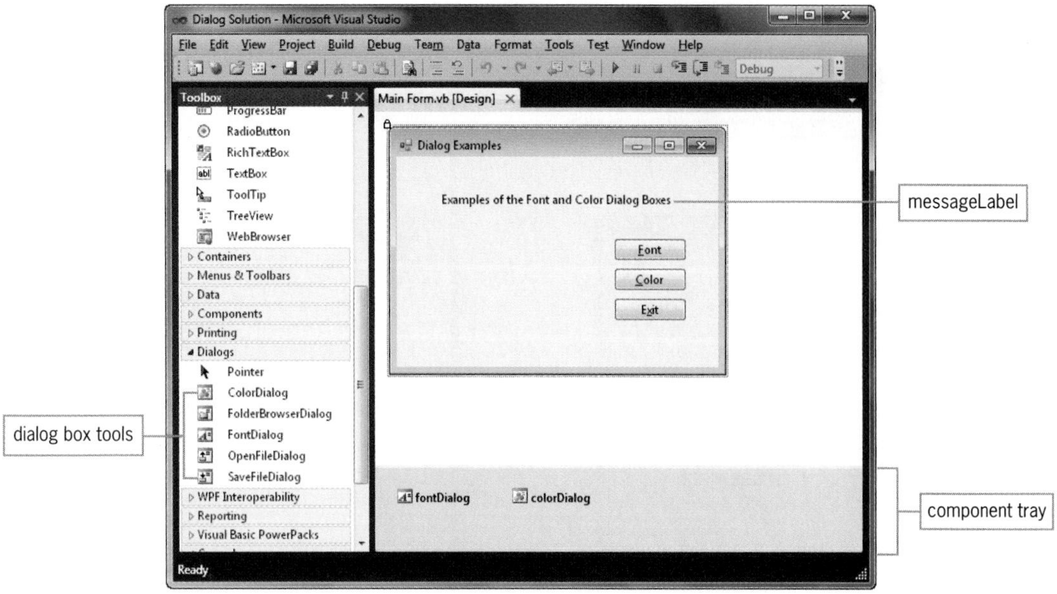

Figure 2-22 Font and Color dialog box controls in the component tray

The Font button in the interface allows the user to change the form's Font property values. The code entered in the button's Click event procedure is shown in Figure 2-23. When the user clicks the Font button, the assignment statement on Line 9 assigns the form's Font property values (name, style, size, and so on) to the fontDialog control's Font property. By doing this, the form's values will be selected in the Font dialog box when the dialog box appears on the screen. The `fontDialog.ShowDialog()` statement on Line 10 uses the ShowDialog method to show (in other words, open) the Font dialog box. Figure 2-24 shows an example of an open Font dialog box. As are all of the dialog boxes created by the dialog tools in the toolbox, the Font dialog box is **modal**, which means it remains on the screen until the user closes it. While it is on the screen, no input from the keyboard or mouse can occur in the application's primary window; however, you can access other applications. You close a modal dialog box by selecting either the OK button or the Cancel button, or by clicking the Close button on the dialog box's title bar. When the Font dialog box closes, the assignment statement on Line 11 in the Click event procedure assigns the values selected in the dialog box to the form's Font property.

```
8     Private Sub fontButton_Click(ByVal sender As O
9         fontDialog.Font = Me.Font
10        fontDialog.ShowDialog()
11        Me.Font = fontDialog.Font
12
13    End Sub
```

sets the dialog box's initial values (Line 9)
opens the dialog box (Line 10)
assigns the dialog box choices to the form's Font property (Line 11)

Figure 2-23 Code entered in the Font button's Click event procedure

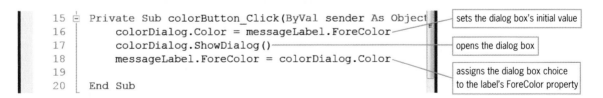

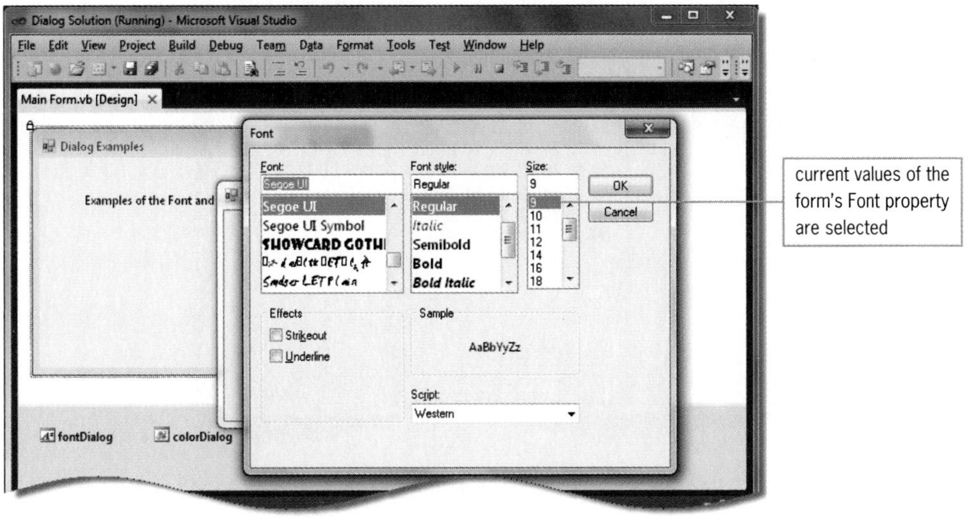

Figure 2-24 Font dialog box created by the FontDialog tool

The Color button in the interface shown earlier in Figure 2-22 allows the user to change the color of the messageLabel's text. The color of an object's text is determined by the object's ForeColor property. (The background color of an object is determined by the object's BackColor property.) The code entered in the Color button's Click event procedure is shown in Figure 2-25. When the user clicks the Color button, the assignment statement on Line 16 assigns the current value of the messageLabel's ForeColor property to the colorDialog control's Color property. This assignment statement ensures that the Fore-Color's value is selected in the Color dialog box when the dialog box appears on the screen. The `colorDialog.ShowDialog()` statement on Line 17 shows (opens) the Color dialog box. An example of an open Color dialog box is shown in Figure 2-26. When the Color dialog box closes, the assignment statement on Line 18 in the Click event procedure assigns the color selected in the Color dialog box to the messageLabel's ForeColor property.

```
15  Private Sub colorButton_Click(ByVal sender As Object
16      colorDialog.Color = messageLabel.ForeColor
17      colorDialog.ShowDialog()
18      messageLabel.ForeColor = colorDialog.Color
19
20  End Sub
```

sets the dialog box's initial value

opens the dialog box

assigns the dialog box choice to the label's ForeColor property

Figure 2-25 Code entered in the Color button's Click event procedure

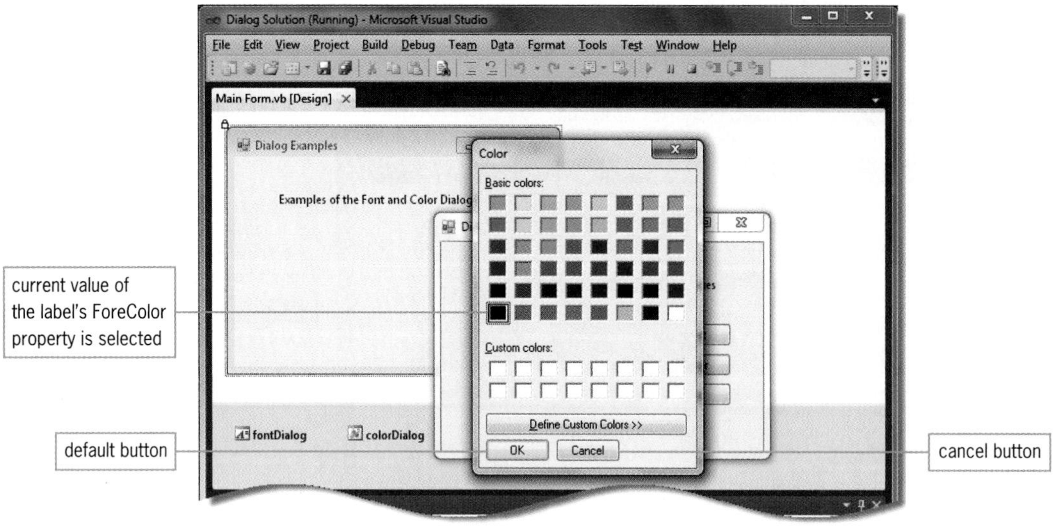

Figure 2-26 Color dialog box created by the ColorDialog tool

If you want to try the Font and Color dialog boxes, open the solution contained in the Try It 3! folder. Then use the information shown in Figures 2-22 through 2-26.

Notice that the OK button in the Color dialog box in Figure 2-26 has a darkened border, even though it does not have the focus. (The black square in the color palette has the focus.) This is because the OK button is the dialog box's default button. Like other buttons, a default button can be selected by clicking it or by pressing the Enter key when the button has the focus. However, unlike other buttons, a **default button** can also be selected by pressing the Enter key when the button does *not* have the focus. Not all default buttons are captioned OK. For example, the Open button is the default button in the Open dialog box, and the Save button is the default button in the Save As dialog box. In addition to a default button, most dialog boxes also have a cancel button, which usually is captioned Cancel. A **cancel button** can be selected in one of three ways: by clicking it, by pressing the Enter key when the button has the focus, or by pressing the Esc key when the button does *not* have the focus.

Designating the Default Button on a Form

In the previous section, you learned about the default button found in dialog boxes. A primary window created using the Windows Form template also can have a default button. You specify the default button by setting the form's AcceptButton property to the name of the button. For example, to make the Calculate Order button the default button on the MainForm in the Sunshine Cellular application, you set the MainForm's AcceptButton property to calcButton. Doing this allows the user to select the Calculate Order button without having to take his or her hands off the keyboard. A form does not have to have a default button. However, if one is used, it should be the button that is most often selected by the user, except in cases where the tasks performed by the button are both destructive and irreversible. For example, a button that deletes information should not be designated as the default button. A form can have only one default button. The default button has a darkened border during design time, as shown in Figure 2-27, and also during run time.

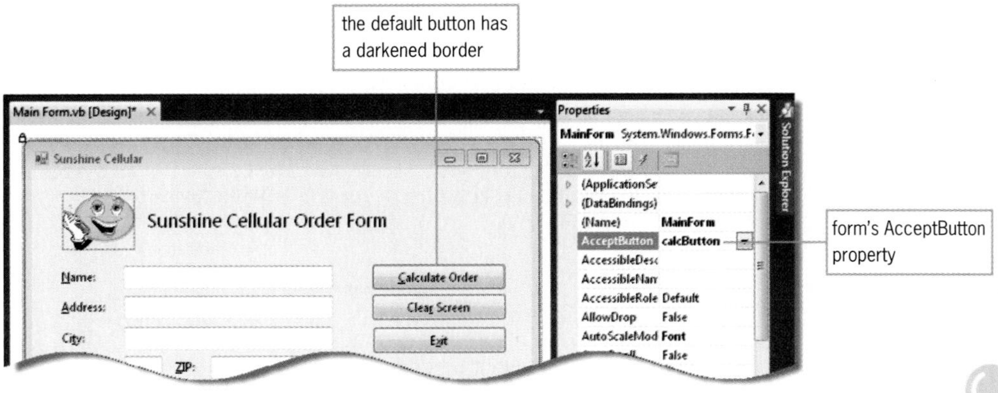

Figure 2-27 Default button during design time

Although rarely done, you also can designate a cancel button in a primary window. You do this by setting the form's CancelButton property.

Printing an Interface During Run Time

Visual Basic provides the PrintForm tool for printing an interface during run time. The tool is contained in the Visual Basic PowerPacks section of the toolbox. When you drag the PrintForm tool to the form, the instantiated PrintForm control appears in the component tray, as shown in Figure 2-28. The Print Preview button in the interface sends the printer output to the Print preview window, whereas the Print button sends it directly to the printer. Figure 2-29 shows the code entered in the Click event procedures for both of these buttons. The first line in each procedure specifies the output destination, and the second line starts the print operation.

You learned how to print an interface during design time in Chapter 1.

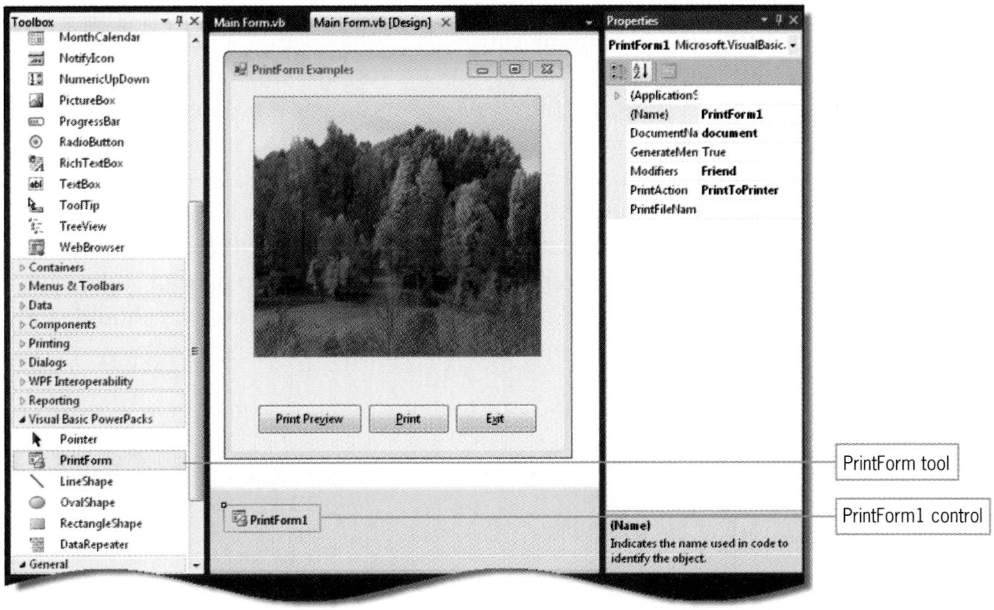

Figure 2-28 PrintForm Examples interface

```
Private Sub printPreviewButton_Click(ByVal sender As Object, ByVal e As S
    PrintForm1.PrintAction = Printing.PrintAction.PrintToPreview
    PrintForm1.Print()

End Sub

Private Sub printButton_Click(ByVal sender As Object, ByVal e As System.E
    PrintForm1.PrintAction = Printing.PrintAction.PrintToPrinter
    PrintForm1.Print()

End Sub
```

starts the print operation

destination

destination

Figure 2-29 Code entered in the Click event procedures

If you want to try the PrintForm tool, open the solution contained in the Try It 4! folder. Then use the information shown in Figures 2-28 and 2-29.

We'll wrap up this chapter with a fun and easy topic, and one that you will use in both programming tutorials at the end of this chapter: playing audio files.

Playing Audio Files

Some applications contain an audio component, such as music, sound effects, or spoken text. Figure 2-30 shows the syntax you use to include audio in a Visual Basic application. The keyword `My` in the syntax refers to Visual Basic's **My feature**—a feature that exposes a set of commonly-used objects to the programmer. One of the objects exposed by the My feature is the Computer object, which represents your computer. The Computer object provides access to other objects available on your computer, such as your computer's Audio object. To have the Audio object play an audio file, you use its Play method. Following the Play method in the syntax is a set of parentheses containing the text, *fileName*. Items within parentheses after a method's name are called **arguments** and represent information that the method needs to perform its task. In this case, the *fileName* argument represents the name of the audio file you want played. The file must be a WAV file, which is an audio file whose filename extension is .wav. You enclose the *fileName* argument in quotation marks. If the audio file is not in the project's bin\Debug folder, you will need to include the path to the file in the *fileName* argument. Also shown in Figure 2-30 is an example of using the syntax to play an audio file named GoodMorning.wav. (As mentioned in the Overview, you should study the information in How To boxes that contain syntax and examples while you are reading the chapter.)

If you want to try playing an audio file, open the solution contained in the Try It 5! folder. Then use the information shown in Figure 2-30.

HOW TO Play an Audio File

Syntax
My.Computer.Audio.Play(*fileName*)

if the file is not contained in the project's bin\Debug folder, you will need to specify the path to the file

Example
```
My.Computer.Audio.Play("GoodMorning.wav")
```

Figure 2-30 How to play an audio file

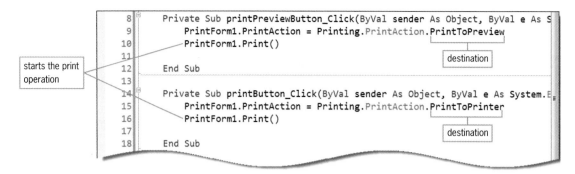

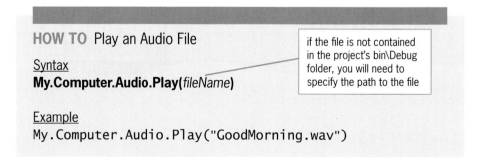

Mini-Quiz 2-4

The answers to Mini-Quiz questions are located in Appendix A.

1. In most cases, a splash screen's title bar contains ______________.
   a. the Control menu box
   b. Minimize and Maximize buttons
   c. the Close button
   d. none of the above
2. In most cases, a dialog box's title bar contains ______________.
   a. the Control menu box
   b. Minimize and Maximize buttons
   c. the Close button
   d. all of the above
3. The default button on a form can be selected by ______________.
   a. clicking it
   b. pressing the Enter key when the button has the focus
   c. pressing the Enter key when the button does not have the focus
   d. all of the above
4. If a form contains the PrintForm1 control, which of the following statements can be used to start the print operation?
   a. `PrintForm1.Go()`
   b. `PrintForm1.Print()`
   c. `PrintForm1.Start()`
   d. none of the above
5. The My.Computer.Audio object can play ______________ files only.
   a. .aud
   b. .avi
   c. .wav
   d. .wmv

You have completed the concepts section of Chapter 2. The Programming Tutorial section is next. Recall that the first tutorial in each chapter contains more detailed step-by-step instructions than does the second tutorial.

PROGRAMMING TUTORIAL 1

Creating the Color Game Application

The Ch02ProgTut1 video demonstrates all of the steps in Programming Tutorial 1.

In this tutorial, you create an application that can be used to teach the Spanish names for nine different colors. The application's TOE chart and MainForm are shown in Figures 2-31 and 2-32, respectively. The MainForm contains a table layout panel, label, and 13 buttons. It also uses a PrintForm control and a FontDialog control, which do not appear on the form. The application also uses the splash screen shown in Figure 2-33.

If you are in a computer lab, your instructor (or the lab supervisor) may not want you to play the audio files for this tutorial because doing so might be disruptive to other students.

Task	**Object**	**Event**
1. Change the button's background to the appropriate color 2. Display the appropriate Spanish word on the button's face 3. Play an audio file of the Spanish word's pronunciation	redButton, blueButton, greenButton, yellowButton, brownButton, pinkButton, purpleButton, grayButton, orangeButton	Click
Change the background of the nine color buttons to white	startOverButton	Click
Send a printout of the interface to the Print preview window	printButton, PrintForm1	Click, None
Show the Font dialog box to allow the user to change the form's font	fontButton, fontDialog	Click, None
End the application	exitButton	Click

Figure 2-31 TOE chart for the Color Game application

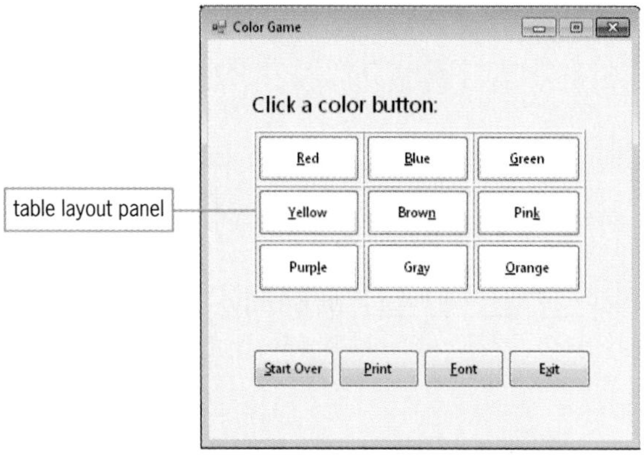

Figure 2-32 MainForm for the Color Game application

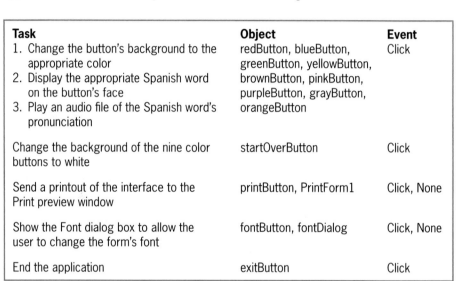

Figure 2-33 SplashScreenForm for the Color Game application

Completing the MainForm's Interface

Included in the data files for this book is a partially completed Color Game application. Before you begin coding the application, you will need to complete the MainForm's interface by adding a table layout panel, font dialog, and PrintForm control.

To complete the MainForm's user interface:

1. Start Visual Studio or the Express Edition of Visual Basic. If necessary, open the Toolbox and Solution Explorer windows.
2. If the access keys are not underlined on your screen, press the **Alt** key.
3. Open the **Color Game Solution** (**Color Game Solution.sln**) file, which is contained in the VbReloaded2010\Chap02\Color Game Solution folder. If necessary, open the designer window. The partially completed MainForm appears on the screen.
4. If necessary, open the Properties window.
5. Set the MainForm's StartPosition property to **CenterScreen**.
6. In this application, you will not allow the user to maximize the MainForm. Set the MainForm's **MaximizeBox** property to False.
7. Use the TableLayoutPanel tool, which is located in the Containers section of the toolbox, to add a table layout panel control to the form. You can move the control to a different location on the form by placing your mouse pointer on the control's move box and then dragging the control to the desired location. If necessary, click the **task box** to open the task list. See Figure 2-34.

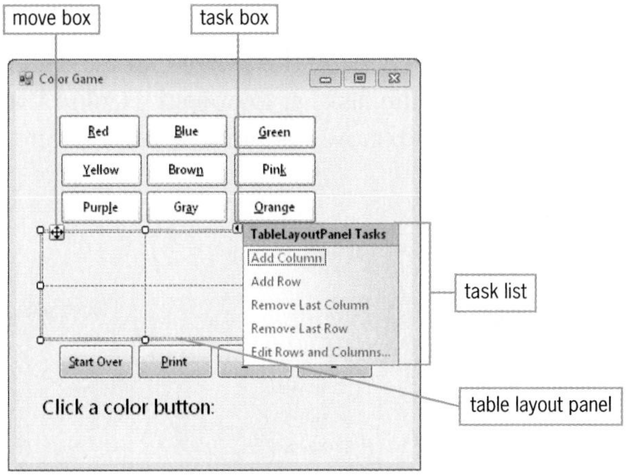

Figure 2-34 Table layout panel added to the form

8. Click **Add Column** on the task list to add another column to the table layout panel, and then click **Add Row** to add another row to the control. The control now contains three rows and three columns.
9. Next, you will make each column the same size. Click **Edit Rows and Columns** on the task list to open the Column and Row Styles dialog box.

10. Press and hold down the **Shift** key as you click **Column3** in the Member list. The three entries in the Member list are selected. Click the **Percent** radio button in the Size Type section of the dialog box. As Figure 2-35 shows, the Value column in the dialog box indicates that each of the three columns will occupy 50.00% (one-half) of the table, which is impossible. The three columns, if sized the same, would each occupy 33.33% (one-third) of the table.

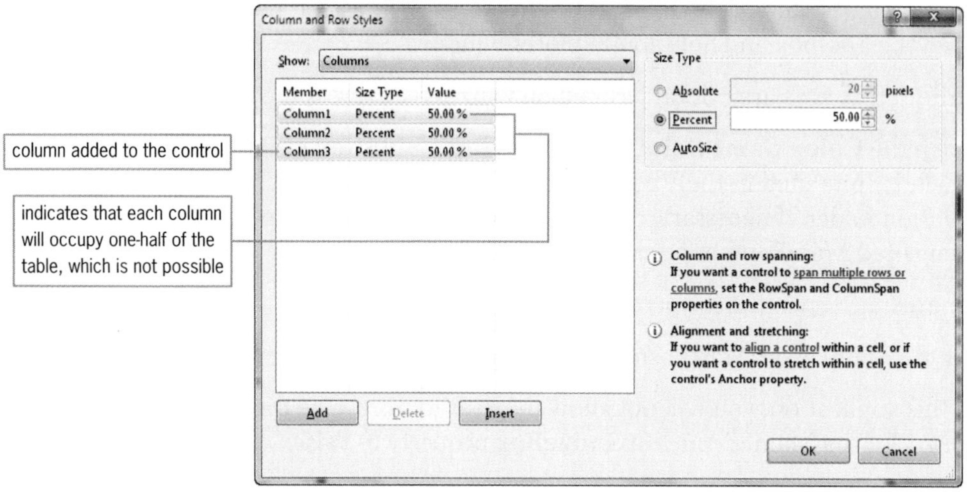

Figure 2-35 Column and Row Styles dialog box

11. You can enter the appropriate percentage for each column manually, using the text box that appears next to the Percent radio button. Or, you can let the computer change the percentages for you. Click the **OK** button to have the computer change the percentages. The Column and Row Styles dialog box closes.

12. Now verify that the computer changed the percentages to 33.33%. Click **Edit Rows and Columns** on the task list to open the Column and Row Styles dialog box. The dialog box now contains the correct percentages. See Figure 2-36.

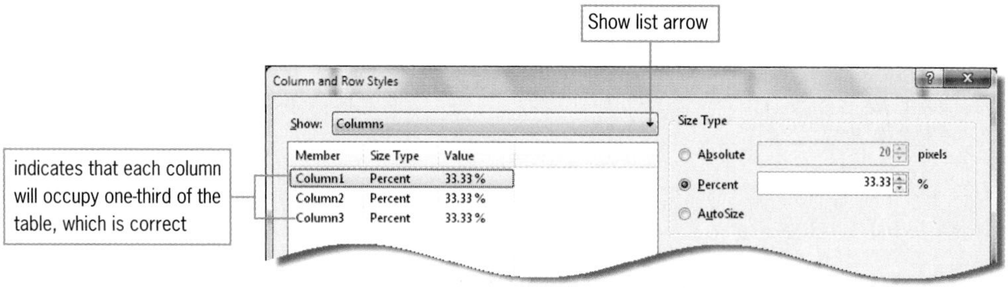

Figure 2-36 Correct percentages shown in the Column and Row Styles dialog box

13. Next, you will make the rows the same size. Click the **list arrow** in the Show box, and then click **Rows**. Press and hold down the **Shift** key as you click **Row3** in the Member list. Click the **Percent** radio button in the Size Type section of the dialog box, and then click the **OK** button.

14. On your own, verify that each row's percentage is now 33.33% in the Column and Row Styles dialog box, and then close the dialog box.

15. Next, you will put a border around each cell in the table layout panel. A cell is an intersection of a row and column. The table layout panel contains nine cells. Click **CellBorderStyle** in the Properties window, and then change the property's setting to **OutsetDouble**.

16. Now you will make the table layout panel larger. Click **Size** in the Properties window, then type **300, 146** and press **Enter**.

17. Drag the Red button into the first cell in the table layout panel. The button appears in the upper-left corner of the cell, because its Anchor property is set to the default, which is "Top, Left". The Anchor property determines how a control is anchored to its container. If you want the Red button centered within its container (in this case, the cell), you would change its Anchor property to None. However, if you want the button to fill the entire cell, you would change its Anchor property to "Top, Bottom, Left, Right"; this setting anchors each of the button's borders to its associated border within the cell. In the next step, you will have the button fill the entire cell.

18. Click **Anchor** in the Properties list, and then click the property's **list arrow**. The left and top bars are already selected. Click the **right and bottom bars**. All four bars are now selected, as shown in Figure 2-37.

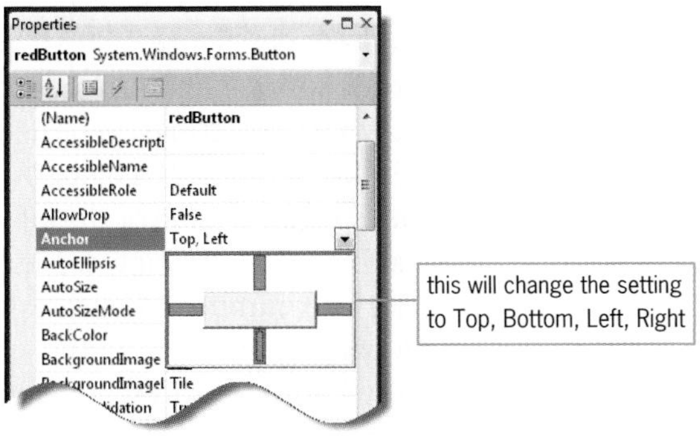

Figure 2-37 Bars selected in the Anchor property

19. Press **Enter** to close the Anchor property's box. The Anchor property is now set to "Top, Bottom, Left, Right", and the Red button fills the cell.

20. Select the remaining eight color buttons, and then set their Anchor properties to **Top, Bottom, Left, Right**.

21. Click the **form** to deselect the buttons. Next, drag each of the remaining eight color buttons into its own cell in the table layout panel. As you drag the buttons, try placing more than one button in the same cell. You will find that each cell in the table layout panel accepts only one control. (If you need to put several controls in a cell, you can do so by first putting the controls in a panel control, and then placing the panel control in the cell.) Figure 2-38 shows the correct placement of the buttons in the table layout panel.

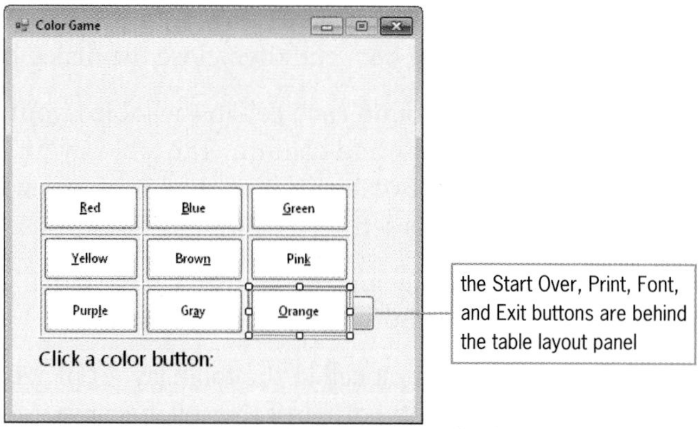

Figure 2-38 Color buttons positioned in the table layout panel

22. Now you will position the table layout panel and label controls appropriately. Click the **table layout panel**, and then set its Location property to **41, 78**. Click the **Label1** control (which contains the text "Click a color button:"), and then set its Location property to **35, 43**.

23. Click the **Start Over** button, and then set its Location property to **41, 269**. Now use the Format menu to align the top borders of the Print, Font, and Exit buttons with the top border of the Start Over button.

24. Right-click the **form**, and then click **Lock Controls**.

25. Next, use the Tab Order option on the View menu to set each control's TabIndex property to the values shown in Figure 2-39. (If you are using the Express Edition, the Tab Order option might not be available until you click Tools on the menu bar, point to Settings, and then click Expert Settings.) Notice that the TabIndex values of the color buttons begin with the number 4, which is the TabIndex value of the table layout panel. (The table layout panel's TabIndex value is not visible because the Red button fills the entire first cell.) The number 4 indicates that the buttons belong to the table layout panel rather than to the form. If you move or delete the table layout panel, the controls that belong to it also will be moved or deleted. The numbers that appear after the period in the color buttons' TabIndex values indicate the order in which each button will receive the focus within the table layout panel.

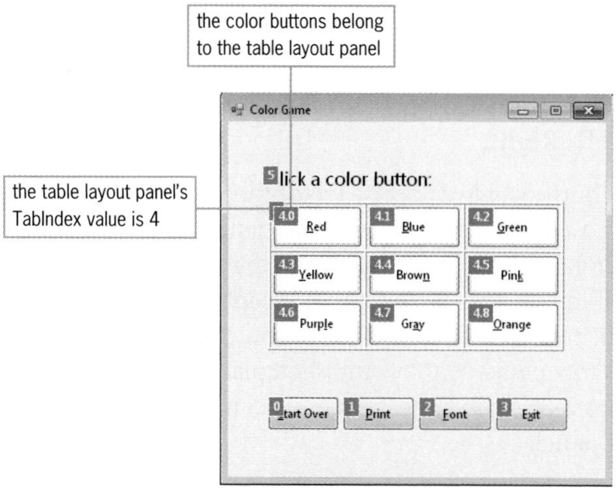

Figure 2-39 Tab order for the controls in the interface

26. Press the **Esc** key to remove the tab order boxes from the form.

27. Click **FontDialog** in the Dialogs section of the toolbox, and then drag a font dialog control to the form. The control appears in the component tray. Change the control's name to **fontDialog**.

28. Click **PrintForm** in the Visual Basic PowerPacks section of the toolbox, and then drag a PrintForm control to the form. The control appears in the component tray.

29. The MainForm's interface is now complete. Auto-hide the Toolbox, Solution Explorer, and Properties windows. Save the solution by clicking **File** on the menu bar, and then clicking **Save All**.

Coding the Color Buttons

According to the TOE chart shown earlier in Figure 2-31, each color button's Click event procedure must perform three tasks. The first task is to change the button's background to the appropriate color. The background color of an object is specified in the object's BackColor property. To change the value stored in the BackColor property while an application is running, you use an assignment statement in the following format: *objectName*.**BackColor** = *color*.

To begin coding the color buttons' Click event procedures:

1. Open the Code Editor window. Notice that the exitButton's Click event procedure already contains the `Me.Close()` instruction.

2. Open the code template for the blueButton's Click event procedure, and then type **blueButton.BackColor = Color.LightBlue** and press **Enter**.

3. On your own, code the Click event procedures for the remaining eight color buttons. Assign the following colors to the buttons' BackColor properties: Color.Brown, Color.Gray, Color.Green, Color.Orange, Color.Pink, Color.MediumPurple, Color.Red, and Color.Yellow.

4. Save the solution, and then start the application. Click **each of the color buttons** to verify that the code you entered is working correctly. See Figure 2-40. (If the access keys do not appear in the interface, press the Alt key on your keyboard.)

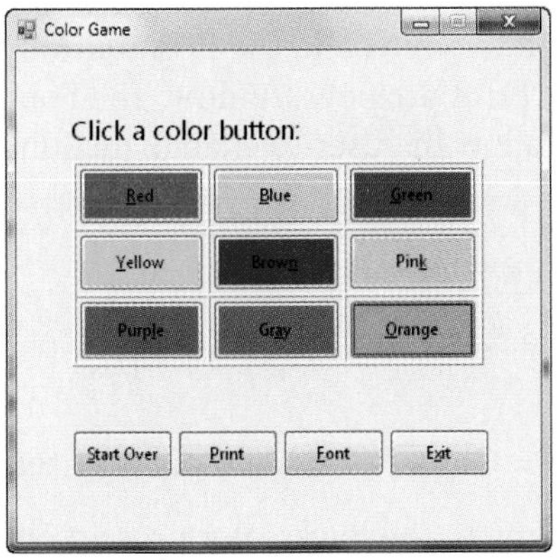

Figure 2-40 Result of clicking each color button

5. Click the **Exit** button to end the application.

Each color button also should display the appropriate Spanish word on the button's face and then play an audio file containing the pronunciation of the Spanish word. The audio files are located in the current project's bin\Debug folder. Figure 2-41 lists the Spanish words, as well as the names of the audio files, associated with each button.

Button	Spanish word	Audio file
Blue	Azul	blue.wav
Brown	Marron	brown.wav
Gray	Gris	gray.wav
Green	Verde	green.wav
Orange	Anaranjado	orange.wav
Pink	Rosa	pink.wav
Purple	Morado	purple.wav
Red	Rojo	red.wav
Yellow	Amarillo	yellow.wav

Figure 2-41 Spanish words and audio files for the color buttons

Playing audio files in a computer lab might be disruptive to other students. If your instructor (or the lab supervisor) does not want you to play the audio files for this tutorial, don't enter the Play method in the color buttons' Click event procedures.

To finish coding each color button's Click event procedure:

1. Locate the code template for the blueButton's Click event procedure. In the blank line below the assignment statement, type **blueButton.Text = "Azul"** and press **Enter**. If you are allowed to play audio files, type **My.Computer.Audio.Play("blue.wav")** and press **Enter**.
2. Save the solution, and then start the application. Click the **Blue** button. Azul, which is the Spanish word for "blue," appears on the button's face. In addition, you hear the message "Blue, Azul."
3. Click the **Exit** button.
4. Using the information listed in Figure 2-41, finish coding the Click event procedures for the remaining eight color buttons.
5. Save the solution, and then start the application. Click **each of the color buttons** to verify that the code you entered is working correctly.

Coding the Start Over, Print, and Font Buttons

According to the application's TOE chart, the Start Over button should change each color button's background to white, and the Print button should send a printout of the interface to the Print preview window. The Font button should show the Font dialog box and allow the user to change the font used to display the text on the form.

To code the Start Over button's Click event procedure:

1. Open the code template for the startOverButton's Click event procedure.
2. Type **blueButton.BackColor = Color.White** and press **Enter**.
3. On your own, assign Color.White to the BackColor property of the remaining eight color buttons.

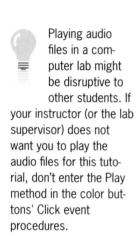

4. Save the solution, and then start the application. Click **each of the color buttons**, and then click the **Start Over** button. The background of each color button is now white.
5. Click the **Exit** button to end the application.

To code the Print button's Click event procedure:

1. Open the code template for the printButton's Click event procedure.
2. Type **PrintForm1.PrintAction = Printing.PrintAction.PrintToPreview** to specify that the printout should be sent to the Print preview window, and then press **Enter**.
3. Type **PrintForm1.Print()** and then press **Enter**.
4. Save the solution, and then start the application. Click the **Print button**. The printout of the interface appears in the Print preview window. Click the **Zoom button** list arrow, and then click **75%**. See Figure 2-42.

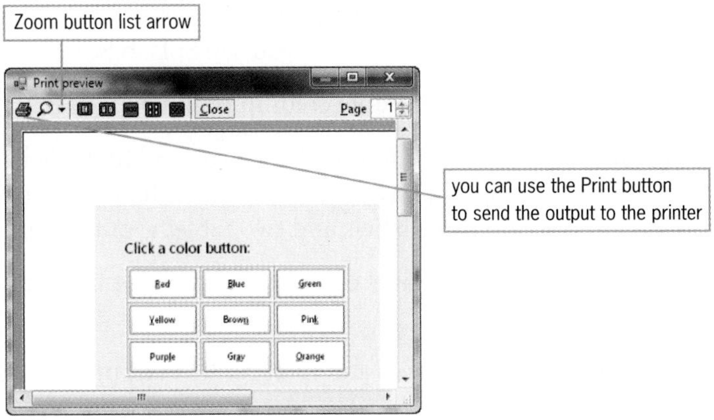

Figure 2-42 Print preview window

5. Click the **Close** button in the Print preview window, and then click the **Exit** button to end the application.

To code the Font button's Click event procedure:

1. Open the code template for the fontButton's Click event procedure.
2. First, assign the current values of the form's Font property to the font dialog control. By doing this, the values will be selected in the Font dialog box when it opens. Type **fontDialog.Font = Me.Font** and press **Enter**.
3. Next, show the Font dialog box. Type **fontDialog.ShowDialog()** and press **Enter**.
4. Finally, assign the values selected in the dialog box to the form's Font property. Type **Me.Font = fontDialog.Font** and press **Enter**.
5. Save the solution, and then start the application. Click the **Font** button to open the Font dialog box. Select a different font, style, or

size, and then click the **OK** button. Your changes affect all of the text except the text in the Label1 control. This is because the Label1 control's Font property was changed individually.

6. Click the **Exit** button to end the application.

Adding a Splash Screen to the Color Game Project

In the next set of steps, you will add a splash screen to the application. Recall that the Add New Item dialog box provides a template that is already configured as a splash screen.

To add a new splash screen to the Color Game project:

1. Display the Solution Explorer and Properties windows.
2. Click **Project** on the menu bar, and then click **Add New Item**.
3. *If you are using Visual Studio 2010,* expand the Common Items node in the Installed Templates list (if necessary), and then click **Windows Forms**. *If you are using Visual Basic 2010 Express Edition,* scroll the middle column of the dialog box until you see Splash Screen.
4. Click **Splash Screen** in the middle column of the dialog box.
5. Type **SplashScreenForm.vb** in the Name box, and then click the **Add** button to add a splash screen to the project. Included on the SplashScreenForm are three labels and two table layout panels.
6. Click the **ApplicationTitle** label control, and then set its Font property to **Segoe UI, 18pt**.
7. Click the **Version** label control, and then set its Font property to **Segoe UI, 9pt**.
8. Click the **Copyright** label control, and then set its Font property to **Segoe UI, 9pt**.
9. Right-click **My Project** in the Solution Explorer window, and then click **Open** to open the Project Designer window. Click the **Splash screen** list arrow in the Application pane, and then click **SplashScreenForm** in the list.
10. Click the **Assembly Information** button in the Application pane to open the Assembly Information dialog box. Change the text in the Title box to **Color Game**. If necessary, change the year in the Copyright box to **2012**. See Figure 2-43.

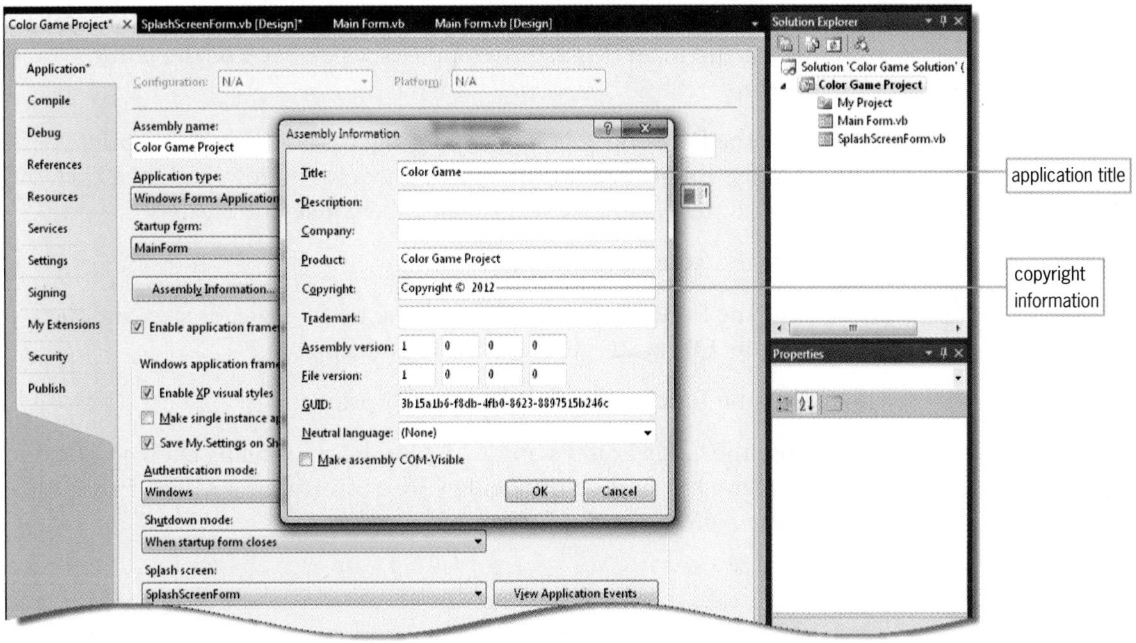

Figure 2-43 Project Designer window and Assembly Information dialog box

11. Click the **OK** button to close the Assembly Information dialog box. Save the solution, and then close the Project Designer window.

Testing the Application

When you are finished with an application, you should always test it to verify that it is working correctly.

To test the application:

1. Start the application. The splash screen shown in Figure 2-44 appears first.

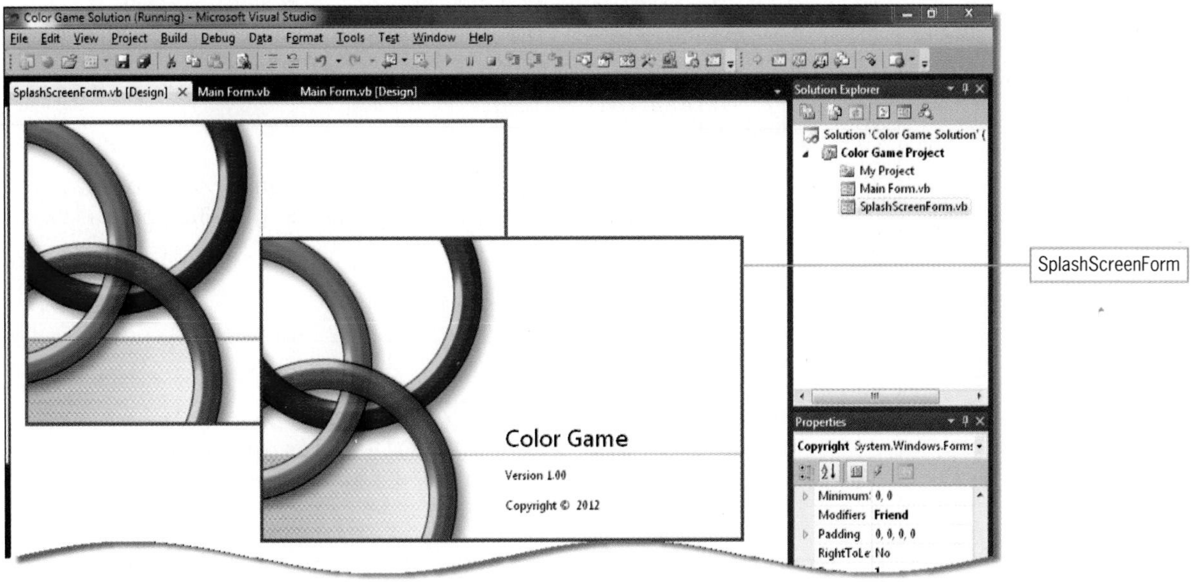

Figure 2-44 The splash screen appears first

2. After a few seconds have elapsed, the splash screen disappears and the startup form (MainForm) appears. Click **each of the color buttons**.
3. Click the **Print** button. If your computer is connected to a printer, click the **Print** button in the Print preview window, and then click the **Close** button. Otherwise, just click the **Close** button.
4. Click the **Start Over** button.
5. Click the **Font** button. Select a different font, style, or size, and then click the **OK** button to close the Font dialog box.
6. Click the **Exit** button to end the application.
7. Close the Code Editor window. Close the solution by clicking **File** on the menu bar, and then clicking **Close Solution** (or **Close Project**). Figure 2-45 shows the Color Game application's code.

```
Public Class MainForm

    Private Sub exitButton_Click(ByVal sender As Object,
    ByVal e As System.EventArgs) Handles exitButton.Click
        Me.Close()

    End Sub

    Private Sub blueButton_Click(ByVal sender As Object,
    ByVal e As System.EventArgs) Handles blueButton.Click
        blueButton.BackColor = Color.LightBlue
        blueButton.Text = "Azul"
        My.Computer.Audio.Play("blue.wav")

    End Sub

    Private Sub brownButton_Click(ByVal sender As Object,
    ByVal e As System.EventArgs) Handles brownButton.Click
        brownButton.BackColor = Color.Brown
        brownButton.Text = "Marron"
        My.Computer.Audio.Play("brown.wav")

    End Sub

    Private Sub grayButton_Click(ByVal sender As Object,
    ByVal e As System.EventArgs) Handles grayButton.Click
        grayButton.BackColor = Color.Gray
        grayButton.Text = "Gris"
        My.Computer.Audio.Play("gray.wav")

    End Sub

    Private Sub greenButton_Click(ByVal sender As Object,
    ByVal e As System.EventArgs) Handles greenButton.Click
        greenButton.BackColor = Color.Green
        greenButton.Text = "Verde"
```

Figure 2-45 Color Game application's code *(continues)*

(continued)

```
        My.Computer.Audio.Play("green.wav")

    End Sub

    Private Sub orangeButton_Click(ByVal sender As Object,
    ByVal e As System.EventArgs) Handles orangeButton.Click
        orangeButton.BackColor = Color.Orange
        orangeButton.Text = "Anaranjado"
        My.Computer.Audio.Play("orange.wav")

    End Sub

    Private Sub pinkButton_Click(ByVal sender As Object,
    ByVal e As System.EventArgs) Handles pinkButton.Click
        pinkButton.BackColor = Color.Pink
        pinkButton.Text = "Rosa"
        My.Computer.Audio.Play("pink.wav")

    End Sub

    Private Sub purpleButton_Click(ByVal sender As Object,
    ByVal e As System.EventArgs) Handles purpleButton.Click
        purpleButton.BackColor = Color.MediumPurple
        purpleButton.Text = "Morado"
        My.Computer.Audio.Play("purple.wav")

    End Sub

    Private Sub redButton_Click(ByVal sender As Object,
    ByVal e As System.EventArgs) Handles redButton.Click
        redButton.BackColor = Color.Red
        redButton.Text = "Rojo"
        My.Computer.Audio.Play("red.wav")

    End Sub

    Private Sub yellowButton_Click(ByVal sender As Object,
    ByVal e As System.EventArgs) Handles yellowButton.Click
        yellowButton.BackColor = Color.Yellow
        yellowButton.Text = "Amarillo"
        My.Computer.Audio.Play("yellow.wav")

    End Sub

    Private Sub startOverButton_Click(ByVal sender As Object,
    ByVal e As System.EventArgs) Handles startOverButton.Click
        blueButton.BackColor = Color.White
        brownButton.BackColor = Color.White
        grayButton.BackColor = Color.White
        greenButton.BackColor = Color.White
        orangeButton.BackColor = Color.White
        pinkButton.BackColor = Color.White
        purpleButton.BackColor = Color.White
        redButton.BackColor = Color.White
        yellowButton.BackColor = Color.White

    End Sub
```

Figure 2-45 Color Game application's code *(continues)*

(continued)

```
    Private Sub printButton_Click(ByVal sender As Object,
    ByVal e As System.EventArgs) Handles printButton.Click
        PrintForm1.PrintAction =
            Printing.PrintAction.PrintToPreview
        PrintForm1.Print()

    End Sub

    Private Sub fontButton_Click(ByVal sender As Object,
    ByVal e As System.EventArgs) Handles fontButton.Click
        fontDialog.Font = Me.Font
        fontDialog.ShowDialog()
        Me.Font = fontDialog.Font

    End Sub
End Class
```

Figure 2-45 Color Game application's code

PROGRAMMING TUTORIAL 2

Creating the Music Sampler Application

In this tutorial, you create an application that allows the user to preview a song by playing several seconds of it. The application's TOE chart and MainForm are shown in Figures 2-46 and 2-47, respectively. The MainForm contains a table layout panel, seven labels, and nine buttons. The application also uses the splash screen shown in Figure 2-48.

If you are in a computer lab, your instructor (or the lab supervisor) may not want you to play the audio files for this tutorial because doing so might be disruptive to other students.

Task	**Object**	**Event**
Play an audio file that contains a preview of the song associated with the button	breakawayButton, boomButton, sydneyButton, thrillerbutton, treysonButton, feelingButton	Click
Show the Color dialog box to allow the user to change the background color of the form	colorButton, colorDialog	Click, None
Send a printout of the interface to the Print preview window	printButton, PrintForm1	Click, None
End the application	exitButton	Click

Figure 2-46 TOE chart for the Music Sampler application

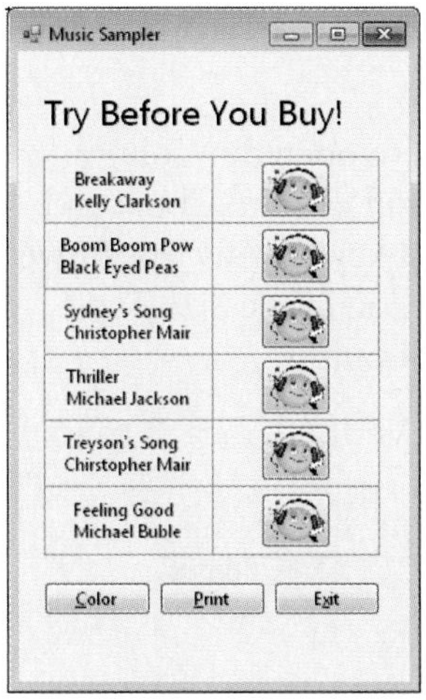

Figure 2-47 MainForm for the Music Sampler application

Figure 2-48 SplashScreenForm for the Music Sampler application

Completing the MainForm's Interface

Included in the data files for this book is a partially completed Music Sampler application. Before you begin coding the application, you will need to complete the MainForm's interface by adding a table layout panel, color dialog, and PrintForm control.

To complete the MainForm's user interface:

1. Start Visual Studio or the Express Edition of Visual Basic. If necessary, open the Toolbox and Solution Explorer windows.
2. If the access keys are not underlined on your screen, press the **Alt** key.
3. Open the **Music Sampler Solution** (**Music Sampler Solution.sln**) file, which is contained in the VbReloaded2010\Chap02\Music Sampler Solution folder. If necessary, open the designer window. The partially completed MainForm appears on the screen.
4. If necessary, open the Properties window.
5. The MainForm should be centered on the screen when it first appears. Set the appropriate property.

6. Add a table layout panel control to the form. Using the control's task list, add four additional rows to the control.
7. Click **Edit Rows and Columns** on the task list to open the Column and Row Styles dialog box. Click the **list arrow** in the Show box, and then click **Rows**. Press and hold down the **Shift** key as you click **Row6** in the Member list. Click the **Percent** radio button in the Size Type section of the dialog box, and then click the **OK** button.
8. Open the Column and Row Styles dialog box. Verify that each row's percentage is 16.67%, as shown in Figure 2-49.

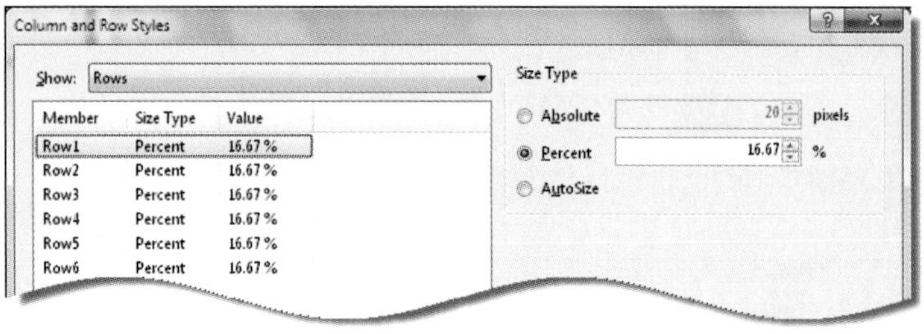

Figure 2-49 Row percentages in the Column and Row Styles dialog box

9. Close the Column and Row Styles dialog box.
10. Use the Properties window to change the table layout panel's CellBorderStyle property to **Single**.
11. Make the table layout panel larger by dragging its bottom and right borders. See Figure 2-50.

Figure 2-50 Correct size of the table layout panel

12. Drag the **Label2** control into the first cell in the table layout panel. The label appears in the upper-left corner of the cell, because its Anchor property is set to the default, which is "Top, Left". The Anchor property determines how a control is anchored to its container. If you want the Label2 control to fill the entire cell (its container), you would change its Anchor property to "Top, Bottom, Left, Right"; this setting

anchors each of the label's borders to its associated border within the cell. However, if you want the label centered within the cell, you would change its Anchor property to None. In the next step, you will center the label within the entire cell.

13. Click **Anchor** in the Properties list, and then click the property's **list arrow**. Click the **left and top bars** to deselect them, and then press **Enter** to close the Anchor property's box. The Anchor property is now set to None.

14. Select the remaining five labels, and then set their Anchor properties to **None**.

15. Click the **form** to deselect the controls. Now drag each of the remaining five labels into its own cell in the table layout panel. As you drag the labels, try placing more than one label in the same cell. You will find that each cell in the table layout panel accepts only one control. (If you need to put several controls in a cell, you can do so by first putting the controls in a panel control, and then placing the panel control in the cell.) Figure 2-51 shows the correct placement of the labels in the table layout panel.

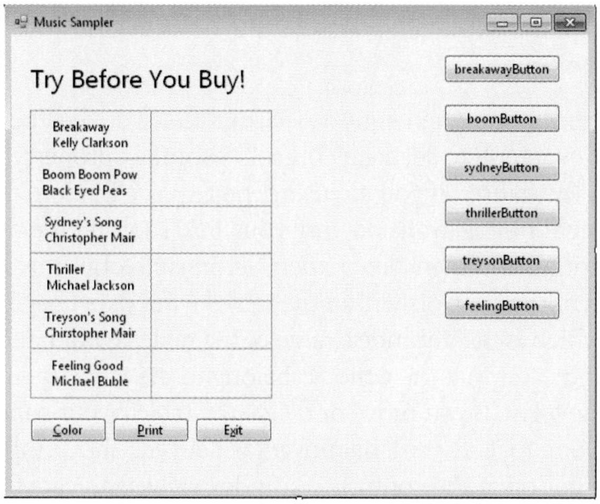

Figure 2-51 Correct placement of the labels in the table layout panel

16. Select the six buttons located on the right side of the form. Set their Anchor properties to **None**. Also set their BackgroundImage properties to **j0440430.wmf** and their BackgroundImageLayout properties to **Stretch**. The j0440430.wmf file is contained in the current project's bin\Debug folder. (The j0440430.wmf file is from Microsoft's Clip Art collection and was downloaded from *www.office.microsoft.com/en-us/clipart.*)

17. Click the **form** to deselect the six buttons.

18. Next, delete the text stored in the Text property of the six buttons. You will need to do each of the six buttons individually.

19. Make the breakawayButton smaller, as shown in Figure 2-52.

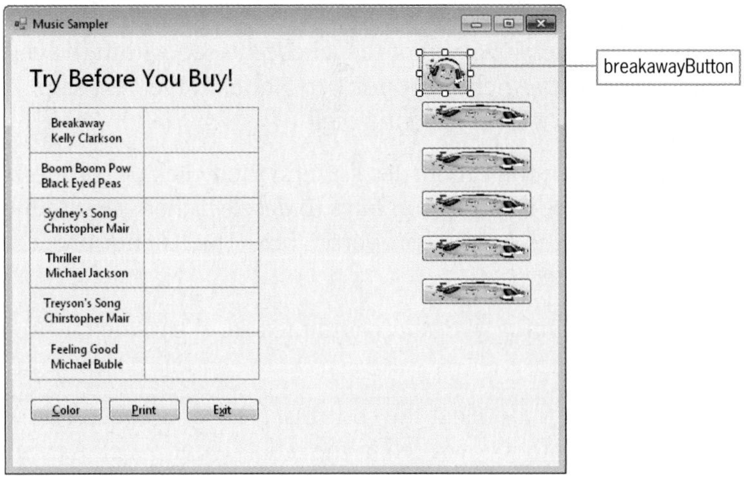

Figure 2-52 New size for the breakawayButton

20. Use the Format menu to make the other five buttons the same size as the breakawayButton, and then click the **form** to deselect the selected buttons.

21. Drag the breakawayButton into the first cell in the second column of the table layout panel. Now drag each of the other five buttons into their appropriate cells.

22. Next, size the form as shown in Figure 2-53, and then use the Tab Order option on the View menu to set each control's TabIndex property to the values shown in the figure. (If you are using the Express Edition, the Tab Order option might not be available until you click Tools on the menu bar, point to Settings, and then click Expert Settings.) Notice that the TabIndex values of the controls within the table layout panel begin with the number 3, which is the TabIndex value of the table layout panel. The number 3 indicates that the controls belong to the table layout panel rather than to the form. If you move or delete the table layout panel, the controls that belong to it also will be moved or deleted. The numbers that appear after the period in the controls' TabIndex values indicate the order in which each control will receive the focus within the table layout panel.

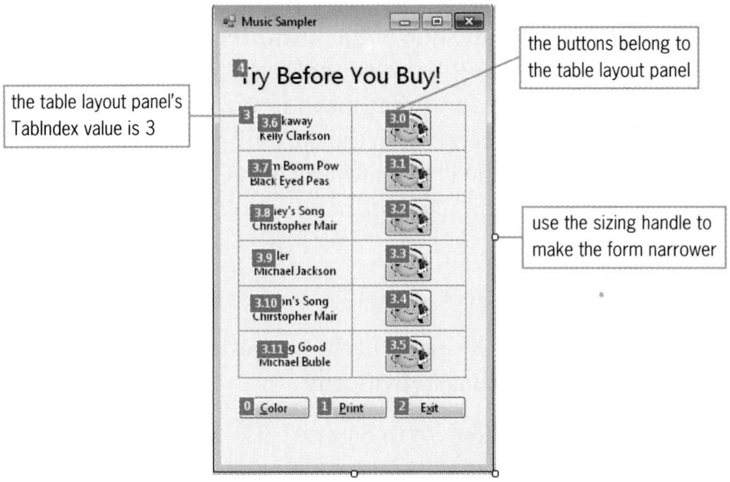

Figure 2-53 TabIndex values

23. Remove the tab order boxes from the form, and then lock the controls.
24. Add a color dialog control to the form. The control appears in the component tray. Change the control's name to **colorDialog**.
25. Add a PrintForm control to the form. The control appears in the component tray.
26. The MainForm's interface is now complete. Auto-hide the Toolbox, Solution Explorer, and Properties windows. Save the solution by clicking **File** on the menu bar, and then clicking **Save All**.

Coding the Buttons Within the Table Layout Panel

According to the TOE chart shown earlier in Figure 2-46, the six buttons contained in the table layout panel should play an audio file when they are clicked. The audio files are contained in the current project's bin\Debug folder.

To code the Click event procedures for the six buttons:

1. Open the Code Editor window. Notice that the exitButton's Click event procedure already contains the `Me.Close()` instruction.
2. Open the code template for the boomButton's Click event procedure. If you are allowed to play audio files, enter the instruction to play the BoomBoomPow.wav file. If you need help, refer to the How To box shown earlier in Figure 2-30.
3. On your own (and only if you are allowed to play audio files), code the Click event procedures for the breakawayButton, feelingButton, sydneyButton, thrillerButton, and treysonButton. The files associated with each button are named Breakaway.wav, FeelingGood.wav, Sydney.wav, Thriller.wav, and Treyson.wav.
4. Save the solution, and then start the application. Click **each of the buttons within the table layout panel** to verify that the code you entered is working correctly.
5. Click the **Exit** button to end the application.

Playing audio files in a computer lab might be disruptive to other students. If your instructor (or the lab supervisor) does not want you to play the audio files for this tutorial, don't enter the Play methods in Steps 2 and 3.

Coding the Color and Print Buttons

According to the application's TOE chart, the Color button should show the Color dialog box and allow the user to change the background color of the form. The background color of an object is specified in the object's BackColor property. The Print button should send a printout of the interface to the Print preview window.

To code the Color button's Click event procedure:

1. Open the code template for the colorButton's Click event procedure.
2. First, enter the instruction to assign the current value of the form's BackColor property to the color dialog control's Color property. (Recall that you refer to the form using the keyword `Me`.)

3. Next, enter the instruction to show the Color dialog box.
4. Finally, enter the instruction to assign the value selected in the Color dialog box to the form's BackColor property.
5. Save the solution, and then start the application. Click the **Color** button to open the Color dialog box. Select a different color square, and then click the **OK** button. The background color of the form changes to the color you selected.
6. Click the **Exit** button to end the application.

To code the Print button's Click event procedure:

1. Open the code template for the printButton's Click event procedure.
2. First, enter the instruction to specify that the printout should be sent to the Print preview window. If you need help, refer to Figure 2-29 in the chapter.
3. Next, enter the instruction to tell the computer to start the print operation.
4. Save the solution, and then start the application. Click the **Print** button. The printout of the interface appears in the Print preview window. Click the **Zoom button** list arrow, and then click **50%**. See Figure 2-54.

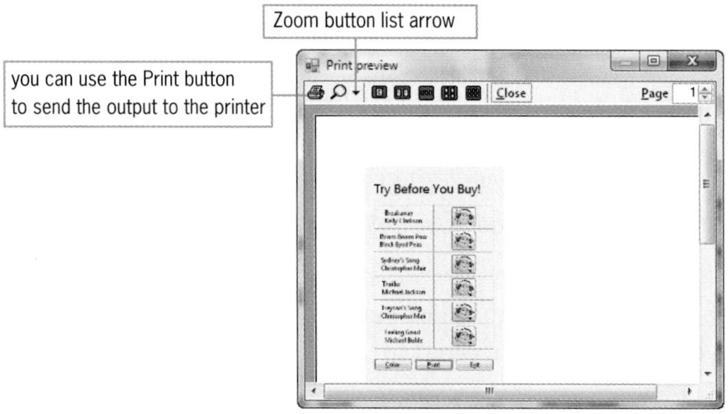

Figure 2-54 The Print preview window

5. Click the **Close** button in the Print preview window, and then click the **Exit** button to end the application.

Adding a Splash Screen to the Music Sampler Project

In the next set of steps, you will add a splash screen to the application. Recall that the Add New Item dialog box provides a template that is already configured as a splash screen.

To add a new splash screen to the Music Sampler project:

1. Add a new splash screen to the project. Name the splash screen **SplashScreenForm**. If you need help, refer to the How To box shown earlier in Figure 2-14.
2. Set the Font property of the ApplicationTitle label control to **Segoe UI, 18pt**.
3. Set the Font properties of the Version and Copyright label controls to **Segoe UI, 9pt**.
4. Specify that the SplashScreenForm is the splash screen for the project. If you need help, refer to the How To box shown earlier in Figure 2-17.
5. Open the Project Designer window, if necessary. Click the **Assembly Information** button in the Application pane to open the Assembly Information dialog box. Change the text in the Title box to **Music Sampler**. If necessary, change the year in the Copyright box to **2012**.
6. Click the **OK** button to close the Assembly Information dialog box. Save the solution, and then close the Project Designer window.

Testing the Application

When you are finished with an application, you should always test it to verify that it is working correctly.

To test the application:

1. Start the application. The splash screen shown earlier in Figure 2-48 appears first.
2. After a few seconds have elapsed, the splash screen disappears and the startup form (MainForm) appears. Click **each of the buttons within the table layout panel**.
3. Click the **Color** button. Select a different color, and then click the **OK** button to close the Color dialog box.
4. Click the **Print** button. If your computer is connected to a printer, click the **Print** button in the Print preview window, and then click the **Close** button. Otherwise, just click the **Close** button.
5. Click the **Exit** button to end the application.
6. Close the Code Editor window. Close the solution by clicking **File** on the menu bar, and then clicking **Close Solution** (or **Close Project**). Figure 2-55 shows the Music Sampler application's code.

```
Public Class MainForm

    Private Sub exitButton_Click(ByVal sender As Object,
    ByVal e As System.EventArgs) Handles exitButton.Click
        Me.Close()

    End Sub

    Private Sub boomButton_Click(ByVal sender As Object,
    ByVal e As System.EventArgs) Handles boomButton.Click
        My.Computer.Audio.Play("BoomBoomPow.wav")

    End Sub

    Private Sub breakawayButton_Click(ByVal sender As Object,
    ByVal e As System.EventArgs) Handles breakawayButton.Click
        My.Computer.Audio.Play("Breakaway.wav")
    End Sub

    Private Sub feelingButton_Click(ByVal sender As Object,
    ByVal e As System.EventArgs) Handles feelingButton.Click
        My.Computer.Audio.Play("FeelingGood.wav")

    End Sub

    Private Sub sydneyButton_Click(ByVal sender As Object,
    ByVal e As System.EventArgs) Handles sydneyButton.Click
        My.Computer.Audio.Play("Sydney.wav")

    End Sub

    Private Sub thrillerButton_Click(ByVal sender As Object,
    ByVal e As System.EventArgs) Handles thrillerButton.Click
        My.Computer.Audio.Play("Thriller.wav")

    End Sub

    Private Sub treysonButton_Click(ByVal sender As Object,
    ByVal e As System.EventArgs) Handles treysonButton.Click
        My.Computer.Audio.Play("Treyson.wav")

    End Sub

    Private Sub colorButton_Click(ByVal sender As Object,
    ByVal e As System.EventArgs) Handles colorButton.Click
        colorDialog.Color = Me.BackColor
        colorDialog.ShowDialog()
        Me.BackColor = colorDialog.Color

    End Sub

    Private Sub printButton_Click(ByVal sender As Object,
    ByVal e As System.EventArgs) Handles printButton.Click
        PrintForm1.PrintAction = Printing.PrintAction.
            PrintToPreview
        PrintForm1.Print()

    End Sub
End Class
```

Figure 2-55 Color Game application's code

PROGRAMMING EXAMPLE

Moonbucks Coffee

Create an interface that allows the user to enter the following customer information: name, address, city, state, ZIP code, the number of pounds of regular coffee ordered, and the number of pounds of decaffeinated coffee ordered. The interface will need to display the total number of pounds of coffee ordered and the total price of the order. Use the following names for the solution, project, and form file: Moonbucks Solution, Moonbucks Project, and Main Form.vb. Save the files in the VbReloaded2010\Chap02 folder. In this chapter, you will code only the Exit and Print buttons' Click event procedures. You will code the Click event procedures for the Calculate Order and Clear Order buttons in Chapter 3. See Figures 2-56 through 2-60.

Task	Object	Event
1. Calculate the total pounds of coffee ordered and the total price of the order 2. Display the total pounds of coffee ordered and the total price of the order in totalPoundsLabel and totalPriceLabel	calcButton	Click
Send a printout of the interface to the Print preview window	printButton, PrintForm1	Click, None
Clear screen for the next order	clearButton	Click
End the application	exitButton	Click
Display the total pounds of coffee ordered (from calcButton)	totalPoundsLabel	None
Display the total price of the order (from calcButton)	totalPriceLabel	None
Get and display the order information	nameTextBox, addressTextBox, cityTextBox, stateTextBox, zipTextBox, regularTextBox, decafTextBox	None

Figure 2-56 TOE chart

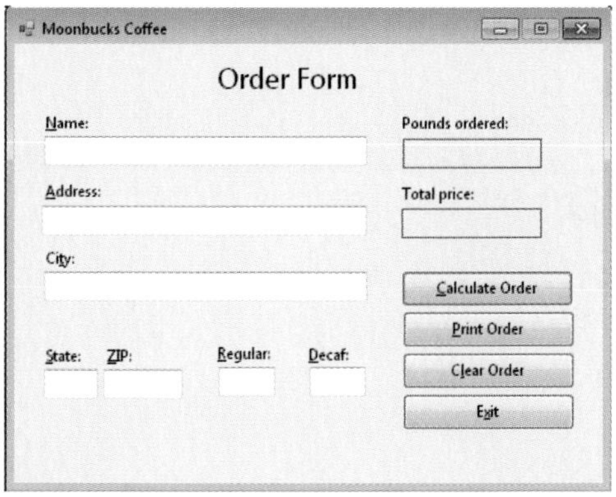

Figure 2-57 User interface

Object	Property	Setting
Form1	Name	MainForm
	AcceptButton	calcButton
	Font	Segoe UI, 9 point
	MaximizeBox	False
	StartPosition	CenterScreen
	Text	Moonbucks Coffee
Label1	Font	Segoe UI, 16 point
	Text	Order Form
Label2	Text	&Name:
Label3	Text	&Address:
Label4	Text	Ci&ty:
Label5	Text	&State:
Label6	Text	&ZIP:
Label7	Text	&Regular:
Label8	Text	&Decaf:
Label9	Text	Pounds ordered:
Label10	Text	Total price:
Label11	Name	totalPoundsLabel
	AutoSize	False
	BorderStyle	FixedSingle
	Text	(empty)
	TextAlign	MiddleCenter
Label12	Name	totalPriceLabel
	AutoSize	False
	BorderStyle	FixedSingle
	Text	(empty)
	TextAlign	MiddleCenter
TextBox1	Name	nameTextBox
TextBox2	Name	addressTextBox
TextBox3	Name	cityTextBox
TextBox4	Name	stateTextBox
	CharacterCasing	Upper (changes entry to uppercase)
	MaxLength	2 (allows the user to enter a maximum of 2 characters)
TextBox5	Name	zipTextBox
TextBox6	Name	regularTextBox
TextBox7	Name	decafTextBox
Button1	Name	calcButton
	Text	&Calculate Order
Button2	Name	printButton
	Text	&Print Order
Button3	Name	clearButton
	Text	C&lear Order
Button4	Name	exitButton
	Text	E&xit
PrintForm1		

Figure 2-58 Objects, properties, and settings

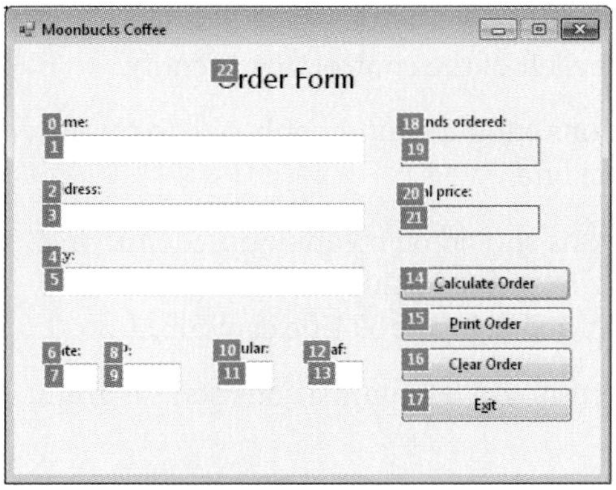

Figure 2-59 Tab order

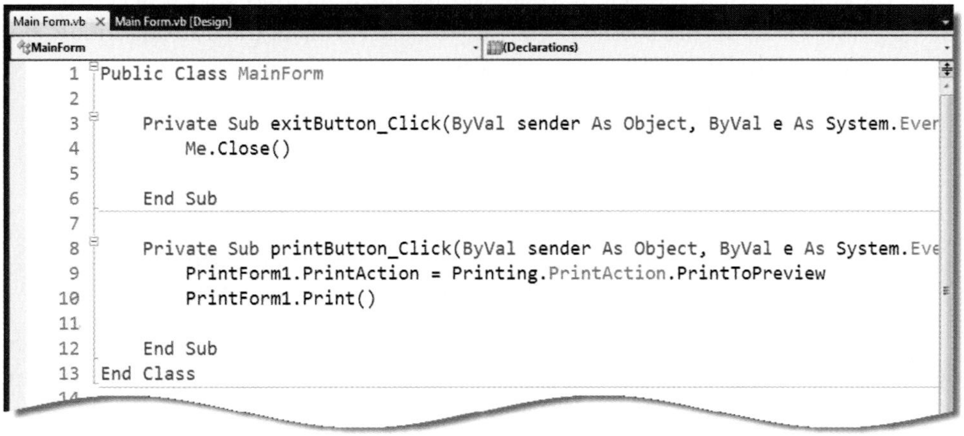

Figure 2-60 Code

Summary

- You should plan an application jointly with the user to ensure that the application meets the user's needs.
- Planning an application requires that you identify the application's tasks, objects, and events. You then build the interface. You can record the tasks, objects, and events in a TOE chart.
- Not all objects will need an event to occur for them to perform their assigned task.
- You use a text box control to give the user an area in which to enter data.
- In Western countries, you should organize the user interface so that the information flows either vertically or horizontally, with the most important information always located in the upper-left corner of the screen.
- You can group related controls together using either white (empty) space or one of the tools located in the Containers section of the toolbox.

- Labels that identify other controls (such as text boxes) should be left-aligned and positioned either above or to the left of the control they identify.
- Identifying labels and button captions should contain only one to three words, which should appear on one line.
- Identifying labels and button captions should be meaningful. Identifying labels should end with a colon and be entered using sentence capitalization. Button captions should be entered using book title capitalization.
- When positioning the controls, you should maintain a consistent margin from the edges of the form.
- Related controls typically are placed close together in the interface.
- When buttons are positioned horizontally on the form, all the buttons should be the same height; their widths, however, may vary if necessary. When buttons are stacked vertically on the form, all the buttons should be the same height and the same width.
- Align the borders of the controls wherever possible to minimize the number of different margins used in the interface.
- Graphics and color should be used sparingly in an interface.
- Avoid using italics and underlining in an interface, and limit the use of bold text to titles, headings, and key items that you want to emphasize.
- You can use an object's Font property to change the type, style, and size of the font used to display the text in the object. You should use only one font type and not more than two different font sizes for the text in an interface. The Segoe UI (9 point) font is the recommended font for Windows 7 and Windows Vista applications.
- It's helpful to change the form's Font property *before* adding controls to the form.
- In most cases, label controls that identify other controls have a BorderStyle property setting of None and an AutoSize property setting of True. Label controls that display program output typically have a BorderStyle property setting of FixedSingle and an AutoSize property setting of False.
- You should assign access keys to each of the controls that can accept user input (such as text boxes and buttons). You assign an access key by including an ampersand (&) in the control's caption or identifying label.
- To always display access keys, click the Start button on the Windows 7 taskbar. Click Control Panel, and then click Appearance and Personalization. In the Ease of Access Center section, click Turn on easy access keys. Select the Underline keyboard shortcuts and access keys check box, and then click the OK button. Close the Control Panel window.
- The TabIndex property determines the order in which a control receives the focus when the user either presses the Tab key or employs an access key during run time. The TabIndex property of a text box should be set to a value that is one number more than the value stored in the TabIndex property of its identifying label.

- You can use the Add New Item dialog box to add a splash screen to a project. You specify the name of a project's splash screen in the Project Designer window.
- The primary viewing and editing of your application's data takes place in a primary window. Dialog boxes are used to support and supplement a user's activities in a primary window.
- The form's FormBorderStyle property specifies its border style. The form's ControlBox, MinimizeBox, and MaximizeBox properties determine the status of the form's Control menu box, Minimize button, and Maximize button.
- The Dialogs section of the toolbox provides tools for creating commonly-used dialog boxes. The dialog boxes are modal and contain both default and cancel buttons. The controls instantiated from these tools appear in the component tray in the IDE.
- You use a form's AcceptButton property to designate a default button. A form can have only one default button.
- The Visual Basic PowerPacks section of the toolbox provides the PrintForm tool for instantiating a PrintForm control. The instantiated control appears in the component tray in the IDE. You can use the PrintForm control to print the interface during run time.
- You can use the Play method of the My.Computer.Audio object to play a WAV file during run time.

Key Terms

Access key—the underlined character in an object's identifying label or caption; allows the user to select the object using the Alt key in combination with the underlined character

Arguments—the items within parentheses after a method's name; represent information that the method needs to perform its task

Book title capitalization—the capitalization used for the text on a button's face; refers to capitalizing the first letter in each word, except for articles, conjunctions, and prepositions that do not occur at either the beginning or the end of the text

Cancel button—a button that can be selected by pressing the Esc key

Default button—a button that can be selected by pressing the Enter key even when it does not have the focus

Dialog boxes—windows that support and supplement a user's activities in a primary window

Focus—indicates that a control is ready to accept user input

Modal—refers to the fact that the dialog box remains on the screen until the user closes it; while it is on the screen, no input from the keyboard or mouse can occur in the application's primary window; however, you can access other applications

My feature—the Visual Basic feature that exposes a set of commonly-used objects (such as the Computer object) to the programmer

Primary window—the window in which the primary viewing and editing of your application's data takes place

Sentence capitalization—the capitalization used for identifying labels; refers to capitalizing only the first letter in the first word and in any words that are customarily capitalized

Text box—a control that provides an area in the form for the user to enter data

Review Questions

1. Which of the following statements is false?
   a. A button's caption should appear on one line.
   b. A button's caption should be from one to three words only.
   c. A button's caption should be entered using book title capitalization.
   d. A button's caption should end with a colon (:).

2. Which of the following statements is false?
   a. The text that identifies a text box should be aligned on the left in a label control.
   b. An identifying label should be positioned either above or to the left of the control it identifies.
   c. Labels that identify controls should be entered using book title capitalization.
   d. Labels that identify text boxes should end with a colon (:).

3. Which property determines the order in which a control receives the focus when the user employs an access key?
   a. OrderTab
   b. SetOrder
   c. TabIndex
   d. TabOrder

4. You assign an access key using a control's ______________ property.
   a. Access
   b. Caption
   c. KeyAccess
   d. Text

5. You use the _______________ property to designate a default button in the interface.

   a. button's AcceptButton

   b. button's DefaultButton

   c. form's AcceptButton

   d. form's DefaultButton

6. If a text box's TabIndex value is 7, its identifying label's TabIndex value should be _______________.

   a. 6

   b. 7

   c. 8

   d. 9

7. Which of the following changes the background color of the blueTextBox to blue?

   a. `blueTextBox.BackGround = Color.Blue`

   b. `blueTextBox.BackGroundColor = Color.Blue`

   c. `blueTextBox.Color = Color.Blue`

   d. none of the above

8. A _______________ dialog box remains on the screen until the user closes it.

   a. modal

   b. perpetual

   c. sticky

   d. none of the above

9. Which of the following tells the PrintForm1 control to start the print operation?

   a. `Print.PrintForm1()`

   b. `PrintForm1.Begin()`

   c. `PrintForm1.Start()`

   d. none of the above

10. Which of the following tells the computer to play the Hello.wav file, which is contained in the project's bin\Debug folder?

    a. `My.Audio.Play("Hello.wav")`

    b. `My.Computer.Audio.Play("Hello.wav")`

    c. `My.Computer.Play.Audio("Hello.wav")`

    d. none of the above

Exercises

Pencil and Paper

INTRODUCTORY

1. Define the following two terms: book title capitalization and sentence capitalization.

INTRODUCTORY

2. List the four steps you should follow when planning a Visual Basic application.

INTRODUCTORY

3. Explain the procedure for choosing a control's access key.

INTRODUCTORY

4. Explain how you give users keyboard access to a text box.

INTERMEDIATE

5. Write the Visual Basic instruction to change the color of the text in the redLabel to red.

INTERMEDIATE

6. Write the Visual Basic instruction to specify that the PrintForm1 control should send a printout of the interface directly to the printer.

ADVANCED

7. Six of the labels in Figure 2-51 contain two lines of text. How do you enter more than one line of text in a label?

SWAT THE BUGS

8. Correct the following line of code, which should play the Hello.wav file contained in the Music folder on the F drive: `My.Computer.Music.Play("Hello.wav")`.

Computer

MODIFY THIS

9. If necessary, create the Color Game application from this chapter's Programming Tutorial 1. Add three buttons to the form. Change their Anchor properties to "Top, Bottom, Left, Right". Make the buttons the same size and color as the Red button. Name the buttons goldButton, maroonButton, and turquoiseButton. Use the following captions for the buttons: Gold, Maroon, Turquoise. Add another row to the table layout panel. You may need to adjust the size of the form and the location of the Start Over, Print, Font, and Exit buttons. Drag the Gold, Maroon, and Turquoise buttons into the new cells in the table layout panel. Code the new buttons using the following Spanish words and WAV files: Dorado, gold.wav, Granate, maroon.wav, Turquesa, turquoise.wav. The WAV files are contained in the VbReloaded2010\Chap02 folder. You will need to copy the files to the current project's bin\Debug folder. Modify the Start Over button's Click event procedure. Save the solution and then start and test the application. Close the solution. Locate the application's .exe file. Run the file from the Run dialog box in Windows.

MODIFY THIS

10. If necessary, create the Music Sampler application from this chapter's Programming Tutorial 2. Add a label and button to the form. Set their Anchor properties to None. Enter Bleeding Love on the first line

in the label and Leona Lewis on the second line. Name the button bleedingButton. Set its BackgroundImage and BackgroundImageLayout properties, and then delete the text from its Text property. Add another row to the table layout panel. You may need to adjust the size of the form and the location of the Color, Print, and Exit buttons. Move the label and button into the table layout panel, and then size the button. Code the bleedingButton using the Bleeding.wav file. The file is contained in the VbReloaded2010\Chap02 folder. You will need to copy the file to the current project's bin\Debug folder. Save the solution and then start and test the application. Close the solution. Locate the application's .exe file. Run the file from the Run dialog box in Windows.

MODIFY THIS

11. If necessary, create the Moonbucks Coffee application from this chapter's Programming Example, and then close the solution. Use Windows to make a copy of the Moonbucks Solution folder. Rename the folder Moonbucks Solution-Modified.

    a. Open the Moonbucks Solution (Moonbucks Solution.sln) file contained in the VbReloaded2010\Chap02\Moonbucks Solution-Modified folder.

    b. Add four labels to the form. Two of the labels will display the price of the order without any sales tax and the sales tax amount. The other two labels will be identifying labels. Use appropriate captions for the identifying labels.

    c. Place the four labels from Step b, as well as the four labels that display the pounds ordered and total price, in a table layout panel. If necessary, reset the interface's tab order.

    d. Modify the TOE chart shown in Figure 2-56.

    e. Save the solution, and then start the application. If your computer is connected to a printer, use the Print Order button to print the interface. Click the Exit button, and then close the solution. (You do not need to code the Calculate Order or Clear Order buttons.)

MODIFY THIS

12. Open the Time Solution (Time Solution.sln) file contained in the VbReloaded2010\Chap02\Time Solution folder. Lay out and organize the interface so that it follows all of the design guidelines specified in this chapter. Save the solution, and then start the application. Click the Exit button, and then close the solution. (You do not need to code the Calculate Hours button.)

INTRODUCTORY

13. Karen Scott wants an application that calculates and displays the amount to tip a waiter at a restaurant. The application should allow Karen to enter her total bill and the tip percentage. It also should allow her to send a printout of the interface to the Print preview window. Prepare a TOE chart ordered by object. Create a Windows application. Use the following names for the solution, project, and form file: Tip Solution, Tip Project, and Main Form.vb. Save the application in the VbReloaded2010\Chap02 folder. Code only the Print and Exit buttons. Save the solution and then start and test the application. Close the solution.

INTRODUCTORY

14. Party-On sells individual hot/cold cups and dessert plates for parties. The store manager wants an application that allows him to enter the price of a cup, the price of a plate, the number of cups purchased, and the number of plates purchased. The application will need to calculate and display the total cost of the purchase. It also should allow the store manager to send a printout of the interface to the Print preview window. In addition, the store manager should be allowed to change the background color of the form. Prepare a TOE chart ordered by object. Create a Windows application. Use the following names for the solution, project, and form file: Party Solution, Party Project, and Main Form.vb. Save the application in the VbReloaded2010\Chap02 folder. Include a table layout panel in the interface. Code only the Print, Color, and Exit buttons. Save the solution and then start and test the application. Close the solution.

INTERMEDIATE

15. The manager of Rent A Van wants an application that calculates and displays the total cost of renting a van. Customers pay a base fee plus a charge per mile. The application should allow the manager to send a printout of the interface to the Print preview window. In addition, the manager should be allowed to change the form's font. Prepare a TOE chart ordered by object. Create a Windows application. Use the following names for the solution, project, and form file: Van Solution, Van Project, and Main Form.vb. Save the application in the VbReloaded2010\Chap02 folder. Include a splash screen in the application. Code only the Print, Font, and Exit buttons. Save the solution and then start and test the application. Close the solution.

ADVANCED

16. In this exercise, you create an application that plays five quotes from either a movie or TV show. Download any five WAV files from the Internet. You can find free WAV files at *www.thefreesite.com/Free_Sounds/Free_WAVs*. Create a Windows application that allows the user to play each WAV file. Use the following names for the solution, project, and form file: Quotes Solution, Quotes Project, and Main Form.vb. Save the application in the VbReloaded2010\Chap02 folder. Code the application. Save the solution and then start and test the application. Close the solution.

DISCOVERY

17. In this exercise, you learn how to bypass a control in the tab order when the user is tabbing.

    a. Open the Johnson Solution (Johnson Solution.sln) file contained in the VbReloaded2010\Chap02\Johnson Solution folder. Start the application. Press the Tab key several times and notice where the focus is placed each time. Click the Exit button.

    b. Most of Johnson's customers are located in California. Enter CA in the stateTextBox's Text property. Find a way to bypass (skip over) the stateTextBox when the user is tabbing. If the user needs to place the focus in the stateTextBox—perhaps to change the control's contents—he or she will need to click or double-click the control, or use its access key.

c. Save the solution and then start and test the application. Click the Exit button, and then close the solution.

18. Open the Debug Solution (Debug Solution.sln) file contained in the VbReloaded2010\Chap02\Debug Solution folder. Start the application. Test all of the access keys in the interface. So that you can test its access key, the Calculate Total button's Click event procedure contains a line of code. Notice that not all of the access keys are working. Stop the application. Locate and then correct any errors. Save the solution and then start and test the application. Close the solution.

SWAT THE BUGS

Case Projects

Crispies Bagels and Bites

Create a TOE chart and interface for an application that allows the user to enter the number of bagels, donuts, and cups of coffee a customer orders. The interface will need to display the total price of the order. Name the solution, project, and form file Crispies Solution, Crispies Project, and Main Form.vb, respectively. Save the application in the VbReloaded2010\Chap02 folder. You can create either your own interface or the one shown in Figure 2-61. The Color button should allow the user to change the background color of the label that displays the total price of the order. The Font button should allow the user to change the form's font. Code the Click event procedures for the Color, Font, and Exit buttons only.

Figure 2-61 Sample interface for the Crispies Bagels and Bites application

Perry Primary School

Create a TOE chart and interface for an application that allows the user to enter two numbers. The interface will need to display both the sum of and difference between both numbers. Name the solution, project, and form file Perry Solution, Perry Project, and Main Form.vb, respectively. Save the application in the VbReloaded2010\Chap02 folder. Include a splash screen in the application. You can create either your own interface or the one shown in Figure 2-62. The Print Preview button should send a printout of the interface to the Print preview window. Code the Click event procedures for the Print Preview and Exit buttons only.

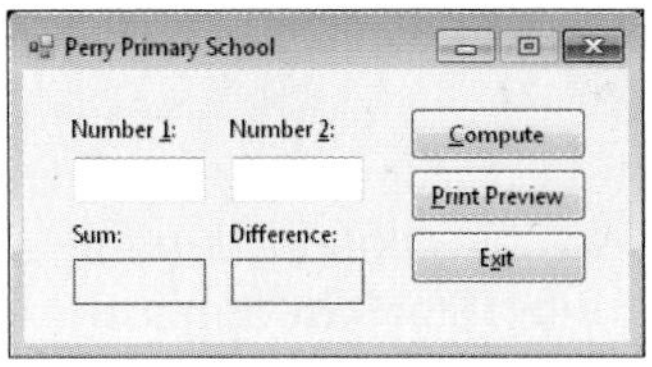

Figure 2-62 Sample interface for the Perry Primary School application

Jasper Health Foods

Create a TOE chart and interface for an application that allows the user to enter the sales amounts for four states: Illinois, Indiana, Kentucky, and Ohio. The interface will need to display the total sales and the sales commission earned. Name the solution, project, and form file Jasper Solution, Jasper Project, and Main Form.vb, respectively. Save the solution in the VbReloaded2010\Chap02 folder. You can create either your own interface or the one shown in Figure 2-63. The Font button should allow the user to change the form's font. The Print button should send a printout of the interface to the Print preview window. Code the Click event procedures for the Font, Print, and Exit buttons only. Include a splash screen in the application.

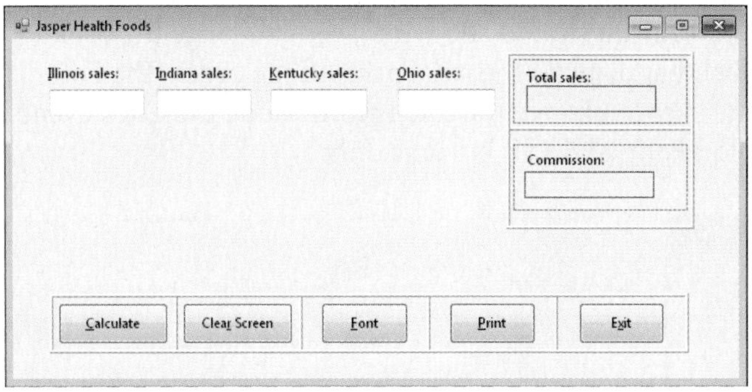

Figure 2-63 Sample interface for the Jasper Health Foods application

Sophia's Italian Deli

Sophia's offers the following items on its lunch menu: Italian sub, meatball sandwich, slice of pizza, sausage sandwich, meatball/sausage combo, chicken fingers, ravioli plate, lasagna plate, bowl of soup, Caesar salad, calamari, spumoni, and cheesecake. Create a TOE chart and interface for an application that allows the user to enter a customer's lunch order. The interface will need to display the price of the order without sales tax, the sales tax amount, and the total price of the order. Name the solution, project, and form file Sophia Solution, Sophia Project, and Main Form.vb, respectively. Save the solution in the VbReloaded2010\Chap02 folder. Include Calculate, Clear, About, and Exit buttons in the interface. Use the Windows Forms About Box template in the Add New Item dialog box to include an About Box form in the application. The form should display as a modal form when the user clicks the About button. Code the Click event procedures for the About and Exit buttons only.

CHAPTER 3

Memory Locations and Calculations

After studying Chapter 3, you should be able to:

- Declare variables and named constants
- Assign data to an existing variable
- Convert data to the appropriate type using the TryParse method and the Convert class methods
- Write arithmetic expressions
- Understand the scope and lifetime of variables and named constants
- Understand the purpose of the Option statements
- Use a TOE chart, pseudocode, and a flowchart to code an application
- Clear the contents of a control's Text property during run time
- Send the focus to a control during run time
- Explain the difference between syntax errors and logic errors
- Format an application's numeric output

Internal Memory

Inside every computer is a component called internal memory. The internal memory of a computer is composed of memory locations, with each memory location having a unique numeric address. It may be helpful to picture memory locations as storage bins, similar to the ones illustrated in Figure 3-1. However, unlike the storage bins shown in the figure, each storage bin (memory location) inside a computer can hold only one item at a time. Examples of items stored in memory locations include numbers, strings, and Visual Basic instructions.

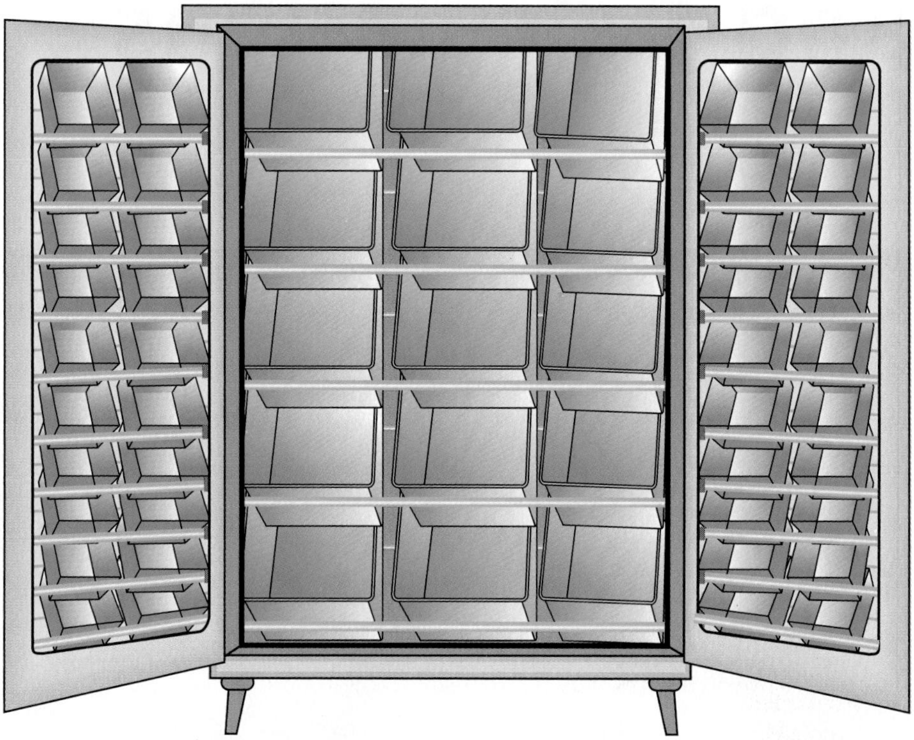

Figure 3-1 Illustration of storage bins

A programmer can reserve memory locations for use in a program. Reserving a memory location is also referred to as declaring the memory location. You declare a memory location using a Visual Basic instruction that assigns a name, data type, and initial value to the location. The name allows the programmer to refer to the memory location using one or more descriptive words, rather than a cryptic numeric address. The **data type** indicates the type of data—for example, numeric or string—the memory location will store. There are two types of memory locations that a programmer can declare: variables and named constants. You will learn about variables first. Named constants are covered in the *Named Constants* section in this chapter.

Variables

Variables are computer memory locations where programmers can temporarily store data while an application is running. The data might be entered by the user at the keyboard. It also might be read from a file or be the result of a calculation made by the computer. The memory locations are called variables because their contents can change (vary) during run time. Each variable used in a Visual Basic application must be assigned a name by the programmer. The name should be meaningful in that it should describe the variable's contents. For example, a variable that stores the name of a city should be named `city` rather than just `c`. Although not required by the Visual Basic language, most programmers enter variable names using camel case. Recall that camel case means you enter the first word in the name in lowercase and then capitalize the first letter of each subsequent word in the name. Following this convention, a programmer might assign either the name `sales` or the name `salesAmount` to a variable that stores a sales amount. Besides being meaningful, a variable name must follow the rules listed in Figure 3-2. The figure also includes examples of valid and invalid variable names.

HOW TO Name a Variable

1. The name must begin with a letter or an underscore.
2. The name can contain only letters, numbers, and the underscore character. No punctuation characters, special characters, or spaces are allowed in the name.
3. Although the name can contain thousands of characters, 32 characters is the recommended maximum number of characters to use.
4. The name cannot be a reserved word, such as `Date`.

Valid names
`income2012, lastName, northSales`

Invalid names	Problem
`2012Income`	the name must begin with a letter or an underscore
`last Name`	the name cannot contain a space
`north.Sales`	the name cannot contain punctuation
`north$Sales`	the name cannot contain a special character

Figure 3-2 How to name a variable

Like storage bins, memory locations come in different types and sizes. The type and size you use depends on the item you want the memory location to store. Some memory locations can store a number, while others can hold a string, a date, or a Boolean value (True or False). The item that a memory location will accept for storage is determined by the location's data type, which the programmer assigns to the location when he or she declares it in code. Figure 3-3 describes most of the basic data types available in Visual Basic. Each data type listed in the figure is a class, which means that each data type is a pattern from which objects—in this case, variables—are instantiated. As the figure indicates, variables assigned the Integer, Long, or Short data type can store **integers**, which are whole numbers—positive or negative numbers without any decimal places. The differences among these three data types are in the range of integers each type can store and the amount of memory each type needs to store the integer. Decimal, Double, and Single variables, on the other hand, can store **real numbers**, which are numbers that contain a decimal place. Here again, the differences among these three data types are in the range of numbers each type can store and the amount of memory each type needs to store the numbers. However, calculations involving Decimal variables are not subject to the small rounding errors that may occur when using Double or Single variables. In most cases, the small rounding errors do not create any problems in an application. One exception to this is when the application contains complex equations dealing with money, where you need accuracy to the penny. In those cases, the Decimal data type is the best type to use.

Also listed in Figure 3-3 are the Char, String, Boolean, Date, and Object data types. The Char data type can store one Unicode character, while the String data type can store from zero to approximately two billion Unicode characters. **Unicode** is the universal coding scheme for characters. It assigns a unique numeric value to each character used in the written languages of the world. (For more information, see The Unicode Standard at *www.unicode.org*.) You use a Boolean variable to store a Boolean value (either True or False), and a Date variable to store date and time information. The Object data type can store any type of data. However, your application will pay a price for this flexibility: it will run more slowly, because the computer has to determine the type of data currently stored in an Object variable. It is best to avoid using the Object data type.

Data type	Stores	Memory required
Boolean	a logical value (True, False)	2 bytes
Char	one Unicode character	2 bytes
Date	date and time information Date range: January 1, 0001 to December 31, 9999 Time range: 0:00:00 (midnight) to 23:59:59	8 bytes
Decimal	a number with a decimal place Range with no decimal place: +/−79,228,162,514,264,337,593,543,950,335 Range with a decimal place: +/−7.9228162514264337593543950335	16 bytes
Double	a number with a decimal place Range: +/−4.94065645841247 x 10^{-324} to +/−1.79769313486231 x 10^{308}	8 bytes
Integer	integer Range: −2,147,483,648 to 2,147,483,647	4 bytes
Long	integer Range: −9,223,372,036,854,775,808 to 9,223,372,036,854,775,807	8 bytes
Object	data of any type	4 bytes
Short	integer Range: −32,768 to 32,767	2 bytes
Single	a number with a decimal place Range: +/−1.401298 x 10^{-45} to +/−3.402823 x 10^{38}	4 bytes
String	text; 0 to approximately 2 billion Unicode characters	

Figure 3-3 Basic data types in Visual Basic

In this book, you will use the Integer data type for variables that will store integers used in calculations, even when the integers are small enough to fit into a Short variable. This is because a calculation containing Integer variables takes less time to process than the equivalent calculation containing Short variables. You will use either the Decimal or Double data type for real numbers that are used in calculations. You will use the String data type for variables that contain either text or numbers not used in calculations, and the Boolean data type to store Boolean values.

Declaring a Variable in Code

You use a declaration statement to declare a variable in code. The declaration statement reserves a small section of the computer's internal memory. The size of the section is determined by the variable's data type. Figure 3-4 shows the syntax of a declaration statement and includes several examples of declaring variables. The {Dim | Private | Static} portion of the syntax indicates that you can select only one of the keywords appearing within the braces. In most instances, you declare a variable using the `Dim` keyword. *VariableName* and *dataType* are the variable's name and data type, respectively. As mentioned earlier, a variable is considered an object in Visual Basic and is an instance of the class specified in the *dataType* information. The `Dim hours As Integer` statement, for example, declares an object named `hours`; the object is an instance of the Integer class. *InitialValue* in the syntax is the value you want stored in the variable when it is created in the computer's internal memory. The square brackets in the syntax indicate that the = *initialValue* part of a declaration statement is optional. If you do not assign an initial value to a variable when it is declared, the computer stores a default value in the variable; the default value depends on the variable's data type. A variable declared using one of the numeric data types is automatically initialized to—in other words, given a beginning value of—the number 0. The computer automatically initializes a Boolean variable using the keyword `False`, and a Date variable to 1/1/0001 12:00:00 AM. Object and String variables are automatically initialized using the keyword `Nothing`. Variables initialized to `Nothing` do not actually contain the word "Nothing"; rather, they contain no value at all.

The `Private` and `Static` keywords are covered in the *Variables with Class Scope* and *Static Variables* sections, respectively, in this chapter.

Dim comes from the word "dimension," which is how programmers in the 1960s referred to the process of allocating the computer's memory. "Dimension" refers to the "size" of something.

HOW TO Declare a Variable

Syntax
{Dim | Private | Static} *variableName* **As** *dataType* [= *initialValue*]

Example 1
```
Dim hours As Integer
Dim payRate As Double
```
declares an Integer variable named `hours` and a Double variable named `payRate`; the variables are automatically initialized to 0

Figure 3-4 How to declare a variable *(continues)*

(continued)

Example 2
`Dim discount As Decimal`
declares a Decimal variable named `discount`; the variable is automatically initialized to 0

Example 3
`Dim isDataOk As Boolean = True`
declares a Boolean variable named `isDataOk` and initializes it using the keyword `True`

Example 4
`Dim message As String = "Good Morning"`
declares a String variable named `message` and initializes it using the string "Good Morning"

Figure 3-4 How to declare a variable

The answers to Mini-Quiz questions are located in Appendix A.

Mini-Quiz 3-1

1. A variable can store ______________ at a time.
   a. only one item
   b. a maximum of two items
   c. an unlimited number of items
2. Which of the following is a valid name for a variable?
   a. `jan.Sales`
   b. `2ndQuarterIncome`
   c. `commission_rate`
   d. `march$`
3. Write a Dim statement that declares a Double variable named `pricePerItem`.
4. Write a Dim statement that declares an Integer variable named `counter` and initializes the variable to the number 1.

Assigning Data to an Existing Variable

In the previous chapters, you used an assignment statement to assign a value to a control's property while an application is running. You also can use an assignment statement to assign a value to a variable during run time; the syntax for doing this is shown in Figure 3-5. In the syntax, *expression* represents the value you want assigned to the variable. The expression can contain items such as literal constants, object properties, variables, keywords, or arithmetic operators. A **literal constant** is an item of data whose value does not change during run time; examples include the string literal constant "James" and the numeric literal constant 650. When the computer processes an assignment statement, it assigns the value of the expression that appears on the right side of the assignment operator to the variable (memory location) whose name appears on the left side of the assignment operator. In other words, the computer evaluates the expression first and then stores the result in the variable, replacing the variable's existing data. (Recall that a variable can store only one item of data at a time.)

Recall from Chapter 1 that the equal sign in an assignment statement is called the assignment operator.

The data type of the value assigned to a variable should be the same data type as the variable itself. Figure 3-5 shows examples of assigning values to variables having the same data type. The assignment statement in Example 1 stores the numeric literal constant 650, an integer, in an Integer variable named `quantity`. Similarly, the assignment statement in Example 2 stores the string literal constant "James" in a String variable named `firstName`. Notice that string literal constants are enclosed in quotation marks, but numeric literal constants and variable names are not. The quotation marks differentiate a string from both a number and a variable name. In other words, "650" is a string, but 650 is a number. Similarly, "James" is a string, but James (without the quotation marks) would be interpreted by the computer as the name of a variable. When the computer processes an assignment statement that assigns a string to a String variable, it assigns only the characters that appear between the quotation marks; it does not assign the quotation marks themselves. The assignment statement in Example 3 assigns the contents of the zipTextBox to a String variable named `zipCode`. A String variable is appropriate in this case because the value contained in an object's Text property is always treated as a string in Visual Basic. The assignment statement in Example 4 assigns the Double number .05 to a Double variable named `discountPercent`. This is because a numeric literal constant that has a decimal place is automatically treated as a Double number in Visual Basic. When entering a numeric literal constant, you do not enter a comma or special characters, such as the dollar sign or percent sign. If you want to include a percentage in an assignment statement, you do so using its decimal equivalent; for example, you enter .05 rather than 5%.

HOW TO Assign a Value to a Variable

Syntax
variableName = *expression*

Example 1
```
Dim quantity As Integer
quantity = 650
```
The assignment statement assigns the integer 650 to the `quantity` variable.

Figure 3-5 How to assign a value to a variable *(continues)*

(continued)

Example 2
```
Dim firstName As String
firstName = "James"
```
The assignment statement assigns the string "James" to the `firstName` variable.

Example 3
```
Dim zipCode As String
zipCode = zipTextBox.Text
```
The assignment statement assigns the string contained in the zipTextBox's Text property to the `zipCode` variable.

Example 4
```
Dim discountPercent As Double
discountPercent = .05
```
The assignment statement assigns the Double number .05 to the `discountPercent` variable.

Figure 3-5 How to assign a value to a variable

In all of the assignment statements in Figure 3-5, the data type of the value matches the data type of the variable to which the value is assigned. At times, however, the value's data type might be different from the variable's data type. You can change the value's data type to match the variable's data type using either the TryParse method or one of the methods in the Convert class.

Using the TryParse Method

As you learned earlier, each data type in Visual Basic is a class. Most classes have one or more methods that perform a specific task for the class. For example, all of the Visual Basic numeric data types (such as Double, Decimal, or Integer) have a **TryParse method** whose task is to convert a string to that particular data type. Figure 3-6 shows the basic syntax of the TryParse method along with examples of using the method. In the syntax, *dataType* is one of the numeric data types available in Visual Basic. The dot member access operator in the syntax indicates that the TryParse method is a member of the *dataType* class. The method's arguments (*string* and *numericVariableName*) represent information that the method needs to perform its task. The *string* argument is the string you want converted to a number of the *dataType* type and typically is either the Text property of a control or the name of a String variable. The *numericVariableName* argument is the name of a numeric variable in which the TryParse method can store the number. The numeric variable must have the same data type as specified in the *dataType* portion of the syntax. In other words, when using the TryParse method to convert a string to a Double number, you need to provide the method with the name of a Double variable in which to store the number. The TryParse method parses the string, which means it looks at each character in the string, to determine whether the string can be converted to a number of the specified data type. If the string can be converted, the TryParse method converts the string to a number and stores the number in the variable specified in the *numericVariableName* argument. If the TryParse method determines that the string cannot be converted to the appropriate data type, it assigns the number 0 to the variable.

HOW TO Use the Basic Syntax of the TryParse Method

Basic syntax

dataType.**TryParse(***string*, *numericVariableName***)**

Example 1

```
Dim sales As Double
Double.TryParse(salesTextBox.Text, sales)
```

If the string contained in the Text property can be converted to a Double number, the TryParse method converts the string and then stores the result in the `sales` variable; otherwise, it stores 0 in the `sales` variable.

Example 2

```
Dim gross As Decimal
Decimal.TryParse(grossTextBox.Text, gross)
```

If the string contained in the Text property can be converted to a Decimal number, the TryParse method converts the string and then stores the result in the `gross` variable; otherwise, it stores 0 in the `gross` variable.

Example 3

```
Dim inputNumber As String = "34"
Dim number As Integer
Integer.TryParse(inputNumber, number)
```

The TryParse method converts the string contained in the `inputNumber` variable to an Integer number and then stores the result (34) in the `number` variable.

Figure 3-6 How to use the basic syntax of the TryParse method

Figure 3-7 shows how the TryParse method of the Double, Decimal, and Integer data types would convert various strings. As the figure indicates, the three methods can convert a string that contains only numbers. They also can convert a string that contains a leading sign, as well as one that contains leading or trailing spaces. In addition, the Double.TryParse and Decimal.TryParse methods can convert a string that contains a decimal point or a comma. However, none of the three methods can convert a string that contains a dollar sign, a percent sign, a letter, or a space within the string.

String	Double.TryParse	Decimal.TryParse	Integer.TryParse
"62"	62.0	62.0	62
-9	-9.0	-9.0	-9
"12.55"	12.55	12.55	0
"-4.23"	-4.23	-4.23	0
"1,457	1457.0	1457.0	0
" 33 "	33.0	33.0	33
"$5"	0	0	0
"7%"	0	0	0
"122a"	0	0	0
"1 345"	0	0	0
empty string	0	0	0

Figure 3-7 Result of the TryParse method for the Double, Decimal, and Integer data types

Using the Convert Class Methods

At times, you may need to convert a number (rather than a string) from one data type to another. Visual Basic provides several ways of accomplishing this task. For example, you can use the Visual Basic conversion functions, which are listed in Appendix D in this book. You also can use one of the methods defined in the **Convert class**. In this book you will use the Convert class methods, because they have an advantage over the conversion functions: the methods can be used in any of the languages built into Visual Studio, whereas the conversion functions can be used only in the Visual Basic language. The more commonly used methods in the Convert class are the ToDouble, ToDecimal, ToInt32, and ToString methods. The methods convert a value to the Double, Decimal, Integer, and String data types, respectively.

The syntax for using the Convert class methods is shown in Figure 3-8. In most cases, the *value* argument is a numeric value that you want converted either to the String data type or to a different numeric data type (for example, from Double to Decimal). Although you can use the Convert methods to convert a string to a numeric data type, the TryParse method is the recommended method to use for that task. This is because, unlike the Convert methods, the TryParse method does not produce an error when it tries to convert the empty string; instead, the TryParse method assigns the number 0 to its *numericVariableName* argument. Also included in Figure 3-8 are examples of using the Convert class methods. The Convert.ToDecimal method in Example 1 converts the Double number .15 to Decimal, storing the result in the `taxRate` variable. (Recall that a number with a decimal place is automatically treated as a Double number in Visual Basic.) The Convert.ToString method in Example 2 converts the integer stored in the `totalScore` variable to String and assigns the result to the totalLabel's Text property.

HOW TO Use the Convert Class Methods

Syntax
Convert.*method***(***value***)**

Example 1
```
Dim taxRate As Decimal
taxRate = Convert.ToDecimal(.15)
```
converts the Double number .15 to Decimal and then assigns the result to the `taxRate` variable

Example 2
```
Dim totalScore As Integer = 73
totalLabel.Text = Convert.ToString(totalScore)
```
converts the integer stored in the `totalScore` variable to String and then assigns the result to the totalLabel's Text property

Figure 3-8 How to use the Convert class methods

The dot member access operator in Figure 3-8 indicates that the *method* is a member of the Convert class.

Mini-Quiz 3-2

The answers to Mini-Quiz questions are located in Appendix A.

1. Which of the following assigns the city name Paris to a String variable named `city`?
   a. `city = 'Paris'`
   b. `city = "Paris"`
   c. `city = Paris`
   d. `city As String = "Paris"`

2. Which of the following assigns the number 50 to an Integer variable named `amount`?
   a. `amount = '50'`
   b. `amount = "50"`
   c. `amount = 50`
   d. `amount As Integer = 50`

3. Which of the following can be used to store the contents of a String variable named `inputPop` in an Integer variable named `population`?
   a. `inputPop.TryParse(String, population)`
   b. `Integer.TryParse(inputPop, population)`
   c. `String.TryParse(inputPop, population)`
   d. `inputPop = TryParse(String, population)`

4. Which of the following assigns the number 25.67 to a Decimal variable named `cost`?

   a. `cost = Convert.ToDecimal(25.67)`

   b. `Convert.ToDecimal(25.67, cost)`

   c. `cost = TryParse.ToDecimal(25.67)`

   d. `TryParse.ToDecimal(25.67, cost)`

Including Variables in Arithmetic Expressions

Most applications require the computer to perform at least one calculation. You instruct the computer to perform a calculation by writing an arithmetic expression, which is an expression that contains one or more arithmetic operators. The expression also can contain any of the following: variables, literal constants, named constants, or methods. When an expression contains a variable or named constant, the computer uses the value stored inside the memory location to process the expression. Figure 3-9 lists the most commonly used arithmetic operators available in Visual Basic, along with their precedence numbers. The precedence numbers indicate the order in which the computer performs the operation in an expression. Operations with a precedence number of 1 are performed before operations with a precedence number of 2, which are performed before operations with a precedence number of 3, and so on. However, you can use parentheses to override the order of precedence, because operations within parentheses are always performed before operations outside of parentheses.

Operator	Operation	Precedence number
^	exponentiation (raises a number to a power)	1
–	negation	2
*, /	multiplication and division	3
\	integer division	4
Mod	modulus	5
+, –	addition and subtraction	6

Figure 3-9 Most commonly used arithmetic operators

Although the negation and subtraction operators listed in Figure 3-9 use the same symbol (a hyphen), there is a difference between both operators: the negation operator is unary, whereas the subtraction operator is binary. Unary and binary refer to the number of operands required by the operator. Unary operators require one operand; binary operators require two operands. For example, the expression –7 uses the negation operator to turn its one operand (the positive number 7) into a negative number. The expression 9 – 4, on the other hand, uses the subtraction operator to subtract its second operand (the number 4) from its first operand (the number 9).

Two of the arithmetic operators listed in Figure 3-9 might be less familiar to you: the integer division operator (\) and the modulus operator (Mod). You use the **integer division operator** to divide two integers and then return the result as an integer. For instance, the expression 211 \ 4 results in 52, which is the integer result of dividing 211 by 4. (If you use the standard division operator [/] to divide 211 by 4, the result is 52.75 rather than 52.) You might use the integer division operator in a program that determines the number of quarters, dimes, and nickels to return as change to a customer. For example, if a customer should receive 53 cents in change, you could use the expression 53 \ 25 to determine the number of quarters to return; the expression evaluates to 2. The **modulus operator** also is used to divide two numbers, but the numbers do not have to be integers. After dividing the numbers, the modulus operator returns the remainder of the division. For instance, 211 Mod 4 equals 3, which is the remainder of 211 divided by 4. A common use for the modulus operator is to determine whether a number is even or odd. If you divide the number by 2 and the remainder is 0, the number is even; if the remainder is 1, however, the number is odd. Figure 3-10 shows several examples of using the integer division and Mod operators.

HOW TO Use the Integer Division and Mod Operators

Examples	Results
211 \ 4	52
211 Mod 4	3
53 \ 25	2
53 Mod 25	3
75 \ 2	37
75 Mod 2	1
100 \ 2	50
100 Mod 2	0

Figure 3-10 How to use the integer division and Mod operators

You may have noticed that some of the operators listed in Figure 3-9 have the same precedence number. For example, both the addition and subtraction operators have a precedence number of 6. When an expression contains more than one operator having the same priority, those operators are evaluated from left to right. In the expression 7 – 8 / 2 + 5, for instance, the division (/) is performed first, then the subtraction (–), and then the addition (+). The result of the expression is the number 8, as shown in Figure 3-11. You can use parentheses to change the order in which the operators in an expression are evaluated. For example, as Figure 3-11 shows, the expression 7 – (8 / 2 + 5) evaluates to –2 rather than to 8. This is because the parentheses tell the computer to perform the division first, then the addition, and then the subtraction.

Original expression	7 – 8 / 2 + 5
The division is performed first	7 – 4 + 5
The subtraction is performed next	3 + 5
The addition is performed last	8
Original expression	7 – (8 / 2 + 5)
The division is performed first	7 – (4 + 5)
The addition is performed next	7 – 9
The subtraction is performed last	–2

Figure 3-11 Expressions containing more than one operator having the same precedence

Most times, you will want to save the result of an arithmetic expression. You do this by assigning the resulting value to a variable. The variable should have the same data type as the value being assigned to it, as shown in the examples in Figure 3-12. The assignment statements in Examples 1 and 2, for instance, assign the Integer results of their arithmetic expressions to Integer variables. The assignment statement in Example 3 assigns the Double result of its arithmetic expression to a Double variable. When processing the assignment statement in Example 4, the computer first converts the Double number 1.04 to Decimal before multiplying the number by the contents of the Decimal `price` variable. It then assigns the Decimal result (20.8) to the `price` variable. When processing the assignment statement in Example 5, the computer first multiplies the contents of the Double `sales` variable by the Double number .1. It then converts the Double result (207.5) to String before assigning the result to the bonusLabel's Text property.

HOW TO Use Variables and Arithmetic Operators

Example 1
```
Dim age As Integer = 35
age = age + 1
```
adds the integer 1 to the contents of the Integer `age` variable and then assigns the result (36) to the `age` variable

Example 2
```
Dim dimes As Integer
Dim change As Integer = 123
dimes = change \ 10
```
divides the contents of the Integer `change` variable by the integer 10 and then assigns the result (12) to the Integer `dimes` variable

Example 3
```
Dim sales As Double = 2075
Dim bonus As Double
bonus = sales * .1
```
multiplies the contents of the Double `sales` variable by the Double number .1 and then assigns the result (207.5) to the Double `bonus` variable

Figure 3-12 How to use variables and arithmetic operators *(continues)*

(continued)

Example 4
```
Dim price As Decimal = 20
price = price * Convert.ToDecimal(1.04)
```
converts the Double number 1.04 to Decimal, then multiplies the Decimal result by the contents of the Decimal `price` variable, and then assigns the result (20.8) to the `price` variable

Example 5
```
Dim sales As Double = 2075
bonusLabel.Text = Convert.ToString(sales * .1)
```
multiplies the contents of the Double `sales` variable by the Double number .1, then converts the result (207.5) to the String data type, and then assigns the String result ("207.5") to the bonusLabel's Text property

Figure 3-12 How to use variables and arithmetic operators

Arithmetic Assignment Operators

In addition to the standard arithmetic operators listed earlier in Figure 3-9, Visual Basic also provides several arithmetic assignment operators. The **arithmetic assignment operators** allow you to abbreviate an assignment statement that contains an arithmetic operator, as long as the assignment statement has the following format, in which *variableName* is the name of the same variable: *variableName* = *variableName arithmeticOperator value*. For example, you can use the addition assignment operator (+=) to abbreviate the statement `age = age + 1` as follows: `age += 1`. Both statements tell the computer to add the number 1 to the contents of the `age` variable and then store the result in the `age` variable. Figure 3-13 shows the syntax of a Visual Basic statement that uses an arithmetic assignment operator. The figure also lists the most commonly used arithmetic assignment operators, and it includes examples of using arithmetic assignment operators to abbreviate assignment statements. Notice that each arithmetic assignment operator consists of an arithmetic operator followed immediately by the assignment operator (=). The arithmetic assignment operators do not contain a space. In other words, the multiplication assignment operator is *=, not * =.

It's easy to abbreviate an assignment statement. Simply remove the variable name that appears on the left side of the assignment operator (=) in the statement, and then put the assignment operator immediately after the arithmetic operator.

HOW TO Use the Arithmetic Assignment Operators

Syntax
variableName arithmeticAssignmentOperator value

Operator	Purpose
+=	addition assignment
−=	subtraction assignment
*=	multiplication assignment
/=	division assignment

Figure 3-13 How to use the arithmetic assignment operators *(continues)*

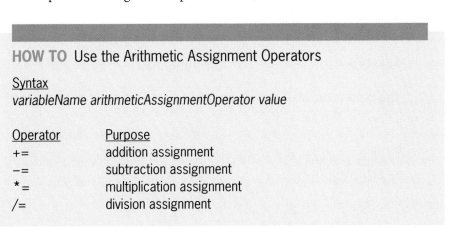

(continued)

Example 1
Original statement: `age = age + 1`
Abbreviated statement: `age += 1`
Both statements add 1 to the number stored in the `age` variable and then assign the result to the variable.

Example 2
Original statement: `price = price - discount`
Abbreviated statement: `price -= discount`
Both statements subtract the number stored in the `discount` variable from the number stored in the `price` variable and then assign the result to the `price` variable.

Example 3
Original statement: `sales = sales * 1.05`
Abbreviated statement: `sales *= 1.05`
Both statements multiply the number stored in the `sales` variable by 1.05 and then assign the result to the variable.

Example 4
Original statement: `price = price / 2`
Abbreviated statement: `price /= 2`
Both statements divide the number stored in the `price` variable by 2 and then assign the result to the variable.

Figure 3-13 How to use the arithmetic assignment operators

The answers to Mini-Quiz questions are located in Appendix A.

Mini-Quiz 3-3

1. The expression 7 + 4 / 2 * 4.5 evaluates to ______________.
   a. 1.222222
   b. 7.444444
   c. 16
   d. 24.75

2. The expression 131 \ 4 evaluates to ______________.
   a. 3
   b. 32
   c. 32.75
   d. 33

3. Which of the following is equivalent to the statement `counter = counter + 1`?
   a. `counter += 1`
   b. `counter =+ 1`
   c. `1 += counter`
   d. both a and c

To review what you learned about arithmetic expressions in assignment statements, view the Ch03Arithmetic-Expressions video.

If you want to practice writing assignment statements that contain arithmetic expressions, open the solution contained in the Try It 1! folder.

The Scope and Lifetime of a Variable

Besides a name, data type, and initial value, every variable also has a scope and a lifetime. A variable's **scope** indicates where the variable can be used in the application's code, and its **lifetime** indicates how long the variable remains in the computer's internal memory. Variables can have class scope, procedure scope, or block scope. However, most of the variables used in an application will have procedure scope. This is because fewer unintentional errors occur in applications when the variables are declared using the minimum scope needed, which usually is procedure scope. A variable's scope and lifetime are determined by where you declare the variable—in other words, where you enter the variable's declaration statement. Typically, you enter the declaration statement either in a procedure (such as an event procedure) or in the Declarations section of a form. A form's Declarations section is located between the `Public Class` and `End Class` clauses in the Code Editor window. Variables declared in a procedure have either procedure scope or block scope, depending on where in the procedure they are declared. Variables declared in a form's Declarations section have class scope. In the following two sections, you will learn about procedure scope variables and class scope variables. Variables having block scope are covered in Chapter 4.

Variables also can have namespace scope and are referred to as namespace variables, global variables, or public variables. Such variables can lead to unintentional errors in a program and should be avoided, if possible. For this reason, they are not covered in this book.

Variables with Procedure Scope

When you declare a variable in a procedure, the variable is called a **procedure-level variable** and it has **procedure scope**, because only that procedure can use the variable. Procedure-level variables typically are declared at the beginning of a procedure, and they remain in the computer's internal memory only while that procedure is running. Procedure-level variables are removed from memory when the procedure in which they are declared ends. In other words, a procedure-level variable has the same lifetime as the procedure that declares it. As mentioned earlier, most of the variables in your applications will be procedure-level variables.

Procedure-level variables are also called local variables and their scope is often referred to as local scope.

The Sales Tax Calculator application that you view next illustrates the use of procedure-level variables. As the interface shown in Figure 3-14 indicates, the application allows the user to enter a sales amount. It then calculates and displays either a 2% sales tax or a 5% sales tax, depending on the button selected by the user.

In the *Static Variables* section of this chapter, you will learn how to declare a procedure-level variable that remains in the computer's memory even when the procedure in which it is declared ends.

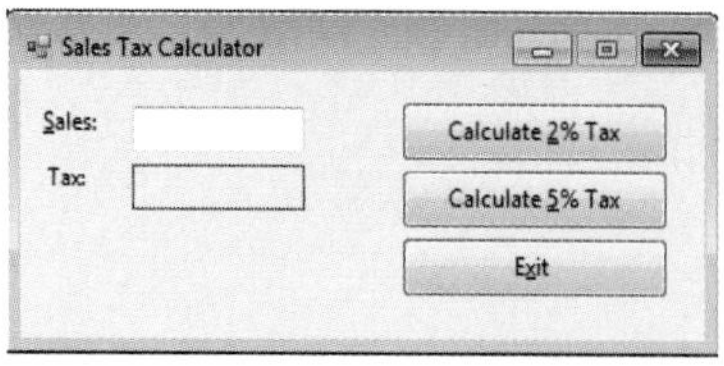

Figure 3-14 User interface for the Sales Tax Calculator application

Figure 3-15 shows the Click event procedures for the Calculate 2% Tax and Calculate 5% Tax buttons. The green lines of text in each procedure are called comments. Programmers use **comments** to document a procedure's purpose and also to explain various sections of a procedure's code, because comments make the code more readable and easier to understand by anyone viewing it. You create a comment in Visual Basic by typing an apostrophe (`'`) before the text that represents the comment. The computer ignores everything that appears after the apostrophe on that line. Although it is not required, some programmers use a space to separate the apostrophe from the comment text, as shown in the figure. When the user clicks the Calculate 2% Tax button in the interface, the Dim statements in the button's Click event procedure create and initialize two procedure-level Double variables named `sales` and `tax2`; both variables can be used only by that procedure. Next, the TryParse method converts the sales amount entered in the salesTextBox to Double and then stores the result in the `sales` variable. The first assignment statement in the procedure multiplies the contents of the Double `sales` variable by the Double number .02 and then stores the result in the `tax2` variable. The last assignment statement in the procedure converts the contents of the `tax2` variable to String, assigning the result to the taxLabel's Text property. When the calcTax2Button's Click event procedure ends, the computer removes the `sales` and `tax2` variables from memory. The variables will be created again the next time the user clicks the Calculate 2% Tax button. A similar process is followed when the user clicks the Calculate 5% Tax button, except the variable that stores the tax amount is named `tax5` and the tax is calculated using a rate of .05 rather than .02.

comments begin with an apostrophe

procedure-level variables declared in the calcTax2Button's Click event procedure

```
Private Sub calcTax2Button_Click(ByVal sender As Object,
     ByVal e As System.EventArgs) Handles calcTax2Button.Click
     ' calculates a 2% sales tax

     ' declare variables
     Dim sales As Double
     Dim tax2 As Double

     ' calculate and display the sales tax
     Double.TryParse(salesTextBox.Text, sales)
     tax2 = sales * 0.02
     taxLabel.Text = Convert.ToString(tax2)
End Sub
```

Figure 3-15 Examples of using procedure-level variables *(continues)*

(continued)

```
Private Sub calcTax5Button_Click(ByVal sender As Object,
     ByVal e As System.EventArgs) Handles calcTax5Button.Click
     ' calculates a 5% sales tax

     ' declare variables
     Dim sales As Double
     Dim tax5 As Double

     ' calculate and display the sales tax
     Double.TryParse(salesTextBox.Text, sales)
     tax5 = sales * 0.05
     taxLabel.Text = Convert.ToString(tax5)
End Sub
```

procedure-level variables declared in the calcTax5Button's Click event procedure

Figure 3-15 Examples of using procedure-level variables

If you want to experiment with the Sales Tax Calculator application, open the solution contained in the Try It 2! folder.

Notice that both procedures in Figure 3-15 declare a variable named `sales`. When you use the same name to declare a variable in more than one procedure, each procedure creates its own variable when the procedure is invoked. Each procedure also destroys its own variable when the procedure ends. In other words, although the `sales` variables in both procedures have the same name, they are not the same variable. Rather, each refers to a different section in the computer's internal memory, and each is created and destroyed independently from the other.

Variables with Class Scope

In addition to declaring a variable in a procedure, you also can declare a variable in the form's Declarations section, which begins with the `Public Class` clause and ends with the `End Class` clause. When you declare a variable in the form's Declarations section, the variable is called a **class-level variable** and it has **class scope**. Class-level variables can be used by all of the procedures in the form, including the procedures associated with the controls contained on the form, and they retain their values and remain in the computer's internal memory until the application ends. In other words, a class-level variable has the same lifetime as the application itself. Unlike a procedure-level variable, which is declared using the `Dim` keyword, you declare a class-level variable using the `Private` keyword. You typically use a class-level variable when you need more than one procedure in the same form to use the same variable. However, a class-level variable also can be used when a procedure needs to retain a variable's value after the procedure ends. The Total Sales application, which you view next, illustrates this use of a class-level variable. The application's interface is shown in Figure 3-16. As the interface indicates, the application calculates and displays the total of the sales amounts entered by the user.

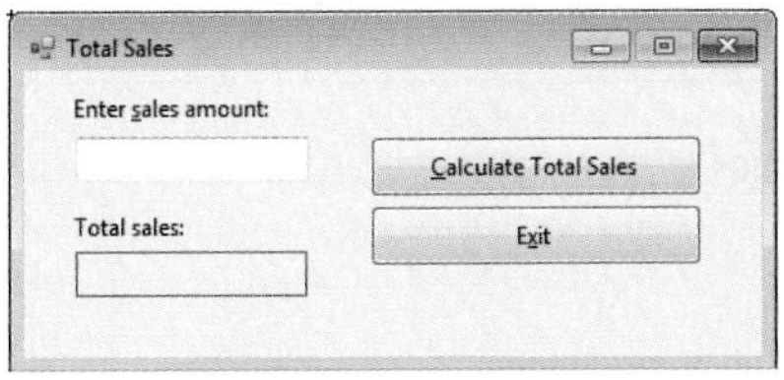

Figure 3-16 User interface for the Total Sales application

Figure 3-17 shows the Total Sales application's code. The code uses a class-level variable named `totalSales` to accumulate (add together) the sales amounts entered by the user. Class-level variables should be declared after the `Public Class` clause, but before the first `Private Sub` clause, in the form's Declarations section. When the Total Sales application is started, the `Private totalSales As Decimal` statement in the form's Declarations section is processed first. The statement creates and initializes a Decimal variable named `totalSales`. The variable is created and initialized only once, when the application is first started. It remains in the computer's internal memory until the application ends. Each time the user clicks the Calculate Total Sales button in the interface, the button's Click event procedure creates and initializes a procedure-level variable named `salesAmount`. Next, the TryParse method in the procedure converts the sales amount entered in the salesTextBox to Decimal, storing the result in the `salesAmount` variable. The first assignment statement in the procedure adds the contents of the procedure-level `salesAmount` variable to the contents of the class-level `totalSales` variable. At this point, the `totalSales` variable contains the sum of all of the sales amounts entered so far. The last assignment statement in the procedure converts the contents of the `totalSales` variable to String and then assigns the result to the totalSalesLabel. When the procedure ends, the computer removes the procedure-level `salesAmount` variable from its memory; however, it does not remove the class-level `totalSales` variable. The `totalSales` variable is removed from the computer's memory only when the application ends.

If you want to experiment with the Total Sales application, open the solution contained in the Try It 3! folder.

class-level variable declared in the form's Declarations section

procedure-level variable declared in the calcButton's Click event procedure

you also can write this as `totalSales += salesAmount`

```
Public Class MainForm

    ' class-level variable used to store the total sales
    Private totalSales As Decimal

    Private Sub calcButton_Click(ByVal sender As Object,
       ByVal e As System.EventArgs) Handles calcButton.Click
       ' calculates the total sales

       ' declare variables
       Dim salesAmount As Decimal

       ' calculate and display the total sales
       Decimal.TryParse(salesTextBox.Text, salesAmount)
       totalSales = totalSales + salesAmount
       totalSalesLabel.Text = Convert.ToString(totalSales)
    End Sub

    Private Sub exitButton_Click(ByVal sender As Object,
       ByVal e As System.EventArgs) Handles exitButton.Click
       Me.Close()
    End Sub
End Class
```

Figure 3-17 Example of using a class-level variable

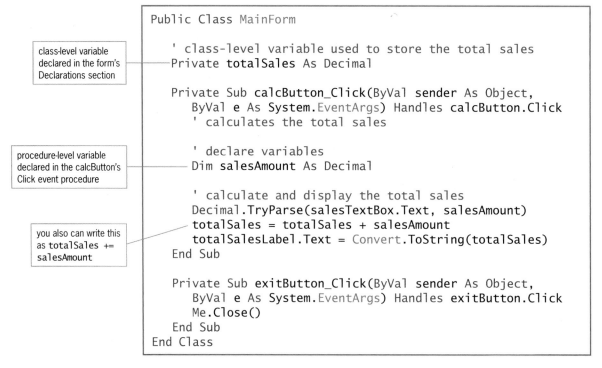

Static Variables

Recall that you can declare a variable using the `Dim`, `Private`, or `Static` keywords. You already know how to use the `Dim` and `Private` keywords to declare procedure-level and class-level variables, respectively. In this section, you will learn how to use the `Static` keyword to declare a special type of procedure-level variable, called a static variable. A **static variable** is a procedure-level variable that remains in memory, and also retains its value, even when the procedure in which it is declared ends. Like a class-level variable, a static variable is not removed from the computer's internal memory until the application ends. However, unlike a class-level variable, which can be used by all of the procedures in a form, a static variable can be used only by the procedure in which it is declared. In other words, a static variable has a narrower scope than does a class-level variable. As mentioned earlier, you can prevent many unintentional errors from occurring in an application by declaring the variables using the minimum scope needed.

The `Static` keyword can be used only in a procedure.

In the previous section, you viewed the interface (Figure 3-16) and code (Figure 3-17) for the Total Sales application. Recall that the application uses a class-level variable to accumulate the sales amounts entered by the user. Rather than using a class-level variable for that purpose, you also can use a static variable. Figure 3-18 shows the Total Sales application's code using a static variable. The first time the user clicks the Calculate Total Sales button in the interface, the button's Click event procedure creates and initializes (to 0) a procedure-level variable named `salesAmount` and a static variable named `totalSales`. Next, the TryParse method converts the sales amount entered in the salesTextBox to Decimal, storing the result in the `salesAmount` variable. The first assignment statement in the procedure adds the contents of the `salesAmount` variable to the contents of the `totalSales` variable. The last assignment statement in the procedure converts the contents of the `totalSales` variable to String and assigns the result to the totalSalesLabel. When the procedure ends, the computer removes from its internal memory the variable declared using the `Dim` keyword (`salesAmount`). But it does not remove the variable declared using the `Static` keyword (`totalSales`). Each subsequent time the user clicks the Calculate Total Sales button, the computer re-creates and re-initializes the `salesAmount` variable declared in the button's Click event procedure. However, it does not re-create or re-initialize the `totalSales` variable because that variable, as well as its current value, is still in the computer's memory. After re-creating and re-initializing the `salesAmount` variable, the computer processes the remaining instructions contained in the button's Click event procedure. Here again, each time the procedure ends, the `salesAmount` variable is removed from the computer's internal memory. The `totalSales` variable is removed only when the application ends.

If you want to experiment with this version of the Total Sales application, open the solution contained in the Try It 4! folder.

static variable declared in the calcButton's Click event procedure

you also can write this as `totalSales += salesAmount`

```
Public Class MainForm

    Private Sub calcButton_Click(ByVal sender As Object,
        ByVal e As System.EventArgs) Handles calcButton.Click
        ' calculates the total sales

        ' declare variables
        Dim salesAmount As Decimal
        Static totalSales As Decimal

        ' calculate and display the total sales
        Decimal.TryParse(salesTextBox.Text, salesAmount)
        totalSales = totalSales + salesAmount
        totalSalesLabel.Text = Convert.ToString(totalSales)
    End Sub

    Private Sub exitButton_Click(ByVal sender As Object,
        ByVal e As System.EventArgs) Handles exitButton.Click
        Me.Close()
    End Sub
End Class
```

Figure 3-18 Example of using a static variable

Named Constants

In addition to using literal constants and variables in your code, you also can use named constants. Like a variable, a **named constant** is a memory location inside the computer. However, unlike a variable's value, a named constant's value cannot be changed while the application is running. You create a named constant using the **Const statement**. Figure 3-19 shows the syntax of the Const statement and includes examples of declaring named constants. To differentiate the name of a constant from the name of a variable, many programmers enter the names of constants using Pascal case (rather than camel case), as shown in the examples in the figure. (Recall that Pascal case means you capitalize the first letter in the name and the first letter of each subsequent word in the name.) The Const statement stores the value of the *expression* in the named constant. The expression can contain a literal constant, another named constant, or an arithmetic operator; however, it cannot contain a variable or a method. The expression's value must have the same data type as the named constant. When entered in a procedure, the Const statements shown in the first three examples in Figure 3-19 create procedure-level named constants. To create a class-level named constant, you precede the `Const` keyword with the `Private` keyword, as shown in Example 4. In addition, you enter the Const statement in the form's Declarations section. Notice the letter D that appears after the number .05 in Example 3. The letter D is one of the literal type characters in Visual Basic. A **literal type character** forces a literal constant to assume a data type other than the one its form indicates. In this case, the letter D forces the Double number .05 to assume the Decimal data type. At this point, you may be wondering why the Convert.ToDecimal method was not used to convert the Double number to the Decimal data type, like this: `Const TaxRate As Decimal = Convert.ToDecimal(.05)`. This is because, as you learned earlier, the expression assigned to a named constant cannot contain a method.

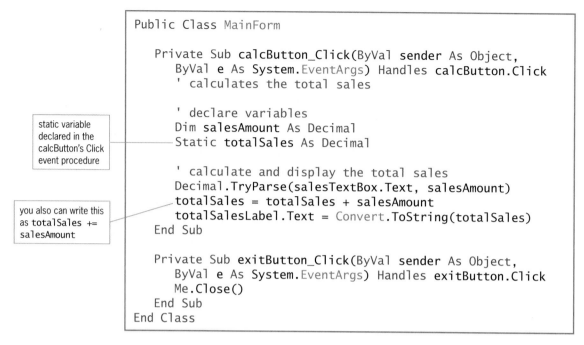

HOW TO Declare a Named Constant

<u>Syntax</u>
Const *constantName* **As** *dataType* = *expression*

<u>Example 1</u>
```
Const Pi As Double = 3.141593
```
declares `Pi` as a Double named constant and initializes it to the Double number 3.141593

<u>Example 2</u>
```
Const MaxHours As Integer = 40
```
declares `MaxHours` as an Integer named constant and initializes it to the integer 40

<u>Example 3</u>
```
Const TaxRate As Decimal = .05D
```
(the D literal type character changes the number to the Decimal data type)

declares `TaxRate` as a Decimal named constant and initializes it to the Decimal number .05

<u>Example 4</u>
```
Private Const Heading As String = "ABC Company"
```
declares Heading as a String named constant and initializes it to the string "ABC Company"

Figure 3-19 How to declare a named constant

Named constants make code more self-documenting and easier to modify, because they allow you to use meaningful words in place of values that are less clear. The named constant `Pi`, for example, is much more meaningful than is the number 3.141593, which is the value of pi rounded to six decimal places. Once you create a named constant, you then can use the constant's name, rather than its value, in the application's code. Unlike the value stored in a variable, the value stored in a named constant cannot be inadvertently changed while the application is running. Using a named constant to represent a value has another advantage: if the value changes in the future, you will need to modify only the Const statement in the program, rather than all of the program statements that use the value. The Area Calculator application that you view next illustrates the use of a named constant. The application's interface is shown in Figure 3-20. As the interface indicates, the application allows the user to enter the radius of a circle. It then calculates and displays the circle's area. The formula for calculating the area of a circle is πr^2, where π stands for pi (3.141593).

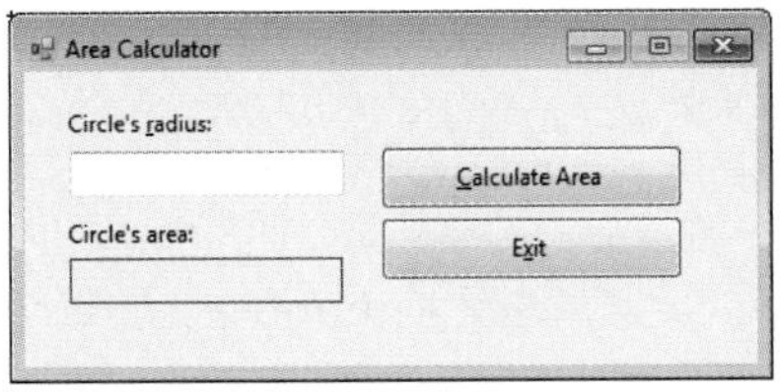

Figure 3-20 Area Calculator application's interface

You also can write the first assignment statement in Figure 3-21 as `area = Pi * radius ^ 2`.

If you want to experiment with the Area Calculator application, open the solution contained in the Try It 5! folder.

Figure 3-21 shows the code for the Calculate Area button's Click event procedure. The declaration statements in the procedure create and initialize a named constant and two variables. Next, the TryParse method converts (to Double) the radius value entered in the radiusTextBox, and it stores the result in the `radius` variable. The first assignment statement in the procedure calculates the circle's area using the values stored in the `Pi` named constant and `radius` variable; it then assigns the result to the `area` variable. The second assignment statement displays the contents of the `area` variable (converted to String) in the areaLabel. When the procedure ends, the computer removes the named constant and two variables from its internal memory.

```
Private Sub calcButton_Click(ByVal sender As Object,
   ByVal e As System.EventArgs) Handles calcButton.Click
      ' calculates the area of a circle

      ' declare named constant and variables
     Const Pi As Double = 3.141593
     Dim radius As Double
     Dim area As Double

      ' calculate and display the area
     Double.TryParse(radiusTextBox.Text, radius)
     area = Pi * radius * radius
     areaLabel.Text = Convert.ToString(area)
End Sub
```

named constant declaration statement (callout: Const Pi As Double = 3.141593)

assignment statement containing the named constant (callout: area = Pi * radius * radius)

Figure 3-21 Example of using a named constant

The answers to Mini-Quiz questions are located in Appendix A.

Mini-Quiz 3-4

1. Most of the variables used in an application will have ________ scope.
   a. block
   b. class
   c. general
   d. procedure

2. ________ variables are declared in the form's General Declarations section using the `Private` keyword.
   a. Block-level
   b. Class-level
   c. General-level
   d. Procedure-level

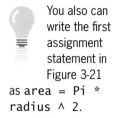

3. Which of the following declares a procedure-level variable that retains its value until the application ends?
   a. `Dim Static score As Integer`
   b. `Private Static score As Integer`
   c. `Static score As Integer`
   d. `Static Dim score As Integer`

4. Which of the following declares and initializes a class-level named constant called `title`?
   a. `Private Const title As String = "Coach"`
   b. `Static title As String = "Coach"`
   c. `Const Private title As String = "Coach"`
   d. `Const Class title As String = "Coach"`

Option Explicit, Option Infer, and Option Strict

It is important to declare the memory locations used in an application, because doing so allows you to control their data type. It also makes the application more self-documenting, which means it will be clearer and easier to understand by anyone reading your code. A word of caution is in order at this point: In Visual Basic you can create variables "on the fly," which means that if your code contains the name of an undeclared variable, Visual Basic creates the variable for you and assigns the Object data type to it. (An undeclared variable is a variable that does not appear in a declaration statement, such as a Dim statement.) Recall that the Object data type is not a very efficient data type, and its use should be limited. Because it is so easy to forget to declare a variable—and so easy to misspell a variable's name while coding, thereby inadvertently creating an undeclared variable—Visual Basic provides a way that prevents you from using undeclared variables in your code. You simply enter the statement `Option Explicit On` in the General Declarations section of the Code Editor window. The General Declarations section is located above the `Public Class` clause. (You can look ahead to Figure 3-23 to see the location of the General Declarations section.) Then if your code contains the name of an undeclared variable, the Code Editor informs you of the error. When you also enter the `Option Infer Off` statement in the General Declarations section, the Code Editor ensures that every variable and named constant is declared with a data type. In other words, the statement tells the computer not to infer (or assume) a memory location's data type based on the data assigned to the memory location.

As you learned earlier, the data type of the value assigned to a memory location (variable or named constant) should be the same as the data type of the memory location itself. If the value's data type does not match the memory location's data type, the computer uses a process called **implicit type**

conversion to convert the value to fit the memory location. For example, when processing the statement `Dim sales As Double = 453`, the computer converts the integer 453 to a Double number before storing the value in the variable. It does this by appending a decimal point and the number 0 to the end of the integer. In this case, the integer 453 will be converted to the Double number 453.0 before the number is assigned to the Double `sales` variable. When a value is converted from one data type to another data type that can store either larger numbers or numbers with greater precision, the value is said to be **promoted**. In this case, if the Double `sales` variable is used subsequently in a calculation, the results of the calculation will not be adversely affected by the implicit promotion of the number 453 to the number 453.0. However, if you inadvertently assign a Double number to a variable that can store only integers—as does the statement `Dim score As Integer = 3.2`—the computer converts the Double number to an integer before storing the value in the variable. It does this by rounding the number to the nearest whole number and then truncating (dropping off) the decimal portion of the number. In this case, the computer converts the Double number 3.2 to the integer 3, which then is assigned to the Integer `score` variable. When a value is converted from one data type to another data type that can store only smaller numbers or numbers with less precision, the value is said to be **demoted**. If the `score` variable is used subsequently in a calculation, the results of the calculation will probably be adversely affected by the implicit demotion of the number 3.2 to the number 3. More than likely, the demotion will cause the calculated results to be incorrect.

With implicit type conversions, data loss can occur when a value is converted from one data type to a narrower data type, which is a data type with less precision or smaller capacity. You can eliminate the problems that occur as a result of implicit type conversions by entering the `Option Strict On` statement in the General Declarations section of the Code Editor window. When the `Option Strict On` statement appears in an application's code, the computer uses the type conversion rules listed in Figure 3-22. The figure also includes examples of applying these rules. According to the first rule, the computer will not implicitly convert a string to a number. As a result, the Code Editor will issue the warning "Option Strict On disallows implicit conversions from 'String' to 'Double'" when your code contains the statement `hours = hoursTextBox.Text`, because the statement tells the computer to store a string in the Double `hours` variable. As you learned earlier, you should use the TryParse method to explicitly convert a string to the Double data type before assigning it to a Double variable. In this case, the appropriate statement to use is `Double.TryParse(hoursTextBox.Text, hours)`. According to the second rule, the computer will not implicitly convert a number to a string. Therefore, the Code Editor will issue the warning "Option Strict On disallows implicit conversions from 'Decimal' to 'String' when your code contains the statement `grossLabel.Text = grossPay`, because the statement assigns a number to a string. Recall that you can use one of the Convert class methods to explicitly convert a number to the String data type. The appropriate statement to use here is `grossLabel.Text = Convert.ToString(grossPay)`. The third rule states that wider data types will not be implicitly demoted to narrower data types. A data type is wider than another data type if it can store either larger numbers or numbers with greater precision. Because of this rule, a Double number will not be implicitly demoted to the Decimal or Integer data types. If your code contains the statement `Dim rate As Decimal = .05`, the Code Editor will issue the "Option Strict On disallows implicit conversions from 'Double' to 'Decimal'" warning, because the statement assigns a Double number to a Decimal variable. The correct statement to use in this case is either `Dim rate As Decimal = Convert.ToDecimal(.05)` or `Dim rate As Decimal = .05D`. According to the last rule listed in Figure 3-22, the computer will implicitly convert narrower data types to wider data types. For example, when processing the `average = total / num` statement, in which `average` and `total` are Double variables and `num` is an Integer variable, the computer will implicitly promote the contents of the `num` variable to Double before dividing it into the contents of the `total` variable. The result, a Double number, will be assigned to the `average` variable.

Type conversion rules

1. Strings will not be implicitly converted to numbers. The Code Editor will display a warning message when a statement attempts to use a string where a number is expected.

```
            Dim hours As Double
Incorrect:  hours = hoursTextBox.Text
Correct:    Double.TryParse(hoursTextBox.Text, hours)
```

2. Numbers will not be implicitly converted to strings. The Code Editor will display a warning message when a statement attempts to use a number where a string is expected.

```
            Dim grossPay As Decimal = 235.67
Incorrect:  grossLabel.Text = grossPay
Correct:    grossLabel.Text = Convert.ToString(grossPay)
```

3. Wider data types will not be implicitly demoted to narrower data types. The Code Editor will display a warning message when a statement attempts to use a wider data type where a narrower data type is expected.

```
Incorrect:  Dim rate As Decimal = .05
Correct:    Dim rate As Decimal = .05D
Correct:    Dim rate As Decimal = Convert.ToDecimal(.05)
```

4. Narrower data types will be implicitly promoted to wider data types.

```
            Dim num As Integer = 3
            Dim total As Double = 45.15
            Dim average As Double
Correct:    average = total / num
```

Figure 3-22 Rules and examples of type conversions

Figure 3-23 shows the three Option statements entered in the Area Calculator application, which you viewed earlier in Figures 3-20 and 3-21. The statements are entered in the General Declarations section of the Code Editor window, below the comments that document the project's name and purpose, the programmer's name, and the date the code was either created or revised. If a project contains more than one form, the statements must be entered in each form's Code Editor window.

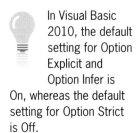

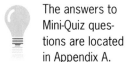

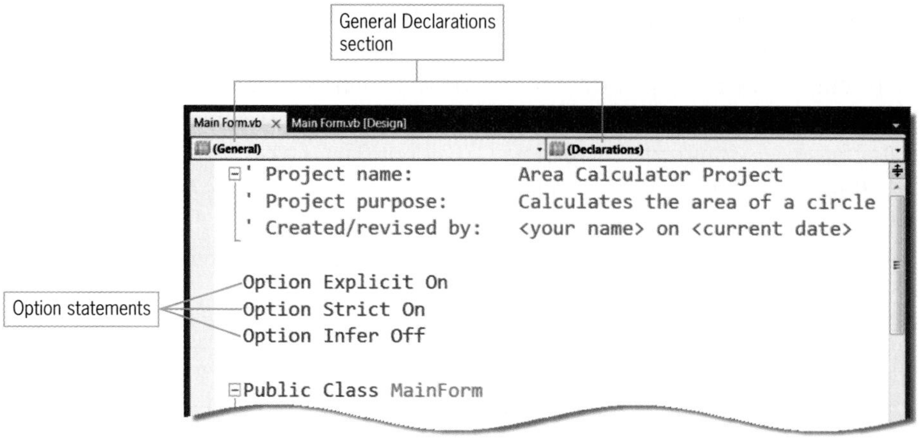

Figure 3-23 Option statements entered in the General Declarations section

In Visual Basic 2010, the default setting for Option Explicit and Option Infer is On, whereas the default setting for Option Strict is Off.

Rather than entering the Option statements in the Code Editor window, you also can set the options using either the Project Designer window or the Options dialog box. However, it is strongly recommended that you enter the Option statements in the Code Editor window, because doing so ensures that the options are set appropriately; it also makes your code more self-documenting. The steps for setting the options in the Project Designer window and Options dialog box are located in the Summary section at the end of this chapter.

Beginning with the next section, you will use what you learned about variables, constants, and calculations to code the Sunshine Cellular application from Chapter 2. You also will learn how programmers plan a procedure's code.

The answers to Mini-Quiz questions are located in Appendix A.

Mini-Quiz 3-5

1. When entered in the General Declarations section of the Code Editor window, the ______________ statement prevents you from using an undeclared variable in your code.
   a. `Option Explicit On`
   b. `Option Infer On`
   c. `Option Undeclared Off`
   d. `Option Declared On`

2. If your code contains the `Option Strict On` statement, which of the following is the correct way to assign the contents of the salesTextBox to a Double variable named `sales`?
   a. `sales = salesTextBox.Text`
   b. `sales = Double.TryParse(salesTextBox.Text)`
   c. `Double.TryParse(salesTextBox.Text, sales)`
   d. `Double.TryParse(sales, salesTextBox.Text)`

3. The `sales` and `commission` variables in the following assignment statement have the Double data type, whereas the `commRate` variable has the Decimal data type: `commission = sales * commRate`. If your code contains the `Option Strict On` statement, how will the computer process the assignment statement?

Coding the Sunshine Cellular Application

In Chapter 2, you created a TOE chart and user interface for the Sunshine Cellular application. As you may remember, the company takes orders for cell phones by phone. The cell phones are priced at $100 each and are available in two colors: silver and blue. The application needs to both calculate and display the total number of phones ordered and the total price of the phones, including a 5% sales tax. The interface and TOE chart created in Chapter 2 are shown in Figures 3-24 and 3-25, respectively.

You can watch the Sunshine Cellular application being coded by viewing the Ch03Sunshine video.

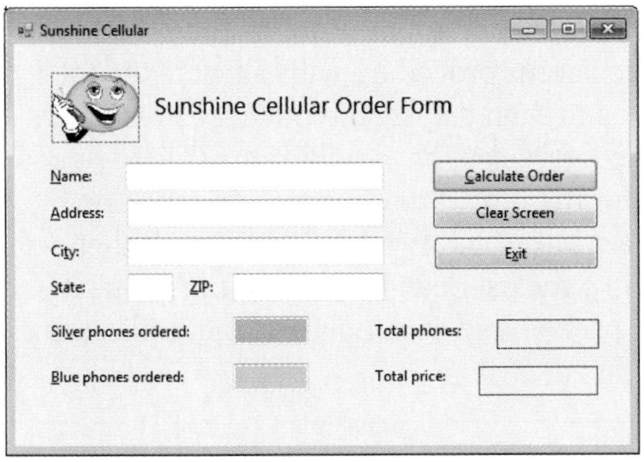

Figure 3-24 Sunshine Cellular interface from Chapter 2

Task	Object	Event
1. Calculate total phones ordered and total price 2. Display total phones ordered and total price in totalPhonesLabel and totalPriceLabel	calcButton	Click
Clear screen for the next order	clearButton	Click
End the application	exitButton	Click
Display total phones ordered (from calcButton)	totalPhonesLabel	None
Display total price (from calcButton)	totalPriceLabel	None
Get and display the order information	nameTextBox, addressTextBox, cityTextBox, stateTextBox, zipTextBox, silverTextBox, blueTextBox	None

Figure 3-25 Sunshine Cellular TOE chart from Chapter 2

After planning an application and building its interface, you then can begin coding the application. You code an application so that the objects in the interface perform their assigned tasks when the appropriate event occurs. The objects and events that need to be coded, as well as the tasks assigned to each object and event, are listed in the application's TOE chart. The TOE chart in Figure 3-25 indicates that only the three buttons require coding, as they are the only objects with an event listed in the third column of the chart. Before you begin coding an object's event procedure, you should plan it. Many programmers use planning tools such as pseudocode or flowcharts. You do not need to create both a flowchart and pseudocode for a procedure; you need to use only one of these planning tools. The tool you use is really a matter of personal preference. For simple procedures, pseudocode works just fine. When a procedure becomes more complex, however, the procedure's steps may be easier to understand in a flowchart.

Using Pseudocode to Plan a Procedure

Pseudocode uses short phrases to describe the steps a procedure must take to accomplish its goal. Figure 3-26 shows the pseudocode for the procedures that need to be coded in the Sunshine Cellular application. As the pseudocode indicates, the calcButton's Click event procedure will calculate the total phones ordered and the total price, and then display the calculated results in the appropriate label controls in the interface. The clearButton's Click event procedure will prepare the screen for the next order by removing the previous order's information from the text boxes and two label controls. It then will send the focus to the nameTextBox so the user can begin entering the next order. The exitButton's Click event procedure will simply end the application.

```
calcButton Click event procedure
1. assign user input (silver phones ordered and blue phones ordered) to variables
2. total phones ordered = silver phones ordered + blue phones ordered
3. subtotal = total phones ordered * phone price
4. sales tax = subtotal * sales tax rate
5. total price = subtotal + sales tax
6. display total phones ordered and total price in totalPhonesLabel and totalPriceLabel

clearButton Click event procedure
1. clear the Text property of the 7 text boxes
2. clear the Text property of the totalPhonesLabel and totalPriceLabel
3. send the focus to the nameTextBox so the user can begin entering the next order

exitButton Click event procedure
end the application
```

Figure 3-26 Pseudocode for the Sunshine Cellular application

Using a Flowchart to Plan a Procedure

Unlike pseudocode, which consists of short phrases, a **flowchart** uses standardized symbols to show the steps a procedure must follow to reach its goal. Figure 3-27 shows the flowcharts for the procedures that need to be coded in the Sunshine Cellular application. The logic illustrated in the flowcharts is the same as the logic shown in the pseudocode in Figure 3-26. The flowcharts in Figure 3-27 contain three different symbols: an oval, a rectangle, and a parallelogram. The oval symbol is called the **start/stop symbol**. The start and stop ovals indicate the beginning and end, respectively, of the flowchart. The rectangles that appear between the start and stop ovals are called **process symbols**. You use the process symbol to represent tasks such as making assignments and calculations. The parallelogram in a flowchart is called the **input/output symbol** and is used to represent input tasks (such as getting information from the user) and output tasks (such as displaying information). The parallelogram in Figure 3-27 represents an output task. The lines connecting the symbols in a flowchart are called **flowlines**.

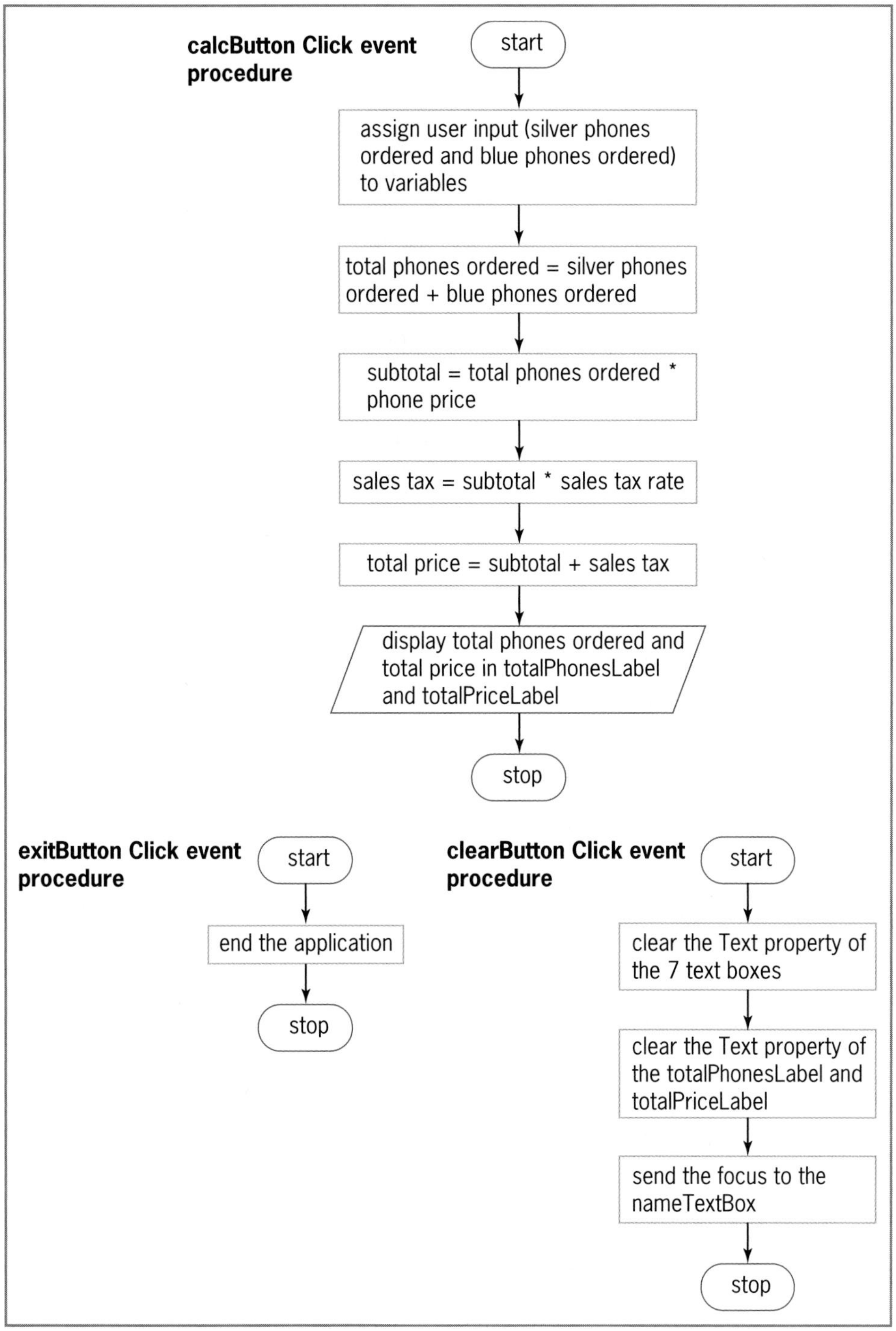

Figure 3-27 Flowcharts for the Sunshine Cellular application

Coding the Calculate Order Button's Click Event Procedure

The programmer uses either the procedure's pseudocode or its flowchart as a guide when coding the procedure. In this chapter, you will use the pseudocode. Figure 3-28 shows the pseudocode for the calcButton's Click event procedure.

```
calcButton Click event procedure
1. assign user input (silver phones ordered and blue phones ordered) to variables
2. total phones ordered = silver phones ordered + blue phones ordered
3. subtotal = total phones ordered * phone price
4. sales tax = subtotal * sales tax rate
5. total price = subtotal + sales tax
6. display total phones ordered and total price in totalPhonesLabel and totalPriceLabel
```

Figure 3-28 Pseudocode for the calcButton's Click event procedure

Before you begin coding a procedure, you first study the procedure's pseudocode (or flowchart) to determine any variables and named constants the procedure will require. When determining the named constants, look for items whose value will be the same each time the procedure is invoked. In the calcButton's Click event procedure, for instance, the phone price and sales tax rate will always be $100 and .05 (the decimal equivalent of 5%), respectively. Therefore, you will assign both values to named constants. You will declare the named constants using the names `PhonePrice` and `TaxRate`, and the Decimal data type. At this point, you may be wondering why the `PhonePrice` constant is declared using the Decimal data type rather than the Integer data type. Although the price of a phone does not currently contain any decimal places, it is possible that the price may include a decimal place in the future. By using the Decimal data type now, you can change the named constant's value to include a decimal place without having to remember to also change its data type.

When determining the variables a procedure will use, look in the pseudocode (or flowchart) for items whose value probably will change each time the procedure is processed. In the calcButton's Click event procedure, the numbers of silver and blue phones ordered, as well as the total number of phones ordered, the subtotal, the sales tax, and the total price, probably will be different each time the procedure is processed; therefore, you will use variables to store the values. You will use Integer variables to store the number of silver phones ordered, the number of blue phones ordered, and the total number of phones ordered, because those values can be whole numbers only. You will use Decimal variables to store the subtotal, sales tax, and total price of the order, because those amounts may contain a decimal place. Figure 3-29 lists the names, data types, and values of the two named constants. It also lists the names and data types of the six variables, as well as the source of their values.

Named constants	**Data type**	**Value**
`PhonePrice`	Decimal	100
`TaxRate`	Decimal	.05
Variables	**Data type**	**Value source**
`silverPhones`	Integer	user input (silverTextBox)
`bluePhones`	Integer	user input (blueTextBox)
`totalPhones`	Integer	procedure calculation
`subtotal`	Decimal	procedure calculation
`salesTax`	Decimal	procedure calculation
`totalPrice`	Decimal	procedure calculation

Figure 3-29 Named constants and variables for the calcButton's Click event procedure

Figure 3-30 shows the declaration statements entered in the calcButton's Click event procedure. The green jagged lines indicate that, at this point, the named constants and variables do not appear in any other statement in the code.

```
Main Form.vb* ×  Main Form.vb [Design]*
calcButton                              Click
    Private Sub calcButton_Click(ByVal sender As Object, ByVa
        ' calculates the total number of phones
        ' ordered and the total price

        ' declare constants and variables
        Const PhonePrice As Decimal = 100D
        Const TaxRate As Decimal = 0.05D
        Dim silverPhones As Integer
        Dim bluePhones As Integer
        Dim totalPhones As Integer
        Dim subtotal As Decimal
        Dim salesTax As Decimal
        Dim totalPrice As Decimal

    End Sub
150 %
```

green jagged line

Figure 3-30 Declaration statements entered in the procedure

Next, you code each of the steps in the pseudocode (or each symbol in the flowchart), one at a time. However, keep in mind that some steps (symbols) may require more than one line of code. The first step listed in the pseudocode shown earlier in Figure 3-28 is to assign the user input to the appropriate variables. In this case, the user input is the number of silver phones ordered and the number of blue phones ordered. The user enters those values in the silverTextBox and blueTextBox in the interface. You can use the TryParse methods shown in Figure 3-31 to convert the Text properties of the two text boxes to the Integer data type and then store the results in the `silverPhones` and `bluePhones` variables.

```
        ' assign user input to variables
        Integer.TryParse(silverTextBox.Text, silverPhones)
        Integer.TryParse(blueTextBox.Text, bluePhones)
```

Figure 3-31 User input stored in variables

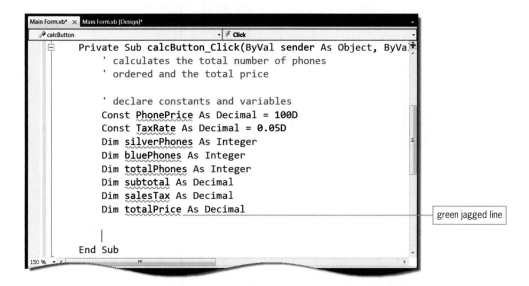

Step 2 in the pseudocode is to calculate the total number of phones ordered by adding together the number of silver phones ordered and the number of blue phones ordered. You can perform this task using the statement `totalPhones = silverPhones + bluePhones`. Step 3 is to calculate the subtotal by multiplying the total number of phones ordered by the phone price. The correct statement to use here is `subtotal = totalPhones * PhonePrice`. Step 4 is to calculate the sales tax; this step is accomplished with the statement `salesTax = subtotal * TaxRate`. Step 5 is to calculate the total price of the order. You do this with the statement `totalPrice = subtotal + salesTax`. The last step in the pseudocode is to display the total number of phones ordered and the total price of the order in the appropriate label controls. You accomplish this task using assignment statements along with the Convert.ToString method. Figure 3-32 shows the completed Click event procedure for the calcButton.

```
Private Sub calcButton_Click(ByVal sender As Object,
ByVal e As System.EventArgs) Handles calcButton.Click
     ' calculates the total number of phones
     ' ordered and the total price

     ' declare constants and variables
     Const PhonePrice As Decimal = 100D
     Const TaxRate As Decimal = 0.05D
     Dim silverPhones As Integer
     Dim bluePhones As Integer
     Dim totalPhones As Integer
     Dim subtotal As Decimal
     Dim salesTax As Decimal
     Dim totalPrice As Decimal

     ' assign user input to variables
     Integer.TryParse(silverTextBox.Text, silverPhones)
     Integer.TryParse(blueTextBox.Text, bluePhones)

     ' perform calculations
     totalPhones = silverPhones + bluePhones
     subtotal = totalPhones * PhonePrice
     salesTax = subtotal * TaxRate
     totalPrice = subtotal + salesTax

     ' display calculated amounts
     totalPhonesLabel.Text = Convert.ToString(totalPhones)
     totalPriceLabel.Text = Convert.ToString(totalPrice)
End Sub
```

Figure 3-32 Completed calcButton's Click event procedure

Completing the Sunshine Cellular Application

To complete the Sunshine Cellular application, you still need to code the Click event procedures for the exitButton and clearButton. According to its pseudocode (shown earlier in Figure 3-26), the exitButton's Click event procedure should end the application. You accomplish that task using the `Me.Close()` statement. The pseudocode for the clearButton's Click event procedure is shown in Figure 3-33. The procedure does not perform any tasks that require user input or calculations; therefore, it will not need any named constants or variables.

clearButton Click event procedure
1. clear the Text property of the 7 text boxes
2. clear the Text property of the totalPhonesLabel and totalPriceLabel
3. send the focus to the nameTextBox so the user can begin entering the next order

Figure 3-33 Pseudocode for the clearButton's Click event procedure

Steps 1 and 2 in the pseudocode are to clear the Text property of the text boxes and two of the labels in the interface. You can clear the Text property by assigning an empty string to the property. An **empty string**, also referred to as a **zero-length string**, is a set of quotation marks with nothing between them, like this: "". You also can clear an object's Text property by assigning the value **String.Empty** to it. When you do this, the computer assigns an empty string to the Text property, thereby removing its contents. Step 3 in the pseudocode is to send the focus to the nameTextBox. You can accomplish this task using the **Focus method**. The method's syntax is *object*.**Focus()**, in which *object* is the name of the object to which you want the focus sent. Figure 3-34 shows the completed code for the Sunshine Cellular application.

```
' Project name:          Sunshine Cellular Project
' Project purpose:       Calculates the total number of phones
'                        ordered and the total price
' Created/revised by:    <your name> on <current date>

Option Explicit On
Option Strict On
Option Infer Off

Public Class MainForm

   Private Sub calcButton_Click(ByVal sender As Object,
   ByVal e As System.EventArgs) Handles calcButton.Click
      ' calculates the total number of phones
      ' ordered and the total price

      ' declare constants and variables
      Const PhonePrice As Decimal = 100D
      Const TaxRate As Decimal = 0.05D
      Dim silverPhones As Integer
      Dim bluePhones As Integer
      Dim totalPhones As Integer
      Dim subtotal As Decimal
      Dim salesTax As Decimal
      Dim totalPrice As Decimal

      ' assign user input to variables
      Integer.TryParse(silverTextBox.Text, silverPhones)
      Integer.TryParse(blueTextBox.Text, bluePhones)

      ' perform calculations
      totalPhones = silverPhones + bluePhones
      subtotal = totalPhones * PhonePrice
      salesTax = subtotal * TaxRate
      totalPrice = subtotal + salesTax
```

Figure 3-34 Sunshine Cellular application's code *(continues)*

(continued)

```

        ' display calculated amounts
        totalPhonesLabel.Text = Convert.ToString(totalPhones)
        totalPriceLabel.Text = Convert.ToString(totalPrice)
End Sub

    Private Sub exitButton_Click(ByVal sender As Object,
    ByVal e As System.EventArgs) Handles exitButton.Click
        Me.Close()
    End Sub

    Private Sub clearButton_Click(ByVal sender As Object,
    ByVal e As System.EventArgs) Handles clearButton.Click
        ' prepares the screen for the next order

        nameTextBox.Text = String.Empty
        addressTextBox.Text = String.Empty
        cityTextBox.Text = String.Empty
        stateTextBox.Text = String.Empty
        zipTextBox.Text = String.Empty
        silverTextBox.Text = String.Empty
        blueTextBox.Text = String.Empty
        totalPhonesLabel.Text = String.Empty
        totalPriceLabel.Text = String.Empty
        nameTextBox.Focus()
    End Sub
End Class
```

Figure 3-34 Sunshine Cellular application's code

Testing and Debugging the Application

After coding an application, you then test it to verify that the code works correctly. You begin by choosing a set of sample data for the input values. You then use the sample data to manually compute the expected output. Next, you start the application and enter your sample data. You then compare the application's output with the expected output; both should be the same. If the outputs are not the same, it indicates that your code contains one or more errors. You will need to locate and then correct the errors before giving the application to the user. Recall that errors in a program's code are called bugs, and the process of locating and correcting the bugs is referred to as debugging. As you learned in Chapter 1, the bugs in a program are usually caused by either syntax errors or logic errors. Recall that a syntax error occurs when an instruction in your code breaks one of the programming language's rules. The Code Editor detects most syntax errors as you enter the instructions. Unlike syntax errors, logic errors are much more difficult to find, because they do not trigger an error message from the Code Editor. A **logic error** can occur for a variety of reasons, such as forgetting to enter an instruction or entering the instructions in the wrong order. Some logic errors occur as a result of calculation statements that are correct syntactically but incorrect mathematically. For example, consider the statement `average = num1 + num2 / 2`, which is supposed to calculate the average of two numbers.

The statement's syntax is correct, but it is incorrect mathematically. This is because it tells the computer to divide the contents of the `num2` variable by 2 and then add the quotient to the contents of the `num1` variable. (Recall that division is performed before addition in an arithmetic expression.) The correct instruction for calculating the average of two numbers is `average = (num1 + num2) / 2`. The parentheses tell the computer to add the contents of the `num1` variable to the contents of the `num2` variable before dividing the sum by 2.

You should use both valid and invalid data when testing an application. **Valid data** is data that the application is expecting the user to enter, whereas **invalid data** is data that the application is not expecting the user to enter. The Sunshine Cellular application, for instance, expects the user to enter a numeric value in the silverTextBox; it does not expect the user to enter a letter. In most cases, invalid data is a result of a typing error made by the user. Figure 3-35 shows two sets of sample data for the Sunshine Cellular application. Each item in the first set is valid. The second set, however, contains an invalid item—namely, the letter t as the number of silver phones ordered. Although two sets of sample data are shown in the figure, you should use multiple sets of valid and invalid data, because you want to test the application as thoroughly as possible. Doing this helps to ensure that the application displays the correct output when valid data is entered, and does not end abruptly when invalid data is entered.

	Set 1	**Set 2**
Input values		
Name	Jasper Jones	Jasper Jones
Address	123 Main St.	123 Main St.
City	Any City	Any City
State	IL	IL
ZIP	Any ZIP	Any ZIP
Silver phones ordered	10	t (invalid data)
Blue phones ordered	5	7
Calculations		
	10	t
	+ 5	+ 7
total phones ordered	15	7
	* 100	* 100
subtotal	1500	700
	* .05	* .05
sales tax	75	35
	+ 1500	+ 700
total price	1575	735

Figure 3-35 Sample test data for the Sunshine Cellular application

Figure 3-36 shows the result of clicking the Calculate Order button after entering the data from Set 1 in Figure 3-35. The interface indicates that a total of 15 phones were ordered at a cost of 1575.00; both amounts agree with the manual calculations shown in Figure 3-35.

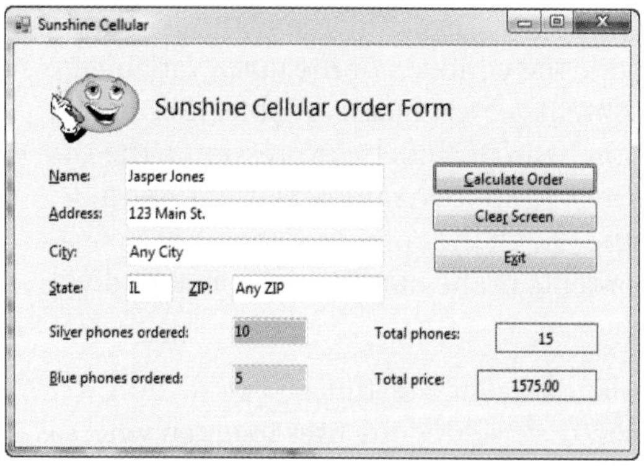

Figure 3-36 Result of using the data from Set 1 in Figure 3-35

Figure 3-37 shows the result of clicking the Calculate Order button after entering the data from Set 2 in Figure 3-35. In this case, the interface indicates that a total of 7 phones were ordered at a cost of 735.00; this agrees with the manual calculations performed earlier. Notice that, although a letter was entered as the number of silver phones ordered, the application does not end with an error. This is because the `Integer.TryParse(silverTextBox.Text, silverPhones)` statement in the calcButton's Click event procedure stores the number 0 (rather than the letter t) in the `silverPhones` variable.

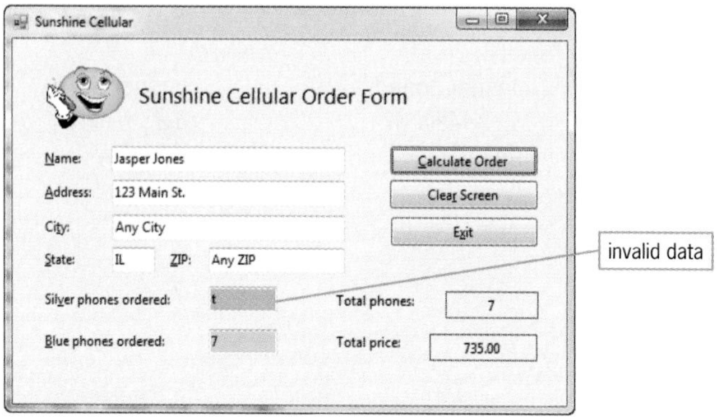

Figure 3-37 Result of using the data from Set 2 in Figure 3-35

Formatting Numeric Output

Numbers representing monetary amounts are usually displayed with either zero or two decimal places and may include a dollar sign and a thousands separator. Similarly, numbers representing percentage amounts are usually displayed with zero or more decimal places and a percent sign. Specifying the number of decimal places and the special characters to display in a number is called **formatting**. You can format a number in Visual Basic using the ToString method, whose syntax is shown in Figure 3-38. In the syntax, *variableName* is the name of a numeric variable. The **ToString method** formats the number stored in the numeric variable and then returns the result as a string. The *formatString* argument in the syntax specifies the format you want to use. The *formatString* argument must take the form *"Axx"*, where *A* is an alphabetic character called the format specifier, and *xx* is a sequence of digits called the precision specifier. The format specifier must be one of the built-in format characters. The most commonly used format characters are listed in Figure 3-38. Notice that you can use either an uppercase letter or a lowercase letter as the format specifier. When used with one of the format characters listed in Figure 3-38, the precision specifier controls the number of digits that will appear after the decimal point in the formatted number. Also included in Figure 3-38 are several examples of using the ToString method.

HOW TO Format a Number

Syntax
variableName.**ToString(***formatString***)**

Format specifier (Name)	Description
C or c (Currency)	displays the string with a dollar sign; includes a thousands separator (if appropriate); negative values are enclosed in parentheses
N or n (Number)	similar to the Currency format, but does not include a dollar sign and negative values are preceded by a minus sign
F or f (Fixed-point)	same as the Number format, but does not include a thousands separator
P or p (Percent)	multiplies the value by 100 and displays the result with a percent sign; negative values are preceded by a minus sign

Example 1
```
Dim commission As Integer = 1250
commissionLabel.Text = commission.ToString("C2")
```
assigns the string "$1,250.00" to the commissionLabel's Text property

Example 2
```
Dim total As Decimal = 123.675
totalLabel.Text = total.ToString("N2")
```
assigns the string "123.68" to the totalLabel's Text property

Example 3
```
Dim rate As Double = .06
rateLabel.Text = rate.ToString("P0")
```
assigns the string "6 %" to the rateLabel's Text property

Figure 3-38 How to format a number

In the Sunshine Cellular application, you can include a dollar sign, a thousands separator, and two decimal places in the total price by changing the `totalPriceLabel.Text = Convert.ToString(totalPrice)` statement in the calcButton's Click event procedure to `totalPriceLabel.Text = totalPrice.ToString("C2")`. Figure 3-39 shows the modified procedure, and Figure 3-40 shows the formatted output in the interface.

```
Private Sub calcButton_Click(ByVal sender As Object,
 ByVal e As System.EventArgs) Handles calcButton.Click
     ' calculates the total number of phones
     ' ordered and the total price

     ' declare constants and variables
     Const PhonePrice As Decimal = 100D
     Const TaxRate As Decimal = 0.05D
     Dim silverPhones As Integer
     Dim bluePhones As Integer
     Dim totalPhones As Integer
     Dim subtotal As Decimal
     Dim salesTax As Decimal
     Dim totalPrice As Decimal

     ' assign user input to variables
     Integer.TryParse(silverTextBox.Text, silverPhones)
     Integer.TryParse(blueTextBox.Text, bluePhones)

     ' perform calculations
     totalPhones = silverPhones + bluePhones
     subtotal = totalPhones * PhonePrice
     salesTax = subtotal * TaxRate
     totalPrice = subtotal + salesTax

     ' display calculated amounts
     totalPhonesLabel.Text = Convert.ToString(totalPhones)
     totalPriceLabel.Text = totalPrice.ToString("C2")
End Sub
```

formats the total price with a dollar sign, a thousands separator, and two decimal places

Figure 3-39 The calcButton's modified Click event procedure

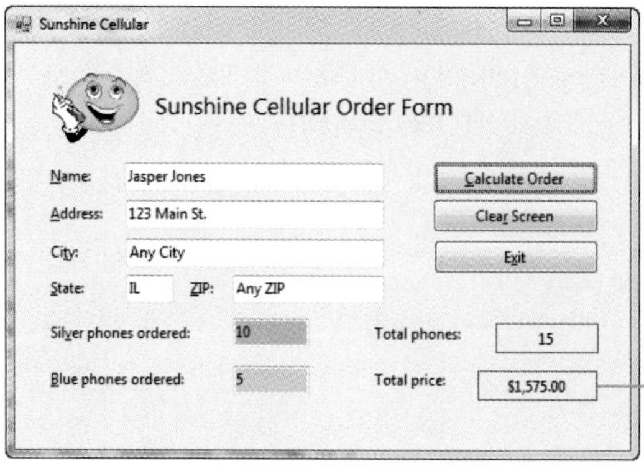

formatted total price

Figure 3-40 Formatted output shown in the interface

If you want to experiment with the Sunshine Cellular application, open the solution contained in the Try It 6! folder.

Mini-Quiz 3-6

The answers to Mini-Quiz questions are located in Appendix A.

1. The rectangle in a flowchart is called the ____________ symbol.
   a. input
   b. output
   c. process
   d. start/stop

2. Which of the following can be used to clear the contents of the salesTextBox?
   a. `salesTextBox.Text = ""`
   b. `salesTextBox.Text = String.Empty`
   c. `salesTextBox.Text = String.Clear`
   d. both a and b

3. Which of the following sends the focus to the clearButton?
   a. `clearButton.Focus()`
   b. `clearButton.SendFocus()`
   c. `clearButton.SetFocus()`
   d. none of the above

4. If the `commission` variable contains the number 1325.5, which of the following assigns the string "1,325.50" to the commLabel?
   a. `commLabel.Text = commission.Format("N2")`
   b. `commLabel.Text = commission.ToString("N2")`
   c. `commLabel.Text = commission.ToFormat("C2")`
   d. `commLabel.Text = commission.ToString("C2")`

You have completed the concepts section of Chapter 3. The Programming Tutorial section is next.

PROGRAMMING TUTORIAL 1

Creating the Color Mixer Application

The Ch03ProgTut1 video demonstrates all of the steps in Programming Tutorial 1.

The colors displayed on a computer screen are created using a mixture of three primary colors: red, green, and blue. The difference in each screen color is due to the amount, or intensity, of each primary color it contains. The intensity can range from 0 to 255, with 0 meaning an absence of the primary color. Figure 3-41 lists several colors along with their red, green, and blue values. The combination of a color's red, green, and blue values is called its RGB value. For example, the color yellow's RGB value is 255, 255, 0. You can make the yellow lighter by adding some blue to its RGB value, like this: 255, 255, 100.

Color	**Red value**	**Green value**	**Blue value**
Black	0	0	0
White	255	255	255
Red	255	0	0
Green	0	255	0
Blue	0	0	255
Yellow	255	255	0
Light yellow	255	255	100
Light gray	192	192	192

Figure 3-41 Colors and their RGB values

In this tutorial, you create an application that allows the user to enter three numbers that represent an RGB value. The application will display the color associated with the RGB value in an oval shape in the interface. It will do this by assigning the RGB value to the oval shape's BackColor property. You assign the RGB value using the Color class's **FromArgb method**, whose syntax is **Color.FromArgb(*redValue*, *greenValue*, *blueValue*)**. The method's three arguments must be integers. The application's TOE chart and MainForm are shown in Figures 3-42 and 3-43, respectively. The MainForm contains three labels, three text boxes, two buttons, and an oval shape.

Task	**Object**	**Event**
Change the background color of the colorOvalShape to match the RGB values entered in the text boxes	viewButton	Click
End the application	exitButton	Click
Get and display the RGB values	redTextBox, greenTextBox, blueTextBox	None
Display the appropriate color (from viewButton)	colorOvalShape	None

Figure 3-42 Color Mixer application's TOE chart

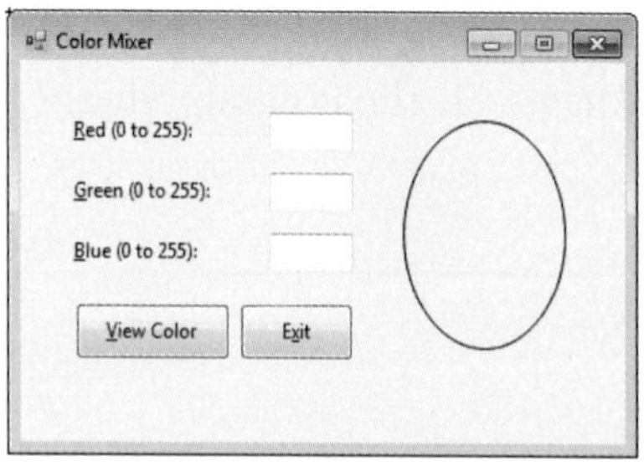

Figure 3-43 MainForm for the Color Mixer application

Completing the MainForm's Interface

Included in the data files for this book is a partially completed Color Mixer application. Before you begin coding the application, you will need to complete the MainForm's interface by adding an oval shape.

To complete the MainForm's interface:

1. Start Visual Studio or the Express Edition of Visual Basic. If necessary, open the Toolbox and Solution Explorer windows.
2. Open the **Color Mixer Solution** (**Color Mixer Solution.sln**) file, which is contained in the VbReloaded2010\Chap03\Color Mixer Solution folder. If necessary, open the designer window. The partially completed MainForm appears on the screen.
3. If necessary, open the Properties window.
4. Use the OvalShape tool, which is located in the Visual Basic PowerPacks section of the toolbox, to add an oval shape control to the form. Figure 3-43 shows the appropriate size and location for the control.
5. Set the oval shape's Name and BackStyle properties to **colorOvalShape** and **Opaque**, respectively.
6. The MainForm's interface is now complete. Lock the controls on the form.
7. Auto-hide the Toolbox, Solution Explorer, and Properties windows, and then save the solution.

Including Comments and the Option Statements in the General Declarations Section

In the General Declarations section of the Code Editor window, many programmers include comments that document the project's name and purpose, the programmer's name, and the date the program was either created or revised. As you learned in the chapter, you create a comment by typing an apostrophe before the text that represents the comment. The computer ignores everything that appears after the apostrophe on that line.

To include comments in the General Declarations section:

1. Right-click the **form** and then click **View Code** to open the Code Editor window.
2. Press **Enter** to insert a blank line above the `Public Class MainForm` clause.
3. Enter the comments shown in Figure 3-44 and then position the insertion point as shown in the figure. Be sure to replace <your name> and <current date> with your name and the current date, respectively.

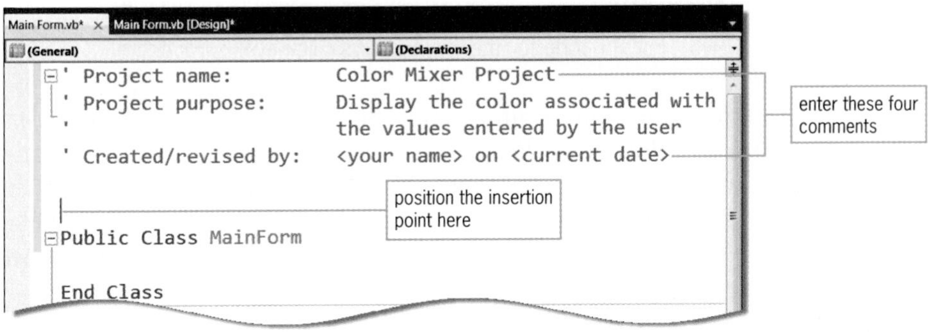

Figure 3-44 Comments entered in the General Declarations section

The Color Mixer application will use variables, so the General Declarations section should also contain the three Option statements you learned in the chapter. Recall that the `Option Explicit On` statement tells the Code Editor window to warn you if your code contains the name of an undeclared variable. The `Option Infer Off` statement tells the Code Editor to warn you if you forget to include a data type when declaring a variable or named constant. The `Option Strict On` statement tells the computer not to perform any implicit type conversions that may lead to a loss of data.

To include the Option statements in the General Declarations section:

1. Enter the three Option statements shown in Figure 3-45, and then save the solution.

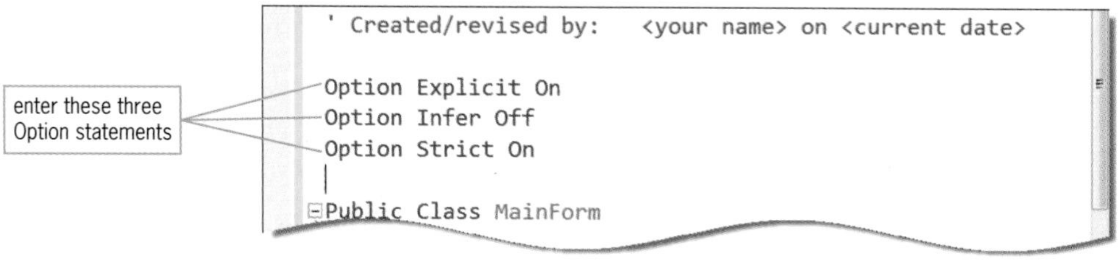

Figure 3-45 Option statements entered in the General Declarations section

Coding the Exit and View Color Buttons

According to the application's TOE chart (shown earlier in Figure 3-42), the Exit button should end the application when it is clicked by the user.

To code the Exit button's Click event procedure:

1. Open the code template for the exitButton's Click event procedure.
2. Type **Me.Close()** and press **Enter**.

The application's TOE chart indicates that the View Color button should change the background color of the colorOvalShape to match the RGB values entered in the text boxes. The pseudocode for the button's Click event procedure is shown in Figure 3-46.

<u>viewButton Click event procedure</u>
1. assign the contents of the three text boxes to Integer variables
2. assign the contents of the Integer variables to the colorOvalShape's BackColor property

Figure 3-46 Pseudocode for the viewButton's Click event procedure

Recall that before you begin coding a procedure, you first study the procedure's pseudocode (or flowchart) to determine any variables or named constants the procedure will require. In this case, the viewButton's Click event procedure will not need any named constants. However, it will need three Integer variables to store the RGB values entered in the text boxes. The variables are listed in Figure 3-47.

Variables	Data type	Value source
inputRed	Integer	user input (redTextBox)
inputGreen	Integer	user input (greenTextBox)
inputBlue	Integer	user input (blueTextBox)

Figure 3-47 Variables for the viewButton's Click event procedure

To code the View Color button's Click event procedure:

1. Open the code template for the viewButton's Click event procedure.
2. Type **' change the oval's color** and press **Enter** twice.
3. Enter the comment and declaration statements shown in Figure 3-48, and then position the insertion point as shown in the figure.

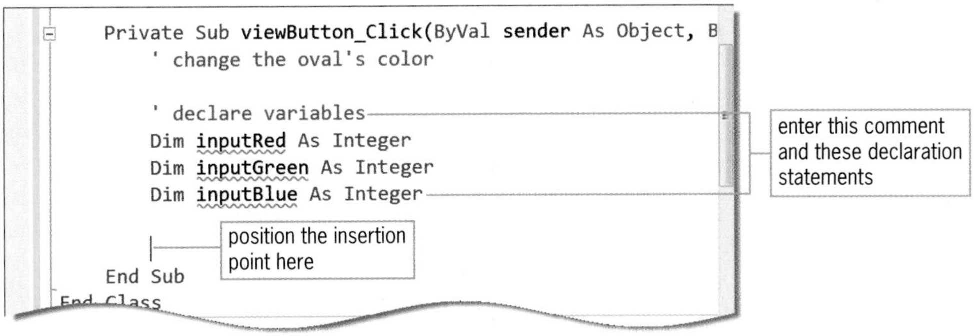

Figure 3-48 Comment and declaration statements entered in the procedure

4. Step 1 in the pseudocode is to assign the contents of the three text boxes to the Integer variables. Enter the comment and three TryParse methods shown in Figure 3-49, and then position the insertion point as shown in the figure.

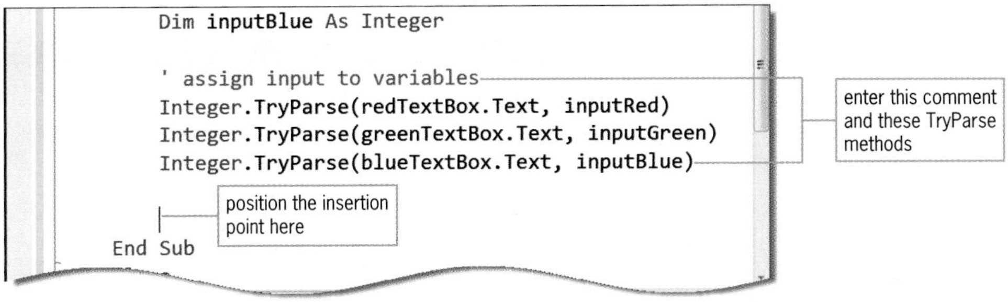

Figure 3-49 Comment and TryParse methods entered in the procedure

5. Step 2 in the pseudocode is to assign the contents of the Integer variables to the colorOvalShape's BackColor property. Enter the comment and assignment statement shown in Figure 3-50.

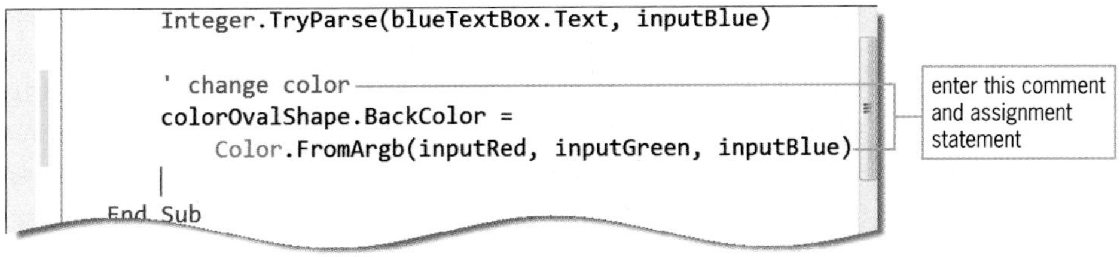

Figure 3-50 Comment and assignment statement entered in the procedure

Testing and Debugging the Application

After coding an application, you then test it to verify that the code works correctly. Recall that you should use both valid and invalid test data.

To test the application using both valid and invalid data:

1. Save the solution, and then start the application. Type **255** in the Red text box and then press **Tab**. Type **255** in the Green text box and then press **Tab**. Type **0** in the Blue text box and then click the **View Color** button. The background color of the oval shape turns to yellow. See Figure 3-51.

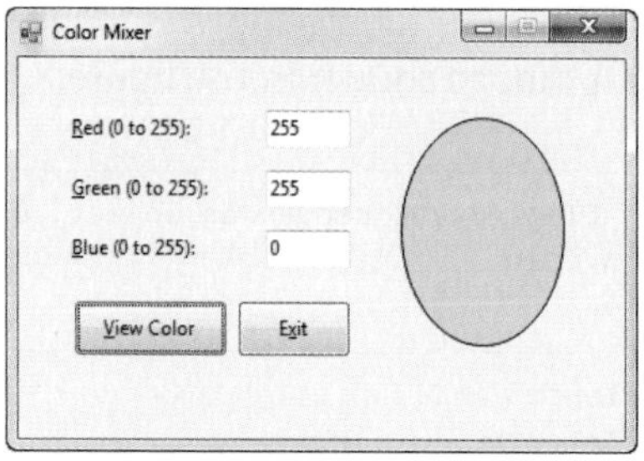

Figure 3-51 Result of entering 255, 255, and 0 as the RGB values

2. Change the contents of the Blue text box from 0 to **100** and then click the **View Color** button. The background color of the oval shape turns to a light yellow.

3. Next, you will test the application using invalid data. Change the contents of the Red text box to **256** and then click the **View Color** button. The application ends abruptly and a box containing an error message appears, as shown in Figure 3-52. The error message states the following: "Value of '256' is not valid for 'red'. 'red' should be greater than or equal to 0 and less than or equal to 255."

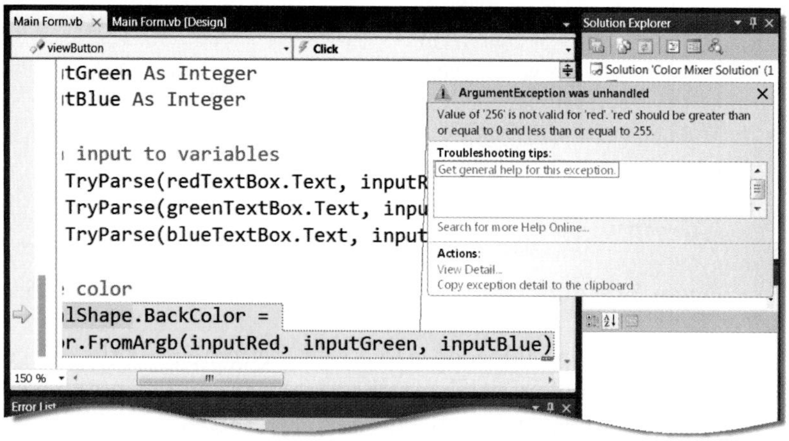

Figure 3-52 Result of entering 256 in the Red text box

4. Click **Debug** on the menu bar and then click **Stop Debugging**. In Chapter 4, you will learn how to prevent the application from ending abruptly with an error when the user enters an invalid RGB value.

5. Start the application again. On your own, test the application using different RGB values. However, be sure to use numbers from 0 through 255 only.

6. Click the **Exit** button to end the application. Close the Code Editor window and then close the solution. Figure 3-53 shows the Color Mixer application's code.

```
' Project name:         Color Mixer Project
' Project purpose:      Display the color associated with
'                       the values entered by the user
' Created/revised by:   <your name> on <current date>

Option Explicit On
Option Infer Off
Option Strict On

Public Class MainForm

    Private Sub exitButton_Click(ByVal sender As Object,
    ByVal e As System.EventArgs) Handles exitButton.Click
        Me.Close()

    End Sub

    Private Sub viewButton_Click(ByVal sender As Object,
    ByVal e As System.EventArgs) Handles viewButton.Click
        ' change the oval's color

        ' declare variables
        Dim inputRed As Integer
        Dim inputGreen As Integer
        Dim inputBlue As Integer

        ' assign input to variables
        Integer.TryParse(redTextBox.Text, inputRed)
        Integer.TryParse(greenTextBox.Text, inputGreen)
        Integer.TryParse(blueTextBox.Text, inputBlue)

        ' change color
        colorOvalShape.BackColor =
            Color.FromArgb(inputRed, inputGreen, inputBlue)

    End Sub
End Class
```

Figure 3-53 Color Mixer application's code

PROGRAMMING TUTORIAL 2

Coding the Vans & More Depot Application

In this tutorial, you create an application for the Vans & More Depot, which rents vans for company outings. Each van can transport 10 people. The application's interface should allow the user to enter the number of people attending the outing. The application should calculate and display both the number of vans that can be filled completely and the number of people who will need to arrange for their own transportation. The application's TOE chart and MainForm are shown in Figures 3-54 and 3-55, respectively. The MainForm contains five labels, one text box, and two buttons.

Task	Object	Event
Get and display the number of attendees	attendeesTextBox	None
1. Calculate the number of filled vans 2. Calculate the number of people remaining 3. Display the calculated results in the vansLabel and remainingLabel 4. Send the focus to the attendeesTextBox	calcButton	Click
End the application	exitButton	Click
Display the number of filled vans (from calcButton)	vansLabel	None
Display the number of people remaining (from calcButton)	remainingLabel	None

Figure 3-54 TOE chart for the Vans & More Depot application

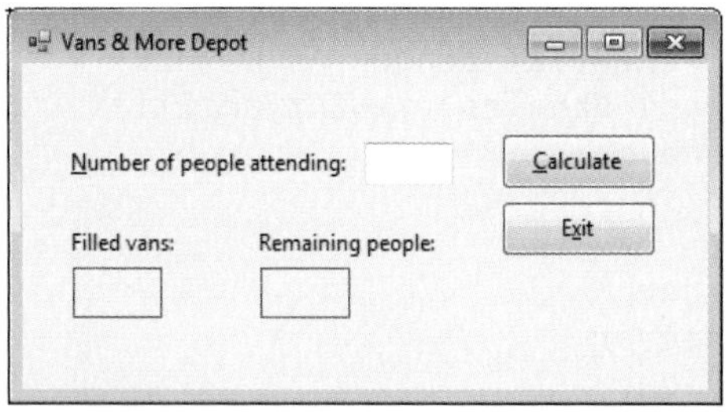

Figure 3-55 MainForm for the Vans & More Depot application

Opening the Vans & More Depot Solution

Included in the data files for this book is a partially completed Vans & More Depot application. To complete the application, you just need to code it.

To open the Vans & More Depot solution:

1. Start Visual Studio or the Express Edition of Visual Basic. If necessary, open the Solution Explorer window.
2. Open the **Vans Solution (Vans Solution.sln)** file, which is contained in the VbReloaded2010\Chap03\Vans Solution folder. If necessary, open the designer window. The MainForm shown earlier in Figure 3-55 appears on the screen.

Including Comments and the Option Statements in the General Declarations Section

In the General Declarations section of the Code Editor window, you will enter comments that document the project's name and purpose, the programmer's name, and the date the program was either created or revised.

To include comments in the General Declarations section:

1. Auto-hide the Solution Explorer window and then open the Code Editor window.
2. Enter the comments shown in Figure 3-56 and then position the insertion point as shown in the figure. Be sure to replace <your name> and <current date> with your name and the current date, respectively.

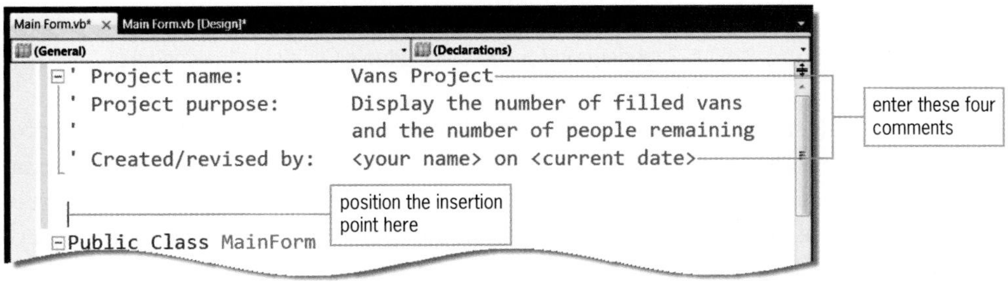

Figure 3-56 Comments entered in the General Declarations section

The application will use variables, so the General Declarations section should also contain the three Option statements you learned in the chapter.

To include the Option statements in the General Declarations section:

1. Enter the three Option statements you learned in the chapter. (If you need help, you can look ahead to Figure 3-62.)
2. Save the solution.

Coding the Exit and Calculate Buttons

According to the application's TOE chart (shown earlier in Figure 3-54), the Exit button should end the application when it is clicked.

To code the Exit button's Click event procedure:

1. Open the code template for the exitButton's Click event procedure.
2. Enter the instruction to end the application.

The application's TOE chart indicates that the Calculate button's Click event procedure is responsible for calculating and displaying both the number of filled vans and the number of people remaining. The procedure's pseudocode is shown in Figure 3-57. Notice the calculation tasks in Steps 2 and 3. To calculate the number of filled vans, you divide the number of attendees by the maximum number of people that a van can transport (in this case, 10). Because you are interested only in the integer result of the division, you will use the integer division operator rather than the standard division operator. Using the integer division operator, the quotient will be 4 when the number of attendees is 48; it would be 4.8 if you used the standard division operator. You can use the Mod operator to calculate the number of people remaining. The Mod operator will return the remainder after dividing the number of attendees by the maximum number of people that a van can transport.

<u>calcButton Click event procedure</u> 1. assign the number of attendees entered in the text box to an Integer variable 2. number of filled vans = number of attendees \ maximum number of people that a van can transport 3. number of people remaining = number of attendees Mod maximum number of people that a van can transport 4. display number of filled vans and number of people remaining in vansLabel and remainingLabel 5. send the focus to the attendeesTextBox

Figure 3-57 Pseudocode for the calcButton's Click event procedure

Recall that before you begin coding a procedure, you first study the procedure's pseudocode (or flowchart) to determine any variables or named constants the procedure will require. In this case, the calcButton's Click event procedure will use one named constant to store the maximum number of people that a van can transport: 10. It also will use three Integer variables to store the number of attendees, the number of filled vans, and the number of people remaining. The named constant and variables are listed in Figure 3-58.

Named constant	**Data type**	**Value**
`MaxInVan`	Integer	10
Variables	**Data type**	**Value source**
`attendees`	Integer	user input (attendeesTextBox)
`vans`	Integer	procedure calculation
`remaining`	Integer	procedure calculation

Figure 3-58 Named constant and variables for the calcButton's Click event procedure

To code the Calculate button's Click event procedure:

1. Open the code template for the calcButton's Click event procedure.
2. Enter the comments shown in Figure 3-59 and then position the insertion point as shown in the figure.

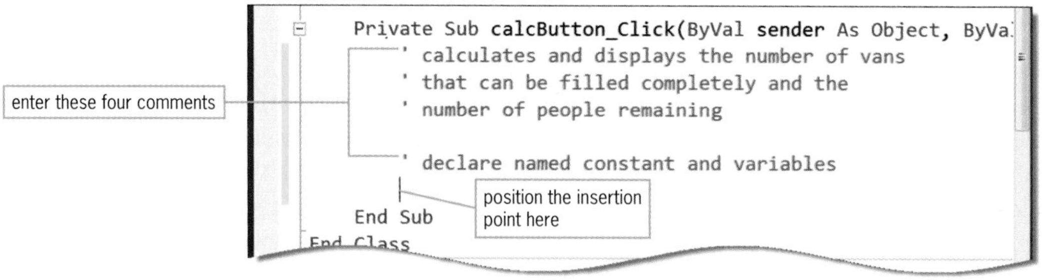

Figure 3-59 Comments entered in the calcButton's Click event procedure

3. Enter the statement to declare an Integer named constant whose value is 10. Name the constant `MaxInVan`.
4. Enter the statements to declare three Integer variables named `attendees`, `vans`, and `remaining`. Press **Enter** twice after typing the last declaration statement.

5. The first step in the pseudocode shown earlier in Figure 3-57 is to assign the number of attendees to a variable. Type **' store user input in a variable** and press **Enter**. Now, enter a TryParse method that converts the contents of the attendeesTextBox to Integer and then stores the result in the `attendees` variable. Press **Enter** twice after typing the TryParse method.
6. The second step in the pseudocode is to calculate the number of filled vans. Type **' make calculations** and press **Enter**. As the pseudocode indicates, you calculate the number of filled vans using the integer division operator to divide the number of attendees by the maximum number of people that a van can transport. The result should be assigned to the `vans` variable. Enter the appropriate assignment statement.
7. Step 3 in the pseudocode is to calculate the number of people remaining. You do this using the Mod operator to divide the number of attendees by the maximum number of people that a van can transport. Type the appropriate assignment statement and then press **Enter** twice.
8. Step 4 in the pseudocode is to display the number of filled vans and number of people remaining in the vansLabel and remainingLabel controls, respectively. Type **' display output** and press **Enter**, and then enter the appropriate assignment statements. Press **Enter** twice after typing the last assignment statement.
9. The last step in the pseudocode is to send the focus to the attendeesTextBox. Enter the appropriate statement.
10. Save the solution.

Testing and Debugging the Application

After coding an application, you then test it to verify that the code works correctly. Recall that you should use both valid and invalid test data.

To test the application using both valid and invalid data:

1. Start the application. Type **48** in the Number of people attending text box and then click the **Calculate** button. The interface indicates that 4 vans can be filled completely, and 8 people will need to arrange for their own transportation. See Figure 3-60.

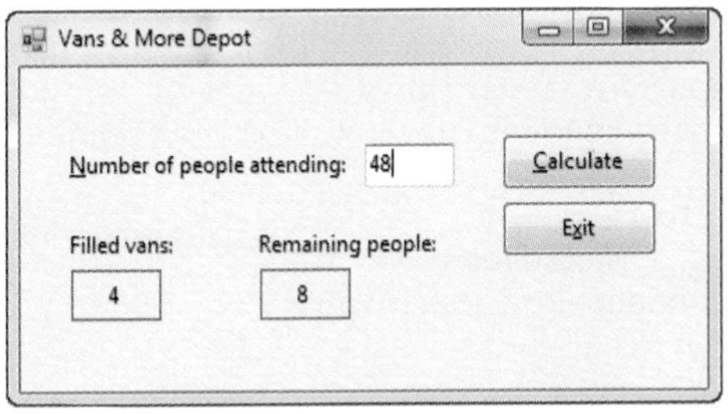

Figure 3-60 Result of testing the application using valid data

2. Now, you will test the application using invalid data. Change the contents of the text box to **4$a** and then click the **Calculate** button. The number 0 appears in the label controls, as shown in Figure 3-61.

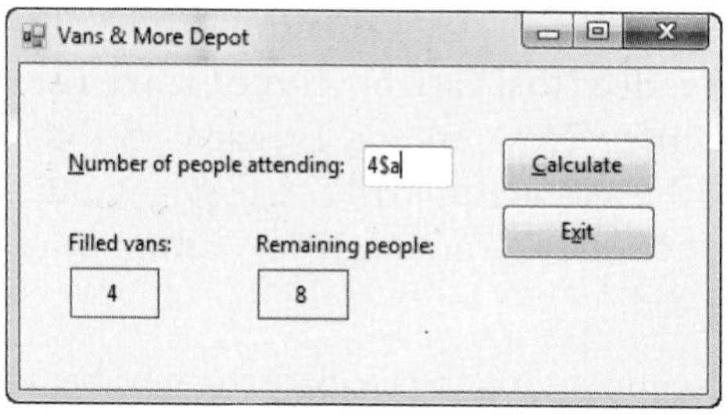

Figure 3-61 Result of testing the application using invalid data

3. Click the **Exit** button to end the application. Close the Code Editor window and then close the solution. Figure 3-62 shows the Vans & More Depot application's code. (In Lines 36 and 37, you can use the Convert class's ToString method rather than the Integer data type's ToString method, like this: `Convert.ToString(vans)` and `Convert.ToString(remaining)`.)

```
 1 ' Project name:          Vans Project
 2 ' Project purpose:       Display the number of filled vans
 3 '                        and the number of people remaining
 4 ' Created/revised by:    <your name> on <current date>
 5
 6 Option Explicit On
 7 Option Infer Off
 8 Option Strict On
 9
10 Public Class MainForm
11
12     Private Sub exitButton_Click(ByVal sender As Object,
       ByVal e As System.EventArgs) Handles exitButton.Click
13         Me.Close()
14
15     End Sub
16
17     Private Sub calcButton_Click(ByVal sender As Object,
       ByVal e As System.EventArgs) Handles calcButton.Click
18         ' calculates and displays the number of vans
19         ' that can be filled completely and the
20         ' number of people remaining
21
22         ' declare named constant and variables
23         Const MaxInVan As Integer = 10
24         Dim attendees As Integer
25         Dim vans As Integer
26         Dim remaining As Integer
27
28         ' store user input in a variable
29         Integer.TryParse(attendeesTextBox.Text, attendees)
30
31         ' make calculations
32         vans = attendees \ MaxInVan
33         remaining = attendees Mod MaxInVan
34
35         ' display output
36         vansLabel.Text = vans.ToString()
37         remainingLabel.Text = remaining.ToString()
38
39         attendeesTextBox.Focus()
40
41     End Sub
42 End Class
```

Figure 3-62 Vans & More Depot application's code

PROGRAMMING EXAMPLE

Completing the Moonbucks Coffee Application

In this Programming Example, you will complete the Moonbucks Coffee application from Chapter 2's Programming Example. The application's TOE chart and user interface are shown in Figures 2-56 and 2-57, respectively, in Chapter 2. According to the TOE chart, the Click event procedures for the four button controls need to be coded. You coded the printButton and exitButton controls' Click event procedures in Chapter 2. You will code the Click event procedures for the remaining two buttons in this chapter. The pseudocode for both procedures is shown in Figure 3-63. Figure 3-64 lists the named constant and variables used in the calcButton's Click event procedure. (Moonbucks charges $11.15 for a pound of coffee.) Open the Moonbucks Solution (Moonbucks Solution.sln) file contained in the VbReloaded2010\Chap03\Moonbucks Solution folder. Open the designer window (if necessary) and then open the Code Editor window. In the General Declarations section, enter the comments and Option statements shown in Figure 3-65. Also enter the appropriate code in the Click event procedures for the clearButton and calcButton. Save the solution and then start and test the application. Figure 3-66 shows a sample run of the application.

```
clearButton Click event procedure
1. clear the Text property of the 7 text boxes
2. clear the Text property of the totalPoundsLabel and totalPriceLabel
3. send the focus to the nameTextBox

calcButton Click event procedure
1. assign number of regular pounds ordered and number of decaffeinated pounds
   ordered to variables
2. total pounds ordered = regular pounds ordered + decaffeinated pounds ordered
3. total price = total pounds ordered * price per pound
4. display total pounds ordered and total price in totalPoundsLabel and totalPriceLabel
5. send the focus to the clearButton
```

Figure 3-63 Pseudocode

Named constant	**Data type**	**Value**
`PricePerPound`	Double	11.15
Variables	**Data type**	**Value source**
`regularCoffee`	Integer	user input (regularTextBox)
`decafCoffee`	Integer	user input (decafTextBox)
`totalPounds`	Integer	procedure calculation
`totalPrice`	Double	procedure calculation

Figure 3-64 Named constant and variables for the calcButton's Click event procedure

```
' Project name:          Moonbucks Project
' Project purpose:       Calculates the total pounds of coffee
'                        ordered and the total price
' Created/revised by:    <your name> on <current date>

Option Explicit On
Option Strict On
Option Infer Off

Public Class MainForm

   Private Sub exitButton_Click(ByVal sender As Object,
   ByVal e As System.EventArgs) Handles exitButton.Click
        Me.Close()

   End Sub

   Private Sub printButton_Click(ByVal sender As Object,
   ByVal e As System.EventArgs) Handles printButton.Click
        PrintForm1.PrintAction =
             Printing.PrintAction.PrintToPreview
        PrintForm1.Print()

   End Sub

   Private Sub clearButton_Click(ByVal sender As Object,
   ByVal e As System.EventArgs) Handles clearButton.Click
        ' prepares the screen for the next order

        nameTextBox.Text = String.Empty
        addressTextBox.Text = String.Empty
        cityTextBox.Text = String.Empty
        stateTextBox.Text = String.Empty
        zipTextBox.Text = String.Empty
        regularTextBox.Text = String.Empty
        decafTextBox.Text = String.Empty
        totalPoundsLabel.Text = String.Empty
        totalPriceLabel.Text = String.Empty
        nameTextBox.Focus()

   End Sub

   Private Sub calcButton_Click(ByVal sender As Object,
   ByVal e As System.EventArgs) Handles calcButton.Click
        ' calculates total pounds ordered and total price

        ' declare constant and variables
        Const PricePerPound As Double = 11.15
        Dim regularCoffee As Integer
        Dim decafCoffee As Integer
        Dim totalPounds As Integer
        Dim totalPrice As Double

        ' assign input to variables
        Integer.TryParse(regularTextBox.Text, regularCoffee)
        Integer.TryParse(decafTextBox.Text, decafCoffee)

```

Figure 3-65 Moonbucks Coffee application's code *(continues)*

(continued)

```
        ' perform calculations
        totalPounds = regularCoffee + decafCoffee
        totalPrice = totalPounds * PricePerPound

        ' display calculated results
        totalPoundsLabel.Text = Convert.ToString(totalPounds)
        totalPriceLabel.Text = totalPrice.ToString("C2")

        clearButton.Focus()

    End Sub
End Class
```

Figure 3-65 Moonbucks Coffee application's code

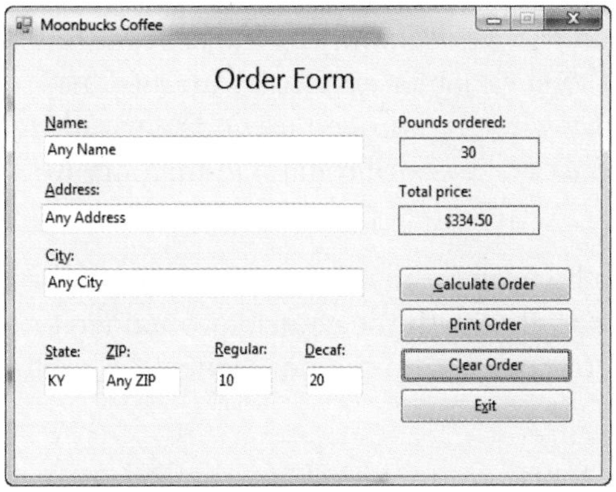

Figure 3-66 Sample run of the Moonbucks Coffee application

Summary

- Each memory location in the computer's internal memory has a unique numeric address, and each can store only one item at a time.
- Variables and named constants are computer memory locations that the programmer uses to store data while an application is running. During run time, the contents of a variable can change, whereas the contents of a named constant cannot change.
- All variables and named constants have a name, data type, initial value, scope, and lifetime.
- The name assigned to a memory location (variable or named constant) should describe the memory location's contents.
- You use a declaration statement to declare a variable. A variable declared in a procedure has procedure scope, and its declaration statement begins with either the keyword `Dim` or the keyword `Static`. A variable declared in a form's Declarations section has class scope, and its declaration statement begins with the keyword `Private`.

- You can use an assignment statement to assign a value to an existing variable during run time. The data type of the value should be the same as the data type of the variable.
- Unlike variables and named constants, which are computer memory locations, a literal constant is an item of data. The value of a literal constant does not change during run time.
- String literal constants are enclosed in quotation marks ("").
- You can use the TryParse method to convert a string to a number.
- The Convert class contains methods that convert values to a specified data type.
- When an arithmetic expression contains the name of a memory location (variable or named constant), the computer uses the value stored inside the memory location to evaluate the expression.
- A procedure-level memory location can be used only by the procedure in which it is declared. Procedure-level variables declared with the `Dim` keyword are removed from memory when the procedure ends. Procedure-level variables declared with the `Static` keyword remain in memory until the application ends.
- A class-level memory location can be used by all of the procedures in the form, including the procedures associated with the controls contained on the form. Class-level variables are removed from memory when the application ends.
- It is a good programming practice to use comments to internally document your application's code. Comments begin with an apostrophe.
- You use the Const statement to declare a named constant.
- The `Option Explicit On` statement tells the Code Editor to warn you if your code contains the name of an undeclared variable.
- The `Option Infer Off` statement tells the Code Editor to warn you if you fail to include a data type when declaring a variable or named constant.
- The `Option Strict On` statement tells the computer not to perform any implicit type conversions that may lead to a loss of data.
- Programmers commonly use either pseudocode (short phrases) or a flowchart (standardized symbols) when planning a procedure's code.
- While an application is running, you can remove the contents of a text box or label by assigning either the empty string ("") or the `String.Empty` value to the control's Text property.
- You can use the Focus method to move the focus to a control during run time.
- After coding an application, you should test the application, using both valid and invalid data, to verify that the code works correctly.
- You can use the ToString method to format an application's numeric output so that it displays special characters (such as dollar signs and percent signs) and a specified number of decimal places.

To set the Option statements for an entire project, open the project, right-click My Project in the Solution Explorer window, click Open, and then click the Compile tab. To set the Option statements for all new projects, click Tools on the Visual Studio menu bar, click Options, expand the Project and Solutions node, and then click VB Defaults.

Key Terms

Arithmetic assignment operators—composed of an arithmetic operator followed by the assignment operator; used to abbreviate an assignment statement that has the following format, in which *variableName* is the name of the same variable: *variableName = variableName arithmeticOperator value*

Class scope—the scope of a class-level variable; refers to the fact that the variable can be used by any procedure in the form

Class-level variable—a variable declared in the form's Declarations section; the variable has class scope

Comments—used to document a program internally; created by placing an apostrophe (') before the text you want to treat as a comment

Const statement—the statement used to create a named constant

Convert class—contains methods that return the result of converting a value to a specified data type

Data type—indicates the type of data a memory location (variable or named constant) can store

Demoted—the process of converting a value from one data type to another data type that can store only smaller numbers or numbers with less precision

Empty string—a set of quotation marks with nothing between them (""); also called a zero-length string

Flowchart—a planning tool that uses standardized symbols to show the steps a procedure must take to accomplish its goal

Flowlines—the lines connecting the symbols in a flowchart

Focus method—used to move the focus to a control during run time

Formatting—specifying the number of decimal places and the special characters to display in a number

FromArgb method—a member of the Color class; used to assign RGB values

Implicit type conversion—the process by which a value is automatically converted to fit the memory location to which it is assigned

Input/output symbol—the parallelogram in a flowchart; used to represent input and output tasks

Integer division operator—represented by a backslash (\); divides two integers and then returns the quotient as an integer

Integers—whole numbers; positive or negative numbers without any decimal places

Invalid data—data that an application is not expecting the user to enter

Lifetime—indicates how long a variable or named constant remains in the computer's internal memory

Literal constant—an item of data whose value does not change during run time

Literal type character—a character (such as the letter D) appended to a literal constant for the purpose of forcing the literal constant to assume a different data type (such as Decimal)

Logic error—occurs when you neglect to enter an instruction or enter the instructions in the wrong order; also occurs as a result of calculation statements that are correct syntactically but incorrect mathematically

Modulus operator—represented by the keyword `Mod`; divides two numbers and then returns the remainder of the division

Named constant—a computer memory location whose contents cannot be changed during run time; created using the Const statement

Procedure scope—the scope of a procedure-level variable; refers to the fact that the variable can be used only by the procedure in which it is declared

Procedure-level variable—a variable declared in a procedure; the variable has procedure scope

Process symbol—the rectangle symbol in a flowchart; used to represent assignment and calculation tasks

Promoted—the process of converting a value from one data type to another data type that can store either larger numbers or numbers with greater precision

Pseudocode—a planning tool that uses phrases to describe the steps a procedure must take to accomplish its goal

Real numbers—numbers that contain a decimal place

Scope—indicates where a memory location (variable or named constant) can be used in the application's code

Start/stop symbol—the oval symbol in a flowchart; used to indicate the beginning and end of the flowchart

Static variable—a procedure-level variable that remains in memory, and also retains its value, until the application (rather than the procedure) ends

String.Empty—the value that represents the empty string in Visual Basic

ToString method—formats a number stored in a numeric variable and then returns the result as a string

TryParse method—used to convert a string to a number

Unicode—the universal coding scheme that assigns a unique numeric value to each character used in the written languages of the world

Valid data—data that an application is expecting the user to enter

Variables—computer memory locations where programmers can temporarily store data, as well as change the data, while an application is running

Zero-length string—a set of quotation marks with nothing between them (""); also called an empty string

Review Questions

1. Every variable and named constant has ______________.
   a. a data type
   b. a lifetime
   c. a scope
   d. all of the above
2. Which of the following statements stores the string contained in the `inputValue` variable in a Double variable named `number`?
   a. `Double.TryParse(number, inputValue)`
   b. `Double.TryParse(inputValue, number)`
   c. `number = Double.TryParse(inputValue)`
   d. `number = TryParse.Double(inputValue)`
3. What will be assigned to the Integer `answer` variable when the `answer = 45 Mod 6` statement is processed?
   a. 3
   b. 7
   c. 7.5
   d. none of the above
4. Static variables can be declared in ______________.
   a. the form's Declarations section
   b. the General Declarations section
   c. a procedure
   d. all of the above
5. Which of the following is a valid variable name?
   a. `income.94`
   b. `inc_94`
   c. `income$Tax`
   d. all of the above
6. A ______________ is a data item whose value does not change during run time.
   a. literal constant
   b. literal variable
   c. named constant
   d. variable

7. Which of the following assigns the sum of two Integer variables (named `score1` and `score2`) to the Text property of the answerTextBox? (The application contains the `Option Strict On` statement.)
   a. `answerTextBox.Text = Convert.ToString(score1) + Convert.ToString(score2)`
   b. `answerTextBox.Text = Convert.ToString(score1 + score2)`
   c. `answerTextBox.Text = score1 + score2`
   d. all of the above

8. Which of the following declares a Decimal named constant? (The application contains the `Option Strict On` statement.)
   a. `Const Rate As Decimal = .09`
   b. `Const Rate As Decimal = Convert.ToDecimal(.09)`
   c. `Const Rate As Decimal = .09D`
   d. both b and c

9. Which of the following statements adds the number 5 to the contents of the `order` variable?
   a. `order += 5`
   b. `order =+ 5`
   c. `5 += order`
   d. both a and c

10. Which of the following sends the focus to the numberTextBox?
    a. `numberTextBox.Focus()`
    b. `numberTextBox.SendFocus()`
    c. `numberTextBox.SetFocus()`
    d. `SetFocus(numberTextBox)`

Exercises

Pencil and Paper

INTRODUCTORY

1. A procedure needs to store an inventory item's name, height, and weight. The height may have a decimal place. The weight will be whole numbers only. Write the Dim statements to create the necessary procedure-level variables.

INTRODUCTORY

2. Write an assignment statement that adds the contents of the `sales1` variable to the contents of the `sales2` variable and then assigns the sum to an existing variable named `totalSales`. All of the variables have the Decimal data type.

3. Write the statement to declare a procedure-level named constant named `TaxRate` whose value is .2. The named constant should have the Double data type. INTRODUCTORY

4. Write the statement to store the contents of the unitsTextBox in an Integer variable named `numberOfUnits`. INTRODUCTORY

5. Write the statement to assign the contents of an Integer variable named `numberOfUnits` to the unitsLabel. INTRODUCTORY

6. Write the statement to declare a class-level named constant named `BonusRate` whose value is .05. The named constant should have the Decimal data type. INTERMEDIATE

7. Write the statement to declare a String variable that can be used by two procedures in the same form. Name the variable `employeeName`. Also specify where you will need to enter the statement and whether the variable is a procedure-level or class-level variable. INTERMEDIATE

8. Write the statement to assign to the payLabel the value stored in a Decimal variable named `grossPay`. The value should be displayed with a dollar sign and two decimal places. INTERMEDIATE

9. Write the statement to add together the contents of two Decimal variables named `westSales` and `eastSales` and then assign the sum to a String variable named `totalSales`. ADVANCED

10. Write two versions of an assignment statement that multiplies the contents of the `salary` variable by the number 1.5 and then assigns the result to the `salary` variable. The `salary` variable has the Decimal data type. Use the standard multiplication and assignment operators in one of the statements. Use the appropriate arithmetic assignment operator in the other statement. ADVANCED

Computer

11. If necessary, complete the Moonbucks Coffee application from this chapter's Programming Example, and then close the solution. Use Windows to make a copy of the Moonbucks Solution folder. Rename the folder Moonbucks Solution-Modified. MODIFY THIS
    a. Open the Moonbucks Solution (Moonbucks Solution.sln) file contained in the VbReloaded2010\Chap03\Moonbucks Solution-Modified folder.
    b. Modify the application so that it adds a 2% sales tax and a $5 shipping charge to the total price. (Don't charge sales tax on the shipping.)
    c. Save the solution and then start and test the application. (If the customer orders a total of 15 pounds of coffee, the total price should be $175.60.) Close the solution.

MODIFY THIS

12. Open the Sunshine Cellular Solution (Sunshine Cellular Solution.sln) file contained in the VbReloaded2010\Chap03\Sunshine Cellular Solution folder. Remove any references to the `subtotal` and `salesTax` variables in the calcButton's Click event procedure. Next, make the appropriate modifications to the statement that calculates the total price. Save the solution and then start and test the application. Close the solution.

MODIFY THIS

13. Open the Static Solution (Static Solution.sln) file contained in the VbReloaded2010\Chap03\Static Solution folder. Start the application. Click the Count button several times. The message indicates the number of times the Count button was clicked. Click the Exit button. Modify the application's code so that it uses a static variable rather than a class-level variable. Save the solution and then start and test the application. Close the solution.

INTRODUCTORY

14. Open the Time Solution (Time Solution.sln) file contained in the VbReloaded2010\Chap03\Time Solution folder. Open the Code Editor window and enter the `Option Explicit On`, `Option Strict On`, and `Option Infer Off` statements. The application should calculate and display the total number of weekday hours and the total number of weekend hours. Write the pseudocode and then code the application. Save the solution and then start and test the application. Close the solution.

INTRODUCTORY

15. Open the Property Tax Solution (Property Tax Solution.sln) file contained in the VbReloaded2010\Chap03\Property Tax Solution folder. Open the Code Editor window and enter the `Option Explicit On`, `Option Strict On`, and `Option Infer Off` statements. The application should calculate the annual property tax. Currently, the property tax rate is $1.02 for each $100 of a property's assessed value. Write the pseudocode and then code the application. Save the solution and then start and test the application. Close the solution.

INTRODUCTORY

16. Colfax Industries needs an application that allows the shipping clerk to enter the quantity of an item in inventory and the quantity that can be packed in a box for shipping. When the shipping clerk clicks a button, the application should compute and display the number of full boxes that can be packed and the number of items left over.

    a. Prepare a TOE chart ordered by object.

    b. Create a Windows application. Use the following names for the solution, project, and form file: Colfax Solution, Colfax Project, and Main Form.vb. Save the application in the VbReloaded2010\Chap03 folder.

    c. Build the interface.

d. Write the pseudocode and then code the application. Be sure to include comments and the Option statements.

e. Save the solution and then start and test the application. Colfax has 45 skateboards in inventory. If six skateboards can fit into a box for shipping, how many full boxes could the company ship, and how many skateboards will remain in inventory?

f. Close the solution.

INTRODUCTORY

17. In this exercise, you create an application that calculates the amount to tip a waiter at a restaurant. The interface should allow the user to enter the amount of the bill. The application should calculate and display a 10% tip, 15% tip, and 20% tip.

a. Prepare a TOE chart ordered by object.

b. Create a Windows application. Use the following names for the solution, project, and form file: Tip Solution, Tip Project, and Main Form.vb. Save the application in the VbReloaded2010\Chap03 folder.

c. Build the interface.

d. Write the pseudocode and then code the application. Be sure to include comments and the Option statements.

e. Save the solution and then start and test the application. Close the solution.

INTERMEDIATE

18. The River Bend Hotel needs an application that calculates a customer's total bill. Each customer pays a room charge that is based on a per-night rate of $55. For example, if the customer stays two nights, the room charge is $110. Customers also may be billed a room service charge and a telephone charge. In addition, each customer pays an entertainment tax, which is 10% of the room charge only. The application's interface should allow the hotel manager to enter the number of nights, the total charge for room service, and the total charge for using the telephone. It should display the room charge, the entertainment tax, and the total bill. The application should allow the manager to send a printout of the interface to the Print preview window.

a. Prepare a TOE chart ordered by object.

b. Create a Windows application. Use the following names for the solution, project, and form file: River Bend Solution, River Bend Project, and Main Form.vb. Save the application in the VbReloaded2010\Chap03 folder.

c. Build the interface.

d. Draw the flowcharts and then code the application.

e. Save the solution and then start and test the application. Close the solution.

INTERMEDIATE

19. If necessary, create the Vans & More Depot application from this chapter's Programming Tutorial 2, and then close the solution. Use Windows to make a copy of the Vans Solution folder. Rename the folder Vans Solution-Modified.

    a. Open the Vans Solution (Vans Solution.sln) file contained in the VbReloaded2010\Chap03\Vans Solution-Modified folder.

    b. In addition to renting vans, Vans & More Depot also rents cars. Each van can transport 10 people, and each car can transport five people. The modified application should calculate and display three values: the number of filled vans, the number of filled cars, and the number of people remaining. Make the appropriate modifications to the interface and code.

    c. Save the solution and then start and test the application. Close the solution.

ADVANCED

20. Create an application that can help students in grades 1 through 6 learn how to make change. Name the solution, project, and form file Change Solution, Change Project, and Main Form.vb, respectively. The interface should allow the student to enter the amount of money a customer owes and the amount of money the customer paid. It also should include a button for clearing the screen. The application should calculate the amount of change, as well as the number of dollars, quarters, dimes, nickels, and pennies to return to the customer. Code the application. Save the solution and then start and test the application. Close the solution.

SWAT THE BUGS

21. Open the Debug Solution (Debug Solution.sln) file contained in the VbReloaded2010\Chap03\Debug Solution folder. Start and then test the application. Locate and then correct any errors. When the application is working correctly, close the solution.

Case Projects

Willow Pools

Create an application that allows the user to enter the length, width, and height of a rectangle. The application should calculate and display the volume of the rectangle. Name the solution, project, and form file Willow Pools Solution, Willow Pools Project, and Main Form.vb, respectively. Save the application in the VbReloaded2010\Chap03 folder. You can create either your own user interface or the one shown in Figure 3-67. Test the application using the following data: the swimming pool at a health club is 100 feet long, 30 feet wide, and 4 feet deep. How many cubic feet of water will the pool contain?

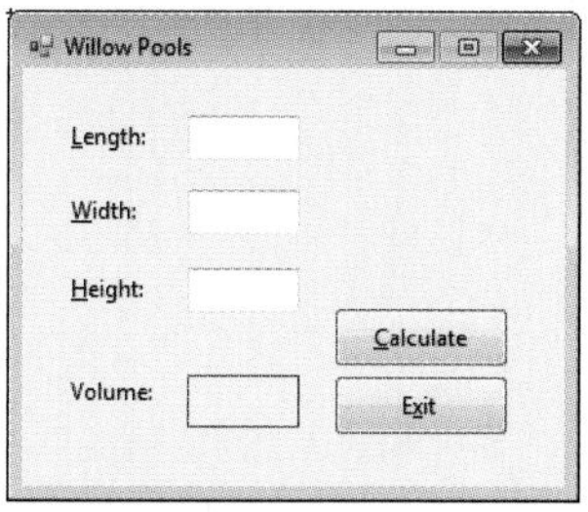

Figure 3-67 Sample interface for the Willow Pools application

Currency Calculator

Create an application that converts American dollars to British pounds, Mexican pesos, Canadian dollars, and Japanese yen. The application should make the appropriate calculations and then display the results (formatted with three decimal places) on the screen. Name the solution, project, and form file Currency Calculator Solution, Currency Calculator Project, and Main Form.vb, respectively. Save the application in the VbReloaded2010\Chap03 folder. You can create either your own user interface or the one shown in Figure 3-68. Use the following conversion rates for one American dollar: 0.670388 British pounds, 12.7525 Mexican pesos, 1.05479 Canadian dollars, and 89.22 Japanese yen.

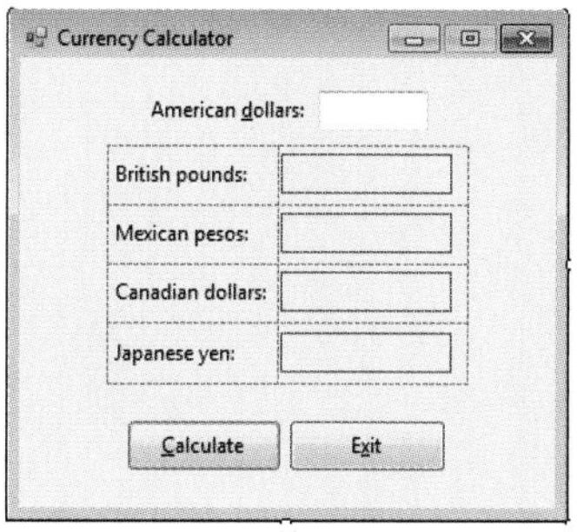

Figure 3-68 Sample interface for the Currency Calculator application

Tile Limited

Create an application that allows the user to enter the length and width (in feet) of a rectangle and the price of a square foot of tile. The application should calculate and display the area of the rectangle and the total price of the tile. Name the solution, project, and form file Tile Limited Solution, Tile Limited Project, and Main Form.vb, respectively. Save the application in the VbReloaded2010\Chap03 folder. You can create either your own user interface or the one shown in Figure 3-69. Test the application using the following data. Susan Caper, one of Tile Limited's customers, is tiling a floor in her home. The floor is 12 feet long and 14 feet wide. The price of a square foot of tile is $1.59. What is the area of the floor and how much will the tile cost?

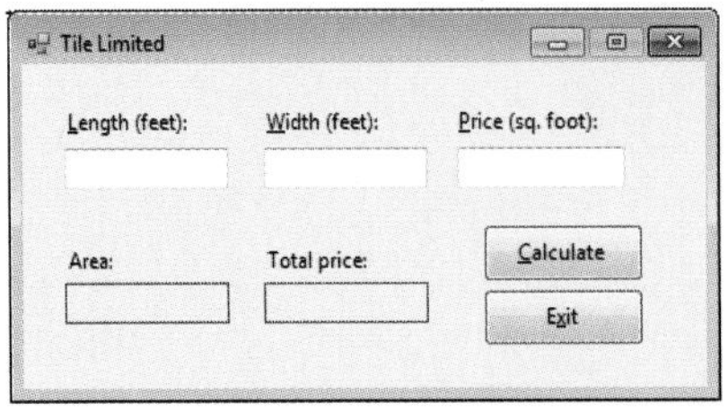

Figure 3-69 Sample interface for the Tile Limited application

Quick Loans

Create an application that allows the user to enter the amount of a loan, the interest rate, and the term of the loan (in years). The application should calculate and display the total amount of interest and the total amount to be repaid. (Hint: Research Visual Basic's Financial.Pmt method.) Name the solution, project, and form file Quick Loans Solution, Quick Loans Project, and Main Form.vb, respectively. Save the application in the VbReloaded2010\Chap03 folder. Test the application using the following data. You visit Quick Loans because you want to borrow $9000 to buy a new car. The loan is for three years at an annual interest rate of 12%. How much will you pay in interest over the three years, and what is the total amount you will repay?

CHAPTER 4

Making Decisions in a Program

After studying Chapter 4, you should be able to:

- Include the selection structure in pseudocode and in a flowchart
- Explain the difference between single-alternative and dual-alternative selection structures
- Code a selection structure using the If...Then...Else statement
- Include comparison and logical operators in a selection structure's condition
- Create a block-level variable
- Concatenate strings
- Use the `ControlChars.NewLine` constant
- Change the case of a string
- Include a check box in an interface
- Generate random numbers

The Selection Structure

All of the procedures in an application are written using one or more of three basic control structures: sequence, selection, and repetition. The procedures in the previous chapters used the sequence structure only. When one of the procedures was invoked during run time, the computer processed its instructions sequentially—in other words, in the order the instructions appeared in the procedure. Every procedure you write will contain the sequence structure. Many times, however, a procedure will need the computer to make a decision before selecting the next instruction to process. A procedure that calculates an employee's gross pay, for example, typically has the computer determine whether the number of hours the employee worked is greater than 40. The computer then would select either an instruction that computes regular pay only or an instruction that computes regular pay plus overtime pay. Procedures that need the computer to make a decision require the use of the selection structure (also called the decision structure). The **selection structure** indicates that a decision (based on some condition) needs to be made, followed by an appropriate action derived from that decision. There are three types of selection structures: single-alternative, dual-alternative, and multiple-alternative. You will learn about single-alternative and dual-alternative selection structures in this chapter. Multiple-alternative selection structures are covered in Chapter 5.

Although the idea of using the selection structure in a procedure is new to you, you already are familiar with the concept of the selection structure because you use it each day to make hundreds of decisions. Figure 4-1 shows examples of selection structures you might use today. The examples are written in pseudocode. Each example contains a **condition** that specifies the decision you are making. The condition must be phrased so that it results in either a true or false answer only. The selection structure in Example 1 is a **single-alternative selection structure**, because it requires a specific set of tasks to be performed only when the condition is true. The tasks to perform when the condition is true are called the **true path**. Example 2 contains a **dual-alternative selection structure**, because it contains one set of tasks to perform when the condition is true, but a different set of tasks to perform when the condition is false. The tasks to perform when the condition is false are called the **false path**. When writing pseudocode, most programmers use the words "if" and "end if" to denote the beginning and end, respectively, of a selection structure, and the word "else" to denote the beginning of the false path. They also indent the instructions within the selection structure, as shown in the figure.

<u>Example 1 – single-alternative selection structure</u>

condition

```
if it is raining
    wear a raincoat
    bring an umbrella
end if
```

true path

Figure 4-1 Selection structures you might use today *(continues)*

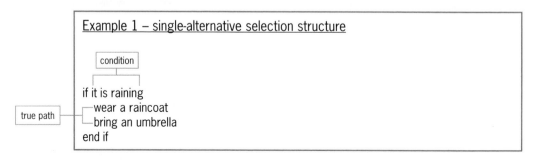

(continued)

Example 2 – dual-alternative selection structure

```
condition

if you have a test tomorrow
        study tonight ——————— true path
else
        watch a movie ——————— false path
end if
```

Figure 4-1 Selection structures you might use today

But how does a programmer determine whether a procedure in an application requires a selection structure? The answer to this question is by studying the problem specification. The first problem specification you will examine in this chapter is for Mountain Biking. The problem specification is shown in Figure 4-2.

> Mountain Biking wants an application that allows the store clerk to enter an item's price and the quantity purchased by a customer. The application should calculate the total amount the customer owes by multiplying the price by the quantity purchased. It then should display the total amount owed.

Figure 4-2 Problem specification for Mountain Biking

Figure 4-3 shows an appropriate interface for the Mountain Biking application, and Figure 4-4 shows the pseudocode for the Calculate button's Click event procedure. The procedure requires only the sequence structure. It does not need a selection structure because no decisions are necessary to calculate and display the total amount owed.

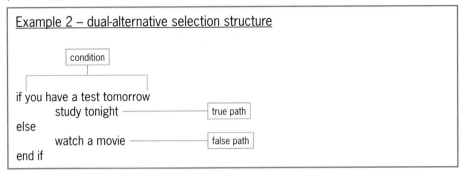

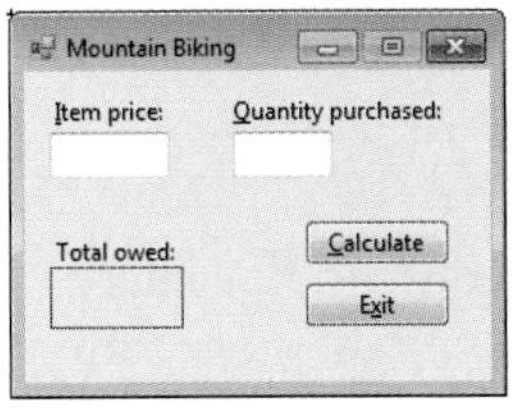

Figure 4-3 Interface for the Mountain Biking application

calcButton Click event procedure
1. store user input (price and quantity purchased) in variables
2. total owed = price * quantity purchased
3. display total owed in totalLabel

Figure 4-4 Pseudocode containing only the sequence structure

Now we'll make a slight change to the problem specification from Figure 4-2. This time, Mountain Biking offers a 10% discount when the quantity purchased is over five. Consider the changes you will need to make to the

Calculate button's original pseudocode, which is shown in Figure 4-4. The first two steps in the original pseudocode are to store the user input in variables and then calculate the total owed by multiplying the price by the quantity purchased. The modified pseudocode will still need both of these steps. Step 3 in the original pseudocode is to display the total owed in the totalLabel. Before the modified procedure can display the total owed, it will need to make a decision regarding the number of items purchased. More specifically, the modified procedure will need to determine whether the quantity purchased is over five; if it is, the modified procedure will need to calculate the discount and then subtract the discount from the total owed. The modified problem specification and pseudocode are shown in Figure 4-5. The pseudocode contains a single-alternative selection structure. In this case, a single-alternative selection structure is appropriate because the procedure needs to perform a special set of actions only when the condition is true, which occurs when the customer purchases more than five of the item.

Mountain Biking wants an application that allows the store clerk to enter an item's price and the quantity purchased by a customer. The application should calculate the total amount the customer owes by multiplying the price by the quantity purchased and then subtracting any discount. It then should display the total amount owed. Mountain Biking gives customers a 10% discount when the quantity purchased is over five.

```
calcButton Click event procedure
1. store user input (price and quantity purchased) in variables
2. total owed = price * quantity purchased
3. if the quantity purchased is over 5
       discount = total owed * .1
       total owed = total owed – discount
   end if
4. display total owed in totalLabel
```

condition (points to: if the quantity purchased is over 5)

true path (points to: discount = total owed * .1 / total owed = total owed – discount)

Figure 4-5 Modified problem specification and pseudocode containing a single-alternative selection structure

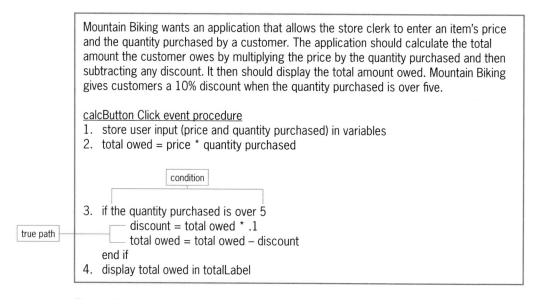

Figure 4-6 shows the Calculate button's Click event procedure in flowchart form. Recall that the oval in a flowchart is the start/stop symbol, the rectangle is the process symbol, and the parallelogram is the input/output symbol. The diamond in a flowchart is called the **decision symbol**, because it is used to represent the condition (decision) in both the selection and repetition structures. The diamond in Figure 4-6 represents the condition in a selection structure. (You will learn how to use the diamond to represent a repetition structure's condition in Chapter 6.) The condition in Figure 4-6's diamond checks whether the customer purchased more than five items. Notice that the condition results in an answer of either true or false only. Also notice that the diamond has one flowline entering it and two flowlines leaving it. One of the flowlines leading out of the diamond in a flowchart should be marked with a T (for true) and the other should be marked with an F (for false). The T flowline points to the next instruction to be processed when the condition is true. In Figure 4-6, the next instruction calculates the 10% discount. The F flowline points to the next instruction to be processed when the condition is false. In Figure 4-6, that instruction displays the total owed. The flowchart in Figure 4-6 illustrates a single-alternative selection structure, because only the true path contains a special set of actions.

You also can mark the flowlines leading out of a diamond with a Y and an N (for yes and no).

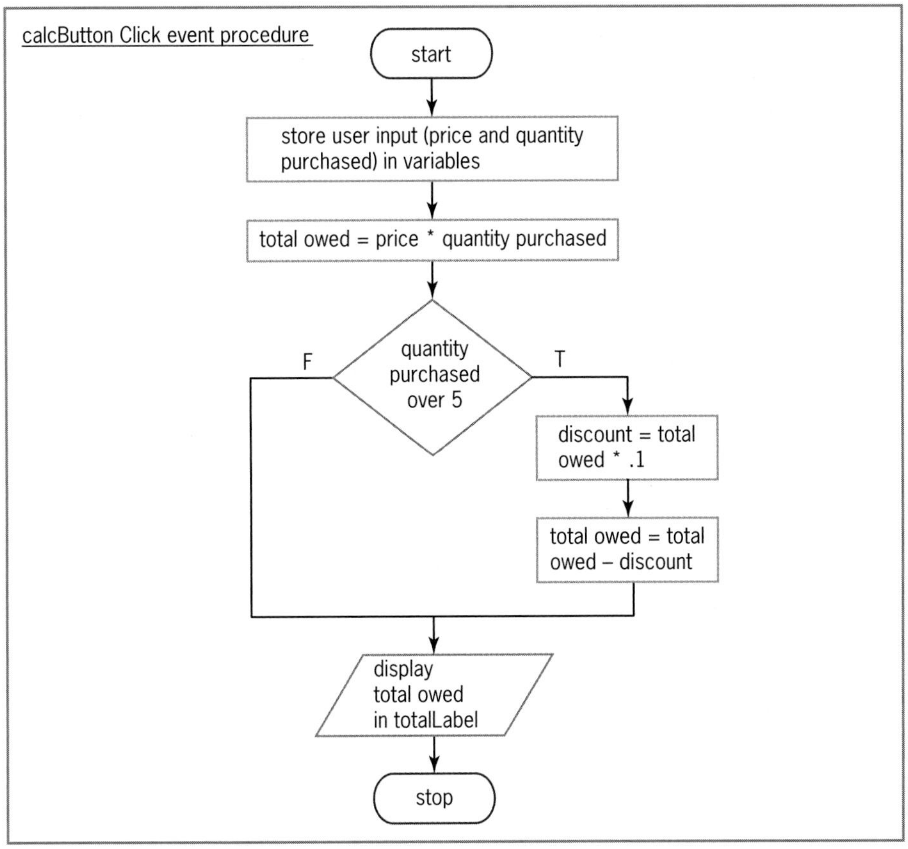

Figure 4-6 Single-alternative selection structure shown in a flowchart

Next, we'll modify the Mountain Biking problem specification one more time. In addition to the 10% discount for purchasing more than five of an item, Mountain Biking is now offering a 5% discount when the quantity purchased is five or less. The modified problem specification and pseudocode are shown in Figure 4-7, and the corresponding flowchart is shown in Figure 4-8. The pseudocode and flowchart contain a dual-alternative selection structure. In this case, a dual-alternative selection structure is appropriate because the procedure needs to perform one action when the condition is true, but a different action when the condition is false. The condition will be true when the customer purchases more than five of the item, and false when the customer purchases five or less of the item.

Mountain Biking wants an application that allows the store clerk to enter an item's price and the quantity purchased by a customer. The application should calculate the total amount the customer owes by multiplying the price by the quantity purchased and then subtracting the discount. It then should display the total amount owed. Mountain Biking gives customers a 10% discount when the quantity purchased is over five; otherwise, it gives a 5% discount.

<u>calcButton Click event procedure</u>

```
1. store user input (price and quantity purchased) in variables
2. total owed = price * quantity purchased
3. if the quantity purchased is over 5          [condition]
        discount rate = .1                      [true path]
   else
        discount rate = .05                     [false path]
   end if
4. discount = total owed * discount rate
5. total owed = total owed – discount
6. display total owed in totalLabel
```

Figure 4-7 Modified problem specification and pseudocode containing a dual-alternative selection structure

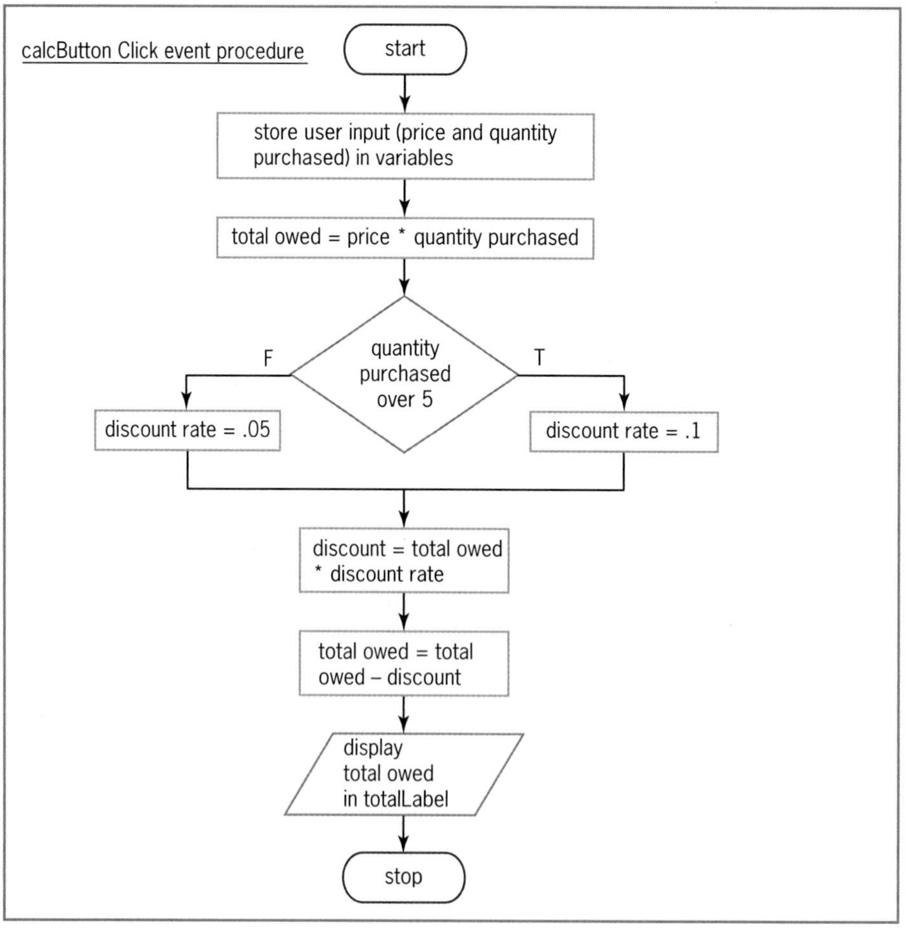

Figure 4-8 Dual-alternative selection structure shown in a flowchart

Mini-Quiz 4-1

The answers to Mini-Quiz questions are located in Appendix A.

1. Every procedure in an application contains the selection structure.
   a. True
   b. False
2. A dual-alternative selection structure contains instructions in ________________.
   a. its true path only
   b. its false path only
   c. both its true and false paths
3. The true path in a single-alternative selection structure can contain only one instruction.
   a. True
   b. False
4. Which of the following is the decision symbol in a flowchart?
   a. diamond
   b. oval
   c. parallelogram
   d. rectangle

Coding Single-Alternative and Dual-Alternative Selection Structures

Visual Basic provides the **If...Then...Else statement** for coding single-alternative and dual-alternative selection structures. The statement's syntax is shown in Figure 4-9. The square brackets in the syntax indicate that the Else portion, referred to as the Else clause, is optional. Boldfaced items in a statement's syntax are required. In this case, the keywords `If`, `Then`, and `End If` are required. The `Else` keyword is necessary only in a dual-alternative selection structure. Italicized items in a statement's syntax indicate where the programmer must supply information. In the If...Then...Else statement, the programmer must supply the *condition* that the computer needs to evaluate before further processing can occur. The condition must be a Boolean expression, which is an expression that results in a Boolean value (either True or False). The condition can contain variables, constants, properties, methods, arithmetic operators, comparison operators, and logical operators. (You will learn about comparison operators and logical operators in this chapter.) Besides providing the condition, the programmer must provide the statements to be processed in the true path and (optionally) in the false path. The set of statements contained in each path is referred to as a **statement block**.

Also included in Figure 4-9 are two examples of using the If...Then...Else statement to code selection structures. Example 1 shows how you use the statement to code the single-alternative selection structure shown earlier in Figures 4-5 and 4-6. Example 2 shows how you use the statement to code the dual-alternative selection structure shown earlier in Figures 4-7 and 4-8.

If you want to experiment with the Mountain Biking application, open the solution contained in the Try It 1! folder.

To review what you learned so far about selection structures, view the Ch04Selection-Structure video.

HOW TO Use the If...Then...Else Statement

Syntax

If *condition* **Then**
statement block to be processed when the condition is true
[Else
statement block to be processed when the condition is false]
End If

Example 1

```
Dim price As Double
Dim quantity As Integer
Dim total As Double
Dim discount As Double
Double.TryParse(priceTextBox.Text, price)
Integer.TryParse(quantityTextBox.Text, quantity)

total = price * quantity
If quantity > 5 Then
     discount = total * .1
     total = total - discount
End If
totalLabel.Text = total.ToString("C2")
```

single-alternative selection structure

Example 2

```
Dim price As Double
Dim quantity As Integer
Dim total As Double
Dim discount As Double
Dim discountRate As Double
Double.TryParse(priceTextBox.Text, price)
Integer.TryParse(quantityTextBox.Text, quantity)

total = price * quantity
If quantity > 5 Then
     discountRate = .1
Else
     discountRate = .05
End If
discount = total * discountRate
total = total - discount
totalLabel.Text = total.ToString("C2")
```

dual-alternative selection structure

Figure 4-9 How to use the If...Then...Else statement

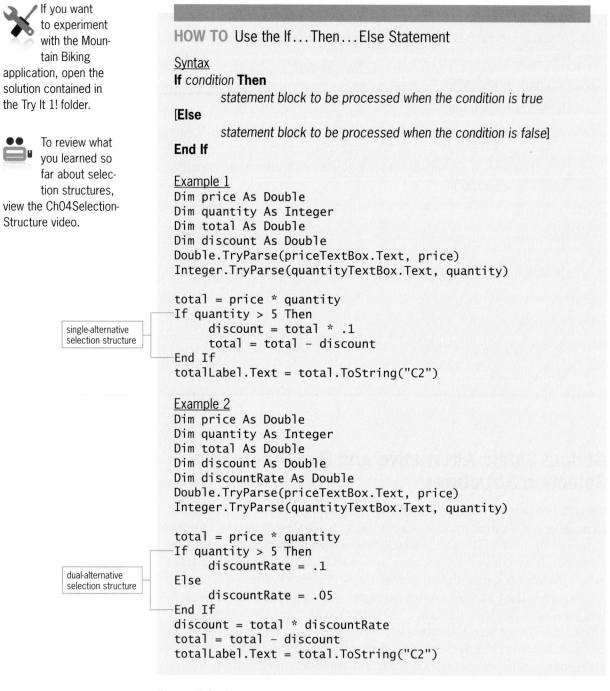

Comparison Operators

As mentioned earlier, the condition in an If...Then...Else statement can contain comparison operators. The operators are called **comparison operators** because they are used to compare two values. The comparison always results in a Boolean value. Figure 4-10 lists the most commonly used comparison operators in Visual Basic and includes examples of using the operators in an If...Then...Else statement's condition.

Comparison operators are also referred to as relational operators.

Keep in mind that = is the opposite of <>, > is the opposite of <=, and < is the opposite of >=.

HOW TO Use Comparison Operators in a Condition

Comparison operator	Operation
=	equal to
>	greater than
>=	greater than or equal to
<	less than
<=	less than or equal to
<>	not equal to

Example 1

```
If northSales = southSales Then
```

The condition evaluates to True when both variables contain the same value; otherwise, it evaluates to False.

Example 2

```
If age >= 21 Then
```

The condition evaluates to True when the `age` variable's value is greater than or equal to 21; otherwise, it evaluates to False.

Example 3

```
If price < 35.99D Then
```

The condition evaluates to True when the value stored in the Decimal `price` variable is less than 35.99; otherwise, it evaluates to False. You also can write the condition as `price < Convert.ToDecimal(35.99)`.

Example 4

```
If state <> "TN" Then
```

The condition evaluates to True when the `state` variable does not contain the string "TN"; otherwise, it evaluates to False.

Figure 4-10 How to use comparison operators in a condition

Unlike arithmetic operators, comparison operators do not have an order of precedence. When an expression contains more than one comparison operator, the computer evaluates the comparison operators from left to right in the expression, similar to what is done with arithmetic operators. Comparison operators are evaluated after any arithmetic operators in an expression. For example, when processing the expression 12 / 2 * 3 < 7 + 4, the computer will evaluate the three arithmetic operators before it evaluates the comparison operator. The result of the expression is the Boolean value False, as shown in Figure 4-11.

Original expression	12 / 2 * 3 < 7 + 4
The division is performed first	6 * 3 < 7 + 4
The multiplication is performed next	18 < 7 + 4
The addition is performed next	18 < 11
The < comparison is performed last	False

Figure 4-11 Evaluation steps for an expression containing arithmetic and comparison operators

Comparing Numeric Values

Figure 4-12 shows a sample run of the Auction House application, which displays the lowest and highest of two bids entered by the user. Figures 4-13 and 4-14 show the pseudocode and flowchart, respectively, for the Display button's Click event procedure. The procedure contains a single-alternative selection structure that determines whether the first bid entered by the user is greater than the second bid, and then takes the appropriate action if it is.

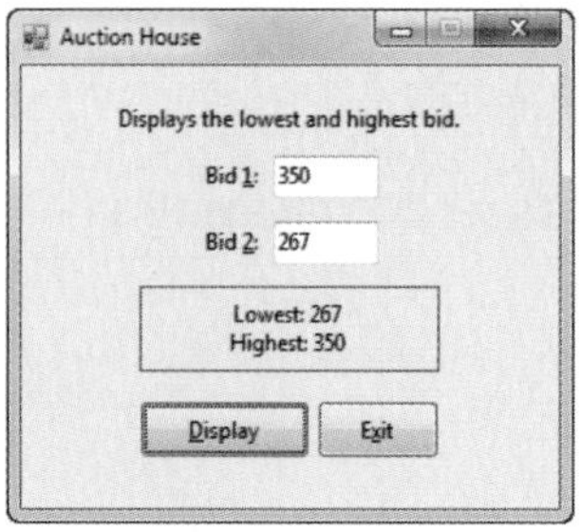

Figure 4-12 Sample run of the Auction House application

```
displayButton Click event procedure
1. store user input (bid 1 and bid 2) in variables
2. if the bid in the first variable is greater than the bid in the second variable
         swap both bids so that the first variable contains the lowest of the two bids
   end if
3. display the lowest bid and the highest bid in the messageLabel
```

Figure 4-13 Pseudocode containing a single-alternative selection structure

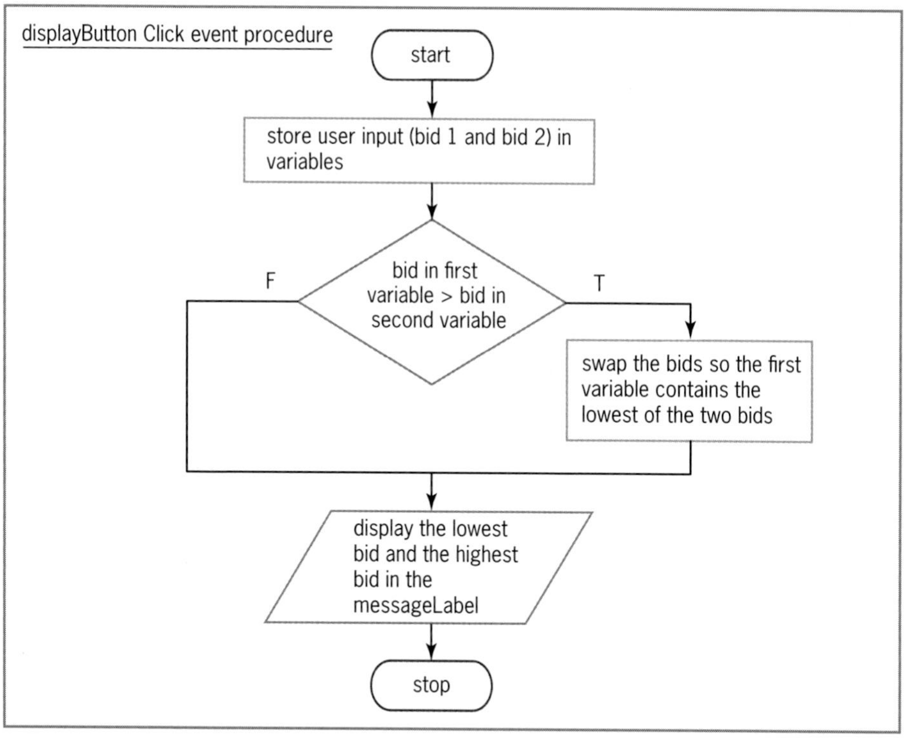

Figure 4-14 Flowchart containing a single-alternative selection structure

Figure 4-15 shows the code entered in the Display button's Click event procedure. The `bid1 > bid2` condition in the If clause compares the contents of the `bid1` variable with the contents of the `bid2` variable. If the value in the `bid1` variable is greater than the value in the `bid2` variable, the condition evaluates to True and the four instructions in the If...Then...Else statement's true path swap both values. Swapping the values places the smaller bid in the `bid1` variable and places the larger bid in the `bid2` variable. If the condition evaluates to False, on the other hand, the instructions in the true path are skipped over because the `bid1` variable already contains a number that is smaller than (or possibly equal to) the number stored in the `bid2` variable.

```
Private Sub displayButton_Click(ByVal sender As Object,
ByVal e As System.EventArgs) Handles displayButton.Click
      ' displays the lowest and highest bid

      Dim bid1 As Integer
      Dim bid2 As Integer

      ' assign input to variables
      Integer.TryParse(bid1TextBox.Text, bid1)
      Integer.TryParse(bid2TextBox.Text, bid2)
```

Figure 4-15 Code entered in the Display button's Click event procedure *(continues)*

(continued)

```
        ' swap bids, if necessary
        If bid1 > bid2 Then
            Dim temp As Integer
            temp = bid1
            bid1 = bid2
            bid2 = temp
        End If

        ' display lowest and highest bid
        messageLabel.Text = "Lowest: " & bid1.ToString() &
            ControlChars.NewLine & "Highest: " & bid2.ToString()

End Sub
```

single-alternative selection structure

comparison operator

Figure 4-15 Code entered in the Display button's Click event procedure

Study closely the instructions used to swap the values stored in the `bid1` and `bid2` variables. The first instruction is a Dim statement that declares a variable named `temp`. Like the variables declared at the beginning of a procedure, variables declared within a statement block—referred to as **block-level variables**—remain in memory until the procedure ends. However, unlike variables declared at the beginning of a procedure, block-level variables have block scope rather than procedure scope. As you know, a variable that has procedure scope can be used anywhere within the procedure. A variable that has **block scope**, however, can be used only within the statement block in which it is declared. More specifically, it can be used only below its declaration statement within the statement block. In this case, the `bid1` and `bid2` variables can be used anywhere within the Display button's Click event procedure, but the `temp` variable can be used only after the `Dim temp As Integer` statement within the If…Then…Else statement's true path. You may be wondering why the `temp` variable is not declared at the beginning of the procedure, along with the other variables. Although there is nothing wrong with declaring all variables at the beginning of a procedure, the `temp` variable is not needed unless a swap is necessary, so there is no reason to create the variable ahead of time. The second instruction in the If…Then…Else statement's true path assigns the value in the `bid1` variable to the `temp` variable. If you do not store the `bid1` variable's value in the `temp` variable, the value will be lost when the computer processes the next statement, `bid1 = bid2`, which replaces the contents of the `bid1` variable with the contents of the `bid2` variable. Finally, the `bid2 = temp` instruction assigns the `temp` variable's value to the `bid2` variable; this completes the swap. Figure 4-16 illustrates the concept of swapping, assuming the user enters the numbers 350 and 267 in the bid1TextBox and bid2TextBox, respectively.

	bid1	bid2	temp
values stored in the variables immediately before the `temp = bid1` statement is processed	350	267	0
result of the `temp = bid1` statement	350	267	350
result of the `bid1 = bid2` statement	267	267	350
result of the `bid2 = temp` statement	267	350	350

the values were swapped

Figure 4-16 Illustration of the swapping concept

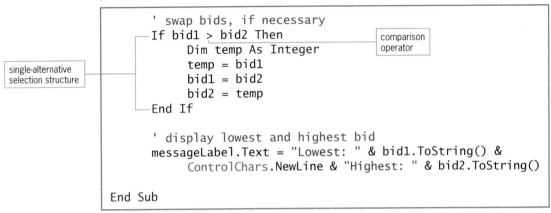

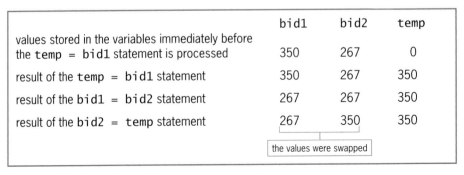

The code shown earlier in Figure 4-15 contains two items that were not covered in the previous three chapters: the concatenation operator (&) and the `ControlChars.NewLine` constant. You use the **concatenation operator** to concatenate (connect or link together) strings. When concatenating strings, you must be sure to include a space before and after the ampersand; otherwise, the Code Editor will not recognize the ampersand as the concatenation operator. Figure 4-17 shows the syntax you use when concatenating strings. It also includes examples of string concatenation.

If you want to practice concatenating strings, open the solution contained in the Try It 2! folder.

HOW TO Concatenate Strings

Syntax
string **&** *string* [**&** *string*...]

Variables	Data type	Contents
`firstName`	String	Jacob
`lastName`	String	Mopenski
`salary`	Integer	56000

Concatenated string	Result
`firstName & lastName`	JacobMopenski
`firstName & " " & lastName`	Jacob Mopenski
`lastName & ", " & firstName`	Mopenski, Jacob
`firstName & " earns " & salary.ToString("C0")`	Jacob earns $56,000

Figure 4-17 How to concatenate strings

The concatenation operator appears four times in the `messageLabel.Text = "Lowest: " & bid1.ToString() & ControlChars.NewLine & "Highest: " & bid2.ToString()` statement. The statement concatenates five strings: the string "Lowest: ", the contents of the `bid1` variable converted to a string, the `ControlChars.NewLine` constant, the string "Highest: ", and the contents of the `bid2` variable converted to a string. The **ControlChars.NewLine constant** advances the insertion point to the next line in the messageLabel and is the reason that the "Highest: 350" text appears on the second line in the label, as shown earlier in Figure 4-12.

If you want to experiment with the Auction House application, open the solution contained in the Try It 3! folder.

Comparing Strings

Figure 4-18 shows a sample run of the Addition and Subtraction Calculator application, which displays either the sum of two numbers entered by the user or the difference between both numbers. Figures 4-19 and 4-20 show the pseudocode and flowchart, respectively, for the Calculate button's Click event procedure. The procedure uses a dual-alternative selection structure to determine the appropriate arithmetic operation to perform.

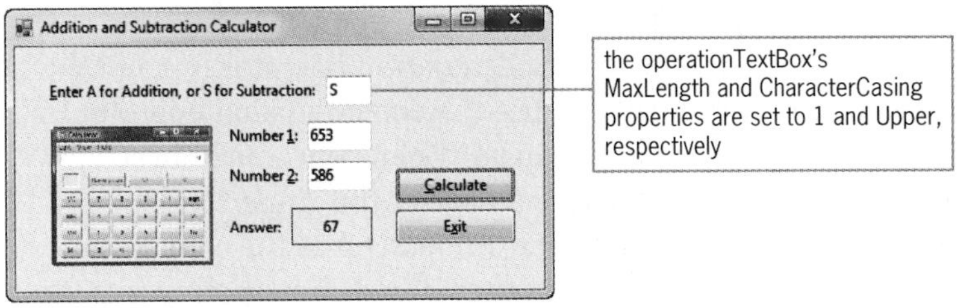

Figure 4-18 Sample run of the Addition and Subtraction Calculator application

calcButton Click event procedure
1. store user input (operation, number 1, and number 2) in variables
2. if the operation is "A"
   answer = number 1 + number 2
   else
   answer = number 1 – number 2
   end if
3. display the answer in the answerLabel

Figure 4-19 Pseudocode containing a dual-alternative selection structure

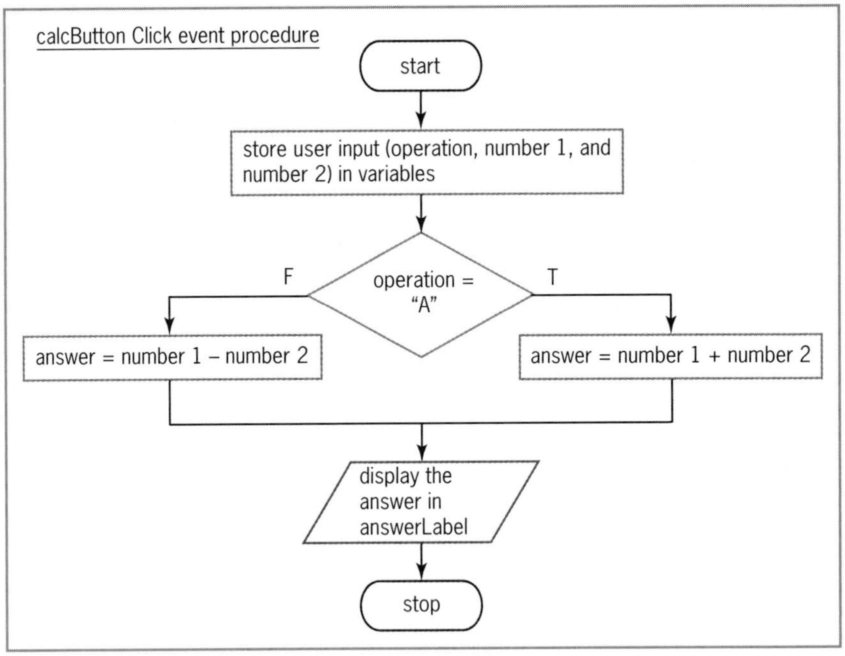

Figure 4-20 Flowchart containing a dual-alternative selection structure

Figure 4-21 shows the code entered in the Calculate button's Click event procedure. The Dim statements in the procedure declare a String variable named `operation` and three Double variables. The next statement (`operation = operationTextBox.Text`) assigns the contents of the operationTextBox's Text property to the `operation` variable. In this case, the Text property contains one uppercase character; this is because the operationTextBox's MaxLength and CharacterCasing properties are set to 1 and Upper, respectively, in the Properties window. A text box's **MaxLength property** specifies the maximum number of characters that the user can enter in the text box, and its **CharacterCasing property** indicates whether the text should remain as typed or be converted to either uppercase or lowercase. The TryParse methods in the procedure convert the contents of both the num1TextBox and num2TextBox to Double, storing the results in the `num1` and `num2` variables, respectively. The condition in the If clause then compares the contents of the `operation` variable with the string "A". In this case, the condition will evaluate to True only when the `operation` variable contains the uppercase letter A. It will evaluate to False when the `operation` variable contains anything other than the uppercase letter A. If the condition evaluates to True, the statement in the selection structure's true path assigns the sum of the numbers entered by the user to the `answer` variable. If the condition evaluates to False, the statement in the selection structure's false path assigns the difference between both numbers to the `answer` variable. When the selection structure ends, the last assignment statement in the procedure displays the contents of the `answer` variable, converted to String, in the answerLabel.

```
Private Sub calcButton_Click(ByVal sender As Object,
ByVal e As System.EventArgs) Handles calcButton.Click
      ' calculates either the sum of or the
      ' difference between two numbers

      Dim operation As String
      Dim num1 As Double
      Dim num2 As Double
      Dim answer As Double

      ' assign operation input to a variable
      operation = operationTextBox.Text

      ' convert number input to Double
      Double.TryParse(num1TextBox.Text, num1)
      Double.TryParse(num2TextBox.Text, num2)

      ' calculate and display the sum or the difference
      If operation = "A" Then
            answer = num1 + num2
      Else
            answer = num1 - num2
      End If
      answerLabel.Text = answer.ToString()
End Sub
```

comparison operator

dual-alternative selection structure

Figure 4-21 Calculate button's Click event procedure

Now assume that, rather than being set to Upper, the operationTextBox's CharacterCasing property is left at its default value, which is Normal. If the user enters an uppercase letter A in the text box, the `operation = operationTextBox.Text` statement assigns an uppercase letter A to the `operation` variable. When the variable contains an uppercase letter A, the selection structure's condition evaluates to True and the statement in its true path calculates the sum of the numbers entered by the user, which is correct. However, if the user enters a lowercase letter a in the text box, the `operation = operationTextBox.Text` statement assigns a lowercase letter a to the `operation` variable. In this case, the selection structure's condition evaluates to False and the statement in its false path calculates the difference between the numbers entered by the user, which is

The uppercase letter A and the lowercase letter a have different Unicode values. Therefore, as far as the computer is concerned, both characters are not the same.

probably not what the user is expecting. The `operation = "A"` condition evaluates to False when the `operation` variable contains a lowercase letter a because string comparisons in Visual Basic are case-sensitive. This means that an uppercase letter is not the same as its lowercase counterpart. Visual Basic provides two methods that you can use to solve the case problems that occur when comparing strings: ToUpper and ToLower.

The ToUpper and ToLower Methods

As already mentioned, string comparisons in Visual Basic are case-sensitive, which means that the string "Yes" is not the same as either the string "YES" or the string "yes". A problem occurs when a comparison needs to include a string that is either entered by the user or read from a file, because you cannot always control the case of the string. Although you can change a text box's CharacterCasing property from its default value of Normal to either Upper (which converts the user's entry to uppercase) or Lower (which converts the user's entry to lowercase), you may not want to change the case of the user's entry as he or she is typing it. And it's entirely possible that you may not be aware of the case of strings that are read from a file. Before using a string in a comparison, you can convert it to either uppercase or lowercase and then use the converted string in the comparison. You use the **ToUpper method** to convert a string to uppercase, and the **ToLower method** to convert a string to lowercase. The ToUpper and ToLower methods affect only characters that represent letters of the alphabet, as these are the only characters that have uppercase and lowercase forms.

Figure 4-22 shows the syntax of the ToUpper and ToLower methods and includes examples of using the methods. In each syntax, *string* typically is either the name of a String variable or the Text property of an object. Both methods temporarily convert the *string* to the specified case. When using the ToUpper method in a comparison, be sure that everything you are comparing is uppercase; otherwise, the comparison will not evaluate correctly. For example, the condition `letter.ToUpper = "p"` is not correct: the condition will always evaluate to False, because the uppercase letter P will never be equal to a lowercase letter p. Likewise, when using the ToLower method in a comparison, be sure that everything you are comparing is lowercase. You also can use the ToUpper and ToLower methods to permanently convert the contents of either a String variable or a control's Text property to uppercase or lowercase, respectively. You do this using an assignment statement, as shown in Example 6 in Figure 4-22.

HOW TO Use the ToUpper and ToLower Methods

Syntax
string.**ToUpper**
string.**ToLower**

Example 1
```
If letter.ToUpper = "P" Then
```
compares the uppercase version of the string stored in the `letter` variable with the uppercase letter P

Figure 4-22 How to use the ToUpper and ToLower methods *(continues)*

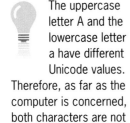

(continued)

Example 2
```
If item1.ToUpper = item2.ToUpper Then
```
compares the uppercase version of the string stored in the `item1` variable with the uppercase version of the string stored in the `item2` variable

Example 3
```
If letter.ToLower > "r" Then
```
compares the lowercase version of the string stored in the `letter` variable with the lowercase letter r

Example 4
```
If "london" = cityTextBox.Text.ToLower Then
```
compares the lowercase string "london" with the lowercase version of the string stored in the cityTextBox's Text property

Example 5
```
nameLabel.Text = customer.ToUpper
```
assigns the uppercase version of the string stored in the `customer` variable to the nameLabel's Text property

Example 6
```
firstName = firstName.ToUpper
stateTextBox.Text = stateTextBox.Text.ToLower
```
changes the contents of the firstName variable to uppercase, and changes the contents of the stateTextBox's Text property to lowercase

Figure 4-22 How to use the ToUpper and ToLower methods

As mentioned earlier, if the CharacterCasing property of the operationTextBox in Figure 4-18 is left at its default value (Normal), the code shown earlier in Figure 4-21 will not work correctly when the user enters a lowercase letter a in the text box. Recall that the code will calculate and display the difference between the two numbers entered by the user, rather than the sum of both numbers. Figure 4-23 shows two examples of using the ToUpper method to fix this problem. In Example 1, the ToUpper method is included in the statement that assigns the text box value to the `operation` variable. After the statement is processed, the variable will contain an uppercase letter (assuming the user entered a letter). In Example 2, the ToUpper method is included in the If...Then...Else statement's condition. The `operation.ToUpper` portion of the condition will change the `operation` variable's value to uppercase only temporarily. After the comparison is made, the variable will still contain its original value. In this instance, neither way is better than the other; both simply represent two different ways of performing the same task.

If you want to experiment with the Addition and Subtraction Calculator application, open the solution contained in the Try It 4! folder.

Example 1

```
Private Sub calcButton_Click(ByVal sender As Object,
ByVal e As System.EventArgs) Handles calcButton.Click
      ' calculates either the sum of or the
      ' difference between two numbers

      Dim operation As String
      Dim num1 As Double
      Dim num2 As Double
      Dim answer As Double

      ' assign operation input to a variable
      operation = operationTextBox.Text.ToUpper

      ' convert number input to Double
      Double.TryParse(num1TextBox.Text, num1)
      Double.TryParse(num2TextBox.Text, num2)

      ' calculate and display the sum or the difference
      If operation = "A" Then
            answer = num1 + num2
      Else
            answer = num1 - num2
      End If
      answerLabel.Text = answer.ToString()
End Sub
```

ToUpper method

Example 2

```
Private Sub calcButton_Click(ByVal sender As Object,
ByVal e As System.EventArgs) Handles calcButton.Click
      ' calculates either the sum of or the
      ' difference between two numbers

      Dim operation As String
      Dim num1 As Double
      Dim num2 As Double
      Dim answer As Double

      ' assign operation input to a variable
      operation = operationTextBox.Text

      ' convert number input to Double
      Double.TryParse(num1TextBox.Text, num1)
      Double.TryParse(num2TextBox.Text, num2)

      ' calculate and display the sum or the difference
      If operation.ToUpper = "A" Then
            answer = num1 + num2
      Else
            answer = num1 - num2
      End If
      answerLabel.Text = answer.ToString()
End Sub
```

ToUpper method

Figure 4-23 Examples of using the ToUpper method in the calcButton Click event procedure

Comparing Boolean Values

Figure 4-24 shows a different interface for the Addition and Subtraction Calculator application. In this interface, the user does not need to enter a letter to indicate the arithmetic operation. Instead, the default operation is addition; however, the interface provides a check box for changing the operation to subtraction. You add a check box to an interface using the CheckBox tool in the toolbox. An interface can contain any number of check boxes, and any number of them can be selected at the same time. **Check boxes** are used to offer the user one or more independent and nonexclusive items from which to choose. Each check box in an interface should be labeled to make its purpose obvious. You enter the label using sentence capitalization in the check box's Text property. Each check box also should have a unique access key. During run time, you can determine whether a check box is selected or unselected by looking at the value in its Checked property. If the property contains the Boolean value True, the check box is selected. If it contains the Boolean value False, the check box is not selected.

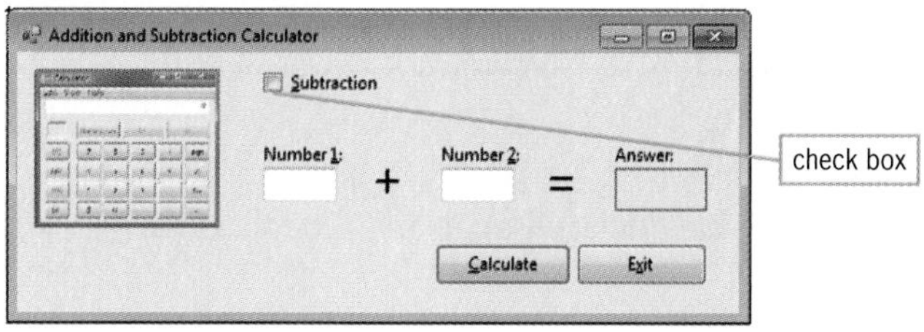

Figure 4-24 A different interface for the Addition and Subtraction Calculator application

If you want to experiment with this version of the Addition and Subtraction Calculator application, open the solution contained in the Try It 5! folder.

Figure 4-25 shows the Click event procedures for the subtractionCheckBox and calcButton. Both procedures contain a dual-alternative selection structure whose condition compares the check box's Checked property with a Boolean value. The conditions are shaded in the figure.

You can omit `= True` in the If clause in Figure 4-25.

```
Private Sub subtractionCheckBox_Click(ByVal sender As Object,
ByVal e As System.EventArgs) Handles subtractionCheckBox.Click
      ' assigns the appropriate arithmetic operator
      ' to the operationLabel

      If subtractionCheckBox.Checked = True Then
            operationLabel.Text = "-"
      Else
            operationLabel.Text = "+"
      End If
End Sub

Private Sub calcButton_Click(ByVal sender As Object,
ByVal e As System.EventArgs) Handles calcButton.Click
      ' calculates either the sum of or the
      ' difference between two numbers
```

Figure 4-25 Click event procedures for the subtractionCheckBox and calcButton *(continues)*

(continued)

```
        Dim num1 As Double
        Dim num2 As Double
        Dim answer As Double

        ' convert number input to Double
        Double.TryParse(num1TextBox.Text, num1)
        Double.TryParse(num2TextBox.Text, num2)

        ' calculate and display the sum or the difference
        If subtractionCheckBox.Checked = False Then
              answer = num1 + num2
        Else
              answer = num1 - num2
        End If
        answerLabel.Text = answer.ToString()
End Sub
```

Figure 4-25 Click event procedures for the subtractionCheckBox and calcButton

The answers to Mini-Quiz questions are located in Appendix A.

Mini-Quiz 4-2

1. What is the scope of a variable declared in an If…Then…Else statement's false path?
   a. the entire application
   b. the procedure in which the If…Then…Else statement appears
   c. the entire If…Then…Else statement
   d. only the false path in the If…Then…Else statement

2. Which of the following determines whether the value contained in the `sales` variable is at least $450.67?
   a. `If sales >= 450.67 Then`
   b. `If sales <= 450.67 Then`
   c. `If sales > 450.67 Then`
   d. `If sales < 450.67 Then`

3. Which of the following concatenates the "Do they live in " message, the contents of the String `state` variable, and a question mark?
   a. `"Do they live in " & state & "?"`
   b. `"Do they live in & state & ?"`
   c. `Do they live in & state & ?`
   d. `"Do they live in " # state # "?"`

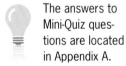

4. Which of the following methods temporarily converts the string stored in the `item` variable to lowercase?

   a. `item.Lower`

   b. `item.ToLower`

   c. `LowerCase(item)`

   d. `Lower(item)`

5. If a check box is selected, its ______________ property contains the Boolean value True.

   a. Checked

   b. Checkbox

   c. Selected

   d. Selection

To review what you learned about comparison operators, view the Ch04ComparisonOperator video.

Logical Operators

An If...Then...Else statement's condition can also contain logical operators, often referred to as Boolean operators. **Logical operators** allow you to combine two or more conditions, called sub-conditions, into one compound condition. The compound condition will always evaluate to either True or False. Figure 4-26 lists the two most commonly used logical operators available in Visual Basic, along with their order of precedence. Keep in mind, however, that logical operators are evaluated after any arithmetic or comparison operators in an expression. Also included in Figure 4-26 are examples of using logical operators in an If...Then...Else statement's condition.

Also available in Visual Basic are the Not, And, Or, and Xor logical operators.

HOW TO Use Logical Operators in a Condition

Logical operator	Operation	Precedence number
AndAlso	all sub-conditions must be true for the compound condition to evaluate to True	1
OrElse	only one of the sub-conditions needs to be true for the compound condition to evaluate to True	2

Figure 4-26 How to use logical operators in a condition *(continues)*

(continued)

Example 1
```
Dim quantity As Integer
Integer.TryParse(quantityTextBox.Text, quantity)
If quantity > 0 AndAlso quantity < 50 Then
```
The compound condition evaluates to True when the `quantity` variable's value is greater than zero and, at the same time, less than 50; otherwise, it evaluates to False.

Example 2
```
Dim age As Integer
Integer.TryParse(ageTextBox.Text, age)
If age = 21 OrElse age > 55 Then
```
The compound condition evaluates to True when the `age` variable's value is either equal to 21 or greater than 55; otherwise, it evaluates to False.

Example 3
```
Dim quantity As Integer
Dim price As Double
Integer.TryParse(quantityTextBox.Text, quantity)
Double.TryParse(priceTextBox.Text, price)
If quantity < 100 AndAlso price < 10.35 Then
```
The compound condition evaluates to True when the `quantity` variable's value is less than 100 and, at the same time, the `price` variable's value is less than 10.35; otherwise, it evaluates to False.

Example 4
```
Dim quantity As Integer
Dim state As String
Integer.TryParse(quantityTextBox.Text, quantity)
state = stateTextBox.Text.ToUpper
If quantity > 0 AndAlso quantity < 100 OrElse state = "KY" Then
```
The compound condition evaluates to True when either (or both) of the following is true: the `quantity` variable's value is between 0 and 100 or the `state` variable contains the string "KY"; otherwise, it evaluates to False. (The AndAlso operator is evaluated before the OrElse operator, because it has a higher precedence.)

Figure 4-26 How to use logical operators in a condition

All expressions containing a logical operator evaluate to a Boolean value: either True or False. The tables shown in Figure 4-27, called **truth tables**, summarize how the computer evaluates the logical operators in an expression. As the figure indicates, when you use the **AndAlso operator** to combine two sub-conditions, the resulting compound condition evaluates to True only when both sub-conditions are True. If either sub-condition is False or if both sub-conditions are False, then the compound condition evaluates to False. When you use the **OrElse operator** to combine two sub-conditions, the compound condition evaluates to False only when both sub-conditions are False. If either sub-condition is True or if both sub-conditions are True, then the compound condition evaluates to True.

Truth table for the AndAlso operator

sub-condition1	sub-condition2	sub-condition1 AndAlso sub-condition2
True	True	True
True	False	False
False	True (not evaluated)	False
False	False (not evaluated)	False

Truth table for the OrElse operator

sub-condition1	sub-condition2	sub-condition1 OrElse sub-condition2
True	True (not evaluated)	True
True	False (not evaluated)	True
False	True	True
False	False	False

Figure 4-27 Truth tables for the AndAlso and OrElse logical operators

As indicated in Figure 4-27, when the computer evaluates the "sub-condition1 AndAlso sub-condition2" expression, it will not evaluate sub-condition2 when sub-condition1 is False. Because both sub-conditions combined with the AndAlso operator need to be True for the compound condition to be True, there is no need to evaluate sub-condition2 when sub-condition1 is False. When the computer evaluates the "sub-condition1 OrElse sub-conditon2" expression, on the other hand, it will not evaluate sub-condition2 when sub-condition1 is True. Because only one of the sub-conditions combined with the OrElse operator needs to be True for the compound condition to be True, there is no need to evaluate sub-condition2 when sub-condition1 is True. The concept of evaluating sub-condition2 based on the result of sub-condition1 is referred to as **short-circuit evaluation**.

Using the Truth Tables

A procedure needs to calculate a bonus for each A-rated salesperson whose monthly sales are more than $8000. The procedure uses a String variable named `rating` and an Integer variable named `sales` to store the salesperson's rating and sales amount, respectively. Therefore, you can phrase sub-condition1 as `rating = "A"` and phrase sub-condition2 as `sales > 8000`. Which logical operator should you use to combine both sub-conditions into one compound condition? You can use the truth tables from Figure 4-27 to help you answer this question. For a salesperson to receive a bonus, both sub-condition1 and sub-condition2 must be True at the same time. If either sub-condition is False or if both sub-conditions are False, then the compound condition should be False and the salesperson should not receive a bonus. According to the truth tables, both logical operators evaluate a compound condition as True when both sub-conditions are True. However, only the AndAlso operator evaluates a compound condition as False when either one or both of the sub-conditions are False. Therefore, the correct compound condition to use in this case is `rating = "A" AndAlso sales > 8000`.

Now assume you want to send a letter to all A-rated salespeople and all B-rated salespeople. If the rating is stored in the `rating` variable, you can phrase sub-condition1 as `rating = "A"` and phrase sub-condition2 as `rating = "B"`. Now which logical operator should you use to combine both sub-conditions? At first it might appear that the AndAlso operator is the correct one to use, because the example says to send the letter to "all A-rated salespeople and all B-rated salespeople." In everyday conversations, people sometimes use the word "and" when what they really mean is "or." Although both words do not mean the same thing, using "and" instead of "or" generally does not cause a problem, because we are able to infer what another person means. Computers, however, cannot infer anything; they simply process the directions you give them, word for word. In this case, you actually want to send a letter to all salespeople with either an A rating or a B rating (a salesperson can have only one rating), so you need to use the OrElse operator. As the truth tables indicate, the OrElse operator is the only operator that evaluates the compound condition as True when at least one of the sub-conditions is True. Therefore, the correct compound condition to use in this case is `rating = "A" OrElse rating = "B"`.

The Carroll Company Application

Carroll Company wants an application that calculates and displays an employee's gross pay. No one at the company works more than 40 hours per week and everyone earns the same hourly rate, $10.65. Before making the gross pay calculation, the procedure should verify that the number of hours entered by the user is greater than or equal to zero, but less than or equal to 40. Programmers refer to the process of verifying that the input data is within the expected range as **data validation**. In this case, if the number of hours is valid, the procedure should calculate and display the gross pay; otherwise, it should display an error message alerting the user that the input data is incorrect. Figure 4-28 shows two ways of writing the Visual Basic code for the procedure; both contain a dual-alternative selection structure whose compound condition includes a logical operator. The compound condition in Example 1 uses the AndAlso operator to determine whether the value stored in the `hours` variable is greater than or equal to zero and, at the same time, less than or equal to 40. If the compound condition evaluates to True, the selection structure calculates and displays the gross pay; otherwise, it displays the "Error" message. The compound condition in Example 2 uses the OrElse operator to determine whether the value stored in the `hours` variable is either less than zero or greater than 40. If the compound condition evaluates to True, the selection structure displays the "Error" message; otherwise, it calculates and displays the gross pay. Both examples in Figure 4-28 produce the same result and simply represent two different ways of performing the same task. Figures 4-29 and 4-30 show sample runs of the Carroll Company application.

Example 1 – using the AndAlso operator

```
Private Sub calcButton_Click(ByVal sender As Object,
ByVal e As System.EventArgs) Handles calcButton.Click
     ' calculates and displays a gross pay amount
     ' or an error message

     Dim hours As Double
     Dim grossPay As Double

     Double.TryParse(hoursTextBox.Text, hours)
```

Figure 4-28 Two ways of writing the calcButton Click event procedure *(continues)*

(continued)

```
    If hours >= 0 AndAlso hours <= 40 Then
        ' calculate and display gross pay
        grossPay = hours * 10.65
        grossLabel.Text = grossPay.ToString("C2")
    Else
        ' display an error message
        grossLabel.Text = "Error"
    End If
End Sub
```

Example 2 – using the OrElse operator

```
Private Sub calcButton_Click(ByVal sender As Object,
ByVal e As System.EventArgs) Handles calcButton.Click
    ' calculates and displays a gross pay amount
    ' or an error message

    Dim hours As Double
    Dim grossPay As Double

    Double.TryParse(hoursTextBox.Text, hours)

    If hours < 0 OrElse hours > 40 Then
        ' display an error message
        grossLabel.Text = "Error"
    Else
      ' calculate and display gross pay
        grossPay = hours * 10.65
        grossLabel.Text = grossPay.ToString("C2")
    End If
End Sub
```

Figure 4-28 Two ways of writing the calcButton Click event procedure

Recall that < is the opposite of >=, and > is the opposite of <=.

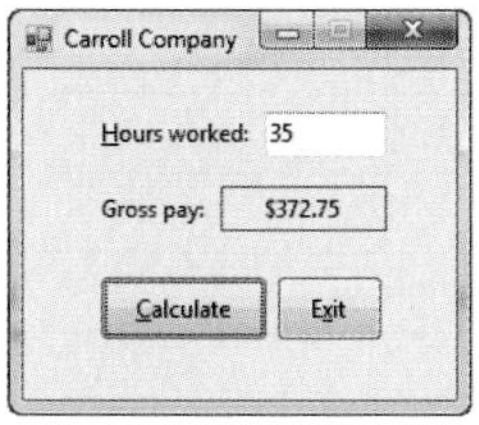

Figure 4-29 Sample run of the Carroll Company application using valid data

If you want to experiment with the Carroll Company application, open the solution contained in the Try It 6! folder.

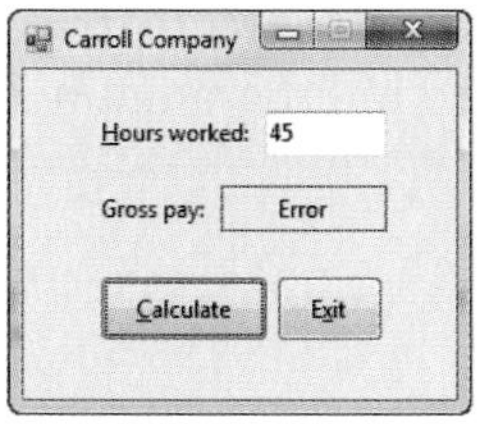

Figure 4-30 Sample run of the Carroll Company application using invalid data

To review what you learned about logical operators, view the Ch04LogicalOperator video.

Summary of Operators

Figure 4-31 contains a listing of the arithmetic, concatenation, comparison, and logical operators you have learned so far, along with their order of precedence. Notice that arithmetic operators are evaluated first, followed by the concatenation operator, comparison operators, and logical operators. As a result, the expression 30 > 75 / 3 AndAlso 5 < 10 * 2 will evaluate to True, as shown in the example in the figure.

Operator	**Operation**	**Precedence number**
^	exponentiation (raises a number to a power)	1
–	negation	2
*, /	multiplication and division	3
\	integer division	4
Mod	modulus	5
+, –	addition and subtraction	6
&	concatenation	7
=, >, >=, <, <=, <>	equal to, greater than, greater than or equal to, less than, less than or equal to, not equal to	8
AndAlso	all sub-conditions must be true for the compound condition to evaluate to True	9
OrElse	only one of the sub-conditions needs to be true for the compound condition to evaluate to True	10

Example

Evaluation steps	Result
Original expression	30 > 75 / 3 AndAlso 5 < 10 * 2
75 / 3 is evaluated first	30 > 25 AndAlso 5 < 10 * 2
10 * 2 is evaluated second	30 > 25 AndAlso 5 < 20
30 > 25 is evaluated third	True AndAlso 5 < 20
5 < 20 is evaluated fourth	True AndAlso True
True AndAlso True is evaluated last	True

Figure 4-31 Listing of arithmetic, concatenation, comparison, and logical operators

The last concept covered in this chapter is how to generate random integers. You will use random integers in the game application coded in Programming Tutorial 1.

Generating Random Integers

Some applications require the use of random numbers; examples include game applications, lottery applications, and applications used to practice elementary math skills. Most programming languages provide a **pseudo-random number generator**, which is a device that produces a sequence of numbers that meet certain statistical requirements for randomness. Pseudo-random numbers are chosen with equal probability from a finite set of numbers. The chosen numbers are not completely random, because a definite mathematical algorithm is used to select them. However, they are sufficiently random for practical purposes. The pseudo-random number generator in Visual Basic is an object whose data type is Random. Figure 4-32 shows the syntax for generating random integers, and it includes examples of using the syntax. As the figure indicates, you first create a **Random object** to represent the pseudo-random number generator. You create the Random object by declaring it in a Dim statement. You enter the Dim statement in the procedure that will use the number generator. After the Random object is created, you can use the object's Random.Next method to generate random integers. In the method's syntax, *randomObjectName* is the name of the Random object. The *minValue* and *maxValue* arguments in the syntax must be integers, and *minValue* must be less than *maxValue*. The **Random.Next method** returns an integer that is greater than or equal to *minValue*, but less than *maxValue*.

HOW TO Generate Random Integers

Syntax

Dim *randomObjectName* **As New Random**

randomObjectName.**Next(***minValue*, *maxValue***)**

Example 1

```
Dim number As Integer
Dim randomGenerator As New Random
number = randomGenerator.Next(1, 51)
```

The Dim statements create an Integer variable named `number` and a Random object named `randomGenerator`. The assignment statement generates a random integer that is greater than or equal to one, but less than 51, and then assigns the random integer to the `number` variable.

Example 2

```
Dim number As Integer
Dim randomGenerator As New Random
number = randomGenerator.Next(-10, 0)
```

The Dim statements create an Integer variable named `number` and a Random object named `randomGenerator`. The assignment statement generates a random integer that is greater than or equal to –10, but less than zero, and then assigns the random integer to the `number` variable.

Figure 4-32 How to generate random integers

In Computer Exercise 22, you learn how to use the Random.NextDouble method to generate a random number containing a decimal place.

Figure 4-33 shows a sample run of the Random Integers application. Figure 4-34 shows the code for the Generate Random Integer button's Click event procedure, which generates and displays a random number from 1 through 10.

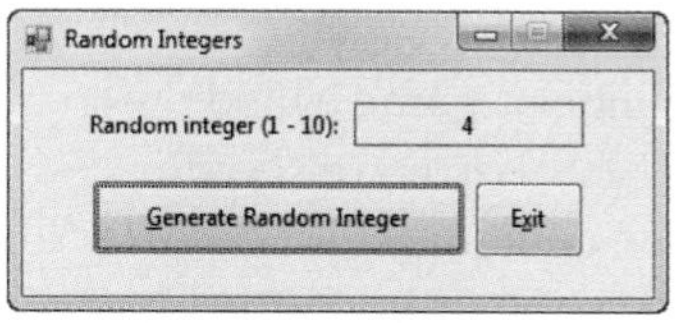

Figure 4-33 Sample run of the Random Integers application

If you want to experiment with the Random Integers application, open the solution contained in the Try It 7! folder.

```
Private Sub generateButton_Click(ByVal sender As Object,
ByVal e As System.EventArgs) Handles generateButton.Click
     ' displays random numbers from 1 through 10

     Dim number As Integer
     Dim randomGenerator As New Random

     ' generate and display random number
     number = randomGenerator.Next(1, 11)
     randomLabel.Text = Convert.ToString(number)
End Sub
```

Figure 4-34 Generate button's Click event procedure

The answers to Mini-Quiz questions are located in Appendix A.

Mini-Quiz 4-3

1. If the value of sub-condition1 is True and the value of sub-condition2 is False, then the value of sub-condition1 OrElse sub-condition2 is ______________.
   a. True
   b. False
2. The compound condition 7 > 3 AndAlso 5 < 2 will evaluate to ______________.
3. The compound condition 3 + 4 * 2 > 12 AndAlso 4 < 15 will evaluate to ______________.
4. Which of the following declares an object to represent the pseudo-random number generator?
   a. `Dim ranGen As New Generator`
   b. `Dim ranGen As New Random`
   c. `Dim ranGen As New RandomGenerator`
   d. `Dim ranGen As New RandomObject`

You have completed the concepts section of Chapter 4. The Programming Tutorial section is next.

The Ch04ProgTut1 video demonstrates all of the steps in Programming Tutorial 1.

PROGRAMMING TUTORIAL 1

Creating the Find the Mouse Game Application

In this tutorial, you create an application that simulates a game called Find the Mouse. The application's TOE chart and MainForm are shown in Figures 4-35 and 4-36, respectively. The interface contains eight picture boxes, a label, and two buttons. When the user clicks the Start Game button, the button's Click event procedure will display the "Is the mouse here?" image in the five empty picture boxes located at the top of the form. It also will generate a random number from 1 through 5. The random number will indicate which of the five picture boxes will display the mouse picture when clicked. For example, if the random number is 1 and the user clicks the first of the five picture boxes, the mouse image will appear in the picture box. However, if the user clicks the second of the five picture boxes, the "Not Here!" message will appear in the picture box. The player's task is to find the mouse picture, using as few guesses as possible. (The mouse image was contributed by the photographer, Jean Scheijen. You can browse Jean's other images at *www.vierdrie.nl.*)

Task	Object	Event
1. Generate a random number from 1 through 5 2. Display the "Is the mouse here?" image in PictureBox1, PictureBox2, PictureBox3, PictureBox4, and PictureBox5	startButton	Click
Use the random number generated by the startButton to display either the mouse image or the "Not Here!" image	PictureBox1, PictureBox2, PictureBox3, PictureBox4, PictureBox5	Click
End the application	exitButton	Click
Store the "Is the mouse here?" image	questionPictureBox	None
Store the "Not Here!" image	notHerePictureBox	None
Store the mouse image	mousePictureBox	None

Figure 4-35 TOE chart for the Find the Mouse Game application

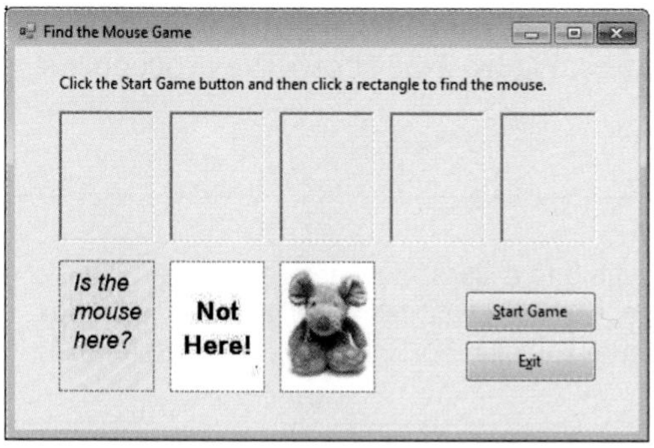

Figure 4-36 MainForm for the Find the Mouse Game application

Coding the Find the Mouse Game Application

Included in the data files for this book is a partially completed Find the Mouse Game application. To complete the application, you just need to code it. According to the application's TOE chart, the Click event procedures for the startButton, exitButton, and five of the picture boxes need to be coded.

To begin coding the application:

1. Start Visual Studio or the Express Edition of Visual Basic. If necessary, open the Solution Explorer window.
2. Open the **Mouse Game Solution** (**Mouse Game Solution.sln**) file, which is contained in the VbReloaded2010\Chap04\Mouse Game Solution folder. Open the designer window (if necessary), and then auto-hide the Solution Explorer window.
3. Open the Code Editor window. Notice that the exitButton's Click event procedure has already been coded for you.
4. In the comments that appear in the General Declarations section, replace <your name> and <current date> with your name and the current date.
5. The application will use variables, so you should enter the appropriate Option statements in the General Declarations section. Enter the Option statements shown in Figure 4-37.

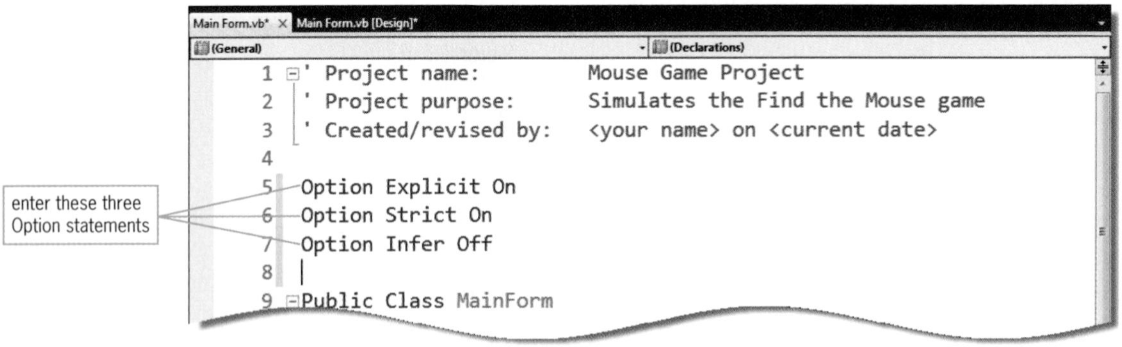

Figure 4-37 Option statements entered in the General Declarations section

The startButton's Click event procedure is responsible for generating a random number from 1 through 5. It also must display the "Is the mouse here?" image in five of the picture boxes. Figure 4-38 shows the procedure's pseudocode.

<u>startButton Click event procedure</u> 1. assign a random number from 1 through 5 to a class-level variable 2. assign the "Is the mouse here?" image, which is contained in the questionPictureBox, to the Image properties of the PictureBox1, PictureBox2, PictureBox3, PictureBox4, and PictureBox5 controls

Figure 4-38 Pseudocode for the startButton's Click event procedure

The procedure will use two variables: a Random variable to represent the pseudo-random number generator, and an Integer variable to store the random integer. You will name the Random variable `randomGenerator`, and name the Integer variable `randomNumber`. The `randomGenerator` variable will be a procedure-level variable, because it will be used only within the startButton's Click event procedure. The `randomNumber` variable will be a class-level variable, because it will be used by the Click event procedures for the startButton and the five picture boxes.

To declare the class-level variable and then code the startButton's Click event procedure:

1. In the blank line below the `' class-level variable for storing a random number` comment, type **Private randomNumber As Integer** and press **Enter**.
2. Open the code template for the startButton's Click event procedure. Type the comment **' prepares the interface for a new game** and press **Enter** twice.
3. Next, type **Dim randomGenerator As New Random** and press **Enter** twice.
4. The first step in the pseudocode is to assign a random number from 1 through 5 to the `randomNumber` variable. Type **' generate random number from 1 through 5** and press **Enter**, and then type **randomNumber = randomGenerator.Next(1, 6)** and press **Enter** twice.
5. Step 2 in the pseudocode is to assign the image contained in the questionPictureBox to five picture boxes. Enter the following comment and code:

   ' display the "Is the mouse here?" image
   PictureBox1.Image = questionPictureBox.Image
   PictureBox2.Image = questionPictureBox.Image
   PictureBox3.Image = questionPictureBox.Image
   PictureBox4.Image = questionPictureBox.Image
   PictureBox5.Image = questionPictureBox.Image

6. Save the solution.

According to the application's TOE chart, the PictureBox1's Click event procedure will use the random number generated by the startButton to display either the mouse image or the "Not Here!" image in the picture box. The pseudocode for the PictureBox1's Click event procedure is shown in Figure 4-39.

```
PictureBox1 Click event procedure
if the random number generated by the startButton is 1
        assign the mouse image, which is contained in the mousePictureBox, to the Image
        property of the PictureBox1 control
else
        assign the "Not Here!" image, which is contained in the notHerePictureBox, to the
        Image property of the PictureBox1 control
end if
```

Figure 4-39 Pseudocode for the PictureBox1's Click event procedure

To code the PictureBox1's Click event procedure:

1. Open the code template for the PictureBox1's Click event procedure. Type **' displays the appropriate image** and press **Enter** twice.
2. Now, enter the following code. (You will notice that when you press Enter after typing the If clause, the Code Editor will automatically enter the End If clause for you.)

```
If randomNumber = 1 Then
    PictureBox1.Image = mousePictureBox.Image
Else
    PictureBox1.Image = notHerePictureBox.Image
End If
```

3. Save the solution.

The Click event procedures for the other four picture boxes are almost identical to the PictureBox1's Click event procedure. The only exception is that the PictureBox2's Click event procedure will display the mouse image in the PictureBox2 control when the random number is 2 (rather than 1). Similarly, the PictureBox3's Click event procedure will display the mouse image in the PictureBox3 control when the random number is 3, and so on.

To finish coding the application and then test it:

1. Open the code template for the PictureBox2's Click event procedure. Copy the comment and code from the PictureBox1's Click event procedure to the PictureBox2's Click event procedure.
2. In the PictureBox2's Click event procedure, change the number 1 in the If...Then...Else statement's condition to **2**. Also change PictureBox1 in both the true path and false path to **PictureBox2**.
3. On your own, enter the appropriate code in the PictureBox3, PictureBox4, and PictureBox5 Click event procedures.
4. Save the solution, and then start the application.
5. Click the **Start Game** button. The "Is the mouse here?" image appears in the five picture boxes, as shown in Figure 4-40.

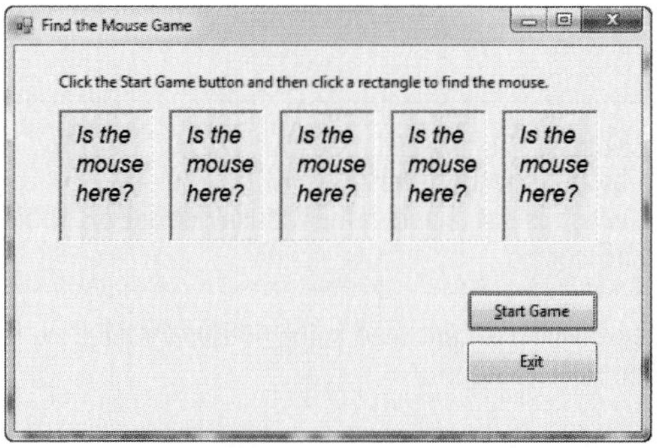

Figure 4-40 Result of clicking the Start Game button

6. Click **one of the "Is the mouse here?" rectangles**. One of two images appears: either the "Not Here!" image or the mouse image. If you found the mouse, the game is over.

7. Click each of the remaining four rectangles. Figure 4-41 shows a sample run of the application. Because the application uses a random number, the mouse image may be in a different rectangle on your screen.

Figure 4-41 Sample run of the Find the Mouse Game application

8. Click the **Start Game** button, and then play the game again.

9. Click the **Exit** button. Close the Code Editor window, and then close the solution. Figure 4-42 shows the application's code.

```
' Project name:          Mouse Game Project
' Project purpose:       Simulates the Find the Mouse game
' Created/revised by:    <your name> on <current date>

Option Explicit On
Option Strict On
Option Infer Off

Public Class MainForm

  ' class-level variable for storing a random number
  Private randomNumber As Integer

  Private Sub exitButton_Click(ByVal sender As Object,
  ByVal e As System.EventArgs) Handles exitButton.Click
     Me.Close()

  End Sub

  Private Sub startButton_Click(ByVal sender As Object,
  ByVal e As System.EventArgs) Handles startButton.Click
     ' prepares the interface for a new game

     Dim randomGenerator As New Random

     ' generate random number from 1 through 5
     randomNumber = randomGenerator.Next(1, 6)

```

Figure 4-42 Find the Mouse Game application's code *(continues)*

(continued)

```
    ' display the "Is the mouse here?" image
    PictureBox1.Image = questionPictureBox.Image
    PictureBox2.Image = questionPictureBox.Image
    PictureBox3.Image = questionPictureBox.Image
    PictureBox4.Image = questionPictureBox.Image
    PictureBox5.Image = questionPictureBox.Image

End Sub

Private Sub PictureBox1_Click(ByVal sender As Object,
ByVal e As System.EventArgs) Handles PictureBox1.Click
    ' displays the appropriate image

    If randomNumber = 1 Then
        PictureBox1.Image = mousePictureBox.Image
    Else
        PictureBox1.Image = notHerePictureBox.Image
    End If
End Sub

Private Sub PictureBox2_Click(ByVal sender As Object,
ByVal e As System.EventArgs) Handles PictureBox2.Click
    ' displays the appropriate image

    If randomNumber = 2 Then
        PictureBox2.Image = mousePictureBox.Image
    Else
        PictureBox2.Image = notHerePictureBox.Image
    End If
End Sub

Private Sub PictureBox3_Click(ByVal sender As Object,
ByVal e As System.EventArgs) Handles PictureBox3.Click
    ' displays the appropriate image

    If randomNumber = 3 Then
        PictureBox3.Image = mousePictureBox.Image
    Else
        PictureBox3.Image = notHerePictureBox.Image
    End If
  End Sub

Private Sub PictureBox4_Click(ByVal sender As Object,
ByVal e As System.EventArgs) Handles PictureBox4.Click
    ' displays the appropriate image

    If randomNumber = 4 Then
        PictureBox4.Image = mousePictureBox.Image
    Else
        PictureBox4.Image = notHerePictureBox.Image
    End If
End Sub

```

Figure 4-42 Find the Mouse Game application's code *(continues)*

(continued)

```
   Private Sub PictureBox5_Click(ByVal sender As Object,
   ByVal e As System.EventArgs) Handles PictureBox5.Click
      ' displays the appropriate image

      If randomNumber = 5 Then
          PictureBox5.Image = mousePictureBox.Image
      Else
          PictureBox5.Image = notHerePictureBox.Image
      End If
   End Sub
End Class
```

Figure 4-42 Find the Mouse Game application's code

PROGRAMMING TUTORIAL 2

Coding the Greenview Health Club Application

In this tutorial, you create an application for the Greenview Health Club. The application calculates and displays a club member's monthly dues. The interface provides a text box for entering the member's basic monthly fee. It also provides check boxes for specifying whether the member is entitled to use the club's tennis and racquetball courts. The additional monthly charge for using the tennis court is $20. The additional monthly charge for using the racquetball court is $10. The application's TOE chart and MainForm are shown in Figures 4-43 and 4-44, respectively. The MainForm contains three labels, one text box, two check boxes, and two buttons.

Task	**Object**	**Event**
Get and display the basic monthly fee	basicTextBox	None
Specify whether the member should be charged for using the tennis and racquetball courts	tennisCheckBox, racquetballCheckBox	None
1. Calculate the monthly dues, which include the basic monthly fee and optional additional charges for tennis and racquetball 2. Display the monthly dues in the monthlyDuesLabel	calcButton	Click
End the application	exitButton	Click
Display the monthly dues (from calcButton)	monthlyDuesLabel	None

Figure 4-43 TOE chart for the Greenview Health Club application

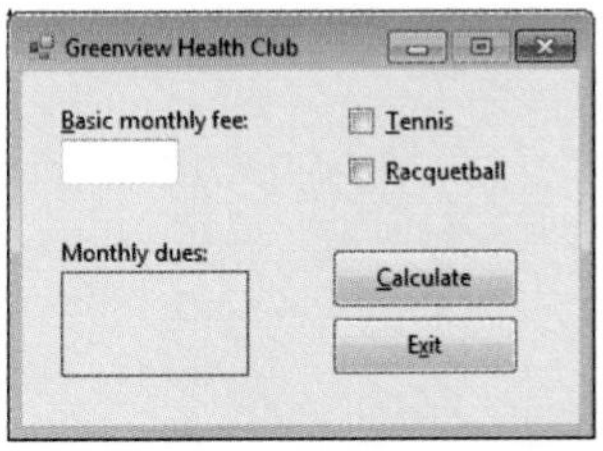

Figure 4-44 MainForm for the Greenview Health Club application

Coding the Greenview Health Club Application

Included in the data files for this book is a partially completed Greenview Health Club application. To complete the application, you just need to code it. According to the application's TOE chart, the Click event procedures for the calcButton and exitButton need to be coded.

To begin coding the application:

1. Start Visual Studio or the Express Edition of Visual Basic. If necessary, open the Solution Explorer window.
2. Open the **Greenview Solution** (**Greenview Solution.sln**) file, which is contained in the VbReloaded2010\Chap04\Greenview Solution folder. Open the designer window (if necessary), and then auto-hide the Solution Explorer window.
3. Open the Code Editor window. Notice that the exitButton's Click event procedure has already been coded for you.
4. In the comments that appear in the General Declarations section, replace <your name> and <current date> with your name and the current date.
5. Enter the appropriate Option statements in the General Declarations section.

The application's TOE chart indicates that the Calculate button's Click event procedure is responsible for calculating and displaying the monthly dues. The procedure's pseudocode is shown in Figure 4-45.

```
calcButton Click event procedure
1. assign the basic fee entered in the text box as the monthly dues
2. if the Tennis check box is selected
       add the additional tennis charge to the monthly dues
   end if
3. if the Racquetball check box is selected
       add the additional racquetball charge to the monthly dues
   end if
4. display the monthly dues in monthlyDuesLabel
```

Figure 4-45 Pseudocode for the calcButton's Click event procedure

Recall that before you begin coding a procedure, you first study the procedure's pseudocode (or flowchart) to determine any variables or named constants the procedure will require. In this case, the calcButton's Click event procedure will use two named constants to store the charges for using the tennis and racquetball courts. It also will use an Integer variable to keep track of the monthly dues. The named constants and variable are listed in Figure 4-46.

Named constants	Data type	Value
TennisChg	Integer	20
RacquetballChg	Integer	10
Variable	**Data type**	**Value source**
monthlyDues	Integer	user input (basicTextBox)

Figure 4-46 Named constants and variable for the calcButton's Click event procedure

To code the Calculate button's Click event procedure, and then test the application:

1. Open the code template for the calcButton's Click event procedure.
2. Enter the following two comments. Press **Enter** twice after typing the second comment.

   ' calculates the monthly dues, which include
   ' a basic fee and optional additional charges

3. Enter the statements to declare the three memory locations listed in Figure 4-46. Press **Enter** twice after typing the last declaration statement.
4. The first step in the pseudocode shown earlier in Figure 4-45 is to assign the basic fee entered in the text box as the monthly dues. Enter a TryParse method that converts the contents of the basicTextBox to Integer and then stores the result in the `monthlyDues` variable. Press **Enter** twice after typing the TryParse method.
5. The second step in the pseudocode is a single-alternative selection structure that determines whether the Tennis check box is selected. If it is selected, the selection structure's true path should add the tennis charge to the monthly dues. Type **' add any additional charges to the monthly dues** and press **Enter**. Now enter the appropriate If...Then...Else statement.
6. Step 3 in the pseudocode is another single-alternative selection structure. This selection structure determines whether the Racquetball check box is selected. If it is selected, the selection structure's true path should add the racquetball charge to the monthly dues. If necessary, insert a blank line between the End If clause and the End Sub clause. In the blank line, enter the appropriate If...Then...Else statement.
7. The last step in the pseudocode is to display the monthly dues. If necessary, insert two blank lines between the second End If clause and the End Sub clause. In the blank line above the End Sub clause, type **' display the monthly dues** and press **Enter**. Then enter the assignment statement to display the monthly dues, formatted with a dollar sign and two decimal places, in the monthlyDuesLabel.
8. Save the solution, and then start the application.
9. Type **50** in the Basic monthly fee box, and then click the **Racquetball** check box to select it. Click the **Calculate** button. $60.00 appears in the Monthly dues box, as shown in Figure 4-47.

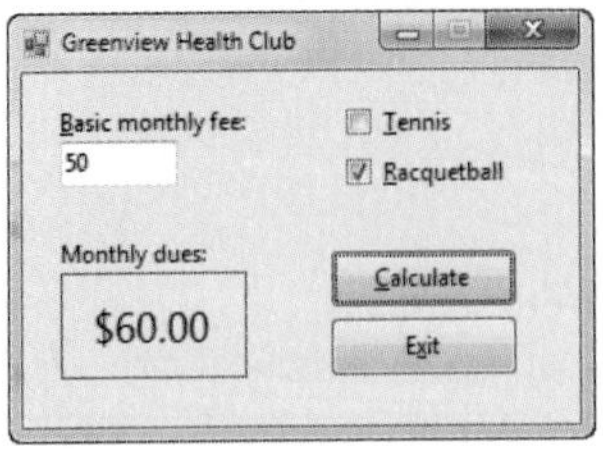

Figure 4-47 The monthly dues appears in the interface

10. Click the **Tennis** check box to select it, and then click the **Calculate** button. The monthly dues are now $80.00.
11. Click the **Racquetball** check box to deselect it, and then click the **Calculate** button. The monthly dues are now $70.00.
12. Click the **Tennis** check box to deselect it, and then click the **Calculate** button. The monthly dues are now $50.00.
13. Click the **Exit** button to end the application. Close the Code Editor window and then close the solution. Figure 4-48 shows the Greenview Health Club application's code. (You also can write the assignment statements in Lines 27 and 30 as `monthlyDues = monthlyDues + TennisChg` and `monthlyDues = monthlyDues + RacquetballChg`, respectively.)

```
 1 ' Project name:          Greenview Project
 2 ' Project purpose:       Displays a member's monthly dues
 3 ' Created/revised by:    <your name> on <current date>
 4
 5 Option Explicit On
 6 Option Strict On
 7 Option Infer Off
 8
 9 Public Class MainForm
10
11   Private Sub exitButton_Click(ByVal sender As Object,
     ByVal e As System.EventArgs) Handles exitButton.Click
12       Me.Close()
13   End Sub
14
15   Private Sub calcButton_Click(ByVal sender As Object,
     ByVal e As System.EventArgs) Handles calcButton.Click
16      ' calculates the monthly dues, which include
17      ' a basic fee and optional additional charges
18
19      Const TennisChg As Integer = 20
20      Const RacquetballChg As Integer = 10
21      Dim monthlyDues As Integer
22
23      Integer.TryParse(basicTextBox.Text, monthlyDues)
24
25      ' add any additional charges to the monthly dues
26      If tennisCheckBox.Checked = True Then
27        monthlyDues += TennisChg
28      End If
```

Figure 4-48 Greenview Health Club application's code *(continues)*

(continued)

```
        If racquetballCheckBox.Checked = True Then
           monthlyDues += RacquetballChg
        End If

        ' display the monthly dues
        monthlyDuesLabel.Text = monthlyDues.ToString("C2")

    End Sub
End Class
```

Figure 4-48 Greenview Health Club application's code

PROGRAMMING EXAMPLE

Fat Calculator Application

Create an interface that allows the user to enter the total number of calories and grams of fat contained in a specific food. The interface will need to display two values: the food's fat calories and its fat percentage. A food's fat calories are the number of calories attributed to fat. You calculate the fat calories by multiplying the grams of fat by 9. A food's fat percentage is the ratio of its fat calories to its total calories. The interface also should display the message "This food is high in fat." when the fat percentage is over 30%; otherwise, it should display the message "This food is not high in fat." Use the following names for the solution, project, and form file: Fat Calculator Solution, Fat Calculator Project, and Main Form.vb. Save the files in the VbReloaded2010\Chap04 folder. See Figures 4-49 through 4-54. Test the application using 150 and 6 as the number of calories and grams of fat, respectively. The fat calories should be 54 and the fat percentage should be 36.0 %. In addition, the "This food is high in fat." message should appear.

Task	Object	Event
Get and display the calories and fat grams	caloriesTextBox, fatGramsTextBox	None
1. Calculate the fat calories 2. Calculate the fat percentage 3. Display the fat calories and fat percentage in fatCalsLabel and fatPercentLabel 4. Display the appropriate message in messageLabel	calcButton	Click
End the application	exitButton	Click
Display the fat calories, fat percentage, and appropriate message (from calcButton)	fatCalsLabel, fatPercentLabel, messageLabel	None

Figure 4-49 TOE chart for the Fat Calculator application

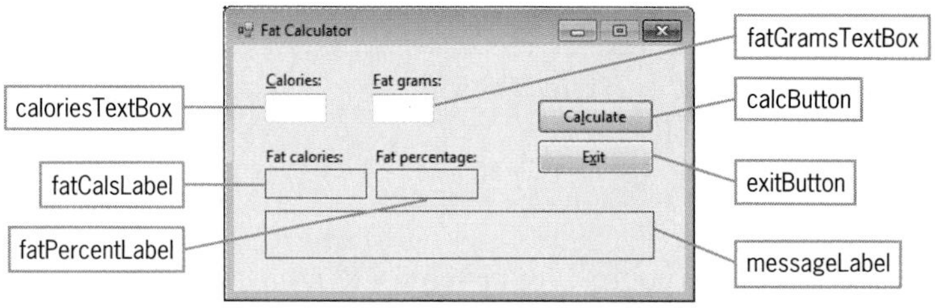

Figure 4-50 MainForm in the Fat Calculator application

Object	**Property**	**Setting**
Form1	Name	MainForm
	AcceptButton	calcButton
	Font	Segoe UI, 9 point
	StartPosition	CenterScreen
	Text	Fat Calculator
fatCalsLabel	AutoSize	False
	BorderStyle	FixedSingle
	Text	(empty)
	TextAlign	MiddleCenter
fatPercentLabel	AutoSize	False
	BorderStyle	FixedSingle
	Text	(empty)
	TextAlign	MiddleCenter
messageLabel	AutoSize	False
	BorderStyle	FixedSingle
	Text	(empty)
	TextAlign	MiddleCenter

Figure 4-51 Objects, properties, and settings

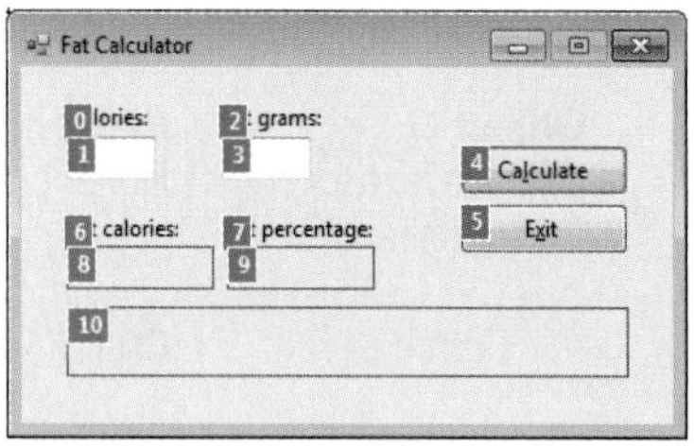

Figure 4-52 Tab order

<u>exitButton Click event procedure</u>
close the application

<u>calcButton Click event procedure</u>
1. assign user input (total calories and fat grams) to variables
2. fat calories = fat grams * 9
3. fat percentage = fat calories / total calories

Figure 4-53 Pseudocode *(continues)*

(continued)

4. display fat calories and fat percentage in fatCalsLabel and fatPercentLabel
5. if fat percentage is over 30%
      display "This food is high in fat." message in messageLabel
   else
      display "This food is not high in fat." message in messageLabel
   end if

Figure 4-53 Pseudocode

```
' Project name:        Fat Calculator Project
' Project purpose:     Allows the user to enter a food's
'                      calories and grams of fat. It
'                      then calculates the food's fat
'                      calories and fat percentage.
' Created/revised by:  <your name> on <current date>

Option Explicit On
Option Strict On
Option Infer Off

Public Class MainForm

  Private Sub exitButton_Click(ByVal sender As Object,
  ByVal e As System.EventArgs) Handles exitButton.Click
       Me.Close()
  End Sub

  Private Sub calcButton_Click(ByVal sender As Object,
  ByVal e As System.EventArgs) Handles calcButton.Click
       ' calculates fat calories and fat percentage

       Dim calories As Double
       Dim fatGrams As Double
       Dim fatCalories As Double
       Dim fatPercent As Double

       ' assign user input to variables
       Double.TryParse(caloriesTextBox.Text, calories)
       Double.TryParse(fatGramsTextBox.Text, fatGrams)

       ' calculate and display fat calories and
       ' fat percentage
       fatCalories = fatGrams * 9
       fatPercent = fatCalories / calories
       fatCalsLabel.Text = Convert.ToString(fatCalories)
       fatPercentLabel.Text = fatPercent.ToString("P1")

       ' display message indicating whether the food is
       ' or is not high in fat
       If fatPercent > 0.3 Then
           messageLabel.Text = "This food is high in fat."
       Else
           messageLabel.Text = "This food is not high in fat."
       End If
  End Sub
End Class
```

Figure 4-54 Code

Summary

- The selection structure allows a procedure to make a decision (based on some condition) and then take the appropriate action.
- There are three types of selection structures: single-alternative, dual-alternative, and multiple-alternative.
- The condition in a selection structure must result in an answer of either true or false. In a single-alternative selection structure, a specific set of tasks is performed only when the condition is true. In a dual-alternative selection structure, one set of tasks is performed when the condition is true, but a different set of tasks is performed when it is false.
- A selection structure's condition is represented in a flowchart by a diamond, which is called the decision symbol. The decision symbol has one flowline entering the symbol, and two flowlines (marked with a "T" and "F") leaving the symbol.
- Visual Basic provides the If…Then…Else statement for coding single-alternative and dual-alternative selection structures.
- All expressions containing a comparison operator evaluate to a Boolean value: either True or False.
- Comparison operators do not have an order of precedence in Visual Basic. Rather, they are evaluated from left to right in an expression and are evaluated after any arithmetic operators in the expression.
- Variables declared in a statement block (for example, in the true or false path of a selection structure) have block scope and are referred to as block-level variables. A block-level variable can be used only within the statement block in which it is defined, and only after its declaration statement.
- You connect (or link) strings together using the concatenation operator, which is the ampersand (&).
- The `ControlChars.NewLine` constant advances the insertion point to the next line in a control.
- String comparisons in Visual Basic are case-sensitive. When comparing strings, you can use either the ToUpper method or the ToLower method to temporarily convert the strings to uppercase or lowercase, respectively.
- You can use check boxes in an interface to provide the user with one or more independent and nonexclusive items from which to choose. The value in a check box's Checked property indicates whether the check box is selected (True) or unselected (False).
- You use logical operators to combine two or more sub-conditions into one compound condition. The compound condition always evaluates to a Boolean value: either True or False.
- Like arithmetic operators, logical operators have an order of precedence. For example, the AndAlso operator is evaluated before the OrElse operator in an expression. Logical operators are evaluated after any arithmetic and comparison operators in an expression.

- You use the pseudo-random number generator in Visual Basic to generate random numbers. The pseudo-random number generator is an object whose data type is Random.

Key Terms

AndAlso operator—one of the logical operators in Visual Basic; when used to combine two sub-conditions, the resulting compound condition evaluates to True only when both sub-conditions are true

Block scope—the scope of a variable declared within a statement block; a variable with block scope can be used only within the statement block in which it is declared, and only after its declaration statement

Block-level variables—variables declared within a statement block; the variables have block scope

CharacterCasing property—the text box property that indicates whether the case of the text should remain as typed or be converted to either uppercase or lowercase

Check boxes—controls used to offer the user one or more independent and nonexclusive choices

Comparison operators—operators used to compare values in an expression; also called relational operators

Concatenation operator—the ampersand (&); used to concatenate strings; must be both preceded and followed by a space character

Condition—specifies the decision you are making and must be phrased so that it evaluates to a Boolean value: either True or False

ControlChars.NewLine constant—used to advance the insertion point to the next line in a control

Data validation—the process of verifying that a program's input data is within the expected range

Decision symbol—the diamond in a flowchart; used to represent the condition in selection and repetition structures

Dual-alternative selection structure—a selection structure that requires the computer to perform one set of actions when the structure's condition is true, but a different set of actions when the structure's condition is false

False path—contains the instructions to be processed when a selection structure's condition evaluates to False

If...Then...Else statement—used to code the single-alternative and dual-alternative forms of the selection structure in Visual Basic

Logical operators—operators used to combine two or more sub-conditions into one compound condition; also called Boolean operators

MaxLength property—the text box property that specifies the maximum number of characters that the user can enter in the text box

OrElse operator—one of the logical operators in Visual Basic; when used to combine two sub-conditions, the resulting compound condition evaluates to False only when both sub-conditions are false

Pseudo-random number generator—a device that produces a sequence of numbers that meet certain statistical requirements for randomness; the pseudo-random number generator in Visual Basic is an object whose data type is Random

Random object—represents the pseudo-random number generator in Visual Basic

Random.Next method—used to generate a random integer that is greater than or equal to a minimum value, but less than a maximum value

Selection structure—one of the three basic control structures; tells the computer to make a decision based on some condition and then select the appropriate action; also called the decision structure

Short-circuit evaluation—refers to the way the computer evaluates two sub-conditions connected by a logical operator; when the logical operator is AndAlso, the computer does not evaluate sub-condition2 when sub-condition1 is false; when the logical operator is OrElse, the computer does not evaluate sub-condition2 when sub-condition1 is true

Single-alternative selection structure—a selection structure that requires the computer to perform a special set of actions only when the structure's condition is true

Statement block—in a selection structure, the set of statements terminated by an Else or End If clause

ToLower method—temporarily converts a string to lowercase

ToUpper method—temporarily converts a string to uppercase

True path—contains the instructions to be processed when a selection structure's condition evaluates to True

Truth tables—tables that summarize how the computer evaluates the logical operators in an expression

Review Questions

1. Which of the following is a valid condition for an If...Then...Else statement?
   a. `priceLabel.Text > 0 AndAlso priceLabel.Text < 10`
   b. `age > 30 OrElse < 50`
   c. `number > 100 AndAlso number <= 1000`
   d. `state.ToUpper = "Alaska" OrElse state.ToUpper = "Hawaii"`

2. Which of the following conditions should you use in an If...Then...Else statement to compare the string contained in the firstTextBox with the name Joe? (Be sure the condition will handle Joe, JOE, joe, and so on.)

a. `firstTextBox.Text = ToUpper("JOE")`

b. `firstTextBox.Text = ToUpper("Joe")`

c. `ToUpper(firstTextBox.Text) = "JOE"`

d. `firstTextBox.Text.ToUpper = "JOE"`

3. The expression `3 < 6 AndAlso 7 > 4` evaluates to____________.

   a. True

   b. False

4. The computer will perform short-circuit evaluation when processing which of the following If clauses?

   a. `If 3 * 2 < 4 AndAlso 5 > 3`

   b. `If 6 < 9 OrElse 5 > 3`

   c. `If 12 > 4 * 4 AndAlso 6 < 2`

   d. all of the above

5. The expression `7 >= 3 + 4 AndAlso 6 < 4 OrElse 2 < 5` evaluates to ______________.

   a. True

   b. False

6. The expression `5 * 3 > 3 ^ 2 AndAlso True OrElse False` evaluates to ______________.

   a. True

   b. False

7. Which of the following generates a random integer from 10 to 55, inclusive? (The Random object is named `randGen`.)

   a. `randGen.Next(10, 56)`

   b. `randGen.Next(10, 55)`

   c. `randGen.Next(9, 55)`

   d. `randGen.Next(9, 56)`

8. The `city` variable contains the string "Boston" and the `state` variable contains the string "MA". Which of the following will display the string "Boston, MA" (the city, a comma, a space, and the state) in the addressLabel?

   a. `addressLabel.Text = "city" & ", " & "state"`

   b. `addressLabel.Text = city $ ", " $ state`

   c. `addressLabel.Text = city & ", " & state`

   d. `addressLabel.Text = "city," & "state"`

9. A procedure contains an If...Then...Else statement. If the `x` variable is declared immediately after the statement's `Else` clause, where can the variable be used?

   a. in any instruction in the entire procedure

   b. in any instruction after the declaration statement in the procedure

   c. in any instruction in the false path

   d. in any instruction in the If...Then...Else statement

10. Which of the following conditions evaluates to True when the `initial` variable contains the letter A in either uppercase or lowercase?

    a. `initial = "A" OrElse initial = "a"`

    b. `initial = "A" AndAlso initial = "a"`

    c. `initial = "A" OrElse "a"`

    d. `initial = "A" AndAlso "a"`

Exercises

Pencil and Paper

INTRODUCTORY

1. Draw the flowchart that corresponds to the following pseudocode:

```
if the years employed are less or equal to 2
      display "1 week vacation"
else
      display "2 weeks vacation"
end if
```

INTRODUCTORY

2. Write the If...Then...Else statement that corresponds to the partial flowchart shown in Figure 4-55. Use the following variable names: `sold` and `bonus`. Display the appropriate message and bonus amount (formatted with a dollar sign and two decimal places) in the messageLabel.

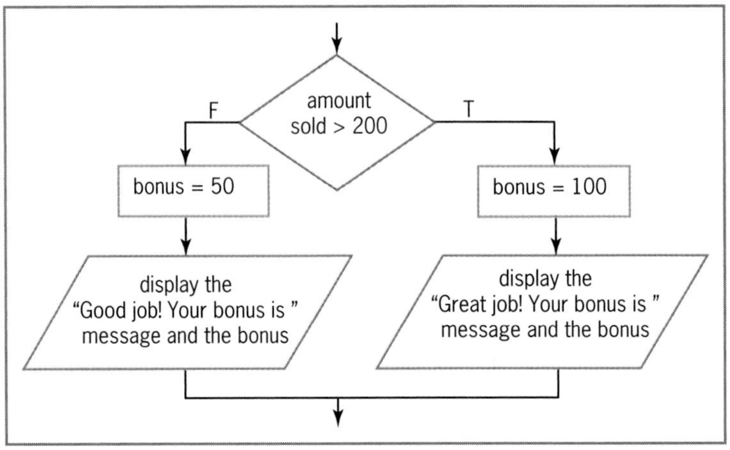

Figure 4-55 Flowchart

3. Write an If...Then...Else statement that displays the string "350Z" in the carLabel when the carTextBox contains the string "Nissan" (entered using any case). INTRODUCTORY

4. Write an If...Then...Else statement that displays the string "Reorder" in the messageLabel when the `quantity` variable's value is less than 10; otherwise, display the string "Sufficient quantity". INTRODUCTORY

5. Write an If...Then...Else statement that assigns the number 25 to the `bonus` variable when the `sales` variable's value is less than or equal to $500; otherwise, assign the number 40. INTRODUCTORY

6. Write an If...Then...Else statement that assigns the number 100 to the `shipping` variable when the `state` variable contains the string "Hawaii" (entered using any case); otherwise, assign the number 65. INTRODUCTORY

7. Write an If...Then...Else statement that assigns the number 15 to the `reward` variable when the `state` variable contains the string "IL" (entered using any case) and the `sales` variable contains a number that is greater than 2000; otherwise, assign the number 5. INTRODUCTORY

8. Write an If...Then...Else statement that displays the string "Winner" in the messageLabel when the `status` variable contains either the uppercase letter X or the uppercase letter Y. INTRODUCTORY

9. Write an If...Then...Else statement that displays the string "Please enter your ZIP code" in the messageLabel when the zipTextBox does not contain any data. INTERMEDIATE

10. Write an If...Then...Else statement that calculates a 5% sales tax when the `code` variable contains the string "3", and calculates a 4.5% sales tax when the `code` variable contains anything other than "3". Calculate the sales tax by multiplying the tax rate by the contents of the Double `sales` variable. Assign the sales tax to the Double `tax` variable. Also write the code to display the sales tax in the taxLabel. Display the sales tax with a dollar sign and two decimal places. INTERMEDIATE

11. In Figure 4-25 in the chapter, you viewed the Click event procedures for the subtractionCheckBox and calcButton in the Addition and Subtraction Calculator application. Rather than writing the If clause in the subtractionCheckBox's Click event procedure as `If subtractionCheckBox.Checked = True Then`, you also can write it as simply `If subtractionCheckBox.Checked Then`. Research the Not logical operator. Then use it to rewrite the If clause in the calcButton's Click event procedure. ADVANCED

Computer

MODIFY THIS

12. If necessary, complete the Greenview Health Club application from this chapter's Programming Tutorial 2, and then close the solution. Use Windows to make a copy of the Greenview Solution folder. Rename the folder Greenview Solution-Modified.

    a. Open the Greenview Solution (Greenview Solution.sln) file contained in the VbReloaded2010\Chap04\Greenview Solution-Modified folder.

    b. Include a Golf check box in the interface. The monthly charge for using the golf course is $35. Modify the application's code.

    c. Save the solution and then start and test the application. Close the solution.

MODIFY THIS

13. In this exercise, you modify the Color Mixer application from Chapter 3's Programming Tutorial 1. Open the Color Mixer Solution (Color Mixer Solution.sln) file contained in the VbReloaded2010\Chap04\Color Mixer Solution folder. Add a label at the bottom of the form. Change the label's Name property to messageLabel. Remove its Text property value. (If necessary, you can use the Properties window's Object box to access the label.) Modify the View Color button's Click event procedure so that it uses one dual-alternative selection structure to determine whether the text box entries are valid. A valid entry is a number from 0 through 255. If one or more entries are not valid, display the message "Invalid color code" in the messageLabel; otherwise, change the oval shape to the appropriate color and remove any message from the messageLabel. Save the solution and then start and test the application. Close the solution.

INTRODUCTORY

14. Open the Random Swap Solution (Random Swap Solution.sln) file contained in the VbReloaded2010\Chap04\Random Swap Solution folder. The application should generate two random integers from 1 through 250. It then should display the lowest and highest number in the interface. Draw the flowchart, and then code the application. Save the solution and then start and test the application. Close the solution.

INTRODUCTORY

15. Open the Bonus Solution (Bonus Solution.sln) file contained in the VbReloaded2010\Chap04\Bonus Solution folder. The application should calculate and display a salesperson's bonus. Salespeople selling more than $3500 in products receive a 5% bonus; otherwise, the bonus rate is 4%. Display the bonus with a dollar sign and two decimal places. Write the pseudocode and then code the application. Save the solution and then start and test the application. Close the solution.

INTERMEDIATE

16. Open the Computer Workshop Solution (Computer Workshop Solution.sln) file contained in the VbReloaded2010\Chap04\Computer Workshop Solution folder. Computer Workshop offers programming seminars to companies. The price per person depends on the number of people the company registers. The price for the first 10 registrants is $80 per person; thereafter, it is $70 per person. Therefore, if the company

registers seven people, the total cost is $560. If the company registers 12 people, the total cost is $940. Display the total cost (formatted with a dollar sign and no decimal places) in the totalLabel. Save the solution and then start and test the application. Close the solution.

17. Jacques Cousard has been playing the lottery for four years. Unfortunately, he has yet to win any money. He wants an application that will select the six lottery numbers for him. Each lottery number can range from 1 through 54 only. (An example of six lottery numbers would be: 4, 8, 35, 15, 20, 3.) Create a Windows application. Use the following names for the solution, project, and form file: Lottery Solution, Lottery Project, and Main Form.vb. Save the application in the VbReloaded2010\Chap04 folder. Build an appropriate interface. Code the application. For now, do not worry if the lottery numbers are not unique. You will learn how to display unique numbers in Chapter 9 in this book. Save the solution and then start and test the application. Close the solution.

INTERMEDIATE

18. Open the Shipping Solution (Shipping Solution.sln) file contained in the VbReloaded2010\Chap04\Shipping Solution folder. The application should display the appropriate shipping charge. The shipping charge for the following ZIP codes is $32: 60618, 60620, and 60632. All other ZIP codes are charged $37.75. Code the application. Save the solution and then start and test the application. Close the solution.

INTERMEDIATE

19. In this exercise, you modify the Moonbucks Coffee application from Chapter 3's Programming Example.

INTERMEDIATE

    a. Open the Moonbucks Solution (Moonbucks Solution.sln) file contained in the VbReloaded2010\Chap04\Moonbucks Solution folder.

    b. Add a check box to the form. Change the text box's Name property to employeeCheckBox, and change its Text property to &Employee. Modify the code so that it charges $10 per pound when the check box is selected, and charges $11.15 per pound when it is not selected.

    c. Also modify the code so that it gives a 2% discount when a total of at least 10 pounds is ordered.

    d. Save the solution and then start and test the application. Close the solution.

20. In this exercise, you modify the Color Game application from Chapter 2's Programming Tutorial 1. Open the Color Game Solution (Color Game Solution.sln) file contained in the VbReloaded2010\Chap04\Color Game Solution folder. Add a check box to the form. When the user selects the check box, its Click event procedure should change the Text property of each color button to the appropriate Spanish word. When the user deselects the check box, its Click event procedure should change the Text property of each color button to the appropriate English word. Make the appropriate modifications to the code. Save the solution and then start and test the application. Close the solution.

INTERMEDIATE

ADVANCED

21. Open the Color Mixer Solution (Color Mixer Solution.sln) file contained in the VbReloaded2010\Chap04\Color Mixer Solution-Advanced folder. Add a label at the bottom of the form. Change the label's Name property to messageLabel. Remove its Text property value. (If necessary, you can use the Properties window's Object box to access the label.) Modify the View Color button's Click event procedure so that it determines whether each text box entry is valid. A valid entry is a number from 0 through 255. If the Red text box's entry is invalid, display the message "Invalid Red code" in the messageLabel. If the Green text box's entry is invalid, display the message "Invalid Green code" in the messageLabel. If the Blue text box's entry is invalid, display the message "Invalid Blue code" in the messageLabel. If more than one entry is incorrect, the messageLabel should display each message on a separate line. Change the oval shape to the appropriate color only when all three entries are correct. Save the solution and then start and test the application. Close the solution.

DISCOVERY

22. In this exercise, you learn how to generate and display random real numbers, which are numbers that contain a decimal place.
    a. Open the Random Float Solution (Random Float Solution.sln) file contained in the VbReloaded2010\Chap04\Random Float Solution folder.
    b. You can use the Random.NextDouble method to return a random real number that is greater than or equal to 0.0, but less than 1.0. The syntax of the Random.NextDouble method is *randomObjectName*.**NextDouble**. Code the Display Random Number button's Click event procedure so that it displays a random real number in the numberLabel.
    c. Save the solution and then start the application. Click the Display Random Number button several times. Each time you click the button, a random number that is greater than or equal to 0.0, but less than 1.0, appears in the numberLabel. Click the Exit button to end the application.
    d. You can use the following formula to generate random real numbers within a specified range: **(***maxValue* – *minValue* **+ 1.0) *** *randomObjectName***.NextDouble +** *minValue*. For example, the formula `(10.0 - 1.0 + 1.0) * randomGenerator.NextDouble + 1.0` generates real numbers that are greater than or equal to 1.0, but less than 11.0. Modify the Display Random Number button's Click event procedure so that it displays a random real number that is greater than or equal to 25.0, but less than 51.0. Display two decimal places in the number.
    e. Save the solution and then start the application. Click the Display Random Number button several times to verify that the code you entered is working correctly. Close the solution.

SWAT THE BUGS

23. Open the Debug Solution (Debug Solution.sln) file contained in the VbReloaded2010\Chap04\Debug Solution folder. Read the comments in the Code Editor window. Start and then test the application. Locate and then correct any errors. When the application is working correctly, close the solution.

Case Projects

Allenton Water Department

Create an application that calculates a customer's water bill. The user will enter the current meter reading and the previous meter reading. The application should calculate and display the number of gallons of water used and the total charge for the water. The charge for water is $1.75 per 1000 gallons, or .00175 per gallon. Make the calculations only when the current meter reading is greater than or equal to the previous meter reading; otherwise, display an appropriate error message. Name the solution, project, and form file Allenton Solution, Allenton Project, and Main Form.vb, respectively. Save the solution in the VbReloaded2010\Chap04 folder. You can create either your own user interface or the one shown in Figure 4-56.

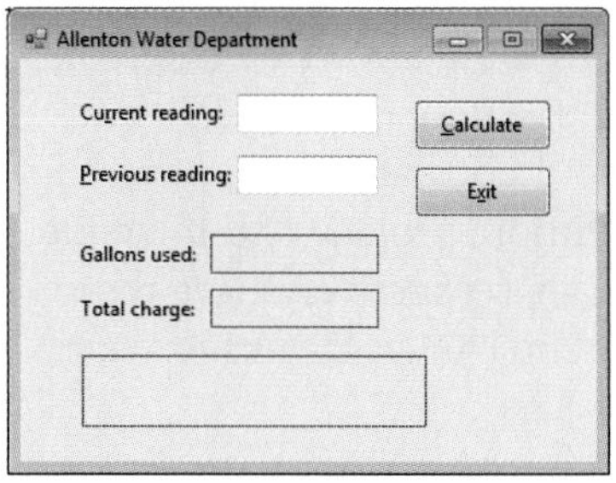

Figure 4-56 Sample interface for the Allenton Water Department application

Novelty Warehouse

Novelty Warehouse needs an application that allows the user to enter an item's price. When the user clicks a button in the interface, the button's Click event procedure should add the price to the total of the prices already entered; this amount represents the subtotal owed by the customer. The application should display the subtotal on the screen. It also should display a 3% sales tax, the shipping charge, and the grand total owed by the customer. The grand total is calculated by adding together the subtotal, the 3% sales tax, and a $15 shipping charge. For example, if the user enters 26.75 as the price and then clicks the button, the button's Click event procedure should display 26.75 as the subtotal, .80 as the sales tax, 15.00 as the shipping charge, and 42.55 as the grand total. If the user subsequently enters 30.00 as the price and then clicks the button, the button's Click event procedure should display 56.75 as the subtotal, 1.70 as the sales tax, 15.00 as the shipping charge, and 73.45 as the grand total. However, when the subtotal is at least $100, the shipping charge is 0 (zero). Name the solution, project, and form file Novelty Solution, Novelty Project, and Main Form.vb, respectively. Save the solution in the VbReloaded2010\Chap04 folder. You can create either your own user interface or the one shown in Figure 4-57.

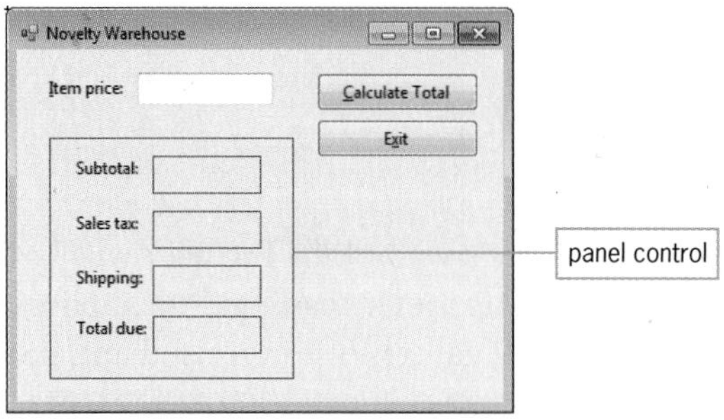

Figure 4-57 Sample interface for the Novelty Warehouse application

Marcy's Department Store

Marcy's is having a BoGoHo (Buy One, Get One Half Off) sale. Create an application that allows the user to enter the prices of two items. The application should calculate the total owed. The half-off should always be taken on the item having the lowest price. For example, if one item costs $24.99 and the second item costs $12.50, the $12.50 item would be half off. (In other words, the item would cost $6.25.) Name the solution, project, and form file Marcy Solution, Marcy Project, and Main Form.vb, respectively. Save the solution in the VbReloaded2010\Chap04 folder. You can create either your own user interface or the one shown in Figure 4-58.

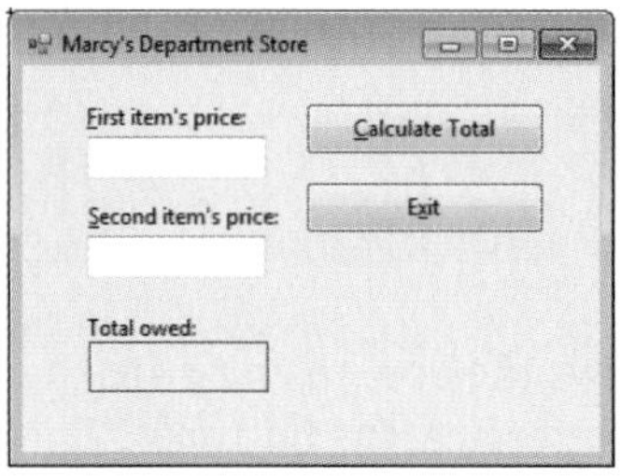

Figure 4-58 Sample interface for the Marcy's Department Store application

Addition Practice

Create an application that displays two random integers from 1 through 10 in the interface. The application should allow the user to enter the sum of both numbers. It then should check whether the user's answer is correct. Display an appropriate message (or image) when the answer is correct. Also display an appropriate message (or image) when the answer is incorrect. Name the solution, project, and form file Addition Practice Solution, Addition Practice Project, and Main Form.vb, respectively. Save the solution in the VbReloaded2010\Chap04 folder.

CHAPTER 5

More on the Selection Structure

After studying Chapter 5, you should be able to:

- Include a nested selection structure in pseudocode and in a flowchart
- Code a nested selection structure
- Include a multiple-alternative selection structure in pseudocode and in a flowchart
- Code a multiple-alternative selection structure
- Include radio buttons in an interface
- Display a message in a message box
- Prevent the entry of invalid characters in a text box

Making More Than One Decision

In Chapter 4, you learned that you use the selection structure when you want the computer to make a decision and then select the appropriate path—either the true path or the false path—based on the result. Both paths in a selection structure can include instructions that declare variables, perform calculations, and so on. In this chapter, you will learn that both paths also can include other selection structures. When either a selection structure's true path or its false path contains another selection structure, the inner selection structure is referred to as a **nested selection structure**, because it is contained (nested) within the outer selection structure. You already are familiar with the concept of nested selection structures, examples of which are shown in Figure 5-1. The examples are written in pseudocode. Example 1 contains an outer single-alternative selection structure and a nested dual-alternative selection structure. The outer selection structure begins with "if the customer orders a cup of coffee", and it ends with the last "end if". The nested selection structure begins with "if the customer wants regular coffee" and ends with the first "end if". The "else" in Example 1 separates the nested selection structure's true path from its false path. Notice that the instructions in both paths are indented within the nested selection structure. Indenting in this manner clearly indicates the instructions to be followed when the condition is true, as well as the ones to be followed when the condition is false.

Example 2 in Figure 5-1 contains an outer dual-alternative selection structure and a nested dual-alternative selection structure. The outer selection structure begins with "if the video store has *The Shining* in stock", and it ends with the last "end if". The first "else" belongs to the outer selection structure. The nested selection structure begins with "if the video store has *Misery* in stock" and ends with the first "end if". The second "else" belongs to the nested selection structure. Keep in mind that for a nested selection structure to work correctly, it must be contained entirely within one of the paths in the outer selection structure. The nested selection structure in Example 1, for instance, appears entirely within the outer selection structure's true path. The nested selection structure in Example 2, on the other hand, appears entirely within the outer selection structure's false path.

Example 1 – nested selection structure in the true path

```
if the customer orders a cup of coffee
        ask the customer if he/she wants regular or decaffeinated coffee
        if the customer wants regular coffee
                pour regular coffee into a cup
        else
                pour decaffeinated coffee into a cup
        end if
        give the customer the cup of coffee
end if
```

nested selection structure

Figure 5-1 Selection structures containing nested selection structures *(continues)*

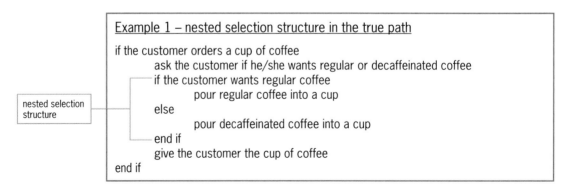

(continued)

Example 2 – nested selection structure in the false path

```
if the video store has The Shining in stock
        rent The Shining
else
        if the video store has Misery in stock
                rent Misery
        else
                watch Pet Sematary on DVR
        end if
end if
```

nested selection structure

Figure 5-1 Selection structures containing nested selection structures

The Voter Eligibility Application

Figure 5-2 shows the problem specification for the Voter Eligibility application. The application determines whether a person can vote and then displays one of three different messages. The appropriate message depends on the person's age and voter registration status. For example, if the person is younger than 18 years old, the application should display the message "You are too young to vote." However, if the person is at least 18 years old, the application should display one of two messages; the correct message is determined by the person's voter registration status. If the person is registered, then the appropriate message is "You can vote."; otherwise, it is "You must register before you can vote." Notice that determining the person's voter registration status is important only *after* his or her age is determined. Because of this, the decision regarding the age is considered the primary decision, while the decision regarding the registration status is considered the secondary decision, because whether it needs to be made depends on the result of the primary decision. A primary decision is always made by an outer selection structure, while a secondary decision is always made by a nested selection structure.

The Harrisburg city manager wants an application that determines voter eligibility and displays one of three messages. The messages and criteria for displaying each message are as follows:

Message	Criteria
You are too young to vote.	person is younger than 18 years old
You can vote.	person is at least 18 years old and is registered to vote
You must register before you can vote.	person is at least 18 years old but is not registered to vote

Figure 5-2 Problem specification for the Voter Eligibility application

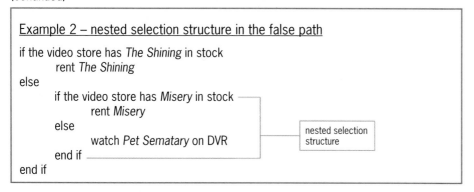

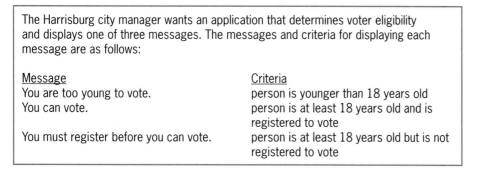

Figure 5-3 shows a sample run of the Voter Eligibility application, and Figure 5-4 shows the flowchart for the Display button's Click event procedure. The first diamond in the flowchart represents the outer selection structure's condition, which checks whether the age entered by the user is greater than or equal to 18. If the condition evaluates to False, it means that the person is not old enough to vote. In that case, the outer selection structure's false path displays the "You are too young to vote." message before the outer selection structure ends. However, if the outer selection structure's condition evaluates to True, it means that the person *is* old enough to vote. In that case, the nested selection structure in the procedure determines the person's registration status. The nested selection structure's condition is represented by the second diamond in Figure 5-4. If the person is registered, the nested selection structure's true path displays the "You can vote." message; otherwise, its false path displays the "You must register before you can vote." message. After the appropriate message is displayed, the outer and nested selection structures end. Notice that the nested selection structure is processed only when the outer selection structure's condition evaluates to True.

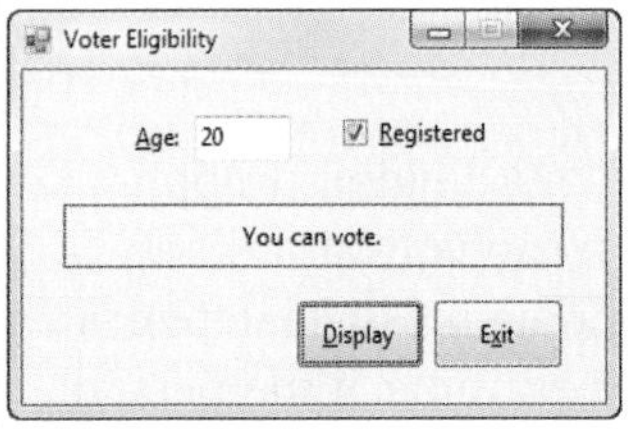

Figure 5-3 Sample run of the Voter Eligibility application

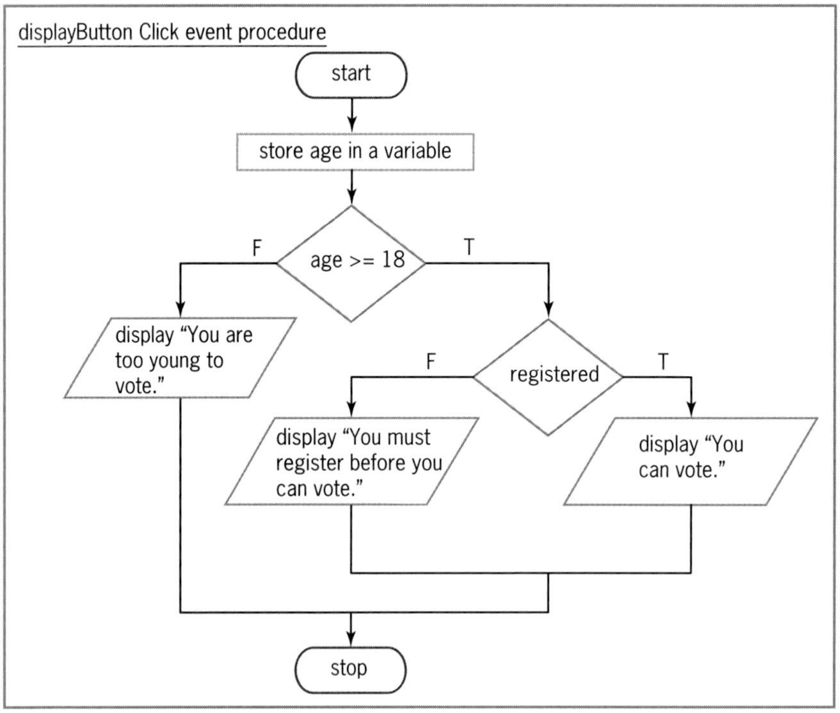

Figure 5-4 Flowchart showing the nested selection structure in the true path

Even small procedures can have more than one solution. Figure 5-5 shows another version of the Display button's Click event procedure, also in flowchart form. As in the previous solution, the outer selection structure in this solution determines the age (the primary decision), and the nested selection structure determines the voter registration status (the secondary decision).

In this solution, however, the outer selection structure's condition checks whether the age is less than 18. In addition, the nested selection structure appears in the outer selection structure's false path in this solution, which means it will be processed only when the outer selection structure's condition evaluates to False. The solutions in Figures 5-4 and 5-5 produce the same result. Neither solution is better than the other. Each simply represents a different way of solving the same problem.

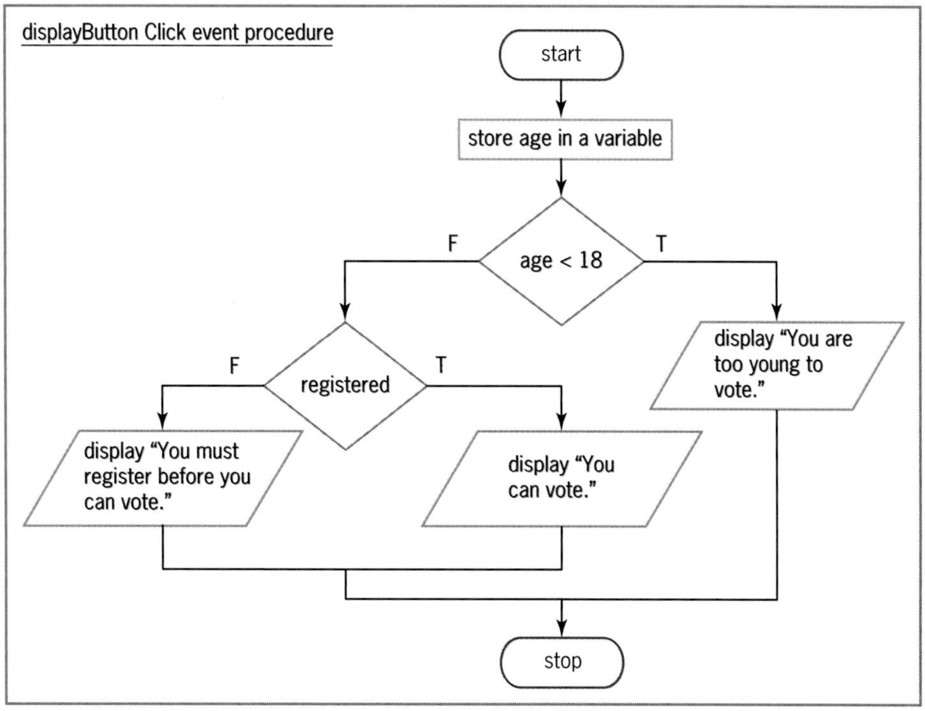

Figure 5-5 Flowchart showing the nested selection structure in the false path

Figure 5-6 shows the code corresponding to the flowcharts in Figures 5-4 and 5-5.

<u>Code for the flowchart in Figure 5-4</u>

```
Private Sub displayButton_Click(ByVal sender As Object,
ByVal e As System.EventArgs) Handles displayButton.Click
     ' displays a message based on a person's
     ' age and registration status

     Const VoteMsg As String = "You can vote."
     Const RegisterMsg As String =
          "You must register before you can vote."
     Const TooYoungMsg As String = "You are too young to vote."
     Dim age As Integer

     ' store age in a variable
     Integer.TryParse(ageTextBox.Text, age)
```

Figure 5-6 Code for the flowcharts in Figures 5-4 and 5-5 *(continues)*

(continued)

the nested selection structure is contained in the outer selection structure's true path

```
    ' display appropriate message
    If age >= 18 Then
        If registeredCheckBox.Checked = True Then
            messageLabel.Text = VoteMsg
        Else
            messageLabel.Text = RegisterMsg
        End If
    Else
        messageLabel.Text = TooYoungMsg
    End If
End Sub
```

Code for the flowchart in Figure 5-5

```
Private Sub displayButton_Click(ByVal sender As Object,
ByVal e As System.EventArgs) Handles displayButton.Click
    ' displays a message based on a person's
    ' age and registration status

    Const VoteMsg As String = "You can vote."
    Const RegisterMsg As String =
        "You must register before you can vote."
    Const TooYoungMsg As String = "You are too young to vote."
    Dim age As Integer

    ' store age in a variable
    Integer.TryParse(ageTextBox.Text, age)

    ' display appropriate message
    If age < 18 Then
        messageLabel.Text = TooYoungMsg
    Else
        If registeredCheckBox.Checked = True Then
            messageLabel.Text = VoteMsg
        Else
            messageLabel.Text = RegisterMsg
        End If
    End If
End Sub
```

the nested selection structure is contained in the outer selection structure's false path

Figure 5-6 Code for the flowcharts in Figures 5-4 and 5-5

If you want to experiment with the Voter Eligibility application, open the solution contained in the Try It 1! folder.

To review what you learned about nested selection structures, view the Ch05Nested video.

The answers to Mini-Quiz questions are located in Appendix A.

Mini-Quiz 5-1

1. The manager of a golf club wants an application that displays the appropriate fee to charge a golfer. Club members pay a $5 fee. Non-members golfing on Monday through Thursday pay $15. Non-members golfing on Friday through Sunday pay $25. The condition in the outer selection structure should check the ______________, while the condition in its nested selection structure should check the ______________.

    a. membership status, day of the week

    b. day of the week, membership status

    c. membership status, fee

    d. fee, day of the week

2. Write the pseudocode for the outer and nested selection structures from Question 1.

3. Draw a flowchart for the outer and nested selection structures from Question 1.

4. Write the Visual Basic code corresponding to the selection structures from Questions 2 and 3. If the memberCheckBox in the interface is selected, it means that the person is a member. The day of the week is stored in an Integer variable named `dayNum`. The `dayNum` values range from 1 (Monday) through 7 (Sunday). Display the fee in the feeLabel.

Multiple-Alternative Selection Structures

At times, you may need to create a selection structure that can choose from several alternatives. Such selection structures are referred to as **multiple-alternative selection structures**. The Yardley Theater application is an example of an application that requires a multiple-alternative selection structure. The application's problem specification is shown in Figure 5-7, and a sample run of the application is shown in Figure 5-8. The application displays either the ticket price associated with the code entered by the user or an error message. To determine the appropriate output, the Display button's Click event procedure will use a multiple-alternative selection structure to compare the user's code with one or more of the theater's codes.

Multiple-alternative selection structures are also called extended selection structures.

The manager of the Yardley Theater wants an application that displays either the price of a concert ticket or an error message. The ticket price is based on the following codes:

Code	Ticket price
1	$15
2	$15
3	$25
4	$35
Other	Invalid code

Figure 5-7 Problem specification for the Yardley Theater application

Figure 5-8 Sample run of the Yardley Theater application

Figures 5-9 and 5-10 show the pseudocode and flowchart, respectively, for the Display button's Click event procedure. The diamond in the flowchart represents the multiple-alternative selection structure's condition. As you already know, the diamond is also used to represent the condition in both the single-alternative and dual-alternative selection structures. However, unlike the diamond in both of those selection structures, the diamond in a multiple-alternative selection structure has several flowlines (rather than only two flowlines) leading out of the symbol. Each flowline represents a possible path and must be marked appropriately, indicating the value or values necessary for the path to be chosen.

```
displayButton Click event procedure
1. store the code in a variable
2. if the code is one of the following:
        1 or 2  display "$15"
        3       display "$25"
        4       display "$35"
   else
        display "Invalid code"
   end if
```

Figure 5-9 Pseudocode for the Display button's Click event procedure

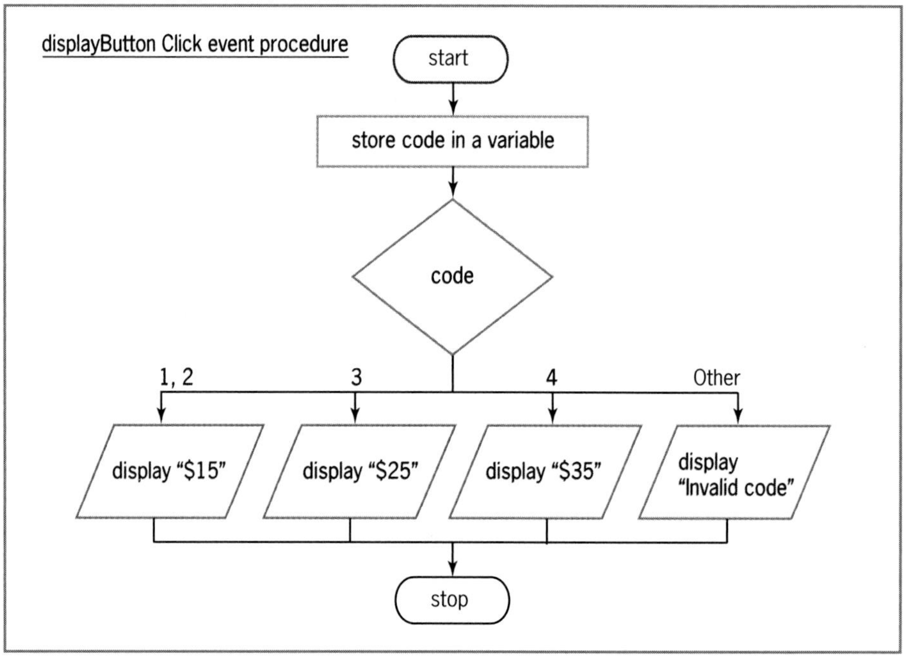

Figure 5-10 Flowchart for the Display button's Click event procedure

Figure 5-11 shows two versions of the code for the Display button's Click event procedure. Both versions use If...Then...Else statements and both produce the same result. The second version is simply a more convenient and compact way of writing a multiple-alternative selection structure.

Version 1—multiple-alternative selection structure

```
Private Sub displayButton_Click(ByVal sender As Object,
ByVal e As System.EventArgs) Handles displayButton.Click
     ' displays the ticket price

     Dim code As Integer
     Integer.TryParse(codeTextBox.Text, code)

     ' display appropriate price
     If code = 1 OrElse code = 2 Then
          priceLabel.Text = "$15"
     Else
          If code = 3 Then
               priceLabel.Text = "$25"
          Else
               If code = 4 Then
                    priceLabel.Text = "$35"
               Else
                    priceLabel.Text = "Invalid code"
               End If
          End If
     End If
End Sub
```

you get here when the code is not 1 and not 2

you get here when the code is not 1, 2, or 3

you get here when the code is not 1, 2, 3, or 4

three End If clauses are required

Version 2—multiple-alternative selection structure

```
Private Sub displayButton_Click(ByVal sender As Object,
ByVal e As System.EventArgs) Handles displayButton.Click
     ' displays the ticket price

     Dim code As Integer
     Integer.TryParse(codeTextBox.Text, code)

     ' display appropriate price
     If code = 1 OrElse code = 2 Then
          priceLabel.Text = "$15"
     ElseIf code = 3 Then
          priceLabel.Text = "$25"
     ElseIf code = 4 Then
          priceLabel.Text = "$35"
     Else
          priceLabel.Text = "Invalid code"
     End If
End Sub
```

only one End If clause is required

Figure 5-11 Two versions of the code corresponding to Figures 5-9 and 5-10

If you want to experiment with the Yardley Theater application, open the solution contained in the Try It 2! folder.

The Select Case Statement

When a multiple-alternative selection structure has many paths from which to choose, it is often simpler and clearer to code the selection structure using the **Select Case statement** rather than several If...Then...Else statements. The Select Case statement's syntax is shown in Figure 5-12. The figure also shows how you can use the Select Case statement to code the multiple-alternative selection structure from Figure 5-11. The Select Case statement begins with the keywords `Select Case`, followed by a *selectorExpression*. The selectorExpression can contain any combination of variables, constants, methods, operators, and properties. In the example in Figure 5-12, the selectorExpression is an Integer variable named `code`. The Select Case statement ends with the End Select clause. Between the Select Case and End Select clauses are the individual Case clauses. Each Case clause represents a different path that the computer can follow. It is customary to indent each Case clause and the instructions within each Case clause, as shown in the figure. You can have as many Case clauses as necessary in a Select Case statement. However, if the Select Case statement includes a Case Else clause, the Case Else clause must be the last clause in the statement. Each of the individual Case clauses, except the Case Else clause, must contain an *expressionList*, which can include one or more expressions. To include more than one expression in an expressionList, you separate each expression with a comma, as in the expressionList `Case 1, 2`. The selectorExpression needs to match only one of the expressions listed in an expressionList. The data type of the expressions must be compatible with the data type of the selectorExpression. If the selectorExpression is numeric, the expressions in the Case clauses should be numeric. Likewise, if the selectorExpression is a string, the expressions should be strings. In the example in Figure 5-12, the selectorExpression (`code`) is an integer, and so are the expressions: 1, 2, 3, and 4.

HOW TO Use the Select Case Statement

Syntax

Select Case *selectorExpression*
    Case *expressionList1*
        instructions for the first Case
    [**Case** *expressionList2*
        instructions for the second Case]
    [**Case** *expressionListN*
        instructions for the Nth Case]
    [**Case Else**
        instructions for when the selectorExpression does not match any of the expressionLists]
End Select

Example

```
Select Case code
    Case 1, 2
        priceLabel.Text = "$15"
    Case 3
        priceLabel.Text = "$25"
    Case 4
        priceLabel.Text = "$35"
    Case Else
        priceLabel.Text = "Invalid code"
End Select
```

Figure 5-12 How to use the Select Case statement

When processing the Select Case statement, the computer first compares the value of the selectorExpression with the values listed in expressionList1. If a match is found, the computer processes the instructions for the first Case, stopping when it reaches either another Case clause or the End Select clause; it then skips to the instruction following the End Select clause. For example, if the `code` variable contains the number 1, the Select Case statement in Figure 5-12 will assign the string "$15" to the priceLabel before the statement ends. If a match is not found in expressionList1, the computer skips to the second Case clause, where it compares the selectorExpression with the values listed in expressionList2. If a match is found, the computer processes the instructions for the second Case clause and then skips to the instruction following the End Select clause. If a match is not found, the computer skips to the third Case clause, and so on.

If a Case clause contains more than one value, as does the `Case 1, 2` clause, the selectorExpression needs to match only one of the values. As a result, the Select Case statement in Figure 5-12 will assign the string "$15" when the `code` variable contains either the number 1 or the number 2. If the selectorExpression does not match any of the values listed in any of the expressionLists, the computer processes the instructions listed in the Case Else clause (if there is one) and then skips to the instruction following the End Select clause. Keep in mind that if the selectorExpression matches a value in more than one Case clause, only the instructions in the first match are processed.

Specifying a Range of Values in a Case Clause

In addition to specifying one or more discrete values in a Case clause, you also can specify a range of values, such as the values from 1 through 5 or values greater than 10. You do this using either the keyword `To` or the keyword `Is`. You use the `To` keyword when you know both the upper and lower values in the range. The `Is` keyword is appropriate when you know only one end of the range (either the upper or lower end). Figure 5-13 shows the syntax for using both keywords. It also contains an example of a Select Case statement that assigns a price based on the number of items ordered. According to the price chart in the figure, the price for 1 to 5 items is $25 each. Using discrete values, the first Case clause would look like this: `Case 1, 2, 3, 4, 5`. However, a more convenient way of writing that range of numbers is to use the `To` keyword, like this: `Case 1 To 5`. The expression `1 To 5` specifies the range of numbers from 1 to 5, inclusive. The expression `6 To 10` in the second Case clause specifies the range of numbers from 6 through 10. Notice that both Case clauses state both the lower (1 and 6) and upper (5 and 10) values in each range. The third Case clause, `Case Is > 10`, contains the `Is` keyword rather than the `To` keyword. Recall that you use the `Is` keyword when you know only one end of the range of values. In this case you know only the lower end of the range, 10. The `Is` keyword is always used in combination with one of the following comparison operators: =, <, <=, >, >=, <>. The `Case Is > 10` clause specifies all numbers greater than the number 10. Because `ordered` is an Integer variable, you also can write this Case clause as `Case Is >= 11`. The Case Else clause in the example is processed only when the `ordered` variable contains a value that is not included in any of the previous Case clauses.

If you neglect to type the `Is` keyword in an expression—for example, if you enter `Case > 10`—the Code Editor will change the expression to `Case Is > 10`.

Be sure to test your code thoroughly, because the computer will not display an error message when the value preceding `To` in a Case clause is greater than the value following `To`. Instead, the Select Case statement will not give the correct results.

HOW TO Specify a Range of Values in a Case Clause

Syntax
Case *smallest value in the range* **To** *largest value in the range*
Case Is *comparisonOperator value*

Example
ABC Corporation Price Chart

Number ordered	Price per item
1 - 5	$25
6 - 10	$23
More than 10	$20
Less than 1	$0

```
Select Case ordered
    Case 1 To 5
        price = 25
    Case 6 To 10
        price = 23
    Case Is > 10
        price = 20
    Case Else
        price = 0
End Select
```

Figure 5-13 How to specify a range of values in a Case clause

If you want to experiment with the ABC Corporation application, open the solution contained in the Try It 3! folder.

To review what you learned about multiple-alternative selection structures, view the Ch05Multiple-Alternative video.

The answers to Mini-Quiz questions are located in Appendix A.

Mini-Quiz 5-2

1. A Select Case statement's selectorExpression is a String variable named `colorCode`. Which of the following Case clauses will process the same instructions for color codes from 1 through 4?
   a. `Case 1, 2, 3, 4`
   b. `Case "1", "2", "3", "4"`
   c. `Case "4" To "1"`
   d. both b and c

2. A Select Case statement's selectorExpression is an Integer variable named `colorCode`. Which of the following Case clauses will process the same instructions for color codes from 10 through 15?
   a. `Case 10, 11, 12, 13, 14, 15`
   b. `Case 15 To 10`
   c. `Case Is >= 10 AndAlso <= 15`
   d. all of the above

3. You can code a multiple-alternative selection structure using either If... Then... Else statements or the Select Case statement.
   a. True
   b. False

Using Radio Buttons in an Interface

Multiple-alternative selection structures are commonly used in applications whose interfaces contain several radio buttons. You add a radio button to a form using the RadioButton tool in the toolbox. **Radio buttons** allow you to limit the user to only one choice from a group of two or more related but mutually exclusive choices. The interface shown in Figure 5-14 contains six radio buttons. Each radio button is labeled so that the user knows its purpose. You enter the label using sentence capitalization in the radio button's Text property. Each radio button also has a unique access key that allows the user to select the button using the keyboard. Notice that the radio buttons are separated into two groups: one group contains the four state radio buttons and the other contains the two delivery radio buttons. To include two groups of radio buttons in an interface, at least one of the groups must be placed within a container, such as a group box, panel, or table layout panel. Otherwise, the radio buttons are considered to be in the same group and only one can be selected at any one time. In this case, the radio buttons pertaining to the state choice are contained in the GroupBox1 control, and the radio buttons pertaining to the delivery choice are contained in the GroupBox2 control.

To learn how to add group box controls and radio buttons to a form, view the Ch05GroupRadioButton video.

You add a **group box** to a form using the GroupBox tool in the toolbox. Placing each group of radio buttons in a separate group box allows the user to select one button from each group. Keep in mind that the minimum number of radio buttons in a group is two, because the only way to deselect a radio button is to select another radio button. The recommended maximum number of radio buttons in a group is seven. It is customary in Windows applications to have one of the radio buttons in each group already selected when the interface first appears. The automatically selected button is called the **default radio button** and is either the radio button that represents the user's most likely choice or the first radio button in the group. You designate the default radio button by setting the button's Checked property to the Boolean value True. When you set the Checked property to True in the Properties window, a colored dot appears inside the button's circle to indicate that the button is selected. The Alabama radio button is the default button in the State group in Figure 5-14; the Standard radio button is the default button in the Delivery group.

You also can use a list box, checked list box, or combo box to limit the user to only one choice from a group of related but mutually exclusive choices.

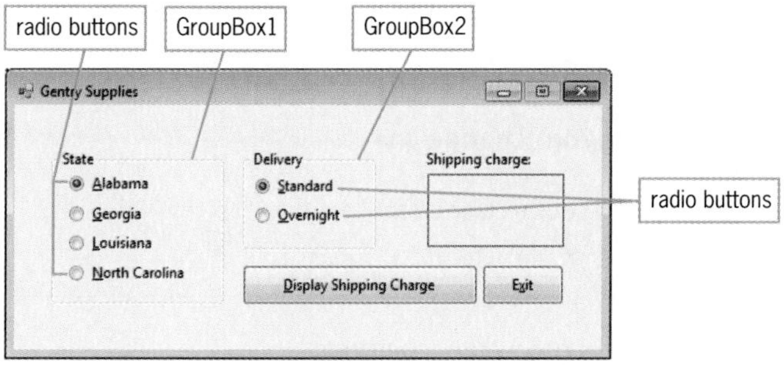

Figure 5-14 Gentry Supplies application's interface

You can omit the = True in the multiple-alternative selection structure in Version 1 in Figure 5-15. You also can omit the = True in the single-alternative selection structure in both versions.

If you want to experiment with the Gentry Supplies application, open the solution contained in the Try It 4! folder.

When the user clicks the Display Shipping Charge button, the button's Click event procedure should calculate and display the appropriate shipping charge. The shipping charge information is shown in Figure 5-15, along with two versions of the Display Shipping Charge button's code: one using If...Then...Else statements and the other using the Select Case statement. Notice that both versions of the code use the Checked property to determine the radio button selected in each group.

Gentry Supplies Shipping Chart

State	Standard delivery charge
Alabama	$20
Georgia	$35
Louisiana	$30
North Carolina	$28
Overnight delivery	add $10 to the standard delivery charge

Version 1 – If...Then...Else statements

```
Private Sub displayButton_Click(ByVal sender As Object,
ByVal e As System.EventArgs) Handles displayButton.Click
     ' displays the appropriate shipping charge

     Dim shipCharge As Integer

     ' determine state shipping charge
     If alabamaRadioButton.Checked = True Then
          shipCharge = 20
     ElseIf georgiaRadioButton.Checked = True Then
          shipCharge = 35
     ElseIf louisianaRadioButton.Checked = True Then
          shipCharge = 30
     Else
          shipCharge = 28
     End If

     ' add $10 for overnight delivery
     If overnightRadioButton.Checked = True Then
          shipCharge = shipCharge + 10
     End If

     ' display shipping charge
     shipLabel.Text = shipCharge.ToString("C2")
End Sub
```

you also can write this statement as `shipCharge += 10`

Version 2 – Select Case statement

```
Private Sub displayButton_Click(ByVal sender As Object, ByVal e As
System.EventArgs) Handles displayButton.Click
     ' displays the appropriate shipping charge

     Dim shipCharge As Integer

     ' determine state shipping charge
     Select Case True
          Case alabamaRadioButton.Checked
               shipCharge = 20
```

Figure 5-15 Display button's Click event procedure *(continues)*

(continued)

```
        Case georgiaRadioButton.Checked
            shipCharge = 35
        Case louisianaRadioButton.Checked
            shipCharge = 30
        Case Else
            shipCharge = 28
    End Select

    ' add $10 for overnight delivery
    If overnightRadioButton.Checked = True Then
        shipCharge = shipCharge + 10
    End If

    ' display shipping charge
    shipLabel.Text = shipCharge.ToString("C2")
End Sub
```

you also can write this statement as `shipCharge += 10`

Figure 5-15 Display button's Click event procedure

The MessageBox.Show Method

At times, an application may need to communicate with the user during run time. For instance, before calculating an employee's gross pay, the application should alert the user when the hoursTextBox does not contain any data. One means of communicating with the user is through a message box. You display the message box using the **MessageBox.Show method**. The message box contains text, one or more buttons, and an icon. Figure 5-16 shows the method's syntax and lists the meaning of each argument. The figure also includes examples of using the method. Figures 5-17 and 5-18 show the message boxes created by the two examples.

HOW TO Use the MessageBox.Show Method

Syntax
MessageBox.Show(text**,** *caption***,** *buttons***,** *icon*[**,** *defaultButton*]**)**

Argument	Meaning
text	text to display in the message box; use sentence capitalization
caption	text to display in the message box's title bar; use book title capitalization

buttons	buttons to display in the message box; can be one of the following constants:
	`MessageBoxButtons.AbortRetryIgnore`
	`MessageBoxButtons.OK` (default setting)
	`MessageBoxButtons.OKCancel`
	`MessageBoxButtons.RetryCancel`
	`MessageBoxButtons.YesNo`
	`MessageBoxButtons.YesNoCancel`

Figure 5-16 How to use the MessageBox.Show method *(continues)*

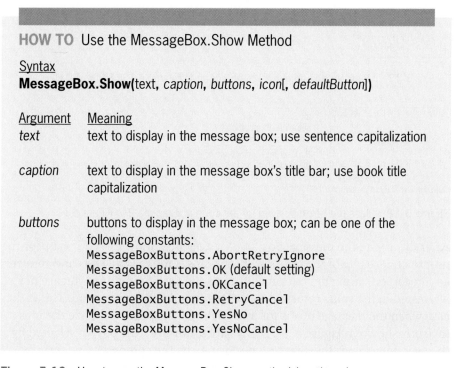

(continued)

icon — icon to display in the message box; typically, one of the following constants:
`MessageBoxIcon.Exclamation`
`MessageBoxIcon.Information`
`MessageBoxIcon.Question`
`MessageBoxIcon.Stop`

defaultButton — button automatically selected when the user presses Enter; can be one of the following constants:
`MessageBoxDefaultButton.Button1` (default setting)
`MessageBoxDefaultButton.Button2`
`MessageBoxDefaultButton.Button3`

Example 1

```
MessageBox.Show("Record deleted.", "Payroll",
     MessageBoxButtons.OK, MessageBoxIcon.Information)
```

displays an informational message box that contains the message "Record deleted."

Example 2

```
MessageBox.Show("Delete this record?", "Payroll",
     MessageBoxButtons.YesNo, MessageBoxIcon.Exclamation,
     MessageBoxDefaultButton.Button2)
```

displays a warning message box that contains the message "Delete this record?"

Figure 5-16 How to use the MessageBox.Show method

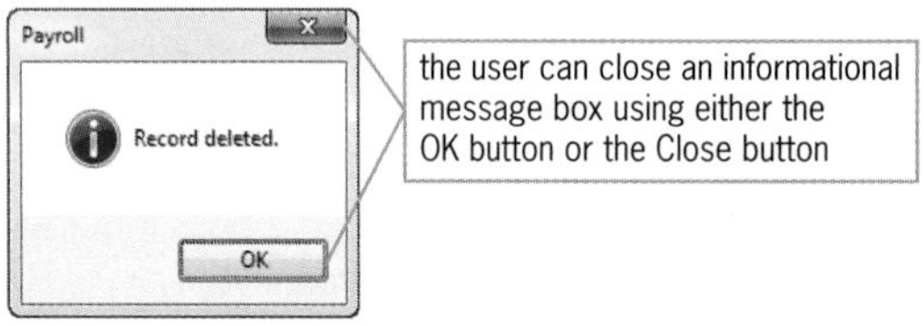

Figure 5-17 Message box displayed by the code in Example 1 in Figure 5-16

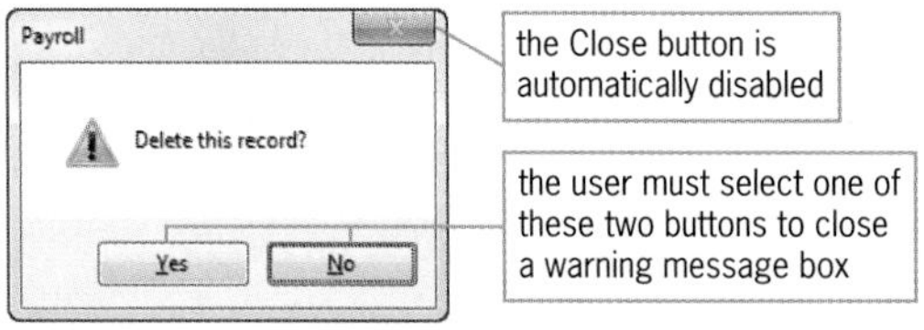

Figure 5-18 Message box displayed by the code in Example 2 in Figure 5-16

After displaying the message box, the MessageBox.Show method waits for the user to choose one of the buttons. It then closes the message box and returns an integer indicating the button chosen by the user. Sometimes you are not interested in the value returned by the MessageBox.Show method. This is the case when the message box is for informational purposes only, like the message box shown in Figure 5-17. Many times, however, the button selected by the user determines the next task performed by the computer. For example, selecting the Yes button in the message box shown in Figure 5-18 tells the computer to delete the record; selecting the No button tells it *not* to delete the record. Figure 5-19 lists the integer values returned by the MessageBox.Show method. Each value is associated with a button that can appear in a message box. The figure also lists the DialogResult values assigned to each integer, and the meaning of the integers and DialogResult values. As the figure indicates, the MessageBox.Show method returns the integer 6 when the user selects the Yes button. The integer 6 is represented by the DialogResult value, `DialogResult.Yes`. When referring to the method's return value in code, you should use the DialogResult values rather than the integers, because the values make the code more self-documenting and easier to understand.

Figure 5-19 also contains two examples of using the value returned by the MessageBox.Show method. In the first example, the return value is assigned to a DialogResult variable named `button`. The selection structure in the example compares the value in the `button` variable with the `DialogResult.Yes` value. In the second example, the method's return value is not stored in a variable. Instead, the method appears in a selection structure's condition, where its return value is compared with the `DialogResult.Yes` value. The selection structure in Example 2 performs one set of tasks when the user selects the Yes button in the message box, but a different set of tasks when the user selects the No button. It is a good programming practice to document the Else portion of the selection structure as shown in the figure, because it makes it clear that the Else portion is processed only when the user selects the No button.

HOW TO Use the MessageBox.Show Method's Return Value

Integer	DialogResult value	Meaning
1	`DialogResult.OK`	user chose the OK button
2	`DialogResult.Cancel`	user chose the Cancel button
3	`DialogResult.Abort`	user chose the Abort button
4	`DialogResult.Retry`	user chose the Retry button
5	`DialogResult.Ignore`	user chose the Ignore button
6	`DialogResult.Yes`	user chose the Yes button
7	`DialogResult.No`	user chose the No button

Example 1
```
Dim button As DialogResult
button = MessageBox.Show("Delete this record?", "Payroll",
     MessageBoxButtons.YesNo, MessageBoxIcon.Exclamation,
     MessageBoxDefaultButton.Button2)
If button = DialogResult.Yes Then
     instructions to delete the record
End If
```

Example 2
```
If MessageBox.Show("Play another game?", "Math Monster",
     MessageBoxButtons.YesNo,
     MessageBoxIcon.Exclamation) = DialogResult.Yes Then
     instructions to start another game
Else   ' No button
     instructions to close the game application
End If
```

Figure 5-19 How to use the MessageBox.Show method's return value

If you want to experiment with the MessageBox.Show method, open the solution contained in the Try It 5! folder.

To review what you learned about the MessageBox.Show method, view the Ch05MessageBox video.

The last topic covered in this chapter is the KeyPress event, which you can use to prevent a text box from accepting an inappropriate character. You will use the KeyPress event in this chapter's Programming Example.

Using the KeyPress Event

Earlier, in Figure 5-3, you viewed a sample run of the Voter Eligibility application, which provides a text box for the user to enter a person's age. The user should enter the age as an integer. The age should not contain any letters, spaces, punctuation marks, or special characters. Unfortunately, you can't stop the user from trying to enter an inappropriate character into a text box. However, you can prevent the text box from accepting the character; you do this by coding the text box's KeyPress event procedure. A control's **KeyPress event** occurs each time the user presses a key while the control has the focus. When the KeyPress event occurs, a character corresponding to the pressed key is sent to the KeyPress event's `e` parameter, which appears between the parentheses in the event's procedure header. For example, when the user presses the period (.) while entering data into a text box, the text box's KeyPress event occurs and a period is sent to the event's `e` parameter. Similarly, when the Shift key along with a letter is pressed, the uppercase version of the letter is sent to the `e` parameter. To prevent a text box from accepting an inappropriate character, you first use the `e` parameter's **KeyChar property** to determine the pressed key. (KeyChar stands for "key character.") You then use the `e` parameter's **Handled property** to cancel the key if it is an inappropriate one. You cancel the key by setting the Handled property to True, like this: `e.Handled = True`.

In the Voter Eligibility application, the ageTextBox's KeyPress event procedure should allow the text box to accept only numbers and the Backspace key, which is used for editing. You refer to the Backspace key on your keyboard using Visual Basic's **ControlChars.Back constant**. Figure 5-20 shows two versions of the KeyPress event procedure's code. The If clause in both versions determines whether the value stored in the KeyChar property is inappropriate for the text box. In this case, an inappropriate value is one that is either less than "0" or greater than "9" and, at the same time, is not the Backspace key. You can enter the entire If clause on one line in the Code Editor window. Or, you can split the clause into two lines, as shown in both versions in the figure. Depending on where you break a line of code, you may or may not need a line continuation character. The **line continuation character** is the underscore shown in Version 2. Examples of places where you can break a line of code without using the line continuation character include the following: after a comma, after an opening parenthesis, before a closing parenthesis, and after an operator (arithmetic, assignment, comparison, logical, or concatenation operator). The line continuation character must be immediately preceded by a space and appear at the end of a physical line of code in the Code Editor window.

HOW TO Use the KeyPress Event to Cancel Invalid Characters

Version 1

```
Private Sub ageTextBox_KeyPress(ByVal sender As Object,
ByVal e As System.Windows.Forms.KeyPressEventArgs
) Handles ageTextBox.KeyPress
     ' allows the text box to accept only numbers
     ' and the Backspace key

     If (e.KeyChar < "0" OrElse e.KeyChar > "9") AndAlso
          e.KeyChar <> ControlChars.Back Then
          e.Handled = True
     End If
End Sub
```

Version 2

```
Private Sub ageTextBox_KeyPress(ByVal sender As Object,
ByVal e As System.Windows.Forms.KeyPressEventArgs
) Handles ageTextBox.KeyPress
        ' allows the text box to accept only numbers
        ' and the Backspace key

        If (e.KeyChar < "0" OrElse e.KeyChar > "9") _
              AndAlso e.KeyChar <> ControlChars.Back Then
            e.Handled = True
        End If
    End Sub
```

line continuation character

Figure 5-20 How to use the KeyPress event to cancel invalid characters

If you want to experiment with the KeyPress event, open the solution contained in the Try It 6! folder.

The KeyPress event automatically allows the use of the Delete key for editing.

To review what you learned about the KeyPress event, view the Ch05KeyPress video.

Mini-Quiz 5-3

1. The Backspace key is represented by the ______________ constant.
   a. `Control.Back`
   b. `Control.Backspace`
   c. `ControlKey.Back`
   d. `ControlChars.Back`

2. You designate a default radio button by setting its ______________ property to True.
   a. Checked
   b. Chosen
   c. Default
   d. Selected

The answers to Mini-Quiz questions are located in Appendix A.

3. The Abort button in a message box is represented by which of the following values?

   a. `Button.Abort`

   b. `Dialog.Abort`

   c. `DialogResult.Abort`

   d. `Result.Abort`

4. When entered in a text box's KeyPress event procedure, which of the following statements cancels the key pressed by the user?

   a. `e.Cancel = True`

   b. `e.Handled = True`

   c. `e.KeyCancel = True`

   d. `e.KeyChar = True`

You have completed the concepts section of Chapter 5. The Programming Tutorial section is next.

PROGRAMMING TUTORIAL 1

Creating the Rock, Paper, Scissors Game Application

The Ch05ProgTut1 video demonstrates all of the steps in Programming Tutorial 1.

In this tutorial, you create an application that simulates a game called Rock, Paper, Scissors. The game is meant to be played with two people. However, you will program the game so that one person can play against the computer. "Rock, Paper, Scissors" refers to the three choices each player can indicate using hand gestures. To play the game, the players face each other, call out "Rock, paper, scissors, shoot," and then make the hand gesture corresponding to their choice: a fist (rock), a flat hand (paper), or two fingers forming a V shape (scissors). The rules for determining a win are listed in Figure 5-21. Figures 5-22 and 5-23 show the application's TOE chart and MainForm, respectively. The interface contains five picture boxes, four labels, one table layout panel, and one button. (The three images were downloaded from the Stock.XCHNG site and were contributed by the photographer, Laura Kennedy. You can browse and optionally download other free images at *www.sxc.hu*.)

Rock breaks scissors, so rock wins
Paper covers rock, so paper wins
Scissors cut paper, so scissors win

Figure 5-21 Rules for the Rock, Paper, Scissors game

Task	Object	Event
1. Display the appropriate image in the playerPictureBox 2. Generate a random number from 1 through 3 to represent the computer's choice 3. Use the random number to display the rock, paper, or scissors image in the computerPictureBox 4. Determine whether the game is tied or there is a winner, and then display an appropriate message in the winnerLabel	rockPictureBox, paperPictureBox, scissorsPictureBox	Click
End the application	exitButton	Click
Display a message indicating either the winner or a tie game (from rockPictureBox, paperPictureBox, or scissorsPictureBox)	winnerLabel	None
Display the image corresponding to the player's choice	playerPictureBox	None
Display the image corresponding to the computer's choice (from rockPictureBox, paperPictureBox, or scissorsPictureBox)	computerPictureBox	None

Figure 5-22 TOE chart for the Rock, Paper, Scissors Game application

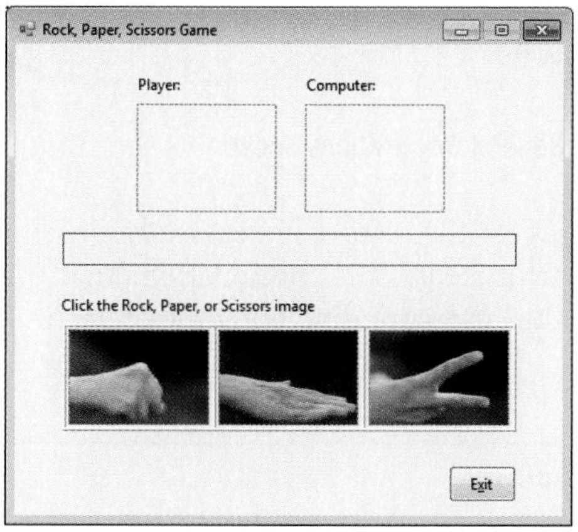

Figure 5-23 MainForm for the Rock, Paper, Scissors Game application

Coding the Rock, Paper, Scissors Game Application

Included in the data files for this book is a partially completed Rock, Paper, Scissors Game application. To complete the application, you just need to code it. According to the application's TOE chart, the Click event procedures for the rockPictureBox, paperPicturebox, scissorsPictureBox, and exitButton need to be coded.

To begin coding the application:

1. Start Visual Studio or the Express Edition of Visual Basic. If necessary, open the Solution Explorer window.
2. Open the **RockPaperScissorsGame Solution** (**RockPaperScissors-Game Solution.sln**) file, which is contained in the VbReloaded2010\

Chap05\RockPaperScissorsGame Solution folder. Open the designer window (if necessary), and then auto-hide the Solution Explorer window.

3. Open the Code Editor window. Notice that the exitButton's Click event procedure has already been coded for you.

4. In the comments that appear in the General Declarations section, replace <your name> and <current date> with your name and the current date.

5. The application will use variables, so you should enter the appropriate Option statements in the General Declarations section. Enter the Option statements shown in Figure 5-24. (It's not necessary for you to display the line numbers in the Code Editor window.)

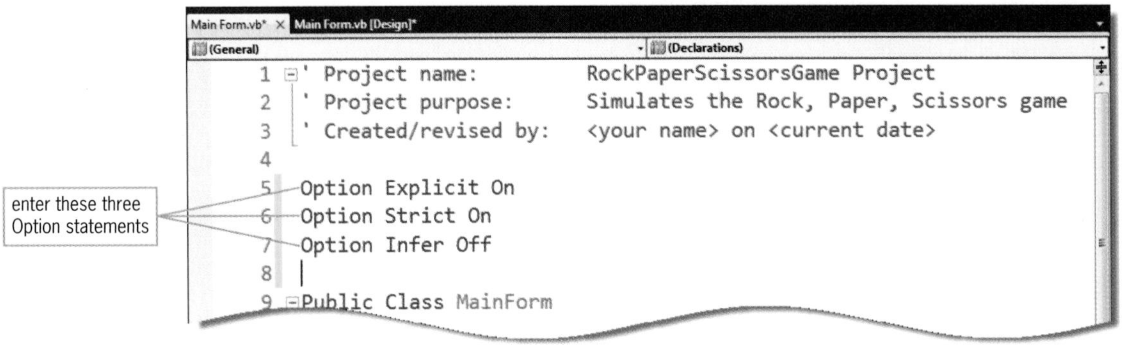

Figure 5-24 Option statements entered in the General Declarations section

Before coding the Click event procedures for the picture boxes, study closely the chart shown in Figure 5-25. The chart indicates the combinations that can occur when playing the game, and the corresponding outcome of each combination.

Player's choice	Computer's choice	Outcome
Rock	Rock	Tie
	Paper	Computer wins because paper covers rock
	Scissors	Player wins because rock breaks scissors
Paper	Rock	Player wins because paper covers rock
	Paper	Tie
	Scissors	Computer wins because scissors cut paper
Scissors	Rock	Computer wins because rock breaks scissors
	Paper	Player wins because scissors cut paper
	Scissors	Tie

Figure 5-25 Chart showing combinations and outcomes

Now study the pseudocode shown in Figure 5-26. The pseudocode indicates the tasks to be performed by the rockPictureBox's Click event procedure.

```
rockPictureBox Click event procedure
1. display the rockPictureBox image, which represents the player's choice, in the playerPictureBox
2. generate a random number from 1 through 3 to represent the computer's choice
3. if the random number is one of the following:
        1  display the rockPictureBox image in the computerPictureBox
           display the string "Tie" in the winnerLabel
        2  display the paperPictureBox image in the computerPictureBox
           display the string "Computer wins because paper covers rock." in the winnerLabel
        3  display the scissorsPictureBox image in the computerPictureBox
           display the string "Player wins because rock breaks scissors." in the winnerLabel
   end if
```

Figure 5-26 Pseudocode for the rockPictureBox's Click event procedure

To code the rockPictureBox's Click event procedure and then test the procedure's code:

1. Open the code template for the rockPictureBox's Click event procedure. Type **' determines whether the game is tied or the winner** and press **Enter** twice.

2. The procedure will need a Random object to represent the pseudo-random number generator. It will use an Integer variable to store the random number. Enter the following two Dim statements. Press **Enter** twice after typing the second Dim statement.

   Dim randomGenerator As New Random
   Dim computerChoice As Integer

3. The first step in the pseudocode is to display the rockPictureBox image, which represents the player's choice, in the playerPictureBox. Enter the following comment and assignment statement. Press **Enter** twice after typing the assignment statement.

   ' display the player's choice
   playerPictureBox.Image = rockPictureBox.Image

4. The next step is to generate a random number from 1 through 3. You will assign the random number to the `computerChoice` variable. Enter the following comment and assignment statement.

   ' generate a random number from 1 through 3
   computerChoice = randomGenerator.Next(1, 4)

5. The last step in the pseudocode is to use the random number to display the appropriate image and message in the computerPictureBox and winnerLabel, respectively. Enter the additional comment and code shown in Figure 5-27.

```
Private Sub rockPictureBox_Click(ByVal sender As Object, ByVal e As System.
    ' determines whether the game is tied or the winner

    Dim randomGenerator As New Random
    Dim computerChoice As Integer

    ' display the player's choice
    playerPictureBox.Image = rockPictureBox.Image

    ' generate a random number from 1 through 3
    computerChoice = randomGenerator.Next(1, 4)
    ' display the computer's choice and the outcome
    Select Case computerChoice
        Case 1
            computerPictureBox.Image = rockPictureBox.Image
            winnerLabel.Text = "Tie"
        Case 2
            computerPictureBox.Image = paperPictureBox.Image
            winnerLabel.Text = "Computer wins because paper covers rock."
        Case 3
            computerPictureBox.Image = scissorsPictureBox.Image
            winnerLabel.Text = "Player wins because rock breaks scissors."
    End Select
End Sub
```

enter this comment and the Select Case statement

Figure 5-27 Completed Click event procedure for the rockPictureBox

6. Save the solution and then start the application. Click the **rockPictureBox** several times to verify that its Click event procedure is working properly. Figure 5-28 shows a sample run of the application. (Because the procedure generates a random number for the computer's choice, a different image and message might appear in the computerPictureBox and winnerLabel controls on your screen.)

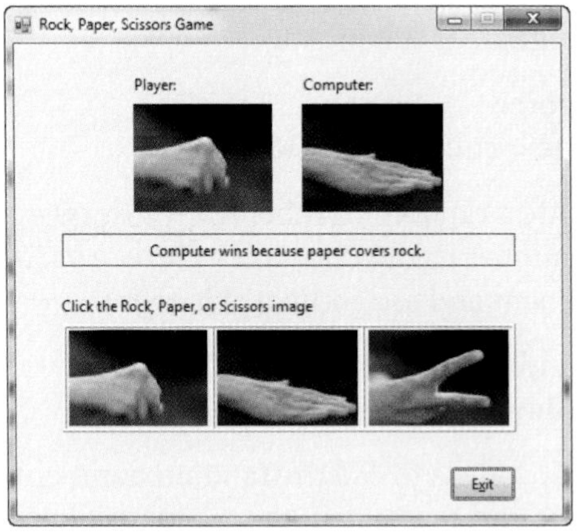

Figure 5-28 Sample run of the Rock, Paper, Scissors Game application

7. Click the **Exit** button to end the application.

Next, you will code the Click event procedure for the paperPictureBox. The procedure's pseudocode is shown in Figure 5-29.

<u>paperPictureBox Click event procedure</u>
1. display the paperPictureBox image, which represents the player's choice, in the playerPictureBox
2. generate a random number from 1 through 3 to represent the computer's choice
3. if the random number is one of the following:
   1 display the rockPictureBox image in the computerPictureBox
     display the string "Player wins because paper covers rock." in the winnerLabel
   2 display the paperPictureBox image in the computerPictureBox
     display the string "Tie" in the winnerLabel
   3 display the scissorsPictureBox image in the computerPictureBox
     display the string "Computer wins because scissors cut paper." in the winnerLabel
   end if

Figure 5-29 Pseudocode for the paperPictureBox's Click event procedure

To code the paperPictureBox's Click event procedure and then test the procedure's code:

1. Open the code template for the paperPictureBox's Click event procedure.
2. Copy the comments and code from the rockPictureBox's Click event procedure to the paperPictureBox's Click event procedure. (Do not copy the procedure header or footer.)
3. Make the appropriate modifications to the paperPictureBox's Click event procedure.
4. Save the solution and then start the application. Click the **paper-PictureBox** several times to verify that its Click event procedure is working properly.
5. Click the **Exit** button to end the application.

Finally, you will code the Click event procedure for the scissorsPictureBox. The procedure's pseudocode is shown in Figure 5-30.

<u>scissorsPictureBox Click event procedure</u>
1. display the scissorsPictureBox image, which represents the player's choice, in the playerPictureBox
2. generate a random number from 1 through 3 to represent the computer's choice
3. if the random number is one of the following:
   1 display the rockPictureBox image in the computerPictureBox
     display the string "Computer wins because rock breaks scissors." in the winnerLabel
   2 display the paperPictureBox image in the computerPictureBox
     display the string "Player wins because scissors cut paper." in the winnerLabel
   3 display the scissorsPictureBox image in the computerPictureBox
     display the string "Tie" in the winnerLabel
   end if

Figure 5-30 Pseudocode for the scissorsPictureBox's Click event procedure

To code the scissorsPictureBox's Click event procedure and then test the procedure's code:

1. Open the code template for the scissorsPictureBox's Click event procedure.
2. Copy the comments and code from the rockPictureBox's Click event procedure to the scissorsPictureBox's Click event procedure. (Do not copy the procedure header or footer.)
3. Make the appropriate modifications to the scissorsPictureBox's Click event procedure.
4. Save the solution and then start the application. Click the **scissorsPictureBox** several times to verify that its Click event procedure is working properly.
5. Click the **Exit** button to end the application. Close the Code Editor window, and then close the solution. Figure 5-31 shows the application's code.

```
' Project name:        RockPaperScissorsGame Project
' Project purpose:     Simulates the Rock, Paper, Scissors game
' Created/revised by:  <your name> on <current date>

Option Explicit On
Option Strict On
Option Infer Off

Public Class MainForm

  Private Sub exitButton_Click(ByVal sender As Object,
  ByVal e As System.EventArgs) Handles exitButton.Click
     Me.Close()
  End Sub

  Private Sub rockPictureBox_Click(ByVal sender As Object,
  ByVal e As System.EventArgs) Handles rockPictureBox.Click
     ' determines whether the game is tied or the winner

     Dim randomGenerator As New Random
     Dim computerChoice As Integer

     ' display the player's choice
     playerPictureBox.Image = rockPictureBox.Image

     ' generate a random number from 1 through 3
     computerChoice = randomGenerator.Next(1, 4)
     ' display the computer's choice and the outcome
     Select Case computerChoice
        Case 1
           computerPictureBox.Image = rockPictureBox.Image
           winnerLabel.Text = "Tie"
        Case 2
           computerPictureBox.Image = paperPictureBox.Image
           winnerLabel.Text = "Computer wins because paper covers rock."
```

Figure 5-31 Code for the Rock, Paper, Scissors Game application *(continues)*

(continued)

```
        Case 3
            computerPictureBox.Image = scissorsPictureBox.Image
            winnerLabel.Text = "Player wins because rock breaks scissors."
    End Select
End Sub

Private Sub paperPictureBox_Click(ByVal sender As Object,
ByVal e As System.EventArgs) Handles paperPictureBox.Click
    ' determines whether the game is tied or the winner

    Dim randomGenerator As New Random
    Dim computerChoice As Integer

    ' display the player's choice
    playerPictureBox.Image = paperPictureBox.Image

    ' generate a random number from 1 through 3
    computerChoice = randomGenerator.Next(1, 4)
    ' display the computer's choice and the outcome
    Select Case computerChoice
        Case 1
            computerPictureBox.Image = rockPictureBox.Image
            winnerLabel.Text = "Player wins because paper covers rock."
        Case 2
            computerPictureBox.Image = paperPictureBox.Image
            winnerLabel.Text = "Tie"
        Case 3
            computerPictureBox.Image = scissorsPictureBox.Image
            winnerLabel.Text = "Computer wins because scissors cut paper."
    End Select
End Sub

Private Sub scissorsPictureBox_Click(ByVal sender As Object,
ByVal e As System.EventArgs) Handles scissorsPictureBox.Click
    ' determines whether the game is tied or the winner

    Dim randomGenerator As New Random
    Dim computerChoice As Integer

    ' display the player's choice
    playerPictureBox.Image = scissorsPictureBox.Image

    ' generate a random number from 1 through 3
    computerChoice = randomGenerator.Next(1, 4)
    ' display the computer's choice and the outcome
    Select Case computerChoice
        Case 1
            computerPictureBox.Image = rockPictureBox.Image
            winnerLabel.Text = "Computer wins because rock breaks scissors."
        Case 2
            computerPictureBox.Image = paperPictureBox.Image
            winnerLabel.Text = "Player wins because scissors cut paper."
        Case 3
            computerPictureBox.Image = scissorsPictureBox.Image
            winnerLabel.Text = "Tie"
    End Select
End Sub
End Class
```

Figure 5-31 Code for the Rock, Paper, Scissors Game application

PROGRAMMING TUTORIAL 2

Coding the Charleston Cable Company Application

In this tutorial, you create an application for the Charleston Cable Company. The application calculates and displays a customer's monthly cable bill, which is based on the information shown in Figure 5-32. The application's TOE chart and MainForm are shown in Figures 5-33 and 5-34, respectively. The MainForm provides radio buttons and check boxes for selecting the cable package and additional features, respectively.

Packages/Additional features	Charge
Basic	39.99
Bronze	44.99
Silver	59.99
Gold	74.99
HBI movie channels	10.00
Showtimer movie channels	11.50
Cinematic movie channels	12.00
Local stations	5.00

Figure 5-32 Charleston Cable Company's rates

Task	Object	Event
Specify the cable package	basicRadioButton, bronzeRadioButton, silverRadioButton, goldRadioButton	None
Specify any additional charges	hbiCheckBox, showtimerCheckBox, cinematicCheckBox, localCheckBox	None
1. Calculate the cable bill 2. Display the cable bill in a message box	calcButton	Click
End the application	exitButton	Click

Figure 5-33 TOE chart for the Charleston Cable Company application

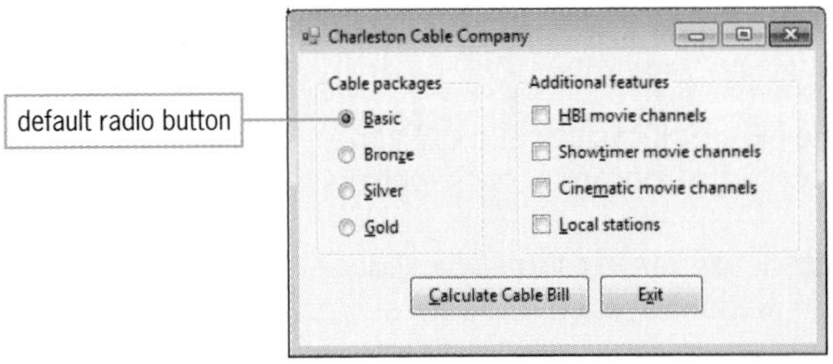

Figure 5-34 MainForm for the Charleston Cable Company application

Coding the Charleston Cable Company Application

Included in the data files for this book is a partially completed Charleston Cable Company application. To complete the application, you just need to code it. According to the application's TOE chart, the Click event procedures for the calcButton and exitButton need to be coded.

To begin coding the application:

1. Start Visual Studio or the Express Edition of Visual Basic. If necessary, open the Solution Explorer window.
2. Open the **Charleston Cable Solution** (**Charleston Cable Solution.sln**) file, which is contained in the VbReloaded2010\Chap05\Charleston Cable Solution folder. Open the designer window (if necessary), and then auto-hide the Solution Explorer window.
3. Open the Code Editor window. Notice that the exitButton's Click event procedure has already been coded for you.
4. In the comments that appear in the General Declarations section, replace <your name> and <current date> with your name and the current date.
5. Enter the appropriate Option statements in the General Declarations section.

The application's TOE chart indicates that the Calculate Cable Bill button's Click event procedure is responsible for calculating and displaying the cable bill. The procedure's pseudocode is shown in Figure 5-35.

```
calcButton Click event procedure
1. if one of the following radio buttons is selected in the Cable packages group:
        Basic              cable bill = 39.99
        Bronze             cable bill = 44.99
        Silver             cable bill = 59.99
        Gold               cable bill = 74.99
   end if
2. if the HBI movie channels check box is selected
        add 10 to the cable bill
   end if
3. if the Showtimer movie channels check box is selected
        add 11.50 to the cable bill
   end if
4. if the Cinematic movie channels check box is selected
        add 12 to the cable bill
   end if
5. if the Local stations check box is selected
        add 5 to the cable bill
   end if
6. display the cable bill in a message box
```

Figure 5-35 Pseudocode for the calcButton's Click event procedure

As you know, before you begin coding a procedure, you first study the procedure's pseudocode (or flowchart) to determine any variables or named constants the procedure will require. In this case, the calcButton's Click event procedure will use eight named constants to store the package and additional charges. It also will use a Double variable to keep track of the cable bill. The named constants and variable are listed in Figure 5-36.

Named constants	**Data type**	**Value**
`Basic`	Double	39.99
`Bronze`	Double	44.99
`Silver`	Double	59.99
`Gold`	Double	74.99
`Hbi`	Double	10.00
`Showtimer`	Double	11.50
`Cinematic`	Double	12.00
`Local`	Double	5.00
Variable	**Data type**	**Value source**
`cableBill`	Double	procedure calculation

Figure 5-36 Named constants and variable for the calcButton's Click event procedure

To code the Calculate button's Click event procedure, and then test the application:

1. Open the code template for the calcButton's Click event procedure.
2. Type **' calculates a monthly cable bill** and press **Enter** twice.
3. Enter the statements to declare the nine memory locations listed in Figure 5-36. Press **Enter** twice after typing the last declaration statement.
4. Step 1 in the pseudocode (shown earlier in Figure 5-35) determines the radio button selected in the Cable packages group, and then assigns the appropriate charge as the cable bill. Type **' determine package charge** and press **Enter**. Next, enter a multiple-alternative selection structure to assign the appropriate charge to the `cableBill` variable. Use the If...Then...Else statement.
5. Steps 2 through 5 in the pseudocode determine whether the customer should be charged for any additional features. Insert two blank lines above the End Sub clause. In the blank line above the End Sub clause, type **' add any additional charges** and press **Enter**. Now enter four single-alternative selection structures to add the additional charges (if any) to the cable bill.
6. The last step in the pseudocode displays the cable bill in a message box. Insert two blank lines between the last End If clause and the End Sub clause. In the blank line above the End Sub clause, type **' display the cable bill** and press **Enter**. Now enter an appropriate MessageBox.Show method. The message box should contain the message "Your monthly cable bill is " followed by the contents of the `cableBill` variable, formatted with a dollar sign and two decimal places. The message box should also contain an OK button and the Information icon. The company's name, Charleston Cable Company, should appear in the message box's title bar.

7. Save the solution, and then start the application. Notice that the Basic radio button, which is the default radio button, is already selected in the interface.

8. Click the **Silver** radio button, and then click the **Local stations** check box. Click the **Calculate Cable Bill** button. The monthly cable bill appears in a message box, as shown in Figure 5-37.

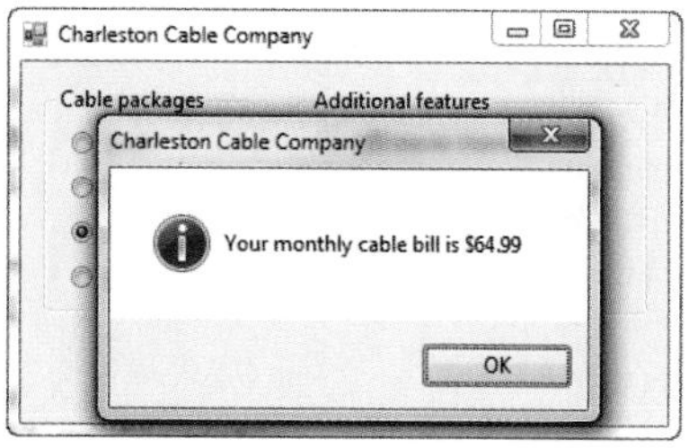

Figure 5-37 Message box showing the monthly cable bill

9. Click the **OK** button to close the message box.

10. Click the **Local stations** check box to deselect it. Click the **Basic** radio button, the **HBI movie channels** check box, and the **Showtimer movie channels** check box. Click the **Calculate Cable Bill** button. The message box indicates that the monthly cable bill is $61.49.

11. Close the message box. Click the **Exit** button to end the application. Close the Code Editor window and then close the solution. Figure 5-38 shows the code for the Charleston Cable Company application.

```
' Project name:          Charleston Cable Project
' Project purpose:       Displays a customer's cable bill
' Created/revised by:    <your name> on <current date>

Option Explicit On
Option Strict On
Option Infer Off

Public Class MainForm

  Private Sub exitButton_Click(ByVal sender As Object,
  ByVal e As System.EventArgs) Handles exitButton.Click
     Me.Close()
  End Sub

  Private Sub calcButton_Click(ByVal sender As Object,
  ByVal e As System.EventArgs) Handles calcButton.Click
     ' calculates a monthly cable bill

     Const Basic As Double = 39.99
     Const Bronze As Double = 44.99
     Const Silver As Double = 59.99
     Const Gold As Double = 74.99
```

Figure 5-38 Code for the Charleston Cable Company application *(continues)*

The = `True` in the selection structures is not required.

(continued)

```
        Const Hbi As Double = 10.0
        Const Showtimer As Double = 11.5
        Const Cinematic As Double = 12.0
        Const Local As Double = 5.0
        Dim cableBill As Double

        ' determine package charge
        If basicRadioButton.Checked = True Then
                cableBill += Basic
        ElseIf bronzeRadioButton.Checked = True Then
                cableBill += Bronze
        ElseIf silverRadioButton.Checked = True Then
                cableBill += Silver
        Else
                cableBill += Gold
        End If

        ' add any additional charges
        If hbiCheckBox.Checked = True Then
                cableBill += Hbi
        End If
        If showtimerCheckBox.Checked = True Then
                cableBill += Showtimer
        End If
        If cinematicCheckBox.Checked = True Then
                cableBill += Cinematic
        End If
        If localCheckBox.Checked = True Then
                cableBill += Local
        End If

        ' display the cable bill
        MessageBox.Show("Your monthly cable bill is " &
                        cableBill.ToString("C2"),
                        "Charleston Cable Company",
                        MessageBoxButtons.OK,
                        MessageBoxIcon.Information)

    End Sub
End Class
```

Figure 5-38 Code for the Charleston Cable Company application

PROGRAMMING EXAMPLE

CD Emporium Application

Each CD at CD Emporium costs $11.99. If a customer has a CD Emporium coupon, he or she is entitled to a 5% discount when purchasing three or less CDs, but a 10% discount when purchasing more than three CDs. Create an interface that provides a text box for the sales clerk to enter the number of CDs purchased. The text box should accept only numbers and the Backspace key. Use a message box to ask the sales clerk whether the customer has a coupon. Display the amount of the discount and the total price in labels on the form. Use the following names for the solution, project, and form file:

CD Emporium Solution, CD Emporium Project, and Main Form.vb. Save the files in the VbReloaded2010\Chap05 folder. See Figures 5-39 through 5-45. Test the application using the data shown in Figure 5-44. The figure also shows the correct results. Using the first set of test data, the application should show $0.00 and $23.98 as the discount and total price, respectively. Using the second set of test data, the application should show $1.20 and $22.78 as the discount and total price, and so on.

Task	Object	Event
1. Determine whether the customer gets a discount 2. Calculate the discount (if necessary) 3. Calculate the total price 4. Display the discount and total price in discountLabel and totalLabel	calcButton	Click
End the application	exitButton	Click
Display the discount (from calcButton)	discountLabel	None
Display the total price (from calcButton)	totalLabel	None
Get and display the number of CDs purchased	cdsTextBox	None
Allow the text box to accept only numbers and the Backspace key		KeyPress

Figure 5-39 TOE chart for the CD Emporium application

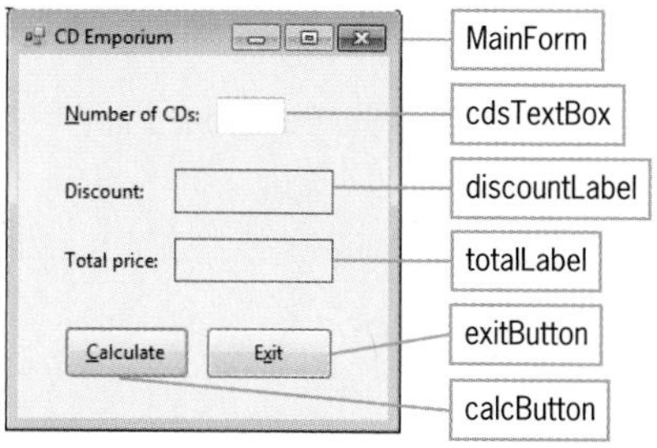

Figure 5-40 MainForm in the CD Emporium application

Object	Property	Setting
MainForm	AcceptButton	calcButton
	Font	Segoe UI, 9 point
	StartPosition	CenterScreen
	Text	CD Emporium
discountLabel	AutoSize	False
	BorderStyle	FixedSingle
	Text	(empty)
	TextAlign	MiddleCenter
totalLabel	AutoSize	False
	BorderStyle	FixedSingle
	Text	(empty)
	TextAlign	MiddleCenter

Figure 5-41 Objects, properties, and settings

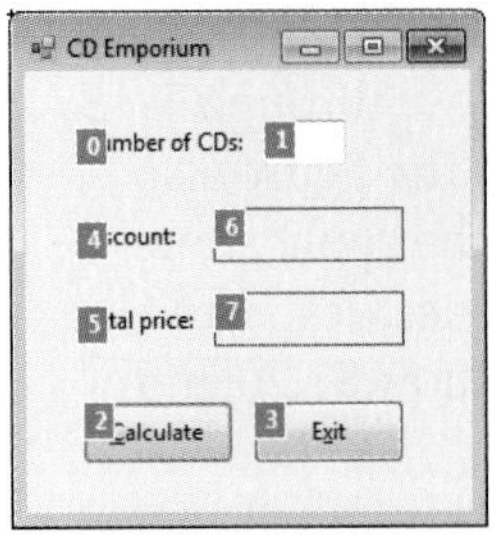

Figure 5-42 Tab order

```
exitButton Click event procedure
close the application

calcButton Click event procedure
1. assign user input (number of CDs) to a variable
2. total price = number of CDs * CD price
3. use a message box to ask the user whether the customer has a coupon
4. if the customer has a coupon
        if the number of CDs is over 3
              discount = total price * 10%
        else
              discount = total price * 5%
        end if
        total price = total price – discount
   end if
5. display the discount in discountLabel
6. display the total price in totalLabel

cdsTextBox KeyPress event procedure
if the user pressed a key that is not a number from 0 through 9 or the Backspace key
        cancel the key
end if
```

Figure 5-43 Pseudocode

Number of CDs	Coupon	Discount	Total price
2	No	$0.00	$23.98
2	Yes	$1.20	$22.78
4	No	$0.00	$47.96
4	Yes	$4.80	$43.16

Figure 5-44 Test data and results

```
' Project name:          CD Emporium Project
' Project purpose:       Displays the discount and total price.
' Created/revised by:    <your name> on <current date>

Option Explicit On
Option Strict On
Option Infer Off

Public Class MainForm

```

Figure 5-45 Code *(continues)*

(continued)

```
    Private Sub exitButton_Click(ByVal sender As Object,
    ByVal e As System.EventArgs) Handles exitButton.Click
        Me.Close()
    End Sub

    Private Sub cdsTextBox_KeyPress(ByVal sender As Object,
    ByVal e As System.Windows.Forms.KeyPressEventArgs
    ) Handles cdsTextBox.KeyPress
        ' allows the text box to accept only numbers
        ' and the Backspace key for editing

        If (e.KeyChar < "0" OrElse e.KeyChar > "9") AndAlso
            e.KeyChar <> ControlChars.Back Then
            e.Handled = True
        End If
    End Sub

    Private Sub calcButton_Click(ByVal sender As Object,
    ByVal e As System.EventArgs) Handles calcButton.Click
        ' calculates and displays the
        ' discount and total price

        Const CdPrice As Double = 11.99
        Const CouponQuestion As String =
                "Does the customer have a coupon?"
        Const RateOverThree As Double = 0.1
        Const RateThreeOrLess As Double = 0.05

        Dim numCds As Integer
        Dim discount As Double
        Dim totalPrice As Double
        Dim button As DialogResult

        ' convert user input to integer
        Integer.TryParse(cdsTextBox.Text, numCds)

        ' calculate the total before any discount
        totalPrice = numCds * CdPrice

        ' ask whether the customer has a coupon
        button = MessageBox.Show(CouponQuestion,
                                 "CD Emporium",
                                 MessageBoxButtons.YesNo,
                                 MessageBoxIcon.Exclamation)

        ' if the customer has a coupon, calculate the
        ' discount and then subtract it from the total price
        If button = DialogResult.Yes Then
            If numCds > 3 Then
                discount = totalPrice * RateOverThree
            Else
                discount = totalPrice * RateThreeOrLess
            End If
            totalPrice = totalPrice - discount
        End If

        ' display the discount and total price
        discountLabel.Text = discount.ToString("C2")
        totalLabel.Text = totalPrice.ToString("C2")
    End Sub
End Class
```

Figure 5-45 Code

Summary

- You can nest selection structures, which means you can place one selection structure in either the true or false path of another selection structure.
- The primary decision is always made by an outer selection structure. The secondary decision is always made by a nested selection structure.
- You can code a multiple-alternative selection structure using either If…Then…Else statements or the Select Case statement.
- In a flowchart, a diamond is used to represent the condition in a multiple-alternative selection structure. The diamond has several flowlines leading out of the symbol. Each flowline represents a possible path.
- In a Select Case statement, the data type of the expressions in the Case clauses should match the data type of the statement's selectorExpression.
- A Case clause in a Select Case statement can contain more than one expression. The selectorExpression needs to match only one of the expressions for the instructions in that Case to be processed.
- You use the keyword `To` in a Case clause's expressionList when you know both the upper and lower values of the range you want to specify. You use the keyword `Is` when you know only one end of the range.
- Radio buttons allow you to limit the user to only one choice from a group of two or more related but mutually exclusive choices.
- If you need to include two groups of radio buttons in an interface, at least one of the groups must be placed within a container, such as a group box, panel, or table layout panel.
- It is customary to have one radio button in each group of radio buttons selected when the interface first appears. The selected radio button is called the default radio button.
- If a radio button is selected, its Checked property contains the Boolean value True; otherwise, it contains the Boolean value False.
- The MessageBox.Show method allows an application to communicate with the user while the application is running.
- The MessageBox.Show method displays a message box that contains text, one or more buttons, and an icon. It then returns an integer indicating the button chosen by the user. You should use the DialogResult value associated with the integer when referring to the return value in code.
- Use sentence capitalization for the text argument in the MessageBox.Show method, but book title capitalization for the caption argument.
- You can code a text box's KeyPress event procedure to prevent the text box from accepting an inappropriate character. The character is stored in the `e` parameter's KeyChar property. To cancel the character, you set the `e` parameter's Handled property to True.

Key Terms

ControlChars.Back constant—the Visual Basic constant that represents the Backspace key on your keyboard

Default radio button—the radio button that is automatically selected when an interface first appears

Group box—a control that is used to contain other controls; instantiated using the GroupBox tool, which is located in the Containers section of the toolbox

Handled property—a property of the KeyPress event procedure's `e` parameter; used to cancel the key pressed by the user

KeyChar property—a property of the KeyPress event procedure's `e` parameter; stores the character associated with the key pressed by the user

KeyPress event—occurs each time the user presses a key while the control has the focus

Line continuation character—an underscore that is immediately preceded by a space and located at the end of a physical line of code; used to split a long instruction into two or more physical lines in the Code Editor window

MessageBox.Show method—displays a message box that contains text, one or more buttons, and an icon; allows an application to communicate with the user during run time

Multiple-alternative selection structures—selection structures that contain several alternatives; also called extended selection structures; can be coded using either If...Then...Else statements or the Select Case statement

Nested selection structure—a selection structure that is wholly contained (nested) within either the true or false path of another selection structure

Radio buttons—used in an interface to limit the user to only one choice from a group of two or more related but mutually exclusive choices

Select Case statement—used to code a multiple-alternative selection structure

Review Questions

1. A nested selection structure can appear in ______________ of another selection structure.
   a. only the true path
   b. only the false path
   c. either the true path or the false path

2. If a Select Case statement's selectorExpression is an Integer variable named `code`, which of the following Case clauses is valid?
   a. `Case Is > 7`
   b. `Case 3, 5`
   c. `Case 1 To 4`
   d. all of the above

Use the code shown in Figure 5-46 to answer Questions 3 through 5.

```
If number <= 100 Then
     number *= 2
Else
     If number > 500 Then
          number *= 3
     End If
End If
```

Figure 5-46 Code for Questions 3 through 5

3. The **number** variable contains the number 90 before the code in Figure 5-46 is processed. What value will be in the **number** variable after the code is processed?
   a. 0
   b. 90
   c. 180
   d. 270

4. The **number** variable contains the number 1000 before the code in Figure 5-46 is processed. What value will be in the **number** variable after the code is processed?
   a. 0
   b. 1000
   c. 2000
   d. 3000

5. The **number** variable contains the number 200 before the code in Figure 5-46 is processed. What value will be in the **number** variable after the code is processed?
   a. 0
   b. 200
   c. 400
   d. 600

Use the code shown in Figure 5-47 to answer Questions 6 through 9.

```
If job = "A" Then
      employee = "Janet"
ElseIf job = "C" OrElse job = "T" Then
      employee = "George"
ElseIf job = "R" Then
      employee = "Jerry"
Else
      employee = "Sue"
End If
```

Figure 5-47 Code for Questions 6 through 9

6. When the `job` variable contains the letter T, what will the code in Figure 5-47 assign to the `employee` variable?

   a. George

   b. Janet

   c. Jerry

   d. Sue

7. When the `job` variable contains the letter R, what will the code in Figure 5-47 assign to the `employee` variable?

   a. George

   b. Janet

   c. Jerry

   d. Sue

8. When the `job` variable contains the letter C, what will the code in Figure 5-47 assign to the `employee` variable?

   a. George

   b. Janet

   c. Jerry

   d. Sue

9. When the `job` variable contains the letter X, what will the code in Figure 5-47 assign to the `employee` variable?

   a. George

   b. Janet

   c. Jerry

   d. Sue

Use the code shown in Figure 5-48 to answer Questions 10 through 12.

```
Select Case id
      Case 1
            city = "Paris"
      Case 2 To 4
            city = "Madrid"
      Case 5, 7
            city = "London"
      Case Else
            city = "Rome"
End Select
```

Figure 5-48 Code for Questions 10 through 12

10. When the `id` variable contains the number 2, what will the code in Figure 5-48 assign to the `city` variable?

    a. London

    b. Madrid

    c. Paris

    d. Rome

11. When the `id` variable contains the number 3, what will the code in Figure 5-48 assign to the `city` variable?

    a. London

    b. Madrid

    c. Paris

    d. Rome

12. When the `id` variable contains the number 6, what will the code in Figure 5-48 assign to the `city` variable?

    a. London

    b. Madrid

    c. Paris

    d. Rome

13. If the user clicks the OK button in a message box, the MessageBox.Show method returns the number 1, which is equivalent to which of the following values?

    a. `DialogResult.OK`

    b. `DialogResult.OKButton`

    c. `MessageBox.OK`

    d. `MessageResult.OK`

14. A Select Case statement's selectorExpression is an Integer variable. Which of the following Case clauses tells the computer to process the instructions when the Integer variable contains one of the following numbers: 1, 2, 3, 4, or 5?

    a. Case 1, 2, 3, 4, And 5

    b. Case 1 To 5

    c. Case Is > 1 And < 5

    d. all of the above

15. A text box's _______________ event occurs when a user presses a key while the text box has the focus.
    a. Key
    b. KeyPress
    c. Press
    d. PressKey

Exercises

Pencil and Paper

INTRODUCTORY

1. Write the code to display the message "Entry error" in the msgLabel when the value in the Integer `units` variable is less than or equal to 0. Otherwise, calculate the total owed as follows: If the value stored in the `units` variable is less than 20, multiply the value by $10; otherwise, multiply it by $5. Store the total owed in the `total` variable. Use the If...Then...Else statement.

INTRODUCTORY

2. A procedure stores sales amounts in two Integer variables named `region1Sales` and `region2Sales`. Write the code to display the message "Both regions sold the same amount" when both variables contain the same number. If the variables contain different numbers, the code should compare the numbers and then display either the message "Region 1 sold more than region 2" or the message "Region 2 sold more than region 1". Use the If...Then...Else statement. Display the appropriate message in the msgLabel.

INTRODUCTORY

3. A selection structure needs to display the name of the month associated with a number. The number is stored in an Integer variable named `monthNum`. If the `monthNum` variable contains the number 1, the selection structure should display the string "January" in the monthLabel. If the `monthNum` variable contains the number 2, the selection structure should display the string "February", and so on. If the month number is not 1 through 12, the selection structure should display the "Incorrect month number" message in the monthLabel. Write two versions of the selection structure's code. In the first version, use the If...Then...Else statement. Use the Select Case statement in the second version.

INTRODUCTORY

4. Write two versions of the code to compare the contents of an Integer variable named `ordered` with the number 10. When the `ordered` variable contains the number 10, display the string "Equal". When the `ordered` variable contains a number that is greater than 10, display the string "Over 10". When the `ordered` variable contains a number that is less than 10, display the string "Not over 10". Display the appropriate message in the msgLabel. In the first version, use the Select Case statement. Use the If...Then...Else statement in the second version.

INTRODUCTORY

5. Write two versions of the code to display the message "Great!" when a student's test score is at least 90. When the test score is from 70 through 89, display the message "Good job". For all other test scores, display the message "Retake the test". The test score is stored in an Integer variable named `score`. Display the appropriate message in the msgLabel. In the first version, use the If...Then...Else statement. Use the Select Case statement in the second version.

INTERMEDIATE

6. A procedure uses a String variable named `department` and two Double variables named `salary` and `raise`. The `department` variable contains one of the following letters (entered in either uppercase or lowercase): A, B, C, or D. Employees in departments A and B are receiving a 2% raise. Employees in department C are receiving a 1.5% raise, and employees in department D are receiving a 3% raise. Write two versions of the code to calculate the appropriate raise amount. In the first version, use the Select Case statement. Use the If...Then...Else statement in the second version.

INTERMEDIATE

7. Code the partial flowchart shown in Figure 5-49. Use an Integer variable named `code` and a Double variable named `rate`. Display the rate formatted with a percent sign and no decimal places. Use the Select Case statement to code the multiple-alternative selection structure in the figure.

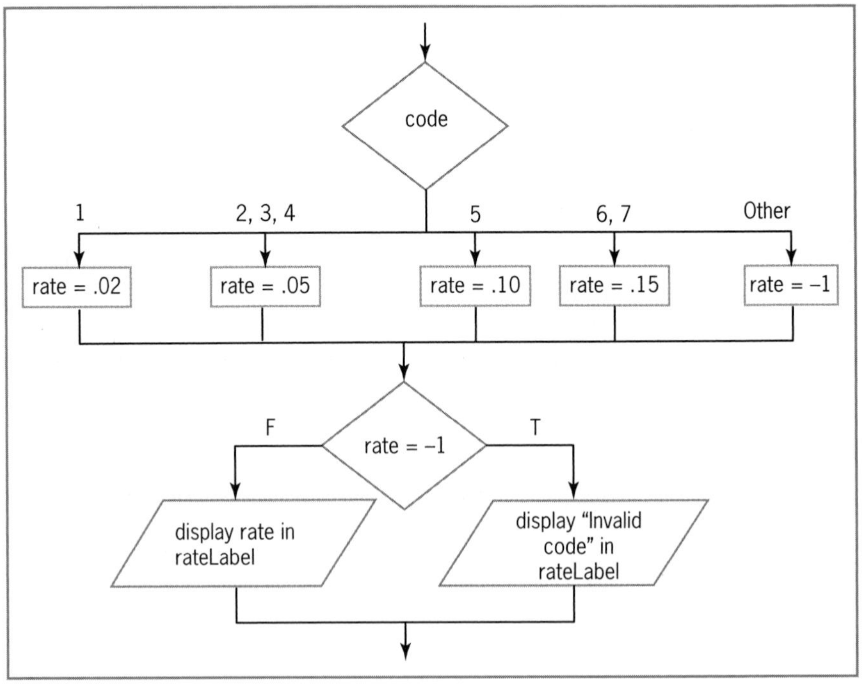

Figure 5-49 Flowchart

ADVANCED

8. The answerTextBox should accept only the letters Y, y, N, or n, and the Backspace key. Write the appropriate selection structure for the text box's KeyPress event procedure.

Computer

9. If necessary, complete the Rock, Paper, Scissors Game application from this chapter's Programming Tutorial 1, and then close the solution. Use Windows to make a copy of the RockPaperScissorsGame Solution folder. Rename the folder RockPaperScissorsGame Solution-Modified. MODIFY THIS

   a. Open the RockPaperScissorsGame Solution (RockPaperScissorsGame Solution.sln) file contained in the VbReloaded2010\Chap05\RockPaperScissorsGame Solution-Modified folder.

   b. Change the Select Case statements to If...Then...Else statements.

   c. Save the solution and then start and test the application. Close the solution.

10. If necessary, complete the Charleston Cable Company application from this chapter's Programming Tutorial 2, and then close the solution. Use Windows to make a copy of the Charleston Cable Solution folder. Rename the folder Charleston Cable Solution-Modified. MODIFY THIS

    a. Open the Charleston Cable Solution (Charleston Cable Solution.sln) file contained in the VbReloaded2010\Chap05\Charleston Cable Solution-Modified folder.

    b. Change the multiple-alternative selection structure in the calcButton's Click event procedure to a Select Case statement.

    c. Save the solution and then start and test the application. Close the solution.

11. Use Windows to make a copy of the AddSub Solution folder, which is contained in the VbReloaded2010\Chap05 folder. Rename the folder AddSub Solution-Modified. MODIFY THIS

    a. Open the AddSub Solution (AddSub Solution.sln) file contained in the VbReloaded2010\Chap05\AddSub Solution-Modified folder.

    b. Set the operationTextBox's MaxLength property to 1.

    c. The operationTextBox should accept only the letters A, a, S, or s, and the Backspace key. Code the appropriate event procedure.

    d. Modify the calcButton's Click event procedure to display "N/A" in the answerLabel when the operationTextBox is empty.

    e. Save the solution and then start and test the application. Close the solution.

12. Use Windows to make a copy of the AddSub Solution folder, which is contained in the VbReloaded2010\Chap05 folder. Rename the folder AddSub Solution-RadioButtons. MODIFY THIS

    a. Open the AddSub Solution (AddSub Solution.sln) file contained in the VbReloaded2010\Chap05\AddSub Solution-RadioButtons folder.

    b. Provide the user with radio buttons, rather than a text box, for entering the mathematical operation.

c. Make the appropriate modifications to the code.

d. Save the solution and then start and test the application. Close the solution.

INTRODUCTORY

13. Open the Shipping Solution (Shipping Solution.sln) file contained in the VbReloaded2010\Chap05\Shipping Solution folder. The application should display the appropriate shipping charge, which is based on the state selected by the user. The states and shipping charges are shown in Figure 5-50. Code the application. Save the solution and then start and test the application. Close the solution.

State	Shipping charge
Alaska	$50
California	$40
Hawaii	$80
North Dakota	$40
Oregon	$40
Texas	$35
Wyoming	$45

Figure 5-50 States and shipping charges

INTRODUCTORY

14. Open the Bonus Solution (Bonus Solution.sln) file contained in the VbReloaded2010\Chap05\Bonus Solution folder.

a. The user will enter the sales amount in the salesTextBox. The sales amount will always be an integer. The salesTextBox should accept only numbers and the Backspace key. Code the appropriate event procedure.

b. Code the calcButton's Click event procedure so that it calculates the salesperson's bonus. A salesperson selling from $0 through $3500 in products receives a 1% bonus. A salesperson selling from $3501 through $10000 in products receives a 5% bonus. A salesperson selling more than $10000 in products receives a 10% bonus. Display the bonus, formatted with a dollar sign and two decimal places, in the bonusLabel. No calculations should be made when the salesTextBox is empty; rather, display an appropriate message.

c. Save the solution and then start and test the application. Close the solution.

INTRODUCTORY

15. Open the Random Swap Solution (Random Swap Solution.sln) file contained in the VbReloaded2010\Chap05\Random Swap Solution folder. The application should generate two random integers from 1 through 10. It then should display the lowest and highest number in the interface. If both numbers are equal, the application should display the numbers in the interface and also display an appropriate message in the messageLabel. Draw the flowcharts, and then code the application. Save the solution and then start and test the application. Close the solution.

INTERMEDIATE

16. The JK Department Store has five departments, which are listed in Figure 5-51. The store manager wants an application that displays a

department's telephone extension. Create a Windows application. Use the following names for the solution, project, and form file: JK Department Store Solution, JK Department Store Project, and Main Form.vb. Save the files in the VbReloaded2010\Chap05 folder. Build an appropriate interface. Provide the user with radio buttons for selecting the department. Save the solution and then start and test the application. Close the solution.

Department	Extension
Apparel	582
Electronics	340
Small Appliances	168
Pharmacy	456
Toys	233

Figure 5-51 Departments and extensions

17. The manager of the Barren Community Center wants an application that displays a seminar fee. The fee is based on a person's membership status and age. Non-members who are at least 65 years old pay $20. All other non-members pay $50. Members who are at least 65 years old pay $5. All other members pay $10. Create a Windows application. Use the following names for the solution, project, and form file: Barren Solution, Barren Project, and Main Form.vb. Save the files in the VbReloaded2010\Chap05 folder. Build an appropriate interface. Provide a text box for entering the age. The text box should accept only numbers and the Backspace key. Use a message box to ask the user whether the person is a member. Code the application. Display an appropriate message if the text box is empty. Save the solution and then start and test the application. Close the solution.

INTERMEDIATE

18. Create a Windows application. Use the following names for the solution, project, and form file: Currency Solution, Currency Project, and Main Form.vb. Save the application in the VbReloaded2010\Chap05 folder. The application's interface should provide a text box for the user to enter the number of U.S. dollars, and radio buttons for the seven currencies listed in Figure 5-52. The text box should accept only numbers and the Backspace key. The interface should convert the US dollars to the selected currency and then display the result (formatted to three decimal places). Use the exchange rates shown in Figure 5-52. Code the application. Save the solution and then start and test the application. Close the solution.

INTERMEDIATE

Currency	Exchange rate
Canada Dollar	1.01615
Eurozone Euro	.638490
India Rupee	40.1798
Japan Yen	104.390
Mexico Peso	10.4613
South Africa Rand	7.60310
United Kingdom Pound	.504285

Figure 5-52 Currencies and exchange rates

ADVANCED

19. Open the Computer Workshop Solution (Computer Workshop Solution.sln) file contained in the VbReloaded2010\Chap05\Computer Workshop Solution folder. Computer Workshop offers programming seminars to companies. The price per person depends on the number of people the company registers. The price for the first 10 registrants is $80 per person. The price for the 11th through 25th registrants is $70 per person. Starting with the 26th registrant, the price per person is $65. Therefore, if the company registers seven people, the total cost is $560. If the company registers 12 people, the total cost is $940. If the company registers 26 people, the total cost is $1,915. Display the total cost (formatted with a dollar sign and no decimal places) in the totalLabel. The numberTextBox should accept only numbers and the Backspace key. No calculations should be made when the numberTextBox is empty; rather, display an appropriate message. Save the solution and then start and test the application. Close the solution.

ADVANCED

20. Golf Pro, a U.S. company, sells golf equipment both domestically and abroad. Each of Golf Pro's salespeople receives a commission based on the total of his or her domestic and international sales. The sales manager wants an application that allows him to enter two amounts: the salesperson's domestic sales and his or her international sales. Both amounts may contain decimal places. The application should calculate the salesperson's bonus, using the information shown in Figure 5-53. It then should display the bonus, formatted with a dollar sign and two decimal places. Create a Windows application. Use the following names for the solution, project, and form file: Golf Pro Solution, Golf Pro Project, and Main Form.vb. Save the application in the VbReloaded2010\Chap05 folder. Build an appropriate interface. Code the application. Save the solution and then start and test the application. Close the solution.

Sales ($)	**Commission rate**
0 – 100,000	2% of sales
100,000.01 – 400,000	$2000 + 5% * sales over $100,000
Over 400,000	$17000 + 10% * sales over $400,000
Less than 0	0

Figure 5-53 Sales and commission rates

ADVANCED

21. If necessary, complete the Rock, Paper, Scissors Game application from this chapter's Programming Tutorial 1, and then close the solution. Use Windows to make a copy of the RockPaperScissorsGame Solution folder. Rename the folder RockPaperScissorsGame Solution-Advanced.

    a. Open the RockPaperScissorsGame Solution (RockPaperScissorsGame Solution.sln) file contained in the VbReloaded2010\Chap05\RockPaperScissorsGame Solution-Advanced folder.

b. Modify the interface to display the number of times the player wins and the number of times the computer wins. Make the appropriate modifications to the code.

c. Save the solution and then start and test the application. Close the solution.

22. In this exercise, you learn about the SelectAll method and a text box control's Enter event. DISCOVERY

a. Open the Name Solution (Name Solution.sln) file contained in the VbReloaded2010\Chap05\Name Solution folder.

b. Start the application. Type your first name in the First text box and then press Tab. Type your last name in the Last text box and then click the Concatenate Names button. Your full name appears in the Full name label.

c. Press Tab twice to move the focus to the First text box. Notice that the insertion point appears after your first name in the text box. It is customary in Windows applications to have a text box's existing text selected (highlighted) when the text box receives the focus. You can select a text box's existing text by entering the text box's SelectAll method in the text box's Enter event procedure. The Enter event occurs when the text box receives the focus.

d. Click the Exit button to end the application. Open the Code Editor window. Enter the SelectAll method in the Enter event procedures for the firstTextBox and lastTextBox controls. The method's syntax is *object*.**SelectAll**.

e. Save the solution, and then start the application. Type your first name in the First text box and then press Tab. Type your last name in the Last text box and then click the Concatenate Names button. Your full name appears in the Full name label.

f. Press Tab twice to move the focus to the First text box. Notice that your first name is selected in the text box. Press Tab to move the focus to the Last text box. Notice that your last name is selected in the text box. End the application, and then close the solution.

23. Open the Debug Solution (Debug Solution.sln) file contained in the VbReloaded2010\Chap05\Debug Solution folder. The application should display the total amount a customer owes; however, it does not always work correctly. Open the Code Editor window and review the existing code. Start and then test the application. Locate and then correct any errors. When the application is working correctly, close the solution. SWAT THE BUGS

Case Projects

Shoppers Paradise

Shoppers Paradise wants an application that displays the number of reward points a customer earns each month. The reward points are based on the customer's membership type and total monthly purchase amount, as shown in Figure 5-54. Name the solution, project, and form file Shoppers Paradise Solution, Shoppers Paradise Project, and Main Form.vb, respectively. Save the solution in the VbReloaded2010\Chap05 folder. You can create either your own user interface or the one shown in Figure 5-55. Display the reward points without any decimal places.

Membership type	Total monthly purchase ($)	Reward points
Basic	Less than 75	5% of the total monthly purchase
	75 – 149.99	7.5% of the total monthly purchase
	150 and over	10% of the total monthly purchase
Standard	Less than 150	6% of the total monthly purchase
	150 and over	13% of the total monthly purchase
Premium	Less than 200	7% of the total monthly purchase
	200 and over	15% of the total monthly purchase

Figure 5-54 Reward points chart

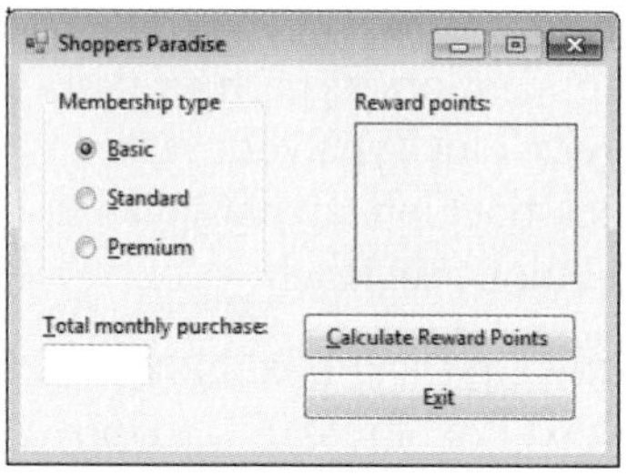

Figure 5-55 Sample interface for the Shoppers Paradise application

Willow Health Club

The personal trainer at Willow Health Club wants an application that displays the number of daily calories a person needs to maintain his or her current weight. The number of calories is based on the person's gender, activity level, and weight, as shown in Figure 5-56. Name the solution, project, and form file Willow Solution, Willow Project, and Main Form.vb, respectively. Save the solution in the VbReloaded2010\Chap05 folder. You can create either your own user interface or the one shown in Figure 5-57.

Gender	Activity level	Total daily calories formula
Female	Moderately active	weight * 12 calories per pound
Female	Relatively inactive	weight * 10 calories per pound
Male	Moderately active	weight * 15 calories per pound
Male	Relatively inactive	weight * 13 calories per pound

Figure 5-56 Daily calories chart

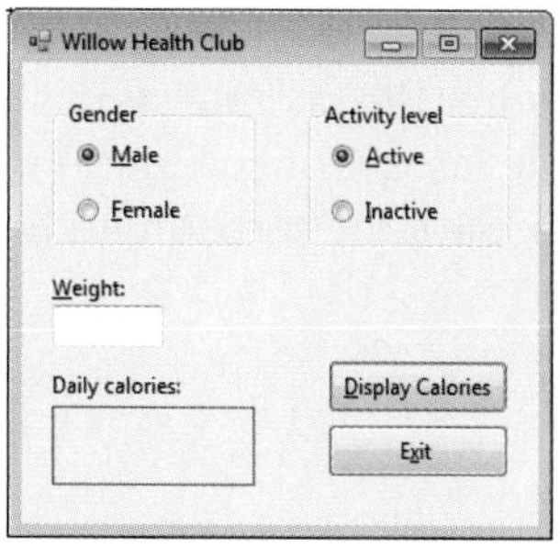

Figure 5-57 Sample interface for the Willow Health Club application

Johnson Supply

The manager of Johnson Supply wants an application that displays the price of an order. The price is based on the number of units ordered and the customer's status (either wholesaler or retailer), as shown in Figure 5-58. Name the solution, project, and form file Johnson Solution, Johnson Project, and Main Form.vb, respectively. Save the solution in the VbReloaded2010\Chap05 folder. You can create either your own user interface or the one shown in Figure 5-59.

Wholesaler		**Retailer**	
Number of units	Price per unit ($)	Number of units	Price per unit ($)
1 – 4	10	1 – 3	15
5 and over	9	4 – 8	14
		9 and over	12

Figure 5-58 Price per unit chart

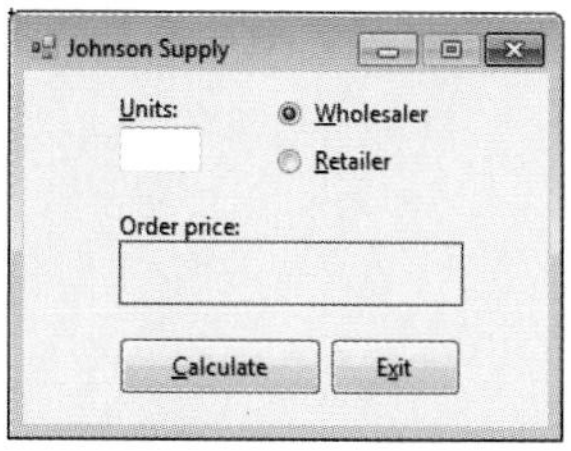

Figure 5-59 Sample interface for the Johnson Supply application

Jason's Coffee Shop

Jason's Coffee Shop sells coffee by the pound. Each pound of coffee costs $12. The coffee comes in the following flavors: Hazelnut, French Vanilla, Breakfast Blend, Mocha, and Amaretto. Create an application that displays the total pounds of coffee a customer orders, the sales tax, and the total price of the order. The user will need to enter the number of pounds of each flavor ordered by the customer. He or she will also need to specify whether the customer should be charged any sales tax and, if so, whether the tax rate should be 5% or 6%. Name the solution, project, and form file Jason Coffee Solution, Jason Coffee Project, and Main Form.vb, respectively. Save the solution in the VbReloaded2010\Chap05 folder.

CHAPTER 6

Repeating Program Instructions

After studying Chapter 6, you should be able to:

- Differentiate between a pretest loop and a posttest loop
- Include pretest and posttest loops in pseudocode and in a flowchart
- Write a Do...Loop statement
- Utilize counters and accumulators
- Display a dialog box using the InputBox function
- Include a list box in an interface
- Enable and disable a control
- Refresh the screen
- Delay program execution

The Repetition Structure

Recall that all procedures are written using one or more of three basic control structures: sequence, selection, and repetition. You learned about the sequence and selection structures in previous chapters. This chapter provides an introduction to the repetition structure. Programmers use the **repetition structure**, referred to more simply as a **loop**, when they need the computer to repeatedly process one or more program instructions. If and for how long the instructions are repeated is determined by the loop's condition. Like the condition in a selection structure, the condition in a loop must evaluate to either True or False. The condition is evaluated with each repetition (or iteration) of the loop and can be phrased in one of two ways: it can specify either the requirement for repeating the instructions or the requirement for *not* repeating them. The requirement for repeating the instructions is referred to as the **looping condition**, because it indicates when the computer should continue "looping" through the instructions. The requirement for *not* repeating the instructions is referred to as the **loop exit condition**, because it tells the computer when to exit (or stop) the loop. An example may help illustrate the difference between the looping condition and the loop exit condition. You've probably heard the old adage "Make hay while the sun shines." The "while the sun shines" is the looping condition, because it tells you when to continue making hay. The adage also could be phrased as "Make hay until the sun stops shining." In this case, the "until the sun stops shining" is the loop exit condition, because it indicates when you should stop making hay. Every looping condition has an opposing loop exit condition; in other words, one is the opposite of the other. See Figure 6-1.

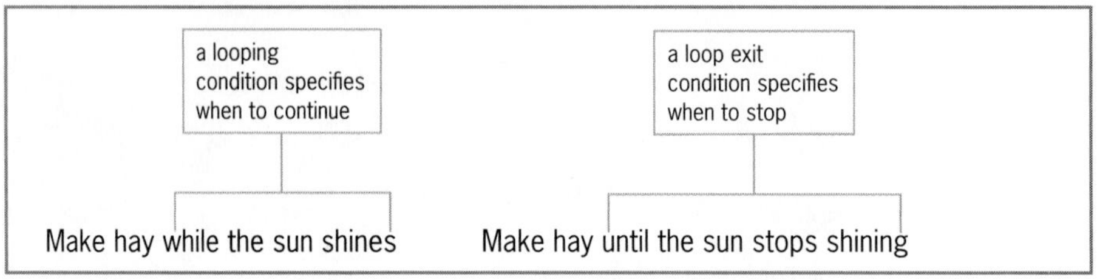

Figure 6-1 Example of a looping condition and a loop exit condition

The programmer determines whether a problem's solution requires a loop by studying the problem specification. The first problem specification you will examine in this chapter is for the Getting to a Million Club. The problem specification is shown in Figure 6-2.

> The Getting to a Million Club wants an application that allows a club member to enter two items: the amount of money deposited into a savings account at the beginning of the year and the annual interest rate. The application should display the balance in the savings account at the end of the year, assuming the interest is compounded annually and no withdrawals or additional deposits are made.

Figure 6-2 Problem specification for the Getting to a Million Club application

Figure 6-3 shows a sample run of the Getting to a Million Club application. The .00 entered in the Annual interest rate (.00): label indicates that the user should enter the interest rate in decimal form. Figure 6-4 shows the pseudocode for the Calculate button's Click event procedure. The procedure requires only the sequence structure. It does not need a selection structure or a loop, because no decisions need to be made and no instructions need to be repeated to calculate and display the account balance at the end of one year.

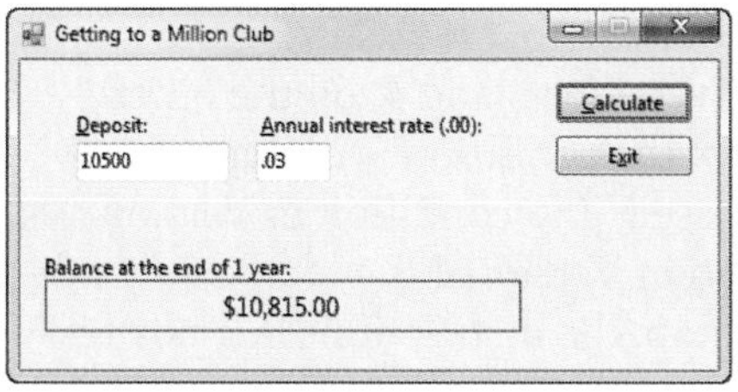

Figure 6-3 Sample run of the Getting to a Million Club application

calcButton Click event procedure
1. store deposit in balance variable
2. store rate in rate variable
3. interest = balance * rate
4. add interest to balance
5. display balance

Figure 6-4 Pseudocode containing only the sequence structure

Next, we'll make a slight change to the problem specification from Figure 6-2. The Getting to a Million Club application will now need to display the number of years required for the savings account to reach one million dollars, and the balance in the account at that time. Consider the changes you will need to make to the Calculate button's original pseudocode (shown in Figure 6-4). The first two steps in the original pseudocode are to store the input items (deposit and interest rate) in variables; the modified pseudocode will still need both of these steps. Steps 3 and 4 are to calculate the interest and then add the interest to the savings account balance. The modified pseudocode will need to repeat both of those steps either while the balance is less than one million dollars (looping condition) or until the balance is greater than or equal to one million dollars (loop exit condition). Notice that the loop exit condition is the opposite of the looping condition. The loop in the modified pseudocode also will need to keep track of the number of times the instructions in Steps 3 and 4 are processed, because each time represents a year. The last step in the original pseudocode is to display the account balance. The modified pseudocode will need to display the account balance and the number of years.

The modified problem description is shown in Figure 6-5 along with four versions of the modified pseudocode. (As mentioned in Chapter 5, even small procedures can have more than one solution.) Only the loop is different in each version. In Versions 1 and 2, the loop is a pretest loop. In a **pretest loop**, the condition is evaluated *before* the instructions within the loop are processed. The condition in Version 1 is a looping condition,

The condition appears at the beginning of a pretest loop, but at the end of a posttest loop. For that reason, pretest and posttest loops are also called top-driven and bottom-driven loops, respectively.

You can nest loops, which means you can place one loop within another loop. Nested loops are covered in Chapter 7.

because it tells the computer when to continue repeating the loop instructions. Version 2's condition, on the other hand, is a loop exit condition, because it tells the computer when to *stop* repeating the instructions. Depending on the result of the evaluation, the instructions in a pretest loop may never be processed. For example, if the user enters a deposit that is greater than or equal to one million, the looping condition in Version 1 will evaluate to False and the loop instructions will be skipped over. Similarly, the loop exit condition in Version 2 will evaluate to True, causing the loop instructions to be bypassed. The loops in Versions 3 and 4, on the other hand, are posttest loops. In a **posttest loop**, the condition is evaluated *after* the instructions within the loop are processed. The condition in Version 3 is a looping condition, whereas the condition in Version 4 is a loop exit condition. Unlike the instructions in a pretest loop, the instructions in a posttest loop will always be processed at least once. In this case, if the user enters a deposit that is greater than or equal to one million, the instructions in the two posttest loops will be processed once before the loop ends. Posttest loops should be used only when you are certain that the loop instructions should be processed at least once.

The Getting to a Million Club wants an application that allows a club member to enter two items: the amount of money deposited into a savings account at the beginning of the year and the annual interest rate. The application should display the number of years required for the balance in the savings account to reach one million dollars, assuming the interest is compounded annually and no withdrawals or additional deposits are made. It also should display the account balance at that time.

Version 1 – pretest loop

```
1. store deposit in balance variable
2. store rate in rate variable
3. repeat while balance < 1,000,000
       interest = balance * rate
       add interest to balance
       add 1 to number of years
   end repeat while
4. display number of years and balance
```

looping condition specifies when to continue

Version 2 – pretest loop

```
1. store deposit in balance variable
2. store rate in rate variable
3. repeat until balance >= 1,000,000
       interest = balance * rate
       add interest to balance
       add 1 to number of years
   end repeat until
4. display number of years and balance
```

loop exit condition specifies when to stop

Version 3 – posttest loop

```
1. store deposit in balance variable
2. store rate in rate variable
3. repeat
       interest = balance * rate
       add interest to balance
       add 1 to the number of years
   end repeat while balance < 1,000,000
4. display number of years and balance
```

looping condition specifies when to continue

Version 4 – posttest loop

```
1. store deposit in balance variable
2. store rate in rate variable
3. repeat
       interest = balance * rate
       add interest to balance
       add 1 to the number of years
   end repeat until balance >= 1,000,000
4. display number of years and balance
```

loop exit condition specifies when to stop

Figure 6-5 Modified problem specification and pseudocode containing a loop

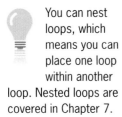

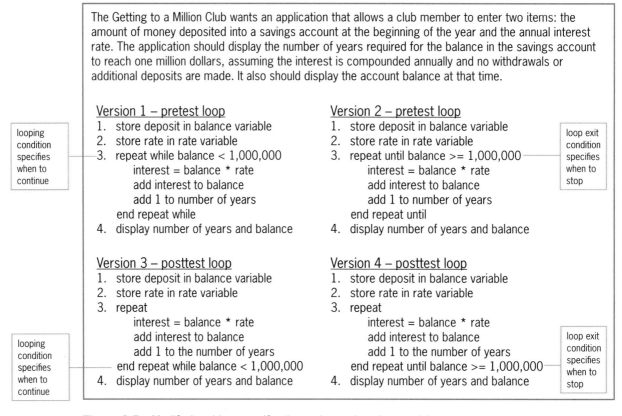

Mini-Quiz 6-1

1. It's possible that the instructions in a _____________ loop may never be processed.
   a. posttest
   b. pretest
2. The "repeat until your hair is clean" instruction is an example of a _____________ condition.
   a. looping
   b. loop exit
3. A _____________ condition tells the computer when to continue repeating the loop instructions.
   a. looping
   b. loop exit

The answers to Mini-Quiz questions are located in Appendix A.

The Visual Basic language provides three different statements for coding loops: Do...Loop, For...Next, and For Each...Next. The Do...Loop statement can be used to code both pretest and posttest loops, whereas the For...Next and For Each...Next statements are used only for pretest loops. You will learn about the Do...Loop statement in this chapter. The For...Next and For Each...Next statements are covered in Chapters 7 and 9, respectively.

The Do...Loop Statement

You can use the **Do...Loop statement** to code both pretest and posttest loops. Figure 6-6 shows two versions of the statement's syntax: one for coding a pretest loop and the other for coding a posttest loop. In both versions of the syntax, the statement begins with the Do clause and ends with the Loop clause. Between both clauses, you enter the instructions you want the computer to repeat. The instructions between the Do and Loop clauses are referred to as the **loop body**. The {While | Until} portion in each syntax indicates that you can select only one of the keywords appearing within the braces. You follow the keyword with a *condition*, which can be phrased as either a looping condition or a loop exit condition. You use the `While` keyword in a looping condition to specify that the loop body should be processed *while* (in other words, as long as) the condition is true. You use the `Until` keyword in a loop exit condition to specify that the loop body should be processed *until* the condition becomes true, at which time the loop should stop. Like the condition in an If...Then...Else statement, the condition in a Do...Loop statement can contain variables, constants, properties, methods, and operators; it also must evaluate to a Boolean value. The condition is evaluated with each repetition of the loop and determines whether the computer processes the loop body. Notice that the keyword (either `While` or `Until`) and the condition

You can use the `Exit Do` statement to exit the Do...Loop statement prematurely, which means to exit it before the loop has finished processing. You may need to do this if the computer encounters an error when processing the loop instructions.

appear in the Do clause in a pretest loop, but they appear in the Loop clause in a posttest loop. Also included in Figure 6-6 are examples of using both syntax versions to display the numbers 1, 2, and 3 in message boxes.

HOW TO Use the Do...Loop Statement

Syntax for a pretest loop

Do {**While** | **Until**} *condition*
loop body instructions, which will be processed either while the condition is true or until the condition becomes true
Loop

Pretest loop example

```
Dim number As Integer = 1
Do While number <= 3
    MessageBox.Show(number.ToString)
    number += 1
Loop
```

loop body

Syntax for a posttest loop

Do
loop body instructions, which will be processed either while the condition is true or until the condition becomes true
Loop {**While** | **Until**} *condition*

Posttest loop example

```
Dim number As Integer = 1
Do
    MessageBox.Show(number.ToString)
    number += 1
Loop Until number > 3
```

loop body

Figure 6-6 How to use the Do...Loop statement

Included in the data files for this book is a file named Processing Steps for Figure 6-6.pdf. The file describes the way the computer processes the code shown in the examples in Figure 6-6. The file is contained in the VbReloaded2010\Chap06 folder.

It's often easier to understand loops when viewed in flowchart form. Figures 6-7 and 6-8 show the flowcharts associated with the pretest and posttest loop examples from Figure 6-6. The loop's condition in a flowchart is represented by the decision symbol, which is a diamond. Inside each diamond is a comparison that evaluates to either True or False only. Recall that the result of the comparison determines whether the instructions within the loop are processed. The diamonds in both figures have one flowline entering the symbol and two flowlines leaving the symbol. The two flowlines leading out of the diamond should be marked so that anyone reading the flowchart can distinguish the true path from the false path. You mark the flowline leading to the true path with a T and the flowline leading to the false path with an F. You also can mark the flowlines leading out of the diamond with a Y and an N (for yes and no). In the pretest loop's flowchart, the flowline entering the diamond, along with the diamond and the symbols and flowlines within the true path, form a circle or loop. In the posttest loop's flowchart, the loop is formed by all of the symbols and flowlines in the false path. It is this loop, or circle, that distinguishes the repetition structure from the selection structure in a flowchart.

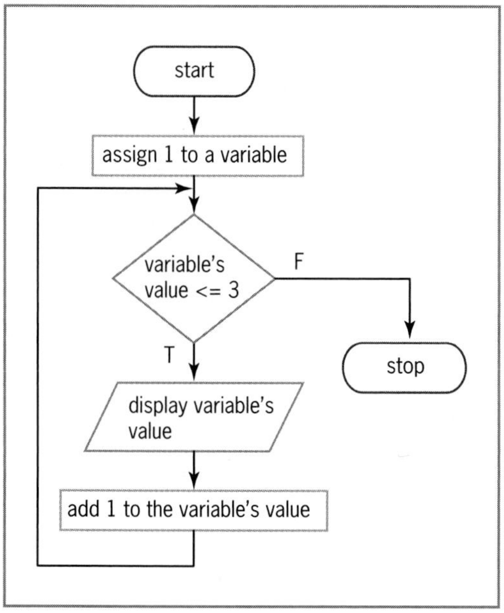

Figure 6-7 Flowchart for the pretest loop example from Figure 6-6

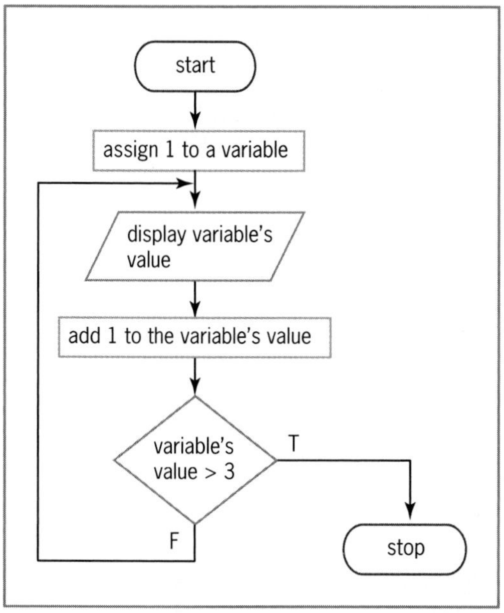

Figure 6-8 Flowchart for the posttest loop example from Figure 6-6

Counters and Accumulators

Some procedures require you to calculate a subtotal, a total, or an average. You make these calculations using a loop that includes a counter, an accumulator, or both. A **counter** is a numeric variable used for counting something, such as the number of employees paid in a week. An **accumulator** is a numeric variable used for accumulating (adding together) something, such as the total dollar amount of a week's payroll. Two tasks are associated with counters and accumulators: initializing and updating. **Initializing** means to assign a beginning value to the counter or accumulator. Typically, counters and accumulators are initialized to the number 0. However, they can be initialized to any number, depending on the value required by the procedure. The initialization task is performed before the loop is processed, because it needs to be performed only once. **Updating**, often referred to as **incrementing**, means adding a number to the value stored in the counter or accumulator. The number can be either positive or negative, integer or non-integer. A counter is always updated by a constant value—typically the number 1—whereas an accumulator is updated by a value that varies. The assignment statement that updates a counter or an accumulator is placed within the loop body, because the update task must be performed each time the loop instructions are processed. You will use a counter to code the Getting to a Million Club application.

Coding the Getting to a Million Club Application

Figure 6-9 shows Version 1 of the modified pseudocode from Figure 6-5, along with its associated Visual Basic code, and Figure 6-10 shows a sample run of the modified application. The `Dim years As Integer` statement in the code declares and initializes a counter variable to keep track of the number of years. The `years += 1` statement in the loop body updates the counter variable by adding the number 1 to it. (You also can write the statement as `years = years + 1`.) The counter variable will be updated each time the loop body is processed. The looping condition in the Do clause tells the computer to repeat the loop body as long as (or while) the number in the `balance` variable is less than one million. Rather than using a looping condition in the Do clause, you also can use a loop exit condition, as follows: `Do Until balance >= 1000000`. (Recall that >= is the opposite of <.)

Version 1 – pretest loop (pseudocode from Figure 6-5)

```
1. store deposit in balance variable
2. store rate in rate variable
3. repeat while balance < 1,000,000          <- looping condition
       interest = balance * rate
       add interest to balance
       add 1 to number of years
   end repeat while
4. display number of years and balance
```

Visual Basic code

```
Private Sub calcButton_Click(ByVal sender As Object,
ByVal e As System.EventArgs) Handles calcButton.Click
    ' display account balance and number of years

    Dim balance As Double
    Dim rate As Double
    Dim interest As Double
    Dim years As Integer ' counter initialization      <- declares and initializes the counter

    Double.TryParse(depositTextBox.Text, balance)
    Double.TryParse(rateTextBox.Text, rate)

    Do While balance < 1000000                          <- looping condition
        interest = balance * rate
        balance += interest
        years += 1 ' counter update                     <- updates the counter
```

Figure 6-9 Modified pseudocode and code for the calcButton's Click event procedure *(continues)*

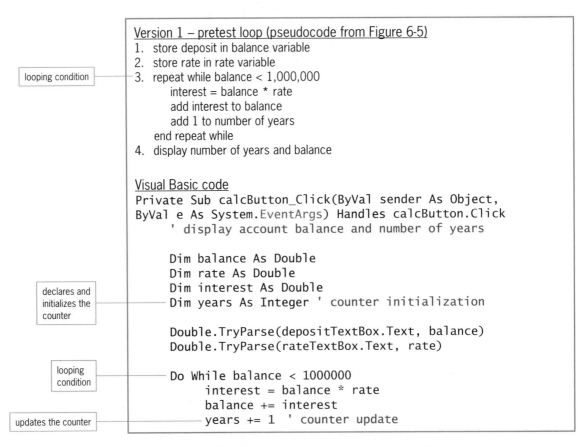

(continued)

```
        Loop

        balanceLabel.Text = "You will have " &
              balance.ToString("C2") &
              " in " & years.ToString & " years."
  End Sub
```

Figure 6-9 Modified pseudocode and code for the calcButton's Click event procedure

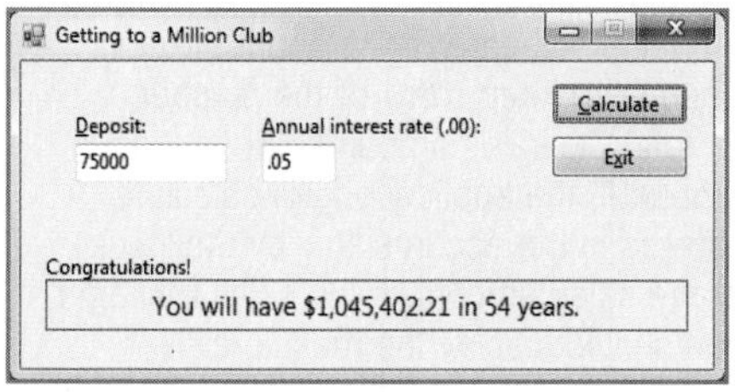

Figure 6-10 Sample run of the modified Getting to a Million Club application

If you want to experiment with the modified Getting to a Million Club application, open the solution contained in the Try It 1! folder.

The answers to Mini-Quiz questions are located in Appendix A.

Mini-Quiz 6-2

1. Which of the following clauses will stop the loop when the `age` variable contains a number that is greater than 21?
   a. `Do While age <= 21`
   b. `Do Until age > 21`
   c. `Loop Until age > 21`
   d. all of the above
2. Write an assignment statement that updates an accumulator variable named `sum` by the value in the `score` variable. Both variables have the Double data type.
3. Write an assignment statement that updates a counter variable named `numValues` by 5.
4. Write an assignment statement that updates a counter variable named `numItems` by –1 (a negative 1).

The Sales Express Company Application

Figure 6-11 shows the problem specification for the Sales Express Company application, which uses a loop, a counter, and an accumulator to calculate the average sales amount entered by the sales manager. Figure 6-12 shows a sample run of the application, assuming the sales manager entered the following four sales amounts: 2000, 13000, 4550, and 9750. The salesTextBox in the interface has its Multiline and ReadOnly properties set to True, and its ScrollBars property set to Vertical. When a text box's **Multiline property** is set to True, the text box can both accept and display multiple lines of text; otherwise, only one line of text can be entered in the text box. Changing a text box's **ReadOnly property** from its default value (False) to True prevents the user from changing the contents of the text box during run time. A text box's **ScrollBars property** specifies whether the text box has no scroll bars (the default), a horizontal scroll bar, a vertical scroll bar, or both horizontal and vertical scroll bars.

The Sales Express Company wants an application that displays the average amount the company sold during the prior year. The sales manager will enter the amount of each salesperson's sales. The application will use a counter to keep track of the number of sales amounts entered and an accumulator to total the sales amounts. When the sales manager has finished entering the sales amounts, the application will calculate the average sales amount by dividing the value stored in the accumulator by the value stored in the counter. It then will display the average sales amount. If the sales manager does not enter any sales amounts, the application should display the message "N/A" (for "not available").

Figure 6-11 Problem specification for the Sales Express Company application

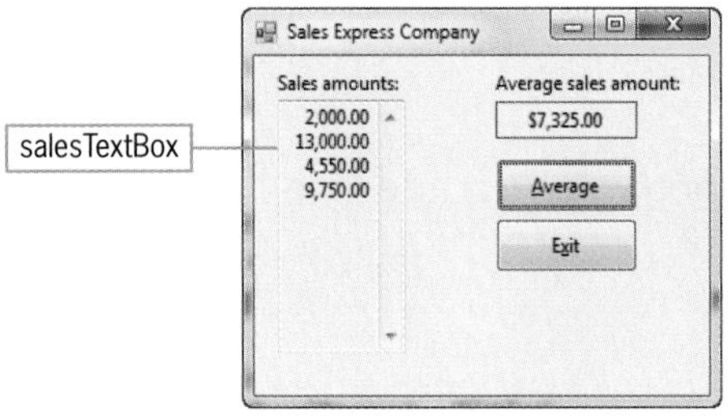

Figure 6-12 Sample run of the Sales Express Company application

Figure 6-13 shows the pseudocode for the Average button's Click event procedure. Step 1 in the pseudocode is to remove the contents of the salesTextBox, and Step 2 is to get a sales amount from the user. Step 3 is a pretest loop whose loop body is processed as long as the user enters a sales amount. The first instruction in the loop body adds the number 1 to the counter, which keeps track of the number of sales. The second instruction adds the sales amount to the accumulator, which keeps track of the total sales. The third instruction in the loop body displays the sales amount in the salesTextBox, and the fourth instruction requests another sales amount from the user. The loop then checks whether a sales amount was entered; this is necessary to determine whether the loop body should be processed again. When the user has finished entering sales amounts, the loop ends and processing continues with Step 4 in the pseudocode. Step 4 is a selection structure whose condition verifies that the value stored in the sales counter is greater than the number 0. This verification is necessary because the first instruction in the selection structure's true path uses the sales counter as the divisor when calculating the average sales amount. Before using a counter variable (or any variable) as the divisor in an expression, you always should verify that the variable does not contain the number 0 because, as in mathematics, division by 0 is not possible. Dividing by 0 in a procedure will cause the application to end abruptly with an error. As Step 4 indicates, if the sales counter's value is greater than 0, the average sales amount is calculated and then displayed; otherwise, the string "N/A" is displayed.

```
averageButton Click event procedure
1. remove the contents of the salesTextBox
2. get a sales amount from the user                    [priming read]
3. repeat while the user entered a sales amount
      add 1 to the number of sales counter
      add the sales amount to the total sales accumulator
      display the sales amount in the salesTextBox
      get a sales amount from the user                 [update read]
   end repeat while
4. if the number of sales counter is greater than 0
      average sales = total sales accumulator / number of sales counter
      display average sales in averageLabel
   else
      display "N/A" in averageLabel
   end if
```

Figure 6-13 Pseudocode for the Average button's Click event procedure

Notice that the pseudocode in Figure 6-13 contains two "get a sales amount from the user" instructions. One of the instructions appears above the loop, and the other appears as the last instruction in the loop body. The "get a sales amount from the user" instruction above the loop is referred to as the **priming read**, because it is used to prime (prepare or set up) the loop. The priming read initializes the loop condition by providing its first value. In this case, the priming read gets only the first sales amount from the user. Because the loop in Figure 6-13 is a pretest loop, the first sales amount determines whether the instructions in the loop body are processed at all. If the loop body instructions are processed, the "get a sales amount from the user" instruction in the loop body gets the remaining sales amounts (if any) from the user. The "get a sales amount from the user" instruction in the loop body is referred to as the **update read**, because it allows the user to update the value of the input item (in this case, the sales amount) that controls the loop's condition. The update read is often an exact copy of the priming read. Keep in mind that if you don't include the update read in the loop body, there will be no way to enter a value that will stop the loop after it has been processed the first time. This is because the priming read is processed only once and gets only the first sales amount from the user. A loop that has no way to end is called an **infinite loop** or an **endless loop**. You can stop a program that has an infinite loop by clicking Debug on the menu bar and then clicking Stop Debugging.

Figure 6-14 shows the Average button's Click event procedure in flowchart form. Notice that the priming read's parallelogram is located above the loop's condition, while the update read's parallelogram is located at the end of the loop body.

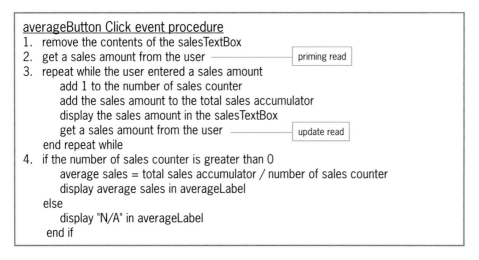

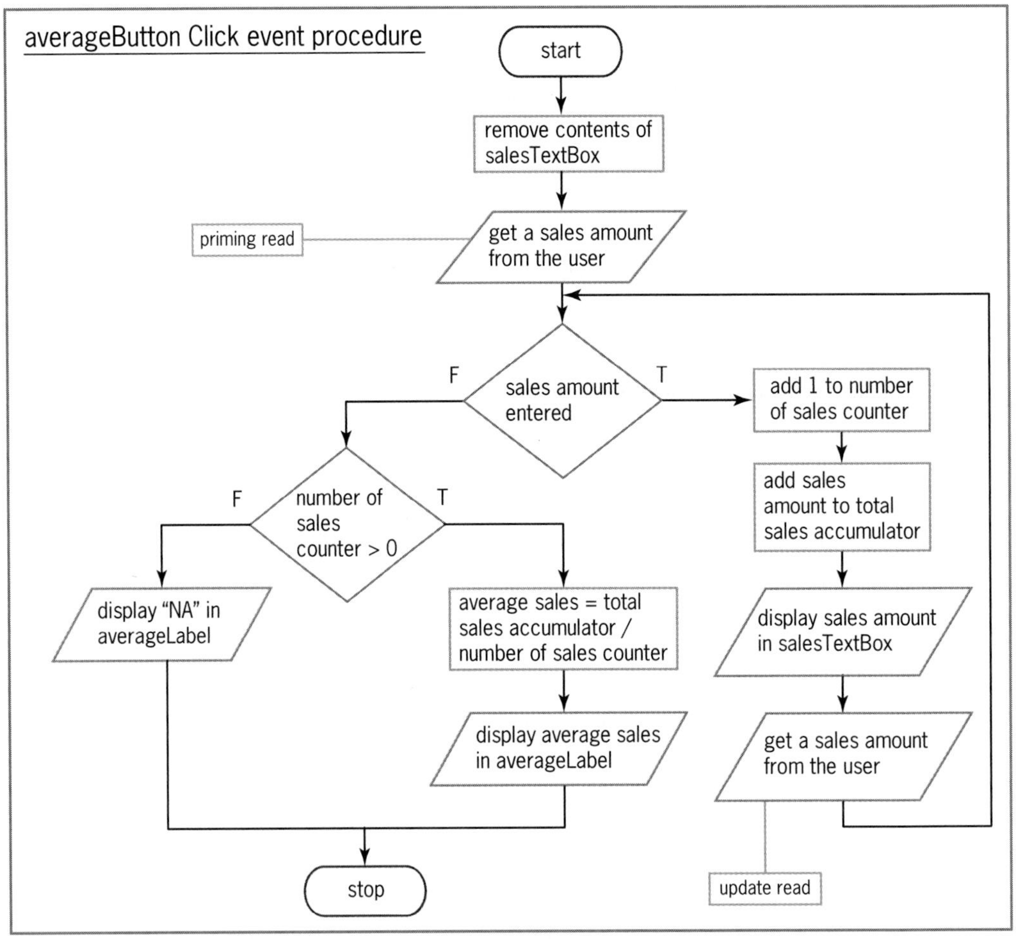

Figure 6-14 Flowchart for the Average button's Click event procedure

You may have noticed that the Sales Express Company's interface, shown earlier in Figure 6-12, does not provide a text box for the user to enter the sales amounts. Rather than using a text box, the application will use an input dialog box. You display an input dialog box using Visual Basic's InputBox function.

The InputBox Function

The **InputBox function** displays an input dialog box, which is one of the standard dialog boxes available in Visual Basic. An example of an input dialog box is shown in Figure 6-15. The input dialog box contains a message, an OK button, a Cancel button, and an input area where the user can enter information. The message in the dialog box should prompt the user to enter the appropriate information in the input area. The user closes the dialog box by clicking the OK button, Cancel button, or Close button. The value returned by the InputBox function depends on the button the user chooses. If the user clicks the OK button, the InputBox function returns the value contained in the input area of the dialog box; the return value is always treated as a string. If the user clicks either the Cancel button in the dialog box or the Close button on the dialog box's title bar, the InputBox function returns an empty (or zero-length) string.

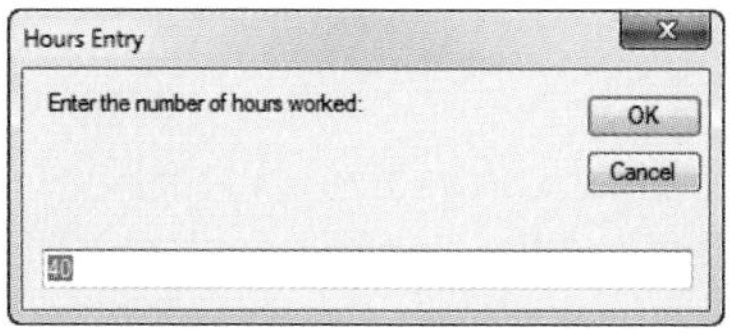

Figure 6-15 Example of an input dialog box

Figure 6-16 shows the basic syntax of the InputBox function. The *prompt* argument contains the message to display inside the dialog box. The optional *title* and *defaultResponse* arguments control the text that appears in the dialog box's title bar and input area, respectively. If you omit the title argument, the project name appears in the title bar. If you omit the defaultResponse argument, a blank input area appears when the dialog box opens. In the input dialog box shown in Figure 6-15, "Enter the number of hours worked:" is the prompt, "Hours Entry" is the title, and "40" is the defaultResponse. When entering the InputBox function in the Code Editor window, the prompt, title, and defaultResponse arguments must be enclosed in quotation marks, unless that information is stored in a String named constant or a String variable. The Windows standard is to use sentence capitalization for the prompt, but book title capitalization for the title. The capitalization (if any) you use for the defaultResponse depends on the text itself. In most cases, you assign the value returned by the InputBox function to a String variable, as shown in the first three examples in Figure 6-16.

The InputBox function's syntax also includes *XPos* and *YPos* arguments, which allow you to specify the horizontal and vertical positions, respectively, of the dialog box on the screen. Both arguments are optional; if omitted, the dialog box appears centered on the screen.

HOW TO Use the InputBox Function

Syntax

InputBox(*prompt*[**,** *title*][**,** *defaultResponse*]**)**

Example 1

```
Dim inputHours As String
inputHours = InputBox("Enter the number of hours worked:",
                      "Hours Entry", "40")
```

The InputBox function displays the input dialog box shown in Figure 6-15. When the user closes the dialog box, the assignment statement assigns the user's response to a String variable named `inputHours`.

Example 2

```
Dim first As String
first = InputBox("First name:", "Name Entry")
```

The InputBox function displays an input dialog box that shows First name: as the prompt, Name Entry in the title bar, and an empty input area. When the user closes the dialog box, the assignment statement assigns the user's response to a String variable named `first`.

Example 3

```
Const Prompt As String = "Enter the interest rate:"
Const Title As String = "Interest Rate"
Dim rate As String
rate = InputBox(Prompt, Title, ".00")
```

Figure 6-16 How to use the InputBox function *(continues)*

(continued)

The InputBox function displays an input dialog box that shows the contents of the `Prompt` constant as the prompt, the contents of the `Title` constant in the title bar, and .00 in the input area. When the user closes the dialog box, the assignment statement assigns the user's response from String to a String variable named `rate`.

Example 4

```
Dim age As Integer
Integer.TryParse(InputBox("How old are you?",
                          "Discount Verification"), age)
```

The InputBox function displays an input dialog box that shows How old are you? as the prompt, Discount Verification in the title bar, and an empty input area. When the user closes the dialog box, the TryParse method converts the user's response from String to Integer and then stores the result in an Integer variable named `age`.

Figure 6-16 How to use the InputBox function

You will use the InputBox function to code the Average button's Click event procedure in the Sales Express Company application. Figure 6-17 shows the code associated with the procedure's pseudocode and flowchart, shown earlier in Figures 6-13 and 6-14, respectively. (A sample run of the application appears earlier in Figure 6-12.)

```
Private Sub averageButton_Click(ByVal sender As Object,
ByVal e As System.EventArgs) Handles averageButton.Click
    ' calculates and displays the average sales amount

    Const Prompt As String = "Enter a sales amount. " &
        ControlChars.NewLine &
        "Click Cancel or leave blank to end."
    Const Title As String = "Sales Entry"
    Dim inputSales As String
    Dim sales As Double
    Dim salesCounter As Integer
    Dim salesAccumulator As Double
    Dim salesAverage As Double

    ' remove contents of text box
    salesTextBox.Text = ""

    ' get first sales amount
    inputSales = InputBox(Prompt, Title)

    ' repeat as long as the user enters a sales amount
    Do While inputSales <> String.Empty
        ' convert the sales amount to a number
        Double.TryParse(inputSales, sales)

        ' update the counter and accumulator
        salesCounter = salesCounter + 1
        salesAccumulator = salesAccumulator + sales
```

priming read

Figure 6-17 Code associated with the pseudocode and flowchart shown in Figures 6-13 and 6-14, respectively *(continues)*

(continued)

```
        ' display the sales amount in the text box
        salesTextBox.Text = salesTextBox.Text &
              sales.ToString("N2") & ControlChars.NewLine

        ' get the next sales amount
        inputSales = InputBox(Prompt, Title)        update read
    Loop

    ' verify that the salesCounter is greater than 0
    If salesCounter > 0 Then
        salesAverage = salesAccumulator / salesCounter
        averageLabel.Text = salesAverage.ToString("C2")
    Else
        averageLabel.Text = "N/A"
    End If
End Sub
```

Figure 6-17 Code associated with the pseudocode and flowchart shown in Figures 6-13 and 6-14, respectively

To review what you learned about loops, counters, accumulators, and the InputBox function, view the Ch06SalesExpress video.

If you want to experiment with the Sales Express Company application, open the solution contained in the Try It 2! folder.

The answers to Mini-Quiz questions are located in Appendix A.

Mini-Quiz 6-3

1. Which of the following properties allows a text box to accept and display multiple lines of text?
   a. Multiline
   b. MultipleLine
   c. MultipleLines
   d. none of the above
2. The priming read appears ______________ the loop.
   a. above
   b. within
3. How do you stop an endless loop?
4. Which of the following statements prompts the user for the name of a city and then assigns the user's response to a String variable named `myCity`?
   a. `InputBox("City name:", "City Entry", myCity)`
   b. `Input("City name:", "City Entry", myCity)`
   c. `myCity = Input("City name:", "City Entry")`
   d. `myCity = InputBox("City name:", "City Entry")`

Including a List Box in an Interface

The Do...Loop statement is often used to assign values to a list box. You add a list box to an interface using the ListBox tool in the toolbox. A **list box** displays a list of choices from which the user can select zero choices, one choice,

You can learn more about the SelectionMode property in Computer Exercise 32 at the end of this chapter.

If you have only two choices to offer the user, use two radio buttons rather than a list box.

or multiple choices. The number of choices the user can select is controlled by the list box's **SelectionMode property**. The default value for the property is One, which allows the user to select only one choice at a time. You can make a list box any size you want. However, the Windows standard for list boxes is to display a minimum of three choices and a maximum of eight choices at a time. If you have more items than can fit into the list box, the control automatically displays a scroll bar for viewing the complete list of items. You should use a label control to provide keyboard access to the list box. For the access key to work correctly, you must set the label's TabIndex property to a value that is one less than the list box's TabIndex value.

Adding Items to a List Box

The items in a list box belong to a collection called the **Items collection**. A **collection** is a group of individual objects treated as one unit. The first item in the Items collection appears as the first item in the list box, the second item in the collection appears as the second item in the list box, and so on. You can use the String Collection Editor window to specify the list box items during design time. You can open the window by clicking Edit Items on the list box's task list, as was done in Figure 6-18. Or, you can click the ellipsis button in the Items property in the Properties list.

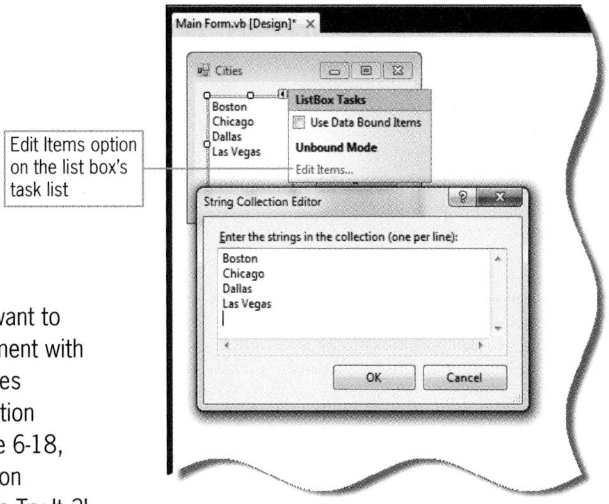

Figure 6-18 String Collection Editor window

If you want to experiment with the Cities application shown in Figure 6-18, open the solution contained in the Try It 3! folder.

You also can add items to a list box using the Items collection's **Add method**. Figure 6-19 shows the method's syntax and includes examples of using the method. In the syntax, *object* is the name of the list box control, and the *item* argument is the text you want to add to the control's list. The three Add methods in Example 1 will add the strings "Dog", "Cat", and "Horse" to the animalListBox. In Example 2, the Add method appears in the body of a pretest loop that repeats its instructions for `code` values of 100 through 105. As a result, the Add method will add the values 100, 101, 102, 103, 104, and 105 (each converted to the String data type) to the codeListBox. (You also can write the Add method in Example 2 as follows: `codeListBox.Items.Add(Convert.ToString(code))`.)

HOW TO Use the Items Collection's Add Method

Syntax
object.**Items.Add(***item***)**

Example 1
```
animalListBox.Items.Add("Dog")
animalListBox.Items.Add("Cat")
animalListBox.Items.Add("Horse")
```
adds Dog, Cat, and Horse to the animalListBox

Example 2
```
Dim code As Integer = 100
Do While code <= 105
     codeListBox.Items.Add(code.ToString)
     code += 1
Loop
```
adds 100, 101, 102, 103, 104, and 105 to the codeListBox

Figure 6-19 How to use the Items collection's Add method

To learn about the Items collection's Insert, Remove, RemoveAt, and Clear methods, complete Computer Exercise 33 at the end of this chapter.

In most cases, you enter the Add methods in the Load event procedure of a form, as shown in Figure 6-20. You open the Load event procedure by clicking (MainForm Events) in the Class Name list box in the Code Editor window, and then clicking Load in the Method Name list box. A form's **Load event** occurs when an application is started. Any code contained in the Load event procedure is processed before the form is displayed on the screen. In this case, the Add methods in Figure 6-20 ensure that the animalListBox and codeListBox display their values when the interface comes into view. Figure 6-21 shows the animalListBox and codeListBox after the Add methods are processed.

If your form is not named MainForm, you open its Load event by clicking (*formName* Events) in the Class Name list box, where *formName* is the name of your form.

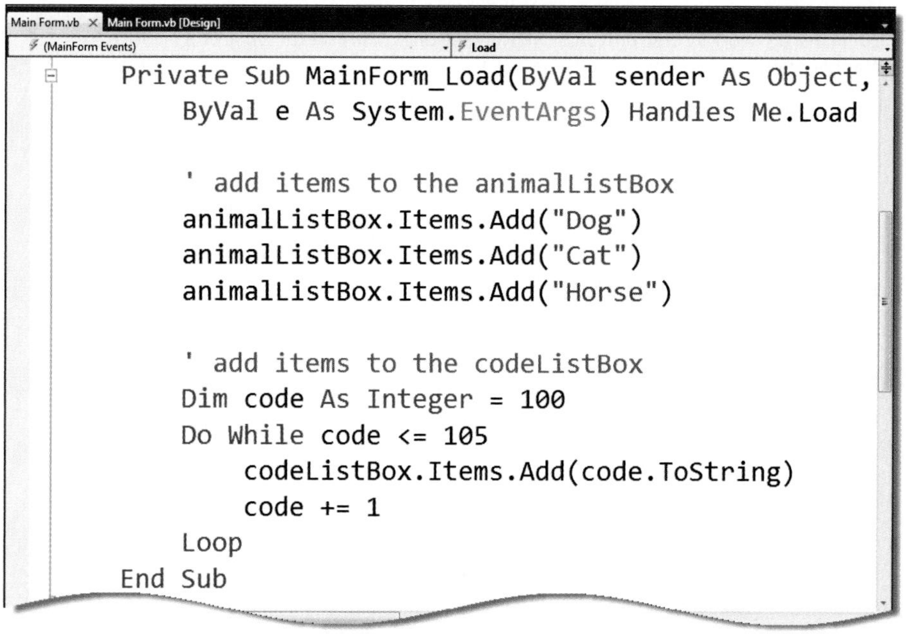
Main Form.vb
Main Form.vb [Design]
(MainForm Events)
Load
Private Sub MainForm_Load(ByVal sender As Object,
ByVal e As System.EventArgs) Handles Me.Load
' add items to the animalListBox
animalListBox.Items.Add("Dog")
animalListBox.Items.Add("Cat")
animalListBox.Items.Add("Horse")
' add items to the codeListBox
Dim code As Integer = 100
Do While code <= 105
codeListBox.Items.Add(code.ToString)
code += 1
Loop
End Sub

Figure 6-20 Add methods entered in the MainForm's Load event procedure

If you want to experiment with the Add Method Examples application shown in Figure 6-21, open the solution contained in the Try It 4! folder.

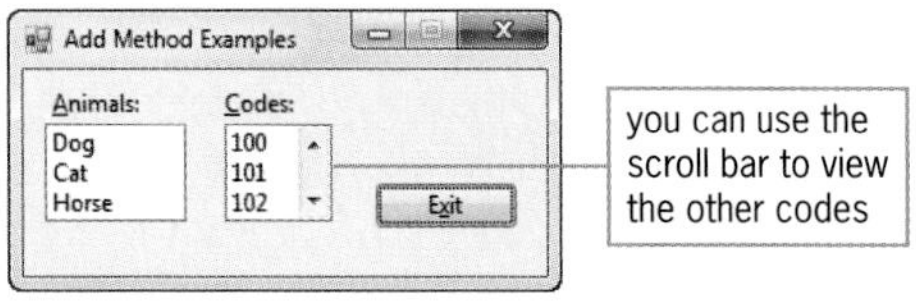

Figure 6-21 Result of processing the Add methods in Figure 6-20

At times, you may want to allow the user to add items to a list box during run time. The Jasper's Food Hut application accomplishes this by providing a text box for entering an item, and a button for adding the item to the list box. Figure 6-22 shows a sample run of the application, and Figure 6-23 shows the code entered in the Add to List button's Click event procedure. The procedure uses the Add method to add the contents of the nameTextBox to the workerListBox.

If you want to experiment with the Jasper's Food Hut application shown in Figure 6-22, open the solution contained in the Try It 5! folder.

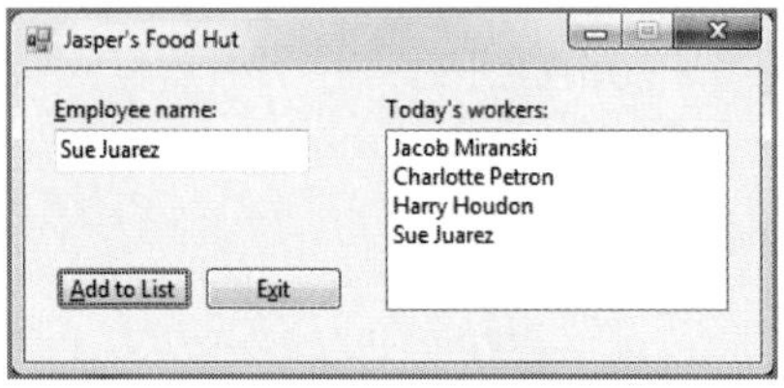

Figure 6-22 Sample run of the Jasper's Food Hut application

```
Private Sub addButton_Click(ByVal sender As Object,
ByVal e As System.EventArgs) Handles addButton.Click
      ' adds the name entered in the text box
      ' to the list box

      workerListBox.Items.Add(nameTextBox.Text)
End Sub
```

Figure 6-23 Add to List button's Click event procedure in the Jasper's Food Hut application

The Clark's Chicken application uses a different approach to allow the user to add items to a list box during run time. Figure 6-24 shows a sample run of the application, and Figure 6-25 shows the code entered in the Add to List button's Click event procedure. The procedure uses the Add method, a pretest loop, and the InputBox function.

If you want to experiment with the Clark's Chicken application shown in Figure 6-24, open the solution contained in the Try It 6! folder.

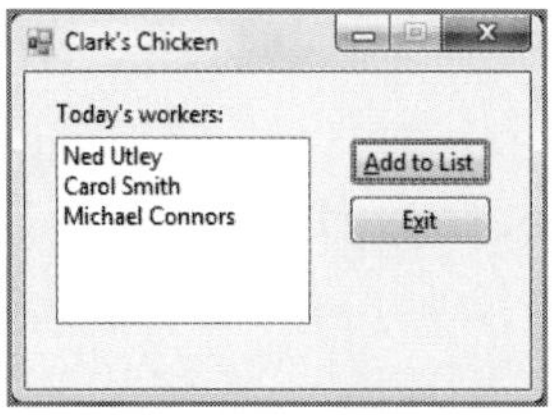

Figure 6-24 Sample run of the Clark's Chicken application

```
Private Sub addButton_Click(ByVal sender As Object,
ByVal e As System.EventArgs) Handles addButton.Click
     ' adds items to the list box

     Dim worker As String

     worker = InputBox("Who is working today?", "Name")        priming read
     Do While worker <> String.Empty
          workerListBox.Items.Add(worker)
          worker = InputBox("Who else is working?", "Name")     update read
     Loop
End Sub
```

Figure 6-25 Add to List button's Click event procedure in the Clark's Chicken application

The Sorted Property

The position of an item in a list box depends on the value stored in the list box's **Sorted property**. When the Sorted property is set to False (the default value), the item is added at the end of the list. When the Sorted property is set to True, the item is sorted along with the existing items and then placed in its proper position in the list. Visual Basic sorts the list box items in dictionary order, which means that numbers are sorted before letters, and a lowercase letter is sorted before its uppercase equivalent. The items in a list box are sorted based on the leftmost characters in each item. As a result, the items "Personnel", "Inventory", and "Payroll" will appear in the following order when the departmentListBox's Sorted property is set to True: Inventory, Payroll, and Personnel. Likewise, the items 1, 2, 3, and 10 will appear in the following order when the numberListBox's Sorted property is set to True: 1, 10, 2, and 3. Both list boxes are shown in Figure 6-26.

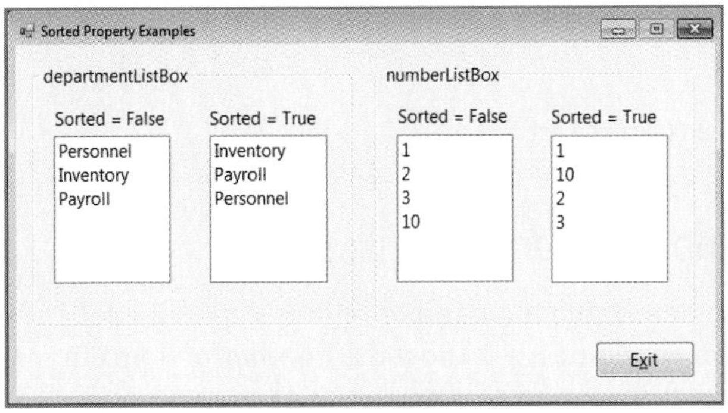

Figure 6-26 Examples of the list box's Sorted property

The requirements of the application you are creating determine whether you display the list box items in either sorted order or the order in which they are added to the list box. If several list items are selected much more frequently than other items, you typically leave the list box's Sorted property set to False and then add the frequently used items first; doing this ensures that the items appear at the beginning of the list. However, if the list box items are selected fairly equally, you typically set the list box's Sorted property to True, because it is easier to locate items when they appear in a sorted order.

Accessing Items in a List Box

A unique number called an **index** identifies each item in the Items collection. The first item in the collection (which also is the first item in the list box) has an index of 0. The second item's index is 1, and so on. The index allows you to access a specific item in the list box; you do this using the syntax shown in Figure 6-27. The figure also includes examples of using the syntax to assign list box items to variables. Notice that you need to convert the list box item to the variable's data type.

HOW TO Access an Item in a List Box

Syntax
object.**Items(***index***)**

Example 1
```
Dim animalType As String
animalType = animalListBox.Items(0).ToString
```
Assigns the first item in the animalListBox to a String variable named `animalType`. You also can use the `animalType = Convert.ToString(animalListBox.Items(0))` statement.

Example 2
```
Dim myCode As Integer
myCode = Convert.ToInt32(codeListBox.Items(2))
```
Assigns the third item in the codeListBox to an Integer variable named `myCode`. You also can use the `Integer.TryParse(codeListBox.Items(2).ToString, myCode)` statement.

Figure 6-27 How to access an item in a list box

Determining the Number of Items in a List Box

At times, you may need to determine the number of items contained in a list box. For example, you would need to know the number of items in order to search the list box, from top to bottom, looking for a specific item. The number of items in a list box is stored in the Items collection's **Count property**. The property's value is always one number more than the last index in the list box; this is because the first index in a list box is 0. For example, the highest index in the animalListBox shown earlier in Figure 6-21 is 2, but the Count property contains 3. Figure 6-28 shows the syntax of the Count property and includes examples of using the property. Notice that the loop instructions in Example 2 will be processed as long as the `index` variable contains a value that is less than the number of items in the codeListBox. This is because the codeListBox's highest index is 4, but its Count property contains 5.

HOW TO Determine the Number of Items in a List Box

Syntax
object.**Items.Count**

Example 1
```
Dim numAnimals As Integer
numAnimals = animalListBox.Items.Count
```
The assignment statement assigns the number 3, which is the number of items contained in the animalListBox (shown earlier in Figure 6-21), to an Integer variable named `numAnimals`.

Example 2
```
Dim numCodes As Integer
Dim index As Integer
numCodes = codeListBox.Items.Count
Do While index < numCodes
     MessageBox.Show(codeListBox.Items(index).ToString)
     index += 1
Loop
```
The loop displays the codeListBox items in message boxes. You also can use the `MessageBox.Show(Convert.ToString(animalListBox.Items(index)))` statement. (Recall that the codeListBox, which is shown earlier in Figure 6-21, contains 100, 101, 102, 103, 104, and 105.)

Figure 6-28 How to determine the number of items in a list box

The SelectedItem and SelectedIndex Properties

When you select an item in a list box, the item appears highlighted in the list, as shown in Figure 6-29. In addition, the computer stores the item's value (in this case, Dog) and its index (in this case, 0) in the list box's SelectedItem and SelectedIndex properties, respectively.

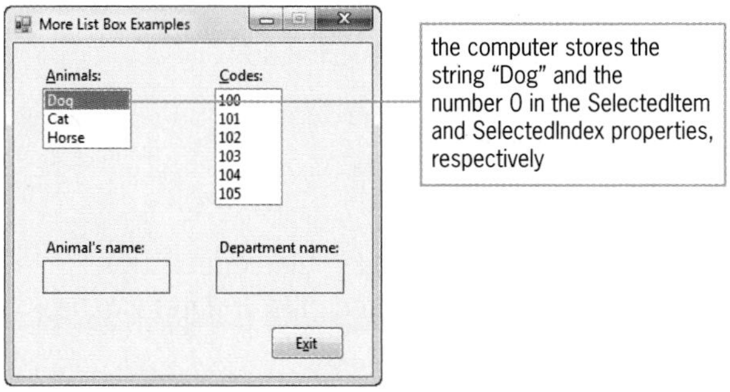

Figure 6-29 Item selected in the animalListBox

You can use either the **SelectedItem property** or the **SelectedIndex property** to determine whether an item is selected in a list box. When no item is selected, the SelectedItem property contains the empty string, and the SelectedIndex property contains the number –1 (negative 1). Otherwise, the SelectedItem and SelectedIndex properties contain the value of the selected item and the item's index, respectively. Figure 6-30 shows examples of using the SelectedItem and SelectedIndex properties.

HOW TO Use the SelectedItem and SelectedIndex Properties

Example 1 (SelectedItem property)

```
animalLabel.Text = Convert.ToString(animalListBox.
SelectedItem)
```

The assignment statement converts the item selected in the animalListBox to String and then assigns the result to the animalLabel's Text property.

Example 2 (SelectedItem property)

```
If Convert.ToInt32(codeListBox.SelectedItem) = 103 Then
```

The If clause converts the item selected in the codeListBox to Integer and then compares the result with the integer 103. The condition evaluates to True when item 103 is selected in the codeListBox; otherwise, it evaluates to False. You also can convert the item to String and then compare the result with the string "103" as follows:

```
If Convert.ToString(codeListBox.SelectedItem) = "103"
```

Example 3 (SelectedItem property)

```
If Convert.ToString(codeListBox.SelectedItem)
<> String.Empty Then
```

The If clause converts the item selected in the codeListBox to String and then compares the result to the empty string. The condition evaluates to True when an item is selected in the codeListBox; otherwise, it evaluates to False.

Example 4 (SelectedIndex property)

```
MessageBox.Show(animalListBox.SelectedIndex.ToString)
```

The MessageBox.Show method displays (in a message box) the index of the item selected in the animalListBox. You also can use the `MessageBox.Show(Convert.ToString(animalListBox.SelectedIndex))` statement.

Example 5 (SelectedIndex property)

```
If codeListBox.SelectedIndex = 0 Then
```

The If clause compares the index of the item selected in the codeListBox with the number 0. The condition evaluates to True when the first item in the list box is selected; otherwise, it evaluates to False.

Figure 6-30 How to use the SelectedItem and SelectedIndex properties

If a list box allows the user to make only one selection, it is customary in Windows applications to have one of the list box items already selected when the interface appears. The selected item, called the **default list box item**, should be either the item selected most frequently or the first item in the list. You can use either the SelectedItem property or the SelectedIndex property to select the default list box item from code, as shown in the examples in Figure 6-31. In most cases, you enter the appropriate code in the form's Load event procedure. (You can look ahead to Figure 6-32 to see the location of the code.)

HOW TO Select the Default List Box Item

Example 1 (SelectedItem property)

```
animalListBox.SelectedItem = "Cat"
```

selects the Cat item in the animalListBox

Example 2 (SelectedItem property)

```
codeListBox.SelectedItem = "101"
```

selects the 101 item in the codeListBox

Example 3 (SelectedIndex property)

```
codeListBox.SelectedIndex = 2
```

selects the third item in the codeListBox

Figure 6-31 How to select the default list box item

The SelectedValueChanged and SelectedIndexChanged Events

Each time either the user or a statement selects an item in a list box, both the list box's **SelectedValueChanged event** and its **SelectedIndexChanged event** occur. You can use the procedures associated with these events to perform one or more tasks when the selected item has changed. Figure 6-32 shows the code entered in the SelectedValueChanged and SelectedIndexChanged procedures for the animalListBox and codeListBox, respectively. It also includes the code entered in the form's Load event procedure. The animalListBox's SelectedValueChanged procedure uses the list box's SelectedItem property to determine the item selected in the list box. It then uses that information to display the name of the animal associated with the selected item. The codeListBox's SelectedIndexChanged procedure, on the other hand, uses the list box's SelectedIndex property to determine the index of the code selected in the list box. It then uses that information to display the name of the department associated with the selected code. It's not necessary to use the SelectedItem property in the SelectedValueChanged procedure; you also can use the SelectedIndex property. Similarly, you can use the SelectedItem property, rather than the SelectedIndex property, in the SelectedIndexChanged procedure.

```
Private Sub MainForm_Load(ByVal sender As Object,
ByVal e As System.EventArgs) Handles Me.Load

     ' add items to the animalListBox
     animalListBox.Items.Add("Dog")
     animalListBox.Items.Add("Cat")
     animalListBox.Items.Add("Horse")

     ' add items to the codeListBox
     Dim code As Integer = 100
     Do While code <= 105
          codeListBox.Items.Add(code.ToString)
          code += 1
     Loop

     ' select the default list box item
     animalListBox.SelectedIndex = 0
     codeListBox.SelectedItem = "100"
End Sub

Private Sub animalListBox_SelectedValueChanged(
ByVal sender As Object, ByVal e As System.EventArgs
) Handles animalListBox.SelectedValueChanged
     ' displays the animal's name

     Dim animal As String
     animal = Convert.ToString(animalListBox.SelectedItem)

     Select Case animal
          Case "Dog"
               animalLabel.Text = "Rover"
          Case "Cat"
               animalLabel.Text = "Fluffy"
          Case Else
               animalLabel.Text = "Poco"
     End Select
End Sub

Private Sub codeListBox_SelectedIndexChanged(ByVal sender As Object,
ByVal e As System.EventArgs) Handles codeListBox.SelectedIndexChanged
     ' displays the department name

     Select Case codeListBox.SelectedIndex
          Case 0
               deptLabel.Text = "Personnel"
          Case 1
               deptLabel.Text = "Payroll"
          Case 2
               deptLabel.Text = "Budget"
          Case 3
               deptLabel.Text = "Inventory"
          Case 4
               deptLabel.Text = "Security"
          Case Else
               deptLabel.Text = "Accounting"
     End Select
End Sub
```

selects the default item in each list box

SelectedValueChanged event procedure

SelectedIndexChanged event procedure

Figure 6-32 Code showing the SelectedValueChanged and SelectedIndexChanged event procedures

When the application containing the code shown in Figure 6-32 is started, the Add methods in the form's Load event procedure fill the two list boxes with values. The `animalListBox.SelectedIndex = 0` and `codeListBox.SelectedItem = "100"` statements then select the first item in each list box; doing this invokes each list box's SelectedValueChanged event procedure followed by its SelectedIndexChanged event procedure. As a result, Rover and Personnel appear in the animalLabel and deptLabel, respectively, as shown in Figure 6-33.

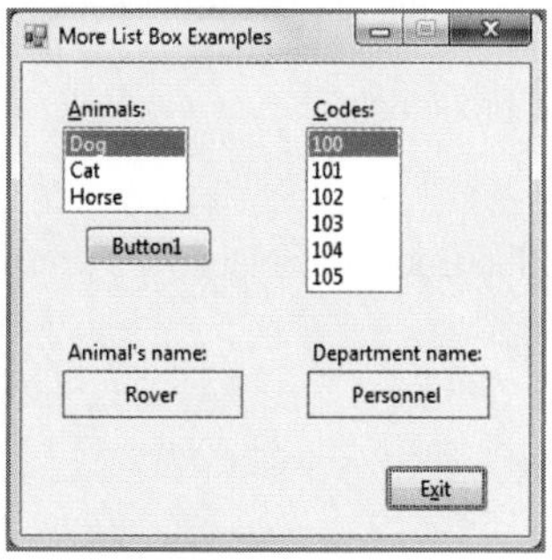

Figure 6-33 Result of processing the code shown in Figure 6-32

If you want to experiment with the application shown in Figure 6-33, open the solution contained in the Try It 7! folder.

To review what you learned about list boxes, view the Ch06ListBox video.

The Product Finder Application

The Product Finder application demonstrates most of what you learned about list boxes. The application also provides another example of using a repetition structure. The application allows the user to enter a product ID. It then searches for the ID in a list box that contains the valid product IDs. If the product ID is included in the list box, the application highlights (selects) the ID in the list. If the product ID is not in the list box, the application ensures that no ID is highlighted in the list box, and it displays a message indicating that the ID was not found. Figures 6-34 and 6-35 show sample runs of the application.

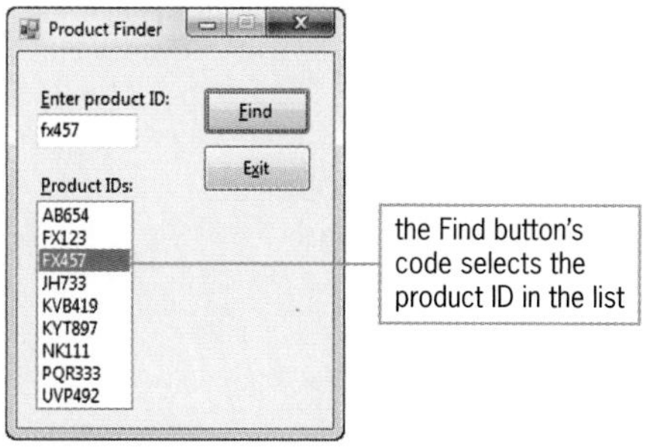

Figure 6-34 Sample run of the application when the product ID is found

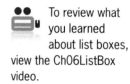

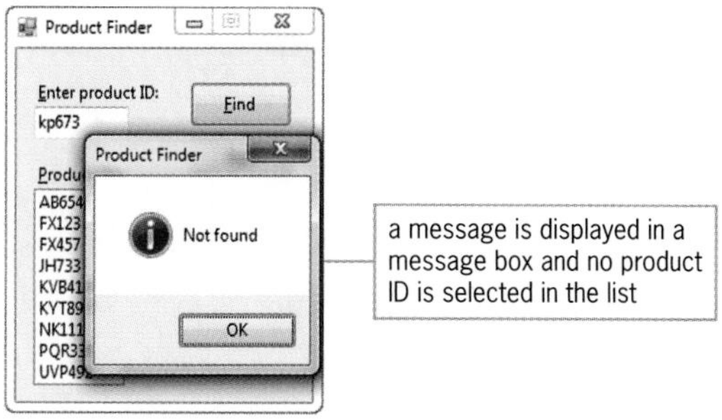

Figure 6-35 Sample run of the application when the product ID is not found

Figure 6-36 shows the pseudocode for the Find button's Click event procedure, and Figure 6-37 shows the application's code.

```
findButton Click event procedure
1. assign the product ID entered by the user to a variable
2. assign the number of list box items to a variable
3. repeat while the list box item's index is less than the number of items in the list and,
   at the same time, the product ID has not been found
        if the product ID entered by the user is the same as the current item in the list box
               indicate that the product ID was found by assigning True to a Boolean variable
        else
               continue the search by adding 1 to the list box index
        end if
   end repeat
4. if the product ID was found (indicated by a True value in the Boolean variable)
        select the product ID in the list box
   else
        clear any selection in the list box
        display the "Not found" message in a message box
   end if
```

Figure 6-36 Pseudocode for the Find button's Click event procedure

```
' Project name:          Products Project
' Project purpose:       Search a list box for a product ID
' Created/revised by:    <your name> on <current date>

Option Explicit On
Option Strict On
Option Infer Off

Public Class MainForm

  Private Sub exitButton_Click(ByVal sender As Object,
  ByVal e As System.EventArgs) Handles exitButton.Click
    Me.Close()
  End Sub

  Private Sub MainForm_Load(ByVal sender As Object,
  ByVal e As System.EventArgs) Handles Me.Load
     ' fills the list box with IDs

     idListBox.Items.Add("FX123")
     idListBox.Items.Add("AB654")
     idListBox.Items.Add("JH733")
     idListBox.Items.Add("FX457")
     idListBox.Items.Add("NK111")
     idListBox.Items.Add("KYT897")
     idListBox.Items.Add("KVB419")
     idListBox.Items.Add("PQR333")
     idListBox.Items.Add("UVP492")
  End Sub

```

Figure 6-37 Product Finder application's code *(continues)*

(continued)

```
Private Sub findButton_Click(ByVal sender As Object,
ByVal e As System.EventArgs) Handles findButton.Click
   ' searches a list box for a specific ID

   Dim isFound As Boolean
   Dim index As Integer
   Dim numItems As Integer
   Dim id As String

   ' assign ID and number of list box
   ' items to variables
   id = idTextBox.Text.ToUpper
   numItems = idListBox.Items.Count

   ' search the list box, stopping either after the
   ' last item or when the item is found
   Do While index < numItems AndAlso isFound = False
      If id = idListBox.Items(index).ToString.ToUpper Then
         isFound = True
      Else
         index = index + 1
      End If
   Loop

   If isFound = True Then
      idListBox.SelectedIndex = index
   Else
      idListBox.SelectedIndex = -1
      MessageBox.Show("Not found", "Product Finder",
            MessageBoxButtons.OK,
            MessageBoxIcon.Information)
   End If
 End Sub
End Class
```

Figure 6-37 Product Finder application's code

If you want to experiment with the Product Finder application, open the solution contained in the Try It 8! folder.

The last concepts covered in this chapter involve enabling and disabling a control, refreshing the screen, and pausing program execution. You will use these concepts in the Color Viewer application coded in the next section. You also will use the concepts in the game application coded in Programming Tutorial 1.

The Color Viewer Application

Figure 6-38 shows the MainForm in the Color Viewer application. When the user clicks the View Colors button, the button's Click event procedure should disable the button while the procedure is running, and then enable it when the procedure is finished. You disable a control by changing its Enabled property from its default value (True) to False. When a control's **Enabled property** is set to False, the control appears dimmed (grayed out) during run time, indicating that it is not currently available to the user. After disabling the button, the button's Click event procedure should change the background color of the colorLabel to blue, then to yellow, and then to red. You change the background color by setting the colorLabel's BackColor property to `Color.Blue`,

`Color.Yellow`, and `Color.Red`. Finally, the Click event procedure should enable the button to make it available to the user once again.

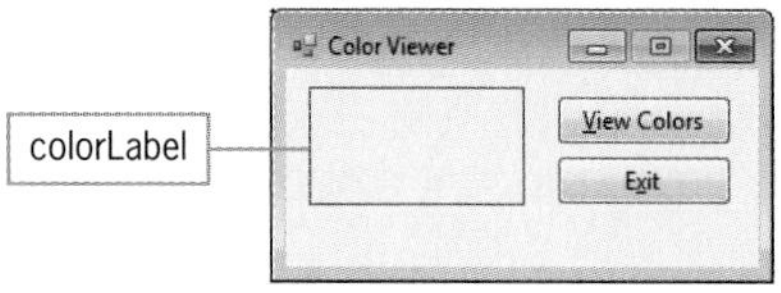

Figure 6-38 MainForm in the Color Viewer application

> If you want to experiment with the Color Viewer application shown in Figure 6-38, open the solution contained in the Try It 9! folder.

Figure 6-39 shows the code entered in the View Colors button's Click event procedure. The `Me.Refresh()` statement uses the form's Refresh method to refresh the interface. (Recall that the `Me` keyword refers to the current form.) The **Refresh method** ensures that the computer processes any previous lines of code that affect the interface's appearance. The `SystemThreading.Thread.Sleep(1000)` statement uses the **Sleep method** to delay program execution for one second. The Sleep method's syntax is **System.Threading.Thread.Sleep(*milliseconds*)**, in which the *milliseconds* argument is the number of milliseconds to suspend the program. A millisecond is 1/1000 of a second; in other words, there are 1000 milliseconds in a second. If you do not refresh the screen and delay program execution before switching from one color to the next, the user will see only the last color (in this case, red) in the colorLabel when the View Colors button is clicked. This is due to the speed at which the computer executes a procedure's instructions. The Refresh and Sleep methods in Figure 6-39 will pause program execution for one second between color changes.

```
Private Sub viewButton_Click(ByVal sender As Object,
ByVal e As System.EventArgs) Handles viewButton.Click
     ' changes the background color of the colorLabel

     ' disable the button
     viewButton.Enabled = False

     ' change the colors
     colorLabel.BackColor = Color.Blue
     Me.Refresh()
     System.Threading.Thread.Sleep(1000)

     colorLabel.BackColor = Color.Yellow
     Me.Refresh()
     System.Threading.Thread.Sleep(1000)

     colorLabel.BackColor = Color.Red

     ' enable the button
     viewButton.Enabled = True
End Sub
```

Figure 6-39 View Colors button's Click event procedure

Mini-Quiz 6-4

The answers to Mini-Quiz questions are located in Appendix A.

1. You can use the _____________ method to add items to a list box.
   a. Add
   b. AddList
   c. Item
   d. ItemAdd
2. The items in a list box belong to the _____________ collection.
   a. ItemList
   b. Items
   c. List
   d. ListItems
3. When an item is selected in a list box, the computer stores the item's index in the _____________ property.
   a. Index
   b. ItemIndex
   c. SelectedIndex
   d. SelectedItem
4. Which of the following will delay program execution for two seconds?
   a. `System.Threading.Thread.Sleep(2)`
   b. `System.Threading.Thread.Sleep(200)`
   c. `System.Threading.Thread.Sleep(2000)`
   d. `System.Threading.Thread.Sleep(20000)`

You have completed the concepts section of Chapter 6. The Programming Tutorial section is next.

PROGRAMMING TUTORIAL 1

Creating the Roll 'Em Game Application

The Ch06ProgTut1 video demonstrates all of the steps in Programming Tutorial 1.

In this tutorial, you create an application that simulates a dice game called Roll 'Em. The game is played using two dice. Each player takes a turn at rolling the dice. The first player who rolls the same number on both dice wins the game. Figures 6-40 and 6-41 show the application's TOE chart and MainForm, respectively. The images at the bottom of the user interface represent the six sides of a die. The application will use random numbers to display the appropriate image in the firstDiePictureBox and secondDiePictureBox controls. For example, if the random numbers are 6 and 3, the application will display the image containing six dots in the firstDiePictureBox, and display the image containing three dots in the secondDiePictureBox. The images in the firstDiePictureBox and secondDiePictureBox controls will correspond to a roll of the dice.

Task	Object	Event
1. Keep track of the current player 2. Display the current player's number in the messageLabel 3. Generate two random numbers from 1 through 6 4. Use the random numbers to display the appropriate images in the firstDiePictureBox and secondDiePictureBox controls 5. Determine whether the current player won and display an appropriate message in the messageLabel	rollButton	Click
End the application	exitButton	Click
Display a message indicating either the current player or the winner (from rollButton)	messageLabel	None
Display the image corresponding to the first die (from rollButton)	firstDiePictureBox	None
Display the image corresponding to the second die (from rollButton)	secondDiePictureBox	None

Figure 6-40 TOE chart for the Roll 'Em Game application

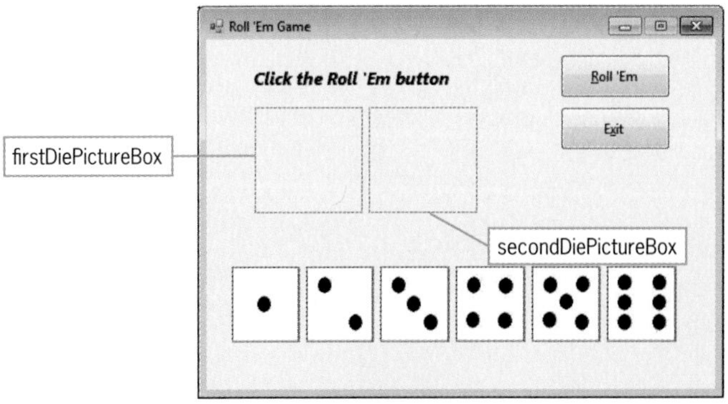

Figure 6-41 MainForm for the Roll 'Em Game application

Coding the Roll 'Em Game Application

Included in the data files for this book is a partially completed Roll 'Em Game application. To complete the application, you just need to code it. According to the application's TOE chart, only the Click event procedures for the rollButton and exitButton need to be coded.

To begin coding the application:

1. Start Visual Studio or the Express Edition of Visual Basic. If necessary, open the Solution Explorer window.
2. Open the **Roll Em Game Solution** (**Roll Em Game Solution.sln**) file, which is contained in the VbReloaded2010\Chap06\Roll Em Game Solution folder. Open the designer window (if necessary), and then auto-hide the Solution Explorer window.
3. Open the Code Editor window. Notice that the exitButton's Click event procedure has already been coded for you. In addition, the Option statements have already been entered in the General Declarations section.
4. In the comments that appear in the General Declarations section, replace <your name> and <current date> with your name and the current date.

Figure 6-42 shows the pseudocode for the rollButton's Click event procedure. As the pseudocode indicates, the procedure will use a static variable to keep track of the player number (either 1 or 2). In addition, it will use two random numbers to display the appropriate images in the firstDiePictureBox and secondDiePictureBox.

```
rollButton Click event procedure
1. initialize a static variable to 1, because player 1 rolls first
2. remove any existing images from firstDiePictureBox and secondDiePictureBox
3. display a message (in the messageLabel) indicating the current player
4. generate two random numbers from 1 through 6
5. if the first random number is one of the following:
        1  display dot1PictureBox image in firstDiePictureBox
        2  display dot2PictureBox image in firstDiePictureBox
        3  display dot3PictureBox image in firstDiePictureBox
        4  display dot4PictureBox image in firstDiePictureBox
        5  display dot5PictureBox image in firstDiePictureBox
        6  display dot6PictureBox image in firstDiePictureBox
   end if
6. if the second random number is one of the following:
        1  display dot1PictureBox image in secondDiePictureBox
        2  display dot2PictureBox image in secondDiePictureBox
        3  display dot3PictureBox image in secondDiePictureBox
        4  display dot4PictureBox image in secondDiePictureBox
        5  display dot5PictureBox image in secondDiePictureBox
        6  display dot6PictureBox image in secondDiePictureBox
   end if
```

Figure 6-42 Pseudocode for the rollButton's Click event procedure *(continues)*

(continued)

```
7. if both random numbers are equal
        display a message (in the messageLabel) indicating the winning player
   end if
8. if the static variable contains the number 1
        assign the number 2 to the static variable, because it's player 2's turn next
   else
        assign the number 1 to the static variable, because it's player 1's turn next
   end if
```

Figure 6-42 Pseudocode for the rollButton's Click event procedure

To code the rollButton's Click event procedure and then test the procedure's code:

1. Open the code template for the rollButton's Click event procedure. Type **' simulates the Roll 'Em game** and press **Enter** twice.

2. The procedure will need a Random object to represent the pseudo-random number generator, and two Integer variables to store the two random numbers. Enter the following three Dim statements:

   Dim randomGenerator As New Random
   Dim random1 As Integer
   Dim random2 As Integer

3. The first step in the pseudocode is to initialize a static variable to 1. Type the following declaration statement and then press **Enter** twice:

   Static player As Integer = 1

4. Steps 2 and 3 remove any existing images from the firstDiePictureBox and secondDiePictureBox controls and then display a message indicating the current player. You can remove an image from a picture box by assigning the keyword `Nothing` to the control's Image property. Enter the following comment and assignment statements. Press **Enter** twice after typing the last assignment statement.

   ' clear images and display message
   firstDiePictureBox.Image = Nothing
   secondDiePictureBox.Image = Nothing
   messageLabel.Text = "Player " &
   player.ToString & " rolled:"

5. The next step is to generate two random numbers from 1 through 6. You will assign the random numbers to the `random1` and `random2` variables. Enter the following comment and assignment statements. Press **Enter** twice after typing the last assignment statement.

   ' generate two random numbers from 1 through 6
   random1 = randomGenerator.Next(1, 7)
   random2 = randomGenerator.Next(1, 7)

6. Step 5 in the pseudocode is a multiple-alternative selection structure that uses the first random number to display the appropriate image in the firstDiePictureBox. Enter the additional comment and code shown in Figure 6-43, and then position the insertion point as indicated in the figure. (You do not need to display the line numbers.)

```
        ' generate two random numbers from 1 through 6
        random1 = randomGenerator.Next(1, 7)
        random2 = randomGenerator.Next(1, 7)

        ' display appropriate image in firstDiePictureBox
        Select Case random1
            Case 1
                firstDiePictureBox.Image = dot1PictureBox.Image
            Case 2
                firstDiePictureBox.Image = dot2PictureBox.Image
            Case 3
                firstDiePictureBox.Image = dot3PictureBox.Image
            Case 4
                firstDiePictureBox.Image = dot4PictureBox.Image
            Case 5
                firstDiePictureBox.Image = dot5PictureBox.Image
            Case Else
                firstDiePictureBox.Image = dot6PictureBox.Image
        End Select


    End Sub
```

enter this comment and the Select Case statement

position the insertion point here

Figure 6-43 First selection structure entered in the procedure

7. Step 6 is a multiple-alternative selection structure that uses the second random number to display the appropriate image in the secondDiePictureBox. Enter the additional comment and code shown in Figure 6-44, and then position the insertion point as indicated in the figure.

rollButton | Click

```
                firstDiePictureBox.Image = dot6PictureBox.Image
        End Select

        ' display appropriate image in secondDiePictureBox
        Select Case random2
            Case 1
                secondDiePictureBox.Image = dot1PictureBox.Image
            Case 2
                secondDiePictureBox.Image = dot2PictureBox.Image
            Case 3
                secondDiePictureBox.Image = dot3PictureBox.Image
            Case 4
                secondDiePictureBox.Image = dot4PictureBox.Image
            Case 5
                secondDiePictureBox.Image = dot5PictureBox.Image
            Case Else
                secondDiePictureBox.Image = dot6PictureBox.Image
        End Select


    End Sub
```

enter this comment and the Select Case statement

position the insertion point here

Figure 6-44 Second selection structure entered in the procedure

8. Step 7 is a single-alternative selection structure that compares both random numbers for equality. If both numbers are equal, the selection structure's true path should display a message indicating the winning player. Enter the additional comment and code shown in Figure 6-45, and then position the insertion point as indicated in the figure.

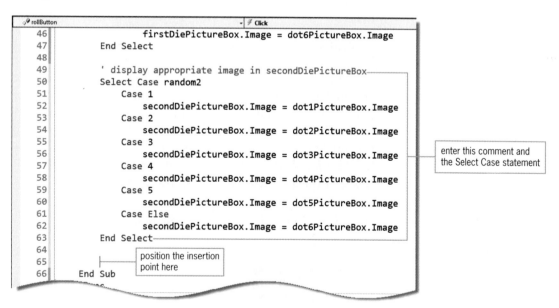

enter this comment and the single-alternative selection structure

position the insertion point here

```
                secondDiePictureBox.Image = dot6PictureBox.Image
        End Select

        ' check if there is a winner
        If random1 = random2 Then
            messageLabel.Text = "Congratulations, player " &
                player.ToString
        End If

    End Sub
```

Figure 6-45 Third selection structure entered in the procedure

9. The last step in the pseudocode is a dual-alternative selection structure that uses the static variable to determine the current player, and then resets the variable's value accordingly. If the static variable contains the number 1, it indicates that the first player rolled the dice. Therefore, the selection structure's true path assigns the number 2 to the variable to indicate that it's the second player's turn. Otherwise, the selection structure's false path assigns the number 1 to the static variable to indicate that it's the first player's turn. Type the following comment and selection structure:

```
' reset the current player
If player = 1 Then
    player = 2
Else
    player = 1
End If
```

10. Save the solution and then start the application. Click the **Roll 'Em** button. Figure 6-46 shows the result of player 1 rolling the dice. Because random numbers determine the images assigned to the firstDiePictureBox and secondDiePictureBox controls, your application might display different images than those shown in the figure. In addition, the "Congratulations, player 1" message, rather than the "Player 1 rolled:" message, may appear on your screen.

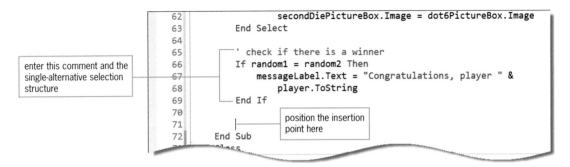

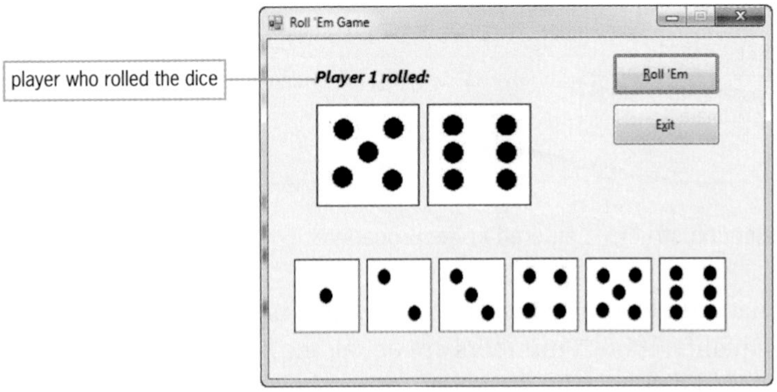

Figure 6-46 Player 1's roll of the dice

11. Click the **Roll 'Em** button again. Notice that the message (either "Player 2 rolled:" or "Congratulations, player 2") refers to player 2.

12. Click the **Roll 'Em** button several times until there is a winner. Figure 6-47 shows a sample of the interface when player 2 wins.

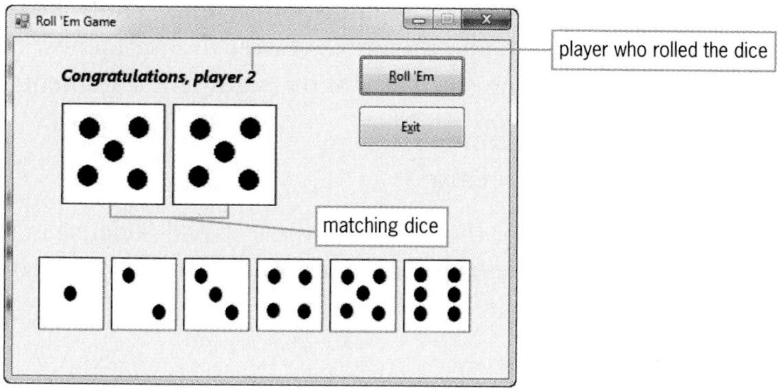

Figure 6-47 Result of player 2 winning

13. Click the **Exit** button to end the application.

14. There is no need to show the six images at the bottom of the form during run time. Make the Designer window the active window. Unlock the controls on the form, then drag the form's bottom border until it hides the six images, and then lock the controls again.

15. Save the solution.

Modifying the Application

In this section, you are going to modify the rollButton's Click event procedure to make the application a bit more exciting. First, you will have the procedure delay program execution after displaying the "Player *x* rolled:" message, but before displaying the dice images. The delay will give the player a short time to anticipate the roll. You will delay the execution for one second, which is 1000 milliseconds.

To modify the rollButton's code and then test the code:

1. Make the Code Editor window the active window. Click the **blank line** above the `' generate two random numbers from 1 through 6` comment, and then press **Enter** to insert a new blank line. Enter the following comment and statements:

```
' refresh form and then delay execution
Me.Refresh()
System.Threading.Thread.Sleep(1000)
```

2. Save the solution and then start the application.

3. Click the **Roll 'Em** button. Notice that there is a slight delay from when the message appears to when the dice images appear. Click the **Exit** button to end the application.

4. The disadvantage of the delay between the message and the dice images is that it might cause the user to click the Roll 'Em button before the dice images appear. You can fix this problem by disabling the Roll 'Em button after it has been clicked, and then enabling it after all of the code in its Click event procedure is processed. Click the **blank line** above the `' refresh form and then delay execution` comment, and then press **Enter** to insert a new blank line. Enter the following comment and assignment statement:

   ' disable Roll 'Em button
   rollButton.Enabled = False

5. Click immediately after the letter **f** in the last End If clause in the procedure, and then press **Enter** twice. Enter the following comment and assignment statement:

   ' enable Roll 'Em button
   rollButton.Enabled = True

6. Save the solution, and then start the application. Click the **Roll 'Em** button. Notice that the Roll 'Em button is disabled until after the dice images appear. Click the **Exit** button to end the application.

You will make one final modification to the rollButton's Click event procedure. Specifically, you will use a loop to make the Congratulations message blink several times when a player wins the game. You can make a control blink by switching its Visible property from True to False and then back again several times. However, switching the Visible property isn't all that is needed. Because the computer will process the switching instructions so rapidly, you won't even notice that the control is blinking. To actually see the control blink, you will need to refresh the form and then delay program execution each time you switch the Visible property's setting. Figure 6-48 shows two ways of writing the code to make the Congratulations message blink five times. Version 2 uses the **Not logical operator**, which reverses the truth value of the messageLabel's Visible property. If the Visible property contains True when the `messageLabel.Visible = Not messageLabel.Visible` statement is processed, the `Not messageLabel.Visible` expression evaluates to False; as a result, the statement assigns False to the Visible property. On the other hand, if the Visible property contains False when the statement is processed, the `Not messageLabel.Visible` expression evaluates to True and the statement assigns True to the Visible property.

Version 1
```
Dim count As Integer = 1
Do While count <= 10
     If messageLabel.Visible = True Then
          messageLabel.Visible = False
     Else
          messageLabel.Visible = True
     End If
     Me.Refresh()
     System.Threading.Thread.Sleep(100)
     count += 1
Loop
```

Figure 6-48 Two ways of writing the blinking code *(continues)*

(continued)

```
Version 2
Dim count As Integer = 1
Do While count <= 10
     messageLabel.Visible = Not messageLabel.Visible
     Me.Refresh()
     System.Threading.Thread.Sleep(100)
     count += 1
Loop
```

Figure 6-48 Two ways of writing the blinking code

To complete the rollButton's Click event procedure, and then test the procedure's code:

1. Locate the single-alternative selection structure in the procedure. Click immediately after the letter **g** in the `player.ToString` line and then press **Enter** to insert a blank line.
2. Enter either version of the code shown in Figure 6-48. (If you find the Not operator confusing, definitely enter Version 1 of the code.)
3. Save the solution and then start the application. Click the **Roll 'Em** button several times until one player wins, which causes the messageLabel to blink.
4. Click the **Exit** button to end the application. Close the Code Editor window, and then close the solution. Figure 6-49 shows the application's code. (The figure contains Version 2 of the code shown in Figure 6-48. Your code may contain Version 1.)

```
' Project name:          Roll Em Game Project
' Project purpose:       Simulates the Roll 'Em game
' Created/revised by:    <your name> on <current date>

Option Explicit On
Option Strict On
Option Infer Off

Public Class MainForm

  Private Sub exitButton_Click(ByVal sender As Object,
  ByVal e As System.EventArgs) Handles exitButton.Click
     Me.Close()
  End Sub

  Private Sub rollButton_Click(ByVal sender As Object,
  ByVal e As System.EventArgs) Handles rollButton.Click
     ' simulates the Roll 'Em game

     Dim randomGenerator As New Random
     Dim random1 As Integer
     Dim random2 As Integer
     Static player As Integer = 1

```

Figure 6-49 Code for the Roll 'Em Game application *(continues)*

(continued)

```
    ' clear images and display message
    firstDiePictureBox.Image = Nothing
    secondDiePictureBox.Image = Nothing
    messageLabel.Text = "Player " &
        player.ToString & " rolled:"

    ' disable Roll 'Em button
    rollButton.Enabled = False

    ' refresh form and then delay execution
    Me.Refresh()
    System.Threading.Thread.Sleep(1000)

    ' generate two random numbers from 1 through 6
    random1 = randomGenerator.Next(1, 7)
    random2 = randomGenerator.Next(1, 7)

    ' display appropriate image in firstDiePictureBox
    Select Case random1
       Case 1
          firstDiePictureBox.Image = dot1PictureBox.Image
       Case 2
          firstDiePictureBox.Image = dot2PictureBox.Image
       Case 3
          firstDiePictureBox.Image = dot3PictureBox.Image
       Case 4
          firstDiePictureBox.Image = dot4PictureBox.Image
       Case 5
          firstDiePictureBox.Image = dot5PictureBox.Image
       Case Else
          firstDiePictureBox.Image = dot6PictureBox.Image
    End Select

       ' display appropriate image in secondDiePictureBox
       Select Case random2
       Case 1
          secondDiePictureBox.Image = dot1PictureBox.Image
       Case 2
          secondDiePictureBox.Image = dot2PictureBox.Image
       Case 3
          secondDiePictureBox.Image = dot3PictureBox.Image
       Case 4
          secondDiePictureBox.Image = dot4PictureBox.Image
       Case 5
          secondDiePictureBox.Image = dot5PictureBox.Image
       Case Else
          secondDiePictureBox.Image = dot6PictureBox.Image
    End Select

    ' check if there is a winner
    If random1 = random2 Then
       messageLabel.Text = "Congratulations, player " &
           player.ToString
       Dim count As Integer = 1
       Do While count <= 10
          messageLabel.Visible = Not messageLabel.Visible
```

Figure 6-49 Code for the Roll 'Em Game application *(continues)*

(continued)

```
            Me.Refresh()
            System.Threading.Thread.Sleep(100)
            count += 1
         Loop
      End If

      ' reset the current player
      If player = 1 Then
         player = 2
      Else
         player = 1
      End If

      ' enable Roll 'Em button
      rollButton.Enabled = True

   End Sub
End Class
```

Figure 6-49 Code for the Roll 'Em Game application

PROGRAMMING TUTORIAL 2

Coding the Just Birthdays Application

In this tutorial, you create an application for the Just Birthdays store, which sells unique supplies for birthday parties. The store's price list is shown in Figure 6-50. The application calculates and displays a customer's total charge, which is based on the type of party and the number of guests. The application's TOE chart and MainForm are shown in Figures 6-51 and 6-52, respectively. The MainForm provides a text box for entering the number of guests and a list box for selecting the party type.

Birthday party	Charge per guest
Kid's	$11
21st	$20
40th	$25
Other	$15

Figure 6-50 Just Birthdays' price list

Task	Object	Event
Get and display the number of guests	guestsTextBox	None
Allow the user to enter only numbers and the Backspace key		KeyPress
Specify the party type	typeListBox	None
Display the birthday types in the typeListBox	MainForm	Load
1. Calculate the total charge 2. Display the total charge in totalLabel	calcButton	Click
Display the total charge (from calcButton)	totalLabel	None
End the application	exitButton	Click

Figure 6-51 TOE chart for the Just Birthdays application

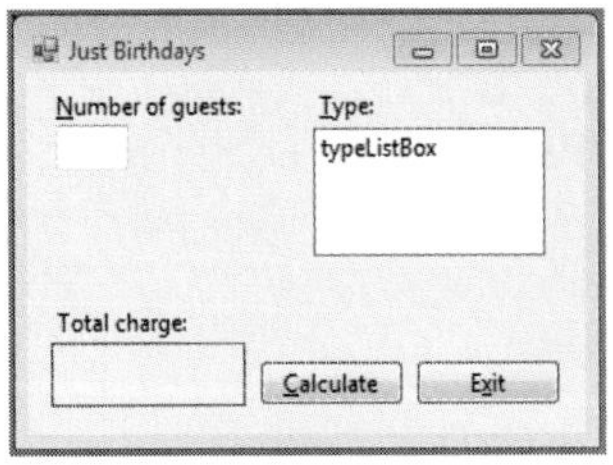

Figure 6-52 MainForm for the Just Birthdays application

Coding the Just Birthdays Application

Included in the data files for this book is a partially completed Just Birthdays application. To complete the application, you just need to code it. According to the application's TOE chart, the guestsTextBox's KeyPress event procedure, the MainForm's Load event procedure, and the Click event procedures for the calcButton and exitButton need to be coded.

To begin coding the application:

1. Start Visual Studio or the Express Edition of Visual Basic. If necessary, open the Solution Explorer window.
2. Open the **Just Birthdays Solution (Just Birthdays Solution.sln)** file, which is contained in the VbReloaded2010\Chap06\Just Birthdays Solution folder. Open the designer window (if necessary), and then auto-hide the Solution Explorer window.
3. Open the Code Editor window. Notice that the exitButton's Click event procedure and the guestsTextBox's KeyPress event procedure have already been coded for you. In addition, the Option statements have already been entered in the General Declarations section.
4. In the comments that appear in the General Declarations section, replace <your name> and <current date> with your name and the current date.

The application's TOE chart indicates that the MainForm's Load event procedure is responsible for displaying the birthday types in the typeListBox.

To code the MainForm's Load event procedure, and then test the code:

1. Open the code template for the MainForm's Load event procedure. Recall that you do this by selecting (MainForm Events) in the Class Name list box and Load in the Method Name list box.
2. Type **' fills the list box and selects the first item** and press **Enter** twice.
3. Enter the following four Add methods:

```
typeListBox.Items.Add("Kid's Birthday")
typeListBox.Items.Add("21st Birthday")
typeListBox.Items.Add("40th Birthday")
typeListBox.Items.Add("Other Birthdays")
```

4. Next, enter a statement that uses the SelectedIndex property to select the first item in the typeListBox.
5. Save the solution and then start the application. Four items appear in the Type list box. The first item is selected (highlighted), as shown in Figure 6-53.

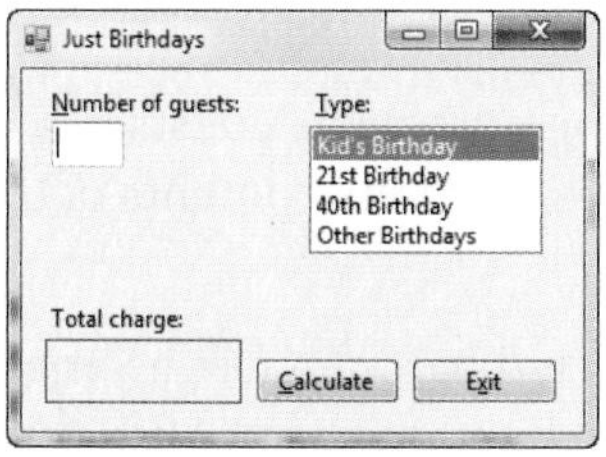

Figure 6-53 Result of processing the MainForm's Load event procedure

6. Click the **Exit** button to end the application.

According to the application's TOE chart, the Calculate button's Click event procedure is responsible for calculating and displaying the total charge. The procedure's pseudocode is shown in Figure 6-54.

```
calcButton Click event procedure
1. store the number of guests in a variable
2. store the index of the selected party type in a variable
3. if the party type index is one of the following:
       0 (Kid's Birthday)        price per guest = 11
       1 (21st Birthday)         price per guest = 20
       2 (40th Birthday)         price per guest = 25
       3 (Other Birthdays)       price per guest = 15
   end if
4. total charge = number of guests * price per guest
5. display the total charge in totalLabel
```

Figure 6-54 Pseudocode for the calcButton's Click event procedure

As you know, before you begin coding a procedure, you first study the procedure's pseudocode (or flowchart) to determine any variables or named constants the procedure will require. In this case, the calcButton's Click event procedure will use the four Integer variables listed in Figure 6-55.

Variables	Data type	Value source
guests	Integer	user input (guestsTextBox)
typeIndex	Integer	user input (index of item selected in the typeListBox)
guestPrice	Integer	assigned in the procedure
totalCharge	Integer	procedure calculation

Figure 6-55 Variables for the calcButton's Click event procedure

To code the Calculate button's Click event procedure, and then test the code:

1. Open the code template for the calcButton's Click event procedure.
2. Type **' displays the total charge** and press **Enter** twice.
3. Enter the statements to declare the four variables listed in Figure 6-55. Press **Enter** twice after typing the last declaration statement.
4. Step 1 in the pseudocode is to store the number of guests in a variable. Enter a TryParse method that will store the contents of the guestsTextBox in the `guests` variable.
5. Step 2 is to store the index of the selected party type in a variable. Enter the appropriate assignment statement to accomplish this task. Store the index in the `typeIndex` variable. Press **Enter** twice after typing the assignment statement.
6. Step 3 is a multiple-alternative selection structure that uses the party type index to determine the price per guest. Type **' determine the price per guest** and press **Enter.** Now, enter the appropriate Select Case statement. Assign the price per guest to the `guestPrice` variable. Use comments to make the Select Case statement more self-documenting. For example, enter `Case 0 ' Kid's Birthday` for the first Case clause.
7. Step 4 is to calculate the total charge by multiplying the number of guests by the price per guest. If necessary, insert two blank lines between the End Select clause and the End Sub clause. In the blank line above the End Sub clause, type **' calculate and display the total charge** and press **Enter.** Now, enter the assignment statement to calculate the total charge. Assign the total charge to the `totalCharge` variable.
8. The last step in the pseudocode displays the total charge in the totalLabel. Enter the appropriate assignment statement. Display the total charge with a dollar sign and no decimal places.
9. Save the solution, and then start the application. Type **10** in the Number of guests box and then click **40th Birthday** in the list box. Click the **Calculate** button. $250 appears in the interface, as shown in Figure 6-56.

Figure 6-56 Interface showing the total charge

10. On your own, test the application using different values for the number of guests and birthday types.
11. Click the **Exit** button to end the application.

Generating Test Data for the Just Birthdays Application

As you know, you should test an application as thoroughly as possible, because you don't want to give the user an application that either produces incorrect output or ends abruptly with an error. For all of the applications you have created so far, you were either given the test data or expected to create your own test data. However, it's also possible to have the computer create a set of test data for you. As you will learn in the next set of steps, you do this using a loop and the random number generator.

To modify the user interface:

1. Make the Designer window the active window.
2. Unlock the controls on the form. Make the form larger by dragging its bottom border. Stop dragging when you see the testDataLabel and Generate Test Data button. See Figure 6-57.

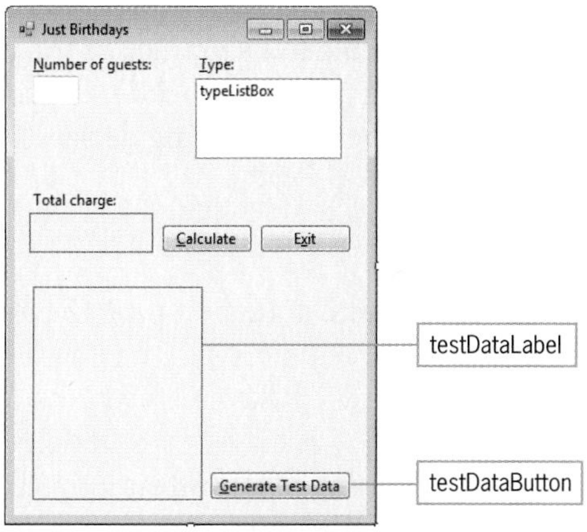

Figure 6-57 Interface showing the additional label and button

3. Lock the controls on the form.

   The Generate Test Data button's Click event procedure will be responsible for generating 10 sets of random test data. The procedure's pseudocode is shown in Figure 6-58.

```
testDataButton Click event procedure
1. assign the number 1 to a counter variable
2. clear the contents of the testDataLabel
3. repeat
       generate a random number from 1 through 50 to represent the number of guests
       generate a random number from 0 through 3 to represent the party type index
       if the party type index is one of the following:
               0 (Kid's Birthday)          price per guest = 11
               1 (21st Birthday)           price per guest = 20
               2 (40th Birthday)           price per guest = 25
               3 (Other Birthdays)         price per guest = 15
       end if
       total charge = number of guests * price per guest
       display the party type index, number of guests, and total charge in the testDataLabel
       add 1 to the counter variable
   end repeat until the counter variable is greater than 10
```

Figure 6-58 Pseudocode for the Generate Test Data button's Click event procedure

To code the Generate Test Data button's Click event procedure, and then test the code:

1. Make the Code Editor window the active window. Highlight the comments and code contained in the calcButton's Click event procedure, beginning with the `Dim guests As Integer` statement and ending with the blank line above the End Sub clause. Click **Edit** on the menu bar and then click **Copy**.
2. Open the testDataButton's Click event procedure. Click **Edit** on the menu bar and then click **Paste**.
3. The testDataButton's Click event procedure will need a Random object to represent the random number generator. Click the **blank line** below the `Dim totalCharge As Integer` statement, and then enter the following declaration statement:

   Dim randomGen As New Random
4. The procedure will use a counter variable to keep track of the number of test data sets. According to Step 1 in the pseudocode, the counter variable should be initialized to 1. Type the following declaration statement and then press **Enter** twice:

   Dim setCounter As Integer = 1
5. Step 2 is to clear the contents of the testDataLabel. Type the following statement and then press **Enter** twice:

   testDataLabel.Text = String.Empty
6. Step 3 in the pseudocode is the beginning of a posttest loop. Type **Do** and press **Enter**, and then change the Loop clause to **Loop Until setCounter > 10**.
7. Delete the statement containing the TryParse method. Also delete the statement that assigns the SelectedIndex value to the typeIndex variable.
8. Now you can start coding the loop body. According to the pseudocode, the first instruction in the loop body should generate a random number from 1 through 50 to represent the number of guests. Click the **blank line** between the Do and Loop clauses, and then enter the following statement:

   guests = randomGen.Next(1, 51)
9. The next instruction in the loop body should generate a random number from 0 through 3 to represent the party type index. Type the following statement and then press **Enter** twice:

   typeIndex = randomGen.Next(0, 4)
10. The procedure already contains the code corresponding to the selection structure and calculation task shown in the pseudocode. You just need to move that code into the loop. Highlight all of the comments and code, beginning with the `' determine the price per guest` comment and ending with the blank line below the last assignment statement. Click **Edit** on the menu bar and then click **Cut**.

11. Click the **blank line** above the Loop clause. Click **Edit** on the menu bar and then click **Paste**.

12. After calculating the total charge, the procedure will need to display the party type index, number of guests, and total charge in the testDataLabel. Change the `totalLabel.Text = totalCharge.ToString("C0")` statement in the loop body to the following (There are four spaces within the first two sets of quotation marks.):

```
testDataLabel.Text = testDataLabel.Text &
    typeIndex.ToString & "    " &
    guests.ToString & "    " &
    totalCharge.ToString("C0") &
    ControlChars.NewLine
```

13. The last instruction in the loop body is to update the counter variable by 1. Enter the following statement in the blank line above the Loop clause:

```
setCounter += 1
```

14. Save the solution and then start the application. Click the **Generate Test Data** button. The test data appears in the testDataLabel. See Figure 6-59.

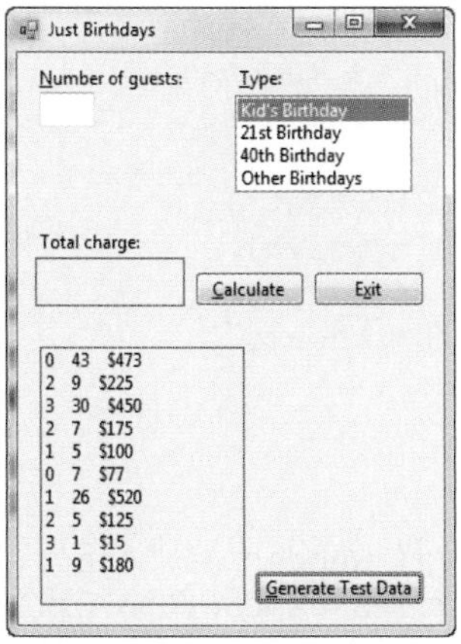

Figure 6-59 Test data generated by the Generate Test Data button

15. Now, manually calculate the total charges using the values shown in the first two columns of the testDataLabel, and then compare your answers with the values in the third column. For example, the first set of test data shown in Figure 6-59 (0 and 43) indicates a Kid's birthday party with 43 guests. The price per guest for a Kid's birthday party is $11. If you multiply 43 by 11, the result is 473, which agrees with the value shown in the third column for this set of test data.

16. Click the **Exit** button. Close the Code Editor window and then close the solution. Figure 6-60 shows the code for the Just Birthdays application.

```
' Project name:         Just Birthdays Project
' Project purpose:      Displays the total charge for
'                       a birthday party
' Created/revised by:   <your name> on <current date>

Option Explicit On
Option Strict On
Option Infer Off

Public Class MainForm

  Private Sub exitButton_Click(ByVal sender As Object,
  ByVal e As System.EventArgs) Handles exitButton.Click
     Me.Close()
  End Sub

  Private Sub guestsTextBox_KeyPress(ByVal sender As Object,
  ByVal e As System.Windows.Forms.KeyPressEventArgs
  ) Handles guestsTextBox.KeyPress
     ' allows only numbers and the Backspace key

     If (e.KeyChar < "0" OrElse e.KeyChar > "9") AndAlso
         e.KeyChar <> ControlChars.Back Then
         e.Handled = True
     End If
  End Sub

  Private Sub MainForm_Load(ByVal sender As Object,
  ByVal e As System.EventArgs) Handles Me.Load
     ' fills the list box and selects the first item

     typeListBox.Items.Add("Kid's Birthday")
     typeListBox.Items.Add("21st Birthday")
     typeListBox.Items.Add("40th Birthday")
     typeListBox.Items.Add("Other Birthdays")
     typeListBox.SelectedIndex = 0

  End Sub

  Private Sub calcButton_Click(ByVal sender As Object,
  ByVal e As System.EventArgs) Handles calcButton.Click
     ' displays the total charge

     Dim guests As Integer
     Dim typeIndex As Integer
     Dim guestPrice As Integer
     Dim totalCharge As Integer

     Integer.TryParse(guestsTextBox.Text, guests)
     typeIndex = typeListBox.SelectedIndex

     ' determine the price per guest
     Select Case typeIndex
         Case 0  ' Kid's Birthday
              guestPrice = 11
```

Figure 6-60 Code for the Just Birthdays application *(continues)*

(continued)

```
            Case 1  ' 21st Birthday
                guestPrice = 20
            Case 2  ' 40th Birthday
                guestPrice = 25
            Case Else   ' other birthdays
                guestPrice = 15
        End Select

        ' calculate and display the total charge
        totalCharge = guests * guestPrice
        totalLabel.text = totalCharge.ToString("C0")

    End Sub

    Private Sub testDataButton_Click(ByVal sender As Object,
    ByVal e As System.EventArgs) Handles testDataButton.Click
        Dim guests As Integer
        Dim typeIndex As Integer
        Dim guestPrice As Integer
        Dim totalCharge As Integer
        Dim randomGen As New Random
        Dim setCounter As Integer = 1

        testDataLabel.Text = String.Empty

        Do
            guests = randomGen.Next(1, 51)
            typeIndex = randomGen.Next(0, 4)

            ' determine the price per guest
            Select Case typeIndex
                Case 0  ' Kid's Birthday
                    guestPrice = 11
                Case 1  ' 21st Birthday
                    guestPrice = 20
                Case 2  ' 40th Birthday
                    guestPrice = 25
                Case Else   ' other birthdays
                    guestPrice = 15
            End Select

            ' calculate and display the total charge
            totalCharge = guests * guestPrice
            testDataLabel.Text = testDataLabel.Text &
                typeIndex.ToString & "     " &
                guests.ToString & "     " &
                totalCharge.ToString("C0") &
                ControlChars.NewLine
            setCounter += 1

        Loop Until setCounter > 10

    End Sub
End Class
```

Figure 6-60 Code for the Just Birthdays application

PROGRAMMING EXAMPLE

Grade Calculator Application

Create an application that allows the user to enter the number of points a student earns on four projects and two tests. Each project is worth 50 points and each test is worth 100 points. The application should total the number of points earned and then assign the appropriate grade using the information shown in Figure 6-61. After assigning the grade, the application should display the total points earned and the grade. Use the following names for the solution, project, and form file: Grade Calculator Solution, Grade Calculator Project, and Main Form.vb. Save the application in the VbReloaded2010\Chap06 folder. See Figures 6-61 through 6-67.

Total points earned	**Grade**
360 – 400	A
320 – 359	B
280 – 319	C
240 – 279	D
Less than 240	F

Figure 6-61 Grade scale

Task	**Object**	**Event**
1. Get points earned on 4 projects and 2 tests 2. Calculate the total points earned 3. Display the total points earned in totalLabel 4. Display the grade in gradeLabel	assignButton	Click
End the application	exitButton	Click
Display the total points earned (from assignButton)	totalLabel	None
Display the grade (from assignButton)	gradeLabel	None

Figure 6-62 TOE chart for the Grade Calculator application

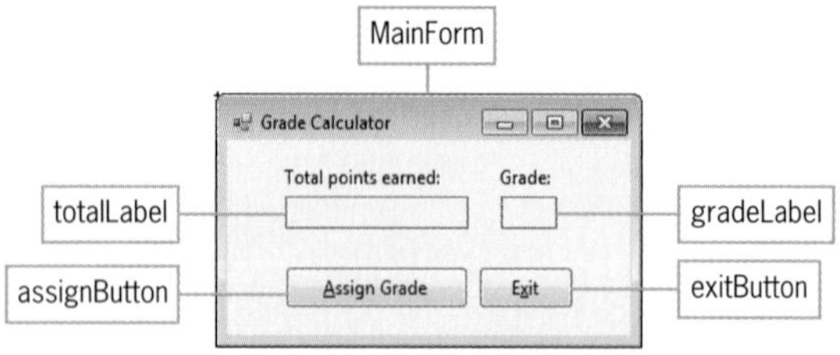

Figure 6-63 MainForm in the Grade Calculator application

Object	Property	Setting
MainForm	Font	Segoe UI, 9 point
	StartPosition	CenterScreen
	Text	Grade Calculator
totalLabel	AutoSize	False
	BorderStyle	FixedSingle
	Text	(empty)
	TextAlign	MiddleCenter
gradeLabel	AutoSize	False
	BorderStyle	FixedSingle
	Text	(empty)
	TextAlign	MiddleCenter

Figure 6-64 Objects, properties, and settings

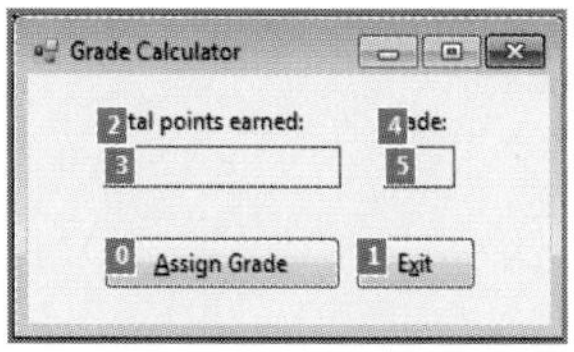

Figure 6-65 Tab order

<u>exitButton Click event procedure</u>
close the application

<u>assignButton Click event procedure</u>
1. repeat while the number of projects counter is less than 5
      get the points earned on the project
      add 1 to the number of projects counter
      add the project points to the total points accumulator
   end repeat
2. repeat while the number of tests counter is less than 3
      get the points earned on the test
      add 1 to the number of tests counter
      add the test points to the total points accumulator
   end repeat
3. if the total points accumulator is one of the following:
      >= 360 grade = A
      >= 320 grade = B
      >= 280 grade = C
      >= 240 grade = D
      < 240 grade = F
4. display the total points accumulator's value in totalLabel
5. display the grade in gradeLabel

Figure 6-66 Pseudocode

```
' Project name:         Grade Calculator Project
' Project purpose:      Displays the total points earned
'                       and the grade
' Created/revised by:   <your name> on <current date>

Option Explicit On
Option Strict On
Option Infer Off

Public Class MainForm

  Private Sub exitButton_Click(ByVal sender As Object,
  ByVal e As System.EventArgs) Handles exitButton.Click
       Me.Close()
  End Sub

  Private Sub assignButton_Click(ByVal sender As Object,
  ByVal e As System.EventArgs) Handles assignButton.Click
       ' calculates the total points earned, then displays
       ' the total points earned and the appropriate grade

       Const title As String = "Grade Calculator"
       Dim inputProjectPoints As String
       Dim inputTestPoints As String
       Dim grade As String
       Dim projectPoints As Integer
       Dim testPoints As Integer
       Dim totalAccumulator As Integer
       Dim projectCounter As Integer = 1
       Dim testCounter As Integer = 1

       ' get and accumulate the project points
       Do While projectCounter < 5
          inputProjectPoints =
             InputBox("Points earned on project " &
             projectCounter & " (0-50)", title)
          Integer.TryParse(inputProjectPoints, projectPoints)
          projectCounter += 1
          totalAccumulator += projectPoints
       Loop

       ' get and accumulate the test points
       Do While testCounter < 3
          inputTestPoints =
             InputBox("Points earned on test " &
             testCounter & " (0-100)", title)
          Integer.TryParse(inputTestPoints, testPoints)
          testCounter = testCounter + 1
          totalAccumulator += testPoints
       Loop

       ' assign grade
       Select Case totalAccumulator
          Case Is >= 360
               grade = "A"
          Case Is >= 320
               grade = "B"
```

Figure 6-67 Code *(continues)*

(continued)

```
            Case Is >= 280
                grade = "C"
            Case Is >= 240
                grade = "D"
            Case Else
                grade = "F"
        End Select

        ' display the total points earned and the grade
        totalLabel.Text = totalAccumulator.ToString
        gradeLabel.Text = grade
    End Sub
End Class
```

Figure 6-67 Code

Summary

- The three basic control structures are sequence, selection, and repetition.
- You use the repetition structure, also called a loop, to repeatedly process one or more program instructions while the looping condition is true (or until the loop exit condition has been met). A loop's condition must result in an answer of true or false only.
- A repetition structure can be either a pretest loop or a posttest loop. Depending on the loop condition, the instructions in a pretest loop may never be processed. The instructions in a posttest loop are always processed at least once.
- You can use the Do...Loop statement to code both pretest loops and posttest loops. The condition used in the Do...Loop statement must evaluate to a Boolean value.
- When used in the Do...Loop statement, the keyword `While` indicates that the loop instructions should be processed *while* (as long as) the condition is true. The keyword `Until` indicates that the loop instructions should be processed *until* the condition becomes true.
- In a flowchart, the loop condition is represented by the decision symbol, which is a diamond.
- You use a counter and/or an accumulator to calculate subtotals, totals, and averages.
- All counters and accumulators must be initialized and updated. The initialization is done outside of the loop that uses the counter or accumulator, and the updating is done within the loop. Counters are updated by a constant value, whereas accumulators are usually updated by an amount that varies.

- The input instruction located above a pretest loop's condition is referred to as the priming read. The input instruction within the loop body is referred to as the update read. The priming read gets only the first value from the user. The update read gets the remaining values (if any).
- The InputBox function displays an input dialog box that contains a message, an OK button, a Cancel button, and an input area. The function's return value is always treated as a string.
- In the InputBox function, you should use sentence capitalization for the prompt, but book title capitalization for the title.
- Before using a variable as the divisor in an expression, you first should verify that the variable does not contain the number 0. Dividing by 0 is mathematically impossible and will cause the application to end abruptly with an error.
- A list box displays a list of choices from which the user can select zero choices, one choice (the default), or multiple choices, depending on the value of its SelectionMode property.
- Use a label control to provide keyboard access to a list box. Set the label's TabIndex property to a value that is one number less than the list box's TabIndex value.
- You can use the String Collection Editor window to add items to a list box during design time. You can add items to a list box during run time using the Items collection's Add method.
- The code contained in a form's Load event procedure will be processed before the form appears on the screen.
- List box items are either arranged by use, with the most used entries appearing first in the list, or sorted in ascending order.
- You use a list box item's index to access the item. The index of the first item in a list box is 0.
- The number of items in a list box control is contained in the control's Items collection's Count property. The value in the Count property is always one number more than the list box's highest index.
- When an item is selected in a list box, the item appears highlighted in the list. The item's value is stored in the list box's SelectedItem property, and the item's index is stored in the list box's SelectedIndex property.
- If a list box allows the user to make only one selection at a time, then a default item should be selected in the list box when the interface first appears. The default item should be either the item selected most frequently or the first item in the list.
- A list box's SelectedItem property and its SelectedIndex property can be used both to determine the item selected in the list box and to select a list box item from code.
- When you select an item in a list box, the list box's SelectedValueChanged and SelectedIndexChanged events occur.
- You use a control's Enabled property to enable or disable the control.

- You can use the Sleep method to delay program execution. The method's syntax is **System.Threading.Thread.Sleep(*milliseconds*)**.
- You use the Refresh method to refresh (redraw) the form. The method's syntax is **Me.Refresh()**.

Key Terms

Accumulator—a numeric variable used for accumulating (adding together) something

Add method—the Items collection's method used to add items to a list box

Collection—a group of individual objects treated as one unit

Counter—a numeric variable used for counting something

Count property—a property of the Items collection; stores the number of items contained in a list box

Default list box item—the item automatically selected in a list box when the interface appears on the screen

Do...Loop statement—a Visual Basic statement that can be used to code both pretest loops and posttest loops

Enabled property—used to enable and display a control

Endless loop—a loop whose instructions are processed indefinitely; also called an infinite loop

Incrementing—another name for updating

Index—the unique number that identifies each item in a collection; used to access an item in a list box; the first index in a list box is 0

Infinite loop—another name for an endless loop

Initializing—the process of assigning a beginning value to a memory location, such as a counter or accumulator variable

InputBox function—a Visual Basic function that displays an input dialog box containing a message, OK and Cancel buttons, and an input area

Items collection—the collection composed of the items in a list box

List box—a control used to display a list of choices from which the user can select zero choices, one choice, or multiple choices

Load event—the event that occurs when an application is started and the form is displayed the first time

Loop—another name for the repetition structure

Loop body—the instructions within a loop

Loop exit condition—the requirement that must be met for the computer to stop processing the loop body instructions

Looping condition—the requirement that must be met for the computer to continue processing the loop body instructions

Multiline property—determines whether a text box can accept and display only one line of text or multiple lines of text

Not logical operator—reverses the truth value of a condition

Posttest loop—a loop whose condition is evaluated *after* the instructions in its loop body are processed

Pretest loop—a loop whose condition is evaluated *before* the instructions in its loop body are processed

Priming read—the input instruction that appears above the loop that it controls; used to get the first input item from the user

ReadOnly property—controls whether the user is allowed to change the contents of a text box during run time

Refresh method—refreshes (redraws) a form

Repetition structure—the control structure used to repeatedly process one or more program instructions; also called a loop

ScrollBars property—a property of a text box; specifies whether the text box has scroll bars

SelectedIndexChanged event—occurs when an item is selected in a list box

SelectedIndex property—stores the index of the item selected in a list box

SelectedItem property—stores the value of the item selected in a list box

SelectedValueChanged event—occurs when an item is selected in a list box

SelectionMode property—determines the number of choices that can be selected in a list box

Sleep method—used to delay program execution

Sorted property—specifies whether the list box items should appear in the order they are entered or in sorted order

Update read—the input instruction that appears within a loop and is associated with the priming read

Updating—the process of adding a number to the value stored in a counter or accumulator variable; also called incrementing

Review Questions

1. Which of the following clauses will stop the loop when the value in the `order` variable is less than the number 0?
   a. `Do While order >= 0`
   b. `Do Until order < 0`
   c. `Loop While order >= 0`
   d. all of the above

2. How many times will the MessageBox.Show method in the following code be processed?

```
Dim counter As Integer
Do While counter > 3
   MessageBox.Show("Hello")
   counter = counter + 1
Loop
```

a. 0

b. 1

c. 3

d. 4

3. How many times will the MessageBox.Show method in the following code be processed?

```
Dim counter As Integer
Do
   MessageBox.Show("Hello")
   counter = counter + 1
Loop While counter > 3
```

a. 0

b. 1

c. 3

d. 4

Refer to Figure 6-68 to answer Questions 4 through 7.

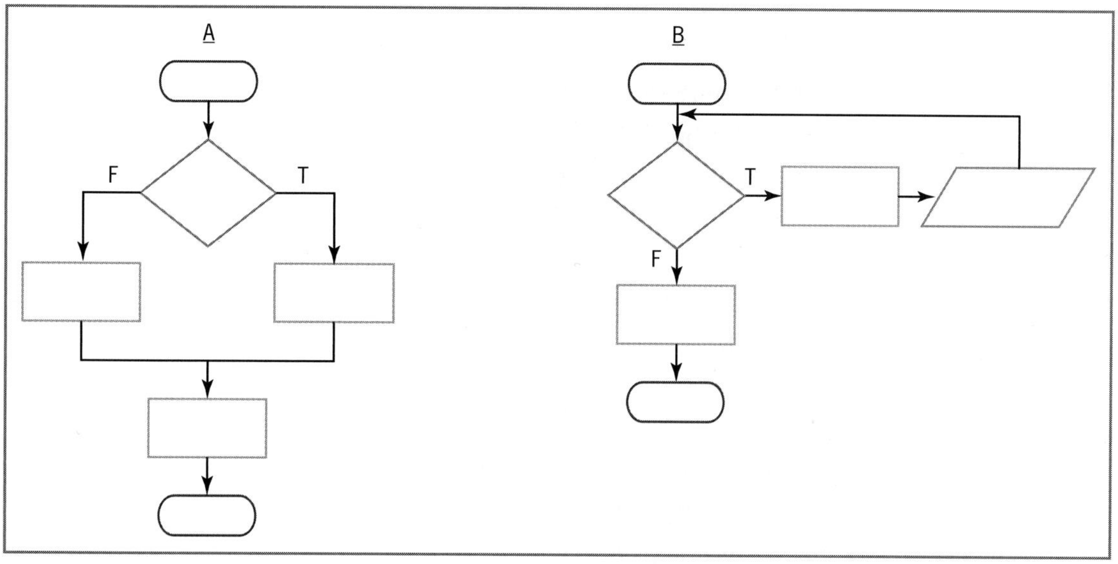

Figure 6-68 Flowcharts for Questions 4 through 7 *(continues)*

(continued)

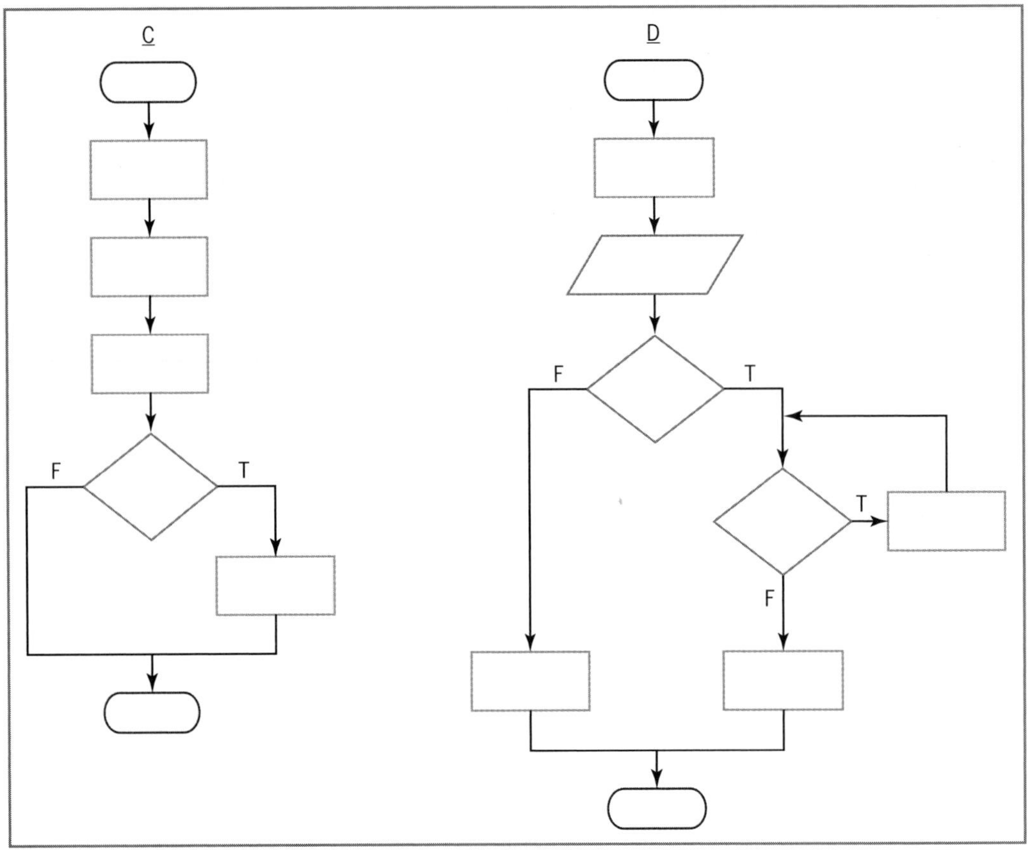

Figure 6-68 Flowcharts for Questions 4 through 7

4. Which of the following control structures are used in flowchart A in Figure 6-68? (Select all that apply.)
   a. sequence
   b. selection
   c. repetition

5. Which of the following control structures are used in flowchart B in Figure 6-68? (Select all that apply.)
   a. sequence
   b. selection
   c. repetition

6. Which of the following control structures are used in flowchart C in Figure 6-68? (Select all that apply.)
   a. sequence
   b. selection
   c. repetition

7. Which of the following control structures are used in flowchart D in Figure 6-68? (Select all that apply.)

   a. sequence

   b. selection

   c. repetition

8. A procedure allows the user to enter one or more numbers. The first input instruction will get the first number only and is referred to as the _______________ read.

   a. entering

   b. initializer

   c. priming

   d. starter

9. When the user clicks the Cancel button in an InputBox function's dialog box, the function returns _______________.

   a. the number 0

   b. the empty string

   c. an error message

   d. none of the above

10. The _______________ property stores the index of the item selected in a list box.

    a. Index

    b. SelectedIndex

    c. Selection

    d. SelectionIndex

11. Which of the following selects the third item in the animalListBox?

    a. `animalListBox.SelectedIndex = 2`

    b. `animalListBox.SelectedIndex = 3`

    c. `animalListBox.SelectedItem = 2`

    d. `animalListBox.SelectedItem = 3`

12. The _______________ event occurs when the user selects an item in a list box.

    a. SelectionChanged

    b. SelectedItemChanged

    c. SelectedValueChanged

    d. none of the above

Exercises

Pencil and Paper

INTRODUCTORY

1. Write a Visual Basic Do clause that processes the loop instructions as long as the value in the `quantity` variable is greater than the number 0. Use the `While` keyword. Then rewrite the Do clause using the `Until` keyword.

INTRODUCTORY

2. Write a Visual Basic Do clause that stops the loop when the value in the `inStock` variable is less than or equal to the value in the `reorder` variable. Use the `Until` keyword. Then rewrite the Do clause using the `While` keyword.

INTRODUCTORY

3. Write an assignment statement that updates the `quantity` variable by 2.

INTRODUCTORY

4. Write an assignment statement that updates the `total` variable by –3.

INTRODUCTORY

5. Write an assignment statement that updates the `totalPurchases` variable by the value stored in the `purchases` variable.

INTRODUCTORY

6. Write an assignment statement that updates the `salesReturns` variable by subtracting the contents of the `sales` variable.

INTERMEDIATE

7. Write a Visual Basic Loop clause that processes the loop instructions as long as the value in the `letter` variable is either Y or y. Use the `While` keyword. Then rewrite the Loop clause using the `Until` keyword.

INTERMEDIATE

8. Write a Visual Basic Do clause that processes the loop instructions as long as the value in the `empName` variable is not "Done" (in any case). Use the `Until` keyword. Then rewrite the Do clause using the `While` keyword.

INTERMEDIATE

9. What will the following code display in message boxes?

```
Dim x As Integer
Do While x < 5
     MessageBox.Show(x.ToString)
     x += 1
Loop
```

INTERMEDIATE

10. What will the following code display in message boxes?

```
Dim x As Integer
Do
     MessageBox.Show(x.ToString)
     x += 1
Loop Until x > 5
```

11. What will the following code display in message boxes?

INTERMEDIATE

```
Dim totalEmp As Integer
Do While totalEmp <= 5
     MessageBox.Show(totalEmp.ToString)
     totalEmp += 2
Loop
```

12. What will the following code display in message boxes?

INTERMEDIATE

```
Dim totalEmp As Integer = 1
Do
    MessageBox.Show(totalEmp.ToString)
    totalEmp += 2
    Loop Until totalEmp >= 3
```

13. Write two different statements that you can use to select the fifth item in the deptListBox. The fifth item is Security.

INTERMEDIATE

14. Write the Visual Basic code that corresponds to the flowchart shown in Figure 6-69. Display the calculated results in the numberListBox.

ADVANCED

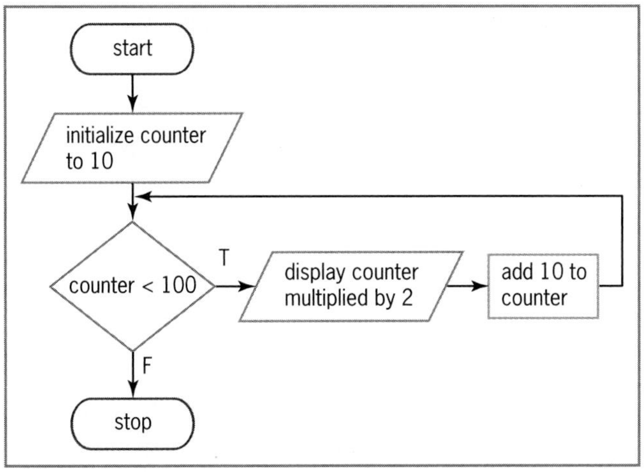

Figure 6-69 Flowchart for Exercise 14

15. The following code should display the numbers 1 through 4, but it is not working correctly. Correct the code.

SWAT THE BUGS

```
Dim number As Integer = 1
Do While number < 5
     MessageBox.Show(number.ToString)
Loop
```

16. The following code should display the numbers 10 through 1, but it is not working correctly. Correct the code.

SWAT THE BUGS

```
Dim number As Integer = 10
Do
    MessageBox.Show(number.ToString)
Loop Until number = 0
```

Computer

MODIFY THIS

17. If necessary, complete the Roll 'Em Game application from this chapter's Programming Tutorial 1, and then close the solution. Use Windows to make a copy of the Roll Em Game Solution folder. Rename the folder Roll Em Game Solution-Modified.
    a. Open the Roll Em Game Solution (Roll Em Game Solution.sln) file contained in the VbReloaded2010\Chap06\Roll Em Game Solution-Modified folder.
    b. Modify the code to allow three people to play the game.
    c. Save the solution and then start and test the application. Close the solution.

MODIFY THIS

18. If necessary, complete the Just Birthdays application from this chapter's Programming Tutorial 2, and then close the solution. Use Windows to make a copy of the Just Birthdays Solution folder. Rename the folder Just Birthdays Solution-Modified.
    a. Open the Just Birthdays Solution (Just Birthdays Solution.sln) file contained in the VbReloaded2010\Chap06\Just Birthdays Solution-Modified folder.
    b. Modify the testDataButton's Click event procedure so that it displays the type of party, rather than the party type's index, in the testDataLabel. (In other words, display "Kid's Birthday" rather than 0.) Modify the interface accordingly.
    c. Save the solution and then start and test the application. Close the solution.

MODIFY THIS

19. If necessary, complete the Grade Calculator application from this chapter's Programming Example, and then close the solution. Use Windows to make a copy of the Grade Calculator Solution folder. Rename the folder Grade Calculator Solution-Modified.
    a. Open the Grade Calculator Solution (Grade Calculator Solution.sln) file contained in the VbReloaded2010\Chap06\Grade Calculator Solution-Modified folder.
    b. Currently the Assign Grade button's Click event procedure uses two pretest loops containing looping conditions. Change both pretest loops to posttest loops, and change both conditions to loop exit conditions.
    c. Save the solution and then start and test the application. Close the solution.

INTRODUCTORY

20. Open the Even Number Solution (Even Number Solution.sln) file contained in the VbReloaded2010\Chap06\Even Number Solution folder.
    a. Code the Do...Loop Pretest button's Click event procedure so that it uses a pretest loop to display the even integers between 1 and 9. Display each even integer on a separate line in the evenNumsLabel.

b. Code the Do...Loop Posttest button's Click event procedure so that it uses a posttest loop to display the even integers between 21 and 39. Display each even integer on a separate line in the evenNumsLabel.

c. Save the solution and then start and test the application. Close the solution.

INTRODUCTORY

21. Open the Even Squares Solution (Even Squares Solution.sln) file contained in the VbReloaded2010\Chap06\Even Squares Solution folder. Code the Display button's Click event procedure so that it uses a pretest loop to display the squares of the even integers from 2 through 12. Display each square on a separate line in the squaresLabel. Save the solution and then start and test the application. Close the solution.

INTRODUCTORY

22. Open the Gwen Solution (Gwen Solution.sln) file contained in the VbReloaded2010\Chap06\Gwen Solution folder. Code the Calculate button's Click event procedure so that it allows the user to enter as many sales amounts as he or she wants to enter. Use the InputBox function to get the sales amounts. When the user has completed entering the sales amounts, the procedure should display the total sales in the totalSalesLabel. It also should display a 10% bonus in the bonusLabel. Save the solution and then start the application. Test the application using the following six sales amounts: 600.50, 4500.75, 3500, 2000, 1000, and 6500. Then test it again using the following four sales amounts: 75, 67, 88, and 30. Close the solution.

INTRODUCTORY

23. Open the Colfax Solution (Colfax Solution.sln) file contained in the VbReloaded2010\Chap06\Colfax Solution folder. Code the Add button's Click event procedure so that it adds the amount entered in the salesTextBox to an accumulator variable, and then displays the variable's value in the totalSalesLabel. Display the total sales with a dollar sign and two decimal places. Save the solution and then start the application. Test the application using the following sales amounts: 1000, 2000, 3000, and 4000. Close the solution.

INTERMEDIATE

24. In this exercise, you create an application for Premium Paper. The application allows the sales manager to enter the company's income and expense amounts. The number of income and expense amounts may vary each time the application is started. For example, the user may enter five income amounts and three expense amounts. Or, he or she may enter 20 income amounts and 30 expense amounts. The application should calculate and display the company's total income, total expenses, and profit (or loss). Use the InputBox function to get the individual income and expense amounts.

a. Create a Windows application. Use the following names for the solution, project, and form file: Premium Solution, Premium Project, and Main Form.vb. Save the files in the VbReloaded2010\Chap06 folder.

b. Design an appropriate interface. Use label controls to display the total income, total expenses, and profit (loss). Display the calculated amounts with a dollar sign and two decimal places. If the company experienced a loss, display the amount of the loss using a red font; otherwise, display the profit using a black font.

c. Code the application. Keep in mind that the income and expense amounts may contain decimal places.

d. Save the solution and then start the application. Test the application twice using the following data, and then close the solution.

First test:	Income amounts: 57.75, 83.23 Expense amounts: 200
Second test:	Income amounts: 5000, 6000, 35000, 78000 Expense amounts: 1000, 2000, 600

INTERMEDIATE

25. Open the SumOddEven Solution (SumOddEven Solution.sln) file contained in the VbReloaded2010\Chap06\SumOddEven Solution folder. The application should allow the user to enter a series of integers. It then should display the sum of the odd integers and the sum of the even integers. Code the application. Use the InputBox function to get the input. Save the solution and then start the application. Test the application using the following integers: 45, 2, 34, 7, 55, 90, and 32. The sum of the odd and even integers should be 107 and 158, respectively. Now test it again using the following integers: 5, 7, and 33. Close the solution.

INTERMEDIATE

26. Create a Windows application. Use the following names for the solution, project, and form file: Gentry Supplies Solution, Gentry Supplies Project, and Main Form.vb. Save the files in the VbReloaded2010\Chap06 folder. The interface should provide a list box that contains the following state names: Alabama, Georgia, Louisiana, and North Carolina. When a state name is selected in the list box, the application should display the appropriate shipping charge. Alabama's shipping charge is $20, Georgia's shipping charge is $35, Louisiana's shipping charge is $30, and North Carolina's shipping charge is $28. Code the application. Save the solution and then start and test the application. Close the solution.

INTERMEDIATE

27. Open the Phone Solution (Phone Solution.sln) file contained in the VbReloaded2010\Chap06\Phone Solution folder.

a. The items in the list box should be sorted. Set the appropriate property.

b. Code the form's Load event procedure so that it adds the following five names to the nameListBox, and also selects the first name in the list.

Smith, Joe
Jones, Mary
Adkari, Joel
Lin, Sue
Li, Vicky

c. Code the list box's SelectedValueChanged event procedure so that it assigns the item selected in the nameListBox to a variable. The procedure then should use the Select Case statement to determine the telephone extension corresponding to the name stored in the variable. Joe's extension is 3388, Mary's is 3356, Joel's is 2487, Sue's is 1111, and Vicky's is 2222.

d. Save the solution and then start and test the application. Close the solution.

e. Use Windows to make a copy of the Phone Solution folder. Rename the folder Phone Solution-Modified.

f. Open the Phone Solution (Phone Solution.sln) file contained in the VbReloaded2010\Chap06\Phone Solution-Modified folder. Modify the list box's SelectedValueChanged event procedure so that it assigns the index of the item selected in the nameListBox to a variable. Then, modify the Select Case statement so that it determines the telephone extension corresponding to the index stored in the variable.

g. Save the solution and then start and test the application. Close the solution.

28. Open the Fibonacci Solution (Fibonacci Solution.sln) file contained in the VbReloaded2010\Chap06\Fibonacci Solution folder. Code the application so that it displays the first 10 Fibonacci numbers (1, 1, 2, 3, 5, 8, 13, 21, 34, and 55). Notice that, beginning with the third number in the series, each Fibonacci number is the sum of the prior two numbers. In other words, 2 is the sum of 1 plus 1, 3 is the sum of 1 plus 2, 5 is the sum of 2 plus 3, and so on. Save the solution and then start and test the application. Close the solution. ADVANCED

29. Open the Multiplication Solution (Multiplication Solution.sln) file contained in the VbReloaded2010\Chap06\Multiplication Solution folder. Code the application so that it displays a multiplication table similar to the one shown in Figure 6-70. Save the solution and then start and test the application. Close the solution. ADVANCED

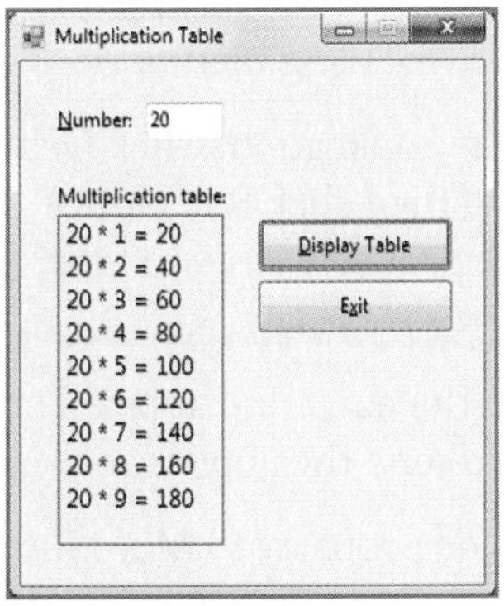

Figure 6-70 Multiplication table for Exercise 29

ADVANCED

30. Create a Windows application. Use the following names for the solution, project, and form file: GPA Solution, GPA Project, and Main Form.vb. Save the files in the VbReloaded2010\Chap06 folder. Create an interface that allows the user to enter the gender (either F or M) and GPA (0.0 through 4.0) for any number of students. Use list boxes for this purpose. The application should calculate the average GPA for all students, the average GPA for male students, and the average GPA for female students. Save the solution and then start and test the application. Close the solution.

ADVANCED

31. If necessary, complete the Roll 'Em Game application from this chapter's Programming Tutorial 1, and then close the solution. Use Windows to make a copy of the Roll Em Game Solution folder. Rename the folder Roll Em Game Solution-Advanced.
    a. Open the Roll Em Game Solution (Roll Em Game Solution.sln) file contained in the VbReloaded2010\Chap06\Roll Em Game Solution-Advanced folder.
    b. Modify the interface and code so the application rolls three dice rather than two. In addition, include labels on the form to keep track of the number of times each player has won.
    c. Save the solution and then start and test the application. Close the solution.

DISCOVERY

32. In this exercise, you learn how to create a list box that allows the user to select more than one item at a time.
    a. Open the Multi Solution (Multi Solution.sln) file contained in the VbReloaded2010\Chap06\Multi Solution folder. The interface contains a list box named namesListBox. The list box's Sorted and SelectionMode properties are set to True and One, respectively.
    b. Open the Code Editor window. Notice that the form's Load event procedure adds five names to the namesListBox. Code the singleButton's Click event procedure so that it displays, in the resultLabel, the item selected in the namesListbox. For example, if the user clicks Debbie in the list box and then clicks the Single Selection button, the name Debbie should appear in the resultLabel. (Hint: Use the Convert.ToString method.)
    c. Save the solution and then start the application. Click Debbie in the list box, then click Ahmad, and then click Bill. Notice that, when the list box's SelectionMode property is set to One, you can select only one item at a time in the list.
    d. Click the Single Selection button. The name Bill appears in the resultLabel. Click the Exit button to end the application.
    e. Change the list box's SelectionMode property to MultiSimple. Save the solution and then start the application. Click Debbie in the list box, then click Ahmad, then click Bill, and then click Ahmad. Notice that, when the list box's SelectionMode property is set to MultiSimple, you can select more than one item at a time in the list. Also notice that you click to both select and deselect an item. (You also can use Ctrl+click and Shift+click, as well as

press the Spacebar, to select and deselect items when the list box's SelectionMode property is set to MultiSimple.) Click the Exit button to end the application.

f. Change the list box's SelectionMode property to MultiExtended. Save the solution and then start the application. Click Debbie in the list, and then click Jim. Notice that, in this case, clicking Jim deselects Debbie. When a list box's SelectionMode property is set to MultiExtended, you use Ctrl+click to select multiple items in the list. You also use Ctrl+click to deselect items in the list. Click Debbie in the list, then Ctrl+click Ahmad, and then Ctrl+click Debbie.

g. Next, click Bill in the list, and then Shift+click Jim; this selects all of the names from Bill through Jim. Click the Exit button to end the application.

h. As you know, when a list box's SelectionMode property is set to One, the item selected in the list box is stored in the SelectedItem property, and the item's index is stored in the SelectedIndex property. However, when a list box's SelectionMode property is set to either MultiSimple or MultiExtended, the items selected in the list box are stored (as strings) in the SelectedItems property, and the indices of the items are stored (as integers) in the SelectedIndices property. Code the multiButton's Click event procedure so that it first clears the contents of the resultLabel. The procedure should then display the selected names (which are stored in the SelectedItems property) on separate lines in the resultLabel.

i. Save the solution and then start the application. Click Ahmad in the list box, and then Shift+click Jim. Click the Multi-Selection button. The five names should appear on separate lines in the resultLabel. Close the solution.

33. In this exercise, you learn how to use the Items collection's Insert, Remove, RemoveAt, and Clear methods.

DISCOVERY

a. Open the Items Solution (Items Solution.sln) file contained in the VbReloaded2010\Chap06\Items Solution folder.

b. The Items collection's Insert method allows you to add an item at a desired position in a list box during run time. The Insert method's syntax is *object*.**Items.Insert(***position*, *item***)**, where *position* is the index of the item. Code the Insert button's Click event procedure so it adds your name as the fourth item in the list box.

c. The Items collection's Remove method allows you to remove an item from a list box during run time. The Remove method's syntax is *object*.**Items.Remove(***item***)**, where *item* is the item's value. Code the Remove button's Click event procedure so it removes your name from the list box.

d. Like the Remove method, the Items collection's RemoveAt method also allows you to remove an item from a list box while an application is running. However, in the RemoveAt method, you specify the item's index rather than its value. The RemoveAt method's syntax is ***object*.Items.RemoveAt(*index*)**, where ***index*** is the item's index. Code the Remove At button's Click event procedure so it removes the second name from the list box.

e. The Items collection's Clear method allows you to remove all items from a list box during run time. The Clear method's syntax is ***object*.Items.Clear()**. Code the Clear button's Click event procedure so it clears the items from the list box.

f. Code the Count button's Click event procedure so it displays (in a message box) the number of items in the list box.

g. Save the solution and then start and test the application. Close the solution.

SWAT THE BUGS

34. Open the Debug Solution (Debug Solution.sln) file contained in the VbReloaded2010\Chap06\Debug Solution folder. Open the Code Editor window and review the existing code. Start and then test the application. Locate and then correct any errors. When the application is working correctly, close the solution.

Case Projects

Sonheim Manufacturing Company

Create an application that the company's accountant can use to calculate an asset's annual depreciation. Use the following names for the solution, project, and form file: Sonheim Solution, Sonheim Project, and Main Form.vb. Save the solution in the VbReloaded2010\Chap06 folder. You can create either your own interface or the one shown in Figure 6-71. The figure shows a sample depreciation schedule for an asset with a cost of $1000, a useful life of four years, and a salvage value of $100. The accountant will enter the asset's cost, useful life (in years), and salvage value (which is the value of the asset at the end of its useful life). Use a list box to allow the user to select the useful life. Display the numbers from 3 through 20 in the list box. The application should use the double-declining balance method to calculate the annual depreciation amounts. You can use the Financial.DDB method to calculate the depreciation. The method's syntax is **Financial.DDB(*cost, salvage, life, period*)**. In the syntax, the *cost, salvage*, and *life* arguments are the asset's cost, salvage value, and useful life, respectively. The *period* argument is the period for which you want the depreciation amount calculated. The method returns the depreciation amount as a Double number. The Asset cost and Salvage value text boxes shown in Figure 6-71 should accept only numbers, the period, and the Backspace key. Below the Depreciation schedule label is a text box whose Multiline and ReadOnly properties are set to True, and whose ScrollBars property is set to Vertical.

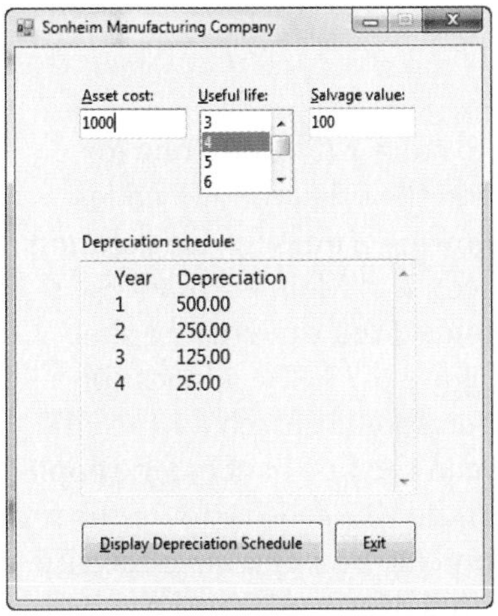

Figure 6-71 Sample interface and depreciation schedule for the Sonheim Manufacturing Company

Cook College

Create an application that displays the total credit hours and GPA for a student during one semester. Use the following names for the solution, project, and form file: Cook Solution, Cook Project, and Main Form.vb. Save the solution in the VbReloaded2010\Chap06 folder. You can create either your own interface or the one shown in Figure 6-72. The figure, which shows a sample run of the application, uses three labels for the output: one for the total credit hours, one for the GPA, and one for the number of grades entered. When the user clicks the Enter Data button, two input boxes should appear in succession: one for the number of credit hours (such as 3) and the next for the corresponding letter grade (such as A). One credit hour of A is worth 4 grade points, an hour of B is worth 3 grade points, and so on. The Enter Data button's Click event procedure should allow the user to enter as many sets of credit hours and grades as desired. The labels on the form should be updated after the user enters the letter grade. (The sample output shown in Figure 6-72 is a result of the user entering 3 as the credit hours, A as the grade, 5 as the credit hours, and B as the grade.)

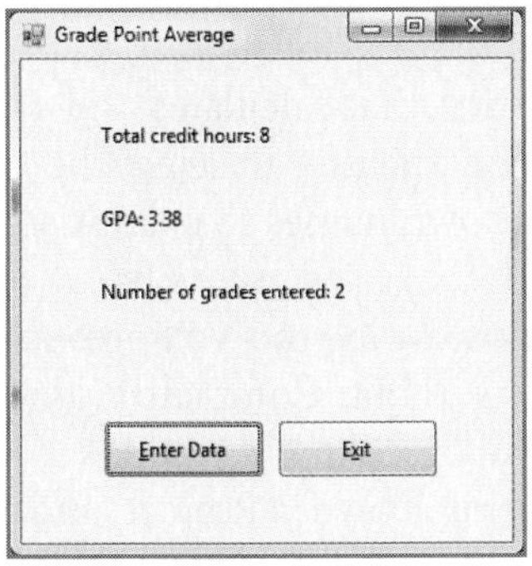

Figure 6-72 Sample interface and output for the Cook College application

Ship With Us

Create an application that uses two list boxes to store ZIP codes: one for ZIP codes associated with a $15 shipping fee and the other for ZIP codes associated with a $20 shipping fee. Use the following names for the solution, project, and form file: Ship Solution, Ship Project, and Main Form.vb. Save the solution in the VbReloaded2010\Chap06 folder. You can create either your own user interface or the one shown in Figure 6-73. The application should allow the user to enter a ZIP code. It then should search for the ZIP code in the first list box. If it finds the ZIP code in the first list box, the application should display $15 as the shipping fee. If the ZIP code is not in the first list box, the application should search the second list box. If it finds the ZIP code in the second list box, the application should display $20 as the shipping fee. If the ZIP code is not included in either list box, the application should display an appropriate message. Use the following ZIP codes for the first list box: 60611, 60234, 56789, 23467, 60543, 60561, 55905, and 89567. Use the following ZIP codes for the second list box: 50978, 78432, 98432, 97654, and 20245.

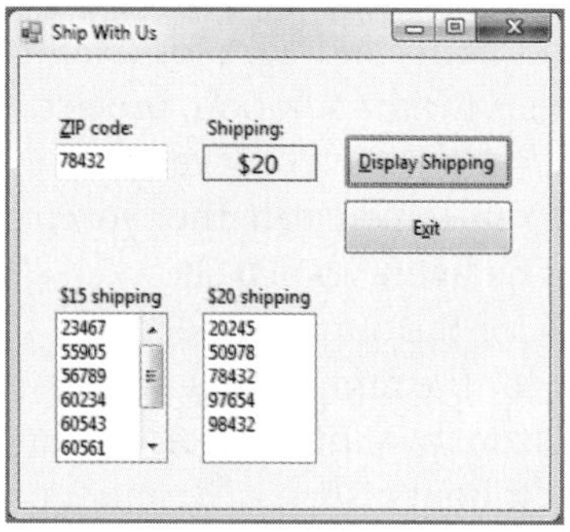

Figure 6-73 Sample interface for the Ship With Us application

Powder Skating Rink

Powder Skating Rink holds a weekly ice-skating competition. Competing skaters must perform a two-minute program in front of a panel of six judges. At the end of a skater's program, each judge assigns a score of 0 through 10 to the skater. The manager of the ice rink wants an application that calculates and displays a skater's average score. Use list boxes to allow the user to select the names of the judges. (You will need to make up your own names to use.) Also use a list box to allow the user to select the score. After a judge's score has been recorded, remove his/her name from the list box. Doing this will prevent the user from entering a judge's score more than once. (Hint: Complete Computer Exercise 33 before coding this application.) Use the following names for the solution, project, and form file: Powder Solution, Powder Project, and Main Form.vb. Save the solution in the VbReloaded2010\Chap06 folder.

CHAPTER 7

More on the Repetition Structure

After studying Chapter 7, you should be able to:

- Code a counter-controlled loop using the For...Next statement
- Nest repetition structures
- Calculate a periodic payment using the Financial.Pmt method
- Select the existing text in a text box
- Code the TextChanged event procedure for a text box
- Code a list box's SelectedValueChanged and SelectedIndexChanged event procedures
- Include a combo box in an interface
- Code the TextChanged event procedure for a combo box
- Store images in an image list control
- Display an image stored in an image list control

The For...Next Statement

As mentioned in Chapter 6, Visual Basic provides three different statements for coding repetition structures (loops): Do...Loop, For...Next, and For Each...Next. You learned about the Do...Loop statement in Chapter 6; recall that the statement can be used to code both pretest and posttest loops. In this chapter, you will learn how to use the **For...Next statement** to code a specific type of pretest loop, called a counter-controlled loop. A **counter-controlled loop** is just what its name implies: it's a loop whose processing is controlled by a counter. You use a counter-controlled loop when you want the computer to process the loop instructions a precise number of times. Although you also can use the Do...Loop statement to code a counter-controlled loop, the For...Next statement provides a more compact and convenient way of writing that type of loop.

The For Each... Next statement is covered in Chapter 9.

Figure 7-1 shows the For...Next statement's syntax and includes examples of using the statement. You enter the loop body, which contains the instructions you want the computer to repeat, between the statement's For and Next clauses. Notice that *counterVariableName* appears in both clauses. *CounterVariableName* is the name of a numeric variable that the computer can use to keep track of (in other words, count) the number of times it processes the loop body. Although, technically, you do not need to specify the name of the counter variable in the Next clause, doing so is highly recommended because it makes your code more self-documenting.

You can use the `As` *dataType* portion of the For clause to declare the counter variable, as shown in the first two examples in Figure 7-1. When you declare a variable in the For clause, the variable has block scope and can be used only within the For...Next loop. Alternatively, you can declare the counter variable in a Dim statement, as shown in Example 3 in Figure 7-1. As you know, a variable declared in a Dim statement at the beginning of a procedure has procedure scope and can be used within the entire procedure. When deciding where to declare the counter variable, keep in mind that if the variable is needed only by the For...Next loop, then it is a better programming practice to declare the variable in the For clause. As mentioned in Chapter 3, fewer unintentional errors occur in applications when the variables are declared using the minimum scope needed. Block-level variables have the smallest scope, followed by procedure-level variables, followed by class-level variables. You should declare the counter variable in a Dim statement only when its value is required by statements outside the For...Next loop in the procedure.

The *startValue*, *endValue*, and *stepValue* items in the For clause control the number of times the loop body is processed. The startValue and endValue tell the computer where to begin and end counting, respectively. The stepValue tells the computer how much to count by—in other words, how much to add to the counter variable each time the loop body is processed. If you omit the stepValue, a stepValue of positive 1 is used. In Example 1 in Figure 7-1, the startValue is 10, the endValue is 13, and the stepValue (which is omitted) is 1. Those values tell the computer to start counting at 10 and, counting by 1s, stop at 13—in other words, count 10, 11, 12, and 13. The computer will process the instructions in Example 1's loop body four times. The startValue, endValue, and stepValue items must be numeric and can be either positive or negative, integer or non-integer. If the stepValue is a positive number, the startValue must be less than or equal to the endValue for the loop instructions to be processed. For instance, the `For price As Integer = 10 To 13` clause is correct, but the `For price As Integer = 13 To 10` clause is not correct because you cannot count from 13 (the startValue) to 10 (the endValue) by adding increments of 1 (the stepValue). If, on the other hand, the stepValue is a negative number, then the startValue must be greater than or equal to the endValue for the loop instructions to be processed. As a result, the `For num As Integer = 5 To 1 Step -1` clause is correct, but the `For num As Integer = 1 To 5 Step -1` clause is not correct because you cannot count from 1 to 5 by adding increments of negative 1. Adding increments of a negative number is referred to as **decrementing**. In other words, adding increments of negative 1 is the same as decrementing by 1. In addition to the syntax and examples of the For...Next statement, Figure 7-1 also shows the tasks performed by the computer when processing the statement.

You can use the `Exit For` statement to exit the For...Next statement prematurely, which means to exit it before the loop has finished processing. You may need to do this if the computer encounters an error when processing the loop instructions.

HOW TO Use the For...Next Statement

Syntax

For *counterVariableName* [**As** *dataType*] = *startValue* **To** *endValue* [**Step** *stepValue*]
    loop body instructions

If the stepValue is a positive number, the computer will process the loop body instructions while the counter variable's value is less than or equal to the endValue. It will stop processing the instructions when the counter variable's value is greater than the endValue.

If the stepValue is a negative number, the computer will process the loop body instructions while the counter variable's value is greater than or equal to the endValue. It will stop processing the instructions when the counter variable's value is less than the endValue.

Next *counterVariableName*

Example 1

```
For price As Integer = 10 To 13
     priceListBox.Items.Add(price.ToString)     ' loop body
Next price
```

adds 10, 11, 12, and 13 to the priceListBox

Example 2

```
Dim city As String
For num As Integer = 5 To 1 Step -1
     city = InputBox("City name:", "City Entry")     ' loop body
     cityListBox.Items.Add(city)
Next num
```

adds the five city names entered by the user to the cityListBox

Figure 7-1 How to use the For...Next statement *(continues)*

(continued)

Example 3

```
Dim rate As Double
For rate = .05 To .1 Step .01
    rateListBox.Items.Add(rate.ToString("P0"))
Next rate
```

loop body

adds 5 %, 6 %, 7 %, 8 %, 9 %, and 10 % to the rateListBox

Processing tasks

1. If the counter variable is declared in the For clause, the computer creates and then initializes the variable to the startValue; otherwise, it just performs the initialization task. This is done only once, at the beginning of the loop.
2. The computer evaluates the loop condition by comparing the value in the counter variable with the endValue. If the stepValue is a positive number, the comparison determines whether the counter variable's value is greater than the endValue. If the stepValue is a negative number, the comparison determines whether the counter variable's value is less than the endValue. Notice that the computer evaluates the loop condition before processing the instructions within the loop.
3. If the loop condition evaluates to True, the computer stops processing the loop; processing continues with the statement following the Next clause. If the loop condition evaluates to False, the computer processes the loop body and then task 4 is performed.
4. Task 4 is performed only when the loop condition evaluates to False. In this task, the computer adds the stepValue to the contents of the counter variable. It then repeats tasks 2, 3, and 4 until the loop condition evaluates to True.

Figure 7-1 How to use the For...Next statement

Figure 7-2 describes the steps the computer follows when processing the loop shown in Example 1 in Figure 7-1. As Step 2 indicates, the loop's condition is evaluated before the loop body is processed. This is because the loop created by the For...Next statement is a pretest loop. Notice that the `price` variable contains the number 14 when the For...Next statement ends. The number 14 is the first integer that is greater than the loop's endValue of 13.

Processing steps for Example 1

1. The computer creates the `price` variable and initializes it to 10.
2. The computer checks whether the `price` variable's value is greater than 13. It's not, so the computer displays the number 10 in the priceListBox and then increments the `price` variable's value by 1, giving 11.
3. The computer again checks whether the `price` variable's value is greater than 13. It's not, so the computer displays the number 11 in the priceListBox and then increments the `price` variable's value by 1, giving 12.

Figure 7-2 Processing steps for Example 1 in Figure 7-1 *(continues)*

(continued)

4. The computer again checks whether the `price` variable's value is greater than 13. It's not, so the computer displays the number 12 in the priceListBox and then increments the `price` variable's value by 1, giving 13.
5. The computer again checks whether the `price` variable's value is greater than 13. It's not, so the computer displays the number 13 in the priceListBox and then increments the `price` variable's value by 1, giving 14.
6. The computer again checks whether the `price` variable's value is greater than 13. It is, so the computer stops processing the loop body. Processing continues with the statement following the Next clause.

Figure 7-2 Processing steps for Example 1 in Figure 7-1

You will use the For...Next statement to code the Savings Account application. The problem specification and a sample run of the application are shown in Figures 7-3 and 7-4, respectively.

Create an application that allows the user to enter two items: the amount of money deposited into a savings account at the beginning of the year and the annual interest rate. The application should display the account balance at the end of three years, assuming the interest is compounded annually and no withdrawals or additional deposits are made.

Figure 7-3 Problem specification for the Savings Account application

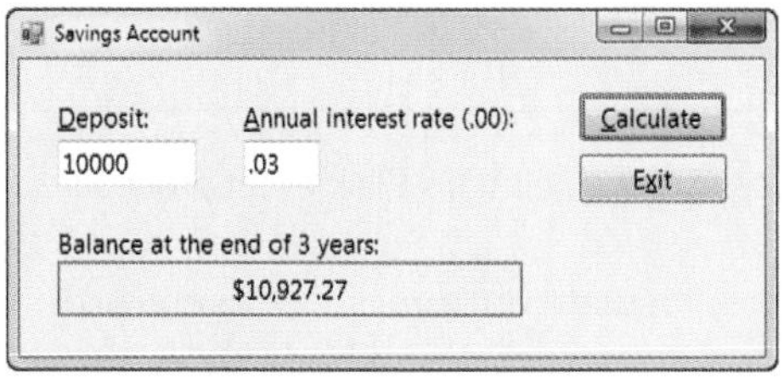

Figure 7-4 Sample run of the Savings Account application

If you want to experiment with the Savings Account application, open the solution contained in the Try It 1! folder.

Figure 7-5 shows the pseudocode and flowchart for the Calculate button's Click event procedure. Many programmers use a hexagon, which is a six-sided figure, to represent the For clause in a flowchart. Within the hexagon, you record the four items contained in a For clause: *counterVariableName, startValue, endValue,* and *stepValue.* The counterVariableName and stepValue are placed at the top and bottom, respectively, of the hexagon. The startValue and endValue are placed on the left and right side, respectively. The hexagon in Figure 7-5 indicates that the counterVariableName is `years`, the startValue is 1, the endValue is 3, and the stepValue is 1. Notice that a less than or equal to sign (<=) precedes the endValue in the hexagon. The <= sign indicates that the loop body will be processed as long as the counter variable's value is less than or equal to 3.

calcButton Click event procedure

1. store deposit in balance variable
2. store rate in rate variable
3. repeat for years from 1 through 3 in increments of 1
    interest = balance * rate
    add interest to balance
   end repeat for
4. display balance

calcButton Click event procedure

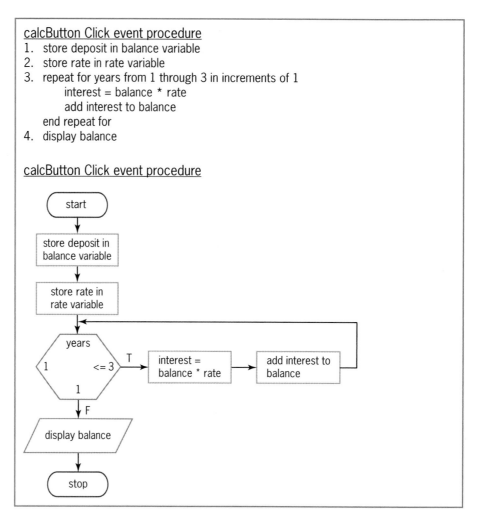

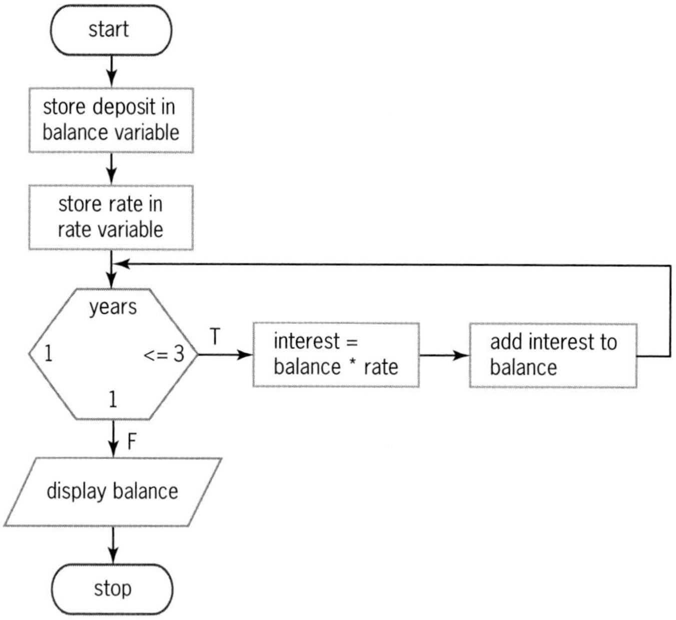

Figure 7-5 Pseudocode and flowchart for the Calculate button's Click event procedure

Figure 7-6 shows the code entered in the Calculate button's Click event procedure. The For clause tells the computer to repeat the loop body three times.

calcButton Click event procedure

```
Private Sub calcButton_Click(ByVal sender As Object,
ByVal e As System.EventArgs) Handles calcButton.Click
    ' display account balance at the end of 3 years

    Dim balance As Double
    Dim rate As Double
    Dim interest As Double

    Double.TryParse(depositTextBox.Text, balance)
    Double.TryParse(rateTextBox.Text, rate)

    For years As Integer = 1 To 3
        interest = balance * rate
        balance += interest
    Next years

    balanceLabel.Text = balance.ToString("C2")
End Sub
```

loop body

you also can use `balance = balance + interest`

Figure 7-6 Calculate button's Click event procedure

As mentioned earlier, you can code a counter-controlled loop using either the For...Next statement or the Do...Loop statement; however, the For...Next statement is more convenient to use. Figure 7-7 shows the For...Next statement from Figure 7-6 along with its comparable Do...Loop statement. Notice that, when using the Do...Loop statement to code a counter-controlled loop, you must include a statement to declare and initialize the counter variable, as well as a statement to update the counter variable. In addition, you must include the appropriate comparison in the Do clause. In a For...Next statement, the declaration, initialization, update, and comparison tasks are handled by the For clause.

To review what you learned about the For...Next statement, view the Ch07ForNext video.

declares, initializes, compares, and updates the counter variable

For...Next statement

```
For years As Integer = 1 To 3
      interest = balance * rate
      balance += interest
Next years
```

Do...Loop statement

```
Dim years As Integer = 1
Do While years <= 3
      interest = balance * rate
      balance += interest
      years += 1
Loop
```

declares and initializes the counter variable

compares the counter variable

updates the counter variable

Figure 7-7 Comparison of the For...Next and Do...Loop statements

Mini-Quiz 7-1

The answers to Mini-Quiz questions are located in Appendix A.

1. Which of the following For clauses processes the loop body as long as the `x` variable's value is less than or equal to the number 100?

   a. `For x As Integer = 10 To 100 Step 10`

   b. `For x As Integer = 1 To 100`

   c. `For x As Integer = 3 To 100 Step 2`

   d. all of the above

2. A For...Next statement contains the following For clause: `For x As Integer = 5 To 11 Step 2`. The computer will stop processing the loop body when the `x` variable contains the number ______________.

   a. 11

   b. 12

   c. 13

   d. none of the above

3. Write a For...Next statement that displays the integers 6, 5, 4, 3, 2, and 1 in the numListBox. Use `num` as the counter variable's name.

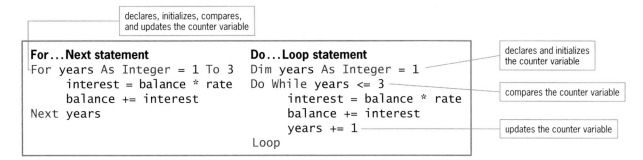

Nested Repetition Structures

Like selection structures, repetition structures can be nested. In other words, you can place one loop (called the nested or inner loop) within another loop (called the outer loop). Both loops can be pretest loops, or both can be posttest loops. Or, one can be a pretest loop and the other a posttest loop. You already are familiar with the concept of nested loops, because a clock uses nested loops to keep track of the time. For simplicity, consider a clock's minute and second hands only. The second hand on a clock moves one position, clockwise, for every second that has elapsed. After the second hand moves 60 positions, the minute hand moves one position, also clockwise. The second hand then begins its journey around the clock again. Figure 7-8 shows three versions of the logic used by a clock's minute and second hands. In each version, an outer loop controls the minute hand, while an inner (nested) loop controls the second hand. Notice that the entire nested loop is contained within the outer loop in each version. This must be true for the loop to be nested and work correctly.

```
Version 1
repeat for minutes from 0 through 59
      repeat for seconds from 0 through 59          (nested loop)
            move second hand 1 position, clockwise
      end repeat for seconds
      move minute hand 1 position, clockwise
end repeat for minutes

Version 2
1. start minutes at 0
2. repeat while minutes are less than 60
      start seconds at 0
      repeat while seconds are less than 60         (nested loop)
            move second hand 1 position, clockwise
            add 1 to seconds
      end repeat while seconds
      move minute hand 1 position, clockwise
      add 1 to minutes
   end repeat while minutes

Version 3
1. start minutes at 0
2. repeat
      repeat for seconds from 0 through 59          (nested loop)
            move second hand 1 position, clockwise
      end repeat for seconds
      move minute hand 1 position, clockwise
      add 1 to minutes
   end repeat until minutes = 60
```

Figure 7-8 Three versions of the logic used by a clock's minute and second hands

If you want to experiment with the logic shown in Figure 7-8, open the solution contained in the Try It 2! folder.

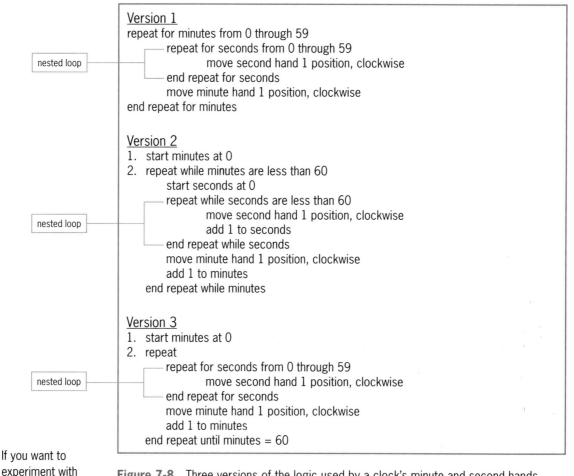

You will use a nested loop to code a modified version of the Savings Account application, which you viewed earlier in the chapter. In the original version, the application displays the account balance at the end of three years, using

the annual interest rate entered by the user. The modified application also will display the account balance at the end of three years; however, it will do so using annual interest rates of 3%, 4%, and 5%. The modified problem specification and a sample run of the modified application are shown in Figures 7-9 and 7-10, respectively. Figure 7-11 shows just two ways of coding the Calculate button's Click event procedure.

If you want to experiment with the modified Savings Account application, open the solutions contained in the Try It 3!-Version 1 and Try It 3!-Version 2 folders.

> Create an application that allows the user to enter the amount of money deposited into a savings account at the beginning of the year. The application should display the account balance at the end of three years, assuming the interest is compounded annually and no withdrawals or additional deposits are made. Display the account balance using annual interest rates of 3%, 4%, and 5%.

Figure 7-9 Modified problem specification for the Savings Account application

In both versions in Figure 7-11, you can write the `balance += interest` statement as `balance = balance + interest`. In version 2, you can write the `rates += .01` statement as `rates = rates + .01`.

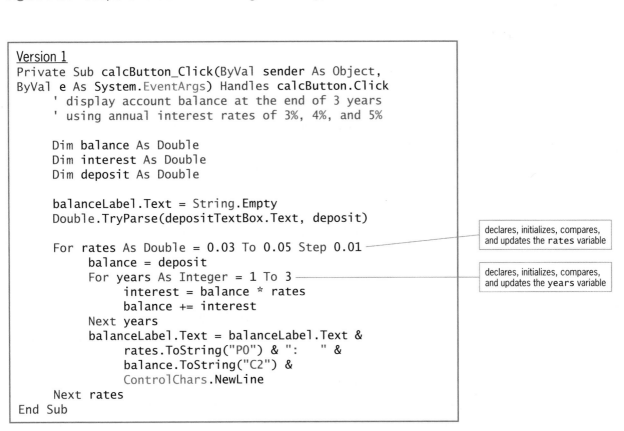

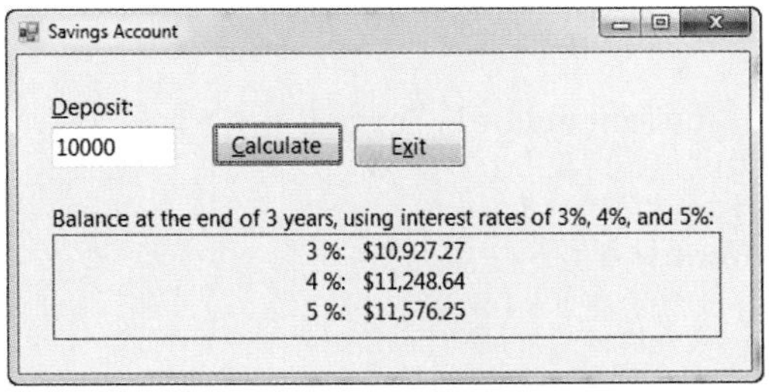

Figure 7-10 Sample run of the modified Savings Account application

Version 1

```
Private Sub calcButton_Click(ByVal sender As Object,
ByVal e As System.EventArgs) Handles calcButton.Click
     ' display account balance at the end of 3 years
     ' using annual interest rates of 3%, 4%, and 5%

     Dim balance As Double
     Dim interest As Double
     Dim deposit As Double

     balanceLabel.Text = String.Empty
     Double.TryParse(depositTextBox.Text, deposit)

     For rates As Double = 0.03 To 0.05 Step 0.01
          balance = deposit
          For years As Integer = 1 To 3
               interest = balance * rates
               balance += interest
          Next years
          balanceLabel.Text = balanceLabel.Text &
               rates.ToString("P0") & ":    " &
               balance.ToString("C2") &
               ControlChars.NewLine
     Next rates
End Sub
```

declares, initializes, compares, and updates the `rates` variable

declares, initializes, compares, and updates the `years` variable

Figure 7-11 Two versions of the Calculate button's Click event procedure *(continues)*

To review what you learned about nested loops, view the Ch07NestedLoops video.

(continued)

declares and initializes the rates variable

compares the rates variable

declares, initializes, compares, and updates the years variables

updates the rates variable

Version 2

```
Private Sub calcButton_Click(ByVal sender As Object,
ByVal e As System.EventArgs) Handles calcButton.Click
     ' display account balance at the end of 3 years
     ' using annual interest rates of 3%, 4%, and 5%

     Dim balance As Double
     Dim interest As Double
     Dim deposit As Double
     Dim rates As Double = .03

     balanceLabel.Text = String.Empty
     Double.TryParse(depositTextBox.Text, balance)

     Do While rates <= .05
          balance = deposit
          For years As Integer = 1 To 3
               interest = balance * rates
               balance += interest
          Next years
          balanceLabel.Text = balanceLabel.Text &
               rates.ToString("P0") & ":    " &
               balance.ToString("C2") &
               ControlChars.NewLine
          rates += .01
     Loop
End Sub
```

Figure 7-11 Two versions of the Calculate button's Click event procedure

The answers to Mini-Quiz questions are located in Appendix A.

Mini-Quiz 7-2

1. A nested loop can be ______________.
   a. a pretest loop only
   b. a posttest loop only
   c. either a pretest loop or a posttest loop
2. For ______________ loop to work correctly, it must be contained entirely within the ______________ loop.
   a. a nested, outer
   b. an outer, nested
3. A clock's hour hand is controlled by a(n) ______________ loop, while its minute hand is controlled by a(n) ______________ loop.
   a. nested, outer
   b. outer, nested

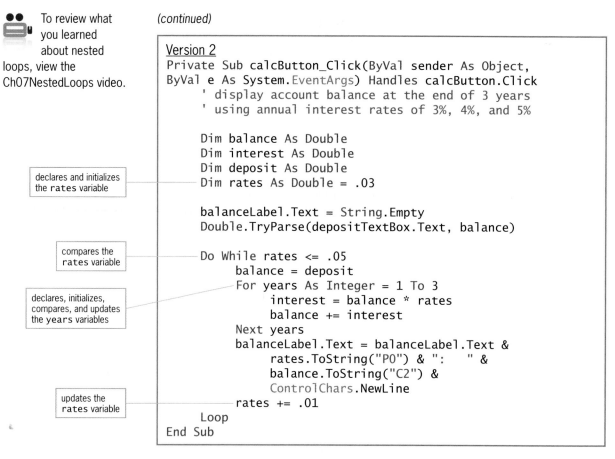

The Payment Calculator Application

Figure 7-12 shows the problem specification for the Payment Calculator application, which requires a loop, and Figure 7-13 shows a sample run of the application.

> Tyrone Johnson needs to take out a loan to buy a new car. He wants an application that allows him to enter the loan amount and the number of years he has to pay off the loan (called the term). The term can be 2 years, 3 years, 4 years, or 5 years only. The application should calculate and display his monthly car payment, using annual interest rates of 5%, 6%, 7%, 8%, 9%, and 10%.

Figure 7-12 Problem specification for the Payment Calculator application

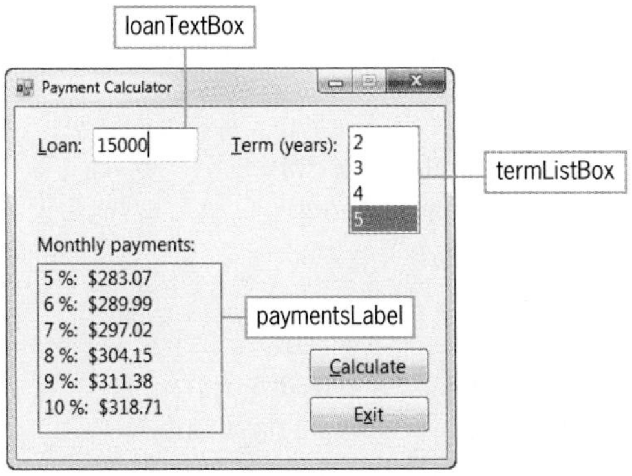

Figure 7-13 Sample run of the Payment Calculator application

Before you can code the Payment Calculator application, you need to learn how to calculate a monthly payment on a loan. You can make the calculation using Visual Basic's Financial.Pmt method.

The Financial.Pmt Method

The **Financial.Pmt method** calculates a periodic payment on either a loan or an investment, and it returns the calculated value as a Double number. Figure 7-14 shows the method's basic syntax and lists the meaning of each argument. The *Rate* and *NPer* (number of periods) arguments must be expressed using the same units. If Rate is a monthly interest rate, then NPer must specify the number of monthly payments. Likewise, if Rate is an annual interest rate, then NPer must specify the number of annual payments. Figure 7-14 also includes examples of using the Financial.Pmt method. Example 1 calculates the annual payment for a loan of $9000 for 3 years at 5% interest. As the example indicates, the annual payment rounded to the nearest cent is –3304.88. This means that if you borrow $9000 for 3 years at 5% interest, you will need to make three annual payments of $3304.88 to pay off the loan. Notice that the Financial.Pmt method returns a negative number. You can change the negative number to a positive number by preceding the method with the negation operator, like this: `-Financial.Pmt(.05, 3, 9000)`. As you learned in Chapter 3, the purpose of the negation operator is

"Pmt" stands for "payment".

to reverse the sign of a number. A negative number preceded by the negation operator becomes a positive number, and vice versa. The Financial.Pmt method shown in Example 2 calculates the monthly payment for a loan of $12000 for 5 years at 6% interest. In this example, the Rate and NPer arguments are expressed in monthly terms rather than in annual terms. You change an annual rate to a monthly rate by dividing the annual rate by 12. You change the term from years to months by multiplying the number of years by 12. The monthly payment for the loan in Example 2, rounded to the nearest cent and expressed as a positive number, is 231.99.

You can use the PMT function in Microsoft Excel to verify that the payments shown in Figure 7-14 are correct.

HOW TO Use the Financial.Pmt Method

Syntax
Financial.Pmt(*Rate*, *NPer*, *PV***)**

Argument	Meaning
Rate	interest rate per period
NPer	total number of payment periods (the term)
PV	present value of the loan (the loan amount)

Example 1
```
Financial.Pmt(.05, 3, 9000)
```
Calculates the annual payment for a loan of $9000 for 3 years at 5% interest. *Rate* is .05, *NPer* is 3, and *PV* is 9000. The annual payment (rounded to the nearest cent) is –3304.88.

Example 2
```
-Financial.Pmt(.06 / 12, 5 * 12, 12000)
```
Calculates the monthly payment for a loan of $12000 for 5 years at 6% interest. *Rate* is .06 / 12, *NPer* is 5 * 12, and *PV* is 12000. The monthly payment (rounded to the nearest cent and expressed as a positive number) is 231.99.

Figure 7-14 How to use the Financial.Pmt method

You will use the Financial.Pmt method to calculate the monthly car payments in the Payment Calculator application. Figure 7-15 shows both the pseudocode and code for the Calculate button's Click event procedure.

```
calcButton Click event procedure
1. store user input (loan and term) in variables
2. clear the paymentsLabel
3. repeat for rate from .05 through .1 in increments of .01
        calculate monthly payment (using the loan, rate, and term)
        display rate and monthly payment in paymentsLabel
   end repeat for
4. send focus to the loanTextBox
```

Figure 7-15 Pseudocode and code for the Calculate button's Click event procedure *(continues)*

(continued)

```
Private Sub calcButton_Click(ByVal sender As Object,
ByVal e As System.EventArgs) Handles calcButton.Click
    ' calculates the monthly payments on a loan
    ' using interest rates of 5% through 10%

        Dim term As Integer
        Dim loan As Double
        Dim monthlyPayment As Double

        ' assign input to variables
        Double.TryParse(loanTextBox.Text, loan)
        term = Convert.ToInt32(termListBox.SelectedItem)

        ' clear contents of the paymentsLabel
        paymentsLabel.Text = String.Empty

        ' calculate and display monthly payments
        For rate As Double = 0.05 To 0.1 Step 0.01
            monthlyPayment =
                -Financial.Pmt(rate / 12, term * 12, loan)
            paymentsLabel.Text = paymentsLabel.Text &
                rate.ToString("P0") & ":  " &
                monthlyPayment.ToString("C2") &
                ControlChars.NewLine
        Next rate

        loanTextBox.Focus()
End Sub
```

calculates a monthly payment

Figure 7-15 Pseudocode and code for the Calculate button's Click event procedure

Before the Calculate button's Click event procedure ends, it sends the focus to the loanTextBox. Doing this places the cursor after the existing text in the text box, as shown earlier in Figure 7-13. However, it is customary in Windows applications to select (highlight) the existing text when a text box receives the focus.

Selecting the Existing Text in a Text Box

When the text in a text box is selected, the user can remove it simply by pressing a key on the keyboard, such as the letter n; the pressed key—in this case, the letter n—replaces the selected text. Visual Basic provides the **SelectAll method** for selecting a text box's existing text. The method's syntax is shown in Figure 7-16 along with an example of using the method. In the syntax, *textBox* is the name of the text box whose contents you want to select.

HOW TO Use the SelectAll Method

<u>Syntax</u>
textBox.**SelectAll()**

<u>Example</u>
`nameTextBox.SelectAll()`
selects the contents of the nameTextBox

Figure 7-16 How to use the SelectAll method

You can use the SelectAll method to select the contents of the Loan text box when the text box receives the focus. You do this by entering the SelectAll method in the text box's Enter event procedure. A text box's **Enter event** occurs when the text box receives the focus, which can happen as a result of the user either tabbing to the control or using the control's access key. It also occurs when the Focus method is used to send the focus to the control. Figure 7-17 shows the Loan text box's Enter event procedure, and Figure 7-18 shows the result of the computer processing the procedure's code.

```
Private Sub loanTextBox_Enter(ByVal sender As Object,
ByVal e As System.EventArgs) Handles loanTextBox.Enter
     ' selects the existing text when the text box
     ' receives the focus

     loanTextBox.SelectAll()
End Sub
```

processed when the text box's Enter event occurs

Figure 7-17 Loan text box's Enter event procedure

the existing text is selected when the text box receives the focus

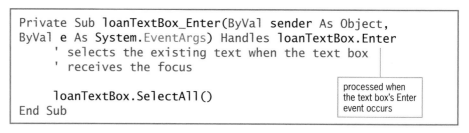

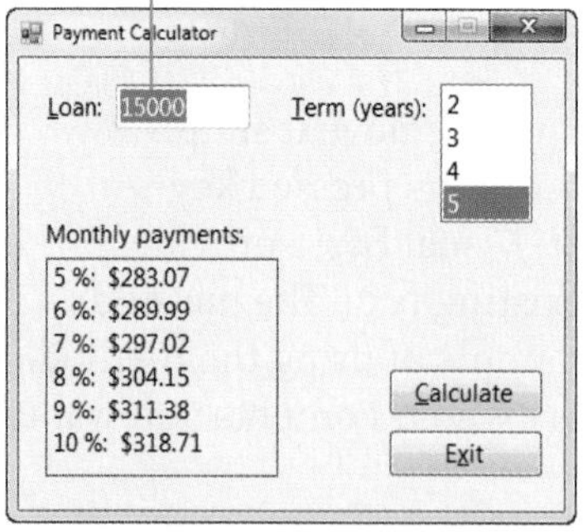

Figure 7-18 Result of processing the text box's Enter event procedure

Now consider what happens when the user enters the number 25000 in the Loan text box, as shown in Figure 7-19. Notice that, even though the loan amount has changed, the Monthly payments label still lists the monthly payments for a $15000 loan. The monthly payments for a $25000 loan will not appear in the label until the user clicks the Calculate button. To prevent any confusion, it would be better to clear the contents of the Monthly payments label when the user enters a different value in the Loan text box. You can do this by coding the Loan text box's TextChanged event procedure.

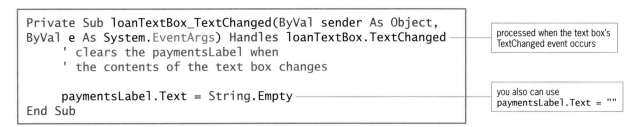

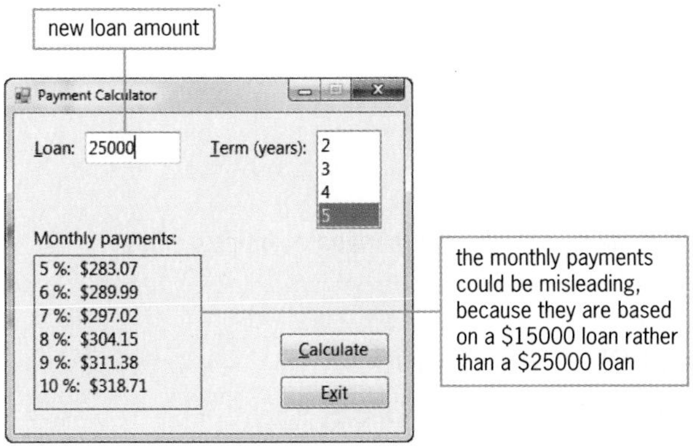

Figure 7-19 New loan amount entered in the Loan text box

Coding the TextChanged Event Procedure

A control's **TextChanged event** occurs when a change is made to the contents of the control's Text property. This can happen as a result of either the user entering data into the control or the application's code assigning data to the control's Text property. In the Payment Calculator application, you will code the Loan text box's TextChanged event procedure so that it removes the monthly payments from the Monthly payments label when the user changes the loan amount. Figure 7-20 shows the procedure's code, and Figure 7-21 shows a sample run of the application. In the sample run, the user enters the number 2 in the Loan text box after calculating the monthly payments for a $15000 loan. Notice that the monthly payments no longer appear in the Monthly payments box.

```
Private Sub loanTextBox_TextChanged(ByVal sender As Object,
ByVal e As System.EventArgs) Handles loanTextBox.TextChanged
    ' clears the paymentsLabel when
    ' the contents of the text box changes

    paymentsLabel.Text = String.Empty
End Sub
```

processed when the text box's TextChanged event occurs

you also can use `paymentsLabel.Text = ""`

Figure 7-20 Loan text box's TextChanged event procedure

the 2 invokes the text box's TextChanged event

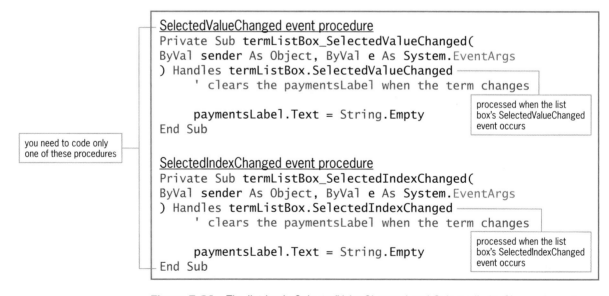

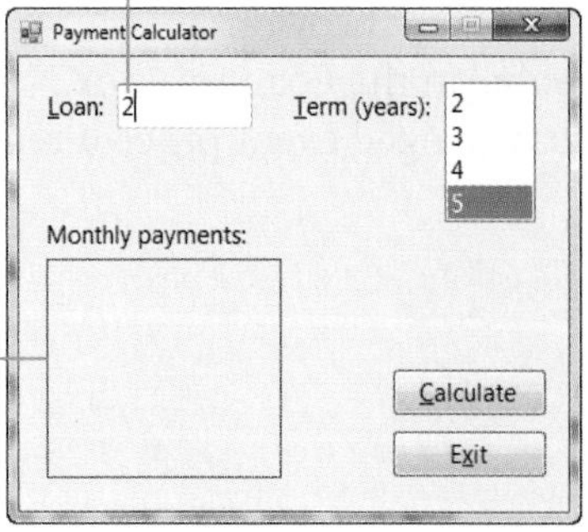

the label is cleared when the user enters a value in the text box

Figure 7-21 Result of processing the text box's TextChanged event procedure

Coding the SelectedValueChanged and SelectedIndexChanged Event Procedures

If you want to experiment with the Payment Calculator application, open the solution contained in the Try It 4! folder.

The Monthly payments label also should be cleared when the user selects a different term in the termListBox. You can accomplish this by entering the `paymentsLabel.Text = String.Empty` statement in either the termListBox's SelectedValueChanged event procedure or its SelectedIndexChanged event procedure. Both procedures are shown in Figure 7-22. However, you need to enter the `paymentsLabel.Text = String.Empty` statement in only one of the procedures.

SelectedValueChanged event procedure

```
Private Sub termListBox_SelectedValueChanged(
ByVal sender As Object, ByVal e As System.EventArgs
) Handles termListBox.SelectedValueChanged
    ' clears the paymentsLabel when the term changes

    paymentsLabel.Text = String.Empty
End Sub
```

processed when the list box's SelectedValueChanged event occurs

you need to code only one of these procedures

SelectedIndexChanged event procedure

```
Private Sub termListBox_SelectedIndexChanged(
ByVal sender As Object, ByVal e As System.EventArgs
) Handles termListBox.SelectedIndexChanged
    ' clears the paymentsLabel when the term changes

    paymentsLabel.Text = String.Empty
End Sub
```

processed when the list box's SelectedIndexChanged event occurs

Figure 7-22 The list box's SelectedValueChanged and SelectedIndexChanged event procedures

Including a Combo Box in an Interface

In many interfaces, combo boxes are used in place of list boxes. You use the ComboBox tool in the toolbox to add a combo box to an interface. A **combo box** is similar to a list box in that it allows the user to select from a list of choices. However, unlike a list box, the full list of choices in a combo box can be hidden, allowing you to save space on the form. Also unlike a list box, a combo box contains a text field. Depending on the style of the combo box, the text field may or may not be editable by the user.

Three styles of combo boxes are available in Visual Basic. The style is controlled by the combo box's **DropDownStyle property**, which can be set to Simple, DropDown (the default), or DropDownList. Each style of combo box contains a text portion and a list portion. When the DropDownStyle property is set to either Simple or DropDown, the text portion of the combo box is editable. However, in a Simple combo box the list portion is always displayed, while in a DropDown combo box the list portion appears only when the user clicks the combo box's list arrow. When the DropDownStyle property is set to the third style, DropDownList, the text portion of the combo box is not editable and the user must click the combo box's list arrow to display the list of choices. Figure 7-23 shows an example of each combo box style. You should use a label control to provide keyboard access to the combo box, as shown in the figure. For the access key to work correctly, you must set the label's TabIndex property to a value that is one number less than the combo box's TabIndex value. Like the items in a list box, the items in the list portion of a combo box are either arranged by use, with the most used entries listed first, or sorted in ascending order. To sort the items in the list portion of a combo box, you set the combo box's Sorted property to True.

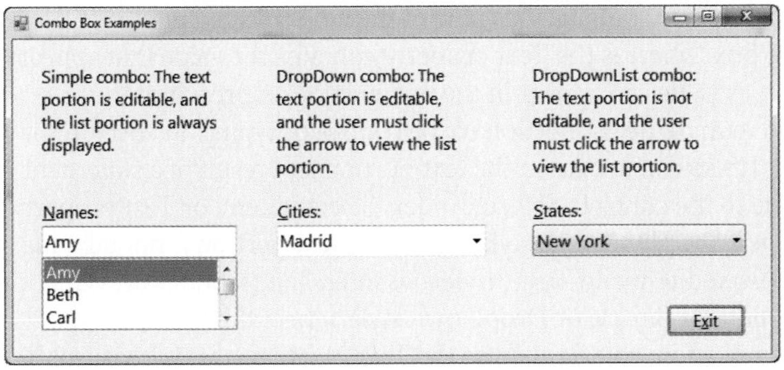

Figure 7-23 Examples of the three styles of combo boxes

You can use the String Collection Editor window to specify the combo box items during design time. You can open the window by clicking Edit Items on the combo box's task list. Or, you can click the ellipsis button in the Items property in the Properties list. During run time, you use the Items collection's Add method to add an item to a combo box, as shown in the code in Figure 7-24. Like the first item in a list box, the first item in a combo box has an index of 0. You can use any of the following properties to select a default item, which will appear in the text portion of the combo box: SelectedIndex, SelectedItem, or Text. If no item is selected, the SelectedItem and Text properties contain the empty string, and the SelectedIndex property contains the number –1 (negative one). To determine the number of items in the list portion of a combo box, you use the Items collection's Count property. The property's value will always be one number more than the combo box's highest index.

```
Private Sub MainForm_Load(ByVal sender As Object,
ByVal e As System.EventArgs) Handles Me.Load
     ' fills the combo boxes with values

     nameComboBox.Items.Add("Amy")
     nameComboBox.Items.Add("Beth")
     nameComboBox.Items.Add("Carl")
     nameComboBox.Items.Add("Dan")
     nameComboBox.Items.Add("Jan")
     nameComboBox.SelectedIndex = 0

     cityComboBox.Items.Add("London")
     cityComboBox.Items.Add("Madrid")
     cityComboBox.Items.Add("Paris")
     cityComboBox.SelectedItem = "Madrid"

     stateComboBox.Items.Add("Alabama")
     stateComboBox.Items.Add("Maine")
     stateComboBox.Items.Add("New York")
     stateComboBox.Items.Add("South Dakota")
     stateComboBox.Text = "New York"
End Sub
```

Items collection's Add method

you can use any of these properties to select the default item in a combo box

If you want to experiment with the Combo Box Examples application, open the solution contained in the Try It 5! folder.

Figure 7-24 Code used to fill the combo boxes in Figure 7-23 with values

It is easy to confuse a combo box's SelectedItem property with its Text property. The SelectedItem property contains the value of the item selected in the list portion of the combo box, whereas the Text property contains the value that appears in the text portion. A value can appear in the text portion as a result of the user either selecting an item in the list portion of the control or typing an entry in the text portion itself. It also can appear in the text portion as a result of a statement that assigns a value to the control's SelectedIndex, SelectedItem, or Text property. If the combo box is a DropDownList style, where the text portion is not editable, you can use the SelectedItem and Text properties interchangeably. However, if the combo box is either a Simple or DropDown style, where the user can type an entry in the text portion, you should use the Text property; this is because the Text property contains the value either selected or entered by the user.

Figure 7-25 shows a sample run of the Payment Calculator application using a DropDown combo box rather than a list box, and Figure 7-26 shows most of the application's code. Notice that the contents of the paymentsLabel are cleared in the combo box's TextChanged event procedure. A combo box's TextChanged event occurs when the user either selects an item in the list portion or types a value in the text portion.

If you want to experiment with this version of the Payment Calculator application, open the solution contained in the Try It 6! folder.

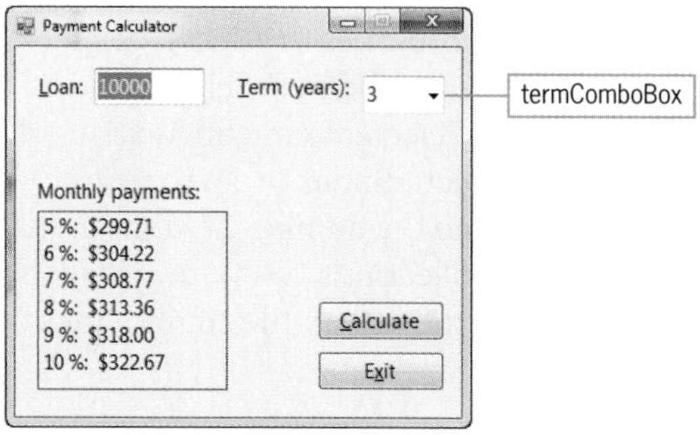

Figure 7-25 Sample run of the Payment Calculator application using a combo box

```
Private Sub MainForm_Load(ByVal sender As Object,
ByVal e As System.EventArgs) Handles Me.Load
     ' fills the termComboBox with terms of 2, 3,
     ' 4, and 5 years

     For term As Integer = 2 To 5
          termComboBox.Items.Add(term.ToString)
     Next term

     ' select the 4-year term
     termComboBox.SelectedItem = "4"
End Sub

Private Sub calcButton_Click(ByVal sender As Object,
ByVal e As System.EventArgs) Handles calcButton.Click
     ' calculates the monthly payments on a loan
     ' using interest rates of 5% through 10%

     Dim term As Integer
     Dim loan As Double
     Dim monthlyPayment As Double

     ' assign input to variables
     Double.TryParse(loanTextBox.Text, loan)
     term = Convert.ToInt32(termComboBox.Text)

     ' clear contents of the paymentsLabel
     paymentsLabel.Text = String.Empty

     ' calculate and display monthly payments
     For rate As Double = 0.05 To 0.1 Step 0.01
        monthlyPayment =
           -Financial.Pmt(rate / 12, term * 12, loan)
        paymentsLabel.Text = paymentsLabel.Text &
           rate.ToString("P0") & ":  " &
           monthlyPayment.ToString("C2") &
           ControlChars.NewLine
     Next rate

     loanTextBox.Focus()
End Sub

Private Sub loanTextBox_Enter(ByVal sender As Object,
ByVal e As System.EventArgs
) Handles loanTextBox.Enter
     ' selects the existing text when the text box
     ' receives the focus

     loanTextBox.SelectAll()
End Sub

Private Sub loanTextBox_TextChanged(
ByVal sender As Object, ByVal e As System.EventArgs
) Handles loanTextBox.TextChanged
     ' clears the paymentsLabel when
     ' the contents of the text box changes

     paymentsLabel.Text = String.Empty

End Sub

Private Sub termComboBox_TextChanged(
ByVal sender As Object, ByVal e As System.EventArgs
) Handles termComboBox.TextChanged
     ' clears the paymentsLabel when the term changes

     paymentsLabel.Text = String.Empty
End Sub
```

use the combo box's Text property to determine the value

the text box's TextChanged event procedure

the combo box's TextChanged event procedure

Figure 7-26 Code for the Payment Calculator application shown in Figure 7-25

The last concept covered in this chapter is how to use an image list control. You will use an image list control in the Slot Machine application, which you will code in Programming Tutorial 1.

Using an Image List Control

You instantiate an image list control using the ImageList tool, which is located in the Components section of the toolbox. An image list control does not appear on the form; rather, it appears in the component tray, as shown in the Image Viewer application in Figure 7-27.

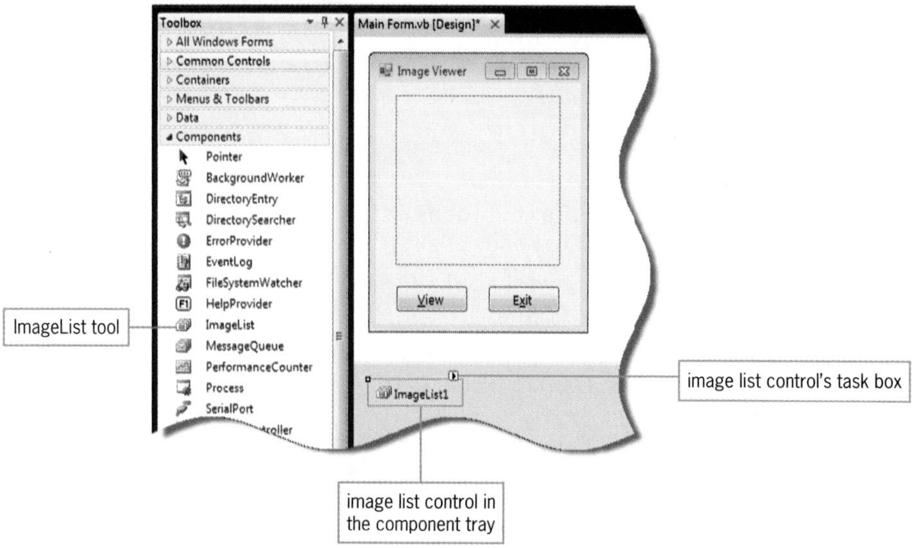

Figure 7-27 Image Viewer application

The purpose of an **image list control** is to store a collection of images. The collection is called the Images collection. You add images to the control's collection using the Images Collection Editor window. The steps for doing this are listed in Figure 7-28. Figure 7-29 shows the completed Images Collection Editor window in the Image Viewer application.

HOW TO Add Images to an Image List Control's Images Collection

1. Open the Images Collection Editor window. To open the window, you can click the task box on the image list control and then click Choose images. Or, you can click Images in the Properties window and then click the ellipsis (...) button in the Settings box.
2. Click the Add button in the Images Collection Editor window. Click the name of the image file in the Open dialog box and then click the Open button.
3. Repeat Step 2 for each image you want to add to the control. When you are finished adding images, click the OK button to close the Images Collection Editor window.

Figure 7-28 How to add images to an image list control's Images collection

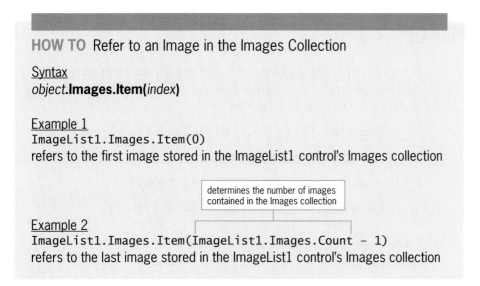

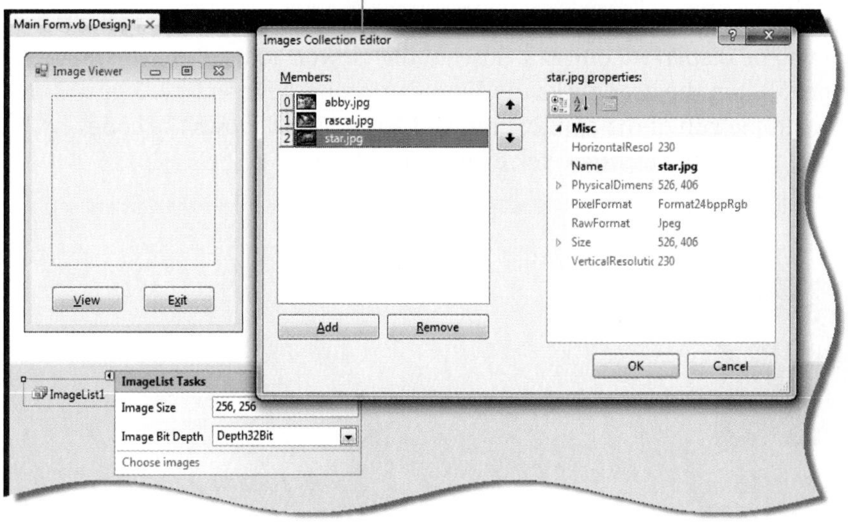

Figure 7-29 Completed Images Collection Editor window in the Image Viewer application

Each image in the Images collection has a unique index. The index of the first image in the Images collection is 0, the second is 1, and so on. Figure 7-30 shows the syntax you use to refer to an image in the Images collection. In the syntax, *object* is the name of the image list control, Images is the name of the collection, Item is a property of the Images collection, and *index* is the index of the image you want to access. Figure 7-30 also includes examples of using the syntax. Example 1 shows how you refer to the first image stored in the ImageList1 control's Images collection. Example 2 shows how you refer to the last image stored in the ImageList1 control's Images collection. The code in Example 2 uses the Images collection's Count property to determine the number of images stored in the collection. The index of the last image in the collection will always be one number less than the value in the Count property.

HOW TO Refer to an Image in the Images Collection

Syntax
object.**Images.Item(***index***)**

Example 1
```
ImageList1.Images.Item(0)
```
refers to the first image stored in the ImageList1 control's Images collection

determines the number of images contained in the Images collection

Example 2
```
ImageList1.Images.Item(ImageList1.Images.Count - 1)
```
refers to the last image stored in the ImageList1 control's Images collection

Figure 7-30 How to refer to an image in the Images collection

An image list control merely stores the images; it does not display the images. To display the images, you need to use another control, such as a picture box. In the Image Viewer application, the images stored in the ImageList1 control will be displayed, one at a time, in the viewerPictureBox. The images will appear when the user clicks the View button in the interface. Figure 7-31 shows a sample run of the application, and Figure 7-32 shows the code entered in the View button's Click event procedure.

Figure 7-31 Sample run of the Image Viewer application

```
Private Sub viewButton_Click(ByVal sender As Object,
ByVal e As System.EventArgs) Handles viewButton.Click
     ' view images, one at a time

     Dim numImages As Integer = ImageList1.Images.Count

     For index As Integer = 0 To numImages - 1
          viewerPictureBox.Image =
               ImageList1.Images.Item(index)
          Me.Refresh()
          System.Threading.Thread.Sleep(500)
     Next index
End Sub
```

Figure 7-32 Code entered in the View button's Click event procedure

If you want to experiment with the Image Viewer application, open the solution contained in the Try It 7! folder.

The answers to Mini-Quiz questions are located in Appendix A.

Mini-Quiz 7-3

1. Which of the following calculates the monthly payment on a $5000 loan for 2 years using an annual interest rate of 4%? Payments should be expressed as a positive number.
   a. `-Financial.Pmt(5000, .04 / 12, 24)`
   b. `-Financial.Pmt(24, .04 / 12, 5000)`
   c. `-Financial.Pmt(.04 / 12, 24, 5000)`
   d. `-Financial.Pmt(5000, 24, .04 / 12)`
2. Write the statement to select all of the text contained in the cityTextBox.

3. You use the ______________ method to add items to a combo box.
   a. Add
   b. AddItem
   c. AddList
   d. ItemAdd
4. Write the statement to refer to the second image stored in the ImageList1 control's Images collection.

You have completed the concepts section of Chapter 7. The Programming Tutorial section is next.

PROGRAMMING TUTORIAL 1

Creating the Slot Machine Application

In this tutorial, you create an application that simulates a slot machine. Figures 7-33 and 7-34 show the application's TOE chart and MainForm, respectively. The MainForm contains a table layout panel, three picture boxes, and two buttons. The application will store six different images in an image list control. When the user clicks the Click Here button, the button's Click event procedure will generate 10 sets of three random numbers. The random numbers will be used to select images from the image list control. The selected images will be displayed, one at a time, in the three picture boxes. If the final three random numbers are the same, the picture boxes will contain the same image. When that happens, the Click event procedure will display the message "Congratulations!" in a message box.

The Ch07ProgTut1 video demonstrates all of the steps in Programming Tutorial 1.

Task	Object	Event
1. Display 10 random images from the ImageList1 control, one at a time, in the leftPictureBox, centerPictureBox, and rightPictureBox 2. Display "Congratulations!" in a message box when the leftPictureBox, centerPictureBox, and rightPictureBox contain the same image	clickHereButton	Click
End the application	exitButton	Click
Store 6 different images	ImageList1	None
Display random ImageList1 images (from clickHereButton)	leftPictureBox, centerPictureBox, rightPictureBox	None

Figure 7-33 TOE chart for the Slot Machine application

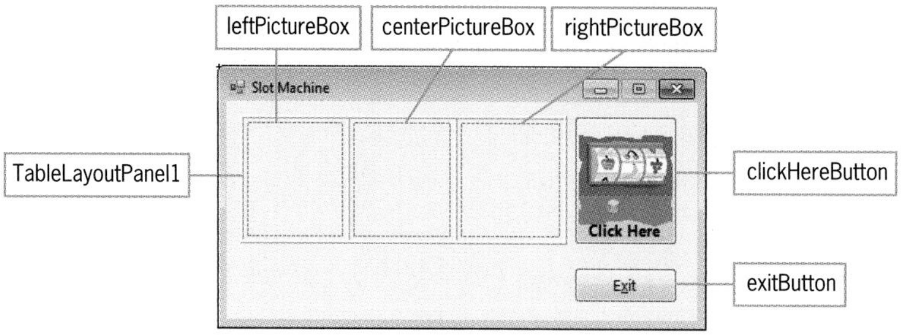

Figure 7-34 MainForm in the Slot Machine application

Instantiating the ImageList1 Control

Included in the data files for this book is a partially completed Slot Machine application. Before you begin coding the application, you will need to instantiate the ImageList1 control and then store the six images in its Images collection. (All of the images used in the application are from Microsoft's Clip Art collection and were downloaded from *www.office.microsoft.com/en-us/clipart.*)

To instantiate the ImageList1 control and then store images in its Images collection:

1. Start Visual Studio or the Express Edition of Visual Basic. If necessary, open the Solution Explorer window.
2. Open the **Slot Machine Solution** (**Slot Machine Solution.sln**) file, which is contained in the VbReloaded2010\Chap07\Slot Machine Solution folder. Open the designer window (if necessary), and then auto-hide the Solution Explorer window.
3. If necessary, open the Toolbox window and expand the Components section. Click **ImageList** and then drag an image list control to the form. Release the mouse button. The ImageList1 control appears in the component tray.
4. Click the ImageList1 control's **task box** and then click **Choose images** to open the Images Collection Editor window. Click the **Add** button. Open the VbReloaded2010\Chap07\Slot Machine Solution\Slot Machine Project\Resources folder. Click **j0436899.png** in the list of filenames. (The file contains an image of a strawberry.) Click the **Open** button. The filename and a small image appear in the Members list section of the Images Collection Editor window.
5. On your own, add the following five image files: j0436903.png (watermelon),j0441708.png (apple), j0441718.png (bananas), j0441719.png (cherries), and j0441720.png (orange). The completed Images Collection Editor window is shown in Figure 7-35.

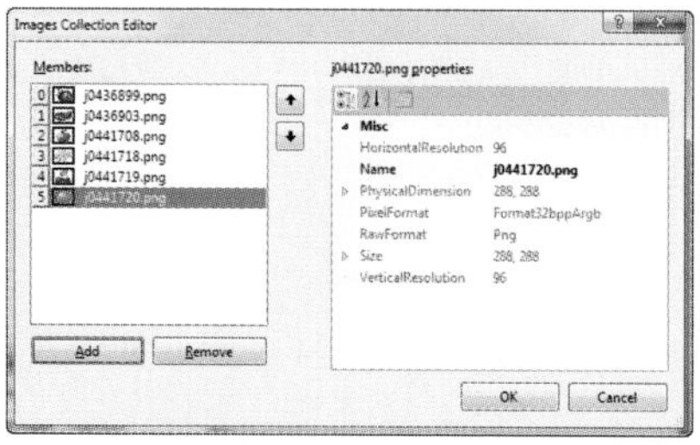

Figure 7-35 Completed Images Collection Editor window

6. Click the **OK** button to add the six images to the ImageList1 control's Images collection.
7. Change the Image Size in the ImageList Tasks box to **85, 96** (which is the size of the picture boxes on the form). Change the Image Bit Depth in the ImageList Tasks box to **Depth32Bit**.
8. Click the **form** to close the ImageList Tasks box. Close the Toolbox window and then save the solution.

Coding the Slot Machine Application

To complete the application, you just need to code it. According to the application's TOE chart, only the Click event procedures for the clickHereButton and exitButton need to be coded.

To begin coding the application:

1. Open the Code Editor window. Notice that the exitButton's Click event procedure has already been coded for you. In addition, the Option statements have already been entered in the General Declarations section.
2. In the comments that appear in the General Declarations section, replace <your name> and <current date> with your name and the current date.

Figure 7-36 shows the pseudocode for the clickHereButton's Click event procedure. As the pseudocode indicates, the procedure will use random numbers to display the appropriate images in the leftPictureBox, centerPictureBox, and rightPictureBox. It then will compare the random numbers to determine whether the "Congratulations!" message should be displayed.

```
clickHereButton Click event procedure
1. disable the clickHereButton
2. repeat for spins from 1 through 10 in increments of 1
        generate a random number from 0 through 5 and store it in a variable named leftIndex
        use the leftIndex variable to display the appropriate ImageList1 image in the leftPictureBox
        refresh the screen and pause the application

        generate a random number from 0 through 5 and store it in a variable named centerIndex
        use the centerIndex variable to display the appropriate ImageList1 image in the centerPictureBox
        refresh the screen and pause the application

        generate a random number from 0 through 5 and store it in a variable named rightIndex
        use the rightIndex variable to display the appropriate ImageList1 image in the rightPictureBox
        refresh the screen and pause the application
   end repeat for
3. if the leftIndex, centerIndex, and rightIndex variables contain the same number
        display "Congratulations!" in a message box
   end if
4. enable the clickHereButton
```

Figure 7-36 Pseudocode for the clickHereButton's Click event procedure

To code the clickHereButton's Click event procedure and then test the procedure's code:

1. Open the code template for the clickHereButton's Click event procedure. Type **' simulates a slot machine** and press **Enter** twice.
2. The procedure will need a Random object to represent the pseudo-random number generator, and three Integer variables to store the random numbers. Enter the following four Dim statements. Press **Enter** twice after typing the last Dim statement.

   ```
   Dim randGen As New Random
   Dim leftIndex As Integer
   Dim centerIndex As Integer
   Dim rightIndex As Integer
   ```

3. The first step in the pseudocode is to disable the clickHereButton. Enter the following assignment statement:

   ```
   clickHereButton.Enabled = False
   ```

4. Step 2 in the pseudocode is a counter-controlled loop that repeats the loop body 10 times. Enter the following For clause:

   ```
   For spins As Integer = 1 To 10
   ```

5. Notice that the Code Editor enters the `Next` clause for you. Change the `Next` clause to **Next spins** and press **Enter**.
6. The first instruction in the loop body should generate a random number from 0 through 5 and store it in the `leftIndex` variable. In the blank line between the For and Next clauses, enter the following assignment statement:

   ```
   leftIndex = randGen.Next(0, 6)
   ```

7. The second instruction in the loop body should use the value in the `leftIndex` variable to display the appropriate image in the leftPictureBox. Enter the following assignment statement:

   ```
   leftPictureBox.Image =
       ImageList1.Images.Item(leftIndex)
   ```

8. Next, the loop body should refresh the screen and pause the application. Enter the following two statements. Press **Enter** twice after typing the second statement.

   ```
   Me.Refresh()
   System.Threading.Thread.Sleep(50)
   ```

9. The next three instructions in the pseudocode are to generate a random number and store it in the `centerIndex` variable, then use the variable's value to display the appropriate image in the centerPictureBox, and then refresh the screen and pause the application. Enter the following statements. Press **Enter** twice after typing the last statement.

   ```
   centerIndex = randGen.Next(0, 6)
   centerPictureBox.Image =
       ImageList1.Images.Item(centerIndex)
   Me.Refresh()
   System.Threading.Thread.Sleep(50)
   ```

10. The last three instructions in the loop body are to generate a random number and store it in the `rightIndex` variable, then use the variable's value to display the appropriate image in the rightPictureBox, and then refresh the screen and pause the application. Enter the following statements:

```
rightIndex = randGen.Next(0, 6)
rightPictureBox.Image =
    ImageList1.Images.Item(rightIndex)
Me.Refresh()
System.Threading.Thread.Sleep(50)
```

11. Step 3 in the pseudocode is a single-alternative selection structure that determines whether the "Congratulations!" message should be displayed. Click the **blank line** below the `Next spins` clause and then press **Enter** to insert another blank line. Enter the following selection structure:

```
If leftIndex = centerIndex AndAlso
    leftIndex = rightIndex Then
    MessageBox.Show("Congratulations!", "Winner"
            MessageBoxButtons.OK,
            MessageBoxIcon.Information)
 End If
```

12. The last step in the pseudocode is to enable the clickHereButton. Click immediately after the letter **f** in the End If clause and then press **Enter**. Enter the following assignment statement:

```
clickHereButton.Enabled = True
```

13. Save the solution and then start the application. Click the **Click Here** button. See Figure 7-37. Because random numbers determine the images assigned to the three picture boxes, your application might display different images than those shown in the figure. In addition, the "Congratulations!" message may appear in a message box on your screen. If necessary, click the **OK** button to close the message box.

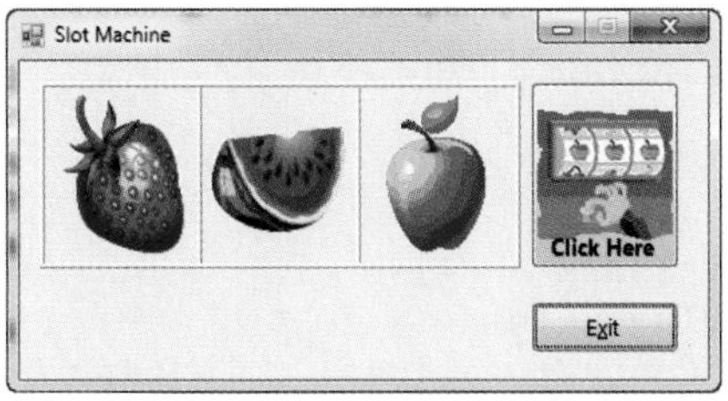

Figure 7-37 Result of clicking the Click Here button

14. Click the **Click Here** button until there is a winner. (You may need to click the button many times.) Then click the **OK** button to close the message box.

15. Click the **Exit** button to end the application. Close the Code Editor window, and then close the solution. Figure 7-38 shows the application's code.

```
' Project name:         Slot Machine Project
' Project purpose:      Simulates a slot machine
' Created/revised by:   <your name> on <current date>

Option Explicit On
Option Strict On
Option Infer Off

Public Class MainForm

  Private Sub exitButton_Click(ByVal sender As Object,
  ByVal e As System.EventArgs) Handles exitButton.Click
     Me.Close()
  End Sub

  Private Sub clickHereButton_Click(ByVal sender As Object,
  ByVal e As System.EventArgs) Handles clickHereButton.Click
     ' simulates a slot machine

     Dim randGen As New Random
     Dim leftIndex As Integer
     Dim centerIndex As Integer
     Dim rightIndex As Integer

     clickHereButton.Enabled = False
     For spins As Integer = 1 To 10
        leftIndex = randGen.Next(0, 6)
        leftPictureBox.Image =
            ImageList1.Images.Item(leftIndex)
        Me.Refresh()
        System.Threading.Thread.Sleep(50)

        centerIndex = randGen.Next(0, 6)
        centerPictureBox.Image =
            ImageList1.Images.Item(centerIndex)
        Me.Refresh()
        System.Threading.Thread.Sleep(50)

        rightIndex = randGen.Next(0, 6)
        rightPictureBox.Image =
            ImageList1.Images.Item(rightIndex)
        Me.Refresh()
        System.Threading.Thread.Sleep(50)

     Next spins

     If leftIndex = centerIndex AndAlso
        leftIndex = rightIndex Then
        MessageBox.Show("Congratulations!", "Winner",
                         MessageBoxButtons.OK,
                         MessageBoxIcon.Information)
     End If
     clickHereButton.Enabled = True

    End Sub
End Class
```

Figure 7-38 Code for the Slot Machine application

PROGRAMMING TUTORIAL 2

Creating the Birmingham Sales Application

In this tutorial, you create an application for Birmingham Sales. The company's sales territories are divided into three regions. Each region has four stores. The application should use the InputBox function to allow the user to enter each store's sales. It should calculate and display the total sales made in each region and the total company sales. The application's TOE chart and MainForm are shown in Figures 7-39 and 7-40, respectively.

Task	**Object**	**Event**
1. Get the sales amounts made in each of the 4 stores in each of the 3 regions 2. Calculate each region's sales by accumulating the sales made in each of its 4 stores 3. Display each region's sales in regionLabel 4. Calculate the company's sales by accumulating the sales made in each of the 3 regions 5. Display the company's sales in companyLabel	calcButton	Click
Display each region's sales (from calcButton)	regionLabel	None
Display the company's sales (from calcButton)	companyLabel	None
End the application	exitButton	Click

Figure 7-39 TOE chart for the Birmingham Sales application

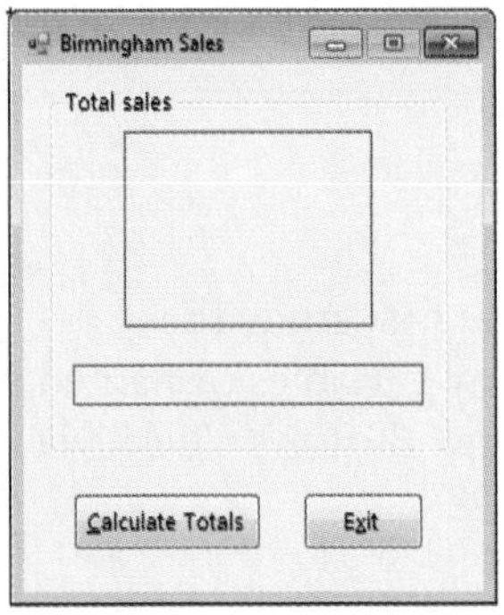

Figure 7-40 MainForm for the Birmingham Sales application

Coding the Birmingham Sales Application

Included in the data files for this book is a partially completed Birmingham Sales application. To complete the application, you just need to code it. According to the application's TOE chart, only the Click event procedures for the calcButton and exitButton need to be coded.

To begin coding the application:

1. Start Visual Studio or the Express Edition of Visual Basic. If necessary, open the Solution Explorer window.

2. Open the **Birmingham Sales Solution** (**Birmingham Sales Solution.sln**) file, which is contained in the VbReloaded2010\Chap07\Birmingham Sales Solution folder. Open the designer window (if necessary), and then auto-hide the Solution Explorer window.

3. Open the Code Editor window. Notice that the exitButton's Click event procedure has already been coded for you. In addition, the Option statements have already been entered in the General Declarations section.

4. In the comments that appear in the General Declarations section, replace <your name> and <current date> with your name and the current date.

According to the application's TOE chart, the Calculate Totals button's Click event procedure is responsible for getting and accumulating the sales made in the four stores in each region. It also must display each region's sales and the company sales. The procedure's pseudocode is shown in Figure 7-41.

```
calcButton Click event procedure
1. clear the regionLabel and companyLabel
2. repeat for regions from 1 through 3 in increments of 1
       repeat for stores from 1 through 4 in increments of 1
           get the store's sales
           add the store's sales to the region sales
       end repeat for stores

       add the region sales to the company sales
       display the region sales in regionLabel
       reset the region sales to 0
   end repeat for regions
3. display the company sales in companyLabel
```

Figure 7-41 Pseudocode for the calcButton's Click event procedure

As you know, before you begin coding a procedure, you first study the procedure's pseudocode (or flowchart) to determine any variables or named constants the procedure will require. In this case, the calcButton's Click event procedure will use the four variables listed in Figure 7-42.

Variables	Data type	Value source
`inputSales`	String	user input (InputBox function)
`storeSales`	Double	user input converted to Double
`regionAccumulator`	Double	procedure calculation
`companyAccumulator`	Double	procedure calculation

Figure 7-42 Variables for the calcButton's Click event procedure

To code the Calculate Totals button's Click event procedure, and then test the code:

1. Open the code template for the calcButton's Click event procedure.

2. Type **' displays the region and company sales** and press **Enter** twice.

3. Enter the statements to declare the four variables listed in Figure 7-42. Press **Enter** twice after typing the last declaration statement.
4. Step 1 in the pseudocode is to clear the regionLabel and companyLabel. Type **‘ clear the regionLabel and companyLabel** and press **Enter**. Now, enter the appropriate assignment statements. Press **Enter** twice after typing the second assignment statement.
5. Step 2 is a counter-controlled loop that repeats its loop body three times—once for each of the three regions. Enter an appropriate For clause. Use `regions` as the counter variable's name. Be sure to change the `Next` clause to **Next regions**, and then press **Enter**.
6. The first instruction in the loop body is a nested counter-controlled loop that repeats its loop body four times—once for each store. Enter an appropriate For clause. Use `stores` as the counter variable's name. Be sure to change the `Next` clause to **Next stores**, and then press **Enter**.
7. The first instruction in the nested loop is to get the store's sales. Click the **blank line** between the nested loop's For and Next clauses, and then enter the following assignment statement:

   inputSales = InputBox("Sales for store " &
   stores.ToString, "Region " &
   regions.ToString

8. The last instruction in the nested loop is to add the store's sales to the region sales. However, before you can do that, you need to convert the store's sales to the Double data type. Enter the appropriate TryParse method.
9. Now, type **‘ add store sales to region sales** and press **Enter**, and then enter an assignment statement to handle this task.
10. The instruction below the nested loop in the pseudocode is to add the region sales to the company sales. Click the **blank line** below the `Next stores` clause and then press **Enter**. Type **‘ add region sales to company sales** and press **Enter**, and then enter an assignment statement to accomplish this task.
11. Next, you need to display the region sales in the regionLabel. Enter the following comment and assignment statement:

    ‘ display region sales
    regionLabel.Text = regionLabel.Text &
    "Region " & regions.ToString & ": " &
    regionAccumulator.ToString("N2") &
    ControlChars.NewLine

12. The last step in the outer loop is to reset the region sales to 0. Type **‘ reset region sales for next region** and press **Enter**, and then enter an assignment statement to accomplish this task.
13. Step 3 in the pseudocode is to display the company sales in the companyLabel. Click the **blank line** above the `End Sub` clause and then press **Enter**. Enter the following comment and assignment statement:

    ‘ display company sales
    companyLabel.Text = "Company sales: " &
    companyAccumulator.ToString("C2")

14. Save the solution, and then start the application. Click the **Calculate Totals** button. Type **2450.67** as Region 1's first store sales and press **Enter**. Now, enter the following sales amounts for the remaining three stores in Region 1:

    7500.45
    230.84
    760.23

15. Next, enter the following four sales amounts for Region 2's stores:

    9456.78
    1234.56
    5555.89
    1234.89

16. Finally, enter the following four sales amounts for Region 3's stores:

    7632.67
    9998.88
    234.45
    8320.78

17. The region and company sales appear in the interface, as shown in Figure 7-43. On your own, manually check the region and company sales amounts to verify that they are correct.

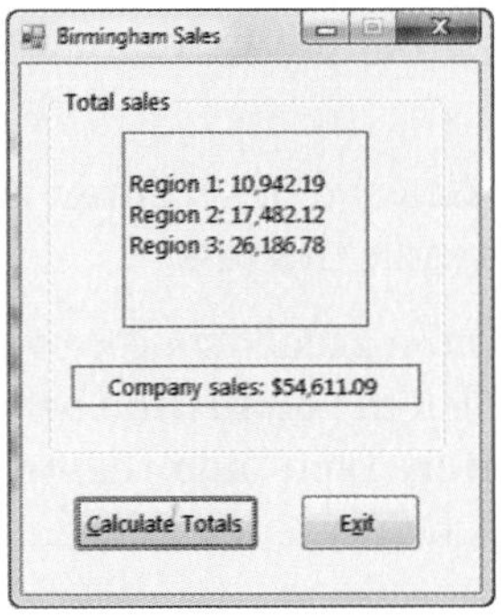

Figure 7-43 Interface showing the region and company sales

18. On your own, test the application using different values for the store sales.

19. Click the **Exit** button to end the application. Close the Code Editor window and then close the solution. Figure 7-44 shows the code for the Birmingham Sales application.

```
' Project name:         Birmingham Sales Project
' Project purpose:      Displays the total sales made
'                       in each region and the grand total
' Created/revised by:   <your name> on <current date>

Option Explicit On
Option Strict On
Option Infer Off

Public Class MainForm

  Private Sub exitButton_Click(ByVal sender As Object,
  ByVal e As System.EventArgs) Handles exitButton.Click
     Me.Close()
  End Sub

  Private Sub calcButton_Click(ByVal sender As Object,
  ByVal e As System.EventArgs) Handles calcButton.Click
     ' displays the region and company sales

     Dim inputSales As String
     Dim storeSales As Double
     Dim regionAccumulator As Double
     Dim companyAccumulator As Double

     ' clear the regionLabel and companyLabel
     regionLabel.Text = String.Empty
     companyLabel.Text = String.Empty

     For regions As Integer = 1 To 3
         For stores As Integer = 1 To 4
            inputSales = InputBox("Sales for store " &
                 stores.ToString, "Region " &
                 regions.ToString)
            Double.TryParse(inputSales, storeSales)
            ' add store sales to region sales
            regionAccumulator += storeSales

         Next stores

         ' add region sales to company sales
         companyAccumulator += regionAccumulator
         ' display region sales
         regionLabel.Text = regionLabel.Text &
            "Region " & regions.ToString & ": " &
            regionAccumulator.ToString("N2") &
            ControlChars.NewLine
         ' reset region sales for next region
         regionAccumulator = 0

     Next regions

     ' display company sales
     companyLabel.Text = "Company sales: " &
        companyAccumulator.ToString("C2")

  End Sub

End Class
```

Figure 7-44 Code for the Birmingham Sales application

PROGRAMMING EXAMPLE

Raise Calculator Application

Create an interface that allows the user to enter two items: a salary amount and a raise percentage entered in decimal form. The interface should provide a text box for entering the salary amount, and a combo box for entering the raise percentage. The combo box should contain the following numbers: .03, .04, .05, and .06. However, the user also should be able to enter a different raise percentage. The application should calculate and display two amounts: the raise and the new salary. Use the following names for the solution, project, and form file: Raise Solution, Raise Project, and Main Form.vb. Save the application in the VbReloaded2010\Chap07 folder. See Figures 7-45 through 7-50.

Task	Object	Event
1. Fill the combo box with items 2. Select the first item in the combo box	MainForm	Load
1. Calculate the raise 2. Calculate the new salary 3. Display the raise in raiseLabel 4. Display the new salary in newSalaryLabel	calcButton	Click
End the application	exitButton	Click
Display the raise (from calcButton)	raiseLabel	None
Display the new salary (from calcButton)	newSalaryLabel	None
Get the salary Select the existing text Allow numbers, period, and Backspace Clear raiseLabel and newSalaryLabel	salaryTextBox	None Enter KeyPress TextChanged
Get the raise percentage Clear raiseLabel and newSalaryLabel	raiseRateComboBox	None TextChanged

Figure 7-45 TOE chart for the Raise Calculator application

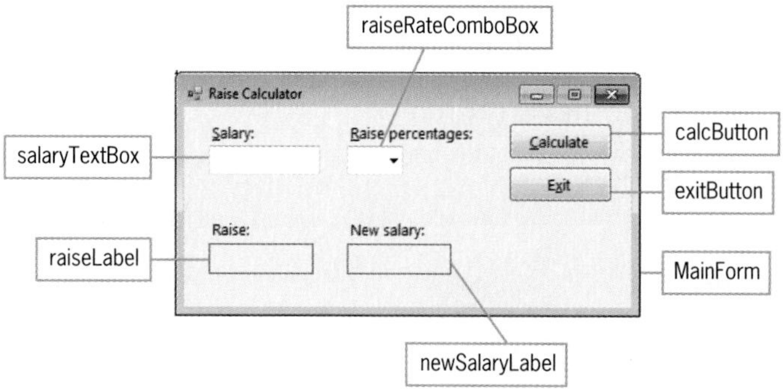

Figure 7-46 MainForm in the Raise Calculator application

Object	Property	Setting
MainForm	Font	Segoe UI, 10 point
	MaximizeBox	False
	StartPosition	CenterScreen
	Text	Raise Calculator
raiseLabel	AutoSize	False
	BorderStyle	FixedSingle
	Text	(empty)
	TextAlign	MiddleCenter
newSalaryLabel	AutoSize	False
	BorderStyle	FixedSingle
	Text	(empty)
	TextAlign	MiddleCenter

Figure 7-47 Objects, properties, and settings

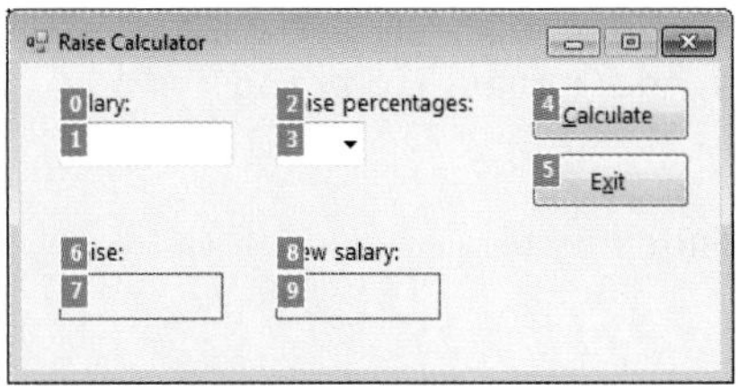

Figure 7-48 Tab order

<u>exitButton Click event procedure</u>
close the application

<u>MainForm Load event procedure</u>
1. repeat for rates from .03 through .06 in increments of .01
   add the current rate to the raiseRateComboBox
   end repeat for
2. select the first rate in the raiseRateComboBox

<u>salaryTextBox Enter event procedure</u>
select the text box's text

<u>salaryTextBox KeyPress event procedure</u>
allow only numbers, the period, and the Backspace key

<u>salaryTextBox TextChanged event procedure</u>
clear the contents of the raiseLabel and newSalaryLabel

<u>raiseRateComboBox TextChanged event procedure</u>
clear the contents of the raiseLabel and newSalaryLabel

<u>calcButton Click event procedure</u>
1. store user input (salary and raise percentage) in variables
2. calculate the raise by multiplying the salary by the raise percentage
3. calculate the new salary by adding the raise to the salary
4. display the raise in raiseLabel
5. display the new salary in newSalaryLabel
6. send the focus to the salaryTextBox

Figure 7-49 Pseudocode

```
' Project name:         Raise Project
' Project purpose:      Display the raise and new salary
' Created/revised by:   <your name> on <current date>

Option Explicit On
Option Strict On
Option Infer Off

Public Class MainForm

  Private Sub exitButton_Click(ByVal sender As Object,
  ByVal e As System.EventArgs) Handles exitButton.Click
     Me.Close()
  End Sub

  Private Sub MainForm_Load(ByVal sender As Object,
  ByVal e As System.EventArgs) Handles Me.Load
     ' fill combo box with item

     For rates As Decimal = 0.03D To 0.06D Step 0.01D
         raiseRateComboBox.Items.Add(rates.ToString)
     Next rates
     ' select first item
     raiseRateComboBox.SelectedIndex = 0
  End Sub

  Private Sub salaryTextBox_Enter(ByVal sender As Object,
  ByVal e As System.EventArgs) Handles salaryTextBox.Enter
     ' select existing text

     salaryTextBox.SelectAll()
  End Sub

  Private Sub salaryTextBox_KeyPress(
  ByVal sender As Object,
  ByVal e As System.Windows.Forms.KeyPressEventArgs
  ) Handles salaryTextBox.KeyPress
     ' allow only numbers, the period, and the Backspace key

     If (e.KeyChar < "0" OrElse e.KeyChar > "9") AndAlso
         e.KeyChar <> "." AndAlso
         e.KeyChar <> ControlChars.Back Then
         e.Handled = True
     End If
  End Sub

  Private Sub salaryTextBox_TextChanged(
  ByVal sender As Object, ByVal e As System.EventArgs
  ) Handles salaryTextBox.TextChanged
     ' clear calculated amounts from labels

     raiseLabel.Text = String.Empty
     newSalaryLabel.Text = String.Empty
  End Sub


```

Figure 7-50 Code *(continues)*

(continued)

```
    Private Sub raiseRateComboBox_TextChanged(
    ByVal sender As Object, ByVal e As System.EventArgs
    ) Handles raiseRateComboBox.TextChanged
        ' clear calculated amounts from labels

        raiseLabel.Text = String.Empty
        newSalaryLabel.Text = String.Empty
    End Sub

    Private Sub calcButton_Click(
    ByVal sender As Object, ByVal e As System.EventArgs
    ) Handles calcButton.Click
        ' calculate the raise and new salary

        Dim salary As Decimal
        Dim raiseRate As Decimal
        Dim raise As Decimal
        Dim newSalary As Decimal

        Decimal.TryParse(salaryTextBox.Text, salary)
        Decimal.TryParse(raiseRateComboBox.Text, raiseRate)

        raise = salary * raiseRate
        newSalary = salary + raise

        raiseLabel.Text = raise.ToString("N2")
        newSalaryLabel.Text = newSalary.ToString("N2")

        salaryTextBox.Focus()
    End Sub
End Class
```

Figure 7-50 Code

Summary

- You can use the For...Next statement to code a specific type of pretest loop, called a counter-controlled loop. You also can code a counter-controlled loop using the Do...Loop statement; however, the For...Next statement is more convenient to use.
- A variable declared in a For clause has block scope and can be used only within the For...Next loop.
- The For clause's startValue, stepValue, and endValue items can be positive or negative numbers, integer or non-integer.
- Many programmers use a hexagon to represent the For clause in a flowchart. Inside the hexagon, you record the counter variable's name and its startValue, stepValue, and endValue.
- For a nested loop to work correctly, it must be contained entirely within the outer loop.

- You can use the Financial.Pmt method to calculate a periodic payment on a loan.
- It is customary in Windows applications to highlight (select) the existing text in a text box when the text box receives the focus. You can do this by entering the SelectAll method in the text box's Enter event procedure.
- A control's TextChanged event occurs when either the user or the application's code changes the contents of the control's Text property.
- A list box's SelectedValueChanged and SelectedIndexChanged events occur when either the user or the application's code selects a different item in the list box.
- Combo boxes are similar to list boxes in that they allow the user to select from a list of choices. However, combo boxes also have a text field that may or may not be editable.
- Three styles of combo boxes are available. The style is specified in a combo box's DropDownStyle property. You can use a combo box to save space in an interface.
- You should use a label control to provide keyboard access to a combo box. Set the label's TabIndex property to a value that is one number less than the combo box's TabIndex value.
- You use the Items collection's Add method to add an item to a combo box during run time. You can use the String Collection Editor window to add an item to a combo box during design time.
- You can use the SelectedIndex, SelectedItem, or Text property to select the default item in a combo box.
- The number of items in the list portion of a combo box is stored in the Items collection's Count property.
- You can use the Sorted property to sort the items listed in a combo box.
- A combo box's SelectedItem property contains the value of the item selected in the list portion of the combo box. A combo box's Text property contains the value that appears in the text portion of the combo box.
- A combo box's TextChanged event occurs when the user either selects an item in the list portion or types a value in the text portion.
- The images stored in an image list control belong to the Images collection. Each image in the collection has a unique index. The index of the first image is 0.
- You access an image in the Images collection using the collection's Item property along with the index of the image you want to access.
- You use the Images collection's Count property to determine the number of images in the collection.
- You need to use another control, such as a picture box, to display an image contained in an image list control.

Key Terms

Combo box—a control that allows the user to select from a list of choices and also has a text field that may or may not be editable

Counter-controlled loop—a loop whose processing is controlled by a counter; the loop body will be processed a precise number of times

Decrementing—adding increments of a negative number

DropDownStyle property—determines the style of a combo box

Enter event—occurs when a control receives the focus, which can happen as a result of the user either tabbing to the control or using the control's access key; also occurs when the Focus method is used to send the focus to the control

Financial.Pmt method—used to calculate a periodic payment on either a loan or an investment

For...Next statement—used to code a specific type of pretest loop, called a counter-controlled loop

Image list control—used to store the Images collection, which is simply a collection of images

SelectAll method—used to select all of the text contained in a text box

TextChanged event—occurs when a change is made to the contents of a control's Text property

Review Questions

1. How many times will the computer process the MessageBox.Show method in the following code?

```
For counter As Integer = 4 To 11 Step 2
   MessageBox.Show("Hello")
Next counter
```

   a. 3

   b. 4

   c. 5

   d. 8

2. What value will cause the loop in Question 1 to stop?

   a. 10

   b. 11

   c. 12

   d. 13

   Use the code in Figure 7-51 to answer Review Questions 3 through 5.

```
For x As Integer = 1 To 2
     For y As Integer = 1 To 3
          msgLabel.Text = msgLabel.Text & "*"
     Next y
     msgLabel.Text = msgLabel.Text & ControlChars.NewLine
Next x
```


Figure 7-51 Code for Review Questions 3 through 5

3. What will the code in Figure 7-51 display in the msgLabel?

   a. ***
      ***

   b. ***
      ***
      ***

   c. **
      **
      **

   d. ****
      ****
      ****
      ****

4. What value will terminate the outer loop in Figure 7-51?
   a. 2
   b. 3
   c. 4
   d. none of the above

5. What value will terminate the nested loop in Figure 7-51?
   a. 2
   b. 3
   c. 4
   d. none of the above

   Use the code in Figure 7-52 to answer Review Question 6.

```
Dim sum As Integer
Dim y As Integer
Do While y < 3
     For x As Integer = 1 To 4
          sum += x
     Next x
     y += 1
Loop
msgLabel.Text = sum.ToString
```

Figure 7-52 Code for Review Question 6

6. What number will the code in Figure 7-52 display in the msgLabel?

   a. 5

   b. 8

   c. 15

   d. 30

7. Which of the following calculates an annual payment on a $50000 loan? The term is 10 years and the annual interest rate is 3%.

   a. `-Financial.Pmt(.03 / 12, 10, 50000)`

   b. `-Financial.Pmt(.03 / 12, 10 * 12, 50000)`

   c. `-Financial.Pmt(.03, 10, 50000)`

   d. `-Financial.Pmt(.03, 10 * 12, 50000)`

8. Which of the following selects the "Cat" item, which is the third item in the animalComboBox?

   a. `animalComboBox.SelectedIndex = 2`

   b. `animalComboBox.SelectedItem = "Cat"`

   c. `animalComboBox.Text = "Cat"`

   d. all of the above

9. The item entered by the user in the text field of a combo box is stored in the ______________ property.

   a. SelectedItem

   b. SelectedValue

   c. Text

   d. TextItem

10. Which of the following refers to the third item in the ImageList1 control?

    a. `ImageList1.Images.Item(2)`

    b. `ImageList1.Images.Item(3)`

    c. `ImageList1.Item.Images(2)`

    d. `ImageList1.ItemImages(3)`

Exercises

Pencil and Paper

INTRODUCTORY

1. When processing the For...Next statement, the computer performs the following three tasks. Put these tasks in their proper order by placing the numbers 1 through 3 on the line to the left of the task.

   ______________ Adds the stepValue to the counter variable

   ______________ Initializes the counter variable to the startValue

   ______________ Checks whether the counter variable's value is greater (less) than the endValue

INTRODUCTORY

2. Create a chart (similar to the one shown earlier in Figure 7-2) that lists the processing steps for the code shown in Example 2 in Figure 7-1.

INTRODUCTORY

3. Create a chart (similar to the one shown earlier in Figure 7-2) that lists the processing steps for the code shown in Example 3 in Figure 7-1.

INTRODUCTORY

4. Write the code to calculate the annual payment on a loan of $6000 for 3 years at 9% interest. Payments should be expressed as a negative number.

INTRODUCTORY

5. Write the statement to select the existing text in the itemTextBox.

INTERMEDIATE

6. Write three different statements that you can use to select the first item in a combo box named deptComboBox. The first item is "Accounting."

INTERMEDIATE

7. Write the code to calculate the quarterly payment on a loan of $6000 for 3 years at 9% interest. Payments should be expressed as a positive number.

INTERMEDIATE

8. Write the code for a pretest loop that uses the For...Next statement and an Integer variable named `evenNum` to display the even integers from 2 through 10 on separate lines in the numbersLabel. Then rewrite the code using the Do...Loop statement.

INTERMEDIATE

9. Write an assignment statement that displays (in the msgLabel) the number of images contained in the ImageList1 control.

INTERMEDIATE

10. Write a For...Next statement that displays the images stored in the ImageList1 control. Display the images, one at a time, in the imagePictureBox. Display the images in reverse order; in other words, display the last image first. Refresh the screen and pause the application for 100 milliseconds between images.

11. Write the code to display the following pattern of asterisks in the asterisksLabel. Use two For...Next statements. INTERMEDIATE

```
*****
*****
*****
```

12. Rewrite the code from Exercise 11 using two Do...Loop statements. Both loops should be pretest loops. INTERMEDIATE

13. Rewrite the code from Exercise 11 using two Do...Loop statements. Both loops should be posttest loops. ADVANCED

14. Rewrite the code from Exercise 11 using a For...Next statement for the outer loop, and a Do...Loop statement for the nested loop. The nested loop should be a posttest loop. ADVANCED

15. The following code should display three rows of percent signs in the msgLabel. The first row should contain one percent sign, the second row should contain two percent signs, and the third row should contain three percent signs. However, the code is not working correctly. Correct the code. SWAT THE BUGS

```
For row As Integer = 1 To 3
     For percent As Integer = 1 To 3
          msgLabel.Text = msgLabel.Text & "%"
     Next percent
Next row
```

Computer

16. Use Windows to make a copy of the Savings Solution folder. Rename the folder Savings Solution-ComboBox. Open the Savings Solution (Savings Solution.sln) file contained in the VbReloaded2010\Chap07\Savings Solution-ComboBox folder. MODIFY THIS

    a. Replace the rateTextBox with a combo box named rateComboBox. Be sure to reset the tab order. The combo box should list annual interest rates from .03 to .1 in increments of .01. However, the user also should be allowed to enter an interest rate that is not on the list.

    b. Before ending, the Calculate button's Click event procedure should send the focus to the depositTextBox.

    c. Clear the balanceLabel when a change is made to either the text box or the combo box.

    d. The text box's existing text should be selected when the text box receives the focus.

    e. Remove the rateTextBox's KeyPress event procedure, and code the rateComboBox's KeyPress event procedure.

    f. Save the solution and then start and test the application. Close the solution.

MODIFY THIS

17. Use Windows to make a copy of the Savings Solution-Nested folder. Rename the folder Savings Solution-PretestDoLoop. Open the Savings Solution (Savings Solution.sln) file contained in the VbReloaded2010\Chap07\Savings Solution-PretestDoLoop folder. Change both For...Next statements to Do...Loop statements. Both loops should be pretest loops. Save the solution and then start and test the application. Close the solution.

MODIFY THIS

18. Use Windows to make a copy of the Savings Solution-Nested folder. Rename the folder Savings Solution-PosttestDoLoop. Open the Savings Solution (Savings Solution.sln) file contained in the VbReloaded2010\Chap07\Savings Solution-PosttestDoLoop folder. Change both For...Next statements to Do...Loop statements. Both loops should be posttest loops. Save the solution and then start and test the application. Close the solution.

MODIFY THIS

19. Use Windows to make a copy of the Savings Solution-Nested folder. Rename the folder Savings Solution-Formula. Open the Savings Solution (Savings Solution.sln) file contained in the VbReloaded2010\Chap07\Savings Solution-Formula folder. Replace the interest and balance calculations with the following formula: $balance = loan * (1 + rate)^{numPeriods}$. Save the solution and then start and test the application. Close the solution.

MODIFY THIS

20. If necessary, complete the Slot Machine application from this chapter's Programming Tutorial 1, and then close the solution. Use Windows to make a copy of the Slot Machine Solution folder. Rename the folder Slot Machine Solution-Modified. Open the Slot Machine Solution (Slot Machine Solution.sln) file contained in the VbReloaded2010\Chap07\Slot Machine Solution-Modified folder. Modify the code so that it uses a counter to keep track of the number of times the user clicked the Click Here button before the "Congratulations!" message appeared. Display the counter's value in a label on the form. Be sure to reset the counter after the user wins. Save the solution and then start and test the application. Close the solution.

MODIFY THIS

21. If necessary, complete the Birmingham Sales application from this chapter's Programming Tutorial 2, and then close the solution. Use Windows to make a copy of the Birmingham Sales Solution folder. Rename the folder Birmingham Sales Solution-Modified. Open the Birmingham Solution (Birmingham Solution.sln) file contained in the VbReloaded2010\Chap07\Birmingham Sales Solution-Modified folder. Change the two For...Next statements to two pretest Do...Loop statements. Save the solution and then start and test the application. Close the solution.

MODIFY THIS

22. If necessary, complete the Raise Calculator application from this chapter's Programming Example, and then close the solution. Use Windows to make a copy of the Raise Solution folder. Rename the folder Raise Solution-Modified. Open the Raise Solution (Raise Solution.sln) file contained in the VbReloaded2010\Chap07\Raise Solution-Modified folder. Change the For...Next statement in the Load event procedure to a posttest Do...Loop statement. Save the solution and then start and test the application. Close the solution.

23. Open the Car Solution (Car Solution.sln) file contained in the VbReloaded2010\Chap07\Car Solution folder. When the Click Me button is clicked, the "I WANT THIS CAR!" message should blink 10 times. In other words, it should disappear and then reappear, disappear and then reappear, and so on, 10 times. Code the button's Click event procedure using the For...Next statement. Save the solution and then start and test the application. Close the solution.

INTRODUCTORY

24. Open the Odd Squares Solution (Odd Squares Solution.sln) file contained in the VbReloaded2010\Chap07\Odd Squares Solution folder. Code the Display button's Click event procedure so that it displays the squares of the odd integers from 1 through 9 in the squaresLabel. Display each square on a separate line in the control. Use the For...Next statement. Save the solution and then start and test the application. Close the solution.

INTERMEDIATE

25. Open the Gentry Supplies Solution (Gentry Supplies Solution.sln) file contained in the VbReloaded2010\Chap07\Gentry Supplies Solution folder.

INTERMEDIATE

a. Add the state names listed in Figure 7-53 to the combo box.

b. The combo box's TextChanged event procedure should display the following message in the msgLabel: "The shipping charge for *state* is *charge*.", in which *state* is the name of the state either selected or entered in the combo box, and *charge* is the shipping charge. The shipping charges are listed in Figure 7-53.

c. Save the solution and then start and test the application. Close the solution.

State	Shipping charge
Alabama	$20
Georgia	$35
Louisiana	$30
North Carolina	$28
All other entries	$15

Figure 7-53 Shipping information for Exercise 25

26. In this exercise, you code an application that allows the user to enter two integers. The application then displays all of the odd numbers between both integers and all of the even numbers between both integers. Open the OddEven Solution (OddEven Solution.sln) file contained in the VbReloaded2010\Chap07\OddEven Solution folder. Code the application. Use the For...Next statement. Save the solution and then start the application. Test the application using the following integers: 6 and 25. The application should display the following odd numbers: 7, 9, 11, 13, 15, 17, 19, 21, and 23. It also should display the following even numbers: 8, 10, 12, 14, 16, 18, 20, 22, and 24. Now test it again using the following integers: 10 and 3. Close the solution.

ADVANCED

ADVANCED

27. Open the Numbers Table Solution (Numbers Table Solution.sln) file contained in the VbReloaded2010\Chap07\Numbers Table Solution folder. Code the application so that it displays a table consisting of four rows and six columns. The first column should contain the numbers 1 through 4. The second and subsequent columns should contain the result of multiplying the number in the first column by the numbers 0 through 4. The table will look similar to the one shown in Figure 7-54. However, don't be concerned about the alignment of the numbers within each column. Use two For...Next statements. Save the solution and then start and test the application. Close the solution.

1	0	1	2	3	4
2	0	2	4	6	8
3	0	3	6	9	12
4	0	4	8	12	16

Figure 7-54 Sample output for Exercise 27

SWAT THE BUGS

28. Open the Debug Solution (Debug Solution.sln) file contained in the VbReloaded2010\Chap07\Debug Solution folder. Open the Code Editor window and review the existing code. Start and then test the application. Locate and then correct any errors. When the application is working correctly, close the solution.

Case Projects

Principal and Interest Calculator

Create an application that displays a monthly payment on a loan of $5000 for 1 year at 6% interest. The application also should display the amount applied to the loan's principal each month and the amount that represents interest. Use the following names for the solution, project, and form file: Principal and Interest Solution, Principal and Interest Project, and Main Form.vb. Save the solution in the VbReloaded2010\Chap07 folder. You can create either your own interface or the one shown in Figure 7-55. The figure shows a sample run of the application. You can use the Financial.PPmt method to calculate the portion of the payment applied to the principal each month. The method's syntax is **Financial.PPmt(*Rate*, *Per*, *NPer*, *PV*)**. In the syntax, *Rate* is the interest rate, *NPer* is the number of payment periods, and *PV* is the present value of the loan. The *Per* argument is the payment period for which you want to calculate the portion applied to the principal. The *Per* argument must be a number from 1 through *NPer*. The method returns the calculated value as a Double number. The text box located below the Monthly payment label has its Multiline and ReadOnly properties set to True.

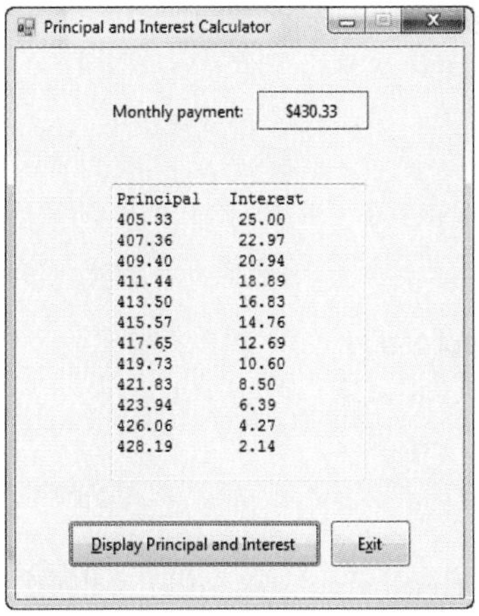

Figure 7-55 Sample run of the Principal and Interest Calculator application

Kenton Incorporated

The payroll manager at Kenton Incorporated wants an application that allows her to enter five payroll amounts for each of three stores: Store 1, Store 2, and Store 3. Use the InputBox function. The application should calculate and display each store's total payroll and the total company payroll. Display the payroll amounts with a dollar sign and two decimal places. Use the following names for the solution, project, and form file: Kenton Solution, Kenton Project, and Main Form.vb. Save the solution in the VbReloaded2010\Chap07 folder. You can create either your own interface or the one shown in Figure 7-56.

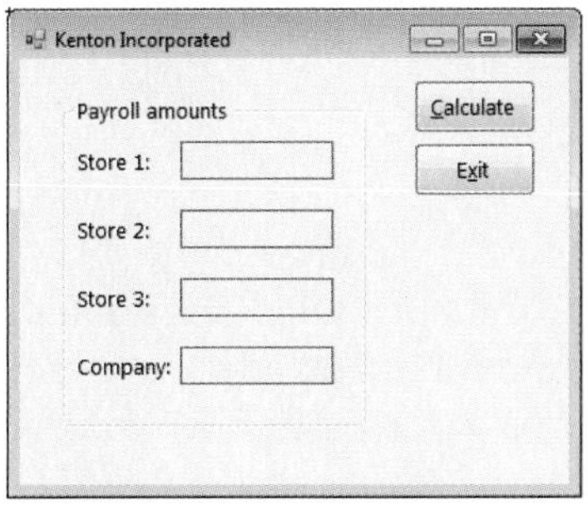

Figure 7-56 Sample interface for the Kenton Incorporated application

Happy Temps

Happy Temps has hired you as a temporary worker for 10 days. The company offers you two pay options. Option 1 doubles your pay each day; however, the first day's pay is only $1. In other words, you would earn $1 the first day, $2 the second day, $4 the third day, $8 the fourth day, and so on. Option 2 is to be paid $100 per day. Create an application that calculates and displays the total amount you would earn under each pay plan. Use the following names for the solution, project, and form file: Happy Temps Solution, Happy Temps Project, and Main Form.vb. Save the solution in the VbReloaded2010\Chap07 folder. You can create either your own interface or the one shown in Figure 7-57.

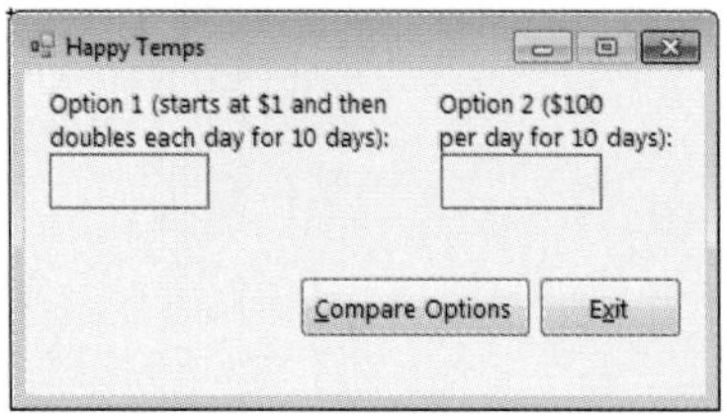

Figure 7-57 Sample interface for the Happy Temps application

South Central Investments

South Central Investments wants an application that calculates and displays the amount a customer needs to save each month to accumulate a specific amount. The user will enter three items of information: the amount he or she wants to accumulate, the term (in years), and the annual interest rate. The interface should provide a text box for entering the desired ending amount. It also should provide combo boxes for the term and annual interest rate. The term combo box should display terms from 1 through 50, and it should not allow the user to enter a different term. The interest rate combo box should display annual interest rates from .02 to .11; however, it should allow the user to enter a different interest rate. Research the full syntax of the Financial.Pmt method. Display the monthly amount as a positive number. Use the following names for the solution, project, and form file: South Central Solution, South Central Project, and Main Form.vb. Save the solution in the VbReloaded2010\Chap07 folder.

CHAPTER 8

Sub and Function Procedures

After studying Chapter 8, you should be able to:

- Explain the difference between Sub and Function procedures
- Create a Sub procedure
- Pass information to a procedure
- Explain the difference between passing data *by value* and passing data *by reference*
- Explain the purpose of the `sender` and `e` parameters
- Associate a procedure with more than one object and event
- Create a Function procedure
- Convert an Object variable to a different type using the TryCast operator
- Utilize a timer control

Procedures

As you already know, a procedure is a block of program code that performs a specific task. Most procedures in Visual Basic are either Sub procedures or Function procedures. The difference between both types of procedures is that a **Function procedure** returns a value after performing its assigned task, whereas a **Sub procedure** does not return a value. All of the applications coded in previous chapters contain Sub procedures that are predefined in Visual Basic, such as the Click, TextChanged, and KeyPress event procedures. In this chapter, you will learn how to create and use your own Sub procedures. You also will learn how to create and use Function procedures.

You also can create Property procedures in Visual Basic. Property procedures are covered in Chapter 12.

Sub Procedures

There are two types of Sub procedures in Visual Basic: event procedures and independent Sub procedures. The procedures coded in the previous chapters were event procedures. An event procedure is a Sub procedure that is associated with a specific object and event, such as a button's Click event or a text box's TextChanged event. The computer automatically processes an event procedure when the event occurs. An **independent Sub procedure**, on the other hand, is a procedure that is independent of any object and event. An independent Sub procedure is processed only when called (invoked) from code. Programmers use independent Sub procedures for several reasons. First, they allow the programmer to avoid duplicating code when different sections of a program need to perform the same task. Rather than enter the same code in each of those sections, the programmer can enter the code in a procedure and then have each section call the procedure to perform its task when needed. Second, consider an event procedure that must perform many tasks. To keep the event procedure's code from getting unwieldy and difficult to understand, the programmer can assign some of the tasks to one or more independent Sub procedures. Doing this makes the event procedure easier to code, because it allows the programmer to concentrate on one small piece of the code at a time. And finally, independent Sub procedures are used extensively in large and complex programs, which typically are written by a team of programmers. The programming team will break up the program into small and manageable tasks, and then assign some of the tasks to different team members to be coded as independent Sub procedures. Doing this allows more than one programmer to work on the program at the same time, decreasing the time it takes to write the program.

Figure 8-1 shows the syntax for creating an independent Sub procedure in Visual Basic. It also includes an example of an independent Sub procedure, as well as the steps for entering an independent Sub procedure in the Code Editor window. Some programmers enter independent Sub procedures above the first event procedure, while others enter them below the last event procedure. Still others enter them either immediately above or immediately below the procedure from which they are invoked. In this book, the independent Sub procedures will usually be entered above the first event procedure in the Code Editor window.

When you enter a procedure below the last event procedure in the Code Editor window, be sure to enter it above the End Class clause.

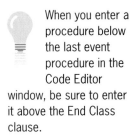

As the syntax in Figure 8-1 shows, independent Sub procedures have both a procedure header and a procedure footer. In most cases, the procedure header begins with the `Private` keyword, which indicates that the procedure can be used only within the current Code Editor window. Following the `Private` keyword is the `Sub` keyword, which identifies the procedure as a Sub procedure. After the `Sub` keyword is the procedure name. The rules for naming an independent Sub procedure are the same as those for naming variables; however, procedure names are usually entered using Pascal case. The Sub procedure's name should indicate the task the procedure performs. It is a common practice to begin the name with a verb. For example, a good name for a Sub procedure that clears the contents of the label controls in an interface is ClearLabels.

Using Pascal case, you capitalize the first letter in the procedure name and the first letter of each subsequent word in the name.

Following the procedure name in the procedure header is a set of parentheses that contains an optional *parameterList*. The *parameterList* lists the data type and name of one or more memory locations, called parameters. The **parameters** store the information passed to the procedure when it is invoked. If the procedure does not require any information to be passed to it, as is the case with the ClearLabels procedure in Figure 8-1, an empty set of parentheses follows the procedure name in the procedure header. You will learn more about parameters later in this chapter. A Sub procedure ends with its procedure footer, which is always `End Sub`. Between the procedure header and procedure footer, you enter the instructions to be processed when the procedure is invoked.

HOW TO Create an Independent Sub Procedure

Syntax

Private Sub *procedureName*(**[***parameterList***]**) — procedure header
    statements
End Sub — procedure footer

Example

```
Private Sub ClearLabels()
     regularLabel.Text = String.Empty
     overtimeLabel.Text = String.Empty
     grossLabel.Text = String.Empty
End Sub
```

(clears the contents of the labels)

Steps

1. Click a blank line in the Code Editor window. The blank line can be anywhere between the Public Class and End Class clauses. However, it must be outside any other Sub or Function procedure.
2. Type the Sub procedure header and then press Enter. The Code Editor automatically enters the End Sub clause for you.

Figure 8-1 How to create an independent Sub procedure

You can invoke an independent Sub procedure using the **Call statement**. Figure 8-2 shows the statement's syntax and includes an example of using the statement to invoke the ClearLabels procedure from Figure 8-1. In the syntax, *procedureName* is the name of the procedure you are calling (invoking), and *argumentList* (which is optional) is a comma-separated list of arguments you want passed to the procedure. If you have no information to pass to the procedure that you are calling, as is the case with the ClearLabels

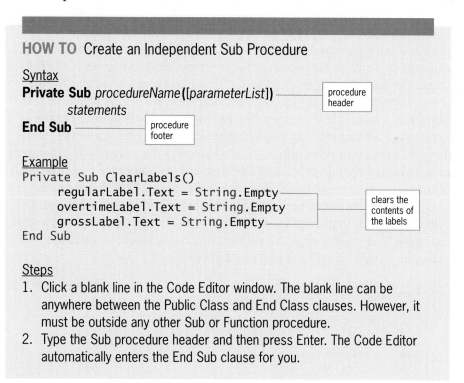

The `Call` keyword is optional when invoking a Sub procedure. Therefore, you also can call the ClearLabels procedure using the statement `ClearLabels()`.

procedure, you include an empty set of parentheses after the *procedureName* in the Call statement. The ClearLabels procedure is used in the Gadis Antiques application, which you view in the next section.

HOW TO Call an Independent Sub Procedure

Syntax
Call *procedureName*(*[argumentList]*)

Example
```
Call ClearLabels()
```

Figure 8-2 How to call an independent Sub procedure

The Gadis Antiques Application

If you want to experiment with the Gadis Antiques application, open the solution contained in the Try It 1! folder.

The manager at Gadis Antiques wants an application that calculates an employee's regular pay, overtime pay, and gross pay. Employees are paid on an hourly basis and receive time and one-half for the hours worked over 40. Figure 8-3 shows a sample run of the Gadis Antiques application, and Figure 8-4 shows a portion of the application's code. When the user clicks the Clear button in the interface, the button's Click event procedure should clear the contents of the regularLabel, overtimeLabel, and grossLabel. The labels also should be cleared in the TextChanged event procedures for the two combo boxes. Recall that the TextChanged event occurs when the text portion of a combo box changes. You can clear the labels by entering the appropriate assignment statements in the Click event procedure and in both TextChanged event procedures. Or, you can enter the assignment statements in an independent Sub procedure and then call the Sub procedure from each of the three event procedures, as shown in Figure 8-4. Entering the code in an independent Sub procedure saves you from having to enter the same statements more than once. In addition, if you subsequently need to assign the string "0.00" rather than the empty string to the labels, you will need to make the change in only one place in the code.

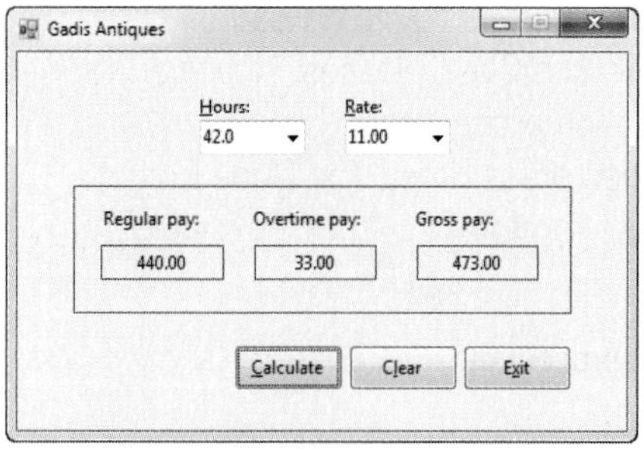

Figure 8-3 Sample run of the Gadis Antiques application

```
Public Class MainForm

    Private Sub ClearLabels()
        regularLabel.Text = String.Empty
        overtimeLabel.Text = String.Empty
        grossLabel.Text = String.Empty

    End Sub

    Private Sub MainForm_Load...

    Private Sub exitButton_Click...

    Private Sub calcButton_Click...

    Private Sub clearButton_Click(ByVal sender As Object,
    ByVal e As System.EventArgs) Handles clearButton.Click
        Call ClearLabels()
    End Sub

    Private Sub hoursComboBox_TextChanged(
    ByVal sender As Object, ByVal e As System.EventArgs
    ) Handles hoursComboBox.TextChanged
        Call ClearLabels()
    End Sub

    Private Sub rateComboBox_TextChanged(
    ByVal sender As Object, ByVal e As System.EventArgs
    ) Handles rateComboBox.TextChanged
        Call ClearLabels()
    End Sub
End Class
```

ClearLabels procedure

invokes the ClearLabels procedure

invokes the ClearLabels procedure

invokes the ClearLabels procedure

Figure 8-4 Partial code for the Gadis Antiques application

Notice that the ClearLabels procedure is entered above the event procedures in the code shown in Figure 8-4.

When the computer processes the `Call ClearLabels()` statement in the clearButton's Click event procedure, it temporarily leaves the procedure to process the code in the ClearLabels procedure. The assignment statements in the ClearLabels procedure remove the contents of the regularLabel, overtimeLabel, and grossLabel. After processing the assignment statements, the computer processes the ClearLabels procedure's End Sub clause, which ends the procedure. The computer then returns to the clearButton's Click event procedure and processes the line of code located immediately below the Call statement—in this case, the event procedure's End Sub clause. A similar process is followed when either combo box's TextChanged event occurs. The computer temporarily leaves the event procedure to process the code contained in the ClearLabels procedure. When the ClearLabels procedure ends, the computer returns to the event procedure and processes the code immediately below the Call statement.

Mini-Quiz 8-1

The answers to Mini-Quiz questions are located in Appendix A.

1. An event procedure is a Sub procedure that is associated with a specific object and event.

   a. True

   b. False

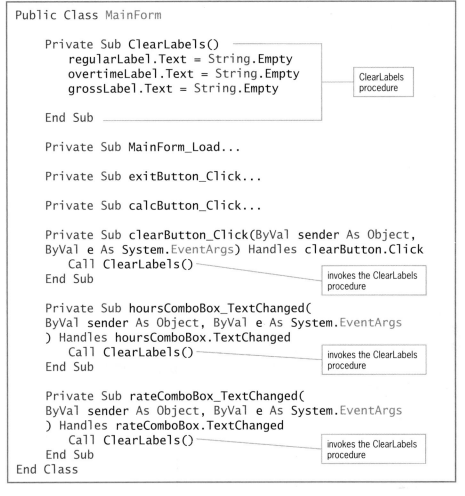

2. If the DisplayMessage procedure does not require any information to be passed to it, its procedure header should be ____________.
   a. `Private Sub DisplayMessage`
   b. `Private Sub DisplayMessage()`
   c. `Private Sub DisplayMessage(none)`
   d. `Private Sub DisplayMessage[]`

3. Which of the following invokes the DisplayMessage procedure from Question 2?
   a. `Call DisplayMessage`
   b. `Call Sub DisplayMessage()`
   c. `Call DisplayMessage(none)`
   d. `Call DisplayMessage()`

Including Parameters in an Independent Sub Procedure

As mentioned earlier, an independent Sub procedure can contain one or more parameters in its procedure header; each parameter stores an item of data. The data is passed to the procedure through the *argumentList* in the Call statement. The number of arguments in the Call statement's argumentList should agree with the number of parameters in the procedure's parameterList. If the parameterList contains one parameter, then the argumentList should have one argument. Similarly, a procedure that contains three parameters requires three arguments in the Call statement. (Refer to the first Tip on this page for an exception to this general rule.) In addition to having the same number of arguments as parameters, the data type and position of each argument should agree with the data type and position of its corresponding parameter. For example, if the first parameter has a data type of String and the second a data type of Double, then the first argument in the Call statement should have the String data type and the second should have the Double data type. This is because, when the procedure is called, the computer stores the value of the first argument in the procedure's first parameter, the value of the second argument in the second parameter, and so on. An argument can be a literal constant, named constant, keyword, or variable; however, in most cases, it will be a variable.

Visual Basic allows you to specify that an argument in the Call statement is optional. To learn more about optional arguments, complete Computer Exercise 29 at the end of this chapter.

Passing Variables

The internal memory of a computer is similar to a large post office. Like each post office box, each memory cell has a unique address.

Every variable has both a value and a unique address that represents its location in the computer's internal memory. Visual Basic allows you to pass either a copy of the variable's value or the variable's address to the receiving procedure. Passing a copy of the variable's value is referred to as **passing**

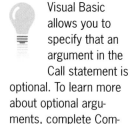

by value. Passing a variable's address is referred to as **passing by reference**. The method you choose—*by value* or *by reference*—depends on whether you want the receiving procedure to have access to the variable in memory. In other words, it depends on whether you want to allow the receiving procedure to change the variable's contents.

Although the idea of passing information *by value* and *by reference* may sound confusing at first, it is a concept with which you already are familiar. To illustrate, assume you have a savings account at a local bank. During a conversation with your friend Jake, you mention the amount of money you have in the account. Sharing this information with Jake is similar to passing a variable *by value*. Knowing your account balance does not give Jake access to your bank account. It merely provides information that he can use to compare to the balance in his savings account. The savings account example also provides an illustration of passing information *by reference*. To deposit money to or withdraw money from your account, you must provide the bank teller with your account number. The account number represents the location of your account at the bank and allows the teller to change the account balance. Giving the teller your bank account number is similar to passing a variable *by reference*. The account number allows the teller to change the contents of your bank account, similar to the way the variable's address allows the receiving procedure to change the contents of the variable.

Passing Variables by Value

To pass a variable *by value*, you include the keyword `ByVal` before the name of its corresponding parameter in the receiving procedure's parameterList. When you pass a variable *by value*, the computer passes a copy of the variable's contents to the receiving procedure. When only a copy of the contents is passed, the receiving procedure is not given access to the variable in memory. Therefore, it cannot change the value stored inside the variable. It is appropriate to pass a variable *by value* when the receiving procedure needs to *know* the variable's contents, but it does not need to *change* the contents. Unless you specify otherwise, variables in Visual Basic are automatically passed *by value*.

The Pet Information application provides an example of passing variables *by value*. Figure 8-5 shows a sample run of the application, and Figure 8-6 shows the code entered in two of the application's procedures: an independent Sub procedure named ShowMsg and the displayButton's Click event procedure. The Call statement in the Click event procedure passes two variables, *by value*, to the ShowMsg procedure: a String variable and an Integer variable. Notice that the number, data type, and sequence of the arguments in the Call statement match the number, data type, and sequence of the corresponding parameters in the ShowMsg procedure header. Also notice that the names of the arguments do not need to be identical to the names of the corresponding parameters. In fact, to avoid confusion, it usually is better to use different names for the arguments and parameters. The parameters in a procedure header have procedure scope, which means they can be used only by the procedure.

If you want to experiment with the Pet Information application, open the solution contained in the Try It 2! folder.

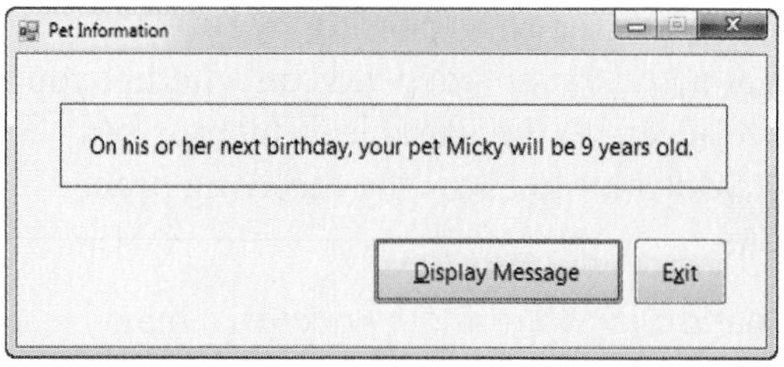

Figure 8-5 Sample run of the Pet Information application

The Call statement does not indicate whether a variable is being passed to a procedure *by value* or *by reference*. To make that determination, you need to look at the receiving procedure's header.

parameterList

```
Private Sub ShowMsg(ByVal pet As String, ByVal age As Integer)
      ' calculates age on next birthday, and
      ' displays name and next age in a message

      age = age + 1
      msgLabel.Text = "On his or her next birthday," &
            " your pet " & pet & " will be " &
            age & " years old."
End Sub


Private Sub displayButton_Click(ByVal sender As Object,
ByVal e As System.EventArgs) Handles displayButton.Click
      ' gets the pet information, then calls
      ' a procedure to display the information

      Dim inputName As String
      Dim inputAge As String
      Dim currentAge As Integer

      inputName = InputBox("Pet's name:", "Name")
      inputAge = InputBox("Pet's age (years):", "Age")
      Integer.TryParse(inputAge, currentAge)

      Call ShowMsg(inputName, currentAge)
End Sub
```

you also can use age += 1

argumentList

Figure 8-6 ShowMsg procedure and displayButton Click event procedure

The InputBox functions in the displayButton's Click event procedure prompt the user to enter the pet's name and age. If the user enters Micky as the name and 8 as the age, the functions store the strings "Micky" and "8" in the `inputName` and `inputAge` variables, respectively. The TryParse method then converts the contents of the String `inputAge` variable to Integer and stores the result in the Integer `currentAge` variable. Next, the Call statement calls the ShowMsg procedure, passing it the `inputName` and `currentAge` variables *by value*. You can tell that the variables are passed *by value* because the keyword `ByVal` appears before each variable's corresponding parameter in the ShowMsg procedure header. Passing both variables *by value* means that only a copy of the contents of both variables—in this case, the string "Micky" and the integer 8—are passed to the procedure. At this point, the computer temporarily leaves the displayButton's Click event procedure to process the ShowMsg procedure.

The parameterList in the ShowMsg procedure header tells the computer to create two procedure-level variables: a String variable named `pet` and an Integer variable named `age`. The computer stores a copy of the information passed to the procedure in those variables. In this case, it stores the string "Micky" in the `pet` variable and the integer 8 in the `age` variable. Next, the computer processes the statements contained within the procedure. The first statement adds the number 1 to the contents of the `age` variable and then assigns the sum (9) to the `age` variable. The last statement in the procedure displays a message that contains the values stored in the `pet` and `age` variables. As shown earlier in Figure 8-5, the statement displays the message "On his or her next birthday, your pet Micky will be 9 years old." The ShowMsg procedure footer is processed next and ends the procedure. At this point, the `pet` and `age` variables are removed from the computer's internal memory. (Recall that a procedure-level variable is removed from the computer's memory when the procedure ends.) The computer then returns to the displayButton's Click event procedure to process the line of code immediately following the Call statement. In this case, the line of code is the End Sub clause, which ends the event procedure. The computer then removes the `inputName`, `inputAge`, and `currentAge` procedure-level variables from its internal memory.

Passing Variables by Reference

Instead of passing a copy of a variable's value to a procedure, you can pass the variable's address. In other words, you can pass the variable's location in the computer's internal memory. As you learned earlier, passing a variable's address is referred to as passing *by reference*, and it gives the receiving procedure access to the variable being passed. You pass a variable *by reference* when you want the receiving procedure to change the contents of the variable. To pass a variable *by reference* in Visual Basic, you include the keyword `ByRef` before the name of its corresponding parameter in the receiving procedure's parameterList. The `ByRef` keyword tells the computer to pass the variable's address rather than a copy of its contents.

The Gross Pay application provides an example of passing a variable *by reference*. Figure 8-7 shows a sample run of the application, and Figure 8-8 shows the code entered in two of the application's procedures: an independent Sub procedure named CalcGrossPay and the calcButton's Click event procedure. Here again, notice that the number, data type, and sequence of the arguments in the Call statement match the number, data type, and sequence of the corresponding parameters in the procedure header. Also notice that the names of the arguments are not identical to the names of their corresponding parameters. The parameterList indicates that the first two variables in the argumentList are passed *by value*, and the third variable is passed *by reference*.

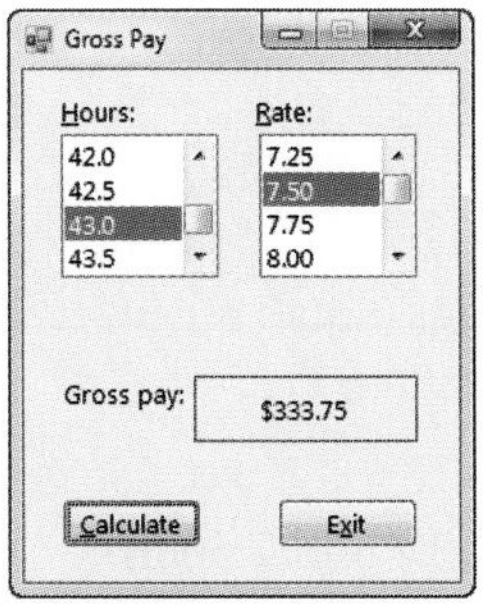

Figure 8-7 Sample run of the Gross Pay application

If you want to experiment with the Gross Pay application, open the solution contained in the Try It 3! folder.

```
Private Sub CalcGrossPay(ByVal hours As Double,
                         ByVal rate As Double,
                         ByRef gross As Double)
    ' calculates the gross pay

    gross = hours * rate
    ' add overtime, if necessary
    If hours > 40 Then
        gross = gross + (hours - 40) * rate / 2
    End If
End Sub


Private Sub calcButton_Click(ByVal sender As Object,
ByVal e As System.EventArgs) Handles calcButton.Click
    ' displays gross pay

    Dim hoursWkd As Double
    Dim rateOfPay As Double
    Dim grossPay As Double

    hoursWkd =
        Convert.ToDouble(hoursListBox.SelectedItem)
    rateOfPay =
        Convert.ToDouble(rateListBox.SelectedItem)

    ' use a Sub procedure to calculate the gross pay
    Call CalcGrossPay(hoursWkd, rateOfPay, grossPay)

    grossLabel.Text = grossPay.ToString("C2")
End Sub
```

parameterList

passed by value

passed by reference

Figure 8-8 CalcGrossPay procedure and calcButton Click event procedure

Desk-checking the procedures shown in Figure 8-8 will help clarify the difference between passing *by value* and passing *by reference.* **Desk-checking** refers to the process of reviewing the program instructions while seated at your desk rather than in front of the computer. Desk-checking is also called **hand-tracing**, because you use a pencil and paper to follow each of the instructions by hand. Before you begin the desk-check, you first choose a set of sample data for the input values, which you then use to manually compute the expected output values. You will desk-check Figure 8-8's procedures using 43 and $7.50 as the hours worked and rate of pay, respectively. The expected gross pay amount is $333.75, as shown in Figure 8-9.

43	hours worked
* 7.50	hourly pay rate
322.50	regular pay for 43 hours
+ 11.25	overtime pay for 3 hours at $3.75 per hour
333.75	gross pay

Figure 8-9 Gross pay calculation using sample input values

When the user clicks the Calculate button after selecting 43.0 and 7.50 in the hoursListBox and rateListBox, respectively, the Dim statements in the button's Click event procedure create and initialize three Double variables. Next, the two Convert.ToDouble methods convert the items selected in the list boxes to Double, storing the results in the `hoursWkd` and `rateOfPay` variables. Figure 8-10 shows the contents of the variables before the Call statement is processed.

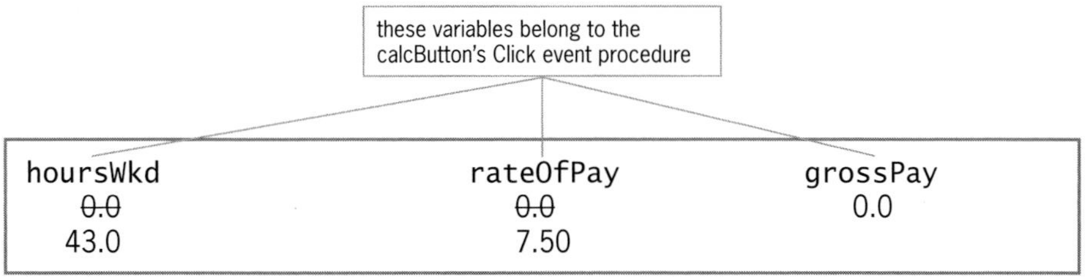

Figure 8-10 Desk-check table before the Call statement is processed

The computer processes the Call statement next. The Call statement invokes the CalcGrossPay procedure, passing it three arguments. At this point, the computer temporarily leaves the Click event procedure to process the code contained in the CalcGrossPay procedure; the procedure header is processed first. The `ByVal` keyword indicates that the first two parameters are receiving values from the Call statement—in this case, copies of the numbers stored in the `hoursWkd` and `rateOfPay` variables. As a result, the computer creates the `hours` and `rate` variables listed in the parameterList, and stores the numbers 43.0 and 7.50, respectively, in the variables. The `ByRef` keyword indicates that the third parameter is receiving the address of a variable. When you pass a variable's address to a procedure, the computer uses the address to locate the variable in its internal memory. It then assigns the parameter name to the memory location. In this case, the computer locates the `grossPay` variable in memory and assigns the name `gross` to it. At this point, the memory location has two names: one assigned by the calcButton's Click event procedure and the other assigned by the CalcGrossPay procedure, as indicated in Figure 8-11. Notice that two of the variables in the figure belong strictly to the Click event procedure, and two belong strictly to the CalcGrossPay procedure. One memory location, however, belongs to both procedures. Although both procedures can access the memory location, each procedure uses a different name to do so. The Click event procedure uses the name `grossPay`, whereas the CalcGrossPay procedure uses the name `gross`.

Although the `grossPay` and `gross` variables refer to the same location in memory, the `grossPay` variable is recognized only within the calcButton's Click event procedure. Similarly, the `gross` variable is recognized only within the CalcGrossPay procedure.

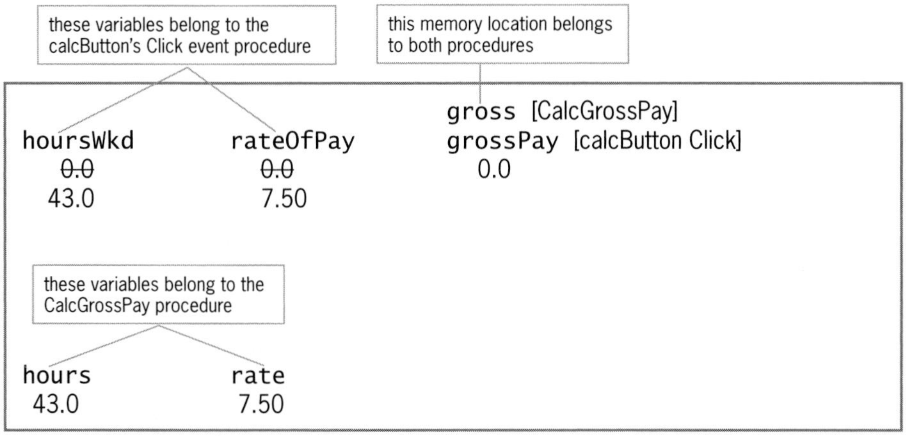

Figure 8-11 Desk-check table after the Call statement and CalcGrossPay procedure header are processed

After processing the CalcGrossPay procedure header, the computer processes the code contained in the procedure. The first statement calculates the gross pay by multiplying the contents of the `hours` variable (43.0) by the contents of the `rate` variable (7.50), and then assigns the result (322.50) to the `gross` variable. Figure 8-12 shows the desk-check table after the statement is processed. Notice that when the value in the `gross` variable changes, the value in the `grossPay` variable also changes. This happens because the names `gross` and `grossPay` refer to the same location in the computer's internal memory.

changing the value in the `gross` variable also changes the value in the `grossPay` variable

hoursWkd	rateOfPay	gross [CalcGrossPay] grossPay [calcButton Click]
~~0.0~~	~~0.0~~	~~0.0~~
43.0	7.50	322.50
hours	**rate**	
43.0	7.50	

Figure 8-12 Desk-check table after the first statement in the CalcGrossPay procedure is processed

The `hours` variable contains a value that is greater than 40, so the statement in the selection structure's true path calculates the overtime pay (11.25) and adds it to the regular pay (322.50); it assigns the result (333.75) to the `gross` variable. The result agrees with the manual calculation performed earlier. Figure 8-13 shows the desk-check table after the statement is processed.

hoursWkd	rateOfPay	gross [CalcGrossPay] grossPay [calcButton Click]
~~0.0~~	~~0.0~~	~~0.0~~
43.0	7.50	~~322.50~~
		333.75
hours	**rate**	
43.0	7.50	

Figure 8-13 Desk-check table after the statement in the selection structure's true path is processed

The CalcGrossPay procedure's End Sub clause is processed next and ends the procedure. At this point, the computer removes the `hours` and `rate` variables from memory. It also removes the `gross` name from the appropriate location in memory, as indicated in Figure 8-14. Notice that the `grossPay` memory location now has only one name: the name assigned to it by the calcButton's Click event procedure.

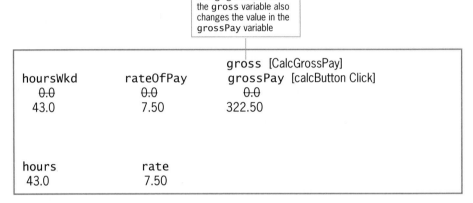

		~~gross [CalcGrossPay]~~
hoursWkd	rateOfPay	grossPay [calcButton Click]
~~0.0~~	~~0.0~~	~~0.0~~
43.0	7.50	~~322.50~~
		333.75
~~hours~~	~~rate~~	
~~43.0~~	~~7.50~~	

Figure 8-14 Desk-check table after the CalcGrossPay procedure ends

After the CalcGrossPay procedure ends, the computer returns to the line of code below the Call statement in the calcButton's Click event procedure. In this case, it returns to the `grossLabel.Text = grossPay.ToString("C2")` statement, which formats the contents of the `grossPay` variable and displays the result ($333.75) in the grossLabel, as shown earlier in Figure 8-7. Finally, the computer processes the Click event procedure's End Sub clause. When the Click event procedure ends, the computer removes the procedure's variables (`hoursWkd`, `rateOfpay`, and `grossPay`) from memory.

Mini-Quiz 8-2

The answers to Mini-Quiz questions are located in Appendix A.

1. Which of the following is a valid procedure header for a procedure that receives a copy of the values stored in two String variables?
   a. `Private Sub Display(ByRef x As String, ByRef y As String)`
   b. `Private Sub Display(ByVal x As String, ByVal y As String)`
   c. `Private Sub Display(ByValue x As String, ByValue y As String)`
   d. `Private Sub Display(ByCopy x As String, ByCopy y As String)`

2. Which of the following indicates that the procedure will receive two items of data: an integer and the address of a Double variable?
   a. `Private Sub Calc(ByVal x As Integer, ByRef y As Double)`
   b. `Private Sub Calc(Value x As Integer, Address y As Double)`
   c. `Private Sub Calc(ByInt x As Integer, ByAdd y As Double)`
   d. `Private Sub Calc(ByCopy x As Integer, ByAdd y As Double)`

3. Which of the following invokes the Calc procedure from Question 2, passing it an Integer variable named `sales` and a Double variable named `bonus`?

   a. `Call Calc(ByVal sales, ByRef bonus)`

   b. `Call Calc(sales, bonus)`

   c. `Call Calc(bonus, sales)`

   d. both b and c

Associating a Procedure with Different Objects and Events

As you learned in Chapter 1, the Handles clause in an event procedure's header indicates the object and event associated with the procedure. The `Handles clearButton.Click` clause in Figure 8-15, for example, indicates that the clearButton_Click procedure is associated with the Click event of the clearButton. As a result, the procedure will be processed when the clearButton's Click event occurs. Although an event procedure's name—in this case, clearButton_Click—contains the names of its associated object and event, that is not a requirement. You can change the name of an event procedure to any name that follows the naming rules for procedures. For example, you can change the name clearButton_Click to Clear and the procedure will still work correctly. This is because the Handles clause, rather than the event procedure's name, determines when the procedure is processed.

```
Private Sub ClearLabels()
     regularLabel.Text = String.Empty
     overtimeLabel.Text = String.Empty
     grossLabel.Text = String.Empty
End Sub

Private Sub clearButton_Click(ByVal sender As Object,
ByVal e As System.EventArgs) Handles clearButton.Click
     Call ClearLabels()
End Sub

Private Sub hoursComboBox_TextChanged(
ByVal sender As Object, ByVal e As System.EventArgs
) Handles hoursComboBox.TextChanged
     Call ClearLabels()
End Sub

Private Sub rateComboBox_TextChanged(
ByVal sender As Object, ByVal e As System.EventArgs
) Handles rateComboBox.TextChanged
     Call ClearLabels()
End Sub
```

procedure name

the Handles clause determines when the procedure is processed

Figure 8-15 Some of the Gadis Antiques application's code from Figure 8-4

You can associate a procedure with more than one object and event, as long as each event contains the same parameters in its procedure header. In the code shown in Figure 8-15, for instance, you can associate the ClearLabels procedure with the clearButton's Click event and the TextChanged events for the two combo boxes. This is because the three event procedures have the same parameters in their procedure header: `sender` and `e`. You may have noticed that all event procedures contain the `sender` and `e` parameters in their procedure header. The **sender parameter** contains the memory address of the object that raised the event (in other words, caused the event to occur). For example, when the clearButton's Click event occurs, the button's address in memory is stored in the `sender` parameter. Similarly, when the TextChanged event occurs for either of the combo boxes, the corresponding combo box's memory address is stored in the `sender` parameter. The **e parameter** in an event procedure's header contains additional information provided by the object that raised the event. The `e` parameter in the KeyPress event procedure's header, for instance, contains a character that corresponds to the key pressed by the user. You can determine the items of information contained in an event procedure's `e` parameter by viewing its properties. You do this by displaying the event procedure's code template in the Code Editor window, and then typing the letter e followed by a period. The Code Editor displays a list that includes the `e` parameter's properties.

You learned about a text box's KeyPress event in Chapter 5.

To associate a procedure with more than one object and event, you enter the appropriate parameters in the procedure's parameterList, and then enter each object and event in the procedure's Handles clause. You use commas to separate each parameter and also to separate each object and event. In the ClearLabels procedure in Figure 8-16, the Handles clause tells the computer to process the procedure's code when any of the following occurs: the clearButton's Click event, the hoursComboBox's TextChanged event, or the rateComboBox's TextChanged event. The ClearLabels procedure in Figure 8-16 can be used in place of the ClearLabels, clearButton_Click, hoursComboBox_TextChanged, and rateComboBox_TextChanged procedures shown in Figure 8-15.

If you want to experiment with the code shown in Figure 8-16, open the solution contained in the Try It 4! folder.

```
Private Sub ClearLabels(ByVal sender As Object,
                        ByVal e As System.EventArgs
                        ) Handles clearButton.Click,
                        hoursComboBox.TextChanged,
                        rateComboBox.TextChanged
    regularLabel.Text = String.Empty
    overtimeLabel.Text = String.Empty
    grossLabel.Text = String.Empty
End Sub
```

parameterList

the Handles clause associates the procedure with three objects and events

Figure 8-16 ClearLabels procedure

Function Procedures

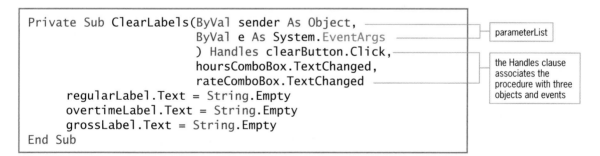

In addition to creating Sub procedures in Visual Basic, you also can create Function procedures. Recall that the difference between both types of procedures is that a Function procedure returns a value after performing its assigned task, whereas a Sub procedure does not return a value. Function procedures are referred to more simply as **functions**. Figure 8-17 shows the syntax for creating a function in Visual Basic. The header and footer in a function are almost identical to the header and footer in a Sub procedure, except the function's header and footer contain the `Function` keyword rather than the `Sub` keyword. Also different from a Sub procedure header, a function's header includes the `As` *dataType* section, which specifies the data type of the value returned by the function. As is true with a Sub procedure, a function can receive information either *by value* or *by reference*. The information it receives is listed in the parameterList in the header. Between the function's header and footer, you enter the instructions to process when the function is invoked. In most cases, the **Return statement** is the last statement within a function. The Return statement's syntax is `Return` *expression*, where *expression* represents the one and only value that will be returned to the statement invoking the function. The data type of the *expression* must agree with the data type specified in the `As` *dataType* section.

In addition to the syntax, Figure 8-17 also includes two examples of a function, as well as the steps you follow to enter a function in the Code Editor window. As with Sub procedures, you can enter your functions above the first event procedure, below the last event procedure, or immediately above or below the procedure from which they are invoked. In this book, you usually will enter the functions above the first event procedure. Like Sub procedure names, function names are entered using Pascal case and typically begin with a verb. The name should indicate the task the function performs. For example, a good name for a function that returns the area of a circle is GetCircleArea.

HOW TO Create a Function Procedure

<u>Syntax</u>

Private Function *procedureName*(*[parameterList]*) **As** *dataType*
    statements
    Return *expression*
End Function

function header
function footer
specifies the data type of the return value

<u>Example 1</u>

```
Private Function GetCircleArea(ByVal radius As Double) As Double
    Dim area As Double
    area = 3.141593 * radius ^ 2
    Return area
End Function
```

returns the `area` variable's value to the statement that called the function

<u>Example 2</u>

```
Private Function GetCircleArea(ByVal radius As Double) As Double
    Return 3.141593 * radius ^ 2
End Function
```

calculates and returns the area to the statement that called the function

<u>Steps</u>

1. Click a blank line in the Code Editor window. The blank line can be anywhere between the Public Class and End Class clauses. However, it must be outside any other Sub or Function procedure.
2. Type the Function procedure header and then press Enter. The Code Editor automatically enters the End Function clause for you.

Figure 8-17 How to create a Function procedure

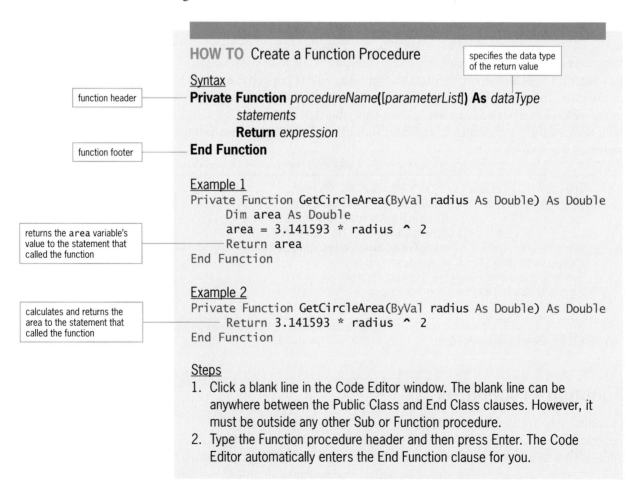

You can invoke a function from one or more places in an application's code. You invoke a function that you create in exactly the same way as you invoke one of Visual Basic's built-in functions, such as the InputBox function. You do this by including the function's name and arguments (if any) in a statement. The number, data type, and position of the arguments should agree with the number, data type, and position of the function's parameters. In most cases, the statement that invokes a function assigns the function's return value to a variable. However, it also may use the return value in a calculation or simply display the return value. Figure 8-18 shows examples of invoking the GetCircleArea function from Figure 8-17. The `GetCircleArea(circleRadius)` entry in each example invokes the function, passing it the value stored in the `circleRadius` variable.

HOW TO Invoke a Function Procedure

Example 1 – assign the return value to a variable
```
circleArea = GetCircleArea(circleRadius)
```

Example 2 – use the return value in a calculation
```
halveArea = GetCircleArea(circleRadius) / 2
```
the assignment statement divides the function's return value by 2 and assigns the result to the `halveArea` variable

Example 3 – display the return value
```
areaLabel.Text = GetCircleArea(circleRadius).ToString
```

Figure 8-18 How to invoke a Function procedure

The Circle Area Calculator Application

If you want to experiment with the Circle Area Calculator application, open the solution contained in the Try It 5! folder.

The Circle Area Calculator application uses the GetCircleArea function from the previous section to calculate the area of a circle. It then displays the area in the areaLabel. Figure 8-19 shows a sample run of the application, and Figure 8-20 shows a portion of the application's code.

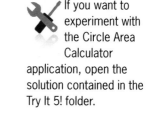

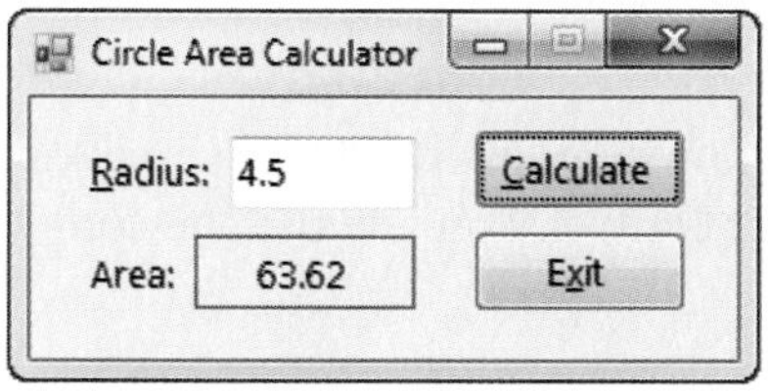

Figure 8-19 Sample run of the Circle Area Calculator application

GetCircleArea function

invokes the GetCircleArea function and assigns the return value to the circleArea variable

```
Private Function GetCircleArea(ByVal radius As Double) As Double
     Dim area As Double
     area = 3.141593 * radius ^ 2
     Return area
End Function

Private Sub calcButton_Click(ByVal sender As Object,
ByVal e As System.EventArgs) Handles calcButton.Click
     Dim circleRadius As Double
     Dim circleArea As Double

     Double.TryParse(radiusTextBox.Text, circleRadius)
     circleArea = GetCircleArea(circleRadius)
     areaLabel.Text = circleArea.ToString("N2")
End Sub
```

Figure 8-20 Partial code for the Circle Area Calculator application

The `circleArea = GetCircleArea(circleRadius)` statement in the calcButton's Click event procedure calls the GetCircleArea function, passing it the value stored in the `circleRadius` variable. The computer stores the value in the `radius` variable listed in the function's header. After processing the header, the computer processes the statements contained in the function. The Dim statement in the function creates and initializes the Double `area` variable. Next, the assignment statement calculates the circle's area, using the radius value passed to the function, and assigns the result to the `area` variable. The `Return area` statement then returns the contents of the `area` variable to the statement that invoked the function. That statement is the `circleArea = GetCircleArea(circleRadius)` statement in the calcButton's Click event procedure. The End Function clause is processed next and ends the function. At this point, the computer removes the `radius` and `area` variables from its internal memory.

To review what you learned about Sub and Function procedures, view the Ch08SubAndFunction video.

The `circleArea = GetCircleArea(circleRadius)` statement in the calcButton's Click event procedure assigns the function's return value to the `circleArea` variable. The next statement in the event procedure displays the contents of the `circleArea` variable in the areaLabel, as shown earlier in Figure 8-19. The End Sub clause is processed next and ends the procedure. The computer then removes the `circleRadius` and `circleArea` variables from its internal memory.

The last concepts covered in this chapter are how to convert Object variables to a different data type and how to use a timer control. You will use the concepts in this chapter's programming tutorials.

Converting Object Variables

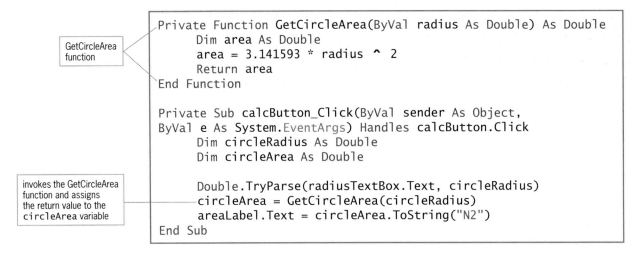

Every event procedure contains the `ByVal sender As Object` code in its procedure header. The code creates a variable named `sender` and assigns the Object data type to it. As you learned in Chapter 3, an Object variable can store any type of data. In this case, the `sender` variable contains the address of the object that raised the event. Unlike variables declared using the String and numeric data types, variables declared using the Object data type do not have a set of properties. This is because there are no common attributes for all of the different types of data that can be stored in an Object variable. If you need to access the properties of the object whose address is stored in the `sender` variable, you must convert the variable to the appropriate data type. The process of converting a variable from one data type to another is sometimes referred to as **type casting** or, more simply, as **casting**. You can cast a variable from the Object data type to a different data type using the **TryCast operator**. The operator's syntax is shown in Figure 8-21, along with examples of using the operator.

HOW TO Use the TryCast Operator

Syntax
TryCast(*object, dataType***)**

Example 1
```
Dim thisTextBox As TextBox
thisTextBox = TryCast(sender, TextBox)
thisTextBox.SelectAll()
```
The assignment statement casts (converts) the `sender` variable to the TextBox data type and assigns the result to a TextBox variable named `thisTextBox`. The SelectAll method selects (highlights) the contents of the text box whose address is stored in the `thisTextBox` variable.

Example 2
```
Dim clickedButton As Button
clickedButton = TryCast(sender, Button)
MessageBox.Show(clickedButton.Text)
```
The assignment statement casts (converts) the `sender` variable to the Button data type and assigns the result to a Button variable named `clickedButton`. The MessageBox.Show method displays the Text property of the button whose address is stored in the `clickedButton` variable.

Figure 8-21 How to use the TryCast operator

The Full Name Application

The Full Name application allows the user to enter a first name and a last name. It then concatenates both names and displays the result in the interface. When a text box in the interface receives the focus, the application's code selects the text box's existing text. Figure 8-22 shows a sample run of the application, and Figure 8-23 shows two ways of writing the code for each text box's Enter event. As shown in Version 1, you can enter the appropriate SelectAll method in each text box's Enter event procedure. Or, as Version 2 indicates, you can associate each text box's Enter event with the SelectText procedure and then enter the TryCast operator and SelectAll method in that procedure.

If you want to experiment with the Full Name application, open the solution contained in the Try It 6! folder.

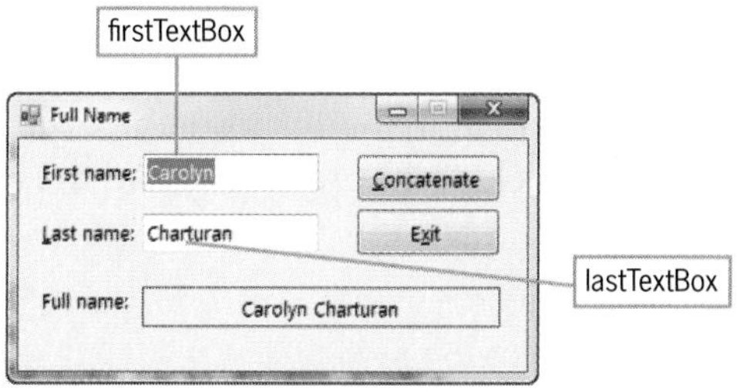

Figure 8-22 Sample run of the Full Name application

Version 1

```
Private Sub firstTextBox_Enter(ByVal sender As Object,
ByVal e As System.EventArgs) Handles firstTextBox.Enter
      ' selects the existing text

      firstTextBox.SelectAll()
End Sub

Private Sub lastTextBox_Enter(ByVal sender As Object,
ByVal e As System.EventArgs) Handles lastTextBox.Enter
      ' selects the existing text

      lastTextBox.SelectAll()
End Sub
```

Version 2

```
Private Sub SelectText(ByVal sender As Object,
                       ByVal e As System.EventArgs
                       ) Handles firstTextBox.Enter,
                       lastTextBox.Enter
      ' selects the existing text

      Dim thisTextBox As TextBox
      thisTextBox = TryCast(sender, TextBox)
      thisTextBox.SelectAll()
End Sub
```

selects the firstTextBox's text

selects the lastTextBox's text

assigns the text box that raised the Enter event to the `thisTextBox` variable, and then selects the text box's text

Figure 8-23 Two ways of writing the Enter event procedures for both text boxes

Using a Timer Control

The game application in Programming Tutorial 2 requires you to use a timer control. You instantiate a timer control using the Timer tool, which is located in the Components section of the toolbox. Timer controls are not placed on the form; instead, they are placed in the component tray. Recall that the component tray stores controls that do not appear in the user interface during run time. The purpose of a **timer control** is to process code at one or more regular intervals. The length of each interval is specified in milliseconds and entered in the timer's **Interval property**. As you learned in Chapter 6, a millisecond is 1/1000 of a second. In other words, there are 1000 milliseconds in a second. The timer's state—either running or stopped—is determined by its Enabled property. When its Enabled property is set to True, the timer is running; when it is set to False, the timer is stopped. If the timer is running, its **Tick event** occurs each time an interval has elapsed. Each time the Tick event occurs, the code contained in the Tick event procedure is processed. If the timer is stopped, the Tick event does not occur; as a result, the code entered in the Tick event procedure is not processed.

The Timer Example application uses a timer to blink a label 10 times. Figure 8-24 shows the application's interface, and Figure 8-25 shows the code entered in two procedures: the Blink button's Click event procedure and the timer's Tick event procedure.

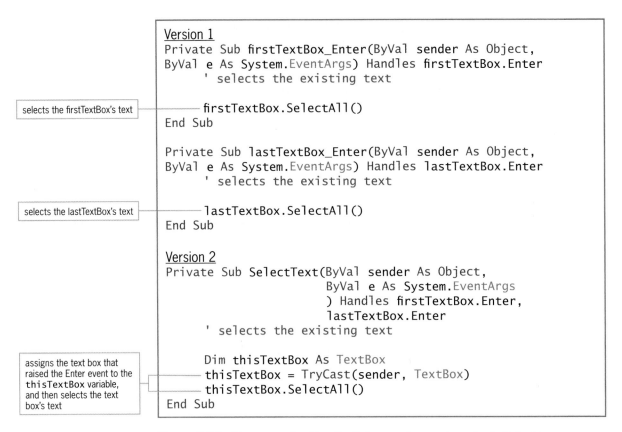

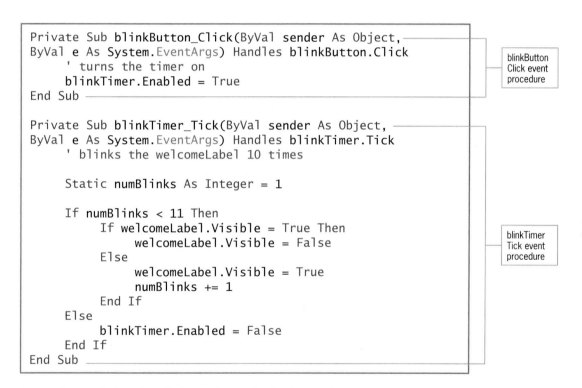

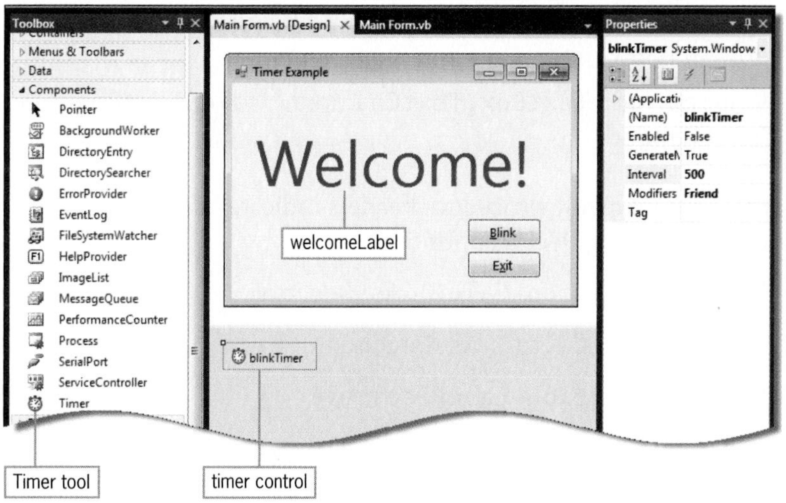

Figure 8-24 Interface for the Timer Example application

If you want to experiment with the Timer Example application, open the solution contained in the Try It 7! folder.

```
Private Sub blinkButton_Click(ByVal sender As Object,
ByVal e As System.EventArgs) Handles blinkButton.Click
     ' turns the timer on
     blinkTimer.Enabled = True
End Sub

Private Sub blinkTimer_Tick(ByVal sender As Object,
ByVal e As System.EventArgs) Handles blinkTimer.Tick
     ' blinks the welcomeLabel 10 times

     Static numBlinks As Integer = 1

     If numBlinks < 11 Then
          If welcomeLabel.Visible = True Then
               welcomeLabel.Visible = False
          Else
               welcomeLabel.Visible = True
               numBlinks += 1
          End If
     Else
          blinkTimer.Enabled = False
     End If
End Sub
```

blinkButton Click event procedure

blinkTimer Tick event procedure

Figure 8-25 Code entered in two of the application's procedures

Mini-Quiz 8-3

The answers to Mini-Quiz questions are located in Appendix A.

1. Which of the following Handles clauses associates a procedure with the TextChanged events of the nameTextBox and salesTextBox?
   a. `Handles nameTextBox_TextChanged, salesTextBox_TextChanged`
   b. `Handles nameTextBox.TextChanged AndAlso salesTextBox.TextChanged`

c. `Handles nameTextBox-TextChanged, salesTextBox-TextChanged`

d. `Handles nameTextBox.TextChanged, salesTextBox.TextChanged`

2. Which of the following procedure headers indicates that the procedure returns a Decimal number?

   a. `Private Function Calc() As Decimal`

   b. `Private Sub Calc() As Decimal`

   c. `Private Function Calc(Decimal)`

   d. both a and b

3. A function can return ______________.

   a. zero or more values

   b. one or more values

   c. one value only

4. Which of the following converts the `sender` parameter to the Label data type, assigning the result to a Label variable named `currentLabel`?

   a. `TryCast(sender, Label, currentLabel)`

   b. `currentLabel = TryCast(sender, Label)`

   c. `currentLabel = TryCast(Label, sender)`

   d. `sender = TryCast(currentLabel, Label)`

5. To turn on a timer, you set its ______________ property to True.

   a. Enabled

   b. Running

   c. Start

   d. none of the above

You have completed the concepts section of Chapter 8. The Programming Tutorial section is next.

PROGRAMMING TUTORIAL 1

Coding the Tri-County Electricity Application

In this tutorial, you code an application for the Tri-County Electricity Company. Figures 8-26 and 8-27 show the application's TOE chart and MainForm, respectively. The MainForm contains a group box, two radio buttons, two text boxes, six labels, and two buttons. The interface allows the user to enter three items of data: the rate code, previous meter reading, and current meter reading. When the user clicks the Calculate button, the button's Click event procedure should verify that the current meter reading is greater than or equal to the previous meter reading. If it is, the application should both calculate and display the number of electrical units used during the month and the total charge. The total charge is based on the number of units used and the rate code. Residential customers are charged $0.09 per unit, with a minimum charge of $17.65. Commercial customers are charged $0.11 per unit, with a minimum charge of $21.75. If the current meter reading is less than the previous meter reading, the application should display an appropriate message.

Task	Object	Event
End the application	exitButton	Click
Get the rate code	residentialRadioButton, commercialRadioButton	None
Get and display the current meter reading and previous meter reading	currentTextBox, previousTextBox	None
Select the existing text	currentTextBox, previousTextBox	Enter
Allow only numbers and the Backspace key	currentTextBox, previousTextBox	KeyPress
Clear usageLabel and totalLabel	currentTextBox, previousTextBox	TextChanged
	residentialRadioButton, commercialRadioButton	Click
1. Determine whether the current meter reading is greater than or equal to the previous meter reading 2. If necessary, calculate the monthly usage and total charge and then display the results in the usageLabel and totalLabel 3. If necessary, display "The current reading must be greater than or equal to the previous reading." message in a message box	calcButton	Click
Display monthly usage (from calcButton)	usageLabel	None
Display total charge (from calcButton)	totalLabel	None

Figure 8-26 TOE chart for the Tri-County Electricity application

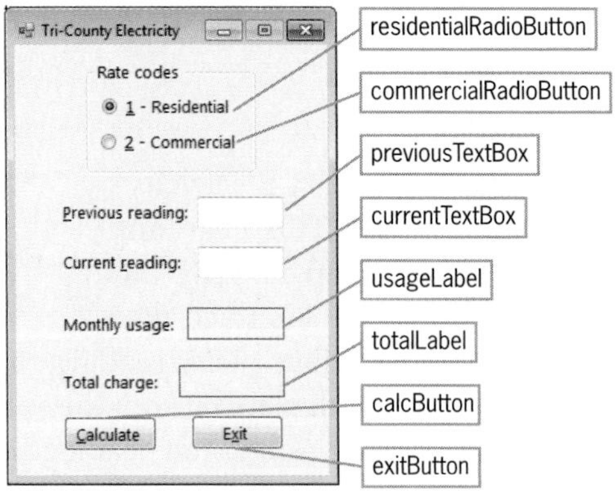

Figure 8-27 MainForm in the Tri-County Electricity application

Coding the Application

Included in the data files for this book is a partially completed Tri-County Electricity application. To complete the application, you just need to code it. According to the application's TOE chart, the Click event procedures for the two buttons and two radio buttons need to be coded. Each text box's Enter, KeyPress, and TextChanged event procedures also need to be coded.

To open the Tri-County Electricity application:

1. Start Visual Studio or the Express Edition of Visual Basic. If necessary, open the Solution Explorer window.
2. Open the **Tri-County Electricity Solution** (**Tri-County Electricity Solution.sln**) file, which is contained in the VbReloaded2010\Chap08\Tri-County Electricity Solution folder. Open the designer window (if necessary), and then auto-hide the Solution Explorer window.
3. Open the Code Editor window. Notice that the exitButton's Click event procedure has already been coded for you. In addition, the Option statements have already been entered in the General Declarations section.
4. In the comments that appear in the General Declarations section, replace <your name> and <current date> with your name and the current date.

First, you will code the Enter event procedures for both text boxes. The procedures should select the text box's existing text when the text box receives the focus. You can code each text box's Enter event procedure individually. Or, you can enter the code in a Sub procedure and then associate both Enter events with the procedure; this is the method you will use.

To code each text box's Enter event procedure:

1. Open the code template for the currentTextBox's Enter event procedure. In the procedure header, change `currentTextBox_Enter` to **SelectText**.
2. Change the Handles clause in the procedure header to the following:

   Handles currentTextBox.Enter, previousTextBox.Enter
3. In the blank line below the procedure header, type **' select existing text** and press **Enter** twice.

4. Now, enter the following code:

   Dim thisTextBox As TextBox
   thisTextBox = TryCast(sender, TextBox)
   thisTextBox.SelectAll()

5. Save the solution and then start the application. Type **12** in the Previous reading box, press **Tab**, and then type **200** in the Current reading box. Press **Tab** four times to move the focus to the Previous reading box; doing this selects the text entered in the box. Press **Tab** again to move the focus to the Current reading box, which selects that box's text.

6. Click the **Exit** button.

Next, you will code the KeyPress event procedures for both text boxes. Each procedure should allow its text box to accept only numbers and the Backspace key. Here again, you can code each KeyPress event procedure separately. Or, you can enter the code in a Sub procedure that is associated with both KeyPress events.

To code each text box's KeyPress event procedure:

1. Open the code template for the currentTextBox's KeyPress event procedure. In the procedure header, change `currentTextBox_KeyPress` to **CancelKeys**.

2. Change the Handles clause in the procedure header to the following:

   Handles currentTextBox.KeyPress, previousTextBox.KeyPress

3. In the blank line below the procedure header, type **' allow only numbers and the Backspace** and press **Enter** twice.

4. Now, enter the following code (the Code Editor will automatically enter the End If clause for you):

   If (e.KeyChar < "0" OrElse e.KeyChar > "9") AndAlso
   e.KeyChar <> ControlChars.Back Then
   e.Handled = True

5. Save the solution and then start the application. On your own, test the KeyPress event procedures. You can do this by trying to enter characters other than numbers into each text box. Also be sure to verify that the text boxes accept numbers and the Backspace key.

6. Click the **Exit** button.

Next, you will code the TextChanged event procedures for both text boxes and the Click event procedures for both radio buttons. The procedures should clear the contents of the usageLabel and totalLabel when either of those events occurs. Here too, you can code each TextChanged event procedure individually. Or, you can enter the code in a Sub procedure that is associated with both TextChanged events.

To code each text box's TextChanged event procedure and each radio button's Click event procedure:

1. Open the code template for the currentTextBox's TextChanged event procedure. In the procedure header, change `currentTextBox_TextChanged` to **ClearLabels**.

2. Change the Handles clause in the procedure header to the following:

   Handles currentTextBox.TextChanged, previousTextBox.TextChanged, residentialRadioButton.Click, commercialRadioButton.Click

3. In the blank line below the procedure header, type **' clear calculated value** and press **Enter** twice.

4. Now, enter the following code:

   usageLabel.Text = String.Empty
   totalLabel.Text = String.Empty

5. Save the solution. You won't be able to test the ClearLabels procedure until the calcButton's Click event procedure is coded.

Completing the Application's Code

Figure 8-28 shows the pseudocode for the calcButton's Click event procedure. As the pseudocode indicates, the procedure will use a Sub procedure to calculate the total charge for residential customers, and a function to calculate the total charge for commercial customers. A Sub procedure and function were chosen, rather than two Sub procedures or two function procedures, simply to allow you to practice with both types of procedures. The pseudocode for both procedures is included in Figure 8-28.

```
calcButton Click event procedure
1. assign user input (previous reading and current reading) to variables
2. if current reading is greater than or equal to previous reading
       usage = current reading – previous reading

       if the residentialRadioButton is selected
              call CalcResidentialTotal Sub procedure to calculate
              the total charge; pass the procedure the usage value
              and a variable in which to store the total charge
       else
              total charge = call the GetCommercialTotal function; pass
              the function the usage value
       end if
       display the usage and total charge in usageLabel and totalLabel
   else
       display message in a message box
   end if

CalcResidentialTotal procedure (receives the usage value and the address of a variable in which to store the total charge)
1. declare constants to store the unit charge (.09) and the minimum fee (17.65)
2. total charge = usage value * unit charge
3. if total charge is less than the minimum fee
       total charge = minimum fee
   end if

GetCommercialTotal function (receives the usage value)
1. declare constants to store the unit charge (.12) and the minimum fee (21.75)
2. declare a variable to store the total charge
3. total charge = usage value * unit charge
4. if total charge is less than the minimum fee
       total charge = minimum fee
   end if
5. return total charge
```

Figure 8-28 Pseudocode for three procedures in the Tri-County Electricity application

You will code the CalcResidentialTotal Sub procedure first. According to its pseudocode, the procedure will receive two items of data from the statement that calls it: the usage value and the address of a variable where it can place the total charge after it has been calculated. The procedure will store the information it receives in two parameters named `units` and `charge`.

To code the CalcResidentialTotal Sub procedure:

1. Scroll to the top of the Code Editor window. Click the **blank line** below the `Public Class MainForm` clause and then press **Enter** to insert a new blank line. Enter the following procedure header and comments. Press **Enter** twice after typing the second comment. (When you press Enter after typing the procedure header, the Code Editor automatically enters the End Sub clause for you.)

```
Private Sub CalcResidentialTotal(ByVal units As Integer,
                                  ByRef charge As Double)

    ' calculates the total charge for a
    ' residential customer
```

2. Step 1 in the pseudocode is to declare constants to store the unit charge and minimum fee. Enter the following declaration statements. Press **Enter** twice after typing the second declaration statement.

```
Const UnitCharge As Double = .09
Const MinFee As Double = 17.65
```

3. Step 2 is to calculate the total charge. Enter the following assignment statement:

```
    charge = units * UnitCharge
```

4. Step 3 is a single-alternative selection structure that compares the total charge with the minimum fee. If the total charge is less than the minimum fee, the selection structure's true path assigns the minimum fee as the total charge. Enter the following code (the Code Editor will automatically enter the End If clause for you):

```
If charge < MinFee Then
    charge = MinFee
```

5. Save the solution.

Next, you will code the GetCommercialTotal function. According to its pseudocode, the function will receive one item of data from the statement that calls it: the usage value. The function will store the usage value in a parameter named `units`.

To code the GetCommercialTotal function:

1. Click immediately after the letter **b** in the CalcResidentialTotal procedure's End Sub clause, and then press **Enter** twice.

2. Enter the following function header and comments. Press **Enter** twice after typing the second comment. (When you press Enter after typing the function header, the Code Editor automatically enters the End Function clause for you. Don't be concerned about the jagged line

that appears below the clause; it will disappear when you enter the Return statement.)

```
Private Function GetCommercialTotal(ByVal units As Integer) As Double
    ' calculates the total charge for a
    ' commercial customer
```

3. Step 1 in the pseudocode is to declare constants to store the unit charge and minimum fee. Enter the following declaration statements:

```
Const UnitCharge As Double = .12
Const MinFee As Double = 21.75
```

4. Step 2 is to declare a variable to store the total charge. Type the following declaration statement and then press **Enter** twice:

```
Dim charge As Double
```

5. Step 3 is to calculate the total charge. Enter the following assignment statement:

```
    charge = units * UnitCharge
```

6. Step 4 is a single-alternative selection structure that compares the total charge with the minimum fee. If the total charge is less than the minimum fee, the selection structure's true path assigns the minimum fee as the total charge. Enter the following code (the Code Editor will automatically enter the End If clause for you):

```
If charge < MinFee Then
   charge = MinFee
```

7. The final step in the pseudocode is to return the total charge. Click immediately after the letter **f** in the End If clause and then press **Enter** twice. Enter the following statement:

```
Return charge
```

8. Save the solution.

The last procedure you need to code is the calcButton's Click event procedure.

To code the calcButton's Click event procedure and then test the code:

1. Open the code template for the calcButton's Click event procedure. Type **' displays the monthly usage and total charge** and press **Enter** twice.

2. The procedure will use three Integer variables to store the previous reading, current reading, and usage amount. It also will use a Double variable to store the total charge. Enter the following declaration statements. Press **Enter** twice after typing the last declaration statement.

```
Dim previous As Integer
Dim current As Integer
Dim usage As Integer
Dim total As Double
```

3. The first step in the pseudocode is to assign the user input to variables. Enter the following TryParse methods. Press **Enter** twice after typing the last TryParse method.

   Integer.TryParse(previousTextBox.Text, previous)
   Integer.TryParse(currentTextBox.Text, current)

4. Step 2 in the pseudocode is a dual-alternative selection structure that determines whether the current reading is greater than or equal to the previous reading. If the selection structure's condition evaluates to True, the first instruction in the true path calculates the usage amount. Enter the additional code shown in Figure 8-29, and then position the insertion point as shown in the figure.

```
        Integer.TryParse(previousTextBox.Text, previous)
        Integer.TryParse(currentTextBox.Text, current)

        If current >= previous Then
            usage = current - previous
            |
        End If
    End Sub
```

enter these lines of code

position the insertion point here

Figure 8-29 Additional code entered in the calcButton's Click event procedure

5. The next instruction in the true path is a nested dual-alternative selection structure. The nested selection structure's condition determines whether the residentialRadioButton is selected in the interface. If the condition evaluates to True, the nested selection structure's true path calls the CalcResidentialTotal Sub procedure, passing it the `usage` and `total` variables. Recall that the `usage` variable is passed *by value*, whereas the `total` variable is passed *by reference*. If the condition evaluates to False, on the other hand, the nested selection structure's false path invokes the GetCommercialTotal function, passing it the `usage` variable *by value*, and then assigns the return value to the `total` variable. Enter the nested selection structure shown in Figure 8-30, and then position the insertion point as shown in the figure.

```
        If current >= previous Then
            usage = current - previous
            If residentialRadioButton.Checked = True Then
                Call CalcResidentialTotal(usage, total)
            Else
                total = GetCommercialTotal(usage)
            End If

            |
        End If
    End Sub
```

enter the nested selection structure

position the insertion point here

Figure 8-30 Nested selection structure entered in the calcButton's Click event procedure

6. The last instruction in the outer selection structure's true path is to display the usage and total charge in the usageLabel and totalLabel, respectively. Enter the following two assignment statements:

   usageLabel.Text = usage.ToString("N0")
   totalLabel.Text = total.ToString("C2")

7. Finally, you need to enter the appropriate code in the outer selection structure's false path. The code should display a message in a message box. Enter the additional code shown in Figure 8-31.

```
            usageLabel.Text = usage.ToString("N0")
            totalLabel.Text = total.ToString("C2")
        Else
            MessageBox.Show("The current reading must " &
                "be greater than or equal to the " &
                "previous reading.",
                "Tri-County Electricity",
                MessageBoxButtons.OK,
                MessageBoxIcon.Information)

        End If
    End Sub
```

enter these lines of code

Figure 8-31 Outer selection structure's false path entered in the calcButton's Click event procedure

8. Save the solution and then start the application. Type **2500** in the Previous reading box. Press **Tab** and then type **3500** in the Current reading box. Click the **Calculate** button. The monthly usage and total charge appear in the interface, as shown in Figure 8-32.

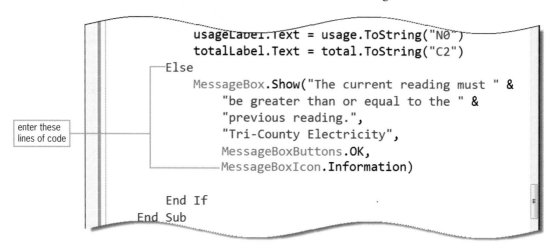

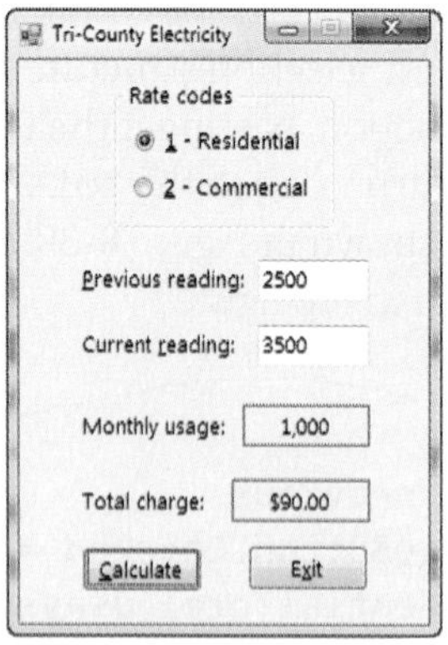

Figure 8-32 Interface showing the monthly usage and total charge

9. Click the **2 - Commercial** radio button. The radio button's Click event procedure clears the contents of the Monthly usage and Total charge boxes. Click the **Calculate** button. The interface shows that the monthly usage and total charge are 1,000 and $120.00, respectively.

10. Press **Tab** three times to place the focus in the Previous reading box. Type **4**. The previousTextBox's TextChanged event procedure clears the contents of the Monthly usage and Total charge boxes. Click the **Calculate** button.

11. Press **Tab** four times to place the focus in the Current reading box. Type **2**. The currentTextBox's TextChanged event procedure clears the contents of the Monthly usage and Total charge boxes. Click the **Calculate** button.

12. The message "The current reading must be greater than or equal to the previous reading." appears in a message box. Close the message box.

13. Click the **Exit** button to end the application. Close the Code Editor window, and then close the solution. Figure 8-33 shows the application's code.

```
' Project name:         Tri-County Electricity Project
' Project purpose:      Displays the monthly electric bill
' Created/revised by:   <your name> on <current date>

Option Explicit On
Option Strict On
Option Infer Off

Public Class MainForm

  Private Sub CalcResidentialTotal(ByVal units As Integer,
                                   ByRef charge As Double)
    ' calculates the total charge for a
    ' residential customer

    Const UnitCharge As Double = 0.09
    Const MinFee As Double = 17.65

    charge = units * UnitCharge
    If charge < MinFee Then
        charge = MinFee
    End If
 End Sub

  Private Function GetCommercialTotal(ByVal units As Integer)
  As Double
    ' calculates the total charge for a
    ' commercial customer

    Const UnitCharge As Double = 0.12
    Const MinFee As Double = 21.75
    Dim charge As Double

    charge = units * UnitCharge
    If charge < MinFee Then
        charge = MinFee
    End If

    Return charge

  End Function
```

Figure 8-33 Code for the Tri-County Electricity application *(continues)*

(continued)

```
Private Sub exitButton_Click(ByVal sender As Object,
ByVal e As System.EventArgs) Handles exitButton.Click
     Me.Close()
End Sub

Private Sub SelectText(ByVal sender As Object,
ByVal e As System.EventArgs) Handles currentTextBox.Enter,
previousTextBox.Enter
  ' select existing text

  Dim thisTextBox As TextBox
  thisTextBox = TryCast(sender, TextBox)
  thisTextBox.SelectAll()

End Sub

Private Sub CancelKeys(ByVal sender As Object,
ByVal e As System.Windows.Forms.KeyPressEventArgs
) Handles currentTextBox.KeyPress,
previousTextBox.KeyPress
  ' allow only numbers and the Backspace

  If (e.KeyChar < "0" OrElse e.KeyChar > "9") AndAlso
      e.KeyChar <> ControlChars.Back Then
      e.Handled = True

  End If
End Sub

Private Sub ClearLabels(ByVal sender As Object,
ByVal e As System.EventArgs
) Handles currentTextBox.TextChanged,
previousTextBox.TextChanged,
residentialRadioButton.Click,
commercialRadioButton.Click
  ' clear calculated values

  usageLabel.Text = String.Empty
  totalLabel.Text = String.Empty

End Sub

Private Sub calcButton_Click(ByVal sender As Object,
ByVal e As System.EventArgs) Handles calcButton.Click
  ' displays the monthly usage and total charge

  Dim previous As Integer
  Dim current As Integer
  Dim usage As Integer
  Dim total As Double

  Integer.TryParse(previousTextBox.Text, previous)
  Integer.TryParse(currentTextBox.Text, current)

  If current >= previous Then
      usage = current - previous
      If residentialRadioButton.Checked = True Then
```

Figure 8-33 Code for the Tri-County Electricity application *(continues)*

(continued)

```
            Call CalcResidentialTotal(usage, total)
        Else
            total = GetCommercialTotal(usage)
        End If

        usageLabel.Text = usage.ToString("N0")
        totalLabel.Text = total.ToString("C2")
    Else
    MessageBox.Show("The current reading must " &
            "be greater than or equal to the " &
            "previous reading.",
            "Tri-County Electricity",
            MessageBoxButtons.OK,
            MessageBoxIcon.Information)

    End If
  End Sub
End Class
```

Figure 8-33 Code for the Tri-County Electricity application

PROGRAMMING TUTORIAL 2

Coding the Concentration Game Application

In this tutorial, you code an application that simulates a game called Concentration. The game board contains 16 labels. Scattered among the labels are eight pairs of matching words that are hidden from view. The user begins by clicking one of the labels to reveal a word. He or she then clicks another label to reveal another word. If the two words match, the words remain on the screen. If the words do not match, they are hidden once again. The game is over when all of the matching words are revealed. The user can start a new game by clicking the New Game button in the interface. In each game, the words will appear in different locations on the game board. This is accomplished using an independent Sub procedure that generates random numbers and then uses the random numbers to shuffle the words. The application's TOE chart and MainForm are shown in Figures 8-34 and 8-35, respectively.

Task	Object	Event
1. Fill the list box with 8 pairs of matching words 2. Call a procedure to shuffle the words in the wordListBox	MainForm	Load
End the application	exitButton	Click
1. Clear the label controls and then enable them 2. Reset the counter, which is used by the 16 labels, to 0 3. Call a procedure to shuffle the words in the wordListBox	newButton	Click
1. Enable the boardTableLayoutPanel 2. Disable the matchTimer	matchTimer	Tick
1. Clear the words from the chosen labels 2. Enable the boardTableLayoutPanel 3. Disable the noMatchTimer	noMatchTimer	Tick

Figure 8-34 TOE chart for the Concentration Game application *(continues)*

(continued)

Task	Object	Event
1. Use a counter to keep track of whether this is the first or second label clicked 2. If this is the first label clicked, display a word from the wordListBox in the label 3. If this is the second label clicked, disable the boardTableLayoutPanel, display a word from the wordListBox in the label, and then compare both words 4. If both words match, disable both labels and then turn on the matchTimer 5. If both words do not match, turn on the noMatchTimer 6. Reset the counter, which is used by the 16 labels, to 0	16 labels	Click
Store the 16 words	wordListBox	None
Display the game board	boardTableLayoutPanel	None

Figure 8-34 TOE chart for the Concentration Game application

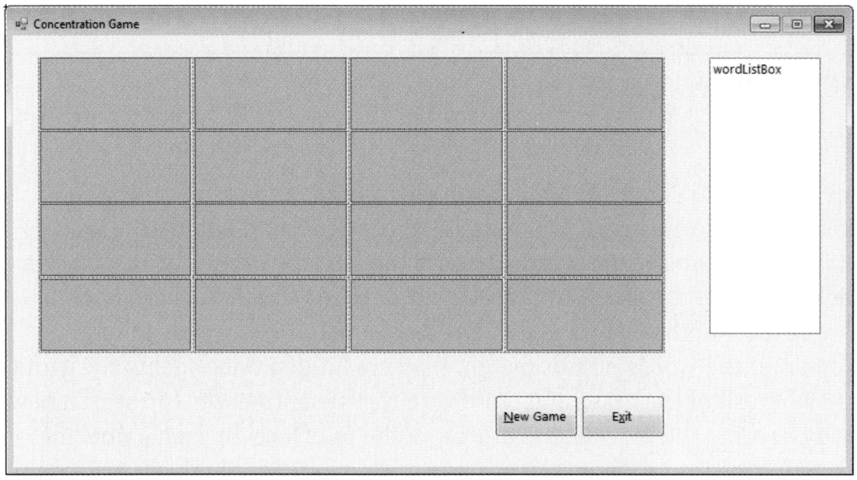

Figure 8-35 MainForm for the Concentration Game application

Coding the Concentration Game Application

Included in the data files for this book is a partially completed Concentration Game application. To complete the application, you just need to code it. According to the application's TOE chart, the MainForm's Load event procedure and the Click event procedures for the exitButton, newButton, and 16 labels need to be coded. You also need to code the Tick event procedures for the two timers. (If you need help while coding the application, you can look ahead to Figure 8-45.)

To begin coding the application:

1. Start Visual Studio or the Express Edition of Visual Basic. If necessary, open the Solution Explorer and Properties windows.
2. Open the **Concentration Game Solution** (**Concentration Game Solution.sln**) file, which is contained in the VbReloaded2010\Chap08\Concentration Game Solution folder. Open the designer

window (if necessary), and then auto-hide the Solution Explorer window. The MainForm contains a table layout panel, 16 labels, two buttons, and a list box. The component tray contains two timers.

3. On your own, click **each of the labels** in the table layout panel, one at a time. Notice that the TabIndex values in the Properties window range from 0 through 15. The TabIndex values will be used to access the appropriate word in the wordListBox, whose indexes also range from 0 through 15. Auto-hide the Properties window.
4. Open the Code Editor window, which already contains some of the application's code.
5. In the comments that appear in the General Declarations section, replace <your name> and <current date> with your name and the current date.

First, you will complete the MainForm's Load event procedure. The procedure is responsible for filling the wordListBox with eight pairs of matching words and then reordering the words. The list box provides the words that will appear on the game board. The procedure's pseudocode is shown in Figure 8-36.

```
MainForm Load event procedure
1. fill the wordListBox with 8 pairs of matching words
2. call the ShuffleWords procedure to reorder the words in the wordListBox
```

Figure 8-36 Pseudocode for the MainForm's Load event procedure

To complete the MainForm's Load event procedure:

1. Scroll down the Code Editor window (if necessary) to view the code already entered in the MainForm's Load event procedure. Notice that the first eight statements in the procedure add eight unique words to the wordListBox control, and the last eight statements duplicate the words in the control.
2. Save the solution and then start the application. The Load event procedure adds the 16 words to the list box, as shown in Figure 8-37. The words appear in the order in which they are added in the Load event procedure.

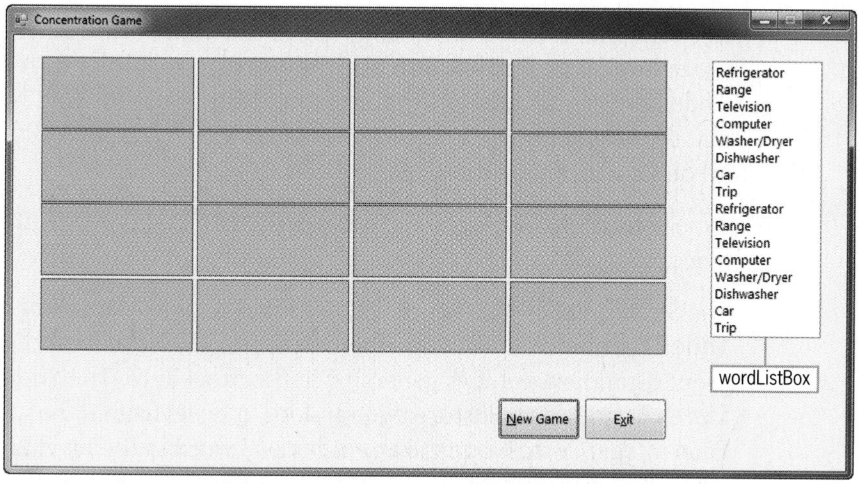

Figure 8-37 Sixteen words added to the wordListBox

3. Click the **Exit** button to end the application.

4. To complete the Load event procedure, you just need to enter a statement to call the ShuffleWords procedure, which will reorder (or shuffle) the words in the wordListBox. If you do not shuffle the words, they will appear in the exact same location on the game board each time the application is started. Shuffling the words makes the game more challenging, because the user will never be sure exactly where each word will appear on the game board. The ShuffleWords procedure will be a Sub procedure, because it will not need to return a value. The procedure will not be passed any data when it is invoked. Click the **blank line** above the End Sub clause in the Load event procedure, and then enter the appropriate Call statement. (Do not be concerned about the jagged line that appears below ShuffleWords in the Call statement. The line will disappear when you create the procedure in the next section.)

Coding the ShuffleWords Procedure

The ShuffleWords procedure is responsible for reordering the words in the wordListBox. Reordering the words will ensure that most of the words appear in different locations in each game. An easy way to reorder a list of words is to swap one word with another word. For example, you can swap the word that appears at the top of the list with the word that appears in the middle of the list. In this application, you will use random numbers to select the positions of the two words to be swapped. You will perform the swap 20 times to ensure that the words are sufficiently reordered. The procedure's pseudocode is shown in Figure 8-38.

```
ShuffleWords procedure
1. repeat 20 times
        generate two random numbers from 0 through 15
        use the random numbers to swap words in the wordListBox
   end repeat
```

Figure 8-38 Pseudocode for the ShuffleWords procedure

To code the ShuffleWords procedure and then test the procedure:

1. Click the **blank line** immediately above the MainForm's Load event procedure. Type **Private Sub ShuffleWords()** and press **Enter**. The Code Editor enters the procedure footer (`End Sub`) for you. Notice that the jagged line no longer appears below the ShuffleWords name in the Load event procedure.

2. Type **' shuffles the words in the wordListBox** and press **Enter** twice.

3. The ShuffleWords procedure will use four variables named `randGen`, `index1`, `index2`, and `temp`. The `randGen` variable will represent the pseudo-random number generator in the procedure. The `index1` and `index2` variables will store two random integers from 0 through 15. Each integer corresponds to the index of a word in the wordListBox.

The `temp` variable will be used during the swapping process. Enter the following Dim statements. Press **Enter** twice after typing the last Dim statement.

Dim randGen As New Random
Dim index1 As Integer
Dim index2 As Integer
Dim temp As String

4. The first step in the pseudocode is a loop that repeats its instructions 20 times. Enter the following For clause:

   For counter As Integer = 1 to 20

5. Change the Next clause to **Next counter**.

6. The first instruction in the loop is to generate two random numbers from 0 through 15. Click the **blank line** below the For clause, and then enter the following comment and assignment statements:

   ‘ generate two random numbers
   index1 = randGen.Next(0, 16)
   index2 = randGen.Next(0, 16)

7. The second instruction in the loop is to use the random numbers to swap the words in the wordListBox. You learned how to swap the contents of two variables in Chapter 4. You can use a similar process to swap two words in the wordListBox. The `index1` variable contains the index of the first word you want to swap. You begin by storing that word in the `temp` variable. Enter the following comment and assignment statement:

   ‘ swap two words
   temp = wordListBox.Items(index1).ToString

8. Next, you replace the word located in the `index1` position in the wordListBox with the word located in the `index2` position. Enter the following assignment statement:

   wordListBox.Items(index1) =
   wordListBox.Items(index2)

9. Finally, you replace the word located in the `index2` position in the wordListBox with the word stored in the `temp` variable. On your own, enter the appropriate assignment statement.

10. Save the solution and then start the application. The 16 words appear in the wordListBox. This time, however, they do not appear in the order in which they are entered in the Load event procedure. Instead, they appear in a random order. Click the **Exit** button to end the application.

Coding the Labels’ Click Event Procedures

Next, you will code the Click event procedures for the 16 labels in the interface. Each label is associated with a word in the list box. The first label is associated with the first word, the second label with the second word, and so on. When the user clicks a label, the label’s Click event procedure will access the appropriate word in the wordListBox and then display the word in the label. For example, if the user clicks the first label on the game board, the Click event procedure will assign the first word in the list box to the label's Text property. After the user selects two labels, the procedure will determine whether the labels contain matching words. If the words match, they will remain visible in their respective labels. If the words do not match, the user will be given a short amount of time to memorize the location of the words before the words are hidden again. The pseudocode for the labels' Click event procedures is shown in Figure 8-39.

```
16 Labels' Click event procedure
1. add 1 to the selection counter, which keeps track of whether this is the first or
   second label selected on the game board
2. if this is the first label selected
       assign the current label's TabIndex property to an Integer variable named index1

       use the index1 variable to access the appropriate word in the wordListBox, and
       then display the word in the current label

   else (which means it is the second label selected)
       disable the game board to prevent the user from making another selection

       assign the current label's TabIndex property to an Integer variable named index2

       use the index2 variable to access the appropriate word in the wordListBox, and
       then display the word in the current label

       if the first label and second label contain the same word
             disable both labels on the game board
             turn the matchTimer on

       else
             turn the noMatchTimer on
       end if
       reset the selection counter to 0
   end if
```

Figure 8-39 Pseudocode for the 16 labels' Click event procedures

To code the Click event procedures for the 16 labels:

1. Locate the TestForMatch procedure in the Code Editor window. The Handles clause indicates that the procedure will be processed when the Click event occurs for any of the 16 labels.
2. The TestForMatch procedure will use two Integer variables named `index1` and `index2` to store the TabIndex property values associated with the two labels clicked by the user. The procedure will use the values to access the corresponding word in the wordListBox. For example, if the user clicks the Label1 control, which is located in the upper-left corner of the game board, the procedure will assign the control's TabIndex value—in this case, 0—to the `index1` variable. It then will use the value in the `index1` variable to access the appropriate word in the list box. The appropriate word is the one whose index value matches the TabIndex value. Click the **blank line** above the End Sub clause in the TestForMatch procedure, and then enter

the following Dim statements. Press **Enter** twice after typing the last Dim statement.

Dim index1 As Integer
Dim index2 As Integer

3. The procedure also will use three class-level variables named `selectionCounter`, `firstLabel`, and `secondLabel`. The variables need to be class-level variables, because they will be used by more than one procedure in the application. The `selectionCounter` variable will keep track of whether the user has clicked one or two labels. The `firstLabel` and `secondLabel` variables will keep track of the labels the user clicked. Click the **blank line** below the Public Class MainForm clause and then press **Enter** to insert another blank line. Enter the following Private statements:

   Private selectionCounter As Integer
   Private firstLabel As Label
   Private secondLabel As Label

4. The first step in the pseudocode shown in Figure 8-39 is to add the number 1 to the selection counter. Click the **blank line** above the End Sub clause in the TestForMatch procedure. Enter the following comment and assignment statement. Press **Enter** twice after typing the assignment statement.

   ' update the selection counter
   selectionCounter += 1

5. The next step is a dual-alternative selection structure that determines whether this is the first label control selected. Type the following comments and If clause:

   ' determine whether this is the first
   ' or second selection
   If selectionCounter = 1 Then

6. If this is the first of two labels selected on the game board, the selection structure's true path should assign the label's TabIndex value to the `index1` variable. First, however, you will need to use the `sender` parameter to determine the label that was clicked. Recall that the parameter contains the address of the object that raised the event. Enter an assignment statement that uses the TryCast method to convert the `sender` parameter to the Label data type, and then assigns the result to the `firstLabel` variable. (Remember that if you need help, you can look ahead to Figure 8-45.)

7. Now, enter a statement that assigns the label's TabIndex property value to the `index1` variable.

8. Next, enter a statement that uses the `index1` variable to access the appropriate word in the wordListBox. The appropriate word is the one whose index matches the value contained in the `index1` variable. Assign the word to the label's Text property.

9. You have finished coding the selection structure's true path; you will code its false path next. Type **Else** and press **Tab**. Type **' second label selected** and press **Enter**.

10. If this is the second of two labels selected on the game board, the procedure will need to compare the contents of both labels before the user makes the next selection. Therefore, you will disable the game board, temporarily. Enter an assignment statement that changes the boardTableLayoutPanel control's Enabled property to **False**.

11. Next, enter an assignment statement that uses the TryCast method to convert the `sender` parameter to the Label data type, and then assigns the result to the `secondLabel` variable.

12. Now, enter a statement that assigns the label's TabIndex property value to the `index2` variable.

13. Next, enter a statement that uses the `index2` variable to access the appropriate word in the wordListBox. The appropriate word is the one whose index matches the value contained in the `index2` variable. Assign the word to the label's Text property.

14. The next instruction in the false path is a nested dual-alternative selection structure whose condition compares the contents of both labels. If both labels contain the same word, the nested selection structure's true path will disable the labels to prevent them from responding if the user inadvertently clicks them again. It also will turn on the matchTimer. If the labels do not contain the same word, the nested selection structure's false path will turn on the noMatchTimer. Enter the following comment and selection structure:

```
' compare words in both labels
If firstLabel.Text = secondLabel.Text Then
    firstLabel.Enabled = False
    secondLabel.Enabled = False
    matchTimer.Enabled = True
Else
    noMatchTimer.Enabled = True
End If
```

15. Click immediately after the letter **f** in the nested selection structure's End If clause, and then press **Enter** twice.

16. The last instruction in the pseudocode (shown earlier in Figure 8-39) is to reset the selection counter to 0. Recall that the selection counter keeps track of whether the user has clicked one or two labels. Type **'reset the selection counter** and press **Enter**, then enter an assignment statement to assign the number 0 to the `selectionCounter` variable.

17. Save the solution.

Coding Each Timer's Tick Event Procedure

Figure 8-40 shows the pseudocode for the matchTimer's Tick event procedure, which performs two tasks. First, it enables the game board so the user can make another selection. Second, it turns off the matchTimer. Turning off the timer stops the timer's Tick event and prevents its code from being processed again. The matchTimer's Tick event procedure will not be processed again until the timer is turned back on, which happens when the user locates a matching pair of words on the game board.

<u>matchTimer Tick event procedure</u>
1. enable the game board
2. turn the matchTimer off

Figure 8-40 Pseudocode for the matchTimer's Tick event procedure

To code the matchTimer's Tick event procedure:

1. Locate the matchTimer's Tick event procedure in the Code Editor window.
2. Click the **blank line** above the procedure's End Sub clause. Enter an assignment statement to enable the boardTableLayoutPanel.
3. Next, enter an assignment statement to disable the matchTimer.

Figure 8-41 shows the pseudocode for the noMatchTimer's Tick event procedure, which performs three tasks. The first task clears the contents of the labels whose addresses are stored in the `firstLabel` and `secondLabel` variables. The second task enables the game board so the user can make another selection. The third task turns off the noMatchTimer to prevent the timer's Tick event from occurring and prevent its code from being processed. The noMatchTimer's Tick event procedure will not be processed again until the timer is turned back on, which happens when the two labels selected by the user contain different words.

<u>noMatchTimer Tick event procedure</u>
1. clear the contents of the labels associated with the firstLabel and secondLabel variables
2. enable the game board
3. turn the noMatchTimer off

Figure 8-41 Pseudocode for the noMatchTimer's Tick event procedure

To code the noMatchTimer's Tick event procedure:

1. Locate the noMatchTimer's Tick event procedure in the Code Editor window.
2. Click the **blank line** above the procedure's End Sub clause.
3. Enter two assignment statements to clear the Text properties of the labels associated with the `firstLabel` and `secondLabel` variables.
4. Enter an assignment statement to enable the boardTableLayoutPanel.
5. Next, enter an assignment statement to disable the noMatchTimer.
6. Save the solution.

Coding the New Game Button's Click Event Procedure

The last procedure you need to code is the newButton's Click event procedure. The procedure's pseudocode is shown in Figure 8-42. The first two steps have already been coded for you in the Code Editor window.

<u>newButton Click event procedure</u>
1. clear the contents of the 16 labels
2. enable the 16 labels
3. reset the selection counter to 0
4. call the ShuffleWords procedure to reorder the words in the wordListBox

Figure 8-42 Pseudocode for the newButton's Click event procedure

To complete the newButton's Click event procedure:

1. Locate the newButton's Click event procedure in the Code Editor window. Click the **blank line** above the procedure's End Sub clause.
2. Enter an assignment statement to assign the number 0 to the `selectionCounter` variable.
3. Enter a statement to call the ShuffleWords procedure.
4. Save the solution.

Testing the Concentration Game Application

In this section, you will test the application to verify that it is working correctly.

To test the Concentration Game application:

1. Start the application. Click the **label in the upper-left corner of the game board**. The TestForMatch procedure (which is associated with the label's Click event) assigns the first word in the wordListBox to the label's Text property. See Figure 8-43. Recall that the ShuffleWords procedure uses random numbers to reorder the list of words in the list box. Therefore, the first word in your list box, as well as the word in the Label1 control, might be different from the one shown in the figure.

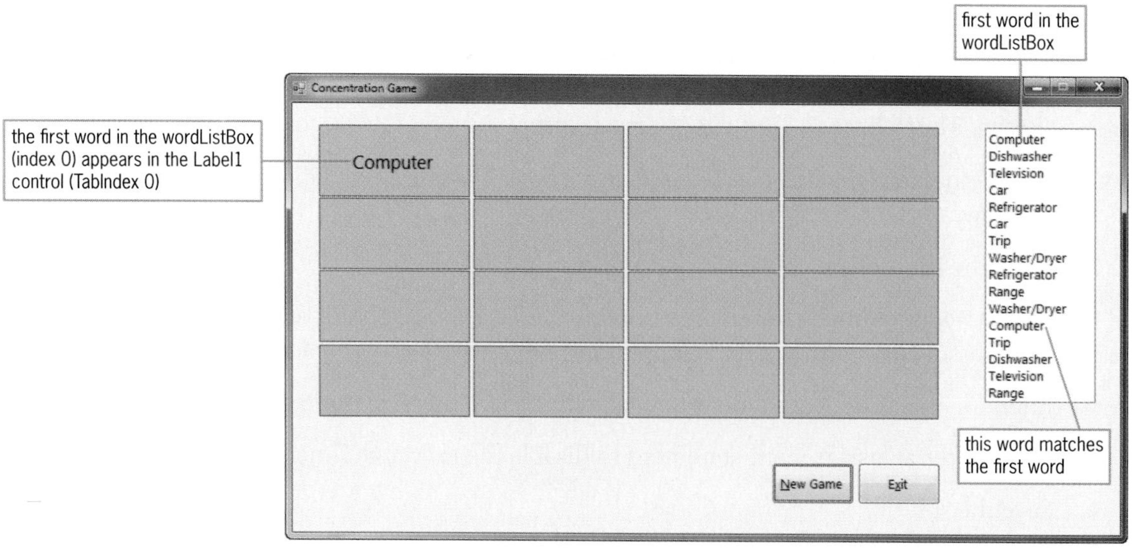

Figure 8-43 First word appears in the label on the game board

2. First, you will test the code that handles two matching words. To do this, you will need to find the word in the list box that matches the first

word, and then click its associated label on the game board. Count down the list of words in the list box, stopping when you reach the word that matches the first word in your list box. In Figure 8-43, the word that matches the first word (Computer) is the twelfth word in the list box.

3. Now count each label, from left to right, beginning with the first row on the game board. Stop counting when you reach the label whose number is the same as in the previous step. In Figure 8-43, for example, you would stop counting when you reached the twelfth label, which is located in the fourth column of the third row. Click the **label associated with the matching word**. See Figure 8-44.

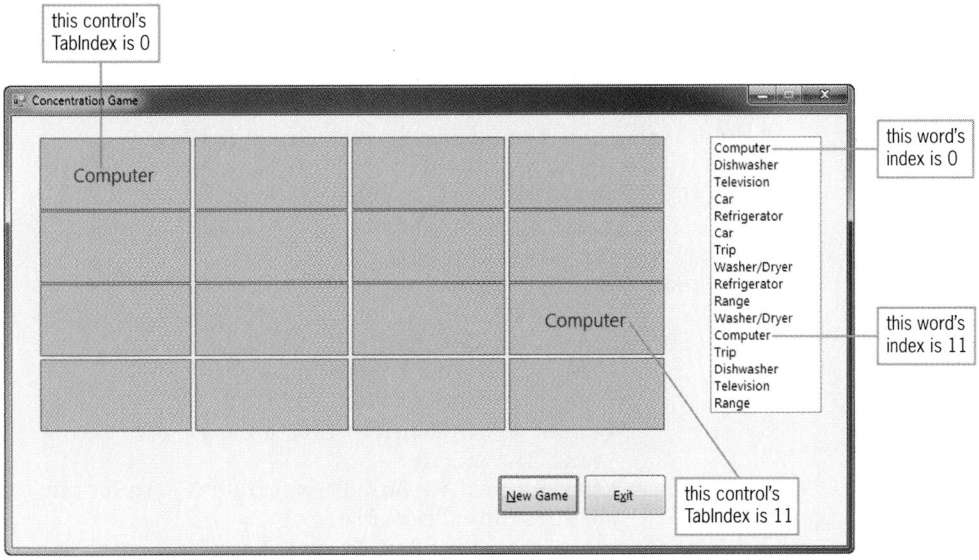

Figure 8-44 Both labels contain the same word

4. Click the **Label1 control** again. Nothing happens because the TestForMatch procedure disables the label when its matching word is found.

5. Now, you will test the code that handles two words that do not match. Click a **blank label control on the game board**, and then click **another blank label control**. However, be sure that the second label's word is not the same as the first label's word. Because both words are not the same, they are hidden after a short time.

6. Finally, verify that the code entered in the newButton's Click event procedure works correctly. Click the **New Game** button. The button's Click event procedure clears the contents of the label controls and also enables them. In addition, it resets the selection counter to 0 and calls the ShuffleWords procedure to reorder the words in the list box.

7. On your own, test the application several more times. When you are finished, click the **Exit** button to end the application.

8. Now that you know that the application works correctly, you can resize the form to hide the list box. Close the Code Editor window. Unlock the controls on the form and then drag the form's right border so that it hides the list box. Lock the controls on the form.

9. Save the solution, and then close the solution. Figure 8-45 shows the code for the Concentration Game application.

```
' Project name:          Concentration Game Project
' Project purpose:       Simulates the Concentration game,
'                        where a player tries to find
'                        matching pairs of words
' Created/revised by:    <your name> on <current date>

Option Explicit On
Option Strict On
Option Infer Off

Public Class MainForm

Private selectionCounter As Integer
Private firstLabel As Label
Private secondLabel As Label

  Private Sub ShuffleWords()
    ' shuffles the words in the wordListBox

    Dim randGen As New Random
    Dim index1 As Integer
    Dim index2 As Integer
    Dim temp As String

    For counter As Integer = 1 To 20
         ' generate two random numbers
         index1 = randGen.Next(0, 16)
         index2 = randGen.Next(0, 16)
         'swap two words
         temp = wordListBox.Items(index1).ToString
         wordListBox.Items(index1) =
               wordListBox.Items(index2)
         wordListBox.Items(index2) = temp

    Next counter
  End Sub
  Private Sub MainForm_Load(ByVal sender As Object,
  ByVal e As System.EventArgs) Handles Me.Load
    ' fills the list box with 8 pairs of matching
    ' words, then calls a procedure to shuffle
    ' the words

    wordListBox.Items.Add("Refrigerator")
    wordListBox.Items.Add("Range")
    wordListBox.Items.Add("Television")
    wordListBox.Items.Add("Computer")
    wordListBox.Items.Add("Washer/Dryer")
    wordListBox.Items.Add("Dishwasher")
    wordListBox.Items.Add("Car")
    wordListBox.Items.Add("Trip")
    wordListBox.Items.Add("Refrigerator")
    wordListBox.Items.Add("Range")
    wordListBox.Items.Add("Television")
    wordListBox.Items.Add("Computer")
    wordListBox.Items.Add("Washer/Dryer")
    wordListBox.Items.Add("Dishwasher")
    wordListBox.Items.Add("Car")
    wordListBox.Items.Add("Trip")

```

Figure 8-45 Code for the Concentration Game application *(continues)*

(continued)

```
      Call ShuffleWords()

    End Sub

    Private Sub exitButton_Click(ByVal sender As Object,
    ByVal e As System.EventArgs) Handles exitButton.Click
      Me.Close()
    End Sub

    Private Sub newButton_Click(ByVal sender As Object,
    ByVal e As System.EventArgs) Handles newButton.Click
      ' removes any words from the label controls, then
      ' enables the label controls, then resets the
      ' selection counter, and then calls a procedure
      ' to shuffle the words

      Label1.Text = String.Empty
      Label2.Text = String.Empty
      Label3.Text = String.Empty
      Label4.Text = String.Empty
      Label5.Text = String.Empty
      Label6.Text = String.Empty
      Label7.Text = String.Empty
      Label8.Text = String.Empty
      Label9.Text = String.Empty
      Label10.Text = String.Empty
      Label11.Text = String.Empty
      Label12.Text = String.Empty
      Label13.Text = String.Empty
      Label14.Text = String.Empty
      Label15.Text = String.Empty
      Label16.Text = String.Empty

      Label1.Enabled = True
      Label2.Enabled = True
      Label3.Enabled = True
      Label4.Enabled = True
      Label5.Enabled = True
      Label6.Enabled = True
      Label7.Enabled = True
      Label8.Enabled = True
      Label9.Enabled = True
      Label10.Enabled = True
      Label11.Enabled = True
      Label12.Enabled = True
      Label13.Enabled = True
      Label14.Enabled = True
      Label15.Enabled = True
      Label16.Enabled = True

      selectionCounter = 0
      Call ShuffleWords()

    End Sub

    Private Sub TestForMatch(ByVal sender As Object,
    ByVal e As System.EventArgs) Handles Label1.Click,
```

Figure 8-45 Code for the Concentration Game application *(continues)*

(continued)

```
Label2.Click, Label3.Click, Label4.Click, Label5.Click,
Label6.Click, Label7.Click,
Label8.Click, Label9.Click, Label10.Click, Label11.Click,
Label12.Click, Label13.Click,
Label14.Click, Label15.Click, Label16.Click
  ' displays the appropriate words and determines
  ' whether the user selected a matching pair

  Dim index1 As Integer
  Dim index2 As Integer

  ' update the selection counter
  selectionCounter += 1

  ' determine whether this is the first
  ' or second selection
  If selectionCounter = 1 Then
      firstLabel = TryCast(sender, Label)
      index1 = firstLabel.TabIndex
      firstLabel.Text = wordListBox.Items(index1).ToString
  Else    ' second label selected
      boardTableLayoutPanel.Enabled = False
      secondLabel = TryCast(sender, Label)
      index2 = secondLabel.TabIndex
      secondLabel.Text = wordListBox.Items(index2).ToString
      ' compare words in both labels
      If firstLabel.Text = secondLabel.Text Then
         firstLabel.Enabled = False
         secondLabel.Enabled = False
         matchTimer.Enabled = True
      Else
         noMatchTimer.Enabled = True
      End If

      ' reset the selection counter
      selectionCounter = 0

  End If
End Sub

Private Sub matchTimer_Tick(ByVal sender As Object,
ByVal e As System.EventArgs) Handles matchTimer.Tick
  ' when the two words match, the game board is
  ' enabled and the timer is turned off

  boardTableLayoutPanel.Enabled = True
  matchTimer.Enabled = False

End Sub

Private Sub noMatchTimer_Tick(ByVal sender As Object,
ByVal e As System.EventArgs) Handles noMatchTimer.Tick
  ' when the words do not match, the words are
  ' removed from the labels, the game board is
  ' enabled, and the timer is turned off

  firstLabel.Text = String.Empty
```

Figure 8-45 Code for the Concentration Game application *(continues)*

(continued)

```
    secondLabel.Text = String.Empty
    boardTableLayoutPanel.Enabled = True
    noMatchTimer.Enabled = False

  End Sub
End Class
```

Figure 8-45 Code for the Concentration Game application

PROGRAMMING EXAMPLE

Rainfall Calculator Application

Create an interface that provides a text box for the user to enter monthly rainfall amounts. The application should calculate and display two amounts: the total rainfall and the average rainfall. Use the following names for the solution, project, and form file: Rainfall Solution, Rainfall Project, and Main Form.vb. Save the application in the VbReloaded2010\Chap08 folder. See Figures 8-46 through 8-51.

Task	**Object**	**Event**
1. Use a counter and accumulator to keep keep track of the number of rainfall amounts entered and the total rainfall 2. Call a procedure to calculate the average rainfall 3. Display the total rainfall and average rainfall in totalLabel and averageLabel 4. Send the focus to the monthTextBox 5. Select the monthTextBox's existing text	calcButton	Click
End the application	exitButton	Click
Display the total rainfall amount (from calcButton)	totalLabel	None
Display the average rainfall amount (from calcButton)	averageLabel	None
Get and display the monthly rainfall amounts Select the existing text Allow numbers, period, and Backspace Clear totalLabel and averageLabel	monthTextBox	None Enter KeyPress TextChanged

Figure 8-46 TOE chart for the Rainfall Calculator application

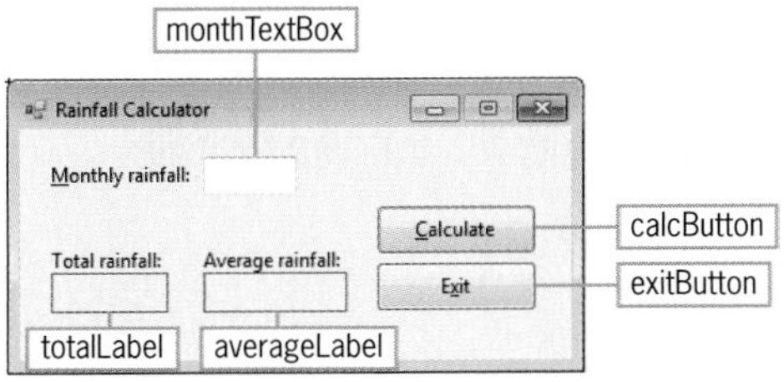

Figure 8-47 MainForm in the Rainfall Calculator application

Object	Property	Setting
MainForm	AcceptButton	calcButton
	Font	Segoe UI, 10 point
	MaximizeBox	False
	StartPosition	CenterScreen
	Text	Rainfall Calculator
totalLabel	AutoSize	False
	BorderStyle	FixedSingle
	Text	(empty)
	TextAlign	MiddleCenter
averageLabel	AutoSize	False
	BorderStyle	FixedSingle
	Text	(empty)
	TextAlign	MiddleCenter

Figure 8-48 Objects, properties, and settings

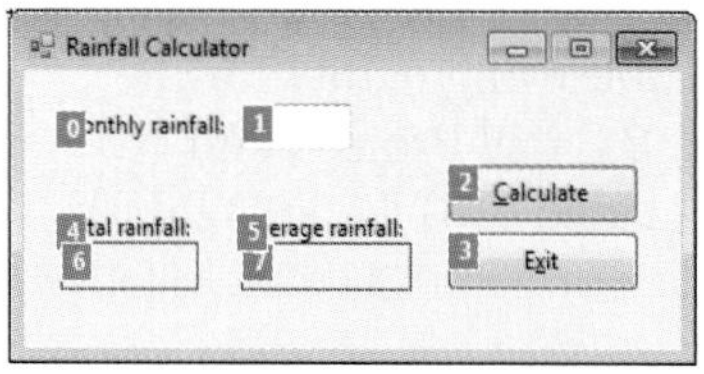

Figure 8-49 Tab order

<u>exitButton Click event procedure</u>
close the application

<u>monthTextBox Enter event procedure</u>
select the existing text

<u>monthTextBox KeyPress event procedure</u>
allow only numbers, the period, and the Backspace key

<u>monthTextBox TextChanged event procedure</u>
clear the contents of the totalLabel and averageLabel

<u>calcButton Click event procedure</u>

1. if the monthTextBox is not empty
        add the monthly rainfall to the total rainfall accumulator
        add 1 to the rainfall counter
    end if
2. Call the CalcAverage procedure to calculate the average rainfall; pass the procedure the rainfall counter and rainfall accumulator values and the address of a variable in which to store the average rainfall
3. send the focus to the monthTextBox
4. select the existing text in the monthTextBox

<u>CalcAverage procedure (receives the rainfall counter and rainfall accumulator values and the address of a variable in which to store the average rainfall)</u>
if the rainfall counter > 0
    average rainfall = rainfall accumulator / rainfall counter
else
    average rainfall = 0
end if

Figure 8-50 Pseudocode

```
' Project name:         Rainfall Project
' Project purpose:      Displays the total and average
'                       rainfall amounts
' Created/revised by:   <your name> on <current date>

Option Explicit On
Option Strict On
Option Infer Off

Public Class MainForm

    Private Sub CalcAverage(ByVal counter As Integer,
                            ByVal accumulator As Decimal,
                            ByRef avg As Decimal)
        ' calculates the average rainfall amount

        If counter > 0 Then
            avg = accumulator / counter
        Else
            avg = 0
        End If
    End Sub

    Private Sub exitButton_Click(ByVal sender As Object,
    ByVal e As System.EventArgs) Handles exitButton.Click
       Me.Close()
    End Sub

    Private Sub calcButton_Click(ByVal sender As Object,
    ByVal e As System.EventArgs) Handles calcButton.Click
       ' displays the total and average rainfall amount

       Static rainCounter As Integer
       Static rainAccum As Decimal
       Dim monthRain As Decimal
       Dim avgRain As Decimal

       If monthTextBox.Text <> String.Empty Then
            Decimal.TryParse(monthTextBox.Text, monthRain)
            ' update the accumulator and counter
            rainAccum += monthRain
            rainCounter += 1
       End If

       ' calculate the average
       Call CalcAverage(rainCounter, rainAccum, avgRain)

       totalLabel.Text = rainAccum.ToString("N2")
       averageLabel.Text = avgRain.ToString("N2")
       monthTextBox.Focus()
       monthTextBox.SelectAll()
    End Sub

    Private Sub monthTextBox_Enter(ByVal sender As Object,
    ByVal e As System.EventArgs) Handles monthTextBox.Enter
       monthTextBox.SelectAll()
    End Sub

```

Figure 8-51 Code *(continues)*

(continued)

```
    Private Sub monthTextBox_KeyPress(ByVal sender As Object,
    ByVal e As System.Windows.Forms.KeyPressEventArgs
    ) Handles monthTextBox.KeyPress
       ' allow numbers, period, and Backspace

       If (e.KeyChar < "0" OrElse e.KeyChar > "9") AndAlso
       e.KeyChar <> "." AndAlso e.KeyChar <> ControlChars.Back Then
       e.Handled = True
       End If
    End Sub

    Private Sub monthTextBox_TextChanged(ByVal sender As Object,
    ByVal e As System.EventArgs) Handles monthTextBox.TextChanged
       totalLabel.Text = String.Empty
       averageLabel.Text = String.Empty
    End Sub
End Class
```

Figure 8-51 Code

Summary

- The difference between a Sub procedure and a Function procedure is that a Function procedure returns a value, whereas a Sub procedure does not return a value.
- An event procedure is a Sub procedure that is associated with one or more objects and events.
- Independent Sub procedures and Function procedures are not associated with any specific object or event. The names of independent Sub procedures and Function procedures typically begin with a verb.
- Procedures allow programmers to avoid duplicating code in different parts of a program. They also allow the programmer to concentrate on one small piece of a program at a time. In addition, they allow a team of programmers to work on large and complex programs.
- You can use the Call statement to invoke an independent Sub procedure. The Call statement allows you to pass arguments to the Sub procedure.
- When calling a procedure, the number of arguments listed in the argumentList should agree with the number of parameters listed in the parameterList in the procedure header. Also, the data type and position of each argument in the argumentList should agree with the data type and position of its corresponding parameter in the parameterList.
- You can pass information to a Sub or Function procedure either *by value* or *by reference*. To pass a variable *by value*, you precede the variable's corresponding parameter with the keyword `ByVal`. To pass a variable *by reference*, you precede the variable's corresponding parameter with the keyword `ByRef`. The procedure header indicates whether a variable is being passed *by value* or *by reference*.

- When you pass a variable *by value*, only a copy of the variable's contents is passed. When you pass a variable *by reference*, the variable's address is passed.
- Variables that appear in the parameterList in a procedure header have procedure scope, which means they can be used only by the procedure.
- You can use an event procedure's Handles clause to associate the procedure with more than one object and event.
- You invoke a Function procedure, also called a function, by including its name and any arguments in a statement. Usually the statement assigns the function's return value to a variable. However, it also may use the return value in a calculation or display the return value.
- You can use the TryCast operator to convert an Object variable to a different data type.
- The purpose of a timer control is to process code at one or more specified intervals. You start a timer by setting its Enabled property to True. You stop a timer by setting its Enabled property to False. You use a timer's Interval property to specify the number of milliseconds that must elapse before the timer's Tick event occurs.

Key Terms

Call statement—the statement used to invoke an independent Sub procedure in a Visual Basic program

Casting—another term for type casting

Desk-checking—the process of manually walking through your code, using sample data; also called hand-tracing

e parameter—one of the parameters in an event procedure's header; contains additional information provided by the object that raised the event

Function procedure—a procedure that returns a value after performing its assigned task

Functions—another term for Function procedures

Hand-tracing—another term for desk-checking

Independent Sub procedure—a procedure that is not associated with any specific object or event and is processed only when invoked (called) from code

Interval property—a property of a timer control; stores the length of each interval

Parameters—the memory locations listed in a procedure header

Passing by reference—the process of passing a variable's address to a procedure

Passing by value—the process of passing a copy of a variable's value to a procedure

Return statement—the Visual Basic statement that returns a function's value to the statement that invoked the function

sender parameter—one of the parameters in an event procedure's header; contains the memory address of the object that raised the event

Sub procedure—a procedure that does not return a value after performing its assigned task

Tick event—one of the events of a timer control; occurs each time an interval has elapsed

Timer control—the control used to process code at one or more regular intervals

TryCast operator—used to convert an Object variable to a different data type

Type casting—the process of converting a variable from one data type to another; also called casting

Review Questions

1. To determine whether a variable is being passed to a procedure *by value* or *by reference*, you will need to examine ______________.
   a. the Call statement
   b. the procedure header
   c. the statements entered in the procedure
   d. either a or b

2. Which of the following statements invokes the CalcArea Sub procedure, passing it two variables *by value*?
   a. `Call CalcArea(length, width)`
   b. `Call CalcArea(ByVal length, ByVal width)`
   c. `Invoke CalcArea ByVal(length, width)`
   d. `CalcArea(length, width) As Double`

3. Which of the following is a valid header for a procedure that receives an integer followed by a number with a decimal place?
   a. `Private Sub CalcFee(base As Integer, rate As Decimal)`
   b. `Private Sub CalcFee(ByRef base As Integer, ByRef rate As Decimal)`
   c. `Private Sub CalcFee(ByVal base As Integer, ByVal rate As Decimal)`
   d. none of the above

4. Which of the following indicates that the procedure should be processed when the user clicks either the firstCheckBox or the secondCheckBox?
   a. `Private Sub Clear(ByVal sender As Object, ByVal e As System.EventArgs) Handles firstCheckBox.Click, secondCheckBox.Click`

b. `Private Sub Clear(ByVal sender As Object, ByVal e As System.EventArgs) Handles firstCheckBox_Click, secondCheckBox_Click`

c. `Private Sub Clear_Click(ByVal sender As Object, ByVal e As System.EventArgs) Handles firstCheckBox, secondCheckBox`

d. `Private Sub Clear(ByVal sender As Object, ByVal e As System.EventArgs) Handles firstCheckBox.Click AndAlso secondCheckBox.Click`

5. Which of the following is false?

   a. The sequence of the arguments listed in the Call statement should agree with the sequence of the parameters listed in the receiving procedure's header.

   b. The data type of each argument in the Call statement should match the data type of its corresponding parameter in the procedure header.

   c. The name of each argument in the Call statement should be identical to the name of its corresponding parameter in the procedure header.

   d. When you pass information to a procedure *by value,* the procedure stores the value of each item it receives in a separate memory location.

6. Which of the following instructs a function to return the contents of the `stateTax` variable?

   a. `Return stateTax`

   b. `Return stateTax ByVal`

   c. `Return ByVal stateTax`

   d. `Return ByRef stateTax`

7. Which of the following is a valid header for a procedure that receives the value stored in an Integer variable first, and the address of a Decimal variable second?

   a. `Private Sub CalcFee(ByVal base As Integer, ByAdd rate As Decimal)`

   b. `Private Sub CalcFee(base As Integer, rate As Decimal)`

   c. `Private Sub CalcFee(ByVal base As Integer, ByRef rate As Decimal)`

   d. none of the above

8. Which of the following is false?

   a. When you pass a variable *by reference,* the receiving procedure can change its contents.

   b. To pass a variable *by reference* in Visual Basic, you include the keyword `ByRef` before the variable's name in the Call statement.

c. When you pass a variable *by value*, the receiving procedure creates a procedure-level variable that it uses to store the value passed to it.

d. Unless you specify otherwise, all variables in Visual Basic are passed *by value*.

9. A Sub procedure named CalcEndingInventory is passed four Integer variables named `begin`, `sales`, `purchases`, and `ending`. The procedure should calculate the ending inventory using the beginning inventory, sales, and purchase amounts passed to the procedure. The result should be stored in the `ending` variable. Which of the following procedure headers is correct?

a. `Private Sub CalcEndingInventory(ByVal b As Integer, ByVal s As Integer, ByVal p As Integer, ByRef final As Integer)`

b. `Private Sub CalcEndingInventory(ByVal b As Integer, ByVal s As Integer, ByVal p As Integer, ByVal final As Integer)`

c. `Private Sub CalcEndingInventory(ByRef b As Integer, ByRef s As Integer, ByRef p As Integer, ByVal final As Integer)`

d. `Private Sub CalcEndingInventory(ByRef b As Integer, ByRef s As Integer, ByRef p As Integer, ByRef final As Integer)`

10. Which of the following statements should you use to call the CalcEndingInventory procedure described in Question 9?

a. `Call CalcEndingInventory(begin, sales, purchases, ending)`

b. `Call CalcEndingInventory(ByVal begin, ByVal sales, ByVal purchases, ByRef ending)`

c. `Call CalcEndingInventory(ByRef begin, ByRef sales, ByRef purchases, ByRef ending)`

d. `Call CalcEndingInventory(ByVal begin, ByVal sales, ByVal purchases, ByVal ending)`

Exercises

Pencil and Paper

INTRODUCTORY

1. Explain the difference between a Sub procedure and a function.

INTRODUCTORY

2. Explain the difference between passing a variable *by value* and passing it *by reference*.

3. Explain the difference between invoking a Sub procedure and invoking a function. INTRODUCTORY

4. Write the code for a Sub procedure that receives an integer passed to it. The procedure should divide the integer by 2 and then display the result in the numLabel. Name the procedure DivideByTwo. Then write a statement to invoke the procedure, passing it the number 120. INTRODUCTORY

5. Write the code for a Sub procedure that prompts the user to enter the name of a city and then stores the user's response in the String variable whose address is passed to the procedure. Name the procedure GetCity. Then write a statement to invoke the procedure, passing it the `city` variable. INTRODUCTORY

6. Write the code for a function that prompts the user to enter the name of a state and then returns the user's response. Name the function GetState. Then write a statement to invoke the GetState function. Display the function's return value in a message box. INTRODUCTORY

7. Write the code for a Sub procedure that receives three Double variables: the first two *by value* and the last one *by reference*. The procedure should divide the first variable by the second variable and then store the result in the third variable. Name the procedure CalcQuotient. INTRODUCTORY

8. Write the code for a function that receives a copy of the value stored in an Integer variable. The procedure should divide the value by 2 and then return the result, which may contain a decimal place. Name the function GetQuotient. Then write an appropriate statement to invoke the function, passing it the `number` variable. Assign the function's return value to the `answer` variable. INTRODUCTORY

9. Write the code for a function that receives a copy of the contents of four Integer variables. The function should calculate the average of the four integers and then return the result, which may contain a decimal place. Name the function GetAverage. Then write a statement to invoke the function, passing it the `num1`, `num2`, `num3`, and `num4` variables. Assign the function's return value to a Double variable named `average`. INTERMEDIATE

10. Write the code for a Sub procedure that receives four Integer variables: the first two *by value* and the last two *by reference*. The procedure should calculate the sum of and the difference between the two variables passed *by value*, and then store the results in the variables passed *by reference*. When calculating the difference, subtract the contents of the second variable from the contents of the first variable. Name the procedure GetSumAndDiff. Then write an appropriate statement to invoke the procedure, passing it the `first`, `second`, `sum`, and `difference` variables. INTERMEDIATE

INTERMEDIATE

11. Write the procedure header for a Sub procedure named CalculateTax. The procedure should be invoked when any of the following occurs: the rate1Button's Click event, the rate2Button's Click event, and the salesListBox's SelectedValueChanged event.

INTERMEDIATE

12. Write the statement to convert the `sender` parameter to a radio button. Assign the result to a RadioButton variable named `currentRadioButton`.

Computer

MODIFY THIS

13. In this exercise, you experiment with passing variables *by value* and *by reference.*

    a. Open the Passing Solution (Passing Solution.sln) file contained in the VbReloaded2010\Chap08\Passing Solution folder. Open the Code Editor window and review the existing code. Notice that the `myName` variable is passed *by value* to the GetName procedure. Start the application. Click the Display Name button. When prompted to enter a name, type your name and press Enter. Explain why the button's Click event procedure does not display your name in the nameLabel. Stop the application.

    b. Modify the Display Name button's Click event procedure so that it passes the `myName` variable *by reference* to the GetName procedure. Save the solution and then start the application. Click the Display Name button. When prompted to enter a name, type your name and press Enter. This time, your name appears in the nameLabel. Explain why the button's Click event procedure now works correctly. Close the solution.

MODIFY THIS

14. Open the Gross Pay Solution (Gross Pay Solution.sln) file contained in the VbReloaded2010\Chap08\Gross Pay Solution-Ex14 folder. Modify the code so that it uses one procedure to clear the contents of the grossLabel when the SelectedValueChanged event occurs for either list box. Save the solution and then start and test the application. Close the solution.

MODIFY THIS

15. If necessary, complete the Tri-County Electricity application from this chapter's Programming Tutorial 1, and then close the solution. Use Windows to make a copy of the Tri-County Electricity Solution folder. Rename the folder Tri-County Electricity Solution-Modified. Open the Tri-County Electricity Solution (Tri-County Electricity Solution.sln) file contained in the VbReloaded2010\Chap08\Tri-County Electricity Solution-Modified folder. Modify the code so that it uses a function named GetResidentialTotal (rather than the CalcResidentialTotal Sub procedure) to calculate the charge for residential customers. Also modify the code so that it uses a Sub procedure named CalcCommercialTotal (rather than the GetCommercialTotal function) to calculate the charge for commercial customers. Save the solution and then start and test the application. Close the solution.

16. If necessary, complete the Concentration Game application from this chapter's Programming Tutorial 2, and then close the solution. Use Windows to make a copy of the Concentration Game Solution folder. Rename the folder Concentration Game Solution-Color. Open the Concentration Game Solution (Concentration Game Solution.sln) file contained in the VbReloaded2010\Chap08\Concentration Game Solution-Color folder. When the user finds a matching pair of words, change the BackColor property of the corresponding labels to a different color. Be sure to return the labels to their original color when the user clicks the New Game button. Also modify the application so that it displays the message "Game Over" when the user has located all of the matching pairs. Save the solution and then start and test the application. Close the solution.

MODIFY THIS

17. If necessary, complete the Rainfall Calculator application from this chapter's Programming Example, and then close the solution. Use Windows to make a copy of the Rainfall Solution folder. Rename the folder Rainfall Solution-Modified. Open the Rainfall Solution (Rainfall Solution.sln) file contained in the VbReloaded2010\Chap08\Rainfall Solution-Modified folder. Replace the CalcAverage procedure with a function named GetAverage. Save the solution and then start and test the application. Close the solution.

MODIFY THIS

18. Open the Gross Pay Solution (Gross Pay Solution.sln) file contained in the VbReloaded2010\Chap08\Gross Pay Solution-Ex18 folder. Replace the CalcGrossPay procedure with a function named GetGrossPay. Save the solution and then start and test the application. Close the solution.

INTRODUCTORY

19. Open the Bonus Calculator Solution (Bonus Calculator Solution.sln) file contained in the VbReloaded2010\Chap08\Bonus Calculator Solution folder. Code the application, using a Sub procedure to both calculate and display a 10% bonus. Also use a Sub procedure named ClearLabel to clear the contents of the bonusLabel when the TextChanged event occurs for either text box. In addition, code each text box's Enter event procedure. Save the solution and then start and test the application. Close the solution.

INTRODUCTORY

20. Open the Car Solution (Car Solution.sln) file contained in the VbReloaded2010\Chap08\Car Solution folder. When the Click Me button is clicked, the "I WANT THIS CAR!" message should blink 14 times. Add a timer control to the application. Code the control's Tick event procedure. Save the solution and then start and test the application. Close the solution.

INTRODUCTORY

21. If necessary, complete the Rainfall Calculator application from this chapter's Programming Example, and then close the solution. Use Windows to make a copy of the Rainfall Solution folder. Rename the folder Rainfall Solution-Intermediate. Open the Rainfall Solution (Rainfall Solution.sln) file contained in the VbReloaded2010\Chap08\Rainfall Solution-Intermediate folder. Modify the code so that it

INTERMEDIATE

uses two functions rather than the CalcAverage procedure. One of the functions should calculate and return the total rainfall; the other should calculate and return the average rainfall. Save the solution and then start and test the application. Close the solution.

INTERMEDIATE

22. Use Windows to make a copy of the Temperature Solution folder. Rename the folder Temperature Solution-Subs. Open the Temperature Solution (Temperature Solution.sln) file contained in the VbReloaded2010\Chap08\Temperature Solution-Subs folder. Code the application so that it uses two independent Sub procedures: one to convert a temperature from Fahrenheit to Celsius, and the other to convert a temperature from Celsius to Fahrenheit. Save the solution and then start and test the application. Close the solution.

INTERMEDIATE

23. Use Windows to make a copy of the Temperature Solution folder. Rename the folder Temperature Solution-Functions. Open the Temperature Solution (Temperature Solution.sln) file contained in the VbReloaded2010\Chap08\Temperature Solution-Functions folder. Code the application so that it uses two functions: one to convert a temperature from Fahrenheit to Celsius, and the other to convert a temperature from Celsius to Fahrenheit. Save the solution and then start and test the application. Close the solution.

INTERMEDIATE

24. Open the Translator Solution (Translator Solution.sln) file contained in the VbReloaded2010\Chap08\Translator Solution folder. Code the application so that it uses functions to translate the English words into French, Spanish, or Italian. Save the solution and then start and test the application. Close the solution.

INTERMEDIATE

25. If necessary, complete the Concentration Game application from this chapter's Programming Tutorial 2, and then close the solution. Use Windows to make a copy of the Concentration Game Solution folder. Rename the folder Concentration Game Solution-Wild. Open the Concentration Game Solution (Concentration Game Solution.sln) file contained in the VbReloaded2010\Chap08\Concentration Game Solution-Wild folder. Replace the Washer/Dryer values in the list box with two Wild Card values. A Wild Card value matches any other value on the game board. The game is over either when all of the words are revealed or when two unmatched words remain on the game board. Make the appropriate modifications to the code. Save the solution and then start and test the application. Close the solution.

ADVANCED

26. If necessary, complete the Tri-County Electricity application from this chapter's Programming Tutorial 1, and then close the solution. Use Windows to make a copy of the Tri-County Electricity Solution folder. Rename the folder Tri-County Electricity Solution-Advanced1. Open the Tri-County Electricity Solution (Tri-County Electricity Solution.sln) file contained in the VbReloaded2010\Chap08\Tri-County Electricity Solution-Advanced1 folder. Replace the CalcResidentialTotal Sub procedure and the GetCommercialTotal function with a Sub procedure named CalcTotal. Modify the Calculate button's

Click event procedure so that it uses the CalcTotal procedure for both residential and commercial customers. Save the solution and then start and test the application. Close the solution.

27. If necessary, complete the Tri-County Electricity application from this chapter's Programming Tutorial 1, and then close the solution. Use Windows to make a copy of the Tri-County Electricity Solution folder. Rename the folder Tri-County Electricity Solution-Advanced2. Open the Tri-County Electricity Solution (Tri-County Electricity Solution.sln) file contained in the VbReloaded2010\Chap08\Tri-County Electricity Solution-Advanced2 folder. Replace the CalcResidentialTotal Sub procedure and the GetCommercialTotal function with a function named GetTotal. Modify the Calculate button's Click event procedure so that it uses the GetTotal function for both residential and commercial customers. Save the solution and then start and test the application. Close the solution.

ADVANCED

28. If necessary, complete the Concentration Game application from this chapter's Programming Tutorial 2, and then close the solution. Use Windows to make a copy of the Concentration Game Solution folder. Rename the folder Concentration Game Solution-Counters. Open the Concentration Game Solution (Concentration Game Solution.sln) file contained in the VbReloaded2010\Chap08\Concentration Game Solution-Counters folder. Modify the application so that it displays (in two labels) the number of times the user selects a matching pair of words, and the number of times the user does not select a matching pair of words. Save the solution and then start and test the application. Close the solution.

ADVANCED

29. In this exercise, you learn how to specify that one or more arguments are optional in a Call statement. Open the Optional Solution (Optional Solution.sln) file contained in the VbReloaded2010\Chap08\Optional Solution folder.

DISCOVERY

   a. Open the Code Editor window and review the existing code. The calcButton's Click event procedure contains two Call statements. The first Call statement passes three variables to the CalcBonus procedure. The second call statement, however, passes only two variables to the procedure. (Do not be concerned about the jagged line that appears below the second Call statement.) Notice that the `rate` variable is omitted from the second Call statement. You indicate that the `rate` variable is optional in the Call statement by including the keyword `Optional` before the variable's corresponding parameter in the procedure header; you enter the `Optional` keyword before the `ByVal` keyword. You also assign a default value that the procedure will use for the missing parameter when the procedure is called. You assign the default value by entering the assignment operator and the default value after the parameter in the procedure header. In this case, you will assign the number .1 as the default value for the `rate` variable. (Optional parameters must be listed at the end of the procedure header.)

b. Change the `ByVal bonusRate As Double` in the procedure header appropriately. Save the solution and then start the application. Calculate the bonus for a salesperson with an "a" code, $1000 in sales, and a rate of .05. The `Call CalcBonus(sales, bonus, rate)` statement calls the CalcBonus procedure, passing it the number 1000, the address of the `bonus` variable, and the number .05. The CalcBonus procedure stores the number 1000 in the `totalSales` variable. It also assigns the name `bonusAmount` to the `bonus` variable and stores the number .05 in the `bonusRate` variable. The procedure then multiplies the contents of the `totalSales` variable (1000) by the contents of the `bonusRate` variable (.05), assigning the result (50) to the `bonusAmount` variable. The `bonusLabel.Text = bonus.ToString("C2")` statement then displays $50.00 in the bonusLabel.

c. Now calculate the bonus for a salesperson with a code of "b" and a sales amount of $2000. The `Call CalcBonus(sales, bonus)` statement calls the CalcBonus procedure, passing it the number 2000 and the address of the `bonus` variable. The CalcBonus procedure stores the number 2000 in the `totalSales` variable and assigns the name `bonusAmount` to the `bonus` variable. Because the Call statement did not supply a value for the `bonusRate` variable, the default value (.1) is assigned to the variable. The procedure then multiplies the contents of the `totalSales` variable (2000) by the contents of the `bonusRate` variable (.1), assigning the result (200) to the `bonusAmount` variable. The `bonusLabel.Text = bonus.ToString("C2")` statement then displays $200.00 in the bonusLabel. Close the solution.

SWAT THE BUGS

30. Open the Debug Solution (Debug Solution.sln) file contained in the VbReloaded2010\Chap08\Debug Solution folder. Open the Code Editor window and review the existing code. Start and then test the application. Locate and then correct any errors. When the application is working correctly, close the solution.

Case Projects

Car Shoppers Inc.

In an effort to boost sales, Car Shoppers Inc. is offering buyers a choice of either a large cash rebate or an extremely low financing rate, much lower than the rate most buyers would pay by financing the car through their local bank. Jake Miller, the manager of Car Shoppers Inc., wants you to create an application that helps buyers decide whether to take the lower financing rate from his dealership, or take the rebate and then finance the car through their local bank. Be sure to use one or more independent Sub or Function procedures in the application. (Hint: Use the Financial.Pmt method to calculate the payments.) Use the following names for the solution, project, and form file: Car Shoppers Solution, Car Shoppers

Project, and Main Form.vb. Save the solution in the VbReloaded2010\Chap08\ folder. You can create either your own interface or the one shown in Figure 8-52.

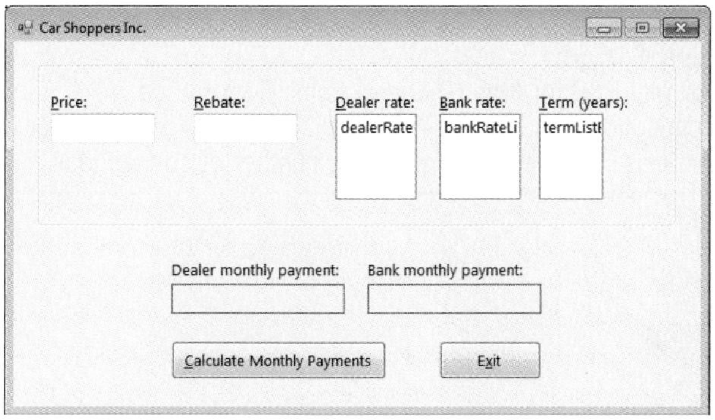

Figure 8-52 Sample interface for the Car Shoppers Inc. application

Wallpaper Warehouse

Last year, Johanna Liu opened a new wallpaper store named Wallpaper Warehouse. Johanna would like you to create an application that the salesclerks can use to quickly calculate and display the number of single rolls of wallpaper required to cover a room. Be sure to use one or more independent Sub or Function procedures in the application. Use the following names for the solution, project, and form file: Wallpaper Warehouse Solution, Wallpaper Warehouse Project, and Main Form.vb. Save the solution in the VbReloaded2010\Chap08 folder. You can create either your own interface or the one shown in Figure 8-53.

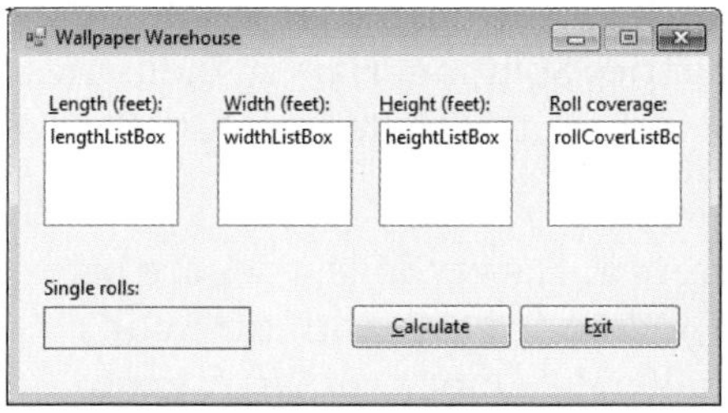

Figure 8-53 Sample interface for the Wallpaper Warehouse application

Cable Direct

Sharon Barrow, the billing supervisor at Cable Direct (a local cable company), has asked you to create an application that calculates and displays a customer's bill. The cable rates are shown in Figure 8-54. Business customers must have at least one connection. Be sure to use one or more independent Sub or Function procedures in the application. Use the following names for the solution, project, and form file: Cable Direct Solution, Cable Direct Project, and Main Form.vb. Save the solution in the VbReloaded2010\Chap08 folder. You can create either your own interface or the one shown in Figure 8-55.

Residential customers:
- Processing fee: $4.50
- Basic service fee: $30
- Premium channels: $5 per channel

Business customers:
- Processing fee: $16.50
- Basic service fee: $80 for first 10 connections; $4 for each additional connection
- Premium channels: $50 per channel for any number of connections

Figure 8-54 Cable Direct rates

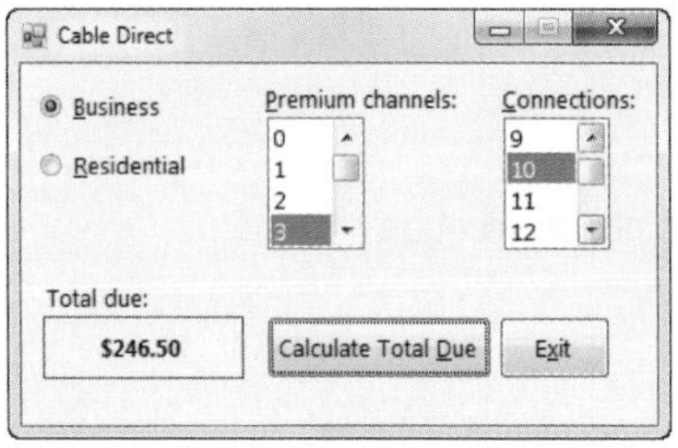

Figure 8-55 Sample run of the Cable Direct application

Harvey Industries

Khalid Patel, the payroll manager at Harvey Industries, manually calculates each employee's weekly gross pay, Social Security and Medicare (FICA) tax, federal withholding tax (FWT), and net pay—a very time-consuming process and one that is prone to mathematical errors. Mr. Patel has asked you to create an application that performs the payroll calculations both efficiently and accurately. Use the following names for the solution, project, and form file: Harvey Industries Solution, Harvey Industries Project, and Main Form.vb. Save the solution in the VbReloaded2010\Chap08 folder.

Create an appropriate interface. Employees at Harvey Industries are paid every Friday. All employees are paid on an hourly basis, with time and one-half paid for the hours worked over 40. The amount of FICA tax to deduct from an employee's weekly gross pay is calculated by multiplying the gross pay amount by 7.65%. The amount of FWT to deduct from an employee's weekly gross pay is based on the employee's filing status—either single (including head of household) or married—and his or her weekly taxable wages. You calculate the weekly taxable wages by first multiplying the number of withholding allowances by $70.19 (the value of a withholding allowance), and then subtracting the result from the weekly gross pay. For example, if your weekly gross pay is $400 and you have two withholding allowances, your weekly taxable wages are $259.62. You use the weekly taxable wages, along with the filing status and the appropriate weekly Federal Withholding Tax table, to determine the amount of FWT to withhold. The weekly tax tables for the year 2010 are shown in Figure 8-56. Be sure to use one or more independent Sub or Function procedures in the application.

FWT Tables – Weekly Payroll Period

Single person (including head of household)

If the taxable wages are: The amount of income tax to withhold is:

Over	But not over	Base amount	Percentage	Of excess over
	$ 116	0		
$ 116	$ 200	0	10%	$ 116
$ 200	$ 693	$ 8.40 plus	15%	$ 200
$ 693	$1,302	$ 82.35 plus	25%	$ 693
$1,302	$1,624	$ 234.60 plus	27%	$1,302
$1,624	$1,687	$ 321.54 plus	30%	$1,624
$1,687	$3,344	$ 340.44 plus	28%	$1,687
$3,344	$7,225	$ 804.40 plus	33%	$3,344
$7,225		$2,085.13 plus	35%	$7,225

Married person

If the taxable wages are: The amount of income tax to withhold is:

Over	But not over	Base amount	Percentage	Of excess over
	$ 264	0		
$ 264	$ 471	0	10%	$ 264
$ 471	$1,457	$ 20.70 plus	15%	$ 471
$1,457	$1,809	$ 168.80 plus	25%	$1,457
$1,809	$2,386	$ 256.60 plus	27%	$1,809
$2,386	$2,789	$ 412.39 plus	25%	$2,386
$2,789	$4,173	$ 513.14 plus	28%	$2,789
$4,173	$7,335	$ 900.66 plus	33%	$4,173
$7,335		$1,944.12 plus	35%	$7,335

Figure 8-56 Weekly FWT tables

CHAPTER 9

Arrays

After studying Chapter 9, you should be able to:

- Declare and initialize a one-dimensional array
- Store data in a one-dimensional array
- Determine the number of array elements and the highest subscript
- Traverse a one-dimensional array
- Code a loop using the For Each…Next statement
- Compute the total and average of a one-dimensional array's contents
- Find the highest value in a one-dimensional array
- Associate a list box with a one-dimensional array
- Use a one-dimensional array as an accumulator
- Sort a one-dimensional array
- Create and initialize a two-dimensional array
- Store data in a two-dimensional array
- Sum the values in a two-dimensional array
- Search a two-dimensional array

Arrays

All of the variables you have used so far have been simple variables. A **simple variable**, also called a **scalar variable**, is one that is unrelated to any other variable in memory. At times, however, you will encounter situations in which some of the variables in a program *are* related to each other. In those cases, it is easier and more efficient to treat the related variables as a group. You already are familiar with the concept of grouping. The clothes in your closet probably are separated into groups, such as coats, sweaters, shirts, and so on. Grouping your clothes in this manner allows you to easily locate your favorite sweater, because you just need to look through the sweater group rather than through the entire closet. You also probably have your CD (compact disc) collection grouped by either music type or artist. If your collection is grouped by artist, it will take only a few seconds to find all of your Michael Jackson CDs and, depending on the number of Michael Jackson CDs you own, only a short time after that to locate a particular CD.

When you group together related variables, the group is referred to as an array of variables or, more simply, an **array**. You might use an array of 50 variables to store the population of each U.S. state. Or, you might use an array of four variables to store the sales made in each of your company's four sales regions. As you will learn in this chapter, the variables in an array can be used just like any other variables. You can assign values to them, use them in calculations, display their contents, and so on.

Storing data in an array increases the efficiency of a program, because data can be both stored in and retrieved from the computer's internal memory much faster than it can be written to and read from a file on a disk. In addition, after the data is entered into an array, which typically is done at the beginning of a program, the program can use the data as many times as necessary without having to enter the data again. Your company's sales program, for example, can use the sales amounts stored in an array to calculate the total company sales and the percentage that each region contributed to the total sales. It also can use the sales amounts in the array either to calculate the average sales amount or to simply display the sales made in a specific region.

It takes longer for the computer to access the information stored in a disk file, because the computer must wait for the disk drive to first locate the needed information and then read the information into internal memory.

The most commonly used arrays in business applications are one-dimensional and two-dimensional. Arrays having more than two dimensions are used mostly in scientific and engineering applications and are beyond the scope of this book. At this point, it's important to point out that arrays are one of the more challenging topics for beginning programmers. Therefore, it is important for you to read and study each section in this chapter thoroughly before moving on to the next section. If you still feel overwhelmed by the end of the chapter, try reading the chapter again, paying particular attention to the examples and procedures shown in the figures.

One-Dimensional Arrays

The variables in an array are stored in consecutive locations in the computer's internal memory. Each variable in an array has the same name and data type. You distinguish one variable in a **one-dimensional array** from another variable in the same array using a unique number. The unique number, which is always an integer, is called a subscript. The **subscript** indicates the variable's position in the array and is assigned by the computer when the array is created in internal memory. The first variable in a one-dimensional array is assigned a subscript of 0, the second a subscript of 1, and so on. You refer to each variable in an array by the array's name and the variable's subscript, which is specified in a set of parentheses immediately following the array name. To refer to the first variable in a one-dimensional array named `sales`, you use `sales(0)`—read "`sales` sub zero." Similarly, to refer to the second variable in the `sales` array, you use `sales(1)`. If the `sales` array contains four variables, you refer to the fourth (and last) variable using `sales(3)`. Notice that the last subscript in an array is always one number less than the total number of variables in the array; this is because array subscripts start at 0. Figure 9-1 illustrates the variables contained in the one-dimensional `sales` array using the storage bin analogy from Chapter 3. The `age`, `rate`, and `unitCharge` variables included in the figure are scalar variables.

A subscript is also called an index.

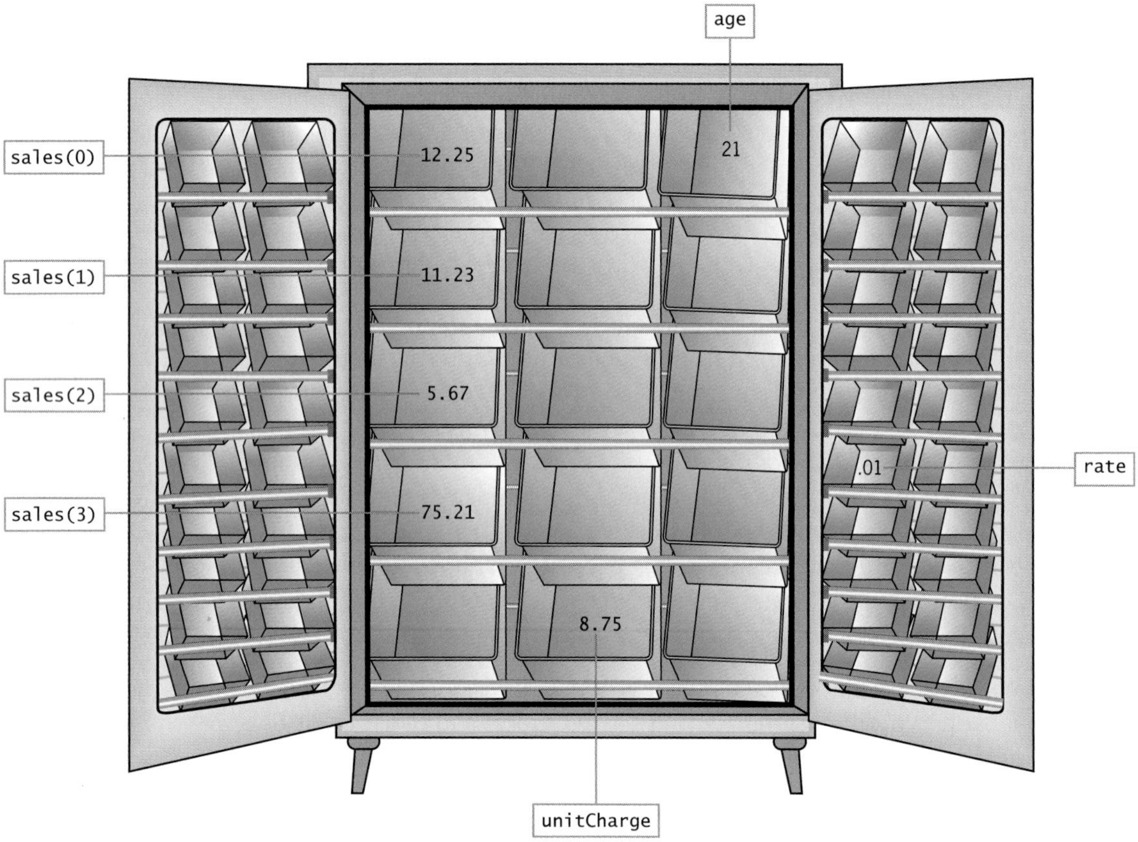

Figure 9-1 Illustration of the naming convention for the one-dimensional `sales` array

Before you can use an array, you first must declare (create) it. Figure 9-2 shows two versions of the syntax for declaring a one-dimensional array in Visual Basic. The {Dim | Private | Static} portion in each version indicates that you can select only one of the keywords appearing within the braces. The appropriate keyword depends on whether you are creating a procedure-level array or a class-level array. *ArrayName* is the name of the array, and *dataType* is the type of data the array variables, referred to as **elements**, will store. In Version 1 of the syntax, *highestSubscript* is an integer that specifies the highest subscript in the array. When the array is created, it will contain one element more than the number specified in the highestSubscript argument. This is because the first element in a one-dimensional array has a subscript of 0. In Version 2 of the syntax, *initialValues* is a comma-separated list of values you want assigned to the array elements. Also included in Figure 9-2 are examples of using both versions of the syntax.

HOW TO Declare a One-Dimensional Array

Syntax – Version 1
{**Dim** | **Private** | **Static**} *arrayName*(*highestSubscript*) **As** *dataType*

Syntax – Version 2
{**Dim** | **Private** | **Static**} *arrayName*() **As** *dataType* = {*initialValues*}

Example 1
`Dim cities(15) As String`
declares a 16-element procedure-level array named `cities`; each element is automatically initialized using the keyword `Nothing`

Example 2
`Static numbers(4) As Decimal`
declares a static, five-element procedure-level array named `numbers`; each element is automatically initialized to 0

Example 3
`Private scores(5) As Integer`
declares a six-element class-level array named `scores`; each element is automatically initialized to 0

Example 4
`Private sales() As Double = {12.25, 11.23, 5.67, 75.21}`
declares and initializes a four-element class-level array named `sales`

Figure 9-2 How to declare a one-dimensional array

When you use Version 1 of the syntax, the computer automatically initializes each element in the array when the array is created. If the array's data type is String, each element in the array is initialized using the keyword `Nothing`. As you learned in Chapter 3, variables initialized to `Nothing` do not actually contain the word "Nothing"; rather, they contain no data at all. Elements in a numeric array are initialized to the number 0, and elements in a Boolean array are initialized using the Boolean keyword `False`. Date array elements are initialized to 12:00 AM January 1, 0001.

Rather than having the computer use a default value to initialize each array element, you can use Version 2 of the syntax to specify each element's initial value when the array is declared. Assigning initial values to an array is often referred to as **populating the array**. You list the initial values in the initial-Values section of the syntax, using commas to separate the values, and you enclose the list of values in braces ({}). Notice that Version 2's syntax does not include the highestSubscript argument; instead, an empty set of parentheses follows the array name. The computer automatically calculates the highest subscript based on the number of values listed in the initialValues section. Because the first subscript in a one-dimensional array is the number 0, the highest subscript is always one number less than the number of values listed in the initialValues section. The `Private sales() As Double = {12.25, 11.23, 5.67, 75.21}` statement in Example 4 in Figure 9-2, for instance, creates a four-element array with subscripts of 0, 1, 2, and 3. The computer assigns the number 12.25 to the `sales(0)` element, 11.23 to the `sales(1)` element, 5.67 to the `sales(2)` element, and 75.21 to the `sales(3)` element, as illustrated earlier in Figure 9-1.

After an array is declared, you can use another statement to store a different value in an array element. Examples of such statements include assignment statements and statements that contain the TryParse method. Figure 9-3 shows examples of both types of statements.

HOW TO Store Data in a One-Dimensional Array

Example 1
```
cities(0) = "Madrid"
```
assigns the string "Madrid" to the first element in the `cities` array

Example 2
```
For x As Integer = 1 To 5
    numbers(x - 1) = x ^ 2
Next x
```
assigns the squares of the numbers from 1 through 5 to the `numbers` array

Example 3
```
Dim subscript As Integer
Do While subscript <= 5
    scores(subscript) = 100
    subscript += 1
Loop
```
assigns the number 100 to each element in the `scores` array

Example 4
```
sales(1) *= .1
```
multiplies the contents of the second element in the `sales` array by .1 and then assigns the result to the second element; you also can write this statement as `sales(1) = sales(1) * .1`

Example 5
```
Double.TryParse(salesTextBox.Text, sales(2))
```
assigns either the value entered in the salesTextBox (converted to Double) or the number 0 to the third element in the `sales` array

Figure 9-3 How to store data in a one-dimensional array

The number of elements in a one-dimensional array is stored, as an integer, in the array's **Length property**. Figure 9-4 shows the property's syntax and includes an example of using the property.

HOW TO Use a One-Dimensional Array's Length Property

Syntax
arrayName.**Length**

Example
```
Dim cities(15) As String
Dim numElements As Integer
numElements = cities.Length
```
assigns the number 16 to the `numElements` variable

Figure 9-4 How to use a one-dimensional array's Length property

You can determine the highest subscript in a one-dimensional array by subtracting the number 1 from the array's Length property. This is because the highest subscript in a one-dimensional array is always one number less than the number of array elements. You also can use the array's GetUpperBound method. Figure 9-5 shows the method's syntax and includes an example of using the method. The **GetUpperBound method** returns an integer that represents the highest subscript in the specified dimension in the array. When used with a one-dimensional array, the specified dimension is always 0.

HOW TO Use a One-Dimensional Array's GetUpperBound Method

Syntax
arrayName.**GetUpperBound(0)**

the specified dimension for a one-dimensional array is always 0

Example
```
Dim cities(15) As String
Dim highestSub As Integer
highestSub = cities.GetUpperBound(0)
```
assigns the number 15 to the `highestSub` variable

Figure 9-5 How to use a one-dimensional array's GetUpperBound method

Mini-Quiz 9-1

The answers to Mini-Quiz questions are located in Appendix A.

1. Which of the following declares a one-dimensional String array named `letters`? The array should have four elements.

   a. `Dim letters(3) As String`

   b. `Dim letters() As String = "A", "B", "C", "D"`

   c. `Dim letters(3) As String = {"A", "B", "C", "D"}`

   d. all of the above

2. Which of the following assigns to the `numElements` variable the number of elements contained in a one-dimensional array named `items`?

   a. `numElements = items.Length`

   b. `numElements = items.GetUpperBound(0) + 1`

   c. `numElements = items.GetNumItems(0)`

   d. both a and b

3. Which of the following assigns the string "Scottsburg" to the fifth element in a one-dimensional array named `cities`?

   a. `cities(4) = "Scottsburg"`

   b. `cities(5) = "Scottsburg"`

   c. `cities[4] = "Scottsburg"`

   d. `cities[5] = "Scottsburg"`

Traversing a One-Dimensional Array

At times, you may need to traverse an array, which means to look at each array element, one by one, beginning with the first element and ending with the last element. You traverse an array using a loop. Figure 9-6 shows two examples of loops that traverse the `months` array, displaying each element's value in the monthsListBox. The loop in Example 1 is coded using the For...Next statement; Example 2's loop uses the Do...Loop statement.

HOW TO Traverse a One-Dimensional Array

```
Dim months() As String = {"Jan", "Feb", "Mar",
                          "Apr", "May", "Jun",
                          "Jul", "Aug", "Sep",
                          "Oct", "Nov", "Dec"}
```

Example 1

you also can use `Dim highSub As Integer = months.Length - 1`

```
Dim highSub As Integer = months.GetUpperBound(0)
For subscript As Integer = 0 to highSub
    monthsListBox.Items.Add(months(subscript))
Next subscript
```

displays the contents of the `months` array in the monthsListBox

Example 2

you also can use `Dim highSub As Integer = months.GetUpperBound(0)`

```
Dim highSub As Integer = months.Length - 1
Dim subscript As Integer
Do While subscript <= highSub
    monthsListBox.Items.Add(months(subscript))
    subscript += 1
Loop
```

displays the contents of the `months` array in the monthsListBox

Figure 9-6 How to traverse a one-dimensional array

Recall that Visual Basic provides three statements for coding a loop: Do ... Loop, For ... Next, and For Each ... Next. You already know how to use the Do ... Loop and For ... Next statements. You will learn about the For Each ... Next statement in the next section.

The For Each ... Next Statement

Visual Basic provides the **For Each ... Next statement** for coding a loop whose instructions you want processed for each element in a group, such as for each variable in an array. An advantage of using the For Each ... Next statement to process an array is that your code does not need to keep track of the array subscripts or even know the number of array elements. However, unlike the loop instructions in a Do ... Loop or For ... Next statement, the instructions in a For Each ... Next statement can only read the array values; they cannot modify the values. Figure 9-7 shows the For Each ... Next statement's syntax, which begins with the For Each clause and ends with the Next clause. The *elementVariableName* that appears in both clauses is the name of a variable that the computer can use to keep track of each element in the *group*. The variable's data type is specified in the `As` *dataType* portion of the For Each clause and must be the same as the group's data type. A variable declared in the For Each clause has block scope and is recognized only by the instructions within the For Each ... Next loop. You enter the loop body, which contains the instructions you want the computer to repeat, between the For Each and Next clauses. The example in Figure 9-7 shows how to write the loops from Figure 9-6 using the For Each ... Next statement.

HOW TO Use the For Each ... Next Statement

Syntax

For Each *elementVariableName* **As** *dataType* **In** *group*
    loop body instructions
Next *elementVariableName*

Example

```
For Each monthElement As String In months
     monthsListBox.Items.Add(months(subscript))
Next monthElement
```

displays the contents of the `months` array in the monthsListBox

Figure 9-7 How to use the For Each ... Next statement

Although you do not need to specify the *elementVariableName* in the Next clause, doing so is highly recommended because it makes your code more self-documenting.

Starward Coffee—Calculating a Total and an Average

Figure 9-8 shows the problem specification for the Starward Coffee application, and Figure 9-9 shows a sample run of the application.

The store manager at Starward Coffee wants an application that displays two items: the total number of pounds of coffee used during a 12-month period and the average number of pounds used each month. Last year, the monthly usage amounts were as follows: 400.5, 450, 475.5, 336.5, 457, 325, 220.5, 276, 300, 320.5, 400.5, and 415. The application will store the monthly amounts in a 12-element one-dimensional array. It then will calculate the total usage and average monthly usage. The total usage is calculated by accumulating the array values. The average monthly usage is calculated by dividing the total usage by the number of array elements.

Figure 9-8 Problem specification for the Starward Coffee application

If you want to experiment with the Starward Coffee application, open the solution contained in the Try It 1! folder.

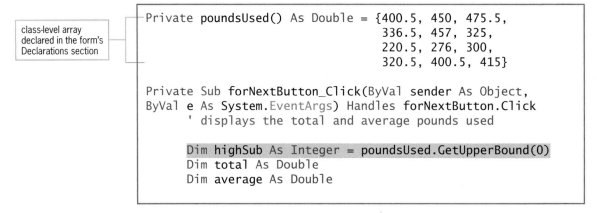

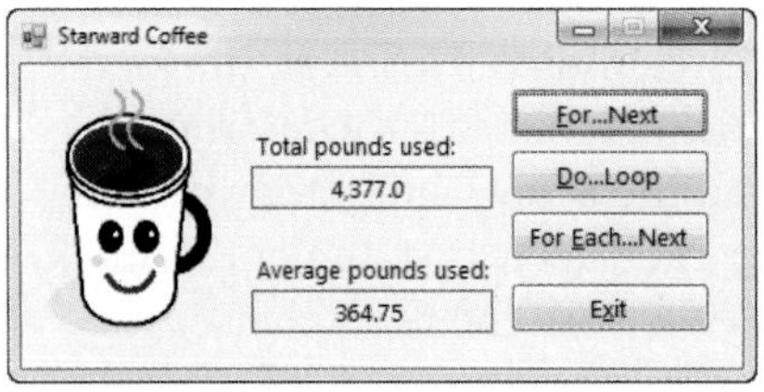

Figure 9-9 Sample run of the Starward Coffee application

Figure 9-10 shows most of the application's code. The Private statement in the MainForm's Declarations section declares and initializes a class-level Double array named `poundsUsed`; the array contains 12 elements. Each button's Click event procedure uses a loop to traverse the `poundsUsed` array, adding each array element's value to the `total` variable. The code pertaining to each loop is shaded in the figure. Notice that you need to specify the highest array subscript in the For ... Next and Do ... Loop statements, but not in the For Each ... Next statement. The For ... Next and Do ... Loop statements also must keep track of the array subscripts; this task is not necessary in the For Each ... Next statement. When each loop has finished processing, the `total` variable contains the total number of pounds used during the 12-month period. After accumulating the array values, each button's Click event procedure calculates the average monthly usage. The calculation is made by dividing the value stored in the `total` variable by the number of elements in the array. Each procedure then displays the total and average amounts on the form, as shown in Figure 9-9.

class-level array declared in the form's Declarations section

```
Private poundsUsed() As Double = {400.5, 450, 475.5,
                                   336.5, 457, 325,
                                   220.5, 276, 300,
                                   320.5, 400.5, 415}

Private Sub forNextButton_Click(ByVal sender As Object,
ByVal e As System.EventArgs) Handles forNextButton.Click
      ' displays the total and average pounds used

      Dim highSub As Integer = poundsUsed.GetUpperBound(0)
      Dim total As Double
      Dim average As Double
```

Figure 9-10 Partial code for the Starward Coffee application *(continues)*

(continued)

```
        ' accumulate pounds used
        For subscript As Integer = 0 To highSub
            total += poundsUsed(subscript)
        Next subscript
        ' calculate average
        average = total / poundsUsed.Length

        totalLabel.Text = total.ToString("N1")
        averageLabel.Text = average.ToString("N2")
End Sub

Private Sub doLoopButton_Click(ByVal sender As Object,
ByVal e As System.EventArgs) Handles doLoopButton.Click
        ' displays the total and average pounds used

        Dim highSub As Integer = poundsUsed.GetUpperBound(0)
        Dim total As Double
        Dim average As Double
        Dim subscript As Integer

        ' accumulate pounds used
        Do While subscript <= highSub
            total += poundsUsed(subscript)
            subscript += 1
        Loop
        ' calculate average
        average = total / poundsUsed.Length

        totalLabel.Text = total.ToString("N1")
        averageLabel.Text = average.ToString("N2")
End Sub

Private Sub forEachNextButton_Click(ByVal sender As Object,
ByVal e As System.EventArgs) Handles forEachNextButton.Click
        ' displays the total and average pounds used

        Dim total As Double
        Dim average As Double

        ' accumulate pounds used
        For Each pound As Double In poundsUsed
            total += pound
        Next pound
        ' calculate average
        average = total / poundsUsed.Length

        totalLabel.Text = total.ToString("N1")
        averageLabel.Text = average.ToString("N2")
End Sub
```

Figure 9-10 Partial code for the Starward Coffee application

Car-Mart—Finding the Highest Value

Figure 9-11 shows the problem specification for the Car-Mart application, and Figure 9-12 shows a sample run of the application.

The sales manager at Car-Mart wants an application that displays two items: the highest commission amount earned during the month and the number of salespeople who earned that amount. Last month, the following commission amounts were paid to the 16 salespeople: 1000, 2000, 4500, 100, 5000, 100, 6700, 5000, 780, 890, 150, 5100, 6700, 5100, 3000, and 200. The application will store the commission amounts in a 16-element one-dimensional array. It then will examine each element in the array, looking for the highest commission amount. It will use a counter variable to keep track of the number of salespeople earning that amount.

Figure 9-11 Problem specification for the Car-Mart application

Figure 9-12 Sample run of the Car-Mart application

If you want to experiment with the Car-Mart application, open the solution contained in the Try It 2! folder.

Figure 9-13 shows the Get Highest button's Click event procedure. The first Dim statement declares and initializes a procedure-level Integer array named `commission`; the array contains 16 elements. The second Dim statement declares an Integer variable named `highSub` and initializes it to the highest subscript in the `commission` array (15). The third Dim statement declares and initializes an Integer variable named `highestComm`. The procedure will use the `highestComm` variable to keep track of the highest value in the array. When searching an array for the highest (or lowest) value, it's a common programming practice to initialize the variable to the value stored in the first array element. In this case, the `highestComm` variable is initialized to the value stored in the `commission(0)` element; that value represents the first salesperson's commission. The fourth Dim statement declares and initializes an Integer variable named `salespeople`. The `salespeople` variable will be used as a counter variable to keep track of the number of salespeople whose commission matches the amount stored in the `highestComm` variable. The Dim statement initializes the `salespeople` variable to 1 because, at this point, one salesperson (the first one) has earned the amount currently stored in the `highestComm` variable.

Notice that the loop in Figure 9-13 searches the second through the last element in the `commission` array. The first element is not included in the search, because its value is assigned to the `highestComm` variable when the variable is declared. The loop body contains an outer selection structure and a nested selection structure. The first time the loop body is processed, the outer selection structure's condition compares the value stored in the current array element with the value stored in the `highestComm` variable. If both values are equal, the outer selection structure's true path adds 1 to the `salespeople` counter variable; otherwise, the nested selection structure in its false path is processed. The nested selection structure's condition determines whether the value stored in the current array element is greater than the value stored in the `highestComm` variable. If it is, the nested selection structure's true path assigns the current array element's value to the `highestComm` variable. It also assigns the number 1 to the `salespeople` counter variable because, at this point, only one salesperson has earned that commission amount. After both selection structures end, the loop proceeds to the next element in the array. When the loop has finished processing, the last two assignment statements in the procedure display the highest commission ($6,700) and the number of people earning that commission (2) in the interface, as shown earlier in Figure 9-12.

```
Private Sub highestButton_Click(ByVal sender As Object,
ByVal e As System.EventArgs) Handles highestButton.Click
      ' displays the highest commission amount and the
      ' number of salespeople who earned that amount

      Dim commission() As Integer = {1000, 2000, 4500, 100,
                                      5000, 100, 6700, 5000,
                                      780, 890, 150, 5100,
                                      6700, 5100, 3000, 200}

      Dim highSub As Integer = commission.GetUpperBound(0)
      Dim highestComm As Integer = commission(0)
      Dim salespeople As Integer = 1

      For x As Integer = 1 To highSub
            If commission(x) = highestComm Then
                  salespeople += 1
            Else
                  If commission(x) > highestComm Then
                        highestComm = commission(x)
                        salespeople = 1
                  End If
            End If
      Next x

      highestLabel.Text = highestComm.ToString("C0")
      salespeopleLabel.Text = salespeople.ToString("N0")
End Sub
```

assign the first array element's value and the number 1 to the `highestComm` and `salespeople` variables, respectively

search the second through the last array elements

Figure 9-13 Get Highest button's Click event procedure

Hunt Auditorium—Arrays and Collections

Figure 9-14 shows the problem specification for the Hunt Auditorium application, and Figure 9-15 shows a sample run of the application.

The theater manager at Hunt Auditorium wants an application that displays the price of a ticket. The price is based on the seating section, as shown in the chart below. The application's interface will provide a list box from which the user can select the seating section. The application will store the prices in a four-element one-dimensional array. It will use the index of the item selected in the list box to access the appropriate price from the array.

Section	Price ($)
A	150
B	100
C	95
D	85

Figure 9-14 Problem specification for the Hunt Auditorium application

If you want to experiment with the Hunt Auditorium application, open the solution contained in the Try It 3! folder.

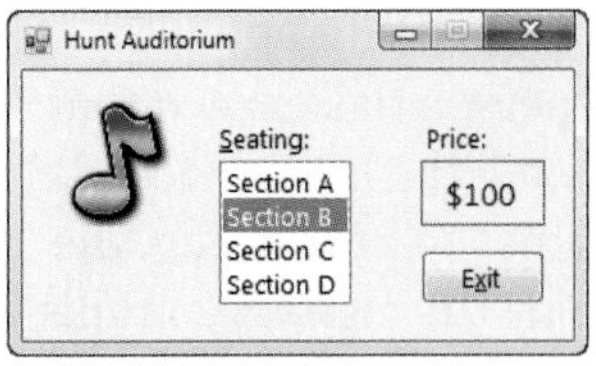

Figure 9-15 Sample run of the Hunt Auditorium application

Recall that the items in a list box belong to the Items collection.

It's not uncommon for programmers to associate the items in a list box with the values stored in an array. This is because the items in a list box belong to a collection, and collections and arrays have several things in common. First, each is a group of individual objects treated as one unit. Second, each individual object in the group is identified by a unique number. The unique number is called an index when referring to a collection, but a subscript when referring to an array. Third, both the first index in a collection and the first subscript in an array are 0. These commonalities allow you to associate the list box items and array elements by their positions within their respective groups. In other words, you can associate the first item in a list box with the first element in an array, the second item with the second element, and so on. To associate a list box with an array, you first add the appropriate items to the list box. You then store each item's related value in its corresponding position in the array.

Figure 9-16 shows most of the Hunt Auditorium application's code. The MainForm's Load event procedure adds the seating sections to the seatingListBox and then selects the first item in the list. The Private statement in the form's Declarations section initializes the first element in the `prices` array to 150, which is the price associated with the first item in the list box (Section A). The remaining array elements are initialized to the prices corresponding to their list box items. The relationship between the list box and `prices` array is illustrated in Figure 9-16. The list box's SelectedIndexChanged event procedure uses the index of the item selected in the list box to access the appropriate price from the `prices` array. If the second item (Section B) is selected in the list box, the first assignment statement in the procedure assigns the number 1 to the `subscript` variable. The next assignment statement then uses the `subscript` variable to access the corresponding price (100) from the `prices` array.

class-level array declared in the form's Declarations section

```
Private prices() As Integer = {150, 100, 95, 85}

Private Sub MainForm_Load(ByVal sender As Object,
ByVal e As System.EventArgs) Handles Me.Load
      ' fill list box with values

      seatingListBox.Items.Add("Section A")
      seatingListBox.Items.Add("Section B")
      seatingListBox.Items.Add("Section C")
      seatingListBox.Items.Add("Section D")
      seatingListBox.SelectedIndex = 0
End Sub
```

Figure 9-16 Partial code and an illustration for the Hunt Auditorium application *(continues)*

(continued)

```
Private Sub seatingListBox_SelectedIndexChanged(
ByVal sender As Object, ByVal e As System.EventArgs
) Handles seatingListBox.SelectedIndexChanged
      ' displays the price

      Dim subscript As Integer
      subscript = seatingListBox.SelectedIndex
      priceLabel.Text = prices(subscript).ToString("C0")
End Sub

      seatingListBox      prices array
      Section A           150
      Section B           100
      Section C            95
      Section D            85
```

uses the selected item's index as the array subscript

the indexes are 0, 1, 2, and 3

the subscripts are 0, 1, 2, and 3

Figure 9-16 Partial code and an illustration for the Hunt Auditorium application

Hinsbrook School—Accumulator Array

Figure 9-17 shows the problem specification for the Hinsbrook School application, and Figure 9-18 shows a sample run of the application.

> Hinsbrook School is having its annual Chocolate Fund Raiser event. Students sell the following five candies: Chocolate Bar, Chocolate Bar-Peanuts, Kit Kat, Peanut Butter Cups, and Take 5 Bar. The school principal wants an application that she can use to enter the amount of each candy sold by each student. The application should display the total number sold for each candy. The interface will provide a list box for the user to select the candy, and a text box for entering the amount sold by a student. The application will use a five-element one-dimensional array to accumulate the amounts sold.

Figure 9-17 Problem specification for the Hinsbrook School application

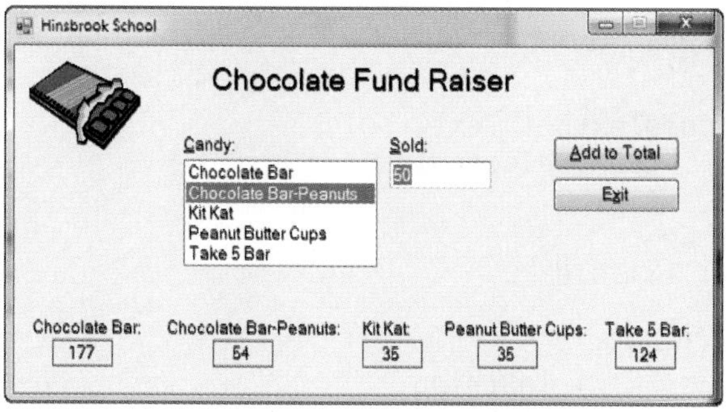

Figure 9-18 Sample run of the Hinsbrook School application

If you want to experiment with the Hinsbrook School application, open the solution contained in the Try It 4! folder.

Figure 9-19 shows most of the Hinsbrook School application's code. The MainForm's Load event procedure adds the five candy names to the candyListBox and then selects the first name in the list. The Static statement in the addButton's Click event procedure declares a one-dimensional Integer array named `candies`. The `candies` array has five elements; each element corresponds to an item listed in the candyListBox. The first array element corresponds to the Chocolate Bar item, the second array element to the Chocolate Bar-Peanuts item, and so on. Each array element will be used to accumulate the sales of its corresponding list box item. Like static variables, which you learned about in Chapter 3, static arrays remain in memory and retain their values until the application ends.

The two Dim statements in the Click event procedure shown in Figure 9-19 declare and initialize two Integer variables named `sold` and `subscript`. The TryParse method stores the contents of the soldTextBox, converted to Integer, in the `sold` variable. The first assignment statement in the procedure assigns to the `subscript` variable the index of the item selected in the list box. The `candies(subscript) += sold` statement uses the number stored in the `subscript` variable to locate the appropriate element in the `candies` array; it then adds the contents of the `sold` variable to the element's contents. The last five assignment statements in the procedure display the contents of the array in the interface. The last statement in the procedure sends the focus to the soldTextBox.

```
Private Sub MainForm_Load(ByVal sender As Object,
ByVal e As System.EventArgs) Handles Me.Load
      ' fill the list box with values

      candyListBox.Items.Add("Chocolate Bar")
      candyListBox.Items.Add("Chocolate Bar-Peanuts")
      candyListBox.Items.Add("Kit Kat")
      candyListBox.Items.Add("Peanut Butter Cups")
      candyListBox.Items.Add("Take 5 Bar")
      candyListBox.SelectedIndex = 0
End Sub

Private Sub addButton_Click(ByVal sender As Object,
ByVal e As System.EventArgs) Handles addButton.Click
      ' add amount sold to the appropriate total

      Static candies(4) As Integer
      Dim sold As Integer
      Dim subscript As Integer

      Integer.TryParse(soldTextBox.Text, sold)
      subscript = candyListBox.SelectedIndex

      ' update array value
      candies(subscript) += sold

      ' display array values
      cbLabel.Text = candies(0).ToString
      cbpLabel.Text = candies(1).ToString
      kkLabel.Text = candies(2).ToString
      pbcLabel.Text = candies(3).ToString
      t5bLabel.Text = candies(4).ToString

      soldTextBox.Focus()
End Sub
```

static procedure-level array

uses the selected item's index as the array subscript

Figure 9-19 Partial code for the Hinsbrook School application

Sorting a One-Dimensional Array

In some applications, you might need to arrange the contents of an array in either ascending or descending order. Arranging data in a specific order is called **sorting**. When an array is sorted in ascending order, the first element in the array contains the smallest value and the last element contains the largest value. When an array is sorted in descending order, on the other hand, the first element contains the largest value and the last element contains the smallest value. You can use the **Array.Sort method** to sort the elements in a one-dimensional array in ascending order. To sort a one-dimensional array in descending order, you first use the Array.Sort method to sort the array in ascending order, and then use the **Array.Reverse method** to reverse the array elements. Figure 9-20 shows the syntax of both methods. In each syntax, *arrayName* is the name of a one-dimensional array.

HOW TO Use the Array.Sort and Array.Reverse Methods

Syntax
Array.Sort(*arrayName***)**
Array.Reverse(*arrayName***)**

Example 1
```
Dim scores As Integer = {78, 83, 75, 90}
Array.Sort(scores)
```
sorts the contents of the array in ascending order, as follows: 75, 78, 83, and 90

Example 2
```
Dim scores As Integer = {78, 83, 75, 90}
Array.Reverse(scores)
```
reverses the contents of the array, placing the values in the following order: 90, 75, 83, and 78

Example 3
```
Dim scores As Integer = {78, 83, 75, 90}
Array.Sort(scores)
Array.Reverse(scores)
```
sorts the contents of the array in ascending order and then reverses the contents, placing the values in descending order as follows: 90, 83, 78, and 75

Figure 9-20 How to use the Array.Sort and Array.Reverse methods

If you want to experiment with sorting a one-dimensional array, open the solution contained in the Try It 5! folder.

To review what you learned about one-dimensional arrays, view the Ch09OneDimensional video.

Mini-Quiz 9-2

The answers to Mini-Quiz questions are located in Appendix A.

1. The `scores` array is a one-dimensional Integer array that contains five elements. Write a For Each... Next statement that totals the array values. Store the total in an Integer variable named `totalScores`. Use `scoreElement` as the elementVariableName in the For Each clause.

2. Rewrite the code from Question 1 using a For... Next statement. Use `subscript` as the counterVariableName in the For clause.

3. Rewrite the code from Question 2 using a Do ... Loop statement.

4. Write the code to sort the `scores` array in ascending order.

Two-Dimensional Arrays

As you learned earlier, the most commonly used arrays in business applications are one-dimensional and two-dimensional. You can visualize a one-dimensional array as a column of variables in memory, similar to the column of storage bins shown earlier in Figure 9-1. A **two-dimensional array**, on the other hand, resembles a table in that the variables (elements) are in rows and columns. You can determine the number of elements in a two-dimensional array by multiplying the number of its rows by the number of its columns. An array that has four rows and three columns, for example, contains 12 elements.

Each element in a two-dimensional array is identified by a unique combination of two subscripts that the computer assigns to the element when the array is created. The subscripts specify the element's row and column positions in the array. Elements located in the first row in a two-dimensional array are assigned a row subscript of 0. Elements in the second row are assigned a row subscript of 1, and so on. Similarly, elements located in the first column in a two-dimensional array are assigned a column subscript of 0. Elements in the second column are assigned a column subscript of 1, and so on.

You refer to each element in a two-dimensional array by the array's name and the element's row and column subscripts, with the row subscript listed first and the column subscript listed second. The subscripts are separated by a comma and specified in a set of parentheses immediately following the array name. For example, to refer to the element located in the first row, first column in a two-dimensional array named `orders`, you use `orders(0, 0)`—read "`orders` sub zero comma zero." Similarly, to refer to the element located in the second row, third column, you use `orders(1, 2)`. Notice that the subscripts are one number less than the row and column in which the element is located. This is because the row and column subscripts start at 0 rather than at 1. You will find that the last row subscript in a two-dimensional array is always one number less than the number of rows in the array. Likewise, the last column subscript is always one number less than the number of columns in the array. Figure 9-21 illustrates the elements contained in the two-dimensional `orders` array using the storage bin analogy. The `rating` and `numSold` variables included in the figure are scalar variables.

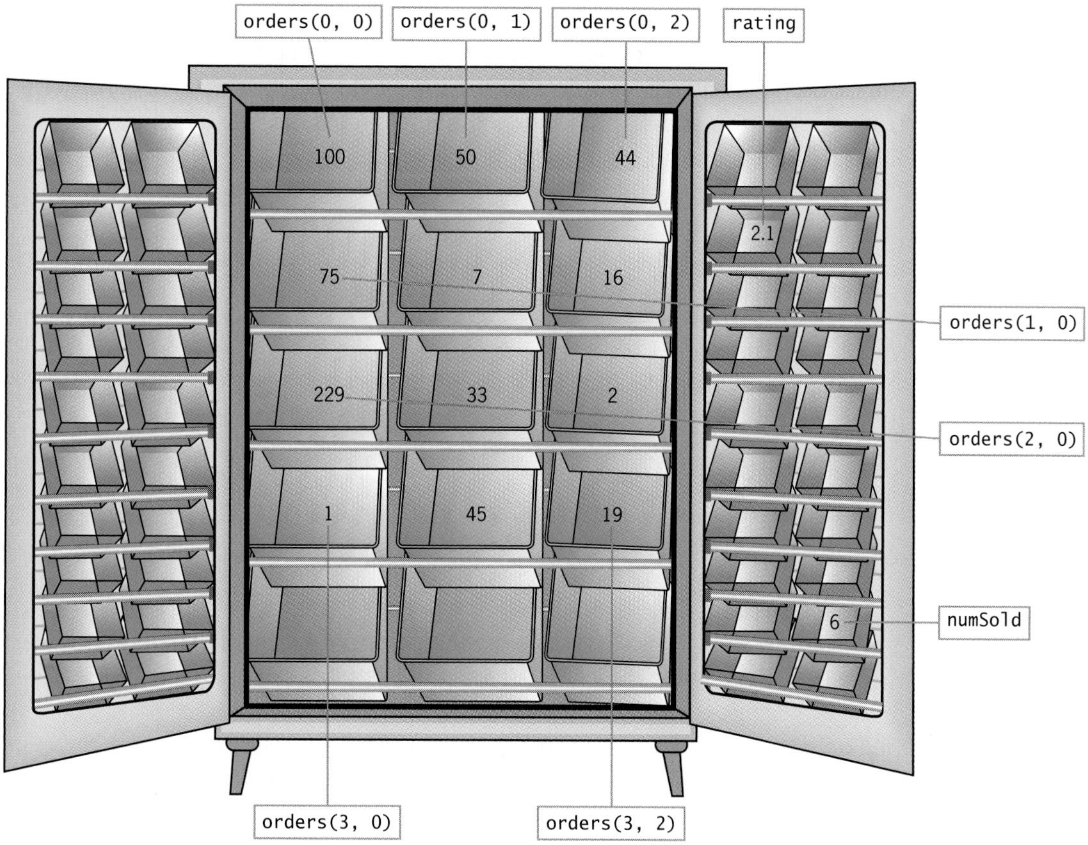

Figure 9-21 Names of some of the variables contained in the two-dimensional `orders` array

Figure 9-22 shows two versions of the syntax for declaring a two-dimensional array in Visual Basic. In each version, *arrayName* is the name of the array and *dataType* is the type of data the array variables will store. In Version 1's syntax, *highestRowSubscript* and *highestColumnSubscript* are integers that specify the highest row and column subscripts, respectively, in the array. When the array is created, it will contain one row more than the number specified in the highestRowSubscript argument and one column more than the number specified in the highestColumnSubscript argument. This is because the first row and column subscripts in a two-dimensional array are 0. When you declare a two-dimensional array using the syntax shown in Version 1, the computer automatically initializes each element in the array when the array is created.

You would use Version 2's syntax when you want to specify each variable's initial value. You do this by including a separate *initialValues* section, enclosed in braces, for each row in the array. If the array has two rows, then the statement that declares and initializes the array should have two initialValues sections. If the array has five rows, then the declaration statement should have five initialValues sections. Within the individual initialValues sections, you enter one or more values separated by commas. The number of values to enter corresponds to the number of columns in the array. If the array contains 10 columns, then each individual initialValues section should contain 10 values. In addition to the set of braces enclosing each individual initialValues section, Version 2's syntax also requires all of the initialValues sections to be enclosed in a set of braces. When using

Version 2's syntax, be sure to include a comma within the parentheses that follow the array's name. The comma indicates that the array is a two-dimensional array. (Recall that a comma is used to separate the row subscript from the column subscript in a two-dimensional array.) Also included in Figure 9-22 are examples of using both syntax versions.

HOW TO Declare a Two-Dimensional Array

Syntax – Version 1
{**Dim** | **Private** | **Static**} *arrayName*(*highestRowSubscript*, *highestColumnSubscript*) **As** *dataType*

Syntax – Version 2
{**Dim** | **Private** | **Static**} *arrayName*(**,**) **As** *dataType* = **{{***initialValues***}**, ... **{***initialValues***}}**

Example 1
```
Dim states(5, 3) As String
```
declares a six-row, four-column procedure-level array named `states`; each element is automatically initialized using the keyword `Nothing`

Example 2
```
Private orders(,) As Integer = {{100, 50, 44},
                                {75, 7, 16},
                                {229, 33, 2},
                                {1, 45, 19}}
```
declares a four-row, three-column class-level array named `orders`; initializes orders(0, 0) to 100, orders(0, 1) to 50, orders(0, 2) to 44, orders(1, 0) to 75, orders(1, 1) to 7, orders(1, 2) to 16, orders(2, 0) to 229, orders(2, 1) to 33, orders(2, 2) to 2, orders(3, 0) to 1, orders(3, 1) to 45, and orders(3, 2) to 19

Figure 9-22 How to declare a two-dimensional array

After a two-dimensional array is declared, you can use another statement to store a different value in an array element. Examples of such statements include assignment statements and statements that contain the TryParse method. Figure 9-23 shows examples of both types of statements.

HOW TO Store Data in a Two-Dimensional Array

Example 1
```
states(0, 1) = "Kansas"
```
assigns the string "Kansas" to the element located in the first row, second column in the `states` array

Figure 9-23 How to store data in a two-dimensional array *(continues)*

(continued)

Example 2
```
For row As Integer = 0 To 3
     For column As Integer = 0 To 2
           orders(row, column) += 1
     Next column
Next row
```
adds the number 1 to each element in the `orders` array

Example 3
```
Dim row As Integer
Dim column As Integer
Do While row <= 3
     column = 0
     Do While column <= 2
          orders(row, column) = 0
          column += 1
     Loop
     row += 1
Loop
```
assigns the number 0 to each element in the `orders` array

Example 4
```
Integer.TryParse(orderTextBox.Text, orders(2, 1))
```
assigns either the value entered in the orderTextBox (converted to Integer) or the number 0 to the element located in the third row, second column in the `orders` array

Figure 9-23 How to store data in a two-dimensional array

Earlier, you learned how to use the GetUpperBound method to determine the highest subscript in a one-dimensional array. You also can use the GetUpperBound method to determine the highest row and column subscripts in a two-dimensional array, as shown in Figure 9-24.

HOW TO Use a Two-Dimensional Array's GetUpperBound Method

Syntax to determine the highest row subscript

arrayName.**GetUpperBound(0)**

the row dimension is always 0

Syntax to determine the highest column subscript

arrayName.**GetUpperBound(1)**

the column dimension is always 1

Example
```
Dim products(10, 3) As String
Dim highestRowSub As Integer
Dim highestColumnSub As Integer
highestRowSub = products.GetUpperBound(0)
highestColumnSub = products.GetUpperBound(1)
```
assigns the numbers 10 and 3 to the `highestRowSub` and `highestColumnSub` variables, respectively

Figure 9-24 How to use a two-dimensional array's GetUpperBound method

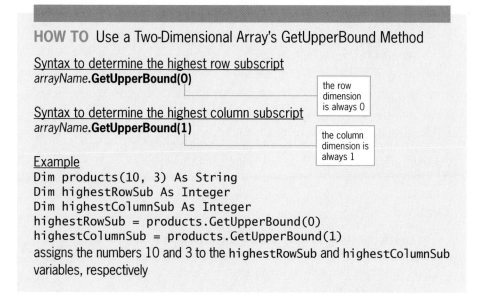

Traversing a Two-Dimensional Array

Recall that you use a loop to traverse a one-dimensional array. To traverse a two-dimensional array, you typically use two loops: an outer loop and a nested loop. One of the loops keeps track of the row subscript and the other keeps track of the column subscript. You can code the loops using either the For ... Next statement or the Do ... Loop statement. Rather than using two loops, you also can traverse a two-dimensional array using one For Each ... Next loop. However, recall that the instructions in a For Each ... Next loop can only read the array values; they cannot modify the values. Figure 9-25 shows examples of loops that traverse the `months` array, displaying each element's value in the monthsListBox.

HOW TO Traverse a Two-Dimensional Array

```
Private months(,) As String = {{"Jan", "31"},
                               {"Feb", "28"},
                               {"Mar", "31"},
                               {"Apr", "30"}}
```

Example 1

```
Dim highRow As Integer = months.GetUpperBound(0)
Dim highCol As Integer = months.GetUpperBound(1)
For row As Integer = 0 To highRow
    For col As Integer = 0 To highCol
        monthsListBox.Items.Add(months(row, col))
    Next col
Next row
```

displays the contents of the `months` array in the monthsListBox; the contents are displayed row by row, as follows: Jan, 31, Feb, 28, Mar, 31, Apr, and 30

Example 2

```
Dim highRow As Integer = months.GetUpperBound(0)
Dim highCol As Integer = months.GetUpperBound(1)
Dim row As Integer
Dim col As Integer
Do While col <= highCol
    row = 0
    Do While row <= highRow
        monthsListBox.Items.Add(months(row, col))
        row += 1
    Loop
    col += 1
Loop
```

displays the contents of the `months` array in the monthsListBox; the contents are displayed column by column, as follows: Jan, Feb, Mar, Apr, 31, 28, 31, and 30

Example 3

```
For Each monthElement As String In months
    monthsListBox.Items.Add(monthElement)
Next monthElement
```

displays the contents of the `months` array in the monthsListBox; the contents are displayed as follows: Jan, 31, Feb, 28, Mar, 31, Apr, and 30

Figure 9-25 How to traverse a two-dimensional array

If you want to experiment with the code shown in Figure 9-25, open the solution contained in the Try It 6! folder.

Jenko Booksellers—Calculating a Total

Figure 9-26 shows the problem specification for the Jenko Booksellers application, and Figure 9-27 shows a sample run of the application.

Jenko Booksellers sells paperback and hardcover books in each of its three stores. The sales manager wants an application that displays the total sales made in the previous month. The sales amounts for the previous month are shown in the chart below. The application will store the sales amounts in a two-dimensional array that has three rows and two columns. Each row will contain the data pertaining to one of the three stores. The sales amounts for paperback books will be stored in the first column. The second column will contain the sales amounts for hardcover books. The application will need to accumulate the array values.

	Paperback sales ($)	Hardcover sales ($)
Store 1	1200.33	2350.75
Store 2	3677.80	2456.05
Store 3	750.67	1345.99

Figure 9-26 Problem specification for the Jenko Booksellers application

Figure 9-27 Sample run of the Jenko Booksellers application

If you want to experiment with the Jenko Booksellers application, open the solution contained in the Try It 7! folder.

Figure 9-28 shows the Calculate button's Click event procedure. The first Dim statement declares and initializes a procedure-level Double array named `sales`; the array has three rows and two columns. The paperback book sales are stored in column 1 in the array, and the hardcover book sales are stored in column 2. The second Dim statement declares and initializes a Double variable named `total`. The `total` variable will be an accumulator variable; it will accumulate the sales amounts stored in the array. The For Each…Next loop adds each array element's value to the `total` accumulator variable. When the loop ends, the last statement in the procedure displays the total sales ($11,781.59) in the interface.

```
Private Sub calcButton_Click(ByVal sender As Object,
ByVal e As System.EventArgs) Handles calcButton.Click
      ' display the total sales

      Dim sales(,) As Double = {{1200.33, 2350.75},
                                {3677.8, 2456.05},
                                {750.67, 1345.99}}
      Dim total As Double

      ' accumulate array values
      For Each saleElement As Double In sales
           total += saleElement
      Next saleElement

      totalLabel.Text = total.ToString("C2")
End Sub
```

Figure 9-28 Calculate button's Click event procedure

O'Reilly Studios—Searching a Two-Dimensional Array

Figure 9-29 shows the problem specification for the O'Reilly Studios application, and Figure 9-30 shows a sample run of the application.

O'Reilly Studios sells paintings for local artists. The studio manager wants an application that allows him to enter the number of paintings a customer orders. The application should display the total cost of the order. The price per painting depends on the number of paintings ordered, as shown in the chart below. Notice that each price in the chart is associated with a range of values. The minimum value in the first range is 1, and the maximum value is 5. The minimum and maximum values in the second range are 6 and 10, respectively. The third range has only a minimum value, 11. The application will store each range's minimum value and price in a two-dimensional array. The array will have three rows and two columns. The first column will contain the minimum values for the three ranges; the second column will contain the prices. The application will need to search the first column in the array, row by row, looking for the minimum value associated with the quantity ordered. The appropriate price can be found in the same row as the minimum value, but in the second column.

Minimum order	Maximum order	Price per painting ($)
1	5	100
6	10	90
11		75

Figure 9-29 Problem specification for the O'Reilly Studios application

If you want to experiment with the O'Reilly Studios application, open the solution contained in the Try It 8! folder.

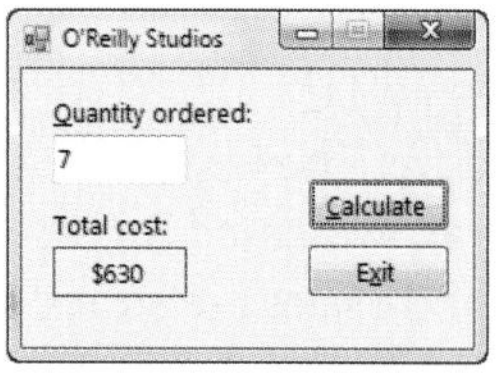

Figure 9-30 Sample run of the O'Reilly Studios application

Figure 9-31 shows most of the code for the O'Reilly Studios application. The Private statement in the MainForm's Declarations section declares and initializes a class-level Integer array named `priceChart`; the array contains three rows and two columns. Notice that the minimum values, which appear in ascending order in Figure 9-29, are entered in the array in descending order. Although the `priceChart` array is used only by the calcButton's Click event procedure, it is declared as a class-level array (rather than a procedure-level array) for efficiency. In this application, the Calculate button probably will be clicked many times while the application is running. If the array is declared in the button's Click event procedure, it will need to be recreated each time the button is clicked. By declaring it as a class-level array, it will be created only once, when the application first starts.

The first three Dim statements in the calcButton's Click event procedure declare and initialize the `quantity`, `pricePerPainting`, and `totalCost` variables, which will store the quantity ordered, price per painting, and total cost, respectively. The next three Dim statements declare the `row`, `highRow`, and `found` variables; these variables will be used to search the array. The `row` variable will keep track of the row subscripts in the array, and the `highRow` variable will keep track of the highest row subscript in the array.

The **found** variable will keep track of whether the appropriate minimum value is located in the first column in the array. Next, the TryParse method converts the contents of the quantityTextBox to Integer and stores the result in the **quantity** variable. The Do clause then tells the computer to repeat the loop body while the current row subscript is less than or equal to the highest row subscript and, at the same time, the **found** variable contains False. Within the loop body is a dual-alternative selection structure. The selection structure's condition compares the quantity ordered with the value stored in the first column in the current row of the array. If the quantity is greater than or equal to the array value, the selection structure's true path is processed. The true path contains two instructions. The first instruction assigns the price from the second column in the current row of the array to the **pricePerPainting** variable. The second instruction assigns the Boolean value True to the **found** variable to indicate that the appropriate range was located. On the other hand, if the quantity is not greater than or equal to the array value, the instruction in the selection structure's false path is processed. That instruction updates the row subscript by 1, allowing the loop to search the next row in the array. When the loop ends, the procedure calculates the total price and then displays the result in the interface. As shown earlier in Figure 9-30, the procedure displays $630 when the user enters 7 in the Quantity ordered box.

Recall that Boolean variables are automatically initialized to False.

To review what you learned about two-dimensional arrays, view the Ch09TwoDimensional video.

minimum values | prices

```
Private priceChart(,) As Integer = {{11, 75},
                                     {6, 90},
                                     {1, 100}}

Private Sub calcButton_Click(ByVal sender As Object,
ByVal e As System.EventArgs) Handles calcButton.Click
      ' display the total price

      Dim quantity As Integer
      Dim pricePerPainting As Integer
      Dim totalCost As Integer

      Dim row As Integer
      Dim highRow As Integer =
           priceChart.GetUpperBound(0)
      Dim found As Boolean

      Integer.TryParse(quantityTextBox.Text, quantity)

      ' search the first column in each row
      Do While row <= highRow AndAlso found = False
           If quantity >= priceChart(row, 0) Then
                pricePerPainting = priceChart(row, 1)
                found = True
           Else
                row += 1
           End If
      Loop

      totalCost = quantity * pricePerPainting
      totalLabel.Text = totalCost.ToString("C0")
End Sub
```

class-level array declared in the form's Declarations section

searches the first column in the current row

assigns the price from the second column in the current row

Figure 9-31 Partial code for the O'Reilly Studios application

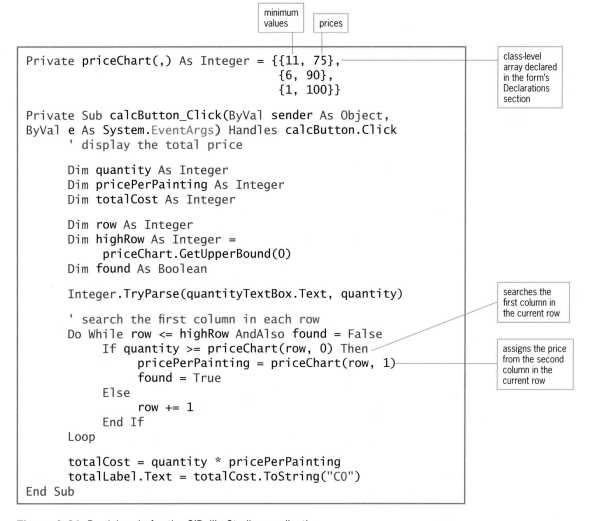

The answers to Mini-Quiz questions are located in Appendix A.

Mini-Quiz 9-3

1. Which of the following declares a two-dimensional String array named `letters`? The array should contain four rows and two columns.
   a. `Dim letters(3, 1) As String`
   b. `Private letters(3, 1) As String`
   c. `Dim letters(,) As String = {{"A", "B"}, {"C", "D"}, {"E", "F"}, {"G", "H"}}`
   d. all of the above

2. Which of the following assigns the Boolean value True to the element located in the third row, first column of a two-dimensional Boolean array named `testAnswers`?
   a. `testAnswers(0, 2) = True`
   b. `testAnswers(2, 0) = True`
   c. `testAnswers(3, 1) = True`
   d. `testAnswers(1, 3) = True`

3. Write the code that assigns to the `highCol` variable the highest column subscript in a two-dimensional array named `people`.

You have completed the concepts section of Chapter 9. The Programming Tutorial section is next.

PROGRAMMING TUTORIAL 1

Creating the Lottery Game Application

In this tutorial, you code the Lottery Game application. Figures 9-32 and 9-33 show the application's TOE chart and MainForm, respectively. The MainForm contains a picture box, two labels, and two buttons. When the user clicks the Get Numbers button, the button's Click event procedure generates and displays six unique random numbers. Each number can range from 1 through 54 only.

Task	Object	Event
1. Generate random numbers from 1 through 54 2. Store six unique random numbers in a one-dimensional array 3. Display the contents of the array in the lotteryLabel	getButton	Click
End the application	exitButton	Click
Display the six unique random numbers (from getButton)	lotteryLabel	None

Figure 9-32 TOE chart for the Lottery Game application

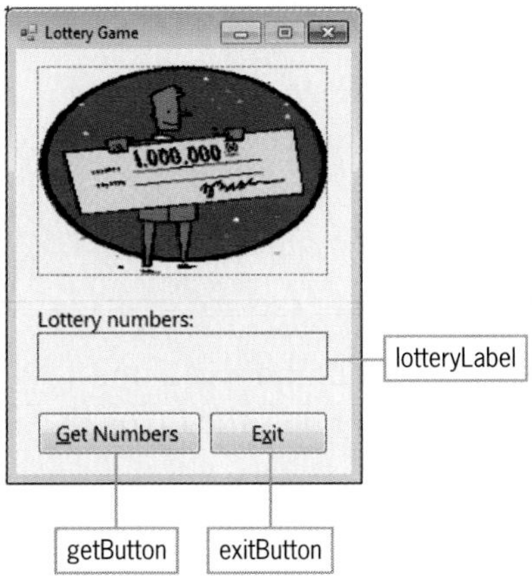

Figure 9-33 MainForm in the Lottery Game application

Coding the Application

Included in the data files for this book is a partially completed Lottery Game application. To complete the application, you just need to code it. According to the application's TOE chart, only the Click event procedures for the two buttons need to be coded.

To open the Lottery Game application:

1. Start Visual Studio or the Express Edition of Visual Basic. If necessary, open the Solution Explorer window.
2. Open the **Lottery Game Solution** (**Lottery Game Solution.sln**) file, which is contained in the VbReloaded2010\Chap09\Lottery Game Solution folder. Open the designer window (if necessary), and then auto-hide the Solution Explorer window.
3. Open the Code Editor window. Notice that the exitButton's Click event procedure has already been coded for you. In addition, the Option statements have already been entered in the General Declarations section.
4. In the comments that appear in the General Declarations section, replace <your name> and <current date> with your name and the current date.

Figure 9-34 shows the pseudocode for the Get Numbers button's Click event procedure, which is responsible for generating and displaying six unique lottery numbers.

```
getButton Click event procedure
1.  declare a six-element Integer array named numbers
2.  generate a random number from 1 through 54 and then store it in the first array element
3.  repeat until all of the remaining array elements contain a unique random number
          generate a random number from 1 through 54

          search the array elements that contain numbers

          if the random number is not already in the array
                store the random number in the current array element and
                then continue with the next array element
          end if
    end repeat
4.  display the contents of the array in the lotteryLabel
```

Figure 9-34 Pseudocode for the Get Numbers button's Click event procedure

To begin coding the Get Numbers button's Click event procedure:

1. Open the code template for the getButton's Click event procedure. Enter the following two comments. Press **Enter** twice after typing the second comment.

   ' generates and displays six unique random
   ' numbers from 1 through 54

2. The procedure will store the six unique lottery numbers in a one-dimensional Integer array that has six elements. Enter the following Dim statement:

   Dim numbers(5) As Integer

3. Next, declare a Random object to represent the pseudo-random number generator in the procedure. Enter the following Dim statement:

   Dim randGen As New Random

4. The procedure will store the random numbers generated by the pseudo-random number generator in an Integer variable named `randomNum`. Enter the following Dim statement:

   Dim randomNum As Integer

5. While the procedure's loop is filling the array with values, it will use an Integer variable to keep track of the array subscripts. Enter the following Dim statement:

   Dim subscript As Integer

6. The procedure's loop will use another Integer variable to keep track of the array subscripts while the array is being searched. Enter the following Dim statement:

   Dim searchSubscript As Integer

7. The procedure will use a Boolean variable to indicate whether the current random number is already contained in the array. Enter the following Dim statement:

   Dim isFound As Boolean

8. The last variable you need to declare will store the highest subscript in the `numbers` array. Type the following statement and then press **Enter** twice:

   Dim highestSub As Integer = numbers.GetUpperBound(0)

9. The first step in the pseudocode shown earlier in Figure 9-34 is to declare the `numbers` array. That step has already been coded. The second step is to generate a random number from 1 through 54 and then store it in the first array element. Enter the following comments and assignment statement. Press **Enter** three times after typing the assignment statement.

   ' generate the first random number and
   ' store it in the first array element
   numbers(0) = randGen.Next(1, 55)

10. Next, the procedure should fill the remaining array elements with unique random numbers. The remaining elements have subscripts of 1 through 5. Enter the following comments and lines of code. (The Code Editor will automatically enter the Loop clause for you.) Press **Enter** twice after typing the last assignment statement.

```
' fill remaining array elements with
' unique random numbers
subscript = 1
Do While subscript <= highestSub
    randomNum = randGet.Next(1, 55)
```

11. Save the solution.

Next, the procedure needs to search the array to verify that it does not contain the newly generated random number, which is stored in the `randomNum` variable. Only the array elements that already contain numbers need to be searched. Those elements have subscripts starting with 0 and ending with the subscript that is one less than the current subscript. In other words, if the current subscript is 1, you need to search only the `numbers(0)` element, because that is the only element that contains a number. Similarly, if the current subscript is 4, you need to search only the `numbers(0)`, `numbers(1)`, `numbers(2)`, and `numbers(3)` elements.

To finish coding the Click event procedure and then test the code:

1. Enter the following comments:

```
' search the array for the random number
' stop the search when there are no more
' elements or when the random number is found
```

2. The search should begin with the first array element. Enter the following statement:

```
searchSubscript = 0
```

3. Before the search begins, the procedure will assume that the newly generated random number is not already in the array. Enter the following statement:

```
isFound = False
```

4. The procedure should continue searching as long as there are array elements to search and, at the same time, the random number has not been found in the array. Enter the following code. (The Code Editor will automatically enter the Loop clause for you.)

```
Do While searchSubscript < subscript AndAlso
    isFound = False
```

5. Now, enter the following comments and code. (The Code Editor will automatically enter the End If clause for you.)

```
' if the random number is in the current
' array element, assign True to isFound
' otherwise, examine the next element
If numbers(searchSubscript) = randomNum Then
    isFound = True
Else
    searchSubscript += 1
```

6. If the newly generated random number is not in the array, the procedure should assign the random number to the current array element and then prepare to fill the next element. Insert two blank lines between the two Loop clauses, and then position the insertion point in the second blank line. Enter the following comments and selection structure. (The Code Editor will automatically enter the End If clause for you.)

```
' if the random number is not in the array
' assign the random number to the current array
' element and then move to the next element
If isFound = False Then
    numbers(subscript) = randomNum
    subscript += 1
```

7. The last step in the procedure's pseudocode is to display the contents of the `numbers` array, which now contains the six lottery numbers. Insert two blank lines between the outer Loop clause and the End Sub clause. In the blank line above the End Sub clause, enter the following comment and code. Be sure to include two spaces between the quotation marks. Also be sure to change the Next clause to `Next numElement`.

```
' display the contents of the array
lotteryLabel.Text = String.Empty
For Each numElement As Integer In numbers
    lotteryLabel.Text = lotteryLabel.Text &
            "  " & numElement.ToString
Next numElement
```

8. Save the solution and then start the application. Click the **Get Numbers** button. Six unique numbers appear in the Lottery numbers box. See Figure 9-35. Because the application generates random numbers, your numbers might be different from those shown in the figure.

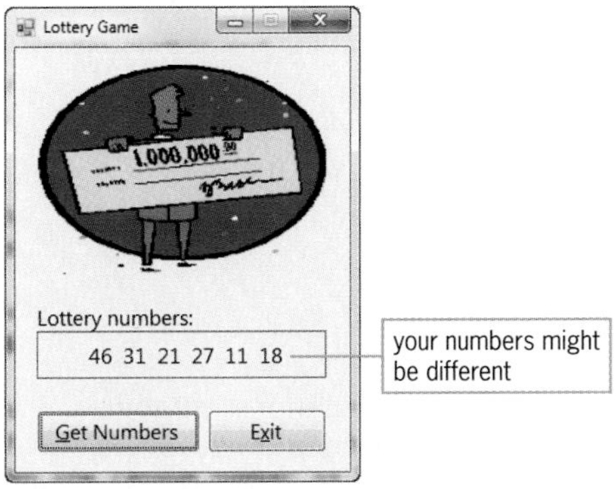

Figure 9-35 Interface showing the six unique lottery numbers

9. Click the **Get Numbers** button several times to continue testing the code.
10. Click the **Exit** button to end the application. Close the Code Editor window, and then close the solution. Figure 9-36 shows the application's code.

```
' Project name:          Lottery Game Project
' Project purpose:       Displays six unique random
'                        numbers from 1 through 54
' Created/revised by:    <your name> on <current date>

Option Explicit On
Option Strict On
Option Infer Off

Public Class MainForm

  Private Sub exitButton_Click(ByVal sender As Object,
  ByVal e As System.EventArgs) Handles exitButton.Click
     Me.Close()
  End Sub

  Private Sub getButton_Click(ByVal sender As Object,
  ByVal e As System.EventArgs) Handles getButton.Click
     ' generates and displays six unique random
     ' numbers from 1 through 54

     Dim numbers(5) As Integer
     Dim randGen As New Random
     Dim randomNum As Integer
     Dim subscript As Integer
     Dim searchSubscript As Integer
     Dim isFound As Boolean
     Dim highestSub As Integer = numbers.GetUpperBound(0)

     ' generate the first random number and
     ' store it in the first array element
     numbers(0) = randGen.Next(1, 55)
```

Figure 9-36 Code for the Lottery Game application *(continues)*

(continued)

```
        ' fill remaining array elements with
        ' unique random numbers
        subscript = 1
        Do While subscript <= highestSub
            randomNum = randGen.Next(1, 55)

            ' search the array for the random number
            ' stop the search when there are no more
            ' elements or when the random number is found
            searchSubscript = 0
            isFound = False
            Do While searchSubscript < subscript AndAlso
               isFound = False
               ' if the random number is in the current
               ' array element, assign True to isFound
               ' otherwise, examine the next element
               If numbers(searchSubscript) = randomNum Then
                    isFound = True
               Else
                    searchSubscript += 1
               End If
            Loop

            ' if the random number is not in the array
            ' assign the random number to the current array
            ' element and then move to the next element
            If isFound = False Then
               numbers(subscript) = randomNum
               subscript += 1
            End If
        Loop

        ' display the contents of the array
        lotteryLabel.Text = String.Empty
        For Each numElement As Integer In numbers
            lotteryLabel.Text = lotteryLabel.Text &
                "  " & numElement.ToString
        Next numElement
     End Sub
 End Class
```

Figure 9-36 Code for the Lottery Game application

PROGRAMMING TUTORIAL 2

Creating the Stay Fit Health Club Application

In this tutorial, you code an application for the Stay Fit Health Club. The application displays the monthly fees for three different membership levels: Gold, Silver, and Bronze. The monthly fees are based on the membership type, which can be Single, Family, or Senior. The appropriate fees are listed in Figure 9-37. The application's TOE chart and MainForm are shown in Figures 9-38 and 9-39, respectively.

Membership type	Membership level	Fee ($)
Single	Gold	125
	Silver	95
	Bronze	60
Family	Gold	150
	Silver	120
	Bronze	90
Senior	Gold	105
	Silver	80
	Bronze	50

Figure 9-37 Stay Fit Health Club's monthly membership fees

Task	Object	Event
Declare and initialize a class-level two-dimensional array named feeTable; the array should have three rows and three columns	MainForm	Declarations section
1. Fill the membershipListBox with the membership types 2. Select the first membership type in the membershipListBox		Load
End the application	exitButton	Click
Display the membership types	membershipListBox	None
Get the membership type		None
Use the index of the item selected in the membershipListBox to display the fees for the three membership levels in the goldLabel, silverLabel, and bronzeLabel		SelectedIndexChanged
Display the fees for the three membership levels (from membershipListBox)	goldLabel, silverLabel, bronzeLabel	None

Figure 9-38 TOE chart for the Stay Fit Health Club application

Figure 9-39 MainForm for the Stay Fit Health Club application

Coding the Stay Fit Health Club Application

Included in the data files for this book is a partially completed Stay Fit Health Club application. To complete the application, you just need to code it. According to the application's TOE chart, three event procedures need to be coded: the MainForm's Load event procedure, the exitButton's Click event procedure, and the membershipListBox's SelectedIndexChanged event procedure. You also need to declare and initialize a two-dimensional array in the MainForm's Declarations section. (If you need help while coding the application, you can look ahead to Figure 9-41.)

To begin coding the application:

1. Start Visual Studio or the Express Edition of Visual Basic. If necessary, open the Solution Explorer window.
2. Open the **Stay Fit Solution** (**Stay Fit Solution.sln**) file, which is contained in the VbReloaded2010\Chap09\Stay Fit Solution folder. Open the designer window (if necessary), and then auto-hide the Solution Explorer window. The MainForm contains a group box, a list box, eight labels, and one button.
3. Open the Code Editor window. Notice that the exitButton's Click event procedure has already been coded for you. In addition, the Option statements have already been entered in the General Declarations section.
4. In the comments that appear in the General Declarations section, replace <your name> and <current date> with your name and the current date.

First, you will complete the MainForm's Load event procedure. The procedure is responsible for filling the membershipListBox with the three membership types and then selecting the first type.

To code the MainForm's Load event procedure:

1. Open the code template for the MainForm's Load event procedure. Type **' fills the list box** and then press **Enter** twice.
2. Enter the statements to add the following three membership types to the membershipListBox: Single, Family, and Senior.
3. Enter the statement to select the first item in the membershipListBox.
4. Save the solution and then start the application. The three membership types appear in the membershipListBox, with the first type selected in the list.
5. Click the **Exit** button to end the application.

Next, you will declare the `feeTable` array in the MainForm's Declarations section. The array should have three rows and three columns. Each row represents a membership type (Single, Family, and Senior), and each column represents a membership level (Gold, Silver, and Bronze).

To declare and initialize the array:

1. Click the **blank line** above the exitButton_Click procedure header. Enter the statement to declare a three-row, three-column Integer array named `feeTable`. Initialize the array using the fees shown earlier in Figure 9-37.
2. Save the solution.

The last procedure you need to code is the list box's SelectedIndexChanged procedure.

To code the list box's SelectedIndexChanged procedure, and then test the code:

1. Open the code template for the membershipListBox's SelectedIndexChanged event procedure. Type **' display membership fees** and then press **Enter** twice.
2. Next, enter the statement to declare an Integer variable named `row`. The statement should initialize the variable to the index of the item selected in the list box.
3. Now, enter three assignment statements. Each assignment statement should assign the appropriate fees to the goldLabel, silverLabel, and bronzeLabel controls in the interface. Format the fees with a dollar sign and no decimal places.
4. Save the solution, and then start the application. The fees for a Single membership appear in the interface, as shown in Figure 9-40.

Figure 9-40 Sample run of the Stay Fit Health Club application

5. Click **Family** in the list box. The fees for a Family membership ($150, $120, and $90) appear in the interface.
6. Click **Senior** in the list box. The fees for a Senior membership ($105, $80, and $50) appear in the interface.
7. Click the **Exit** button to end the application. Close the Code Editor window, and then close the solution. Figure 9-41 shows the code for the Stay Fit Health Club application.

```
' Project name:          Stay Fit Project
' Project purpose:       Display the membership fees
' Created/revised by:    <your name> on <current date>

Option Explicit On
Option Strict On
Option Infer Off

Public Class MainForm

  Private feeTable(,) As Integer = {{125, 95, 60},
                                     {150, 120, 90},
                                     {105, 80, 50}}

```

Figure 9-41 Code for the Stay Fit Health Club application *(continues)*

(continued)

```
    Private Sub exitButton_Click(ByVal sender As Object,
    ByVal e As System.EventArgs) Handles exitButton.Click
        Me.Close()
    End Sub

    Private Sub MainForm_Load(ByVal sender As Object,
    ByVal e As System.EventArgs) Handles Me.Load
        ' fills the list box

         membershipListBox.Items.Add("Single")
         membershipListBox.Items.Add("Family")
         membershipListBox.Items.Add("Senior")
         membershipListBox.SelectedIndex = 0

    End Sub

    Private Sub membershipListBox_SelectedIndexChanged(
    ByVal sender As Object, ByVal e As System.EventArgs
    ) Handles membershipListBox.SelectedIndexChanged
        ' display membership fees

        Dim row As Integer =
               membershipListBox.SelectedIndex
        goldLabel.Text = feeTable(row, 0).ToString("C0")
        silverLabel.Text = feeTable(row, 1).ToString("C0")
        bronzeLabel.Text = feeTable(row, 2).ToString("C0")

    End Sub
End Class
```

Figure 9-41 Code for the Stay Fit Health Club application

PROGRAMMING EXAMPLE

Professor Coleman Application

Create an interface that allows the user to select a letter grade from a list box. The letter grades are as follows: A, B, C, D, and F. The application should display the names of the students who earned the selected letter grade. The application should store each student's name and letter grade in a two-dimensional array that has 11 rows and two columns. The first column should contain the student names, and the second column should contain the grades. Use the following names for the solution, project, and form file: Coleman Solution, Coleman Project, and Main Form.vb. Save the application in the VbReloaded2010\Chap09 folder. See Figures 9-42 through 9-46.

Task	Object	Event
Declare and initialize a class-level two-dimensional array named studentInfo; the array should have 11 rows and two columns	MainForm	Declarations section
1. Fill the gradeListBox with the letter grades 2. Select the first letter grade in the gradeListBox		Load
End the application	exitButton	Click
Display the letter grades	gradeListBox	None
Get the letter grades		None
Clear the studentsLabel		SelectedIndexChanged
1. Search the studentInfo array for the letter grade selected in the gradeListBox 2. Display the names of students who earned the selected letter grade in the studentsLabel	findButton	Click
Display the names of students who earned the grade selected in the gradeListBox (from findButton)	studentsLabel	None

Figure 9-42 TOE chart for the Professor Coleman application

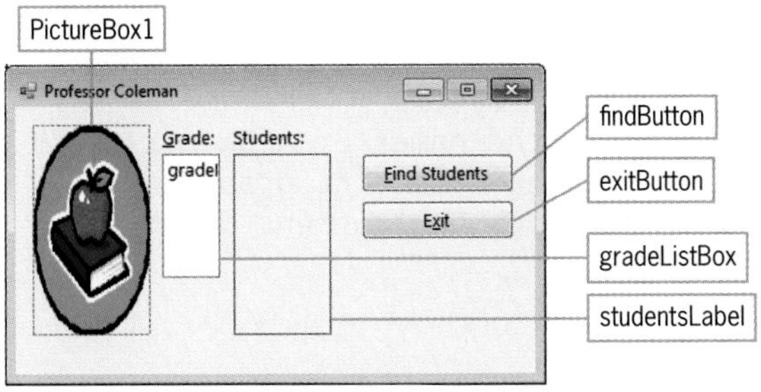

Figure 9-43 MainForm in the Professor Coleman application

Object	Property	Setting
MainForm	Font MaximizeBox StartPosition Text	Segoe UI, 10 point False CenterScreen Professor Coleman
Label1	TabIndex Text	0 &Grade:
gradeListBox	TabIndex	1
Label2	TabIndex Text	4 Students:
studentsLabel	AutoSize BorderStyle TabIndex Text	False FixedSingle 5 (empty)
findButton	TabIndex	2
exitButton	TabIndex	3
PictureBox1	Image SizeMode	VbReloaded2010\Chap09\j0397995.wmf StretchImage

Figure 9-44 Objects, properties, and settings

exitButton Click event procedure
close the application

gradeListBox SelectedIndexChanged event procedure
clear the studentsLabel

MainForm Load event procedure
1. fill the list box with the following letter grades: A, B, C, D, and F
2. select the first letter grade in the list box

findButton Click event procedure
1. declare a variable named studentNames that can be used to keep track of the student names
2. assign the grade selected in the gradeListBox to a variable named searchGrade
3. repeat for array rows from 0 through the highest row subscript
   if the grade stored in the second column in the current row matches the grade stored in the searchGrade variable
      concatenate the student name, which is stored in the first column in the current row, to the existing names (if any) in the studentNames variable
   end if
   end repeat for
4. display the contents of the studentNames variable in the studentsLabel

Figure 9-45 Pseudocode

```
' Project name:         Coleman Project
' Project purpose:      Display the names of students
'                       who earned a specific grade
' Created/revised by:   <your name> on <current date>

Option Explicit On
Option Strict On
Option Infer Off

Public Class MainForm

    Private studentInfo(,) As String = {{"Carol", "A"},
                 {"Toby", "C"}, {"George", "A"},
                 {"Elaine", "B"}, {"Francisco", "C"},
                 {"Khalid", "B"}, {"Jack", "D"},
                 {"Carl", "F"}, {"Susan", "B"},
                 {"Mark", "A"}, {"Monica", "B"}}

    Private Sub exitButton_Click(ByVal sender As Object,
    ByVal e As System.EventArgs) Handles exitButton.Click
        Me.Close()
    End Sub

    Private Sub gradeListBox_SelectedIndexChanged(
    ByVal sender As Object, ByVal e As System.EventArgs
    ) Handles gradeListBox.SelectedIndexChanged
        ' clear student names

        studentsLabel.Text = String.Empty
    End Sub

```

Figure 9-46 Code *(continues)*

(continued)

```
Private Sub MainForm_Load(ByVal sender As Object,
ByVal e As System.EventArgs) Handles Me.Load
    ' fills the list box

    gradeListBox.Items.Add("A")
    gradeListBox.Items.Add("B")
    gradeListBox.Items.Add("C")
    gradeListBox.Items.Add("D")
    gradeListBox.Items.Add("F")
    gradeListBox.SelectedIndex = 0
End Sub

Private Sub findButton_Click(ByVal sender As Object,
ByVal e As System.EventArgs) Handles findButton.Click
    ' displays the names of students who earned the
    ' grade selected in the list box

    Dim highRowSub As Integer =
            studentInfo.GetUpperBound(0)
    Dim searchGrade As String
    Dim studentNames As String = String.Empty

    searchGrade = gradeListBox.SelectedItem.ToString
    For row As Integer = 0 To highRowSub
      If studentInfo(row, 1) = searchGrade Then
          ' concatenate the student name with
          ' the existing names (if any)
          studentNames = studentNames &
             studentInfo(row, 0) & ControlChars.NewLine
      End If
    Next row
    ' display the student names
    studentsLabel.Text = studentNames
End Sub
End Class
```

Figure 9-46 Code

Summary

- Programmers use arrays to temporarily store related data in the internal memory of the computer.
- All of the variables in an array have the same name and data type.
- When declaring a one-dimensional array, you provide either the highest subscript or the initial values.
- Each element in a one-dimensional array is identified by a unique subscript that appears in parentheses after the array's name. The first subscript in a one-dimensional array is 0.
- You refer to an element in a one-dimensional array using the array's name followed by the element's subscript.

- Examples of statements that you can use to change the data stored in an array include assignment statements and statements that contain the TryParse method.
- A one-dimensional array's Length property contains an integer that represents the number of elements in the array. The number of elements is always one more than the array's highest subscript.
- A one-dimensional array's GetUpperBound method returns an integer that represents the highest subscript in the array. The highest subscript is always one number less than the number of array elements.
- You use a loop to traverse a one-dimensional array. You can code the loop using the For ... Next, Do ... Loop, or For Each ... Next statements. However, keep in mind that the instructions within a For Each ... Next loop can only read the array values; the instructions cannot change the values.
- You can associate the items in a list box with the elements in an array. You do this using the list box's index and the array's subscript, both of which start at 0.
- You can use the variables in an array as accumulators.
- The Array.Sort method sorts the elements in a one-dimensional array in ascending order. The Array.Reverse method reverses the elements in a one-dimensional array.
- A two-dimensional array resembles a table in that the variables (elements) are in rows and columns.
- When declaring a two-dimensional array, you provide either the highest row and column subscripts or the initial values.
- The number of rows in a two-dimensional array is one number more than its highest row subscript. Likewise, the number of columns is one number more than its highest column subscript.
- You can determine the number of elements in a two-dimensional array by multiplying the number of its rows by the number of its columns.
- Each element in a two-dimensional array is identified by a unique combination of two subscripts: a row subscript and a column subscript. The subscripts appear in parentheses after the array's name. You list the row subscript first, followed by a comma and the column subscript. The first row subscript in a two-dimensional array is 0. Likewise, the first column subscript also is 0.
- You refer to an element in a two-dimensional array using the array's name followed by the element's row and column subscripts, which are separated by a comma.
- You can use a two-dimensional array's GetUpperBound method to determine the highest row subscript and highest column subscript in the array.
- You can traverse a two-dimensional array using either two loops (coded with the For ... Next or Do ... Loop statements) or one loop (coded with the For Each ... Next statement). However, recall that the instructions in a For Each ... Next loop can only read the array values; they cannot modify the values.

Key Terms

Array—a group of related variables that have the same name and data type

Array.Reverse method—reverses the order of the elements in a one-dimensional array

Array.Sort method—sorts the elements in a one-dimensional array in ascending order

Elements—the variables in an array

For Each ... Next statement—used to code a loop whose instructions you want processed for each element in a group

GetUpperBound method—returns an integer that represents the highest subscript in a specified dimension; the dimension is 0 for a one-dimensional array; for a two-dimensional array, the dimension is 0 for the row subscript, but 1 for the column subscript

Length property—one of the properties of an array; stores an integer that represents the number of array elements

One-dimensional array—an array whose elements are identified by a unique subscript

Populating the array—refers to the process of initializing the elements in an array

Scalar variable—another term for a simple variable

Simple variable—a variable that is unrelated to any other variable in the computer's internal memory; also called a scalar variable

Sorting—the process of arranging data in a specific order

Subscript—a unique number that identifies the position of an element in an array

Two-dimensional array—an array made up of rows and columns; each element has the same data type and is identified by a unique combination of two subscripts: a row subscript and a column subscript

Review Questions

1. Which of the following declares a five-element array named `prices`?
   a. `Dim prices(4) As Decimal`
   b. `Dim prices(5) As Decimal`
   c. `Dim prices() As Decimal = {3.55D, 6.7D, 8D, 4D, 2.34D}`
   d. both a and c

2. The `items` array is declared using the `Dim items(20) As String` statement. The `x` variable keeps track of the array subscripts and is initialized to 0. Which of the following Do clauses will process the loop instructions for each element in the array?

a. `Do While x > 20`

b. `Do While x < 20`

c. `Do While x >= 20`

d. `Do While x <= 20`

Use the information shown in Figure 9-47 to answer Review Questions 3 through 7.

```
Dim sales() As Integer = {10000, 12000, 900, 500, 20000}
```

Figure 9-47 Code for Review Questions 3 through 7

3. The `sales(3) += 10` statement will replace the number __________.

a. 500 with 10

b. 500 with 510

c. 900 with 10

d. 900 with 910

4. The `sales(4) = sales(4 - 2)` statement will replace the number __________.

a. 20000 with 900

b. 20000 with 19998

c. 500 with 12000

d. 500 with 498

5. Which of the following If clauses verifies that the array subscript stored in the `x` variable is valid for the `sales` array?

a. `If sales(x) >= 0 AndAlso sales(x) < 4 Then`

b. `If sales(x) >= 0 AndAlso sales(x) <= 4 Then`

c. `If x >= 0 AndAlso x < 4 Then`

d. `If x >= 0 AndAlso x <= 4 Then`

6. Which of the following will correctly add 100 to each element in the `sales` array? The `x` variable was declared using the `Dim x As Integer` statement.

a.
```
Do While x <= 4
     x += 100
Loop
```

b.
```
Do While x <= 4
     sales += 100
Loop
```

c.
```
Do While sales < 5
      sales(x) += 100
Loop
```

d.
```
Do While x < 5
      sales(x) += 100
      x += 1
Loop
```


7. Which of the following statements sorts the `sales` array in ascending order?

   a. `Array.Sort(sales)`

   b. `sales.Sort()`

   c. `Sort(sales)`

   d. `SortArray(sales)`

Use the information shown in Figure 9-48 to answer Review Question 8.

```
Dim numbers() As Double = {10, 5, 7, 2}
Dim x As Integer
Dim total As Double
Dim avg As Double
```

Figure 9-48 Code for Review Question 8

8. Which of the following will correctly calculate the average of the elements included in the `numbers` array?

   a.
```
Do While x < 4
      numbers(x) = total + total
      x += 1
Loop
avg = total / x
```

   b.
```
Do While x < 4
      total += numbers(x)
      x += 1
Loop
avg = total / x
```

   c.
```
Do While x < 4
      total += numbers(x)
      x += 1
Loop
avg = total / x - 1
```

   d.
```
Do While x < 4
      total += numbers(x)
      x += 1
Loop
avg = total / (x - 1)
```

9. Which of the following statements creates a two-dimensional array that contains three rows and four columns?

    a. `Dim temps(2, 3) As Decimal`

    b. `Dim temps(3, 4) As Decimal`

    c. `Dim temps(3, 2) As Decimal`

    d. `Dim temps(4, 3) As Decimal`

Use the information shown in Figure 9-49 to answer Review Questions 10 and 11.

```
Dim sales(,) As Decimal = {{1000, 1200, 900, 500, 2000},
                           {350, 600, 700, 800, 100}}
```

Figure 9-49 Code for Review Questions 10 and 11

10. The `sales(1, 3) += 10` statement will replace the number ______________.

    a. 900 with 910

    b. 500 with 510

    c. 700 with 710

    d. 800 with 810

11. Which of the following If clauses verifies that the array subscripts stored in the `r` and `c` variables are valid for the `sales` array?

    a. `If sales(r, c) >= 0 AndAlso sales(r, c) < 5 Then`

    b. `If sales(r, c) >= 0 AndAlso sales(r, c) <= 5 Then`

    c. `If r >= 0 AndAlso r < 3 AndAlso c >= 0 AndAlso c < 6 Then`

    d. `If r >= 0 AndAlso r < 2 AndAlso c >= 0 AndAlso c < 5 Then`

12. Which of the following assigns the string "California" to the variable located in the third column, fifth row of the `states` array?

    a. `states(3, 5) = "California"`

    b. `states(5, 3) = "California"`

    c. `states(4, 2) = "California"`

    d. `states(2, 4) = "California"`

Exercises

Pencil and Paper

1. Write the Dim statement to declare a one-dimensional Integer array named `inventory` that has 20 elements. Then write the statement to store the number 7 in the second element in the array. INTRODUCTORY

2. Write the code to display the contents of the `inventory` array from Pencil and Paper Exercise 1 in the inventoryListBox. Use the For Each ... Next statement. Then rewrite the code using the For ... Next statement. INTRODUCTORY

3. Write the Private statement to declare and initialize a one-dimensional Double array named `rates` that has five elements. Use the following numbers to initialize the array: 6.5, 8.3, 4.0, 2.0, and 10.5. INTRODUCTORY

4. Write the code to display the contents of the `rates` array from Pencil and Paper Exercise 3 in the ratesListBox. Use the Do ... Loop statement. Then rewrite the code using the For Each ... Next statement. INTRODUCTORY

5. Write the statement that determines the number of elements in a one-dimensional array named `flowerTypes`. The statement should assign the number to an Integer variable named `numTypes`. INTRODUCTORY

6. Write the statement that determines the highest subscript in a one-dimensional array named `flowerTypes`. The statement should assign the number to an Integer variable named `highSub`. INTRODUCTORY

7. Write the code to multiply by 2 the number stored in the first element in a one-dimensional Integer array named `nums`. Store the result in the `numDoubled` variable. INTRODUCTORY

8. Write the code to add together the numbers stored in the first and second elements in a one-dimensional Integer array named `nums`. Display the sum in the sumLabel. INTRODUCTORY

9. Write the Private statement to declare a two-dimensional Double array named `balances` that has four rows and six columns. INTRODUCTORY

10. Write the code to display the contents of a two-dimensional String array named `parts` in the partsListBox. Use the For Each ... Next statement. Then rewrite the code using two For ... Next statements to display the array, row by row. INTERMEDIATE

11. Write the statements that determine the highest row and highest column subscripts in a two-dimensional array named `dogTypes`. The statements should assign the numbers to Integer variables named `highRow` and `highColumn`. INTERMEDIATE

INTERMEDIATE

12. Write the statement that determines the number of elements in a two-dimensional array named `dogTypes`. The statement should assign the number to an Integer variable named `numTypes`.

INTERMEDIATE

13. Write the code to subtract the number 1 from each element in a one-dimensional Integer array named `quantities`. Use the Do ... Loop statement.

INTERMEDIATE

14. The `sales` array is a two-dimensional Double array. Write the statement to total the numbers stored in the following three array elements: the first row, first column; the second row, third column; and the third row, fourth column. Assign the sum to the `total` variable.

INTERMEDIATE

15. The `quantities` array is a two-dimensional Integer array. Write the code to subtract the number 1 from each array element. Use two For ... Next statements.

ADVANCED

16. The `orders` array is a two-dimensional Integer array. Write the code to determine the largest number stored in the first column of the array. Use the For ... Next statement.

Computer

MODIFY THIS

17. Open the Starward Coffee Solution (Starward Coffee Solution.sln) file contained in the VbReloaded2010\Chap09\Starward Coffee Solution folder. Modify the interface and code so that each button (except the Exit button) also displays the lowest and highest values stored in the `poundsUsed` array. Save the solution, and then start and test the application. Close the solution.

MODIFY THIS

18. Open the Car-Mart Solution (Car-Mart Solution.sln) file contained in the VbReloaded2010\Chap09\Car-Mart Solution folder. Replace the For ... Next statement in the code with the For Each ... Next statement. Save the solution, and then start and test the application. Close the solution.

MODIFY THIS

19. Open the Jenko Booksellers Solution (Jenko Booksellers Solution.sln) file contained in the VbReloaded2010\Chap09\Jenko Booksellers Solution folder. Modify the interface and code so that it displays three sales amounts: the total paperback book sales, the total hardcover book sales, and the total sales. Save the solution, and then start and test the application. Close the solution.

MODIFY THIS

20. If necessary, complete the Stay Fit Health Club application from this chapter's Programming Tutorial 2, and then close the solution. Use Windows to make a copy of the Stay Fit Solution folder. Rename the folder Stay Fit Solution-Modified. Open the Stay Fit Solution (Stay Fit Solution.sln) file contained in the VbReloaded2010\Chap09\Stay Fit Solution-Modified folder. The health club has just announced a new membership type: Military. The fees for the Gold, Silver, and Bronze levels are $80, $60, and $45, respectively. Modify the interface and code to accommodate the new membership type. Save the solution and then start and test the application. Close the solution.

21. In this exercise, you code an application that sums the values contained in a two-dimensional array. Open the Inventory Solution (Inventory Solution.sln) file, which is contained in the VbReloaded2010\Chap09\Inventory Solution folder. Code the Display Total button's Click event procedure so that it adds together the values stored in the `inventory` array. Display the sum in the totalLabel.

INTRODUCTORY

22. Open the Update Prices Solution (Update Prices Solution.sln) file contained in the VbReloaded2010\Chap09\Update Prices Solution folder. In the form's Declarations section, declare a one-dimensional Double array named `prices`. Initialize the array using the following 10 prices: 6.75, 12.50, 33.50, 10.00, 9.50, 25.50, 7.65, 8.35, 9.75, and 3.50. Open the code template for the Increase button's Click event procedure. The procedure should ask the user for a percentage amount by which each price in the array should be increased. It then should increase each price by that amount and display the increased prices in the list box. (Hint: You can clear the contents of a list box using the Items collection's Clear method.) Save the solution and then start the application. Click the Increase button. Increase each price by 5%. Close the solution.

INTRODUCTORY

23. In this exercise, you modify the application from Computer Exercise 22. The modified application allows the user to update a specific price.

INTERMEDIATE

    a. Use Windows to make a copy of the Update Prices Solution folder, which is contained in the VbReloaded2010\Chap09 folder. Rename the folder Update Prices Solution-Modified.
    b. Open the Update Prices Solution (Update Prices Solution.sln) file contained in the VbReloaded2010\Chap09\Update Prices Solution-Modified folder.
    c. Modify the Increase button's Click event procedure so that it also asks the user to enter a number from 1 through 10. If the user enters the number 1, the procedure should update the first price in the array. If the user enters the number 2, the procedure should update the second price in the array, and so on.
    d. Save the solution and then start the application. Click the Increase button. Increase the second price by 10%. Click the Increase button again. This time, increase the tenth price by 2%. (The second price in the list box should still reflect the 10% increase.) Close the solution.

24. In this exercise, you code an application that allows Professor Carver to display a student's grade based on the number of points he enters. The grading scale is shown in Figure 9-50. Open the Carver Solution (Carver Solution.sln) file contained in the VbReloaded2010\Chap09\Carver Solution folder. In the form's Declarations section, declare a one-dimensional Integer array named `points` and a one-dimensional String array named `grades`. Store the minimum points in the `points` array, and the corresponding grades in the `grades` array. Code the Display Grade button's Click event procedure so that it searches the `points` array and then displays the corresponding grade from the

INTERMEDIATE

`grades` array. Save the solution and then start the application. Enter 455 in the Points box and then click the Display Grade button. The letter A appears in the Grade box. Enter 210 in the Points box and then click the Display Grade button. The letter F appears in the Grade box. Close the solution.

Minimum points	Maximum points	Grade
0	299	F
300	349	D
350	399	C
400	449	B
450	500	A

Figure 9-50 Grading scale for Professor Carver's class

INTERMEDIATE

25. In this exercise, you code an application that displays the highest score earned on the midterm exam and the highest score earned on the final exam. Open the Highest Solution (Highest Solution.sln) file, which is contained in the VbReloaded2010\Chap09\Highest Solution folder. Code the Display Highest button's Click event procedure so that it displays (in the appropriate label controls) the highest score earned on the midterm exam and the highest score earned on the final exam. Save the solution, and then start and test the application. Close the solution.

INTERMEDIATE

26. In this exercise, you code an application that allows Ms. Laury to display a shipping charge based on the number of items ordered by a customer. The shipping charges are shown in Figure 9-51. Open the Laury Solution (Laury Solution.sln) file contained in the VbReloaded2010\Chap09\Laury Solution folder. In the form's Declarations section, declare a two-dimensional Integer array to store the minimum order amounts and shipping charges. Code the Display Shipping Charge button's Click event procedure so that it displays the appropriate shipping charge with a dollar sign and two decimal places. Save the solution, and then start and test the application. Close the solution.

Minimum order	Maximum order	Shipping
1	10	15
11	50	10
51	100	5
101	No maximum	0

Figure 9-51 Shipping charges for the Laury application

ADVANCED

27. In this exercise, you code an application that displays the number of students earning a specific score.

    a. Open the Scores Solution (Scores Solution.sln) file contained in the VbReloaded2010\Chap09\Scores Solution folder. In the form's Declarations section, declare a one-dimensional Integer array named `scores`. Initialize the array using the following 20 numbers: 88, 72, 99, 20, 66, 95, 99, 100, 72, 88, 78, 45, 57, 89, 85, 78, 75, 88, 72, and 88.

b. Open the code template for the Display button's Click event procedure. Code the procedure so that it prompts the user to enter a score from 0 through 100. The procedure then should display (in a message box) the number of students who earned that score.

c. Save the solution and then start the application. Use the application to answer the following questions: How many students earned a score of 72? How many students earned a score of 88? How many students earned a score of 20? How many students earned a score of 99? Close the solution.

28. In this exercise, you modify the application from Computer Exercise 27. The modified application allows the user to display the number of students earning a score within a specific range.

ADVANCED

a. Use Windows to make a copy of the Scores Solution folder, which is contained in the VbReloaded2010\Chap09 folder. Rename the folder Scores Solution-Modified.

b. Open the Scores Solution (Scores Solution.sln) file contained in the VbReloaded2010\Chap09\Scores Solution-Modified folder. Modify the Display button's Click event procedure so that it prompts the user to enter a minimum score and a maximum score. The procedure then should display (in a message box) the number of students who earned a score within that range.

c. Save the solution and then start the application. Use the application to answer the following questions: How many students earned a score from 70 through 79? How many students earned a score from 65 through 85? How many students earned a score from 0 through 50? Close the solution.

29. In this exercise, you code an application that displays the number of times a value appears in a two-dimensional array. Open the Count Solution (Count Solution.sln) file contained in the VbReloaded2010\Chap09\Count Solution folder. Code the Display Counts button's Click event procedure so that it displays the number of times each of the numbers from 1 through 9 appears in the `numbers` array. (Hint: Store the counts in a one-dimensional array.) Save the solution, and then start and test the application. Close the solution.

ADVANCED

30. In this exercise, you learn about the ReDim statement.

DISCOVERY

a. Research the Visual Basic ReDim statement. What is the purpose of the statement? What is the purpose of the `Preserve` keyword?

b. Open the ReDim Solution (ReDim Solution.sln) file contained in the VbReloaded2010\Chap09\ReDim Solution folder. Open the Code Editor window and view the displayButton's Click event procedure. Study the existing code, and then modify the procedure so that it stores any number of sales amounts in the `sales` array.

c. Save the solution, and then start the application. Click the Display Sales button, and then enter the following sales amounts, one at a time: 700, 550, and 800. Click the Cancel button in the input box. The three sales amounts should appear in the list box.

d. Click the Display Sales button again and then enter the following sales amounts, one at a time: 5, 9, 45, 67, 8, and 0. Click the Cancel button in the input box. This time, six sales amounts should appear in the list box. Close the solution.

SWAT THE BUGS

31. Open the Debug Solution (Debug Solution.sln) file contained in the VbReloaded2010\Chap09\Debug Solution folder. Open the Code Editor window and review the existing code. Start and then test the application. Locate and then correct any errors. When the application is working correctly, close the solution.

Case Projects

JM Sales

JM Sales employs five salespeople. The sales manager wants an application that allows him to enter any number of sales amounts for each of the five salespeople. The application should accumulate the sales amounts in a one-dimensional array. The application also should display a report similar to the one shown in Figure 9-52. The report contains each salesperson's ID and total sales. It also contains the total company sales. Use the following names for the solution, project, and form file: JM Sales Solution, JM Sales Project, and Main Form.vb. Save the application in the VbReloaded2010\Chap09 folder. You can create either your own interface or the one shown in Figure 9-52. The text box that displays the report has its BorderStyle property set to Fixed3D, its Font property set to Courier New 10 point, its MultiLine and ReadOnly properties set to True, and its ScrollBars property set to Vertical.

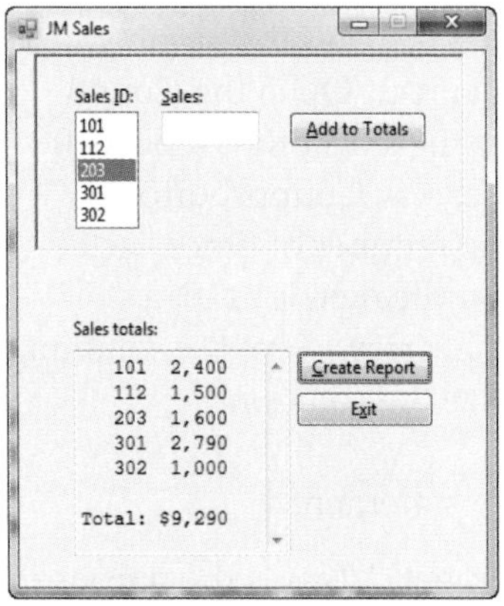

Figure 9-52 Sample interface for the JM Sales application

Waterglen Horse Farms

Each year, Sabrina Cantrell, the owner of Waterglen Horse Farms, enters four of her horses in five local horse races. She uses the table shown in Figure 9-53 to keep track of her horses' performances in each race. In the table, a 1 indicates that the horse won the race, a 2 indicates second place, and a

3 indicates third place. A 0 indicates that the horse did not finish in the top three places. Sabrina wants an application that displays a summary of each horse's individual performance, as well as the performances of all the horses. For example, according to the table shown in Figure 9-53, horse 1 won one race, finished second in one race, finished third in one race, and didn't finish in the top three in two races. Overall, Sabrina's horses won four races, finished second in three races, finished third in three races, and didn't finish in the top three in 10 races. Be sure to use one or more arrays in the application. Use the following names for the solution, project, and form file: Waterglen Solution, Waterglen Project, and Main Form.vb. Save the application in the VbReloaded2010\Chap09 folder. You can create either your own interface or the one shown in Figure 9-54.

each column represents a race

each row represents a horse

	1	2	3	4	5
1	0	1	0	3	2
2	1	0	2	0	0
3	0	3	0	1	0
4	3	2	1	0	0

Figure 9-53 Table for keeping track of each horse race

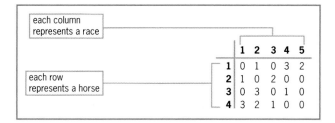

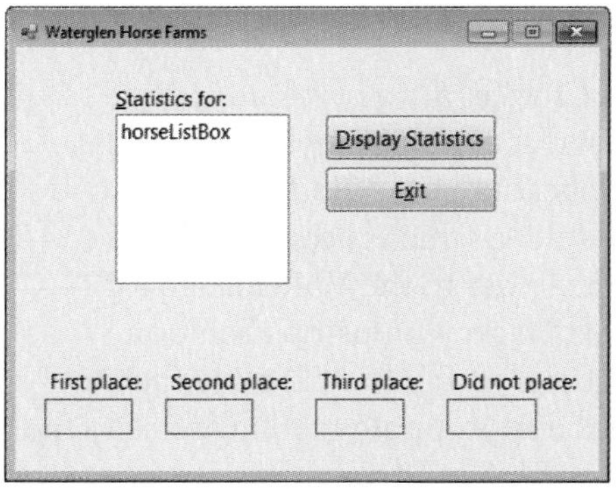

Figure 9-54 Sample interface for the Waterglen Horse Farms application

Conway Enterprises

Conway Enterprises has both domestic and international sales operations. The company's sales manager wants an application that she can use to display the total domestic, total international, and total company sales made during a six-month period. The sales amounts are shown in Figure 9-55. Be sure to use one or more arrays in the application. Use the following names for the solution, project, and form file: Conway Solution, Conway Project, and Main Form.vb. Save the application in the VbReloaded2010\Chap09 folder. You can create either your own interface or the one shown in Figure 9-56.

Month	Domestic	International
1	100,000	150,000
2	90,000	120,000
3	75,000	210,000
4	88,000	50,000
5	125,000	220,000
6	63,000	80,000

Figure 9-55 Sales amounts for Conway Enterprises

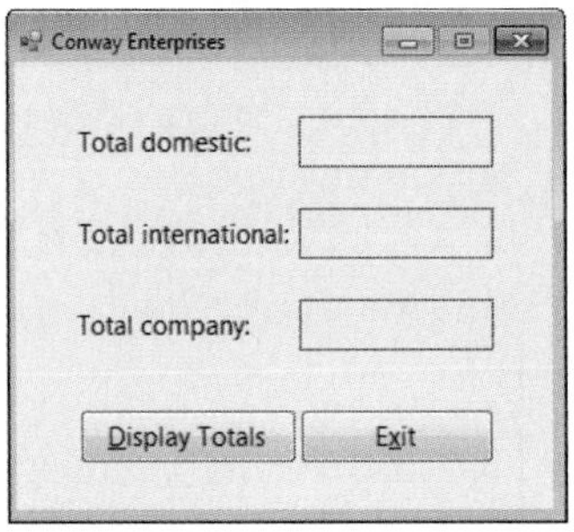

Figure 9-56 Sample interface for the Conway Enterprises application

Modified Harvey Industries

In the Harvey Industries Case Project in Chapter 8, you created an application for Khalid Patel, the payroll manager at Harvey Industries. If you completed the Harvey Industries application, use Windows to make a copy of the Harvey Industries Solution folder, which is contained in the VbReloaded2010\Chap08 folder. Copy the folder to the VbReloaded2010\Chap09 folder, and then rename the folder Harvey Industries Solution-Modified. Store the weekly Federal Withholding Tax (FWT) tables in two two-dimensional arrays, and then make the appropriate modifications to the code. The FWT tables are shown in Figure 8-56 in Chapter 8.

Tic-Tac-Toe

Create an application that simulates the Tic-Tac-Toe game, which requires two players. Be sure to use one or more arrays in the application. Use the following names for the solution, project, and form file: TicTacToe Solution, TicTacToe Project, and Main Form.vb. Save the application in the VbReloaded2010\Chap09 folder. (Hint: You may find it helpful to create an array of Label controls.)

CHAPTER 10

String Manipulation and Menus

After studying Chapter 10, you should be able to:

- Determine the number of characters in a string
- Remove characters from a string
- Insert characters in a string
- Search a string
- Access the characters in a string
- Align the characters in a string
- Compare strings using pattern-matching
- Add a menu to a form
- Code a menu item's Click event procedure

Working with Strings

Many times, an application will need to manipulate (process) string data in some way. For example, it may need to look at the first character in an inventory part number to determine the part's location in the warehouse. Or, it may need to search an address to determine the street name. In this chapter, you will learn several ways of manipulating strings in Visual Basic. You will begin by learning how to determine the number of characters in a string.

Determining the Number of Characters in a String

If an application expects the user to enter a seven-digit phone number or a five-digit ZIP code, you should verify that the user entered the required number of characters. The number of characters contained in a string is stored as an integer in the string's **Length property**. Figure 10-1 shows the syntax of the Length property and includes examples of using the property. In the syntax, *string* can be a String variable, a String named constant, or the Text property of a control.

HOW TO Determine the Number of Characters in a String

Syntax
string.**Length**

Example 1
```
Dim custName As String = "Kevin Jameswell"
Dim numChars As Integer = custName.Length
```
assigns the number 15 to the `numChars` variable

Example 2
```
Dim numChars As Integer
numChars = phoneTextBox.Text.Length
```
assigns the number of characters in the phoneTextBox's Text property to the `numChars` variable

Example 3
```
Dim zip As String
Do
     zip = InputBox("5-digit ZIP code", "ZIP")
Loop Until zip.Length = 5
```
continues prompting the user for a ZIP code until the user enters exactly five characters

Figure 10-1 How to determine the number of characters in a string

Removing Characters from a String

Visual Basic provides the Trim and Remove methods for removing characters from a string. You can use the **Trim method** to remove (trim) any space characters from both the beginning and end of a string. You can use the **Remove method**, on the other hand, to remove a specified number of characters located anywhere in a string. Figure 10-2 shows the syntax of both methods and includes examples of using the methods. In each syntax, *string* can be a String variable, a String named constant, or the Text property of a control. When processing the Trim and Remove methods, the computer first makes a temporary copy of the *string* in memory. It then performs the specified removal on the copy only. In other words, neither method removes any characters from the original *string*. Both methods return a string with the appropriate characters removed.

The Trim method also can remove other characters from the beginning and end of a string. To learn more about the Trim method, as well as its companion TrimStart and TrimEnd methods, complete Computer Exercise 33 at the end of this chapter.

The *startIndex* argument in the Remove method is the index of the first character you want removed from the copy of the *string*. A character's index is an integer that indicates the character's position in the string. The first character in a string has an index of 0; the second character has an index of 1, and so on. The optional *numCharsToRemove* argument is the number of characters you want removed. To remove only the first character from a string, you use 0 as the startIndex and 1 as the numCharsToRemove. To remove the fourth through eighth characters, you use 3 as the startIndex and 5 as the numCharsToRemove. If the numCharsToRemove argument is omitted, the Remove method removes all of the characters from the startIndex position through the end of the string, as shown in Example 3 in Figure 10-2.

HOW TO Remove Characters from a String

Syntax
string.**Trim**
string.**Remove(***startIndex*[, *numCharsToRemove*]**)**

Example 1
```
Dim city As String
city = cityTextBox.Text.Trim
```
assigns the contents of the cityTextBox's Text property, excluding any leading and trailing spaces, to the `city` variable

Example 2
```
Dim fullName As String = "Cheryl Jones"
lastTextBox.Text = fullName.Remove(0, 7)
```
assigns the string "Jones" to the lastTextBox's Text property

Example 3
```
Dim fullName As String = "Roberta Jones"
firstTextBox.Text = fullName.Remove(7)
```
assigns the string "Roberta" to the firstTextBox's Text property; you also can write the assignment statement as
```
firstTextBox.Text = fullName.Remove(7, 6)
```

Example 4
```
Dim firstName As String = "John"
firstName = firstName.Remove(2, 1)
```
assigns the string "Jon" to the `firstName` variable

Figure 10-2 How to remove characters from a string

Inserting Characters in a String

Visual Basic's **Insert method** allows you to insert characters anywhere in a string. The method's syntax is shown in Figure 10-3 along with examples of using the method. In the syntax, *string* can be a String variable, a String named constant, or the Text property of a control. When processing the Insert method, the computer first makes a temporary copy of the *string* in memory. It then performs the specified insertion on the copy only. In other words, the method does not affect the original *string*. The *startIndex* argument in the Insert method is an integer that specifies where in the string's copy you want the *value* inserted. The integer represents the character's index—in other words, its position in the string. To insert the value at the beginning of a string, you use a startIndex of 0, as shown in Example 1 in Figure 10-3. To insert the value beginning with the sixth character in the string, you use a startIndex of 5, as shown in Example 2. The Insert method returns a string with the appropriate characters inserted.

HOW TO Insert Characters in a String

Syntax
string.**Insert(***startIndex*, *value***)**

Example 1
```
Dim phone As String = "111-2222"
phone = phone.Insert(0, "(877) ")
```
assigns the string "(877) 111-2222" to the phone variable

Example 2
```
Dim fullName As String = "Jose Munoz"
fullName = fullName.Insert(5, "C. ")
```
assigns the string "Jose C. Munoz" to the fullName variable

Figure 10-3 How to insert characters in a string

If you want to experiment with the Length property and the Trim, Remove, and Insert methods, open the solution contained in the Try It 1! folder.

The answers to Mini-Quiz questions are located in Appendix A.

Mini-Quiz 10-1

1. Which of the following assigns the number of characters stored in the msgLabel to the `numChars` variable?

   a. `numChars = Len(msgLabel.Text)`

   b. `numChars = Length(msgLabel.Text)`

   c. `numChars = msgLabel.Length.Text`

   d. `numChars = msgLabel.Text.Length`

2. Which of the following changes the contents of the `state` variable from Illinois to Il?

   a. `state = state.Remove(2)`

   b. `state = state.Remove(3)`

   c. `state = state.Remove(3, 6)`

   d. both b and c

3. Which of the following changes the contents of the `state` variable from Dakota to South Dakota?

   a. `state = state.Insert(0, "South ")`

   b. `state = state.Insert(1, "South ")`

   c. `state = state.Insert("South ", 0)`

   d. `state = state.Insert("South", 1)`

Searching a String

If you need to determine whether a string contains a specific sequence of characters, you can use either the Contains method or the IndexOf method. Figure 10-4 shows the syntax of both methods. In each syntax, *string* can be a String variable, a String named constant, or the Text property of a control. When processing the Contains and IndexOf methods, the computer first makes a temporary copy of the *string* in memory. It then performs the specified search on the copy only. The *subString* argument in each syntax represents the sequence of characters for which you are searching. Both methods perform a case-sensitive search, which means the case of the subString must match the case of the string in order for both to be considered equal.

The **Contains method** returns the Boolean value True when the subString is contained anywhere in the string; otherwise, it returns the Boolean value False. The Contains method always begins the search with the first character in the string. The Contains method is used in Examples 1 through 3 in Figure 10-4. The **IndexOf method**, on the other hand, returns an integer—either −1 if the subString is not contained in the string or the character index that represents the starting position of the subString in the string. Unless you specify otherwise, the IndexOf method starts the search with the first character in the string. To specify a different starting location, you use the optional *startIndex* argument. The IndexOf method is used in Examples 4 through 6 in Figure 10-4. Notice that two methods appear in the expression in Example 3: ToUpper and Contains. Two methods also appear in the expression in Example 6: ToLower and IndexOf. When an expression contains more than one method, the computer processes the methods from left to right. In this case, the computer will process the ToUpper method before the Contains method in Example 3, and process the ToLower method before the IndexOf method in Example 6.

HOW TO Search a String

Syntax
string.**Contains(***subString***)**
string.**IndexOf(***subString*[, *startIndex*]**)**

Example 1
```
Dim cityState As String = "Nashville, TN"
Dim isContained As Boolean
isContained = cityState.Contains("TN")
```
assigns True to the `isContained` variable, because the string "TN" appears in the `cityState` variable

Example 2
```
Dim cityState As String = "Nashville, TN"
Dim isContained As Boolean
isContained = cityState.Contains("Tn")
```
the Contains method performs a case-sensitive search

assigns False to the `isContained` variable, because the string "Tn" does not appear in the `cityState` variable

Example 3
```
Dim address As String = "345 Main Ave."
If address.ToUpper.Contains("MAIN AVE.") Then
```
the ToUpper method is evaluated before the Contains method

the condition evaluates to True because the string "MAIN AVE." appears in the `address` variable when the variable's contents are temporarily converted to uppercase

Example 4
character index 11
```
Dim cityState As String = "Nashville, TN"
Dim charIndex As Integer
charIndex = cityState.IndexOf("TN")
```
assigns the number 11 to the `charIndex` variable because the string "TN" appears in the `cityState` variable, beginning with the character whose index is 11

Example 5
```
Dim cityState As String = "Nashville, TN"
Dim charIndex As Integer
charIndex = cityState.IndexOf("Tn")
```
the IndexOf method performs a case-sensitive search

assigns the number –1 to the `charIndex` variable because the string "Tn" does not appear in the `cityState` variable

Example 6
```
Dim address As String = "345 Main Ave."
Dim charIndex As Integer
charIndex = address.ToLower.IndexOf("main ave.", 5) Then
```
the ToLower method is evaluated before the IndexOf method

assigns the number –1 to the `charIndex` variable because the string "main ave." does not appear in the `address` variable when the search starts with the character whose index is 5 (the letter a)

Figure 10-4 How to search a string

Accessing the Characters in a String

Visual Basic provides the **Substring method** for accessing any number of characters in a string. Figure 10-5 shows the method's syntax and includes examples of using the method. In the syntax, *string* can be a String variable, a String named constant, or the Text property of a control. When processing the Substring method, the computer first makes a temporary copy of the *string* in memory. It then accesses the specified number of characters in the copy only. The *startIndex* argument in the syntax is the index of the first character you want to access in the string's copy. As you already know, the first character in a string has an index of 0. The optional *numCharsToAccess* argument specifies the number of characters you want to access. The Substring method returns a string that contains the number of characters specified in the numCharsToAccess argument, beginning with the character whose index is startIndex. If you omit the numCharsToAccess argument, the Substring method returns all characters from the startIndex position through the end of the string.

HOW TO Access Characters in a String

Syntax

string.**Substring(***startIndex*[,*numCharsToAccess*]**)**

Example 1

character index 0 | character index 7

```
Dim full As String = "Herman Gutierez"
Dim first As String = full.Substring(0, 6)
Dim last As String = full.Substring(7)
```

assigns the string "Herman" to the `first` variable and the string "Gutierez" to the `last` variable; you also can write the last Dim statement as

```
Dim last As String = full.Substring(7, 8)
```

Example 2

character index 2

```
Dim employeeNum As String = "38F45"
Dim dept As String = employeeNum.Substring(2, 1)
```

assigns the string "F" to the `dept` variable

Figure 10-5 How to access characters in a string

If you want to experiment with the Contains, IndexOf, and Substring methods, open the solution contained in the Try It 2! folder.

Aligning the Characters in a String

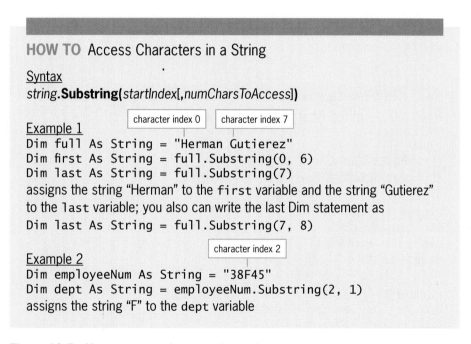

You can use Visual Basic's PadLeft and PadRight methods to align the characters in a string. The methods do this by inserting (padding) the string with zero or more characters until the string is a specified length; each method then returns the padded string. Figure 10-6 shows the syntax of both methods. In each syntax, *string* can be a String variable, a String named constant, or the Text property of a control. When processing the PadLeft and PadRight methods, the computer first makes a temporary copy of the *string* in memory; it then pads the copy only. The *totalChars* argument in each syntax is an integer that represents the total number of characters you want the string's copy to contain. The optional *padCharacter* argument is the character that each method uses to pad the string until it reaches the desired number of characters. If the padCharacter argument is omitted, the default padding character is the space character.

The **PadLeft method** pads the string on the left, which means it inserts the padded characters at the beginning of the string; doing this right-aligns the characters within the string. The **PadRight method**, on the other hand, pads the string on the right, which means it inserts the padded characters at the end of the string and left-aligns the characters within the string. Examples of using both methods are included in Figure 10-6. Notice that Example 3's expression contains the ToString and PadLeft methods. Recall that when an expression contains more than one method, the computer processes the methods from left to right. In this case, the computer will process the ToString method before processing the PadLeft method. Also notice the letter c that appears at the end of the *padCharacter* argument in Example 3. The letter c is one of the literal type characters in Visual Basic. As you learned in Chapter 3, a literal type character forces a literal constant to assume a data type other than the one its form indicates. In this case, the letter c forces the "*" string in the padCharacter argument to assume the Char (character) data type.

If you want to experiment with the PadLeft and PadRight methods, open the solution contained in the Try It 3! folder.

HOW TO Align the Characters in a String

Syntax
string.**PadLeft(***totalChars*[, *padCharacter*]**)**
string.**PadRight(***totalChars*[, *padCharacter*]**)**

Example 1
```
Dim num As String = "73"
num = num.PadLeft(5)
```
assigns the string "   73" to the `num` variable
3 spaces

Example 2
```
Dim first As String = "Sue"
first = first.PadRight(10)
```
assigns the string "Sue   " to the `first` variable
7 spaces

Example 3
```
Dim netPay As Double = 645.75
Dim formattedPay As String
formattedPay = netPay.ToString("C2").PadLeft(10, "*"c)
```
assigns the string "***$645.75" to the `formattedPay` variable (Many companies use this type of formatting on their employee paychecks, because it makes it more difficult for someone to change the amount.)

Figure 10-6 How to align the characters in a string

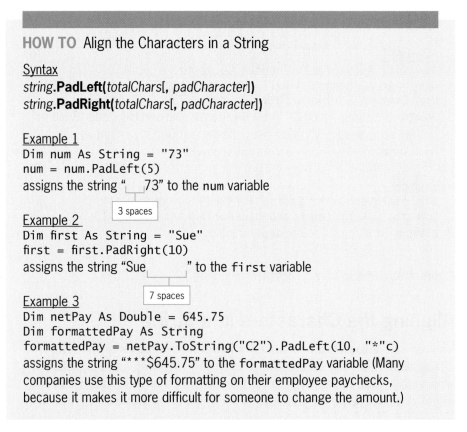

Mini-Quiz 10-2

1. If the `restaurant` variable contains the string "Anna's Greek Restaurant", what will the `restaurant.ToUpper.Contains("GREEK")` method return?
   a. 7
   b. 8
   c. True
   d. False

2. If the `restaurant` variable contains the string "Anna's Greek Restaurant", what will the `restaurant.ToUpper.IndexOf("GREEK")` method return?
   a. 7
   b. 8
   c. True
   d. False

3. If the `restaurant` variable contains the string "Anna's Greek Restaurant", which of the following assigns the string "GREEK" to the `foodType` variable?
   a. `foodType = restaurant.ToUpper.Substring(8, 5)`
   b. `foodType = restaurant.ToUpper.Substring(7, 5)`
   c. `foodType = restaurant.Substring(7, 5).ToUpper`
   d. both b and c

4. Which of the following changes the contents of the `grade` variable from A to A++++?
   a. `grade = grade.PadRight("+"c, 5)`
   b. `grade = grade.PadRight(5, "+"c)`
   c. `grade = grade.Insert(1, "++++")`
   d. both b and c

The answers to Mini-Quiz questions are located in Appendix A.

Using Pattern-Matching to Compare Strings

The **Like operator** allows you to use pattern-matching characters to determine whether one string is equal to another string. Figure 10-7 shows the Like operator's syntax. In the syntax, *string* can be a String variable, a String named constant, or the Text property of a control. *Pattern* is a String expression containing one or more of the pattern-matching characters listed in the figure. As the figure indicates, the question mark (?) character in a pattern represents one character only, whereas the asterisk (*) character represents zero or more characters. To represent a single digit in a pattern, you use the number sign (#) character. The last two pattern-matching characters listed in Figure 10-7 contain a *characterList*, which is simply a listing of characters. "[A9M]" is a characterList that contains three characters: A, 9, and M. You also can include a range of values in a characterList. You do this using a hyphen to separate the lowest value in the range from the highest value in the range. For example, to include all lowercase letters in a characterList, you use "[a-z]". To include both lowercase and uppercase letters in the characterList, you use "[a-zA-Z]".

The Like operator compares the string to the pattern; the comparison is case-sensitive. If the string matches the pattern, the Like operator returns the Boolean value True; otherwise, it returns the Boolean value False. Examples of using the Like operator are included in Figure 10-7.

HOW TO Use Pattern-Matching to Compare Strings

Syntax
string **Like** *pattern*

Pattern-matching characters	Matches in *string*
?	any single character
*	zero or more characters
#	any single digit (0 through 9)
[*characterList*]	any single character in the characterList (for example, "[A9M]" matches A, 9, or M, whereas "[a-z]" matches any lowercase letter)
[!*characterList*]	any single character *not* in the characterList (for example, "[!A9M]" matches any character other than A, 9, or M, whereas "[!a-z]" matches any character that is not a lowercase letter)

Example 1
```
If firstName.ToUpper Like "B?LL" Then
```
The condition evaluates to True when the string stored in the `firstName` variable (converted to uppercase) begins with the letter B followed by one character and then the two letters LL; otherwise, it evaluates to False. Examples of strings that would make the condition evaluate to True include "Bill", "Ball", "bell", and "bull". Examples of strings for which the condition would evaluate to False include "BPL", "BLL", and "billy".

Example 2
```
If stateTextBox.Text Like "K*" Then
```
The condition evaluates to True when the value in the stateTextBox's Text property begins with the letter K followed by zero or more characters; otherwise, it evaluates to False. Examples of strings that would make the condition evaluate to True include "KANSAS", "Ky", and "Kentucky".

Figure 10-7 How to use pattern-matching to compare strings *(continues)*

(continued)

Examples of strings for which the condition would evaluate to False include "kansas" and "ky".

Example 3

```
Do While id Like "###*"
```

The condition evaluates to True when the string stored in the `id` variable begins with three digits followed by zero or more characters; otherwise, it evaluates to False. Examples of strings that would make the condition evaluate to True include "178" and "983Ab". Examples of strings for which the condition would evaluate to False include "X34" and "34Z5".

Example 4

```
If firstName.ToUpper Like "T[OI]M" Then
```

The condition evaluates to True when the string stored in the `firstName` variable (converted to uppercase) is either "TOM" or "TIM". When the variable does not contain "TOM" or "TIM"—for example, when it contains "Tam" or "Tommy"—the condition evaluates to False.

Example 5

```
If letter Like "[a-z]" Then
```

The condition evaluates to True when the string stored in the `letter` variable is one lowercase letter; otherwise, it evaluates to False.

Example 6

```
For index As Integer = 0 to userEntry.Length - 1
     If userEntry.Substring(index, 1) Like "[!a-zA-Z]" Then
          nonLetter += 1
     End If
Next index
```

Compares each character in the `userEntry` variable with the lowercase and uppercase letters of the alphabet, and counts the number of characters that are not letters.

Example 7

```
If userEntry Like "*.*" Then
     MessageBox.Show("The entry contains a period.")
End If
```

The condition evaluates to True when a period appears anywhere in the `userEntry` variable; otherwise, it evaluates to False.

Example 8

```
If userEntry.ToUpper Like "[A-Z][A-Z]##" Then
```

The condition evaluates to True when the value in the `userEntry` variable (converted to uppercase) is two letters followed by two numbers; otherwise, it evaluates to False.

Figure 10-7 How to use pattern-matching to compare strings

If you want to experiment with the Like operator, open the solution contained in the Try It 4! folder.

The answers to Mini-Quiz questions are located in Appendix A.

Mini-Quiz 10-3

1. Which of the following evaluates to True when the `partNum` variable contains the string "123X45"?
   a. `partNum Like "999[A-Z]99"`
   b. `partNum Like "######"`
   c. `partNum Like "###[A-Z]##"`
   d. `partNum Like "*[A-Z]"`

2. Which of the following determines whether a comma appears anywhere in the salesTextBox's Text property?
   a. `salesTextBox.Text Like ","`
   b. `salesTextBox.Text Like "*,*"`
   c. `salesTextBox.Text Like "[*,*]"`
   d. none of the above

3. Which of the following determines whether a percent sign (%) appears as the last character in the rateTextBox's Text property?
   a. `rateTextBox.Text Like "%"`
   b. `rateTextBox.Text Like "*%*"`
   c. `rateTextBox.Text Like "*%"`
   d. none of the above

Adding a Menu to a Form

To watch a demonstration of creating a menu, view the Ch10Menu video.

The Menus & Toolbars section of the toolbox contains a MenuStrip tool for instantiating a menu strip control. You use a **menu strip control** to include one or more menus on a Windows form. Each menu contains a menu title, which appears on the menu bar at the top of the form. When you click a menu title, its corresponding menu opens and displays a list of options, called menu items. The menu items can be commands (such as Open or Exit), separator bars, or submenu titles. As in all Windows applications, clicking a command on a menu executes the command, and clicking a submenu title opens an additional menu of options. Each of the options on a submenu is referred to as a submenu item. You can use a separator bar to visually group together related items on a menu or submenu. Figure 10-8 identifies the location of these menu elements.

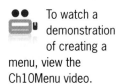

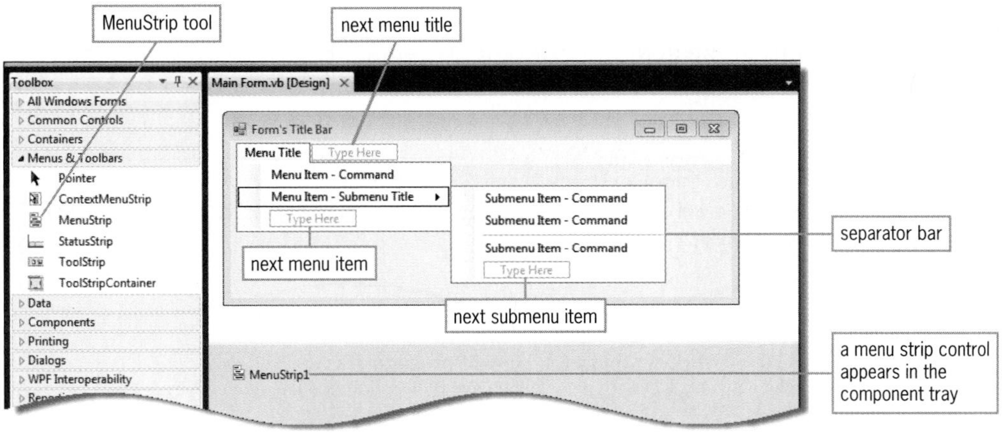

Figure 10-8 Location of menu elements

Each menu element is considered an object; therefore, each has a set of properties associated with it. The most commonly used properties for a menu element are the Name and Text properties. The programmer uses the Name property to refer to the menu element in code. The Text property stores the menu element's caption, which is the text that the user sees when he or she is working with the menu. The caption indicates the purpose of the menu element. Examples of familiar captions for menu elements include Edit, Save As, Copy, and Exit.

Menu title captions should be one word only, with the first letter capitalized. Each menu title should have a unique access key. The access key allows the user to open the menu by pressing the Alt key in combination with the access key. Unlike the captions for menu titles, the captions for menu items typically consist of one to three words. The Windows standard is to use book title capitalization for the menu item captions. Each menu item should have an access key that is unique within its menu. The access key allows the user to select the item by pressing the access key when the menu is open.

Commonly used menu items should be assigned shortcut keys. The **shortcut keys** appear to the right of the menu item and allow the user to select the item without opening the menu. Examples of familiar shortcut keys include Ctrl+X and Ctrl+V. In Windows applications that have an Edit menu, Ctrl+X and Ctrl+V are used to select the Cut and Paste commands, respectively, when the Edit menu is closed. You specify a menu item's shortcut keys in the ShortcutKeys property in the Properties window.

A menu item's access key can be used only when the menu is open. A menu item's shortcut keys can be used only when the menu is closed.

Figure 10-9 shows the Game menu you will create in Programming Tutorial 1. The menu contains two menu items: New Game and Exit. The menu title and both menu items have access keys. In addition, shortcut keys are provided for the New Game menu item.

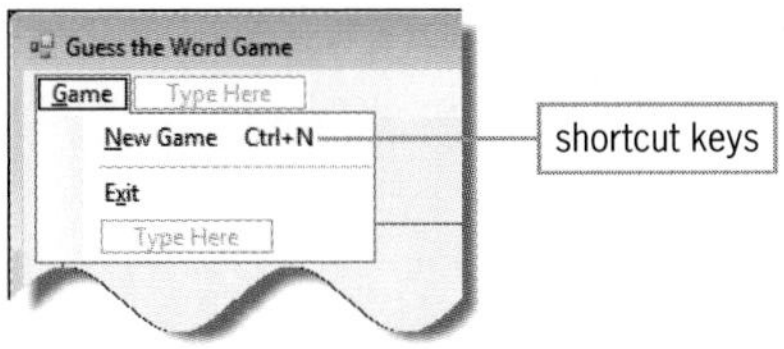

Figure 10-9 Game menu

If an item on a menu or submenu is a command, you enter the appropriate instructions in the item's Click event procedure. Figure 10-10 shows the Click event procedure for the Exit command from Figure 10-9.

```
Private Sub gameExitMenuItem_Click(ByVal sender As Object,
    ByVal e As System.EventArgs) Handles gameExitMenuItem.Click
    Me.Close()
End Sub
```

Figure 10-10 Exit command's Click event procedure

You have completed the concepts section of Chapter 10. The Programming Tutorial section is next.

PROGRAMMING TUTORIAL 1

Creating the Guess the Word Game Application

In this tutorial, you code the Guess the Word Game application, which is played by two people. Figures 10-11 and 10-12 show the application's TOE chart and MainForm, respectively. The MainForm contains four labels, a panel, and 26 buttons. It also contains a Game menu that has two options: New Game and Exit. When the user clicks the New Game option, the option's Click event procedure will prompt player 1 to enter a five-letter word. Player 2 will then be given 10 chances to guess the word, letter by letter. If player 2 guesses the word, the application will display the "Great guessing!" message. If player 2 does not guess the word, the application will display the message "Sorry, the word is" followed by the word.

Task	Object	Event
1. prepare for a new game by clearing the contents of the wordLabel and incorrectLabel and setting the number of incorrect guesses to 0 2. get a 5-letter word from player 1 3. validate the word, which should contain 5 letters 4. if the word is not valid, display the "Please enter 5 letters only" message; otherwise, display 5 dashes in the wordLabel and enable the 26 letter buttons	gameNewMenuItem	Click
End the application	gameExitMenuItem	Click
1. disable the letter button that raised the Click event to indicate that the letter has already been guessed 2. search the 5-letter word for the letter entered by player 2 3. if the letter is contained in the 5-letter word, replace the corresponding dash (or dashes) in the wordLabel with the letter 4. if a dash was replaced in the wordLabel, determine whether the wordLabel contains another dash 5. if the wordLabel doesn't contain another dash, the game is over; therefore, display the "Great guessing!" message in a messagebox and disable the 26 letter buttons; otherwise, add 1 to the number of incorrect guesses and then display the number of incorrect guesses in the incorrectLabel	26 letter buttons	Click

Figure 10-11 TOE chart for the Guess the Word Game application *(continues)*

(continued)

Task	Object	Event
6. If player 2 made 10 incorrect guesses, the game is over; therefore, display the "Sorry, the word is" message and the word in a message box and then disable the 26 letter buttons		
Display the word entered by player 1; this may be dashes, a combination of dashes and letters, or all letters (from gameNewMenuItem and the 26 letter buttons)	wordLabel	None
Display the number of incorrect guesses (from the 26 letter buttons)	incorrectLabel	None
Display the Game menu	MenuStrip1	None

Figure 10-11 TOE chart for the Guess the Word Game application

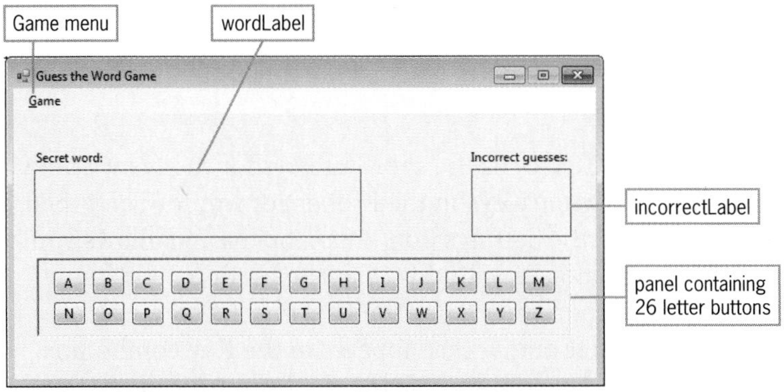

Figure 10-12 MainForm in the Guess the Word Game application

Completing the Interface

Included in the data files for this book is a partially completed Guess the Word Game application. Before you can code the application, you need to add the Game menu to the form.

To add the Game menu to the form:

1. Start Visual Studio or the Express Edition of Visual Basic. If necessary, open the Solution Explorer window.
2. Open the **Guess the Word Solution** (**Guess the Word Solution.sln**) file, which is contained in the VbReloaded2010\Chap10\Guess the Word Solution folder. Open the designer window (if necessary), and then auto-hide the Solution Explorer window.
3. Open the Toolbox window (if necessary), and then click **MenuStrip** in the Menus and Toolbars section. Drag a menu strip control to the form. When you release the mouse button, the MenuStrip1 control will appear in the component tray.
4. Auto-hide the Toolbox window and then display the Properties window (if necessary). Click the **Type Here** box on the menu bar, and then type **&Game**. See Figure 10-13. You use the Type Here box that appears below the menu title to add a menu item to the Game menu. You use the Type Here box that appears to the right of the menu title to add another menu title to the menu bar.

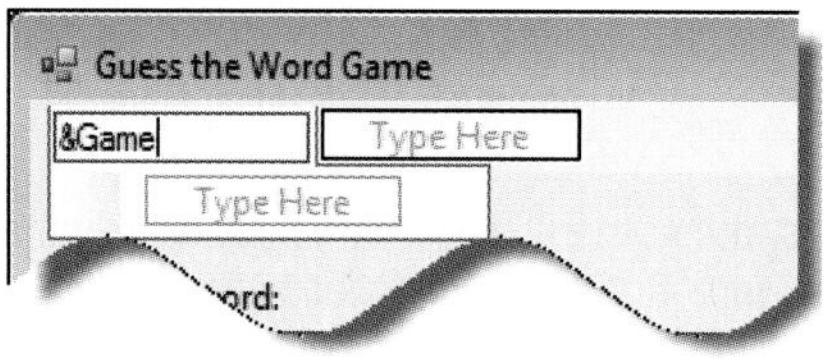

Figure 10-13 Game menu title added to the menu bar

5. Press **Enter** and then click the **Game** menu title. Scroll the Properties window until you see the Text property; notice that the property contains &Game.
6. Scroll to the top of the Properties window and then click **(Name)**. Type **gameMenuTitle** and press **Enter**.
7. Click the **Type Here** box that appears below the Game menu title. Type **&New Game** and press **Enter**.
8. Click the **New Game** menu item. Change the menu item's name to **gameNewMenuItem**.
9. Next, you will assign Ctrl+N as the shortcut keys for the New Game menu item. Click **ShortcutKeys** in the Properties window, and then click the **list arrow** in the Settings box. A box opens and allows you to specify a modifier and a key. In this case, the modifier and key will be Ctrl and N, respectively. Click the **Ctrl** check box to select it, and then click the **list arrow** that appears in the Key combo box. An alphabetical list of keys appears. Scroll the list until you see the letter N, and then click **N** in the list. See Figure 10-14.

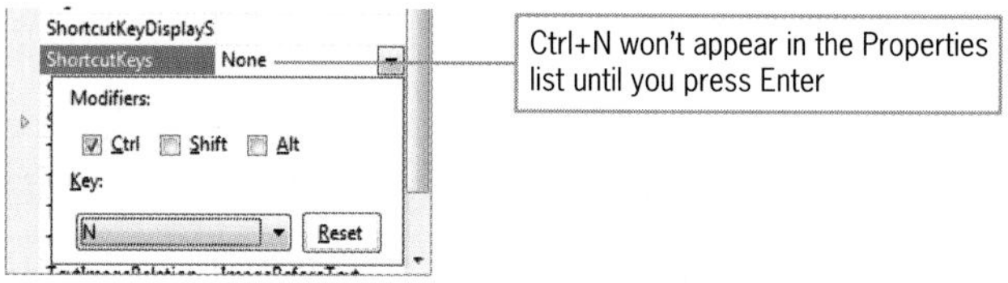

Figure 10-14 Ctrl+N shortcut keys specified in the ShortcutKeys box

10. Press **Enter**. Ctrl+N appears in the ShortcutKeys property in the Properties list. It also appears to the right of the New Game menu item.
11. Next, you will add a separator bar to the Game menu. Place your mouse pointer on the Type Here box that appears below the New Game menu item, but don't click the box. Instead, click the **list arrow** that appears inside the box. See Figure 10-15.

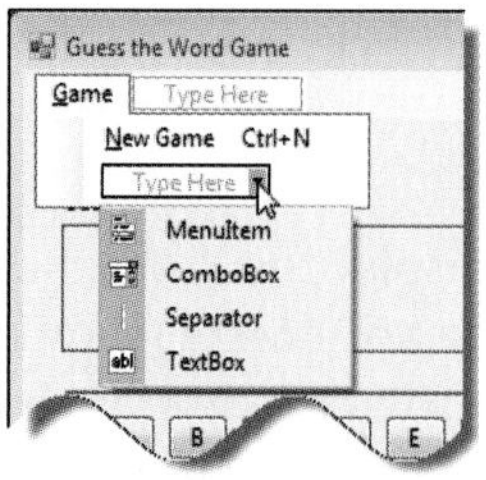

Figure 10-15 Result of clicking the list arrow in the Type Here box

12. Click **Separator** in the list. A horizontal line, called a separator bar, appears below the New Game menu item.
13. Click the **Type Here** box that appears below the separator bar. Type **E&xit** and press **Enter**. Click the **Exit** menu item. Change the menu item's Name to **gameExitMenuItem**.
14. Save the solution and then start the application. Click **Game** on the menu bar. The Game menu opens and offers two options separated by a separator bar. See Figure 10-16.

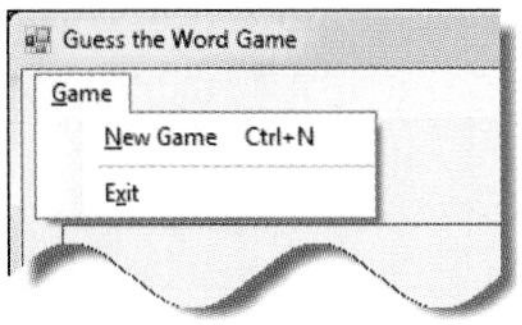

Figure 10-16 Open Game menu during run time

15. Click the **Close** button on the form's title bar.

Coding the Application

Now that the interface is complete, you can begin coding the application. According to the application's TOE chart, the Click event procedures for the two menu items and the 26 letter buttons need to be coded. You'll begin by coding the Exit item's Click event procedure.

To begin coding the Guess the Word Game application:

1. Open the Code Editor window, which already contains some of the application's code.
2. Notice the EnableDisableButtons procedure, which is an independent Sub procedure. According to its procedure header, the EnableDisableButtons procedure will receive a Boolean value from the statement that calls it. The procedure uses the Boolean value (either True or False) to set each letter button's Enabled property. As you learned in Chapter 6, the Enabled property determines whether the control is available to the user.
3. Scroll the Code Editor window (if necessary) until you see the CheckStatus procedure. The procedure header indicates that the procedure will receive a Boolean value when it is called. You will code the procedure later in this tutorial.
4. Locate the LetterButtons procedure in the Code Editor window. Notice that the procedure is associated with the Click event procedures for the 26 letter buttons. You will code the procedure later in this tutorial.
5. In the comments that appear in the General Declarations section, replace <your name> and <current date> with your name and the current date.

6. Open the code template for the gameExitMenuItem's Click event procedure. Type **Me.Close()** and press **Enter**.
7. Now you will test the Exit item's code. Save the solution and then start the application. Click **Game** on the menu bar and then click **Exit**.

Next, you will code the New Game item's Click event procedure. The procedure's pseudocode is shown in Figure 10-17 along with the pseudocode for an independent Sub procedure named EnableDisableButtons. The Click event procedure calls the independent Sub procedure to enable the 26 letter buttons. This is necessary because the buttons are disabled when the form first appears on the screen. They also will be disabled when the game ends, which happens when player 2 either guesses the word or makes 10 incorrect guesses.

```
gameNewMenuItem Click event procedure
1. clear the contents of the wordLabel and incorrectLabel
2. assign 0 to the variable that keeps track of the number of incorrect guesses
3. get a 5-letter word from player 1 and convert it to uppercase
4. if the word does not contain exactly 5 letters
         display the "Please enter 5 letters only" message in a message box
   else
         display 5 dashes in the wordLabel
         call the EnableDisableButtons procedure to enable the 26 letter
         buttons; pass the procedure the Boolean value True
   end if

EnableDisableButtons procedure (receives a Boolean value that indicates the desired
state of the 26 letter buttons)
assign the Boolean value to the Enabled property of each of the 26 letter buttons
```

Figure 10-17 Pseudocode for the Click event and EnableDisableButtons procedures

To code the New Game item's Click event procedure and then test the code:

1. The procedure will use two class-level variables. One of the variables will store the word entered by player 1, and the other will store the number of incorrect guesses. Locate the EnableDisableButtons procedure in the Code Editor window and then click the **blank line** above its procedure header. Enter the following comment and Private statements:

   ' class-level variables
   Private word As String
   Private incorrect As Integer

2. Open the code template for the gameNewMenuItem's Click event procedure. Type **' prepares the application for a new game** and press **Enter** twice.
3. The first step in the procedure's pseudocode is to clear the contents of the wordLabel and incorrectLabel. Enter the following assignment statements:

   wordLabel.Text = String.Empty
   incorrectLabel.Text = String.Empty

4. The next step is to assign 0 to the variable that keeps track of the number of incorrect guesses. Type the following assignment statement and then press **Enter** twice:

   incorrect = 0

5. Step 3 in the pseudocode is to get a 5-letter word from player 1 and convert it to uppercase. Enter the following assignment statement:

   ```
   word = InputBox("Enter a 5-letter word:",
                   "Player 1").ToUpper
   ```

6. Step 4 in the pseudocode is a dual-alternative selection structure that determines whether player 1's word is valid. You can use the `word` variable's Length property to determine whether the word contains exactly five characters. You can use the Like operator to verify that each character in the word is a letter. Enter the following comment and If clause. (The Code Editor will automatically enter the End If clause.)

   ```
   ' validate the word
   If word.Length <> 5 OrElse word Like "*[!A-Z]*" Then
   ```

7. If the `word` variable does not contain five letters, the selection structure's true path should display the "Please enter 5 letters only" message. Enter the following lines of code:

   ```
   MessageBox.Show("Please enter 5 letters only",
        "Guess the Word", MessageBoxButtons.OK,
        MessageBoxIcon.Information)
   ```

8. On the other hand, if the `word` variable does contain five letters, the selection structure's false path should perform two tasks. First, it should display five dashes (hyphens) in the wordLabel. Enter the following Else clause and assignment statement:

   ```
   Else
      wordLabel.Text = "-----"
   ```

9. Next, the selection structure's false path should call the EnableDisableButtons procedure to enable the 26 letter buttons. The Call statement will pass the procedure the Boolean value True, which the procedure will use to enable the buttons. Enter the following Call statement:

   Call EnableDisableButtons(True)

10. Save the solution and then start the application. Notice that the 26 letter buttons are dimmed (grayed out), indicating that they are not available to the user.

11. First, you will enter a word that contains only three letters. Click **Game** on the menu bar and then click **New Game**. Type **bas** and press **Enter**. The "Please enter 5 letters only" message appears in a message box. Close the message box.

12. Now, you will enter a word that contains four letters and one number. Click **Game** and then click **New Game**. Type **basi2** and press **Enter**. The "Please enter 5 letters only" message appears in a message box. Close the message box.

13. Finally, you will enter a word that contains five letters. Press **Ctrl+n** to select the New Game item on the Game menu. Type **basic** and press **Enter**. Five dashes (hyphens) appear in the Secret word box and the 26 letter buttons are enabled.
14. Click **Game** on the menu bar and then click **Exit**.

Now, you will code the Click event procedures for the 26 letter buttons. Recall that the Click event procedures are associated with the LetterButtons procedure in the Code Editor window. The pseudocode for the LetterButtons procedure is shown in Figure 10-18 along with the code for an independent Sub procedure named CheckStatus. The CheckStatus procedure is called by the LetterButtons procedure.

```
LetterButtons procedure (associated with the Click event procedures for the 26 letter buttons)
1. disable the button that raised the Click event to indicate that the letter has already been guessed
2. search the 5-letter word for the letter entered by player 2, as follows:
   repeat for index from 0 through 4 in increments of 1
        if the current letter in the word matches the button's Text property
              replace the associated dash in the wordLabel with the letter
              selected by player 2

              assign True to a Boolean variable named dashReplaced to
              indicate that a dash was replaced in the wordLabel
        end if
   end repeat for
3. call the CheckStatus procedure; pass the procedure the value stored in the dashReplaced variable

CheckStatus procedure (receives a Boolean value that indicates whether a dash was replaced in the wordLabel)
if the Boolean value is True (indicating that a dash was replaced in the wordLabel)
        if the wordLabel doesn't contain another dash, the game is over
              display the "Great guessing!" message in a message box

              call the EnableDisableButtons procedure to disable the 26 letter
              buttons; pass the procedure the Boolean value False
        end if
else
        add 1 to the number of incorrect guesses

        display the number of incorrect guesses in the incorrectLabel

        if the number of incorrect guesses is 10, the game is over
              display the "Sorry, the word is" and the word in a
              message box

              call the EnableDisableButtons procedure to disable the
              26 letter buttons; pass the procedure the Boolean value False
        end if
end if
```

Figure 10-18 Pseudocode for the LetterButtons and CheckStatus procedures

To code the LetterButtons procedure, which is associated with the 26 letter buttons:

1. Locate the LetterButtons procedure in the Code Editor window. Click the **blank line** immediately below the procedure header. Type the following comments and then press **Enter** twice:

   ' determines whether the button's letter
   ' is in the word

2. The procedure will use two procedure-level variables. One of the variables will store the result of casting (converting) the `sender` variable from the Object data type to the Button data type. (You learned about casting in Chapter 8.) The other variable will keep track of whether a dash was replaced in the wordLabel. Enter the following two Dim statements. Press **Enter** twice after typing the second Dim statement.

   Dim clickedButton As Button
   Dim dashReplaced As Boolean

3. Step 1 in the pseudocode is to disable the button that raised the Click event procedure. You are doing this to indicate that the letter associated with the button has already been used. Enter the following two statements. Press **Enter** twice after typing the second statement.

   clickedButton = TryCast(sender, Button)
   clickedButton.Enabled = False

4. Step 2 in the pseudocode is to search the 5-letter word, looking for the letter entered by player 2. You can do this using a loop that repeats its loop body for each letter in the word. Enter the following For clause:

   For index As Integer = 0 To 4

5. Change the Next clause to **Next index**.

6. The loop body contains a single-alternative selection structure whose condition determines whether the current letter in the word matches the letter selected by player 2. Click the **blank line** below the For clause. Enter the following comments and If clause:

   ' if the current letter in the word
   ' matches player 2's letter, replace the
   ' associated dash in the wordLabel with
   ' player 2's letter and then indicate
   ' that a replacement was made
   If word.Substring(index, 1) =
   clickedButton.Text Then

7. According to the pseudocode, the selection structure's true path should replace the dash in the wordLabel with the letter selected by player 2. You can do this by first removing the dash from the wordLabel and then inserting the letter in the same position. Enter the following two assignment statements:

   wordLabel.Text =
   wordLabel.Text.Remove(index, 1)
   wordLabel.Text =
   wordLabel.Text.Insert(index, clickedButton.Text)

8. The selection structure's true path also should assign True to the `dashReplaced` variable to indicate that a dash was replaced in the wordLabel. Enter the following assignment statement:

   dashReplaced = True

9. Step 3 in the pseudocode is to call the CheckStatus procedure, passing it the value stored in the `dashReplaced` variable. Insert a blank line between the Next index and End Sub clauses, and then enter the following Call statement:

   Call CheckStatus(dashReplaced)

The last procedure you need to code is the CheckStatus procedure, which is called by the LetterButtons procedure.

To code the CheckStatus procedure and then test the code:

1. Locate the CheckStatus procedure in the Code Editor window. Click the **blank line** below the procedure header. Type **' determines whether the game is over** and press **Enter** twice.

2. According to its pseudocode (shown earlier in Figure 10-18), the procedure begins with a dual-alternative selection structure. The selection structure's condition determines whether the LetterButtons procedure replaced a dash in the wordLabel. You can make this determination by looking at the contents of the `dashStatus` variable declared in the CheckStatus procedure header. If the variable contains the Boolean value True, at least one dash was replaced; otherwise, no dashes were replaced. Enter the following If clause:

   If dashStatus = True Then

3. The selection structure's true path contains a nested single-alternative selection structure. The nested selection structure's condition determines whether the wordLabel contains any more dashes. You can make this determination using the Contains method. Enter the following If clause:

   If wordLabel.Text.Contains("-") = False Then

4. If the wordLabel doesn't contain any dashes, the game is over. Therefore, the nested selection structure's true path displays the "Great guessing!" message and then calls the EnableDisableButtons procedure to disable the 26 letter buttons. Enter the following comments and code:

```
' the game is over because the
' word was guessed
MessageBox.Show("Great guessing!",
    "Game Over", MessageBoxButtons.OK,
    MessageBoxIcon.Information)
Call EnableDisableButtons(False)
```

5. On the other hand, if a dash was not replaced in the wordLabel, the outer selection structure's false path should add 1 to the number of incorrect guesses and then display the number of incorrect guesses in the incorrectLabel. Insert a blank line between the two End If clauses, and then enter the following Else clause and assignment statements:

```
Else
    incorrect += 1
    incorrectLabel.Text = incorrect.ToString
```

6. The next instruction in the outer selection structure's false path is a nested single-alternative selection structure. The nested selection structure's condition determines whether the user has made 10 incorrect guesses. If 10 incorrect guesses were made, the game is over. Therefore, the nested selection structure's true path displays the "Sorry, the word is" message and the word in a message box. It then calls the EnableDisableButtons procedure to disable the 26 letter buttons. Enter the following selection structure:

```
If incorrect = 10 Then
    MessageBox.Show("Sorry, the word is " &
            word, "Game Over",
            MessageBoxButtons.OK,
            MessageBoxIcon.Information)
    Call EnableDisableButtons(False)
End If
```

7. Save the solution and then start the application. Click **Game** on the menu bar and then click **New Game**. Type **puppy** and then press **Enter**. Click the **E** button. The E button is disabled and the number 1 appears in the Incorrect guesses label. Click the **P** button. The P button is disabled and three of the dashes in the Secret word box are replaced with the letter P. See Figure 10-19.

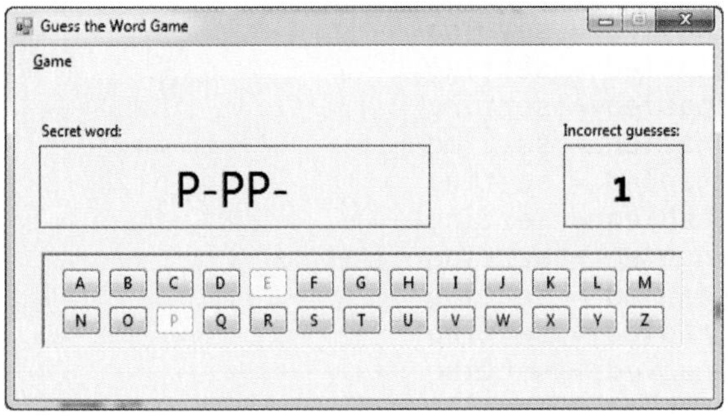

Figure 10-19 Result of guessing the letters E and P

8. Now click the following four buttons: **A**, **T**, **U**, and **G**. Notice that each time you click a correct button, the button's letter appears in the appropriate position in the Secret word label. Each time you click an incorrect button, the number in the Incorrect guesses box increases by 1.

9. Click the **Y** button. The word "PUPPY" appears in the Secret word box and the "Great guessing!" message appears in a message box. Close the message box. Notice that the 26 letter buttons are now disabled.

10. Press **Ctrl+n** to start a new game. Notice that the 26 letter buttons are now enabled. Type **basic** and press **Enter**. Now click the following 11 buttons: **D**, **E**, **F**, **G**, **H**, **I**, **J**, **K**, **L**, **M**, and **N**. A message box opens and displays the "Sorry, the word is BASIC" message. Close the message box. The Incorrect guesses box contains the number 10 and the 26 letter buttons are disabled once again.

11. Click **Game** on the menu bar and then click **Exit** to end the application. Close the Code Editor window and then close the solution. Figure 10-20 shows the application's code.

```
' Project name:          Guess the Word Project
' Project purpose:       Simulates the Guess the
'                        Word game
' Created/revised by:    <your name> on <current date>

Option Explicit On
Option Strict On
Option Infer Off

Public Class MainForm

  ' class-level variables
  Private word As String
  Private incorrect As Integer

  Private Sub EnableDisableButtons(ByVal setting As Boolean)
    ' enable or disable letter buttons

    aButton.Enabled = setting
    bButton.Enabled = setting
    cButton.Enabled = setting
    dButton.Enabled = setting
    eButton.Enabled = setting
    fButton.Enabled = setting
    gButton.Enabled = setting
    hButton.Enabled = setting
    iButton.Enabled = setting
    jButton.Enabled = setting
    kButton.Enabled = setting
    lButton.Enabled = setting
    mButton.Enabled = setting
    nButton.Enabled = setting
    oButton.Enabled = setting
    pButton.Enabled = setting
    qButton.Enabled = setting
    rButton.Enabled = setting
    sButton.Enabled = setting
    tButton.Enabled = setting
    uButton.Enabled = setting
    vButton.Enabled = setting
    wButton.Enabled = setting
    xButton.Enabled = setting
    yButton.Enabled = setting
    zButton.Enabled = setting
  End Sub

  Private Sub CheckStatus(ByVal dashStatus As Boolean)
    ' determines whether the game is over

    If dashStatus = True Then
      If wordLabel.Text.Contains("-") = False Then
          ' the game is over because the
```

Figure 10-20 Code for the Guess the Word Game application *(continues)*

(continued)

```
            ' word was guessed
            MessageBox.Show("Great guessing!",
               "Game Over", MessageBoxButtons.OK,
               MessageBoxIcon.Information)
            Call EnableDisableButtons(False)

        End If
    Else
        incorrect += 1
        incorrectLabel.Text = incorrect.ToString
        If incorrect = 10 Then
            MessageBox.Show("Sorry, the word is " &
                word, "Game Over",
                MessageBoxButtons.OK,
                MessageBoxIcon.Information)
            Call EnableDisableButtons(False)
        End If
    End If
End Sub

Private Sub LetterButtons(ByVal sender As Object,
ByVal e As System.EventArgs) Handles aButton.Click,
bButton.Click, cButton.Click, dButton.Click,
eButton.Click, jButton.Click, iButton.Click,
hButton.Click,
gButton.Click, fButton.Click, oButton.Click,
nButton.Click, mButton.Click, lButton.Click,
kButton.Click,
tButton.Click, sButton.Click, rButton.Click,
qButton.Click, pButton.Click, yButton.Click,
xButton.Click,
wButton.Click, vButton.Click, uButton.Click,
zButton.Click
    ' determines whether the button's letter
    ' is in the word

    Dim clickedButton As Button
    Dim dashReplaced As Boolean

    clickedButton = TryCast(sender, Button)
    clickedButton.Enabled = False

    For index As Integer = 0 To 4
        ' if the current letter in the word
        ' matches player 2's letter, replace the
        ' associated dash in the wordLabel with
        ' player 2's letter and then indicate
        ' that a replacement was made
        If word.Substring(index, 1) =
            clickedButton.Text Then
            wordLabel.Text =
                wordLabel.Text.Remove(index, 1)
            wordLabel.Text =
                wordLabel.Text.Insert(index,
                clickedButton.Text)
            dashReplaced = True

```

Figure 10-20 Code for the Guess the Word Game application *(continues)*

(continued)

```
101         End If
102       Next index
103       Call CheckStatus(dashReplaced)
104
105     End Sub
106
107     Private Sub gameExitMenuItem_Click(
        ByVal sender As Object, ByVal e As System.EventArgs
        ) Handles gameExitMenuItem.Click
108       Me.Close()
109
110     End Sub
111
112     Private Sub gameNewMenuItem_Click(
        ByVal sender As Object, ByVal e As System.EventArgs
        ) Handles gameNewMenuItem.Click
113       ' prepares the application for a new game
114
115       wordLabel.Text = String.Empty
116       incorrectLabel.Text = String.Empty
117       incorrect = 0
118
119       word = InputBox("Enter a 5-letter word:",
120                       "Player 1").ToUpper
121       ' validate the word
122       If word.Length <> 5 OrElse word Like "*[!A-Z]*" Then
123          MessageBox.Show("Please enter 5 letters only",
124                  "Guess the Word", MessageBoxButtons.OK,
125                  MessageBoxIcon.Information)
126       Else
127          wordLabel.Text = "-----"
128          Call EnableDisableButtons(True)
129
130       End If
131     End Sub
132 End Class
```

You also can write Line 122 as follows: `if word Like "[A-Z][A-Z][A-Z][A-Z][A-Z]" Then`. However, you then would need to swap the instructions in the true and false paths.

Figure 10-20 Code for the Guess the Word Game application

PROGRAMMING TUTORIAL 2

Creating the Bucky Burgers Application

In this tutorial, you code an application for the manager of the Bucky Burgers restaurant. The application's interface provides a text box for entering the names of employees who worked the previous day. Each name is added, using proper case, to a list box. Proper case means that the first and last names begin with an uppercase letter, while the remaining letters in the names are lowercase. The application allows the manager to print the interface. The application's TOE chart and MainForm are shown in Figures 10-21 and 10-22, respectively.

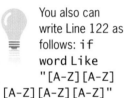

Task	Object	Event
Display the File menu	MenuStrip1	None
End the application	fileExitMenuItem	Click
Print the interface	PrintForm1, filePrintMenuItem	None Click
Get the employee's name Select the text box's existing text	nameTextBox	None Enter
Display the employee names (from addButton)	namesListBox	None
1. change the employee name to proper case 2. add the employee name to the namesListBox 3. send the focus to the nameTextBox 4. select the nameTextBox's existing text	addButton	Click

Figure 10-21 TOE chart for the Bucky Burgers application

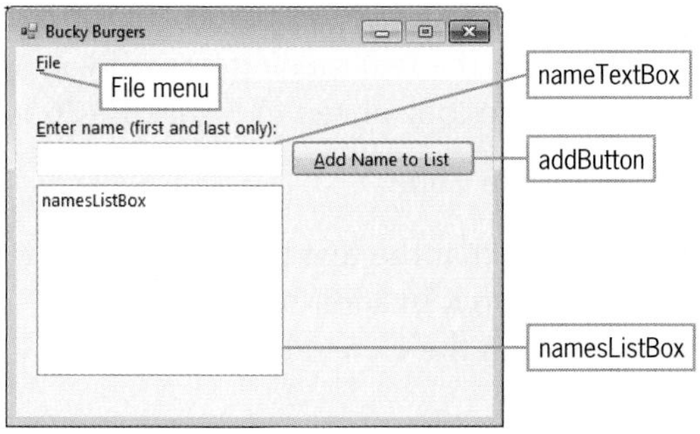

Figure 10-22 MainForm for the Bucky Burgers application

Completing the Interface

Included in the data files for this book is a partially completed Bucky Burgers application. Before you can code the application, you need to add the File menu to the form.

To add the File menu to the form:

1. Start Visual Studio or the Express Edition of Visual Basic. If necessary, open the Solution Explorer window.
2. Open the **Bucky Burgers Solution** (**Bucky Burgers Solution.sln**) file, which is contained in the VbReloaded2010\Chap10\Bucky Burgers Solution folder. Open the designer window (if necessary), and then auto-hide the Solution Explorer window.
3. Open the Toolbox window (if necessary), and then click **MenuStrip** in the Menus and Toolbars section. Drag a menu strip control to the form. When you release the mouse button, the MenuStrip1 control will appear in the component tray.
4. Auto-hide the Toolbox window and then display the Properties window (if necessary). Create the menu shown in Figure 10-23. Use the following names for the menu title and menu items: fileMenuTitle, filePrintMenuItem, and fileExitMenuItem.

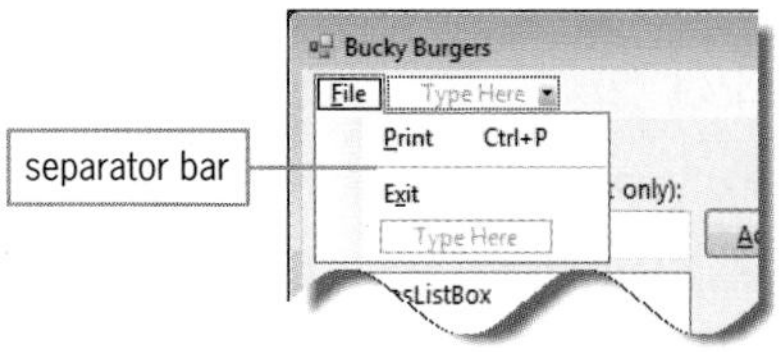

Figure 10-23 File menu

5. Save the solution and then start the application. Click **File** on the menu bar. The File menu opens and offers two options separated by a separator bar.
6. Click the **Close** button on the form's title bar.

Coding the Bucky Burgers Application

According to the application's TOE chart, four event procedures need to be coded: the Click event procedures for the two menu items, the text box's Enter event procedure, and the addButton's Click event procedure. You will begin by coding the Click event procedures for the two menu items. (If you need help while coding the application, you can look ahead to Figure 10-26.)

To code the two menu items and then test the code:

1. Open the Code Editor window. Notice that the text box's Enter event procedure has already been coded for you. In addition, the Option statements have already been entered in the General Declarations section.
2. In the comments that appear in the General Declarations section, replace <your name> and <current date> with your name and the current date.
3. Open the code template for the fileExitMenuItem's Click event procedure. Type **Me.Close()** and press **Enter**.
4. Open the code template for the filePrintMenuItem's Click event procedure. Type **' sends the printout to the Print preview window** and press **Enter** twice. Then enter the following statements:

   ```
   PrintForm1.PrintAction =
       Printing.PrintAction.PrintToPreview
   PrintForm1.Print()
   ```

5. Now you will test the code for both menu items. Save the solution and then start the application. Click **File** on the menu bar and then click **Print**. An image of the interface appears in the Print preview window. Close the Print preview window.
6. Click **File** on the menu bar and then click **Exit** to end the application.

Next, you will code the Add Name to List button's Click event procedure. The procedure's pseudocode is shown in Figure 10-24.

```
addButton Click event procedure
1. assign user input (full name), excluding any leading or trailing spaces, to a variable
2. if the variable is empty
           display the "Please enter a name" message in a message box
   else
           use the IndexOf method to search for the space in the full name; assign
           the space's index to the index variable

           if the full name contains a space
                     use the location of the space to separate the first and last
                     names; assign the first and last names to separate variables

                     change the first name to proper case
                     change the last name to proper case
                     concatenate the first name, a space, and the last name
           else
                     change the full name to proper case
           end if
           add the full name to the namesListBox
   end if
3. send the focus to the nameTextBox
4. select the nameTextBox's existing text
```

Figure 10-24 Pseudocode for the Add Name to List button's Click event procedure

To code the Add Name to List button's Click event procedure:

1. Open the code template for the addButton's Click event procedure. Type **' adds names in proper case to the list box** and then press **Enter** twice.
2. The procedure will use three String variables to store the full name, first name, and last name. Enter the appropriate Dim statements, using the names `fullName`, `firstName`, and `lastName`.
3. The pseudocode indicates that the procedure will search for a space in the full name. The procedure will use an Integer variable named `index` to store the index of the space. Type the appropriate Dim statement and then press **Enter** twice.
4. Step 1 in the pseudocode is to assign the user input, excluding any leading and trailing spaces, to a variable. Enter a statement that assigns the contents of the nameTextBox, excluding any leading and trailing spaces, to the `fullName` variable.
5. Step 2 in the pseudocode is a dual-alternative selection structure whose condition determines whether the `fullName` variable is empty. If it is empty, the selection structure's true path should display the "Please enter a name" message in a message box. Enter an appropriate If clause and MessageBox.Show method.
6. Type **Else** and press **Enter**. If the `fullName` variable is not empty, the selection structure's false path should use the IndexOf method to search for the space in the `fullName` variable. The space's index should be assigned to the `index` variable. Type **' locate the space** and press **Enter**. Then enter the appropriate assignment statement.

7. The next instruction in the false path is a nested dual-alternative selection structure. The nested structure's condition determines whether the IndexOf method located a space in the `fullName` variable. Type the following If clause and then press **Enter**:

   If index > −1 Then

8. If the `fullName` variable contains a space, the nested selection structure's true path should use the location of the space to separate the first and last names. Type **' separate first and last names** and press **Enter**. Now, enter a statement that uses the Substring method to assign the first name to the `firstName` variable. (Hint: The first name starts with index 0 in the `fullName` variable, and it contains the number of characters stored in the `index` variable.)

9. Next, enter a statement that uses the Substring method to assign the last name to the `lastName` variable. (Hint: The last name starts with the character immediately after the space in the `fullName` variable.)

10. The next two instructions in the nested selection structure's true path should change the first and last names to proper case, which means the first letter in each name should be uppercase and the remaining letters should be lowercase. Press **Enter**, and then type **' change first name to proper case** and press **Enter**. Then enter the appropriate code to change the first name to proper case. (Hint: You will need to use the Substring, ToUpper, and ToLower methods.)

11. Next, type **' change last name to proper case** and press **Enter**. Then enter the appropriate code to change the last name to proper case.

12. The last instruction in the nested selection structure's true path is to concatenate the first name, a space, and the last name. Enter a statement that performs the concatenation and assigns the result to the `fullName` variable.

13. It's possible that the user may enter only an employee's first or last name in the nameTextBox. In that case, the `fullName` variable will not contain a space. If that is the case, the nested selection structure's false path should simply change the full name to proper case. Type **Else** and press **Tab** twice. Type **' no space in name** and press **Enter**. Now, enter the code to change the contents of the `fullName` variable to proper case.

14. The last instruction in the outer selection structure's false path is to add the full name to the namesListBox. Insert a blank line between the two End If clauses. Type **' add full name to list box** and press **Enter**. Then enter the appropriate statement.

15. The last two instructions in the pseudocode are to send the focus to the nameTextBox and also select the text box's existing text. Insert a blank line above the End Sub clause and then enter the appropriate statements.

16. Save the solution.

You have finished coding the application, so you can test it to verify that it is working correctly.

To test the Bucky Burgers application's code:

1. Start the application. Click the **Add Name to List** button. The "Please enter a name" message appears in a message box. Close the message box.
2. Type **jerry jones** in the text box and then press **Enter** to select the Add Name to List button, which is the form's default button. The name "Jerry Jones" appears in the list box.
3. Type **cher** in the text box and press **Enter**. The name "Cher" appears in the list box. See Figure 10-25.

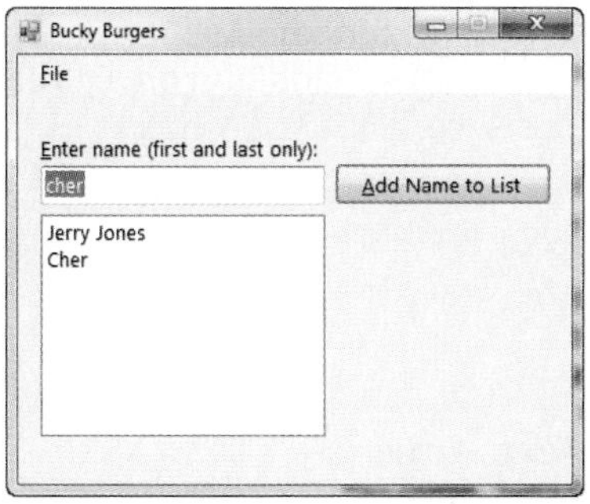

Figure 10-25 Sample run of the Bucky Burgers application

4. Click **File** on the menu bar and then click **Exit** to end the application. Close the Code Editor window, and then close the solution. Figure 10-26 shows the code for the Bucky Burgers application.

```
' Project name:          Bucky Burgers Project
' Project purpose:       Add names in proper case
'                        to a list box and print
'                        the interface
' Created/revised by:    <your name> on <current date>

Option Explicit On
Option Strict On
Option Infer Off

Public Class MainForm

  Private Sub nameTextBox_Enter(ByVal sender As Object,
  ByVal e As System.EventArgs) Handles nameTextBox.Enter
    ' select the existing text

    nameTextBox.SelectAll()
  End Sub

  Private Sub fileExitMenuItem_Click(
  ByVal sender As Object, ByVal e As System.EventArgs
  ) Handles fileExitMenuItem.Click
     Me.Close()

  End Sub

```

Figure 10-26 Code for the Bucky Burgers application *(continues)*

(continued)

```
   Private Sub filePrintMenuItem_Click(
   ByVal sender As Object, ByVal e As System.EventArgs
   ) Handles filePrintMenuItem.Click
      ' sends the printout to the Print preview window

      PrintForm1.PrintAction =
        Printing.PrintAction.PrintToPreview
      PrintForm1.Print()

   End Sub

   Private Sub addButton_Click(ByVal sender As Object,
   ByVal e As System.EventArgs) Handles addButton.Click
      ' adds names in proper case to the list box

      Dim fullName As String
      Dim firstName As String
      Dim lastName As String
      Dim index As Integer

      fullName = nameTextBox.Text.Trim
      If fullName = String.Empty Then
          MessageBox.Show("Please enter a name",
                          "Bucky Burgers",
                          MessageBoxButtons.OK,
                          MessageBoxIcon.Information)
      Else
          ' locate the space
          index = fullName.IndexOf(" ")
          If index > -1 Then
             ' separate first and last names
             firstName = fullName.Substring(0, index)
             lastName = fullName.Substring(index + 1)

             ' change first name to proper case
             firstName =
                firstName.Substring(0, 1).ToUpper &
                firstName.Substring(1).ToLower
             ' change last name to proper case
             lastName =
                lastName.Substring(0, 1).ToUpper &
                lastName.Substring(1).ToLower
             fullName = firstName & " " & lastName
          Else    ' no space in name
             fullName =
                fullName.Substring(0, 1).ToUpper &
                fullName.Substring(1).ToLower

          End If
          ' add full name to list box
          namesListBox.Items.Add(fullName)
      End If
      nameTextBox.Focus()
      nameTextBox.SelectAll()

   End Sub
 End Class
```

Figure 10-26 Code for the Bucky Burgers application

PROGRAMMING EXAMPLE

Yolanda Drapery Application

Create an interface that allows the user to display a report in a list box, but only if the user enters the appropriate password. The password must begin with a lowercase letter, followed by two digits, followed by either the uppercase letter E or the uppercase letter M, followed by the number 3, followed by a lowercase letter from a through d, followed by a digit. Examples of valid passwords include a34E3b9 and z61M3c2. Examples of invalid passwords include A34E3b9 and z61T3c4. The report should list the names of the Yolanda Drapery salespeople in the first column, and each salesperson's bonus amount in the second column. Use the following names for the solution, project, and form file: Yolanda Drapery Solution, Yolanda Drapery Project, and Main Form.vb. Save the application in the VbReloaded2010\Chap10 folder. See Figures 10-27 through 10-31.

Task	Object	Event
1. Declare and initialize a class-level String array named salespeople; the array should have 5 elements 2. Declare and initialize a class-level Integer array named bonus; the array should have 5 elements	MainForm	Declarations section
End the application	exitButton	Click
1. Get the password from the user 2. Determine whether the password is valid 3. If the password is valid, display the report in the reportListBox; otherwise, display the "Invalid password" message in a message box	reportButton	Click
Display the report (from reportButton)	reportListBox	None

Figure 10-27 TOE chart for the Yolanda Drapery application

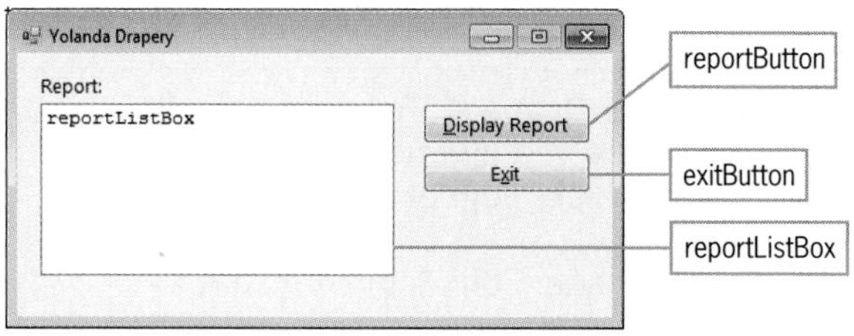

Figure 10-28 MainForm in the Yolanda Drapery application

Object	Property	Setting
MainForm	Font	Segoe UI, 10 point
	MaximizeBox	False
	StartPosition	CenterScreen
	Text	Yolanda Drapery
reportButton	TabIndex	0
exitButton	TabIndex	1
Label1	TabIndex	2
	Text	Report:
reportListBox	Font	Courier New, 10 point
	SelectionMode	None
	TabIndex	3
	TabStop	False

Figure 10-29 Objects, properties, and settings

<u>exitButton Click event procedure</u>
close the application

<u>reportButton Click event procedure</u>
1. declare a variable to store the password entered by the user
2. clear the reportListBox
3. get a password from the user
4. if the password is valid
        display the "Name" and "Bonus $" column headers
        repeat for each element in the salespeople and bonus arrays
                concatenate the current element in both arrays
                and then add the result to the reportListBox
        end repeat for
    else
        display the "Invalid password" message in a message box
    end if

Figure 10-30 Pseudocode

```
' Project name:          Yolanda Drapery Project
' Project purpose:       Displays a report, but only
'                        if the user enters a valid
'                        password
' Created/revised by:    <your name> on <current date>

Option Explicit On
Option Strict On
Option Infer Off

Public Class MainForm

```

Figure 10-31 Code *(continues)*

(continued)

```
   Private salespeople() As String = {"Janice Sterns",
                                      "Lois Kim",
                                      "Robert Pfeiffer",
                                      "Joseph Bonazo",
                                      "Chris Vane"}
   Private bonus() As Integer = {3456, 457, 560, 3000, 425}

   Private Sub exitButton_Click(ByVal sender As Object,
   ByVal e As System.EventArgs) Handles exitButton.Click
      Me.Close()
   End Sub

   Private Sub reportButton_Click(ByVal sender As Object,
   ByVal e As System.EventArgs) Handles reportButton.Click
      ' display either the name or the name and bonus

      Dim passWord As String

      ' clear list box
      reportListBox.Items.Clear()

      ' get password
      passWord = InputBox("Password:", "Password Entry")

      ' determine whether password is valid
      If passWord Like "[a-z]##[EM]3[a-d]#" Then
          Const NameHead As String = "Name"
          Const BonusHead As String = "Bonus $"
          Dim line As String

          ' display column headers
          reportListBox.Items.Add(NameHead.PadRight(20) &
                  BonusHead.PadLeft(8))
          ' display report
          For x As Integer = 0 To 4
              line = salespeople(x).PadRight(20) &
                  bonus(x).ToString("N0").PadLeft(8)
              reportListBox.Items.Add(line)
          Next x
      Else
          MessageBox.Show("Invalid password",
                          "Password Error",
                          MessageBoxButtons.OK,
                          MessageBoxIcon.Information)
      End If
   End Sub
End Class
```

Figure 10-31 Code

Summary

- You use a menu strip control to add one or more menus to a form.
- Each menu title and menu item should have an access key. Commonly used menu items should be assigned a shortcut key.
- Figure 10-32 contains a summary of the string manipulation techniques covered in the chapter.

Technique	Syntax	Purpose
Length property	*string*.**Length**	stores an integer that represents the number of characters contained in a string
Trim method	*string*.**Trim**	removes any spaces from both the beginning and end of a string
Remove method	*string*.**Remove(***startIndex*[**,** *numCharsToRemove*]**)**	removes characters from a string
Insert method	*string*.**Insert(***startIndex***,** *value***)**	inserts characters in a string
Contains method	*string*.**Contains(***subString***)**	determines whether a string contains a specific sequence of characters; returns a Boolean value
IndexOf method	*string*.**IndexOf(***subString*[**,** *startIndex*]**)**	determines whether a string contains a specific sequence of characters; returns either –1 or an integer that indicates the starting position of the characters in the string
Substring method	*string*.**Substring(***startIndex*[**,** *numCharsToAccess*]**)**	accesses one or more characters in a string
PadLeft method	*string*.**PadLeft(***totalChars*[**,** *padCharacter*]**)**	pads the beginning of a string with a character until the string has the specified number of characters; right-aligns the string
PadRight method	*string*.**PadRight(***totalChars*[**,** *padCharacter*]**)**	pads the end of a string with a character until the string has the specified number of characters; left-aligns the string
Like operator	*string* **Like** *pattern*	uses pattern-matching to compare strings

Figure 10-32 String manipulation techniques covered in the chapter

Key Terms

Contains method—determines whether a string contains a specific sequence of characters; returns a Boolean value

IndexOf method—determines whether a string contains a specific sequence of characters; returns either –1 if the string does not contain the sequence of characters or an integer that represents the starting position of the sequence of characters

Insert method—inserts characters anywhere in a string

Length property—stores an integer that represents the number of characters contained in a string

Like operator—uses pattern-matching characters to determine whether one string is equal to another string

Menu strip control—used to include one or more menus on a form

PadLeft method—right-aligns a string by inserting characters at the beginning of the string

PadRight method— left-aligns a string by inserting characters at the end of the string

Remove method—removes a specified number of characters located anywhere in a string

Shortcut keys—appear to the right of a menu item and allow the user to select the item without opening the menu

Substring method—used to access any number of characters contained in a string

Trim method—removes spaces from both the beginning and end of a string

Review Questions

1. The stateTextBox's Text property contains the letters M and I followed by two spaces. Which of the following assigns only the letters M and I to the Text property ?

    a. `state = state.Trim`

    b. `state = Trim(state)`

    c. `state = Trim(state, " ")`

    d. `state = Trim(2, 2)`

2. Which of the following assigns the first three characters in the `partNum` variable to the `code` variable?

    a. `code = partNum.Assign(0, 3)`

    b. `code = partNum.Sub(0, 3)`

    c. `code = partNum.Substring(0, 3)`

    d. `code = partNum.Assign(3, 1)`

3. Which of the following changes the contents of the `product` variable from "Bells" to "Bell"?

    a. `product = product.Remove(4, "s")`

    b. `product = product.Remove(4)`

    c. `product = product.Remove(5, "s")`

    d. `product = product.Remove("s")`

4. Which of the following changes the contents of the `zip` variable from "60121" to "60321"?

   a. `zip = zip.Remove(2, 1)`
      `zip = zip.Insert(2, "3")`

   b. `zip = zip.Insert(2, "3")`
      `zip = zip.Remove(3, 1)`

   c. `zip = zip.Remove(2, 1).Insert(2, "3")`

   d. all of the above

5. If the `msg` variable contains the string "Have a great day", what value will the `msg.IndexOf("day")` method return?

   a. −1

   b. True

   c. 13

   d. 14

6. Which of the following assigns the fifth character in the `word` variable to the `letter` variable?

   a. `letter = word.Substring(4, 1)`

   b. `letter = word.Substring(5, 1)`

   c. `letter = word.Substring(5)`

   d. none of the above

7. Which of the following expressions evaluates to True when the `partNum` variable contains the string "ABC73"?

   a. `partNum Like "[A-Z]99"`

   b. `partNum Like "[A-Z]##"`

   c. `partNum Like "[A-Z][A-Z][A-Z]##"`

   d. none of the above

8. If the `msg` variable contains the string "Today is Monday", which of the following returns the number 9?

   a. `msg.Substring(0, "M")`

   b. `msg.Contains("M")`

   c. `msg.IndexOf("M")`

   d. `msg.IndexOf(0, "M")`

9. Which of the following changes the contents of the `amount` variable from "76.89" to "76.89!!!!"?

   a. `amount = amount.PadRight(4, "!"c)`

   b. `amount = amount.PadRight(9, "!"c)`

c. `amount = amount.PadLeft(4, "!"c)`

d. none of the above

10. Which of the following determines whether the `userEntry` variable contains the dollar sign?

a. `userEntry.Contains("$")`

b. `userEntry.IndexOf("$")`

c. `userEntry.IndexOf("$", 0)`

d. all of the above

11. Which of the following allows you to access a menu item without opening the menu?

a. an access key

b. a menu key

c. shortcut keys

d. none of the above

12. Which of the following is false?

a. Menu titles should be one word only.

b. Each menu title should have a unique access key.

c. You should assign shortcut keys to commonly used menu titles.

d. Menu items should be entered using book title capitalization.

Exercises

Pencil and Paper

1. Write a statement that uses the Trim method to remove the leading and trailing spaces from the addressTextBox. INTRODUCTORY

2. Write a statement that uses the Insert method to change the contents of the `word` variable from "men" to "women". INTRODUCTORY

3. The `productId` variable contains the string "ABCD34G". Write a statement that assigns the string "CD34" from the `productId` variable to the `code` variable. INTRODUCTORY

4. Write a statement that assigns the number of characters in the `msg` variable to the sizeLabel control. INTRODUCTORY

5. Write a statement that uses the Insert method to change the contents of the `word` variable from "mend" to "amend". INTRODUCTORY

INTRODUCTORY ▶ 6. Write a statement that uses the PadLeft method to change the contents of the `pay` variable from "235.67" to "****235.67".

INTRODUCTORY ▶ 7. Write the code that uses the Remove method to change the contents of the `amount` variable from "3,123,560" to "3123560".

INTRODUCTORY ▶ 8. Write a statement that determines whether the `address` variable contains the street name "Maple Street" (entered in uppercase, lowercase, or a combination of uppercase and lowercase). Use the Contains method and assign the method's return value to a Boolean variable named `isContained`.

INTRODUCTORY ▶ 9. Write a statement that determines whether the `address` variable contains the street name "Elm Street" (entered in uppercase, lowercase, or a combination of uppercase and lowercase). Use the IndexOf method and assign the method's return value to an Integer variable named `indexNum`.

INTERMEDIATE ▶ 10. Write the code to change the contents of the `pet` variable from "dog" to "frog".

INTERMEDIATE ▶ 11. Write the code to change the contents of the `word` variable from "mouse" to "mouth".

INTERMEDIATE ▶ 12. Write the code to change the contents of the `amount` variable from "3123560" to "$3,123,560".

INTERMEDIATE ▶ 13. Write an If clause that determines whether the state name stored in the `state` variable is one of the following (entered using any case): New York, New Jersey, or New Mexico. Use the Like operator.

INTERMEDIATE ▶ 14. Write a Do clause that processes the loop body when the `userEntry` variable begins with the two letters J and E (entered using any case) followed by one character. Use the Like operator.

INTERMEDIATE ▶ 15. Write an If clause that determines whether the string stored in the `lastName` variable is either Smith or Smyth (entered using any case). Use the Like operator.

ADVANCED ▶ 16. Write the code to determine the number of lowercase letters stored in the `msg` variable. Assign the result to an Integer variable named `lowercaseLetters`.

ADVANCED ▶ 17. Write an If clause that determines whether the last character in the rateTextBox's Text property is a percent sign (%).

ADVANCED ▶ 18. Write the code to determine the number of commas in the salesTextBox's Text property. Assign the result to an Integer variable named `numCommas`.

Computer

19. If necessary, complete the Guess the Word Game application from this chapter's Programming Tutorial 1, and then close the solution. Use Windows to make a copy of the Guess the Word Solution folder. Rename the folder Guess the Word Solution-Modified. Open the Guess the Word Solution (Guess the Word Solution.sln) file contained in the VbReloaded2010\Chap10\Guess the Word Solution-Modified folder. Modify the application to allow player 1 to enter a word that contains any number of characters. Save the solution, and then start and test the application. Close the solution.

MODIFY THIS

20. If necessary, complete the Guess the Word Game application from this chapter's Programming Tutorial 1, and then close the solution. Use Windows to make a copy of the Guess the Word Solution folder. Rename the folder Guess the Word Solution-Like. Open the Guess the Word Solution (Guess the Word Solution.sln) file contained in the VbReloaded2010\Chap10\Guess the Word Solution-Like folder. Replace the Contains method in the CheckStatus procedure with the Like operator. Save the solution, and then start and test the application. Close the solution.

MODIFY THIS

21. If necessary, complete the Bucky Burgers application from this chapter's Programming Tutorial 2, and then close the solution. Use Windows to make a copy of the Bucky Burgers Solution folder. Rename the folder Bucky Burgers Solution-Modified. Open the Bucky Burgers Solution (Bucky Burgers Solution.sln) file contained in the VbReloaded2010\Chap10\Bucky Burgers Solution-Modified folder. The modified application will allow the user to enter the employee's first, middle, and last names. Remove the "(first and last only)" text from the Label1 control's Text property. Modify the code to display the names using proper case. Save the solution, and then start and test the application. Close the solution.

MODIFY THIS

22. Open the Item Prices Solution (Item Prices Solution.sln) file contained in the VbReloaded2010\Chap10\Item Prices Solution folder. Modify the form's Load event procedure so that it right-aligns the prices listed in the rightComboBox. Save the solution and then start the application. Close the solution.

INTRODUCTORY

23. Open the Zip Solution (Zip Solution.sln) file contained in the VbReloaded2010\Chap10\Zip Solution folder. The Display Shipping Charge button's Click event procedure should display the appropriate shipping charge based on the ZIP code entered by the user. To be valid, the ZIP code must contain exactly five digits, and the first three digits must be either "605" or "606". All ZIP codes beginning with "605" have a $25 shipping charge. All ZIP codes beginning with "606" have a $30 shipping charge. All other ZIP codes are invalid and the procedure should display an appropriate message. Code the procedure. Save the solution and then start the application. Test the application using the following ZIP codes: 60677, 60511, 60344, and 7130. Close the solution.

INTRODUCTORY

INTRODUCTORY

24. Open the Bonus Solution (Bonus Solution.sln) file contained in the VbReloaded2010\Chap10\Bonus Solution folder. Add a File menu to the form. The File menu should contain an Exit menu item that ends the application. Enter the appropriate code in the menu item's Click event procedure. Save the solution, and then start and test the application. Close the solution.

INTRODUCTORY

25. Open the Commission Solution (Commission Solution.sln) file contained in the VbReloaded2010\Chap10\Commission Solution folder. Add a File menu and a Calculate menu to the form. Include an Exit menu item on the File menu. Include two menu items on the Calculate menu: 2% Commission and 5% Commission. Assign shortcut keys to the items on the Calculate menu. When the user clicks the Exit menu item, the application should end. When the user clicks the 2% menu item, the application should calculate and display a 2% commission on the sales entered by the user. When the user clicks the 5% menu item, the application should calculate and display a 5% commission on the sales entered by the user. Code the appropriate procedures. Save the solution, and then start and test the application. Close the solution.

INTERMEDIATE

26. Open the Color Solution (Color Solution.sln) file contained in the VbReloaded2010\Chap10\Color Solution folder. The Display Color button's Click event procedure should display the color of the item whose item number is entered by the user. All item numbers contain exactly five characters. All items are available in four colors: blue, green, red, and purple. The third character in the item number indicates the item's color: b or B is Blue, g or G is green, r or R is Red, and p or P is purple. If the item number does not contain exactly five characters, or if the third character is not one of the valid characters, the procedure should change the colorLabel to white and display "Invalid item number" in the colorLabel. However, if the item number contains exactly five characters and the third character is valid, the procedure should change the colorLabel's background to the appropriate color and also remove any message from the colorLabel. Code the procedure. Save the solution and then start the application. Test the application using the following item numbers: 12x, 12b45, 99G44, abr55, 78p99, and 23abc. Close the solution.

INTERMEDIATE

27. Open the Reverse Name Solution (Reverse Name Solution.sln) file contained in the VbReloaded2010\Chap10\Reverse Name Solution folder. The interface provides a text box for entering a person's first name followed by a space and the person's last name. Code the Reverse Name button's Click event procedure to display the name as follows: the last name followed by a comma, a space, and the first name. Save the solution, and then start and test the application. Close the solution.

ADVANCED

28. Open the Phone Solution (Phone Solution.sln) file contained in the VbReloaded2010\Chap10\Phone Solution folder. The interface provides a text box for entering a phone number. Code the Display button's Click event procedure to display the phone number, excluding any hyphens, spaces, and parentheses, in the phoneLabel. Save the solution and then start the application. Test the application using the following phone numbers: (555) 111-1111, 555-5555, and 123-456-1111. Close the solution.

29. Open the Search Name Solution (Search Name Solution.sln) file contained in the VbReloaded2010\Chap10\Search Name Solution folder. The interface provides text boxes for entering a name (first name followed by a space and the last name) and the search text. If the last name (entered in any case) begins with the search text (entered in any case), the Display Message button's Click event procedure should display the message "The last name begins with" followed by a space and the search text. If the characters in the last name come before the search text, display the message "The last name comes before" followed by a space and the search text. Finally, if the characters in the last name come after the search text, display the message "The last name comes after" followed by a space and the search text. Code the procedure. Save the solution and then start the application. To test the application, enter Helga Swanson as the name and then use the following strings for the search text: g, ab, he, s, SY, sw, swan, and wan. Close the solution.

ADVANCED

30. Open the Sales Tax Solution (Sales Tax Solution.sln) file contained in the VbReloaded2010\Chap10\Sales Tax Solution folder. The interface provides text boxes for entering a sales amount and a tax rate. The Calculate button's Click event procedure should remove any dollar signs, spaces, and commas from the sales amount. It also should verify that the tax rate begins with a period. Code the procedure. Save the solution and then start and test the application. Close the solution.

ADVANCED

31. Open the Sales Bonus Solution (Sales Bonus Solution.sln) file contained in the VbReloaded2010\Chap10\Sales Bonus Solution folder. The interface provides a text box for entering a sales amount. The text box's KeyPress event procedure allows the text box to accept only numbers, the period, and the Backspace key. The Calculate button's Click event procedure should verify that the sales amount contains either no periods or one period. If the sales amount contains more than one period, the procedure should display an appropriate message; otherwise, it should display a 10% bonus. Code the procedure. Save the solution and then start and test the application. Close the solution.

ADVANCED

32. Open the Delivery Solution (Delivery Solution.sln) file contained in the VbReloaded2010\Chap10\Delivery Solution folder. The interface provides a text box for entering a product ID, which should consist of two numbers followed by either one or two letters. The letter(s) represent the delivery method, as follows: SM represents Standard Mail, PM represents Priority Mail, FS represents FedEx Standard, FO represents FedEx Overnight, and U represents UPS. Code the Select Delivery button's Click event procedure so that it selects the appropriate delivery method in the list box; use the Like operator. Display an appropriate message when the product ID does not contain two numbers followed by one or two letters, or when the letter(s) do not represent a valid delivery method. Save the solution and then start the application. Test the application using the following product IDs: 73pm, 34fs, 12u, 78h, 9FO, and 34sm. Close the solution.

ADVANCED

33. Research Visual Basic's Trim, TrimStart, and TrimEnd methods, and then open the Trim Methods Solution (Trim Methods Solution.sln)

DISCOVERY

file contained in the VbReloaded2010\Chap10\Trim Methods Solution folder. Code the Trim, TrimStart, and TrimEnd buttons' Click event procedures. Save the solution, and then start and test the application. Close the solution.

DISCOVERY

34. Research Visual Basic's Replace method, and then open the Replace Method Solution (Replace Method Solution.sln) file contained in the VbReloaded2010\Chap10\Replace Method Solution folder. Code the Replace button's Click event procedure. Save the solution, and then start and test the application. Close the solution.

DISCOVERY

35. Research Visual Basic's StartsWith and EndsWith methods, and then open the StartsWith EndsWith Solution (StartsWith EndsWith Solution.sln) file contained in the VbReloaded2010\Chap10\StartsWith EndsWith Solution folder. Code the StartsWith and EndsWith buttons' Click event procedures. Save the solution, and then start and test the application. Close the solution.

SWAT THE BUGS

36. Open the Debug Solution (Debug Solution.sln) file contained in the VbReloaded2010\Chap10\Debug Solution folder. Open the Code Editor window and review the existing code. Start and then test the application. Locate and then correct any errors. When the application is working correctly, close the solution.

Case Projects

Vita Credit

Each credit card number issued by Vita Credit contains five digits. The last digit is determined by multiplying the second and fourth digits by two and then adding the products to the first and third digits. The last digit in the sum is then appended to the first four digits in the credit card number, as illustrated in Figure 10-33. Create an application that allows the credit manager to enter four digits. The application should calculate the fifth digit and then display the credit card number. Use the following names for the solution, project, and form file: Vita Solution, Vita Project, and Main Form.vb. Save the application in the VbReloaded2010\Chap10 folder. You can create either your own interface or the one shown in Figure 10-34.

Fifth Digit Algorithm

First four digits in credit card number:	1		3		5		7		
Step 1: Multiply the second and fourth digits by 2:			*2				*2		
Result ⟶	1		6		5		14		
Step 2: Add the numbers together:	1	+	6	+	5	+	14	=	26
Step 3: Take the last digit in the sum and append it to the first four digits, resulting in the final credit card number:									13576

Figure 10-33 Illustration of determining the fifth digit

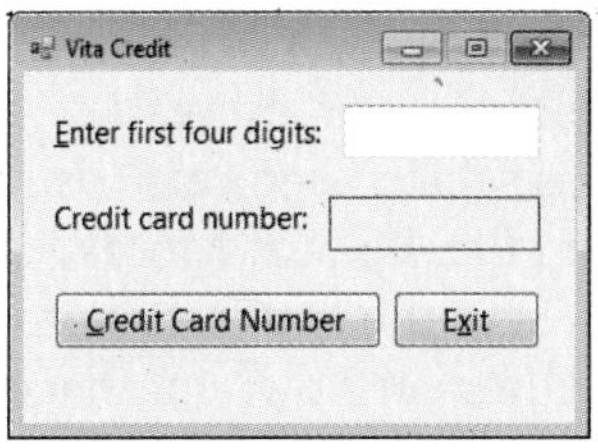

Figure 10-34 Sample interface for the Vita Credit application

Holterback Finance

Create an application that allows the user to enter a password. The password should contain from five to seven characters. The application should create and display a new password using the rules specified in Figure 10-35. Use the following names for the solution, project, and form file: Holterback Solution, Holterback Project, and Main Form.vb. Save the application in the VbReloaded2010\Chap10 folder. You can create either your own interface or the one shown in Figure 10-36.

1. Replace all of the vowels (A, E, I, O, or U) in the original password with a number, as follows:
   - Replace the first vowel with the number 1.
   - Replace the second vowel with the number 2.
   - Replace all other vowels with the number 9.
2. Replace all of the numbers in the original password with the letter Z.
3. Reverse all of the characters in the original password.

Figure 10-35 Rules for creating a new password

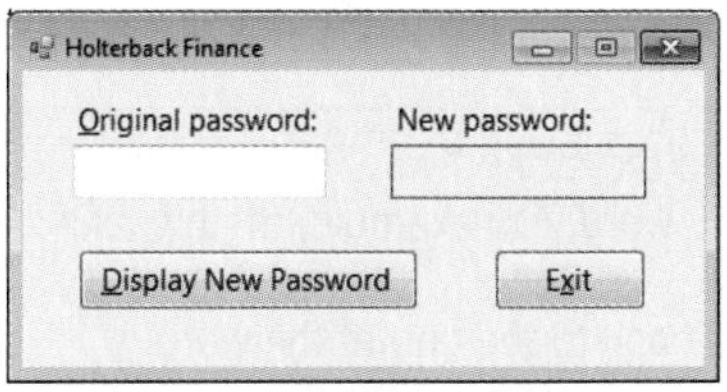

Figure 10-36 Sample interface for the Holterback Finance application

BobCat Motors

Each salesperson at BobCat Motors is assigned an ID number that consists of four characters. The first character is either the letter F or the letter P. The letter F indicates that the salesperson is a full-time employee, whereas the letter P indicates that he or she is a part-time employee. The middle two characters are the salesperson's initials, and the last character is either a 1 or a 2. A 1 indicates that the salesperson sells new cars, and a 2 indicates that the salesperson sells used cars. Create an application that allows the sales manager to enter a salesperson's ID and the number of cars the salesperson sold during the month. The application should allow the sales manager to enter this information for as many salespeople as needed. The application should calculate and display the total number of cars sold by each of the following four categories of employees: full-time employees, part-time employees, employees selling new cars, and employees selling used cars. Use the following names for the solution, project, and form file: BobCat Motors Solution, BobCat Motors Project, and Main Form.vb. Save the application in the VbReloaded2010\Chap10 folder. You can create either your own interface or the one shown in Figure 10-37.

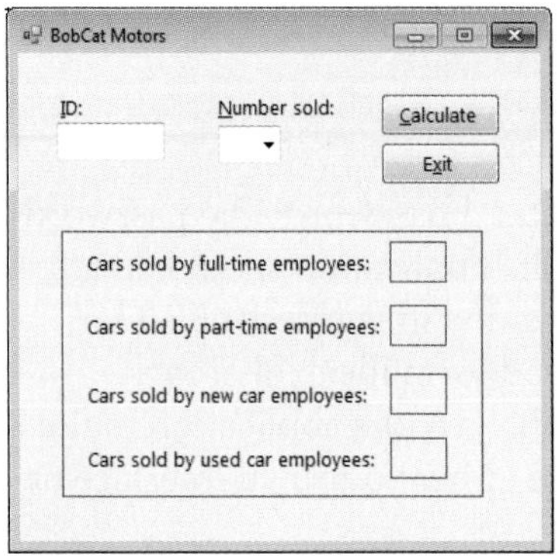

Figure 10-37 Sample interface for the BobCat Motors application

Pig Latin

Create an application that allows the user to enter a word. The application should display the word in pig latin form. The rules for converting a word into pig latin form are shown in Figure 10-38. Use the following names for the solution, project, and form file: Pig Latin Solution, Pig Latin Project, and Main Form.vb. Save the application in the VbReloaded2010\Chap10 folder.

1. If the word begins with a vowel (A, E, I, O, or U), add the string "-way" (a dash followed by the letters w, a, and y) to the end of the word. For example, the pig latin form of the word "ant" is "ant-way".
2. If the word does not begin with a vowel, first add a dash to the end of the word. Then continue moving the first character in the word to the end of the word until the first character is the letter A, E, I, O, U, or Y. Then add the string "ay" to the end of the word. For example, the pig latin form of the word "Chair" is "air-Chay".
3. If the word does not contain the letter A, E, I, O, U, or Y, then add the string "-way" to the end of the word. For example, the pig latin form of "56" is "56-way".

Figure 10-38 Rules for converting a word into pig latin

CHAPTER 11

Structures and Sequential Files

After studying Chapter 11, you should be able to:

- Create a structure
- Declare and use a structure variable
- Pass a structure variable to a procedure
- Create an array of structure variables
- Write data to a sequential access file
- Close a sequential access file
- Read data from a sequential access file
- Use the Exists and Peek methods
- Align columns of information
- Code the FormClosing event procedure
- Write and read records
- Use the Split function

Structures

Most programmers use the Class statement (rather than the Structure statement) to create data types that contain procedures. You will learn about the Class statement in Chapter 12.

You also can include an array in a structure. This topic is explored in Computer Exercises 31 and 32 at the end of the chapter.

The data types used in previous chapters, such as the Integer and Double data types, are built into the Visual Basic language. You also can create your own data types in Visual Basic using the **Structure statement**. Data types created by the Structure statement are referred to as **user-defined data types** or **structures**. Figure 11-1 shows the statement's syntax. Between the Structure and End Structure clauses, you define the members included in the structure. The members can be variables, constants, or procedures. However, in most cases, the members will be variables; such variables are referred to as **member variables**. Each member variable's definition contains the keyword `Public` followed by the variable's name, which typically is entered using Pascal case. Following the structure's name is the keyword `As` and the variable's *dataType*. The dataType identifies the type of data the member variable will store and can be any of the standard data types available in Visual Basic; it also can be another structure (user-defined data type). The Employee structure shown in the example in Figure 11-1 contains four member variables: three String variables and one Double variable. In most applications, you enter the Structure statement in the form's Declarations section, which begins with the Public Class clause and ends with the End Class clause.

HOW TO Define a Structure

Syntax

Structure *structureName*
    Public *memberVariableName1* **As** *dataType*
    [**Public** *memberVariableNameN* **As** *dataType*]
End Structure

Example

```
Structure Employee
      Public id As String
      Public firstName As String
      Public lastName As String
      Public pay As Double
End Structure
```

Figure 11-1 How to define a structure

The Structure statement allows the programmer to group related items into one unit: a structure. However, keep in mind that the Structure statement merely defines the structure members; it does not reserve any memory locations inside the computer. You reserve memory locations by declaring a structure variable.

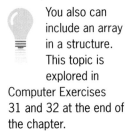

Declaring a Structure Variable

After entering the Structure statement in the Code Editor window, you then can use the structure to declare a variable. Variables declared using a structure are often referred to as **structure variables**. The syntax for creating a structure variable is shown in Figure 11-2. The figure also includes examples of declaring structure variables using the Employee structure from Figure 11-1.

HOW TO Declare a Structure Variable

Syntax
{**Dim** | **Private**} *structureVariableName* **As** *structureName*

Example 1
```
Dim hourly As Employee
```
declares a procedure-level Employee structure variable named `hourly`

Example 2
```
Private salaried As Employee
```
declares a class-level Employee structure variable named `salaried`

Figure 11-2 How to declare a structure variable

Similar to the way the `Dim age As Integer` instruction declares an Integer variable named `age`, the `Dim hourly As Employee` instruction in Example 1 declares an Employee variable named `hourly`. However, unlike the `age` variable, the `hourly` variable contains four member variables. In code, you refer to the entire structure variable by its name—in this case, `hourly`. You refer to a member variable by preceding its name with the name of the structure variable in which it is defined. You use the dot member access operator (a period) to separate the structure variable's name from the member variable's name. For instance, to refer to the member variables within the `hourly` structure variable, you use `hourly.id`, `hourly.firstName`, `hourly.lastName`, and `hourly.pay`. The `Private salaried As Employee` instruction in Example 2 in Figure 11-2 declares a class-level Employee variable named `salaried`. The names of the member variables within the `salaried` variable are `salaried.id`, `salaried.firstName`, `salaried.lastName`, and `salaried.pay`.

The dot member access operator indicates that `id`, `firstName`, `lastName`, and `pay` are members of the `hourly` and `salaried` variables.

The member variables in a structure variable can be used just like any other variables. You can assign values to them, use them in calculations, display their contents, and so on. Figure 11-3 shows various ways of using the member variables created by the statements shown in Figure 11-2.

HOW TO Use a Member Variable

Example 1
`hourly.lastName = "Kent"`
assigns the string "Kent" to the `hourly.lastName` member variable

Example 2
`hourly.pay *= 1.05`
multiplies the contents of the `hourly.pay` member variable by 1.05 and then assigns the result to the member variable; you also can write the statement as `hourly.pay = hourly.pay * 1.05`

Example 3
`salaryLabel.Text = salaried.pay.ToString("C2")`
formats the value contained in the `salaried.pay` member variable and then displays the result in the salaryLabel

Figure 11-3 How to use a member variable

Programmers use structure variables when they need to pass a group of related items to a procedure for further processing, because it's easier to pass one structure variable rather than many individual variables. Programmers also use structure variables to store related items in an array, even when the members have different data types. In the next two sections, you will learn how to pass a structure variable to a procedure and also store a structure variable in an array.

Passing a Structure Variable to a Procedure

The sales manager at Willow Pools wants an application that determines the amount of water required to fill a rectangular pool. To perform this task, the application will need to calculate the volume of the pool. You calculate the volume by first multiplying the pool's length by its width and then multiplying the result by the pool's depth. Assuming the length, width, and depth are measured in feet, this gives you the volume in cubic feet. To determine the number of gallons of water, you multiply the number of cubic feet by 7.48, because there are 7.48 gallons in one cubic foot. Figure 11-4 shows a sample run of the Willow Pools application, and Figure 11-5 shows one way of coding the application without using a structure. Notice that the calcButton's Click event procedure calls the GetGallons function, passing it three variables *by value*. The GetGallons function uses the values to calculate the number of gallons required to fill the pool. The function returns the number of gallons as a Double number to the calcButton's Click event procedure, which assigns the value to the `gallons` variable.

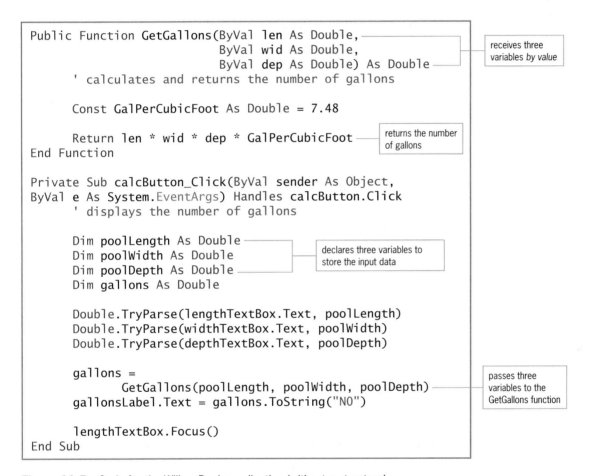

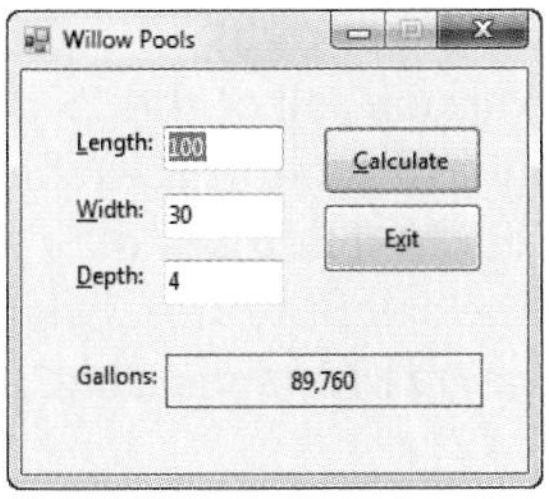

Figure 11-4 Sample run of the Willow Pools application

```
Public Function GetGallons(ByVal len As Double,
                           ByVal wid As Double,
                           ByVal dep As Double) As Double
      ' calculates and returns the number of gallons

      Const GalPerCubicFoot As Double = 7.48

      Return len * wid * dep * GalPerCubicFoot
End Function

Private Sub calcButton_Click(ByVal sender As Object,
ByVal e As System.EventArgs) Handles calcButton.Click
      ' displays the number of gallons

      Dim poolLength As Double
      Dim poolWidth As Double
      Dim poolDepth As Double
      Dim gallons As Double

      Double.TryParse(lengthTextBox.Text, poolLength)
      Double.TryParse(widthTextBox.Text, poolWidth)
      Double.TryParse(depthTextBox.Text, poolDepth)

      gallons =
             GetGallons(poolLength, poolWidth, poolDepth)
      gallonsLabel.Text = gallons.ToString("N0")

      lengthTextBox.Focus()
End Sub
```

receives three variables *by value*

returns the number of gallons

declares three variables to store the input data

passes three variables to the GetGallons function

Figure 11-5 Code for the Willow Pools application (without a structure)

Figure 11-6 shows a more convenient way of writing the code for the Willow Pools application. In this version of the code, a structure named Dimensions is used to group together the input items: length, width, and depth. It's logical to group the three items because they are related; each represents one of the three dimensions of a rectangular pool. The Structure statement that defines the Dimensions structure is entered in the MainForm's Declarations section. The Dimensions structure contains three member variables named `length`, `width`, and `depth`. The first Dim statement in the calcButton's Click event procedure uses the Dimensions structure to declare a structure variable named `poolSize`. The `gallons = GetGallons(poolSize)` statement

If you want to experiment with the code shown in Figure 11-5, open the solution contained in the Try It 1! folder.

in the procedure calls the GetGallons function, passing it the `poolSize` structure variable *by value*. When you pass a structure variable, all of the member variables are automatically passed. The GetGallons function uses the values stored in the member variables to calculate the required number of gallons of water, which it returns as a Double number. The calcButton's Click event procedure assigns the function's return value to the `gallons` variable.

entered in the MainForm's Declarations section

receives a structure variable *by value*

declares a structure variable to store the input data

passes the structure variable to the GetGallons function

```
Structure Dimensions
        Public length As Double
        Public width As Double
        Public depth As Double
End Structure

Public Function GetGallons(ByVal pool As Dimensions) As Double
        ' calculates and returns the number of gallons

        Const GalPerCubicFoot As Double = 7.48

        Return pool.length * pool.width *
            pool.depth * GalPerCubicFoot
End Function

Private Sub calcButton_Click(ByVal sender As Object,
ByVal e As System.EventArgs) Handles calcButton.Click
      ' displays the number of gallons

      Dim poolSize As Dimensions
      Dim gallons As Double

      Double.TryParse(lengthTextBox.Text, poolSize.length)
      Double.TryParse(widthTextBox.Text, poolSize.width)
      Double.TryParse(depthTextBox.Text, poolSize.depth)

      gallons = GetGallons(poolSize)
      gallonsLabel.Text = gallons.ToString("N0")

      lengthTextBox.Focus()
End Sub
```

Figure 11-6 Code for the Willow Pools application (with a structure)

If you want to experiment with the code shown in Figure 11-6, open the solution contained in the Try It 2! folder.

Compare the calcButton's Click event procedure in Figure 11-6 with the same procedure shown earlier in Figure 11-5. Notice that the procedure in Figure 11-5 uses three scalar variables to store the input data, while the procedure in Figure 11-6 uses only one structure variable for this purpose. The procedure in Figure 11-5 also passes three scalar variables (rather than one structure variable) to the GetGallons function, which uses three scalar variables (rather than one structure variable) to accept the data. Imagine if the input data consisted of 20 items rather than just three items! Passing a structure variable would be much easier than passing 20 individual scalar variables.

Creating an Array of Structure Variables

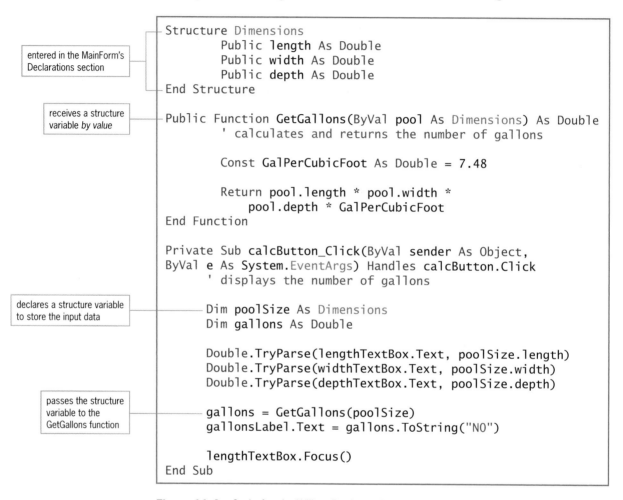

As mentioned earlier, another advantage of using a structure is that a structure variable can be stored in an array, even when its members have different data types. Figure 11-7 shows a sample run of the Treasures Gift Shop application, and Figure 11-8 shows most of the application's code. Notice that the MainForm's Declarations section defines a structure named Item and then uses the structure to declare a five-element one-dimensional array named `gifts`. Each element in the `gifts` array is a structure variable that contains two member variables: a String variable named `id` and an Integer variable named `price`. After the array is declared, the MainForm's Load event procedure populates the array by assigning the appropriate IDs and prices to it. The procedure also adds each product ID stored in the array to the idListBox. You refer to a member variable in an array element using the syntax *arrayName*(*subscript*)**.***memberVariableName*. For example, `gifts(0).price` refers to the `price` member contained in the first element in the `gifts` array. Likewise, `gifts(4).id` refers to the `id` member contained in the last element in the `gifts` array. The Treasures Gift Shop application displays the price associated with the product ID selected in the list box.

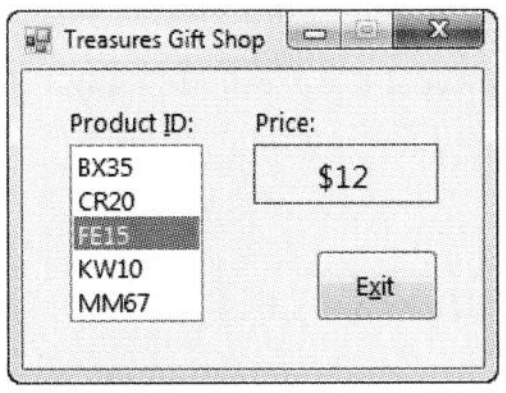

Figure 11-7 Sample run of the Treasures Gift Shop application

```
Structure Item
     Public id As String
     Public price As Integer
End Structure

' declare an array of structure variables
Private gifts(4) As Item

Private Sub MainForm_Load(ByVal sender As Object,
ByVal e As System.EventArgs) Handles Me.Load

     ' assign IDs and prices to the array
     gifts(0).id = "BX35"
     gifts(0).price = 13
     gifts(1).id = "CR20"
     gifts(1).price = 10
     gifts(2).id = "FE15"
     gifts(2).price = 12
     gifts(3).id = "KW10"
     gifts(3).price = 24
     gifts(4).id = "MM67"
     gifts(4).price = 4

     ' assign IDs to the list box
     For index As Integer = 0 To 4
          idListBox.Items.Add(gifts(index).id)
     Next index
     idListBox.SelectedIndex = 0
End Sub
```

entered in the MainForm's Declarations section

fills the member variables in the array

accesses the `id` member in the current array element

Figure 11-8 Partial code for the Treasures Gift Shop application *(continues)*

(continued)

```
Private Sub idListBox_SelectedIndexChanged(
ByVal sender As Object, ByVal e As System.EventArgs
) Handles idListBox.SelectedIndexChanged
     ' displays the price associated with the
     ' ID selected by the user

     Dim index As Integer

     index = idListBox.SelectedIndex
     priceLabel.Text =
          gifts(index).price.ToString("C0")
End Sub
```

accesses the price member in the array element

Figure 11-8 Partial code for the Treasures Gift Shop application

If you want to experiment with the Treasures Gift Shop application, open the solution contained in the Try It 3! folder.

The answers to Mini-Quiz questions are located in Appendix A.

Mini-Quiz 11-1

1. In most applications, the code to define a user-defined data type is entered in the form's ______________.
   a. Declarations section
   b. Definition section
   c. Load event procedure
   d. User-defined section
2. Which of the following assigns the string "Maple" to the `street` member variable within a structure variable named `address`?
   a. `address&street = "Maple"`
   b. `address.street = "Maple"`
   c. `street.address = "Maple"`
   d. none of the above
3. An array is declared using the statement `Dim inventory(4) As Product`. Which of the following assigns the number 100 to the `quantity` member variable contained in the last array element?
   a. `inventory.quantity(4) = 100`
   b. `inventory(4).Product.quantity = 100`
   c. `inventory(3).quantity = 100`
   d. `inventory(4).quantity = 100`

As mentioned in Chapter 9, the values stored in an array usually come from a file on the computer's disk and are assigned to the array after it is declared. In most cases, the file is a sequential access file. You will learn about sequential access files in the next several sections.

Sequential Access Files

In addition to getting data from the keyboard and sending data to the computer screen, an application also can get data from and send data to a file on a disk. Getting data from a file is referred to as "reading the file," and sending data to a file is referred to as "writing to the file." Files to which data is written are called **output files**, because the files store the output produced by an application. Files that are read by the computer are called **input files**, because an application uses the data in these files as input. Most input and output files are composed of lines of text that are both read and written sequentially. In other words, they are read and written in consecutive order, one line at a time, beginning with the first line in the file and ending with the last line in the file. Such files are referred to as **sequential access files**, because of the manner in which the lines of text are accessed. They also are called **text files**, because they are composed of lines of text. Examples of text stored in sequential access files include an employee list, a memo, or a sales report.

Writing Data to a Sequential Access File

An item of data—such as the string "Jacob"—is viewed differently by a human being and a computer. To a human being, the string represents a person's name; to a computer, it is merely a sequence of characters. Programmers refer to a sequence of characters as a **stream of characters**. In Visual Basic, you use a **StreamWriter object** to write a stream of characters to a sequential access file. Before you create the StreamWriter object, you first declare a variable to store the object in the computer's internal memory. Figure 11-9 shows the syntax and an example of declaring a StreamWriter variable. The IO in the syntax stands for Input/Output.

HOW TO Declare a StreamWriter Variable

<u>Syntax</u>
{**Dim** | **Private**} *streamWriterVariableName* **As IO.StreamWriter**

<u>Example</u>
`Dim outFile As IO.StreamWriter`
declares a StreamWriter variable named `outFile`

Figure 11-9 How to declare a StreamWriter variable

After declaring a StreamWriter variable, you can use the syntax shown in Figure 11-10 to create a StreamWriter object. As the figure indicates, creating a StreamWriter object involves opening a sequential access file using one of two methods: CreateText or AppendText. You use the **CreateText method** to open a sequential access file for output. When you open a file for output, the computer creates a new, empty file to which data can be written. If the file already exists, the computer erases the contents of the file before writing any data to it. You use the **AppendText method** to open a sequential access file for append. When a file is opened for append, new data is written after any existing data in the file. If the file does not exist, the computer creates the file for you. In addition to opening the file, both methods automatically create a StreamWriter object to represent the file in the application. You assign the StreamWriter object to a StreamWriter variable, which you use to refer to the file in code.

Also included in Figure 11-10 are examples of using the CreateText and AppendText methods. When processing the statement in Example 1, the computer searches for the employee.txt file in the Chap11 folder on the F drive. If the file exists, its contents are erased and the file is opened for output; otherwise, a new, empty file is created and opened for output. The statement creates a StreamWriter object and assigns it to the `outFile` variable. Unlike the *fileName* argument in Example 1, the *fileName* argument in Example 2 does not contain a folder path. Therefore, the computer will search for the file in the default folder, which is the current project's bin\Debug folder. In this case, if the computer locates the report.txt file in the default folder, it opens the file for append. If it does not find the file, it creates a new, empty file and then opens the file for append. Like the statement in Example 1, the statement in Example 2 creates a StreamWriter object and assigns it to the `outFile` variable.

Although it is not a requirement, the "txt" (short for "text") filename extension typically is used when naming sequential access files. This is because sequential access files contain text.

HOW TO Create a StreamWriter Object

Syntax
IO.File.*method***(***fileName***)**

method	Description
CreateText	opens a sequential access file for output
AppendText	opens a sequential access file for append

Example 1
`outFile = IO.File.CreateText("F:\Chap11\employee.txt")`
opens the employee.txt file for output; creates a StreamWriter object and assigns it to the `outFile` variable

Example 2
`outFile = IO.File.AppendText("report.txt")`
opens the report.txt file for append; creates a StreamWriter object and assigns it to the `outFile` variable

Figure 11-10 How to create a StreamWriter object

Only specify the folder path in the fileName argument when you are sure that the folder path will not change. Keep in mind that a USB drive may have a different letter designation on your computer.

After opening a file for either output or append, you can begin writing data to it. You can write data to a sequential access file using either the **Write method** or the **WriteLine method**; however, in most cases you will use the WriteLine method. The difference between both methods is that the WriteLine method writes a newline character after the data. Figure 11-11 shows the syntax and an example of both methods. As the figure indicates, when using the Write method, the next character written to the file will appear immediately after the letter o in the string "Hello". When using the WriteLine method, however, the next character written to the file will appear on the line immediately below the string. You do not need to include the file's name in either method's syntax, because the data will be written to the file associated with the StreamWriter variable.

HOW TO Write Data to a Sequential Access File

Syntax
streamWriterVariableName.**Write(***data***)**
streamWriterVariableName.**WriteLine(***data***)**

Example 1
```
outFile.Write("Hello")
```

Result
Hello| — the next character will appear immediately after the letter o

Example 2
```
outFile.WriteLine("Hello")
```

Result
Hello
| — the next character will appear on the next line

Figure 11-11 How to write data to a sequential access file

Closing an Output Sequential Access File

You should use the **Close method** to close an output sequential access file as soon as you are finished using it. This ensures that the data is saved and it makes the file available for use elsewhere in the application. The syntax to close an output sequential access file is shown in Figure 11-12 along with an example of using the method. Here again, notice that you use the StreamWriter variable to refer to the file in code.

HOW TO Close an Output Sequential Access File

Syntax
streamWriterVariableName.**Close()**

Example
```
outFile.Close()
```
closes the file associated with the `outFile` variable

Figure 11-12 How to close an output sequential access file

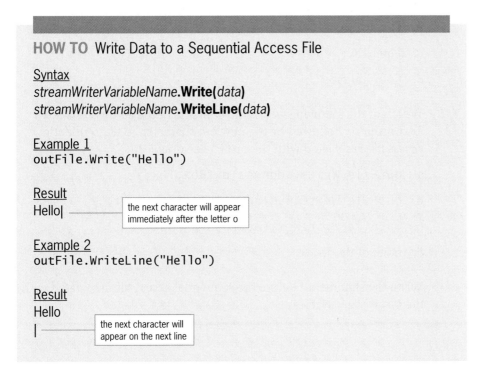

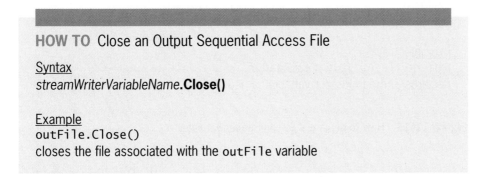

The answers to Mini-Quiz questions are located in Appendix A.

Mini-Quiz 11-2

1. A procedure needs to write information to a sequential access file. Which of the following methods can be used to open the file?
   a. AppendText
   b. CreateText
   c. OpenText
   d. both a and b
2. Which of the following writes the contents of the addressTextBox's Text property, followed by the newline character, to the sequential access file associated with the `outFile` variable?
   a. `outFile.Write(addressTextBox.Text)`
   b. `outFile.WriteLine(addressTextBox.Text)`
   c. `outFile.WriteNext(addressTextBox.Text)`
   d. none of the above
3. Write the statement to close the sequential access file associated with the `outFile` variable.

Reading Data from a Sequential Access File

In Visual Basic, you use a **StreamReader object** to read data from a sequential access file. Before creating the StreamReader object, you first declare a variable to store the object in the computer's internal memory. Figure 11-13 shows the syntax and an example of declaring a StreamReader variable. As mentioned earlier, the IO in the syntax stands for Input/Output.

HOW TO Declare a StreamReader Variable

Syntax
{**Dim** | **Private**} *streamReaderVariableName* **As IO.StreamReader**

Example
`Dim inFile As IO.StreamReader`
declares a StreamReader variable named `inFile`

Figure 11-13 How to declare a StreamReader variable

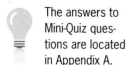

After declaring a StreamReader variable, you can use the **OpenText method** to open a sequential access file for input; doing this automatically creates a StreamReader object. When a file is opened for input, the computer can read the lines of text stored in the file. Figure 11-14 shows the OpenText method's syntax along with an example of using the method. The *fileName* argument in the example does not include a folder path, so the computer will search for the report.txt file in the current project's bin\Debug folder. If the computer finds the file, it opens the file for input; otherwise, a runtime error occurs, causing the application to end abruptly. You assign the StreamReader object created by the OpenText method to a StreamReader variable, which you use to refer to the file in code.

HOW TO Create a StreamReader Object

Syntax
IO.File.OpenText(*fileName***)**

Example
```
inFile = IO.File.OpenText("report.txt")
```
opens the report.txt file for input; creates a StreamReader object and assigns it to the `inFile` variable

Figure 11-14 How to create a StreamReader object

You can use the Exists method to avoid the runtime error that occurs when the computer cannot locate an input file. Figure 11-15 shows the method's syntax and includes an example of using the method. If the *fileName* argument does not include a folder path, the computer searches for the file in the current project's bin\Debug folder. The **Exists method** returns the Boolean value True if the file exists; otherwise, it returns the Boolean value False.

HOW TO Determine Whether a Sequential Access File Exists

Syntax
IO.File.Exists(*fileName***)**

Example
```
If IO.File.Exists("report.txt") Then
```
determines whether the report.txt file exists in the current project's bin\Debug folder; you also can write the If clause as
```
If IO.File.Exists("report.txt") = True Then
```

Figure 11-15 How to determine whether a sequential access file exists

After opening a file for input, you can use the **ReadLine method** to read the file's contents, one line at a time. A **line** is defined as a sequence (stream) of characters followed by the newline character. The ReadLine method returns a string that contains only the sequence of characters in the current line; the string does not include the newline character at the end of the line. In most cases, you assign the string returned by the ReadLine method to a String variable. Figure 11-16 shows the ReadLine method's syntax and includes an example of using the method. The ReadLine method does not require you to provide the file's name, because it uses the file associated with the StreamReader variable.

HOW TO Read Data from a Sequential Access File

Syntax
streamReaderVariableName.**ReadLine**

Example
```
Dim message As String
message = inFile.ReadLine
```
reads a line of text from the sequential access file associated with the `inFile` variable and assigns the line, excluding the newline character, to the `message` variable

Figure 11-16 How to read data from a sequential access file

In most cases, an application will need to read each line of text contained in a sequential access file, one line at a time. You can do this using a loop along with the Peek method. The **Peek method** "peeks" into the file to determine whether the file contains another character to read. If the file contains another character, the Peek method returns the character; otherwise, it returns the number −1 (a negative 1). The Peek method's syntax is shown in Figure 11-17 along with an example of using the method. The Do clause in the example tells the computer to process the loop instructions until the Peek method returns the number −1, which indicates that there are no more characters to read. In other words, the Do clause tells the computer to process the loop instructions until it reaches the end of the file.

HOW TO Use the Peek Method

Syntax
streamReaderVariableName.**Peek**

Example
```
Dim lineOfText As String
Do Until inFile.Peek = -1
     lineOfText = inFile.ReadLine
     MessageBox.Show(lineOfText)
Loop
```
reads each line of text from the sequential access file associated with the `inFile` variable, line by line; each line (excluding the newline character) is assigned to the `lineOfText` variable and is then displayed in a message box

Figure 11-17 How to use the Peek method

Closing an Input Sequential Access File

Just as you do with an output sequential access file, you should use the Close method to close an input sequential access file as soon as you are finished using it. Doing this makes the file available for use elsewhere in the application. The syntax to close an input sequential access file is shown in Figure 11-18 along with an example of using the method. Notice that you use the StreamReader variable to refer to the file in code.

HOW TO Close an Input Sequential Access File

Syntax
streamReaderVariableName.**Close()**

Example
`inFile.Close()`
closes the file associated with the `inFile` variable

Figure 11-18 How to close an input sequential access file

The answers to Mini-Quiz questions are located in Appendix A.

Mini-Quiz 11-3

1. A procedure needs to read information from a sequential access file. Which of the following methods can be used to open the file?
   a. AppendText
   b. CreateText
   c. OpenText
   d. both b and c
2. Which of the following reads a line of text from the sequential access file associated with the `inFile` variable and assigns the line of text (excluding the newline character) to the `msg` variable?
   a. `msg = inFile.Read`
   b. `msg = inFile.ReadLine`
   c. `inFile.ReadLine(msg)`
   d. none of the above
3. Write the statement to close the sequential access file associated with the `inFile` variable.
4. If a sequential access file contains another character to read, what does the Peek method return?

The Game Show Contestants Application

The Game Show Contestants application uses what you have learned so far about sequential access files. The application writes the names of contestants to a sequential access file. It also reads the names and displays them in a list box. Figure 11-19 shows a sample run of the application, and Figure 11-20 shows most of the application's code. The lines of code pertaining to sequential access files are shaded in Figure 11-20.

If you want to experiment with the Game Show Contestants application, open the solution contained in the Try It 4! folder.

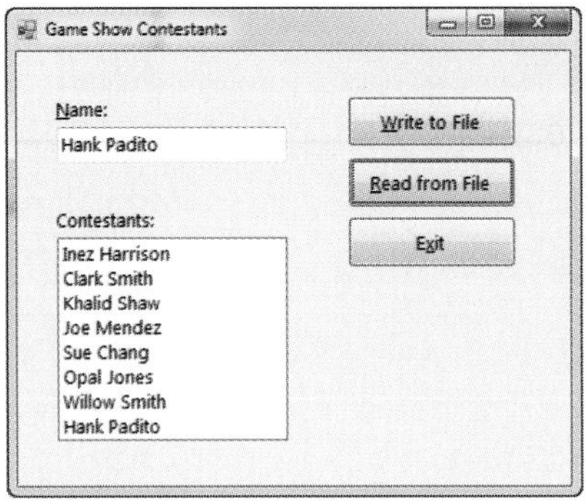

Figure 11-19 Sample run of the Game Show Contestants application

```
Private Sub writeButton_Click(ByVal sender As Object,
ByVal e As System.EventArgs) Handles writeButton.Click
     ' writes a name to a sequential access file

     ' declare a StreamWriter variable
     Dim outFile As IO.StreamWriter

     ' open the file for append
     outFile = IO.File.AppendText("contestants.txt")
     ' write the name on a separate line in the file
     outFile.WriteLine(nameTextBox.Text)
     ' close the file
     outFile.Close()

     ' clear the list box, then set the focus
     contestantsListBox.Items.Clear()
     nameTextBox.Focus()
End Sub

Private Sub readButton_Click(ByVal sender As Object,
ByVal e As System.EventArgs) Handles readButton.Click
     ' reads names from a sequential access file
     ' and displays them in the interface

     Dim inFile As IO.StreamReader
     Dim name As String

     ' clear previous names from the list box
     contestantsListBox.Items.Clear()

     ' determine whether the file exists
     If IO.File.Exists("contestants.txt") Then
          ' open the file for input
          inFile = IO.File.OpenText("contestants.txt")
```

Figure 11-20 Partial code for the Game Show Contestants application *(continues)*

(continued)

```
            ' process loop instructions until end of file
            Do Until inFile.Peek = -1
                ' read a name
                name = inFile.ReadLine
                ' add name to list box
                contestantsListBox.Items.Add(name)
            Loop
            ' close the file
            inFile.Close()
        Else
            MessageBox.Show(
                "Can't find the contestants.txt file",
                "Game Show Contestants",
                MessageBoxButtons.OK,
                MessageBoxIcon.Information)
        End If
    End Sub
```

Figure 11-20 Partial code for the Game Show Contestants application

Figure 11-21 shows the contestants.txt file opened in the IDE. To open a sequential access file in the IDE, you click File on the menu bar and then click Open File. When the Open File dialog box opens, you click the name of the file you want to open and then click the Open button. (Recall that unless you specify otherwise, the sequential access file is saved in the project's bin\Debug folder.)

Figure 11-21 The contestants.txt file opened in the IDE

Aligning Columns of Information

In Chapter 10, you learned how to use the PadLeft and PadRight methods to pad a string with a character until the string is a specified length. Recall that the syntax of the PadLeft method is *string*.**PadLeft(***totalChars*[**,** *padCharacter*]**)**, and the syntax of the PadRight method is *string*.**PadRight(***totalChars*[**,** *padCharacter*]**)**. When processing the PadLeft and PadRight methods, the computer first makes a temporary copy of the *string* in memory; it then pads the copy only. The *totalChars* argument in each syntax is an integer that represents the total number of characters you want the string's copy to contain. The optional *padCharacter* argument is the character that each method uses to pad the string until it reaches the desired number of characters. If the padCharacter argument is omitted, the default padding character is the space character.

In Example 1, you also need to set the priceListBox's Font property to a fixed-space font, such as Courier New. A fixed-space font uses the same amount of space to display each character.

Figure 11-22 shows examples of using the PadLeft and PadRight methods to align columns of information. Example 1 aligns a column of numbers by the decimal point. Notice that you first format each number in the column to ensure that each has the same number of digits to the right of the decimal point. You then use the PadLeft method to insert spaces at the beginning of the number (if necessary); this right-aligns the number within the column. Because each number has the same number of digits to the right of the decimal point, aligning each number on the right will align each by its decimal point.

Example 2 in Figure 11-22 shows how you can align the second column of information when the first column contains strings with varying lengths. First, you use either the PadRight or PadLeft method to ensure that each string in the first column contains the same number of characters. You then concatenate the padded string to the information in the second column. The code in Example 2, for instance, uses the PadRight method to ensure that each name in the first column contains exactly 15 characters. It then concatenates the 15 characters with the string stored in the `city` variable, and then writes the concatenated string to the file. Because each name has 15 characters, each city entry will automatically appear beginning in character position 16 in the file. Example 2 also shows how you can use the **Strings.Space method** to include a specific number of space characters in a string. The method's syntax is **Strings.Space(***number***)**, in which *number* is an integer that represents the number of spaces to include.

HOW TO Align Columns of Information

Example 1

```
Dim formatPrice As String
For price As Decimal = 9D To 11D Step 0.5D
    formatPrice = price.ToString("N2").PadLeft(8)
    priceListBox.Items.Add(formatPrice)
Next price
```

Result

```
 9.00
 9.50
10.00
10.50
11.00
```

Example 2

```
Dim outFile As IO.StreamWriter
Dim heading As String =
    "Name" & Strings.Space(11) & "City"

Dim name As String
Dim city As String

outFile = IO.File.CreateText("example2.txt")
outFile.WriteLine(heading)
```

Strings.Space method

If you want to experiment with the code shown in Figure 11-22, open the solution contained in the Try It 5! folder.

Figure 11-22 How to align columns of information *(continues)*

(continued)

```
name = InputBox("Enter name:", "Name")
Do While name <> String.Empty
    city = InputBox("Enter city:", "City")
    outFile.WriteLine(name.PadRight(15) & city)
    name = InputBox("Enter name:", "Name")
Loop
outFile.Close()
```

Result (when the user enters the following names and cities: Janice, Paris, Sue, Rome)

```
Name          City
Janice        Paris
Sue           Rome
```

Figure 11-22 How to align columns of information

The FormClosing Event

You often will enter code related to files in a form's FormClosing event procedure. The **FormClosing event** occurs when a form is about to be closed. In most cases, this happens when the computer processes the `Me.Close()` statement in the form's code. However, it also occurs when the user clicks the Close button on the form's title bar. Figure 11-23 shows examples of code you might enter in the FormClosing event procedure. Example 1 writes the contents of the namesListBox to the example1.txt file. Example 2 displays the "Do you want to exit?" message in a message box, along with Yes and No buttons. If the user clicks the No button in the message box, it indicates that he or she does not want to exit the application. In that case, the FormClosing event procedure stops the computer from closing the MainForm. You prevent the computer from closing a form by setting the **Cancel property** of the FormClosing procedure's **e** parameter to True.

HOW TO Use the FormClosing Event Procedure

Example 1—writes information to a sequential access file

```
Private Sub MainForm_FormClosing(
ByVal sender As Object,
ByVal e As System.Windows.Forms.FormClosingEventArgs
) Handles Me.FormClosing

    Dim outfile As IO.StreamWriter
    outfile = IO.File.CreateText("example1.txt")
    For Each name As String In namesListBox.Items
         outfile.WriteLine(name)
    Next name
    outfile.Close()
    MessageBox.Show("The names were written to the file.",
                    "FormClosing Examples",
                    MessageBoxButtons.OK,
                    MessageBoxIcon.Information)
End Sub
```

Figure 11-23 How to use the FormClosing event procedure *(continues)*

If you want to experiment with the code shown in Figure 11-23, open the solution contained in the Try It 6! folder.

(continued)

Example 2—verifies that the user wants to exit the application
```
Private Sub MainForm_FormClosing(
ByVal sender As Object,
ByVal e As System.Windows.Forms.FormClosingEventArgs
) Handles Me.FormClosing
    Dim button As DialogResult
    button = MessageBox.Show("Do you want to exit?",
                             "FormClosing Examples",
                             MessageBoxButtons.YesNo,
                             MessageBoxIcon.Exclamation,
                             MessageBoxDefaultButton.Button2)

    If button = DialogResult.No Then
        e.Cancel = True
    End If

End Sub
```


Figure 11-23 How to use the FormClosing event procedure

Writing and Reading Records

In some applications, a sequential access file is used to store fields and records. A **field** is a single item of information about a person, place, or thing. Examples of fields include a name, a salary, a Social Security number, and a price. A **record** is a group of related fields that contain all of the necessary data about a specific person, place, or thing. When writing records to a sequential access file, programmers typically write each record on a separate line in the file. If the records contain more than one field, programmers separate each field with a special character, called a **delimiter character**. The delimiter character allows the computer to distinguish one field from the next when reading the record. Commonly used delimiter characters include the comma and the number sign (#).

Figure 11-24 shows examples of writing records to a sequential access file. The WriteLine method in Example 1 writes a record that contains two fields separated by a comma. The comma separates the city field from the state field. The WriteLine method in Example 2 writes a record that contains three fields, with each field separated by a number sign.

HOW TO Write Records to a Sequential Access File

Example 1
```
Dim city As String = "Raleigh"
Dim state As String = "North Carolina"
outFile.WriteLine(city & "," & state)
```
writes the following record on a separate line in the file associated with the `outFile` variable: Raleigh,North Carolina

Example 2
```
Dim salesperson As String = "Jason Kricky"
Dim sales As Integer = 5000
Dim bonus As Integer = 250
```

Figure 11-24 How to write records to a sequential access file *(continues)*

(continued)

```
outSalesFile.WriteLine(salesperson & "#" &
     sales.ToString & "#" & bonus.ToString)
```
writes the following record on a separate line in the file associated with the `outSalesFile` variable: Jason Kricky#5000#250

Figure 11-24 How to write records to a sequential access file

You can use the **Split function** to read records from a sequential access file. The function's syntax is shown in Figure 11-25. In the syntax, *arrayName* is the name of a one-dimensional String array, and *streamReaderVariableName* is the name of the StreamReader variable associated with the sequential access file. The *delimiterChar* argument specifies the delimiter character that separates the fields in each record. Figure 11-25 also includes examples of using the Split function to read the records from Figure 11-24. In Example 1, the ReadLine method reads a line of text from the file associated with the `inFile` variable. Then, using the delimiter character as a guide, the Split function splits the line of text into two fields and assigns each field to an element in the `cityState` array. The city field (Raleigh) is assigned to the `cityState(0)` element, and the state field (North Carolina) is assigned to the `cityState(1)` element. In Example 2, the ReadLine method reads a line of text associated with the `inFile` variable. The Split function then uses the number sign as a guide when dividing the line of text. In this case, the Split function divides the line of text into three fields and assigns each field to an element in the `salesInfo` array. The salesperson field (Jason Kricky) is assigned to the `salesInfo(0)` element. The sales field (5000) is assigned to the `salesInfo(1)` element, and the bonus field (250) is assigned to the `salesInfo(2)` element. Notice the letter c that appears after the delimiterChar argument in each example. As you learned in Chapter 10, the letter c is one of the literal type characters in Visual Basic. Recall that a literal type character forces a literal constant to assume a data type other than the one its form indicates. In this case, the letter c forces the "," and "#" delimiter characters to assume the Char (character) data type.

HOW TO Read Records from a Sequential Access File

Syntax
arrayName = *streamReaderVariableName*.**ReadLine.Split(***delimiterChar***)**

Example 1
```
Dim cityState() As String
cityState = inFile.ReadLine.Split(","c)
```
reads a record from the file associated with the `inFile` variable and assigns each field to an element in the `cityState` array; using the record written in Example 1 in Figure 11-24, the Split function assigns Raleigh to the `cityState(0)` element and assigns North Carolina to the `cityState(1)` element

Figure 11-25 How to read records from a sequential access file *(continues)*

If you want to experiment with the code shown in Figures 11-24 and 11-25, open the solution contained in the Try It 7! folder.

(continued)

Example 2

```
Dim salesInfo() As String
salesInfo = inFile.ReadLine.Split("#"c)
```

reads a record from the file associated with the `inSalesFile` variable and assigns each field to an element in the `salesInfo` array; using the record written in Example 2 in Figure 11-24, the Split function assigns Jason Kricky to the `salesInfo(0)` element, 5000 to the `salesInfo(1)` element, and 250 to the `salesInfo(2)` element

Figure 11-25 How to read records from a sequential access file

The answers to Mini-Quiz questions are located in Appendix A.

Mini-Quiz 11-4

1. Which of the following concatenates the contents of the `city` variable, 10 spaces, and the contents of the `state` variable, and then assigns the result to the `address` variable?
   a. `address = city & Space(10) & state`
   b. `address = city & Spaces(10) & state`
   c. `address = city & Strings.Space(10) & state`
   d. `address = city & String.Space(10) & state`
2. When entered in the FormClosing event procedure, which of the following prevents the computer from closing the form?
   a. `e.Cancel = True`
   b. `e.Close = False`
   c. `e.Closing = False`
   d. `e.Open = True`
3. A sequential access file contains records whose fields are separated by a dollar sign. Which of the following reads a record from the file and assigns the fields to the `customer` array?
   a. `customer = inFile.ReadLine.Split($)`
   b. `customer = inFile.ReadLine.Split("$"c)`
   c. `customer = inFile.Split("$")`
   d. `customer = inFile.Split.ReadLine("$"c)`

You have completed the concepts section of Chapter 11. The Programming Tutorial section is next.

PROGRAMMING TUTORIAL 1

Modifying the Concentration Game Application

In this tutorial, you modify the Concentration Game application from Chapter 8's Programming Tutorial 2. The modified application will use the words contained in one of four different sequential access files, which will be chosen randomly when the application is started. Three of the files are contained in the Concentration Game project's bin\Debug folder. The three files are named words1.txt, words2.txt, and words3.txt. Figure 11-26 shows the contents of these files. You will create the fourth file, named words4.txt, in this tutorial.

Figure 11-26 Contents of three of the four sequential access files

Creating the words4.txt File

Included in the data files for this book is the Concentration Game application from Chapter 8's Programming Tutorial 2.

To open the Concentration Game application and then create the words4.txt file:

1. Start Visual Studio or the Express Edition of Visual Basic. If necessary, open the Solution Explorer window.
2. Open the **Concentration Game Solution** (**Concentration Game Solution.sln**) file, which is contained in the VbReloaded2010\Chap11\Concentration Game Solution folder. Open the designer window (if necessary), and then auto-hide the Solution Explorer window.
3. Rather than using a StreamWriter object and the WriteLine method to create the words4.txt file, you also can use the Add New Item option on the Project menu. Click **Project** on the menu bar, and then click **Add New Item** to open the Add New Item dialog box.

If necessary, click **Common Items** in the Installed Templates list and then click **Text File** in the middle column of the dialog box. Click the **Add** button. The TextFile1.txt window opens in the IDE.

4. Click **File** and then click **Save TextFile1.txt As** to open the Save File As dialog box. Open the Concentration Game project's bin\Debug folder. Change the name in the File name box to **words4** and then click the **Save** button.
5. Enter the following 16 words. Be sure to press Enter after typing each word.
Apple
Banana
Kiwi
Orange
Watermelon
Peach
Pear
Strawberry
Apple
Banana
Kiwi
Orange
Watermelon
Peach
Pear
Strawberry
6. Save the words4.txt file and then close the words4.txt window.

Modifying the Application's Code

Figure 11-27 shows the code entered in the MainForm's Load event procedure in Chapter 8. (The complete code is shown in Figure 8-45 in Chapter 8.) You will need to modify only the code entered in this procedure. First, you will modify the code so that it uses the words4.txt file to fill the list box with values.

```
Private Sub MainForm_Load(ByVal sender As Object,
ByVal e As System.EventArgs) Handles Me.Load
     ' fills the list box with 8 pairs of matching
     ' words, then calls a procedure to shuffle
     ' the words

     wordListBox.Items.Add("Refrigerator")
     wordListBox.Items.Add("Range")
     wordListBox.Items.Add("Television")
     wordListBox.Items.Add("Computer")
     wordListBox.Items.Add("Washer/Dryer")
     wordListBox.Items.Add("Dishwasher")
     wordListBox.Items.Add("Car")
     wordListBox.Items.Add("Trip")
     wordListBox.Items.Add("Refrigerator")
```

Figure 11-27 MainForm's Load event procedure from Chapter 8 *(continues)*

(continued)

```
        wordListBox.Items.Add("Range")
        wordListBox.Items.Add("Television")
        wordListBox.Items.Add("Computer")
        wordListBox.Items.Add("Washer/Dryer")
        wordListBox.Items.Add("Dishwasher")
        wordListBox.Items.Add("Car")
        wordListBox.Items.Add("Trip")

        Call ShuffleWords()
    End Sub
```

Figure 11-27 MainForm's Load event procedure from Chapter 8

To begin modifying the Load event procedure:

1. Open the Code Editor window. Replace <your name> and <current date> with your name and the current date. Locate the MainForm's Load event procedure. The procedure will use a String variable to store the name of one of the four sequential access files. For now, you will initialize the variable to "words4.txt". Click the **blank line above the first Add method** and then press **Enter** to insert another blank line. Enter the following Dim statement:

   Dim fileName As String = "words4.txt"

2. The procedure will need a StreamReader variable to read the contents of the words4.txt file, line by line. Enter the following Dim statement:

   Dim inFile As IO.StreamReader

3. While reading the words4.txt file, the procedure will store each line in a String variable named `word`. Type the following Dim statement and then press **Enter** twice:

   Dim word As String

4. Next, you will use the Exists method to determine whether the words4.txt file exists. Enter the following If clause. (The Code Editor will automatically enter the End If clause for you.)

   If IO.File.Exists(fileName) Then

5. If the file exists, the selection structure's true path should open the file for input. Enter the following statement:

   inFile = IO.File.OpenText(fileName)

6. Now, you will use a loop to read each line in the file and assign each line to the wordListBox. Enter the following lines of code, but don't press Enter after typing the last line. (The Code Editor will automatically enter the Loop clause for you.)

   Do Until inFile.Peek = –1
   word = inFile.ReadLine
   wordListBox.Items.Add(word)

7. Next, you will close the words4.txt file. Insert a blank line between the Loop and End If clauses, and then enter the following statement:

   inFile.Close()

8. If the words4.txt file does not exist, the selection structure's false path will display an appropriate message. Enter the following lines of code:

```
Else
    MessageBox.Show("Can't find " & fileName,
            "Missing File",
            MessageBoxButtons.OK,
            MessageBoxIcon.Information)
```

9. After displaying the message, the false path will use the 16 existing Add methods to fill the list box with words. Cut the End If clause from its current location and paste it in the blank line above the `Call ShuffleWords()` statement, and then press **Enter**.

10. Save the solution and then start the application. Play the game until all of the words appear on the game board, and then click the **Exit** button.

11. Now, you will test the application using a filename that does not exist. In the Load event procedure, change "words4.txt" in the first Dim statement to **"words5.txt"**.

12. Save the solution and then start the application. The "Can't find words5.txt" message appears in a message box. Close the message box. The Load event procedure uses the 16 Add methods to fill the list box with words. Play the game until all of the words appear on the game board, and then click the **Exit** button.

As mentioned earlier, the Concentration Game application will use the words contained in one of the four sequential access files, which will be chosen randomly when the application is started. The Load event procedure will accomplish this task by assigning the four filenames to an array. It then will use the random number generator to generate a random number from 0 through 3. The random number will be used to select one of the filenames.

To complete the modifications to the Load event procedure and then test the code:

1. Click the **blank line above the first Dim statement** in the Load event procedure and then press **Enter** to insert a new blank line. Enter the following Dim statements:

```
Dim fileList() As String = {"words1.txt",
                            "words2.txt",
                            "words3.txt",
                            "words4.txt"}
Dim randGen As New Random
```

2. Change the `Dim fileName As String = "words5.txt"` statement to the following:

```
Dim fileName As String =
    fileList(randGen.Next(0,4))
```

3. Save the solution and then start the application. Click **any two of the labels** on the game board and then click the **Exit** button.

4. Start the application again. Continue testing the application until each of the four files has been chosen. When you are finished testing the application, close the Code Editor window and then close the solution. Figure 11-28 shows the modified Load event procedure.


```
Private Sub MainForm_Load(ByVal sender As Object,
ByVal e As System.EventArgs) Handles Me.Load
     ' fills the list box with 8 pairs of matching
     ' words, then calls a procedure to shuffle
     ' the words

     Dim fileList() As String = {"words1.txt",
                                 "words2.txt",
                                 "words3.txt",
                                 "words4.txt"}
     Dim randGen As New Random

     Dim fileName As String =
          fileList(randGen.Next(0, 4))
     Dim inFile As IO.StreamReader
     Dim word As String

     If IO.File.Exists(fileName) Then
          inFile = IO.File.OpenText(fileName)
          Do Until inFile.Peek = -1
               word = inFile.ReadLine
               wordListBox.Items.Add(word)
          Loop
          inFile.Close()
     Else
          MessageBox.Show("Can't find " & fileName,
               "Missing File",
               MessageBoxButtons.OK,
               MessageBoxIcon.Information)


          wordListBox.Items.Add("Refrigerator")
          wordListBox.Items.Add("Range")
          wordListBox.Items.Add("Television")
          wordListBox.Items.Add("Computer")
          wordListBox.Items.Add("Washer/Dryer")
          wordListBox.Items.Add("Dishwasher")
          wordListBox.Items.Add("Car")
          wordListBox.Items.Add("Trip")
          wordListBox.Items.Add("Refrigerator")
          wordListBox.Items.Add("Range")
          wordListBox.Items.Add("Television")
          wordListBox.Items.Add("Computer")
          wordListBox.Items.Add("Washer/Dryer")
          wordListBox.Items.Add("Dishwasher")
          wordListBox.Items.Add("Car")
          wordListBox.Items.Add("Trip")
     End If

     Call ShuffleWords()

End Sub
```

Figure 11-28 MainForm's modified Load event procedure

PROGRAMMING TUTORIAL 2

Creating the CD Collection Application

In this tutorial, you code an application that keeps track of a person's CD collection. More specifically, the application saves each CD's name, as well as the artist's name and the CD price, in a sequential access file named cds.txt. The application allows the user to add information to the file and also remove information from the file. The application's TOE chart and MainForm are shown in Figures 11-29 and 11-30, respectively. Figure 11-31 shows the contents of the cds.txt file, which is contained in the CD Collection project's bin\debug folder.

Task	Object	Event
Read the cds.txt file and assign its contents to cdsListBox	MainForm	Load
Save the contents of the cdsListBox in the cds.txt file		FormClosing
End the application	exitButton	Click
1. Get CD name, artist name, and CD price 2. Add CD name, artist name, and CD price to cdsListBox	addButton	Click
Remove the selected CD from cdsListbox	removeButton	Click
Display the CD name, artist name, and CD price	cdsListBox	None

Figure 11-29 TOE chart for the CD Collection application

the list box's Sorted property is set to True, and its Font property is set to Courier New, 10pt

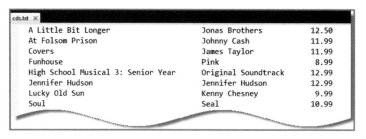

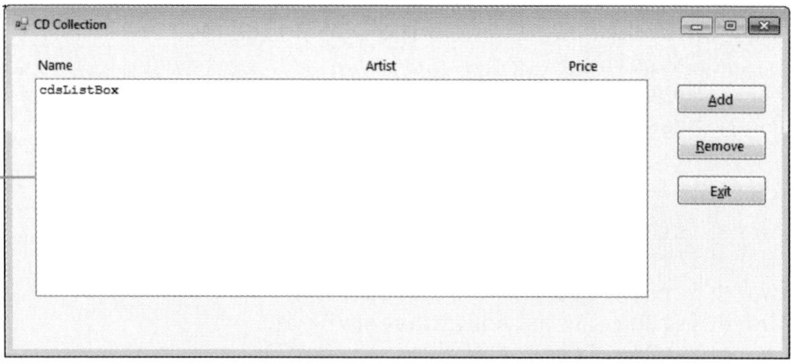

Figure 11-30 MainForm for the CD Collection application

```
cds.txt ×
A Little Bit Longer                  Jonas Brothers        12.50
At Folsom Prison                     Johnny Cash           11.99
Covers                               James Taylor          11.99
Funhouse                             Pink                   8.99
High School Musical 3: Senior Year   Original Soundtrack   12.99
Jennifer Hudson                      Jennifer Hudson       12.99
Lucky Old Sun                        Kenny Chesney          9.99
Soul                                 Seal                  10.99
```

Figure 11-31 Contents of the cds.txt file

Opening the Application

Included in the data files for this book is a partially completed CD Collection application. To complete the application, you just need to code it. According to the application's TOE chart, five event procedures need to be coded: the Click event procedures for the three buttons, the MainForm's Load event procedure, and the MainForm's FormClosing event procedure. (If you need help while coding the application, you can look ahead to Figure 11-38.)

To open the CD Collection application:

1. Start Visual Studio or the Express Edition of Visual Basic. If necessary, open the Solution Explorer window.
2. Open the **CD Collection Solution** (**CD Collection Solution.sln**) file, which is contained in the VbReloaded2010\Chap11\CD Collection Solution folder. Open the designer window (if necessary), and then auto-hide the Solution Explorer window.
3. Open the Code Editor window. Notice that the Exit button's Click event procedure has already been coded for you. In addition, the Option statements have already been entered in the General Declarations section.
4. In the comments that appear in the General Declarations section, replace <your name> and <current date> with your name and the current date.

Coding the MainForm's Load Event Procedure

The first procedure you will code is the MainForm's Load event procedure. The procedure's pseudocode is shown in Figure 11-32.

```
MainForm Load event procedure
if the cds.txt sequential access file exists
        open the file for input
        repeat until the end of the file
                read a line from the file
                add the line to the cdsListBox
        end repeat
        close the file
        select the first line in the cdsListBox
else
        display the "Can't find the cds.txt file" message in a message box
end if
```

Figure 11-32 Pseudocode for the MainForm's Load event procedure

To code the Load event procedure and then test the code:

1. Open the code template for the MainForm's Load event procedure. Enter the following comments. Press **Enter** twice after typing the second comment.

   ' fills the list box with data
   ' stored in a sequential access file

2. Type **' declare variables** and then press **Enter**. The procedure will use a StreamReader variable named `inFile`. Enter the appropriate Dim statement.

3. The procedure will store the cds.txt filename in a String variable named `fileName`. Enter the appropriate Dim statement. Initialize the `fileName` variable to "cds.txt".

4. While reading the cds.txt file, the procedure will use a String variable named `cdInfo` to store each line of text. Type the appropriate Dim statement and then press **Enter** twice.

5. According to its pseudocode, the procedure should verify that the cds.txt file exists. Type **' verify that the file exists** and then press **Enter**. Then enter the appropriate If clause, using the Exists method. (Recall that the filename is stored in the `fileName` variable.)

6. If the cds.txt file exists, the selection structure's true path should open the file for input. Type **' open the file for input** and then press **Enter**. Then enter the appropriate statement to open the file.

7. The next instruction in the pseudocode is a loop that repeats its instructions until the end of the file is reached. Type **' process loop body until end of file** and then press **Enter**. Then enter the appropriate Do clause, using the `Until` keyword and the Peek method.

8. The first instruction in the loop body reads a line from the file. Type **' read a line from the file** and then press **Enter**. Now, enter the appropriate assignment statement. Assign the line to the `cdInfo` variable.

9. The next instruction in the loop body adds the line to the cdsListBox. Type **' add the line to the list box** and then press **Enter**. Then enter the appropriate statement.

10. Next, the procedure needs to close the file. Insert a blank line between the Loop clause and the End If clause. Type **' close the file** and then press **Enter**. Now, enter the appropriate statement.

11. Next, type **' select the first item in the list box** and then press **Enter**, and then enter the appropriate statement.

12. If the cds.txt file does not exist, the selection structure's false path should display the "Can't find the cds.txt file" message in a message box. Type **Else** and then press **Enter**. Now, enter the appropriate MessageBox.Show method.

13. Save the solution and then start the application. The information contained in the cds.txt file appears in the cdsListBox, as shown in Figure 11-33. Click the **Exit** button to end the application.

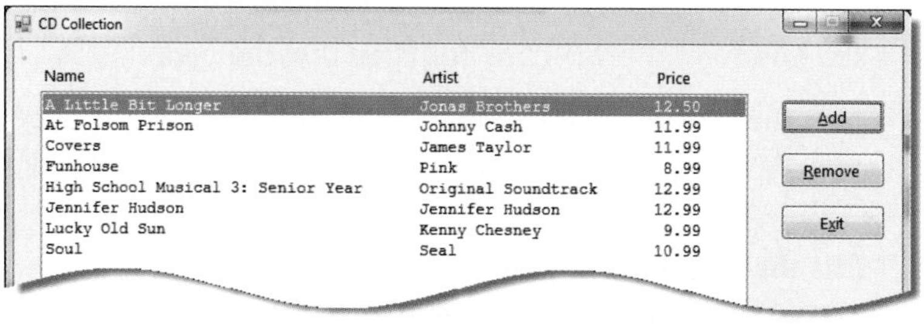

Figure 11-33 The contents of the cds.txt file added to the list box

Coding the Add Button's Click Event Procedure

Next, you will code the Add button's Click event procedure. The procedure's pseudocode is shown in Figure 11-34.

```
addButton Click event procedure
1. use the InputBox function to get the CD name, artist name, and CD price
2. concatenate the CD name, artist name, and CD price
3. add the concatenated string to the cdsListBox
```

Figure 11-34 Pseudocode for the Add button's Click event procedure

To code the Add button's Click event procedure and then test the code:

1. Open the code template for the addButton's Click event procedure. Type **' adds CD information to the list box** and then press **Enter** twice.
2. The procedure will use three String variables to store the CD name, artist name, and CD price. It also will use a String variable to store the concatenated string. Type **' declare variables** and then press **Enter**. Now, enter the appropriate Dim statements, using the names `inputName`, `inputArtist`, `inputPrice`, and `concatenatedInfo`.
3. The procedure will use a Double variable to store the CD price after it has been converted to Double. Type a Dim statement that declares a Double variable named `price` and then press **Enter** twice.
4. The first step in the procedure's pseudocode uses the InputBox function to get the CD name, artist name, and CD price. Type **' get the CD information** and then press **Enter**. Now, enter the appropriate InputBox functions. Assign the functions' return values to the `inputName`, `inputArtist`, and `inputPrice` variables. Press **Enter** twice after typing the last InputBox function.
5. Steps 2 and 3 in the pseudocode concatenate the CD name, artist name, and CD price and then add the concatenated string to the cdsListBox. Enter the following comments:

   ' format the price, then concatenate the
   ' input items, using 40 characters for the
   ' CD name, 25 characters for the artist name,
   ' and 5 characters for the price

6. Now, enter a statement that uses the TryParse method to convert the `inputPrice` variable's value to Double, storing the result in the `price` variable.
7. Next, enter an assignment statement that formats the `price` variable's value to "N2" and assigns the result to the `inputPrice` variable.
8. Enter an assignment statement that concatenates the contents of the following three variables: `inputName`, `inputArtist`, and `inputPrice`. Use the PadRight method to ensure that the CD name and artist name contain 40 and 25 characters, respectively. Use the PadLeft method to ensure that the CD price contains five characters. The statement should assign the concatenated string to the `concatenatedInfo` variable. Press **Enter** twice after typing the statement.

9. Type **' add the information to the list box** and press **Enter**. Finally, enter a statement that adds the contents of the `concatenatedInfo` variable to the cdsListBox.

10. Save the solution and then start the application.

11. Click the **Add** button. Type **Breakout** as the CD name and then press **Enter**. Type **Miley Cyrus** as the artist name and then press **Enter**. Type **8** as the price and then press **Enter**. The Add button's Click event procedure adds the CD information to the list box. The list box's Sorted property is set to True, so the information you entered appears in the third line of the list box, as shown in Figure 11-35. Click the **Exit** button to end the application.

the CD name you entered appears in alphabetical order

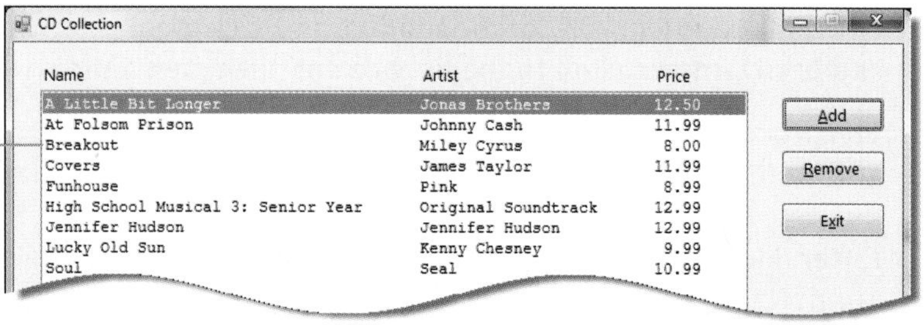

Figure 11-35 CD information added to the list box

Coding the Remove Button's Click Event Procedure

According to the application's TOE chart, the Remove button's Click event procedure should remove the selected CD from the cdsListBox. The procedure's pseudocode is shown in Figure 11-36.

```
removeButton Click event procedure
if a CD is selected in the cdsListBox
        remove the CD from the cdsListBox
end if
```

Figure 11-36 Pseudocode for the Remove button's Click event procedure

To code the Remove button's Click event procedure and then test the code:

1. Open the code template for the removeButton's Click event procedure. Type **' removes the selected CD from the list box** and then press **Enter** twice.

2. The procedure will use an Integer variable to store the index of the CD selected in the cdsListBox. Enter a Dim statement that declares an Integer variable named `index`. Initialize the variable using the list box's SelectedIndex property.

3. The only step in the procedure's pseudocode is a selection structure whose condition determines whether a CD is selected in the cdsListBox. Recall that when no item is selected in a list box, the list box's SelectedIndex property contains the number –1. Enter the following If clause:

   If index <> –1 Then

4. As you learned in Chapter 6's Exercise 33, you can use the Items collection's RemoveAt method to remove a list box item during run time. The method's syntax is *object*.**Items.RemoveAt(***index***)**. Enter the appropriate statement to remove the selected CD from the cdsListBox.
5. Save the solution and then start the application. Notice that the CD information you entered in the previous section does not appear in the list box. This is because you haven't yet entered the instructions to save the list box items to the cds.txt file. Those instructions will be entered in the FormClosing event procedure, which you will code in the next section.
6. Click **Funhouse** in the list box and then click the **Remove** button. The button's Click event procedure removes the Funhouse CD from the list box. Click the **Exit** button to end the application.

Coding the MainForm's FormClosing Event Procedure

The last procedure you need to code is the MainForm's FormClosing event procedure. According to the application's TOE chart, the procedure is responsible for saving the contents of the cdsListBox to the cds.txt file. The procedure's pseudocode is shown in Figure 11-37.

```
MainForm FormClosing event procedure
1. open the cds.txt file for output
2. repeat for each CD in the list box
         write the CD information to the file
   end repeat for
3. close the file
```

Figure 11-37 Pseudocode for the MainForm's FormClosing event procedure

To code the MainForm's FormClosing event procedure and then test the code:

1. Open the code template for the MainForm's FormClosing event procedure. Type **' saves the list box information** and then press **Enter** twice.
2. The procedure will use a StreamWriter variable named `outFile`. Type the appropriate Dim statement and then press **Enter** twice.
3. The first step in the procedure's pseudocode is to open the cds.txt file for output. Type **' open the file for output** and then press **Enter**. Now, enter a statement that uses the CreateText method to open the file.
4. The second step in the pseudocode is a loop that repeats its instructions for each CD in the list box. Enter the following comment and For Each clause:

   ' write each CD in the list box
   For Each cd As String In cdsListBox.Items
5. Change the Next clause to **Next cd**.

6. The instruction in the loop body should write the CD information to the file. In the blank line below the For Each clause, enter a statement that uses the WriteLine method to write the contents of the `cd` variable to the cds.txt file.
7. Step 3 in the pseudocode is to close the file. Insert a blank line between the Next cd and End Sub clauses. Type **' close the file** and then press **Enter**. Finally, enter the statement to close the cds.txt file.
8. Save the solution and then start the application. Click the **Add** button. Type **Breakout** as the CD name and then press **Enter**. Type **Miley Cyrus** as the artist name and then press **Enter**. Type **8** as the price and then press **Enter**. The Add button's Click event procedure adds the CD information to the list box.
9. Click the **Exit** button. The computer processes the `Me.Close()` statement in the button's Click event procedure; doing this invokes the form's FormClosing event. The instructions in the FormClosing event procedure save the contents of the list box to the cds.txt file.
10. Start the application again. Notice that the Breakout CD information appears in the list box. Click **Breakout** in the list box and then click the **Remove** button. The button's Click event procedure removes the Breakout CD information from the list box.
11. Click the **Exit** button. Start the application again. Notice that the Breakout CD information does not appear in the list box. Click the **Exit** button.
12. Close the Code Editor window, and then close the solution. Figure 11-38 shows the code for the CD Collection application.

```
' Project name:          CD Collection Project
' Project purpose:       Allows the user to add and delete
                         list box entries
'                        Reads CD information from a
                         sequential access file
'                        Writes CD information to a
                         sequential access file
' Created/revised by:    <your name> on <current date>

Option Explicit On
Option Strict On
Option Infer Off

Public Class MainForm

   Private Sub exitButton_Click(ByVal sender As Object,
   ByVal e As System.EventArgs) Handles exitButton.Click
       Me.Close()
   End Sub

   Private Sub MainForm_FormClosing(
   ByVal sender As Object,
   ByVal e As System.Windows.Forms.FormClosingEventArgs
   ) Handles Me.FormClosing
       ' saves the list box information
```

Figure 11-38 Code for the CD Collection application *(continues)*

(continued)

```
         Dim outFile As IO.StreamWriter

         ' open the file for output
         outFile = IO.File.CreateText("cds.txt")
         ' write each CD in the list box
         For Each cd As String In cdsListBox.Items
              outFile.WriteLine(cd)

         Next cd
         ' close the file
         outFile.Close()

    End Sub

    Private Sub MainForm_Load(ByVal sender As Object,
    ByVal e As System.EventArgs) Handles Me.Load
         ' fills the list box with data
         ' stored in a sequential access file

         ' declare variables
         Dim inFile As IO.StreamReader
         Dim fileName As String = "cds.txt"
         Dim cdInfo As String

         ' verify that the file exists
         If IO.File.Exists(fileName) Then
            ' open the file for input
            inFile = IO.File.OpenText(fileName)
            ' process loop body until end of file
            Do Until inFile.Peek = -1
               ' read a line from the file
               cdInfo = inFile.ReadLine
               ' add the line to the list box
               cdsListBox.Items.Add(cdInfo)

            Loop
            ' close the file
            inFile.Close()
            ' select the first item in the list box
            cdsListBox.SelectedIndex = 0
         Else
            MessageBox.Show("Can't find the cds.txt file",
                            "CD Collection",
                            MessageBoxButtons.OK,
                            MessageBoxIcon.Information)

         End If
    End Sub

    Private Sub addButton_Click(ByVal sender As Object,
    ByVal e As System.EventArgs) Handles addButton.Click
        ' adds CD information to the list box

        ' declare variables
        Dim inputName As String
        Dim inputArtist As String
```

Figure 11-38 Code for the CD Collection application *(continues)*

(continued)

```
        Dim inputPrice As String
        Dim concatenatedInfo As String
        Dim price As Double

        ' get the CD information
        inputName = InputBox("CD name:", "CD Collection")
        inputArtist = InputBox("Artist:", "CD Collection")
        inputPrice = InputBox("Price:", "CD Collection")

        ' format the price, then concatenate the
        ' input items, using 40 characters for the
        ' CD name, 25 characters for the artist name,
        ' and 5 characters for the price
        Double.TryParse(inputPrice, price)
        inputPrice = price.ToString("N2")
        concatenatedInfo = inputName.PadRight(40) &
           inputArtist.PadRight(25) & inputPrice.PadLeft(5)

        ' add the information to the list box
        cdsListBox.Items.Add(concatenatedInfo)

    End Sub

    Private Sub removeButton_Click(ByVal sender As Object,
    ByVal e As System.EventArgs) Handles removeButton.Click
        ' removes the selected CD from the list box

        Dim index As Integer = cdsListBox.SelectedIndex

        If index <> -1 Then
             cdsListBox.Items.RemoveAt(index)

        End If
    End Sub
End Class
```

Figure 11-38 Code for the CD Collection application

PROGRAMMING EXAMPLE

Glovers Industries Application

Glovers Industries stores the item numbers and prices of its products in a sequential access file named itemInfo.txt. Create an application that displays the item numbers in a list box. When the user selects an item number, the application should display the item's price. Use the following names for the solution, project, and form file: Glovers Solution, Glovers Project, and Main Form.vb. Save the application in the VbReloaded2010\Chap11 folder. You also will need to create the itemInfo.txt sequential access file. Save the itemInfo.txt file in the project's bin\Debug folder. See Figures 11-39 through 11-44.

Task	Object	Event
1. Create a Product structure that has two members: a String member named number and a Decimal member named price 2. Declare and initialize a class-level Product array named items; the array should have 5 rows	MainForm	Declarations section
1. Fill the items array with the item numbers and prices stored in the itemInfo.txt file 2. Fill the numbersListBox with the item numbers stored in the itemInfo.txt file		Load
Display the item numbers	numbersListBox	None
Display the price associated with the selected item number		SelectedIndexChanged
End the application	exitButton	Click
Display the price (from numbersListBox)	priceLabel	None

Figure 11-39 TOE chart for the Glovers Industries application

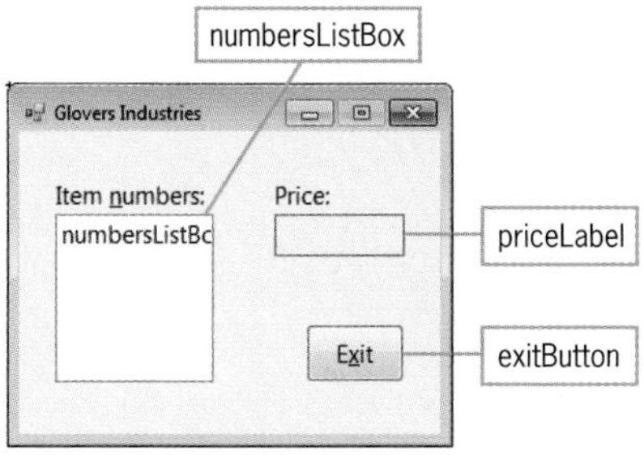

Figure 11-40 MainForm in the Glovers Industries application

Object	Property	Setting
MainForm	Font	Segoe UI, 11 point
	MaximizeBox	False
	StartPosition	CenterScreen
	Text	Glovers Industries
Label1	TabIndex	0
	Text	Item &numbers:
numbersListBox	TabIndex	1
exitButton	TabIndex	2
Label2	TabIndex	3
	Text	Price:
priceLabel	AutoSize	False
	BorderStyle	FixedSingle
	TabIndex	4
	TextAlign	MiddleCenter

Figure 11-41 Objects, properties, and settings

```
itemInfo.txt
12AVX,5
23ABC,8.97
23TWT,4.69
34ZAB,12.5
91BAN,34.67
```

Figure 11-42 The itemInfo.txt sequential access file

<u>MainForm Load event procedure</u>
if the itemInfo.txt file exists
    open the file for input
    repeat until there are no more characters to read in the file
        read a line from the file and split the item number from the price
        assign the item number and price to the current element in the items array
        add the item number to the numbersListBox
        add 1 to the variable that keeps track of the array subscript and list box index
    end repeat
    close the file
    select the first item in the numbersListBox
else
    display an appropriate error message
end if

<u>numbersListBox SelectedIndexChanged event procedure</u>
use the index of the selected item to access the appropriate price from the items array, and then display the price in the priceLabel

<u>exitButton Click event procedure</u>
close the application

Figure 11-43 Pseudocode

```
' Project name:         Glovers Project
' Project purpose:      Display the price of an item
' Created/revised by:   <your name> on <current date>

Option Explicit On
Option Strict On
Option Infer Off

Public Class MainForm

  ' define the Product structure
  Structure Product
     Public number As String
     Public price As Decimal
  End Structure

```

Figure 11-44 Code *(continues)*

(continued)

```
' declare class-level array
Private items(4) As Product

Private Sub MainForm_Load(ByVal sender As Object,
ByVal e As System.EventArgs) Handles Me.Load
   ' fills the items array and numbersListBox
   ' with the data stored in a sequential access file

   Dim inFile As IO.StreamReader
   Dim fileName As String = "itemInfo.txt"
   Dim x As Integer ' subscript and index
   Dim fields() As String

   If IO.File.Exists(fileName) Then
      inFile = IO.File.OpenText(fileName)
      Do Until inFile.Peek = -1
         ' split item number from price
         fields = inFile.ReadLine.Split(","c)
         ' assign item number and price to the array
         items(x).number = fields(0)
         items(x).price = Convert.ToDecimal(fields(1))
         ' add item number to the list box
         numbersListBox.Items.Add(items(x).number)

         ' update variable that keeps track of the
         ' array subscript and list box index
         x += 1
      Loop
      inFile.Close()
      numbersListBox.SelectedIndex = 0
   Else
      MessageBox.Show("Can't find " & fileName,
            "Glovers Industries",
            MessageBoxButtons.OK,
            MessageBoxIcon.Information)

   End If
End Sub

Private Sub numbersListBox_SelectedIndexChanged(
ByVal sender As Object, ByVal e As System.EventArgs
) Handles numbersListBox.SelectedIndexChanged
   ' displays the price corresponding to the
   ' item selected in the list box

   Dim index As Integer =
      numbersListBox.SelectedIndex

   priceLabel.Text = items(index).price.ToString("N2")
End Sub

Private Sub exitButton_Click(ByVal sender As Object,
ByVal e As System.EventArgs) Handles exitButton.Click
   Me.Close()
End Sub
End Class
```

Figure 11-44 Code

Summary

- You can use the Structure statement to define a user-defined data type (or structure) in Visual Basic. You typically enter the Structure statement in the form's Declarations section in the Code Editor window.
- After defining a structure, you can use the structure to declare a structure variable. A structure variable contains one or more member variables. You access a member variable using the structure variable's name, followed by the dot member access operator and the member variable's name.
- The member variables contained in a structure variable can be used just like any other variables.
- A structure variable can be passed to a procedure.
- You can create an array of structure variables. You access a member variable in an array element using the array's name, followed by the element's subscript enclosed in parentheses, the dot member access operator, and the member variable's name, like this: *arrayName(subscript).memberVariableName.*
- An application can write information to a file (called an output file) and also read information from a file (called an input file).
- The information in a sequential access file (also referred to as a text file) is always accessed sequentially. In other words, it is accessed in consecutive order from the beginning of the file through the end of the file.
- You can write data to a sequential access file by first declaring a StreamWriter variable, and then using either the CreateText method or the AppendText method to open the file. You assign the appropriate method's return value to the StreamWriter variable. You then use either the Write method or the WriteLine method to write the data to the file.
- You can read data from a sequential access file by first declaring a StreamReader variable. Before opening the file, you should use the Exists method to determine whether the file exists. If the file exists, you use the OpenText method to open the file. You assign the method's return value to the StreamReader variable. You then use the Peek and ReadLine methods to read the data from the file.
- When a procedure is finished using a sequential access file, it should use the Close method to close the file.
- You can use the PadLeft and PadRight methods to align columns of information that appear in the interface. You also can use the methods to align information written to a sequential access file.
- You can use the Strings.Space method to include a specific number of space characters in a string.
- The FormClosing event occurs when a form is about to be closed. You can prevent a form from being closed by setting the Cancel property of the FormClosing event procedure's `e` parameter to True.

- When writing records to a file, programmers typically write each record on a separate line in the file. They use a delimiter character to separate the fields in each record.
- You can use the Split function to read delimited records from a file.

Key Terms

AppendText method—used with a StreamWriter variable to open a sequential access file for append

Cancel property—a property of the `e` parameter in the FormClosing event procedure; when set to True, it prevents the form from closing

Close method—used with either a StreamWriter variable or a StreamReader variable to close a sequential access file

CreateText method—used with a StreamWriter variable to open a sequential access file for output

Delimiter character—a character used to separate the fields in a record

Exists method—used to determine whether a file exists

Field—a single item of information about a person, place, or thing

FormClosing event—occurs when a form is about to be closed, which can happen as a result of the computer processing the `Me.Close()` statement or the user clicking the Close button on the form's title bar

Input files—files from which an application reads data

Line—a sequence (stream) of characters followed by the newline character

Member variables—the variables contained in a structure

OpenText method—used with a StreamReader variable to open a sequential access file for input

Output files—files to which an application writes data

Peek method—used with a StreamReader variable to determine whether a file contains another character to read

ReadLine method—used with a StreamReader variable to read a line of text from a sequential access file

Record—a group of related fields that contain all of the necessary data about a specific person, place, or thing

Sequential access files—files composed of lines of text that are both read and written sequentially; also called text files

Split function—splits a string into substrings based on a delimiter character and then assigns the substrings to a one-dimensional array

Stream of characters—a sequence of characters

StreamReader object—used to read a sequence (stream) of characters from a sequential access file

StreamWriter object—used to write a sequence (stream) of characters to a sequential access file

Strings.Space method—can be used to include a specific number of spaces in a string

Structure statement—used to create user-defined data types, called structures

Structure variables—variables declared using a structure as the data type

Structures—data types created by the Structure statement; allow the programmer to group related items into one unit; also called user-defined data types

Text files—another term for sequential access files

User-defined data types—data types created by the Structure statement; see Structures

Write method—used with a StreamWriter variable to write data to a sequential access file; differs from the WriteLine method in that it does not write a newline character after the data

WriteLine method—used with a StreamWriter variable to write data to a sequential access file; differs from the Write method in that it writes a newline character after the data

Review Questions

1. Which of the following declares a Country variable named `spain`?
   a. `Private spain As Country`
   b. `Dim spain As Country`
   c. `Dim Country As spain`
   d. both a and b

2. Which of the following assigns the string "Madrid" to the `city` member of a Country variable named `spain`?
   a. `city.spain = "Madrid"`
   b. `Country.city = "Madrid"`
   c. `Country.spain.city = "Madrid"`
   d. `spain.city = "Madrid"`

3. An application uses a structure named Employee. Which of the following statements creates a five-element array of Employee structure variables?
   a. `Dim workers As Employee(4)`
   b. `Dim workers As Employee(5)`
   c. `Dim workers(4) As Employee`
   d. `Dim workers(5) As Employee`

4. Each structure variable in the `items` array contains two members: a String variable named `number` and an Integer variable named `quantity`. Which of the following assigns the inventory number "123XY" to the first element in the array?

   a. `items.number(0) = "123XY"`

   b. `items.number(1) = "123XY"`

   c. `items(0).number = "123XY"`

   d. `items(1).number = "123XY"`

5. Which of the following opens the cities.txt file and allows the computer to write new data to the end of the file's existing data?

   a. `outFile = IO.File.AddText("cities.txt")`

   b. `outFile = IO.File.AppendText("cities.txt")`

   c. `outFile = IO.File.InsertText("cities.txt")`

   d. `outFile = IO.File.OpenText("cities.txt")`

6. If the file to be opened does not exist, the ______________ method results in an error when it is processed by the computer.

   a. AppendText

   b. CreateText

   c. OpenText

   d. WriteText

7. Which of the following reads a line of text from a sequential access file and assigns the line (excluding the newline character) to the `lineOfText` variable?

   a. `lineOfText = inFile.ReadLine`

   b. `lineOfText = ReadLine(inFile)`

   c. `inFile.Read(lineOfText)`

   d. `inFile.ReadLine(lineOfText)`

8. The Peek method returns ______________ when the end of the file is reached.

   a. 0

   b. −1

   c. the last character in the file

   d. the newline character

9. Which of the following If clauses determines whether the employ.txt file exists?

   a. `If IO.File.Exists("employ.txt") Then`

   b. `If IO.File("employ.txt").Exists Then`

   c. `If IO.Exists("employ.txt") = True Then`

   d. `If IO.Exists.File("employ.txt") = True Then`

10. The OpenText method creates a _______________ object.

    a. File

    b. SequenceReader

    c. StreamReader

    d. StreamWriter

11. The AppendText method creates a _______________ object.

    a. File

    b. SequenceReader

    c. StreamReader

    d. StreamWriter

12. Which of the following reads a record from a sequential access file and assigns the fields in each record to the `songs` array? The fields are delimited by a space character.

    a. `songs = inFile.ReadLine.Split(" "c)`

    b. `songs = inFile.ReadLine.SplitBy(" "c)`

    c. `songs = inFile.ReadLine.SplitInto(" "c)`

    d. `songs = inFile.ReadLine.SplitUsing(" "c)`

13. The _______________ event occurs when the computer processes the `Me.Close()` statement or when the user clicks the Close button on the form's title bar.

    a. FormClosing

    b. FormFinish

    c. Finish

    d. none of the above

Exercises

Pencil and Paper

1. Write a Structure statement that defines a structure named Book. The structure contains two String member variables named `title` and `author` and a Decimal member variable named `cost`. Then write a Private statement that declares a Book variable named `fiction`. INTRODUCTORY

2. Write a Structure statement that defines a structure named Tape. The structure contains three String member variables named `name`, `artist`, and `songLength`. It also contains an Integer member variable named `songNum`. Then write a Dim statement that declares a Tape variable named `blues`. INTRODUCTORY

3. An application contains the Structure statement shown here. Write a Dim statement that declares a Computer variable named `homeUse`. Then, write an assignment statement that assigns the string "App75" to the `model` member. Finally, write an assignment statement that assigns the number 1650 to the `cost` member. INTRODUCTORY

```
Structure Computer
   Public model As String
   Public cost As Decimal
End Structure
```

4. An application contains the Structure statement shown here. Write a Dim statement that declares a Friend variable named `school`. Then, write assignment statements that assign the value in the firstTextBox to the `first` member and assign the value in the lastTextBox to the `last` member. Finally, write assignment statements that assign the value in the `last` member to the lastLabel and assign the value in the `first` member to the firstLabel. INTRODUCTORY

```
Structure Friend
   Public last As String
   Public first As String
End Structure
```

5. Write the code to declare a variable named `outFile` that can be used to write data to a sequential access file. Then, write the statement to open a sequential access file named sales.txt for output. INTRODUCTORY

6. Write the code to declare a variable named `inFile` that can be used to read data from a sequential access file. Then, write the statement to open a sequential access file named sales.txt for input. INTRODUCTORY

7. Write the code to close the sequential access file associated with a StreamWriter variable named `outFile`. INTRODUCTORY

8. Write an If clause that determines whether a sequential access file exists. The file's name is sales.txt. INTRODUCTORY

INTRODUCTORY

9. Write a Do clause that determines whether the end of a sequential access file has been reached. The file is associated with a StreamReader variable named `inFile`.

INTERMEDIATE

10. An application contains the Structure statement shown here. Write a Private statement that declares a 10-element one-dimensional array of Computer variables. Name the array `business`. Then, write an assignment statement that assigns the string "Tosh7400" to the `model` member contained in the first array element. Finally, write an assignment statement that assigns the number 4560 to the `cost` member contained in the first array element.

```
Structure Computer
   Public model As String
   Public cost As Decimal
End Structure
```

INTERMEDIATE

11. An application contains the Structure statement shown here. Write a Private statement that declares a five-element one-dimensional array of Friend variables. Name the array `home`. Then, write an assignment statement that assigns the value in the name1TextBox to the `first` member contained in the last array element. Finally, write an assignment statement that assigns the value in the name2TextBox to the `last` member contained in the last array element.

```
Structure Friend
   Public last As String
   Public first As String
End Structure
```

INTERMEDIATE

12. A sequential access file named travel.txt contains records whose fields are delimited by a comma. Write a Dim statement to declare a one-dimensional String array named `travelInfo`. Then, write a statement that reads a line of text from the file and assigns the fields to the `travelInfo` array. The file is associated with a StreamReader variable named `inFile`.

ADVANCED

13. A sequential access file named vacations.txt contains records whose three fields are delimited by a comma. The application that uses the file defines a structure named TravelInfo. The TravelInfo structure contains three members: a String member named `location`, an Integer member named `lengthOfStay`, and a Double member named `cost`.

    a. Write a Private statement to declare a one-dimensional TravelInfo array named `myVacations`. The `myVacations` array should contain 10 elements.

    b. Write a Dim statement to declare a one-dimensional String array named `fields`.

    c. Write a statement that reads a line of text from the vacations.txt file and assigns the fields to the `fields` array. The file is associated with a StreamReader variable named `inFile`.

    d. Write the statements to assign the fields contained in the first element in the `fields` array to the appropriate members in the first element in the `myVacations` array.

Computer

MODIFY THIS

14. If necessary, complete the Concentration Game application from this chapter's Programming Tutorial 1, and then close the solution. Use Windows to make a copy of the Concentration Game Solution folder. Rename the folder Concentration Game Solution-Modified. Open the Concentration Game Solution (Concentration Game Solution.sln) file contained in the Concentration Game Solution-Modified folder. Create a sequential access file named words5.txt. Save the file in the project's bin\Debug folder. The first eight words in the file, as well as the last eight words in the file, should be Alabama, Alaska, Arizona, Arkansas, California, Colorado, Connecticut, and Delaware. Modify the application's code so that it also uses the words5.txt file. Save the solution, and then start and test the application. Close the solution.

MODIFY THIS

15. If necessary, complete the CD Collection application from this chapter's Programming Tutorial 2, and then close the solution. Use Windows to make a copy of the CD Collection Solution folder. Rename the folder CD Collection Solution-Modified. Open the CD Collection Solution (CD Collection Solution.sln) file contained in the CD Collection Solution-Modified folder. Modify the FormClosing event procedure so that it asks the user whether he or she wants to save the list box items to the cds.txt file. The procedure should take the appropriate action based on the user's response. Also modify the Remove button's Click event procedure so that it verifies that the user wants to remove the selected CD from the list box. Use the message "Do you want to remove the *x* CD?", in which *x* is the name of the CD. The procedure should take the appropriate action based on the user's response. Save the solution, and then start and test the application. Close the solution.

MODIFY THIS

16. In this exercise, you will modify the Treasures Gift Shop interface and code from Figures 11-7 and 11-8 in the chapter. Open the Treasures Solution (Treasures Solution.sln) file contained in the VbReloaded2010\Chap11\Treasures Solution-Modified folder. The modified application should display both the name and price corresponding to the product ID selected by the user. The names of the products are shown in Figure 11-45. Make the appropriate modifications to the interface and code. Save the solution, and then start and test the application. Close the solution.

Product ID	Name
BX35	Necklace
CR20	Bracelet
FE15	Jewelry box
KW10	Doll
MM67	Ring

Figure 11-45 Product IDs and names

MODIFY THIS

17. If necessary, complete the Concentration Game application from this chapter's Programming Tutorial 1, and then close the solution. Use Windows to make a copy of the Concentration Game Solution folder. Rename the folder Concentration Game Solution-ListBox. Open the Concentration Game Solution (Concentration Game Solution.sln) file contained in the Concentration Game Solution-ListBox folder. Modify the interface and code to allow the user to change the words used in the game by selecting the desired filename (words1.txt, words2.txt, words3.txt, or words4.txt) from a list box while the application is running. The selected file should be used when the New Game button is clicked. Save the solution, and then start and test the application. Close the solution.

INTRODUCTORY

18. Open the Employee List Solution (Employee List Solution.sln) file contained in the VbReloaded2010\Chap11\Employee List Solution folder. The Write button should write the contents of the employTextBox (excluding any leading or trailing spaces) to a sequential access file named employees.txt. Each name should appear on a separate line in the file. Save the file in the project's bin\Debug folder. The Read button should read the names from the employees.txt file and display each in the list box. Code the appropriate event procedures. Save the solution and then start the application. Test the application by writing five names to the file, and then end the application. Open the employees.txt file to verify that it contains five names. Close the employees.txt window and then close the solution.

INTRODUCTORY

19. Open the Memo Solution (Memo Solution.sln) file contained in the VbReloaded2010\Chap11\Memo Solution folder. The Write button should write the contents of the memoTextBox to a sequential access file named memo.txt. Save the file in the project's bin\Debug folder. Save the solution and then start the application. Test the application by writing the memo shown in Figure 11-46 to the file, and then end the application. Open the memo.txt file to verify that it contains the memo. Close the memo.txt window and then close the solution.

```
To all employees:

The annual picnic will be held at Rogers Park on Saturday, July 13.
Bring your family for a day full of fun!

Carolyn Meyer
Personnel Manager
```

Figure 11-46 Memo

INTRODUCTORY

20. Open the Report Solution (Report Solution.sln) file contained in the VbReloaded2010\Chap11\Report Solution folder. The application stores three state names and sales amounts in an array. Code the application so that it creates the report shown in Figure 11-47. Save the report in a sequential access files named report.txt. Use hyphens for the underline. Use an accumulator to total the sales amounts. Save the solution, and then start and test the application. End the application. Open the report.txt file to verify that it contains the report. Close the report.txt window, and then close the solution.

```
ABC Industries Sales Report

State           Sales
California      15,000
Montana         10,000
Wyoming          7,000
                -------
Total sales:   $32,000
```

Figure 11-47 Report

21. Open the Name Solution (Name Solution.sln) file contained in the VbReloaded2010\Chap11\Name Solution folder. Open the names.txt file contained in the project's bin\Debug folder. The sequential access file contains five names. Close the names.txt window. The Display button should read the five names from the names.txt file and store each in a five-element array. It should sort the array in descending order and then display the contents of the array in the list box. Code the button's Click event procedure. Save the solution, and then start and test the application. Close the solution. (If you need to recreate the names.txt file, open the file in a window in the IDE. Delete the contents of the file, if necessary, and then enter the following five names: Joanne, Zelda, Abby, Ben, and Linda.)

INTERMEDIATE

22. Open the Carver Solution (Carver Solution.sln) file contained in the VbReloaded2010\Chap11\Carver Solution folder. The application should display a grade based on the number of points entered by the user. The grading scale is shown in Figure 11-48. Create a structure that contains two members: an Integer variable for the minimum points and a String variable for the grades. Use the structure to declare a five-element array. Store the minimum points and grades in the array. The application should search the array for the number of points earned and then display the appropriate grade from the array. Code the application. Save the solution, and then start and test the application. Close the solution.

INTERMEDIATE

Minimum points	**Grade**
0	F
300	D
350	C
400	B
450	A

Figure 11-48 Grading scale

23. If necessary, complete Computer Exercise 18, and then close the solution. Use Windows to make a copy of the Employee List Solution folder. Rename the folder Employee List Solution-Modified. Open the Employee List Solution (Employee List Solution.sln) file contained in the Employee List Solution-Modified folder.

INTERMEDIATE

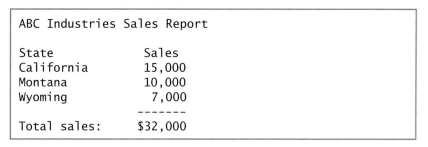

a. Use Windows to delete the employees.txt file contained in the project's bin\Debug folder.

b. The first time the Write button's Click event procedure is processed, it should determine whether the employees.txt file exists. If the file exists, the procedure should use the MessageBox. Show method to ask the user whether the existing file should be replaced. Include Yes and No buttons in the message box. If the user clicks the Yes button, replace the existing file; otherwise, append to the existing file.

c. Save the solution and then start the application. Type Helen in the Name box and then click the Write button. End the application.

d. Start the application again. Type Ginger in the Name box and then click the Write button. The application should ask whether you want the existing file replaced. Click the No button and then end the application.

e. Open the employees.txt file. The file should contain two names: Helen and Ginger. Close the employees.txt window.

f. Start the application again. Type George in the Name box and then click the Write button. Click the Yes button and then end the application.

g. Open the employees.txt file. The file should contain one name: George. Close the employees.txt window and then close the solution.

INTERMEDIATE

24. Open the Salary Solution (Salary Solution.sln) file contained in the VbReloaded2010\Chap11\Salary Solution folder. Open the Code Editor window and study the existing code. The application displays the salary amount associated with the code entered by the user. Currently, the Private statement stores the six salary amounts in the `salaries` array. Modify the application so that it reads the salary amounts from the salary.txt file contained in the project's bin\Debug folder and stores each in the array. Save the solution, and then start and test the application. Close the solution.

INTERMEDIATE

25. If necessary, complete the CD Collection application from this chapter's Programming Tutorial 2, and then close the solution. Use Windows to make a copy of the CD Collection Solution folder. Rename the folder CD Collection Solution-No Duplicate. Open the CD Collection Solution (CD Collection Solution.sln) file contained in the CD Collection Solution-No Duplicate folder. Before prompting the user to enter the artist name and CD price, the Add button's Click event procedure should determine whether the CD name already appears in the list box. If the list box contains the CD name, the procedure should display an appropriate message and then not add the CD to the list. Save the solution, and then start and test the application. Close the solution.

INTERMEDIATE

26. If necessary, complete the CD Collection application from this chapter's Programming Tutorial 2, and then close the solution. Use Windows to make a copy of the CD Collection Solution

folder. Rename the folder CD Collection Solution-Undo. Open the CD Collection Solution (CD Collection Solution.sln) file contained in the CD Collection Solution-Undo folder. Add an Undo Remove button to the interface. The button's Click event procedure should restore the last line removed by the Remove button. Make the necessary modifications to the code. Save the solution, and then start and test the application. Close the solution.

27. If necessary, complete the CD Collection application from this chapter's Programming Tutorial 2, and then close the solution. Use Windows to make a copy of the CD Collection Solution folder. Rename the folder CD Collection Solution-Structure. Open the CD Collection Solution (CD Collection Solution.sln) file contained in the CD Collection Solution-Structure folder. Create a structure and then use the structure in the Add button's Click event procedure. Save the solution, and then start and test the application. Close the solution.

INTERMEDIATE

28. Open the Friends Solution (Friends Solution.sln) file contained in the VbReloaded2010\Chap11\Friends Solution folder. The Add button should add the name entered in the text portion of the combo box control to the list portion of the control, but only if the name is not already in the list. The Remove button should remove (from the list portion of the combo box) the name either entered in the text portion or selected in the list portion. (Hint: Use the Items collection's Remove method.) The form's FormClosing event procedure should save the combo box items in a sequential access file named myFriends.txt. The form's Load event procedure should read the names from the myFriends.txt file and add each name to the combo box. Code the application. Save the solution, and then start and test the application. Close the solution.

ADVANCED

29. Open the Numbers Solution (Numbers Solution.sln) file contained in the VbReloaded2010\Chap11\Numbers Solution folder. The Display button's Click event procedure should read the five numbers stored in the numbers.txt file and display the numbers in the list box. The numbers.txt file is contained in the project's bin\Debug folder. Currently, the file contains the numbers 1 through 5. The Update button's Click event procedure should read the five numbers from the numbers.txt file and store the numbers in an array. It then should increase each number in the array by 1 and write the array contents to an empty numbers.txt file. Code the appropriate procedures. Save the solution and then start the application. Click the Display button. The numbers 1 through 5 appear in the list box. Click the Update button and then click the Display button. The numbers 2 through 6 appear in the list box. Close the solution. (If you need to recreate the numbers.txt file, open the file in a window in the IDE. Delete the contents of the file, if necessary, and then enter the numbers 1 through 5.)

ADVANCED

30. Open the Test Scores Solution (Test Scores Solution.sln) file contained in the VbReloaded2010\Chap11\Test Scores Solution folder. The Save button should save the contents of the nameTextBox and scoreTextBox

ADVANCED

to a sequential access file named scores.txt. The Display button should use the InputBox function to prompt the user to enter a test score. It then should display the names of the students earning that test score. Save the solution and then start the application. Test the application by entering the student records shown in Figure 11-49. Click the Save button after entering each record. Now, click the Display button. Enter 95 and then press Enter. The names of the students whose test score is 95 appear in the list box. Close the solution.

Name	Test score
John Jones	80
Phillip Hawking	95
Kevin Carley	83
Ellie Mayfield	78
Rachael Smith	95
Susan Carkley	99
Harriet Chu	95

Figure 11-49 Student records

DISCOVERY

31. Open the Grades Solution (Grades Solution.sln) file contained in the VbReloaded2010\Chap11\Grades Solution folder. The application should display a student's name and the grades earned on two tests.

    a. Open the Code Editor window. Create a structure named StudentInfo. The structure should contain two members: a String variable for the student's name and a String array for the grades. An array contained in a structure cannot be assigned an initial size, so you will need to include an empty set of parentheses after the array name.

    b. In the getButton's Click event procedure, use the StudentInfo structure to declare a structure variable.

    c. Research the Visual Basic ReDim statement. Use the ReDim statement to declare the array's size in the getButton's Click event procedure. In this case, the array should have two elements. (Keep in mind that the array belongs to the structure variable.)

    d. The getButton's Click event procedure should use three InputBox functions to get the student's name and both grades. (Store each grade in the array.)

    e. The getButton's Click event procedure should display the student's name and grades in the reportLabel.

    f. Save the solution and then start and test the application. Close the solution.

DISCOVERY

32. If necessary, complete Computer Exercise 31, and then close the solution. Use Windows to make a copy of the Grades Solution folder. Rename the folder Grades Solution-Modified. Open the Grades Solution (Grades Solution.sln) file contained in the Grades Solution-Modified folder. The getButton's Click event procedure should allow the user to enter the names and grades for five students.

(Hint: You will need to use an array of structure variables.) Display the five student names and their grades in the reportLabel. You will need to make the reportLabel larger. Save the solution, and then start and test the application. Close the solution.

SWAT THE BUGS

33. Open the Debug Solution (Debug Solution.sln) file contained in the VbReloaded2010\Chap11\Debug Solution folder. Open the Code Editor window and review the existing code. Start the application and then test it using Sue and 1000, and then using Pete and 5000. A run time error occurs. Read the error message. Click Debug on the menu bar and then click Stop Debugging. Open the bonus.txt file contained in the project's bin\Debug folder. Notice that the file is empty. Close the bonus.txt window. Locate and then correct the errors in the code. When the application is working correctly, close the solution.

Case Projects

Warren High School

This year, three students are running for senior class president: Mark Stone, Sheima Patel, and Sam Perez. Create an application that keeps track of the voting. Save the voting information in a sequential access file. The application also should display the number of votes per candidate. Use the following names for the solution, project, and form file: Warren Solution, Warren Project, and Main Form.vb. Save the application in the VbReloaded2010\Chap11 folder. You can create either your own interface or the one shown in Figure 11-50.

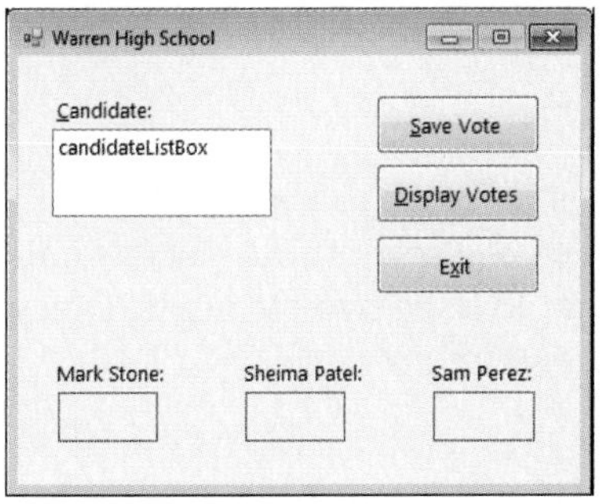

Figure 11-50 Sample interface for the Warren High School application

WKRK-Radio

Each year, WKRK-Radio polls its audience to determine the best Super Bowl commercial. The choices are as follows: Budweiser, FedEx, E*Trade, and Pepsi. Create an application that the station manager can use to save each caller's choice in a sequential access file. The application also should display the number of votes for each commercial. Use the following names for the solution, project, and form file: WKRK Solution, WKRK Project, and Main Form.vb. Save the application in the VbReloaded2010\Chap11 folder. You can create either your own interface or the one shown in Figure 11-51.

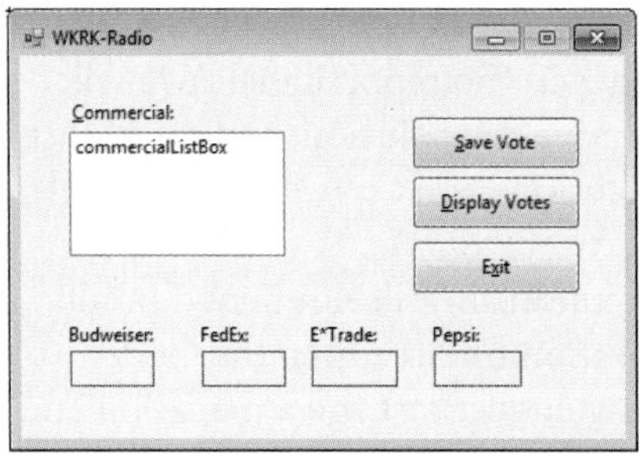

Figure 11-51 Sample interface for the WKRK-Radio application

Political Awareness Organization

During July and August of each year, the Political Awareness Organization (PAO) sends a questionnaire to the voters in its district. The questionnaire asks the voter for his or her political party (Democratic, Republican, or Independent) and age. From the returned questionnaires, the organization's secretary tabulates the number of Democrats, Republicans, and Independents in the district. The secretary wants an application that she can use to save each respondent's information (political party and age) to a sequential access file. The application also should calculate and display the number of voters in each political party. Use the following names for the solution, project, and form file: PAO Solution, PAO Project, and Main Form.vb. Save the application in the VbReloaded2010\Chap11 folder. You can create either your own interface or the one shown in Figure 11-52.

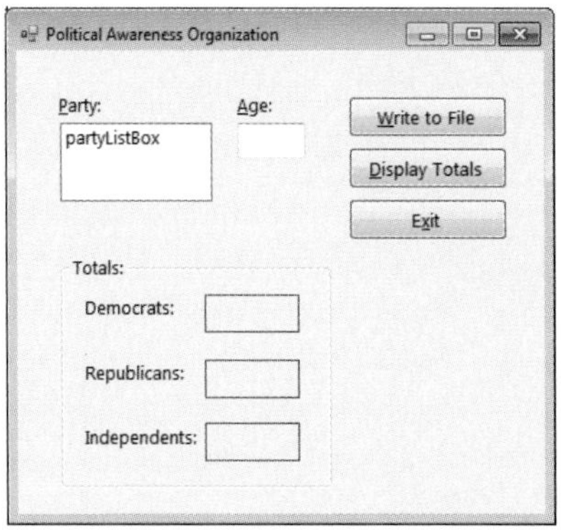

Figure 11-52 Sample interface for the Political Awareness Organization application

Revellos

Revellos has stores located in several states. Create an application that the sales manager can use to enter the following information for each store: the store number, the state in which the store is located, and the store manager's name. The application should save the information in a sequential access file. Each store's information should appear on a separate line in the file. In other words, the first store's number, state name, and manager name should appear on the first line in the file. The application also should allow the sales manager to enter a store number, and then display both the state in which the store is located and the store manager's name. The store information is shown in Figure 11-53. Use the following names for the solution, project, and form file: Revellos Solution, Revellos Project, and Main Form.vb. Save the application in the VbReloaded2010\Chap11 folder.

Number	State	Manager
1004	Texas	Jeffrey Jefferson
1005	Texas	Paula Hendricks
1007	Arizona	Jake Johansen
1010	Arizona	Henry Abernathy
1011	California	Barbara Millerton
1013	California	Inez Baily
1015	California	Sung Lee
1016	California	Lou Chan
1017	California	Homer Gomez
1019	New Mexico	Ingrid Nadkarni

Figure 11-53 Revellos information

CHAPTER 12

Access Databases and LINQ

After studying Chapter 12, you should be able to:

- Define the terms used when talking about databases
- Connect an application to a Microsoft Access database
- Bind table and field objects to controls
- Explain the purpose of the DataSet, BindingSource, TableAdapter, TableAdapterManager, and BindingNavigator objects
- Customize a DataGridView control
- Handle errors using the Try...Catch statement
- Position the record pointer in a dataset
- Access the value stored in a field object
- Query a dataset using LINQ
- Customize a BindingNavigator control
- Use the LINQ aggregate methods

Database Terminology

In order to maintain accurate records, most businesses store information about their employees, customers, and inventory in computer databases. A **computer database** is an electronic file that contains an organized collection of related information. Many products exist for creating computer databases; such products are called database management systems (or DBMS). Some of the most popular database management systems are Microsoft Access, Microsoft SQL Server, and Oracle. You can use Visual Basic to access the data stored in databases created by these database management systems. As a result, companies can use Visual Basic to create a standard interface that allows employees to access information stored in a variety of database formats. Instead of learning each DBMS's user interface, the employee needs to know only one interface. The actual format of the database is unimportant and will be transparent to the user.

You do not have to be a business to make use of a database. Many people use databases to keep track of their medical records, compact disc collections, and even golf scores.

In this chapter, you will learn how to access the data stored in Microsoft Access databases. Databases created using Microsoft Access are relational databases. A **relational database** is one that stores information in tables composed of columns and rows, similar to the format used in a spreadsheet. Each column in a table represents a field and each row represents a record. As you learned in Chapter 11, a **field** is a single item of information about a person, place, or thing—such as a name, a salary amount, a Social Security number, or a price. A **record** is a group of related fields that contain all of the necessary data about a specific person, place, or thing. The college you are attending keeps a student record on you. Examples of fields contained in your student record include your Social Security number, name, address, phone number, credits earned, and grades earned. A group of related records is called a **table**. Each record in a table pertains to the same topic and contains the same type of information. In other words, each record in a table contains the same fields.

The databases are called relational because the information in the tables can be related in different ways. The databases created using SQL Server and Oracle also are relational databases.

A relational database can contain one or more tables. A one-table database would be a good choice for storing information about the college courses you have taken. An example of such a table is shown in Figure 12-1. Each record in the table contains four fields: an ID field that indicates the department name and course number, a course title field, a field listing the number of credit hours, and a grade field. Most tables have a **primary key**, which is a field that uniquely identifies each record. In the table shown in Figure 12-1, you could use either the ID field or the Title field as the primary key, because the data in those fields will be unique for each record.

ID	Title	Hours	Grade
CIS100	Intro to Computers	3	A
ENG100	English Composition	3	B
PHIL105	Philosophy Seminar	2	C
CIS201	Visual Basic 2010	3	A

Figure 12-1 Example of a one-table relational database

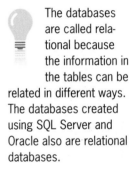

You might use a two-table database to store information about a CD (compact disc) collection. You would store the general information about each CD (such as the CD's name and the artist's name) in one table, and store the information about the songs on each CD (such as their title and track number) in the other table. You then would use a common field—for example, a CD number—to relate the records contained in both tables. Figure 12-2 shows an example of a two-table database that stores CD information. The first table is referred to as the **parent table**, and the second table is referred to as the **child table**. The CdNum field is the primary key in the parent table, because it uniquely identifies each record in the table. The CdNum field in the child table is used solely to link the song title and track information to the appropriate CD in the parent table. In the child table, the CdNum field is called the **foreign key**.

Parent and child tables are also referred to as master and detail tables, respectively.

the two tables are related by the CdNum field

CdNum	Name	Artist
01	Western Way	Dolly Draton
02	Midnight Blue	Paul Elliot

CdNum	SongTitle	Track
01	Country	1
01	Night on the Road	2
01	Old Times	3
02	Lovely Nights	1
02	Colors	2
02	Blue Clouds	3

Figure 12-2 Example of a two-table relational database

Storing data in a relational database offers many advantages. The computer can retrieve data stored in a relational format both quickly and easily, and the data can be displayed in any order. The information in the CD database, for example, can be arranged by artist name, song title, and so on. You also can control the amount of information you want to view from a relational database. You can view all of the information in the CD database, only the information pertaining to a certain artist, or only the names of the songs contained on a specific CD.

The answers to Mini-Quiz questions are located in Appendix A.

Mini-Quiz 12-1

1. A ______________ is an organized collection of related information stored in a computer file.
   a. database
   b. dataset
   c. field
   d. record

2. A ______________ database stores information in tables.
   a. columnar
   b. relational
   c. sorted
   d. tabular

3. Which of the following statements is true about a relational database?
   a. Data stored in a relational database can be retrieved both quickly and easily by the computer.
   b. Data stored in a relational database can be displayed in any order.
   c. A relational database stores data in a column and row format.
   d. all of the above

Connecting an Application to a Microsoft Access Database

In the concepts portion of this chapter, you will use a Microsoft Access database named Employees. The Employees database is stored in the Employees.accdb file, which is located in the VbReloaded2010\Chap12\Access Databases folder. The .accdb filename extension stands for Access Database and indicates that the database was created using Microsoft Access. The Employees database contains one table, which is named tblEmploy. Figure 12-3 shows the table data displayed in a window in the IDE. The table contains seven fields and 14 records. The Emp_Number field is the primary key, because it uniquely identifies each record in the table. The Status field contains the employment status, which is either the letter F (for full-time) or the letter P (for part-time). The Code field identifies the employee's department: 1 for Accounting, 2 for Advertising, 3 for Personnel, and 4 for Inventory.

To open a database table in the IDE, first connect the database to an application, then right-click the table's name in either the Server Explorer (Visual Studio 2010) or Database Explorer (Visual Basic 2010 Express Edition) window, and then click Retrieve Data.

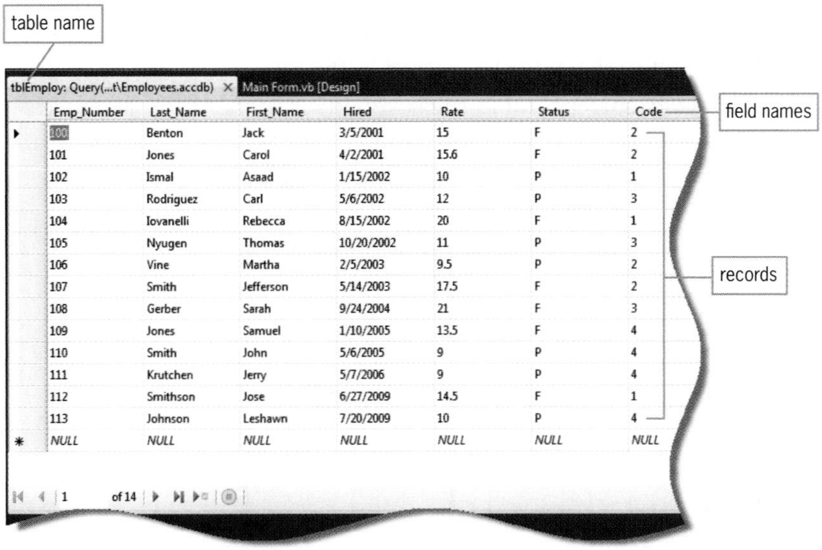

Emp_Number	Last_Name	First_Name	Hired	Rate	Status	Code
100	Benton	Jack	3/5/2001	15	F	2
101	Jones	Carol	4/2/2001	15.6	F	2
102	Ismal	Asaad	1/15/2002	10	P	1
103	Rodriguez	Carl	5/6/2002	12	P	3
104	Iovanelli	Rebecca	8/15/2002	20	F	1
105	Nyugen	Thomas	10/20/2002	11	P	3
106	Vine	Martha	2/5/2003	9.5	P	2
107	Smith	Jefferson	5/14/2003	17.5	F	2
108	Gerber	Sarah	9/24/2004	21	F	3
109	Jones	Samuel	1/10/2005	13.5	F	4
110	Smith	John	5/6/2005	9	P	4
111	Krutchen	Jerry	5/7/2006	9	P	4
112	Smithson	Jose	6/27/2009	14.5	F	1
113	Johnson	Leshawn	7/20/2009	10	P	4
NULL	NULL	NULL	NULL	NULL	NULL	NULL

Figure 12-3 Data contained in the tblEmploy table

You can view the Ch12ConnectingADatabase video and then skim the sections from *Connecting an Application to a Microsoft Access Database to Visual Basic Code*.

In order to access the data stored in a database, an application needs to be connected to the database. You can make the connection using the Data Source Configuration Wizard. The basic procedure for doing this is shown in Figure 12-4. (More detailed steps can be found in Programming Tutorial 1.) The wizard also allows you to specify the data you want to access. The computer makes a copy of the specified data and stores the copy in its internal memory. The copy of the data you want to access is called a **dataset**.

HOW TO Connect an Application to an Access Database

1. Open the application's solution file.
2. *If you are using Visual Studio 2010*, click View on the menu bar and then click Server Explorer to open the Server Explorer window, which lists the available connections.
   If you are using Visual Basic 2010 Express Edition, click View on the menu bar and then click Database Explorer to open the Database Explorer window, which lists the available connections.
3. Click Data on the menu bar and then click Show Data Sources to open the Data Sources window.
4. Click the Add New Data Source link in the Data Sources window to start the Data Source Configuration Wizard, which displays the Choose a Data Source Type screen. If necessary, click Database.
5. Click the Next button and then continue using the wizard to specify the data source and the name of the database file. The data source for an Access database is Microsoft Access Database File (OLE DB).

Figure 12-4 How to connect an application to an Access database

After it connects the application to the database, the Data Source Configuration Wizard adds several files to the project; the filenames appear in the Solution Explorer window. The wizard also lists a connection to the database file in the Server Explorer window and adds a dataset's name to the Data Sources window. Figure 12-5 shows the result of using the wizard to connect the Morgan Industries application to the Employees database. Notice that the EmployeesDataSet contains one table object and seven field objects. The table object is the tblEmploy table contained in the Employees database, and the seven field objects correspond to the seven fields in the table. (If you are using the Express Edition of Visual Basic, your screen will show the Database Explorer window rather than the Server Explorer window.)

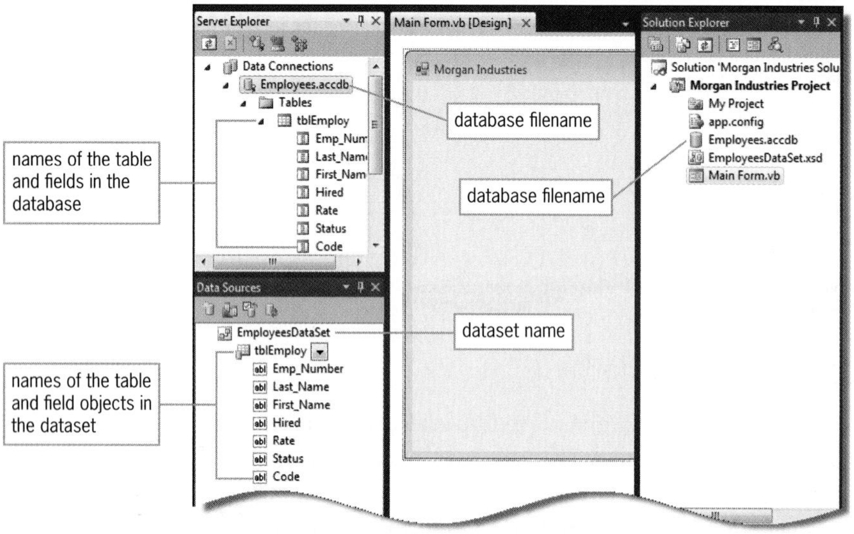

Figure 12-5 Result of running the Data Source Configuration Wizard

After an application is connected to a database, you can use the procedure shown in Figure 12-6 to view the fields and records stored in the dataset. Figure 12-7 shows the result of using the procedure to preview the contents of the EmployeesDataSet. Notice the information that appears in the "Select an object to preview" box in Figure 12-7. EmployeesDataSet is the name of the dataset in the application, and tblEmploy is the name of the table included in the dataset. Fill and GetData are methods. The Fill method populates an existing table with data, while the GetData method creates a new table and populates it with data.

HOW TO Preview the Contents of a Dataset

1. Click the form. Click Data on the menu bar and then click Preview Data to open the Preview Data dialog box.
2. Select the object to preview and then click the Preview button.
3. When you are finished previewing the data, close the dialog box.

Figure 12-6 How to preview the contents of a dataset

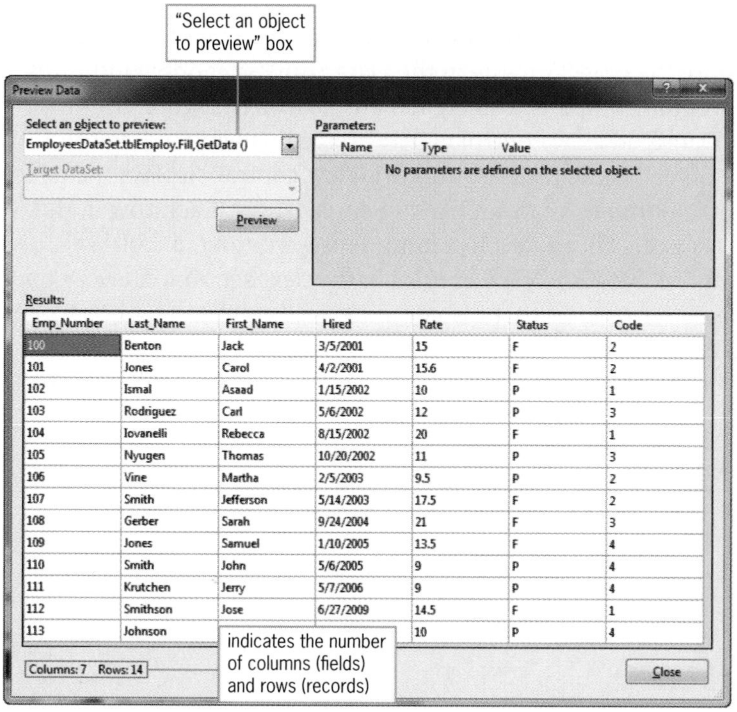

Emp_Number	Last_Name	First_Name	Hired	Rate	Status	Code
100	Benton	Jack	3/5/2001	15	F	2
101	Jones	Carol	4/2/2001	15.6	F	2
102	Ismal	Asaad	1/15/2002	10	P	1
103	Rodriguez	Carl	5/6/2002	12	P	3
104	Iovanelli	Rebecca	8/15/2002	20	F	1
105	Nyugen	Thomas	10/20/2002	11	P	3
106	Vine	Martha	2/5/2003	9.5	P	2
107	Smith	Jefferson	5/14/2003	17.5	F	2
108	Gerber	Sarah	9/24/2004	21	F	3
109	Jones	Samuel	1/10/2005	13.5	F	4
110	Smith	John	5/6/2005	9	P	4
111	Krutchen	Jerry	5/7/2006	9	P	4
112	Smithson	Jose	6/27/2009	14.5	F	1
113	Johnson			10	P	4

Figure 12-7 EmployeesDataSet shown in the Preview Data dialog box

Binding the Objects in a Dataset

For the user to view the contents of a dataset while an application is running, you need to connect one or more objects in the dataset to one or more controls in the interface. Connecting an object to a control is called **binding**, and the connected controls are called **bound controls**. As indicated in Figure 12-8, you can bind the object to a control that the computer creates for you; or, you can bind it to an existing control in the interface.

Bound controls are also referred to as data-aware controls.

HOW TO Bind an Object in a Dataset

To have the computer create a control and then bind an object to it:
In the Data Sources window, click the object you want to bind. If necessary, use the object's list arrow to change the control type. Drag the object to an empty area on the form and then release the mouse button.

To bind an object to an existing control:
In the Data Sources window, click the object you want to bind. Drag the object to the control on the form and then release the mouse button. Alternatively, you can click the control on the form and then use the Properties window to set the appropriate property or properties. (Refer to the *Binding to an Existing Control* section in this chapter.)

Figure 12-8 How to bind an object in a dataset

Having the Computer Create a Bound Control

When you drag an object from a dataset to an empty area on the form, the computer creates a control and automatically binds the object to it. The icon that appears before the object's name in the Data Sources window indicates the type of control the computer will create. The icon in Figure 12-9 indicates that a DataGridView control will be created when you drag the tblEmploy table object to the form. A **DataGridView control** displays the table data in a row and column format, similar to a spreadsheet. Each row in the control represents a record, and each column represents a field. You will learn more about the DataGridView control in the next section. The abl icon shown in Figure 12-9 indicates that the computer will create a text box when you drag a field object to the form.

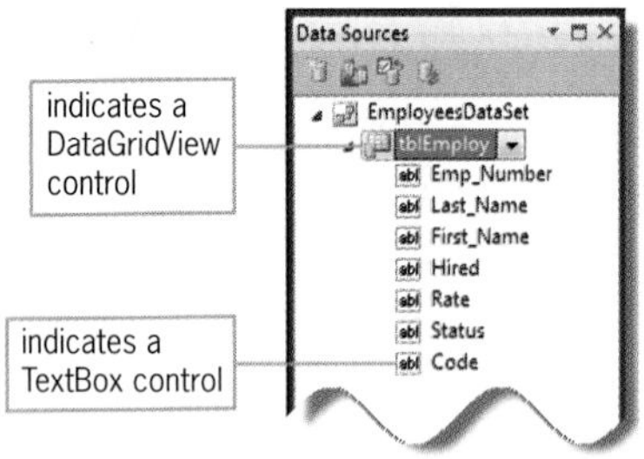

Figure 12-9 Icons in the Data Sources window

When an object is selected in the Data Sources window, you can use the list arrow that appears next to the object's name to change the type of control the computer creates. For example, to display the table data in separate text boxes rather than in a DataGridView control, you click tblEmploy in the Data Sources window and then click the tblEmploy list arrow, as shown in Figure 12-10. Clicking Details in the list tells the computer to create a separate control for each field in the table.

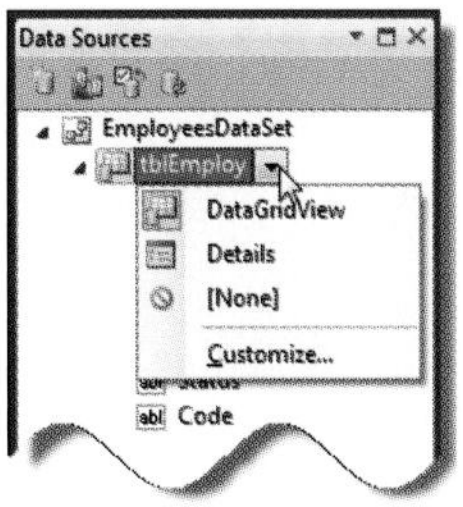

Figure 12-10 Result of clicking the tblEmploy table object's list arrow

Similarly, to display the Last_Name field's data in a label control rather than in a text box, you first click Last_Name in the Data Sources window. You then click the field's list arrow, as shown in Figure 12-11, and then click Label in the list.

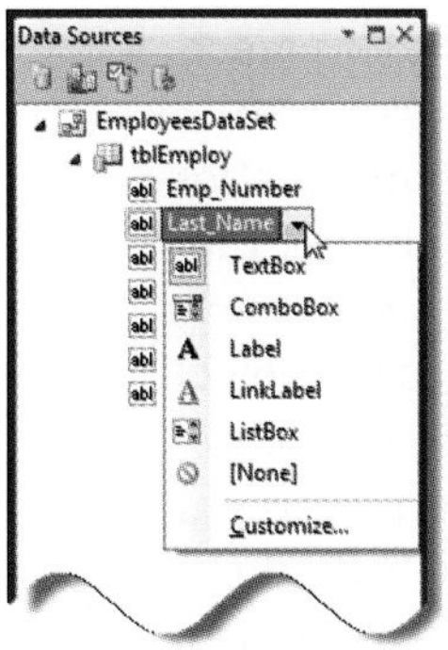

Figure 12-11 Result of clicking the Last_Name field object's list arrow

Figure 12-12 shows the result of dragging the tblEmploy object from the Data Sources window to the MainForm, using the default control type for a table. Besides adding a DataGridView control to the form, the computer also adds a BindingNavigator control. When an application is running, you can use the **BindingNavigator control** to move from one record to the next in the dataset, as well as to add or delete a record and save any changes made to the dataset. The computer also places five objects in the component tray: a DataSet, BindingSource, TableAdapter, TableAdapterManager, and BindingNavigator. As you learned in Chapter 2, the component tray stores objects that do not appear in the user interface while an application is running. An exception to this is the BindingNavigator object, which appears as the BindingNavigator control during both design time and run time.

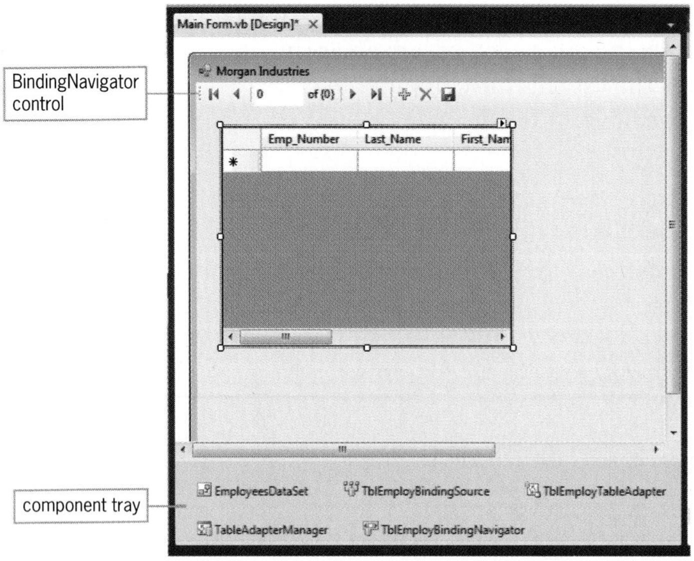

Figure 12-12 Result of dragging the table object to the form

The **TableAdapter object** connects the database to the **DataSet object**, which stores the information you want to access from the database. The TableAdapter is responsible for retrieving the appropriate information from the database and storing it in the DataSet. It also can be used to save to the database any changes made to the data contained in the DataSet. However, in most cases, you will use the **TableAdapterManager object** to save the changes, because it can handle saving data to multiple tables in the DataSet. The **BindingSource object** provides the connection between the DataSet and the bound controls on the form. The TblEmployBindingSource in Figure 12-12 connects the EmployeesDataSet to two bound controls: a DataGridView control and a BindingNavigator control. The TblEmployBindingSource allows the DataGridView control to display the data contained in the EmployeesDataSet. It also allows the BindingNavigator control to access the records stored in the EmployeesDataSet. Figure 12-13 illustrates the relationships among the database, the objects in the component tray, and the bound controls on the form.

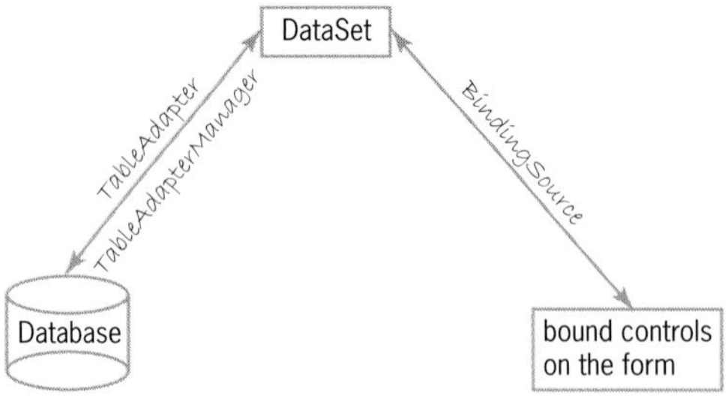

Figure 12-13 Illustration of the relationships among the database, the objects in the component tray, and the bound controls

If a table object's control type is changed from DataGridView to Details, the computer automatically provides the appropriate controls (such as text boxes, labels, and so on) when you drag the table object to the form. It also adds the BindingNavigator control to the form and the five objects to the component tray. The appropriate controls and objects are also automatically included when you drag a field object to an empty area on the form.

The DataGridView Control

The DataGridView control is one of the most popular controls for displaying table data, because it allows you to view a great deal of information at the same time. As mentioned earlier, the control displays the data in a row and column format, similar to a spreadsheet. Each row represents a record, and each column represents a field. The intersection of a row and column in a DataGridView control is called a **cell**. Like the PictureBox control, which you learned about in Chapter 1, the DataGridView control has a task list. The task list appears in Figure 12-14. The first three check boxes on the task list allow you to specify whether the user can add, edit, or delete records during run time. The fourth check box allows you to specify whether the user can reorder the columns in the DataGridView control during run time. Figure 12-15 explains the purpose of each task on the task list.

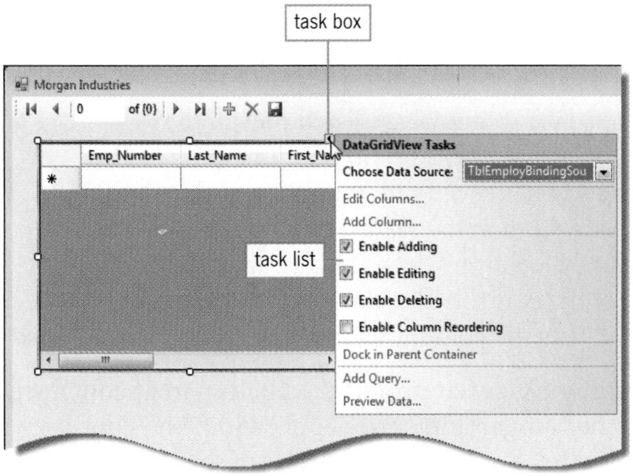

Figure 12-14 Task list for a DataGridView control

Task	**Purpose**
Choose Data Source	select a data source
Edit Columns	open the Edit Columns dialog box (See Figure 12-16)
Add Column	add a new column
Enable Adding	allow/disallow the user to add data
Enable Editing	allow/disallow the user to edit data
Enable Deleting	allow/disallow the user to delete data
Enable Column Reordering	allow/disallow the user to reorder the columns
Dock in Parent Container	bind the borders of the control to the form
Add Query	filter data from a dataset
Preview Data	view the data bound to the control

Figure 12-15 Purpose of each task in the DataGridView's task list

Figure 12-16 shows the Edit Columns dialog box, which opens when you click Edit Columns on the DataGridView control's task list. You can use the Edit Columns dialog box during design time to add and remove columns from the DataGridView control, as well as reorder the columns. You also can use it to set the properties of the bound columns. For example, you can use the DefaultCellStyle property to format a column's data. You also can use the property to change the column's width and alignment. You can use the HeaderText property, on the other hand, to change a column's heading.

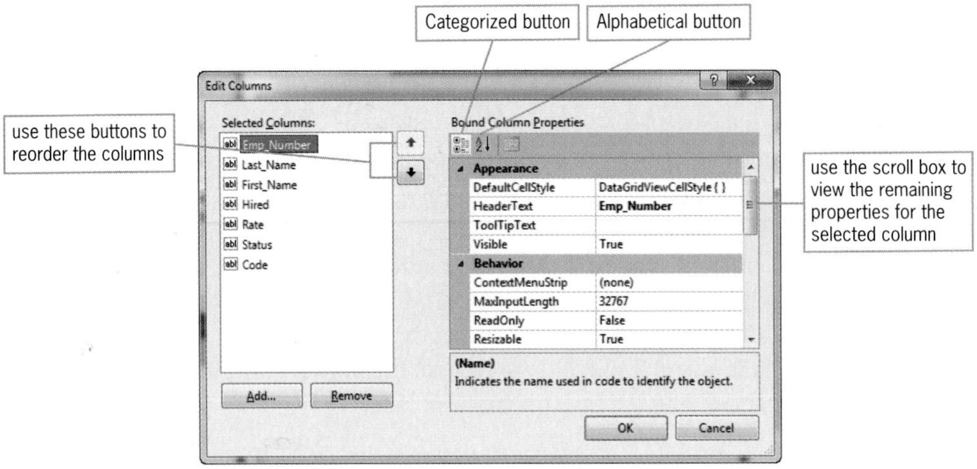

Figure 12-16 Edit Columns dialog box

Some properties of a DataGridView control are listed only in the Properties window. One such property is AutoSizeColumnsMode. The **AutoSizeColumnsMode property** has seven different settings that determine the way the column widths are sized in the DataGridView control. The Fill setting automatically adjusts the column widths so that all of the columns exactly fill the display area of the control. The ColumnHeader setting, on the other hand, automatically adjusts the column widths based on the header text.

Figure 12-17 shows the DataGridView control docked in its parent container, which is the MainForm in the Morgan Industries application. The Edit Columns dialog box was used to change the header text in several columns. It also was used to format and align the data in the Pay Rate column. However, you won't see the effect of the formatting and aligning until the application is started. The Properties window was used to set the control's AutoSizeColumnsMode property to Fill.

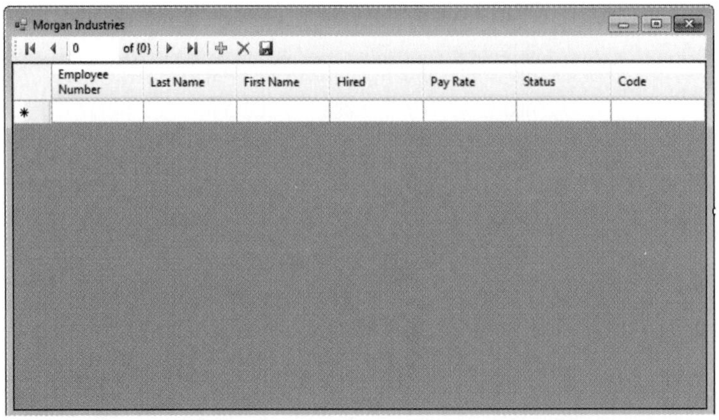

Figure 12-17 DataGridView control after setting some of its properties

Visual Basic Code

In addition to adding the appropriate controls and objects to the application when a table or field object is dragged to the form, the computer also enters some code in the Code Editor window. More specifically, it enters the two event procedures shown in Figure 12-18. The first event procedure, TblEmployBindingNavigatorSaveItem_Click, is processed when you click the Save Data button (the disk) on the BindingNavigator control. The procedure's code validates the changes made to the data before saving the data to the database. Two methods are involved in the save operation: the BindingSource object's EndEdit method and the TableAdapterManager's UpdateAll method. The EndEdit method applies any pending changes (such as new records, deleted records, or changed records) to the dataset. The UpdateAll method commits the dataset changes to the database. The second event procedure in Figure 12-18 is the form's Load event procedure. This procedure uses the TableAdapter object's Fill method to retrieve the data from the database and store it in the DataSet object. In most applications, the code to fill a dataset belongs in the form's Load event procedure. However, as the comments in the Load event procedure indicate, you can either move or delete the code.

```
Private Sub TblEmployBindingNavigatorSaveItem_Click(
ByVal sender As System.Object, ByVal e As System.EventArgs)
     Me.Validate()
     Me.TblEmployBindingSource.EndEdit()
     Me.TableAdapterManager.UpdateAll(Me.EmployeesDataSet)

End Sub

Private Sub MainForm_Load(ByVal sender As System.Object,
ByVal e As System.EventArgs) Handles MyBase.Load
     'TODO: This line of code loads data into the
     'EmployeesDataSet.tblEmploy' table. You can move,
     'or remove it, as needed.
     Me.TblEmployTableAdapter.Fill(Me.EmployeesDataSet.tblEmploy)

End Sub
```

Figure 12-18 Code automatically entered in the Code Editor window

Because it is possible for an error to occur when saving data to a database, it is a good programming practice to add error handling code to the Save Data button's Click event procedure.

Handling Errors in the Code

An error that occurs while an application is running is called an **exception**. If you do not take deliberate steps in your code to handle the exceptions, Visual Basic handles them for you. Typically, it does this by displaying an error message and then abruptly terminating the application. You can prevent your application from behaving in such an unfriendly manner by taking control of the exception handling in your code; you can do this using the **Try...Catch statement**. Figure 12-19 shows the statement's basic syntax and includes examples of using the syntax. The basic syntax contains a Try block and a Catch block. Within the Try block you place the code that could possibly generate an exception. When an exception occurs in the Try block's code, the computer processes the code contained in the Catch block; it then skips

When an error occurs in a procedure's code during run time, programmers say that the procedure "threw an exception."

The Try...Catch statement also has a Finally block. The code in the Finally block is processed whether or not an exception is thrown within the Try block.

to the code following the End Try clause. A description of the exception that occurred is stored in the Message property of the Catch block's `ex` parameter. You can access the description using the code `ex.Message`, as shown in Example 2 in the figure.

HOW TO Use the Try...Catch Statement

Basic syntax

Try
one or more statements that might generate an exception
Catch ex As Exception
one or more statements to execute when an exception occurs
End Try

Example 1

```
Private Sub displayButton_Click(ByVal sender As Object,
ByVal e As System.EventArgs) Handles displayButton.Click

    Dim inFile As IO.StreamReader
    Dim line As String

    Try
        inFile = IO.File.OpenText("names.txt")
        Do Until inFile.Peek = -1
            line = inFile.ReadLine
            nameListBox.Items.Add(line)
        Loop
        inFile.Close()
    Catch ex As Exception
        MessageBox.Show(ex.Message, "JK's",
            MessageBoxButtons.OK,
            MessageBoxIcon.Information)
    End Try
End Sub
```

Example 2

```
Private Sub TblSalesBindingNavigatorSaveItem_Click(
ByVal sender As System.Object, ByVal e As System.EventArgs
) Handles TblSalesBindingNavigatorSaveItem.Click
    Try
        Me.Validate()
        Me.TblSalesBindingSource.EndEdit()
        Me.TableAdapterManager.UpdateAll(Me.SalesDataSet)
    Catch ex As Exception
        MessageBox.Show(ex.Message, "Sales Data",
            MessageBoxButtons.OK,
            MessageBoxIcon.Information)
    End Try
End Sub
```

Figure 12-19 How to use the Try...Catch statement

Figure 12-20 shows a Try...Catch statement entered in the Save Data button's Click event procedure in the Morgan Industries application. If the Try block's code does not produce an exception, the MessageBox.Show method in the block displays the "Changes saved" message. Otherwise, the MessageBox.Show method in the Catch block displays a description of the exception.

```
Private Sub TblEmployBindingNavigatorSaveItem_Click(
ByVal sender As System.Object, ByVal e As System.EventArgs
) Handles TblSalesBindingNavigatorSaveItem.Click
    Try
        Me.Validate()
        Me.TblEmployBindingSource.EndEdit()
        Me.TableAdapterManager.UpdateAll(Me.EmployeesDataSet)
        MessageBox.Show("Changes saved", "Morgan Industries",
            MessageBoxButtons.OK,
            MessageBoxIcon.Information)
    Catch ex As Exception
        MessageBox.Show(ex.Message, "Morgan Industries",
            MessageBoxButtons.OK,
            MessageBoxIcon.Information)
    End Try
End Sub
```

Figure 12-20 Try...Catch statement entered in the Save Data button's Click event procedure

When the Morgan Industries application is started, the statement in the MainForm's Load event procedure (shown earlier in Figure 12-18) retrieves the appropriate data from the Employees database and loads the data into the EmployeesDataSet. The data appears in the DataGridView control because the control is bound to the dataset's tblEmploy object. Figure 12-21 shows the result of starting the Morgan Industries application. Notice that the first cell in the DataGridView control is highlighted (selected). You can use the arrow keys on your keyboard to move the highlight to a different cell in the DataGridView control. When a cell is highlighted, you can modify its contents by simply typing the new data.

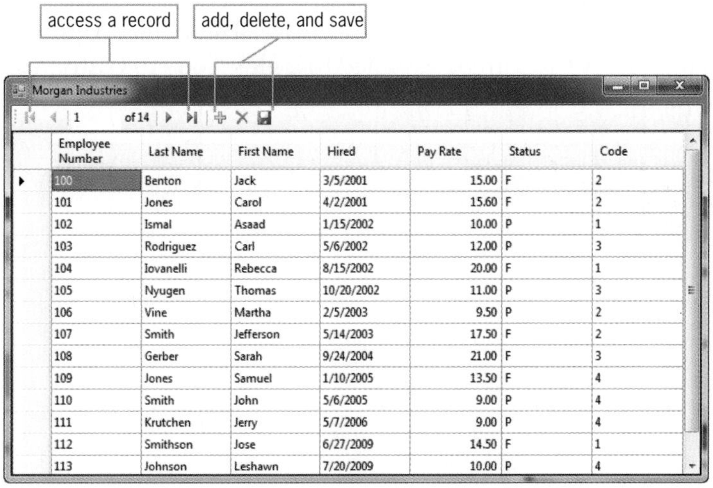

access a record
add, delete, and save
Morgan Industries
1
of 14
Employee Number
Last Name
First Name
Hired
Pay Rate
Status
Code
100 Benton Jack 3/5/2001 15.00 F 2
101 Jones Carol 4/2/2001 15.60 F 2
102 Ismal Asaad 1/15/2002 10.00 P 1
103 Rodriguez Carl 5/6/2002 12.00 P 3
104 Iovanelli Rebecca 8/15/2002 20.00 F 1
105 Nyugen Thomas 10/20/2002 11.00 P 3
106 Vine Martha 2/5/2003 9.50 P 2
107 Smith Jefferson 5/14/2003 17.50 F 2
108 Gerber Sarah 9/24/2004 21.00 F 3
109 Jones Samuel 1/10/2005 13.50 F 4
110 Smith John 5/6/2005 9.00 P 4
111 Krutchen Jerry 5/7/2006 9.00 P 4
112 Smithson Jose 6/27/2009 14.50 F 1
113 Johnson Leshawn 7/20/2009 10.00 P 4

Figure 12-21 Sample run of the Morgan Industries application

A tooltip appears when you hover your mouse pointer over a button on a BindingNavigator control. The tooltip indicates the button's purpose.

As indicated in Figure 12-21, the BindingNavigator control provides buttons for accessing the first, last, previous, and next records in the dataset. You also can use the control to access a record by its record number. The record number for the first record in a dataset is 1; the record number for the second record is 2; and so on. The BindingNavigator control also contains buttons for adding a new record to the dataset, deleting a record from the

If you want to experiment with the DataGridView version of the Morgan Industries application, open the solution contained in the Try It 1! folder. In the solution, the database file's Copy to Output Directory property is set to "Copy if newer."

dataset, and saving the changes made to the dataset. You can add additional items (such as buttons and text boxes) to a BindingNavigator control and also delete items from the control. You will learn how to add items to and delete items from a BindingNavigator control in the *Personalizing a BindingNavigator Control* section in this chapter.

The Copy to Output Directory Property

When the Data Source Configuration Wizard connected the Morgan Industries application to the Employees database, it added the database file (Employees.accdb) to the application's project folder. (You can verify this by referring to the Solution Explorer window shown earlier in Figure 12-5.) A database file contained in a project is referred to as a local database file. The way Visual Basic saves changes to a local database file is determined by the file's **Copy to Output Directory property**. When the property is set to its default setting, Copy always, the file is copied from the project folder to the project folder's bin\Debug folder each time you start the application. In this case, the Employees.accdb file is copied from the Morgan Industries Project folder to the Morgan Industries Project\bin\Debug folder. As a result, the file will appear in two different folders in the solution. When you click the Save Data button on the BindingNavigator control, any changes made in the DataGridView control are recorded only in the file stored in the bin\Debug folder; the file stored in the project folder is not changed. The next time you start the application, the file in the project folder is copied to the bin\Debug folder, overwriting the file that contains the changes. One way to fix this problem is to set the database file's Copy to Output Directory property to "Copy if newer." The "Copy if newer" setting tells the computer to compare the dates on both files to determine which file has the newer (more current) date. If the database file in the project folder has the newer date, the computer should copy it to the bin\Debug folder; otherwise, it shouldn't copy it. Figure 12-22 lists the values that can be assigned to a file's Copy to Output Directory property.

HOW TO Use the Copy to Output Directory Property

Property setting	Meaning
Do not copy	the file in the project folder is never copied to the bin\Debug folder
Copy always	the file in the project folder is copied to the bin\Debug folder each time the application is started
Copy if newer	when an application is started, the computer compares the date on the file in the project folder with the date on the file in the bin\Debug folder; the file from the project folder is copied to the bin\Debug folder only when its date is newer

Figure 12-22 How to use the Copy to Output Directory property

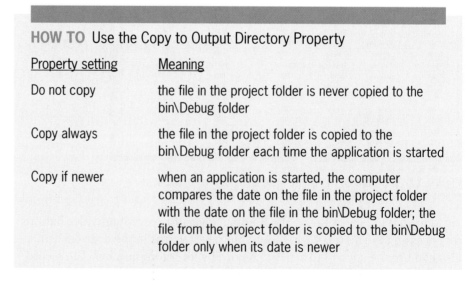

Binding to an Existing Control

As indicated earlier in Figure 12-8, you can bind an object in a dataset to an existing control on the form. The easiest way to do this is by dragging the object from the Data Sources window to the control. However, you also can click the control and then set one or more properties in the Properties window. The appropriate property (or properties) to set depends on the control you are binding. For example, you use the DataSource property to bind a DataGridView control. However, you use the DataSource and DisplayMember properties to bind a ListBox control. To bind label and text box controls, you use the DataBindings/Text property.

When you drag an object from the Data Sources window to an existing control, the computer does not create a new control; instead, it binds the object to the existing control. Because a new control does not need to be created, the computer ignores the control type specified for the object in the Data Sources window. Therefore, it is not necessary to change the control type in the Data Sources window to match the existing control's type. In other words, you can drag an object that is associated with a text box in the Data Sources window to a label control on the form. The computer will bind the object to the label, but it will not change the label to a text box.

Figure 12-23 shows the result of dragging four field objects to four existing label controls in a different version of the Morgan Industries application. In this case, the computer will bind the Emp_Number, Last_Name, Status, and Code field objects to the numberLabel, lastNameLabel, statusLabel, and codeLabel controls, respectively. In addition to binding the field objects to the controls, the computer also adds the DataSet, BindingSource, TableAdapter, and TableAdapterManager objects to the component tray. However, notice that when you drag an object from the Data Sources window to an existing control, the computer does not add a BindingNavigator object to the component tray, nor does it add a BindingNavigator control to the form. You can use the BindingNavigator tool in the toolbox to add a BindingNavigator control and object to the application. You then would set the control's DataSource property to the name of the BindingSource object (in this case, TblEmployBindingSource).

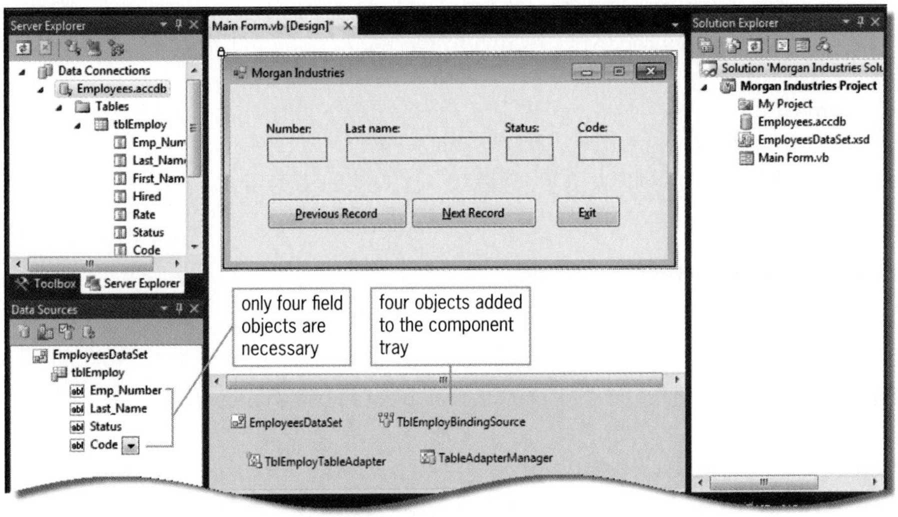

Figure 12-23 Result of dragging field objects to existing controls

When you drag an object from the Data Sources window to an existing control, the computer enters the Load event procedure shown earlier in Figure 12-18. Recall that the procedure uses the TableAdapter object's Fill method to retrieve the data from the database and store it in the DataSet object. Figure 12-24 shows a sample run of this version of the Morgan Industries application. Only the first record in the dataset appears in the interface. Because the form does not contain a BindingNavigator control, which would allow you to move from one record to the next, you will need to code the Next Record and Previous Record buttons to view the remaining records.

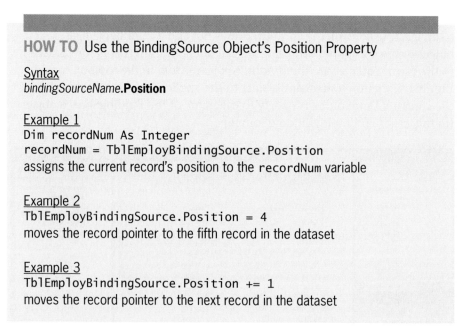

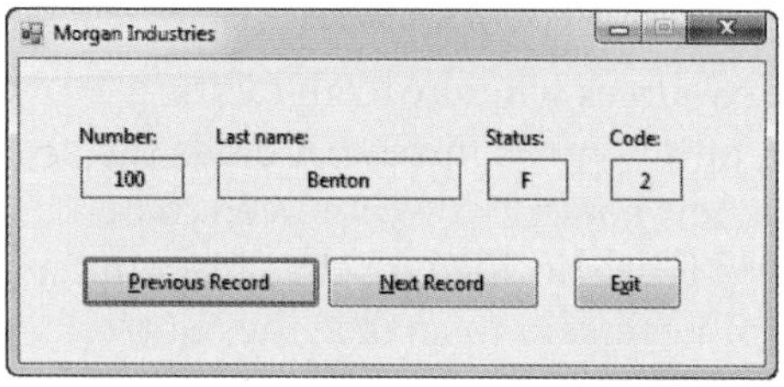

Figure 12-24 Sample run of a different version of the Morgan Industries application

Coding the Next Record and Previous Record Buttons

The BindingSource object uses an invisible record pointer to keep track of the current record in the dataset. It stores the position of the record pointer in its **Position property**. The first record is in position 0; the second is in position 1, and so on. Figure 12-25 shows the Position property's syntax and includes examples of using the property.

HOW TO Use the BindingSource Object's Position Property

Syntax
bindingSourceName.**Position**

Example 1
```
Dim recordNum As Integer
recordNum = TblEmployBindingSource.Position
```
assigns the current record's position to the `recordNum` variable

Example 2
```
TblEmployBindingSource.Position = 4
```
moves the record pointer to the fifth record in the dataset

Example 3
```
TblEmployBindingSource.Position += 1
```
moves the record pointer to the next record in the dataset

Figure 12-25 How to use the BindingSource object's Position property

Rather than using the Position property to position the record pointer in a dataset, you also can use the BindingSource object's Move methods. The **Move methods** move the record pointer to the first, last, next, or previous record in the dataset. Figure 12-26 shows each Move method's syntax and includes examples of using two of the methods.

HOW TO Use the BindingSource Object's Move Methods

Syntax
bindingSourceName.**MoveFirst()**
bindingSourceName.**MoveLast()**
bindingSourceName.**MoveNext()**
bindingSourceName.**MovePrevious()**

Example 1
`TblEmployBindingSource.MoveFirst()`
moves the record pointer to the first record in the dataset

Example 2
`TblEmployBindingSource.MoveNext()`
moves the record pointer to the next record in the dataset

Figure 12-26 How to use the BindingSource object's Move methods

When the user clicks the Next Record button in the Morgan Industries interface, the button's Click event procedure should move the record pointer to the next record in the dataset. Similarly, when the user clicks the Previous Record button, its Click event procedure should move the record pointer to the previous record in the dataset. You can use the TblEmployBindingSource object's MoveNext and MovePrevious methods to code the procedures, as shown in Figure 12-27.

```
Private Sub nextButton_Click(ByVal sender As Object,
ByVal e As System.EventArgs) Handles nextButton.Click
      ' moves the record pointer to the next record

      TblEmployBindingSource.MoveNext()
End Sub

Private Sub previousButton_Click(ByVal sender As Object,
ByVal e As System.EventArgs) Handles previousButton.Click
      ' moves the record pointer to the previous record

      TblEmployBindingSource.MovePrevious()
End Sub
```

Figure 12-27 Code entered in the Click event procedures for the Next Record and Previous Record buttons

If you want to experiment with the Labels version of the Morgan Industries application, open the solution contained in the Try It 2! folder. In the solution, the database file's Copy to Output Directory property is set to "Copy if newer."

Accessing the Value Stored in a Field

At times, you may need to access the value stored in a field object in a dataset. You can do so using the syntax shown in Figure 12-28. The figure also includes examples of accessing some of the fields in the EmployeesDataSet.

HOW TO Access the Value Stored in a Field Object

Syntax
dataSetObjectName.tableName(*recordNumber*).*fieldName*

Example 1
```
Dim last As String
last = EmployeesDataSet.tblEmploy(0).Last_Name
```
assigns the value stored in the first record's Last_Name field (Benton) to the `last` variable

Example 2
```
Dim payRate As Double
payRate = EmployeesDataSet.tblEmploy(4).Rate
```
assigns the value stored in the fifth record's Rate field (20) to the `payRate` variable

Figure 12-28 How to access the value stored in a field object

The answers to Mini-Quiz questions are located in Appendix A.

Mini-Quiz 12-2

1. The _______________ object connects a database to a DataSet object.
   a. BindingSource
   b. DataBase
   c. DataGridView
   d. TableAdapter

2. An application contains the following objects: FriendsDataSet, TblNamesBindingSource, TblNamesTableAdapter, TableAdapterManager, and TblNamesBindingNavigator. Which of the following statements retrieves data from the Friends database and stores it in the FriendsDataSet?
   a. `Me.FriendsDataSet.Fill(Friends.accdb)`
   b. `Me.TblNamesBindingSource.Fill(Me.FriendsDataSet)`
   c. `Me.TblNamesBindingNavigator.Fill(FriendsDataSet.tblNames)`
   d. `Me.TblNamesTableAdapter.Fill(Me.FriendsDataSet.tblNames)`

3. If an application contains the `Catch ex As Exception` clause, you can use _______________ to access the exception's description.
   a. `ex.Description`
   b. `ex.Exception`

c. `ex.Message`

d. `Exception.Description`

4. If the current record is the second record in the dataset, which of the following statements will position the record pointer on the first record?

   a. `TblEmployBindingSource.Position = 0`

   b. `TblEmployBindingSource.Position -= 1`

   c. `TblEmployBindingSource.MoveFirst()`

   d. all of the above

Creating a Query

When used to query a dataset, LINQ is referred to more specifically as LINQ to Datasets.

As you will learn later in this chapter, you also can use LINQ to perform arithmetic calculations (such as a sum or an average) on the data stored in a dataset.

You can arrange the records stored in a dataset in any order. The records in the EmployeesDataSet, for example, can be arranged by employee number, pay rate, status, and so on. You also can control the number of records you want to view at any one time. For example, you can view all of the records in the EmployeesDataSet; or, you can choose to view only the records for the part-time employees. You use a **query** to specify both the records to select in a dataset and the order in which to arrange the records. You can create a query in Visual Basic 2010 using a language feature called **Language Integrated Query** or, more simply, **LINQ**.

Figure 12-29 shows the basic syntax of LINQ when used to select and arrange records in a dataset. The figure also includes examples of using the syntax. In the syntax, *variableName* and *elementName* can be any names you choose, as long as the name follows the naming rules for variables. In other words, there is nothing special about the `records` and `employee` names used in the examples. The Where and Order By clauses are optional parts of the syntax. You use the **Where clause**, which contains a *condition*, to limit the records you want to view. Similar to the *condition* in the If...Then...Else and Do...Loop statements, the *condition* in a Where clause specifies a requirement that must be met for a record to be selected. The **Order By clause** is used to arrange the records in either ascending (the default) or descending order by one or more fields. Notice that the LINQ syntax does not require you to specify the data type of the variable in the Dim statement. Instead, the syntax allows the computer to infer the data type from the value being assigned to the variable. However, for this inference to take place, you must set Option Infer to On (rather than to Off, as you have been doing). You can do this by entering the `Option Infer On` statement in the General Declarations section of the Code Editor window.

HOW TO Use LINQ to Select and Arrange Records in a Dataset

Basic syntax

Dim *variableName* **= From** *elementName* **In** *dataset.table*
    [**Where** *condition*]
    [**Order By** *elementName.fieldName1* [**Ascending** | **Descending**]
        [, *elementName.fieldNameN* [**Ascending** | **Descending**]]]
    Select *elementName*

Figure 12-29 How to use LINQ to select and arrange records in a dataset *(continues)*

(continued)

Example 1
```
Dim records = From employee In EmployeesDataSet.tblEmploy
              Select employee
```
selects all of the records in the dataset

Example 2
```
Dim records = From employee In EmployeesDataSet.tblEmploy
              Order By employee.Code
              Select employee
```
selects all of the records in the dataset and arranges them in ascending order by the Code field

Example 3
```
Dim records = From employee In EmployeesDataSet.tblEmploy
              Where employee.Status.ToUpper = "P"
              Select employee
```
selects only the part-time employee records in the dataset

Example 4
```
Dim records = From employee In EmployeesDataSet.tblEmploy
              Where employee.Status.ToUpper = "P"
              Order By employee.Code Descending
              Select employee
```
selects only the part-time employee records in the dataset and arranges them in descending order by the Code field

If you want to experiment with the code shown in Figures 12-29 and 12-30, open the solution contained in the Try It 3! folder.

Figure 12-29 How to use LINQ to select and arrange records in a dataset

The syntax and examples in Figure 12-29 merely select and/or arrange the appropriate records. To actually view the records, you need to assign the variable's contents to the DataSource property of a BindingSource control. The syntax for doing this is shown in Figure 12-30 along with an example.

HOW TO Assign a LINQ Variable's Contents to a BindingSource Control

Basic syntax
bindingSource.**DataSource** = *variableName*.**AsDataView**

Example
```
TblEmployBindingSource.DataSource = records.AsDataView
```
assigns the contents of the `records` variable (from Figure 12-29) to the TblEmployBindingSource control

Figure 12-30 How to assign a LINQ variable's contents to a BindingSource control

Figure 12-31 provides another example of using LINQ to select records from a dataset. The LINQ code in this example selects records whose Last_Name field begins with one or more letters entered by the user. The condition in the Where clause uses the Like operator and the asterisk pattern-matching character to compare the contents of each record's Last_Name field with the user's entry followed by zero or more characters. You learned about the Like operator and the pattern-matching characters in Chapter 10. Figure 12-32 shows a sample run of the application when the user enters the letter s in the InputBox function's dialog box.

```
Option Explicit On
Option Strict On
Option Infer On

Private Sub findButton_Click(ByVal sender As Object,
ByVal e As System.EventArgs) Handles findButton.Click
    ' selects records whose last name begins with the user's entry

    Const Prompt As String = "One or more letters " &
        "(leave empty to retrieve all records):"

    Dim findName As String =
        InputBox(Prompt, "Find Last Name").ToUpper

    Dim records = From employee In EmployeesDataSet.tblEmploy
        Where employee.Last_Name.ToUpper Like findName & "*"
        Select employee

    TblEmployBindingSource.DataSource = records.AsDataView
End Sub
```

be sure to set Option Infer to On in the General Declarations section

LINQ code to select the records

assigns the LINQ variable to the BindingSource control

Figure 12-31 LINQ code entered in the Find Last Name button's Click event procedure

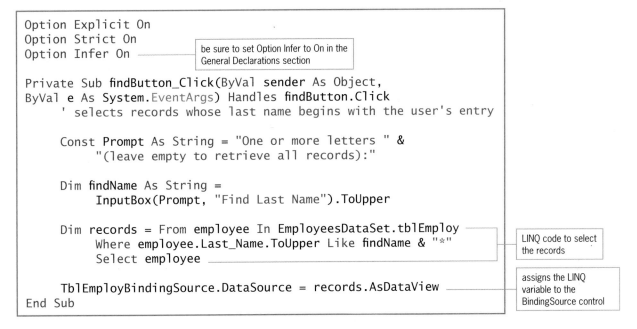

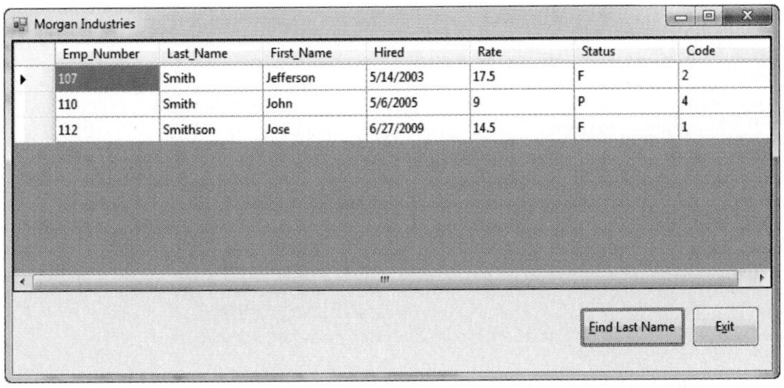

Morgan Industries
Emp_Number
Last_Name
First_Name
Hired
Rate
Status
Code
107 Smith Jefferson 5/14/2003 17.5 F 2
110 Smith John 5/6/2005 9 P 4
112 Smithson Jose 6/27/2009 14.5 F 1
Find Last Name
Exit

Figure 12-32 Employees whose last name begins with the letter S

If you want to experiment with the code shown in Figure 12-31, open the solution contained in the Try It 4! folder.

Personalizing a BindingNavigator Control

As mentioned earlier, the BindingNavigator control contains buttons that allow you to move to a different record in the dataset, as well as to add or delete a record and save any changes made to the dataset. At times, you may want to include additional items—such as another button, a text box, or a drop-down button—on the BindingNavigator control. Figure 12-33 lists the steps for adding and deleting items, and Figure 12-34 shows the Items Collection Editor window.

HOW TO Manipulate the Items on a BindingNavigator Control

To add an item to a BindingNavigator control:

1. Click the BindingNavigator control's task box and then click Edit Items to open the Items Collection Editor window.
2. If necessary, click the "Select item and add to list below" arrow. See Figure 12-34.
3. Click the item you want to add to the BindingNavigator control and then click the Add button.
4. If necessary, you can use the up and down arrows to reposition the item.

To delete an item from a BindingNavigator control:

1. Click the BindingNavigator control's task box and then click Edit Items to open the Items Collection Editor window.
2. In the Members list, click the item you want to remove and then click the *X* button.

Figure 12-33 How to manipulate the items on a BindingNavigator control

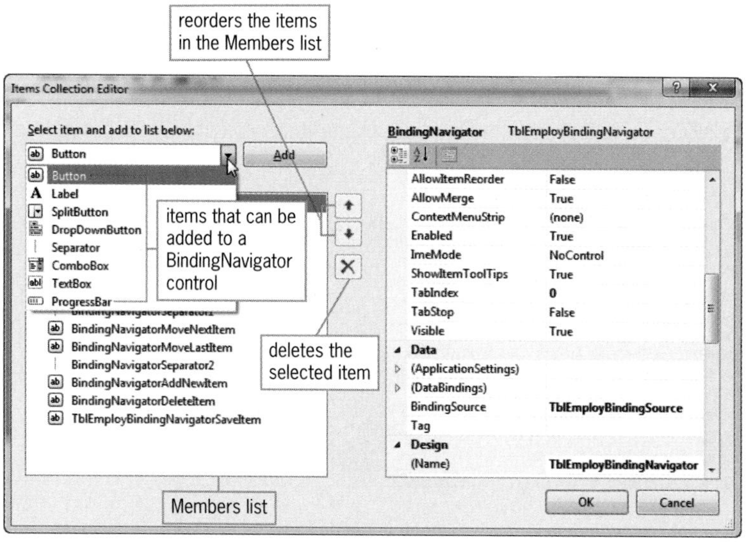

Figure 12-34 Items Collection Editor window

You can watch a demonstration of adding a DropDownButton item to a BindingNavigator control by viewing the Ch12DropDownButton video.

Figure 12-35 shows a DropDownButton on the Morgan Industries BindingNavigator control during design time. The DropDownButton offers a menu that contains three options, called menu items. The menu items allow the user to determine the average pay rate for all employees, part-time employees, or full-time employees. You will learn how to calculate these values in the next section.

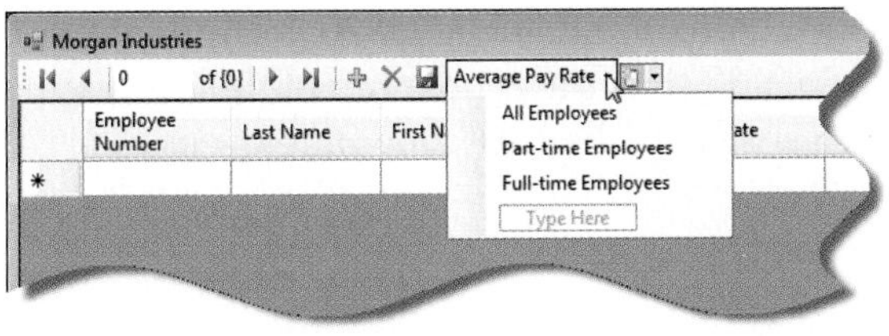

Figure 12-35 DropDownButton added to the BindingNavigator control

Using the LINQ Aggregate Operators

LINQ provides several aggregate operators that you can use when querying a dataset. The most commonly used aggregate operators are Average, Count, Max, Min, and Sum. An **aggregate operator** returns a single value from a group of values. The Sum operator, for example, returns the sum of the values in the group, whereas the Min operator returns the smallest value in the group. You include an aggregate operator in a LINQ statement using the syntax shown in Figure 12-36. The figure also includes examples of using the syntax.

HOW TO Use the LINQ Aggregate Operators

Syntax

Dim *variableName* [**As** *dataType*] =
    Aggregate *elementName* **In** *dataset.table*
    [**Where** *condition*]
    Select *elementName.fieldName*
    Into *aggregateOperator***()**

Example 1

```
Dim avgRate As Double =
     Aggregate employee In EmployeesDataSet.tblEmploy
     Select employee.Rate Into Average()
```

calculates the average of the pay rates in the dataset and assigns the result to the `avgRate` variable

Example 2

```
Dim maxRate As Double =
     Aggregate employee In EmployeesDataSet.tblEmploy
     Where employee.Status.ToUpper = "P"
     Select employee.Rate Into Max()
```

finds the highest pay rate for a part-time employee and assigns the result to the `maxRate` variable

Example 3

```
Dim counter As Integer =
     Aggregate employee In EmployeesDataSet.tblEmploy
     Where employee.Code = 2
     Select employee.Emp_Number Into Count()
```

counts the number of employees whose department code is 2 and assigns the result to the `counter` variable

Figure 12-36 How to use the LINQ aggregate operators

If you want to experiment with the code shown in Figure 12-36, open the solution contained in the Try It 5! folder.

Figure 12-37 shows the code associated with the menu items in the Morgan Industries application, and Figure 12-38 shows a sample run of the Morgan Industries application when the user selects the Part-time Employees item from the DropDownButton.

```
Option Explicit On
Option Strict On
Option Infer On          ← be sure to set Option Infer to On in the General Declarations section

Private Sub avgAllItem_Click(ByVal sender As Object,
ByVal e As System.EventArgs) Handles avgAllItem.Click
     ' displays the average pay rate for all employees

     Dim avgRate As Double =                      ← calculates the average pay rate for all employees
               Aggregate employee In EmployeesDataSet.tblEmploy
               Select employee.Rate Into Average()

     MessageBox.Show("Average pay rate for all employees: " &
               avgRate.ToString("C2"), "Morgan Industries",
               MessageBoxButtons.OK,
               MessageBoxIcon.Information)
End Sub

Private Sub avgParttimeItem_Click(ByVal sender As Object,
ByVal e As System.EventArgs) Handles avgParttimeItem.Click
     ' displays the average pay rate for part-time employees

     Dim avgRate As Double =                      ← calculates the average pay rate for part-time employees
               Aggregate employee In EmployeesDataSet.tblEmploy
               Where employee.Status.ToUpper = "P"
               Select employee.Rate Into Average()

     MessageBox.Show("Average pay rate for part-time employees: " &
               avgRate.ToString("C2"), "Morgan Industries",
               MessageBoxButtons.OK,
               MessageBoxIcon.Information)
End Sub

Private Sub avgFulltimeItem_Click(ByVal sender As Object,
ByVal e As System.EventArgs) Handles avgFulltimeItem.Click
     ' displays the average pay rate for full-time employees

     Dim avgRate As Double =                      ← calculates the average pay rate for full-time employees
               Aggregate employee In EmployeesDataSet.tblEmploy
               Where employee.Status.ToUpper = "F"
               Select employee.Rate Into Average()

     MessageBox.Show("Average pay rate for full-time employees: " &
               avgRate.ToString("C2"), "Morgan Industries",
               MessageBoxButtons.OK,
               MessageBoxIcon.Information)
End Sub
```

Figure 12-37 Code associated with the three items on the DropDownButton

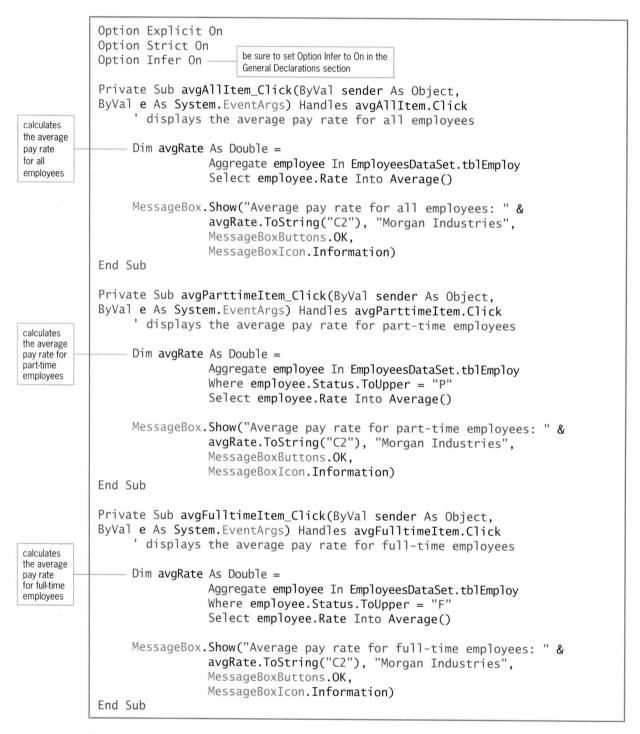

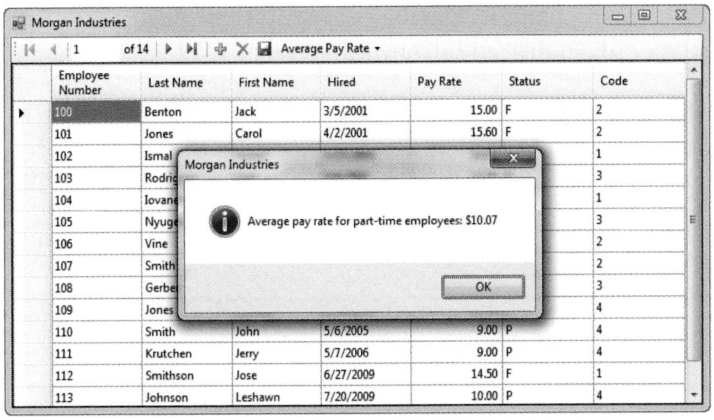

Figure 12-38 Average pay rate for part-time employees

If you want to experiment with the LINQ version of the Morgan Industries application, open the solution contained in the Try It 6! folder.

The answers to Mini-Quiz questions are located in Appendix A.

Mini-Quiz 12-3

1. Which of the following statements selects all of the records in the tblStates table?

a.
```
Dim records =
        From state In StatesDataSet.tblStates
        Select All state
```

b.
```
Dim records =
        From state In StatesDataSet.tblStates
        Select state
```

c.
```
Dim records =
        Select state From StatesDataSet.tblStates
```

d.
```
Dim records =
        From StatesDataSet.tblStates
        Select tblStates.state
```

2. The tblCities table contains a numeric field named Population. Which of the following statements calculates the total population of all the cities in the table?

a.
```
Dim total As Integer =
      Aggregate city In CitiesDataSet.tblCities
      Select city.Population
      Into Sum()
```

b.
```
Dim total As Integer =
      Sum city In CitiesDataSet.tblCities
      Select city.Population
      Into total
```

c.
```
Dim total As Integer =
      Aggregate CitiesDataSet.tblCities.city
      Select city.Population
      Into Sum()
```

d.
```
Dim total As Integer =
      Sum city In CitiesDataSet.tblCities.population
```

3. In a LINQ statement, you can use the ______________ clause to sort the selected records in descending order.
   a. Arrange
   b. Order By
   c. Sort
   d. Where

You have completed the concepts section of Chapter 12. The Programming Tutorial section is next.

PROGRAMMING TUTORIAL 1

Creating the Trivia Game Application

The Ch12ProgTut1 video demonstrates all of the steps in Programming Tutorial 1.

In this tutorial, you create an application that displays trivia questions and answers. The questions and answers are stored in a Microsoft Access database named Trivia.accdb. The database contains one table, which is named tblGame. The table contains nine records. Each record has six fields named Question, AnswerA, AnswerB, AnswerC, AnswerD, and CorrectAnswer. The application displays a question in the interface and then allows the user to answer the question. It keeps track of the number of incorrect responses made by the user, and it displays that information after all nine questions have been answered. Figures 12-39 and 12-40 show the application's TOE chart and MainForm, respectively. The interface contains five text boxes, one label, four radio buttons, and two buttons.

Task	Object	Event
End the application	exitButton	Click
Fill the dataset with data	MainForm	Load
1. Compare the user's answer with the correct answer 2. Keep track of the number of incorrect answers 3. Display the next question and answers from the dataset 4. Display the number of incorrect answers	submitButton	Click
Display questions from the dataset	questionTextBox	None
Display answers from the dataset	aTextBox, bTextBox, cTextBox, dTextBox	None
Get the user's answer	aRadioButton, bRadioButton, cRadioButton, dRadioButton	None

Figure 12-39 TOE chart for the Trivia Game application

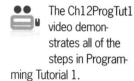

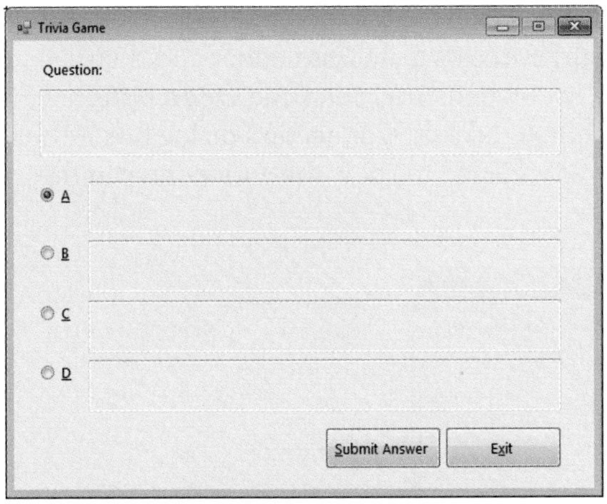

Figure 12-40 MainForm for the Trivia Game application

Connecting the Application to the Trivia Database

Included in the data files for this book is a partially completed Trivia Game application. To complete the application, you need to connect it to the Trivia database and then finish coding it.

To open the Trivia Game application and then connect it to the Trivia database:

1. Start Visual Studio or the Express Edition of Visual Basic. If necessary, open the Solution Explorer window.
2. Open the **Trivia Game Solution** (**Trivia Game Solution.sln**) file, which is contained in the VbReloaded2010\Chap12\Trivia Game Solution folder. Open the designer window, if necessary, and then auto-hide the Solution Explorer window.
3. If necessary, use the View menu to open either the Server Explorer window (Visual Studio) or Database Explorer window (Visual Basic Express Edition).
4. If necessary, open the Data Sources window by clicking **Data** on the menu bar and then clicking **Show Data Sources**.
5. Click **Add New Data Source** in the Data Sources window to start the Data Source Configuration Wizard. If necessary, click **Database** on the Choose a Data Source Type screen.
6. Click the **Next** button to display the Choose a Database Model screen. If necessary, click **Dataset**.
7. Click the **Next** button to display the Choose Your Data Connection screen. Click the **New Connection** button to open the Add Connection dialog box. If Microsoft Access Database File (OLE DB) does not appear in the Data source box, click the **Change** button to open the Change Data Source dialog box, click **Microsoft Access Database File**, and then click the **OK** button.

8. Click the **Browse** button in the Add Connection dialog box. Open the VbReloaded2010\Chap12\Access Databases folder and then click **Trivia.accdb** in the list of filenames. Click the **Open** button. Figure 12-41 shows the completed Add Connection dialog box. (The dialog box in the figure was widened to show the entire entry in the Database file name box.)

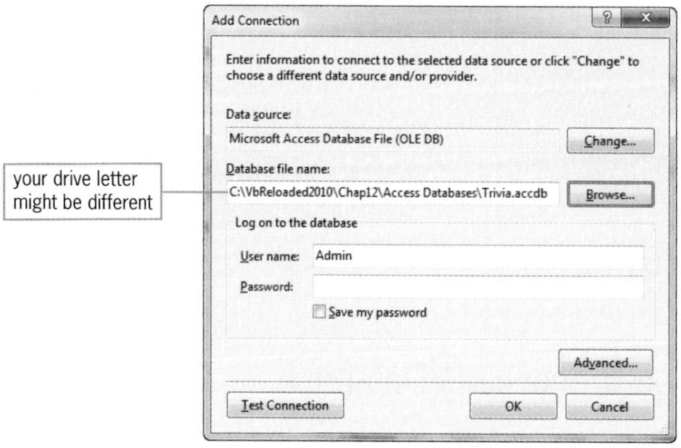

Figure 12-41 Completed Add Connection dialog box

9. Click the **Test Connection** button. The "Test connection succeeded." message appears in a message box. Close the message box.

10. Click the **OK** button to close the Add Connection dialog box. Trivia.accdb appears in the Choose Your Data Connection screen. Click the **Next** button. The message box shown in Figure 12-42 opens. The message asks whether you want to include the database file in the current project. By including the file in the current project, you can more easily copy the application and its database to another computer.

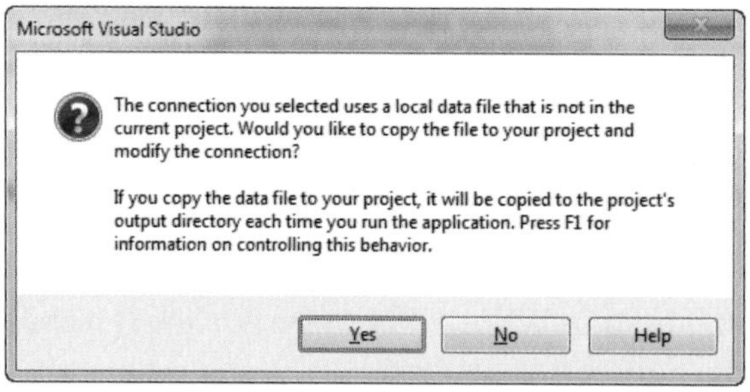

Figure 12-42 Message regarding copying the database file

11. Click the **Yes** button to add the Trivia.accdb file to the application's project folder. The Save the Connection String to the Application Configuration File screen appears next. The name of the connection string, TriviaConnectionString, appears on the screen. If necessary, select the **Yes, save the connection as** check box.

12. Click the **Next** button to display the Choose Your Database Objects screen. Expand the Tables node and then expand the tblGame node. You use this screen to select the table and/or field objects to include in the dataset, which is automatically named TriviaDataSet.

13. In this application, you need the dataset to include all of the fields. Click the **empty box** next to tblGame. Doing this selects the table and field check boxes, as shown in Figure 12-43.

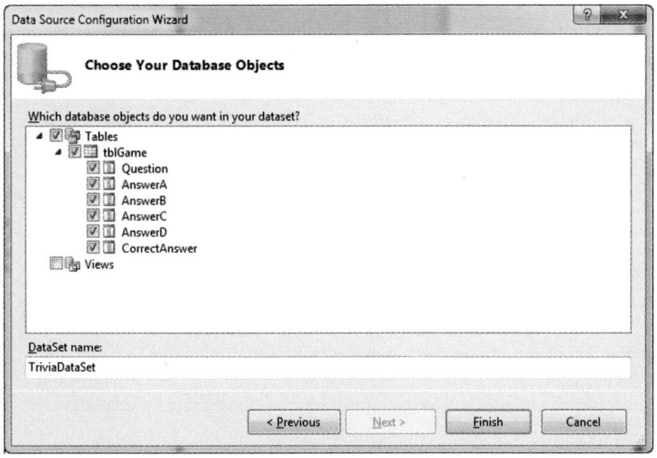

Figure 12-43 Objects selected in the Choose Your Database Objects screen

14. Click the **Finish** button. The computer adds the TriviaDataSet to the Data Sources window. Expand the tblGame node in the Data Sources window. As shown in Figure 12-44, the dataset contains one table and six field objects.

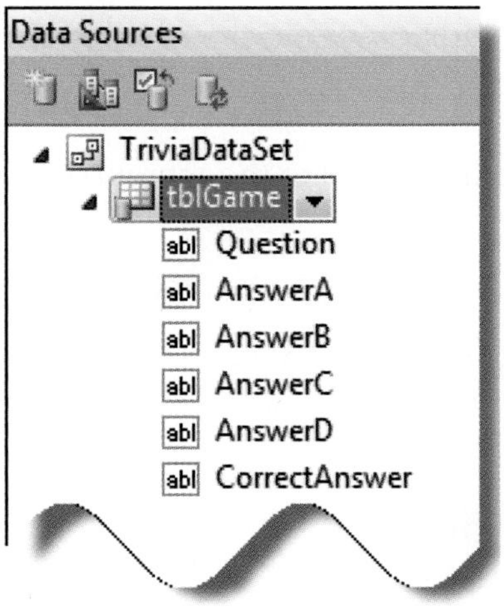

Figure 12-44 TriviaDataSet added to the Data Sources window

15. Now, preview the data contained in the dataset. Click the **form**, click **Data** on the menu bar, and then click **Preview Data** to open the Preview Data dialog box. Click the **Preview** button. See Figure 12-45.

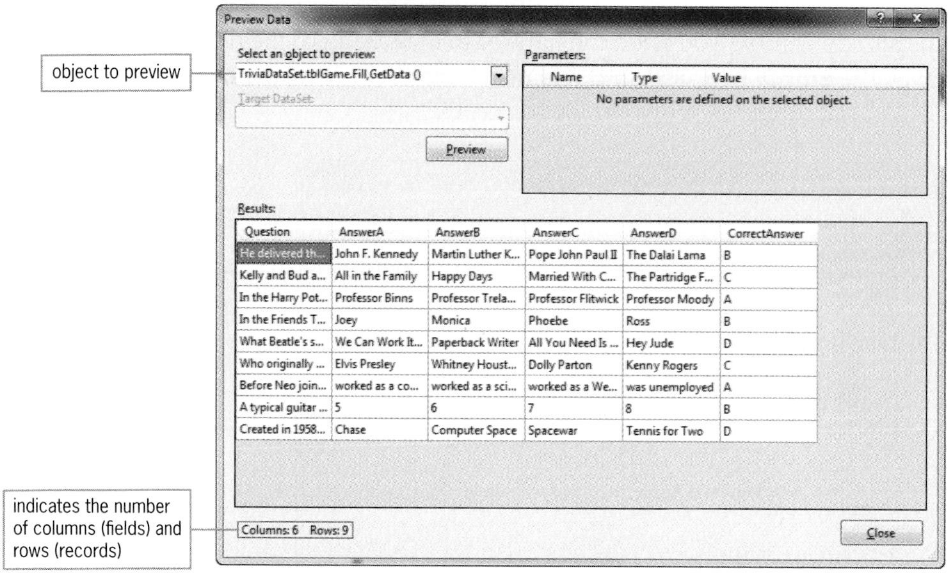

Figure 12-45 Preview Data dialog box

16. Click the **Close** button to close the Preview Data dialog box. If necessary, auto-hide the following windows: Server (Database) Explorer, Solution Explorer, and Properties. In this application, the user will not be adding, deleting, or modifying the records in the dataset, so you do not need to change the database file's Copy to Output Directory property from "Copy always" to "Copy if newer."

Binding the Field Objects to the Text Boxes

Next, you will bind the field objects in the dataset to the appropriate text boxes on the form.

To bind the field objects to the text boxes and then test the application:

1. Click the **Question** field object in the Data Sources window and then drag the field object to the questionTextBox, but don't release the mouse button. See Figure 12-46.

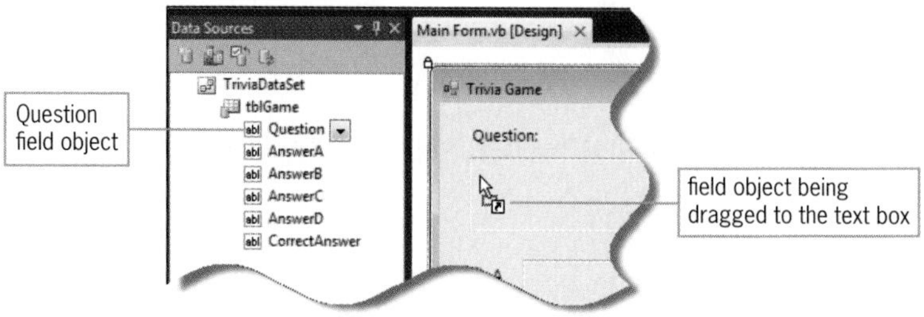

Figure 12-46 Question field object being dragged to the questionTextBox

2. Release the mouse button. The computer binds the Question field object to the questionTextBox. It also adds the TriviaDataSet,

TblGameBindingSource, TblGameTableAdapter, and TableAdapter-Manager objects to the component tray.

3. Drag the AnswerA, AnswerB, AnswerC, and AnswerD field objects to the appropriate text boxes.

4. Save the solution and then start the application. The first record in the dataset appears in the interface. See Figure 12-47.

Figure 12-47 Interface showing the first record

5. Click the **Exit** button to end the application. Auto-hide the Data Sources window.

Coding the Trivia Game Application

According to the application's TOE chart (shown earlier in Figure 12-39), only three event procedures need to be coded: the exitButton's Click event procedure, the MainForm's Load event procedure, and the submitButton's Click event procedure. When you open the Code Editor window, you will notice that the exitButton's Click event procedure has already been coded for you. The MainForm's Load event procedure also contains the appropriate code. Recall that the computer automatically enters the code in the Load event procedure when you drag an object from the Data Sources window to the form. Therefore, the only procedure you need to code is the submitButton's Click event procedure. The procedure's pseudocode is shown in Figure 12-48.

```
submitButton Click event procedure
1. store the position of the record pointer in a variable
2. determine the selected radio button and assign its Text property (without the leading ampersand that designates
   the access key) to a variable named userAnswer
3. if the value in the userAnswer variable does not match the value stored in the current record's CorrectAnswer field
         add 1 to a counter variable named numIncorrect
   end if
4. if the record pointer is not pointing to the last record
         move the record pointer to the next record in the dataset
   else
         display the number of incorrect answers in a message box
   end if
```

Figure 12-48 Pseudocode for the Submit Answer button's Click event procedure

To code the submitButton's Click event procedure and then test the code:

1. Open the Code Editor window. Replace <your name> and <current date> in the comments with your name and the current date.
2. Open the code template for the submitButton's Click event procedure. Enter the following comments. Press **Enter** twice after typing the last comment.

   ' determines whether the user's answer is correct
   ' and the number of incorrect answers

3. The procedure will use an Integer variable to keep track of the record pointer's position in the dataset. It also will use a String variable to store the user's answer (A, B, C, or D) to the current question. Enter the following Dim statements:

   Dim ptrPos As Integer
   Dim userAnswer As String

4. The procedure will use a static Integer variable to keep track of the number of incorrect answers made by the user. Type the following Static statement and then press **Enter** twice:

   Static numIncorrect As Integer

5. The first step in the pseudocode is to store the record pointer's position in a variable. Enter the following comment and assignment statement. Press **Enter** twice after typing the assignment statement.

   ' store record pointer's position
   ptrPos = TblGameBindingSource.Position

6. Next, you need to determine the selected radio button and then assign its Text property (without the leading ampersand) to the `userAnswer` variable. Enter the following comment and Select Case statement. (The Code Editor will enter the End Select clause for you.)

```
' determine selected radio button
Select Case True
    Case aRadioButton.Checked
        userAnswer = aRadioButton.Text.Substring(1, 1)
    Case bRadioButton.Checked
        userAnswer = bRadioButton.Text.Substring(1, 1)
    Case cRadioButton.Checked
        userAnswer = cRadioButton.Text.Substring(1, 1)
    Case Else
        userAnswer = dRadioButton.Text.Substring(1, 1)
End Select
```

7. The next step in the pseudocode is a single-alternative selection structure that compares the value in the `userAnswer` variable with the value in the current record's CorrectAnswer field. If they are not the same, the procedure should add the number 1 to the value in the

numIncorrect variable. Insert two blank lines between the End Select and End Sub clauses. Beginning in the blank line above the End Sub clause, enter the following comment and selection structure. (The Code Editor will enter the End If clause for you.)

```
' if necessary, update the number of incorrect answers
If userAnswer <>
    TriviaDataSet.tblGame(ptrPos).CorrectAnswer Then
        numIncorrect += 1
End If
```

8. The last step in the pseudocode is a dual-alternative selection structure that determines whether the record pointer is pointing to the last record in the dataset. If it's not, the procedure should move the record pointer to the next record; doing this will display that record's question and answers. However, if the record pointer is pointing to the last record, it means that there are no more questions and answers to display. In that case, the procedure should display the number of incorrect answers made by the user. Insert two blank lines between the End If and End Sub clauses. Beginning in the blank line above the End Sub clause, enter the following comment and selection structure. (The Code Editor will enter the End If clause for you.)

```
' determine position of record pointer
If ptrPos < 8 Then
    TblGameBindingSource.MoveNext()
Else
    MessageBox.Show("Number incorrect: " &
            numIncorrect.ToString, "Trivia Game",
            MessageBoxButtons.OK,
            MessageBoxIcon.Information)
End If
```

9. Save the solution and then start the application. You will answer the first question correctly. Click the **B** radio button and then click the **Submit Answer** button.

10. You will answer the second question incorrectly. Click the **D** radio button and then click the **Submit Answer** button.

11. Answer the remaining seven questions on your own. When you have submitted the answer for the last question, the submitButton's Click event procedure displays the number of incorrect responses in a message box.

12. Close the message box and then click the **Exit** button. Close the Code Editor window and then close the solution. Figure 12-49 shows the Trivia Game application's code.

```
' Project name:          Trivia Game Project
' Project purpose:       Displays trivia questions and
'                        answers and the number of incorrect
'                        answers made by the user
' Created/revised by:   <your name> on <current date>

Option Explicit On
Option Strict On
Option Infer Off

Public Class MainForm

   Private Sub exitButton_Click(ByVal sender As Object,
   ByVal e As System.EventArgs) Handles exitButton.Click
      Me.Close()
   End Sub

   Private Sub MainForm_Load(ByVal sender As System.Object,
   ByVal e As System.EventArgs) Handles MyBase.Load
     'TODO: This line of code loads data into the
     'TriviaDataSet.tblGame' table. You can move,
     or remove it, as needed.
     Me.TblGameTableAdapter.Fill(Me.TriviaDataSet.tblGame)

   End Sub

   Private Sub submitButton_Click(ByVal sender As Object,
   ByVal e As System.EventArgs) Handles submitButton.Click
      ' determines whether the user's answer is correct
      ' and the number of incorrect answers

      Dim ptrPos As Integer
      Dim userAnswer As String
      Static numIncorrect As Integer

      ' store record pointer's position
      ptrPos = TblGameBindingSource.Position

      ' determine selected radio button
      Select Case True
          Case aRadioButton.Checked
             userAnswer = aRadioButton.Text.Substring(1, 1)
          Case bRadioButton.Checked
             userAnswer = bRadioButton.Text.Substring(1, 1)
          Case cRadioButton.Checked
             userAnswer = cRadioButton.Text.Substring(1, 1)
          Case Else
             userAnswer = dRadioButton.Text.Substring(1, 1)
     End Select

     ' if necessary, update the number of incorrect answers
     If userAnswer <>
       TriviaDataSet.tblGame(ptrPos).CorrectAnswer Then
          numIncorrect += 1
     End If
```

Figure 12-49 Trivia Game application's code *(continues)*

(continued)

```

      ' determine position of record pointer
      If ptrPos < 8 Then
         TblGameBindingSource.MoveNext()
      Else
         MessageBox.Show("Number incorrect: " &
            numIncorrect.ToString, "Trivia Game",
            MessageBoxButtons.OK,
            MessageBoxIcon.Information)
      End If
   End Sub
End Class
```

Figure 12-49 Trivia Game application's code

PROGRAMMING TUTORIAL 2

Creating the CD Collection Application

In this tutorial, you code an application that uses a database to keep track of a person's CD collection. The CD database is stored in a Microsoft Access file named CD.accdb. The database contains one table, which is named tblCds. The table contains 13 records. Each record contains three fields: CdName, Artist, and Price. The CD Collection application allows the user to add, delete, and modify the records stored in the database. It also allows the user to search for a specific artist.

Connecting the Application to the Database

Included in the data files for this book is a partially completed CD Collection application. First, you will connect the application to the CD database.

To open the CD Collection application and connect it to the CD database:

1. Start Visual Studio or the Express Edition of Visual Basic. If necessary, open the Solution Explorer window.
2. Open the **Cd Collection Solution** (**Cd Collection Solution.sln**) file, which is contained in the VbReloaded2010\Chap12\Cd Collection Solution folder. Open the designer window, if necessary, and then auto-hide the Solution Explorer window.
3. If necessary, open either the Server Explorer window (Visual Studio) or Database Explorer window (Visual Basic Express Edition).
4. If necessary, open the Data Sources window.
5. Click **Add New Data Source** in the Data Sources window to start the Data Source Configuration Wizard. Use the wizard to connect the application to the CD database. The database is stored in the CD.accdb file, which is contained in the VbReloaded2010\Chap12\Access Databases folder. In this application, you need the dataset to include all of the fields in the tblCds table.

6. Now, preview the data contained in the dataset. Click the **form**, click **Data** on the menu bar, and then click **Preview Data** to open the Preview Data dialog box. Click the **Preview** button. See Figure 12-50.

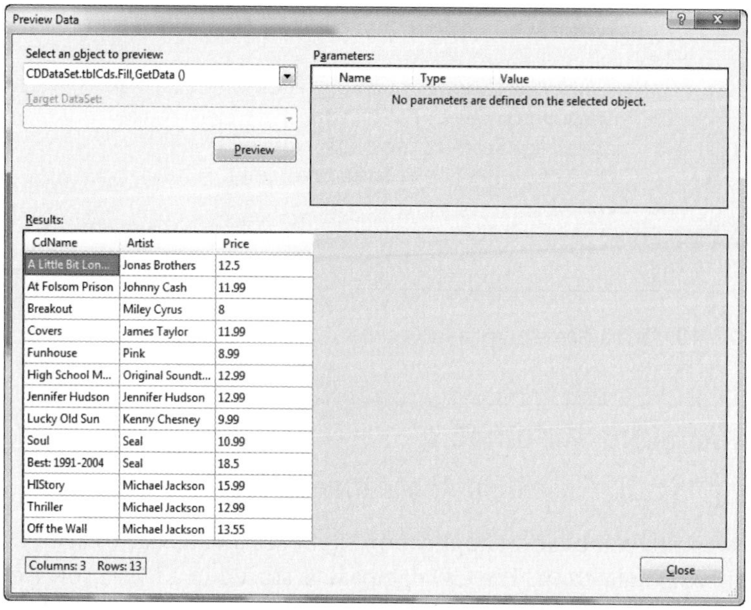

Figure 12-50 Preview Data dialog box showing the data stored in the CDDataSet

7. Close the Preview Data dialog box.

8. In this application, the user will be adding, deleting, or modifying the records in the dataset, so you will need to change the database file's Copy to Output Directory property. Click **CD.accdb** in the Solution Explorer window. Use the Properties window to change the Copy to Output Directory property to **Copy if newer**.

9. Drag the tblCds table object from the Data Sources window to the upper-left corner of the form and then release the mouse button.

10. In the Properties window, set the DataGridView control's AutoSizeColumnsMode to **Fill**.

11. Click the DataGridView control's **task box** and then click **Dock in Parent Container** on the task list.

12. Now, click **Edit Columns** on the task list. Change the CdName column's HeaderText property to **CD Name**.

13. Click **Price** in the Selected Columns list and then click **DefaultCellStyle**. Click the **ellipsis** button in the DefaultCellStyle property to open the CellStyle Builder dialog box. Change the Format property to **Currency** with **2** decimal places and then click the **OK** button to close the Format String Dialog box. Close the CellStyle Builder dialog box and then close the Edit Columns dialog box.

In the next set of steps, you will begin coding the application. If you need help, you can look ahead to Figure 12-53.

To begin coding the application and then test the code:

1. Open the Code Editor window. In the comments that appear in the General Declarations section, replace <your name> and <current date> with your name and the current date.
2. Include an appropriate Try...Catch statement in the TblCdsBindingNavigatorSaveItem_Click event procedure. If an error occurs in the procedure, display a description of the error in a message box.
3. Save the solution and then start the application to display the records in the DataGridView control.
4. Scroll down the DataGridView control until you see the empty row. Enter your own record in the empty row and then click the **Save Data** button (the disk) on the BindingNavigator control. Close the application by clicking the **Close** button on the form's title bar.
5. Start the application again. Verify that the record you entered appears at the end of the DataGridView control. Now, click the **empty box** that appears to the left of your record; doing this highlights (selects) the record. Click the **Delete** button (the *X*) on the BindingNavigator control and then click the **Save Data** button.
6. Close the application and then start the application again. Verify that the record you deleted no longer appears in the DataGridView control.
7. Close the application.

Adding an Item to the BindingNavigator Control

In the next set of steps, you will add a button to the BindingNavigator control. The button will allow the user to display the records associated with a specific artist.

To add a button to the BindingNavigator control:

1. Make the designer window the active window. Click an **empty area** on the TblCdsBindingNavigator control and then click the control's **task box**.
2. Click **Edit Items** on the task list to open the Items Collection Editor dialog box. Click the **Add** button. ToolStripButton1 appears at the bottom of the Members list. Click the **Alphabetical** button to display the property names in alphabetical order. Click **(Name)** in the properties list. Type **artistButton** and press **Enter**. Change the **DisplayStyle** property to **Text**, and then change the **Text** property to **Artist**. See Figure 12-51.

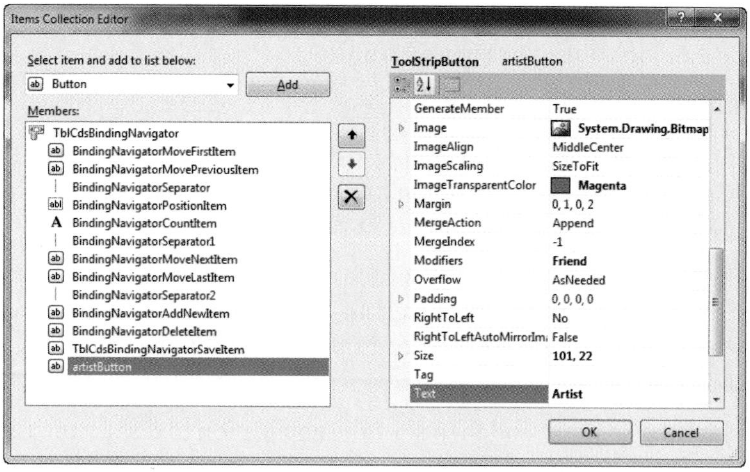

Figure 12-51 artistButton added to the Items Collection Editor dialog box

3. Close the Items Collection Editor dialog box and then click the **form's title bar** to close the BindingNavigator control's task list. The Artist button appears on the BindingNavigator control, as shown in Figure 12-52. Save the solution.

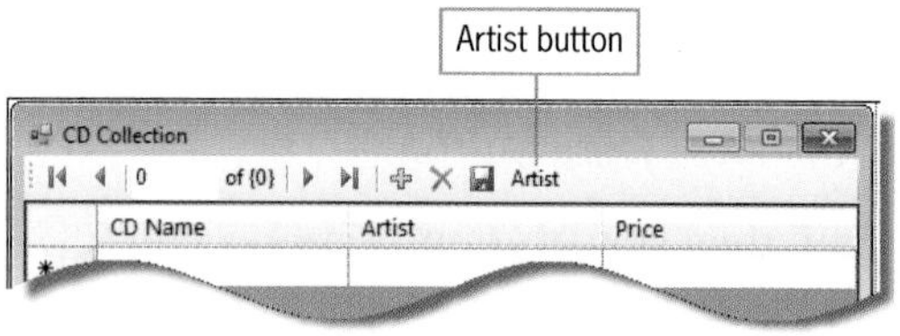

Figure 12-52 Artist button added to the BindingNavigator control

To code the Artist button's Click event procedure and then test the code:

1. Make the Code Editor window the active window.
2. The Artist button's Click event procedure will use LINQ to select the appropriate records. Change `Option Infer Off` in the General Declarations section to **Option Infer On**.
3. Open the code template for the artistButton's Click event procedure. Type the following comment and then press **Enter** twice:

   ' selects records pertaining to a specific artist

4. Enter the following Dim and Const statements. Press **Enter** twice after typing the Const statement.

   Dim artistName As String
   Const Prompt As String = "One or more letters " &
   "(leave empty to retrieve all records):"

5. Next, enter the following comment and assignment statement:

   ' get artist name
   artistName = InputBox(Prompt, "Artist Name")

6. Now, enter a statement that converts the value in the `artistName` variable to uppercase and also removes any leading or trailing spaces from the value. Assign the result to the `artistName` variable. Press **Enter** twice after typing the statement.

7. Enter the following comment:

   ' select records matching artist's name

8. Now, enter the appropriate LINQ statement. The statement should select the records whose Artist field begins with the one or more letters entered by the user. If the user does not enter any letters, the statement should select all of the records. Assign the selected records to a variable named `records`. Press **Enter** twice after typing the statement.

9. Finally, enter a statement that assigns the contents of the `records` variable to the TblCdsBindingSource control. (Hint: Assign `records.AsDataView` to the BindingSource object's DataSource property.)

10. Save the solution and then start the application. Click the **Artist** button. Type **mic** in the input dialog box and then press **Enter**. Only the three Michael Jackson CDs appear in the DataGridView control.

11. Click the **Artist** button and then click the **OK** button to display all of the records in the DataGridView control.

12. Close the application. Close the Code Editor window, and then close the solution. Figure 12-53 shows the CD Collection application's code.

```
' Project name:          Cd Collection Project
' Project purpose:       Allows the user to add, delete,
'                        and modify records and also
'                        search for a specific artist
' Created/revised by:    <your name> on <current date>

Option Explicit On
Option Strict On
Option Infer On

Public Class MainForm

   Private Sub TblCdsBindingNavigatorSaveItem_Click(
   ByVal sender As System.Object, ByVal e As System.EventArgs
   ) Handles TblCdsBindingNavigatorSaveItem.Click
      Try
         Me.Validate()
         Me.TblCdsBindingSource.EndEdit()
         Me.TableAdapterManager.UpdateAll(Me.CDDataSet)
     Catch ex As Exception
          MessageBox.Show(ex.Message, "CD Collection",
             MessageBoxButtons.OK,
             MessageBoxIcon.Information)
     End Try
   End Sub

```

Figure 12-53 Code for the CD Collection application *(continues)*

(continued)

```
    Private Sub MainForm_Load(ByVal sender As System.Object,
    ByVal e As System.EventArgs) Handles MyBase.Load
       'TODO: This line of code loads data into the
       'CDDataSet.tblCds' table. You can move, or
       remove it, as needed.
       Me.TblCdsTableAdapter.Fill(Me.CDDataSet.tblCds)

    End Sub

    Private Sub artistButton_Click(ByVal sender As Object,
    ByVal e As System.EventArgs) Handles artistButton.Click
        ' selects records pertaining to a specific artist

      Dim artistName As String
      Const Prompt As String = "One or more letters " &
         "(leave empty to retrieve all records):"

      ' get artist name
      artistName = InputBox(Prompt, "Artist Name")
      artistName = artistName.ToUpper.Trim

      ' select records matching artist's name
      Dim records = From cd In CDDataSet.tblCds
         Where cd.Artist.ToUpper Like artistName & "*"
         Select cd

      TblCdsBindingSource.DataSource = records.AsDataView

    End Sub
End Class
```

Figure 12-53 Code for the CD Collection application

PROGRAMMING EXAMPLE

Cartwright Industries Application

The sales manager at Cartwright Industries records the item number, name, and price of the company's products in a database named Items. The Items database is stored in the Items.accdb file, which is contained in the VbReloaded2010\Chap12\Access Databases folder. The database contains one table, which is named tblItems. The table contains 10 records, each composed of three fields. The ItemNum and ItemName fields contain text, and the Price field contains numbers. Create an application that displays the records in a DataGridView control. The application should allow the user to select records whose ItemNum field matches the one or more characters entered by the user. Use the following names for the solution, project, and form file: Cartwright Solution, Cartwright Project, and Main Form.vb. Save the application in the VbReloaded2010\Chap12 folder. See Figures 12-54 through 12-57.

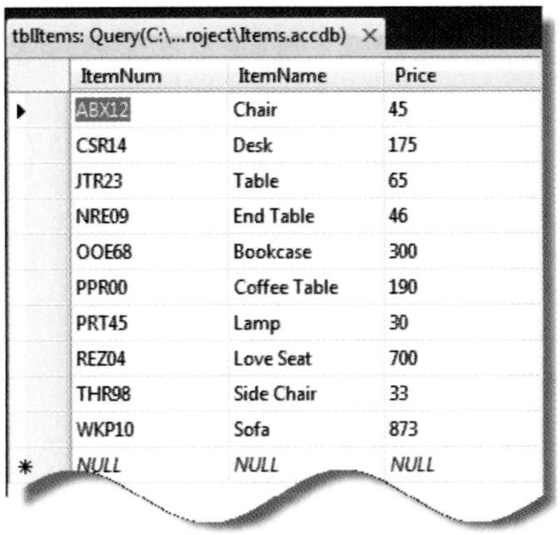

tblItems: Query(C:\...roject\Items.accdb)

ItemNum	ItemName	Price
ABX12	Chair	45
CSR14	Desk	175
JTR23	Table	65
NRE09	End Table	46
OOE68	Bookcase	300
PPR00	Coffee Table	190
PRT45	Lamp	30
REZ04	Love Seat	700
THR98	Side Chair	33
WKP10	Sofa	873
NULL	NULL	NULL

Figure 12-54 Data contained in the tblItems table

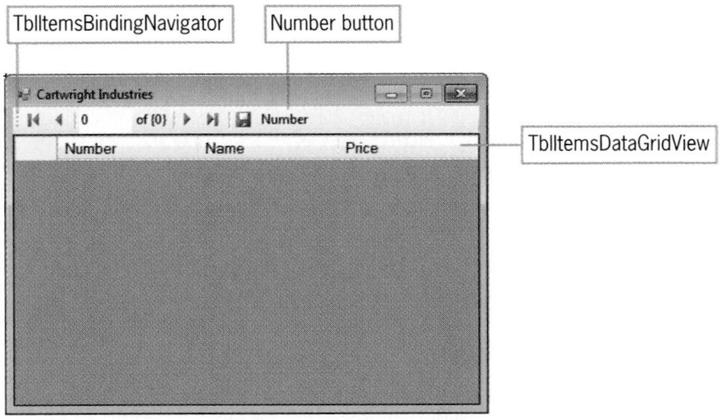

Figure 12-55 MainForm in the Cartwright Industries application

Object	Property	Setting
MainForm	Font	Segoe UI, 10 point
	MaximizeBox	False
	StartPosition	CenterScreen
	Text	Cartwright Industries

Figure 12-56 Objects, properties, and settings

```
' Project name:          Cartwright Project
' Project purpose:       Displays all records from a dataset
'                        and those matching an item number
' Created/revised by:   <your name> on <current date>

Option Explicit On
Option Strict On
Option Infer On

Public Class MainForm

   Private Sub TblItemsBindingNavigatorSaveItem_Click(
   ByVal sender As System.Object,
   ByVal e As System.EventArgs
   ) Handles TblItemsBindingNavigatorSaveItem.Click
      Try
         Me.Validate()
         Me.TblItemsBindingSource.EndEdit()
         Me.TableAdapterManager.UpdateAll(Me.ItemsDataSet)
      Catch ex As Exception
         MessageBox.Show(ex.Message,
              "Cartwright Industries",
              MessageBoxButtons.OK,
              MessageBoxIcon.Information)
      End Try
   End Sub

   Private Sub MainForm_Load(ByVal sender As System.Object,
   ByVal e As System.EventArgs) Handles MyBase.Load
      'TODO: This line of code loads data into the
      'ItemsDataSet.tblItems' table. You can move, or
      remove it, as needed.
      Me.TblItemsTableAdapter.Fill(Me.ItemsDataSet.tblItems)

   End Sub

   Private Sub numButton_Click(ByVal sender As Object,
   ByVal e As System.EventArgs) Handles numButton.Click
      ' displays records matching an item number

      Dim itemNum As String
      Const Prompt As String = "One or more characters " &
         "(leave empty to retrieve all records):"

      ' get item number
      itemNum = InputBox(Prompt, "Item Number")
      itemNum = itemNum.ToUpper.Trim

      ' select records matching item number
      Dim records = From item In ItemsDataSet.tblItems
         Where item.ItemNum.ToUpper Like itemNum & "*"
         Select item

      TblItemsBindingSource.DataSource = records.AsDataView
   End Sub
End Class
```

Figure 12-57 Code

Summary

- You can use Visual Basic to access the data stored in databases created by many different database management systems.
- Databases created by Microsoft Access are relational databases. A relational database can contain one or more tables. Each table consists of rows and columns.
- Most tables contain a primary key that uniquely identifies each record.
- The data in a relational database can be displayed in any order, and you can control the amount of information you want to view.
- To access the data stored in a database, you first connect the application to the database. Doing this creates a dataset that contains objects, such as table objects and field objects.
- You can display the information contained in a dataset by binding one or more of the objects in the dataset to one or more controls in the application's interface.
- A TableAdapter object connects a database to a DataSet object.
- A BindingSource object connects a DataSet object to the bound controls on a form.
- The DataGridView control displays data in a row and column format, similar to a spreadsheet. The intersection of a column and row is called a cell.
- In most applications, the statement to fill a dataset with data is entered in the form's Load event procedure.
- You can use the Try...Catch statement to handle any exceptions that occur while an application is running. A description of the exception is stored in the Message property of the Catch block's `ex` parameter.
- A database file's Copy to Output Directory property determines when and if the file is copied from the project folder to the project folder's bin\Debug folder each time the application is started.
- The BindingSource object uses an invisible record pointer to keep track of the current record in the dataset. The location of the record pointer is stored in the BindingSource object's Position property.
- You can use the BindingSource object's Move methods to move the record pointer in a dataset.
- You can access the value stored in a field object in a dataset.
- You can use LINQ to select and arrange the records in a dataset. LINQ also provides the Average, Sum, Count, Min, and Max aggregate operators.
- You can include additional items, such as text boxes and drop-down buttons, on a BindingNavigator control. You also can delete items from the control.

Key Terms

Aggregate operator—an operator that returns a single value from a group of values; LINQ provides the Average, Count, Max, Min, and Sum aggregate operators

AutoSizeColumnsMode property—determines the way the column widths are sized in a DataGridView control

Binding—the process of connecting an object in a dataset to a control on a form

BindingNavigator control—can be used to move the record pointer from one record to another in a dataset, as well as to add, delete, and save records

BindingSource object—connects a DataSet object to the bound controls on a form

Bound controls—the controls connected to an object in a dataset

Cell—the intersection of a row and column in a DataGridView control

Child table—a table linked to a parent table

Computer database—an electronic file that contains an organized collection of related information

Copy to Output Directory property—a property of a database file; determines when and if the file is copied from the project folder to the project folder's bin\Debug folder

DataGridView control—displays data in a row and column format

Dataset—a copy of the data (database fields and records) that can be accessed by an application

DataSet object—stores the information you want to access from a database

Exception—an error that occurs while an application is running

Field—a single item of information about a person, place, or thing

Foreign key—the field used to link a child table to a parent table

Language Integrated Query—LINQ; the query language built into Visual Basic 2010

LINQ—an acronym for Language Integrated Query

Move methods—methods of a BindingSource object; used to move the record pointer to the first, last, next, or previous record in a dataset

Order By clause—used in LINQ to arrange the records in a dataset

Parent table—a table linked to a child table

Position property—a property of a BindingSource object; stores the position of the record pointer

Primary key—the field that uniquely identifies each record in a table

Query—specifies the records to select in a dataset and the order in which to arrange the records

Record—a group of related fields that contain all of the necessary data about a specific person, place, or thing

Relational database—a database that stores information in tables composed of columns (fields) and rows (records)

Table—a group of related records

TableAdapter object—connects a database to a DataSet object

TableAdapterManager object—handles saving data to multiple tables in a dataset

Try...Catch statement—used for exception handling in a procedure

Where clause—used in LINQ to limit the records you want to view in a dataset

Review Questions

1. The ______________ property stores an integer that represents the location of the record pointer in a dataset.

    a. BindingNavigator object's Position

    b. BindingSource object's Position

    c. TableAdapter object's Position

    d. none of the above

2. If the record pointer is positioned on record number 5 in a dataset, which of the following will move the record pointer to record number 4?

    a. `TblBooksBindingSource.GoPrevious()`

    b. `TblBooksBindingSource.Move(4)`

    c. `TblBooksBindingSource.MovePrevious()`

    d. `TblBooksBindingSource.PositionPrevious()`

3. The ______________ object provides the connection between a DataSet object and a control on a form.

    a. Bound

    b. Binding

    c. BindingSource

    d. Connecting

4. The field that links a child table to a parent table is called the ______________.

    a. foreign key in the child table

    b. foreign key in the parent table

    c. link key in the parent table

    d. primary key in the child table

5. The process of connecting a control to a dataset is called ______________.

   a. assigning

   b. binding

   c. joining

   d. none of the above

6. Which of the following will select only records whose LastName field begins with an uppercase letter A?

   a.
   ```
   Dim records = From name In NamesDataSet.tblNames
           Where name.LastName Like "A*"
           Select name
   ```

   b.
   ```
   Dim records = From NamesDataSet.tblNames
           Select LastName Like "A*"
   ```

   c.
   ```
   Dim records = From tblNames
           Where tblName.LastName Like "A*"
           Select name
   ```

   d.
   ```
   Dim records = From name In NamesDataSet.tblNames
           Where tblName.LastName Like "A*"
           Select name
   ```

7. Which of the following calculates the sum of the values stored in a numeric field named JulySales?

   a.
   ```
   Dim total As Double =
          From sales In SalesDataSet.tblSales
          Select sales.JulySales
          Into Sum()
   ```

   b.
   ```
   Dim total As Double =
          Aggregate sales In SalesDataSet.tblSales
          Select sales.JulySales
          Into Sum()
   ```

   c.
   ```
   Dim total As Double =
          From sales In SalesDataSet.tblSales
          Aggregate sales.JulySales
          Into Sum()
   ```

   d.
   ```
   Dim total As Double =
          From sales In SalesDataSet.tblSales
          Sum sales.JulySales
   ```

8. The tblCities table contains a numeric field named Population. Which of the following statements selects all cities having a population that exceeds 15000?

   a.
   ```
   Dim records = From city In CitiesDataSet.tblCities
           Where Population > 15000
           Select city
   ```

b.
```
Dim records = From city In CitiesDataSet.tblCities
              Select city.Population > 15000
```

c.
```
Dim records = From city In CitiesDataSet.tblCities
              Where city.Population > 15000
              Select city
```

d.
```
Dim records = Select city.Population > 15000 From
   tblCities
```

9. In a LINQ statement, the ______________ clause limits the records that will be selected.

   a. Limit

   b. Order By

   c. Select

   d. Where

10. The Enable Adding check box in a ______________ control's task list determines whether a record can be added to the control.

   a. BindingNavigator

   b. DataGridView

   c. BindingSource

   d. DataBindingNavigator

11. Which of the following determines the number of records in the tblBooks table?

a.
```
Dim num As Integer =
      Aggregate book In BooksDataSet.tblBooks
      In Count()
```

b.
```
Dim num As Integer =
      Aggregate book In BooksDataSet.tblBooks
      Into Count()
```

c.
```
Dim num As Integer =
      Aggregate book In BooksDataSet.tblBooks
      Into Sum()
```

d.
```
Dim num As Integer =
      Aggregate book From BooksDataSet.tblBooks
      Into Counter()
```

Exercises

Pencil and Paper

INTRODUCTORY

1. Write a statement that assigns the location of a dataset's record pointer to an Integer variable named `recNum`. The BindingSource object's name is TblCityBindingSource.

INTRODUCTORY

2. Write a statement that moves the record pointer to the last record in the dataset. The BindingSource object's name is TblCityBindingSource.

INTRODUCTORY

3. The tblMagInfo table contains three fields. The Code and Cost fields are numeric. The Magazine field contains text. The dataset's name is MagsDataSet.
   a. Write a LINQ statement that arranges the records in descending order by the Cost field.
   b. Write a LINQ statement that selects records having a code of 9.
   c. Write a LINQ statement that selects records having a cost of $3 or more.
   d. Write a LINQ statement that selects the Daily Food Guide magazine.

INTERMEDIATE

4. Using the information from Pencil and Paper Exercise 3, write a LINQ statement that selects magazines whose names begin with the letter G (in either uppercase or lowercase). Also write a LINQ statement that calculates the average cost of a magazine.

Computer

MODIFY THIS

5. Open the Morgan Industries Solution (Morgan Industries Solution.sln) file contained in the VbReloaded2010\Chap12\Morgan Industries Solution-Labels folder.
   a. Expand the Employees.accdb node in the Server (Database) Explorer window, and then expand the Tables node. Right-click tblEmploy and then click Retrieve Data. The table data appears in a window in the IDE, as shown in Figure 12-3 in the chapter. Close the window.
   b. Modify the Next Record and Previous Record buttons' Click event procedures to use the Position property rather than the MoveNext and MovePrevious methods. Save the solution, and then start and test the application. Close the solution.

MODIFY THIS

6. If necessary, complete the Trivia Game application from this chapter's Programming Tutorial 1, and then close the solution. Use Windows to make a copy of the Trivia Game Solution folder. Rename

the folder Trivia Game Solution-Modified. Open the Trivia Game Solution (Trivia Game Solution.sln) file contained in the Trivia Game Solution-Modified folder. Display the question number (from 1 through 9) along with the word "Question" in a label control in the interface. Add another button to the interface. The button should allow the user to start a new game. Allow the user to click the New Game button only after he or she has answered all nine questions. Save the solution, and then start and test the application. Close the solution.

7. Open the Morgan Industries Solution (Morgan Industries Solution.sln) file contained in the VbReloaded2010\Chap12\Morgan Industries Solution-ListBox folder.

MODIFY THIS

   a. Unlock the controls and then delete the numberLabel control from the form. Add a list box to the form. Name the list box numberListBox. Lock the controls and then reset the tab order.

   b. Set the list box's DataSource and DisplayMember properties to TblEmployBindingSource and Emp_Number, respectively. Save the solution, and then start and test the application. Close the solution.

8. Open the Morgan Industries Solution (Morgan Industries Solution.sln) file contained in the VbReloaded2010\Chap12\Morgan Industries Solution-DropDownButton folder.

MODIFY THIS

   a. Add a DropDownButton to the BindingNavigator control. Change the DropDownButton's name to deptDropDownButton. Change its DisplayStyle and Text properties to Text and Department, respectively.

   b. Use the DropDownItems property to add four items to the DropDownButton: Accounting (Code 1), Advertising (Code 2), Personnel (Code 3), and Inventory (Code 4). Be sure to change each menu item's name, as well as its DisplayStyle and Text properties. Each item should display (in a message box) the number of employees in the department. Code each item's Click event procedure. Save the solution, and then start and test the application. Close the solution.

9. Sydney Industries records the item number, name, and price of each of its products in a database named Products. The Products database is stored in the Products.accdb file, which is contained in the VbReloaded2010\Chap12\Access Databases folder. The database contains a table named tblProducts. The table contains 10 records, each composed of three fields. The ItemNum and ItemName fields contain text; the Price field contains numbers. Open the Sydney Solution (Sydney Solution.sln) file contained in the VbReloaded2010\Chap12\Sydney Solution folder. Connect the application to the Products database. Bind the appropriate objects to the existing label controls. Open the Code Editor window. Code the Click event procedures for the Next Record and Previous Record buttons. Save the solution, and then start and test the application. Close the solution.

INTRODUCTORY

INTRODUCTORY

10. Open the Magazine Solution (Magazine Solution.sln) file contained in the VbReloaded2010\Chap12\Magazine Solution-Introductory folder. The application is connected to the Magazines database, which is stored in the Magazines.accdb file. The database contains a table named tblMagazine; the table has three fields. The Cost field is numeric. The Code and MagName fields contain text. Start the application to view the records contained in the dataset, and then stop the application. Open the Code Editor window. Code the codeButton's Click event procedure so that it displays the record whose Code field contains PG24. Code the nameButton's Click event procedure so that it displays only the Java record. Code the allButton's Click event procedure to display all of the records. Save the solution, and then start and test the application. Close the solution.

INTRODUCTORY

11. Open the Addison Playhouse Solution (Addison Playhouse Solution.sln) file contained in the VbReloaded\Chap12\Addison Playhouse Solution folder. Connect the application to a Microsoft Access database named Play. The database is contained in the Play.accdb file, which is located in the VbReloaded2010\Chap12\Access Databases folder. The database contains one table named tblReservations. The table has 20 records. Each record has three fields: a numeric field named Seat and two text fields named Patron and Phone. The application should display the contents of the dataset in a DataGridView control. It also should allow the user to add, delete, modify, and save records. Enter the Try...Catch statement in the Save Data button's Click event procedure. Save the solution, and then start and test the application. Close the solution.

INTERMEDIATE

12. Open the Magazine Solution (Magazine Solution.sln) file contained in the VbReloaded2010\Chap12\Magazine Solution-Intermediate folder. The application is connected to the Magazines database, which is stored in the Magazines.accdb file. The database contains a table named tblMagazine; the table has three fields. The Cost field is numeric. The Code and MagName fields contain text. Start the application to view the records contained in the dataset, and then stop the application. Open the Code Editor window. Code the costButton's Click event procedure so that it displays records having a cost of $4 or more. Code the nameButton's Click event procedure so that it displays only magazines whose names begin with the letter C (in either uppercase or lowercase). Code the avgButton's Click event procedure so that it displays the average cost of a magazine. Display the average in a message box. Save the solution, and then start and test the application. Close the solution.

SWAT THE BUGS

13. Open the Debug Solution (Debug Solution.sln) file contained in the VbReloaded2010\Chap12\Debug Solution folder. Open the Code Editor window and review the existing code. Correct the code to remove the jagged line that appears below one of the lines of code. Save the solution, and then start and test the application. Locate and then correct the errors in the code. When the application is working correctly, close the solution.

Case Projects

Modified Trivia Game

If necessary, complete the Trivia Game application from this chapter's Programming Tutorial 1, and then close the solution. Use Windows to make a copy of the Trivia Game Solution folder. Rename the folder Trivia Game Solution-Case Project. Open the Trivia Game Solution (Trivia Game Solution.sln) file contained in the Trivia Game Solution-Case Project folder. Modify the application to allow the user to answer the questions in any order and also to change his or her answers. (You can modify the interface to include additional buttons.) The modified application should display the number of incorrect answers only when the user requests that information. Make the appropriate modifications to the code. Save the solution, and then start and test the application. Close the solution.

College Courses

In this Case Project, you use a Microsoft Access database named Courses. The Courses.accdb database file is located in the VbReloaded2010\Chap12\Access Databases folder. The database contains one table named tblCourses. The table has 10 records. Each record has four fields: ID, Title, CreditHours, and Grade. The CreditHours field is numeric; the other fields contain text. Create an application that allows the user to display the records for a specific grade (A, B, C, D, or F). The user also should be able to display all of the records. Display the records in a DataGridView control. The application should not allow the user to add or delete records. Include a Calculate GPA button on the BindingNavigator control. The button's Click event procedure should display the student's GPA. An A grade is worth 4 points, a B is worth 3 points, and so on. Use the following names for the solution, project, and form file: College Courses Solution, College Courses Project, and Main Form.vb. Save the application in the VbReloaded2010\Chap12 folder.

Political Awareness Organization

During July and August of each year, the Political Awareness Organization (PAO) sends a questionnaire to the voters in its district. The questionnaire asks the voter for his or her political party (Democratic, Republican, or Independent) and age. From the returned questionnaires, the organization's secretary tabulates the number of Democrats, Republicans, and Independents in the district. The secretary wants an application that she can use to save each respondent's information (political party and age) in a database named PAO. The PAO database is contained in the PAO.accdb file, which is located in the VbReloaded2010\Chap12\Access Databases folder. The database contains one table named tblQuestionnaire. The table has 15 records. Each record has a text field named Party and a numeric field named Age. The application also should allow the secretary to edit and delete records, as well as to calculate and display the number of voters in each political party. Use the following names for the solution, project, and form file: PAO Solution, PAO Project, and Main Form.vb. Save the application in the VbReloaded2010\Chap12 folder. Use a DataGridView control in the interface.

The Fiction Bookstore

Jerry Schmidt, the manager of the Fiction Bookstore, uses a Microsoft Access database named Books to keep track of the books in his store. The Books database is stored in the Books.accdb file, which is contained in the VbReloaded2010\Chap12\Access Databases folder. The database has one table named tblBooks. The table has five fields. The BookNumber, Price, and QuantityInStock fields are numeric. The Title and Author fields contain text. Mr. Schmidt wants an application that he can use to enter an author's name (or part of a name) and then display only the titles of books written by the author. Display the information in a DataGridView control; however, don't allow the user to add, delete, modify, or save records. In this application, you need to allow the user to specify the records he or she wants to select while the application is running. Add a text box and a button to the BindingNavigator control. Mr. Schmidt will use the text box to specify the records he wants to select. He will use the button to tell the computer to display the selected records. Mr. Schmidt also wants to display the total value of the books in his store. Use the following names for the solution, project, and form file: Fiction Bookstore Solution, Fiction Bookstore Project, and Main Form.vb. Save the application in the VbReloaded2010\Chap12 folder.

CHAPTER 13

Creating Simple Web Applications

After studying Chapter 13, you should be able to:

- Create a Web application
- View a Web page in a browser window
- Add static text to a Web page
- Format the static text on a Web page
- View a Web page in full screen view
- Add another Web page to an application
- Add controls to a Web page
- Close and open a Web application
- Reposition a control on a Web page
- Code a control on a Web page
- Use a RequiredFieldValidator control (Programming Tutorial 2)

Web Applications

The Internet is the world's largest computer network, connecting millions of computers located all around the world. One of the most popular features of the Internet is the World Wide Web, often referred to simply as the Web. The Web consists of documents called **Web pages** that are stored on Web servers. A **Web server** is a computer that contains special software that "serves up" Web pages in response to requests from client computers. A **client computer** is a computer that requests information from a Web server. The information is requested and subsequently viewed through the use of a program called a Web browser or, more simply, a **browser**. Currently, the two most popular browsers are Microsoft Internet Explorer and Mozilla Firefox.

Many Web pages are static. A **static Web page** is a document whose purpose is merely to display information to the viewer. Static Web pages are not interactive. The only interaction that can occur between static Web pages and the user is through links that allow the user to "jump" from one Web page to another. Figures 13-1 and 13-2 show examples of static Web pages created for the Greenview Toy Store. The Web page in Figure 13-1 shows the store's name, address, and telephone number. The page also provides a link to the Web page shown in Figure 13-2. That page shows the store's business hours and provides a link for returning to the first Web page. You will create both Web pages in Programming Tutorial 1.

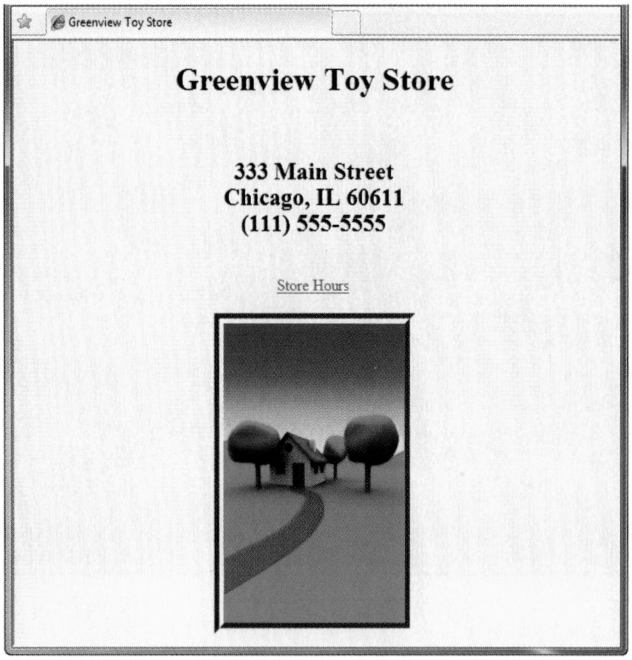

Figure 13-1 First static Web page for the Greenview Toy Store

Figure 13-2 Second static Web page for the Greenview Toy Store

Although static Web pages provide a means for a store to list its location and hours, a company wanting to do business on the Web must be able to do more than just list information: It must be able to interact with customers through its Web site. The Web site should allow customers to submit inquiries, select items for purchase, and submit payment information. It also should allow the company to track customer inquiries and process customer orders. Tasks such as these can be accomplished using dynamic Web pages.

Unlike a static Web page, a **dynamic Web page** is interactive in that it can accept information from the user and also retrieve information for the user. Examples of dynamic Web pages that you might have already used include forms for purchasing merchandise online and for submitting online resumes. Figure 13-3 shows an example of a dynamic Web page that converts American dollars to British pounds. To use the Web page, you enter the number of American dollars in the American dollars box and then click the Submit button. The button's Click event procedure displays the corresponding number of British pounds on the Web page. You will create the Currency Converter Web page in Programming Tutorial 2.

Figure 13-3 Dynamic Currency Converter Web page

The Web applications created in this chapter use a technology called ASP.NET 4.0. **ASP** stands for "active server page" and refers to the type of Web page created by the ASP technology. All ASP pages contain HTML (Hypertext Markup Language) tags that tell the client's browser how to render the page on the computer screen. For example, the instruction `<h1>Hello</h1>` uses the opening <h1> tag and its closing </h1> tag to display the word "Hello" as a heading on the Web page. Many ASP pages also contain ASP tags that specify the controls to include on the Web page. In addition to the HTML and ASP tags, dynamic ASP pages contain code that tells the objects on the Web page how to respond to the user's actions. In this chapter, you will write the appropriate code using the Visual Basic programming language.

When a client computer's browser sends a request for an ASP page, the Web server locates the page and then sends the appropriate HTML instructions to the client. The client's browser uses the instructions to render the Web page on the computer screen. If the Web page is a dynamic one, like the Currency Converter page shown in Figure 13-3, the user can interact with the page by entering data. In most cases, the user then clicks a button on the Web page to submit the data to the server for processing. When the server receives the data, it executes the Visual Basic code associated with the Web page. It then sends back to the client the appropriate HTML, which now includes the result of processing the code and data, for rendering in the browser window. Using the Currency Converter Web page as an example, the user first enters the number of American dollars and then clicks the Submit button, which submits the user's entry to the Web server. The server executes the Visual Basic code to convert the American dollars to British pounds and then sends back the HTML, which now includes the number of British pounds. Notice that the Web page's HTML is interpreted and executed by the client computer, whereas the program code is executed by the Web server. Figure 13-4 illustrates the relationship between the client computer and the Web server.

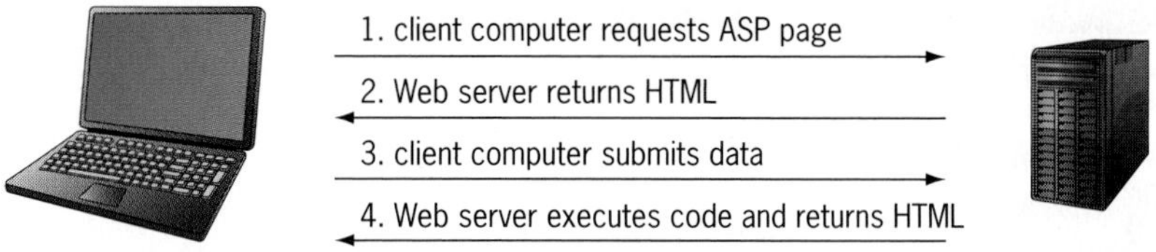

Figure 13-4 Illustration of the relationship between a client computer and a Web server

The answers to Mini-Quiz questions are located in Appendix A.

Mini-Quiz 13-1

1. A computer that requests an ASP page from a Web server is called a _______________ computer.
   a. browser
   b. client
   c. requesting
   d. none of the above

2. A _______________ is a program that uses HTML to render a Web page on the computer screen.
   a. browser
   b. client
   c. server
   d. none of the above

3. A Web page's HTML instructions are processed by the _______________.
   a. client computer
   b. Web server

Creating a Web Application

You create a Web application in Visual Basic using Visual Web Developer 2010, which is available either as a stand-alone product (called Visual Web Developer 2010 Express) or as part of Visual Studio 2010. You can download a free copy of Visual Web Developer 2010 Express from Microsoft's Web site. At the time of this writing, the address is *http://www.microsoft.com/express/Downloads/#2010-Visual-Web-Developer*. Figure 13-5 lists the steps for starting and configuring Visual Web Developer 2010 Express.

HOW TO Start and Configure Visual Web Developer 2010 Express

1. Click the Start button on the Windows 7 taskbar and then point to All Programs.
2. Click Microsoft Visual Studio 2010 Express and then click Microsoft Visual Web Developer 2010 Express.
3. Click Tools on the menu bar, and then click Options to open the Options dialog box. If necessary, select the Show all settings check box.
4. Click the Projects and Solutions node. If necessary, select the following five check boxes: Always show Error List if build finishes with errors, Track Active Item in Solution Explorer, Always show solution, Save new projects when created, and Warn user when the project location is not trusted. If necessary, deselect the following three check boxes: Show advanced build configurations, Show Output window when build starts, and Prompt for symbolic renaming when renaming files.
5. Click the OK button to close the Options dialog box.
6. Click Tools on the menu bar and then point to Settings. If necessary, click Expert Settings to select it.

Figure 13-5 How to start and configure Visual Web Developer 2010 Express

Figure 13-6 lists the steps for creating an empty Web application, and Figure 13-7 shows an example of a completed New Web Site dialog box. (Your dialog box will look slightly different if you are using Visual Web Developer 2010 Express.)

HOW TO Create an Empty Web Application

1. Start Visual Studio 2010 or Visual Web Developer 2010 Express.
2. Click File on the menu bar and then click New Web Site to open the New Web Site dialog box. If necessary, click Visual Basic in the Installed Templates list, and then click ASP.NET Empty Web Site in the middle column of the dialog box.
3. If necessary, change the entry in the Web location box to File System. The File System selection allows you to store your Web application in any folder on either your computer or a network drive.
4. In the box that appears next to the Web location box, enter the location where you want the Web application saved. See Figure 13-7.
5. Click the OK button to close the New Web Site dialog box.

Figure 13-6 How to create an empty Web application

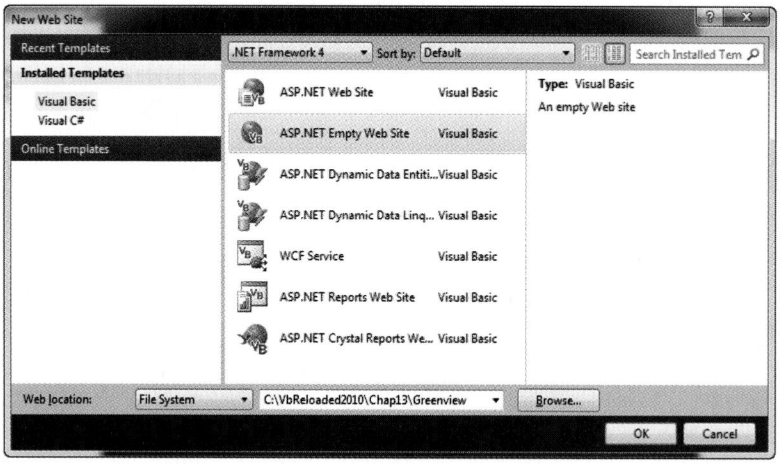

Figure 13-7 Example of a completed New Web Site dialog box in Visual Studio 2010

After creating an empty Web application, you need to add a Web page to it. Figure 13-8 lists the steps for adding a new Web page to an application. As indicated in Step 3 in the figure, you add a new Web page using the Web

Form item in the Add New Item dialog box. Figure 13-9 shows an example of a completed Add New Item dialog box, and Figure 13-10 shows the Default.aspx Web page in Design view. The aspx file contains the instructions for rendering the visual elements on the Web page. (Your dialog box and screen will look slightly different if you are using Visual Web Developer 2010 Express.)

HOW TO Add a New Web Page to a Web Application

1. If necessary, open the Web application.
2. Click Website on the menu bar and then click Add New Item to open the Add New Item dialog box. (If Website does not appear on the menu bar, click the Web application's location and name in the Solution Explorer window.)
3. If necessary, click Visual Basic in the Installed Templates list and then click Web Form in the middle column of the dialog box. Verify that the Place code in separate file check box is selected, and that the Select master page check box is not selected.
4. Enter an appropriate name in the Name box. See Figure 13-9.
5. Click the Add button to display the Web page in the Document window. If necessary, click the Design tab that appears at the bottom of the IDE. You can use Design view to add text and controls to the Web page. Figure 13-10 shows the Default.aspx page in Design view.

Figure 13-8 How to add a new Web page to a Web application

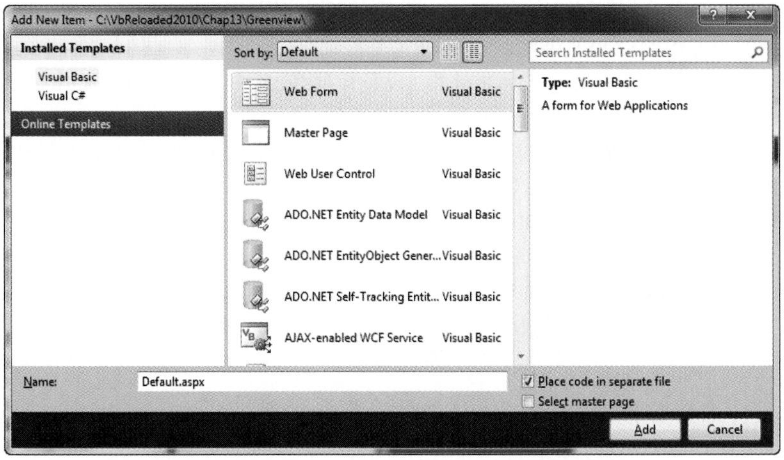

Figure 13-9 Example of a completed Add New Item dialog box

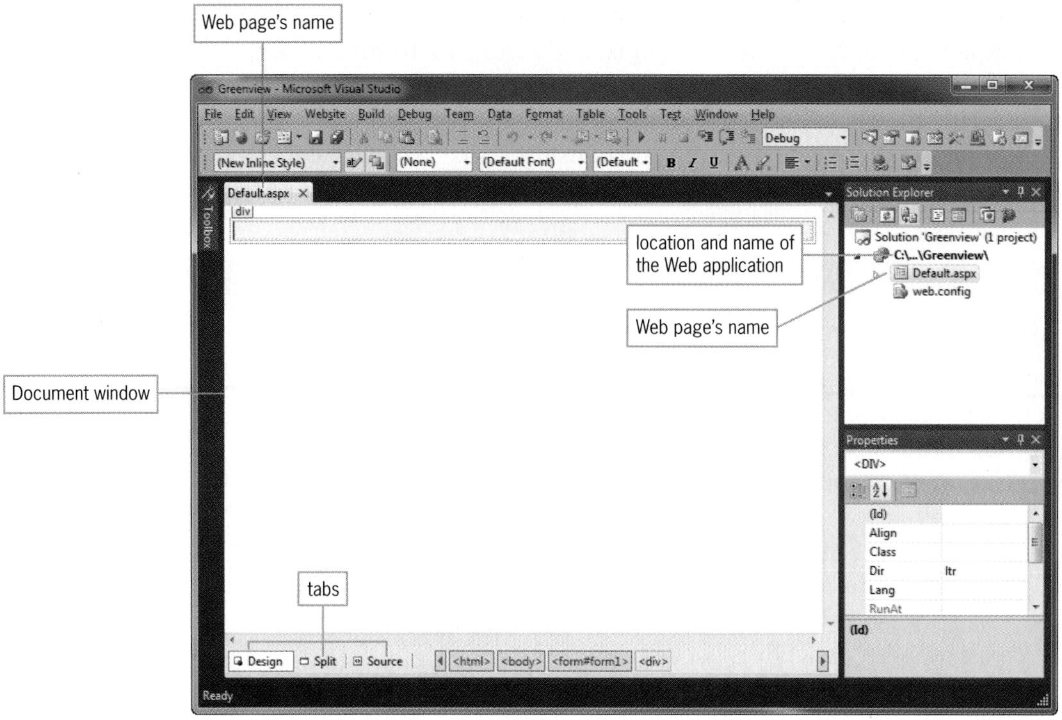

Figure 13-10 Default.aspx Web page

Figure 13-11 lists the steps for adding an existing Web page to a Web application.

HOW TO Add an Existing Web Page to a Web Application

1. If necessary, open the Web application.
2. Click Website on the menu bar and then click Add Existing Item to open the Add Existing Item dialog box. (If Website does not appear on the menu bar, click the Web application's location and name in the Solution Explorer window.)
3. Locate and then click the name of the file that contains the Web page. The filename will end with .aspx.
4. Click the Add button to display the Web page in the Document window. If necessary, click the Design tab that appears at the bottom of the IDE.

Figure 13-11 How to add an existing Web page to a Web application

Customizing a Web Page

You can use the Properties window to customize a Web page. The properties will appear in the Properties window when you select DOCUMENT in the window's Object box. A Web page's Title property, for example, determines the value that appears in the browser's title bar and also on the page's tab in the browser window. Its BgColor property controls the page's background color. The Properties window in Figure 13-12 shows some of the properties of a Web page.

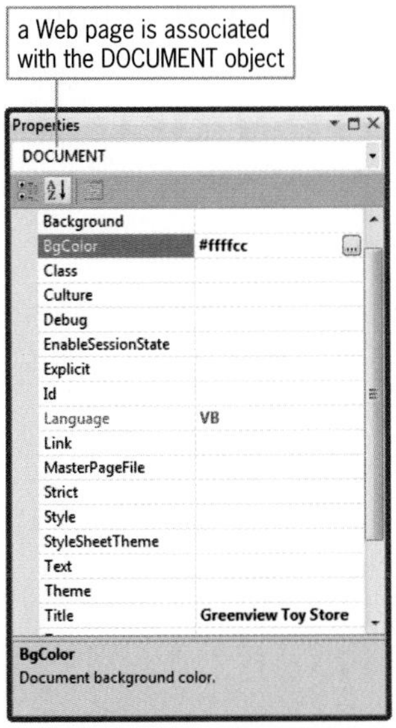

Figure 13-12 Properties window for a Web page

All Web pages contain some text that the user is not allowed to edit, such as a company name or the caption that identifies a text box. Text that cannot be changed by the user is referred to as **static text**. You can add static text to a Web page by simply typing the text on the page itself; or, you can use a label control that you dragged to the Web page from the Toolbox window. See Figure 13-13.

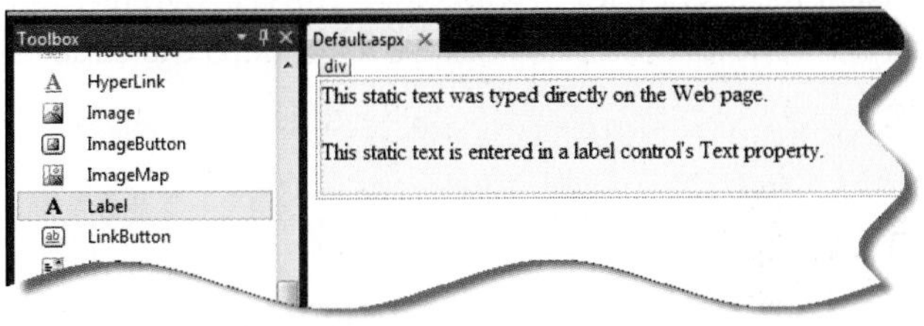

Figure 13-13 Examples of static text on a Web page

You can use either the Format menu or the Formatting toolbar to format the static text on a Web page. Figure 13-14 indicates some of the tools available on the Formatting toolbar.

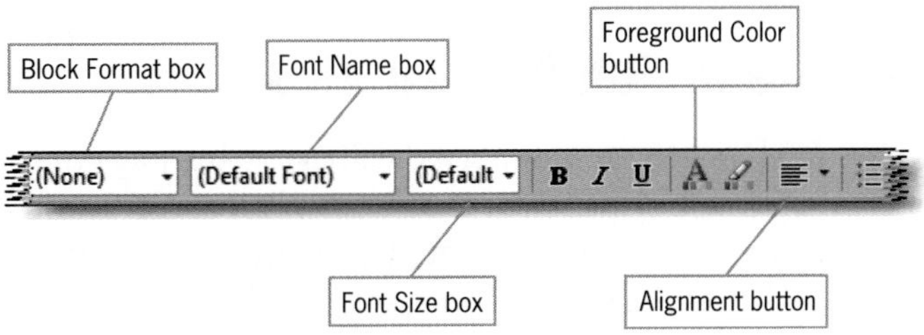

Figure 13-14 Formatting toolbar

You also can customize a Web page by adding controls to it. You do this using the tools provided in the Toolbox window, a portion of which is shown in Figure 13-15. Like Windows controls, Web controls have properties that appear in the Properties window when the control is selected. Unlike Windows controls, however, Web controls have an ID property rather than a Name property.

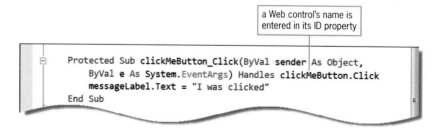

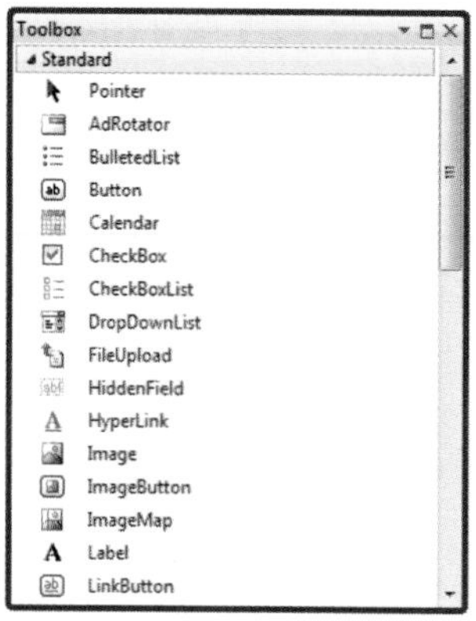

Figure 13-15 Portion of the Toolbox window

Coding the Controls on a Web Page

Like the controls on a Windows form, the controls on a Web page can be coded to perform tasks when a specific event occurs. The clickMeButton_Click procedure shown in Figure 13-16, for example, will display the message "I was clicked" in the messageLabel when the user clicks the Click Me button on the Web page. You enter the code in the Code Editor window. The code is saved in a file whose filename extension is .aspx.vb. The .aspx.vb extension indicates that the file contains the Visual Basic code for a Web page. The .aspx.vb file is commonly referred to as the code-behind file, because it contains the code "behind" the Web page.

a Web control's name is entered in its ID property

```
Protected Sub clickMeButton_Click(ByVal sender As Object,
    ByVal e As System.EventArgs) Handles clickMeButton.Click
    messageLabel.Text = "I was clicked"
End Sub
```

Figure 13-16 Code entered in the Click Me button's Click event procedure

Viewing a Web Page in Full Screen View

While you are designing a Web page, you can periodically view the page in full screen view to determine how it will appear to the user. Full screen view provides a quick and easy way to verify the placement of controls and text on the Web page. Figure 13-17 lists the steps for viewing a Web page in full screen view, and Figure 13-18 shows an example of a Web page displayed in full screen view.

HOW TO View a Web Page in Full Screen View

1. Click View on the menu bar and then click Full Screen. See Figure 13-18.
2. Click the Full Screen button to return to the standard view.

Figure 13-17 How to view a Web page in full screen view

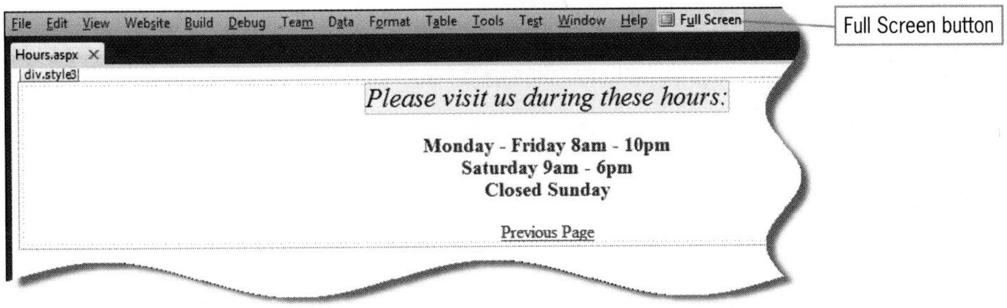

Figure 13-18 Example of a Web page displayed in full screen view

Starting a Web Application

Typically, you start a Web application either by pressing Ctrl+F5 or by clicking the Start Without Debugging option on the Debug menu. The method you use—the shortcut keys or the menu option—is a matter of personal preference. If you prefer to use a menu option, you might need to add the Start Without Debugging option to the Debug menu, because the option is not automatically included on the menu in either Visual Studio or Visual Web Developer Express. Figure 13-19 lists the steps for adding the Start Without Debugging option to the Debug menu, and Figure 13-20 shows the completed Customize dialog box.

HOW TO Add the Start Without Debugging Option to the Debug Menu

1. *If you are using the Express Edition of Visual Web Developer*, click Tools on the menu bar and then point to Settings. If necessary, click Expert Settings to select that option.
2. Click Tools on the menu bar and then click Customize to open the Customize dialog box.
3. Click the Commands tab. The Menu bar radio button should be selected. Click the down arrow in the Menu bar list box. Scroll down the list until you see Debug, and then click Debug.
4. Click the Add Command button to open the Add Command dialog box, and then click Debug in the Categories list. Scroll down the Commands list until you see Start Without Debugging, and then click Start Without Debugging. Click the OK button to close the Add Command dialog box.
5. Click the Move Down button three times. See Figure 13-20.
6. Click the Close button to close the Customize dialog box.

Figure 13-19 How to add the Start Without Debugging option to the Debug menu

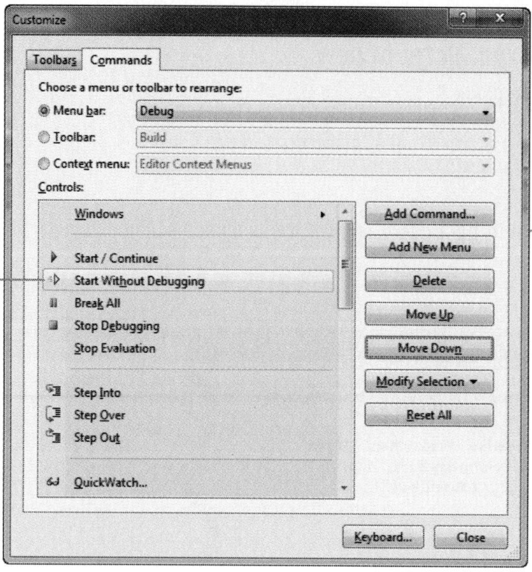

Figure 13-20 Completed Customize dialog box

Opening and Closing an Existing Web Application

You can use the File menu to open and close an existing Web application. Figure 13-21 lists the steps for performing both tasks.

HOW TO Open and Close an Existing Web Application

To open an existing Web application:

1. Click File on the menu bar and then click Open Web Site. If necessary, click the File System button in the Open Web Site dialog box.
2. Click the name of the Web site and then click the Open button.
3. If necessary, right-click the Web page's name in the Solution Explorer window and then click View Designer.

To close an existing Web application:

Click File on the menu bar and then click Close Solution.

Figure 13-21 How to open and close an existing Web application

The answers to Mini-Quiz questions are located in Appendix A.

Mini-Quiz 13-2

1. The Web page in a new Web application is automatically assigned the name ______________.
   a. Default.aspx
   b. Default.vb
   c. Form1.aspx
   d. WebForm1.vb

2. To display a Web page's properties, you first click ______________ in the Properties window's Object box.
   a. DEFAULT
   b. DOCUMENT
   c. PAGE
   d. WEBPAGE

3. Which property determines the background color of a Web page?
   a. BackColor
   b. Background
   c. BackgroundColor
   d. BgColor

You have completed the concepts section of Chapter 13. The Programming Tutorial section is next.

PROGRAMMING TUTORIAL 1

Creating the Greenview Toy Store Web Application

In this tutorial, you create a Web application for the Greenview Toy Store. The application contains the two Web pages shown earlier in Figures 13-1 and 13-2 in the chapter. The Web pages contain static text, an image control, and two link button controls.

The Ch13ProgTut1 video demonstrates all of the steps in Programming Tutorial 1.

To create the Web application:

1. *If you are using Visual Studio 2010,* start Visual Studio 2010. *If you are using Visual Web Developer 2010 Express,* follow the instructions shown earlier in Figure 13-5 to start and (if necessary) configure Visual Web Developer 2010.
2. If necessary, open the Solution Explorer and Properties windows and auto-hide the Toolbox window.
3. Click **File** on the menu bar and then click **New Web Site** to open the New Web Site dialog box. If necessary, click **Visual Basic** in the Installed Templates list. Click **ASP.NET Empty Web Site** in the middle column of the dialog box.
4. If necessary, change the entry in the Web location box to **File System**. Recall that the File System selection allows you to store your Web application in any folder on either your computer or a network drive.
5. In this step, you will be instructed to store the Web application in the C:\VbReloaded2010\Chap13 folder; however, you can use any location. In the box that appears next to the Web location box, replace

the existing text with **C:\VbReloaded2010\Chap13\Greenview**. Figure 13-22 shows the completed New Web Site dialog box. Your dialog box will look slightly different if you are using Visual Web Developer Express.

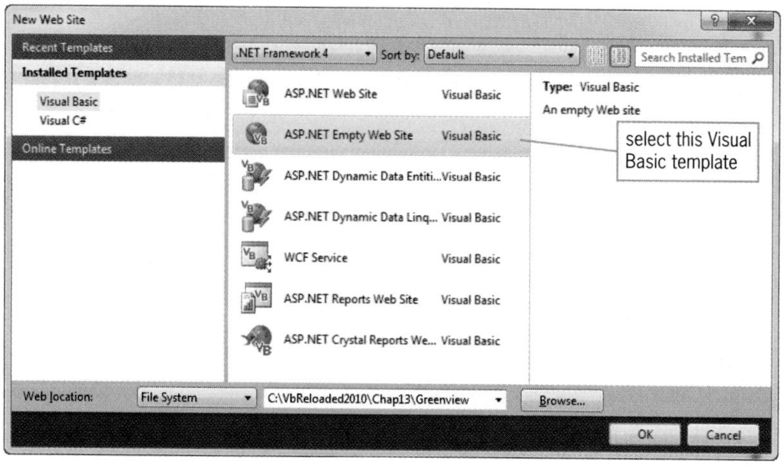

Figure 13-22 New Web Site dialog box

6. Click the **OK** button to close the dialog box. The computer creates the Greenview Web application.
7. Now, you will add a Web page to the application. Click **Website** on the menu bar and then click **Add New Item** to open the Add New Item dialog box. (If Website does not appear on the menu bar, click the Web application's location and name in the Solution Explorer window.)
8. If necessary, click **Visual Basic** in the Installed Templates list and then (if necessary) click **Web Form** in the middle column of the dialog box. Verify that the Place code in separate file check box is selected, and that the Select master page check box is not selected. As indicated in Figure 13-23, the Web page will be named Default.aspx.

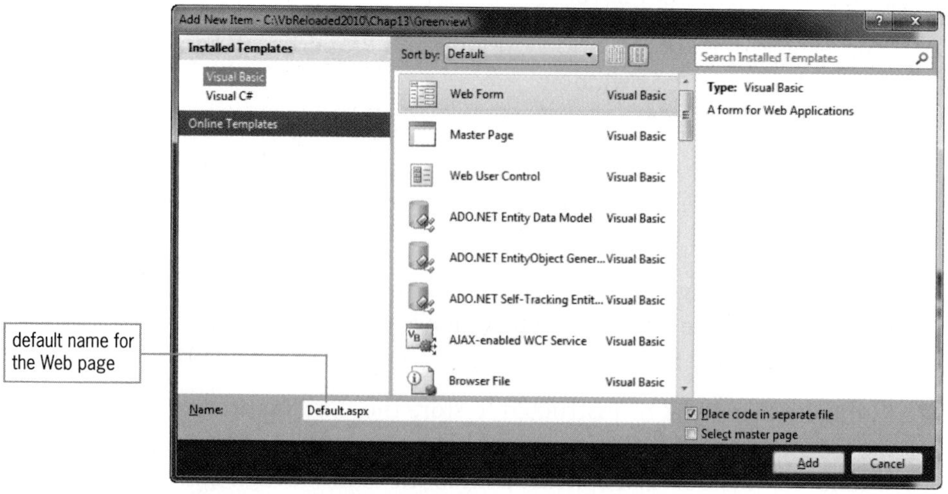

Figure 13-23 Add New Item dialog box

9. Click the **Add** button to display the Default.aspx page in the Document window. If necessary, click the **Design** tab that appears at the bottom of the IDE. When the Design tab is selected, the Web page appears in Design view in the Document window. You can use Design view to add text and controls to the Web page. See Figure 13-24. If the Formatting toolbar does not appear on your screen, click **View** on the menu bar, point to **Toolbars**, and then click **Formatting**. If the div tag does not appear in the Document window, click either the **<div>** button at the bottom of the IDE or the **rectangle** below the body tag.

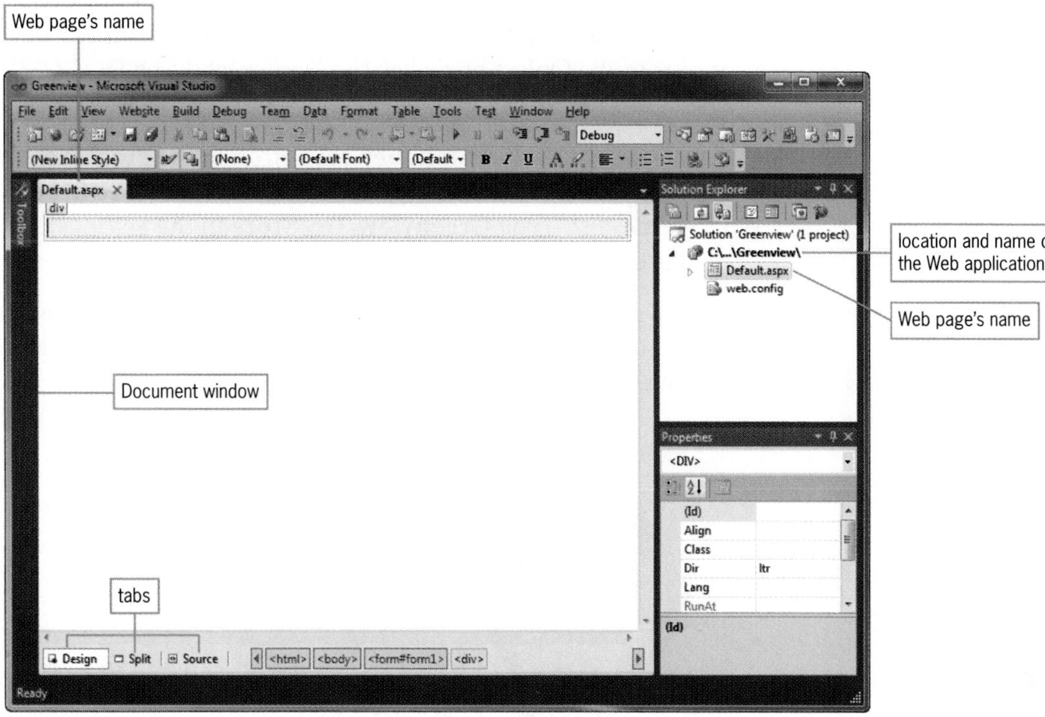

Figure 13-24 Default.aspx Web page shown in Design view

10. Click the **Source** tab to display the Web page in Source view. This view shows the HTML and ASP tags that tell the browser how to render the Web page. The tags are automatically generated for you as you are creating the Web page in Design view. Currently, the Web page contains only HTML tags.

11. Click the **Split** tab to split the Document window into two parts. The upper half displays the Web page in Source view, and the lower half displays it in Design view.

12. Click the **Design** tab to return to Design view. Auto-hide the Solution Explorer window.

Adding a Title and Background Color to the Web Page

In the following set of steps, you will change the Web page's Title to Greenview Toy Store. You also will change its BgColor property to a pale yellow. When a Web page is displayed in a browser, the value stored in its Title property appears in the browser's title bar and also on the page's tab in the browser window. The value stored in the Web page's BgColor property determines the background color of the Web page.

To change the Title and BgColor properties:

1. Click the **down arrow** button in the Properties window's Object box and then click **DOCUMENT** in the list. (If DOCUMENT does not appear in the Object box, click the Design tab.) The DOCUMENT object represents the Web page.
2. If necessary, click the **Alphabetical** button in the Properties window to display the properties in alphabetical order. Click **Title** in the Properties list. Type **Greenview Toy Store** in the Settings box and then press **Enter**.
3. Click **BgColor** in the Properties list and then click the **...** (ellipsis) button to open the More Colors dialog box. Click the **hexagon** indicated in Figure 13-25.

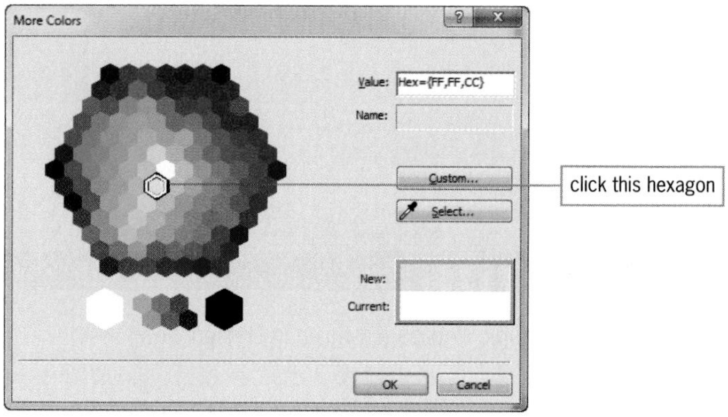

Figure 13-25 More Colors dialog box

4. Click the **OK** button to close the More Colors dialog box. The page's background color changes from white to a pale yellow.
5. Auto-hide the Properties window. Save the solution either by clicking the **Save All** button or by clicking the **Save All** option on the File menu.

Starting a Web Application

As mentioned earlier, you can start a Web application either by pressing Ctrl+F5 or by clicking the Start Without Debugging option on the Debug menu. However, recall that the Start Without Debugging option is not automatically included on the Debug menu in either Visual Studio or Visual Web Developer Express. You can add the option to the menu by performing the next set of steps. If you prefer to use the Ctrl+F5 shortcut keys, you can skip the next set of steps.

To add the Start Without Debugging option to the Debug menu:

1. First, you will verify that your Debug menu does not already contain the Start Without Debugging option. Click **Debug** on the menu bar.
2. If the Debug menu contains the Start Without Debugging option, close the menu by clicking **Debug** again, and then skip the remaining steps in this set of steps.
3. If the Debug menu does not contain the Start Without Debugging option, close the menu by clicking **Debug** again.
4. Click **Tools** on the menu bar and then click **Customize** to open the Customize dialog box.
5. Click the **Commands** tab. The Menu bar radio button should be selected. Click the **down arrow** in the Menu bar list box. Scroll down the list until you see Debug, and then click **Debug**.
6. Click the **Add Command** button to open the Add Command dialog box, and then click **Debug** in the Categories list. Scroll down the Commands list until you see Start Without Debugging, and then click **Start Without Debugging**. Click the **OK** button to close the Add Command dialog box.
7. Click the **Move Down** button three times. The completed Customize dialog box is shown in Figure 13-26. Click the Close button to close the Customize dialog box.

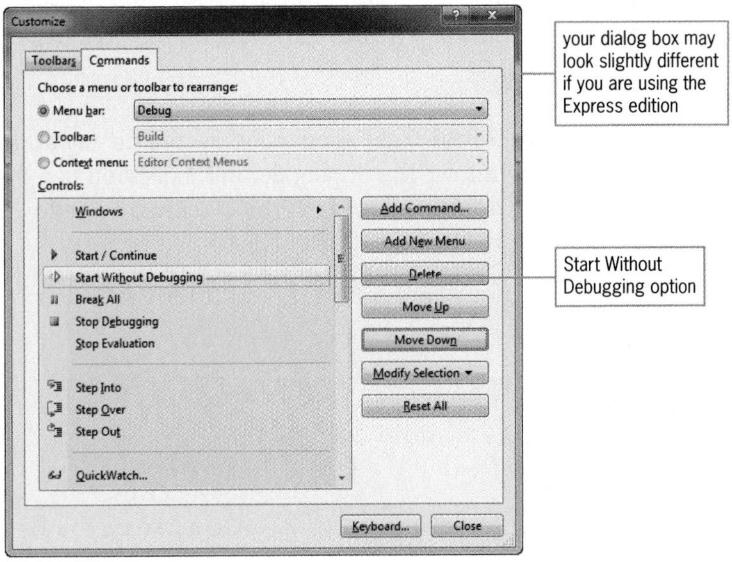

Figure 13-26 Customize dialog box

When you start a Web application in either Visual Studio 2010 or Visual Web Developer 2010 Express, the computer creates a temporary Web server that allows you to view your Web page in a browser. Keep in mind, however, that your Web page will need to be placed on an actual Web server for others to view it.

To start a Web application:

1. Start the Web application. You can do this either by pressing Ctrl+F5 or by clicking the Start Without Debugging option on the Debug menu. The Web page appears in a browser window. Notice that the value in the page's Title property appears in the browser's title bar and on the page's tab in the browser window. See Figure 13-27.

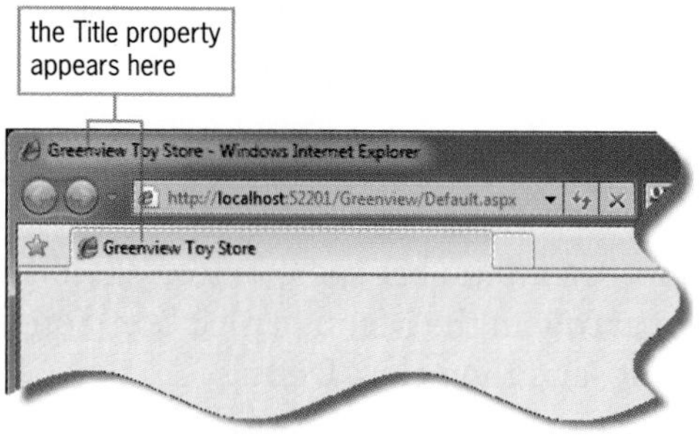

Figure 13-27 Web page showing the effect of the Title and BgColor properties

2. Close the browser window by clicking the **Close** button on its title bar.

Adding Static Text to a Web Page

As you learned in the chapter, all Web pages contain static text, which is text that cannot be changed by the user. Recall that you can add static text to a Web page using a label control; or, you can simply type the text on the page itself. In the following set of steps, you will type the static text on the Web page.

To add static text to the Web page:

1. Click **inside the rectangle** that appears below the div tag at the top of the Document window. The div tag defines a division in a Web page. (If the div tag does not appear in the Document window, click the <div> button at the bottom of the IDE.)
2. Enter the following four lines of text. Press **Enter** twice after typing the last line.

   Greenview Toy Store
   333 Main Street
   Chicago, IL 60611
   (111) 555-5555

3. Save the application.

Formatting the Text on a Web Page

Recall that you can use either the Format menu or the Formatting toolbar to format the static text on a Web page. In the next set of steps, you will use the Formatting toolbar.

To format the static text on the Web page:

1. Select (highlight) the Greenview Toy Store text on the Web page. Click the **down arrow** in the Block Format box on the Formatting toolbar. Click **Heading 1 <h1>**. (If the Formatting toolbar does not appear on your screen, click View on the menu bar, point to Toolbars, and then click Formatting.)
2. Select the address and phone number text on the Web page. Click the **down arrow** in the Block Format box and then click **Heading 2 <h2>**.
3. Now, you will use the Formatting toolbar's alignment button to center all of the static text. Select all of the static text on the Web page and then click the **down arrow** on the Alignment button. See Figure 13-28.

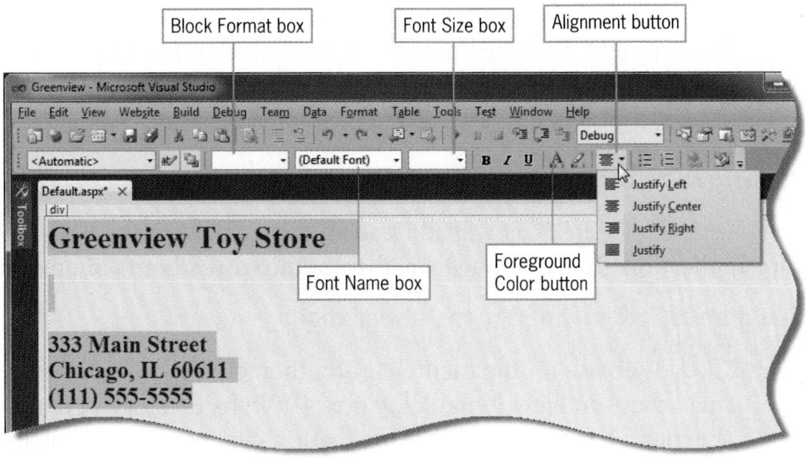

Figure 13-28 Result of clicking the Alignment button on the Formatting toolbar

4. Click **Justify Center**. The selected text appears centered, horizontally, on the Web page. Click **anywhere below the phone number** to deselect the text, and then save the application.

Viewing a Web Page in Full Screen View

While you are designing a Web page, you can periodically view the page in full screen view to determine how it will appear to the user. To view a Web page in full screen view, you use the Full Screen option on the View menu.

To view the Web page using the Full Screen option:

1. Click **View** on the menu bar and then click **Full Screen**. See Figure 13-29. Although not identical to viewing in a browser window, full screen view provides a quick and easy way to verify the placement of controls and text on the Web page.

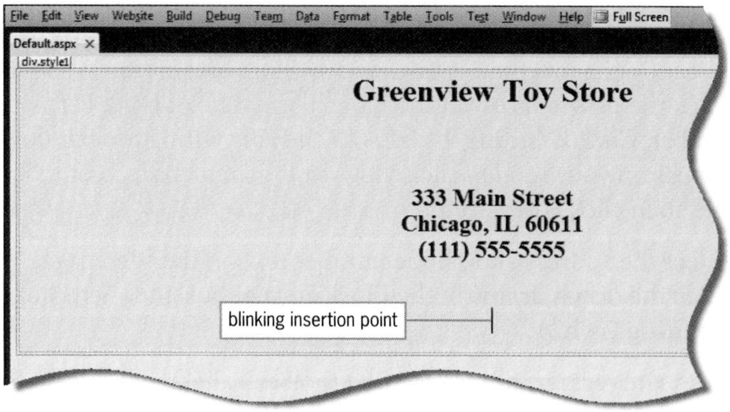

Figure 13-29 Default.aspx Web page displayed in full screen view

2. Click the **Full Screen** button to return to the standard view. (If you mistakenly clicked the window's Close button, click the Full Screen button, right-click Default.aspx in the Solution Explorer window, and then click View Designer.)

Adding Another Web Page to the Application

In the next set of steps, you will add a second Web page to the Greenview Toy Store application. The Web page will display the store's hours of operation.

To add another Web page to the application:

1. Click **Website** on the menu bar and then click **Add New Item** to open the Add New Item dialog box. (If Website does not appear on the menu bar, click the Web application's location and name in the Solution Explorer window.)
2. If necessary, click **Visual Basic** in the Installed Templates list and then (if necessary) click **Web Form** in the middle column of the dialog box. Change the filename in the Name box to **Hours** and then click the **Add** button. The Hours.aspx Web page appears in the Document window.
3. Temporarily display the Solution Explorer window. Notice that the window now contains the Hours.aspx filename.
4. If necessary, click the **Design** tab and then click **inside the rectangle** that appears below the div tag at the top of the Document window. (If the div tag does not appear in the Document window, click either the <div> button at the bottom of the IDE or the **rectangle** below the body tag.) Type **Please visit us during these hours:** and press **Enter** twice.
5. Now, enter the following three lines of text. Press Enter **twice** after typing the last line.

   Monday – Friday 8am – 10pm
   Saturday 9am – 6pm
   Closed Sunday

6. Select the Please visit us during these hours: text. Click the **down arrow** in the Font Size box and then click **x-large (24pt)**. Also click the ***I*** (Italic) button on the Formatting toolbar.

7. Select the three lines of text that contain the store hours. Click the **down arrow** in the Font Size box and then click **large (18pt)**. Also click the **B** (Bold) button on the Formatting toolbar.

8. Now, you will change the color of the selected text. Click the **Foreground Color** button on the Formatting toolbar to open the More Colors dialog box. Click **any dark green hexagon** and then click the **OK** button.

9. Select all of the static text on the Web page. Click the **down arrow** on the Alignment button and then click **Justify Center**.

10. Click **the blank line below the store hours** to deselect the text, and then save the application.

Adding a LinkButton to a Web Page

In the next set of steps, you will add a LinkButton to both Web pages. The LinkButton on the Default.aspx page will display the Hours.aspx page. The LinkButton on the Hours.aspx page will return the user to the Default.aspx Web page.

To add a LinkButton to both Web pages:

1. First, you will add a LinkButton to the Hours.aspx page. Permanently display the Toolbox window and then click the **LinkButton** tool. Drag your mouse pointer to the location shown in Figure 13-30 and then release the mouse button.

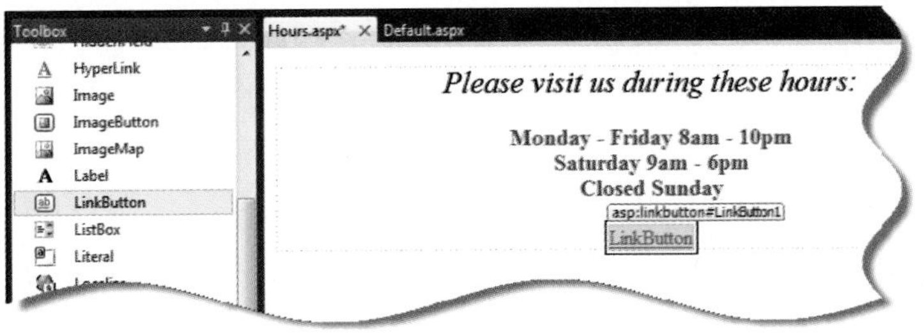

Figure 13-30 LinkButton added to the Hours.aspx Web page

2. Temporarily display the Properties window. Change the control's Text property to **Previous Page** and press **Enter**. Click **PostBackUrl** in the Properties list and then click the **...** (ellipsis) button to open the Select URL dialog box. Click **Default.aspx** in the Contents of folder list. See Figure 13-31.

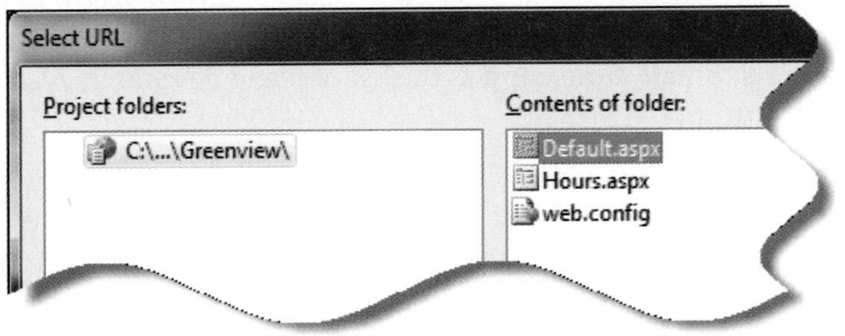

Figure 13-31 Select URL dialog box

3. Click the **OK** button to close the dialog box and then click the **Web page**.

4. Now, you will add a LinkButton to the Default.aspx page. Click the **Default.aspx** tab. Click the **LinkButton** tool. Drag your mouse pointer to the location shown in Figure 13-32 and then release the mouse button.

Figure 13-32 LinkButton added to the Default.aspx Web page

5. Temporarily display the Properties window. Change the control's Text property to **Store Hours** and press **Enter**. Change its PostBackUrl property to **Hours.aspx**.

6. Click the **Web page** and then save the application.

7. Start the application. The Default.aspx page appears in the browser window. Click **Store Hours** to display the Hours.aspx page. Click **Previous Page** to display the Default.aspx page. Close the browser window.

Adding an Image to a Web Page

In the next set of steps, you will add an image to the Default.aspx page. The image is stored in the Small_house.jpg file, which is contained in the VbReloaded2010\Chap13 folder. The image file was downloaded from the Stock.XCHNG site and was generously contributed by photographer Gerrit Schneider. (You can browse and optionally download other free images at *www.sxc.hu*.)

To add an image to the Web page:

1. First, you will need to add the image file to the application. Click **Website** on the menu bar and then click **Add Existing Item**. Open the VbReloaded2010\Chap13 folder. Click the **down arrow** in the box that controls the file types and then click **All Files (*.*)** in the list. Click **Small_house.jpg** in the list of filenames and then click the **Add** button.

2. If necessary, insert a blank line below the Store Hours LinkButton. Click the **blank line** below the Store Hours LinkButton and then press **Enter**. Click the **Image** tool in the toolbox. Drag your mouse pointer to the location shown in Figure 13-33 and then release the mouse button.

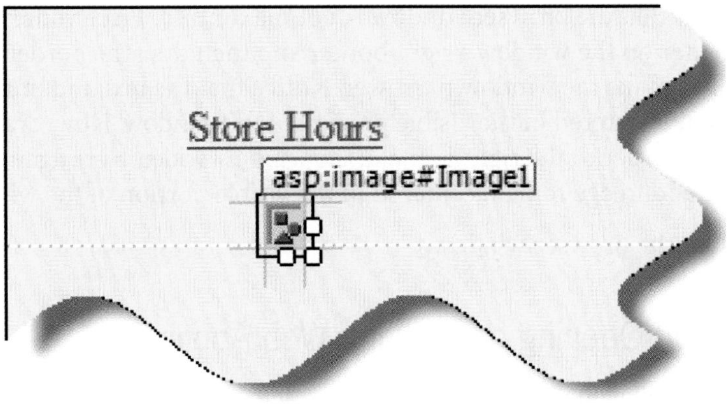

Figure 13-33 Image control added to the Default.aspx Web page

3. Temporarily display the Properties window. Click **ImageUrl** in the Properties list and then click the **...** (ellipsis) button to open the Select Image dialog box. Click **Small_house.jpg** in the Contents of folder section and then click the **OK** button.
4. Next, you will put a colored border around the image control and also change the border's width to 10 pixels. Change the image control's BorderStyle property to **Groove**, and then change its BorderWidth property to **10**. Press **Enter** after typing the number 10.
5. Now, you will change the color of the image's border to match the Web page's color. Click **BorderColor** in the Properties list and then click the **...** (ellipsis) button. When the More Colors dialog box opens, click the same hexagon as you did for the DOCUMENT's BgColor. (If necessary, refer back to Figure 13-25.) Click the **OK** button to close the dialog box and then click the **Web page**.
6. Save and then start the application. See Figure 13-34.

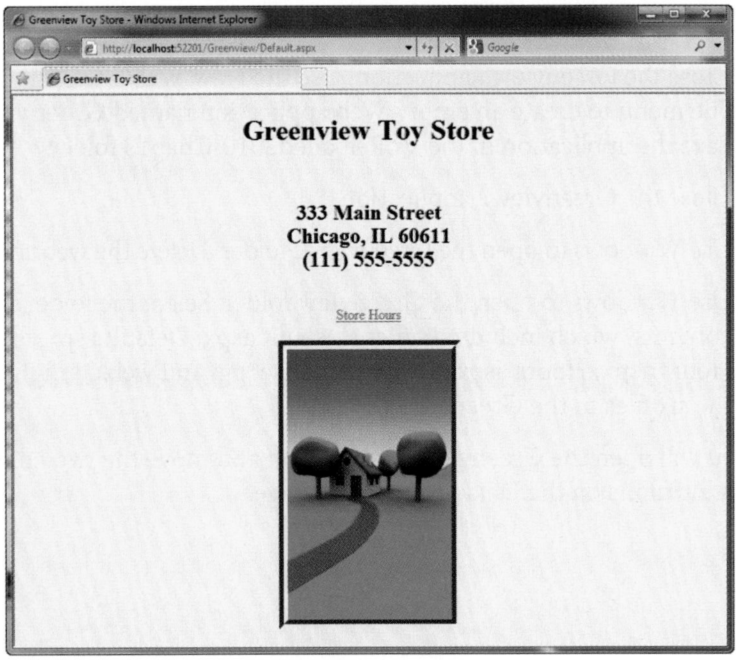

Figure 13-34 Default.aspx Web page displayed in a browser window

7. Verify that the browser window is not maximized. Place your mouse pointer on the window's right border and then drag the border to the left to make the window narrower. Notice that the text and image remain centered in the visible portion of the window. Now, drag the right border to the right to make the window wider. Here again, the text and image remain centered in the visible portion of the window.
8. Close the browser window.

Closing and Opening an Existing Web Application

You can use the File menu to close and also open an existing Web application.

To close and then open the Greenview application:

1. Click **File** on the menu bar and then click **Close Solution** to close the application.
2. Now, you will open the application. Click **File** on the menu bar and then click **Open Web Site**. The Open Web Site dialog box appears. If necessary, click the **File System** button. Click the **Greenview** folder, which is contained in the VbReloaded2010\Chap13 folder, and then click the **Open** button. (If you need to open a Web page in the Document window, right-click the Web page's name in the Solution Explorer window and then click View Designer.)

Repositioning a Control on a Web Page

At times, you may want to reposition a control on a Web page. In this section, you will move the image and link button controls to different locations on the Default.aspx Web page. First, however, you will create a new Web application and then copy the Greenview files to the application.

To create a new Web application and then copy files to the application:

1. Close the Greenview application. Use the New Web Site option on the File menu to create an empty Web application named **Greenview2**. Save the application in the VbReloaded2010\Chap13 folder.
2. Close the Greenview2 application.
3. Use Windows to open the Greenview2 folder. Delete the web.config file.
4. Use Windows to open the Greenview folder. Select the folder's contents, which include six files (Default.aspx, Default.aspx.vb, Hours.aspx, Hours.aspx.vb, Small_house.jpg, and web.config). Copy the six files to the Greenview2 folder.

Now, you will open the Greenview2 application and move the two controls to different locations on the Default.aspx Web page.

To open the Greenview2 application and then move the controls:

1. Open the Greenview2 Web application. Right-click **Default.aspx** in the Solution Explorer window and then click **View Designer**.
2. First, you will move the image control from the bottom of the Web page to the top of the Web page. If necessary, click **immediately before the letter G** in the Greenview Toy Store heading. Press **Enter** to insert a blank line above the heading.
3. Click the **image control** on the Web page. Drag the image control to the blank line immediately above the heading, and then release the mouse button.
4. Next, you will move the link button to the empty area below the store's name. Click the **link button control**. Drag the control to the empty area below the store's name, and then release the mouse button.
5. Save and then start the application. See Figure 13-35.

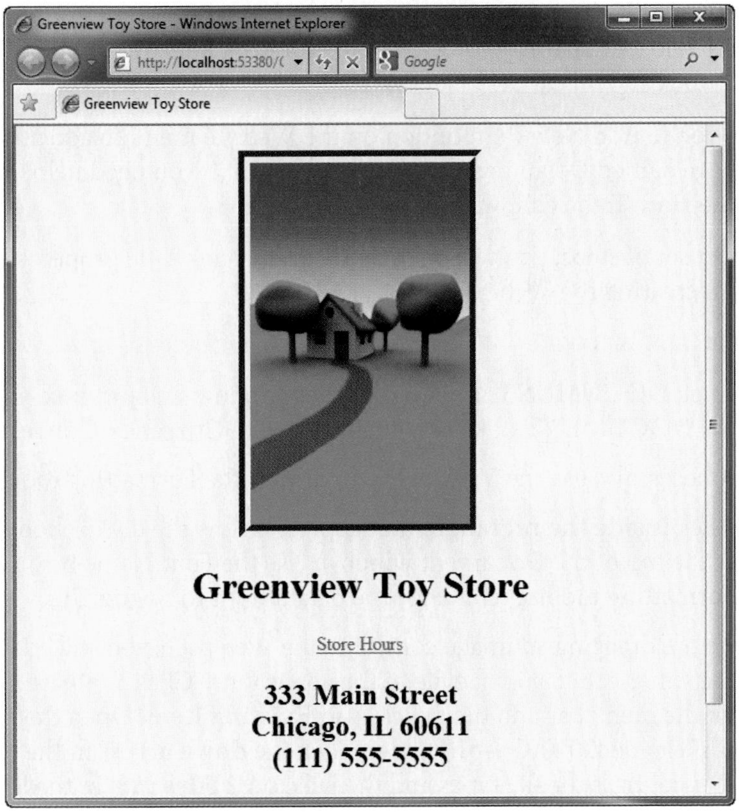

Figure 13-35 Modified Default.aspx Web page

6. Close the browser window and then close the application.

PROGRAMMING TUTORIAL 2

Creating the Currency Converter Application

In this tutorial, you create a Web application that converts U.S. dollars to British pounds. The application contains the dynamic Web page shown earlier in Figure 13-3. The Web page contains static text, an image control, a text box, a label, and a button.

To create the Web application and then add a Web page to it:

1. *If you are using Visual Studio 2010,* start Visual Studio 2010. *If you are using Visual Web Developer 2010 Express,* follow the instructions shown earlier in Figure 13-5 to start and (if necessary) configure Visual Web Developer 2010.
2. If necessary, open the Solution Explorer and Properties windows and auto-hide the Toolbox window.
3. Use the New Web Site option on the File menu to create an empty Web application named Currency. Save the application in the VbReloaded2010\Chap13 folder. If you need help, refer to the How To box shown earlier in Figure 13-6.
4. Use the Add New Item option on the Website menu to add a Web page named Default.aspx to the application. If you need help, refer to the How To box shown earlier in Figure 13-8.

In the next set of steps, you will change the Web page's Title property and also begin creating the Web page.

To change the Web page's Title property and also begin creating the Web page:

1. Click **DOCUMENT** in the Properties window's Object box. Change the DOCUMENT object's Title property to **Currency Converter**.
2. If necessary, use the View menu to display the Formatting toolbar.
3. Click **inside the rectangle** that appears below the div (or body) tag at the top of the Document window. Use the Font Name box on the Formatting toolbar to change the default font to **Segoe UI**.
4. Before dragging an image control to the Web page, you will add the American flag image file to the application. Click **Website** on the menu bar and then click **Add Existing Item**. Open the VbReloaded2010\Chap13 folder. Click the **down arrow** in the box that controls the file types and then click **All Files (*.*)** in the list. Click **USflag.jpg** in the list of filenames and then click the **Add** button.
5. Permanently display the Toolbox window. Drag an image control into the rectangle that appears below the div tag and then release the mouse button. Change the image control's ImageUrl property to **USflag.jpg**.
6. Click an **empty area** to the right of the flag to deselect the image control, and then press **Enter** twice.
7. Next, you will enter the Web page's static text. Press **Tab** twice. Type **Currency Converter** and then press **Enter** twice.
8. Press **Tab** twice. Type **American dollars:**, press the **Spacebar** twice, and then press **Enter** twice.

9. Press **Tab** twice. Type **British pounds:**, press the **Spacebar** twice, and then press **Enter** twice.
10. Press **Tab** twice. Figure 13-36 shows the image control and static text on the Web page.

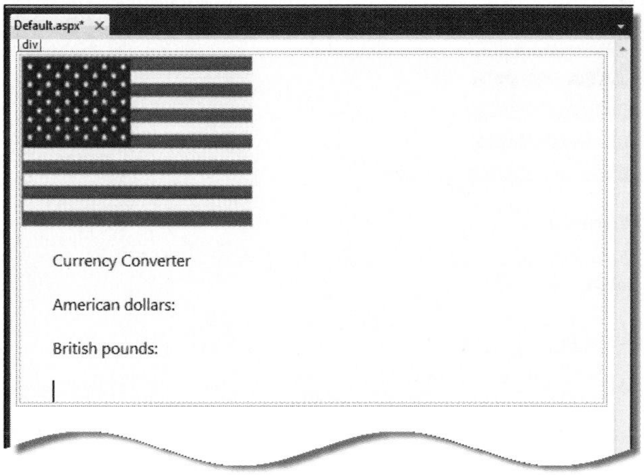

Figure 13-36 Image control and static text on the Web page

In addition to the image control and static text, the Web page will contain a text box, a label, and a button. You will add those controls next.

To add a text box, a label, and a button to the Web page:

1. Drag a text box control to the Web page. Position the control immediately after the two spaces that follow the "American dollars:" text, and then release the mouse button.
2. Unlike Windows controls, Web controls have an ID property rather than a Name property. Use the Properties window to set the TextBox1 control's ID property (which appears at the top of the Properties list) to **dollarsTextBox**. Also set its Width property to **90px**.
3. Drag a label control to the Web page. Position the control immediately after the two spaces that follow the "British pounds:" text, and then release the mouse button. Set the following properties for the Label1 control:

ID	**poundsLabel**
BorderStyle	**Solid**
BorderWidth	**1px**
Text	**0**
Width	**90px**

4. Change the label control's BackColor property to a pale yellow.
5. Finally, drag a button control to the Web page. Position the control two blank lines below the letter B in the "British pounds:" text, and then release the mouse button. Set the following properties for the Button1 control:

ID	**submitButton**
Text	**Submit**

6. Click a **blank area** on the Web page and then save the application. See Figure 13-37.

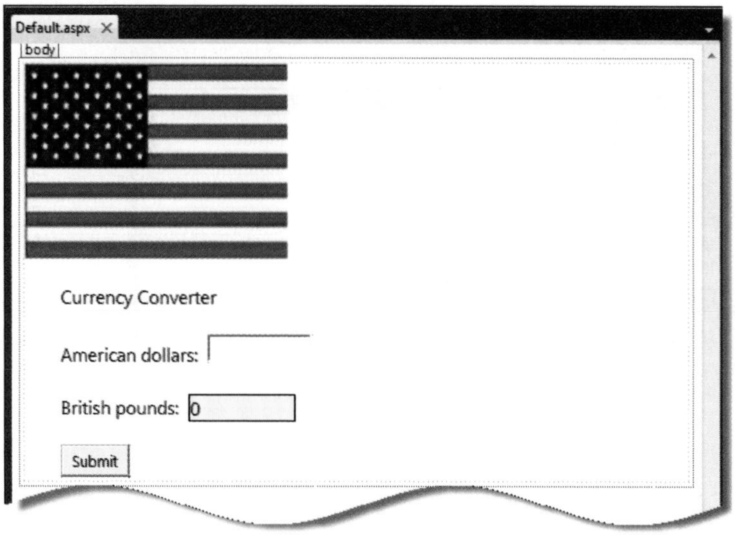

Figure 13-37 Current status of the Web page

Looking back at the Web page shown earlier in Figure 13-3, you will notice that the heading text (Currency Converter) is larger than the other text on the page. Also, the image control is positioned to the left of the static text and controls. You will make these modifications in the next set of steps.

To complete the Web page's interface:

1. Select (highlight) the Currency Converter text. Use the Font Size box on the Formatting toolbar to change the font size to **xx-large (36pt)**.
2. Click the **image control**. Click **Format** on the menu bar, and then click **Position** to open the Position dialog box. See Figure 13-38.

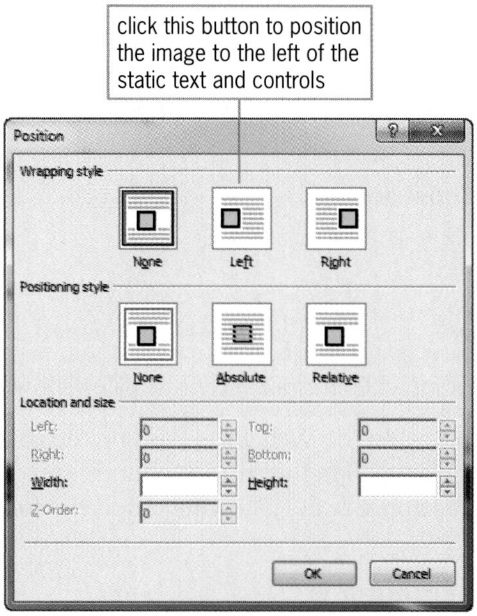

Figure 13-38 Position dialog box

3. The image control should appear on the left side of the static text and controls. Click the **Left** button in the Wrapping style section, and then click the **OK** button.
4. Position your mouse pointer on the image control's lower right sizing handle, as shown in Figure 13-39. Drag the sizing handle until the control is approximately the size shown in the figure. (The number of pixels may be different on your screen. Just be sure that all of the static text and controls appear to the right of the image control.)

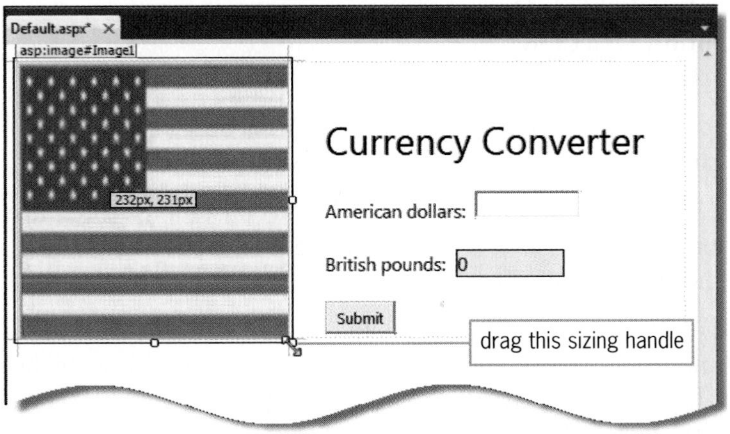

Figure 13-39 Size and position of the image control

5. Click an **empty area** on the Web page to deselect the image control. Save the application and then start it by pressing **Ctrl+F5**. The Web page appears in a browser window. Close the browser window.

Coding the Submit Button's Click Event Procedure

In the following set of steps, you will code the Submit button's Click event procedure so that it converts the number of American dollars to British pounds and then displays the result on the Web page. At the time of this writing, an American dollar was equivalent to approximately .68 British pounds. As you do when coding a control on a Windows form, you enter the code for a control on a Web page in the Code Editor window. (If you need help, you can look ahead to Figure 13-44.)

To code the Submit button's Click event procedure and then test the code:

1. Right-click the **Web page** and then click **View Code** to open the Code Editor window. The Default.aspx.vb window opens. Temporarily display the Solution Explorer window. See Figure 13-40.

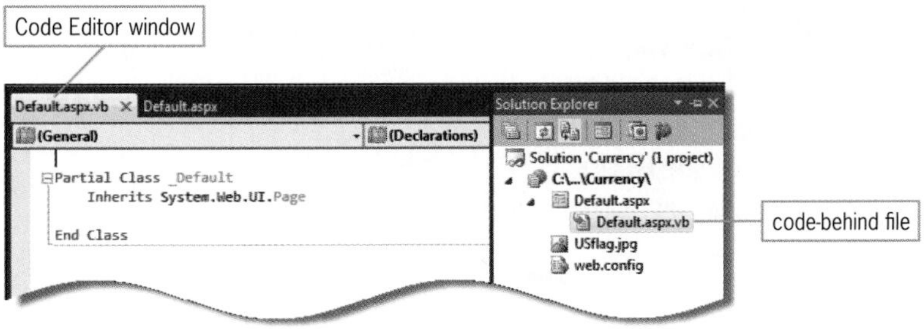

Figure 13-40 Code Editor and Solution Explorer windows

2. Enter the following comments above the Partial Class clause. Replace <your name> and <current date> with your name and the current date. Press **Enter** twice after typing the last comment.

   ' Application name: Currency
   ' Purpose: Convert dollars to pounds
   ' Created/revised by: <your name> on <current date>

3. Now, enter the following Option statements:

   Option Explicit On
   Option Strict On
   Option Infer Off

4. Open the submitButton's Click event procedure. Type **' converts dollars to pounds** and then press **Enter** twice.
5. The procedure will use a Double named constant to store the conversion rate of .68. Enter a Const statement to declare and initialize the `PoundRate` named constant.
6. The procedure will use two Double variables to store the number of American dollars and the number of British pounds. Enter the Dim statements to declare the `dollars` and `pounds` variables. Press **Enter** twice after typing the second Dim statement.
7. Next, enter a statement that uses the TryParse method to convert the contents of the dollarsTextBox to Double, storing the result in the `dollars` variable.
8. Now, enter an assignment statement that converts the dollars to pounds and then assigns the result to the `pounds` variable.
9. Finally, enter an assignment statement that assigns the number of pounds to the poundsLabel's Text property. Format the number of pounds using the "N2" format.
10. Save and then start the application. Click the **American dollars** box and then type **10**. Click the **Submit** button; doing this submits your entry to the server, along with a request for additional services. The server processes the code contained in the button's Click event procedure and then sends the appropriate HTML to the browser for rendering on the screen. See Figure 13-41.

Figure 13-41 Result of clicking the Submit button

11. Close the browser window and then close the Code Editor window.

Validating User Input

The Validation section of the toolbox provides several tools for validating user input. The tools are referred to as **validator tools**. The name, purpose, and important properties of each validator tool are listed in Figure 13-42. In the Currency Converter application, you will use a RequiredFieldValidator control to verify that the user entered the number of American dollars.

Name	Purpose	Properties
CompareValidator	compare an entry with a constant value or the property stored in a control	ControlToCompare ControlToValidate ErrorMessage Type ValueToCompare
CustomValidator	verify that an entry passes the specified validation logic	ClientValidationFunction ControlToValidate ErrorMessage
RangeValidator	verify that an entry is within the specified minimum and maximum values	ControlToValidate ErrorMessage MaximumValue MinimumValue Type
RegularExpressionValidator	verify that an entry matches a specific pattern	ControlToValidate ErrorMessage ValidationExpression
RequiredFieldValidator	verify that a control contains data	ControlToValidate ErrorMessage
ValidationSummary	display all of the validation error messages in a single location on a Web page	DisplayMode HeaderText

Figure 13-42 Validator tools

To verify that the user entered the number of American dollars:

1. If necessary, maximize the Visual Studio (Visual Web Developer) window.
2. Click **on the same line as, but immediately after, the dollarsTextBox** and then press the **Spacebar** three times.
3. If necessary, expand the Validation section in the toolbox. Click the **RequiredFieldValidator** tool and then drag your mouse pointer to the Web page. Position your mouse pointer to the right of the dollarsTextBox and then release the mouse button. Auto-hide the Toolbox window.
4. Set the following properties for the RequiredFieldValidator control:

   ControlToValidate **dollarsTextBox**
   ErrorMessage **Required field**

5. Also set the RequiredFieldValidator control's ForeColor property to red, and then auto-hide the Properties window.
6. Save and then start the application. Click the **Submit** button without entering a value in the dollarsTextBox. The RequiredFieldValidator control displays the "Required field" message. See Figure 13-43.

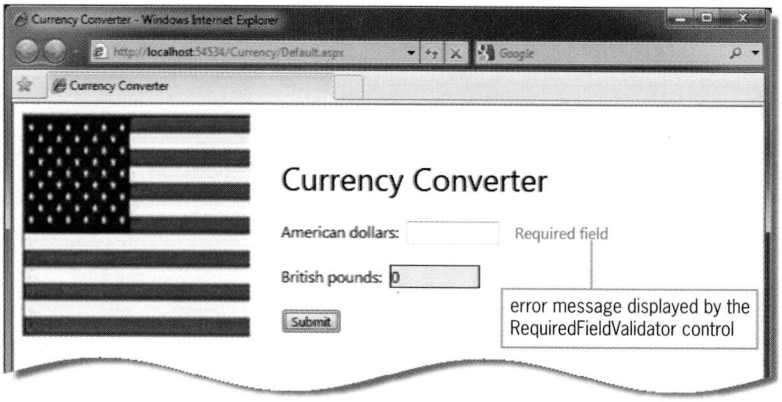

Figure 13-43 Result of clicking the Submit button when the dollarsTextBox is empty

7. Type **20** in the dollarsTextBox and then click the **Submit** button. The error message is removed from the Web page and the number 13.60 appears in the poundsLabel.
8. Close the browser window and then close the application. Figure 13-44 shows the application's code.

```
' Application name:     Currency
' Purpose:              Convert dollars to pounds
' Created/revised by:   <your name> on <current date>

Option Explicit On
Option Strict On
Option Infer Off

Partial Class _Default
    Inherits System.Web.UI.Page

    Protected Sub submitButton_Click(ByVal sender As Object,
    ByVal e As System.EventArgs) Handles submitButton.Click
        ' converts dollars to pounds

        Const PoundRate As Double = 0.68
        Dim dollars As Double
        Dim pounds As Double

        Double.TryParse(dollarsTextBox.Text, dollars)
        pounds = dollars * PoundRate
        poundsLabel.Text = pounds.ToString("N2")

    End Sub
End Class
```

Figure 13-44 Currency application's code

PROGRAMMING EXAMPLE

Multiplication Calculator Application

Create an empty Web application named Multiplication. Save the application in the VbReloaded2010\Chap13 folder. Add a new Web page named Default.aspx to the application. Change the DOCUMENT object's Title property to Multiplication Calculator. Create the Web page shown in Figure 13-45. The X image is contained in the VbReloaded2010\Chap13\Times.jpg file. The Submit button should display the product of the two numbers entered by the user. See Figures 13-45 and 13-46.

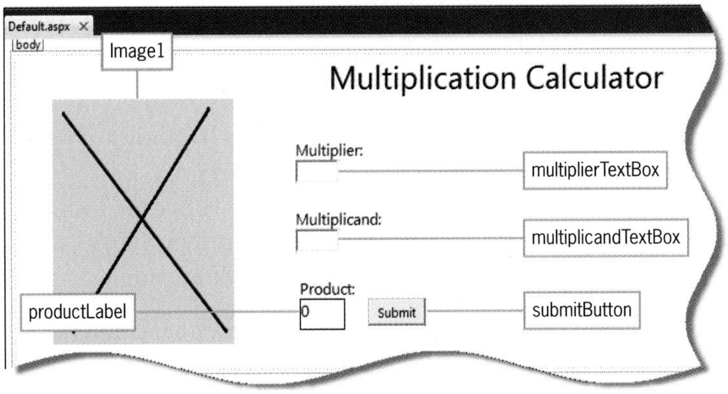

Figure 13-45 Default.aspx Web page

```
' Application name:     Multiplication
' Purpose:              Displays the product of two numbers
' Created/revised by:   <your name> on <current date>

Option Explicit On
Option Strict On
Option Infer Off

Partial Class _Default
   Inherits System.Web.UI.Page

   Protected Sub submitButton_Click(ByVal sender As Object,
   ByVal e As System.EventArgs) Handles submitButton.Click
      ' displays the product of two numbers

      Dim multiplier As Double
      Dim multiplicand As Double
      Dim product As Double

      Double.TryParse(multiplierTextBox.Text, multiplier)
      Double.TryParse(multiplicandTextBox.Text, multiplicand)

      product = multiplier * multiplicand
      productLabel.Text = product.ToString

   End Sub
End Class
```

Figure 13-46 Multiplication Calculator application's code

Summary

- Web pages are stored on Web servers. Client computers use browsers to request Web pages from Web servers. The Web pages are viewed in the browser window.
- Some Web pages are static, while others are dynamic (interactive).
- You can use Visual Web Developer to create Web applications that are composed of one or more Web pages. Visual Web Developer 2010 uses a technology called ASP.NET 4.0. ASP pages contain HTML tags and also may contain ASP tags and Visual Basic code.
- A Web page's HTML and ASP tags are interpreted and executed by the client computer. The program code is executed by the Web server.
- You can add static text and controls to a Web page. Like Windows controls, Web controls have properties, and they can be coded to perform tasks when an action (such as clicking) occurs. However, unlike Windows controls, Web controls have an ID property (rather than a Name property). You use the ID property to refer to the control in code.
- The aspx file contains the instructions for rendering the visual elements on the Web page. The aspx.vb file contains the Web page's code and is referred to as the code-behind file.

Key Terms

ASP—stands for "active server page"

Browser—a program that allows a client computer to request and view Web pages

Client computer—a computer that requests information from a Web server

Dynamic Web page—an interactive document that can accept information from the user and also retrieve information for the user

Static text—text that the user is not allowed to edit

Static Web page—a non-interactive document whose purpose is merely to display information to the viewer

Validator tools—the tools contained in the Validation section of the toolbox; used to validate user input on a Web page

Web pages—the documents stored on Web servers

Web server—a computer that contains special software that "serves up" Web pages in response to requests from client computers

Review Questions

1. An online form that allows you to purchase a product is an example of a _______________ Web page.

   a. dynamic

   b. static

2. ASP stands for _______________.

   a. always special page

   b. active special page

   c. active server product

   d. none of the above

3. Which of the following filenames indicates that the file contains the Visual Basic code associated with a Web page?

   a. Default.aspx.vb

   b. Default.aspx

   c. Default.vb

   d. none of the above

4. In code, you refer to a control on a Web page using the control's _______________ property.

   a. Caption

   b. ID

   c. Name

   d. Text

5. If you want text to appear to the left of the selected image control on a Web form, you would need to click the _______________ button in the Position dialog box.

   a. Align

   b. AlignLeft

   c. Left

   d. Right

6. The Visual Basic code in a Web page is processed by the _______________.

   a. client computer

   b. Web server

7. You can use a ______________ control to verify that a control on a Web page contains data.
   a. RequiredFieldValidator
   b. RequiredField
   c. RequiredValidator
   d. none of the above

8. You can use a ______________ control to verify that an entry on a Web page is within a minimum and maximum value.
   a. MinMaxValidation
   b. MaxMinValidation
   c. EntryValidator
   d. RangeValidator

Exercises

Pencil and Paper

INTRODUCTORY

1. Explain the difference between a static Web page and a dynamic Web page.

INTRODUCTORY

2. Explain the relationship between a client computer and a Web server.

Computer

MODIFY THIS

3. If necessary, complete the Currency Converter application from this chapter's Programming Tutorial 2, and then close the application.
   a. Create an empty Web application named CurrencyRangeValidator. Save the application in the VbReloaded2010\Chap13 folder. Close the CurrencyRangeValidator application.
   b. Use Windows to open the CurrencyRangeValidator folder. Delete the web.config file.
   c. Use Windows to open the Currency folder. Select the folder's contents. Copy the selected contents to the CurrencyRangeValidator folder.
   d. Open the CurrencyRangeValidator application. Right-click Default.aspx in the Solution Explorer window and then click View Designer.
   e. Add a RangeValidator control to the Web page. The control should display an appropriate message when the number of American dollars is less than 1 or greater than 100,000. Be sure to change the control's Type property to Double.

f. Save and then start the application. Test the application. Close the browser window and then close the application.

4. If necessary, complete the Multiplication Calculator application from this chapter's Programming Example, and then close the application.

MODIFY THIS

a. Create an empty Web application named ModifiedMultiplication. Save the application in the VbReloaded2010\Chap13 folder. Close the ModifiedMultiplication application.

b. Use Windows to open the ModifiedMultiplication folder. Delete the web.config file.

c. Use Windows to open the Multiplication folder. Select the folder's contents. Copy the selected contents to the ModifiedMultiplication folder.

d. Open the ModifiedMultiplication application. Right-click Default.aspx in the Solution Explorer window and then click View Designer.

e. Add two RequiredFieldValidator controls to the Web page. Associate the controls with the two text boxes. The controls should display the message "Required field" when their respective text box is empty.

f. Save and then start the application. Test the application. Close the browser window and then close the application.

5. If necessary, complete the Currency Converter application from this chapter's Programming Tutorial 2, and then close the application.

MODIFY THIS

a. Create an empty Web application named CurrencyPesos. Save the application in the VbReloaded2010\Chap13 folder. Close the CurrencyPesos application.

b. Use Windows to open the CurrencyPesos folder. Delete the web.config file.

c. Use Windows to open the Currency folder. Select the folder's contents. Copy the selected contents to the CurrencyPesos folder.

d. Open the CurrencyPesos application. Right-click Default.aspx in the Solution Explorer window and then click View Designer.

e. The Web page also should display the result of converting the number of American dollars to Mexican pesos. Make the appropriate modifications to the Web page and its code. Use 13.58 as the number of pesos for each American dollar.

f. Save and then start the application. Test the application. Close the browser window and then close the application.

6. Create an empty Web application named Johansen. Save the application in the VbReloaded2010\Chap13 folder. Add a new Web page named Default.aspx to the application. Change the DOCUMENT object's Title property to Johansen Pet Supplies. Create a Web page similar to the one shown in Figure 13-47.

INTRODUCTORY

The static text should be centered, horizontally, on the page. Save and then start the application. Close the browser window and then close the application.

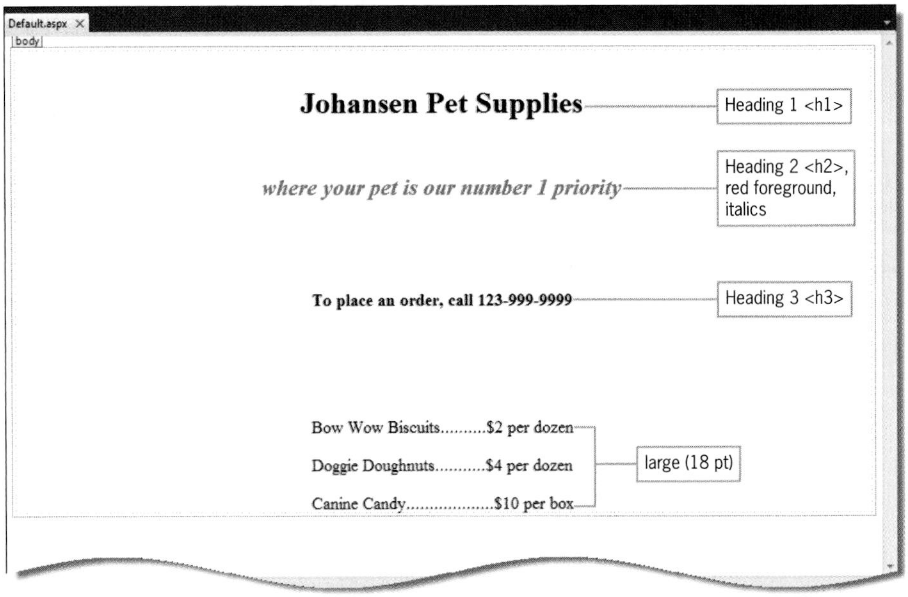

Figure 13-47 Web page for Johansen Pet Supplies

INTRODUCTORY

7. Create an empty Web application named Winterland. Save the application in the VbReloaded2010\Chap13 folder. Add a new Web page named Default.aspx to the application. Change the DOCUMENT object's Title property to Winterland Farms. Change the DOCUMENT object's BgColor property to a light blue. Create a Web page similar to the one shown in Figure 13-48. The winterland.jpg file is contained in the VbReloaded2010\Chap13 folder. Save and then start the application. Close the browser window and then close the solution.

Figure 13-48 Web page for Winterland Farms

8. Create an empty Web application named Gutierrez. Save the application in the VbReloaded2010\Chap13 folder. Add two new Web pages named Default.aspx and Message.aspx to the application. Change the DOCUMENT object's Title property to Gutierrez Heating and Cooling. Create Web pages similar to the ones shown in Figures 13-49 and 13-50. As you are creating the Web pages, periodically view them in full screen view. Save and then start the application. Close the browser window and then close the application.

INTERMEDIATE

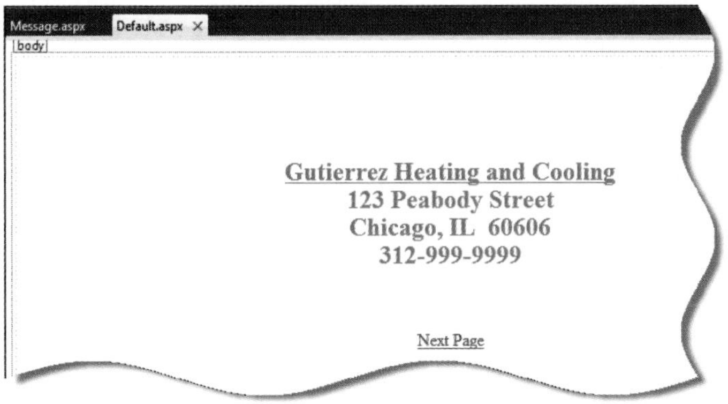

Figure 13-49 Default.aspx Web page for Gutierrez Heating and Cooling

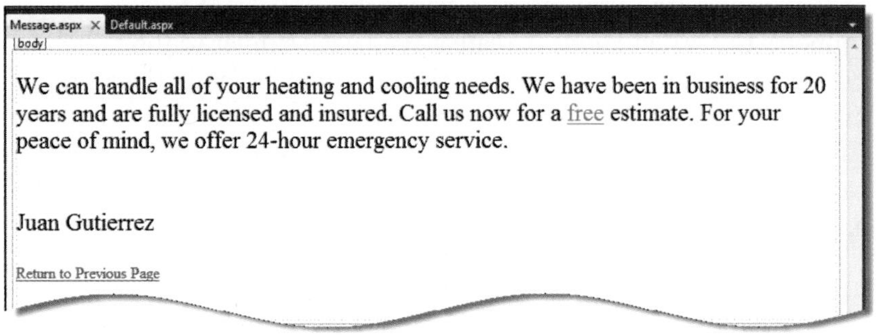

Figure 13-50 Message.aspx Web page for Gutierrez Heating and Cooling

9. Create an empty Web application named ZipCode. Save the application in the VbReloaded2010\Chap13 folder. Add a new Web page named Default.aspx to the application. Change the DOCUMENT object's Title property to ZIP Code Verifier. Create a Web page similar to the one shown in Figure 13-51. Use labels for the static text. Also, use the Segoe UI font for the static text and controls. Verify that the user entered the ZIP code and that the ZIP code is in the appropriate format. (Hint: Use the RegularExpressionValidator control to verify the format.) If the ZIP code is valid, display the message "Your ZIP code is" followed by the ZIP code and a period. Save and then start the application. Test the application by clicking the Submit button without entering a ZIP code. Then test it using the following ZIP codes: 60611, 606123, 60611-3456, and 60611-5. Close the browser window and then close the solution.

INTERMEDIATE

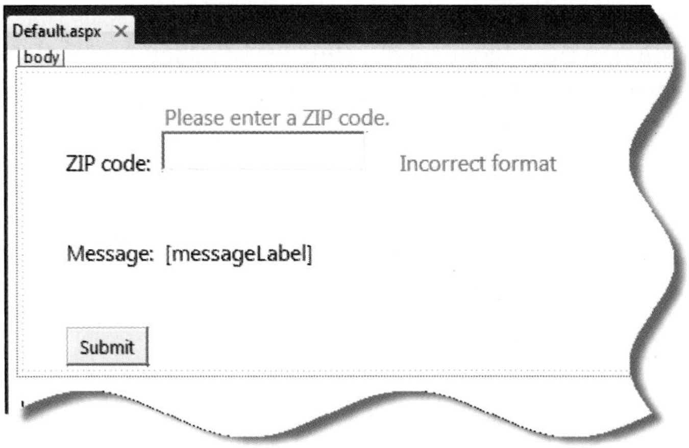

Figure 13-51 Web page for the ZIP Code Verifier application

Case Projects

Market Foods

Create an empty Web application named MarketFoods. Save the application in the VbReloaded2010\Chap13 folder. Add a new Web page named Default.aspx to the application. Change the DOCUMENT object's Title property to Market Foods. Create a Web page similar to the sketch shown in Figure 13-52. The DropDownList control should contain the store numbers listed in Figure 13-53. When the user clicks the Submit button, the button's Click event procedure should display the names of the manager and assistant manager. Code the procedure. Save and then start the application. Test the application and then close it.

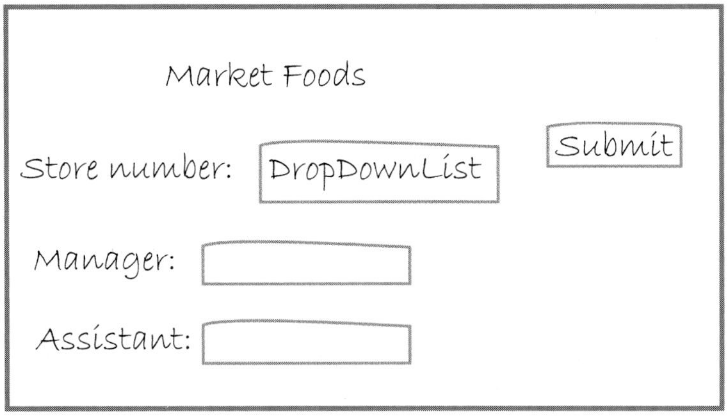

Figure 13-52 Sketch for the Market Foods application

Store number	Manager	Assistant manager
1001	Jeffrey Jefferson	Paula Hendricks
1002	Barbara Millerton	Sung Lee
1003	Inez Baily	Homer Gomez
1004	Lou Chan	Jake Johansen
1005	Henry Abernathy	Ingrid Nadkarni

Figure 13-53 Store information for the Market Foods application

Jeremy Antiques

Create an empty Web application named JeremyAntiques. Save the application in the VbReloaded2010\Chap13 folder. Add a new Web page named Default.aspx to the application. Change the DOCUMENT object's Title property to Jeremy Antiques. Create a Web page that provides a text box for the user to enter a sales amount. Associate a RequiredFieldValidator control with the text box. When the user clicks a button on the Web page, the button's Click event procedure should display both a 5% sales tax and a 6% sales tax. Code the application. Save and then start the application. Test the application and then close it.

Cheap Loans

Create an empty Web application named Cheap Loans. Save the application in the VbReloaded2010\Chap13 folder. Add a new Web page named Default.aspx to the application. Change the DOCUMENT object's Title property to Cheap Loans. Create a Web page that provides text boxes for the user to enter the amount of a loan, the annual interest rate, and the term of the loan (in years). Associate each text box with its own RequiredFieldValidator control. The application should display the monthly payment. Code the application. Save and then start the application. Test the application and then close it.

Skate-Away Sales

Create an empty Web application named SkateAway. Save the application in the VbReloaded2010\Chap13 folder. Add a new Web page named Default.aspx to the application. Change the DOCUMENT object's Title property to Skate-Away Sales. The Skate-Away Sales company sells skateboards by phone. The skateboards are priced at $100 each and are available in two colors: yellow and blue. The application should allow the salesperson to enter the customer's name and the number of blue and yellow skateboards ordered. It should calculate the total number of skateboards ordered and the total price of the order, including a 5% sales tax. Create an appropriate Web page. Code the application. Save and then start the application. Test the application and then close it.

CHAPTER 14

Creating Classes and Objects

After studying Chapter 14, you should be able to:

- Explain the terminology used in object-oriented programming
- Create a class
- Instantiate an object
- Add Property procedures to a class
- Include data validation in a class
- Create default and parameterized constructors
- Include methods other than constructors in a class
- Overload the methods in a class
- Create an auto-implemented property

Object-Oriented Programming Terminology

As you learned in Chapter 1, Visual Basic 2010 is an **object-oriented programming language**, which is a language that allows the programmer to use objects to accomplish a program's goal. Recall that an **object** is anything that can be seen, touched, or used. In other words, an object is nearly any *thing*. The objects used in an object-oriented program can take on many different forms. The text boxes, list boxes, and buttons included in most Windows applications are objects, and so are the application's named constants and variables. An object also can represent something found in real life, such as a wristwatch or a car.

Every object used in an object-oriented program is created from a **class**, which is a pattern that the computer uses to create the object. Using object-oriented programming (**OOP**) terminology, objects are **instantiated** (created) from a class, and each object is referred to as an **instance** of the class. A button control, for example, is an instance of the Button class. The button is instantiated when you drag the Button tool from the toolbox to the form. A String variable, on the other hand, is an instance of the String class and is instantiated the first time you refer to the variable in code. Keep in mind that the class itself is not an object. Only an instance of a class is an object.

Every object has **attributes**, which are the characteristics that describe the object. Attributes are also called properties. Included in the attributes of buttons and text boxes are the Name and Text properties. List boxes have a Name property as well as a Sorted property. In addition to attributes, every object also has behaviors. An object's **behaviors** include methods and events. **Methods** are the operations (actions) that the object is capable of performing. For example, a button can use its Focus method to send the focus to itself. **Events** are the actions to which an object can respond. A button's Click event, for instance, allows it to respond to a mouse click. A class contains—or, in OOP terms, it **encapsulates**—all of the attributes and behaviors of the object it instantiates. The term "encapsulate" means "to enclose in a capsule." In the context of OOP, the "capsule" is a class.

Creating a Class

In previous chapters, you instantiated objects using classes that are built into Visual Basic, such as the TextBox and Label classes. You used the instantiated objects in a variety of ways in many different applications. In some applications, you used a text box to enter a name, while in other applications you used it to enter a sales tax rate. Similarly, you used label controls to identify text boxes and also to display the result of calculations. The ability to use an object for more than one purpose saves programming time and money—an advantage that contributes to the popularity of object-oriented programming. You also can define your own classes in Visual Basic and then create instances (objects) from those classes. Like the Visual Basic classes, your classes must specify the attributes and behaviors of the objects they create.

The creation of a good class, which is one whose objects can be used in a variety of ways by many different applications, requires a lot of planning.

You define a class using the **Class statement**, which you enter in a class file. Figure 14-1 shows the statement's syntax and lists the steps for adding a class file to an open project. Although it is not a requirement, the convention is to use Pascal case for the class name. The names of Visual Basic classes (for example, Integer and TextBox) also follow this naming convention. Within the Class statement, you define the attributes and behaviors of the objects the

You also can include Event procedures in a Class statement. However, that topic is beyond the scope of this book.

class will create. In most cases, the attributes are represented by Private variables and Public properties. The behaviors are represented by methods, which can be Sub or Function procedures. Figure 14-2 shows an example of the Class statement entered in a class file. The three Option statements included in the figure have the same meaning in a class file as they have in a form file.

HOW TO Define a Class

<u>Syntax</u>

Public Class *className*
attributes section
behaviors section
End Class

<u>Adding a class file to an open project</u>

1. Click Project on the menu bar and then click Add Class. The Add New Item dialog box opens with Class selected in the middle column of the dialog box.
2. Type the name of the class followed by a period and the letters vb in the Name box, and then click the Add button.

Figure 14-1 How to define a class

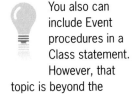

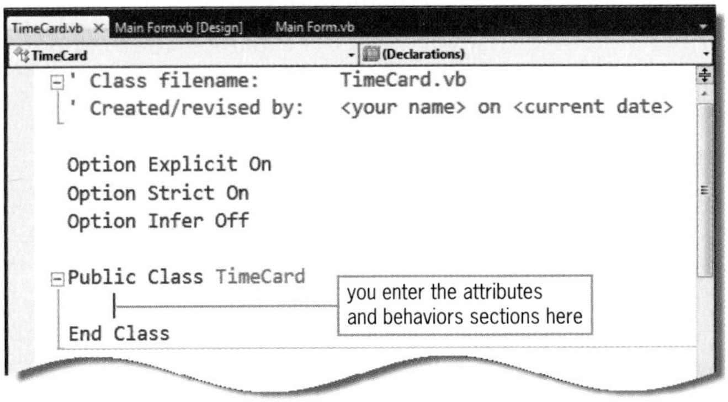

Figure 14-2 Class statement entered in a class file named TimeCard.vb

After you define a class, it then can be used to instantiate one or more objects. Figure 14-3 shows two versions of the syntax for instantiating an object. In both versions, *className* is the name of the class, and *variableName* is the name of a variable that will represent the object. The difference between both versions relates to when the object is actually created. The computer creates the object only when it processes the statement containing the `New` keyword. (You will learn more about the `New` keyword later in this chapter.) Also included in Figure 14-3 is an example of using each version of the syntax. In Example 1, the `Private hoursInfo As TimeCard` instruction creates a class-level variable that can represent a TimeCard object; however, it does not create the object. The object isn't created until the computer processes the `hoursInfo = New TimeCard` statement, which uses the TimeCard class to instantiate a TimeCard object. The statement assigns the object to the `hoursInfo` variable. In Example 2, the `Dim hoursInfo As New TimeCard` instruction creates a procedure-level variable named `hoursInfo`. It also instantiates a TimeCard object and assigns it to the variable.

HOW TO Instantiate an Object from a Class

Syntax – Version 1
{**Dim** | **Private**} *variableName* **As** *className*
variableName = **New** *className*

Syntax – Version 2
{**Dim** | **Private**} *variableName* **As New** *className*

Example 1 (using syntax version 1)

```
Private hoursInfo As TimeCard
hoursInfo = New TimeCard
```

the Private instruction creates a TimeCard variable named `hoursInfo`; the assignment statement instantiates a TimeCard object and assigns it to the `hoursInfo` variable

Example 2 (using syntax version 2)

```
Dim hoursInfo As New TimeCard
```

the Dim instruction creates a TimeCard variable named `hoursInfo` and also instantiates a TimeCard object, which it assigns to the `hoursInfo` variable

Figure 14-3 How to instantiate an object from a class

Mini-Quiz 14-1

The answers to Mini-Quiz questions are located in Appendix A.

1. A class is considered an object.
   a. True
   b. False
2. In Visual Basic, you enter the Class statement in a class file whose filename extension is ______________.
   a. .cla
   b. .cls
   c. .vb
   d. none of the above
3. Which of the following instantiates an Animal object and assigns it to the `dog` variable?
   a. `Dim dog As Animal`
   b. `Dim dog As New Animal`
   c. `Dim dog As Animal`
      `dog = New Animal`
   d. both b and c

In the remainder of this chapter, you will view examples of class definitions, as well as examples of code in which objects are instantiated and used. The first example is a class that contains attributes only, with each attribute represented by a Public variable.

Example 1—A Class that Contains Public Variables Only

In its simplest form, the Class statement can be used in place of the Structure statement, which you learned about in Chapter 11. Like the Structure statement, the Class statement groups related items into one unit. However, the unit is called a class rather than a structure. Figure 14-4 shows a sample run of the Willow Pools application from Chapter 11, and Figure 14-5 shows how you could code the application using a class rather than a structure.

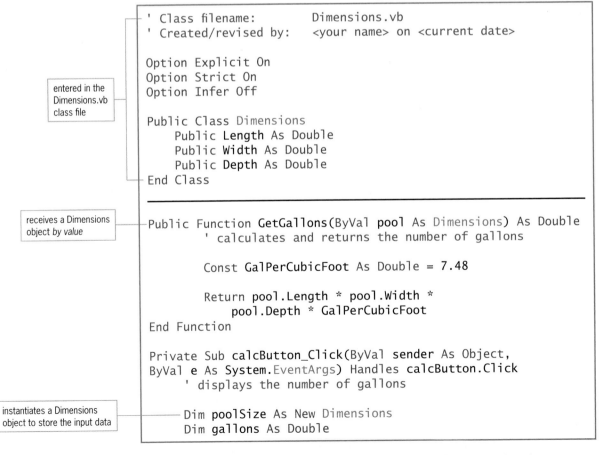

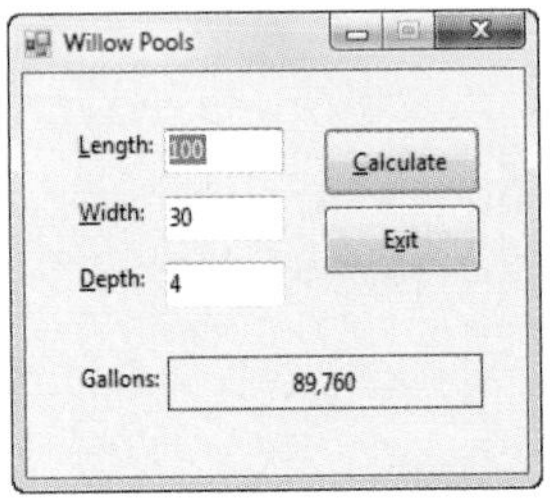

Figure 14-4 Sample run of the Willow Pools application

entered in the Dimensions.vb class file

```
' Class filename:        Dimensions.vb
' Created/revised by:    <your name> on <current date>

Option Explicit On
Option Strict On
Option Infer Off

Public Class Dimensions
    Public Length As Double
    Public Width As Double
    Public Depth As Double
End Class
```

receives a Dimensions object *by value*

instantiates a Dimensions object to store the input data

```
Public Function GetGallons(ByVal pool As Dimensions) As Double
        ' calculates and returns the number of gallons

        Const GalPerCubicFoot As Double = 7.48

        Return pool.Length * pool.Width *
            pool.Depth * GalPerCubicFoot
End Function

Private Sub calcButton_Click(ByVal sender As Object,
ByVal e As System.EventArgs) Handles calcButton.Click
      ' displays the number of gallons

     Dim poolSize As New Dimensions
     Dim gallons As Double
```

Figure 14-5 Code for the Willow Pools application (using a class) *(continues)*

(continued)

```
    Double.TryParse(lengthTextBox.Text, poolSize.Length)
    Double.TryParse(widthTextBox.Text, poolSize.Width)
    Double.TryParse(depthTextBox.Text, poolSize.Depth)

    gallons = GetGallons(poolSize)
    gallonsLabel.Text = gallons.ToString("N0")

    lengthTextBox.Focus()
End Sub
```

fills the Public variables with values

passes the Dimensions object to the GetGallons function

Figure 14-5 Code for the Willow Pools application (using a class)

Comparing the original code shown in Figure 11-6 in Chapter 11 with the code shown in Figure 14-5, you will notice that the Structure statement has been replaced with the Class statement. Unlike the Structure statement, which is entered in the MainForm's Declarations section, the Class statement is entered in a class file named Dimensions.vb. The Class statement defines the three attributes of a Dimensions object. Each attribute in the class is represented by a Public variable. When a variable in a class is declared using the `Public` keyword, it can be accessed by any application that contains an instance of the class. Using OOP terminology, the variables are exposed to the application. The convention is to use Pascal case for the names of the Public variables in a class. This is because Public variables represent properties that will be seen by anyone using an object instantiated from the class. The properties of Visual Basic objects—such as the Text and StartPosition properties—also follow this naming convention. You also will notice that the `Dim poolSize As Dimensions` statement in Figure 11-6 is replaced with the `Dim poolSize As New Dimensions` statement in Figure 14-5. The `Dim poolSize As Dimensions` statement in Figure 11-6 declares a structure variable named `poolSize`, whereas the `Dim poolSize As New Dimensions` statement in Figure 14-5 instantiates a Dimensions object named `poolSize`.

If you want to experiment with the Willow Pools application, open the solution contained in the Try It 1! folder.

Private Variables and Public Property Procedures

Although you can define a class that contains only attributes represented by Public variables—like the Dimensions class shown in Figure 14-5—that is rarely done. The disadvantage of using Public variables in a class is that a class cannot control the values assigned to its Public variables. As a result, the class cannot validate the values to ensure they are appropriate for the variables. Rather than declaring a class's variables using the `Public` keyword, most programmers declare them using the `Private` keyword. Unlike a class's Public variables, its Private variables are not visible to applications that contain an instance of the class. Using OOP terminology, the Private variables are hidden from the application. Because of this, the names of the Private variables will not appear in the IntelliSense list as you are coding, nor will they be recognized within the application's code. A class's Private variables can be used only by instructions within the class itself. The naming convention for a class's Private variables is to use the underscore as the first character in the name and then camel case for the remainder of the name, as in the names `_side`, `_bonus`, and `_annualSale`.

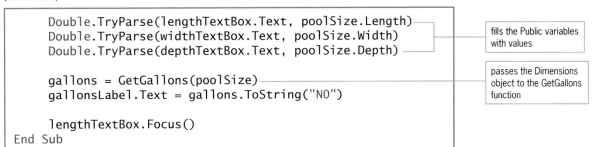

When an application instantiates an object, only the Public members of the object's class are visible to the application; the application cannot access the Private members of the class. For an application to assign data to or retrieve data from a Private variable in a class, it must use a Public property. In other words, an application cannot directly refer to a Private variable in a class. Rather, it must refer to the variable indirectly, through the use of a Public property. You create a Public property using a **Property procedure**. Figure 14-6 shows the syntax of a Property procedure. In most cases, a Property procedure header begins with the keywords `Public Property`. However, as the syntax indicates, the header also can include either the `ReadOnly` keyword or the `WriteOnly` keyword. The `ReadOnly` keyword indicates that the property's value can be retrieved (read) by an application, but the application cannot set (write to) the property. The property would get its value from the class itself rather than from the application. The `WriteOnly` keyword indicates that an application can set the property's value, but it cannot retrieve the value. In this case, the value would be set by the application for use within the class.

A one-dimensional array's Length property, which you learned about in Chapter 9, is an example of a ReadOnly property.

Following the `Property` keyword in the header is the name of the property. You should use nouns and adjectives to name a property and enter the name using Pascal case, as in Side, Bonus, and AnnualSale. Following the property name is a set of parentheses, the keyword `As`, and the property's *dataType.* The dataType must match the data type of the Private variable associated with the Property procedure.

Between a Property procedure's header and footer, you include a Get block of code, a Set block of code, or both Get and Set blocks of code. The appropriate block or blocks of code to include depends on the keywords contained in the procedure header. If the header contains the `ReadOnly` keyword, you include only a Get block of code in the Property procedure. The code contained in the **Get block** allows an application to retrieve the contents of the Private variable associated with the property. In the Property procedure shown in Example 2 in Figure 14-6, the `ReadOnly` keyword indicates that an application can retrieve the contents of the Bonus property, but it cannot set the property's value. If the header contains the `WriteOnly` keyword, you include only a Set block of code in the procedure. The code in the **Set block** allows an application to assign a value to the Private variable associated with the property. In the Property procedure shown in Example 3 in Figure 14-6, the `WriteOnly` keyword indicates that an application can assign a value to the AnnualSale property, but it cannot retrieve the property's contents. If the Property procedure header does not contain the `ReadOnly` or `WriteOnly` keywords, you include both a Get block of code and a Set block of code in the procedure, as shown in Example 1 in Figure 14-6. In this case, an application can both retrieve and set the Side property's value. A Public Property procedure creates a property that is visible to any application that contains an instance of the class.

HOW TO Create a Property Procedure

Syntax

Public [**ReadOnly** | **WriteOnly**] **Property** *propertyName***()** **As** *dataType*
    Get
        [*instructions*]
        Return *privateVariable*
    End Get

Figure 14-6 How to create a Property procedure *(continues)*

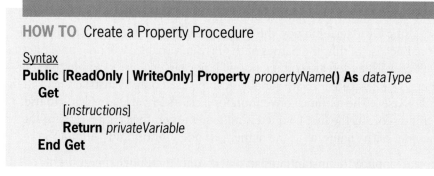

(continued)

Set(ByVal value As *dataType***)**
[instructions]
privateVariable = {**value** | *defaultValue*}
End Set
End Property

Example 1 – an application can both retrieve and set the Side property's value

```
Private _side As Integer

Public Property Side() As Integer
    Get
        Return _side
    End Get
    Set(ByVal value As Integer)
        If value > 0 Then
            _side = value
        Else
            _side = 0
        End If
    End Set
End Property
```

Example 2 – an application can retrieve, but not set, the Bonus property's value

```
Private _bonus As Double

Public ReadOnly Property Bonus() As Double
    Get
        Return _bonus
    End Get
End Property
```

Example 3 – an application can set, but not retrieve, the AnnualSale property's value

```
Private _annualSale As Decimal

Public WriteOnly Property AnnualSale() As Decimal
    Set(ByVal value As Decimal)
        _annualSale = value
    End Set
End Property
```

Figure 14-6 How to create a Property procedure

The Get block contains the **Get statement**, which begins with the keyword `Get` and ends with the keywords `End Get`. Most times, you will enter only the `Return` *privateVariable* instruction within the Get statement. The instruction directs the computer to return the contents of the Private variable associated with the property. In Example 1 in Figure 14-6, the `Return _side` statement tells the computer to return the contents of the `_side` variable, which is the Private variable associated with the Side property. Similarly, the `Return _bonus` statement in Example 2 tells the computer to return the contents of the `_bonus` variable, which is the Private variable associated with the Bonus property. Example 3 does not contain a Get statement, because the AnnualSale property is designated as a `WriteOnly` property.

The Set block contains the **Set statement**, which begins with the keyword `Set` and ends with the keywords `End Set`. The `Set` keyword is followed by a parameter enclosed in parentheses. The parameter begins with the keywords `ByVal value As`. The keywords are followed by a *dataType*, which must match the data type of the Private variable associated with the Property procedure. The `value` parameter temporarily stores the value that is passed to the property by the application. You can enter one or more instructions within the Set statement. One of the instructions should assign the contents of the `value` parameter to the Private variable associated with the property. In Example 3 in Figure 14-6, the `_annualSale = value` statement assigns the contents of the procedure's `value` parameter to the Private `_annualSale` variable. In the Set statement, you often will include instructions to validate the value received from the application before assigning it to the Private variable. The Set statement in Example 1 in Figure 14-6 includes a selection structure that determines whether the side measurement received from the application is valid. In this case, a valid side measurement is an integer that is greater than zero. If the side measurement is valid, the `_side = value` instruction assigns the integer stored in the `value` parameter to the Private `_side` variable. Otherwise, the `_side = 0` instruction assigns a default value (in this case, 0) to the variable. The Property procedure in Example 2 does not contain a Set statement, because the Bonus property is designated as a `ReadOnly` property.

Constructors

Most classes contain at least one constructor. A **constructor** is a class method, always named New, whose sole purpose is to initialize the class's Private variables. Constructors never return a value, so they are always Sub procedures rather than Function procedures. The syntax for creating a constructor is shown in Figure 14-7. Notice that a constructor's *parameterList* is optional. A constructor that has no parameters, like the constructor in Example 1 in Figure 14-7, is called the **default constructor**. A class can have only one default constructor. A class that contains one or more parameters, like the constructor in Example 2, is called a **parameterized constructor**. A class can have as many parameterized constructors as needed; however, the parameterList in each parameterized constructor must be unique within the class. The method name (New) combined with its optional parameterList is called the method's **signature**.

When an object is instantiated, the computer uses one of the class's constructors to initialize the class's Private variables. If a class contains more than one constructor, the computer determines the appropriate constructor by matching the number, data type, and position of the arguments in the statement that instantiates the object with the number, data type, and position of the parameters listed in each constructor's parameterList. Examples of statements that will invoke the default constructor in Figure 14-7 include `Dim mySquare As New Square` and `mySquare = New Square`. The default constructor is used because neither of the statements contains any arguments. Examples of statements that will invoke the parameterized constructor in Figure 14-7 include `Dim mySquare As New Square(10)` and `mySquare = New Square(10)`. In this case, the parameterized constructor is used because both statements contain one argument whose data type is Integer.

Recall that the New keyword tells the computer to instantiate the object.

HOW TO Create a Constructor

Syntax
Public Sub New([*parameterList*]**)**
instructions to initialize the class's Private variables
End Sub

Example 1 (default constructor)
```
Public Sub New()
     _side = 0
End Sub
```
initializes the Private variable directly

Example 2 (parameterized constructor)
```
Public Sub New(ByVal s as Double)
     Side = 0
End Sub
```
uses the Public property to initialize the Private variable indirectly

Figure 14-7 How to create a constructor

The `Dim randomGenerator As New Random` statement from Chapter 4 instantiates a Random object and invokes the class's default constructor.

As Figure 14-7 shows, a default constructor is allowed to initialize the class's Private variables directly. The default constructor in Example 1, for instance, assigns the number 0 to the class's Private `_side` variable. Parameterized constructors, on the other hand, should use the class's Public properties to access the Private variables indirectly. This is because the values passed to a parameterized constructor come from the application rather than from the class itself. Values that originate outside of the class should always be assigned to the Private variables indirectly, through the Public properties. Doing this ensures that the Property procedure's Set block, which typically contains validation code, is processed. The parameterized constructor in Example 2 in Figure 14-7, for instance, uses the Public Side property to initialize the Private `_side` variable indirectly, thereby invoking the validation code in the Side property.

Methods Other Than Constructors

Except for constructors, which must be Sub procedures, the other methods in a class can be either Sub procedures or Function procedures. Recall from Chapter 8 that the difference between both types of procedures is that a Function procedure returns a value after performing its assigned task, whereas a Sub procedure does not return a value. Figure 14-8 shows the syntax for a method that is not a constructor. Like property names, method names should be entered using Pascal case. However, unlike property names, the first word in a method name should be a verb, and any subsequent words should be nouns and adjectives. Figure 14-8 also includes two examples of a method that allows a Square object to calculate its area. Notice that you can write the method as either a Function procedure or a Sub procedure.

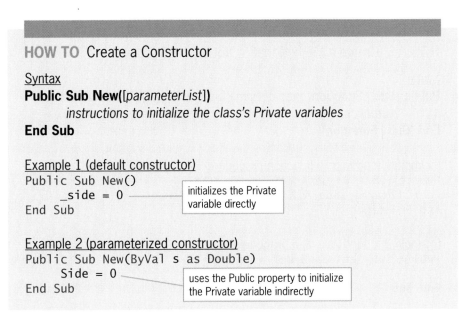

HOW TO Create a Method that Is Not a Constructor

Syntax
Public {**Sub** | **Function**} *methodName*(**[***parameterList***]**) **[As** *dataType***]**
instructions
End {**Sub** | **Function**}

Example 1 (coded as a Function procedure)
```
Public Function GetArea() As Double
      Return _side ^ 2
End Function
```

Example 2 (coded as a Sub procedure)
```
Public Sub GetArea(ByRef a As Double)
      a = _side ^ 2
End Sub
```

Figure 14-8 How to create a method that is not a constructor

Example 2—A Class that Contains Private Variables, Public Properties, and Methods

Figure 14-9 shows a sample run of the Carpet Haven application, which calculates and displays two values: the number of square yards of carpeting required to carpet a rectangular floor and the cost of the carpet. The Calculate button's Click event procedure is shown in Figure 14-10, along with the Rectangle class definition. When the computer processes the `Dim floor As New Rectangle` instruction in the Click event procedure, it instantiates a Rectangle object and uses the default constructor to initialize the Private variables in the class.

If you want to experiment with the code shown in Figure 14-10, open the solution contained in the Try It 2! folder.

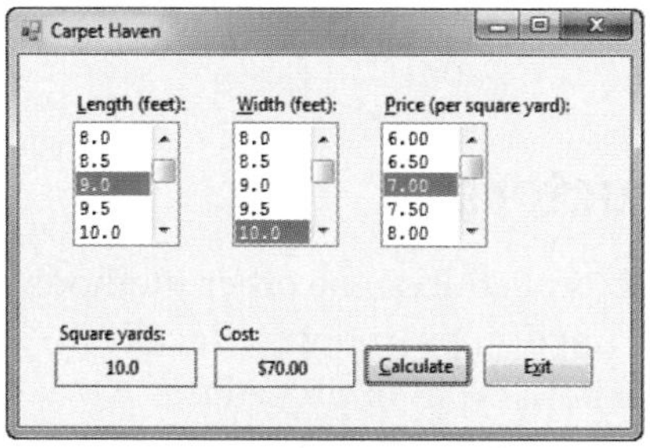

Figure 14-9 Sample run of the Carpet Haven application

beginning of the class definition (entered in the Rectangle.vb file)

```
Public Class Rectangle
    Private _length As Double
    Private _width As Double

    Public Property Length() As Double
        Get
            Return _length
        End Get
        Set(ByVal value As Double)
            If value > 0 Then
```

Figure 14-10 Partial code for the Carpet Haven application *(continues)*

(continued)

```
                _length = value
            Else
                _length = 0
            End If
        End Set
    End Property

    Public Property Width() As Double
        Get
            Return _width
        End Get
        Set(ByVal value As Double)
            If value > 0 Then
                _width = value
            Else
                _width = 0
            End If
        End Set
    End Property

    Public Sub New()
        _length = 0
        _width = 0
    End Sub

    Public Sub New(ByVal l As Double, ByVal w As Double)
        Length = l
        Width = w
    End Sub

    Public Function GetArea() As Double
        Return _length * _width
    End Function

End Class
```

```
Private Sub calcButton_Click(ByVal sender As Object,
ByVal e As System.EventArgs) Handles calcButton.Click
    ' displays the number of square yards
    ' and the cost of the carpet

    Dim floor As New Rectangle
    Dim priceSqYd As Double
    Dim sqYards As Double
    Dim cost As Double

    Double.TryParse(lengthListBox.SelectedItem.ToString, floor.Length)
    Double.TryParse(widthListBox.SelectedItem.ToString, floor.Width)
    Double.TryParse(priceListBox.SelectedItem.ToString, priceSqYd)

    ' calculate required square yards of carpet
    sqYards = floor.GetArea / 9
    ' calculate carpet cost
    cost = priceSqYd * sqYards

    ' display required square yards and carpet cost
    sqYdsLabel.Text = sqYards.ToString("N1")
    costLabel.Text = cost.ToString("C2")
End Sub
```

beginning of the Calculate button's Click event procedure (entered in the Main Form.vb file)

instantiates a Rectangle object, using the default constructor

assigns values to the object's Length and Width properties

invokes the object's GetArea method

Figure 14-10 Partial code for the Carpet Haven application

Figure 14-11 shows another way of coding the Calculate button's Click event procedure. Like the `Dim floor As New Rectangle` instruction in Figure 14-10, the `floor = New Rectangle(roomLength, roomWidth)` instruction in Figure 14-11 tells the computer to instantiate a Rectangle object. However, the two Double arguments in the instruction tell the computer to use the parameterized constructor (rather than the default constructor) to initialize the class's Private variables. In this case, the computer passes the two Double arguments (*by value*) to the parameterized constructor, which stores them in its `l` and `w` parameters. The `Length = l` and `Width = w` instructions in the constructor assign the values stored in the `l` and `w` parameters to the Public Length and Width properties, respectively. When you assign a value to a property, the computer passes the value to the property's Set statement, where it is stored in the Set statement's `value` parameter. In this case, the selection structure in the Length property's Set statement compares the value stored in the `value` parameter with the number 0. If the value is greater than 0, the selection structure's true path assigns the value to the Private `_length` variable; otherwise, its false path assigns the number 0 to the variable. Similarly, the selection structure in the Width property's Set statement compares the value stored in the `value` parameter with the number 0. If the value is greater than 0, the selection structure's true path assigns the value to the Private `_width` variable; otherwise, its false path assigns the number 0 to the variable.

If you want to experiment with the code shown in Figure 14-11, open the solution contained in the Try It 3! folder.

```
Private Sub calcButton_Click(ByVal sender As Object,
ByVal e As System.EventArgs) Handles calcButton.Click
    ' displays the number of square yards
    ' and the cost of the carpet

    Dim floor As Rectangle
    Dim roomLength As Double
    Dim roomWidth As Double
    Dim priceSqYd As Double
    Dim sqYards As Double
    Dim cost As Double

    Double.TryParse(lengthListBox.SelectedItem.ToString, roomLength)
    Double.TryParse(widthListBox.SelectedItem.ToString, roomWidth)
    Double.TryParse(priceListBox.SelectedItem.ToString, priceSqYd)

    floor = New Rectangle(roomLength, roomWidth)

    ' calculate required square yards of carpet
    sqYards = floor.GetArea / 9
    ' calculate carpet cost
    cost = priceSqYd * sqYards

    ' display required square yards and carpet cost
    sqYdsLabel.Text = sqYards.ToString("N1")
    costLabel.Text = cost.ToString("C2")
End Sub
```

instantiates a Rectangle object, using the parameterized constructor

Figure 14-11 A different way of coding the Calculate button's Click event procedure

Example 3—Reusing a Class

In Example 2, you used the Rectangle class to create an object that represented the floor in a room. In this example, you will use the Rectangle class to represent a square pizza. A square is simply a rectangle that has four equal sides. As mentioned earlier, the ability to use an object—in this case, a Rectangle object—for more than one purpose saves programming time and money, which contributes to the popularity of object-oriented programming. Figure 14-12 shows a sample run of the Pizza Roma application, and Figure 14-13 shows the code entered in the Calculate button's Click event procedure. The code uses the Rectangle class from Figure 14-10.

If you want to experiment with the Pizza Roma application, open the solution contained in the Try It 4! folder.

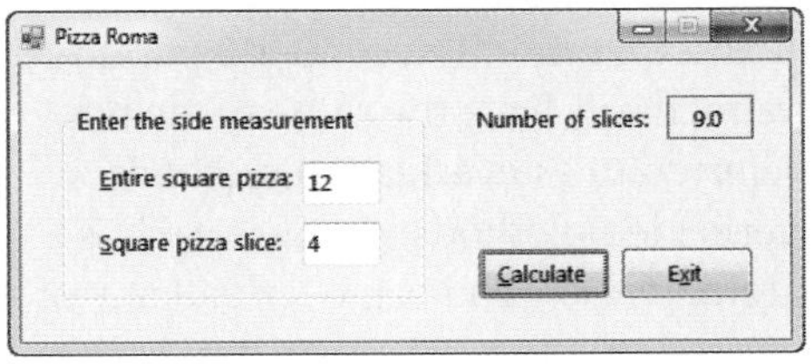

Figure 14-12 Sample run of the Pizza Roma application

```
Private Sub calcButton_Click(ByVal sender As Object,
ByVal e As System.EventArgs) Handles calcButton.Click
     ' displays the number of square pizza slices
     ' that can be cut from a square pizza

     Dim entirePizza As New Rectangle
     Dim pizzaSlice As New Rectangle
     Dim entireArea As Double
     Dim sliceArea As Double
     Dim slices As Double

     Double.TryParse(entirePizzaTextBox.Text, entirePizza.Length)
     Double.TryParse(entirePizzaTextBox.Text, entirePizza.Width)
     Double.TryParse(pizzaSliceTextBox.Text, pizzaSlice.Length)
     Double.TryParse(pizzaSliceTextBox.Text, pizzaSlice.Width)

     ' calculate area of entire pizza and pizza slice
     entireArea = entirePizza.GetArea
     sliceArea = pizzaSlice.GetArea
     ' calculate and display number of slices
     slices = entireArea / sliceArea
     slicesLabel.Text = slices.ToString("N1")
End Sub
```

instantiates two Rectangle objects

assigns values to each object's Length and Width properties

invokes each object's GetArea method

Figure 14-13 Calculate button's Click event procedure

Example 4—A Class that Contains Overloaded Methods

In this example, you will use a class named Employee to instantiate an object. Employee objects have two attributes: an employee number and an employee name. Employee objects also have the following four behaviors:

1. They can initialize their attributes using values provided by the class.
2. They can initialize their attributes using values provided by the application in which they are instantiated.

3. They can calculate and return the gross pay for salaried employees. The gross pay is calculated by dividing the salaried employee's annual salary by 24, because the salaried employees are paid twice per month.

4. They can calculate and return the gross pay for hourly employees. The gross pay is calculated by multiplying the number of hours the employee worked during the week by his or her pay rate.

Figure 14-14 shows the Employee class defined in the Employee.vb file. The class contains two Private variables named `_number` and `_empName`, along with their associated Number and EmpName Property procedures. It also contains four methods. The two New methods are the class's constructors. The first New method is the default constructor and the second is a parameterized constructor. When two or more methods have the same name but different parameters, the methods are referred to as **overloaded methods**. The two constructors are considered overloaded methods, because each is named New and each has a different parameterList. You can overload any of the methods contained in a class, not just constructors. The two GetGross methods in the Employee class are overloaded methods, because they have the same name but a different parameterList.

```
Public Class Employee
  Private _number As String
  Private _empName As String

  Public Property Number() As String
        Get
            Return _number
        End Get
        Set(ByVal value As String)
            _number = value
        End Set
  End Property

  Public Property EmpName() As String
        Get
            Return _empName
        End Get
        Set(ByVal value As String)
            _empName = value
        End Set
  End Property

  Public Sub New()
        _number = String.Empty
        _empName = String.Empty
  End Sub

  Public Sub New(ByVal num As String, ByVal name As String)
        Number = num
        EmpName = name
  End Sub
```

overloaded constructors

Figure 14-14 Employee class definition *(continues)*

(continued)

```
   Public Function GetGross(ByVal salary As Double) As Double
         ' calculates the gross pay for salaried
         ' employees, who are paid twice per month

         Return salary / 24
   End Function

   Public Function GetGross(ByVal hours As Double,
                            ByVal rate As Double) As Double
         ' calculates the weekly gross pay for hourly employees

         Return hours * rate
   End Function
End Class
```

overloaded GetGross methods

Figure 14-14 Employee class definition

You already are familiar with overloaded methods, as you have used several of the overloaded methods built into Visual Basic. Examples of such methods include ToString, TryParse, Convert.ToDecimal, and MessageBox.Show. The Code Editor's IntelliSense feature displays a box that allows you to view a method's signatures, one signature at a time. Recall that a method's signature includes its name and optional parameterList. The box shown in Figure 14-15 displays the first of the ToString method's four signatures. You use the up and down arrows in the box to display the other signatures. The IntelliSense feature also will display the signatures of the overloaded methods contained in the classes you create.

```
grossLabel.Text = gross.ToString(|
                  ▲ 1 of 4 ▼ ToString() As String
                       Converts the numeric value of this instance to its equivalent string representation.
```

Figure 14-15 First of the ToString method's signatures

Overloading is useful when two or more methods require different parameters to perform essentially the same task. Both overloaded constructors in the Employee class, for example, initialize the class's Private variables. However, the default constructor does not need to be passed any information to perform the task, while the parameterized constructor requires two items of information (the employee number and name). Similarly, both GetGross methods in the Employee class calculate and return a gross pay amount. However, the first GetGross method performs its task for salaried employees and requires an application to pass it one item of information: the employee's annual salary. The second GetGross method performs its task for hourly employees and requires two items of information: the number of hours the employee worked and his or her rate of pay. Rather than using two overloaded GetGross methods, you could have used two methods having different names, such as GetSalariedGross and GetHourlyGross. However, by overloading the GetGross method, you need to remember the name of only one method. The Employee class is used in the ABC Company application. Figure 14-16 shows a sample run of the application, and Figure 14-17 shows the code entered in the Calculate button's Click event procedure.

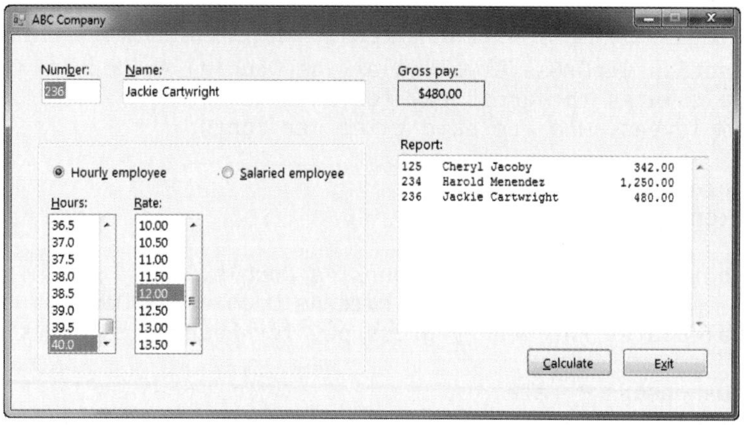

Figure 14-16 Sample run of the ABC Company application

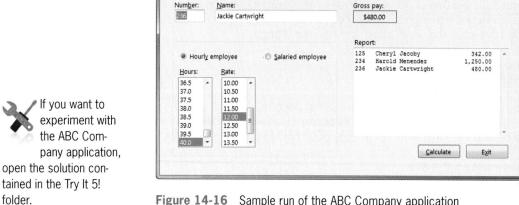

If you want to experiment with the ABC Company application, open the solution contained in the Try It 5! folder.

```
Private Sub calcButton_Click(ByVal sender As Object,
ByVal e As System.EventArgs) Handles calcButton.Click
     ' displays the gross pay and a report

     Dim abcEmployee As Employee
     Dim annualSalary As Double
     Dim hours As Double
     Dim hourRate As Double
     Dim gross As Double

     ' create an Employee object and assign the
     ' employee number and name to the object
     abcEmployee =
          New Employee(numTextBox.Text, nameTextBox.Text)

     ' determine the selected radio button
     If hourlyRadioButton.Checked Then
          ' calculate the gross pay for an hourly employee
          Double.TryParse(hoursListBox.SelectedItem.ToString, hours)
          Double.TryParse(rateListBox.SelectedItem.ToString, hourRate)
          gross = abcEmployee.GetGross(hours, hourRate)
     Else
          ' calculate the gross pay for a salaried employee
          Double.TryParse(salaryListBox.SelectedItem.ToString,
                          annualSalary)
          gross = abcEmployee.GetGross(annualSalary)
     End If

     ' display the gross pay and report, then set the focus
     grossLabel.Text = gross.ToString("C2")
     reportTextBox.Text = reportTextBox.Text &
           abcEmployee.Number.PadRight(6) &
           abcEmployee.EmpName.PadRight(25) &
           gross.ToString("N2").PadLeft(9) & ControlChars.NewLine
     numTextBox.Focus()
End Sub
```

declares a variable to store an Employee object

instantiates an Employee object and provides the initial values

calculates the gross pay for an hourly employee

calculates the gross pay for a salaried employee

Figure 14-17 Code entered in the Calculate button's Click event procedure

Auto-Implemented Properties

A new feature in Visual Basic 2010, called **auto-implemented properties**, enables you to specify the property of a class in one line of code, as shown in Figure 14-18. When you enter the line of code in the Code Editor window, Visual Basic automatically creates a hidden Private variable that it associates with the property; it also automatically creates hidden Get and Set blocks. The Private variable's name will be the same as the property's name, but it will be preceded by an underscore. For example, if you create an auto-implemented property named Address, Visual Basic will create a hidden Private variable named `_Address`. The auto-implemented properties feature provides a shorter syntax for you to use when creating a class: You don't need to create the Private variable associated with a property, nor do you need to enter the property's Get and Set blocks of code. However, keep in mind that you will need to use the standard syntax if you want to add validation code to the Set block, or if you want the property to be either ReadOnly or WriteOnly.

HOW TO Create an Auto-Implemented Property

Syntax
Public Property *propertyName* **As** *dataType*

Example 1
```
Public Property Address As String
```
creates a Public property named Address and a hidden Private variable named `_Address`; also creates hidden Get and Set blocks

Example 2
```
Public Property Sales As Double
```
creates a Public property named Sales and a hidden Private variable named `_Sales`; also creates hidden Get and Set blocks

Figure 14-18 How to create an auto-implemented property

Figure 14-19 shows how to use the auto-implemented properties feature in the Employee class from Figure 14-14.

```
Public Class Employee
  Public Property Number As String
  Public Property EmpName As String

  Public Sub New()
        Number = String.Empty
        EmpName = String.Empty
  End Sub

  Public Sub New(ByVal num As String, ByVal name As String)
        Number = num
        EmpName = name
  End Sub
```

replaces each property's Private variable declaration and its Get and Set blocks

you can use the names of the Public properties

Figure 14-19 Employee class definition using auto-implemented properties *(continues)*

(continued)

```
  Public Function GetGross(ByVal salary As Double) As Double
        ' calculates the gross pay for salaried
        ' employees, who are paid twice per month

      Return salary / 24
  End Function

  Public Function GetGross(ByVal hours As Double,
                           ByVal rate As Double) As Double
        ' calculates the weekly gross pay for hourly employees

       Return hours * rate
  End Function
End Class
```

Figure 14-19 Employee class definition using auto-implemented properties

If you want to experiment with the code shown in Figure 14-19, open the solution contained in the Try It 6! folder.

The answers to Mini-Quiz questions are located in Appendix A.

Mini-Quiz 14-2

1. Some constructors return a value.
   a. True
   b. False
2. A Private variable in a class can be accessed directly by a Public method in the same class.
   a. True
   b. False
3. The name of the default constructor for a class named Animal is _____________.
   a. Animal
   b. AnimalConstructor
   c. Constructor
   d. none of the above
4. Validation code is entered in the _____________ block in a Property procedure.
   a. Assign
   b. Get
   c. Set
   d. Validate

You have completed the concepts section of Chapter 14. The Programming Tutorial section is next.

PROGRAMMING TUTORIAL 1

Creating the Grade Calculator Application

In this tutorial, you create an application that displays a student's grade. The grade is based on two tests whose scores can be from 0 through 100. The grading scale is shown in Figure 14-20. Figures 14-21 and 14-22 show the application's TOE chart and MainForm, respectively. The interface contains four labels, two list boxes, and two buttons.

Points	Grade
at least 180	A
160 – 179	B
140 – 159	C
120 – 139	D
less than 120	F

Figure 14-20 Grading scale for the Grade Calculator application

Task	Object	Event
1. Fill the list boxes with test scores from 0 through 100 2. Select test score 80 in each list box	MainForm	Load
End the application	exitButton	Click
Get the two test scores Clear the gradeLabel	test1ListBox, test2ListBox	None SelectedValueChanged
Display the letter grade in gradeLabel	displayButton	Click
Display the letter grade (from displayButton)	gradeLabel	None

Figure 14-21 TOE chart for the Grade Calculator application

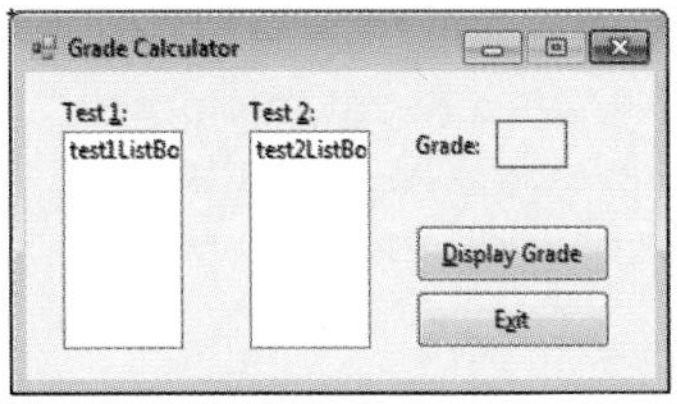

Figure 14-22 MainForm for the Grade Calculator application

Opening the Grade Calculator Application

Included in the data files for this book is a partially completed Grade Calculator application. To complete the application, you just need to code it.

To open the Grade Calculator application:

1. Start Visual Studio or the Express Edition of Visual Basic. If necessary, open the Solution Explorer window.
2. Open the **Grade Solution** (**Grade Solution.sln**) file, which is contained in the VbReloaded2010\Chap14\Grade Solution folder. Open the designer window, if necessary, and then auto-hide the Solution Explorer window.

Creating the CourseGrade Class

First, you will create a class named CourseGrade. The CourseGrade class will contain three attributes: two test scores and a letter grade. It also will contain a default constructor that initializes the test scores to 0 and initializes the letter grade to the empty string. In addition, it will contain a method that determines the appropriate letter grade.

To create the CourseGrade class:

1. Click **Project** on the menu bar and then click **Add Class**. The Add New Item dialog box opens with Class selected in the middle column. Change the entry in the Name box to **CourseGrade.vb** and then click the **Add** button.

2. Press **Enter** to insert a blank line above the Public Class clause. Beginning in the blank line, enter the following two comments, replacing <your name> and <current date> with your name and the current date. Press **Enter** twice after typing the second comment.

   ```
   ' Class filename:       CourseGrade.vb
   ' Created/revised by:   <your name> on <current date>
   ```

3. Now, enter the following three Option statements:

   ```
   Option Explicit On
   Option Strict On
   Option Infer Off
   ```

4. Click the **blank line** below the Public Class clause. The class will not need to validate the two test score attributes, so you can define them using the auto-implemented properties feature. Enter the following lines of code:

   ```
   Public Property Score1 As Integer
   Public Property Score2 As Integer
   ```

5. As mentioned earlier, the class will use a method to determine the appropriate letter grade. The user should not be allowed to change the letter grade, so you will make the letter grade a ReadOnly property. Recall that you must use the standard syntax when creating a ReadOnly property. Type the following line of code and then press **Enter** twice:

   ```
   Private _letterGrade As String
   ```

6. Next, enter the following line of code. When you press Enter, the Code Editor automatically enters the Get statement for you. (Recall that a ReadOnly property contains only the Get block of code.)

   ```
   Public ReadOnly Property LetterGrade() As String
   ```

7. As you learned in the chapter, the Get statement typically contains an instruction that returns the contents of the property's Private variable. Before returning the contents of the `_letterGrade` variable, the LetterGrade property will need to determine the appropriate grade. In the blank line below the Get clause, type the following line of code and then press **Enter** twice:

   ```
   Dim total As Integer
   ```

8. Next, enter the following assignment statement and selection structure:

```
total = Score1 + Score2
Select Case total
    Case Is >= 180
        _letterGrade = "A"
    Case Is >= 160
        _letterGrade = "B"
    Case Is >= 140
        _letterGrade = "C"
    Case Is >= 120
        _letterGrade = "D"
    Case Else
        _letterGrade = "F"
End Select
```

9. Insert a blank line between the End Select and End Get clauses, and then enter the following line of code:

```
Return _letterGrade
```

10. Insert two blank lines between the End Property and End Class clauses. Enter the following default constructor:

```
Public Sub New()
    Score1 = 0
    Score2 = 0
    _letterGrade = String.Empty
End Sub
```

11. Save the CourseGrade.vb file and then close the CourseGrade.vb window.

Coding the Grade Calculator Application

According to the application's TOE chart (shown earlier in Figure 14-21), the following procedures need to be coded: the MainForm's Load event procedure, the Click event procedures for the two buttons, and the SelectedValueChanged procedure for the two list boxes.

To begin coding the application:

1. Open the MainForm's Code Editor window. Notice that the MainForm's Load event procedure, the exitButton's Click event procedure, and the SelectedValueChanged event procedures for the two list boxes have already been coded for you. This means that you will need to code only the Display Grade button's Click event procedure.
2. In the comments that appear in the General Declarations section, replace <your name> and <current date> with your name and the current date.
3. Open the code template for the displayButton's Click event procedure. Type the following comment and then press **Enter** twice:

```
' displays a student's grade
```

4. First, declare a CourseGrade object. Type the following Dim statement and then press **Enter** twice:

   Dim studGrade As New CourseGrade

5. Next, assign the test scores to the object's Public properties. Enter the following comment and assignment statements:

   ' assign test scores
   studGrade.Score1 = Convert.ToInt32(test1ListBox.SelectedItem)
   studGrade.Score2 = Convert.ToInt32(test2ListBox.SelectedItem)

6. Finally, display the letter grade in the gradeLabel. Enter the following comment and assignment statement:

   ' display the letter grade
   gradeLabel.Text = studGrade.LetterGrade

7. Save the solution and then start the application. Click **78** in the Test 1 box and then click **90** in the Test 2 box. Click the **Display Grade** button. The letter B appears in the Grade box. See Figure 14-23.

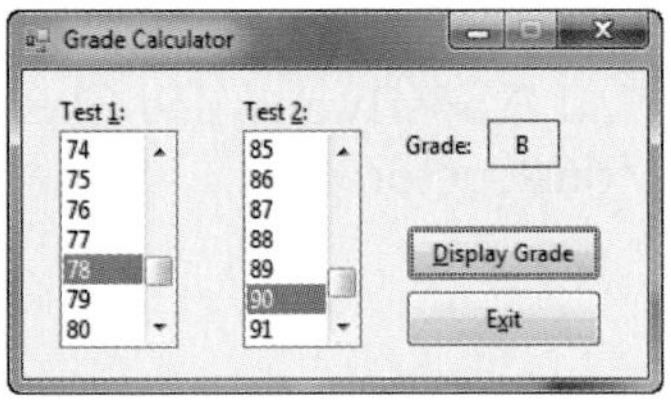

Figure 14-23 Sample run of the Grade Calculator application

8. Click the **Exit** button. Close the Code Editor window and then close the solution. Figure 14-24 shows the application's code. It also includes the code entered in the CourseGrade.vb file.

```
' Class filename:       CourseGrade.vb
' Created/revised by:    <your name> on <current date>

Option Explicit On
Option Strict On
Option Infer Off

Public Class CourseGrade
   Public Property Score1 As Integer
   Public Property Score2 As Integer
   Private _letterGrade As String

   Public ReadOnly Property LetterGrade() As String
     Get
         Dim total As Integer

         total = Score1 + Score2
         Select Case total
            Case Is >= 180
               _letterGrade = "A"
            Case Is >= 160
```

Figure 14-24 Code for the CourseGrade class and Grade Calculator application *(continues)*

(continued)

```
                _letterGrade = "B"
            Case Is >= 140
                _letterGrade = "C"
            Case Is >= 120
                _letterGrade = "D"
            Case Else
                _letterGrade = "F"
        End Select
        Return _letterGrade

    End Get
  End Property

  Public Sub New()
    Score1 = 0
    Score2 = 0
    _letterGrade = String.Empty
  End Sub
End Class
```

```
' Project name:         Grade Project
' Project purpose:      Displays a grade based on two test scores
' Created/revised by:   <your name> on <current date>

Option Explicit On
Option Strict On
Option Infer On

Public Class MainForm

   Private Sub MainForm_Load(ByVal sender As Object,
   ByVal e As System.EventArgs) Handles Me.Load
      ' fills the list boxes with values

      For score As Integer = 0 To 100
         test1ListBox.Items.Add(score.ToString)
         test2ListBox.Items.Add(score.ToString)
      Next score

      test1ListBox.SelectedItem = "80"
      test2ListBox.SelectedItem = "80"
   End Sub

   Private Sub exitButton_Click(ByVal sender As Object,
   ByVal e As System.EventArgs) Handles exitButton.Click
      Me.Close()
   End Sub

   Private Sub ClearLabel(ByVal sender As Object,
   ByVal e As System.EventArgs
   ) Handles test1ListBox.SelectedValueChanged,
   test2ListBox.SelectedValueChanged
      gradeLabel.Text = String.Empty
   End Sub

```

Figure 14-24 Code for the CourseGrade class and Grade Calculator application *(continues)*

(continued)

```
    Private Sub displayButton_Click(ByVal sender As Object,
    ByVal e As System.EventArgs) Handles displayButton.Click
       ' displays a student's grade

       Dim studGrade As New CourseGrade

       ' assign test scores
       studGrade.Score1 = Convert.ToInt32(test1ListBox.SelectedItem)
       studGrade.Score2 = Convert.ToInt32(test2ListBox.SelectedItem)
       ' display the letter grade
       gradeLabel.Text = studGrade.LetterGrade

    End Sub
End Class
```

Figure 14-24 Code for the CourseGrade class and Grade Calculator application

PROGRAMMING TUTORIAL 2

Modifying the Roll 'Em Game Application

In this tutorial, you will modify the Roll 'Em Game application from Chapter 6's Programming Tutorial 1. The modified application will use a class named PairOfDice. The Roll 'Em Game application from Chapter 6 is included in the data files for this chapter. (If you need help while coding the application, you can look ahead to Figure 14-26.)

To open the Roll 'Em Game application:

1. Start Visual Studio or the Express Edition of Visual Basic. If necessary, open the Solution Explorer window.
2. Open the **Roll Em Game Solution** (**Roll Em Game Solution.sln**) file, which is contained in the VbReloaded2010\Chap14\Roll Em Game Solution folder. Open the designer window, if necessary, and then auto-hide the Solution Explorer window.

First, you will create the PairOfDice class.

To create the PairOfDice class:

1. Use the Project menu to add a Class file to the project. Name the class file PairOfDice.vb.
2. Insert a blank line above the Public Class clause. Enter the following comments, replacing <your name> and <current date> with your name and the current date. Press **Enter** twice after typing the second comment.

   ' Class filename: PairOfDice.vb
   ' Created/revised by: <your name> on <current date>

3. Enter the appropriate Option statements.
4. The PairOfDice class should contain two Private Integer variables named `_die1` and `_die2`. Enter the appropriate statements.
5. Enter Property procedures for the two Private variables. The properties should be ReadOnly. Name the properties Die1 and Die2.

6. Enter the default constructor, which should initialize the Private variables to 0.

7. Enter a Public method named RollDice. The RollDice method should be a Sub procedure that generates two random numbers from 1 through 6. The random numbers should be assigned to the class's Private variables.

8. Save the class file and then close the PairOfDice.vb window.

Next, you will modify the code contained in the Roll 'Em button's Click event procedure.

To modify the Roll 'Em button's Click event procedure:

1. Open the MainForm's Code Editor window. In the comments that appear in the General Declarations section, replace <your name> and <current date> with your name and the current date.

2. Locate the rollButton's Click event procedure. Replace the `Dim random1 As Integer` and `Dim random2 As Integer` statements with a Dim statement that declares a PairOfDice variable named `dice`. The Dim statement should also instantiate a PairOfDice object.

3. Replace the two assignment statements that assign values to the `random1` and `random2` variables with a statement that calls the PairOfDice object's RollDice procedure.

4. Replace `random1` in the first Select Case clause with the PairOfDice object's Die1 property.

5. Replace `random2` in the second Select Case clause with the PairOfDice object's Die2 property.

6. Replace `random1` and `random2` in the first If clause with the appropriate properties.

7. Save the solution and then start the application. Click the **Roll 'Em** button. See Figure 14-25. Because random numbers determine the images assigned to the two picture boxes, your application might display different images than those shown in the figure. In addition, the "Congratulations, player 1" message, rather than the "Player 1 rolled" message, may appear on your screen.

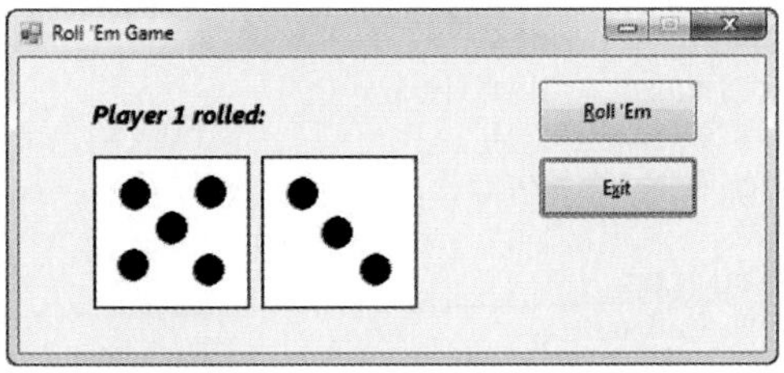

Figure 14-25 Sample run of the modified Roll 'Em Game application

8. Click the **Exit** button. Close the Code Editor window, and then close the solution. Figure 14-26 shows the code entered in the PairOfDice.vb file. It also shows the rollButton's modified Click event procedure. The changes made to the original Click event procedure are shaded in the figure.

```
' Class filename:         PairOfDice.vb
' Created/revised by:     <your name> on <current date>

Option Explicit On
Option Strict On
Option Infer Off

Public Class PairOfDice
  Private _die1 As Integer
  Private _die2 As Integer

  Public ReadOnly Property Die1() As Integer
     Get
       Return _die1
     End Get
  End Property

  Public ReadOnly Property Die2() As Integer
     Get
       Return _die2
     End Get
  End Property

  Public Sub New()
     _die1 = 0
     _die2 = 0
  End Sub

  Public Sub RollDice()
     Dim randomGenerator As New Random
     _die1 = randomGenerator.Next(1, 7)
     _die2 = randomGenerator.Next(1, 7)
  End Sub
End Class
```

```
Private Sub rollButton_Click(ByVal sender As Object,
ByVal e As System.EventArgs) Handles rollButton.Click
  ' simulates the Roll 'Em game

  Dim randomGenerator As New Random
  Dim dice As New PairOfDice
  Static player As Integer = 1

  ' clear images and display message
  firstDiePictureBox.Image = Nothing
  secondDiePictureBox.Image = Nothing
  messageLabel.Text = "Player " &
       player.ToString & " rolled:"

  ' disable Roll 'Em button
  rollButton.Enabled = False

  ' refresh form and then delay execution
  Me.Refresh()
  System.Threading.Thread.Sleep(1000)

  ' generate two random numbers from 1 through 6
  Call dice.RollDice()

```

Figure 14-26 PairOfDice class and Roll 'Em button's Click event procedure *(continues)*

(continued)

```
    ' display appropriate image in firstDiePictureBox
    Select Case dice.Die1
        Case 1
          firstDiePictureBox.Image = dot1PictureBox.Image
        Case 2
          firstDiePictureBox.Image = dot2PictureBox.Image
        Case 3
          firstDiePictureBox.Image = dot3PictureBox.Image
        Case 4
          firstDiePictureBox.Image = dot4PictureBox.Image
        Case 5
          firstDiePictureBox.Image = dot5PictureBox.Image
        Case Else
          firstDiePictureBox.Image = dot6PictureBox.Image
    End Select

    ' display appropriate image in secondDiePictureBox
    Select Case dice.Die2
        Case 1
          secondDiePictureBox.Image = dot1PictureBox.Image
        Case 2
          secondDiePictureBox.Image = dot2PictureBox.Image
        Case 3
          secondDiePictureBox.Image = dot3PictureBox.Image
        Case 4
          secondDiePictureBox.Image = dot4PictureBox.Image
        Case 5
          secondDiePictureBox.Image = dot5PictureBox.Image
        Case Else
          secondDiePictureBox.Image = dot6PictureBox.Image
    End Select

    ' check if there is a winner
    If dice.Die1 = dice.Die2 Then
        messageLabel.Text = "Congratulations, player " &
          player.ToString
        Dim count As Integer = 1
        Do While count <= 10
            messageLabel.Visible = Not messageLabel.Visible
            Me.Refresh()
            System.Threading.Thread.Sleep(100)
            count += 1
        Loop
    End If

    ' reset the current player
    If player = 1 Then
        player = 2
    Else
        player = 1
    End If

    ' enable Roll 'Em button
    rollButton.Enabled = True

End Sub
```

Figure 14-26 PairOfDice class and Roll 'Em button's Click event procedure

PROGRAMMING EXAMPLE

Kessler Landscaping Application

Create an application that estimates the cost of laying sod. Use the following names for the solution, project, and form file: Kessler Solution, Kessler Project, and Main Form.vb. Save the application in the VbReloaded2010\Chap14 folder. Add a new class file named Rectangle.vb to the project. See Figures 14-27 through 14-33.

Task	Object	Event
1. Calculate the area of the rectangle 2. Calculate the total price 3. Display the total price in the totalLabel	calcButton	Click
End the application	exitButton	Click
Display the total price (from calcButton)	totalLabel	None
Get the length in feet	lengthTextBox	None
Get the width in feet	widthTextBox	None
Get the price of the sod per square yard	priceTextBox	None
Clear the contents of the totalLabel Select the existing text	lengthTextBox, widthTextBox, priceTextBox	TextChanged Enter

Figure 14-27 TOE chart for the Kessler Landscaping application

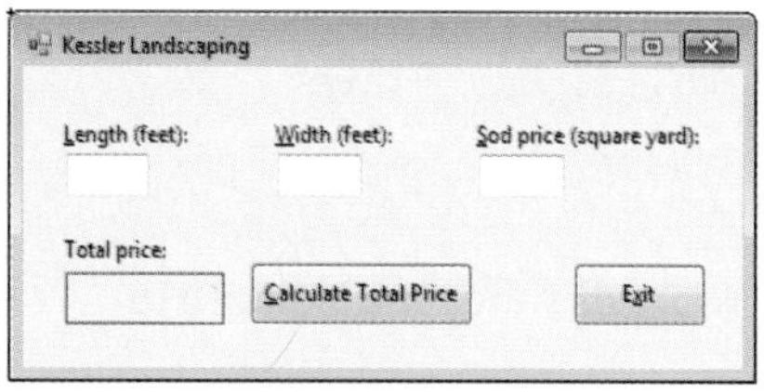

Figure 14-28 MainForm in the Kessler Landscaping application

Object	Property	Setting
MainForm	Font	Segoe UI, 9 point
	MaximizeBox	False
	StartPosition	CenterScreen
	Text	Kessler Landscaping
totalLabel	AutoSize	False
	BorderStyle	FixedSingle
	TextAlign	MiddleCenter

Figure 14-29 Objects, properties, and settings

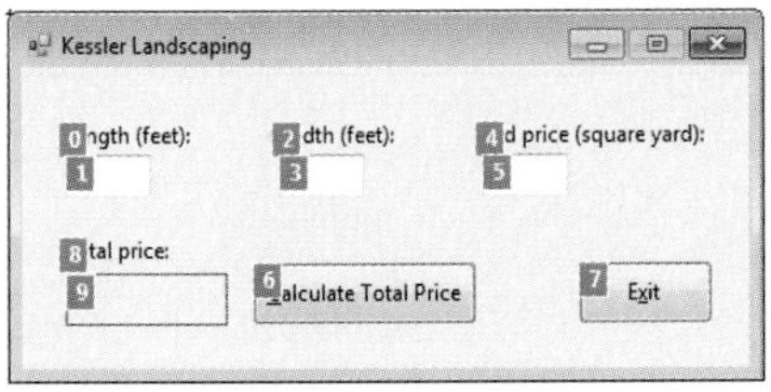

Figure 14-30 Tab order

<u>exitButton Click event procedure</u>
close the application

<u>calcButton Click event procedure</u>
1. instantiate a Rectangle object
2. store the length and width entries in the Rectangle object's Public properties
3. store the sod price in a variable
4. use the Rectangle object's GetArea method to calculate the area of the rectangle
5. calculate the total price of the sod
6. display the total price of the sod in the totalLabel

<u>lengthTextBox, widthTextBox, and priceTextBox TextChanged event procedures</u>
clear the contents of the totalLabel

<u>lengthTextBox, widthTextBox, and priceTextBox Enter event procedures</u>
select the text box's existing text

Figure 14-31 Pseudocode

```
' Class filename:        Rectangle.vb
' Created/revised by:    <your name> on <current date>

Option Explicit On
Option Strict On
Option Infer Off

Public Class Rectangle
  Private _length As Double
  Private _width As Double

  Public Property Length() As Double
     Get
       Return _length
     End Get
     Set(ByVal value As Double)
       If value > 0 Then
            _length = value
       Else
            _length = 0
       End If
     End Set
  End Property

  Public Property Width() As Double
     Get
       Return _width
     End Get
```

Figure 14-32 Code entered in the Rectangle.vb file *(continues)*

(continued)

```
        Set(ByVal value As Double)
          If value > 0 Then
               _width = value
          Else
               _width = 0
          End If
        End Set
    End Property

    Public Sub New()
        _length = 0
        _width = 0
    End Sub

    Public Sub New(ByVal l As Double, ByVal w As Double)
        Length = l
        Width = w
    End Sub

    Public Function GetArea() As Double
        Return _length * _width
    End Function
End Class
```

Figure 14-32 Code entered in the Rectangle.vb file

```
' Project name:          Kessler Project
' Project purpose:       Displays the cost of laying sod
' Created/revised by:    <your name> on <current date>

Option Explicit On
Option Strict On
Option Infer Off

Public Class MainForm

  Private Sub SelectText(ByVal sender As Object,
  ByVal e As System.EventArgs) Handles lengthTextBox.Enter,
  widthTextBox.Enter, priceTextBox.Enter
     Dim thisTextBox As TextBox
     thisTextBox = TryCast(sender, TextBox)
     thisTextBox.SelectAll()
  End Sub

  Private Sub ClearLabel(ByVal sender As Object,
  ByVal e As System.EventArgs) Handles lengthTextBox.TextChanged,
  widthTextBox.TextChanged, priceTextBox.TextChanged
     totalLabel.Text = String.Empty
  End Sub

  Private Sub exitButton_Click(ByVal sender As Object,
  ByVal e As System.EventArgs) Handles exitButton.Click
     Me.Close()
  End Sub

```

Figure 14-33 Code entered in the MainForm.vb file *(continues)*

(continued)

```
    Private Sub calcButton_Click(ByVal sender As Object,
    ByVal e As System.EventArgs) Handles calcButton.Click
        ' calculates the cost of laying sod

        Dim lawn As New Rectangle
        Dim sodPrice As Double
        Dim area As Double
        Dim totalPrice As Double

        Double.TryParse(lengthTextBox.Text, lawn.Length)
        Double.TryParse(widthTextBox.Text, lawn.Width)
        Double.TryParse(priceTextBox.Text, sodPrice)

        ' calculate the area (in square yards)
        area = lawn.GetArea / 9

        ' calculate and display the total price
        totalPrice = area * sodPrice
        totalLabel.Text = totalPrice.ToString("C2")
    End Sub
End Class
```

Figure 14-33 Code entered in the MainForm.vb file

Summary

- The objects used in an object-oriented program are instantiated (created) from classes.
- A class encapsulates (contains) the attributes that describe the object it creates, as well as the behaviors that allow the object to perform tasks and respond to actions.
- In Visual Basic, you use the Class statement to define a class. You enter the class definition in a class file, which you can add to the current project using the Project menu. A class filename ends with .vb.
- It is a good programming practice to enter the `Option Explicit On`, `Option Strict On`, and `Option Infer Off` statements in a class file.
- A class cannot control the values assigned to its Public variables.
- Most classes contain properties and methods.
- When naming the Private variables in a class, many programmers begin the name with the underscore character. Subsequent characters in the name are usually entered using camel case.
- When an object is instantiated in an application, the Public members of the class are exposed to the application; the Private members are hidden from the application.

- An application must use a Public property to assign data to or retrieve data from a Private variable in a class. You create a Public property using a Property procedure.
- In a Property procedure header, the `ReadOnly` keyword indicates that the property's value can be retrieved (read), but not set.
- In a Property procedure header, the `WriteOnly` keyword indicates that the property's value can be set, but not retrieved.
- The names of the properties in a class should be entered using Pascal case. You should use nouns and adjectives in the name.
- The Get block in a Property procedure contains the Get statement, which allows an application to access the contents of the Private variable associated with the property.
- The Set block in a Property procedure contains the Set statement, which allows an application to assign a value to the Private variable associated with the property. The Set statement can contain validation code.
- A class can have one or more constructors. All constructors are Sub procedures that are named New. Each constructor must have a different parameterList (if any).
- A constructor that has no parameters is the default constructor. A class can contain only one default constructor. Constructors that contain parameters are called parameterized constructors.
- The computer processes the constructor whose parameters match (in number, data type, and position) the arguments contained in the statement that instantiates the object.
- The names of the methods in a class should be entered using Pascal case. You should use a verb for the first word in the name, and nouns and adjectives for any subsequent words in the name.
- Values that originate outside of a class should always be assigned to the class's Private variables indirectly, through the Public properties.
- You can overload the methods in a class.
- When you create an auto-implemented property, Visual Basic automatically creates the property's Private variable and its Get and Set blocks of code.

Key Terms

Attributes—the characteristics that describe an object

Auto-implemented properties—a new feature in Visual Basic 2010; enables you to specify the property of a class in one line of code

Behaviors—an object's methods and events

Class—a pattern that the computer follows when instantiating (creating) an object

Class statement—the statement used to define a class in Visual Basic

Constructor—a method whose instructions are automatically processed each time the class instantiates an object; its purpose is to initialize the class's variables; always a Sub procedure named New

Default constructor—a constructor that has no parameters; a class can have only one default constructor

Encapsulates—an OOP term that means "contains"

Events—the actions to which an object can respond

Get block—the section of a Property procedure that contains the Get statement

Get statement—appears in a Get block in a Property procedure; contains the code that allows an application to retrieve the contents of the Private variable associated with the property

Instance—an object created from a class

Instantiated—the process of creating an object from a class

Methods—the actions that an object is capable of performing

Object—anything that can be seen, touched, or used

Object-oriented programming language—a programming language that allows the use of objects to accomplish a program's goal

OOP—an acronym for object-oriented programming

Overloaded methods—methods that have the same name but different parameterLists

Parameterized constructor—a constructor that contains parameters

Property procedure—creates a Public property that an application can use to access a Private variable in a class

Set block—the section of a Property procedure that contains the Set statement

Set statement—appears in a Set block in a Property procedure; contains the code that allows an application to assign a value to the Private variable associated with the property; may also contain validation code

Signature—a method's name combined with its parameterList

Review Questions

1. When two methods have the same name but different parameterLists, the methods are referred to as _______________ methods.
    a. loaded
    b. overloaded
    c. parallel
    d. signature

2. The Product class contains a Private variable named `_price`. The variable is associated with the Public Price property. An application instantiates a Product object and assigns it to a variable named `item`. Which of the following can be used by the application to assign the number 45 to the `_price` variable?

   a. `_price = 45`

   b. `Price = 45`

   c. `_price.item = 45`

   d. `item.Price = 45`

3. The Product class in Review Question 2 also contains a Public method named GetNewPrice. The method is a Function procedure. Which of the following can be used by the application to invoke the GetNewPrice method?

   a. `newPrice = Call GetNewPrice()`

   b. `newPrice = Price.GetNewPrice`

   c. `newPrice = item.GetNewPrice`

   d. `newPrice = item.GetNewPrice(_price)`

4. An application can access the Private variables in a class ______________.

   a. directly

   b. using properties created by Property procedures

   c. through Private procedures contained in the class

   d. none of the above

5. To expose a variable or method contained in a class, you declare the variable or method using the keyword ______________.

   a. Exposed

   b. Private

   c. Public

   d. Viewable

6. The method name combined with the method's optional parameterList is called the method's ______________.

   a. autograph

   b. inscription

   c. signature

   d. statement

7. A constructor is _____________.

   a. a Function procedure

   b. a Property procedure

   c. a Sub procedure

   d. either a Function procedure or a Sub procedure

8. An application creates an Animal object and assigns its address to the `dog` variable. Which of the following calls the DisplayBreed method contained in the Animal class?

   a. `Call Animal.DisplayBreed()`

   b. `Call DisplayBreed.Animal()`

   c. `Call DisplayBreed.Dog`

   d. `Call dog.DisplayBreed()`

9. An application instantiates a MyDate object and assigns it to the `payDate` variable. The MyDate class contains a Public Month property that is associated with a Private String variable named `_month`. Which of the following can be used by the application to assign the number 12 to the Month property?

   a. `payDate.Month = "12"`

   b. `payDate.Month._month = "12"`

   c. `payDate._month = "12"`

   d. `MyDate.Month = "12"`

10. The Return statement is entered in the _____________ block in a Property procedure.

    a. Get

    b. Set

11. A class contains a Private variable named `_capital`. The variable is associated with the Public Capital property. Which of the following is the best way for a parameterized constructor to assign the value stored in its `capName` parameter to the variable?

    a. `_capital = capName`

    b. `Capital = capName`

    c. `_capital.Capital = capName`

    d. none of the above

12. A class can contain only one constructor.

    a. True

    b. False

13. The Salesperson class contains a ReadOnly property named Bonus. The property is associated with the Private `_bonus` variable. A button's Click event procedure instantiates a Salesperson object and assigns it to the `ourSalesperson` variable. Which of the following is valid in the Click event procedure?

    a. `bonusLabel.Text =`
       `ourSalesperson.Bonus.ToString("C2")`

    b. `ourSalesperson.Bonus = sales * .1`

    c. `ourSalesperson._bonus = 500`

    d. all of the above

Exercises

Pencil and Paper

INTRODUCTORY

1. If a class contains more than one constructor, how does the computer determine the appropriate one to use?

INTRODUCTORY

2. What are overloaded methods and why are they used?

INTRODUCTORY

3. Write a Class statement that defines a class named Book. The class contains three Public variables named Title, Author, and Cost. The Title and Author variables are String variables. The Cost variable is a Decimal variable. Then use the syntax shown in Version 1 in Figure 14-3 to declare a variable that can store a Book object; name the variable `fiction`. Also write a statement that instantiates the Book object and assigns it to the `fiction` variable.

INTRODUCTORY

4. Rewrite the Class statement from Pencil and Paper Exercise 3 so that it uses Private variables rather than Public variables. Be sure to include the Property procedures and default constructor. Then rewrite the Class statement using auto-implemented properties.

INTRODUCTORY

5. Write a Class statement that defines a class named Tape. The class contains four Private String variables named `_tapeName`, `_artist`, `_songNumber`, and `_length`. Name the corresponding properties TapeName, Artist, SongNumber, and Length. Then, use the syntax shown in Version 2 in Figure 14-3 to create a Tape object, assigning it to a variable named `blues`.

6. An application contains the class definition shown in Figure 14-34. INTRODUCTORY

   a. Write a Dim statement that creates a Computer object and assigns the object to a variable named `homeUse`.

   b. Using the Computer object from Step a, write an assignment statement that assigns the string "IB-50" to the Model property. Then write an assignment statement that assigns the number 2400 to the Cost property. Finally, write an assignment statement that invokes the GetNewPrice function. Assign the function's return value to a variable named `newPrice`.

```
Public Class Computer
  Public Property Model As String
  Public Property Cost As Double

  Public Sub New()
        Model = String.Empty
        Cost = 0
  End Sub

  Public Function GetNewPrice() As Double
        Return Cost * 1.2
  End Function
End Class
```

Figure 14-34 Computer class definition

7. An application contains the Computer class definition shown in Figure 14-34. Write a parameterized constructor for the class. Then write a Dim statement that creates a Computer object and initializes it using the parameterized constructor. Assign the object to a variable named `companyUse`. Use the following values to initialize the object: "IBM" and 1236.99. INTERMEDIATE

8. Write the Property procedure for a ReadOnly property named BonusRate. The property's data type is Decimal. INTERMEDIATE

9. Write the class definition for a class named Worker. The class should have two attributes: name and salary. The salary may contain a decimal place. Use auto-implemented properties. The class also should contain two constructors: the default constructor and a constructor that allows an application to assign values to the Private variables. INTERMEDIATE

10. Add a method named GetNewSalary to the Worker class from Pencil and Paper Exercise 9. The method should calculate a Worker object's new salary, which is based on a raise percentage provided by the application using the object. Before calculating the new salary, the method should verify that the raise percentage is greater than or equal to zero. If the raise percentage is less than zero, the method should assign the number 0 as the new salary. INTERMEDIATE

Computer

MODIFY THIS

11. Open the Willow Pools Solution (Willow Pools Solution.sln) file contained in the VbReloaded2010\Chap14\Willow Pools Solution folder. Modify the Dimensions class so that it uses Public auto-implemented properties rather than Public variables. Include a default constructor in the class. Save the solution, and then start and test the application. Close the solution.

MODIFY THIS

12. If necessary, complete Computer Exercise 11 and then close the solution. Use Windows to make a copy of the Willow Pools Solution folder. Rename the folder Willow Pools Solution-Modified. Open the Willow Pools Solution (Willow Pools Solution.sln) file contained in the Willow Pools Solution-Modified folder.
    a. Add two labels to the form. Position one of the labels below the Gallons: label, and then change its Text property to Cost:. Position the other label below the gallonsLabel, and then change its Name and TextAlign properties to costLabel and MiddleCenter, respectively.
    b. Right-click Dimensions.vb in the Solution Explorer window, and then click Rename. Change the class file's name to RectangularPool.vb.
    c. Right-click RectangularPool.vb in the Solution Explorer window, and then click View Code. Change the class file's name in the first comment to RectangularPool.vb.
    d. Add a method named GetVolume to the RectangularPool class. The method should calculate and return the volume of a RectangularPool object. Save the solution.
    e. Open the MainForm's Code Editor window. The calcButton's Click event procedure should use the RectangularPool object's GetVolume method to determine the pool's volume. It then should pass the pool's volume to the GetGallons function. Make the necessary modifications to the code.
    f. The calcButton's Click event procedure also should calculate and display the cost of filling the pool with water. The charge for water is $1.75 per 1000 gallons (or .00175 per gallon). Make the necessary modifications to the code.
    g. Save the solution, and then start and test the application. Close the solution.

MODIFY THIS

13. Open the Pizza Roma Solution (Pizza Roma Solution.sln) file contained in the VbReloaded2010\Chap14\Pizza Roma Solution folder. Modify the calcButton's Click event procedure to use the Rectangle class's parameterized constructor. Save the solution, and then start and test the application. Close the solution.

14. Open the Salary Solution (Salary Solution.sln) file contained in the VbReloaded2010\Chap14\Salary Solution folder. Open the Worker.vb class file and then enter the class definition from Computer Exercises 9 and 10. Save the solution and then close the Worker.vb window. Open the MainForm's Code Editor window. Use the comments to enter the missing instructions. Save the solution and then start the application. Test the application by entering your name, a current salary amount of 54000, and a raise percentage of 10 (for 10%). The new salary should be $59,400.00. Close the solution.

INTRODUCTORY

15. In this exercise, you create an application that can be used to calculate the cost of installing a fence around a rectangular area.

INTERMEDIATE

   a. Open the Fence Solution (Fence Solution.sln) file contained in the VbReloaded2010\Chap14\Fence Solution folder. Open the Rectangle.vb class file. Add another method to the class. Name the method GetPerimeter. The GetPerimeter method should calculate and return the perimeter of a rectangle. To calculate the perimeter, the method will need to add together the length and width measurements, and then multiply the sum by 2. Save the solution and then close the Rectangle.vb window.

   b. Open the MainForm's Code Editor window. The application should calculate and display the cost of installing the fence. Code the application.

   c. Save the solution and then start the application. Test the application using 120 feet as the length, 75 feet as the width, and 10 as the cost per linear foot of fencing. The installation cost should be $3,900.00. Close the solution.

16. In this exercise, you define a Triangle class. You also create an application that allows the user to display either a Triangle object's area or its perimeter. The formula for calculating the area of a triangle is 1/2 * *base* * *height*. The formula for calculating the perimeter of a triangle is $a + b + c$. (The a, b, and c are the lengths of the sides.)

INTERMEDIATE

   a. Create a Windows application. Use the following names for the solution, project, and form file: Math Triangle Solution, Math Triangle Project, and Main Form.vb. Save the application in the VbReloaded2010\Chap14 folder.

   b. Create the interface shown in Figure 14-35.

   c. Add a class file to the project. Name the class file Triangle.vb. The Triangle class should verify that the dimensions are greater than 0 before assigning the values to the Private variables. Include a default constructor in the class. The class also should include a method to calculate the area of a triangle and a method to calculate the perimeter of a triangle. Save the solution and then close the Triangle.vb window.

   d. Open the MainForm's Code Editor window. Use the InputBox function to get the appropriate data from the user.

   e. Save the solution and then start and test the application. Close the solution.

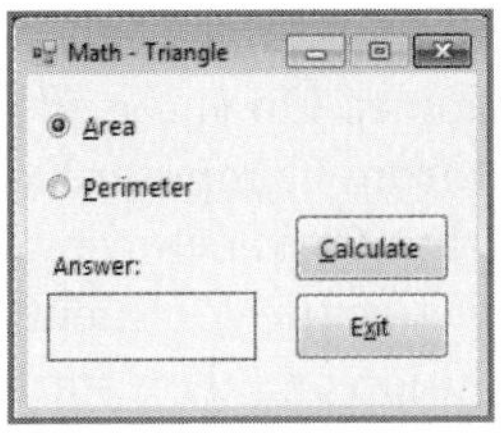

Figure 14-35 Interface for the Math – Triangle application

ADVANCED

17. If necessary, complete the Grade Calculator application from this chapter's Programming Tutorial 1, and then close the solution. Use Windows to make a copy of the Grade Solution folder. Rename the folder Grade Solution-Modified. Open the Grade Solution (Grade Solution.sln) file contained in the Grade Solution-Modified folder.

    a. Open the CourseGrade.vb file. Currently, the maximum number of points a student can earn is 200 (100 points per test). Modify the LetterGrade property so that it accepts the maximum number of points a student can earn. For an A grade, the student must earn at least 90% of the maximum points. For a B, the student must earn at least 80%. For a C, the student must earn at least 70%. For a D, the student must earn at least 60%. If the student earns less than 60% of the maximum points, the grade is F. Make the appropriate modifications to the class's code. Save the solution and then close the CourseGrade.vb window.

    b. Add a label control and a text box to the form. Change the label control's Text property to "&Maximum points". Each list box should display numbers from 0 through 200. Therefore, the maximum number of points the user should enter in the text box is 400.

    c. Open the MainForm's Code Editor window and make the necessary modifications to the code. Save the solution, and then start and test the application. Close the solution.

SWAT THE BUGS

18. Open the Debug Solution (Debug Solution.sln) file contained in the VbReloaded2010\Chap14\Debug Solution folder. Open the Code Editor window and review the existing code. Correct the code to remove the jagged lines. Save the solution, and then start and test the application. Locate and then correct the errors in the code. When the application is working correctly, close the solution.

Case Projects

Glasgow Health Club

Each member of Glasgow Health Club must pay monthly dues that consist of a basic fee and one or more optional charges. The basic monthly fee for a single membership is $50; for a family membership, it is $90. If the member has a single membership, the additional monthly charges are $30 for tennis, $25 for golf, and $20 for racquetball. If the member has a family membership, the additional monthly charges are $50 for tennis, $35 for golf, and $30 for racquetball. The application should display the member's basic fee, additional charges, and monthly dues. Use the following names for the solution, project, and form file: Glasgow Health Solution, Glasgow Health Project, and Main Form.vb. Save the application in the VbReloaded2010\Chap14 folder. You can create either your own interface or the one shown in Figure 14-36. Be sure to use a class in the application.

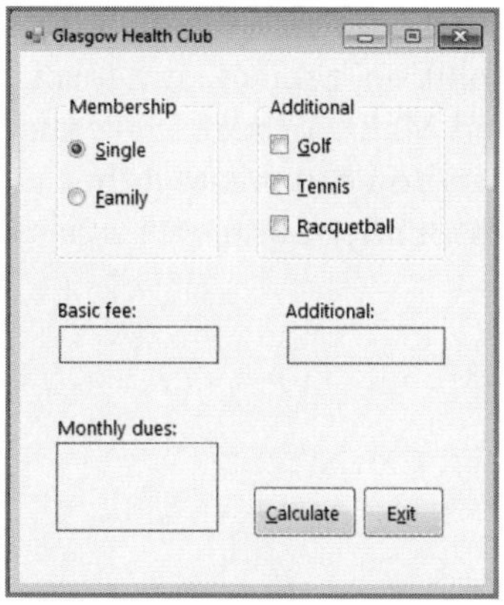

Figure 14-36 Interface for the Glasgow Health Club application

Franklin Calendars

Jeremiah Carter, the manager of the Accounts Payable department at Franklin Calendars, wants an application that keeps track of the checks written by his department. More specifically, he wants to record (in a sequential access file) the check number, date, payee, and amount of each check. Use the following names for the solution, project, and form file: Franklin Calendars Solution, Franklin Calendars Project, and Main Form.vb. Save the application in the VbReloaded2010\Chap14 folder. You can create either your own interface or the one shown in Figure 14-37. Be sure to use a class in the application.

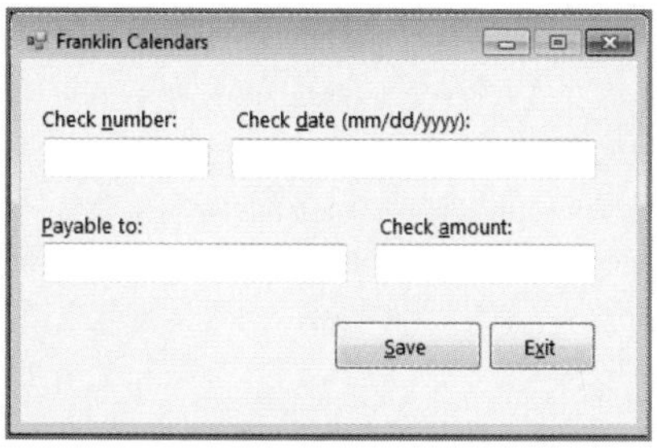

Figure 14-37 Interface for the Franklin Calendars application

Pennington Book Store

Shelly Jones, the manager of Pennington Book Store, wants an application that calculates and displays the total amount a customer owes. A customer can purchase one or more books at either the same price or different prices. The application should keep a running total of the amount the customer owes, and display the total in the Total due box. For example, a customer might purchase two books at $6 and three books at $10. To calculate the total due, Shelly will need to enter 2 in the Quantity box and 6 in the Price box, and then click the Add to Sale button. The Total due box should display $12.00. To complete the order, Shelly will need to enter 3 in the Quantity box and 10 in the Price box, and then click the Add to Sale button. The Total due box should display $42.00. Before calculating the next customer's order, Shelly will need to click the New Order button. Use the following names for the solution, project, and form file: Pennington Solution, Pennington Project, and Main Form.vb. Save the application in the VbReloaded2010\Chap14 folder. You can create either your own interface or the one shown in Figure 14-38. Be sure to use a class in the application.

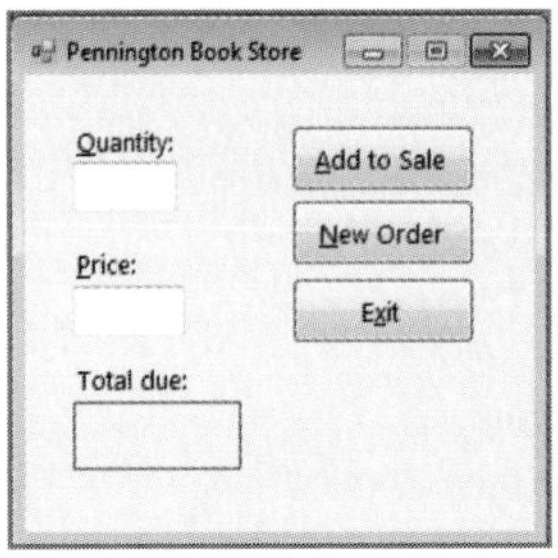

Figure 14-38 Interface for the Pennington Book Store application

Bingo Game

Create an application that simulates the game of Bingo. Use the following names for the solution, project, and form file: Bingo Game Solution, Bingo Game Project, and Main Form.vb. Save the application in the VbReloaded2010\Chap14 folder. You can create either your own interface or the one shown in Figure 14-39. Be sure to use a class in the application.

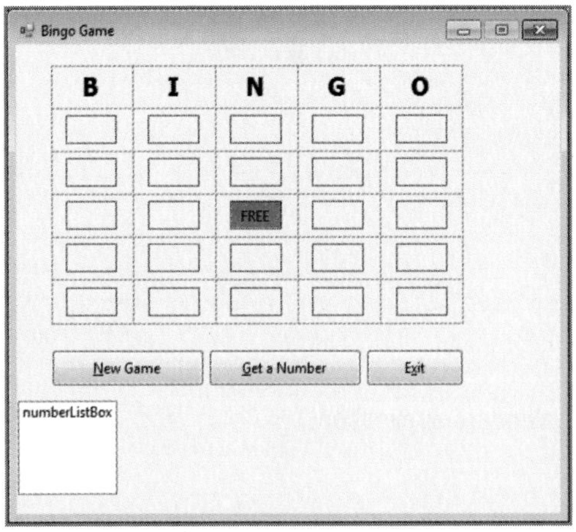

Figure 14-39 Interface for the Bingo Game application

APPENDIX A

Answers to Mini-Quizzes

Chapter 1

Mini-Quiz 1-1

1. d. all of the above
2. You auto-hide a window by clicking the Auto Hide (vertical pushpin) button on the window's title bar.
3. You temporarily display an auto-hidden window by placing your mouse pointer on the window's tab.
4. To reset the windows in the IDE, you click Window on the menu bar, click Reset Window Layout, and then click the Yes button.
5. c. Text
6. a. StartPosition

Mini-Quiz 1-2

1. To delete a control from a form, select the control in the designer window and then press the Delete key.
2. c. label
3. d. all of the above
4. b. Image
5. You should select the Label4 control first.

Mini-Quiz 1-3

1. b. click the Close Solution option on the File menu
2. c. startup
3. b. `Me.Close()`
4. c. `cityLabel.Text = "Las Vegas"`
5. c. debugging

Chapter 2

Mini-Quiz 2-1

1. d. tasks
2. b. False
3. c. text box

Mini-Quiz 2-2

1. a. book title capitalization
2. d. all of the above
3. b. None, True

Mini-Quiz 2-3

1. a. 0
2. c. 3
3. c. Alt+t
4. b. False

Mini-Quiz 2-4

1. d. none of the above
2. c. the Close button
3. d. all of the above
4. b. `PrintForm1.Print()`
5. c. .wav

Chapter 3

Mini-Quiz 3-1

1. a. only one item
2. c. `commission_rate`
3. `Dim pricePerItem As Double`
4. `Dim counter As Integer = 1`

Mini-Quiz 3-2

1. b. `city = "Paris"`
2. c. `amount = 50`
3. b. `Integer.TryParse(inputPop, population)`
4. a. `cost = Convert.ToDecimal(25.67)`

Mini-Quiz 3-3

1. c. 16
2. b. 32
3. a. `counter += 1`

Mini-Quiz 3-4

1. d. procedure
2. b. Class-level
3. c. `Static score As Integer`
4. a. `Private Const title As String = "Coach"`

Mini-Quiz 3-5

1. a. `Option Explicit On`
2. c. `Double.TryParse(salesTextBox.Text, sales)`
3. The computer will promote the contents of the `commRate` variable to Double and then multiply the result by the contents of the `sales` variable. It then will assign the product to the `commission` variable.

Mini-Quiz 3-6

1. c. process
2. d. both a and b
3. a. `clearButton.Focus()`
4. b. `commLabel.Text = commission.ToString("N2")`

Chapter 4

Mini-Quiz 4-1

1. b. False
2. c. both its true and false paths
3. b. False
4. a. diamond

Mini-Quiz 4-2

1. d. only the false path in the If…Then…Else statement
2. a. `If sales >= 450.67 Then`
3. a. `"Do they live in " & state & "?"`
4. b. `item.ToLower`
5. a. Checked

Mini-Quiz 4-3

1. a. True
2. False
3. False
4. b. `Dim ranGen As New Random`

Chapter 5

Mini-Quiz 5-1

1. a. membership status, day of the week

2. if the golfer is a club member
       display $5
   else
       if the day is Monday through Thursday
           display $15
       else
           display $25
       end if
   end if

3.

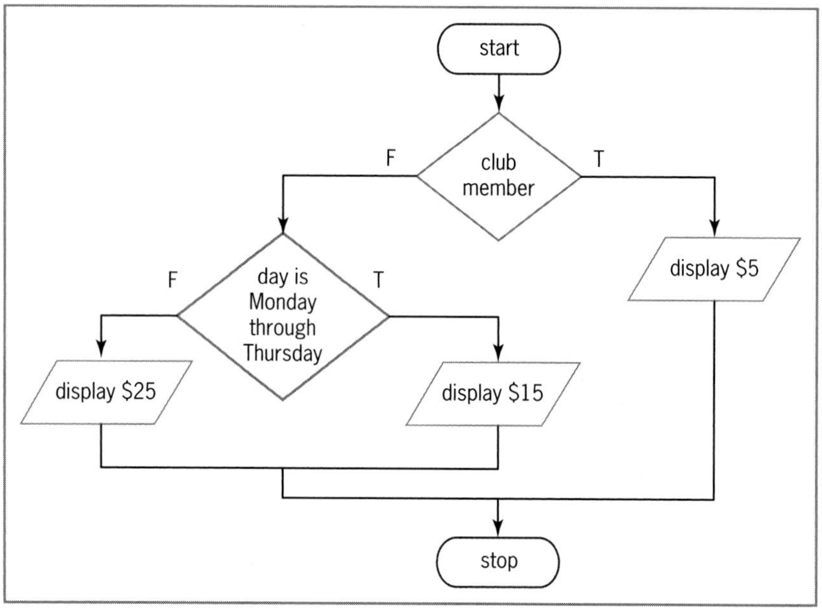

4.
```
If memberCheckBox.Checked = True Then
    feeLabel.Text = "$5"
Else
    If dayNum >= 1 AndAlso dayNum < 5 Then
          feeLabel.Text = "$15"
    Else
          feeLabel.Text = "$25"
    End If
End If
```

Mini-Quiz 5-2

1. b. `Case "1", "2", "3", "4"`
2. a. `Case 10, 11, 12, 13, 14, 15`
3. a. True

Mini-Quiz 5-3

1. d. `ControlChars.Back`
2. a. Checked
3. c. `DialogResult.Abort`
4. b. `e.Handled = True`

Chapter 6

Mini-Quiz 6-1

1. b. pretest
2. b. loop exit
3. a. looping

Mini-Quiz 6-2

1. d. all of the above
2. `sum += score` (or `sum = sum + score`)
3. `numValues += 5` (or `numValues = numValues + 5`)
4. `numItems -= 1` (or `numItems += -1` or `numItems = numItems - 1`)

Mini-Quiz 6-3

1. a. Multiline
2. a. above
3. Click Debug on the menu bar and then click Stop Debugging.
4. d. `myCity = InputBox("City name:", "City Entry")`

Mini-Quiz 6-4

1. a. Add
2. b. Items
3. c. SelectedIndex
4. c. `System.Threading.Thread.Sleep(2000)`

Chapter 7

Mini-Quiz 7-1

1. d. all of the above
2. c. 13
3.
```
For num As Integer = 6 To 1 Step -1
    numListBox.Items.Add(num.ToString)
Next num
```

Mini-Quiz 7-2

1. c. either a pretest loop or a posttest loop
2. a. a nested, outer
3. b. outer, nested

Mini-Quiz 7-3

1. c. `-Financial.Pmt(.04 / 12, 24, 5000)`
2. `cityTextBox.SelectAll()`
3. a. Add
4. `ImageList1.Images.Item(1)`

Chapter 8

Mini-Quiz 8-1

1. a. True
2. b. `Private Sub DisplayMessage()`
3. d. `Call DisplayMessage()`

Mini-Quiz 8-2

1. b. `Private Sub Display(ByVal x As String, ByVal y As String)`
2. a. `Private Sub Calc(ByVal x As Integer, ByRef y As Double)`
3. b. `Call Calc(sales, bonus)`

Mini-Quiz 8-3

1. d. `Handles nameTextBox.TextChanged, salesTextBox.TextChanged`
2. a. `Private Function Calc() As Decimal`
3. c. one value only
4. b. `currentLabel = TryCast(sender, Label)`
5. a. Enabled

Chapter 9

Mini-Quiz 9-1

1. a. `Dim letters(3) As String`
2. d. both a and b
3. a. `cities(4) = "Scottsburg"`

Mini-Quiz 9-2

1.
```
For Each scoreElement In scores
   totalScores += scoreElement
Next scoreElement
```
2.
```
For subscript As Integer = 0 To 4
   totalScores += scores(subscript)
Next subscript
```
3.
```
Dim subscript As Integer
Do While subscript <= 4
   totalScores += scores(subscript)
   subscript += 1
Loop
```
4. `Array.Sort(scores)`

Mini-Quiz 9-3

1. d. all of the above
2. b. `testAnswers(2, 0) = True`
3. `highCol = people.GetUpperBound(1)`

Chapter 10

Mini-Quiz 10-1

1. d. `numChars = msgLabel.Text.Length`
2. a. `state = state.Remove(2)`
3. a. `state = state.Insert(0, "South ")`

Mini-Quiz 10-2

1. c. True
2. a. 7
3. d. both b and c
4. d. both b and c

Mini-Quiz 10-3

1. c. `partNum Like "###[A-Z]##"`
2. b. `salesTextBox.Text Like "*,*"`
3. c. `rateTextBox.Text Like "*%"`

Chapter 11

Mini-Quiz 11-1

1. a. Declarations section
2. b. `address.street = "Maple"`
3. d. `inventory(4).quantity = 100`

Mini-Quiz 11-2

1. d. both a and b
2. b. `outFile.WriteLine(addressTextBox.Text)`
3. `outFile.Close()`

Mini-Quiz 11-3

1. c. OpenText
2. b. `msg = inFile.ReadLine`
3. `inFile.Close()`
4. the character

Mini-Quiz 11-4

1. c. `address = city & Strings.Space(10) & state`
2. a. `e.Cancel = True`
3. b. `customer = inFile.ReadLine.Split("$"c)`

Chapter 12

Mini-Quiz 12-1

1. a. database
2. b. relational
3. d. all of the above

Mini-Quiz 12-2

1. d. TableAdapter
2. d. `Me.TblNamesTableAdapter.Fill(Me.FriendsDataSet.tblNames)`
3. c. `ex.Message`
4. d. all of the above

Mini-Quiz 12-3

1. b.
```
Dim records =
        From state In StatesDataSet.tblStates
        Select state
```
2. a.
```
Dim total As Integer =
        Aggregate city In CitiesDataSet.tblCities
        Select city.population
        Into Sum()
```
3. b. Order By

Chapter 13

Mini-Quiz 13-1

1. b. client
2. a. browser
3. a. client computer

Mini-Quiz 13-2

1. a. Default.aspx
2. b. DOCUMENT
3. d. BgColor

Chapter 14

Mini-Quiz 14-1

1. b. False
2. c. .vb
3. d. both b and c

Mini-Quiz 14-2

1. b. False
2. a. True
3. d. none of the above
4. c. Set

APPENDIX B

How To Boxes

How To	Chapter	Figure
Access an item in a list box	6	6-27
Access characters in a string	10	10-5
Access the value stored in a Field object	12	12-28
Add a control to a form	1	1-16
Add a new splash screen to a project	2	2-14
Add a new Web page to a Web application	13	13-8
Add an existing Web page to a Web application	13	13-11
Add images to an image list control's Images collection	7	7-28
Add the Start Without Debugging option to the Debug menu	13	13-19
Align columns of information	11	11-22
Align the characters in a string	10	10-6
Assign a LINQ variable's contents to a BindingSource control	12	12-30
Assign a value to a variable	3	3-5
Bind an object in a dataset	12	12-8
Call an independent Sub procedure	8	8-2
Close a solution	1	1-31
Close an input sequential access file	11	11-18
Close an output sequential access file	11	11-12
Concatenate strings	4	4-17
Connect an application to an Access database	12	12-4
Create a constructor	14	14-7
Create a Function procedure	8	8-17
Create a method that is not a constructor	14	14-8
Create a Property procedure	14	14-6
Create a StreamReader object	11	11-14
Create a StreamWriter object	11	11-10
Create a Visual Basic 2010 Windows application	1	1-5
Create an auto-implemented property	14	14-18
Create an empty Web application	13	13-6

(continues)

(continued)

How To	Chapter	Figure
Create an independent Sub procedure	8	8-1
Declare a named constant	3	3-19
Declare a one-dimensional array	9	9-2
Declare a StreamReader variable	11	11-13
Declare a StreamWriter variable	11	11-9
Declare a structure variable	11	11-2
Declare a two-dimensional array	9	9-22
Declare a variable	3	3-4
Define a class	14	14-1
Define a structure	11	11-1
Determine the number of characters in a string	10	10-1
Determine the number of items in a list box	6	6-28
Determine whether a sequential access file exists	11	11-15
End an application	1	1-28
Format a number	3	3-38
Generate random integers	4	4-32
Insert characters in a string	10	10-3
Instantiate an object from a class	14	14-3
Invoke a Function procedure	8	8-18
Manage the windows in the IDE	1	1-10
Manipulate the controls on a form	1	1-17
Manipulate the items on a BindingNavigator control	12	12-33
Name a variable	3	3-2
Open an existing solution	1	1-32
Open and close an existing Web application	13	13-21
Open the Code Editor window	1	1-19
Plan an application	2	2-1
Play an audio file	2	2-30
Preview the contents of a dataset	12	12-6
Print the code and interface during design time	1	1-30
Read data from a sequential access file	11	11-16
Read records from a sequential access file	11	11-25
Refer to an image in the Images collection	7	7-30
Remove characters from a string	10	10-2
Save a solution	1	1-23
Search a string	10	10-4
Select the default list box item	6	6-31
Set the TabIndex property using the Tab Order option	2	2-11
Specify a range of values in a Case clause	5	5-13
Specify the splash screen	2	2-17
Specify the startup form	1	1-24
Start an application	1	1-26
Start and configure Visual Web Developer 2010 Express	13	13-5
Start Visual Studio 2010 or Visual Basic 2010 Express Edition	1	1-2
Store data in a one-dimensional array	9	9-3
Store data in a two-dimensional array	9	9-23
Traverse a one-dimensional array	9	9-6
Traverse a two-dimensional array	9	9-25
Use a member variable	11	11-3

(continues)

(continued)

How To	Chapter	Figure
Use a one-dimensional array's GetUpperBound method	9	9-5
Use a one-dimensional array's Length property	9	9-4
Use a two-dimensional array's GetUpperBound method	9	9-24
Use comparison operators in a condition	4	4-10
Use LINQ to select and arrange records in a dataset	12	12-29
Use logical operators in a condition	4	4-26
Use pattern-matching to compare strings	10	10-7
Use the arithmetic assignment operators	3	3-13
Use the Array.Sort and Array.Reverse methods	9	9-20
Use the basic syntax of the TryParse method	3	3-6
Use the BindingSource object's Move methods	12	12-26
Use the BindingSource object's Position property	12	12-25
Use the Convert class methods	3	3-8
Use the Copy to Output Directory property	12	12-22
Use the Do...Loop statement	6	6-6
Use the Financial.Pmt method	7	7-14
Use the For Each...Next statement	9	9-7
Use the For...Next statement	7	7-1
Use the FormClosing event procedure	11	11-23
Use the If...Then...Else statement	4	4-9
Use the InputBox function	6	6-16
Use the integer division and Mod operators	3	3-10
Use the Items collection's Add method	6	6-19
Use the KeyPress event to cancel invalid characters	5	5-20
Use the LINQ aggregate operators	12	12-36
Use the MessageBox.Show method	5	5-16
Use the MessageBox.Show method's return value	5	5-19
Use the Peek method	11	11-17
Use the Select Case statement	5	5-12
Use the SelectAll method	7	7-16
Use the SelectedItem and SelectedIndex properties	6	6-30
Use the ToUpper and ToLower methods	4	4-22
Use the Try...Catch statement	12	12-19
Use the TryCast operator	8	8-21
Use variables and arithmetic operators	3	3-12
View a Web page in full screen view	13	13-17
Write data to a sequential access file	11	11-11
Write records to a sequential access file	11	11-24

APPENDIX C

Most Commonly Used Properties of Objects

Windows Form

AcceptButton	specify a default button that will be selected when the user presses the Enter key
CancelButton	specify a cancel button that will be selected when the user presses the Esc key
ControlBox	indicate whether the form contains the Control box, as well as the Minimize, Maximize, and Close buttons
Font	specify the font to use for text
FormBorderStyle	specify the appearance and behavior of the form's border
MaximizeBox	specify the state of the Maximize button
MinimizeBox	specify the state of the Minimize button
Name	give the form a meaningful name
StartPosition	indicate the starting position of the form
Text	specify the text that appears in the form's title bar and on the taskbar

Button

Enabled	indicate whether the button can respond to the user's actions
Font	specify the font to use for text
Image	specify the image to display on the button's face
ImageAlign	indicate the alignment of the image on the button's face
Name	give the button a meaningful name
TabIndex	indicate the position of the button in the Tab order
Text	specify the text that appears on the button

CheckBox

Checked	indicate whether the check box is selected or unselected
Font	specify the font to use for text
Name	give the check box a meaningful name
TabIndex	indicate the position of the check box in the Tab order
Text	specify the text that appears inside the check box

ComboBox	
DropDownStyle	indicate the style of the combo box
Font	specify the font to use for text
Name	give the combo box a meaningful name
SelectedIndex	get or set the index of the selected item
SelectedItem	get or set the value of the selected item
Sorted	specify whether the items in the list portion are sorted
TabIndex	indicate the position of the combo box in the Tab order
Text	get or set the value that appears in the text portion
DataGridView	
AutoSizeColumnsMode	control the way the column widths are sized
DataSource	indicate the source of the data to display in the control
Dock	define which borders of the control are bound to its container
Name	give the data grid view control a meaningful name
GroupBox	
Name	give the group box a meaningful name
Padding	specify the internal space between the edges of the group box and the edges of the controls contained within the group box
Text	specify the text that appears in the upper-left corner of the group box
Label	
AutoSize	enable/disable automatic sizing
BorderStyle	specify the appearance of the label's border
Font	specify the font to use for text
Name	give the label a meaningful name
TabIndex	specify the position of the label in the Tab order
Text	specify the text that appears inside the label
TextAlign	specify the position of the text inside the label
ListBox	
Font	specify the font to use for text
Name	give the list box a meaningful name
SelectedIndex	get or set the index of the selected item
SelectedItem	get or set the value of the selected item
SelectionMode	indicate whether the user can select zero choices, one choice, or more than one choice
Sorted	specify whether the items in the list are sorted
PictureBox	
Image	specify the image to display
Name	give the picture box a meaningful name
SizeMode	specify how the image should be displayed
Visible	hide/display the picture box
RadioButton	
Checked	indicate whether the radio button is selected or unselected
Font	specify the font to use for text
Name	give the radio button a meaningful name
Text	specify the text that appears inside the radio button

TableLayoutPanel

Name	give the table layout panel a meaningful name
CellBorderStyle	specify whether the table cells have a visible border
ColumnCount	indicate the number of columns in the table
Columns	specify the style of each column in the table
Padding	specify the internal space between the edges of the table layout panel and the edges of the controls contained within the table layout panel
RowCount	indicate the number of rows in the table
Rows	specify the style of each row in the table

TextBox

BackColor	indicate the background color of the text box
CharacterCasing	specify whether the text should remain as is or be converted to either uppercase or lowercase
Font	specify the font to use for text
ForeColor	indicate the color of the text inside the text box
Name	give the text box a meaningful name
MaxLength	specify the maximum number of characters the text box will accept
Multiline	control whether the text can span more than one line
PasswordChar	specify the character to display when entering a password
ReadOnly	specify whether the text can be edited
ScrollBars	indicate whether scroll bars appear on a text box (used with a multiline text box)
TabIndex	specify the position of the text box in the Tab order
TabStop	indicate whether the user can use the Tab key to give focus to the text box
Text	get or set the text that appears inside the text box

Timer

Name	give the timer a meaningful name
Enabled	stop/start the timer
Interval	indicate the number of milliseconds between each Tick event

APPENDIX D

Visual Basic Conversion Functions

This appendix lists the Visual Basic conversion functions. As mentioned in Chapter 3, you can use the conversion functions (rather than the Convert methods) to convert an expression from one data type to another.

Syntax	Return data type	Range for expression
CBool(*expression*)	Boolean	Any valid String or numeric expression
CByte(*expression*)	Byte	0 through 255 (unsigned)
CChar(*expression*)	Char	Any valid String expression; value can be 0 through 65535 (unsigned); only the first character is converted
CDate(*expression*)	Date	Any valid representation of a date and time
CDbl(*expression*)	Double	–1.79769313486231570E+308 through –4.94065645841246544E-324 for negative values; 4.94065645841246544E-324 through 1.79769313486231570E+308 for positive values
CDec(*expression*)	Decimal	+/–79,228,162,514,264,337,593,543,950,335 for zero-scaled numbers, that is, numbers with no decimal places; for numbers with 28 decimal places, the range is +/–7.9228162514264337593543950335; the smallest possible non-zero number is 0.0000000000000000000000000001 (+/–1E-28)
CInt(*expression*)	Integer	–2,147,483,648 through 2,147,483,647; fractional parts are rounded
CLng(*expression*)	Long	–9,223,372,036,854,775,808 through 9,223,372,036,854,775,807; fractional parts are rounded
CObj(*expression*)	Object	Any valid expression
CSByte(*expression*)	SByte (signed Byte)	–128 through 127; fractional parts are rounded
CShort(*expression*)	Short	–32,768 through 32,767; fractional parts are rounded
CSng(*expression*)	Single	–3.402823E+38 through –1.401298E-45 for negative values; 1.401298E-45 through 3.402823E+38 for positive values
CStr(*expression*)	String	Depends on the expression
CUInt(*expression*)	UInt	0 through 4,294,967,295 (unsigned)
CULng(*expression*)	ULng	0 through 18,446,744,073,709,551,615 (unsigned)
CUShort(*expression*)	UShort	0 through 65,535 (unsigned)

Index

S

T